ECONOMETRIC MODELS AND METHODS

ECONOMETRIC MODELS AND METHODS

CARL F. CHRIST

Professor of Political Economy
The Johns Hopkins University

JOHN WILEY & SONS, INC.
New York · London · Sydney

10 9 8 7

Library of Congress Catalog Card Number: 66-21050
Printed in the United States of America
ISBN 0 471 15620 5

To T. C. K. and J. M.

FOREWORD: *A Remark on Econometric Tools*

Why should the tools of inductive inference differ from one empirical discipline to another? In a deeper sense, the tools do not differ. Econometrics shares its logical foundations with psychometrics and biometrics and, for that matter, with meteorology and even with experimental physics. Two or more sets of jointly asserted propositions about observable facts (*not* about mathematics or logic or ethics) are compared to determine which set is, in some sense, in better correspondence with facts. In Harold Hotelling's terminology each set of propositions, or hypotheses, contains a subset which is "considered" (tested) and its complement which is "maintained" (assumed) for the purposes of an individual piece of empirical inquiry. Econometric usage (perhaps since Mann and Wald [1943]) attaches the name "prior" to the maintained propositions, thus extending that old philosophical term to propositions which, although not subjected to test in the particular research piece in question, may well have been derived from previous observations. The "prior" propositions give "specification" (R. A. Fisher's term) of a part, not all, of the properties of the studied phenomena—for example, the form of some functions and possibly the sign, the range, or even the exact numerical value of some of their parameters. To take a crude example, proportionality between two observable variables may be asserted *a priori*, but the choice between rival candidates for the proportionality constant (e.g., between the various estimates of the economists' "velocity of circulation of money") will depend on facts. To be sure, nothing can prevent the facts from discrediting the prior assumption itself.

Some social scientists, including econometricians like Dr. Christ, denote the set of prior propositions by the term "model." I believe this usage is not generally accepted by philosophers of science. But there is hardly much disagreement about the general principle of testing by observations and the usual practice of not testing all propositions at once.

The methodological agreement between social and natural sciences was enhanced when, in the latter, statistical propositions replaced some deterministic ones, and this not only by admitting the randomness of observational "errors" but also (especially since the advent of genetics and statistical physics) by describing in probabilistic terms the phenomenon itself. If all that is asserted in science is a probability distribution, many social hypotheses, even the historical theory presented in *War and Peace*, can claim admission.

So much for common foundations. What about the differences? Does empirical economics have any particular properties that call for special "econometric" methods? Two such properties have been stated. Both are peculiar to economics only in degree but not in essence. First, the standards of the economist's profession require that his empirical results be useful for practical policy, at least over short horizons. Second, many of his prior assumptions are based on vague "common sense" and introspection, rarely amenable to controlled experiment.

The economist is asked to predict how some specified changes (or the absence of changes) in the "environment" will affect "economic variables." These variables represent actions of people in their various economic roles: as producers of, or bidders for, consumer goods, labor, materials, loans, etc. These action variables are supposed to be "endogenous"— that is, to depend on, but not to determine in turn, the environment. Of particular interest are those changes of environment that are deliberate and are called "policies," and those economic variables that are a given policy-maker's "decision criteria," such as the levels of national production and of prices in the case of a goverment's decisions or the level of profit in the case of a single firm. To specify endogenous variables is itself a prior assumption. Less amibitious than Marx, Spengler, or Toynbee, the economist avoids the risk of constructing self-contained social models. He makes, for example, the convenient (yet surely not totally safe) assumption that the growth of population, or the foreign or fiscal policy of a government, influences, but is not influenced by, say, national income.

To predict the effects of a given policy change the economist can seldom rely on experiments. He cannot emulate the engineer's "dry runs." Nor is it easy to synthesize those effects by using help (of psychologists, for example) of the kind offered to meteorologists by physicists who are able to study one variable at a time, controlling all others. He cannot set up a laboratory experiment to study the behaviorial responses of represent- atives of each economic group to changes that would simulate the actions of other groups or changes in the common environment. So far, the economist's main observations have been historical data. Yet he cannot assign future validity to the patterns of the past. For policy change may consist in changing the very mechanism by which the environment influences economic variables. He must therefore peek in the interior of the notorious "black box" that operated in the past and describe policy changes as specific changes of that interior.

In his use of historical data, the economist is also helped by occasional surveys of the expenditures and plans of sampled consumers, producers, etc. Most importantly, he makes full use of his common sense. He is certain, for example, that consumers do not consult steel production statistics before purchasing groceries, and that hog raisers are concerned with the price of corn and of hogs, not of copper. Any knowledge of technology, of legal or habitual constraints, and of the relevant time lags of people's responses must be incorporated.

Using a notation and terminology which differ only slightly from that of Carl Christ, the study of economic time sequences can be said to deal with:

(i) An "endogenous" n-tuple $y(t) = [y_i(t); \ i = 1, \ldots, n]$ and an "exogenous" m-tuple $z(t) = [z_j(t); \ j = 1, \ldots, m]$ of functions of time. For example, $y_1(t)$ may be the rate of savings at time t, and $z_3(t)$ may be a tax rate at time t.

(ii) n functions $\phi_i(i = 1, \ldots, n)$, each having as its argument the quantities
$$[y(t - \lambda), z(t - \mu)]$$

where λ and μ are "time lag" variables ranging from zero to infinity.

(iii) A joint probability distribution $F[u(t)]$ of the n-tuple $u(t)$ of functions of time ("random shocks") defined by

$$u_i(t) \equiv y_i(t) - \phi_i[y(t - \lambda), z(t - \mu)] \qquad i = 1, \ldots, n$$

The values of the $m + n$ functions $y(t)$ and $z(t)$ are observed from time to time. Alternatively, in a more elaborate view occasionally taken from psychologists and sociologists, $y(t)$ and $z(t)$ are "latent" but are statistically related to "manifest" observables in some partly known fashion. (In the simplest case each latent variable differs from a corresponding observable by an additive "error" which enters the distribution function F jointly with the "shocks.")

A *partial* specification of the $n + 1$ functions $F, \phi_1, \ldots, \phi_n$ constitutes a "model." When *fully* specified—or rather estimated—in the light of facts, they constitute a "structure." These "structural functions," together with the exogenous variables $z(t)$, represent the environment. Some changes of environment are deliberate policies. These policies can consist in changing some of the structural functions in a specified way (e.g., when a free market is replaced by rationing or price control of a commodity) or in fixing some of the exogenous variables. It is because of the former type of environmental changes that we need the knowledge of "structure" that prevailed in the observed past. We are then able to formulate the transition to a new structure. But those functions cannot, in general, be obtained ("identified" is the technical term) from observations unless some restrictions are assumed *a priori*. Without sufficient restrictions an infinity of structures may be consistent with a given set of observations.

An important type of such prior restrictions is this: For a given i, the function ϕ_i is independent of $y_k(t - \lambda)$, $z_j(t - \mu)$ $(k = 1, \ldots, n; j = 1, \ldots, m)$ except for a few specified pairs (k, λ), (j, μ). For example, if ϕ_i is linear, all its coefficients are zero, except a few specified ones. Thus the builders' supply of housing will depend, among a few other things, on the interest rate charged on their borrowings, with a time lag (determined by construction technology, customs, and legal regulations) which is ascertainable from experts. The consumers' demand for housing depends on other things, with other time lags. Some of these lags are well known, others very little known.

I submit that very often economists have made more, or stronger, prior assumptions than can be justified by solid knowledge or are needed to make the model identifiable. For example, in many economic models the assumed lags are the first few integers (in years or months). Such arbitrary choice may be quite unrealistic. The choice of time lags not ascertainable from other sources should, at least in part, become a matter of estimation from observed time sequences instead of being imposed *a priori*.

It may be useful to refer here to recent exciting applications of spectral analysis to economics. These have not been concerned, so far, with estimating economic "structures" needed to predict effects of certain policies. To use my earlier phrase, they "assign future validity to the patterns of the past" and have neglected the use of much of available economic "prior knowledge." On the other hand, spectral analysis might help to do away with the unrealistic time lags so cavalierly chosen by practicing econometricians. The frequencies of the major component oscillations of endogenous variables (given the exogenous ones), which can presumably be revealed by such analysis, should be closely related to the prevailing time lags. Is there a way to combine "prior knowledge" of economic models with techniques of spectral analysis?

The historical nature of data is not peculiar to economics alone: consider meteorology. Nor is the stress on policy applications: consider engineering. That these two features occur together is somewhat more distinctive for, though still not unique to, economics. Only by following in detail a book like the present one can we get the peculiar flavor.

One of the merits of the book is its patient use of examples, introducing difficulties step by step. Some methodological problems arise when the simplest economic theory of the freshman classroom (nonstochastic statics) is confronted with available, though generously simplified, facts. New problems of method are added as we ascend to more complex and realistic theories (stochastic dynamics). The reader is then introduced to methods of classical statistical inference. These were developed for the most part in sampling studies outside of economics, and the nature of economic data and tasks creates additional problems (identification, structural estimation, predictive tests) which may not have been noted yet may well arise, and in fact have arisen, in other disciplines. The book should be of great interest to economists. It should also interest students of scientific method applied to nonexperimental data for practical decision purposes, a problem that arises especially, but not exclusively, in social sciences.

I believe the reader will agree that the book reveals the author's exceptional gift of exposition, his experience in matters economic, and his intimate insight into the student's difficulties.

JACOB MARSCHAK

Los Angeles, California
August 1966

PREFACE

Econometrics is a wide and growing field. The aim of this book is not to cover it all, but rather to give the persevering reader a feeling for what econometrics is like and a technical understanding of some of its important models and methods.

Part One (Chapters I–II) is a simple introduction, designed to illustrate most of the main issues in the book in a not very technical manner. A familiar economic example, the effects of an excise tax, is studied.

Part Two (Chapters III–VI) discusses theoretical econometric models, working up from static exact models to dynamic stochastic ones. Empirical work is discussed hardly at all in Part Two.

Part Three (Chapters VII–XI) deals with empirical methods in econometrics, especially with the identification of econometric parameters, statistical estimation, and statistical testing. The last chapter presents a simple illustrative empirical model of the United States economy, with four stochastic equations and three definitions.

Each of the three parts is reasonably self-contained, except that Parts Two and Three make use of some terms defined earlier. Cross references and the index will be helpful in locating relevant definitions. There are questions and problems at the end of each chapter.

Econometrics requires a working knowledge of at least the fundamentals of differential calculus, statistical inference, and matrix algebra. Although the book provides elementary material on these three subjects (in Chapters III, IV, VIII, and Appendix A), there is no pretense that prior knowledge of them is unnecessary. Still, if your knowledge of these

xiii

areas is not too rusty, you should be able to understand the book—if you work at it.

A reader cannot interrupt an author to ask a question. Sometimes, if he could, the answer would be "I'm coming to that." The moral for the reader is that if something is not clear, it is wise to try reading a little further on, or looking in the index, before going back over the difficult passage for the nth time.

I have tried to use a consistent notation throughout the book and to avoid using the same symbol with different meanings in different places. The Latin and Greek alphabets are too short to permit complete success in this endeavor. Where a notation is strictly temporary for a limited context, I have tried to remember to say so. The main principles of notation used are described on pages xxi–xxiii.

The book has many weaknesses of which I am keenly aware, and perhaps more besides. The treatment is at best thin on cross-section studies. There is practically nothing on errors-in-variables models, and nothing on analysis of variance and covariance or on spectral analysis. Mathematical elegance and succinctness have been sacrificed in the quest for interpretive explanation. And so on.

My debts are great. Many economists have helped, too many to mention, either by reading parts of the manuscript or by discussing relevant points, or both. Jacob Marschak suggested the writing of the book, and the many hours he invested in plans and in discussing the early drafts were immensely helpful. He and Tjalling Koopmans taught me much of what I know of econometrics. Koopmans critically read and commented on most of the manuscript. William C. Hood, Marc Nerlove, and John Hooper read the whole manuscript and made many helpful suggestions. James Tobin, Roy Radner, Arnold Harberger, Zvi Griliches, and Curry Gillmore read substantial parts of it and made very useful comments. David Wallace taught me some important points in statistical theory.

Some of the early work was done under a Fulbright Senior Research Fellowship at the Department of Applied Economics, Cambridge, England, and further work was done under a Fellowship at the Center for Advanced Study in the Behavioral Sciences, Stanford, California. The Cowles Foundation for Research in Economics, as a sponsor of the book, provided secretarial and other assistance and arranged for its refereeing. Faithful and skillful typing was done by the Cowles Foundation staff, especially Gloria Turner, Mary M. Stevens, and Mary Markiza, and by Angela Lavarello and Susan Carlin of The Johns Hopkins University. Bibliographical assistance was rendered by Miriam Gallaher and Roger Norton. Computing assistance was given by John Gilbert and Martin Levin. Miss Sarah Redwine did an excellent job as editor. My wife helped with the reading of proof, and my daughter Joan substituted briefly in that task. Unfortunately, there are likely to be some remaining errors, either of substance or typography; the responsibility for them is of course mine.

I hope that readers of this book will experience at least some of the challenge and satisfaction that I have felt in writing it.

CARL F. CHRIST

Baltimore, Maryland
August 1966

Contents

Notation Used in This Book

I have tried to use a consistent notation throughout this book. My original aim was to give no symbol two different meanings in two contexts, but there are not enough Greek and Latin letters to accomplish this without even more subscripts, superscripts, carets, type faces, and so forth, than already grace these pages. At least the most important symbols are almost always used with the same meaning throughout, and I have attempted to warn the reader whenever a symbol is given a meaning that will not be used later on.

The following principles generally apply, but there are exceptions. Below the principles is a list of commonly used symbols with their meanings.

1. Boldface capitals denote matrices, and boldface unprimed lower-case letters denote row vectors. Lightface letters denote scalars. The element in row r and column c of a matrix $\mathbf{A}$ is a_{rc}. If one subscript is to stand for time, the *second* one is used for that, that is, z_{kt} is the value of z_k at time t.

2. In economic contexts (especially Chapters II–VI and XI), capitals denote quantities in *money* terms, and lower-case letters denote quantities in *real* terms. The initial letter of the name of an economic concept is often chosen to symbolize it, for example, c for consumption (but note y for income).

3. Sans serif type is used to denote the deviation of an observation from its sample mean, for example, $\mathsf{y}_t = y_t - \bar{y}$, and $\mathbf{z}_t = \mathbf{z}_t - \bar{\mathbf{z}}$. This usage occurs in VI.3, VIII.5, IX.3-4, and X.7.

4. Greek letters usually refer to parameters or functions. Estimators are usually denoted by the corresponding Latin letter, or by the Greek

letter with some distinguishing mark such as a caret. Thus estimators of α may be denoted by a or $\hat{\alpha}$ or $\tilde{\alpha}$. Among the exceptions are:

δ: in x^δ, the deviation of x from equilibrium as in V.3.

δ: in δ^2/S^2, a serial correlation statistic, as in X.4.

δ: the Kronecker delta, as in X.7.21.

δ: the error of an estimate, as in X.8.11.

Δ: the first difference operator, as in V.3 ff.

ϵ: in x^ϵ, the equilibrium value of x, as in V.3.

ϵ: a probability in the tail of a distribution, as in X.1 ff.

λ: a limited-information test statistic, as in IX.9.

$\sum$: the summation operator as in III.10 ff.

χ^2: the chi-square statistic as in X.1 ff.

5. Latin letters usually refer to observable or unobservable variables (including disturbances), estimators and other statistics, or arbitrary constants. In abstract mathematical or statistical contexts (especially Chapters VIII–XI), disturbances are usually symbolized by u or v, and other variables by x or y or z. Among the exceptions are:

d: the differentiation operator.

e: in x^e, the future expected value of x, as in V.7.

E: the mathematical expectation operator, as in IV.2 ff.

L: the logarithmic likelihood function, as in IX.6.

SOME SYMBOLS COMMONLY USED IN THIS BOOK

GREEK LETTERS   REFERENCE

$\beta, \gamma, \mathbf{B}, \boldsymbol{\Gamma}$	structural coefficients	III.10, IX.2
Δ	first difference operator	V.3
λ	limited-information test statistic	IX.9.18
$\boldsymbol{\Lambda}$	covariance of dependent disturbances	IX.5.7
$\pi, \boldsymbol{\Pi}$	reduced-form coefficients	III.10, IX.2
π or $\underline{\pi}$	ratio of circumference to diameter	IX.3.24
ρ	correlation parameter	IV.3
$\sigma, \boldsymbol{\Sigma}$	structural disturbance variances and covariances	IX.2, IX.6
$\sum$	summation operator	III.10
χ^2	chi-square statistic	X.1
$\omega, \boldsymbol{\Omega}$	reduced-form disturbance variances and covariances	IX.2

LATIN LETTERS

d	differentiation operator	III.5
d	Durbin-Watson statistic	X.4.8
E	mathematical expectation	IV.2
F	F statistic	X.1
G, H	number of jointly dependent variables in the model and in the equation in question	VIII.3.28
$\mathbf{I}$ or $\mathbf{I}_K$	identity matrix (of order K)	A.1
J, K	number of predetermined variables in the equation in question and in the model	VIII.3.28
k	k-class estimator parameter	IX.10.15
l	variance ratio for limited information	IX.9.13
$m, \mathbf{M}$	moments	VI.3, IX.4
r, R	simple and multiple correlation	X.3
t	Student's t statistic	X.3
t	time	V
T	sample size	IX.2
u	structural equation disturbance	IV.4, IX.2
v	reduced-form equation disturbance	IV.4, IX.2
$\mathbf{X}'$	least-squares reduced-form estimate of $(\mathbf{Y}' \quad \mathbf{Z}^{*\prime})$	IX.10.7
$y, \mathbf{y}, \mathbf{Y}$	jointly dependent variables	III.10, IX.2
$z, \mathbf{z}, \mathbf{Z}$	predetermined variables	III.10, IX.2

MODIFIED LETTERS

$f'(x)$	df/dx	III.5
$\mathbf{z}'$ or $\mathbf{Z}'$	transpose of $\mathbf{z}$ or $\mathbf{Z}$	A.1
$\mathbf{z}^*$	z's in the equation in question	IX.9
$\mathbf{z}^{**}$	z's in the model but not in the equation in question	IX.9
$\bar{z}$	sample mean of z	IX.3
$\mathbf{z}_t$	$z_t - \bar{z}$	VI.3
$\mathbf{Z}$	$\mathbf{Z} - \bar{\mathbf{Z}}$	A.1.20
$m^0, \mathbf{M}^0$	moments about zero	IX.4
$\hat{u}, \hat{v}$	calculated disturbances	IX.1
$\hat{y}, \hat{\mathbf{y}}, \hat{\mathbf{Y}}$	calculated values of $y, \mathbf{y}, \mathbf{Y}$	IX.1
$\hat{\beta}$	estimator of β (often denotes maximum-likelihood estimator)	IX.3, IX.9
$\beta^{(k)}$	k-class estimator of β	IX.10.15

Part One

Making the Acquaintance
of Econometrics

CHAPTER I

Econometrics:
Definitions, Objectives, and Approaches

This chapter offers a definition of econometrics, discusses some desirable properties of the economic propositions that econometrics seeks to produce, introduces the general approach to be developed in the book, calls attention to the nonrigorous character of applied econometrics, and introduces some basic concepts including structure and endogenous and exogenous variables.

1 WHAT IS ECONOMETRICS?

1.1 Three leading economists, Samuelson, Koopmans, and Stone, in a report about the journal *Econometrica*, have ably described econometrics as follows:[1]

> ...econometrics may be defined as the quantitative analysis of actual economic phenomena based on the concurrent development of theory and observation, related by appropriate methods of inference.
>
> ...econometrics is a branch of economics....
>
> Without attempting here to define economics, we can say that it is concerned with the study of certain aspects of the actual world of our experience just as is physics or biology. Studies of this kind may be undertaken for their own sake, that is, to obtain a better understanding of the phenomena in question, or to assist in the evaluation, construction, or implementation of

---

[1] Samuelson, Koopmans, and Stone [1954], pp. 141–142. Throughout this book, references to items in the bibliography will be made by means of a date in brackets following the author's name, such as [1954] in this footnote.

3

policy, in Pigou's phrase "for light or for fruit." However this may be, systematic investigation involves certain more or less distinct types of intellectual activity. One of these consists in the development of appropriate concepts and theories in terms of which observable phenomena can be described, classified, and related. This activity, mainly economic theory, results in statements about theoretical counterparts of actual phenomena, which statements may, in principle, be shown by experience to be false or to stand in need of modification. A distinct part of this theory construction, related to applications of economic analysis to policy problems, aims at logical clarification (but not advocation) of ethical precepts or policy objectives.

A second form of intellectual activity consists in the systematic collection of information about actual phenomena and the construction of empirical correlates to theoretical concepts. This activity, descriptive economics and economic statistics, results in a body of observational knowledge against which theories may be checked and from which parameters may be estimated. A third form consists in devising suitable methods which will permit the theories and observations to be related, statements to be made as to the extent to which observations support a belief in the theories and the estimation of the strength of the influence of one variable on another. This activity, drawing mainly on mathematical statistics in the present context, results in a body of tools the purpose of which is to make possible the drawing of inferences about actual economic behavior.

2 OBJECTIVES OF ECONOMETRICS

2.1 In this book the objective of econometrics is taken to be the production of quantitative economic statements that either *explain* the behavior of variables that we have already seen, or *forecast* (i.e., *predict*) behavior that we have not yet seen, or both. (We shall use the terms "forecast" and "prediction" interchangeably to refer to statements about behavior that has not yet been observed by the maker of the statements at the time the statements are made, whether the behavior in question is future behavior, or whether it is past behavior that simply has not been observed yet; an example is the statement that the pyramid of Cheops has another as yet undiscovered chamber.) Such quantitative statements are usually in the form of equations or inequalities, with numerically specified coefficients.[2] There are several desirable properties that we would like our equations to have. They may be called relevance, simplicity, theoretical plausibility, explanatory ability, accuracy of coefficients, and forecasting ability. Sometimes these are mutually exclusive to some extent.

1. *Relevance.* An economic equation should be relevant to an

---

[2] Of course there are many competent studies that do not use equations or inequalities explicitly, that are still econometrics by the definition given above. For two interesting examples, see Tinbergen [1938] and Rees [1951].

important or interesting problem, and not simply a toy that gives intellectual pleasure and nothing else.

2. *Simplicity*. An economic equation should be simple enough so that its meaning can be understood and so that logical and analytical operations can be performed with it. The principle of Occam's razor may be recalled here.

3. *Theoretical plausibility*. If the immediate objective is to make a decision about a real economic problem, for instance, to decide on the selling price of a good or to choose a fiscal policy, then the equation used should be consistent with (plausible in the light of) the relevant parts of well established economic theory. On the other hand, if the immediate objective is to seek truth by testing economic theory, the equations used should be consistent with whatever feature of economic theory we wish to test, be it well established or new and tentative. In either case, it is usually desirable to deal with equations that express or at least are consistent with relevant parts of economic theory.

4. *Explanatory ability*. We prefer equations that are consistent also with available relevant economic data. There is sometimes room for dispute as to whether a given set of data is relevant for a given equation. Clearly it will not do to define as relevant to an equation only those data that are consistent with it. And clearly also an equation is better, other things being equal, the wider the range of data that it can explain.

5. *Accuracy of coefficients*. It is also desirable that our knowledge of the coefficients of the equations be accurate. This is important whenever the value of some one coefficient is critical for the problem being considered, as for example when we want to know the effect of a price change on the quantity demanded.

6. *Forecasting ability*. Perhaps more than anything else, we want equations that can forecast the future. For this purpose "the future" should be interpreted to include anything unknown to the forecaster when he did his work; thus a person might "forecast" some aspect of nineteenth century behavior by means of theory and data derived solely from the twentieth century. The latter sort of forecasting, that is, of temporally past data, can be useful for testing theories,[3] but of course practical interest centers on forecasting the temporal future.

2.2 There are fairly adequate ways, at least in principle, to tell whether the first five desirable properties are present in an equation or not. *Relevance* and *simplicity* are mainly matters of judgment.

2.3 *Consistency with economic theory* is essentially a matter of logic, and as such should be amenable to unambiguous standard tests. But there is much room for error here, as a simple but important example may show.

[3] Provided that when the forecaster did his work he was *really* ignorant of the data to be forecast; see below, in X.6.

Most economists would have said "yes" in 1940 or 1945 if you had asked them whether the following consumption function was consistent with good economic theory:

$$(2.1) \qquad\qquad c_t = \alpha + \beta y_t + u_t$$

where α and β are constant parameters,[4] c_t and y_t are respectively real consumption and real disposable income in year t, and u_t is a random variable called a disturbance (the meaning of the disturbance is explained more fully in later chapters). In fact, many econometric studies were done using just such an equation.[5] When all such studies vastly underestimated the level of consumption in the United States after World War II, more work was done, and substantial improvements were made by Modigliani and Brumberg [1954] and by Friedman [1957] when they changed the interpretation of the income variable from *current* income to a sort of long-range *expected* income concept. Once proposed, the step seems obvious. All economists know that expectations are very important. Yet consumption was regarded as a function of current disposal income for a long time by many economists. This example may help to convince readers that in practice it is not so easy to make sure that econometric equations are consistent with the relevant economic theory.

2.4 For deciding whether an equation is *consistent with a set of data* many techniques are available. Often used is the correlation coefficient. Others involve comparing actual and calculated values of variables at crucial points, such as cyclical turning points. For deciding on the *accuracy of numerical coefficients*, a common method is a statistical test of significance based on the estimated standard deviation of the estimator of the coefficient. These will be discussed in some detail later, especially in Chapter X.

2.5 But it is never possible to tell whether an equation will describe *future* data well or not. For as soon as some "future" data come to us, they are no longer *future* data, and we simply have a larger collection of *available* data against which to try the equation. This may seem sophistical, but it is important to realize that we can never have absolutely certain scientific knowledge about the future. In Chapter X we shall again take up the question of what we can learn from the success or the failure of forecasts.

3 TOOLS AND METHODS OF ECONOMETRICS

3.1 As suggested by the foregoing paragraphs, there are tools that can help economists in the search for equations having the desirable

---

[4] Defined in 5.3 below.

[5] I was guilty too; see Christ [1951].

properties mentioned. But none of these tools is a complete substitute for a good idea as to how economic reality works. This of course is true of the celebrated scientific method itself, for the scientific method is a systematic way of following through and evaluating hypotheses, and not fundamentally a way of arriving at hypotheses. This book is mainly about the tools of econometrics and their use.

3.2 One important tool in econometrics is mathematics, used deductively for stating hypotheses and exploring their logical implications. Chapter III and parts of Chapters IV to VI are devoted to this subject, in an elementary fashion. Another important tool is statistical inference used inductively for getting information from a limited number of cases or observations. It is discussed mainly in Chapters VII to X. Statistical inference proceeds, in its classical form, by starting from some set of statements, often called *a priori knowledge* or the *model*[6] or the *maintained hypothesis*, which is accepted as correct and not questioned during the subsequent inference process. Then data are observed, and with the aid of these data and the maintained hypothesis and probability theory, inferences are drawn about the nature of the world. If probability theory is to be used, the model or maintained hypothesis must at least say that the data were selected by a random process. It must say more besides if much is to be learned. This suggests the following kind of attack on an econometric problem (we shall see presently that this kind of attack is not quite suitable):

(1) State the problem clearly.
(2) Choose an appropriate model or maintained hypothesis to use for this problem.
(3) Observe relevant data.
(4) Using statistical inference techniques based on the maintained hypothesis, draw inferences about the problem from the data.

3.3 This kind of attack would be fine if the correct model or maintained hypothesis were known. In actual econometric practice it is typically impossible to find a sufficiently specific model or maintained hypothesis that we can believe with certainty. The main source of maintained hypotheses in econometrics is economic theory. At best, economic theory can specify what conceptual variables appear in an equation, and sometimes certain homogeneity properties of the equation, and perhaps something about the algebraic signs and sizes of certain partial derivatives. For example, we learn from theory that the quantity of most consumer goods demanded is an increasing function of the demander's current and

---

[6] More about the meaning of the important term "model" will be found in II.1.14, II.2.7, and IV.4.4. The third place contains the definition to be used in the rest of the book.

expected income and of his marketable wealth, and a decreasing function of its own current price, and that it may depend on its own expected price, on the current and expected prices of close substitutes or complements, and on interest rates. We also learn that the demand function should be homogeneous of degree zero in all money incomes and money wealth and money prices; that is, if the general price level were to change and all money magnitudes were to change with it including expectations, in such a way that all opportunities in real terms remained the same, there would be no change in the quantity demanded. But we often do not learn whether the function is linear in real income and relative prices, or linear in their logarithms, or quadratic, or exponential, or of some other form. As suggested by the consumption example in 2.3 above, we do not always learn what empirical data should be used to represent the conceptual variables that are to be included. And we often do not learn whether certain variables of perhaps secondary importance should be included or not. The situation is similar with supply equations, production functions, and other kinds of economic relationships.

3.4 In this situation the economist has several choices. He can give up. The large number of pages remaining in this book suggests that this is not my recommendation. He can somehow choose *one* reasonable form of the equation, on grounds that are in part neither theoretical nor empirical, and use it with relevant data to draw inferences. Or he can try out several different theoretically reasonable forms, in a sort of experimental fashion, confronting each one with relevant data, and then choose among them after he sees how well they fit the data. The last choice is preferable because it offers some more or less objective grounds for preferring one form of an equation to other forms that are about equally reasonable from a theoretical standpoint.

3.5 This experimental approach has dangers, however. First if several forms of an equation appear theoretically reasonable to begin with (i.e., before we have looked at the data), and if the one is selected that fits the available data best according to some rule, then the classical statistical inference procedures do not apply *to those same data* without some adjustment. This is because these classical procedures assume that the maintained hypothesis (which includes the form of the equation) is *known* with certainty, whereas in the experimental procedure that we are discussing the "maintained hypothesis" is *not* known with certainty, but is chosen because it fits the data better than the other maintained hypotheses that have been suggested by *a priori* theory. The effect is essentially as if a systematic nonrandom factor were introduced into the process for selecting samples, that is, as if only those samples that fit the data unusually well were used. Therefore if the classical statistical tests are applied to the same data, we shall too often conclude that the equation is correct, unless some adjustment in the test procedure is made. Often the appropriately adjusted statistical test is not known.

3.6 A second danger in the experimental method is related to the one just discussed. It concerns the problem of how we decide when to stop hunting for additional maintained hypotheses to try out experimentally against the data. Suppose that, to begin with, theoretical considerations have suggested three different possible forms for an economic equation. Assume first that one of these turns out to fit the available data extremely well. Then there is little incentive to look for others. Now assume instead that none of the three forms of the equation fits the data very well. Then there is a strong incentive to look for others. If an economist is clever enough or persistent enough, he can always find an equation that fits the available data fairly well; he may also convince himself that it is a theoretically reasonable equation. The danger lies in the possibility of being too clever or too persistent, and finding an equation that fits the available data well enough but is nevertheless wrong because it describes temporary or accidental features of the available data, rather than the enduring systematic features. (See II.2.2 below for an extreme example of a perfect fit that is wrong.) The best protection we can have against this danger is to test our equations against data that could not have influenced the choice of the equations. The surest way to do this is to use for the test data that we had not seen or known about when we chose the form of the equation. This matter is discussed further in X.6.

4 TWO REALMS IN ECONOMETRICS

4.1 It is important to notice that there are two distinct realms in econometrics, one consisting of a rigorous body of postulates and theorems in mathematical economics and mathematical statistics, and the other consisting of a collection of practical studies of the nature of real economic behavior. Let us call them the rigorous and the applied realms, respectively.

4.2 In the rigorous realm the work and the atmosphere are those of mathematics. Mathematical arguments concerning the logical consequences of assumptions, or the logical conditions necessary for the deduction of certain conclusions, are the stock in trade. A typical theorem, for example, about which we shall hear much in the statistical chapters, concerns assumptions under which the least-squares estimation method yields unbiased estimators of economic parameters.[7] Logic is the main tool used, and except for errors in logic there can be no disagreement about the validity of the propositions found there. (Of course there may be

[7] The least-squares method is described in Chapter IX and unbiasedness is defined in VII.6.2.

disagreement about the *usefulness* of propositions found there, but that already begins to enter the applied realm.)

4.3 In the applied realm the work and the atmosphere are those of any empirical science. The theorems of the rigorous realm are imported into the applied realm and used, but they do not carry the same force here, because here we are interested in whether a statement corresponds to observations about the real world, not simply in whether it follows logically from a given set of premises. When conclusions of theorems from the rigorous realm are carried into the applied realm, they become like guaranteed products that have been used counter to the manufacturer's instructions so that the guarantee no longer holds. The instructions, of course, in this case say "not guaranteed unless used in a situation where the premises are known to be correct." As indicated above, we can never be certain about our maintained hypotheses, and hence we must be ready when necessary to revise them. In the history of econometrics, the transition from the continual use of the least-squares method to the awareness that the so-called simultaneous-equations method are often better is based on such a revision, as will be seen below. Empirical observation plays a central role in the applied realm; while it plays no role in the rigorous realm (except to influence people's choices about what problems to work on and people's intuitions about what theorems may be logically valid). The typical output of the applied realm is a statement about real economic behavior, such as "the price elasticity of total demand for automobiles in the United States in the 1950's was about unity." There can be and sometimes is substantial disagreement about the validity of such propositions, even apart from purely logical errors, because different economists can have different views about what maintained hypothesis is best to use. These differences have narrowed and become negligible in some areas of economics and will continue to do so in others as our knowledge advances. In principle, however, the possibility of such disagreements exists, and there may well be further revolutions in store for us in the applied realm of econometrics.

4.4 This book's pages will be devoted largely to the rigorous realm of econometrics because many important tools are to be found there, but the main interest centers on the applied realm. We shall try to bridge the gap between the two wherever we can.

5 ENDOGENOUS AND EXOGENOUS VARIABLES, STRUCTURE, AND OTHER CONCEPTS

5.1 *Time-series* studies are those based on data coming from the same entity (e.g., the United States) for several periods of time such as months, quarters, and years. It is usual but not necessary for the observations to be successive and equally spaced in time. *Cross-section* studies are those based on data coming from several different members of a population at the same time, such as individual families or firms, industries, and political or geographic subdivisions. Some studies combine time-series and cross-section data,[8] and these of course are richer in data than either time-series or cross-section studies alone.

5.2   Most predictions or forecasts are based in part on empirical observations. In a time-series study the period from which these observations come is called the *observation period* or the *sample period*. The period from which predictions are made is called the *prediction period* or the *forecast period*. It will be convenient to use this same terminology to refer to cross-section studies, and in that case the word "period" will be understood to refer to the set of individuals, firms, regions, or what not that make up the cross section in question. This convention cannot be used in studies that combine time series and cross sections, because then the word "period" is needed to refer explicitly to time; the context will tell whether this convention is being used.

5.3   During a typical period there are changes in some of the economic phenomena being studied, such as prices, outputs, sales, inventories, interest rates, investment, planned investment for the future, consumption, government purchases, tax rates, and subsidies, or sometimes changes in more fundamental economic realities such as consumer tastes, technological knowledge, and known available natural resources. But there are also certain underlying features of the economy that do not change during the same period. [Of course, some of the features that do not change during one period may change during another. For example, the effective Federal income tax rate in the United States was constant (at a level of zero) from 1873 through 1912, but it has been changed every few years since then.] The features of the problem being studied that do change during a period will be called *variables*, and the whole complex of features that do not change will be called the *economic structure* or often simply the *structure*.[9] Numerical constants characterizing the structure are called *structural parameters*. Some parameters of the structure and some variables are observable, and some are not. As we shall see, attention usually centers on discovering the numerical values of unobservable parameters of the structure or the numerical values of certain functions of them. Unobservable variables create difficulties, which are usually dealt with by

---

[8] See, for example, Meyer and Kuh [1957], a study of investment by industry and over time.

[9] It will be necessary to amplify this important definition somewhat, but the meaning given here is sufficient for the present. See II.1.13, II.2.7, and (for the definition to be used throughout the rest of the book) IV.4.2.

assuming that something is known about their behavior so that we can do without observing them. The device of using random variables as disturbances is of this type; it will be dealt with below.

5.4   It is clear from these definitions that we cannot tell which are the variables and which are the parameters of the structure, until we know what problem and what period are being discussed. For example, if the income tax rate entered any problem, it would be a parameter of the structure for periods chosen from the years 1873–1912, but it would be a variable for periods that include any years after 1912 (unless the period were so short that the rate was not changed during the period, in which case it would again be a parameter of the structure). It is also clear that when we say some particular feature (e.g., the demand elasticity) is a parameter of the structure for a certain period (e.g., 1950–1960), we are implicitly including in our maintained hypothesis the assumption that the demand elasticity was constant during the period. If we believe the demand elasticity changed during the period, we should use a maintained hypothesis that permits this, but then the elasticity itself will not be a structural parameter.[10]

5.5   In one sense consumption expenditure is one variable, and income is another variable. Then the income of a certain spending unit in a certain year is one observation of the variable "income," and the income of that spending unit in a different year (or of a different spending unit in the same or a different year) is another observation of the variable "income." The variables thought of in this sense[11] in any econometric problem (other than the random disturbances) will be divided into two groups. The first group includes those variables whose values or levels are required to be explained or predicted, and the second group those whose values or levels are not required to be explained or predicted, because they can be assumed to be determined and known in advance in such a way that they can be regarded as fixed when we analyze the factors determining the variables to be explained or predicted. The first group will be called *endogenous* variables and the second group *exogenous* variables,[12] from the Greek meaning "generated from inside" and

---

[10] More discussion of this point will appear later, but a simple example may be suggestive here. If the demand equation is $q = \beta_0 + \beta_1 p$, where q and p are quantity and price and β_0 and β_1 are constant parameters of the structure, then the elasticity of demand is $\beta_1 p/q$, which is not constant.

[11] In a second sense, to be discussed later, income of a certain spending unit in a certain year is one variable, and income of that same spending unit in *another* year is *another* variable. To anticipate, the concept of a predetermined variable applies to variables in this second sense. See V.3.8 and VI.4.3.

[12] This definition of exogenous variables must be revised somewhat when random variables are introduced into the models. The revised definition, which will be used throughout the rest of the book, appears in IV.4.9. Variables not exogenous are endogenous.

"generated from outside." For example, imagine a theory that claims to be able to make a conditional prediction of national income for next year, given the magnitudes for next year of investment, government purchases, and tax receipts. Then in such a theory national income is an *endogenous variable*; each of the quantities investment, government purchases, and tax receipts is either an *exogenous variable* or a *parameter of the structure*, depending on whether it has varied or stayed constant during the observation period chosen. Any other features of the economy that did not change during the observation period, such as perhaps the marginal propensity to consume, also are parameters of the structure.

5.6 We can now consider two important classes of prediction problems. In one class, called prediction under *unchanged structure*, are all problems in which the structure in the prediction period is the same as in the observation period, that is, the features that do not change during the observation period also do not change during the combined observation and prediction periods. In the other class, called prediction under *changed structure*, are all problems in which the structure changes between the observation and prediction periods, so that the structure in the prediction period is not the same as in the observation period. The difference between the two cases is fundamentally important. In prediction under *unchanged structure*, predictions are to be made about a process that has already been observed in operation. The effect of the exogenous variables upon the endogenous variables (which are the ones we want to explain or predict) can then be deduced from the data of the observation period and applied to the prediction period, so that conditional predictions of the endogenous variables (conditional upon the values of the exogenous variables and the validity of the structure used, that is) can be made. In prediction under *changed structure*, on the other hand, predictions are to be made about a process that (because of the structural change) has some feature(s) that have never been observed before; hence the problem is more difficult. (To anticipate a bit: We shall find that in general it is insoluble unless we know something about the structure before the change and about the character of the change itself.)[13]

5.7 An interesting story[14] of predictions under changed and unchanged structure deals with two students (one a mathematician) who went to Reno a few years ago with $120 and a theory that every roulette wheel has an individuality and slightly prefers some patterns of numbers to others. The students chose a wheel in a casino and observed it continuously for 4 days, spelling each other in shifts so as not to miss anything, and recording the winning number on each spin. This was their observation

[13] See on this topic Marschak [1947] and [1953].

[14] *Time*, Vol. L, No. 22 (December 1, 1947), p. 64. This story illustrates the point in the text, and has the further virtue of showing the possibility of prediction in the case of random events.

period; there were no exogenous variables. On the fifth day they began to bet on the wheel—that is, to predict its behavior. This was prediction under unchanged structure: They were making their predictions about the same wheel that they had observed. After 40 hours of continuous betting, when the $120 had grown to $6000, the casino management introduced a change of structure by replacing the wheel head, and of course the two students were then unable to predict any more.

QUESTIONS AND PROBLEMS

1. Make a case for the proposition that input-output analysis should be regarded as a part of econometrics. Make a case for the opposite proposition.

2. Can you cite examples from the history of economics to show that the attainment of greater simplicity in economic theory does not always result in poorer explanatory ability or decreased relevance?

3. Give several examples of a maintained hypothesis in econometrics, and for each indicate the degree of your confidence in its correctness and the basis upon which that confidence rests.

4. State several economic generalizations about the real world that are supported by empirical evidence, and for each indicate the degree of its certainty and the basis therefor.

5. Can you think of a commodity whose price, in an econometric analysis of its market, is an exogenous variable? Explain.

CHAPTER II

A "Guided Tour" of the Book

This chapter uses a simple economic problem, that of predicting the effects of an excise tax, to exhibit and explore briefly the most important stages of econometric analysis to be treated in the book. Exact and stochastic models, structures, and reduced forms are encountered, as well as the identification concept, prediction under unchanged structure and under changed structure, and the need to re-examine the model when the opportunity arises.

1 A FIRST APPROACH TO A SIMPLE EXCISE-TAX PROBLEM: EXACT EQUATIONS, STRUCTURE, MODEL, AND REDUCED FORM

1.1 When we approach a new subject, it is useful to have an overall view of what it is like, and what are its parts, its important problems, and its main techniques. It is the purpose of this chapter to provide at least a nodding acquaintance with the framework and subject matter of this book. Here we shall examine a familiar simplified excise-tax problem, stripped of many details but still containing most of the important common features of real econometric problems. Using this simplified problem as a vehicle, and using many of the concepts of Chapter I, we shall take a short guided tour of econometrics, carrying the problem at least part way through each of the most important stages of analysis to be treated in the book, without attempting to be rigorous or general. After completing this guided tour, we shall enter upon each type of analysis in some detail in succeeding chapters. Most of this chapter proceeds as if the *a priori*

15

information used were correct, but there will be opportunities for noticing whether data confirm it or cast doubt on it and make its revision desirable.

1.2 The problem we shall discuss is finding what the numerical values of the quantity sold and price will be for a competitively marketed commodity, after an excise tax of E dollars per unit is imposed upon the sellers.[1] We assume, as economists usually do, that the slope is positive for the supply curve and negative for the demand curve. This problem is a familiar one: As compared with the situation when there is no tax, the supply curve is shifted a distance E upward along the vertical price axis, and therefore the price will rise by some amount between zero and E dollars per unit, and the quantity sold will fall, as shown below in Figure 1.1, Section 1.7. The price rise will be greater, and the tax will thus be more completely paid by the buyers, if supply is gently sloping and demand is steeply sloping than if not, and the fall in quantity sold will be greater if both are gently sloping than if not. We deliberately choose such a familiar problem, because it is the econometric approach on which we want to concentrate just now, not the particular problem chosen for illustration.

1.3 We are setting the task of predicting price and quantity sold, conditional upon the excise-tax rate imposed. Hence, using our definitions from I.5.3–5, price and quantity are endogenous variables, and the excise tax rate E is either an exogenous variable or a parameter of the structure, depending on whether it has varied or has remained constant during the observation period used. We shall presently divide the problem into two cases, one corresponding to each of these alternatives. In the first case E is exogenous, having varied during the observation period; here no change of structure is involved at all. In the second case E has been constant (at some rate other than that for which predictions are wanted) during the observation period, and hence is a parameter of the structure by definition; then the change in the rate of the tax represents a change of structure, and the problem is to make a prediction for the period following this change of structure. Of course there are many other types of structural change whose effects might be studied, besides the imposition of an excise tax: changes in consumer preference, decreases in cost due to discovery of new natural resources or new techniques, increases in cost due to political stoppage of imports of raw materials, and so forth. Some of these structural changes are of the sort that can be numerically expressed *before* they happen (such as an excise-tax rate), and some are not. The influence of the latter type, of course, cannot always be predicted quantitatively, but it can often be predicted in *direction* at least. However, we shall confine ourselves in this chapter to the excise-tax rate.

[1] It would also be possible to inquire about the revenue raised by the tax, or the effects on profits in the industry. We shall not go into these questions in the guided tour.

1.4 A straightforward approach to this excise-tax problem is to cast it in terms of the economic theory of supply and demand, and then to pass from that stage to some kind of usable formula that will relate the quantity sold and price of the commodity to the excise-tax rate E. This we shall proceed to do.

1.5 In the interests of simplicity, we shall specify that the demand and supply curves for the commodity are straight lines, that is, that their equations are linear, and also that they are static, that time does not enter at all.[2] We assume that the equations hold exactly, without error or approximation.[3] We assume that the market is cleared, and as said earlier we assume the usual directions of slope: positive for the supply curve and negative for the demand curve. It must be emphasized that these assumptions are made in part because of their plausibility and in part because of their convenience. Later analysis will depend critically on them; and if the empirical results obtained with their aid are not satisfactory, these assumptions must be changed. If we let q^s stand for quantity supplied, q for quantity demanded, p for price, E for excise-tax rate per unit, and Greek letters for the unknown but constant parameters of the equations (we sometimes call these *coefficients*), then we have three equations in the three unknown variables q^s, q, and p:

(1.1) $q^s = \alpha_0 + \alpha_1(p - E)$ $\alpha_1 > 0$

(1.2) $q = \beta_0 + \beta_1 p$ $\beta_1 < 0, \beta_0 > 0, \beta_0 > \alpha_0, \alpha_0 > \alpha_1 \beta_0 / \beta_1$

(1.3) $q^s = q$

The variables q^s, q, and p are endogenous; E is either an exogenous variable or a parameter of the structure, as noted in 1.3. The facts that the supply curve has a positive slope and the demand curve a negative slope are expressed by the inequalities $\alpha_1 > 0$ and $\beta_1 < 0$. The fact that both price and quantity must be positive is expressed by the additional inequalities $\beta_0 > 0$ and $\beta_0 > \alpha_0$ and $\alpha_0 > \alpha_1 \beta_0 / \beta_1$. These equations and inequalities give an explicit picture of what is assumed to be known about the supply side, the demand side, and the market; that is why we begin with them. But they will be easier to work with if we substitute equation

---

[2] If the curves are not linear, they will be approximately linear for short distances on either side of any point we might be interested in, so linearity may not be a bad assumption. But the assumption that they are static is more difficult to justify, except as an expository device. We will keep both assumptions during the guided tour, and relax them later.

[3] This assumption will be replaced later in the book and also in the guided tour by the assumption that each equation is only approximately true, due to the presence of disturbing factors that act in a random (or, as is often said, stochastic) fashion.

(1.3) into (1.1) and (1.2), thus eliminating q^s and obtaining two equations in the two unknown endogenous variables q and p:

(1.4) $\quad q = \alpha_0 + \alpha_1(p - E) \qquad \alpha_1 > 0$

(1.5) $\quad q = \beta_0 + \beta_1 p \qquad\qquad \beta_1 < 0,\ \beta_0 > 0,\ \beta_0 > \alpha_0,\ \alpha_0 > \alpha_1 \beta_0 / \beta_1$

1.6 We now digress briefly to present a numerical illustration. Economic theory, apart from empirical observations, does not tell us the values of the parameters in these equations; it merely tells us the signs of three of them and the sign of two functions of them. Except for these restrictions, it leaves the parameters free to take any values whatever. As a numerical illustration, it might be that $\alpha_0 = 30$, $\alpha_1 = 1$, $\beta_0 = 120$, $\beta_1 = -2$. Then the supply and demand equations (1.4) and (1.5) would become

(1.6) $\qquad\qquad\qquad\qquad q = 30 + (p - E)$

(1.7) $\qquad\qquad\qquad\qquad q = 120 - 2p$

If the parameters have values different from these, the supply and demand equations will differ from (1.6) and (1.7) accordingly. For each set of values of the parameters, there is a corresponding set of equations obtained by substituting the parameter values into (1.4) and (1.5). Each set of equations such as (1.6) and (1.7) describes a structure, since it describes the features of the problem that do not change during the observation period. (Whether E is to be regarded as a variable along with p and q, or a parameter along with the α's and β's, depends upon whether it varied in the observation period, as already noted.)

1.7 We proceed to decide what other information is wanted besides that embodied in the theoretical specification of the supply and demand equations, namely, (1.4) and (1.5). Equations (1.4) and (1.5) determine price p and quantity q, when the parameters and the excise-tax rate E are known. To find p and q for given values of the α's and β's after the tax rate is set at E dollars per unit, it will be helpful to look at Figure 1.1, which illustrates equations (1.4) and (1.5). D is the demand curve, S is the supply curve with no excise tax, and S' is the supply curve with excise tax E. R is the taxless equilibrium point, and R' is the equilibrium after tax. The graph shows the familiar results, namely, that as a result of the tax, price rises and quantity falls. What we need to know are the coordinates of R' in *numerical* terms.

1.8 The same situation can be described in algebraic terms, if we solve the supply and demand equations (1.4) and (1.5) simultaneously for p and q. This can be done by equating their right-hand sides, solving the ensuing equation for p, and substituting the result into either (1.4) or (1.5). This process yields a pair of equations that express the endogenous variables in terms of the exogenous variable (if any, i.e., if E is not a

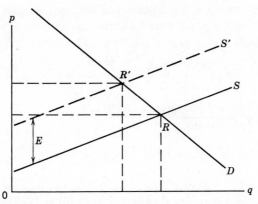

Figure 1.1 Demand curve D and supply curves S and S' before and after imposition of an excise tax of E dollars per unit.

parameter) and the parameters:

(1.8)
$$p = \frac{\beta_0 - \alpha_0}{\alpha_1 - \beta_1} + \frac{\alpha_1}{\alpha_1 - \beta_1} E$$

(1.9)
$$q = \frac{\alpha_1 \beta_0 - \alpha_0 \beta_1}{\alpha_1 - \beta_1} + \frac{\alpha_1 \beta_1}{\alpha_1 - \beta_1} E$$

Let us rewrite them by giving new names to their parameters:

(1.10)
$$p = \gamma_0 + \gamma_1 E$$

(1.11)
$$q = \delta_0 + \delta_1 E$$

where the parameters γ_0, γ_1, δ_0, and δ_1 are defined thus:

(1.12)
$$\gamma_0 = \frac{\beta_0 - \alpha_0}{\alpha_1 - \beta_1}$$

(1.13)
$$\gamma_1 = \frac{\alpha_1}{\alpha_1 - \beta_1}$$

(1.14)
$$\delta_0 = \frac{\alpha_1 \beta_0 - \alpha_0 \beta_1}{\alpha_1 - \beta_1}$$

(1.15)
$$\delta_1 = \frac{\alpha_1 \beta_1}{\alpha_1 - \beta_1}$$

In this algebraic presentation of the problem, clearly what we need to know are the numerical values of the parameters γ_0, γ_1, δ_0, and δ_1 in equations (1.10) and (1.11) in order to find the price and quantity sold of the commodity after a tax rate of E has been set.

1.9 Suppose, just as a numerical illustration, that we know the supply and demand parameters have the values mentioned in 1.6. Then from either (1.8) and (1.9) or (1.10) to (1.15) we shall find

$$(1.16) \qquad p = \frac{120 - 30}{1 - (-2)} + \frac{1}{1 - (-2)} E = 30 + \frac{E}{3}$$

$$(1.17) \qquad q = \frac{1(120) - 30(-2)}{1 - (-2)} + \frac{1(-2)}{1 - (-2)} E = 60 - \frac{2E}{3}$$

Then for several possible values of E we have the results shown in Table 1.1.

TABLE 1.1   Values of Price p and Quantity q for Given Levels of Excise Tax E in Equations (1.16) and (1.17)

E	0	3	6	9	12	15	30	60
p	30	31	32	33	34	35	40	50
q	60	58	56	54	52	50	40	20

1.10 In 1.10 through 1.14 we pause to compare the supply and demand equations (1.4) and (1.5) with the derived equations (1.8) and (1.9) obtained by solving (1.4) and (1.5), and to define several more concepts. The two pairs of equations describe the same situation but from two points of view. The distinguishing characteristic of the supply and demand equations themselves is that each of them describes the behavior of one particular group or sector of economic actors: The supply equation refers only to sellers' behavior and hence is unaffected by any changes that may occur in the demand equation, whereas the demand equation describes only buyers' behavior and hence is unaffected by any changes that may occur in the supply equation. For example, according to (1.5), buyers respond to the price they are charged, and the nature of this response is unaffected by the imposition of an excise tax that changes the supply equation. This property, of being affected only by changes in the behavior of one group or sector in the economy, is referred to as *autonomy*.[4] The derived equations (1.8) and (1.9) do not have it, for both of them are affected by any change in either the buyers' or the sellers' behavior.

1.11 The distinguishing characteristic of the derived equations (1.8) and (1.9) is that each of them contains exactly *one* endogenous variable, expressed in terms of exogenous variables (if any) and parameters. The supply and demand equations do not have this property.

---

[4] See Haavelmo [1944], pp. 26 ff. It will be clear from this definition that there are degrees of autonomy, depending on how large a group or sector is to be described by the equation in question.

1.12   It will be useful to have names for these two kinds of equation systems. The set of autonomous supply and demand equations (1.4) and (1.5) is called a set of *structural equations*; the parameters of these equations are called structural parameters. The set of nonautonomous derived equations (1.8) and (1.9), containing one endogenous variable each, is called the *reduced form*, and its parameters are called reduced-form parameters. It is natural to call the autonomous equations "structural," because it is natural to think of the economy as a "structure" whose component parts are the various groups or sectors, each of which corresponds to an autonomous equation. In later chapters we shall encounter several types of structural equations, each with some degree of autonomy.

1.13   When the values of all the structural parameters in a set of structural equations (not in the reduced form) are specified, the resulting set of equations becomes a *structure*. Thus equations (1.6) and (1.7) above are a structure if E is an exogenous variable rather than a parameter [if E is a parameter, (1.6) and (1.7) becomes a structure only when a numerical value is assigned to E]. What we are doing in effect here is to restrict our original definition of the structure (in I.5.3) somewhat by adding the requirement of autonomy: A *structure* is a set of autonomous relationships describing the complex of economic features that do not change during a given period. An equivalent definition, often used in econometrics, is this: A *structure* is a set of autonomous relationships sufficient to determine the numerical values of the endogenous variables, given the values of the exogenous variables.[5] Thus a structure specifies a numerical value of each structural parameter. The reduced-form equations with numerically specified parameters do not meet these definitions of a structure, but they fail to do so only with regard to autonomy.

1.14   Now that a more satisfactory definition of a structure has been given, it is possible to define a model more carefully. By common usage in econometrics, any set of structural equations is a model. We shall not violate this usage if we follow Koopmans[6] in defining a model as a set of structures. But in this book we shall not call every set of structures a model. In this book a set of structures will be called a *model* if all the structures in the set are alike in these three respects: the number of equations, the lists of endogenous and exogenous variables, and the list of variables that appear in each equation.[7] Thus a model can be described by a list of endogenous variables, a list of exogenous variables, and a list of specifications as to which variables are present in each equation. Some models

---

[5] The definition of structure will be given its final form in IV.4.2. See also I.5.3 and II.2.7.

[6] Koopmans [1949], Section 2.

[7] The definition of model will be given its final form in IV.4.4. See also I.3.2 and II.2.7.

may specify more than this; for example, the supply-and-demand model (1.4) and (1.5) specifies that the equations are linear, that p and $-E$ have the same parameter in the supply function, and that the parameters must satisfy five given inequalities. A model will be called linear it it specifies that all its equations are linear.[8] The information contained in a model is often referred to as *a priori* information, or *a priori* restrictions, or assumptions, or the maintained hypothesis. Some of the later analysis is carried out as if the model were correct, but ultimately the model itself is judged by the empirical results it leads to.

1.15 Returning to the excise-tax problem and using these new definitions, we easily see that what is wanted in order to find the quantity and price corresponding to a given level of the excise-tax rate E are the *numerical values of the parameters of the reduced-form equations* (1.10) and (1.11), namely, γ_0, γ_1, δ_0, and δ_1. What can be learned about these reduced-form parameters by theoretical analysis? We know *a priori* that $\alpha_1 > 0$, $\beta_1 < 0$, $\beta_0 > 0$, $\beta_0 > \alpha_0$, and $\alpha_0 > \alpha_1\beta_0/\beta_1$. From this and equations (1.12) to (1.15) we find that $\gamma_0 > 0$, $\gamma_1 > 0$, $\delta_0 > 0$, and $\delta_1 < 0$. Now γ_1 and δ_1 give the change in p and q respectively, in response to a rise of one dollar in the excise-tax rate. There $\gamma_1 > 0$ and $\delta_1 < 0$ mean that the excise tax raises the price and lowers the quantity sold. From (1.13) we can see that for a given tax rate the rise in price is greater if α_1 is large or if β_1 is numerically small, that is, if the supply curve is gently sloping and the demand curve is steep. Equation (1.15) shows that for a given tax rate the fall in quantity is greater if both α_1 and β_1 are numerically large,[9] that is, if both curves are gently sloping. These results are the mathematical equivalent of the statements in 1.2. The reader may verify them by trying various values for the structural parameters, or by experimenting with different slopes in Figure 1.1.

1.16 Using theoretical analysis of the *a priori* statements, we can go no further than this with the problem. This situation is typical of econometric problems: Economic theory can often lead to *a priori* statements about the *direction* of the economy's response to an imposed change of some kind, and it can sometimes say what makes the response more violent or less violent; but by itself it can rarely lead to quantitative statements.

1.17 At this point we can see the importance of the distinction between the case in which the excise-tax rate E varied in the observation period, thus qualifying as an exogenous variable, and the case in which it did not so vary, thus qualifying as a structural parameter. For if E

---

[8] For a more detailed account of these concepts, see Koopmans and Hood [1953], esp. pp. 113–126.

[9] To see this from (1.15) it is sufficient to rewrite the right-hand side of (1.15) as $1/(1/\beta_1 - 1/\alpha_1)$.

changed during the period for which we have observations, it is possible to learn something more about the parameters γ_0 and γ_1 in (1.10) by analyzing the observed joint behavior of p and E, and similarly to learn more about δ_0 and δ_1 in (1.11) from the observed joint behavior of q and E. But if all our observations pertain to the same value of E, then p and q cannot have varied,[10] and nothing further can be learned from observations about the parameters of the reduced form. Before taking up these problems in separate discussions of the two cases in Sections 4 to 7, we shall consider in Section 2 how *a priori* information and theoretical analysis apply to the excise-tax problem when random disturbing factors are admitted into the equations; and in Section 3 we shall consider briefly how dynamic factors may enter.

2   A SECOND APPROACH TO THE EXCISE-TAX PROBLEM: INEXACT EQUATIONS

2.1   In this section we no longer use exact equations; we introduce additional variables to be called disturbances. Why do economists not use exact theories? The answer is that so far in the history of economics, no exact theory has ever stood up when faced with facts (with the trivial exception of definitional statements such as "total sales revenue equals average price times quantity sold"). However, there are theories that stand up well "on the average," while being wrong by a small amount in nearly every specific instance. For example, consider the data for real consumption expenditure and real disposable income in the United States for 1946–1964, shown in Figure 2.1.[11] There is a certain regularity observable in the graph: The points lie more or less close to the straight line shown. Thus a theory relating real national consumption expenditure to real disposable income for 1946–1964 by a linear equation would be at best approximately correct, disturbances being measured by the distances from the points to the line in the figure. The distances are conventionally taken in the vertical direction since income is supposed to explain consumption. Other and much better theories, using more complicated functional relationships or introducing other variables, have been advanced to explain consumption expenditures.[12] They have been more successful than the above oversimplified bivariate linear theory in that their disturbances (distances from the points to *their* lines) are smaller than those

---

[10] Recall that the equations are assumed exactly true in this section.

[11] See U.S. Department of Commerce [1958] and recent issues of the *Survey of Current Business* for data. See also Table XI.3.1.

[12] For a review and evaluation of some of them, see Ferber [1953]. For more fruitful later work, see Modigliani and Brumberg [1954] and Friedman [1957].

shown in the figure, and in other important ways. None of them, however, has eliminated such disturbances entirely.

2.2   It is very simple to obtain a perfect explanation of the relation between disposable income and consumption, merely by drawing a line on the figure in such a way as to pass through every point. It would be a rather snaky line, but there would be no disturbances then. Such an explanation is vacuous, for it concentrates so intently on the period from

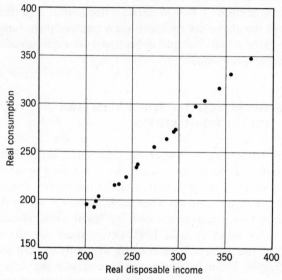

Figure 2.1   Real consumption expenditure and real disposable income, United States, 1946–1964, billions of 1954 dollars. Source: See footnote 11 in text.

1946 to 1964 that it forfeits almost all chance of being even approximately correct for the succeeding years. Suppose, for example, that a polynomial function of 18th degree were used to fit all the points in the figure exactly.[13] This function could be said to describe the income-consumption relationship perfectly for 1946–1964. However, economists rightly have no faith in functions that are made to fit a certain set of data *exactly*, because they know from general experience that economic life is too complex to be exactly described by simple explanations, and because the data for succeeding or preceding years or for other locales never fall exactly on the functions so fitted, and often do not fall even approximately on them. To illustrate this, we can fit a straight line, that is, a first-degree polynomial,

[13] Two points determine a straight line, such as $c = a_0 + a_1 y$; three points determine a parabola such as $c = a_0 + a_1 y + a_2 y^2$; four points determine a cubic equation; and n points determine a polynomial equation of $(n - 1)$th degree. Hence the 19 points for 1946–1964 inclusive determine an 18th-degree polynomial.

to the income-consumption data for 1946–1947, and see whether the data for 1948 and succeeding years fall on it; then we can fit a parabola, that is, a second-degree polynomial, to 1946–1948, and see whether the data for 1949 and later fall on that; and so forth. We shall find that they do not.

2.3 Granted that simple and plausible economic relationships (other than definitions) do not turn out to hold exactly, what is an economist to do who believes that such relationships are nevertheless real and important? The approach to which this book is devoted—an approach that has been very fruitful and promises to continue to be so—is this: Think of an economic relationship as having two parts. One part, a systematic part, expresses the relationship postulated; it does hold exactly and is therefore easy to think about theoretically and handle mathematically. The other part, a nonsystematic one, supplies the link between what the systematic part says and what the real world does. The two parts are typically added together for simplicity, so that the nonsystematic part is simply the algebraic difference between the observed and postulated behavior of the variable being explained, for example, consumption in the case of the consumption function. However, sometimes it may be desirable to combine the two parts by multiplication or in some other way. The factors that are known or are supposed to be important in the relationship are included in the systematic part; they are typically few in number. The other factors, of which there may be more than we can now recognize or measure, are taken to be small or accidental or both; they are not included in the systematic part but are thrown together to form the unsystematic part, called the disturbance. The objective of course is twofold: to make the systematic part simple and plausible, and at the same time to make the nonsystematic part small in size. It is often possible to do well with both of these objectives; and when we are competent or lucky or both, we can obtain a simple plausible systematic relation that has small disturbances not only for the data used to obtain the relation but also for other relevant data to which it may later be "extrapolated." The kinds of disturbing factors that we might expect to find in economic relationships include weather variations (with effects on agricultural supplies and on demand for certain commodities such as ice cream, fuel, and air-conditioning equipment); and variations in the tastes of consumers (with effects on output); not to mention errors in the observation of economic data, which we shall largely ignore in this book.

2.4 There is a set of disturbances corresponding to any systematic relationship among a given set of variables, if data for those variables are given. For each observation,[14] the disturbance is simply equal to the observed value of the variable being explained minus the calculated value

---

[14] If there are n variables, say $x_1, \ldots, x_n$, then "one observation" means a set of n numbers, each being an observed value for one of the n variables for a particular period.

obtained from the systematic relationship. Indeed, as we shall see in more detail in Chapters VII and IX, we choose among alternative systematic relationships in part by examining the disturbances they give rise to, and rejecting those relationships that give rise to implausible disturbances. For this reason it is valuable to have a way of dealing with disturbances. The concept of a chance variable, usually called a *random* or *stochastic* variable, is useful here. By this is meant a variable whose different values on different occasions are determined as if by drawing numbers at random from a hat, there being a particular probability attached to each value.[15] Examples are easy to find. The temperature in Washington at noon on any given July 1 can be thought of as having been drawn from a hat containing tickets, each bearing a number giving the July 1 temperature for some past or future year. Conceptually simpler examples are these: If a coin is tossed, the possible results are one head or no heads, and the probability of either is 1/2. If a die is rolled, the possible results are the integers from 1 to 6, and the probability of each is about 1/6 (unless the die is loaded).

2.5 We shall construct another example of random variables, as follows. And then we shall introduce them into the exact model above and thus transform it into a stochastic model. Suppose there are two dice, A and B. Let us invent a random variable that is equal to -3 if an odd number appears on die A, and $+3$ if an even number appears; we name this random variable u_α. And another randon variable, u_β, which is equal to -6 if die B turns up a 1 or a 2, and $+3$ if it turns up a 3 or greater. Then the probability that $u_\alpha = 3$ is 1/2, and the probability that $u_\alpha = -3$ is 1/2 also. Similarly, for u_β the probabilities are: for $u_\beta = 3$, 2/3; for $u_\beta = -6$, 1/3. Since the results for die A have no connection with those for die B when the two are rolled together, we may expect that on those occasions when $u_\alpha = 3$, u_β will be equal to 3 about two-thirds of the time and to -6 about one-third of the time, and similarly on the occasions when $u_\alpha = -3$. Looking at the matter the other way, we may expect that on the occasions when $u_\beta = 3$, u_α will be equal to 3 about half the time and to -3 about half the time, and similarly when $u_\beta = -6$. Therefore when both dice are rolled together repeatedly, we expect that $u_\alpha = u_\beta = 3$ will occur about one-third of the time; $u_\alpha = 3$ and $u_\beta = -6$, about one-sixth of the time; $u_\alpha = -3$ and $u_\beta = 3$, about one-third of the time; and $u_\alpha = -3$ and $u_\beta = -6$, about one-sixth of the time. All this is summarized in Table 2.1, which shows the probabilities attached to each of the four possible results of rolling the two dice, and also (in the row and column marked "unspecified") the probabilities for u_α and u_β separately. A list of all the possible results of a random event, showing the probability of each, is called a *probability distribution*. Graphs as well

---

[15] See IV.2 below, or any standard text in probability or statistical inference.

TABLE 2.1   A Joint Probability Distribution
for Structural Disturbances u_α and u_β

Values of u_α / Values of u_β	−3	3	Unspecified
−6	1/6	1/6	1/3
3	1/3	1/3	2/3
Unspecified	1/2	1/2	1

as tables can be used to represent probability distributions. Figure 2.2 shows the distributions of u_α and u_β, separately, and also their *joint* distribution. The abbreviation "Pb" stands for probability.

2.6   Now imagine a supply and demand theory made up of two parts, one part systematic like the exact theory we discussed earlier (Section 1 of this chapter) and the other random or stochastic. In such a theory the systematic part shows the average state of affairs, and the random part or disturbance shows the deviations from average, now in

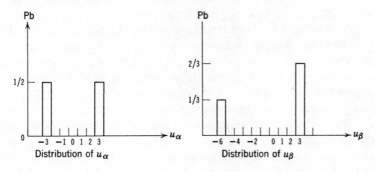

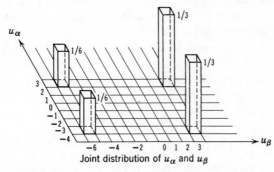

Joint distribution of u_α and u_β

Figure 2.2   Probability distribution of structural disturbances u_α and u_β from Table 2.1.

one direction and now in the other. Let us combine the random variables u_α and u_β with equations (1.4) and (1.5), thus:

(2.1) $q = \alpha_0 + \alpha_1(p - E) + u_\alpha$ $\alpha_1 > 0$

(2.2) $q = \beta_0 + \beta_1 p + u_\beta$ $\beta_1 < 0, \beta_0 > 0, \beta_0 > \alpha_0, \alpha_0 > \alpha_1\beta_0/\beta_1$

Note that although the systematic part of (2.1) is now *never* true in a particular year (or whatever period is used) because of the fact that u_α is always either -3 or $+3$ and never zero, still on the average over many years it will be very close to the truth, because on the average u_α will be close to zero. A similar statement applies to (2.2).

2.7   Equations (2.1) and (2.2) are a *stochastic model*,[16] for they include random variables u_α and u_β. Stochastic models may assert much or little about the distributions of their random variables. Thus equations (2.1) and (2.2) *together with* the above-specified joint probability distribution of u_α and u_β are another stochastic model, a more restrictive one because the distribution of the disturbances is completely specified. A *stochastic structure*[17] is like a nonstochastic structure except that it *specifies completely the joint distribution of random variables.* Thus equations (2.1) and (2.2) together with the completely specified distribution of Table 2.1 can be made into a stochastic structure if all the parameters in (2.1) and (2.2) are assigned numerical values.[18]

2.8   The graph of the stochastic model, Figure 2.3, shows that if $E = 0$ there are *four* possible sets of values of p and q, not just one. (The same is true for any other value of E.) The solid lines show the systematic parts of the supply and demand equations. The dotted lines show the two possible positions of each curve, corresponding to the two possible values of u_α or u_β, and their probabilities are given in parentheses. The four different results correspond to the four intersection points of the dotted lines; these points are marked P_1, P_2, P_3, and P_4 and they have the probabilities shown in the little table inserted in Figure 2.3. If the theory implied in this model is correct, then for any fixed excise-tax rate both the price and quantity will vary randomly among the four values corresponding to the four points shown in the figure, with the probabilities given in the accompanying little table.

2.9   The same thing can be shown algebraically. If (2.1) and (2.2) are solved simultaneously for p and q, the result is the following reduced form, analogous to (1.10) and (1.11):

(2.3) $p = \gamma_0 + \gamma_1 E + v_1$

(2.4) $q = \delta_0 + \delta_1 E + v_2$

---

[16] A stochastic model is defined in IV.4.4. See also I.3.2 and II.1.14.

[17] A stochastic structure is defined in IV.4.2. See also I.5.3 and II.1.13.

[18] See Koopmans and Hood [1953], pp. 113–126. Most stochastic models allow for an infinitely large number of possible values of each random disturbance, and we shall use such models almost exclusively in later chapters.

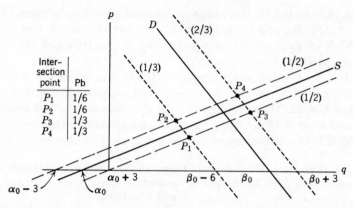

Figure 2.3 Supply and demand equations (2.1) and (2.2) with no tax ($E = 0$) and with the distribution of u_α and u_β as in Table 2.1.

where the γ's and δ's again depend on the α's and β's as given in (1.12) to (1.15), v_1 and v_2 are two new random variables defined by

$$(2.5) \qquad\qquad v_1 = \frac{u_\beta - u_\alpha}{\alpha_1 - \beta_1}$$

$$(2.6) \qquad\qquad v_2 = \frac{\alpha_1 u_\beta - \beta_1 u_\alpha}{\alpha_1 - \beta_1}$$

and all the other symbols have the same meanings as before. Now v_1 has four possible values, corresponding to the four possible *pairs* of values of u_α and u_β; so does v_2. These values with their joint probability distribution are shown in Table 2.2; they are obtained from (2.5) and (2.6) and Table 2.1 (the joint distribution of u_α and u_β). Therefore, for any given value of E, price and quantity may have four different values each, found by substituting the given E and the four values of v_1 and v_2 from Table

TABLE 2.2   Joint Probability Distribution of Reduced-Form Disturbances v_1 and v_2, from Equations (2.5) and (2.6) and Table 2.1

Pairs		Pb	Resulting Pairs	
u_α	u_β		v_1	v_2
3	−6	1/6	$-9/(\alpha_1 - \beta_1)$	$(-6\alpha_1 - 3\beta_1)/(\alpha_1 - \beta_1)$
−3	−6	1/6	$-3/(\alpha_1 - \beta_1)$	$(-6\alpha_1 + 3\beta_1)/(\alpha_1 - \beta_1)$
3	3	1/3	0	3
−3	3	1/3	$6/(\alpha_1 - \beta_1)$	$3(\alpha_1 + \beta_1)/(\alpha_1 - \beta_1)$

2.2 into (2.3) and (2.4). The values so obtained are the coordinates of the points P_1, P_2, P_3, and P_4 in Figure 2.3, for the case when $E = 0$. The probability of each value is the probability of occurrence of the corresponding point.

2.10 As a numerical example, suppose that as in 1.6 and 1.9, $\alpha_0 = 30$, $\alpha_1 = 1$, $\beta_0 = 120$, $\beta_1 = -2$. And suppose first that $E = 0$, then that $E = 12$. The resulting two joint distributions of p and q may be calculated from (1.12)–(1.15), (2.3), (2.4), and Table 2.3. They are shown in Table 2.3. Other illustrations can be constructed by choosing different

TABLE 2.3 Two Joint Distributions of Price p and Quantity q, with Distribution of u_α and u_β as in Table 2.1, Values of Parameters as in Section 2.10, and Tax Levels $E = 0$ and $E = 12$

E	$\gamma_0 + \gamma_1 E$	$\delta_0 + \delta_1 E$	Pairs		Pb	Pairs		Pairs	
			u_α	u_β		v_1	v_2	p	q
0	30	60	3	−6	1/6	−3	0	27	60
			−3	−6	1/6	−1	−4	29	56
			3	3	1/3	0	3	30	63
			−3	3	1/3	2	−1	32	59
12	34	52	3	−6	1/6	−3	0	31	52
			−3	−6	1/6	−1	−4	33	48
			3	3	1/3	0	3	34	55
			−3	3	1/3	2	−1	36	51

values for E and the structural parameters, and each set of values will lead to a new distribution for p and q.

2.11 Thus in the stochastic case, the endogenous variables—price and quantity—become random variables. Their joint distribution is as follows: Their average values are conditional upon the exogenous variable(s) as given by the systematic part of the reduced form [i.e., by (1.10) and (1.11)], and their *deviations* from average are given by functions of the structural disturbances [i.e., by equations (2.5) and (2.6)]. In any real econometric problem the observed data may be viewed as a sample drawn from such a joint conditional distribution of the endogenous variables, given the values of the exogenous variables;[19] and any empirical inferences that are drawn within this framework must be based on that sample.

2.12 In a model like the one just discussed, it would not be possible to predict price and quantity *exactly* for any given year (or whatever period is used), even if E and the structural parameters and the joint distribution

---

[19] This joint conditional distribution is of course the stochastic reduced form.

of u_α and u_β were all known, because of the random nature of the variables. It would be possible to predict their *average* values for a given E over a large number of years, however, and to do rather more than that, but we shall leave this matter until later chapters.

2.13 As for the information required to make the best possible conditional predictions, and how much of it can be obtained by theoretical analysis, the situation is similar to the exact case discussed in 2.1. As there, we need to know the reduced-form parameters γ_0, γ_1, δ_0, and δ_1; their algebraic signs can be found by analyzing (1.12) to (1.15) and (2.1)–(2.2): $\gamma_0 > 0$, $\gamma_1 > 0$, $\delta_0 > 0$, and $\delta_1 < 0$. But here we need to know also the form and parameters of the joint probability distribution of the reduced-form disturbances v_1 and v_2. In some problems it will be impossible to tell anything about the distribution simply by theoretical analysis of *a priori* statements. In other problems (as in this one) enough *a priori* information will be available to determine the distribution almost completely. Table 2.2 shows how much can be learned about it in this problem by theoretical analysis; the only things missing are the values of the structural parameters α_1 and β_1. Even without knowing them, we can see that v_1 has four possible values, and so does v_2, each of which occurs only along with one value of v_1, so that there are just four pairs of values of v_1 and v_2 in the joint distribution. The probability of each pair is determined, and by accident, as shown in Table 2.2, one of the pairs is already known. As in the exact case, nevertheless, theoretical analysis does not tell us all we want to know.

3   DYNAMICS

3.1 Dynamic theory is that into which time enters, in such a way that changes can occur in the endogenous variables even though the structure and exogenous variables (other than time) are constant. Adjustments to new conditions are not instantaneous but take time to work out.

3.2 An example is the familiar cobweb theorem, wherein quantity demanded in a given year[20] depends on the current price, but quantity supplied depends (given a production period of one year) on the price in the preceding year. The price oscillates from year to year (unless the quantities supplied and demanded were equal to begin with), either approaching a fixed limit gradually or else fluctuating ever more widely, depending upon whether the supply or the demand curve is steeper. But no change in structure or exogenous variables (there are none of the latter

---

[20] The terms "year" and "period" do not have the wide meaning in dynamic theory that we assigned to them in I.5.2.

in this simple presentation) is necessary to produce the change in price. The reader may construct numerical illustrations.

3.3 Another example is a model in which it is assumed that the cost of production decreases uniformly because of technological improvements; then, if t represents time in years, we have

(3.1) $q = \alpha_0 + \alpha_1 p + \alpha_2 t$ $\alpha_1 > 0,\ \alpha_2 > 0$

(3.2) $q = \beta_0 + \beta_1 p$ $\beta_1 < 0$

Here also the price changes from year to year via a mechanism built into the model; again the reader may construct numerical illustrations.

3.4 We have presented examples of the two principal types of dynamic models. In one of them some of the equations contain values of variables pertaining to *different periods of time*, or contain *rates of change* of some of the variables; in the other, time appears explicitly as a variable. We shall go no further with dynamics during the guided tour, leaving it instead to later chapters.

4 *EXACT* EQUATIONS IN THE CASE OF *UNCHANGED* STRUCTURE

4.1 We have now carried the analysis of the excise problem as far as possible by theoretical means alone, without resort to data. We have seen that it is necessary to know the values of the reduced-form parameters γ_0, γ_1, δ_0, and δ_1 in equations (2.3) and (2.4) if we are to find the price and quantity associated with a given excise-tax rate E. To be able to make quantitative statements, we must proceed from theory to empirical observation and measurement; we must turn to the "metrics" in econometrics.

4.2 As indicated earlier (in 1.17), when empirical analysis begins, the distinction between the cases of unchanged and changed structure becomes important. We shall take up the case of unchanged structure first, in this section and the next, and the case of changed structure later in Sections 6 and 7. In each case we shall discuss first exact equations (Sections 4 and 6) and then stochastic equations (Sections 5 and 7).

4.3 Consider what can be learned from observed values of the variables p, q, and E when the equations are exact and the structure is not changed (i.e., when E has varied in the observation period). In a typical experiment, certain variables are controlled; they are artifically set at various values, and then the resulting values of the remaining variable(s) are measured. The appropriate experiment here would be to set different values of the excise tax E and observe what happens to price and quantity. Since E has varied during the observation period, we need not actually perform the experiment; the past values of E, together with the accompanying values of p and q, can be observed just *as if* someone had already performed the very experiment we want. This will no longer be true when we come to the case of changes of structure.

4.4 Since the structural equations (1.4) and (1.5) are linear, the reduced-form equations (1.10) and (1.11) are linear too. For easy reference the reduced-form equations are repeated here with new numbers:

(4.1)
$$p = \gamma_0 + \gamma_1 E$$

(4.2)
$$q = \delta_0 + \delta_1 E$$

Two different observed values of E together with the corresponding values of p and q are sufficient to determine exactly the parameters of each

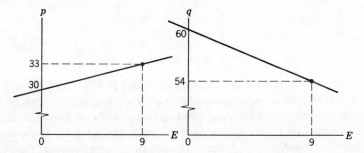

Figure 4.1 Graphs representing reduced-form equations (4.1) and (4.2) with data of 4.4.

equation of the reduced form, because two points from any straight line will locate the line. Graphically, this amounts to taking two observations on each variable, plotting p against E on one graph and q against E on another, and drawing on each graph the straight line determined by the points. The straight lines represent the reduced-form equations. For illustration, suppose that we observed the following two points.

	E	p	q
(1)	0	30	60
(2)	9	33	54

These two points have purposely been chosen to satisfy the structural equations (1.6) and (1.7), so that the same structure given above as a numerical example can be used again below. Then the reduced-form equations would appear as in the graphs in Figure 4.1. The reduced-form parameters can be read from the graph.

4.5 Algebraically we can get the same result. If we substitute two observations of p, q, and E into (4.1) and (4.2), we find that (4.1) yields two simultaneous equations with γ_0 and γ_1 as the unknowns, and (4.2) yields two more simultaneous equations with δ_0 and δ_1 as the unknowns. Then the reduced-form parameters γ_0, γ_1, δ_0, and δ_1 are found by solving these four equations. If we use as an illustration the same hypothetical observations given in 4.4, the equations to be solved are

$$
(4.3) \quad
\begin{aligned}
30 &= \gamma_0 \\
33 &= \gamma_0 + 9\gamma_1 \\
60 &= \delta_0 \\
54 &= \delta_0 + 9\delta_1
\end{aligned}
$$

and the solutions are $\gamma_0 = 30$, $\gamma_1 = \frac{1}{3}$, $\delta_0 = 60$, $\delta_1 = -\frac{2}{3}$. Thus, if the observations were as given, the reduced-form equations would be found to be

$$(4.4) \qquad p = 30 + \tfrac{1}{3}E$$

$$(4.5) \qquad q = 60 - \tfrac{2}{3}E$$

These two equations are the same as (1.16) and (1.17), which we got by solving the structural equations directly. This procedure illustrates the fact that *it is always possible, at least approximately, to infer the values of the reduced-form parameters from observations, as well as from the structure* (of course provided there are enough observations—at least two are required for each variable, in this case).

4.6 The excise-tax problem in this case is thus solved: Equations (4.4) and (4.5) give the solution. Of course if the observations turn out to be different from those used in the illustration, equations (4.3) will have to be changed accordingly, and equations (4.4) and (4.5) may have to be changed too. But in any event, it is clear that this procedure will yield the solution of the problem for the linear static exact case with unchanged structure.

4.7 It was said earlier that two observations are sufficient. In fact if three or more are taken, and if the exact model used [i.e., (1.4) and (1.5)] is correct, the additional equations in the γ's and δ's [like (4.3)] will be redundant and will lead to the same solutions. Why is this so? The model used implies that both reduced-form equations are straight lines with no disturbances and the data given in (4.4) require that those straight lines be exactly as given in (4.4)–(4.5). Therefore, if the model is correct, all possible observations must fall exactly on those straight lines. Of course, if data are observed that do *not* fall on those straight lines, it is obvious that in fact either the economic structure is not linear, or there are disturbances in the equation, or both. Such a result is imcompatible with the model and will force the abandonment or revision of the model. In the stochastic case to be discussed next, it is equally important to look out for the possiblity that the model is rendered implausible by the observed data and to consider revising the model accordingly.

5 *STOCHASTIC* EQUATIONS IN THE CASE OF *UNCHANGED* STRUCTURE

5.1 The use of data with stochastic equations in the case of unchanged structure has important similarities to the analogous problem (just discussed) with exact equations. First, it is still necessary to know the values of the reduced-form parameters to solve the excise-tax problem. Second, it is again as if experiments had already been performed for us by the normal operation of the economy, because of the past changes in E.

5.2 The two important new features that appear in the stochastic case both involve questions that cannot be answered exactly. *First*, since each equation of the reduced form now has a random component in the prediction period as well as the previously discussed systematic component, the price and quantity corresponding to a particular excise-tax rate cannot be predicted exactly, even if the parameters of the systematic part are known exactly. To predict with as little uncertainty as possible, the probability distribution of the random components [the v's in equations (2.3)–(2.6)] must be known completely. *Second*, and again since each equation of the reduced form has a random component, the values of the parameters of the systematic part of the reduced form can no longer be found exactly from two (or any finite number of) observations.[21] The reason is (speaking loosely) that the random disturbances of the observation period jostle the observed values so that they do not always fall exactly on the graph of the systematic part, and therefore it is impossible to tell just where the systematic part belongs among the various observed points. Observe that the former of these difficulties arises from the random variables in the prediction period and the latter from the random variables in the observation period.

5.3 Let us present a numerical illustration. We shall assume the same values for the structural parameters as in previous illustrations ($\alpha_0 = 30$, $\alpha_1 = 1$, $\beta_0 = 120$, $\beta_1 = -2$) and the same set of possible values and probabilities of the structural disturbances ($u_\alpha = -3$ or $+3$, $u_\beta = -6$ or $+3$ and probabilities as shown in Table 2.1 or Figure 2.2), but we

---

[21] To see this, consider whether an equal number of additional observations will *necessarily* give the same result again. Of course they will not, precisely because of the stochastic nature of the problem.

shall assume (as in real problems) that these things are *unknown* to the investigator; he knows that the model is equations (2.1)–(2.2), with u_α and u_β being random variables with unknown distribution. Then the reduced-form disturbances v_1 and v_2 will have the same set of possible values and probabilities as given in Table 2.3. Now consider the attempt to determine γ_0 and γ_1, the parameters of the reduced-form equation (2.3), from data on p and E. If an observation is taken on p when $E = 0$, any one of four values may be found: 27, 29, 30, or 32 (see Table 2.3). Similarly, when $E = 12$, p can be 31, 33, 34, or 36. If these points are plotted as in Figure 5.1, it will be seen that there are sixteen possible lines,

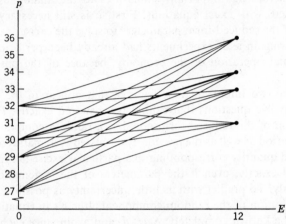

Figure 5.1   Possible estimates of the stochastic reduced-form equation (2.3) based on two observations from the structure shown in Table 2.3.

any of which could be obtained from two observations, one at $E = 0$ and the other at $E = 12$. Only one of the sixteen is the one the investigator is looking for, that is, the systematic part of the price equation (2.3) in the reduced form, and that is the line connecting the price of 30 with the price of 34 (it is drawn heavily on the graph). But fhe investigator *cannot know*, when he obtains a line empirically from two such observations, whether he has obtained the one he wants or not. Furthermore, he can tell nothing so far (i.e., from only two observations) about the distribution of the v's.

    5.4   If he takes some more observations at each of the two values of E (0 and 12), he can learn more. He could guess, in this example, that there are at least four possible values of p for each E (provided he keeps observing long enough so that each one occurs at least once—of course this may be a long time if among the four possible values there is one with a very small probability, such as one in a hundred), and so he could guess that the line he seeks [the systematic component of (2.3)] may be somewhere between the upper and lower lines in Figure 5.1. Furthermore, if he takes many observations, he can begin to feel that he knows something about the probability distribution of p for each of the two given values of E, because values having a high probability can be expected to occur most often, and vice versa. And if he calculates the *average* of p when $E = 0$, and the *average* of p when $E = 12$, and connects these two *averages* by a line on Figure 5.1, he will have a fairly good estimate of the position (and hence the parameters) of the desired systematic component of (2.3), because the random components can be expected roughly to "average out." The more observations he takes, the more likely it is that the random components *will* average out almost completely, and hence the more accurate his estimate is likely to be. The method of least squares is an elaboration of this averaging approach, as are most estimation methods. But there is always the possibility (i.e., small probability) that even in a large (finite) number of observations they will *not* average out; thus without an infinite number of observations the investigator will not know *exactly* and *certainly* the distribution of the random disturbances and the parameters of the systematic component. The approach of this paragraph and the preceding one apply to q just as well as to p.

5.5 If (as is always true in practice) only a finite number of observations is possible, it is helpful to have some *a priori* information about the distribution of disturbances. For example, in the case considered in this section, it would be helpful to know that u_α and u_β each have two possible values, for then we could deduce that v_1 and v_2 each have at most four possible values [equations (2.5)–(2.6) show this]. Of course, if the observed data showed more than four different values of p or of q for a given tax rate, we should have to abandon any model that implied that v_1 and v_2 each have four possible values. But it is best to defer this matter to later chapters, together with other questions of measurement in the stochastic case.

5.6 To sum up Sections 4 and 5: In the case of unchanged structure, data are available just as if appropriate experiments had already been performed. If the exact linear equations (1.4)–(1.5) are used, two observations on each variable suffice to determine the reduced-form parameters exactly, and the problem is solved. If the stochastic linear equations (2.1)–(2.2) are used, no finite number of observations can determine exactly the reduced-form parameters and the distribution of the disturbances; but the larger the number the more nearly correct the estimates of them will probably be, and the less likely the solution will be to err by any given amount. Knowledge of the structure itself is not necessary in order to forecast the effect of a change in the excise-tax rate.[22]

---

[22] In IX.12.4–5 we shall find a case where knowledge of the structure leads to improved reduced-form estimates and improved forecasts.

6 *EXACT* EQUATIONS IN THE CASE OF *CHANGED* STRUCTURE; IDENTIFICATION

6.1 We come now to the case in which the imposition of an excise tax of E dollars per unit represents a change of structure, that is, in which the excise tax has always had a constant value in the observation period, so that there has been no chance to observe its effects. We shall assume for convenience that the constant value was zero, although it really makes no difference to the analysis what the constant value was. In this section we shall discuss exact equations and in Section 7 stochastic equations.

6.2 We shall use the terms "old parameters" and "new parameters" to describe the parameters of the system before and after the structural change, respectively. The old and new parameters of the excise problem

TABLE 6.1   Old and New Parameters in the Excise-Tax Problem
When the Structure Changes

	Supply Curve		Demand Curve		Excise Rate
	Intercept	Slope	Intercept	Slope	
old	α_0	α_1	β_0	β_1	0
new	α_0	α_1	β_0	β_1	E

are as shown in Table 6.1. The structural change in question is clearly shown to be a change in the excise-tax rate from zero to E dollars per unit.

6.3 The analysis of Section 1 applies here in its entirety, except that now we must keep in mind two structures and two reduced forms, the old and the new. The supply equation before the structural change is the same as (1.4), which we have been using all along, except that the excise-tax rate is zero, thus:

$$(6.1) \qquad\qquad q = \alpha_0 + \alpha_1 p \qquad \alpha_1 > 0$$

The demand equation, as before, is

$$(6.2) \qquad q = \beta_0 + \beta_1 p \qquad \beta_1 < 0,\ \beta_0 > 0,\ \beta_0 > \alpha_0,\ \alpha_0 > \alpha_1\beta_0/\beta_1$$

The supply equation *after* the structural change is

$$(6.3) \qquad q = \alpha_0 + \alpha_1(p - E) = (\alpha_0 - \alpha_1 E) + \alpha_1 p \qquad \alpha_1 > 0$$

Therefore the reduced form *after* the structural change is [from solving (6.2) and (6.3)]

(6.4)
$$p = (\gamma_0 + \gamma_1 E) = \frac{\beta_0 - \alpha_0 + \alpha_1 E}{\alpha_1 - \beta_1}$$

(6.5)
$$q = (\delta_0 + \delta_1 E) = \frac{\alpha_1 \beta_0 - \alpha_0 \beta_1 + \alpha_1 \beta_1 E}{\alpha_1 - \beta_1}$$

This looks just like (1.8)–(1.11) except that here E is a structural parameter, and so each reduced-form equation has only one parameter. The reduced form *before* the structural change is obtained by setting $E = 0$ in (6.4)–(6.5), or by solving (6.1)–(6.2). It is[23]

(6.6)
$$p = \gamma_0 = \frac{\beta_0 - \alpha_0}{\alpha_1 - \beta_1}$$

(6.7)
$$q = \delta_0 = \frac{\alpha_1 \beta_0 - \alpha_0 \beta_1}{\alpha_1 - \beta_1}$$

6.4 Let us consider an illustration, assuming the same values for the structural parameters as in previous illustrations: $\alpha_0 = 30$, $\alpha_1 = 1$, $\beta_0 = 120$, $\beta_1 = -2$. Then the old reduced form becomes [using (6.6)–(6.7)]

(6.8)
$$p = 30$$

(6.9)
$$q = 60$$

whereas the new reduced form is

(6.10)
$$p = (30 + \tfrac{1}{3}E)$$

(6.11)
$$q = (60 - \tfrac{2}{3}E)$$

The old reduced form does not give the information we need to predict p and q after the tax is imposed; the new one does.

6.5 The crucial point here is that in order to solve the excise problem in the case of changed structure, it is necessary to know the parameters and distribution of disturbances of the reduced form *as it is after the structural change*, not as it is before; the new parameters and distribution for the reduced form are needed, not the old. This is typical in a problem involving prediction under structural change: Prediction *always* requires a knowledge of the relevant relationships as they will be in the *prediction* period, and for prediction under changed structure this means that the relationships that exist *after* the change are the ones required.[24]

---

[23] It will be seen that the values of γ_0 and δ_0 here agree with those of equations (1.12) and (1.14).

[24] For a good discussion of this point, see Marschak [1947] or [1953].

6.6 Since we are dealing with a case of changed structure, in which the excise-tax rate has *not* been changed during the observation period, the procedure of Section 4 is no longer applicable. Either we shall not be able to get the new reduced-form parameters at all, or we shall have to get them from the structural parameters α_0, α_1, β_0, β_1, and E by means of equations (6.4) and (6.5), because there is no other possible way. It has become necessary for the first time in our discussion to know the *structural* parameters.[25] Note that it is the *new* structural parameters, not the old, that are needed to determine the new reduced-form parameters. In the present problem the new structural parameters are the same as the old except that the excise rate has changed from zero to E.

6.7 Conceptually at least, it would be possible to determine the new structural parameters by experimentation. Consider the demand equation (6.2). If the price were arbitrarily fixed successively at two different values and an unlimited quantity were supplied at each price, the amount demanded at each price could be observed and the two points could be used to determine the parameters β_0 and β_1 of the demand curve, just as was done for the reduced form in 4.4 and 4.5. Or the quantity offered could be fixed successively at two different levels, and the demand price at which those quantities were sold could be observed, to get two points to determine β_0 and β_1. A similar experiment (with E fixed at any known value) would determine the parameters α_0 and α_1 of the old supply equation, (6.1). But to consider the possibility of large-scale experimentation by economists is academic, because our society does not allow us to experiment upon it as we like. Even if it did, there would be serious practical difficulties attendant upon the fact that citizens would realize that arbitrary changes were being made and would speculate on them, thus changing their behavior during the very experiment designed to study it (buying more and selling less than normal amounts when they think the price is low, and vice versa when they think it is high, for instance). Therefore we must often be prepared to proceed without the benefit of experiments.[26]

6.8 We need to know the new structure. But by the assumptions of the problem no observations on the new structure are available, and therefore it has to be approached through (1) the old structure and (2) the manner in which the structural change in question alters the old structure.

[25] Later on, we shall find two other important reasons for wanting to know the values of structural parameters. One is in order to test individual structural equations one by one to improve our models. The other is, in certain cases to be described later, to get better estimates of reduced-form parameters even in the case of unchanged structure than could otherwise be had.

[26] Experiments concerning individual behavior have been made; for example, see Mosteller and Nogee [1951]. The methods described in Sections 4 and 5 for the case of unchanged structure apply.

In our problem we have postulated that the structural change consists solely of an increase in the excise-tax parameter from zero to some known positive value E. Therefore we need only to find the values of the other old structural parameters, α_0, α_1, β_0, and β_1, to be able to solve the problem. We already know from the analysis of the case of unchanged structure (4.4 and 4.5) that it is possible to find the *old reduced-form* parameters (i.e., the reduced-form parameters that existed in the observation period) from nonexperimental observation. Hence we need to inquire whether the old structural parameters can be obtained either from the old reduced form or from observed data directly. Our strategy must then be to try to follow through these steps:

(a) Obtain the old structural parameters, either from the old reduced-form parameters or from observations directly.

(b) Obtain the new structural parameters from the old ones and a knowledge of the nature of the structural change.

(c) Obtain the new reduced-form parameters from the new structural parameters via the right-hand equalities in (6.4)–(6.5).

6.9   Steps (b) and (c) can be done readily, in this problem, as we have seen in the preceding discussions, though step (b) is often troublesome if the structure changes in an imperfectly known way. Let us concentrate upon step (a). The old reduced form by definition gives the observation-period values of the endogenous variables p and q as functions of the exogenous variables, but since E is a parameter there are no exogenous variables here. Hence the old reduced form must simply give the observation-period values of p and q as constants, γ_0 and δ_0, as in the left-hand equalities in (6.6)–(6.7). This is consistent with the results in 6.4; it arises because under our present assumptions nothing happens during the observation period to change p and q. We are required to deduce from the observed p and q the old structural parameters α_0, α_1, β_0, and β_1. If we could solve the right-hand equalities in (6.6)–(6.7) for the α's and β's in terms of γ_0 and δ_0 (which are known from observation) the task would be finished, but it is not possible so to solve because there are only two equations with which to determine the four unknown structural parameters. Step (a) is impossible; hence the excise problem cannot be solved in this case.

6.10   Consider a numerical illustration, in which $\gamma_0 = 30$ and $\delta_0 = 60$. Then the observation period will yield $p = 30$, $q = 60$, by equations (6.6)–(6.7). Any pair of linear supply and demand equations that have the specified directions of slope, and that intersect at $p = 30$ and $q = 60$ during the observation period, would yield these observed values and satisfy all the restrictions of the model [equations (6.1)–(6.2)]. But since there is an infinity of such pairs of equations, the observations do not enable us to tell what the values of the structural parameters were in the observation period. Graphically, the situation is as shown in Figure 6.1. The structures indicated by the solid lines S and D and by the dotted lines S' and D' could equally well have prevailed during the observation period, and the observations cannot determine which (if either) did, for there are still other structures whose equations intersect in the same point. The same indeterminacy is evident from the algebraic approach. The

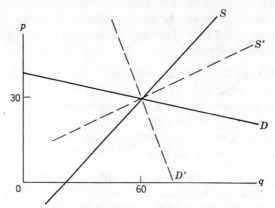

Figure 6.1 Possible supply curves S and S' and demand curves D and D' when the model is (6.1)–(6.2) and the data show price $p = 30$ and quantity $q = 60$.

equations that are to be solved for the structural parameters are [from (6.6)–(6.7)]:

$$(6.12) \qquad 30 = \frac{\beta_0 - \alpha_0}{\alpha_1 - \beta_1}$$

$$(6.13) \qquad 60 = \frac{\alpha_1 \beta_0 - \alpha_0 \beta_1}{\alpha_1 - \beta_1}$$

Here are two conditions that must be met by the four parameters, and the two are insufficient to determine their values. There is an infinite number of sets of structural parameters that are compatible with (6.12)–(6.13).

6.11 The argument of 6.8 to 6.10 has shown that if the *a priori* knowledge and assumptions are as given by equations (6.1)–(6.2), and if the excise-tax rate has remained constant during the observation period, *then it is impossible* to predict the price and quantity that will prevail after an excise tax of a specified rate is imposed—and indeed impossible to predict anything that requires the old structure—because that structure cannot be determined.[27] Situations of this type occur from time to time in econometric research.

[27] Of course anything can be predicted that depends only on whether the true structure belongs to the given model or not, if we are willing to accept the model.

6.12 There are other econometric situations in which the desired predictions *can* be made—in fact we have already discussed one, the excise problem in the case of unchanged structure. But more than this, there are problems involving *structural change* that can be solved. We shall illustrate one briefly here. Suppose that in our problem it is known or assumed *a priori* that the supply equation has unit elasticity so that its graph passes through the origin of coordinates, that is, $\alpha_0 = 0$, and that the demand equation has a slope of unity, that is, $\beta_1 = -1$; while the problem is unchanged in other respects.[28] Then the model (before the structural change in excise-tax rate) becomes, instead of (6.1)–(6.2):

$$(6.14) \qquad q = \alpha_1 p \qquad \alpha_1 > 0$$

$$(6.15) \qquad q = \beta_0 - p \qquad \beta_0 > 0$$

and the old reduced form becomes, instead of (6.6)–(6.7):

$$(6.16) \qquad p = \gamma_0 = \frac{\beta_0}{1 + \alpha_1}$$

$$(6.17) \qquad q = \delta_0 = \frac{\alpha_1 \beta_0}{1 + \alpha_1}$$

If $p = 30$ and $q = 60$ in the observation period, we can solve this old reduced form for the old structural parameters to get $\beta_0 = 90$ and $\alpha_1 = 2$. [There is another solution of these two equations at $\alpha_1 = -1$ and $\beta_0 = 0$ but this does not concern us because it does not satisfy the restrictions on algebraic signs given in (6.1)–(6.2).] The new structure, after the imposition of the excise at a known rate E, will then be

$$(6.18) \qquad q = 2(p - E) = -2E + 2p$$

$$(6.19) \qquad q = 90 - p$$

and the new reduced form obtained from it will be

$$(6.20) \qquad p = 30 + \tfrac{2}{3}E$$

$$(6.21) \qquad q = 60 - \tfrac{2}{3}E$$

Then (6.20)–(6.21) can be used to predict the price and quantity corresponding to any excise-tax rate.

6.13 The essential difference between these two illustrations given in (6.10) and (6.12) of predicting under structural change is as follows: In one (the latter), the *a priori* statements, *together with the observations*, place so many restrictions on the structure that there is only *one* set of

---

[28] Note that we are no longer using the numerical example of structural parameters that we used repeatedly earlier in this chapter, since we are now assuming values different from the earlier ones for α_0 and β_1.

parameter values that is compatible with both the data and the restrictions; in the other (the former), the restrictions imposed on the structure *a priori* and by the observations are so weak that, although many sets of parameter values are excluded, there is still an infinity of possible sets that are compatible with both the data and the restrictions, so the structure cannot be determined. If, with a given model, the structure can be uniquely determined from a sufficient number of observations, it is said to be *identifiable*, or *identified*, with respect to the given model and data. If it cannot be determined no matter how many observations are available, it is said to be unidentifiable, or unidentified, with respect to the given model and data. The general question of identification of linear structures and structural parameters will be systematically discussed in Chapter VIII.

7 *STOCHASTIC* EQUATIONS IN THE CASE OF *CHANGED* STRUCTURE

7.1 The case now to be discussed combines both of the major complications of previous cases; in fact the reason for discussing the previous cases at all is in large part because they lead up to the present case. Now we have a change of structure between the prediction period and the observation period, and we have stochastic disturbances. Hence we need to know the new reduced-form parameters including the distribution of the reduced-form disturbances in order to solve the excise problem. And even if we knew these things, which is the best we could hope for, we would be able to predict only the *probability distribution* of price and quantity that will result from the maintenance of any specified excise-tax rate. We would not be able to predict the exact value in any particular year or market because of the essentially unpredictable character of individual random disturbances in the prediction period.

7.2 As noted already, experiments are proscribed in many economic problems. In such cases the only available approach to the new reduced-form parameters is through the new structure (i.e., the new structural parameters), which in turn can be obtained only from the *old* structure plus specification of the structural change. Hence, as in the exact case, we need to know the old structure. And again it must be obtained, if at all, from nonexperimental observations, either via estimates of the old reduced-form parameters or directly. Thus the same kind of strategy used in the exact case of structural change, and outlined in 6.9, is applicable here. The only two modifications required to adapt that strategy to the stochastic case are: (1) the parameters in the equations are *estimated* instead of determined exactly, because of the presence of random disturbances, and (2) the parameters of the probability distribution of disturbances must be estimated along with the parameters in the equations at each stage. The steps are then:

(a) Obtain estimates of the parameters in the equations and in the distribution of disturbances of the old structure, either from estimates of the old reduced form or from observations directly.

(b) Obtain estimates of the new structure, including parameters of its distribution of disturbances, from the old one and specifications of the nature of the structural change.

(c) Obtain estimates of the new reduced form, including parameters in its distribution of disturbances, from the new structure.

7.3   Again steps (b) and (c) can be done readily in this problem, and step (a), obtaining estimates of the old structure, may be impossible. It will be possible if the structure is identifiable, and not if the structure is not identifiable. We shall defer the more detailed discussion of identification and estimation to later chapters.

8 SUMMARY OF THE GUIDED TOUR

The results to be expected from empirical work for the cases we have discussed in the guided tour are collected in Table 8.1. Any parameters or predictions that are obtained are exact in cases where the applicable

TABLE 8.1 Summary of Prediction under Changed and Unchanged Structure, Showing in Each of Four Cases Whether the Effect on Price and Quantity of a Given Level of Excise Tax Can Be Predicted

Conditions		Conclusions			
Ocurrence of Structural Change	Identification of Structure	Is Knowledge of the Old Structure Needed?	Can the Old Structure Be Estimated?	Can the Effect of the Excise Tax Be Predicted?	Relevant Sections in Ch. II
does not occur	identified	no	yes	yes	4, 5
does not occur	not identified	no	no	yes	4, 5
occurs	identified	yes	yes	yes	6, 7
occurs	not identified	yes	no	no	6, 7

equations are exact,[29] and approximate (with a higher probability of a given level of accuracy if the number of observations is large) in cases where the applicable equations are stochastic. If this is kept in mind, Table 8.1 will serve for both the exact and the stochastic cases. We see, for example, when we look across the third line, that if there is a structural change and the structure is identified, the old structure is needed and can be obtained and the effect of the tax on price and quantity can be predicted at least approximately. The solubility of the problem is of course based on the assumption that the nature of the structural change is known. The sections in which each case is discussed are given in the table, for easy reference. It will become clear as we go along that Table 8.1 describes not only the excise problem of the guided tour but also any econometric prediction problem of the type treated in this book.

QUESTIONS AND PROBLEMS

1.1. Explain and defend each of the inequalities that are given in connection with equations (1.1) and (1.2). (This may be done by considering examples that are constructed to violate them.)

1.2. Find the algebraic and graphical expressions for the supplier's total revenue net of excise tax in the situation described by equations (1.8)–(1.9) and Figure 1.1.

1.3. Verify the signs of γ_0, γ_1, δ_0, and δ_1 that are given in 1.15.

2.1. If α_0, α_1, β_0, and β_1 were numerically specified, would equations (2.1)–(2.2) represent a structure? Explain.

2.2. Verify the entries in the last two columns of Table 2.2.

2.3. Verify the entries in the last five columns of Table 2.3.

2.4. Using the stochastic model in 2.6, choose a different structure (i.e., a different probability distribution for u_α and u_β, and different values of α_0, α_1, β_0, and β_1), and construct joint probability distributions of reduced-form disturbances and of price and quantity.

4.1. Suppose that two observations yielded the following data:

Observation	E	p	q
1	0	30	60
2	10	35	50

What values of the parameters of the exact equations (4.1)–(4.2) are implied by these data? What if a third observation gave the following?

Observation	E	p	q
3	20	40	32

[29] Provided the structural change is of the sort that can be numerically expressed before it occurs, such as a change in a tax rate.

4.2. Suppose you had adopted an exact linear model, and your observed data did not exactly satisfy any exact linear equations. Give at least three possible sources of the difficulty. Indicate how you might try to decide whether each of them is involved, and what you might do to deal with each one that is involved.

5.1. Draw a graph showing possible straight lines resulting from possible pairs of observations of quantity q and tax rate E when the structure is as described in 5.3.

(a) How many possible straight lines are there?

(b) Which, if any, of the lines corresponds to the systematic part of equation (2.4)? Draw this systematic part on your graph and explain.

5.2. How would you deal with question 4.2 if you had adopted a stochastic model?

6.1. Adopt the model given by equations (6.1) and (6.2), and suppose that observed data yield $p = 30$ and $q = 60$ as in 6.3–4. Suppose that during the observation period $E = 0$, that is, there was no excise tax. Suppose that an excise tax is now to be imposed. What can you deduce about the new reduced form, given the model and the fact that when $E = 0$, $p = 30$ and $q = 60$? Explain.

6.2. Suppose the correct model is given by the following supply and demand equations:

$$q = \alpha_0 + \alpha_1 p + \alpha_2 W \qquad \alpha_1 > 0, \; \alpha_2 < 0$$
$$q = \beta_0 + \beta_1 p \qquad \beta_1 < 0, \; \beta_0 > 0, \; \beta_0 > \alpha_0 + \alpha_2 W > \alpha_1 \beta_0 / \beta_1$$

where W is the exogenous wage rate paid by suppliers. Write out the reduced form. What can be determined about the structural parameters (α's and β's) from the model and three observations on each variable? This problem is discussed in detail in VIII.2.

7.1. Offer examples of real-world economic problems that might be solved by the procedure recommended in this section.

7.2. Offer examples that would be difficult or impossible to solve by the procedure of this section, and point out the reasons for the difficulties.

8.1. Offer examples to illustrate each of the four cases represented by the four lines of Table 8.1.

8.2. What kinds of information can be used to discover the new structure when the old structure is known (or has been estimated) and a structural change is thought to have occurred?

Part Two

Theoretical Models

CHAPTER III

Static Theory
with Exact Equations

This chapter first discusses units of measurement and dimensions. Several static exact economic models are presented and discussed. Very simple and brief refreshers are provided concerning differential calculus and determinants. It then uses these mathematical techniques in a comparative statics analysis of several models. Cross-section models are distinguished from time-series models, and some of their special characteristics are discussed. Nonlinear models are discussed, and a technique for dealing with models that are linear in parameters but not in variables is introduced. The summation operator $\sum$ is explained. Some general forms of expressing exact static models are shown.

1 INTRODUCTION; UNITS AND DIMENSIONS

1.1 We shall devote the next two chapters to theoretical analysis of several problems in economic statics and the following two chapters to dynamics. Economic statics is the branch of economic theory in which time does not enter, either as an explicit variable or in the form of lagged variables or rates of change. Statics treats of equilibrium situations, that is, situations which if attained will be maintained. Economic dynamics will be defined and discussed in Chapter V. Chapters III and V will discuss exact theories; Chapters IV and VI will discuss stochastic theories (i.e., theories that include random disturbances). We shall translate economic theories into equation form; state our problems and the relevant *a priori* information; show how to decide what additional information is required; and show how to find as much of the additional information

51

as possible from theoretical analysis. The theories drawn upon may be either micro-economic or macro-economic theories, the former being concerned with particular firms or individuals and the latter with aggregates such as national income and expenditure. The theories drawn upon may belong to different schools of thought, for the method of mathematical models is not prejudiced for or against any economic point of view. Of course, there is no pretense of completeness in our treatment of economic theories; the aim is rather to illustrate how theory can be used in econometrics to prepare the ground for empirical work.

1.2 It is important to specify the units, or at least the dimensions (explained below), in which each economic magnitude is expressed. This practice will be an aid to both clarity and memory. A few simple examples of units are as follows. The price of wheat may be measured in dollars per bushel or per pound or per ton, or in cents or pounds sterling or francs per bushel, etc. In each case the unit of wheat price is some unit of money divided by some unit of wheat quantity. The rate of exchange of sterling for United States money, defined as the price of sterling in terms of United States money, may be expressed in dollars per pound or cents per shilling, etc. In each case its unit is a unit of United States money divided by a unit of sterling. Quantities of goods demanded or supplied are usually expressed in terms of a unit of the good per unit of time, for example, for wheat, bushels per year. Money incomes are expressed in dollars per year, or dollars per month, or billions of dollars per year, in each case the unit being a ratio of a money unit to a time unit. The rate of interest is obtained by dividing an income (for example, in dollars per year) by a capital sum (in dollars) and hence is measured in a unit that is the inverse of a unit of time, "per year," for instance. If the income were expressed in dollars per month instead of dollars per year, the interest rate would be expressed per month instead of per year. Thus a return of $60 a year on an investment of a thousand dollars is the same as $5 a month on that investment. The rate of interest can be expressed equivalently as 6 per cent per year or $\frac{1}{2}$ per cent per month. This is true no matter whether the interest is compounded or not; but if it is compounded the intervals at which it is compounded must be stated separately. Thus 6 per cent a year compounded semiannually is the same as 3 per cent per half year compounded semiannually or as $\frac{1}{2}$ per cent a month compounded every 6 months.

1.3 It is sometimes inconvenient to have to state specific units in which variables are to be measured, particularly in theoretical work. It is possible to specify the *kind* of units to be used, however, for example, money per unit time, instead of dollars or pounds sterling per year or decade. This is called specifying the *dimensions* of the variable. The two major types of dimensions used in economics are *physical* dimensions and *money* dimensions. Physical dimensions include time, distance, weight, volume (which itself has distance cubed as its dimensions), and horse-power, and also ones or pairs or dozens, that is, the simple counted total of objects. Money dimensions include money of the purchasing power that prevailed in a particular period and place, for 1960 money is not the same as 1933 money, and a dollar in Centerville is not a dollar in New York, etc. For some purposes it is convenient to use another dimension—utility.

TABLE 1.1   Dimensions of Some Common Economic Magnitudes
(For an explanation of the notation, see paragraph 1.4)

Economic Magnitude	Dimensions
quantity of stock of a single good	Q or M_o
quantity of flow of a single good	Q/T or M_o/T
price of a single good	M/Q
value of stock of a single good	M
value of flow of a single good	M/T
value of stock of several goods	M
value of flow of several goods, e.g., money income	M/T
price index of several goods	M/M_o
real stock of several goods	M_o
real flow of several goods, e.g., real income	M_o/T
quantity index of several goods	none
value index of several goods	M/M_o
rate of interest	$1/T$
capital coefficient (capital $\div$ income)	T
slope of flow demand or supply curve, $\Delta q/\Delta p$	Q^2/MT or M_o^2/MT
elasticity of flow demand or supply	none
marginal propensity to consume	none
marginal rate of substitution of good i for good j	Q_i/Q_j
elasticity of substitution of good i for good j	none
marginal productivity of good j in producing good i	Q_i/Q_j
average productivity of good j in producing good i	Q_i/Q_j
absolute change in value of flow of goods	M/T
rate of change of value of flow of goods	M/T^2

1.4   Some of the common economic magnitudes and their dimensions are shown in Table 1.1. The symbols used are T for time, Q for other physical quantities, and M for money. M_o refers to money whose purchasing power is that of some comparison-base period or place. Thus the gross national product in current prices is measured as M/T, whereas the real (i.e., deflated) GNP is measured as M_o/T where o is the comparison-base year in which by definition real and money GNP are equal.

1.5 Consistency requires that several rules be observed. Two magnitudes cannot be equal, nor can they be added or subtracted, unless they have the same dimensions. The dimensions of a sum or difference are the same as those of the components. When two magnitudes are multiplied (or divided), the dimensions of the product (or quotient) are obtained as the product (or quotient) of the dimensions of the factors (or dividend and divisor). Thus price times flow quantity equals flow value; and the dimensions of these quantities satisfy the same product rule, thus:

$$(1.1) \qquad \frac{M}{Q}\frac{Q}{T} = \frac{M}{T}$$

Similarly, the slope of a flow-demand curve is the change in quantity divided by the change in price occurring between two chosen points, and the corresponding dimensions satisfy the same quotient rule, thus:

$$(1.2) \qquad \frac{Q/T}{M/Q} = \frac{Q^2}{MT}$$

1.6 The analysis of dimensions leads to a further rule concerning the effects of changes in the units in which economic magnitudes are measured. An actual measurement becomes numerically larger if expressed in a smaller unit, for example, 1 dollar is the same as 100 pennies, or 1 pound sterling is (at the United Kingdom official exchange rate from 1949 to date) the same as $2.80, or 1 year is 12 months. Hence if the units in which any dimension is measured are changed, all numerical magnitudes involving that dimension are changed correspondingly, and no numerical magnitudes not involving it are changed. Thus if the time unit is changed from a year to a month, the numbers representing the following magnitudes do not change because time is not involved in them: prices, stock quantities, stock values, elasticities, marginal rates of substitution. But the number representing the interest rate must be divided by 12; for example, 6 per cent a year becomes $\frac{1}{2}$ per cent a month. And the numbers representing flow quantities must be divided by 12; for example, $240 billion a year is $20 billion a month. And capital coefficients are multiplied by 12; for example, a ratio of $480 billion to $240 billion per year (i.e., 2 years) is the same as the ratio of $480 billion to $20 billion per month (i.e., 24 months). The rule is to replace the old unit (1 year in our example) by its value in terms of the new one (12 months in our example). Thus 6 per cent per year becomes $\frac{1}{2}$ per cent per month by the following process, writing 0.06 per year for 6 per cent per year, etc.:

$$(1.3) \qquad \frac{0.06}{\text{year}} = \frac{0.06}{12 \text{ months}} = \frac{0.005}{\text{month}}$$

The same works with flow quantities, thus:

$$(1.4) \qquad 240 \text{ billion } \frac{\text{dollars}}{\text{year}} = 240 \text{ billion } \frac{\text{dollars}}{12 \text{ months}}$$

$$= 20 \text{ billion } \frac{\text{dollars}}{\text{month}}$$

or with capital coefficients:

$$(1.5) \qquad 2 \text{ years} = 2(12 \text{ months}) = 24 \text{ months}$$

An advantage of elasticities and other dimensionless quantities is that their numerical values are not affected by changes in units.

1.7 It is necessary to be particularly careful when finding the new units of a *rate of change*, for two time dimensions are involved, and both need not be expressed in the same units. Thus United States gross national product data are published quarterly by the Department of Commerce, showing annual rates in billions of dollars per year, during each quarter. Absolute changes in this series from one quarter to another are also expressed in billions of dollars per year, for they are differences between quantities each expressed in those units. For example, gross national product was at the rate of $430 billion per year during the fourth quarter of 1956, and at the rate of $436 billion per year during the first quarter of the following year.[1] The *absolute change* in GNP from the fourth quarter of 1956 to the next quarter was thus $6 billion per year. The *rate of change* between these two quarters was $6 billion per year per quarter, or $1½ billion per quarter per quarter, or $24 billion per year per year.

2 AN OVERSIMPLIFIED TWO-EQUATION NATIONAL INCOME THEORY

2.1 The simplest modern theory of the level of national income goes as follows.[2] Since incomes are payments received by producers of goods and services, total real income is the same as total real output of goods and services. This output can be divided into two components designated as real consumption and real investment. Thus consumption and income are related in that consumption equals income minus investment. They are also related in that consumers spend more when their income after taxes (disposable income) is high. In particular, when disposable income rises, part of the increase goes for consumption, and part

---

[1] U.S. Department of Commerce [1958], p. 121. These figures are seasonally adjusted.

[2] See any recent elementary economics textbook.

goes for savings. This is expressed by the *consumption function*, which assigns a value of the variable "consumption" to each value of the variable "disposable income." Investment (both public and private) is regarded by this simple theory as an exogenous variable whose value in any period can be taken as given. The level of income, therefore, will adjust itself to the level at which the amount consumed plus the given investment is equal to income. Thus investment is the "prime mover" of the system; if investment is increased, a larger income results, and vice versa.

2.2 This theory of income determination can be conveniently expressed in the form of a model with two equations. Here and in later economic models we shall usually follow the notational convention of denoting magnitudes in money terms by capital letters and real magnitudes by lower-case letters. We let c = consumption, i = investment (including public expenditure), y = national income, and t = tax receipts, all in real terms. Then we have

$$(2.1) \qquad c + i = y$$

$$(2.2) \qquad c = \phi(y - t)$$

This model is completed by the specification that c and y are endogenous, and i and t are exogenous. Suppose we wish to find the levels of income y and consumption c that correspond to any given investment i and tax bill t under this model. Then we must solve the equations (2.1)–(2.2) for y and c, that is, find the *reduced form* of the model. Suppose the consumption equation (2.2) is linear, with parameters α and β, thus:

$$(2.3) \qquad c = \alpha(y - t) + \beta$$

Then the solution is easy. The reduced form of (2.1) and (2.3) gives just one value for y and one for c:

$$(2.4) \qquad y = \frac{i + \beta - \alpha t}{1 - \alpha}$$

$$(2.5) \qquad c = \frac{\alpha i + \beta - \alpha t}{1 - \alpha}$$

If the consumption function is not linear, the solution is more difficult.[3] If the form of the consumption function is not specified, as in (2.2), we might say that the solution is impossible except in a very formal way.

---

[3] For some types of functions, a general solution true for all values of i and t may be impossible to write down. Then in order to find the solution for given values of i and t, we use numerical methods of successive approximation. This is the case, for example, if (2.2) is a polynomial equation of the 5th or higher degree in $(y - t)$.

We can say only that y and c are determined by i, t, and the function ϕ. Here it is not simply the value of the function ϕ at some particular value of $y - t$ that matters; it is the *whole function*. If the function ϕ changes, that is, if the curve representing it changes in shape or position, then y and c are likely to be different. (This is sometimes expressed in technical language by saying that y and c are *functionals* of ϕ.)

   2.3   Since nonlinear functions, and unspecified functions such as $\phi(y - t)$, do not give as convenient solutions as do linear functions, we often replace them by linear functions as approximations. For example, if we have a nonlinear function $f(x)$ whose graph is the curve in Figure 2.1,

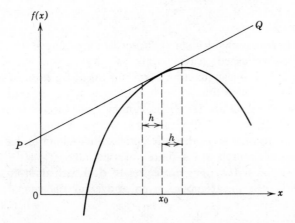

Figure 2.1   Linear approximation of a nonlinear function $f(x)$ near the value $x = x_0$.

we may approximate its values in the neighborhood of the point where $x = x_0$ by a linear function whose equation describes a straight line such as PQ.

   2.4   Since we shall have occasion to do a good deal of linearizing later on in connection with differential calculus, several algebraic examples may be given. To approximate the function $y = x^2$ near the point $x = x_0$, we define a new variable $h = x - x_0$ so that $x = x_0 + h$. Then

$$y = x^2 = (x_0 + h)^2 = x_0^2 + 2x_0 h + h^2.$$

As long as x is near x_0, so that h is small, the term h^2 will be so small that it can be neglected without causing serious error. Thus the function $y = x^2$ can be approximated in the neighborhood of $x = x_0$ by a linear function of h, $y \cong a + bh$, where[4] a and b are constants equal to x_0^2 and $2x_0$ respectively, and where h is small. This linear function of h can

---

[4] The symbol "$\cong$" means "is approximately equal to."

be transformed into a linear function of x if desired, by means of the definition of h, thus: $y \cong a + bh = a + b(x - x_0) = (a - bx_0) + bx = -x_0^2 + 2x_0 x$. The reader may experiment with this approximation by choosing, say, $x_0 = 10$, to see how large the error is in the approximation $y \cong 100 + 20h = -100 + 20x$, where $h = 1$ or $h = \frac{1}{2}$ or $h = 0.1$.

2.5 As another example, suppose $y = x^n$, and a linear approximation to this function is required in the neighborhood of the point x_0. Then using the same transformation $x = x_0 + h$, we find[5]

$$y = x^n = (x_0 + h)^n$$

$$= x_0^n + nx_0^{n-1}h + \frac{n(n-1)}{2} x_0^{n-2}h^2 + \cdots + nx_0 h^{n-1} + h^n.$$

Again, if x is near x_0 so that h is small, the terms containing $h^2, h^3, \ldots, h^{n-1}$, and h^n can be neglected, leaving only two terms, and we will have $y \cong x_0^n + nx_0^{n-1}h$, a linear function of h. This linear function of h can be transformed into a linear function of x, thus: $y \cong x_0^n + nx_0^{n-1}(x - x_0) = x_0^n(1 - n) + nx_0^{n-1}x$. Other functions can be "linearized" in a similar way. As stated above, we shall return to this type of linearizing in order to introduce the techniques of the differential calculus later in this chapter. (The meanings of symbols in 2.4–5 are not used later.)

2.6 Since linear functions are easier to deal with than any others, let us return to the linear model given above for the simple income-determination theory:

(2.1) $$c + i = y$$

(2.3) $$c = \alpha(y - t) + \beta$$

Then as we have seen, the reduced form of this model is equations (2.4)–(2.5), repeated here for easy reference.

(2.4) $$y = \frac{i + \beta - \alpha t}{1 - \alpha}$$

(2.5) $$c = \frac{\alpha i + \beta - \alpha t}{1 - \alpha}$$

It shows us the values of y and c that occur if α, β, i, and t are given. Figure 2.2 illustrates the situation. The line OC represents equation (2.1). The line AB represents the consumption equation (2.3) after i has been

---

[5] This formula is the binomial expansion, so called because it turns a power of a sum such as $(x_0 + h)$ into a sum of terms in x_0 and h. It is discussed in standard elementary algebra books.

added to both sides of it, for some fixed pair of values of i and t. Thus OA is equal to $i + \beta - \alpha t$. The solution, given by the reduced form, is shown by the coordinates of the point P. The reduced form can be used for the theoretical analysis of the effect in this model of a change in any one of these four quantities. For example, if investment (public or private) increases by 1 billion dollars, income increases by $1/(1 - \alpha)$ billion dollars; this is the multiplier effect, and the ratio $1/(1 - \alpha)$ is the multiplier. Since this theory of income shows that α, the marginal propensity to consume, is positive and less than 1 (see 2.1), this simple theoretical

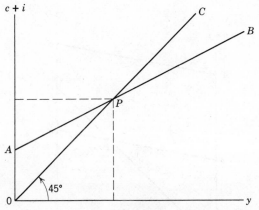

Figure 2.2   Graph of an income-determination model, equations (2.1) and (2.3).

analysis shows that an increase in investment *does* increase income, and by *more* than the investment increment, for $1/(1 - \alpha)$ is positive and greater than 1. As another example, if government expenditures and taxes are each increased by 1 billion dollars at the same time, income will receive a cutback of $\alpha/(1 - \alpha)$ billions because of the extra tax and a rise of $1/(1 - \alpha)$ billions because of the extra expenditure, so that income increases by 1 billion as a net result. This is known as the multiplier effect of a balanced budget.[6]

2.7   The foregoing model says nothing about prices or about the maximum output available with given resources. If the parameters α and β and the exogenous variables i and t are such that the reduced form yields a value of income greater than the actual full-capacity output of the economy, then it is apparent that consumers and private investors and government together are trying to take off the market more goods

[6] See almost any modern book on the theory of income and employment. It might be added that this balanced-budget multiplier theorem (and indeed this model) assumes that additional government expenditures do not cause consumers to spend any more or less from a given disposable income.

than can be produced, that is, there is an inflationary situation. This restriction, that real income cannot exceed the full-capacity output, can be expressed as an inequality,

$$(2.6) \qquad\qquad\qquad\qquad y \leqq y_F$$

where y_F represents capacity output, or what is the same thing, full-employment real income. This inequality (2.6) should be taken account of in the model represented by (2.1) and (2.3). The situation is as shown in Figure 2.3. The bent line OCD represents equation (2.1) with the

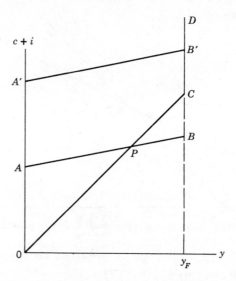

Figure 2.3   Graph of another income-determination model (2.1), (2.3), and (2.6).

restriction of inequality (2.6). The straight lines AB and $A'B'$ represent two possible versions of the demand for goods and services by consumers, investors, and government—equation (2.3) with i added to both sides of it, with given values of i and t. Neither AB nor $A'B'$ is shown extending to the right of y_F, the full-employment income, because y cannot exceed y_F. The equilibrium point corresponding to AB is P. The quantities supplied and demanded corresponding to $A'B'$ are shown by C and B', respectively. Since B' is above C, there is an inflationary gap of CB' representing the excess of goods demanded over goods produced.

2.8   To be quite clear about how (2.6) affects the model, we must distinguish between the *demand* for goods and the amount *actually* produced and acquired. We must also specify how the unsatisfied demand is spread among the various sectors of the economy. If we assume that controls are so applied that consumers are the only ones unable to satisfy their demand during inflation, and if we denote by c_d and y_d the amounts of consumption goods and all goods demanded, respectively, we shall have as our model

(2.7) $$y_d = c_d + i$$

(2.8) $$c_d = \alpha(y - t) + \beta$$

(2.9) $$y = y_d \quad \text{if} \quad y_d \leqq y_F$$

$$y_F \quad \text{if} \quad y_d \geqq y_F$$

(2.10) $$c = y - i$$

The reader may verify that this model represented the situation of Figure 2.3, with the additional condition that it is the consumers who are unsatisfied in case of shortages.

3 SIMPLIFIED VERSIONS OF INCOME AND EMPLOYMENT THEORY USING FUNCTIONS OF ONE VARIABLE; SEGMENTABILITY

3.1 This is not the place for a discussion of Keynes's contributions to the theory of employment.[7] However, it will be instructive to couch his system in the form of a model. We shall do this in two stages, first ignoring and then including the money market and the labor market and employment. In the first stage Keynes's theory can be described briefly as follows:[8] Real consumption is determined by real income in such a way that a given rise in income leads to a smaller rise in consumption (the marginal propensity to consume is less than 1). Real investment is a decreasing function of the interest rate, this function being related to the marginal efficiency of investment. Government expenditures are autonomous. Income is the sum of all spending—consumers', investors', and government's—and is determined by the relationships already mentioned.

3.2 We shall suppose that it is desired to find policies that can maintain income at the full-employment level. Accordingly, we shall be interested in finding what this theory says about the effects on income of changes in exogenous factors: government expenditures, taxes, and the quantity of money.

3.3 Let i now equal *private* real investment only, g = real government purchases, r = interest rate, and other symbols have the same

[7] See Keynes [1936], Pigou [1943], Harris [1947], Patinkin [1951], [1956], and [1965].
[8] See Keynes [1936], pp. 27–28, 183–184.

meanings as before (see 2.2). Then the theory described in 3.1 can be embodied in the following model:

(3.1) $y = c + i + g$ income definition

(3.2) $c = \phi(y - t)$ consumption equation

(3.3) $i = \psi(r)$ investment equation

We are led by economic theory and by experience (cf. 3.1) to assume that ϕ is an upward-sloping function, whereas ψ is downward-sloping. The endogenous variables are y, c, and i. The exogenous variables are g, t, and r.

3.4 This model has a property that makes it quite simple to work with. We shall say it is *segmentable*, since certain small segments of it are complete little models in themselves and can determine certain variables without reference to the remainder of the model. For instance, equation (3.3) is a complete little one-equation model, determining i all by itself, with r exogenous. There is no other equation that is a complete model. And the whole model of equations (3.1)–(3.3) determines i, c, and y. Thus there is a logical chain of determination running through the model, beginning with equation (3.3) and passsing to (3.1) and (3.2).[9] Observe that from the point of view of the two equations (3.1)–(3.2) it is immaterial whether i is regarded as an endogenous variable determined by (3.3) or as exogenous. The logical chain of causation can be represented by a scheme of arrows, thus:

$$(\psi, r) \rightarrow i$$
$$\searrow$$
$$(c, y)$$
$$(\phi, g, t) \nearrow$$

3.5 By following this logical chain of determination, we can trace the effects on y of changes in g, t, and r. Consider r first. A decrease in r, the rate of interest, stimulates investment (ψ is a decreasing function). Now i and r are in effect exogenous to equations (3.1)–(3.2), and we know from our analysis of a two-equation system like this in 2.6 that a rise in investment raises real income. Hence a decrease in r raises real income.

3.6 Consider g and t next. i is determined by (3.3), and so is exogenous to equations (3.1)–(3.2), where the influence of g and t enters. Again our analysis in 2.6 helps us: Increases in g and decreases in t both have the effect of raising y.

---

[9] See Simon [1953] for a careful discussion of the concept of causal priority in economic models, essentially similar to this. When stochastic models are considered in Chapter IV, segmentability will no longer be a sufficient condition for the completeness of such a submodel. See IV.4.9.

3.7   In many discussions of Keynesian theory in the literature,[10] the three relationships corresponding to equations (3.1)–(3.3) above are supplemented by Keynes's familiar liquidity preference equation, and the resulting four equations are used to determine income, consumption, investment, and the rate of interest. We shall argue below in 3.10 that it is not appropriate to do this within the framework of a model so simple that the price level does not appear as an endogenous variable. However, it is such a common expository device that we shall devote a few remarks to it.

3.8   Keynes's liquidity preference equation describes the demand for money to hold, saying that more money is demanded if income increases or if the rate of interest decreases. He was not explicit about what quantities he was expressing in real terms and what in money terms, but his discussion of this equation suggests that he had in mind expressing the *nominal* quantity of money as a function of the rate of interest and *money* income.[11] Such an equation is not acceptable as it stands, because it implies that if the price level were to be, for instance, doubled, with no change in real income, then the demand for nominal money balances that is associated with income would rise, as is reasonable, but the demand for nominal money balances that is associated with the interest rate would not change at all, which is *not* reasonable.[12]

3.9   A rational theory of the demand for money to hold should state that the quantity of *real* money balances demanded (like the quantity of any good in real terms) depends on relative prices (including the interest rate) and real income,[13] so that if the price level and other monetary variables are doubled, leaving real opportunities unchanged, the demand for nominal money balances will also be doubled, ceteris paribus. We denote price level by P, nominal money stock by M, and real money stock by M/P. Thus, in place of Keynes's equation we should have something like $M/P = \lambda(r, y)$. Since we are temporarily dealing with functions of just one variable in this section,[14] we shall here ignore the effect of

[10] See for example Hicks [1937] and Modigliani [1944], pp. 45–61.

[11] The liquidity preference equation is given as $M = L_1(Y) + L_2(r)$ on p. 199 of Keynes [1936]. From the surrounding discussion, particularly that on p. 209, I think it is clear that Y represents *money* income, and M represents *nominal* cash balances. See Patinkin [1956], pp. 465–470 or [1965], pp. 637–642, for a textual analysis in support of this view.

[12] If Keynes's equation were interpreted as expressing the demand for real balances as a function of the interest rate and real income, then it would be acceptable; see (3.4) in the text below and the remarks following.

[13] And also, it should be added, on real assets; this feature will be introduced in the model in Section 4.4 below.

[14] We shall reintroduce income in the liquidity preference equation in 4.4 below.

income on the demand for money, and write

(3.4)
$$\frac{M}{P} = \lambda(r)$$

This equation shows that real balances demanded depend on the interest rate. The value of $\lambda(r)$ increases when r decreases.

3.10   Equation (3.4) can be combined with (3.1)–(3.3) to make a four-equation model in which the endogenous variables are c, i, y, and r, and the exogenous variables are g, t, and M/P. The resulting model is segmentable: (3.4) determines the interest rate r, which is then exogenous to (3.1)–(3.3). The logical structure of these three equations is therefore the same as discussed in 3.3–6. It should be noted, however, that this four-equation model introduces a serious oversimplification concerning the role of monetary authorities, that is, the assumption that it is M/P, *real* cash balances, that are exogenous. Actually, it is more realistic to suppose that *nominal* cash balances M are exogenous, and the price level P and real balances M/P are endogenous. This will be done in the more realistic model of the next section. To see that the oversimple monetary assumption made above is bad economics, consider what happens if the government tries to increase the *real* quantity of money by increasing the *nominal* quantity to a new level and holding it there. It may succeed temporarily but be frustrated eventually, because firms and individuals may not want to hold such large real balances and may accordingly bid up the price level until total real balances are approximately what they were in the first place. This implies that the price level is endogenous.

3.11   We shall now consider two simple and still rather unrealistic alternative ways to complete the four-equation, five-variable model composed of (3.1)–(3.4), the five endogenous variables of course being c, i, y, r, and P. Both ways of completing this model will add three more equations—a production function, a labor demand equation, and a labor supply equation—and two more endogenous variables—employment n and the money wage rate W. The two ways differ only in the labor-supply equation. The production function gives real output y as a function of employment n; the stock of capital and the state of technology should also enter this function, but they will be assumed fixed in the short run. The demand for labor is assumed to depend on the real wage rate W/P (this can be derived from the fact that in a competitive optimum, the marginal product of an input is equal to its real wage). One of the alternative labor supply functions assumes that the labor supply depends on the real wage, that is, that laborers have no money illusion. This alternative is the so-called classical labor-supply equation. The other alternative assumes that the supply of labor is perfectly elastic at a certain money wage rate W_0, that is, that laborers have money illusion. This is the Keynesian labor-supply function.[15] It may be modified by assuming that if employment is increased beyond a certain level n_0, called full employment, the supply price of labor rises according to the classical labor supply just described. Since the Keynesian theory is mainly intended to explain unemployment, we shall assume that the labor-demand curve cuts the Keynesian labor-supply curve in its perfectly elastic part. The corresponding equations are:

(3.1) $y = c + i + g$ income definition

(3.2) $c = \phi(y - t)$ consumption function

(3.3) $i = \psi(r)$ investment function

(3.4) $\dfrac{M}{P} = \lambda(r)$ liquidity preference function

(3.5) $y = \eta(n)$ production function

(3.6) $n = \delta(W/P)$ labor demand

(3.7) $n = \sigma(W/P)$ classical labor supply

(3.8) $W = W_0$ for $n \leqq n_0$ Keynesian labor supply

According to economic theory and experience, it is plausible to assume that η is an upward-sloping function—output increases with more labor input, and δ is a downward-sloping function—the amount of labor demanded decreases with a higher real wage. The labor-supply function σ may be supposed to be either upward sloping, or, if downward sloping, to be steeper than the demand function.

    3.12   Consider first the model containing the classical labor supply, that is, (3.1)–(3.7). The endogenous variables are c, i, y, r, P, n, and W. The exogenous variables are g, t, and M. This model is segmentable. The labor market determines the real wage W/P and employment n, as seen from equations (3.6) and (3.7). Then the production function (3.5) determines real income y from the known level of employment. Then when we come to consider the four equations (3.1)–(3.4), real income y is already determined. Then consumption is determined in (3.2), then investment in (3.1), then the interest rate in (3.3), and then the price level in (3.4). Then the money wage is known from the real wage and the price level. These last four "links" in the causal chain are of course too simple to be realistic, because the consumption and investment functions in this model are too simple. Both should depend on both income and the interest rate (this will be corrected in the model in 4.4).

[15] See Keynes [1936], Ch. 2, passim.

3.13   In this oversimple model (3.1)–(3.7) the chain of causation can be represented by the following arrow scheme:

$$(\delta, \sigma) \longrightarrow \left(\frac{W}{P}, n\right) \longrightarrow y \longrightarrow c \longrightarrow i \longrightarrow r \longrightarrow P \longrightarrow W$$

$$\eta \quad (\phi, t) \quad g \quad \psi \quad (\lambda, M)$$

The exogenous variables M, g, and t and the various behavior functions are at the beginning of this chain of causation, and the endogenous variables are determined successively [except that W/P and n are determined simultaneously by equations (3.6) and (3.7)], beginning with W/P and n and ending with P. The chain can be broken at any arrow, and the endogenous variables appearing before (i.e., to the left of) the break can be regarded as exogenous variables in a smaller model that determines the endogenous variables appearing after (i.e., to the right of) the break. For example, break the chain just to the left of c; then equations (3.1)–(3.4) are a model determining the endogenous variables c, i, r, and P (and hence also W because W/P is already known), on the basis of given values of the exogenous variables M, g, t, W/P, n, and y. One of the first things to be done in analyzing a model is to see whether it is segmentable and, if so, to decompose it into its segments to see what the causal connections implicit in it are.

3.14   The foregoing model, (3.1)–(3.7), is essentially a classical model, even though it does have a liquidity preference equation. It shows that there can be no unemployment in equilibrium, and that the equilibrium levels of real income and employment are unaffected by changes in M, g, or t. The only things that can affect the equilibrium levels of real income and employment, according to this model, are shifts in the labor demand and supply equations and in the production function.

3.15   Now consider the model containing the Keynesian rigid-wage labor supply, that is, equations (3.1)–(3.6) and (3.8). This is essentially a model consisting of the six equations (3.1)–(3.6), with the endogenous variables c, i, y, r, P, and n, and with exogenous variables W, g, t, and M, since the money wage rate W is given by (3.8). This model is not segmentable; it determines the six endogenous variables simultaneously. The amount of unemployment at equilibrium is given by the difference between the full-employment level and the level determined by the model. Real income and employment can be affected by government policy in the forms of changes in g, t, or M and can also be affected by changes in the wage that laborers will accept. In my judgment the labor supply assumed in this model is unrealistic for long-run changes, though it is approximately valid in some short-run situations. The two models discussed in 3.11–3.15 illustrate, in a simple way that ignores the Pigou effect, the now generally agreed-on proposition that unemployment equilibrium cannot exist without rigid wage rates (or prices or both).[16]

3.16 Note that in the model (3.1)–(3.7) there are several types of structural equations. Equations (3.2)–(3.4), (3.6), and (3.7) are *behavior equations*, each describing the behavior of some group in the economy— consumers, entrepreneurs, moneyholders, entrepreneurs again, and laborers, respectively. Equation (3.5) is a *technological restraint*, describing the limitations imposed on output by existing technical and engineering knowledge. Equation (3.1) is a *definition* of total expenditure as the sum of the various kinds of expenditure. There are other types of structural equations that we shall encounter later on; among the most important are *institutional restraints* describing the operations of a law or regulation or custom and *adjustment equations* describing the response of the economy to a disequilibrium in a market. *Equilibrium conditions* specify that the quantities demanded and supplied must be equal; they are a sort of degenerate special case of adjustment equations.[17]

3.17 Note that we have analyzed the model (3.1)–(3.7) without using its reduced form. Instead we have "unraveled" the theory according to the logical chain underlying its segmentation, as discussed in 3.11 to

---

[16] For an excellent discussion of these models see Brownlee [1950] or Bailey [1962].

[17] If we were to examine equation (3.1) carefully, we would find that it is not simply a definition but a mixture of that with an institutional restraint and an equilibrium condition. This system of three equations, from which (3.1) is derived by combination, is as follows (y_d stands for the total amount of goods demanded, y_s for total supply of goods, and other symbols have their previously assigned meanings):

$$\text{(a) } y_d = c + i + g$$

$$\text{(b) } y = \min(y_d, y_s)$$

$$\text{(c) } y_s = y_d$$

Equation (a) is a pure definition, defining the demand for all goods, y_d, as the sum of the various demands. Equation (b) expresses the legal and institutional facts of our economic system that when buyers and sellers do not agree about the quantity to be transacted, the side that favors the *smaller* (minimum) quantity is the side that has its way. If Mr. A wishes to buy up to six of Mr. B's horses for a hundred dollars each, and Mr. B wants to sell only three, and if the price does not change, three are sold, not six; similarly, if Mr. A wants to buy six and Mr. B wants to sell up to twelve, six are sold, not twelve. Equation (c) expresses an equilibrium condition: Quantity supplied and quantity demanded always adjust themselves to each other. If (c) is substituted for y^s in (b), we find that $y = y_d$; and if that is substituted for y_d in (a), we have (3.1) as a result: $y = c + i + g$. If there is a chronic state of excess demand at full capacity output as discussed in 2.7–2.8 above, then (c) must be replaced by a relationship like (2.9) above in the text. This discussion may seem pedantic, but it becomes important if an adjustment equation is used that is not also an equilibrium condition, i.e., if we wish to make our model reflect the reactions of the economy to disequilibrium. Such cases will be considered in Chapter V and beyond.

3.14. With this model, which is segmentable and contains several un-specified functions, it is much easier to do as we did than to try to work through the reduced form. If it is desired to obtain the reduced form, or at least an approximation to it, we can resort to linearizing the model[18] as follows (Greek letters here stand for constant parameters):

$$(3.9) \qquad y = c + i + g$$

$$(3.10) \qquad c = \alpha(y - t) + \beta$$

$$(3.11) \qquad i = \gamma r + \epsilon$$

$$(3.12) \qquad \frac{M}{P} = \zeta r + \theta$$

$$(3.13) \qquad y = \nu n + \mu$$

$$(3.14) \qquad n = \frac{\xi W}{P} + \pi \qquad \text{(labor demand)}$$

$$(3.15) \qquad n = \frac{\rho W}{P} + \tau \qquad \text{(labor supply)}$$

Plausible signs of the parameters, such as might be derived from *a priori* theoretical information, are these: $0 < \alpha < 1$, $\gamma < 0$, $\zeta < 0$, $\nu > 0$, $\xi < 0$, $\rho > \xi$, $\pi > \tau$. On solving (3.13)–(3.15) for y, we obtain as one equation of the reduced form

$$(3.16) \qquad y = \nu \frac{\pi\rho - \tau\xi}{\rho - \xi} + \mu$$

By examining (3.16) we can obtain the results that we got in 3.14, namely, the following: A change in M, g, or t does not affect y. A change in the labor supply or demand function or in the production function, that is, a change in π, τ, ξ, ρ, μ, or ν, will affect y because each of these parameters appears in (3.16).

3.18   The effects of any change, in either an exogenous variable or a parameter, upon any variable of this model can be traced either by the method of linearizing and solving for the reduced form as in 3.17 or by the method of "unraveling" the model into its successive segments as in 3.4 to 3.14. This type of analysis is called *comparative statics*[19] because it deals only with static relationships but analyzes the difference between static equilibrium positions to see the changes in the character of the equilibrium of a system that are associated with changes in the given

---

[18] The model consisting of (3.1)–(3.6) and (3.8) can also be linearized, as can any model, with more or less risk of falsification.

[19] See Samuelson [1947], Ch. 2.

conditions (i.e., in the parameters and exogenous variables). It says nothing about the manner of approach to a new equilibrium. Comparative statics can at best (i.e., when applied to a correct theory) indicate only the *direction and range of magnitudes* of such effects. Their actual magnitudes can be discovered only by having recourse to empirical work.

4 OTHER MACROECONOMIC MODELS; FUNCTIONS OF SEVERAL VARIABLES

4.1 As stated earlier in Section 1, and exemplified in Section 3, the method of mathematical models is not prejudiced for or against particular schools of thought in economics. Almost any economic theory can be expressed in terms of a model. The relations of economic theory often take the form of functions of two or more variables; for example, the amount of investment may be thought to depend on income as well as the rate of interest,[20] or output may be regarded as influenced by both labor input and capital input. Accordingly, it will be well to learn the technique of linearizing functions of several variables.

4.2 Suppose that it is desired to linearize the function $z = xy$ in the neighborhood of the point where $x = x_0$ and $y = y_0$. We define two new variables, $h = x - x_0$ and $k = y - y_0$, so that $x = x_0 + h$ and $y = y_0 + k$. Then $z = (x_0 + h)(y_0 + k) = x_0 y_0 + y_0 h + x_0 k + hk$. Now if x and y are near to x_0 and y_0, respectively, so that h and k are small, the term hk will be very small and can be neglected. Then $z \simeq x_0 y_0 + y_0 h + x_0 k$, a linear function of h and k. If the definitions of h and k are applied, we have $z = -x_0 y_0 + y_0 x + x_0 y$, a linear function of x and y with coefficients that depend only on the chosen values x_0 and y_0. This procedure is the algebraic equivalent of approximating a curved surface in three dimensions by a plane.

4.3 As another example, suppose it is desired to linearize $z = x/y$. Defining h and k as in 4.2, $z = (x_0 + h)/(y_0 + k)$, which is to be approximated by a linear function, for instance, $r + sh + tk$ with coefficients r, s, and t. Our next aim is to express the coefficients r, s, and t in terms of x_0 and y_0. On setting $(x_0 + h)/(y_0 + k)$ equal to $r + sh + tk$ and clearing fractions we obtain $(x_0 + h) = (r + sh + tk)(y_0 + k) = ry_0 + sy_0 h + (r + ty_0)k + shk + tk^2$. Again if h and k are small, the terms in hk and k^2 can be neglected, and we have $x_0 + h = ry_0 + sy_0 h + (r + ty_0)k$. This approximation is supposed to be good for any small values of h and k, and hence should remain good if $h = k = 0$. Substituting $h = 0$ and $k = 0$, we get $x_0 = ry_0$, or $r = x_0/y_0$. That takes care of r. The approximation should also be good if h is small and $k = 0$. Substituting $k = 0$, we

[20] See, for example, Hicks [1937].

get $x_0 + h = x_0 + sy_0h$, or $s = 1/y_0$. That takes care of s. And the approximation should be good if $h = 0$ and k is small. Substituting $h = 0$, we get $x_0 = ry_0 + (r + ty_0)k$, or $t = -r/y_0 = -x_0/y_0^2$. That takes care of t. The linear approximation is then $z = x_0/y_0 + (1/y_0)x - (x_0/y_0^2)y$. The reader may experiment with these approximations to find how close they come to the true value of the function, by choosing various values of x_0, y_0, h, and k. He may also construct linear approximations for other functions by replacing x by $x_0 + h$, y by $y_0 + k$, etc. (The meanings of symbols in this paragraph are not used later.)

4.4   The model of 3.11 can be extended to include other influences, in particular those of interest rate on consumption, income on investment, real income on the demand for real cash balances, and real cash balances on consumption. The system then becomes

(4.1) $$y = c + i + g$$

(4.2) $$c = \phi\left(y - t, r, \frac{M}{P}\right)$$

(4.3) $$i = \psi(y, r)$$

(4.4) $$\frac{M}{P} = \lambda(y, r)$$

(4.5) $$y = \eta(n)$$

(4.6) $$n = \delta\left(\frac{W}{P}\right)$$

(4.7) $$n = \sigma\left(\frac{W}{P}\right)$$

This system can be linearized as indicated above, and then if primed Greek letters are used to denote new parameters it will consist of equations (4.1), (3.13)–(3.15), and the following (α', α'', γ', and ζ' are new parameters):

(4.8) $$c = \alpha(y - t) + \alpha'r + \alpha''\frac{M}{P} + \beta$$

(4.9) $$i = \gamma r + \gamma'y + \epsilon$$

(4.10) $$\frac{M}{P} = \zeta r + \zeta'y + \theta$$

We may postulate from theoretical considerations that consumption responds positively to a change in real balances, investment responds positively to changes in income, and demand for real money balances responds positively to changes in real income. The direction of the effect of an increase in the interest rate upon consumption is not so clear, but consumption will probably decline if r rises. These considerations will determine the signs of the new coefficients in (4.8)–(4.10), thus: $\alpha' < 0$, $\alpha'' > 0$, $\gamma' > 0$, and $\zeta' > 0$.

4.5 Now the question of the effect of an exogenous increase in M, g, or t, or a change in the labor supply function (4.7), upon income y or upon any other endogenous variable can be attacked in either of two ways, as before: first, by trying to find a causal chain in the system in order to unravel it or, second, by solving the linearized model to obtain its reduced form.[21] The unraveling method is applicable here, for the model (4.1)–(4.7) is segmentable. Equations (4.5)–(4.7) determine employment n, the real wage W/P, and real income y, just as discussed in 3.12. The remaining equations (4.1)–(4.4) form a nonsegmentable model that determines c, i, r, and P (and hence also W), given the values of M, g, t, n, W/P, and y.

4.6 It is now generally agreed that for purposes of analyzing long-run equilibrium situations, the model (4.1)–(4.7) is an important improvement on either the crude classical or the crude Keynesian models. It assumes flexible wages and prices and states that the equilibrium values of employment, the real wage, and real income are determined by the labor market and the production function, so that in equilibrium there must be full employment. Government fiscal and monetary policies do not affect the equilibrium values of real income and employment; they do affect the equilibrium price level and allocation of total output among final users. Of course fiscal and monetary policies do affect the actual current values of real income and employment, if not their equilibrium values, and it is precisely because we cannot afford to wait for long-run full-employment equilibrium to re-establish itself after a recession or an inflation that we want to use fiscal and monetary policies to regain full employment and stable prices whenever we start to lose one or the other. These matters are well discussed in Patinkin [1951] and [1956] and [1965].

4.7 A brief comment on the relation between one version of the quantity theory of money and the liquidity preference theory may be interesting. According to the crude quantity theory of money, money income Py is proportional to the nominal quantity of money M, the "constant" of proportionality being the income velocity of circulation of money. According to any reasonable interpretation of the quantity theory, the velocity of circulation is not perfectly constant but may be affected by such variables as the rate of interest, real income, and possibly

---

[21] If the reader wishes to solve the linearized system, (3.13)–(3.15), (4.1) and (4.8)–(4.10) for y, he is advised to use the method of determinants, discussed below in 5.21–5.29.

others. In such a form, the quantity theory of money can be expressed in the same form as the Keynesian liquidity preference equation (4.4) above, and vice versa. For instance, the liquidity preference equation (4.4) says that $M/P = \lambda(y, r)$. The quantity equation says that $M/P = y/V$, where V is income velocity. Equating the two expressions for M/P and solving for velocity, we get $V = y/\lambda(y, r)$, that is, velocity depends on the interest rate and real income. Furthermore, we can see from the negative effect of r on $\lambda(y, r)$ that a rise in interest rate can be expected to produce a rise in velocity. No inference can be drawn from the sign of $\partial\lambda/\partial y$ about the direction of the effect of real income on velocity.

4.8   Of course the systems displayed here do not exhaust the possibilities, even for static models, to which this chapter is confined. Still other theories of consumption, investment, money holding, labor supply, etc., are possible, and many have been used. Other variables may be introduced, such as imports and exports, breakdowns of investment and consumption into their components, and monetary as well as real values, with separate price levels for different economic sectors. We shall encounter some of this variety as we proceed.[22]

5 DIFFERENTIAL CALCULUS AS A TOOL FOR COMPARATIVE STATICS

5.1   In some problems, as we have seen, the model is not segmentable so that it cannot be "unraveled" into a logical chain of determination of the variables. At the same time simple linearization has disadvantages whenever we wish to work in a fairly wide range of the variables, since a linear approximation made for one part of a function is unlikely to be good for other parts. See Figure 5.1, where two linearizations of a function $f(x)$ are shown, one at the point $x = a$ and one at the point $x = b$.

5.2   Where segmentation is impossible and linearization at a single point is not acceptable, a more general linearizing technique, based on differential calculus and determinants, is useful.   In this section and the next we shall set out the features of differential calculus and determinants that are essential to this technique, for the benefit of any readers whose knowledge may be rusty, and we shall illustrate their use in comparative statics as we proceed. The material to be given here is not a good substitute for serious study of the mathematical topics we shall use.[23]

---

[22] For improvements in analysis of the consumption function, see Modigliani and Brumberg [1954] and Friedman [1957]. In particular, these writers substitute consumers' expected long-run average income for current income.

[23] See any standard calculus reference. Courant [1934], [1936] is particularly good. A good calculus reference for economists is Allen [1938].

5.3 The first steps in calculus are very closely related to the process of linearizing with which we are already familiar from the preceding sections. The difference between the linearizing we discussed and the linearizing of calculus lies chiefly in this fact: The type of linearization previously discussed must be made once and for all, and so is useful only in the neighborhood of the particular point for which it is made, whereas the linearization of calculus is flexible and can be applied to *any* point. The principal building block of calculus is called the derivative. We shall look first at its geometric meaning and then at its generally accepted

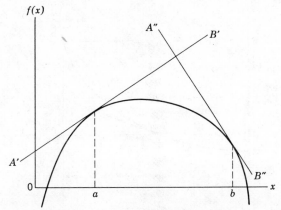

Figure 5.1 Two linearizations of a nonlinear function $f(x)$, at $x = a$ and at $x = b$.

definition. *The derivative of any mathematical function of one variable is another function, and wherever this new function exists its value shows the slope*[24] *of the curve representing the original function.* To be a little more specific, consider a supply function $p = f(x)$, whose graph is shown in Figure 5.2 as the curved line MPQ. At the point P on the curve, where $x = x_0$ and $p = f(x_0)$, the tangent line to the curve is PR. The slope of the curve MPQ at P is by definition the slope of the tangent, namely, the ratio SR/PS. This ratio is equal to the *derivative with respect to x of the function* $f(x)$, evaluated *at the point* $x = x_0$. At some *other* point, the derivative of $f(x)$ would be found by taking the slope of the curve, that is, of the line that is tangent to the curve, at *that* point. Thus the derivative of a function of x is another function of x; for any value of x it tells the *slope* of the curve at that value of x. It is as if the curve were linearized at *every* point, and then a new function of x were formed by taking the *slope* of each linearization and pairing it off with the x-value of the point where that linearization was made; this new function is the derivative.

[24] The slope of a curve at any point is the slope of a straight line tangent to the curve at that point, that is, it is the tangent of the angle between that straight line and the horizontal axis.

5.4 A very familiar example of a derivative is furnished by the speedometer reading on a car. The speedometer gives derivatives of a function that shows distance traveled as a function of time, distance $= f$ (time). At any moment the slope of this function is the instantaneous speed; it tells you how many miles the car would go if it kept on the same rate (slope) for an hour, just as the slope of a curve $f(x)$ tells you how many inches (or dollars or whatever units the function is measured in) you will rise vertically if you move to the right with the same slope for one inch (or one barrel or whatever unit x is measured in).

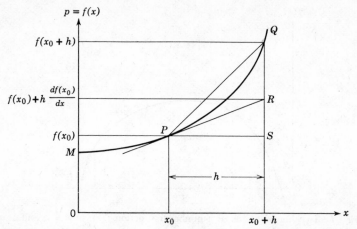

Figure 5.2 Linear approximations to a nonlinear curve MPQ representing $f(x)$.

5.5 It is not always convenient to draw a graph of a function to find its derivative, and in fact there are much more convenient ways of finding some derivatives, based on equations instead of graphs. Look at Figure 5.2 again, at the triangle PQS, and particularly at the slope of the line PQ, which connects the two points on the curve whose x-coordinates are x_0 and $x_0 + h$. (This ought to remind the reader of the linearizing we did in 2.4 and 2.5.) The slope of this line is SQ/PS and can be represented by the important expression

(5.1)
$$\frac{f(x_0 + h) - f(x_0)}{h}$$

It is not equal to SR/PS, the slope of the curve at $x = x_0$, and therefore it is not equal to the derivative at x_0. But if h is not very big, then $[f(x_0 + h) - f(x_0)]/h$ is *approximately* equal to the derivative at x_0. And if h is made smaller and smaller, the point Q will slide down the curve closer and closer to P, and the line PQ will approach the line PR, and $[f(x_0 + h) - f(x_0)]/h$ will come closer to the derivative. The derivative is generally defined as follows: *the limit[25] of $[f(x_0 + h) - f(x_0)]/h$, as h approaches zero, is the derivative of $f(x)$ at x_0, if that limit exists.* It is usually written with the zero subscripts removed to show that it is meant to hold for any value of x for which the limit exists (i.e., the derivative is a function of x), like this:

$$(5.2) \qquad \frac{d}{dx} f(x) = \lim_{h \to 0} \frac{f(x + h) - f(x)}{h}$$

Other common notations for the derivative of f are $df(x)/dx$, df/dx, $f'(x)$, and f'. If, as in the illustration we began with, $f(x) = p$, the derivative is sometimes denoted by dp/dx. Formally speaking, dp/dx is nonsense because p is a variable and not a function. If, when p depends on x, we write $p = p(x)$, thus unwisely using the symbol p for both a function and a variable, then dp/dx or $p'(x)$ can stand for the derivative of $p(x)$. Such usage is common, and we shall sometimes use it.

5.6   Mathematicians usually define the derivative of a function of x by means of the equations (5.2) and explain later that the derivative may be interpreted as a function that tells the slope of the original function for each value of x. That is the more satisfactory procedure from a technical mathematical point of view, and indeed we shall refer to (5.2) whenever we need to find the derivative of any particular function. But we chose to introduce the derivative first as the slope of a curve because that is a more concrete and an easier concept.

5.7   Several facts about derivatives should be noted before we go any further. *First*, the above definition applies only to single-valued functions, that is, to functions that have just one value for each value of x. A somewhat more complicated definition is required for functions like those in Figure 5.3, but we shall not ordinarily encounter such functions. *Second*, the derivatives of certain functions do not exist for some values of x_0 because for those values of x_0 the ratio $[f(x_0 + h) - f(x)]/h$ does not have a limit as $h \to 0$. An example is $f(x) = 1/x$ at the point $x = 0$. *Third*, the definition involves the limit of the ratio $[f(x + h) - f(x)]/h$

---

[25] This is a technical term in calculus, whose precise meaning can be found in any good calculus text. The basic idea of a limit is as follows. Suppose $y = g(h)$, what is the meaning of the statement that A is the limit of y as h approaches zero? It is that no matter how small a nonzero number δ anyone may choose, it is always possible to choose a nonzero number ϵ sufficiently small so that if h is not zero but is between 0 and ϵ or between 0 and $-\epsilon$, the difference between $f(h)$ and A is less than the chosen value δ. This is sometimes expressed by saying that $f(h) - A$ *becomes and remains* less than any nonzero number however small, as h is decreased indefinitely towards zero. Notice that the limit of $f(h)$ as h approaches zero has *nothing whatever* to do with what happens when h is actually equal to zero. Notice also that the limit may or may not exist. Thus the limit of $1/h$ as h approaches zero does not exist. But the limit of $(2h + h^2)/h$ as h approaches zero does exist and is in fact equal to 2, though $(2h + h^2)/h$ itself does not exist when $h = 0$ because division by zero is not permissible.

as $h \to 0$, *not* the value of the ratio when h is actually equal to 0 (that is of course 0/0, which is meaningless). Thus the derivative is *not* the ratio of two numbers $df(x)$ and dx, even though it is conventionally written as df/dx; it is the *limit* of the ratio (5.1) as the denominator approaches zero. *Fourth*, the units in which the derivative is expressed are the units of the function $f(x)$ divided by the units of x itself. Thus, if $f(x)$ is distance in miles and x is time in hours, then df/dx is velocity in miles per hour. Similarly, if $f(x)$ is supply price in dollars per pound, and x is quantity of goods in pounds per week, then df/dx or dp/dx is the slope of the supply curve and is measured in the rather strange units of dollar-weeks per square pound.[26] *Fifth*, the derivative at a point (say where $x = x_0$) can

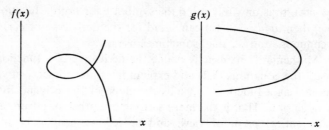

Figure 5.3 Functions that are not single-valued.

be used to approximate linearly the value of a function near that point, thus:

$$(5.3) \qquad f(x) \cong f(x_0) + (x - x_0)\frac{df(x_0)}{dx}$$

where the sign "$\cong$" means "approximately equals" and where $df(x_0)/dx$ means the derivative of the function at the point $x = x_0$. It is understood to mean that we *first* find the derivative df/dx and *then* substitute x_0 for x in the derivative. The same thing is often expressed somewhat differently as follows. Denote the change in the value of x, as it moves from the value x_0 to a new value x, by Δx, that is, let $\Delta x = x - x_0$. Denote the change in the value of the function, as x changes, by Δf, that is, $\Delta f = f(x) - f(x_0) = f(x_0 + \Delta x) - f(x_0)$. Then (5.3) can be solved for $f(x) - f(x_0)$ and written as

$$(5.4) \qquad \Delta f \cong \frac{df(x_0)}{dx}\Delta x$$

This can be illustrated by Figure 5.2, with PS (which was also called h) being equal to Δx, SQ being equal to Δf, and SR being the approximate

[26] $\left(\dfrac{\text{dollars}}{\text{pounds}}\right) \div \left(\dfrac{\text{pounds}}{\text{weeks}}\right) = \dfrac{\text{dollars} \times \text{weeks}}{(\text{pounds})^2}$. Compare equation (1.2) above.

value of Δf obtained from (5.4). This approximation process is exactly what we were using in linearizing functions in 2.4 and 2.5, though there you may not have realized how close we were upon the fundamental concepts of differential calculus. *Sixth*, the process of taking the derivative of a function is called differentiating it. *Seventh*, the complete title of the symbol df/dx is "the derivative of f with respect to x," but in practice the phrase "with respect to x" is often omitted, as in the foregoing pages, wherever there is only one variable with respect to which the derivative can be taken.

5.8　There are several functions that we need to differentiate very often. *It will be convenient to find their derivatives from the definition* (5.2) *and then memorize them*, to save time in their future use. The more important ones are given in the following equations (a and n are any constants, including negative numbers and fractions, and u and v are functions of x):

(5.5)
$$\frac{d}{dx} a = 0$$

(5.6)
$$\frac{d}{dx} af(x) = a \frac{d}{dx} f(x)$$

(5.7)
$$\frac{d}{dx} x^n = nx^{n-1}$$

(5.8)
$$\frac{d}{dx} (u + v) = \frac{du}{dx} + \frac{dv}{dx}$$

(5.9)
$$\frac{d}{dx} uv = u \frac{dv}{dx} + v \frac{du}{dx}$$

(5.10)
$$\frac{d}{dx} \left(\frac{u}{v} \right) = \frac{v(du/dx) - u(dv/dx)}{v^2}$$

(5.11)[27]
$$\frac{d}{dx} \log_e x = \frac{1}{x}$$

(5.12)[27]
$$\frac{d}{dx} e^x = e^x$$

(5.13)
$$\frac{d}{dx} g(u) = \frac{dg}{du} \frac{du}{dx}, \qquad \text{where } u = f(x)$$

Each of the foregoing formulas is proved by appeal to the definition (5.2). For example, equation (5.7) is proved along lines indicated in 2.5, as

----

[27] e is the number 2.71828 approximately, the base of the natural logarithms.

follows. The function $f(x)$ in this case is x^n, and the ratio of Δf to Δx, whose limit we seek is, following (5.2):

$$(5.14) \quad \frac{f(x + h) - f(x)}{h} = \frac{(x + h)^n - x^n}{h}$$

$$= \frac{x^n + nx^{n-1}h + \frac{1}{2}n(n - 1)x^{n-2}h^2 + \cdots + nxh^{n-1} + h^n - x^n}{h}$$

$$= nx^{n-1} + \frac{1}{2}n(n - 1)x^{n-2}h + \cdots + nxh^{n-2} + h^{n-1}$$

Now the limit of this expression as h approaches zero is simply

$$(5.15) \quad \frac{dx^n}{dx} = \lim_{h \to 0} \frac{(x + h)^n - x^n}{h} = nx^{n-1}$$

because all terms in the last expression of (5.14) have h as a factor except the first term, nx^{n-1}; hence all those terms approach zero as h does. Others in the list (5.5)–(5.13) are proved similarly, except for (5.11) and (5.12), which require special treatment.[28] Equation (5.13) is called the function-of-a-function rule because it shows how to differentiate a function $g(u)$ with respect to x, where u is a function $f(x)$.

5.9 A familiar application of differential calculus lies in the relationship connecting marginal revenue, price, and demand elasticity:

$$(5.16) \quad\quad\quad MR = p\left(1 + \frac{1}{\eta}\right)$$

where η is demand elasticity, defined as the per cent change in quantity demanded divided by the per cent change in price that brings it about, thus: $\eta = (p/x)\, dx/dp$. Note that if the demand curve slopes down from left to right, $\eta < 0$. Equation (5.16) is derived as follows. Since marginal revenue MR is the increase in total revenue R per unit of additional sales, it is equal to the derivative of total revenue with respect to quantity sold, that is, $MR = dR/dx$. Now since $R = px$, we have $dR/dx = d(px)/dx$, which by the product rule (5.9) becomes $p\, dx/dx + x\, dp/dx = p + x\, dp/dx = p + p(x/p)\, dp/dx = p[1 + (x/p)\, dp/dx] = p(1 + 1/\eta)$, as in (5.16). This says that when demand is elastic, that is, when $\eta < -1$, marginal revenue is positive; when demand is inelastic, that is, when $\eta > -1$, marginal revenue is negative; and when demand elasticity is -1, marginal revenue is zero.[29] The result is familiar. Many other important applications of calculus center around marginal revenue, marginal cost, and

---

[28] See any standard calculus text for proofs.

[29] The absolute value of any number is always positive, being equal to a if a is positive and equal to $-a$ if a is negative. It is denoted by vertical lines. Thus $|-3| = |3| = 3$. Using this concept, demand is elastic if $|\eta| > 1$, inelastic if $|\eta| < 1$, and of unit elasticity if $|\eta| = 1$.

marginal product, for every marginal quantity is essentially either a derivative or a ratio of two changes such as (5.1).[30]

5.10   An important question arises when we wish to differentiate an equation, that is, to differentiate the expressions on both sides of the equality sign: Does the equation still hold afterward, that is, are the two derivatives equal? Consider the two functions $a^2 + p^2$ and $(a + p)^2 - 2ap$; they are equal *at every value of p*, and their derivatives are equal at every value of p as well. Consider on the other hand a supply function $\sigma(p)$ and a demand function $\delta(p)$, whose values in equilibrium are equal, $\sigma(p) = \delta(p)$ (indeed, it is this very equality that determines the price in a competitive market). Their derivatives are $d\sigma/dp$ and $d\delta/dp$, the slopes of the two functions. Clearly the two slopes may be unequal at every price; in the typical case they are. Why does the differentiating of $a^2 + p^2 = (a + p)^2 - 2ap$ yield an equality, whereas the differentiating of $\delta(p) = \sigma(p)$ does not? The difference lies in the fact that the first equation is true for *every* value of p, whereas the second is *not* true for every value of p, but only for the equilibrium price. An equation that is true for every value of a variable (or variables) is called an *identity* in that variable (or those variables). The rule is, then, that *an equation remains true after differentiation if and only if the equation is an identity in the variable with respect to which the derivative is taken.*

5.11   Often it is necessary, as we have already seen, to deal with functions of two or more variables. The concept of a derivative is applicable here too, with certain modifications. Consider a function of two variables, say a consumption function in which the quantity consumed z depends on both quantity of money held x and income y, so that $z = f(x, y)$. Its graph requires three dimensions, but it might be as shown in perspective by the shaded curved surface $PQRS$ in Figure 5.4. Only a

---

[30] It is interesting and important to note that if an equation is linear in the logarithms of variables, then elasticities in terms of those variables are simply the parameters of the linear equation. Suppose that two variables x and y are related by the equation

$$y = \alpha x^\beta$$

Then, taking logarithms to the base e,

$$\log y = \log \alpha + \beta \log x$$

This is linear in $\log y$ and $\log x$. If the reader will use (5.7) to find the elasticity of y with respect to x in the first equation in this footnote, he will find that it is

$$\frac{x}{y}\frac{dy}{dx} = \frac{x}{\alpha x^\beta}\alpha\beta x^{\beta-1} = \beta$$

Hence this elasticity is equal to

$$\frac{d \log y}{d \log x} = \beta$$

section of the graph of $f(x, y)$ is shown, namely that lying above the rectangle $OABC$ in the xy-plane. Consider the surface at the point P: Its slope depends upon what direction we take from P. The most convenient directions to use are those parallel to Ox and Oy. For the first of these y is held constant at the value corresponding to the point P, and z is treated as a function of the single variable x only; for the second x is held constant at the value corresponding to the point P, and z is treated as a function of y only. *The slopes in these two coordinate directions are equal to the partial derivatives with respect to x and with respect to y,*

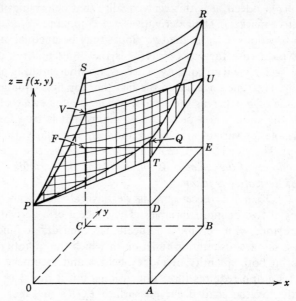

Figure 5.4   Linear approximation to a nonlinear surface $f(x, y)$ at the point P.

respectively, and are denoted by curly d's, thus: $\partial f(x, y)/\partial x$ and $\partial f(x, y)/\partial y$. The partial derivative with respect to x at the point P is equal to the slope of the curve PQ in the plane $OPQA$ at P, whereas the partial derivative with respect to y at P is equal to the slope of the curve PS in the plane $OPSC$ at P. The mathematical definitions of partial derivatives analogous to (5.2) are

$$(5.17) \qquad \frac{\partial}{\partial x} f(x, y) = \lim_{h \to 0} \frac{f(x + h, y) - f(x, y)}{h}$$

$$(5.18) \qquad \frac{\partial}{\partial y} f(x, y) = \lim_{k \to 0} \frac{f(x, y + k) - f(x, y)}{k}$$

Other common notations for the partial derivative of f with respect to x are $\partial f/\partial x, f_x(x, y)$, and f_x. If $f(x, y) = z$, then $\partial z/\partial x$ or z_x may be used also, but these are unwise because they require z to stand for both a variable and a function. All the remarks in 5.7 apply to partial derivatives of functions of several variables, with certain obvious modifications necessitated by the definitions (5.17)–(5.18).

5.12   The manner in which the plane $PTUV$ (tangent to the surface $PQRS$ at P) can be used to obtain the approximate value of the change in z (i.e., in the value of the function f) can be seen from the following three-dimensional discussion of Figure 5.4, analogous to that accompanying (5.3) and (5.4) and Figure 5.2 above. The plane $PTUV$ approximates the surface $PQRS$. Denote the values of x and y at the point P by x_0 and y_0, respectively. Suppose that x increases by an amount $\Delta x = OA$, and y increases by an amount $\Delta y = OC$, so that the value of z increases by an amount $\Delta z = ER$, from its old value OP to the new BR. Then ER, the actual increase in z, will be approximated by the distance EU, which shows how much z would increase if $f(x, y)$ were actually as shown by the plane $PTUV$ instead of the surface $PQRS$. Simple geometry will show that EU is the sum of DT and FV; this can be proved by drawing a line through T parallel to DE, so as to intersect EU, and another line to join this intersection point to F, for example. Let us examine DT and FV. Each of these distances can be evaluated by a formula like (5.4). Thus DT is the approximate increase in the function shown by the curve PQ when x increases by an amount OA; therefore, $DT = OA \cdot \partial f(x_0, y_0)/\partial x$. Similarly, $FV = OC \cdot \partial f(x_0, y_0)/\partial y$. Therefore, remembering that OA is Δx (i.e., the increase in x) and OC is Δy, we can write the analog of (5.4) thus:

$$(5.19) \qquad \Delta z = \Delta f \cong \frac{\partial f(x_0, y_0)}{\partial x} \Delta x + \frac{\partial f(x_0, y_0)}{\partial y} \Delta y$$

This is an important general formulation. It states that the change in a function z of two variables x and y, when x increases by Δx and y increases by Δy from the starting point (x_0, y_0), is approximately equal to the sum of two terms, one showing the effect of Δx when y is constant and the other showing the effect of Δy when x is constant.

5.13   *The rule yielding the partial derivative of a function of, say, x and y with respect to x is to treat the function as if it were a function of x only, that is, as if y were a constant, and then to differentiate it according to the procedure indicated in 5.5 and 5.8.* Thus the partial derivative of $x^2 + 6xy + 9y^2$ with respect to x is $2x + 6y$. The formulas in 5.8 can be used for partial derivatives as well as ordinary derivatives, with this rule in mind.

5.14   The function-of-a-function rule can be used for partial derivatives too, with appropriate important changes. In the next three paragraphs we give three examples. In the first example, let u be a function of x only (say $u = f(x)$, with derivative expressed by du/dx); let v be a function of y only (say $v = g(y)$, with derivative dv/dy); let $\phi(u, v)$ be a function of u and v; and consider how the value of $\phi(u, v)$ depends on x and y. This dependence can be written as follows, where $\psi(x, y)$ expresses the result:

$$(5.20) \qquad \phi(u, v) = \phi[f(x), g(y)] \equiv \psi(x, y)$$

The form of the function ψ clearly depends on the forms of the functions $\phi, f,$ and g.[31] The partial derivatives of $\psi(x, y)$ with respect to x and y are as follows in this case:

$$(5.21) \qquad \frac{\partial \psi(x, y)}{\partial x} = \frac{\partial \phi(u, v)}{\partial x} = \frac{\partial \phi(u, v)}{\partial u} \frac{du}{dx}$$

$$(5.22) \qquad \frac{\partial \psi(x, y)}{\partial y} = \frac{\partial \phi(u, v)}{\partial y} = \frac{\partial \phi(u, v)}{\partial v} \frac{dv}{dy}$$

These equations are directly analogous to the function-of-a-function rule (5.13) above. The first one, (5.21), says that the rate of change of $\psi(x, y)$ per unit change in x, when y is constant, may be found by multiplying together the two derivatives that give (1) the rate of change of $\phi(u, v)$ per unit change in u when v is constant and (2) the rate of change in u per unit change in x. The effect of x on $\psi(x, y)$ is thus decomposed into two multiplicative stages: the effect of x on u, and the effect of u on $\phi(u, v)$ when v is constant. The derivative of $\phi(u, v)$ with respect to u is *partial*, v being held constant, and hence is expressed by the curly d, $\partial \phi(u, v)/\partial u$. The derivative of u with respect to x is an ordinary derivative, not a partial, because u depends only on x via $u = f(x)$; hence the straight d is used, du/dx. Equation (5.22) is similar except that here it is y that affects $\psi(x, y)$, by acting through v. It is important to realize that (5.21)–(5.22) apply *only* if u depends on x alone and v depends on y alone and ϕ depends on u and v, as stated in (5.20).

5.15 A different form of the function-of-a-function rule is required to deal with a function of two (or more) variables, *each of which is itself a function of two (or more) other variables.* In the second example, let u be a function of both x and y, $u = f(x, y)$, with derivatives $\partial u/\partial x$ and $\partial u/\partial y$, and let v also, $v = g(x, y)$, with derivatives $\partial v/\partial x$ and $\partial v/\partial y$. Consider a function $\phi(u, v)$ as before, and its dependence on x and y, as follows:

$$(5.23) \qquad \phi(u, v) = \phi[f(x, y), g(x, y)] \equiv \psi(x, y)$$

[31] Note that ψ and ϕ are *different functions*, except in the degenerate trivial case where f and g are "identity functions" such that $f(x) \equiv x$ and $f(y) \equiv y$ so that $u \equiv x$ and $v \equiv y$. For example, if $\phi(u, v)$ has the form $au + bv$, and if $f(x)$ and $g(y)$ have the forms x^2 and y^3, respectively, then $\psi(x, y)$ is defined as $ax^2 + by^3$, so that ψ is a different function from ϕ. ψ says take the sum of a times the square of the first argument plus b times the cube of the second argument; ϕ says take the sum of a times the first argument plus b times the second.

(Note that the meanings of f and g and ψ here are different from their meanings in the preceding paragraph.) Again ψ and ϕ are in general *different functions*, and again the form of ψ depends on the forms of ϕ, f, and g. The partial derivatives of $\psi(x, y)$ with respect to x and y are as follows in this case:

$$(5.24) \qquad \frac{\partial \psi(x, y)}{\partial x} = \frac{\partial \phi(u, v)}{\partial x} = \frac{\partial \phi(u, v)}{\partial u} \frac{\partial u}{\partial x} + \frac{\partial \phi(u, v)}{\partial v} \frac{\partial v}{\partial x}$$

$$(5.25) \qquad \frac{\partial \psi(x, y)}{\partial y} = \frac{\partial \phi(u, v)}{\partial y} = \frac{\partial \phi(u, v)}{\partial u} \frac{\partial u}{\partial y} + \frac{\partial \phi(u, v)}{\partial v} \frac{\partial v}{\partial y}$$

These equations are analogous to (5.13) above. They are also analogous to (5.19) in that each contains the sum of two terms. Equation (5.24), for example, shows that when y is constant, a unit increase in x affects u at the rate $\partial u / \partial x$ and also affects v at the rate $\partial v / \partial x$, and in turn these two resulting changes in u and v affect $\phi(u, v)$ in the manner explained earlier in (5.19) and Figure 5.4. Similarly, (5.25) shows the effect, with x constant, of a change in y on $f(x, y)$, via the effects of y on u and on v and in turn the effects of u and v on $\phi(u, v)$. It is important to realize that (5.24)–(5.25) are valid *only* for situations described by (5.23).

5.16 Sometimes a situation occurs in which there is a function of two (or more) variables, in which one of those variables is a function of the other (or others). A utility function of quantities consumed, in which the quantity of one good depends via the budget restraint on the quantities chosen of the other goods, is a case in point. In the third example, then, let y depend on x alone via $y = f(x)$, with derivative dy/dx, and consider a function $\phi(x, y)$ and the manner in which it depends on x, as follows:

$$(5.26) \qquad \phi(x, y) = \phi[x, f(x)] \equiv \psi(x)$$

The meanings of the symbols here are all different from those in 5.14 or 5.15. The form of ψ again depends on the forms of ϕ and f. The derivative of $\psi(x)$ with respect to x is an ordinary derivative represented by a straight d, as follows, in this case:

$$(5.27) \qquad \frac{d\psi(x)}{dx} = \frac{d\phi(x, y)}{dx} = \frac{\partial \phi(x, y)}{\partial x} + \frac{\partial \phi(x, y)}{\partial y} \frac{dy}{dx}$$

The straight d is used in the second member of (5.27) because there $\phi(x, y)$ is being regarded as a function of x alone, namely, as $\psi(x)$. The expression $d\phi(x, y)/dx$ is called the *total derivative* of $\phi(x, y)$ with respect to x to distinguish it from the partial derivative $\partial \phi(x, y)/\partial x$, and to call attention to the fact that $\phi(x, y)$ is a function of x alone and *all* the effects of x on $\phi(x, y)$ are being taken into account, both direct effects expressed by $\partial \phi/\partial x$ and indirect effects via $\partial \phi/\partial y$. The *total derivative* of a function of several variables exists only if that function can be expressed as a function of a single variable, as $\phi(x, y)$ can be expressed as $\psi(x)$ above.[32]

5.17 The uses of partial derivatives in economics are manifold. The simplest and most familiar ones are marginal productivities, marginal propensities, and elasticities of various sorts. We shall now return to comparative statics and the two-equation model presented in 2.2, which we previously found difficult to analyze because it is not linear. We shall show how the linearizing technique of calculus makes possible the determination of the effects on income of changes in taxes or government expenditure or investment. We rewrite the model, equations (2.1) and (2.2), separating private investment i and government expenditure g. As before, c = consumption, y = income, and t = tax receipts.

$$(5.28) \qquad\qquad y = c + i + g$$

$$(5.29) \qquad\qquad c = \phi(y - t)$$

Suppose we wish to find the effect on income of a one-billion-dollar increase in government expenditure. The equations (5.28)–(5.29) determine consumption and income if the exogenous variables i, g, and t are given, and we may write these values as

$$(5.30) \qquad\qquad y = f(i, g, t)$$

$$(5.31) \qquad\qquad c = h(i, g, t)$$

What we want to know is the change in y due to a change of one billion dollars in g, that is, $\partial y/\partial g$, or in terms of the function f, $\partial f/\partial g$. We cannot actually solve (5.28)–(5.29) to get (5.30)–(5.31) and then differentiate, because we do not know the form of the consumption function ϕ. Instead, we can differentiate (5.28)–(5.29) *first* [because they are true for every value of g, that is, they are *identities* in g; see Section 5.10], and *then* solve, regarding $\partial y/\partial g$ and $\partial c/\partial g$ as our new variables.

5.18 After partial differentiation according to the rules (5.17)–(5.25), the model (5.28)–(5.29) becomes

$$(5.32) \qquad \frac{\partial y}{\partial g} = \frac{\partial c}{\partial g} + \frac{\partial i}{\partial g} + \frac{\partial g}{\partial g} = \frac{\partial c}{\partial g} + 0 + 1$$

$$(5.33) \qquad \frac{\partial c}{\partial g} = \frac{\partial \phi}{\partial y}\frac{\partial y}{\partial g} + \frac{\partial \phi}{\partial t}\frac{\partial t}{\partial g} = \frac{\partial \phi}{\partial y}\frac{\partial y}{\partial g} + 0$$

[32] *A word of caution to the reader:* Sometimes it is tempting to think of canceling du against ∂u, or canceling ∂u against ∂u, or the like, when one seems to appear in the numerator and the other in the denominator as in (5.21)–(5.27). But the expressions in these equations are *not* ratios, although through unfortunate usage of notation they *look* like ratios [see the third item in (5.27) above], and if the reader will just try such cancellation operations in (5.24) or (5.25) or (5.27) and examine the results he will quickly see what nonsense this can lead to. The fact that sometimes such treatment as a ratio seems warranted, as for example in (5.13) where cancellation of du looks safe, does not make it a safe practice. It is most likely to lead to trouble when *partial* derivatives are involved, but can also lead to trouble when ordinary derivatives are involved.

(The zeros appear because i and t, being exogenous, do not change when g changes.) These equations are linear in the variables $\partial y/\partial g$ and $\partial c/\partial g$, which we are seeking. Considering the right and left member of each, we see that they include as coefficients 1 and $\partial\phi/\partial y$, the latter being the marginal propensity to consume. If we solve them simultaneously, we obtain

(5.34)
$$\frac{\partial y}{\partial g} = \frac{1}{1 - \partial\phi/\partial y}$$

(5.35)
$$\frac{\partial c}{\partial g} = \frac{\partial\phi/\partial y}{1 - \partial\phi/\partial y}$$

Equation (5.34) tells us that the increase in income due to a one-billion-dollar increase in government expenditure is obtained approximately by taking the inverse of the marginal propensity to save; this is the multiplier, and is a generalization of the expression $1/(1 - \alpha)$ obtained in 2.6. Equation (5.35) gives the effect of a change in g on consumption. Similar analysis will show the effect of investment or taxes on income or consumption.

5.19 Since it is reasonable to assume that the marginal propensity to consume is between 0 and 1, we can deduce that $\partial y/\partial g$ in (5.34) is positive, that is, that an increase in g will increase income. We know this much without recourse to empirical work. If we wish to know the numerical magnitude of this multiplier $\partial y/\partial g$, we shall have to appeal to observed data.

5.20 It should be noted that even if all parameters (such as $\partial\phi/\partial y$) are known, the method of 5.17 gives only approximate answers to such questions as "what is the effect on income of a given change in government expenditure?" The approximation is better, the smaller the change contemplated. This is because the value of the marginal propensity to consume, $\partial\phi/\partial y$, is *not* actually constant, and when we treat it as constant in (5.34)–(5.35) we are in effect forming a linear approximation to the consumption function at the point where we evaluate its partial derivative, that is, at the point that describes the levels of c and y just *before* we ask about the effect of a change in g. In Figure 5.1 is shown a nonlinear function, $f(x)$, with a linear approximation to the function at $x = a$ and another at $x = b$. If the analysis of 5.17 were applied to a situation where a was the prevailing level of x, the result predicted would be the same as if the function were the straight line $A'B'$ instead of the curve; similarly for b and $A''B''$.

5.21 In some situations a linear approximation of a function is not accurate enough. In such cases it is often possible to achieve greater accuracy by using quadratic, cubic, or even higher-degree approximations. The mathematical device whereby this is done is known as Taylor's series.

5.22 Differential calculus has another important use in economics and econometrics, in addition to comparative statics. It is called in mathematical terms the maximizing and/or minimizing of functions with respect to the variables upon which they depend. Economics is concerned with maximum profits and outputs and satisfactions, and minimum costs and inputs and sacrifices. These concepts are familiar to the reader.[33] Econometrics is concerned in addition with maximum likelihoods of occurrence of certain statistical events, as we shall see in Chapters VII and IX.

6 DETERMINANTS AND THE SOLUTION
OF LINEAR EQUATIONS[34]

6.1 If the procedure of 5.17–5.19—the partial differentiation of a nonlinear system of equations with respect to a parameter or exogenous variable to obtain a new set of linear equations, which are then solved for derivatives of the original endogenous variables—is applied to a system of several equations, such as the Keynesian or so-called classical systems above, then a system of several linear equations must be solved as the last step. The method of determinants is useful for this, and we shall now review it. Again, the material to be given here is not a good substitute for serious mathematical study.[35]

6.2 Consider first a system of two linear demand and supply equations, where x_1 (quantity) and x_2 (price) are the variables and the six a's with different pairs of subscripts are the coefficients or parameters, thus:

$$(6.1) \qquad a_{11}x_1 + a_{12}x_2 = a_{10} \qquad \text{(supply)}$$

$$(6.2) \qquad a_{21}x_1 + a_{22}x_2 = a_{20} \qquad \text{(demand)}$$

It will be noticed that in either *row* of coefficients in this array, the *first* subscript of the a's is a constant: 1 in the first row and 2 in the second. And in any *column* the *second* subscript of the a's is a constant: 1 for the column of coefficients of x_1, 2 for the column of coefficients of x_2, and 0 for the column of constant terms on the right. If the reader solves the system (6.1)–(6.2) to get its reduced form, either by eliminating one variable or by substituting from one equation into the other, he will obtain the following equilibrium solution, which he should check by substituting it

---

[33] See, for example, Samuelson [1947], Ch. III.

[34] Appendix A gives some material on determinants, but the reader is advised to read this section now rather than that appendix unless he wishes now to take up matrix algebra.

[35] A good reference on determinants is Aitken [1949]. There are many other good references.

back into (6.1)–(6.2). (It is not as hard a job to check this as it looks, because many terms cancel out in the process.)

$$(6.3) \qquad x_1 = \frac{a_{10}a_{22} - a_{20}a_{12}}{a_{11}a_{22} - a_{21}a_{12}}$$

$$(6.4) \qquad x_2 = \frac{a_{11}a_{20} - a_{21}a_{10}}{a_{11}a_{22} - a_{21}a_{12}}$$

6.3 Each of the expressions found in either the numerator or the denominator of (6.3) or (6.4) is called a *determinant*; a determinant is a number, positive or negative or zero. These determinants are said to be of *second order*, because each term contains two a's as factors. Determinants in this form are difficult to remember, but fortunately there is a much more convenient form. Consider the determinant in the denominators of (6.3) and (6.4); it is called the determinant of the system (6.3)–(6.4). It can be written thus:

$$(6.5) \qquad a_{11}a_{22} - a_{21}a_{12} = \begin{vmatrix} a_{11} & a_{12} \\ a_{21} & a_{22} \end{vmatrix}$$

with the understanding that the numerical value of the 2×2 square array on the right is to be found by taking the product of the elements along the northwest-to-southeast diagonal (called the *principal* diagonal) and subtracting from this the product of the elements along the other diagonal. Notice that the array on the right side in (6.5) is formed simply by lifting out the coefficients of the variables in (6.1)–(6.2) *without changing their arrangement*. The numerators of (6.3) and (6.4) can be written in the same form as (6.5), thus:

$$(6.6) \qquad a_{10}a_{22} - a_{20}a_{12} = \begin{vmatrix} a_{10} & a_{12} \\ a_{20} & a_{22} \end{vmatrix}$$

$$(6.7) \qquad a_{11}a_{20} - a_{21}a_{10} = \begin{vmatrix} a_{11} & a_{10} \\ a_{21} & a_{20} \end{vmatrix}$$

Then the solution of (6.1)–(6.2) can be written in this simple schematic form:

$$(6.8), (6.9) \qquad x_1 = \frac{\begin{vmatrix} a_{10} & a_{12} \\ a_{20} & a_{22} \end{vmatrix}}{\begin{vmatrix} a_{11} & a_{12} \\ a_{21} & a_{22} \end{vmatrix}} ; \qquad x_2 = \frac{\begin{vmatrix} a_{11} & a_{10} \\ a_{21} & a_{20} \end{vmatrix}}{\begin{vmatrix} a_{11} & a_{12} \\ a_{21} & a_{22} \end{vmatrix}}$$

The convenience of determinants as a mnemonic device goes even further: The numerator of the solution for any variable is the same as the denominator, except that the column of coefficients of the variable being solved for is replaced by the column of constant terms from the right side of the original equations.

6.4   As an example, consider the system whose graph is shown in Figure 6.1 and whose equations are as follows:

(6.10) $$x_1 - 2x_2 = 1 \qquad \text{(supply)}$$

(6.11) $$x_1 + x_2 = 4 \qquad \text{(demand)}$$

(6.12) $$x_1 = \frac{\begin{vmatrix} 1 & -2 \\ 4 & 1 \end{vmatrix}}{\begin{vmatrix} 1 & -2 \\ 1 & 1 \end{vmatrix}} = \frac{1(1) - 4(-2)}{1(1) - 1(-2)} = \frac{1 - (-8)}{1 - (-2)} = \frac{9}{3} = 3$$

(6.13) $$x_2 = \frac{\begin{vmatrix} 1 & 1 \\ 1 & 4 \end{vmatrix}}{\begin{vmatrix} 1 & -2 \\ 1 & 1 \end{vmatrix}} = \frac{1(4) - 1(1)}{1(1) - 1(-2)} = \frac{4 - 1}{1 - (-2)} = \frac{3}{3} = 1$$

6.5   There is a caution to be observed, and certain useful properties of determinants should be noted. The caution is this: The equations to be

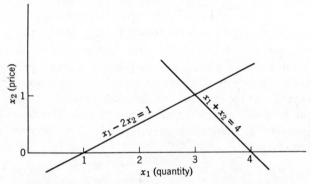

Figure 6.1   Graphical solution of equations (6.10)–(6.11).

solved must be put into the same form as (6.1)–(6.2) before the determinants are pulled out, or errors may result. That is, the equations must be arranged so that *all variables are on one side* of the equality sign and *the constant terms are on the other side*, and then *the terms containing any one variable must be grouped in a single column.*[36] The reader should try violating this rule in the above example and see what results. Four important properties of determinants are:

(a) If any two rows (or any two columns) of a determinant are interchanged, the resulting new determinant is equal to −1 times the original one (from this it follows that if a determinant has two identical rows, or

---

[36] The reader will be able to prove, a little later, that it does not matter in what order the equations are mentioned or in what order the columns corresponding to the variables are arranged, as long as the above rules are obeyed.

columns, then its value must be zero, for the only number that is not changed when multiplied by -1 is zero itself).

(b) If every element (i.e., member) of any row (or column) is multiplied by a constant, k, for instance, the value of the resulting new determinant is k times the original one.

(c) If every element of a row (or column) is altered by the addition to it of a constant (say k) times the corresponding element of some one other chosen row (or column), then the value of the determinant is not changed.

(d) If the array of numbers is replaced by a new array whose first row is the first column of the old array, whose second row is the second column of the old array, etc., the determinant of the new array is the same as that of the old.

The reader may verify these properties with respect to the determinants in (6.12) and (6.13), using any constant of his own choosing.

6.6   Determinants of third order, 3×3 arrays, arise if a system of three linear equations is to be solved. The rule for writing the determinant arrays for the numerator and denominator of the solution for any variable is analogous to that given in 6.3 for systems of two equations. Thus the solution of the system

$$\begin{aligned} a_{11}x_1 + a_{12}x_2 + a_{13}x_3 &= a_{10} \\ a_{21}x_1 + a_{22}x_2 + a_{23}x_3 &= a_{20} \\ a_{31}x_1 + a_{32}x_2 + a_{33}x_3 &= a_{30}. \end{aligned}$$

(6.14)

is written as

(6.15)
$$x_1 = \frac{\begin{vmatrix} a_{10} & a_{12} & a_{13} \\ a_{20} & a_{22} & a_{23} \\ a_{30} & a_{32} & a_{33} \end{vmatrix}}{\begin{vmatrix} a_{11} & a_{12} & a_{13} \\ a_{21} & a_{22} & a_{23} \\ a_{31} & a_{32} & a_{33} \end{vmatrix}}$$

(6.16), (6.17)

$$x_2 = \frac{\begin{vmatrix} a_{11} & a_{10} & a_{13} \\ a_{21} & a_{20} & a_{23} \\ a_{31} & a_{30} & a_{33} \end{vmatrix}}{D} \quad ; \quad x_3 = \frac{\begin{vmatrix} a_{11} & a_{12} & a_{10} \\ a_{21} & a_{22} & a_{20} \\ a_{31} & a_{32} & a_{30} \end{vmatrix}}{D}$$

where D represents the determinant of coefficients of the x's in (6.14), that is, the determinant in the denominator of (6.15). It is called the determinant of the system (6.14).

6.7   The problem remains: How to compute the *numerical value* of 3×3 determinants like those in (6.15)–(6.17)? The simple diagonal rule of 6.3 for 2×2 determinants will not work. A useful rule here involves using several 2×2 determinants to evaluate a 3×3 one and requires the definition of two new terms. Let us illustrate with the determinant D, the denominator of (6.15)–(6.17). For any given element of D there is a corresponding 2×2 determinant obtained by crossing out the row and column of D containing the given element. This 2×2 determinant is called the *minor* of the given element. For instance, the minor of the element a_{12} is obtained from D by crossing out the row and column containing a_{12}, that is, the first row and second column:

$$(6.18) \qquad \text{minor of } a_{12} \text{ in } D = \begin{vmatrix} a_{21} & a_{23} \\ a_{31} & a_{33} \end{vmatrix} = a_{21}a_{33} - a_{31}a_{23}$$

A minor becomes a *cofactor* if its algebraic sign is assigned by the following rule: the *same* as the sign of the minor (i.e., the minor is multiplied by $+1$) if the sum of the number of the row and the number of the column crossed out to obtain it is *even*, and *opposite* to the sign of the minor (i.e., the minor is multiplied by -1) if the sum of the numbers of the row and column crossed out is *odd*.[37] Thus, for example,

$$(6.19) \qquad D_{12} = \operatorname{cof} a_{12} \text{ in } D = - \begin{vmatrix} a_{21} & a_{23} \\ a_{31} & a_{33} \end{vmatrix} = -a_{21}a_{33} + a_{31}a_{23}$$

$$(6.20) \qquad D_{22} = \operatorname{cof} a_{22} \text{ in } D = + \begin{vmatrix} a_{11} & a_{13} \\ a_{31} & a_{33} \end{vmatrix} = a_{11}a_{33} - a_{31}a_{13}$$

D with subscripts is commonly used to denote the cofactor of the element of D having the same subscripts. Note that according to this rule it is *not* the algebraic sign of the number representing the value of the cofactor that must be positive or negative; it is the factor ± 1 by which the minor is multiplied to obtain the cofactor. Thus if the minor of a_{12} in (6.19) is a negative number, D_{12} will be a positive number, because $1 + 2$ is odd.

6.8 We are now ready to find the numerical value of a 3×3 determinant like

$$(6.21) \qquad D = \begin{vmatrix} a_{11} & a_{12} & a_{13} \\ a_{21} & a_{22} & a_{23} \\ a_{31} & a_{32} & a_{33} \end{vmatrix}$$

The rule to be used[38] is this: *Select any row or column of D and move along it, forming the sum of products obtained by multiplying each element*

---

[37] There are other equivalent schemes for determining what sign to affix to a minor in order to make it a cofactor. Among them are: (1) multiply the minor by $(-1)^{r+c}$, where r is the number of the row and c is the number of the column crossed out to obtain it; (2) change the sign of the minor if and only if an *odd* number of moves (vertical or horizontal only) are sufficient to get from the element in the first row and first column to the element in question; (3) change the sign of the minor if and only if, starting from the first row and first column, it is impossible to get to the element in question by diagonal moves only. The reader may choose whichever one seems simplest to him.

[38] There are other equivalent rules; see various algebra references.

of it by the element's cofactor (not its minor). Thus, for example, if D is expanded along the first row, the result is

$$(6.22) \qquad D = a_{11}D_{11} + a_{12}D_{12} + a_{13}D_{13}$$

$$= a_{11} \begin{vmatrix} a_{22} & a_{23} \\ a_{32} & a_{33} \end{vmatrix} - a_{12} \begin{vmatrix} a_{21} & a_{23} \\ a_{31} & a_{33} \end{vmatrix} + a_{13} \begin{vmatrix} a_{21} & a_{22} \\ a_{31} & a_{32} \end{vmatrix}$$

$$= a_{11}a_{22}a_{33} - a_{11}a_{32}a_{23} - a_{12}a_{21}a_{33}$$

$$+ a_{12}a_{31}a_{23} + a_{13}a_{21}a_{32} - a_{13}a_{31}a_{22}$$

The reader may experiment with expansions along other rows or columns and verify that the result is the same. He may also apply the rule to each determinant in (6.15)–(6.17) and thus find the solution of the system of three equations, (6.14).

6.9 Systems of four or more equations are handled in exactly the same way. Each determinant is expanded by selecting a row or column, and taking the sum of products of each element of that row or column times its cofactor. Then, if the cofactors have more than two rows and columns, they in turn are expanded in the same way, and *their* cofactors in turn, etc., until ultimately a set of 2×2 cofactors is obtained. The last set is then evaluated by the rule of (6.5) in 6.3.

6.10 Let us return now to the two-equation system (6.1)–(6.2), which we reproduce here, with its solution:

$$(6.23) \qquad a_{11}x_1 + a_{12}x_2 = a_{10}$$

$$(6.24) \qquad a_{21}x_1 + a_{22}x_2 = a_{20}$$

$$(6.25), (6.26) \qquad x_1 = \frac{\begin{vmatrix} a_{10} & a_{12} \\ a_{20} & a_{22} \end{vmatrix}}{\begin{vmatrix} a_{11} & a_{12} \\ a_{21} & a_{22} \end{vmatrix}} ; \qquad x_2 = \frac{\begin{vmatrix} a_{11} & a_{10} \\ a_{21} & a_{20} \end{vmatrix}}{\begin{vmatrix} a_{11} & a_{12} \\ a_{21} & a_{22} \end{vmatrix}}$$

The values of x_1 and x_2 are definite and unambiguous if the determinant of the system (6.23)–(6.24), that is, the denominator of (6.25) and (6.26), is not zero. The solution may then give positive or negative or zero values for x_1 and x_2 (it will certainly give zero if $a_{10} = a_{20} = 0$, in which case the system is said to be homogeneous). But there is a different story if the determinant of the system is zero. Then both (6.25) and (6.26) have zero denominators, and each is accordingly either meaningless, satisfied by every number, or infinite, satisfied by no number, depending upon whether its numerator is also zero or not.

6.11 The geometry of the situation is this: (1) If the determinant of the system, that is, the denominator of the solutions, is *not* zero, the two lines cross each other somewhere (as in Figure 6.1), and their intersection determines a unique solution (i.e., exactly one solution). In this case we say the system is consistent (because there is no contradiction between the two equations) and determinate (because there is a unique solution). (2) If the determinant of the system *is* zero, the two lines are parallel and there are two cases: (a) If neither numerator is zero, the two parallel lines do not coincide and they never intersect, and there is no point anywhere that will satisfy both equations. In this case we say the system is inconsistent. (b) If both numerators are zero,[39] the two parallel lines coincide, and any point on one of them will satisfy both equations. In this case we say the system is consistent but indeterminate; an infinite number of solutions exists. Similar conditions apply to linear systems of higher order. Accordingly, before trying to solve a linear system of n equations in n variables it is well to check to make sure that its determinant is not zero, that is, that it has a unique solution.

6.12   The properties of systems of linear equations are often phrased in the terms "necessary," "sufficient," and "necessary and sufficient," as are other properties in mathematics, statistics, and logic. We therefore pause a moment to explain their meanings. If we say "proposition A implies proposition B," this means that whenever A is true then B must be true also (note that it does *not* say what happens to B when A is *false*). Thus "A implies B" means "A is a sufficient condition for B"; if we have A, this is *sufficient* to ensure that we have B (though if we do not have A, we may or may not have B). This explains the meaning of a sufficient condition. To return to the original statement, "A implies B": it means also that we cannot have A without having B, so that B is a *necessary* condition for A. This explains the meaning of a necessary condition. Note that "B is a necessary condition for A" means the same as "A is a sufficient condition for B." If C is a necessary and sufficient condition for D, then D implies C (the "necessary" part), *and* C implies D (the "sufficient" part), so that C and D are equivalent statements; one is true if and only if the other is true. To sum up: (1) "A is a necessary condition for B" means the same as "B is a sufficient condition for A," and this means the same as "B implies A." (2) "A is a sufficient condition for B" means the same as "B is a necessary condition for A," and this means the same as "A implies B." (3) "A is a necessary and sufficient condition for B" means the same as "B is a necessary and sufficient condition for A," and this means the same as "A implies B, and also B implies A," which means the same as "A and B are equivalent."

6.13   Thus, for example, a necessary and sufficient condition for the existence of a unique solution of a system of n linear equations in n variables is that the determinant of coefficients of the variables be nonzero. As another example, in a system of n linear equations in n variables the existence of infinitely many solutions implies (i.e., is a sufficient condition

---

[39] It can be shown that if the denominator is zero, neither numerator is zero or else both are; one cannot be zero if the other is not.

for the proposition) that the determinant of the system is zero, but the fact that the determinant is zero does not imply (i.e., is not a sufficient condition for) the existence of infinitely many solutions. As a third example, in a system of linear equations the existence of at least as many equations as variables is a necessary but not sufficient condition for the existence of a unique solution. (Another way of saying the same thing is this: The existence of a unique solution is a sufficient but not necessary condition for the number of equations in a linear system to be at least as great as the number of variables.) Table 6.1 summarizes the situation (without being complete) for linear systems.

6.14 For nonlinear systems the situation is more complicated. No exhaustive treatment will be given here, but rather a few examples of what can happen. First, consider a system with more variables than

TABLE 6.1 Incomplete Summary of Conditions Governing Existence and Uniqueness of Solution to a System of m Linear Equations in n Variables

$m < n$ Fewer Equations than Variables	$m > n$ More Equations than Variables	$m = n$ Same Number of Equations and Variables
There cannot be a unique solution.	There can be a unique solution. A necessary condition is that one can find among the m equations a set of n equations that has a unique solution. A necessary and sufficient condition is the above necessary condition *plus* the condition that the set of m equations is not self-contradictory.	There can be a unique solution. A necessary and sufficient condition is that the determinant of the system is not zero.
There can be an infinity of solutions.	There can be an infinity of solutions.	There can be an infinity of solutions. A necessary condition is that the determinant of the system is zero.
The system can be inconsistent, having no solution.	The system can be inconsistent, having no solution.	The system can be inconsistent, having no solution. A necessary condition is that the determinant of the system is zero.

equations. Unlike the linear case, a unique solution does not require at least as many equations as variables, though it almost does, in the sense that only a very unlikely set of circumstances can provide an exception. Such an exception for two equations in three variables is illustrated by the case of one nonlinear equation representing a sphere and one linear equation representing a plane: If the coefficients of the equations are such that the plane is tangent to the sphere (i.e., touches it at just one point) then the two equations have a unique solution for three variables. A nonlinear system with fewer equations than variables can have infinitely many solutions (consider a single equation in two or more variables), or it can be self-contradictory and have no solution (consider a plane that does not touch or intersect a sphere).

6.15 Second, if there are the same number of equations as variables, the number of solutions may be zero (for a self-contradictory system), one, two, three, or any number, or there may be infinitely many solutions. For an example of two solutions, consider a curve (represented by a non-linear equation) that intersects a straight line at two places. If we encounter a nonlinear system in econometrics and it has several solutions, we can usually discard all but one of the solutions as being economically meaningless or nonsensical, because they involve negative values of variables known to be positive or some other absurdity (see the example in II.6.12 above). If a system has several solutions and two or more of them are economically plausible, then there is real difficulty in deciding what to conclude from the model. Fortunately such cases are rare.

6.16 Third, if there are more equations than variables, there can again be zero, one, two, three, . . . , or an infinity of solutions.

7 COMPARATIVE STATICS IN INCOME AND EMPLOYMENT MODELS[40]

7.1 Let us now use the methods of the two preceding sections to undertake a comparative statics analysis of a simple nonsegmentable model resembling equations (3.1)–(3.3) except that now both consumption and investment are assumed to depend on both income and the rate of interest, as in 4.4. The same result is obtained from (4.1)–(4.3) by dropping the variable M/P. This model is:

$$(7.1) \qquad\qquad y = c + i + g$$

$$(7.2) \qquad\qquad c = \phi(y - t, r)$$

$$(7.3) \qquad\qquad i = \psi(y, r)$$

[40] See Samuelson [1947], Chs. II–III. Examples of this kind of analysis are found, *inter alia*, in Klein [1947], Vickrey [1954], and Patinkin [1956] and [1965].

Let us investigate the effect on real income y of an exogenous change in the interest rate r, with no change in government expenditure g or tax receipts t. We first differentiate each equation of the system partially with respect to r, holding the other exogenous variables (g and t) constant. This yields a new system that is linear, and whose variables are the partial derivatives of the original endogenous variables y, c, and i with respect to r. For brevity of notation we denote these new variables by y_r, c_r, and i_r instead of $\partial y/\partial r$, etc. We apply the rules of 5.10 and equation (5.27). The resulting equations are:

$$(7.4) \qquad\qquad y_r = c_r + i_r$$

$$(7.5) \qquad\qquad c_r = \phi_y y_r + \phi_r$$

$$(7.6) \qquad\qquad i_r = \psi_y y_r + \psi_r$$

Next this system is arranged like (6.1)–(6.2), with all the variables in columns on the left and all the constant terms on the right [the only non-zero constants are ϕ_r and ψ_r in (7.5) and (7.6)], thus:

$$(7.7) \qquad\qquad y_r - c_r - i_r = 0$$

$$(7.8) \qquad\qquad -\phi_y y_r + c_r \qquad = \phi_r$$

$$(7.9) \qquad\qquad -\psi_y y_r \qquad + i_r = \psi_r$$

7.2   The quantity we are looking for is approximately equal to y_r; hence the next step is to solve the system for y_r in terms of the coefficients ϕ_y, ϕ_r, ψ_y, and ψ_r. Using determinants, this is equal to

$$(7.10) \qquad y_r = \frac{\begin{vmatrix} 0 & -1 & -1 \\ \phi_r & 1 & 0 \\ \psi_r & 0 & 1 \end{vmatrix}}{\begin{vmatrix} 1 & -1 & -1 \\ -\phi_y & 1 & 0 \\ -\psi_y & 0 & 1 \end{vmatrix}}$$

A fairly awkward determinant like the ones in (7.10) is easier to evaluate if there is some row or column having only *one* nonzero element because then only one cofactor of the determinant needs to be considered. The second column of the numerator of (7.10) can be made to have only one nonzero element (in the first row) if the first row is added to the second. Then by the rules of 6.8 above, it can be expanded by following down its second column, as follows:

$$(7.11) \qquad \begin{vmatrix} 0 & -1 & -1 \\ \phi_r & 1 & 0 \\ \psi_r & 0 & 1 \end{vmatrix} = \begin{vmatrix} 0 & -1 & -1 \\ \phi_r & 0 & -1 \\ \psi_r & 0 & 1 \end{vmatrix} = -(-1)\begin{vmatrix} \phi_r & -1 \\ \psi_r & 1 \end{vmatrix}$$

$$= \phi_r + \psi_r$$

The denominator of (7.10) can similarly be given a second column with only one nonzero element. The result is

(7.12)

$$\begin{vmatrix} 1 & -1 & -1 \\ -\phi_y & 1 & 0 \\ -\psi_y & 0 & 1 \end{vmatrix} = \begin{vmatrix} 1 & -1 & -1 \\ 1 - \phi_y & 0 & -1 \\ -\psi_y & 0 & 1 \end{vmatrix} = -(-1) \begin{vmatrix} 1 - \phi_y & -1 \\ -\psi_y & 1 \end{vmatrix}$$

$$= 1 - \phi_y - \psi_y$$

Therefore the solution for $\partial y/\partial r$, obtained by substituting these two expressions in the numerator and denominator of (7.10), is this:

(7.13)
$$\frac{\partial y}{\partial r} = \frac{\phi_r + \psi_r}{1 - \phi_y - \psi_y}$$

7.3   The problem now is to tell as much as possible about $\partial y/\partial r$ in (7.13) from theoretical considerations. At first it looks as though nothing can be said, for the numerical values of all the partial derivatives of ϕ and ψ are unknown. For the most part the *algebraic signs* of these derivatives are known; let us see what they can tell us. In the numerator, ϕ_r is expected to be negative, because consumers can be expected to consume less and save more when r rises and makes saving more lucrative. Next, ψ_r is expected to be negative, for a rise in the interest rate will tend to discourage borrowing and investment. Hence it is safe to conclude that the entire numerator is negative. Next, ϕ_y and ψ_y are both taken to be positive, for a rise in income is likely to bring about increases in both consumption and investment. But do ϕ_y and ψ_y together exceed 1, or not? They ordinarily do not, for the marginal propensity to spend (on both consumption and investment together) is ordinarily less than 1, that is, the amount of saving increases faster than the amount of investment when income rises.[41] Hence the denominator in (7.13) is positive. Therefore, putting all of these signs together, we conclude that $\partial y/\partial r$ is negative. In other words, an exogenous rise in the interest rate leads to a fall in real income in the model used here.

7.4   We shall now undertake a comparative statics analysis of a more complex nonsegmentable model, namely, equations (4.1)–(4.6), regarding the money wage rate W as fixed. A comparative statics analysis of (4.1)–(4.7) could also be done, but the segmentability of that model makes it clear that changes in M, g, or t will not affect the equilibrium

[41] Indeed, were this not true, the multiplier would be infinite, and an exogenous increase in spending would generate an infinite increase in the equilibrium level of income.

values of income and employment. The rigid-wages model we analyze here is reproduced below:

$$(7.14) \qquad y = c + i + g$$

$$(7.15) \qquad c = \phi\left(y - t, r, \frac{M}{P}\right)$$

$$(7.16) \qquad i = \psi(y, r)$$

$$(7.17) \qquad \frac{M}{P} = \lambda(y, r)$$

$$(7.18) \qquad y = \eta(n)$$

$$(7.19) \qquad n = \delta\left(\frac{W}{P}\right)$$

Endogenous variables are y, c, i, r, n, and P. Exogenous are W, M, g, and t. Let us now investigate the effect on real income of a change in the nominal quantity of money, M. This is a relevant problem for a monetary policy that seeks to stabilize national income when wages are rigid. We first differentiate each equation of the system partially with respect to M to obtain a new linear system, in which the new variables are the partial derivatives of the original variables with respect to M and are again denoted by y_M, c_M, i_M, etc. This system is shown here with the variables arranged in columns on the left and the constant terms on the right.

$$(7.20) \quad y_M \quad -c_M \quad -i_M \qquad\qquad\qquad\qquad\qquad = 0$$

$$(7.21) \quad -\phi_y y_M \;+c_M \qquad\quad -\phi_r r_M \qquad +\phi_{M/P}\frac{M}{P^2}P_M = \phi_{M/P}\frac{1}{P}$$

$$(7.22) \quad -\psi_y y_M \qquad\quad +i_M \;-\psi_r r_M \qquad\qquad\qquad = 0$$

$$(7.23) \quad \lambda_y y_M \qquad\qquad\qquad\; +\lambda_r r_M \qquad +\frac{M}{P^2}P_M \qquad = \frac{1}{P}$$

$$(7.24) \quad y_M \qquad\qquad\qquad\quad -\eta' n_M \qquad\qquad\qquad = 0$$

$$(7.25) \qquad\qquad\qquad\qquad n_M +\delta'\frac{W}{P^2}P_M \qquad = 0$$

7.5 Then the quantity we seek is given by the solution of this system for the partial derivative $\partial y/\partial M$, or y_M. The determinant form of the solution for y_M is

(7.26)

$$y_M = \frac{\begin{vmatrix} 0 & -1 & -1 & 0 & 0 & 0 \\ \phi_{M/P}\dfrac{1}{P} & 1 & 0 & -\phi_r & 0 & \phi_{M/P}\dfrac{M}{P^2} \\ 0 & 0 & 1 & -\psi_r & 0 & 0 \\ \dfrac{1}{P} & 0 & 0 & \lambda_r & 0 & \dfrac{M}{P^2} \\ 0 & 0 & 0 & 0 & -\eta' & 0 \\ 0 & 0 & 0 & 0 & 1 & \delta'\dfrac{W}{P^2} \end{vmatrix}}{\begin{vmatrix} 1 & -1 & -1 & 0 & 0 & 0 \\ -\phi_y & 1 & 0 & -\phi_r & 0 & \phi_{M/P}\dfrac{M}{P^2} \\ -\psi_y & 0 & 1 & -\psi_r & 0 & 0 \\ \lambda_y & 0 & 0 & \lambda_r & 0 & \dfrac{M}{P^2} \\ 1 & 0 & 0 & 0 & -\eta' & 0 \\ 0 & 0 & 0 & 0 & 1 & \delta'\dfrac{W}{P^2} \end{vmatrix}}$$

The numerator of (7.26) contains a row having only one nonzero element. The denominator contains no such row or column, but this happy condition can be easily produced by adding the first row to the second. Then the second row of the denominator becomes (without change in the other elements)

$$1 - \phi_y \quad 0 \quad -1 \quad -\phi_r \quad 0 \quad \phi_{M/P}\frac{M}{P^2}$$

Then the numerator can be expanded by taking the sole nonzero element of the fifth row and multiplying by its cofactor. The denominator can be expanded along its second column. By repetitions of a similar process, the following result is achieved (the common term $1/P^2$ has not been canceled from numerator and denominator):

(7.27)

$$y_M = \frac{-\eta'\delta'\dfrac{W}{P^3}(\phi_r + \psi_r + \lambda_r\phi_{M/P})}{\dfrac{M}{P^2}(\phi_r + \psi_r + \lambda_r\phi_{M/P}) - \eta'\delta'\dfrac{W}{P^2}[(1 - \phi_y - \psi_y)\lambda_r + (\phi_r + \psi_r)\lambda_y]}$$

The reader should verify this result for himself.

7.6   The problem now is to tell as much about the value of y_M, that is, $\partial y/\partial M$, from (7.27) as possible on theoretical grounds alone. Again let us see what we can do with our knowledge of the algebraic signs of the derivatives of the various functions.

7.7   Let us begin with the numerator. η' is positive because labor has a positive marginal product. δ' is negative because at a higher real wage less labor is demanded. W/P^3 is positive. The expression

$$\phi_r + \psi_r + \lambda_r \phi_{M/P}$$

is negative, because a higher interest rate reduces total real spending and reduces the demand for real balances and a higher level of real balances increases consumption. Therefore the numerator is negative.

7.8   Now let us look at the denominator of (7.27). Its first term is the product of M/P^2, which is positive, and $\phi_r + \psi_r + \lambda_r \phi_{M/P}$, which we saw in the preceding paragraph is negative. In the second term of the denominator, η' is positive as above, δ' is negative as above, and W/P^2 is positive. The expression in the square brackets is negative: $1 - \phi_y - \psi_y$ is the marginal propensity to spend and is positive, whereas λ_r is negative as above; and $\phi_r + \psi_r$ is negative as above whereas λ_y is positive because at higher incomes the demand for real balances is higher. Putting these results together, we see that the second term of the denominator including its minus sign is also negative. Hence the entire denominator, being the sum of two negative terms, is negative.

7.9   Now we can put together the results of the last three paragraphs and conclude that y_M is positive in the rigid-wage model consisting of equations (7.14)–(7.19), since it is the ratio of two negative determinants. In other words, in the rigid-wage world of this model, an increase in the nominal amount of money M will result in an increase in the equilibrium value of real income y. Since y is connected with employment n via (7.18), employment will increase along with real income. Also, as may be readily deduced from the other equations, the price level will rise, the real wage rate will fall, and real private spending will rise.

7.10   We noted in 7.4 that if the rigid-wage assumption of the foregoing model is replaced by the classical postulate that the labor supply depends on the real wage rate, then changes in the quantity of money or in government expenditures and taxes will not affect the equilibrium value of real income, that is, y_M is zero. If all economists do not agree on such questions as whether y_M is positive or zero, it is usually because they do not agree on the fundamental properties of some important function such as the labor-supply function. The comparative statics analysis here exhibited can be used to explore the results of any assumptions.

7.11   If insufficient care is exercised in the setting up of a model, the result may be a system of equations that contains a contradiction. Such a model or system is said to be inconsistent. As an example, consider a model in which real income is determined in the market for consumption and investment goods as in (2.1)–(2.2) above, and in which both the demand and supply of labor depend only on the real wage rate as in the preceding paragraph:

(7.28) $\qquad\qquad\qquad y = c + i + g$

(7.29) $\qquad\qquad\qquad c = \phi(y - t)$

(7.30) $\qquad\qquad\qquad y = \eta(n)$

(7.31) $\qquad\qquad\qquad n = \delta(W/P)$

(7.32) $\qquad\qquad\qquad n = \sigma(W/P)$

This system is inconsistent. It says that real income y is determined by events in the market for final outputs [equations (7.28)–(7.29)], and then it says that real income is determined by the production function (7.30) on the basis of the level of employment determined in the labor market. There is no reason to suppose that these two values of income would be equal (and even if they were, a change in the government budget could change one of them and destroy their equality). This system will not do as a basis for economic analysis.

    7.12 The reader may wish to apply a comparative statics analysis to one of the models discussed above to discover the effect of government spending or taxes on income or consumption or some other variable. Now that he has been through two such problems he will have less trouble with others. As further exercise, he may wish to cast in the form of models some of the verbal arguments in the literature and verify their arguments by means of the techniques presented here.

    7.13 In this chapter so far we have exemplified static models and the technique of comparative statics, whereby it is often possible to discover from theoretical considerations the direction (but not the magnitude) of the effect on endogenous variables of changes in parameters or exogenous variables. If magnitudes as well as directions are sought, then empirical work is necessary.

    7.14 It should be noted that in some models there are derivatives similar to $\partial y/\partial M$ in the model of 7.4, whose algebraic signs cannot be found by purely theoretical methods. These crop up in models that lead to derivatives where the numerator (or denominator) has terms with different signs; it is necessary to estimate the magnitudes of some of the parameters in order to find the sign of such a derivative.[42] Techniques for dealing with this problem when such estimates are not available are worked out by Lancaster [1965].

---

[42] For an example, see Christ [1951a].

8   A SIMPLE MACRO-ECONOMIC MODEL FOR ILLUSTRATIVE EMPIRICAL USE

8.1   We now examine a seven-equation static model that differs from the model of the preceding section, 7.4, in several ways: (a) it is linear; (b) its accounting identities are more detailed and provide for corporate saving, the property-labor income distribution, and two kinds of taxes; (c) there are behavior equations to explain labor income and corporate saving; (d) the monetary and production sectors represented by equations (7.17)–(7.20) are suppressed, with the result that demand conditions (as affected by fiscal policy) are the main determinants of real income, and the price level and monetary phenomena are ignored.

8.2   The endogenous variables in this model are as follows (all in real terms): consumption c, gross private domestic investment i, disposable personal income y, business gross product x_b, labor income in business w_b, property income p, and corporate saving s_c. The exogenous variables (also in real terms) are government purchases g, government wage bill w_g (this is a part of g), personal taxes t_p, business taxes t_b, and depreciation d. The last two always appear together as $(t_b + d)$.

8.3   The static model is:

(8.1)   consumption: $c = \alpha y + \beta$

(8.2)   investment: $i = \delta x_b + \epsilon$

(8.3)   labor: $w_b = \zeta x_b + \eta$

(8.4)   corporate saving: $s_c = \theta p + \lambda$

(8.5)   GNP = expenditure: $x_b + w_g = c + i + g$

(8.6)   GNP = income: $x_b + w_g = y + t_p + s_c + t_b + d$

(8.7)   income distribution: $p + w_b + w_g = y + t_p + s_c$

Note that real GNP is $x_b + w_g$. The consumption function is of the simplest Keynesian type. The investment function recognizes implicitly the relation between capital stock and the output that is to be produced (a dynamic version would include the capital stock at the end of the preceding year; see XI.2 below). The labor equation relates labor input to total output in the business sector. The corporate-saving equation relates corporate saving to property income on the presumption that property income influences corporate profit, which in turn influences corporate saving (see XI.2). The three identities are straightforward; we can think of (8.7) as defining property income as a residual. All the slope parameters (α, δ, ζ, and θ) are presumed to have positive signs. Also, all are expected to be less than 1.

8.4 The reduced-form equation for real gross business product x_b in this model, obtained by solving the system (8.1)–(8.7), is

$$(8.8) \qquad x_b = \frac{(g - w_g) + \alpha w_g - \alpha t_p - \alpha(1 - \theta)(t_b + d) + \mu}{\Delta}.$$

where Δ and μ are functions of parameters only, as follows:

$$(8.9) \qquad\qquad \Delta \equiv 1 - \delta - \alpha[1 - \theta(1 - \zeta)]$$

$$(8.10) \qquad\qquad \mu \equiv \beta + \epsilon - \alpha\lambda + \alpha\theta\eta$$

(Note that $g - w_g$ is government purchases of other than its employees' services, and w_g is government wage payments, and the two add to total government purchases g.) The corresponding reduced-form expression for real GNP, which is equal to $x_b + w_g$, is obtained by adding w_g to (8.8):

$$(8.11) \;\; x_b + w_g = \frac{(g - w_g) + (\alpha + \Delta)w_g - \alpha t_p - \alpha(1 - \theta)(t_b + d) + \mu}{\Delta}$$

Consider the algebraic sign of Δ, given by (8.9). If we look only at the presumed positive signs of α, δ, ζ, and θ, we cannot deduce the sign of Δ. However, it may be presumed to be positive because it represents one minus the marginal propensity to spend out of an increase in real gross business product (also out of real GNP, since the difference between GNP and business product is exogenous). Hence we conclude that Δ is positive. Then it follows from (8.8) that the multiplier $\partial x_b / \partial(g - w_g)$, which is $1/\Delta$, is also positive. The corresponding GNP multiplier from (8.11) is also $1/\Delta$ and positive. Similarly we see that an increase in government wage payments accompanied by no change in purchases of goods will increase gross business product (i.e., $\partial x_b / \partial w_g = \alpha/\Delta > 0$, $g - w_g$ being held constant), and the corresponding real GNP multiplier is $1 + \alpha/\Delta$ and positive. Increases in taxes or depreciation will reduce gross product as is readily seen from (8.8) and (8.11).

8.5 Reduced-form equations for any of the other endogenous variables of the model can be found and analyzed in the same way. In each case the denominator will be Δ as in (8.9), for Δ is the determinant of coefficients of endogenous variables in the system. In Chapter XI a dynamic stochastic model based on this model will be examined empirically.

9 CROSS-SECTION MODELS

9.1 Up to this point all the models presented have been time-series models. That is, they have contained equations supposed to be valid without changes in form or parameters during each of several different (in practice, usually consecutive) time periods, and intended to be used in connection with data describing economic events in these time periods. In I.5 we said that we would use the word "period" loosely, sometimes to refer to an interval of time in a time-series study, and sometimes to refer to a group of firms, individuals, and so forth, in a cross-section study. It is worth devoting a few remarks especially to cross-section models, for although they are not different in basic principle from time-series models, they have certain peculiarities that raise special questions.

9.2 By a "cross-section model" we mean a model containing at least one equation supposed to be valid for each of several different individual firms or consumers or geographical regions or the like, and intended to be used in connection with data describing economic features of those individual firms, consumers, regions, or what not. A time-series model regards all of a certain set of time intervals (e.g., years) as describable by a single general set of equations; a cross-section model regards all of a certain set of individuals (be they consumers, firms, or what not) as describable by a single general set of equations. To take equations of consumer behavior as an example: A time-series consumption equation relating the real consumption (c_t) of a certain consumer in year t to his real income (y_t) in year t might be:

$$(9.1) \qquad c_t = \alpha y_t + \beta$$

In this time-series case the assumption is that this equation applies without change (i.e., that the parameters α and β and the form of the function do not change) from year to year, at least for a certain period of years.[43] A cross-section consumption equation relating real consumption by the ith consumer in a certain year (c_i) to his real income in that year (y_i) might be as follows:

$$(9.2) \qquad c_i = \gamma y_i + \delta$$

In this cross-section case the assumption is that this equation applies for that year without change to all the consumers in question (i.e., that the

---

[43] If we wish to permit the slope α or the intercept β to change with time, or both, this can be done within the framework of an equation that applies without change from year to year, *provided* that the manner of the change in parameters over time is specified. For example, if α and β are both linear functions of time, then we can rewrite the above equation as

$$c_t = (\alpha' + \alpha''t)y_t + \beta' + \beta''t$$

Now even though α and β change, the parameters α', α'', β', and β'' do not, so that the latter equation applies without change.

parameters γ and δ and the form of the equation do not change from one consumer to another).[44]

9.3 It is plain from the definitions used that a model can be both a cross-section model and a time-series model. The same applies to an equation. For example, suppose that in the two preceding equations the slopes α and γ are equal, and the intercepts β and δ are equal. Then let c_{it} and y_{it} be respectively the consumption and income of the ith consumer in year t. Then both the time-series and the cross-section consumption equations above can be expressed in the same way:

$$(9.3) \qquad\qquad c_{it} = \alpha y_{it} + \beta$$

This is a time-series equation because it is supposed to apply to a given consumer without change for several time periods. It is a cross-section equation because it is supposed to apply to a given time period without change for several consumers. We shall use the terms "pure time-series model" and "pure cross-section model" respectively to refer to models that are time series but not cross section and vice versa, and "mixed model" to refer to models that are both.

9.4 For illustration let us set up a very simple pure cross-section model describing individual consumption behavior in an economy containing M individual households. After discussing it we shall modify it so that it becomes a mixed time-series and cross-section model. In this section we shall denote an individual household's real income, real consumption, real net worth, and so forth, by lower-case letters, and the corresponding aggregated real quantities by capital letters, thus temporarily violating our general rule that capital letters correspond to money terms.

9.5 For simplicity, we shall choose a model whose aggregate behavior conforms to the simple multiplier process described in 2.6. That is, aggregate real consumption C is taken to be a linear function of aggregate real income Y, and total real income Y is equated to the sum of total real consumption C and total real investment expenditure Z (assumed exogenous). The ith household's real consumption c_i is assumed to be a linear function of its real income y_i, and the marginal propensities to consume are assumed equal for all households; but the intercepts may differ, reflecting other variables not mentioned directly such as perhaps the household's demographic composition. (No other form of individual consumption function will, when aggregated, yield a linear relation

---

[44] If we wish to permit the slope γ or the intercept δ to vary among consumers, or both, this can be done within the framework of an equation that applies to all consumers without change, *provided* the change from one consumer to another can be described systematically, for example, by a function of the consumers' ages, family sizes, education, etc. This is done by expressing γ or β or both as functions of these variables, in analogy to the preceding footnote.

between total consumption and total income that has constant parameters independent of the income distribution.) Some mechanism for distributing income among households is needed to complete the model. We assume a simple one, which at least has the merit of permitting a household that has saved in the past to have a higher present income than if it had not saved. Each household's real income is assumed to be the sum of two parts: (1) its property income, which is the product of the market rate of return, r, times its real net worth at the end of the preceding period, k_i'; and (2) its real nonproperty income, x_i, which is exogenous (this would be the case if each household's employment and wage rate were exogenous —not necessarily the same for every household). The interest rate r is then determined by the necessity that total property income (which is r times total net worth[45] $\sum_i k_i'$, to be called K') plus total nonproperty income ($\sum_i x_i$, to be called X) add up to total income Y, all in real terms. This is admittedly a strange economy, for total income is determined by aggregate demand and is independent of the stock of capital. The return to a saver depends in no sense on anything like the real productivity of capital. Owning capital merely entitles one to a share in whatever portion of total income is left over (be it positive or negative or zero) after the total exogenous nonproperty income is paid. Nevertheless, such a model will illustrate some features of cross-section models sufficiently to make its examination worth while.

9.6 The pure cross-section model corresponding to the foregoing description is as follows. It is discussed below.

(9.4) $$c_i = \alpha y_i + \gamma + \epsilon_i \qquad i = 1, \ldots, M$$

(9.5) $$y_i = k_i' r + x_i \qquad i = 1, \ldots, M$$

(9.6) $$Y = C + Z$$

(9.7) $$C = \alpha Y + M\gamma$$

(9.8) $$Y = K'r + X$$

This model contains $2M + 3$ independent equations, and the same number of endogenous variables: r, C, Y, $c_1, \ldots, c_M$, and $y_1, \ldots, y_M$. Exogenous variables are Z, X, K', $x_1, \ldots, x_M$, and $k_1', \ldots, k_M'$. The parameters are α, γ, and $\epsilon_1, \ldots, \epsilon_M$. For convenience in writing (9.7) it is assumed that $\sum_i \epsilon_i = 0$. This introduces no restriction since γ in (9.4) can be defined to make it so. There are M households, and survey data yield in principle one observation from each household on each of the variables c_i, y_i, x_i, and k_i', just as time-series data yield one observation from each period on each of the variables in a pure time-series model. The interest-rate

---

[45] The symbol Σ is explained in 10.1.

variable r has only one observed value, associated with *all* the households; there is no direct analog for such a variable in a typical pure time-series analysis.

9.7   The foregoing model does not appear to contain any equations that say explicitly that total consumption and income are obtained by aggregating individual household consumption and income, thus:

$$(9.9) \qquad\qquad\qquad C = \sum_i c_i$$

$$(9.10) \qquad\qquad\qquad Y = \sum_i y_i$$

However, these two equations can be deduced from the model with the help of the relationships $X = \sum_i x_i$ and $K' = \sum_i k_i'$, which govern the exogenous variables. Therefore the $2M + 5$ equations (9.4)–(9.10) contain only $2M + 3$ independent equations. There are many ways to omit two of these equations and leave a set of $2M + 3$ equations that is logically equivalent to (9.4)–(9.8). One way is to omit (9.7)–(9.8) and express the model by (9.4)–(9.6) and (9.9)–(9.10); it is easily seen that then (9.7)–(9.8) follow by aggregating (9.4) and (9.5) respectively. We choose to express the model by means of (9.4)–(9.8) because that permits a somewhat more direct perception of its implications than do the other equivalent forms.

9.8   The variables C and Y can be eliminated from the model (9.4)–(9.8) along with equations (9.7)–(9.8), if desired, by replacing C and Y respectively by $\sum_i c_i$ and $\sum_i y_i$ in (9.6). Then (9.6) becomes

$$(9.11) \qquad\qquad\qquad \sum_i y_i = \sum_i c_i + Z$$

Then (9.4)–(9.5) and (9.11) form a model of $2M + 1$ equations, with $2M + 1$ endogenous variables $r, c_1, \ldots, c_M$, and $y_1, \ldots, y_M$. This model is of course equivalent to (9.4)–(9.8), the difference being that in the one case the aggregates $\sum_i c_i$ and $\sum_i y_i$ have special names (C and Y), and in the other case they do not.

9.9   Notice that in the cross-section consumption function, income y_i cannot be regarded as exogenous, because the total income of the economy is affected by the total demand for consumer goods. There is no possible segmentation of the model (recall the definition in 3.4 above) whereby individual incomes y_i are determined independently of the consumption equation: y_i depends on r in (9.5), r depends on Y in (9.8) and Y depends on $c_1, \ldots, c_M$ via (9.6)–(9.7). This means that the cross-section consumption equation (9.5) cannot be regarded as a complete single-equation model determining household consumption in terms of exogenous forces alone.

9.10   If data are available for several time periods, say from $t = 1$ to $t = T$, we can think of T distinct pure cross-section models, each one applying to a single period and each one determining the $2M + 3$ endogenous variables $r_t, C_t, Y_t, c_{1t}, \ldots, c_{Mt}$, and $y_{1t}, \ldots, y_{Mt}$ (t being constant within any of the cross-section models, but varying from one to another). We may attach subscripts to the parameters to indicate the period to which each applies. For example, α_3 is the marginal propensity to consume for any family in period 3. The pure cross-section model corresponding to period t is just like (9.4)–(9.8) above, except that here each variable and each parameter bears a subscript t to locate it in time.

9.11 The set of distinct cross-section models just described, for periods from $t = 1$ to $t = T$, do not in general constitute a time-series model, because the assumptions made so far do not require that every parameter be constant over all periods (recall the definition in 9.1 above). Let us now impose this requirement. Then $\alpha_1, \ldots, \alpha_T$ all have a common value, say α. This may be expressed concisely by saying $\alpha_t = \alpha$ for $t = 1, \ldots, T$. Similarly $\beta_t = \beta$ and $\epsilon_{it} = \epsilon_i$ for $t = 1, \ldots, T$ and $i = 1, \ldots, M$. In that case the result is a single model, a mixed time-series and cross-section model describing M households during T periods. This mixed model looks like (9.4)–(9.8) with several exceptions. *First*, each variable now must carry a subscript t to locate it in time. *Second*, there is an intertemporal connection in the model that should be stated explicitly: The net capital stock held by any person at the end of any period is equal to the net stock at the beginning of that period plus the net saving during the period. If we interpret the variables y, Y, k', and K' as net not gross of capital consumption [we must do so for k' and K' if (9.8) is to make sense], then for each household

$$(9.12) \quad k'_{it} = y_{i,t-1} - c_{i,t-1} + k'_{i,t-1} \quad i = 1, \ldots, M; \ t = 1, \ldots, T$$

These are dynamic equations, about which we shall have much to say in Chapters V and VI. Since k'_{it} is endogenous in the mixed model, so is K'_t, defined by

$$(9.13) \qquad K'_t = \sum_i k'_{it} \qquad t = 1, \ldots, T$$

The mixed model, consisting of equations (9.4)–(9.8) and (9.12)–(9.13), has $(3M + 4)T$ equations and the same number of endogenous variables: $r_t, C_t, Y_t, K'_t, c_{it}, y_{it}$, and k'_{it}; $i = 1, \ldots, M$ and $t = 1, \ldots, T$.

9.12 There is a two-equation aggregate pure time-series model embedded in the mixed model, as suggested in 9.5. Its equations are (9.6)–(9.7), its endogenous variables are C and Y, and its properties are analyzed in section 2 above.

9.13 We could imagine a pure time-series model for one household alone, containing the consumption function (9.4) for a single value of i, and for $t = 1, \ldots, T$. If such a model contains the income distribution equation (9.5) as well, it cannot explain a single household's behavior without reference to other households, because every household's income then depends on the activities of all other households; the entire mixed model is needed. On the other hand, if the income of one household is not governed by (9.5) but is somehow held fixed instead (through a pension plan or the like), then income can be regarded as exogenous in that household's consumption equation, which then becomes a single-equation pure time-series model with that household's consumption as the endogenous variable. Of course not every household can have a fixed income if the economy's total income is free to vary, as indicated in 9.9.

9.14 Cross-section models become more complicated (as do time-series models) if the output of goods and services is divided into finer classifications, such as consumer durable goods, consumer nondurable goods, and consumer services; or if several different kinds of individual decision makers are taken account of, such as consumers and firms, or consumers and several types of firms. But the general considerations illustrated in the preceding paragraphs still apply, with suitable modification.

9.15 The variables in cross-section and time-series models fall into the following types:

(a) Those that vary with time but are the same for all individuals at any one time, for example, prices, tax schedules, and macro variables or aggregates such as total consumption, total investment, and total tax payments.

(b) Those that vary from one individual to another, but do not change with time (or change only very slowly), such as demographic characteristics and occupation or social class of the head of household.

(c) Those that vary *both* with time *and* from one unit of the population to another, such as household income and household expenditure on each class of output.

Variables of type (a) are purely time-series variables. Those of type (b) are purely cross-section variables. Variables may be endogenous or exogenous, macro or micro, though as a rule the purely cross-section variables [type (b)] are exogenous and micro, and the mixed variables [type (c)] are endogenous and micro.

9.16 The equations of a cross-section model fall into the same types as those of a time-series model (see 3.16), namely *definitions, behavior* equations, *technological* restraints, *institutional* restraints, and *adjustment* equations (including *equilibrium* conditions as a degenerate special case). But in a cross-section model each of these may be further distinguished according to whether it is essentially a micro equation (such as the household consumption equation) or a link between micro and macro variables (such as the income definition, equating aggregate income to the sum of all expenditures by households and other spenders) or a macro equation.

9.17   Cross-section models, whether or not they involve observations from different periods in time, can be subjected to all the techniques discussed in the preceding sections of this chapter—linearizing, segmenting when possible, and comparative statics analysis.

9.18   The decision whether to use cross-section or time-series models or both will depend in practice partly on what kind of data are available at what costs and partly on the objectives of the study in question. The most fortunate situation is one in which data are available individually for a number of economic units over a span of time, so that changes in the behavior of each individual unit and of the group can be traced over time, and differences among units can be studied at any one time. Failing this, we must be satisfied either with repeated cross-section samples in several periods, with different individuals in successive samples, or perhaps even with a single cross-section or a single set of time-series data.

10   GENERAL FORMS OF STATIC EXACT MODELS; MODELS LINEAR IN UNKNOWN PARAMETERS

10.1   In this section we present several general forms, linear and nonlinear, in which static models may be cast. We shall find it convenient to use the accepted notation for a sum of quantities, involving the Greek capital letter $\sum$. For example, a sum of n numbers $a_1, a_2, \ldots, a_n$ is denoted thus:

$$(10.1) \qquad a_1 + a_2 + \cdots + a_n = \sum_{i=1}^{n} a_i$$

The sign $\sum$ indicates that the numbers denoted by the symbol a_i following the $\sum$ are to be added together; the subscript i together with the instructions written directly below and above the $\sum$ are understood to indicate that the sum is to begin with the number called a_1 and is to continue through all the a's up to and including a_n. The right side of (10.1) is read "the sum of a_i over i, with i running from 1 to n," or "the sum of a_i, from a_1 to a_n." Any letter whatsoever may be used instead of i in this expression; it is referred to as the index of summation, and it does not appear in the final result. Similarly, a sum of n products of coefficients and variables can be written in this notation (j is used as the subscript this time for variety):

$$(10.2) \qquad a_1 x_1 + a_2 x_2 + \cdots + a_n x_n = \sum_{j=1}^{n} a_j x_j$$

Hence any linear equation can be written in this notation, if its coefficients are designated by a single letter with consecutive subscripts and its variables by another. For example, equations (6.14) of 6.6 can be so written.

We reproduce them here, first in their original form, and then in the summation notation:

$$a_{11}x_1 + a_{12}x_2 + a_{13}x_3 = a_{10} = \sum_{j=1}^{3} a_{1j}x_j$$

(10.3) $$a_{21}x_1 + a_{22}x_2 + a_{23}x_3 = a_{20} = \sum_{j=1}^{3} a_{2j}x_j$$

$$a_{31}x_1 + a_{32}x_2 + a_{33}x_3 = a_{30} = \sum_{j=1}^{3} a_{3j}x_j$$

Looking at the center and right-hand members of (10.3), we see that the three equations are identical in form, the only difference being that the first subscript of each of the a's in the first equation is 1, in the second equation is 2, and in the third is 3. Why then go to the trouble of writing this form down three times? Instead, we may write it down just once, and leave instructions that we mean it in three different ways, once with 1's, once with 2's, and once with 3's. This is done as follows:

(10.4) $$a_{i0} = \sum_{j=1}^{3} a_{ij}x_j \qquad i = 1, 2, 3$$

The reader is told by the phrase "$i = 1, 2, 3$" in (10.4) that he is to insert 1 for i to get one equation, insert 2 for i to get another, and insert 3 for i to get a third. The system (10.3) is completely expressed by (10.4). It is conventional to have the *first* subscript remain the same along a *row* and the *second* subscript remain the same along a *column*. We have followed this convention.

10.2 We can now express the general linear model in a condensed form similar to (10.4). We let y_i ($i = 1, \ldots, G$) represent endogenous variables, and z_k ($k = 1, \ldots, K$) represent exogenous variables. Thus G is the number of endogenous variables (and the number of equations, if our linear model is to be consistent and determinate and not redundant), and K is the number of exogenous variables. K may be larger than G, or smaller, or the same. We let the parameters of the y's be denoted by β's with two subscripts, which tell respectively the equation and the y to which each β belongs. Thus β_{34} is the parameter of y_4 in the third equation. The parameters of the z's are denoted by γ's with two subscripts having similar meanings. Then any exact linear model can be expressed thus:

$$\beta_{11}y_1 + \beta_{12}y_2 + \cdots + \beta_{1G}y_G + \gamma_{11}z_1 + \cdots + \gamma_{1K}z_K = 0$$
$$\beta_{21}y_1 + \beta_{22}y_2 + \cdots + \beta_{2G}y_G + \gamma_{21}z_1 + \cdots + \gamma_{2K}z_K = 0$$

(10.5)

$$\beta_{G1}y_1 + \beta_{G2}y_2 + \cdots + \beta_{GG}y_G + \gamma_{G1}z_1 + \cdots + \gamma_{GK}z_K = 0$$

It may be disturbing that there appears to be no constant term in these equations. However, a constant term is easily incorporated by defining an exogenous variable, say the last one, z_K, which never varies and is always equal to 1; then its parameters, $\gamma_{1K}, \gamma_{2K}, \ldots, \gamma_{GK}$, are the constant terms. This common device makes the next step neater. We now apply the summation notation to (10.5), and the result is

(10.6)

$$\sum_{i=1}^{G} \beta_{1i} y_i + \sum_{k=1}^{K} \gamma_{1k} z_k = 0$$

$$\sum_{i=1}^{G} \beta_{2i} y_i + \sum_{k=1}^{K} \gamma_{2k} z_k = 0$$

$$\cdot \qquad \cdot \qquad \cdot$$
$$\cdot \qquad \cdot \qquad \cdot$$
$$\cdot \qquad \cdot \qquad \cdot$$

$$\sum_{i=1}^{G} \beta_{Gi} y_i + \sum_{k=1}^{K} \gamma_{Gk} z_k = 0$$

Now if all the G equations in (10.6) are written down at once as in (10.4), we have as the model

(10.7) $$\sum_{i=1}^{G} \beta_{gi} y_i + \sum_{k=1}^{K} \gamma_{gk} z_k = 0 \qquad g = 1, \ldots, G$$

This is the general form of an exact linear model, and by appropriate relabeling of variables and parameters and proper choice of G and K any exact linear model can be made to look like (10.7). This is a great advantage when we wish to discuss properties that all linear models have in common.

    10.3   The reduced form of a model is the result of solving its equations simultaneously for the endogenous variables y_i in terms of the parameters and the exogenous variables z_k. If we are to solve equations (10.7) in this manner, we first arrange them so that all endogenous variables appear on one side, say the left, and all constant terms (which in this case means constant terms and exogenous variables) appear on the right. If the method of determinants is then applied, each y_i will turn out to be a ratio of two determinants. The denominator will have as elements only the parameters β_{gi}, and the numerator will be just like the denominator except that *one column* (the ith column) will consist of elements that are linear functions of the exogenous z's (in fact this column will be simply the column of $-\sum_{k=1}^{K} \gamma_{gk} z_k$ from (10.7), for $g = 1$ to $g = G$). Hence the denominator will have a numerical value independent of the z's—let us call it D—and each y_i will be $(1/D)$ times its numerator determinant. The numerator must itself be a linear function of the z's, as can be seen by expanding it along the column containing the z's. Every cofactor of an element in this column will be a constant because all its elements are constants drawn from among the β_{gi}'s, and so each element of this column will contribute to the value of the numerator a constant times a linear function of z's. Hence each y_i must itself be a linear function of z's. We can then christen the coefficients of these functions as π's, and write the reduced form of (10.7) as

$$
\begin{aligned}
y_1 &= \pi_{11}z_1 + \pi_{12}z_2 + \cdots + \pi_{1K}z_K \\
y_2 &= \pi_{21}z_1 + \pi_{22}z_2 + \cdots + \pi_{2K}z_K
\end{aligned}
$$

(10.8)

$$
y_G = \pi_{G1}z_1 + \pi_{G2}z_2 + \cdots + \pi_{GK}z_K
$$

or as

$$
y_1 = \sum_{k=1}^{K} \pi_{1k}z_k
$$

$$
y_2 = \sum_{k=1}^{K} \pi_{2k}z_k
$$

(10.9)

$$
y_G = \sum_{k=1}^{K} \pi_{Gk}z_k
$$

or as

(10.10)
$$
y_i = \sum_{k=1}^{K} \pi_{ik}z_k \qquad i = 1, \ldots, G
$$

By appropriate relabeling of parameters and variables, and appropriate choice of G and K, any exact linear reduced form [e.g., equations (2.4)–(2.5) in 2.2] can be made to look like (10.10).

10.4 There are varying kinds of linearity that we must now distinguish. By the term "linear model" one of course means a model whose equations contain as terms only constants (parameters) and products of a variable by a constant (parameter). Such a model can be said to be *linear in variables* (because no variable appears to a power other than the first, nor multiplied or divided by any other variable) and *linear in unknown parameters* as well (because no parameter appears as a power or in a product or quotient with another parameter). If a linear model, so defined, is unrealistic in a particular context, usually a model can be used instead that is *nonlinear in variables* but is still *linear in parameters*. A term of such a model must consist either of only a constant (parameter) or of a product of a constant (parameter) by any function of the variables, provided that the function does not itself have any unspecified parameters.

For example, a nonlinear consumption function that is linear in parameters is

(10.11) $$c = \alpha + \beta_1 y + \beta_2 y^2$$

This equation has a quadratic term in y, namely, $\beta_2 y^2$, but each term contains only one parameter and that as a simple factor, so it is linear in parameters. Another example, again of a consumption function, can be obtained by including the deflated value M/P of cash balances M as an influence:[46]

(10.12) $$c = \alpha + \beta_1 y + \beta_3 M/P$$

Here the term M/P is a quotient, but the equation is linear in parameters though not in variables. [Of course, if M and P appeared in the remainder of the model *only* in the quotient M/P, then they would not really be two separate variables from the point of view of the model; M/P itself would be a single variable, and (10.12) would then be a linear equation with the three variables c, y, and M/P.]

10.5 Models linear in parameters but not in variables are less convenient to manipulate than linear models, but they have the advantage of being able to describe curved graphs, by the use of quadratic or logarithmic or other nonlinear functions of the variables. They also have important advantages from a statistical point of view over models that are nonlinear in both parameters and variables, as we shall see in Chapters VII to X. In this book, whenever we are impelled to use nonlinear models in empirical work, we shall always make sure at least that our models are linear in parameters. This limitation does not impair our flexibility very much, for any continuous function whose first $n + 1$ derivatives are continuous in a given region can be approximated in that region by an nth degree Taylor series of linear terms, quadratic terms, cubic terms, and so on. The approximation can usually be improved by continuing the series with higher-order terms.

10.6 As an example of a nonlinear model linear in parameters, consider the following:

(10.13) $$y = c + i + g$$

(10.14) $$c = \alpha_0 + \alpha_1(y - t) + \alpha_2(y - t)^2$$

(10.15) $$i = \beta_0 + \beta_1 r + \beta_2 y + \beta_3 r^2 + \beta_4 ry + \beta_5 y^2$$

Here the endogenous variables are y, c, and i. The exogenous variables are g, t, and r. The first equation is the usual income definition. The second equation is a consumption .function, quadratic in disposable

[46] This equation is used in Christ [1951], following a similar equation in Pigou [1943].

income $y - t$. The third is an investment function of second degree in total income y and interest rate r. This model can be regarded as a linear-in-parameters version of (7.1)–(7.3) in 7.1 above, for the same variables appear in corresponding equations.

10.7 The reduced form of this linear-in-parameters model is non-linear in parameters as well as nonlinear in variables. Its equation for income, y, is obtained by substituting (10.14) and (10.15) into (10.13). When this has been done the result is

$$(10.16) \quad y = \alpha_2(y - t)^2 + \beta_5 y^2 + \alpha_1(y - t)$$
$$+ \beta_2 y + \beta_4 ry + \alpha_0 + \beta_0 + \beta_1 r + \beta_3 r^2 + g$$

Let terms in like powers of y be collected to give a quadratic equation in y of the form

$$(10.17) \quad \gamma_0 + \gamma_1 y + \gamma_2 y^2 = 0$$

We see that γ_2, the coefficient of y^2, is equal to $\alpha_2 + \beta_5$. The coefficient of y, called γ_1, is equal to $\alpha_1 + \beta_2 - 1 + \beta_4 r - 2\alpha_2 t$. And γ_0, the "constant" term, is a nonlinear function of r, g, and t. The solution of this quadratic equation for y will be nonlinear in parameters and nonlinear in exogenous variables. It will clearly not be a convenient equation to deal with, even though we started out with a fairly simple model that is at least linear in parameters.

10.8 As an aid to understanding the nature of a nonlinear model that is linear in parameters, let us convert equations (10.13)–(10.15) into strictly linear form. This can be done by defining each of the nonlinear functions in these equations as a new variable. While we are at it we define $(y - t)$ as a new variable too, for later convenience, thus:[47]

$$(10.18) \quad x_1 = (y - t)$$

$$(10.19) \quad x_2 = (y - t)^2$$

$$(10.20) \quad x_3 = r^2$$

$$(10.21) \quad x_4 = yr$$

$$(10.22) \quad x_5 = y^2$$

Equations (10.13)–(10.15) then become

$$(10.23) \quad y = c + i + g$$

$$(10.24) \quad c = \alpha_0 + \alpha_1 x_1 + \alpha_2 x_2$$

$$(10.25) \quad i = \beta_0 + \beta_1 r + \beta_2 y + \beta_3 x_3 + \beta_4 x_4 + \beta_5 x_5$$

---

[47] Note that x_1, x_2, and x_4, which include both endogenous and exogenous variables from the original set, are endogenous. This is a general rule. Any nonlinear function of exogenous variables *alone* would remain exogenous. The point of defining $(y - t)$ as a new variable is to avoid having two variables with related parameters in an equation (specifically, y and t in (10.14)).

Now equations (10.23)–(10.25) are strictly linear in both variables and parameters. But in order to make them so, we have had to add four new endogenous variables x_2, x_3, x_4, and x_5, so that these three linear equations no longer are a complete model. However, the eight-equation model (10.18)–(10.25) *is* a complete (nonlinear) model, and is in fact equivalent to the original model (10.13)–(10.15).

10.9 The general form of a nonlinear model linear in parameters is as follows:

$$\sum_{i=1}^{G} \beta_{1i} y_i + \sum_{j=1}^{L} \beta_{1,G+j} f_j(y_1, \ldots, y_G) + \sum_{k=1}^{K} \gamma_{1k} z_k = 0$$

(10.26)

$$\sum_{i=1}^{G} \beta_{Gi} y_i + \sum_{j=1}^{L} \beta_{G,G+j} f_j(y_1, \ldots, y_G) + \sum_{k=1}^{K} \gamma_{Gk} z_k = 0$$

or in more concise form:

(10.27)
$$\sum_{i=1}^{G} \beta_{gi} y_i + \sum_{j=1}^{L} \beta_{g,G+j} f_j(y_1, \ldots, y_G) + \sum_{k=1}^{K} \gamma_{gk} z_k = 0$$
$$g = 1, \ldots, G$$

Here $y_1, \ldots, y_G$ are endogenous variables; the β_{gi} are their parameters in the linear terms; the $f_j(y_1, \ldots, y_G)$ are functions of the endogenous variables having no unspecified parameters (these functions may or may not depend on any of the exogenous variables as well, and may be linear like $y - t$ in (10.18) above or nonlinear like y^2); the $\beta_{g,G+j}$ are parameters of these functions; the z_k are exogenous variables (some of these may or may not be functions of others—it makes no difference to their exogenousness); and the γ_{gk} are parameters of the z_k. In most models many of the parameters are equal to zero, meaning that many of the variables and functions do not appear in every equation.

10.10 Let us now define each $f_j(y_1, \ldots, y_G)$ in (10.27) to be a new endogenous variable, thus:

(10.28) $f_j(y_1, \ldots, y_G) = y_{G+j} \qquad j = 1, \ldots, L$

If this is substituted into equations (10.27), then (10.27) will have terms in the original endogenous variables y_i and terms in the new endogenous variables y_{G+j} that can be combined into one sum, and they will hence be linear like this (note that the first sum runs from $i = 1$ to $i = G + L$ now):

(10.29)
$$\sum_{i=1}^{G+L} \beta_{gi} y_i + \sum_{k=1}^{K} \gamma_{gk} z_k = 0 \qquad g = 1, \ldots, G$$

Now (10.29) and (10.28) together are a new nonlinear model of $G + L$ equations in $G + L$ endogenous variables, equivalent to the original model. It will be noticed that the original nonlinear equations (10.27) have been made strictly linear in (10.29) by the addition of the L new equations defining the L new endogenous variables $y_{G+1}, \ldots, y_{G+L}$.

10.11 Sometimes it is convenient to deal with the general form of nonlinear models, in order to investigate the properties they have in common.[48] If y_i and z_k represent endogenous and exogenous variables, respectively, as before, and α_{gi} represent parameters of the gth equation, then a nonlinear model can be expressed thus:

$$f^1(y_1, \ldots, y_G, z_1, \ldots, z_K, \alpha_{11}, \ldots, \alpha_{1L_1}) = 0$$

$$(10.30) \quad f^2(y_1, \ldots, y_G, z_1, \ldots, z_K, \alpha_{21}, \ldots, \alpha_{2L_2}) = 0$$

$$\vdots \qquad \qquad \vdots \qquad \qquad \vdots$$

$$f^G(y_1, \ldots, y_G, z_1, \ldots, z_K, \alpha_{G1}, \ldots, \alpha_{GL_G}) = 0$$

Here $f^1, \ldots, f^G$ represent G different functions, not necessarily all linear, each involving a set of parameters. The number of parameters in an equation (L_1 in the first, L_2 in the second, etc.) bears no necessary relation to G and/or K. The model (10.30) can be written more concisely thus:

$$(10.31) \quad f^g(y_1, \ldots, y_G, z_1, \ldots, z_K, \alpha_{g1}, \ldots, \alpha_{gL_g}) = 0 \qquad g = 1, \ldots, G$$

If we desire to admit the possibility that some parameters appear in more than one equation, there are at least two ways of doing so. First, if, let us say, α_{11} and α_{13} are the same parameter, we can add a restriction to the effect that $\alpha_{11} = \alpha_{13}$, and similarly for any other parameters for which this is appropriate.[49] Alternatively, we can recast the whole model so that every parameter is *formally* included in every equation, and let the form of each function indicate whether a given parameter *effectively* enters it or not. If there are M different parameters in the model altogether, (10.31) then becomes

$$(10.32) \quad F^g(y_1, \ldots, y_G, z_1, \ldots, z_K, \alpha_1, \ldots, \alpha_M) = 0 \qquad g = 1, \ldots, G$$

10.12 The reduced form of a nonlinear model will typically be nonlinear, and may not even be single-valued for all the endogenous

---

[48] For example, in Samuelson [1947], Ch. 2, general nonlinear models are discussed from the point of view of comparative statics.

[49] In empirical work it is sometimes more convenient to avoid this situation by defining a new variable as suggested in footnote 47.

variables y_i.[50] Nevertheless, if one or more solutions exist, we can write down the reduced form of (10.31) thus:

$$(10.33) \quad y_i = h^i(z_1, \ldots, z_K, \alpha_{11}, \ldots, \alpha_{1L_1}, \ldots, \alpha_{G1}, \ldots, \alpha_{GL_G})$$

$$i = 1, \ldots, G$$

Note that every parameter of (10.31) appears in every equation of the reduced form. The advantage, notationally, of (10.32) over (10.31) emerges here, for the reduced form of (10.32) appears as

$$(10.34) \quad y_i = H^i(z_1, \ldots, z_K, \alpha_1, \ldots, \alpha_M) \quad i = 1, \ldots, G$$

10.13   We shall use these general forms of models later in the book, especially the linear-in-parameters ones, when we come to empirical problems. They are presented here in order that the reader may begin to make their acquaintance. He is advised to manipulate them, and in particular to translate some of the concrete models of this chapter into the forms given in this section, particularly (10.6)–(10.10) and (10.26)–(10.31), so that he begins to get the feel of the general approach.

QUESTIONS AND PROBLEMS

1.1.   Assign appropriate dimensions to the following quantities, and give one example of possible units for each:
(a)   The price of pig iron.
(b)   The price of transportation services.
(c)   The relative price of meat as compared with the consumer price index.
(d)   The rate of change of an interest rate.
(e)   The rate of growth of the United States economy.
(f)   The rate of growth of the United States standard of living.
(g)   The marginal utility of bread.
(h)   The marginal utility of money.
(i)   The coefficient of the interest rate in the investment equation.
(j)   The coefficient of the real wage rate in the labor demand equation.
(k)   The coefficient of income in the liquidity preference equation.
(l)   The rate of change of consumption per head.
(m)   The parameters of a Cobb-Douglas production function $x = Ak^b l^c$.
1.2.   List as many dimensionless economic magnitudes as you can.
2.1.   If the function $c = \phi(y - t)$ is a polynomial and is linearized as in Section 2.5, what are the values of α and β that result in (2.3)?
2.2.   What is the value of the balanced-budget multiplier in a model that is similar to (2.1) and (2.3) except that extra government purchases always result in a decline of consumer purchases of the same amount?

---

[50] A system that has an infinite number of solutions is said to be indeterminate, as indicated in 6.11. However, if a system has more than one but less than an infinite number of solutions, it is not usually called indeterminate.

2.3. Write down equations showing how equations (2.7)–(2.10) should be modified if any shortage of goods and services is divided between buyers of consumer and investment goods in the proportions k and $1 - k$, respectively.

2.4. In the model given by equations (2.7)–(2.10), which variables are endogenous and which exogenous? Explain.

2.5. What is the meaning of "small" in 2.4? How is this meaning related to the choice of units for measuring the variables?

2.6. Consider the model consisting of the equations $c = \alpha + \beta(y - t)$ and $y = c + i + g$, where c = consumption, y = income, i = investment, g = government purchases, and t = tax bill, all in real terms. Exogenous variables are i, g, and t. Now suppose the government selects an arbitrary target level for y, chooses t exogenously, and sets g to achieve the target level of y for given i and t.

(a) What level of g is required?

(b) Is y now exogenous and is g now endogenous? Explain.

3.1. From equations (3.1)–(3.4), derive an equation showing how real income and the price level are related to each other when the demand functions for expenditure and real balances are satisfied. Does its graph slope positively or negatively? What does it mean?

3.2. The supply curve as usually drawn has either a positive slope, or (in the case of a backward bending supply curve) a negative slope that is steeper than the demand curve's slope, as specified in 3.11. Is this consistent or inconsistent with the assertion in 3.17 that $\rho > \xi$? Explain.

3.3 Obtain the reduced-form equation for the interest rate in the model in 3.17, and find the direction of its response to an increase in government purchases financed by taxes.

4.1. Obtain the reduced-form equations for real income and the interest rate from the model consisting of equations (4.8)–(4.10), (3.9), and (3.13)–(3.15). How do they respond to changes in g, t, and M?

4.2. From equations (3.9) and (4.8)–(4.10), obtain the equation for the familiar *IS* curve relating the interest rate and real income. Discuss its nature and meaning. Is it a structural equation? A reduced-form equation? Does it have autonomy?

4.3. How would you construct a model to take account of the effect of deficit financing on the stocks of money and bonds outstanding?

5.1. Under what conditions is the linearization of a nonlinear model likely to lead to the most inaccuracy? The least? Explain.

5.2. Why do you suppose the definition of a derivative is restricted to single-valued functions? (See 5.7.)

5.3. In 5.7, the expression $df(x_0)/dx$ was defined as the value taken by the derivative $df(x)/dx$ at the point where $x = x_0$. What happens if one first evaluates $f(x)$ at the point where $x = x_0$, and then takes the derivative of this value with respect to x?

5.4. If df/dx is not the ratio of two numbers, as stated in 5.7, how can it sometimes be legitimate to say that $\dfrac{dz}{dy} \cdot \dfrac{dy}{dx} = \dfrac{dz}{dx}$? How can we tell when it is legitimate and when it is not?

5.5. Prove equation (5.13) and one or two chosen from (5.5)–(5.10).

5.6. For the Cobb-Douglas production function $x = \gamma l^\alpha k^\beta$, prove that
(a) The elasticities of output x with respect to labor and capital l and k are respectively α and β.

(b) The elasticity of substitution is 1 in absolute value. (It is defined as the elasticity of the capital-labor ratio k/l with respect to the slope dk/dl.)

5.7. For the CES production function $x = \gamma[\delta l^{-\rho} + (1 - \delta)k^{-\rho}]^{1/\rho}$, show whether the marginal product of labor can be expressed as a function of x/l only.

5.8. Find an economic example for each of the three cases treated in 5.14, 5.15, and 5.16.

5.9. Since $c + i + g = y$ in (5.28), does it follow that $\dfrac{\partial c}{\partial y} + \dfrac{\partial i}{\partial y} + \dfrac{\partial g}{\partial y} = 1$? Explain.

5.10. What are the meanings of $\partial c/\partial t$ as obtained from the two functions ϕ and h in (5.29) and (5.31)?

6.1. Solve the following systems by determinants:
(a) $\quad 3x_1 - 2x_2 = 0$
$\quad\quad\quad x_1 - 4x_2 = -20$
(b) $\quad\quad\quad x_2 + 12x_3 = 5$
$\quad 3x_1 + 11x_2 - 24x_3 = -8$
$\quad 15x_1 - \quad 7x_2 \quad\quad\quad = 10$

6.2. Show that the solution of a system of simultaneous linear equations by determinants is the same, no matter in what order the equations and variables are arranged. (*Hint*: Use the rules of 6.5.)

6.3. Verify rules (a), (b), (c), and (d) given in 6.5 using any determinant of your choice as an example. Can you give general proofs for the four rules?

6.4. If A implies B, and C is a necessary condition for B, and D is a sufficient condition for A, and the negation of D implies the negation of C, what is the logical relationship of A and C? Of B and D? Of A and B?

6.5. Can you think of one equation in N variables that has a unique solution for all N variables?

7.1. Obtain $\partial c/\partial M$ from the model given by equations (7.14)–(7.19). [You may use (7.20)–(7.25).] Find its sign if possible.

7.2. Obtain $\partial r/\partial g$ from the model given by equations (7.14)–(7.19), and find its sign if possible.

7.3. Set up a model consisting of equations (4.1)–(4.6) and the following supply equation for labor, and analyze its response to changes in M:

$$n = \sigma(W, P)$$

8.1. What algebraic sign would you expect for the partial derivative of real GNP with respect to w_g in equation (8.11)? (Note that g is to be held constant here.)

8.2. Obtain the reduced form of equations (8.1)–(8.7). Obtain the multiplier effects of several of the policy variables on several of the dependent variables; deduce their algebraic signs if possible.

8.3. Introduce a linear tax equation into the model in 8.3, and let the tax bill t be endogenous. Obtain the reduced-form equation for real GNP for this new model, and compare it with equation (8.11).

9.1. Suppose that the ith individual's consumption function is $c_i = \alpha_i y_i + \beta_i$, and that the aggregate consumption function is $C = \alpha Y + \beta$.

(a) Express the aggregate marginal propensity α in terms of the individual marginal propensities α_i (and any other quantities you need).

(b) Show that if $\alpha_i \neq \alpha_j$ then a shift of income from the ith to the jth consumer will change the aggregate marginal propensity to consume.

9.2. Obtain the reduced form of the model in 9.6.

9.3. Derive equations (9.9)–(9.10) from (9.4)–(9.8).

9.4. Construct a simple mixed time-series and cross-section model to describe some particular economic problem, and indicate which variables are pure cross section, pure time series, and mixed. Indicate also which are exogenous and endogenous.

10.1. Express the Cobb-Douglas production function $x = \gamma l^\alpha k^\beta$ in a form linear in parameters.

10.2. Translate the reduced form obtained in exercise 8.2 into the form given by equation (10.8), and indicate carefully which variables and parameters correspond to $y_1, \ldots, y_G, z_1, \ldots, z_K, \pi_{11}, \ldots, \pi_{GK}$.

10.3. Can you transform the following equations into forms that are linear in parameters? (Greek letters as usual denote parameters.)

$$y = \alpha(1 - e^{\beta z})$$
$$x = \gamma[\delta l^{-\rho} + (1 - \delta)k^{-\rho}]^{1/\rho}$$
$$\epsilon = (x - \lambda)(y - \theta)$$

CHAPTER IV

Static Theory
with Stochastic Equations

This chapter first discusses random variables and probability in a brief and elementary way, including the normal distribution and the concepts of regression and correlation. Then several stochastic economic models are presented. The definitions of structure, model, and exogenous variable are revised to apply to the stochastic case. Some problems of cross-section models are discussed.

1 INTRODUCTION

1.1 In this chapter we deal with static models as in the preceding one, but here the models involve random or stochastic variables to represent unsystematic influences on the phenomena being described.

1.2 In II.2.1–4 the rationale for using random variables was set forth briefly, and the reader should read those paragraphs again now. It was pointed out that experience shows that exact theories either fail to explain perfectly any available set of economic data, or, if made to do so, they fail to predict additional data. It was pointed out that the device of a random variable is a fruitful one for bridging the gap between observed data and the systematic theories that conceptually can represent those data at best only approximately.

1.3 Most economic variables are the result of human behavior of some kind. It is too familiar to require much comment that human behavior, even though it exhibits broad underlying uniformities such as the quest for survival, love, power, profit, fun, respect, and so on, appears highly irregular and unpredictable in specific instances. What will be the yield per acre of wheat next year? How many new automobiles will be sold? How many people will be unemployed? What will be the long-term interest rate? Partial answers to all these questions can be given in the light of our knowledge—which is growing in part through the intelligent use of some of the methods discussed in this book—of the relationships among economic variables, but as we have seen these answers are approximate at best. We postulate random components of economic variables to account for the discrepancies between our explanations and the facts. This postulate would be justifiable if in some ultimate sense there "really were" random variables in the economic universe. It would also be justifiable for practical purposes, even if not true in any ultimate sense, if the factors neglected in our systematic relationships were numerous enough and diverse enough and small enough so that the disturbances acted *as if* they were random variables. It is because economists have often been successful in obtaining apparently random disturbances that the postulate of random variables is kept.

1.4 The first part of this chapter is devoted to a review of random variables and probability, and the remainder to models incorporating random variables.

2 PROBABILITY DISTRIBUTIONS AND STOCHASTIC VARIABLES; STATISTICAL INDEPENDENCE; MATHEMATICAL EXPECTATION[1]

2.1 *A random or stochastic variable is a variable that can take on any one of a set of values, each with a given degree of probability.* The simplest examples are related to gambling games. The number of spots showing after a die is thrown is a random variable, for it can take on any integral value from 1 through 6, each with a probability of $1/6$ (if the die is fair). Other random variables are the number of spots showing after two dice are thrown, and the suit of a card dealt from a shuffled deck. (To obtain *numerical* values for the suits we might arrange the four suits in an agreed order, say, ♠ ♡ ◇ ♣, and use three zeros and a one with the *position* of the one indicating the suit; then $(1, 0, 0, 0)$ would mean ♠, $(0, 0, 1, 0)$ would mean ◇, etc. For this reason a random variable has come to be defined in terms of a function whose arguments are possible events and whose values are real numbers.) Many economic variables can be regarded as having random components also, although the probabilities associated with their values are not so easy to discover. Obvious examples are crop yield per acre and the level of prices on the stock

---

[1] See any standard text in probability or statistical inference, e.g., Mood [1950] or Mood and Graybill [1963] or Feller [1957].

market. Less obvious examples are national income, unemployment, and prices of particular commodities.

2.2 Random variables may be either *discrete* (i.e., have a finite number of distinctly separate possible values, like the number of spots showing on a die) or *continuous* (i.e., have an infinite number of possible values infinitesimally close together over a range like crop yield per acre). The gambling examples just cited are discrete: The only possible results of rolling two dice are the eleven integers from 2 to 12 inclusive; and there is a finite number of possible five-card hands. The national income in a year is formally a discrete variable too, since conceptually it is measured in integral multiples of one cent (and actually published as an integral multiple of 1 million dollars), but for all practical purposes it is best regarded as continuous because it has so many possible values. Most economic variables are best regarded as continuous. It is important to note that if there is a random variable, for instance, u, then any function of u is also a random variable. In particular, a constant multiple of u (say ku) and the sum of a constant plus u $(k + u)$ are both random variables. Furthermore, if u_1 and u_2 are two random variables, then new random variables can be obtained from them by taking various functions of them, such as $u_1 + u_2$, $u_1 u_2$, or $k_1 u_1 + k_2 u_2$, where k_1 and k_2 are constants.

2.3 *The probability distribution of a discrete random variable u is defined as a function showing for each possible value of u the probability with which it will occur.* This probability is always a number between zero and one, inclusive, zero for impossible events and one for certainties. The sum of probabilities of all possible values of the variable is 1. Probability distributions, like other functions, are typically expressed in the form of graphs or tables or equations. As an example of a discrete distribution, consider the outcome of rolling a fair die: There are six possible results (the integers from 1 through 6), and the probability of each is 1/6. The distribution of the number of spots turned up, which number we may call x, can be expressed either in the form of a table (Table 2.1) or

TABLE 2.1 Probability Distribution for the Result of Throwing a Fair Die

x = number of spots	1	2	3	4	5	6	total
y = probability of x	1/6	1/6	1/6	1/6	1/6	1/6	1

a graph (Figure 2.1). It may also be expressed in equation form thus:

$$(2.1) \qquad y = (\text{probability of } x) = 1/6 \qquad x = 1, 2, \ldots, 6$$

2.4 Another example of a discrete distribution is given by the results of rolling two fair dice together. The number of spots showing then is

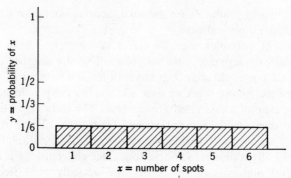

Figure 2.1 Probability distribution for the result of throwing a fair die.

the sum of two random variables distributed as in Figure 2.1 or equation
(2.1); let us call this new variable z. Its possible values are integers from
2 through 12, and its distribution is as shown in Table 2.2 or Figure 2.2.

TABLE 2.2   Probability Distribution for the Result of Throwing Two Fair
Dice

z	2	3	4	5	6	7	8	9	10	11	12	total
Pb(z)	1/36	2/36	3/36	4/36	5/36	6/36	5/36	4/36	3/36	2/36	1/36	1

The symbol Pb stands for "probability." This distribution can also be
represented in equation form:

$$(2.2) \quad \text{Pb}(z) = (\text{probability of } z) = \frac{6 - |z - 7|}{36} \qquad z = 2, 3, \ldots, 12$$

where $|z - 7|$ stands for the *absolute value* of $z - 7$, that is, the numerical
value disregarding sign. A discrete distribution shows the probability
that z will take on any particular value; for example, here the probability that z will be 7 is 6/36, or 1/6. The distribution also shows the

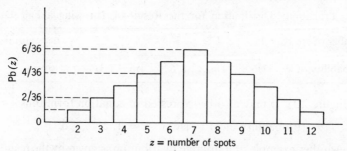

Figure 2.2 Probability distribution for the result of throwing two fair dice.

probability that z will fall between 4 and 7 inclusive is $3/36 + 4/36 + 5/36 + 6/36$, or $1/2$.   Other examples of discrete distributions were given in II.2.4–5, and the reader is referred to them again.

2.5   *The probability distribution of a continuous random variable is defined in a way analogous to that in the discrete case, with certain necessary modifications.* It is like the discrete distribution in that the sum of probabilities of all possible values is 1, and in that it enables us to tell the probability with which the variable will fall between any two preassigned values. It is different in that its graph need not (and in typical cases does not) have steps like those in Figure 2.2, and in that it gives zero as the

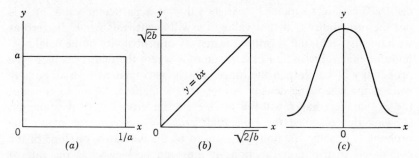

Figure 2.3   Three continuous probability distributions corresponding to equations (2.3)–(2.5).

probability with which the variable will be exactly equal to almost any preassigned value. (This is because a continuous random variable has an infinite number of possible values; if more than a finite number of these had a nonzero probability, the sum of probabilities of all of them could not be 1 but would have to be infinite instead.) Several possible continuous distributions are shown in Figure 2.3. Their respective equations are as follows. The symbol $\phi(x)$ stands for the vertical height of the curve at the point x, which is called the *probability density* of x; a and b are constants, and e is the base of natural logarithms, approximately 2.71828:

(2.3) $$y = \phi(x) = \begin{cases} a \text{ if } 0 \leqq x \leqq 1/a \\ 0 \text{ otherwise} \end{cases}$$

(2.4) $$y = \phi(x) = \begin{cases} bx \text{ if } 0 \leqq x \leqq \sqrt{2/b} \\ 0 \text{ otherwise} \end{cases}$$

(2.5) $$y = \phi(x) = \frac{1}{\sqrt{2\pi}} e^{-\frac{1}{2}x^2}$$

The reader can easily see that the total area under either of the first two curves is 1; the same is true of the third, but the proof is less simple.

2.6 The rule for finding from any of the graphs in Figure 2.3 the probability that x will fall between two preassigned values is to find the area under the curve between two vertical lines drawn at the two given values. The total area under any continuous distribution curve must be 1, because the probability that x will fall somewhere within the range of its possible values is 1. Furthermore, the probability that x will fall below a preassigned value is the area under the curve to the left of a vertical line drawn at that value, and the probability that x will fall above a given value is the area to the right of that value.

2.7 A continuous probability distribution function, such as those shown in Figure 2.3 and equations (2.3)–(2.5), is called a *probability density* function, to indicate that its value at a particular value of x is not the probability that that value of x will occur (this would be zero as we have just seen), but is rather the density of probability in the neighborhood of that value of x. For a range of x where the density is high, the probability of x falling in the range is high, as compared with an equally wide range where the density is low. It is sometimes useful to consider the probability that x will fall at or below a given value; the function showing this is called the *cumulative probability distribution* of x. The probability density function turns out to be the derivative or slope of the cumulative distribution function; it thus can be viewed as the rate at which the cumulative probability is being increased as x increases, or the amount of probability being added per unit increase in x.

2.8 A discrete distribution having a very large number of possible values for its random variable will look almost like a continuous function. If the steps in the discrete distribution in Figure 2.2 were made smaller and more numerous, the graph would come to look even more like a continuous distribution. This is what we mean by saying that a discrete distribution can be approximated by an appropriately chosen continuous distribution, and vice versa. This is an important fact, for it enables us in practice to use whichever type of distribution we wish. We shall use continuous distributions in nearly all of our problems, since they are the easiest to manipulate, but two-valued discrete distributions will sometimes be used too.

2.9 Often it will be convenient to consider two or more random variables at once. We have seen this in one case already in II.2, where we had two equations each containing a random disturbance. The probability distribution of two or more random variables is called a *joint probability* distribution, or a *multivariate* distribution, in contrast to the *univariate* distributions we have discussed so far. Joint distributions can be either discrete or continuous. The discrete distributions give the probability that each possible combination of values of the variables will occur. The continuous distributions give the probability density for each possible combination of values. The graph of a joint distribution of two variables requires three dimensions, two for the variables and one for probability. The *volume* (corresponding to the *area* in the univariate case) under a continuous distribution surface (corresponding to the univariate curve) is equal to 1, which is to say that the sum of probabilities of all possible combinations of values is 1. If the two variables are called x_1 and x_2, then the chance that x_1 will fall between two preassigned values, say α_1 and β_1, while *at the same time* x_2 falls between two other preassigned values, say α_2 and β_2, is found from the volume enclosed under the probability surface by four vertical planes drawn at $x_1 = \alpha_1$, $x_1 = \beta_1$, $x_2 = \alpha_2$, and $x_2 = \beta_2$. This is illustrated in Figure 2.4. The first graph shows a possible continuous joint density function, $F(x_1, x_2)$, and the second shows the

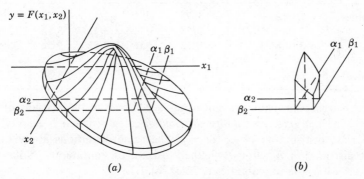

Figure 2.4 Sections of the bivariate normal distribution.

volume under it between α_1 and β_1 and between α_2 and β_2. This volume represents the probability that both $\alpha_1 \leqq x_1 \leqq \beta_1$ and $\alpha_2 \leqq x_2 \leqq \beta_2$. This particular distribution is discussed in 3.11 ff. below.

2.10 Joint distributions can be represented by tables or equations as well as by graphs. A bivariate distribution table, for example, typically has as row headings the values of one variable, and as column headings the values of the other, the probability or probability density for any pair of values being given in the body of the table in the appropriate row and column. Joint distributions can be expressed in the form of cumulative distributions, as can univariate distributions.

2.11 Consider as an example the discrete joint distribution of card suit and card value when a card is drawn at random from a shuffled and cut standard bridge deck. Let us denote the suit by x_1 [formally we use $x_1 = (1, 0, 0, 0)$ for spades, $(0, 1, 0, 0)$ for hearts, $(0, 0, 1, 0)$ for diamonds, and $(0, 0, 0, 1)$ for clubs. But for brevity here we shall simply denote these four values of x_1 by ♠, ♡, ◇, and ♣, respectively.] We denote the card value by x_2 ($x_2 = 1$ for ace, 2 for a face card, and 3 for any other).

The joint probability distribution is then as shown in Table 2.3. It shows, for example, that the probability of drawing a card that is both a diamond and a face card is 3/52, that is, that the probability that $x_1 = \diamondsuit$ and $x_2 = 2$ is 3/52. The last row of the table shows the probabilities of the various values of x_1 when x_2 is ignored, and the last column shows the probabilities of the various values of x_2 when x_1 is ignored; each entry there is the sum of entries in its column or row, respectively. These probabilities are

TABLE 2.3   Bivariate Probability Distribution of Suit (x_1) and Card Value (x_2) of Card Drawn from Shuffled Deck

		Values of x_1 (suit)				
		♠	♡	◇	♣	all
values	1 (ace)	1/52	1/52	1/52	1/52	4/52
of	2 (face card)	3/52	3/52	3/52	3/52	12/52
x_2	3 (other)	9/52	9/52	9/52	9/52	36/52
(card						
value)	all	13/52	13/52	13/52	13/52	52/52

called *marginal* probabilities since they are shown in the margins of the table. The *marginal probability distribution* of x_1 (or x_2) is simply the univariate distribution of x_1 (or x_2). The same definitions apply to all joint distribution functions, whether discrete or continuous. Note that the sum of all the probabilities is 52/52, or 1.

2.12   It will be observed that all the rows in Table 2.3 are proportional to each other, that is, any row (say the first) can be made equal to any other row (say the second) if each of its members is multiplied by a constant (in this case, 3). The same is true of the columns. (Furthermore, the four columns corresponding to the four values of x_1 are equal, but it is only their proportionality that we want to discuss here.) It can also be seen that every probability in the body of the table (i.e., not in the margins) is the product of the two marginal probabilities in its row and column. That is, this particular joint probability distribution of x_1 and x_2 can be obtained by multiplying together the two marginal distributions of x_1 and x_2. If we use f to stand for the joint distribution and f_1 and f_2 for the marginal distributions, we can write for Table 2.3

$$(2.6) \qquad f(x_1, x_2) = f_1(x_1) f_2(x_2)$$

This does not hold for all joint distributions. We shall see that the reason it holds in this case is the proportionality of all the columns and of all the rows in Table 2.3. *Variables having distributions that satisfy equation (2.6) are said to be statistically independent* of each other; the reason for this term will appear shortly.

2.13 Consider now a joint distribution like that in Table 2.3 except that the deck from which the cards are to be drawn has lost its ace of spades. The distribution then appears as in Table 2.4, marginal probabilities again being shown in the last row and column. In this table the rows are *not* proportional. And although the three columns for $x_1 = \heartsuit, \diamondsuit, \clubsuit$ are the same, the other two are not proportional to these three. Here equation (2.6) does not apply; in fact, no probability in the body of the table is the

TABLE 2.4   Bivariate Probability Distribution of Suit (x_1) and Card Value (x_2) of Card Drawn from Shuffled Deck with No Ace of Spades

		Values of x_1 (suit)				
		$\spadesuit$	$\heartsuit$	$\diamondsuit$	$\clubsuit$	all
values of x_2	1 (ace)	0	1/51	1/51	1/51	3/51
(card value)	2 (face card)	3/51	3/51	3/51	3/51	12/51
	3 (other)	9/51	9/51	9/51	9/51	36/51
	all	12/51	13/51	13/51	13/51	51/51

product of the two marginal probabilities in its row and column. This is due to the *lack* of proportionality of rows and of columns.

2.14 Suppose now that a card is drawn from the *complete* deck (Table 2.3) and that it is known beforehand to be a spade. This can be accomplished either by not counting any drawn card that is not a spade (simply putting it aside and drawing another), or by removing all non-spades from the deck beforehand. What is the probability that it will be a face card? There are 13 spades in this deck, of which 3 are face cards; hence the chance of drawing a face card, if it is known that a spade will be drawn, is 3/13. This is called the *conditional* probability of drawing a face card, given the knowledge that a spade will be drawn. If the variables defined above are used, it is the conditional probability that $x_2 = 2$, given that $x_1 = \spadesuit$. It is expressed by the symbol Pb $(x_2 = 2 \mid x_1 = \spadesuit)$. The same procedure and definition hold for any other values of x_1 and x_2, and in fact *the probability distribution of x_2 when x_1 has a given value is called the conditional probability distribution of x_2 given x_1*. It is often written as a function, thus: $g_2(x_2 \mid x_1)$. Observe from Table 2.3 that the conditional probability of a face card, given that it is a spade, 3/13, can be obtained by dividing the joint probability of getting a face card in spades (3/52) by the marginal probability of getting a spade (13/52). This statement holds in general, thus:

(2.7) $$g_2(x_2 \mid x_1) = \frac{f(x_1, x_2)}{f_1(x_1)}$$

Similarly, we may express the conditional distribution function of x_1 given x_2:

$$(2.8) \qquad g_1(x_1 \mid x_2) = \frac{f(x_1, x_2)}{f_2(x_2)}$$

The reader may check equations (2.7) and (2.8) by any pair of values of x_1 and x_2 in Table 2.3.

2.15   Suppose now that the same thing is done with the deck that lacks the ace of spades, that is, a card is drawn with the knowledge that it will be a spade. The conditional probability of drawing a face card, given that a spade will be drawn, is 3/12, since there are 3 face cards among the 12 spades in this deck. Referring to Table 2.4, we see that as before this result can be obtained by dividing the joint probability of getting a spade and a face card (3/51) by the marginal probability of getting a face card (12/51). And as before, this holds for all pairs of values of x_1 and x_2 in Table 2.4, or for *any* discrete bivariate distribution, as the reader may verify.

2.16   Hence equations (2.7) and (2.8) stand up in both Table 2.3 and Table 2.4; their validity is not dependent on the presence of proportionality among the rows or columns. They may be used to obtain two equivalent general expressions for the joint probability distribution $f(x_1, x_2)$, thus:

$$(2.9) \qquad f_1(x_1)\, g_2(x_2 \mid x_1) = f(x_1, x_2) = f_2(x_2)\, g_1(x_1 \mid x_2)$$

Equation (2.9) is true for any pair of random variables. It says that the joint distribution function of x_1 and x_2 is equal to the marginal distribution of x_1 times the conditional distribution of x_2 given x_1, and is also equal to the marginal distribution of x_2 times the conditional distribution of x_1 given x_2. *The two variables x_1 and x_2 are by definition statistically independent of each other if the conditional distribution of one of them given the other is equal to the marginal distribution of the one*, that is, if

$$(2.10) \qquad g_1(x_1 \mid x_2) = f_1(x_1)$$

or if

$$(2.11) \qquad g_2(x_2 \mid x_1) = f_2(x_2)$$

These two equations are equivalent; if either is true, both are. Equation (2.11), for example, says that the conditional distribution of x_2 given x_1 is the same as the marginal distribution of x_2, that is, that the probability distribution of x_2 is unaffected by whether x_1 is specified, and thus is independent of x_1. Referring to Table 2.3, we can see that indeed the probability distribution of x_2 is the same, whether no value or any value

is specified for x_1, and also that the distribution of x_1 is the same regardless of whether anything is specified about x_2. For example,
Pb $(x_2 = 2 \mid x_1 = \spadesuit) = 3/13$ and Pb $(x_2 = 2) = 12/52 = 3/13$, etc.

    2.17   When two variables are *statistically independent*, that is, when
the conditional distribution of one variable given the other is identical to
the marginal distribution of the first variable, then if there is no danger
of confusion with the concepts of linear or (more generally) functional
independence, we shall often say simply that the variables are independent.
Using this definition and equation (2.9), we can see that (2.6) holds if
and only if x_1 and x_2 are independent. That is, *the joint distribution of
two random variables is equal to the product of their marginal distributions
if and only if they are statistically independent*. Thus it is possible to
characterize an important difference between Tables 2.3 and 2.4 in the
remark that in the distribution of Table 2.3, x_1 and x_2 are independent,
whereas in that of Table 2.4 they are not. For example, in Table 2.4,
Pb $(x_2 = 2 \mid x_1 = \spadesuit) = 3/12$, but Pb $(x_2 = 2) = 12/51 = 4/17 \neq 3/12$.

    2.18   Equation (2.6) is often called the *special multiplication theorem
for probabilities*, because it is true only in the special case where x_1 and
x_2 are independent. Equation (2.9) is called the *general multiplication
theorem for probabilities*, since it holds whether the variables are independent or not. Both can be extended readily to joint distributions
involving three or more variables. For example, if x_1, x_2, and x_3 are all
independent of each other, and if their joint distribution function is
denoted by F, then

$$(2.12) \qquad F(x_1, x_2, x_3) = f_1(x_1) f_2(x_2) f_3(x_3)$$

If they are not independent, or if they are but no use is made of the fact,
and the joint conditional distribution of x_2 and x_3 given x_1 is denoted by
G, then

$$(2.13) \quad F(x_1, x_2, x_3) = f_1(x_1)\, G(x_2, x_3 \mid x_1) = f_1(x_1)\, g_2(x_2 \mid x_1)\, g_3(x_3 \mid x_1, x_2)$$

    2.19   The concepts of marginal and conditional distributions and
independence have been presented in connection with the discrete distributions of results of drawing a card from a complete deck and from a
deck that has no ace of spades. However, they apply in an analogous
fashion to any other joint distribution, whether discrete or continuous, and
whether with two variables or more.

    2.20   It has become clear, from the tables and graphs and equations
that have been presented to depict various distributions, that a probability
distribution is a rather cumbersome thing to apprehend. If each distribution could be described by two or three characteristic numbers, we could
refer to these numbers and get an idea of what a distribution's particular
characteristics were, without having to tabulate it or graph it in detail.

Some distributions can be completely described by a few numbers, and some can be only approximately so described. We shall now consider several such characteristic numbers, called *parameters* of a distribution.[2] We shall deal first with univariate distributions.

2.21 One of the most important characteristics of a univariate distribution is some kind of average, called by statisticians the central value of the variable; it is a value that locates the center (in some sense) of the distribution. There are several different possible measures for this.

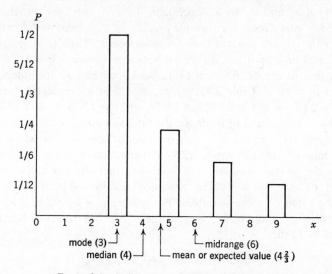

Figure 2.5 A discrete probability distribution.

For example, consider the discrete distribution depicted in Figure 2.5. Halfway from the lowest value ($x = 3$) to the highest ($x = 9$) is the *midrange*, where $x = 6$. The ordinary average of x, called the *arithmetic mean*,[3] or simply the *mean* for short, is $4\frac{2}{3}$. It is also known as the *mathematical expectation* or *expected value* of x. It is obtained by multiplying each value of x by its probability and summing the results:

$$3 \times \frac{1}{2} + 5 \times \frac{1}{4} + 7 \times \frac{1}{6} + 9 \times \frac{1}{12} = 4\frac{2}{3}$$

[2] This usage of the term "parameter" is similar to that given in I.5.3, and in fact the parameters of stochastic models include the parameters of their probability distributions; see 4.2 below.

[3] There are the geometric, harmonic, and other means as well, but we shall make little use of them, and when we simply say "mean" we shall intend to refer to the arithmetic mean.

In symbolic form, if P_i is the probability of x_i, then the mean or expected value of x, conventionally called Ex and also denoted here by μ, is

$$(2.14) \qquad \mu = Ex = \sum_i P_i x_i$$

where the sum includes all values of x. The value of x that is halfway from lowest to highest, in the sense that there is a chance of 1/2 that it will be exceeded by a randomly chosen x, is called the *median*, and is somewhere between 3 and 5; by convention we go half way, so it is 4. The value that is most likely to occur is called the *mode*, and is 3. Of these measures, the midrange is often the simplest to compute, but the mean is the most used because it is of more general interest.

2.22 Another important characteristic of a univariate distribution is its dispersion: the degree to which it is spread out or concentrated around the central value. Again there are several measures that can be used. The simplest is the *range*, the distance from the lowest to the highest value of the variable, which in Figure 2.5 is $9 - 3 = 6$. Another measure is the *average deviation*, that is, the average of the deviations (or mean deviation) from the mean. It would always turn out to be zero if deviations below the mean were regarded as having a negative algebraic sign, and those above a positive sign (see columns 4 and 5 in Table 2.5); hence in order to get a nonzero result we must define the average deviation as the average obtained by disregarding the algebraic signs of the deviations. For the distribution in Figure 2.5, the average deviation is 5/3, as shown in columns 4 and 6 of Table 2.5. Another measure is the *standard deviation*, which is equal to the positive *square root* of the mean or expected value of the *squared* deviations from the mean of the distribution. In symbols, the standard deviation, defined as $\sqrt{E(x - \mu)^2}$, and often denoted by σ, is

$$(2.15) \qquad \sigma = \sqrt{E(x - \mu)^2} = \sqrt{\sum_i P_i (x_i - \mu)^2}$$

where the sum includes all possible values of x. A related measure is the *variance* of x, denoted by[4] σ^2 or var x, and defined as the square of the standard deviation, or as the expected value of the squared deviations from the mean. In symbols, var x is given by (2.15) without the square root sign. Both the standard deviation and the variance are necessarily zero or positive, zero if there is only one possible value of the random variable (i.e., if the random variable is so degenerate that it is a constant), and positive otherwise (because squares are positive). For the distribution in

---

[4] In general, we shall use the notation var x to denote the variance of any random variable x. Sometimes, if a particular variable's variance appears often in a problem, we shall denote it by a special symbol such as σ^2.

TABLE 2.5   The Discrete Probability Distribution of Figure 2.5, with Calculations of Mean, Average Deviation, Variance, Standard Deviation, and Range

Given Information about the Distribution		Calculated Information about the Distribution					
Values of the Variable	Probabilities	Weighted Values	Deviations of x from Mean	Weighted Deviations	Weighted Absolute Deviations	Squared Deviations	Weighted Squared Deviations
x (1)	P (2)	Px (3) $= (1) \times (2)$	$x - 4\frac{2}{3}$ (4) $= (1) - 4\frac{2}{3}$	$P(x - 4\frac{2}{3})$ (5) $= (2) \times (4)$	$P\lvert x - 4\frac{2}{3}\rvert$ (6) $= (2) \times \lvert(4)\rvert$	$(x - 4\frac{2}{3})^2$ (7) $= (4)^2$	$P(x - 4\frac{2}{3})^2$ (8) $= (2) \times (7)$
3	1/2	3/2	−5/3	−5/6	5/6	25/9	25/18
5	1/4	5/4	1/3	1/12	1/12	1/9	1/36
7	1/6	7/6	7/3	7/18	7/18	49/9	49/54
9	1/12	9/12	13/3	13/36	13/36	169/9	169/108
Totals	1	$4\frac{2}{3}$	—	0	5/3	—	35/9

$\mu = Ex$ = mean of distribution = $4\frac{2}{3}$ (total in column 3).

A.D. = average deviation = 5/3 (total in column 6).

$\sigma^2 = E(x - \mu)^2$ = variance = 35/9 (total in column 8).

σ = standard deviation = $\sqrt{35/9} = 1.97$.

R = range = $9 - 3 = 6$ (extreme values in column 1).

Figure 2.5, the variance is 35/9, and the standard deviation is $\sqrt{35/9} =$ 1.97, as shown in columns 4, 7, and 8 of Table 2.5.

2.23 The mean of a distribution has an important property: The expected value of the square of the deviation of a random variable from its mean is less than the expected value of the square of the deviation from any other point. This may be shown easily as follows. Let a be any value of x other than μ, and let P_i be the probability of x_i. Then

(2.16)

$$\sum P_i(x_i - a)^2 = \sum P_i[(x_i - \mu) + (\mu - a)]^2$$

$$= \sum P_i[(x_i - \mu)^2 + 2(x_i - \mu)(\mu - a) + (\mu - a)^2]$$

$$= \sum P_i(x_i - \mu)^2 + 2 \sum P_i(x_i - \mu)(\mu - a) + \sum P_i(\mu - a)^2$$

$$= \sum P_i(x_i - \mu)^2 + 2(\mu - a) \sum P_i(x_i - \mu) + (\mu - a)^2 \sum P_i$$

$$= \sum P_i(x_i - \mu)^2 + (\mu - a)^2$$

The last step involves substituting 0 for $\sum P_i(x_i - \mu)$, and 1 for $\sum P_i$; these are justified by the arguments implied in finding the sums of columns 2 and 5 in Table 2.5. The final expression shows that $EP_i(x_i - a)^2$ is equal to the expression $\sum P_i(x_i - \mu)^2$ *plus* a term that can only be positive (if $a \neq \mu$) or zero (if $a = \mu$); hence the statement is established. In symbols,

(2.17) $$\sum P_i(x_i - \mu)^2 \leqq \sum P_i(x_i - a)^2$$

where a is any number. The equality in (2.17) applies if $a = \mu$, and the inequality applies if $a \neq \mu$. This property of the mean or expected value of a distribution is an important reason for the popularity of the mean as a measure of the central value of a distribution. Later on, when we come to the statistical treatment of econometric models, we shall find analogs of (2.17) for multivariate and conditional distributions. The argument in (2.16) above is typical of many statistical derivations, and it will pay the reader who wants to follow details in the rest of the book to make sure he understands it.

2.24 The expected value of a sum or product is often required in statistical theory. The following rules apply to both discrete and continuous distributions. The expected value of a sum of two random variables x_1 and x_2 is the sum of their expected values, that is,

(2.18) $$E(x_1 + x_2) = Ex_1 + Ex_2$$

The expected value of any constant is equal to that constant itself. The expected value of a constant multiple of a random variable x is equal to that constant times Ex, that is, if α is a constant,

(2.19) $$E(\alpha x) = \alpha Ex$$

If two random variables x_1 and x_2 are independent, then the expected value of the product is the product of their expected values, that is,[5]

(2.20)   If x_1 and x_2 are independent, $E(x_1 x_2) = Ex_1 Ex_2$

2.25 The variance of a sum of two random variables x_1 and x_2 is by definition the expected value of the squared deviation of $x_1 + x_2$ from $E(x_1 + x_2)$, that is, [using (2.18) above],

$$(2.21) \quad \text{var}\,(x_1 + x_2) \equiv E(x_1 - Ex_1 + x_2 - Ex_2)^2$$
$$= E(x_1 - Ex_1)^2 + 2E(x_1 - Ex_1)(x_2 - Ex_2) + E(x_2 - Ex_2)^2$$

If x_1 and x_2 are independent, then this takes a special form [using (2.18) and (2.20) above]:

(2.22)   If x_1 and x_2 are independent,

$$\text{var}\,(x_1 + x_2) = E(x_1 - Ex_1)^2 + 0 + E(x_2 - Ex_2)^2 = \text{var}\,x_1 + \text{var}\,x_2$$

A similar result holds for var $(x_1 - x_2)$, the sign of the cross product only being negative. If x_1 and x_2 are not independent, then the expected value of the cross-product term $(x_1 - Ex_1)(x_2 - Ex_2)$ may fail to be zero in (2.21) and if so (2.22) does not hold. The result in that case is treated in 3.8 below. The variance of a constant multiple of a random variable x is the square of that constant times var (x), that is, if α is a constant,

$$(2.23) \qquad\qquad \text{var}\,\alpha x = \alpha^2 \,\text{var}\,x$$

From (2.22) and (2.23) we can prove an important theorem concerning the variance of the mean of a sample of T independent drawings from a single population. From (2.22), the variance of the sum of T such drawings is the sum of their variances, that is, T times the variance of the population. From (2.23), the variance of $1/T$ times this sum is $1/T^2$ times the variance of this sum, whence the variance of the sample mean $\bar{x}$ is $1/T$ times σ^2, where σ^2 is the variance of the population:

$$(2.24) \qquad\qquad \text{var}\,\bar{x} = \frac{1}{T^2}(T\sigma^2) = \frac{\sigma^2}{T}$$

These theorems will be used repeatedly in later chapters.

2.26 The definition of the mean or expected value of a continuous distribution of x is similar to that for a discrete distribution, except that we do not multiply each value of x by its probability and add the products,

---

[5] If two random variables are not independent, then the expected value of their product is the expected value of the product of either times the conditional expected value of the other given the first, thus:

$$E(x_1, x_2) = E[x_1 E(x_2 \mid x_1)] = E[x_2 E(x_1 \mid x_2)]$$

This expression may be $Ex_1\,Ex_2$ even if x_1 and x_2 are dependent; see 3.8 below.

as in Table 2.5 or equations (2.14) and (2.15). Instead we in effect divide the range of x into small intervals having widths that we may call Δx, then multiply one value of x from each interval (say the mid-point of each) by its probability *density* times Δx, and then add these products. The effect of this process is to replace the smooth-curve continuous distribution with a discrete distribution that is approximately the same, as Figure 2.6 shows. The approximation can be made better if more and smaller intervals are taken—say 100 intervals with $\Delta x = 1/5$, or 100,000 intervals with $\Delta x = 1/5000$, etc. The range from $x = -10$ to $x = 10$ in Figure 2.6 has been divided into 20 segments, of width $\Delta x = 1$. The midpoints of the intervals are $-9.5, -8.5, \ldots, -0.5, +0.5, \ldots, +8.5, +9.5$.

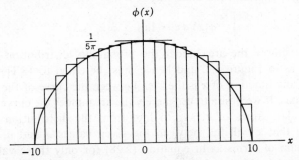

Figure 2.6   A continuous probability distribution approximated by a discrete one.

Let $x_i{}^m$ be the midpoints of the intervals, and $\phi(x_i{}^m)$ be the probability density (height of the curve) at $x_i{}^m$, and $\cong$ mean "equals approximately." Then the approximate mean of the distribution is found from

(2.25)

$$\mu = Ex \cong (-9.5) \times \phi(-9.5) \times 1 + (-8.5) \times \phi(-8.5) \times 1 + \cdots$$

$$+ (-0.5) \times \phi(-0.5) \times 1 + 0.5 \times \phi(0.5) \times 1 + \cdots$$

$$+ 8.5 \times \phi(8.5) \times 1 + 9.5 \times \phi(9.5) \times 1 = \sum x_i{}^m \phi(x_i{}^m) \Delta x$$

In order to obtain an approximation that is perfect, statisticians use the conceptual device of a limit again[6] and define the mean of a distribution by means of (2.25), with the proviso that the number of intervals is to be increased indefinitely and their width is to approach zero; thus

(2.26) $$\mu = \lim_{\Delta x \to 0} \sum x_i{}^m \phi(x_i{}^m) \Delta x$$

There is a special notation in mathematics for this kind of sum, containing the limit of the sum of an indefinitely large number of terms each representing the area of a rectangle whose width is approaching zero. It is

[6] See III.5.5 for the meaning of "limit."

called the *definite integral* of the function $x\phi(x)$ from x_L to x_U and is written thus (see below for explanation of symbols):

$$(2.27) \qquad \mu = Ex = \lim_{\Delta x \to 0} \sum x_i{}^m\, \phi(x_i{}^m)\, \Delta x = \int_{x_L}^{x_U} x\phi(x)\, dx$$

Here the curly line $\int$, a sort of elongated letter S, is the sign for *integration*, replacing the symbol $\sum$ that is used for the sum of a *finite* number of terms; x_U and x_L are the upper and lower limits of the range of x that is included in the integral; and dx is a symbol replacing Δx, and standing for the width of the infinitely narrow and infinitely numerous intervals.[7]

2.27 The definite integral of the function $\phi(x)$, as distinguished from $x\phi(x)$, is found in the same way:

$$(2.28) \qquad \int_{x_L}^{x_U} \phi(x)\, dx = \lim_{\Delta x \to 0} \sum \phi(x_i{}^m)\, \Delta x$$

But this is simply the area under the probability distribution curve of $\phi(x)$, such as in Figure 2.6, and hence must be equal to 1. The definite integral of any function of x is the area between the curve of the function and the x-axis. If we desire to use merely the area under the curve between two particular values of x, say to find from the distribution $\phi(x)$ the probability that x will fall between the given values a and b, then we want the sum of terms as in equation (2.28) for only those values of x between a and b; this is written

$$(2.29) \qquad \mathrm{Pb}\,(a < x < b) = \int_a^b \phi(x)\, dx$$

2.28 It is not an accident that the dx here reminds us of the dx's in our earlier discussions of derivatives. The connection is that integration is the reverse of differentiation, just as squaring is the reverse of taking the square root. Suppose there is a function $y = F(x)$, and we find its derivative, $dy/dx = F'(x)$. This derivative $F'(x)$ is itself a function of x and can be graphed. Suppose we integrate the function $F'(x)$. Since integration is the reverse of differentiation, this should yield $F(x)$ again. The *indefinite integral* of $F'(x)$ is defined as the original function $F(x)$, with an undetermined constant added on. The indefinite integral of a function is expressed by the same curly line $\int$, without any indication of upper and lower limits:

$$(2.30) \qquad \int dy = \int F'(x)\, dx = y + C = F(x) + C$$

The constant C appears because any function of the form $F(x) + C$ will have the same derivative as $F(x)$ has. The integrals in (2.30) are called indefinite because, unlike those in (2.27)–(2.29), they do not carry any

---

[7] For a more detailed discussion of integrals and integral calculus, see Allen [1938] pp. 384 ff., or any standard calculus text, such as Courant [1934] and [1936].

upper and lower values for x. The indefinite integral is a *function of x*, whereas the definite integral is a *number* corresponding to the area under a curve representing a function of x, between two stated values of x. The *fundamental theorem of integral calculus* establishes that these two integrals are the same, in the sense that if the indefinite integral of a function of x is evaluated at two points $x = a$ and $x = b$, and the difference between these two values is computed, it will be equal to the definite integral of the function evaluated between the same two points $x = a$ and $x = b$. Therefore, we are entitled to use the reverse-differentiation process to find the area under a curve.

2.29 As a simple example, suppose that the probability distribution of x were given by the function $f(x)$, where

$$(2.31) \qquad f(x) = \begin{cases} 2x \text{ if } 0 \leq x \leq 1 \\ 0 \text{ elsewhere} \end{cases}$$

as shown in Figure 2.3(*b*) with *b* set equal to 2. What is the integral of $f(x)$ over the whole range of x? It should be equal to 1, since $f(x)$ is a probability distribution.

$$(2.32) \qquad \int f(x)\, dx = \int 2x\, dx = x^2 + C$$

where C is a constant, called the constant of integration. The second step can be taken because $d(x^2 + C)/dx = 2x$. Therefore

$$(2.33) \qquad \int_0^1 f(x)\, dx = \int_0^1 2x\, dx = [x^2 + C]_0^1$$
$$= [1^2 + C] - [0^2 + C] = 1$$

where $[x^2 + C]_0^{\;1}$ means the difference between the values of $x^2 + C$ when $x = 1$ and when $x = 0$. Thus the constant C disappears. Now what is the probability that x will exceed $1/2$ in this distribution? It is $3/4$, as can be seen either from Figure 2.7 or from the following:

$$(2.34) \quad \mathrm{Pb}(1/2 < x) = \int_{\frac{1}{2}}^1 2x\, dx = [x^2 + C]_{\frac{1}{2}}^1 = 1 - 1/4 = 3/4.$$

Other examples can be constructed by the reader.

3 THE NORMAL DISTRIBUTION; CORRELATION AND REGRESSION[8]

3.1 In our future work, one particular probability distribution function plays an extremely important part. It is the so-called *Gaussian*

[8] Concerning this section, see any standard text in statistical theory, e.g., Mood [1950], Mood and Graybill [1963], Kendall [1952], or Kendall and Stuart [1958, 1961].

or *normal distribution*, and a form of it has already appeared in equation (2.5) and Figure 2.3(*c*). Its equation is[9]

$$(3.1) \qquad y = \phi(x) = \frac{1}{\sqrt{2\pi}\alpha} \exp\left[-\frac{1}{2}\left(\frac{x-\beta}{\alpha}\right)^2\right]$$

where π is as usual the ratio of the circumference of a circle to its diameter (3.14159. . .), e is the base of the natural logarithms (2.71828. . .), and α and β are arbitrary constants. [In (2.5) α was 1 and β was zero.] Let us examine this function to discover its properties. First, it is symmetrical with respect to x, the center of symmetry being at the value $x = \beta$. This can be seen from the fact that x appears nowhere except as $(x - \beta)^2$ in the exponent of e, so that two different values of x (one greater than β

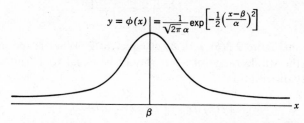

Figure 3.1   The univariate normal distribution with variance α^2 and mean β.

and one less) that differ from β by equal absolute amounts will lead to the same values of y. Second, it has its peak or maximum value at $x = \beta$ and falls off asymptotically toward zero (but never reaching zero) as x increases or decreases from β. This can be seen from the fact that except for a constant factor it is e raised to a negative exponent that increases in absolute magnitude as x deviates further from β. Hence we can draw its graph approximately. It actually appears as in Figure 3.1. Accordingly, both the mode and median are equal to β, and we would guess that the mean is as well. Indeed, by the application of equations (2.27) and (2.35) it can be proved that for the normal distribution of (3.1) and Figure 3.1,

$$(3.2) \qquad \begin{cases} \mu = \beta \\ \sigma = \alpha \end{cases}$$

Hence (2.6) can as well be written with the symbols μ and σ in place of β and α, respectively, and this is usually done:

$$(3.3) \qquad y = \phi(x) = \frac{1}{\sqrt{2\pi}\sigma} \exp\left[-\frac{1}{2}\left(\frac{x-\mu}{\sigma}\right)^2\right]$$

[9] To make the mathematical notation easier to read, e raised to a cumbersome exponent is often written as "exp" followed by a parenthetical expression for the exponent, for example, $e^a = \exp(a)$.

Then the probability that x will fall between two values, a and b, is given by

(3.4) $$\text{Pb}(a < x < b) = \frac{1}{\sqrt{2\pi}\sigma} \int_a^b \exp\left[-\frac{1}{2}\left(\frac{x-\mu}{\sigma}\right)^2\right] dx$$

3.2 This integral happens to be too complicated to obtain by reverse differentiation, and hence its value for different a's and b's must be calculated by numerical approximation procedures, which we cannot go into here. Values of the integral for hundreds of narrowly separated values of a and b have been calculated and tabulated for the special case where $\mu = 0$ and $\sigma = 1$, that is, for cases where the problem is to find

(3.5) $$\text{Pb}(c < z < d) = \frac{1}{\sqrt{2\pi}} \int_c^d e^{-\frac{1}{2}z^2} dz$$

This table may seem to be of no help in case $\mu \neq 0$ or $\sigma \neq 1$, but it actually suffices for all such cases too. The trick is to translate any given normal distribution into the standard form of normal distribution where $\mu = 0$ and $\sigma = 1$, as in (3.5). It may be done by using the following equations to go from x to z:

(3.6) $$z = \frac{x-\mu}{\sigma}, \qquad dz = \frac{dx}{\sigma}$$

or equivalently the following equations to go from z to x:

(3.7) $$x = \mu + \sigma z, \qquad dx = \sigma\, dz$$

where μ and σ are the mean and standard deviation of x, and 0 and 1 are the mean and standard deviation of z, respectively. If (3.6) is substituted into (3.4), the result is (3.5), provided that c and d, the lower and upper values of z, correspond to a and b, the lower and upper values of x, through (3.6) and (3.7), that is, that

(3.8) $$c = \frac{a-\mu}{\sigma}, \qquad d = \frac{b-\mu}{\sigma}$$

Then if we have a normal distribution where, say, $\mu = 50$ and $\sigma = 10$, and we wish to find the probability that x will fall between 50 and 70, we proceed as follows. The lower and upper limits of z are, from (3.8), $(50 - \mu)/\sigma = (50 - 50)/10 = 0$ and $(70 - \mu)/\sigma = (70 - 50)/10 = 2$, respectively. The standard normal table tells us[10] that the probability that

---

[10] The last row of Table 1, Appendix B, shows a part of the normal distribution. It gives the probability as .025 that z will exceed 1.96, i.e., the probability is $.5 - .025 = .475$ that z will fall between 0 and 1.96. Actually, a more detailed table shows that the probability of z falling between 0 and 2 is closer to .477.

z will fall between 0 and 2 is approximately .477, and therefore the probability that x in our example will fall between 50 and 70 is likewise about .477. The equations representing this are

$$(3.9) \quad \text{Pb}(50 < x < 70) = \frac{1}{\sqrt{2\pi}10} \int_{50}^{70} \exp\left[-\frac{1}{2}\left(\frac{x-50}{10}\right)^2\right] dx$$

$$= \frac{1}{\sqrt{2\pi}} \int_{\frac{50-50}{10}}^{\frac{70-50}{10}} e^{-\frac{1}{2}z^2} dz = \frac{1}{\sqrt{2\pi}} \int_0^2 e^{-\frac{1}{2}z^2} dz$$

$$= \text{Pb}(0 < z < 2) = .477 \text{ approximately}$$

3.3 The normal distribution is a convenient approximation to many phenomena in the real world. Errors in physical measurement are often approximately normally distributed. Many physical characteristics of human beings and other organisms are approximately normally distributed—height, weight, and so forth. But even more startling is the fact that either the *sum* or the *average* of a large number of independent random variables having any single distribution whatever (as long as it has a finite variance) is approximately normally distributed, the approximation being better for a larger number of variables, and approaching

TABLE 3.1   Probability Distributions of Results of Throwing
Dice

One Die		Two Dice		Three Dice	
x	Pb(x)	x	Pb(x)	x	Pb(x)
1	1/6	2	1/36	3	1/216
2	1/6	3	2/36	4	3/216
3	1/6	4	3/36	5	6/216
4	1/6	5	4/36	6	10/216
5	1/6	6	5/36	7	15/216
6	1/6	7	6/36	8	21/216
		8	5/36	9	25/216
Σ	1	9	4/36	10	27/216
		10	3/36	11	27/216
		11	2/36	12	25/216
		12	1/36	13	21/216
				14	15/216
		Σ	1	15	10/216
				16	6/216
				17	3/216
				18	1/216
				Σ	1

perfection as the number of variables approaches infinity. This fact is known as the *central limit theorem*; its proof is beyond the techniques used here.[11] It can be illustrated, however, by the distributions of the number of spots turned up when one, two, and three dice are rolled together. These distributions are tabulated in Table 3.1 and graphed in Figure 3.2. Notice that even starting from the so-called rectangular distribution of Figure 3.2(*a*), and adding together as few as three variables thus distributed, the resulting distribution is approximately normal in shape. The importance of this approach to normality is that it entitles us to use the normal distribution as an approximation to the distribution of any quantity with finite variance that we believe to be the result of the

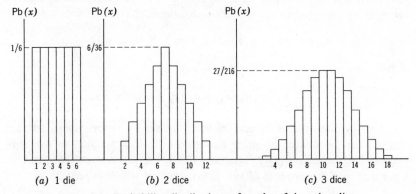

Figure 3.2   Probability distributions of results of throwing dice.

addition of a large number of similar independent small irregular causal forces. Hence economists often assume that the random disturbances to economic equations are normally distributed.

    3.4   We often add several variables together, or multiply each of several variables by a constant and then add the products. The result of the latter process is called a *linear combination* of the variables.[12] It is useful to note that the sum or linear combination of two or more normally distributed random variables is also normal. In particular, suppose that x_1 and x_2 are normally distributed variables, with means μ_1 and μ_2, respectively, and variances σ_1^2 and σ_2^2, respectively. Suppose that y is a linear combination of x_1 and x_2; thus $y = \alpha_1 x_1 + \alpha_2 x_2$, where α_1 and α_2 are constants. Then y is normally distributed, with mean equal to $\alpha_1\mu_1 + \alpha_2\mu_2$ and variance equal to $\alpha_1^2\sigma_1^2 + \alpha_2^2\sigma_2^2 + 2\alpha_1\alpha_2 E(x_1 - \mu_1)(x_2 - \mu_2)$. A similar statement holds for linear combinations of three or more variables.

[11] See Cramer [1946], pp. 213–220.
[12] See Appendix A, paragraph 4.4.

3.5 Let us turn to some of the parameters that can be used to characterize a joint distribution; we shall take a bivariate distribution first, say $f(x_1, x_2)$. Here each variable has a marginal distribution of its own, which is univariate and has a mean and a variance. We may symbolize the respective means of x_1 and x_2 by μ_1 (or Ex_1) and μ_2 (or Ex_2) and the respective variances by $\sigma_1{}^2$ and $\sigma_2{}^2$. Thus there are at least four useful parameters for a bivariate distribution. But these four tell nothing about the relationship between the random variables x_1 and x_2. A significant feature of a joint distribution is whether high values of x_1 are usually accompanied by high values of x_2, or by low values, or by either indiscriminately. This feature is revealed by a fifth parameter, known as the *covariance* of x_1 and x_2, denoted by σ_{12} or σ_{21}, and defined as follows for discrete and continuous distributions, respectively:

$$(3.10) \quad \sigma_{12} = \sigma_{21} = E(x_1 - \mu_1)(x_2 - \mu_2) = \sum_{x_1} \sum_{x_2} f(x_1, x_2)(x_1 - \mu_1)(x_2 - \mu_2)$$

$$(3.10') \quad \sigma_{12} = \sigma_{21} = E(x_1 - \mu_1)(x_2 - \mu_2)$$

$$= \int_{x_{1L}}^{x_{1U}} \int_{x_{2L}}^{x_{2U}} f(x_1, x_2)(x_1 - \mu_1)(x_2 - \mu_2)\, dx_1\, dx_2$$

3.6 Notice that if x_1 and x_2 are statistically independent, so that $f(x_1, x_2)$ can be written by using equation (2.6) as a product of two univariate distributions $f_1(x_1)f_2(x_2)$, then (3.10) for the discrete case can be separated into the product of two sums, each of which is zero, thus:

$$(3.11) \quad \sigma_{12} = \left[\sum_{x_1} f_1(x_1)\,(x_1 - \mu_1) \right]\left[\sum_{x_2} f_2(x_2)\,(x_2 - \mu_2) \right]$$

$$= \left[\sum_{x_1} f_1(x_1)\, x_1 - \sum_{x_1} f_1(x_1)\,\mu_1 \right]\left[\sum_{x_2} f_2(x_2)\, x_2 - \sum_{x_2} f_2(x_2)\,\mu_2 \right]$$

$$= [\mu_1 - \mu_1][\mu_2 - \mu_2] = [0][0] = 0$$

and similarly in the continuous case, if x_1 and x_2 are independent, we have

$$(3.11') \quad \sigma_{12} = \int_{x_{1L}}^{x_{1U}} f_1(x_1)\,(x_1 - \mu_1)\, dx_1 \int_{x_{2L}}^{x_{2U}} f_2(x_2)\,(x_2 - \mu_2)\, dx_2 = 0$$

In other words, if two random variables are statistically independent, then their covariance is zero. This fact was used in (2.22) above. The converse is not necessarily true, however. Statistical independence is a stronger condition than zero covariance, in the sense of implying it but not being implied by it. Examples in which two statistically dependent variables have zero covariance are given presently.

3.7 Notice what happens if above-average values of x_1 are accompanied by above-average values of x_2, and below-average values of x_1 by below-average values of x_2. Then whenever $x_1 - \mu_1$ is positive so is

$x_2 - \mu_2$, and their product is positive. Then also whenever $x_1 - \mu_1$ is negative so is $x_2 - \mu_2$, and their product is again positive. In such a case σ_{12} turns out to be positive. However, if above-average values of x_1 are accompanied by below-average values of x_2 and vice versa, then whenever $x_1 - \mu_1$ is positive $x_2 - \mu_2$ is negative, and vice versa, so that σ_{12} turns out to be negative. Thus the covariance of two random variables tells something about their joint variation. If they usually rise and fall together, the covariance is positive; if one usually rises when the other falls, it is negative; if they are independent, it is zero. The covariance will also be zero for two dependent variables, if their variation is such as to make the terms of the sum in (3.10) or the integral in (3.10′) cancel each other out. When σ_{12} is zero, the two variables are said to be *uncorrelated*.

3.8 In order to have a uniform system of notation, we shall often use the symbol σ_{11} for the variance $\sigma_1{}^2$, and σ_{22} for $\sigma_2{}^2$. Then the variances and covariances of any two variables x_1 and x_2 with means μ_1 and μ_2 can all be expressed in a single formula thus:

$$(3.12) \qquad \sigma_{ij} = E(x_i - \mu_i)(x_j - \mu_j) \qquad i, j = 1, 2$$

If $i = j = 1$, this expresses the variance σ_{11} or $\sigma_1{}^2$ of x_1; if $i = j = 2$, it expresses the variance of x_2; and if $i \neq j$, it expresses the covariance σ_{12} of x_1 and x_2. With this in mind, we can give the general formula for the variance of a sum or difference of two variables x_1 and x_2, derived from (2.21) and (3.10) or (3.10′):

$$(3.13) \qquad \operatorname{var}(x_1 \pm x_2) = \sigma_{11} \pm 2\sigma_{12} + \sigma_{22} = \sigma_1{}^2 \pm 2\sigma_{12} + \sigma_2{}^2$$

The signs $\pm$ must be interpreted as $+$ right through or as $-$ right through. In the special case where x_1 and x_2 are uncorrelated, σ_{12} is zero. It is easily seen that in the case of two uncorrelated variables the expectation of their product is the product of their expectations, and the variance of their sum or difference is the sum of their variances, thus:

$$(3.14) \qquad \text{If } \sigma_{12} = 0, \qquad Ex_1x_2 = Ex_1Ex_2$$

$$(3.15) \qquad \text{If } \sigma_{12} = 0, \qquad \operatorname{var}(x_1 \pm x_2) = \operatorname{var} x_1 + \operatorname{var} x_2$$

These two results are similar to (2.20) and (2.22) except that we now see that they hold for uncorrelated variables whether they are independent or not.

3.9 Another parameter, the *correlation coefficient* ρ_{12} or ρ_{21} or simply ρ, is often used instead of the covariance σ_{12} to describe the relationship between two random variables x_1 and x_2. The relationship between ρ and σ_{12} involves the standard deviations σ_1 and σ_2 and is as follows:

$$(3.16) \qquad \rho = \frac{\sigma_{12}}{\sigma_1\sigma_2}$$

If σ_{12} and the two standard deviations are known, ρ can be found. Likewise if ρ and the two standard deviations are known, σ_{12} can be found. Thus the four parameters μ_1, μ_2, σ_{11}, and σ_{22}, together with either σ_{12} or ρ as a fifth parameter, describe important features of a bivariate distribution.

3.10   The correlation coefficient ρ is always in the range from -1 to $+1$ inclusive. It always has the same sign as σ_{12} and is zero whenever σ_{12} is zero. It is equal to $+1$ or -1 when x_1 and x_2 are related exactly by a *straight line*, $+1$ if the line slopes upward like this $/$ and -1 if it slopes downward like this $\setminus$. In some bivariate distributions the two variables are related exactly but by a line that is not straight; then ρ is not equal to $+1$ or -1 and may even be equal to zero. For instance, if

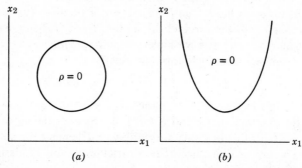

Figure 3.3 Examples illustrating that two variables can be uncorrelated and yet statistically dependent.

the points in the distribution are distributed with uniform probability around a circle, or per unit length of a vertical symmetrical parabola section, as in Figure 3.3, then the relationship is perfect but not linear, and the variables are statistically dependent, and the covariance and the correlation coefficient are zero. This shows that noncorrelation does not imply independence. It is worth noting that when there are three variables, say x, y, and z, if x is uncorrelated with y and y is uncorrelated with z, this does not imply that x is uncorrelated with z. The same statement applies if the word "uncorrelated" is replaced everywhere by "correlated," by "independent," or by "dependent."

3.11   The normal distribution discussed earlier is a univariate one. The normal distribution also has a bivariate form, and we have already presented a picture of it in Figure 2.4. If x_1 and x_2 are each normally distributed with means μ_1 and μ_2 and variances σ_{11} and σ_{22}, then their joint distribution is completely described by these four parameters together with either their covariance or their correlation coefficient. (Most other bivariate distributions are described only incompletely by these five parameters.) The bivariate normal distribution function is much more involved than the univariate one, particularly in the exponent of e. One form of the bivariate normal distribution function is as follows:

(3.17) $f(x_1, x_2)$

$$= \frac{\exp\left(-\dfrac{\sigma_{22}(x_1 - \mu_1)^2 - 2\sigma_{12}(x_1 - \mu_1)(x_2 - \mu_2) + \sigma_{11}(x_2 - \mu_2)^2}{2(\sigma_{11}\sigma_{22} - \sigma_{12}^2)}\right)}{2\pi\sqrt{\sigma_{11}\sigma_{22} - \sigma_{12}^2}}$$

Another form of the bivariate normal distribution, equivalent to (3.17), is as follows:

(3.18) $f(x_1, x_2)$

$$= \frac{\exp\left[-\dfrac{\left(\dfrac{x_1 - \mu_1}{\sigma_1}\right)^2 - 2\rho\left(\dfrac{x_1 - \mu_1}{\sigma_1}\right)\left(\dfrac{x_2 - \mu_2}{\sigma_2}\right) + \left(\dfrac{x_2 - \mu_2}{\sigma_2}\right)^2}{2(1 - \rho^2)}\right]}{2\pi\sigma_1\sigma_2\sqrt{1 - \rho^2}}$$

To prove that (3.17) and (3.18) are equivalent, it is necessary to substitute $\sigma_{12}/\sigma_1\sigma_2$ for ρ in (3.18), or to substitute $\rho\sigma_1\sigma_2$ for σ_{12} in (3.17), and then multiply and divide the exponent by $\sigma_{11}\sigma_{22}$ and the denominator by $\sigma_1\sigma_2$. This function gives the height of the normal probability surface at any point (x_1, x_2), as in Figure 2.4.

3.12 Notice what happens to the bivariate normal distribution when the two variables are uncorrelated, that is, when $\sigma_{12} = \rho = 0$. It then becomes [using the form (3.18)]

(3.19) $f(x_1, x_2) = \dfrac{1}{2\pi\sigma_1\sigma_2} \exp\left\{-\dfrac{1}{2}\left[\left(\dfrac{x_1 - \mu_1}{\sigma_1}\right)^2 + \left(\dfrac{x_2 - \mu_2}{\sigma_2}\right)^2\right]\right\}$

Now this expression can be factored into two parts as follows, since the adding of two exponents of a number (here e) is equivalent to multiplying the separate exponential functions:

(3.20)

$$f(x_1, x_2) = \frac{1}{\sqrt{2\pi}\sigma_1} \exp\left[-\frac{1}{2}\left(\frac{x_1 - \mu_1}{\sigma_1}\right)^2\right] \frac{1}{\sqrt{2\pi}\sigma_2} \exp\left[-\frac{1}{2}\left(\frac{x_2 - \mu_2}{\sigma_2}\right)^2\right]$$

This is simply the product of the two normal univariate marginal distributions of x_1 and x_2, as in equation (2.6). We have already seen that in general the independence of two random variables is sufficient to insure that they are uncorrelated. We now see that in the special case of a normal distribution it is necessary as well. Not all bivariate distributions have this latter property.

3.13 Conditional distributions also can be characterized by "parameters," although of a somewhat different character. As before, let the conditional distribution of x_2 given x_1 be represented by $g_2(x_2 \mid x_1)$. This actually stands for a whole class of distributions of x_2, each one being the result of choosing some particular value of x_1. Each of these distributions has a mean and a variance, and the values of the mean and the variance may depend upon what value of x_1 is chosen. Hence they are called the conditional mean and the conditional variance of x_2, given x_1. They are written this way for discrete distributions:

$$(3.21) \qquad E(x_2 \mid x_1) = \sum x_2\, g_2(x_2 \mid x_1)$$

$$(3.22) \qquad \text{var}\,(x_2 \mid x_1) = \sum [x_2 - E(x_2 \mid x_1)]^2\, g_2(x_2 \mid x_1)$$

and this way for continuous distributions:

$$(3.23) \qquad E(x_2 \mid x_1) = \int_{x_{2L}}^{x_{2U}} x_2\, g_2(x_2 \mid x_1)\, dx_2$$

$$(3.24) \qquad \text{var}\,(x_2 \mid x_1) = \int_{x_{2L}}^{x_{2U}} [x_2 - E(x_2 \mid x_1)]^2\, g_2(x_2 \mid x_1)\, dx_2$$

where x_{2L} and x_{2U} are the extreme lower and upper values of x_2, respectively. Similar definitions apply for $E(x_1 \mid x_2)$ and $\text{var}\,(x_1 \mid x_2)$. Notice that while the parameters of a univariate or a joint distribution (μ_1, μ_2, σ_{11}, σ_{12}, σ_{22}) are all constant numbers, the conditional mean and variance $E(x_2 \mid x_1)$ and $\text{var}\,(x_2 \mid x_1)$ are *not* necessarily constants, but are rather functions of x_1. That is why we referred to them as "parameters" with quotation marks at the beginning of this paragraph; they are not really parameters at all, but functions instead. To find the "parameters" of a conditional distribution we must find the parameters of these functions.

3.14 The conditional mean of x_2 given x_1, or $E(x_2 \mid x_1)$, is called the *regression function* (or simply the *regression*) of x_2 on x_1. Similarly, $E(x_1 \mid x_2)$ is called the regression of x_1 on x_2. It is important not to confuse these two regressions, for only in very special joint distributions (not in general including the normal) are they the same.

3.15 The conditional distribution of x_2 given x_1 can then be thought of as a sort of ridge, as in Figure 3.4, whose vertical cross sections (lying in planes perpendicular to this page, and shown in perspective) at particular values of x_1 are the probability distributions of x_2 for those particular values of x_1. They are here shown as normal, but they need not be so. The line running through the middle of the bottom of the ridge, connecting the means of these univariate distributions of x_2, is the regression of x_2 on x_1, $E(x_2 \mid x_1)$. The fact that it is not a straight horizontal line in the graph indicates that x_1 and x_2 are not independent. The fact that the little conditional distribution curves change shape as we move along the regression line indicates that the conditional variance $\text{var}\,(x_2 \mid x_1)$ is not a constant.

3.16   Notice that the conditional distribution of x_2 given x_1 says nothing at all about the probabilities with which different values of x_1 occur, and indeed x_1 need not even be a random variable. In fact, among the early users of regressions were experimental biologists, using x_1 as a quantity controlled by the experimenter, such as amount of fertilizer or feed, and x_2 was a measure of the growth of plants or animals.

3.17   The most commonly used regression lines are linear, since as we saw in the previous chapter, linear theories are relatively simple to

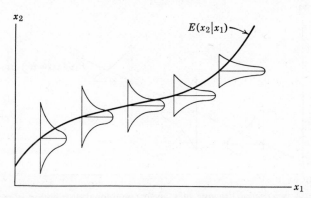

Figure 3.4   A perspective drawing of a conditional distribution of x_2 given x_1.

deal with.[13] Furthermore, a regression obtained from a bivariate normal distribution is always linear. A linear regression of x_2 on x_1 looks like any straight line, thus:

$$(3.25) \qquad E(x_2 \mid x_1) = \alpha + \beta x_1$$

where α and β are constants. They are parameters of the regression, and hence also of the conditional distribution of x_2 given x_1. The most commonly used regressions are assumed to have an additional property, also chosen for simplicity, namely, the conditional variance $\mathrm{var}\,(x_2 \mid x_1)$ is a constant, not changing when x_1 changes.[14] The graph of a conditional distribution of x_2 given x_1, with a linear regression and a constant conditional variance, might look like Figure 3.5. The random variable x_2 can now be said to consist of a sum of two components: a systematic component, $\alpha + \beta x_1$, and a random component whose mean is zero and

[13] Sometimes if a regression line is not linear a simple transformation of variables will make it so. E.g., if $E(x_2 \mid x_1) = \alpha x_1{}^\beta$, then $\log E(x_2 \mid x_1) = \log \alpha + \beta \log x_1$, which is linear in logarithms of the variables.

[14] Sometimes it is more reasonable to assume that $\mathrm{var}\,(x_2 \mid x_1)$ is a simple function of x_1, e.g., a multiple of x_1 or of $x_1{}^2$. Such cases, though less convenient than constant $\mathrm{var}\,(x_2 \mid x_1)$, can be handled.

whose variance is that of the little distribution curves (again imagined to lie in planes perpendicular to this page) in Figure 3.5, the constant var $(x_2 \mid x_1)$, which we may as well call simply σ^2 for brevity. If we regard this random component as a new random variable, and call it u, then we may write the relation between x_2 and x_1 thus:

$$(3.26) \qquad x_2 = \alpha + \beta x_1 + u$$

where u is understood to have a mean of 0 and a variance of σ^2.

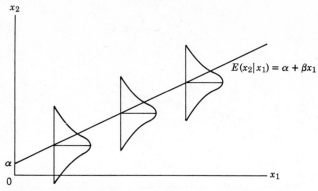

Figure 3.5 A perspective drawing of a linear conditional distribution of x_2 given x_1, with constant conditional variance.

3.18 It is often convenient, as suggested earlier, to use normally distributed random variables. Suppose that u is normal with mean zero and variance σ^2. Then its distribution function is

$$(3.27) \qquad \phi(u) = \frac{1}{\sqrt{2\pi}\sigma}\, e^{-u^2/2\sigma^2}$$

This is derived from the univariate normal distribution (3.3) by substituting 0 for the mean μ and rechristening the variable. The conditional distribution of x_2 given x_1 then becomes normal as well, with mean $\alpha + \beta x_1$ and constant variance σ^2. It is

$$(3.28) \qquad g_2(x_1 \mid x_2) = \frac{1}{\sqrt{2\pi}\sigma} \exp\left[-\frac{(x_2 - \alpha - \beta x_1)^2}{2\sigma^2}\right]$$

This can be obtained from the univariate normal distribution (3.3) by substituting $\alpha + \beta x_1$ for the mean μ and rechristening the variable. It may also be obtained from equation (2.7) as the quotient of the bivariate normal distribution $f(x_1, x_2)$ in equation (3.17) divided by the marginal normal distribution $f_1(x_1)$ as in equation (3.3).

3.19 All of the exposition given so far in this chapter can be extended to joint distributions of three or more variables. The extension is quite straightforward for the most part, but of course the possibilities become more numerous. For example, we encounter the joint conditional distribution of one set of variables $y_1, \ldots, y_n$ given the values of another set of variables $x_1, \ldots, x_m$, thus:

$$\psi(y_1, \ldots, y_n \mid x_1, \ldots, x_m)$$

And the expressions become more complicated, particularly those concerning the joint normal distribution of many variables. But the linear regression equation (3.25) and its companions (3.26) and (3.28) generalize very readily to give the regression of one variable, say x_0, on a set of other variables $x_1, \ldots, x_n$; the value of x_0 in terms of $x_1, \ldots, x_n$ and u; and the conditional distribution of x_0, given $x_1, \ldots, x_n$, all respectively, thus:

(3.29)

$$E(x_0 \mid x_1, \ldots, x_n) = \alpha + \beta_1 x_1 + \cdots + \beta_n x_n = \alpha + \sum_{i=1}^{n} \beta_i x_i$$

(3.30)

$$x_0 = \alpha + \beta_1 x_1 + \cdots + \beta_n x_n + u = \alpha + \sum_{i=1}^{n} \beta_i x_i + u$$

(3.31)

$$h(x_0 \mid x_1, \ldots, x_n) = \frac{1}{\sqrt{2\pi}\,\sigma} \exp\left[-\frac{\left(x_0 - \alpha - \sum_{i=1}^{n} \beta_i x_i \right)^2}{2\sigma^2} \right]$$

3.20   We have now at least made a start on the problem of introducing small unsystematic variations into the type of economic theory we discussed in the previous chapter. We have in effect provided a rationale for the real-world situations in which one economic variable appears to be related to one or more others but with small irregular shifts or disturbances in the relationship over short periods. This has been done by the use of conditional probability distributions, whose means will often be assumed linear, as in equations (3.25) to (3.31).

3.21   There is no reason in principle why the equations used should be linear, or why the shifts should be incorporated in the form of an additive disturbance like u in (3.26) and (3.30) instead of as multiplicative or exponential or logarithmic disturbances or even as errors of measurement of the variables. It is perfectly possible to introduce equations in which the random variable is a multiplicative factor, thus:

(3.32)

$$x_0 = \left(\alpha + \sum_{i=1}^{n} \beta_i x_i \right) u$$

or

(3.33)

$$x_0 = \alpha x_1^{\beta_1} x_2^{\beta_2} u$$

or in which there is a separate random disturbance representing an error of measurement associated with each variable, thus:

(3.34)

$$x_0 = \alpha (x_1 + u_1)^{\beta_1} (x_2 + u_2)^{\beta_2} u$$

Multiplicative disturbances as in (3.33) are particularly appropriate where the variable to be explained has a large amount of variation in the sense that its largest value is several times as large as its smallest value, and where the disturbance's standard deviation is thought to be approximately proportional to the variable to be explained. Equations like (3.33) are relatively easy to handle if we take the logarithm of both sides because the result is linear in logs; in the case of (3.33) this gives

$$(3.35) \qquad \log x_0 = \log \alpha + \beta_1 \log x_1 + \beta_2 \log x_2 + \log u$$

Linearity and additive disturbances are used for simplicity in this relatively young field and will possibly be modified in due course.

3.22   It is important to remember that even if the distribution of a random variable is completely known both as to form and parameters, we cannot predict the value of the variable, or even in general the range within which it will fall; we can only state the probability with which it will fall in any chosen interval, according to equations such as (2.29). When we come to empirical work with our models, this fact will make things difficult for us, because it is only frequencies of occurrence, not probabilities, that are observable. In order to assess the correctness of a theory that says national income next year has a 90 per cent chance of falling between $700 and $712 billion for instance, we would need to observe infinitely many different random drawings from the set of possible national incomes for next year to see whether 90 per cent of them do fall in the given interval; but actually we observe only one. The next best thing is to make predictions for several years with the same theory, each prediction being in the form of an interval designed to have a 90 per cent chance of containing the value of national income for that year, and then check whether and by how much each of the observed values of national incomes for those years falls in or out of the predicted intervals. Even this turns out in practice, however, to give a fairly small number of observations on which to base a test of a theory. Fortunately there are statistical techniques for evaluating, if not eliminating, the risk of error involved in accepting or rejecting a theory on such a basis; these will be discussed in Chapters VII and X.

4   STOCHASTIC STRUCTURES, MODELS, AND REDUCED FORMS; EXOGENOUS VARIABLES[15]

4.1   In this section we shall present several stochastic models, analogous to the models of the previous chapter except that random elements

[15] Concerning this section, see Koopmans and Hood [1953], pp. 113–126; Marschak [1953], pp. 1–15; Haavelmo [1944], pp. 1–59.

are introduced, and we shall explore the modifications that are thereby required or permitted.

4.2 The concept of economic *structure* was defined in I.5.3 as the complex of factors that do not change during a period that is being studied, and in II.1.13 a structure was described as a set of autonomous relationships sufficient to determine uniquely the values of the endogenous variables, conditional upon the values of the exogenous variables. The first definition is applicable to the stochastic case, but the second is too narrow because, as we have just seen, stochastic variables by nature have uncertainty built into their determination. The essential character of the second definition will be retained and its complete equivalence to the first will be secured if it is modified to say that a *structure* is a set of autonomous relationships sufficient to determine uniquely the *conditional probability distributions* of the endogenous variables, given the values of the exogenous variables. Hence a stochastic structure includes the *form and parameters of the distribution of any disturbances* that enter the relationships.

4.3 An example of a stochastic structure is the following simple system of equations[16] in consumption c and income y, and the accompanying distribution function, investment i being exogenous and the mean and variance of the disturbance u being 0 and 16, respectively:

(4.1) $$c = 10 + 0.8y + u$$

(4.2) $$y = c + i$$

(4.3) $$\text{probability density of } u = \phi(u) = \frac{1}{\sqrt{2\pi 4}} e^{-u^2/32}$$

4.4 A *model* was defined in II.1.14 as a set of structures having the same number of equations, the same endogenous and exogenous variables, and the same variables appearing in corresponding equations. This definition applies as it stands to the stochastic case, it being understood of course that a stochastic model is a set of *stochastic* structures.[17] A stochastic model may or may not specify any restriction on the probability distribution of the random disturbances, but for statistical convenience most do. A commonly used stochastic model that includes the structure described by equations (4.1) to (4.3) is as follows:

(4.4) $$c = \alpha + \beta y + u$$

(4.5) $$y = c + i$$

(4.6) $$\text{probability density of } u = \phi(u) = \frac{1}{\sqrt{2\pi}\sigma} e^{-u^2/2\sigma^2}$$

---

[16] Another example appeared in II.2.7.

[17] See I.3.2 for other remarks about the meaning of a model. See II.2.7 for an example of a stochastic model.

where i is again exogenous, and α, β, and σ^2 are unspecified parameters. This model specifies that the distribution of the disturbance u is normal, with a mean of zero. Notice that the assumption that u has a zero mean does not constitute any real restriction, because α is still unspecified. If both α and the mean of u were unspecified, then it might be possible from empirical data to find the value of their sum, as we shall see later, but it would be neither possible nor useful to find either one separately because they always occur together. Hence no real restriction is imposed by making the very convenient assumption that the mean of u is zero, and then denoting the constant term in (4.4) by α.

4.5 Equations (4.4) and (4.5) together form a model too, one that specifies nothing about the probability distribution of u. In econometric work the model that does specify something about the distribution, as the model (4.4)–(4.6) does, is often the more useful. The reasons for this will become clearer later on in Chapters VII–X, but we can anticipate them here by saying that a theory can usually make more specific statements if it has more specific assumptions. If the assumptions are valid, the theory will be better because of them, and of course if they are not the theory may be worse because of them. The remarks in II.2.4 are also relevant here.

4.6 Any of the exact models or structures of Chapter III can be converted into stochastic models or structures by introducing random disturbances together with their distributions. Consider the general exact linear model, given by equations (10.7) in Chapter III and reproduced here:

$$(4.7) \qquad \sum_{i=1}^{G} \beta_{gi} y_i + \sum_{k=1}^{K} \gamma_{gk} z_k = 0 \qquad g = 1, \ldots, G$$

Recall that the endogenous variables are the y_i and the exogenous variables are the z_k. If each of the expressions in (4.7) is assumed to be a normally distributed random disturbance u_g whose mean is zero, instead of being assumed exactly equal to zero, then the result is a general form of linear stochastic model, as in the following equations:

$$(4.8) \qquad \sum_{i=1}^{G} \beta_{gi} y_i + \sum_{k=1}^{K} \gamma_{gk} z_k = u_g \qquad g = 1, \ldots, G$$

$$(4.9) \qquad \phi(u_1, \ldots, u_G) = \text{joint normal density function}$$
$$\text{with each } u_g \text{ having zero mean}$$

The *reduced form* of a model is the algebraic solution that gives each endogenous variable as a linear combination[18] of the exogenous variables z_k and the structural disturbances u_g [compare equations (10.10) in

---

[18] Defined in 3.4 above.

Chapter III]. Since any linear combination of normally distributed random variables is itself a normally distributed random variable, each linear combination of u's in the reduced form is normally distributed. We may call them *reduced-form disturbances* and symbolize them by $v_1, \ldots, v_G$. Each of the v's has a zero mean because the mean of a linear combination of normal variables (such as the u_g) is equal to the same linear combination of their means, which in this case is a linear combination of zeros, that is, zero. The reduced form is then

$$(4.10) \qquad y_i = \sum_{k=1}^{K} \pi_{ik} z_k + v_i \qquad i = 1, \ldots, G$$

$$(4.11) \qquad \psi(v_1, \ldots, v_G) = \text{joint normal density function}$$
$$\text{with each } v_i \text{ having zero mean}$$

4.7 Observe that this stochastic reduced form is a conditional probability distribution; the ith equation of (4.10) together with the corresponding part of (4.11), that is, the marginal distribution of v_i, is the conditional distribution of y_i given the values of all the z's and the parameters of the system. Indeed, the reduced form of any stochastic model is such a conditional distribution.

4.8 Exogenous variables were defined in I.5.5 as variables whose values can be assumed to be determined and known in advance, in such a way that they can be regarded as fixed when we analyze the behavior of the endogenous variables. They then form the fixed conditions under which conditional predictions are made. In exact models this requires only that the equation or equations that determine the variables called exogenous should not contain any of the endogenous variables. That is, the complete set of equations determining *all* the variables, endogenous and exogenous, must be segmentable in the sense defined in III.3.4, with the exogenous variables being determined in a segment that does not include any of the endogenous ones. In the following exact model, z_1 and z_2 meet this condition.

$$(4.12) \qquad \beta_{11} y_1 + \beta_{12} y_2 + \gamma_{11} z_1 \qquad \qquad + \gamma_{10} = 0$$

$$(4.13) \qquad \beta_{21} y_1 + \beta_{22} y_2 \qquad \quad + \gamma_{22} z_2 + \gamma_{20} = 0$$

$$(4.14) \qquad \qquad \qquad \gamma_{31} z_1 + \gamma_{32} z_2 + \gamma_{30} = 0$$

$$(4.15) \qquad \qquad \qquad \gamma_{41} z_1 + \gamma_{42} z_2 + \gamma_{40} = 0$$

Once the parameters $\gamma_{30}, \gamma_{31}, \gamma_{32}, \gamma_{40}, \gamma_{41}$, and γ_{42} are fixed, z_1 and z_2 are determined by (4.14)–(4.15), and the process that determines y_1 and y_2 can be analyzed separately from (4.14)–(4.15). Equations such as (4.14)–(4.15) are ordinarily of no interest to the economist; they are mentioned here by way of demonstrating the meaning of the assumption that z_1 and z_2 are exogenous in the really interesting equations (4.12)–(4.13).

4.9 We want the same heuristic concept of exogenousness to apply to the stochastic case. Now the "segmentability" condition of III.3.4 is no longer sufficient to insure that the process determining the values of one set of variables (the endogenous ones) can be analyzed separately from the process that determines the values of the other set of variables (which we want to regard as exogenous). Consider the stochastic version of the above model:

$$(4.16) \qquad \beta_{11}y_1 + \beta_{12}y_2 + \gamma_{11}z_1 \qquad\qquad + \gamma_{10} = u_1$$

$$(4.17) \qquad \beta_{21}y_1 + \beta_{22}y_2 \qquad\quad + \gamma_{22}z_2 + \gamma_{20} = u_2$$

$$(4.18) \qquad\qquad\qquad\qquad \gamma_{31}z_1 + \gamma_{32}z_2 + \gamma_{30} = u_3$$

$$(4.19) \qquad\qquad\qquad\qquad \gamma_{41}z_1 + \gamma_{42}z_2 + \gamma_{40} = u_4$$

Here, when the parameters of the two equations (4.18) and (4.19) (that contain z_1 and z_2 only) are fixed, the values of z_1 and z_2 are not yet determined; the disturbances u_3 and u_4 also affect them. If we want to be sure that the process determining the y's is separate from the process determining the z's, so that the z's can be regarded as fixed when the determination of the y's is analyzed, we must assume that u_1 and u_2 on the one hand are statistically independent of u_3 and u_4 on the other. If this is not assumed, then the y's and z's are simultaneously determined by all four equations of the model because a change in u_1 or u_2 will be associated with a change in u_3 or u_4 or both, so that the z's are not fixed independently of the y's. If u_1 and u_2 are assumed independent of u_3 and u_4, then no change in u_1 or u_2 will be associated with any change in u_3 or u_4, so that the z's are fixed independently of the y's. An equivalent assumption in this model [since the y's do not appear in (4.18) and (4.19)] is that u_1 and u_2 are independent of the z's. We shall require that in order to be exogenous in a stochastic model, a variable must fulfill two conditions: (1) the variable must be determined in a set of equations in which the endogenous variables do not appear, and (2) the variable must be statistically independent of all random disturbances in the model. Since the second condition implies the first, our revised definition is as follows: *An exogenous variable in a stochastic model is a variable whose value in each period is statistically independent of the values of all the random disturbances in the model in all periods.* In particular, if z is an exogenous variable and u is a disturbance in the same model, then z_t and u_{t-k} are statistically independent for *all* values of k, positive, negative, and zero. Equivalently, u_t is independent of z_{t-k} for all values of k. This definition of an exogenous variable will be used throughout the rest of the book.[19] It follows Koopmans and Hood [1953], pp. 117–120. Exogenous variables may be random, or may be deliberately

[19] In V.3.8 it will be necessary to define a broader class of variables to be known as predetermined, and in VI.4.3 that definition will be extended to the stochastic case. See also Koopmans [1950a].

set by some agency, as by government. Variables that are not exogenous are *endogenous*.

4.10   The importance of the foregoing definition of an exogenous variable in a stochastic model will become clear in Chapters VII and IX when estimation of parameters is discussed. We might note here that in defining exogenous variables, there was a choice to be made between requiring *independence of* and requiring *noncorrelation with* the disturbances. In some cases noncorrelation is too weak a requirement to permit satisfactory estimation, whereas independence is a somewhat stronger requirement than is needed in many cases.[20] Independence has been chosen because it is not much stronger than needed, and it is so simple to work with in logical arguments.

4.11   An example will illustrate these concepts. Consider the consumption equation (4.4), reproduced here for convenience:

$$(4.20) \qquad\qquad c = \alpha + \beta y + u$$

The essential reason why national income should not be treated as exogenous in this equation is that it is impossible to believe that the disturbance u is statistically independent of income. For example, if the linear consumption function in (4.20) is simply a convenient approximation to a function that is really not linear, then u and y will almost certainly not be independent. And even if the consumption function is linear, upward shifts of it (due to positive values of u) will be associated with upward shifts in income.[21] Thus (4.20) is not a complete model, for it has two variables that must be considered endogenous, and only one equation to explain them. Another equation is needed. To carry the matter a step further, if the income definition (4.5) is added to (4.20), then another variable is introduced, investment i. It can be regarded as exogenous if it fulfills the criterion of the definition in 4.9, that is, if u is independent of it. Economists often assume that investment is determined by a system of equations not involving income or consumption (though it is known that expected income, or profit, affects investment). But it is difficult to argue convincingly that u, being that part of the variation in consumption that is unexplained by a linear term in income, is statistically independent of investment. Hence it can be argued that i is not exogenous, and that still another equation should be introduced into the model.

4.12   It is apparent that this view is puristic, and fruitless if pursued too enthusiastically, for there is *no* point in the enlargement of most models

---

[20] If two variables are independent, they must necessarily be uncorrelated. The converse is not true; two variables that are uncorrelated may or may not be independent. This was discussed in 3.6-10 above.

[21] The reader will see this if he will derive the reduced form of any model containing (4.20) and the income definition (4.5), for he will then find that y depends on u with a positive coefficient.

at which a convincing stand can be made against such arguments for the addition of another equation—unless it is the point where all possible variables have already been included, and of course the model would then be utterly unmanageable. What the economist should do in practice, therefore, in my opinion, is to stop adding equations and variables when he believes that the variables he chooses to call exogenous meet the definition *closely enough* so that the errors incurred through the discrepancy are small in comparison with the degree of accuracy that he thinks is desirable for his purpose (or is attainable). This is necessarily a somewhat arbitrary decision, for unlike the other variables, the random disturbances by their nature can never be observed, and hence their statistical relationships to the variables that one would like to treat as exogenous cannot be observed either. These decisions, like other decisions about what the form of each equation is to be and what variables are to be excluded from each, must be made on the basis of whatever presumptions seem plausible in the light of economic theory and experience. The model itself can be definitively tested only after it is confronted with new data. If it proves reasonably accurate all may be well, and if not, it is likely that at least one wrong assumption was made somewhere. But this is anticipating Chapter X.

4.13 It is sometimes argued, by those who are inclined (correctly, in my opinion) to regard simplicity as a virtue in econometric models, that income can be regarded as exogenous for practical purposes in any consumption or demand function that describes the consumption of only a negligible proportion of total output. This is not correct. Consider as an extreme example the demand for shoelaces: it is affected by income, but its ability to affect income in return is very slight, for even a doubling of the purchases of shoelaces would have at most a barely noticeable effect on income. To make the situation clearer, let us denote consumers' real demand for shoelaces by c_1; their real demands for other types of goods by $c_2, \ldots, c_G$; total real consumer demand and income as usual by c and y respectively; and disturbances by $u_1, \ldots, u_G, u$. Then the demand equations for individual consumer goods can be written

$$c_1 = \alpha_1 + \beta_1 y + u_1 \qquad \text{(shoelace demand)}$$

(4.21)

$$c_G = \alpha_G + \beta_G y + u_G$$

The total consumption function is

(4.22)
$$\sum_g c_g = \sum_g \alpha_g + \left(\sum_g \beta_g\right) y + \sum_g u_g$$

$$= c = \alpha + \beta y + u$$

where of course the following relations hold among the individual and aggregate quantities:

$$(4.23) \qquad \sum_g \alpha_g = \alpha, \quad \sum_g \beta_g = \beta, \quad \sum_g u_g = u$$

Furthermore, if i is exogenous real nonconsumption expenditure, we must have

$$(4.24) \qquad y = c + i = \sum_g c_g + i$$

4.14   The question at hand is this: Can y be regarded as exogenous for practical purposes in the first (shoelace) demand equation in (4.21) *by virtue of the fact* that c_1 (the consumption of shoelaces) is such a very small part of total income? The answer is no. Income may or may not be exogenous in the shoelace demand equation, and if it is exogenous, this is unrelated to the fact that income originating in shoelace production is a small part of total income! Furthermore, income cannot be exogenous in *all* the individual-commodity demand equations (4.21), so that if it is exogenous in the shoelace demand equation it must be endogenous in at least one other.

4.15   To demonstrate all this it is helpful to anticipate some of Chapter IX concerning statistical estimation. When an endogenous variable in a model is treated as if it were exogenous, an important part of the harm done usually consists in the introduction of a bias into the statistical estimation of the parameters of the model; this means that the expected value of a statistic used as an estimator is not equal to the value of the parameter being estimated. Let us see whether the shoelace demand parameter β_1 in (4.21) will be practically free of this difficulty or not. It is granted that income is not exogenous in the total consumption equation (4.22) because the disturbance u and income y are correlated. Hence the supposition that income is exogenous will lead to a biased estimator of the propensity to consume, β. Let us suppose that income and the shoelace demand disturbance u_1 are correlated. Then the assumption that income is exogenous in the shoelace demand equation will lead to a biased estimator of β_1. But what we are now asking is a different question: Is the resulting bias for β_1 negligible *simply because shoelaces are so insignificant in the economy*? The answer is no, as already stated. The bias will be small in *absolute* size, but there is no reason for it to be small *in comparison with* β_1. In other words, the *percentage* error expected need not be small just because shoelaces are a small part of the economy. The matter turns on the two facts that the *true* values of all the individual-commodity parameters $\beta_1, \ldots, \beta_G$ add up to β as in (4.23), and that the *estimated* values must add up to the estimated marginal propensity to consume, too. This means that any bias in the estimator of β must be accompanied by an identical bias in the sum of the estimators of $\beta_1, \ldots, \beta_G$. Hence a bias of x per cent in the estimator of β will be accompanied by a bias of x per cent on the average in all the estimators of $\beta_1, \ldots, \beta_G$, and there is no reason to think that *because* β_1 is small it will have a small percentage bias. Only if there is some reason to believe that shoelace demand is not subject to the disturbances that activate consumer demand as a whole can y be regarded as exogenous in the shoelace demand equation. Note that it is necessarily impossible to find such reason for *every* consumer good, because together they make up consumption as a whole, so that $\sum u_g = u$ as in (4.23).[22] Note also that the relative size of the demand for a consumer good in itself gives no clue as to whether that demand is free from the disturbances affecting total demand. Wold and Faxér [1957] is relevant here.

4.16 A similar argument applies to a stochastic model in which all consumers are included and each consumer has a separate individual consumption function, whereby his own consumption depends on his own income, thus:

$$c_1 = \alpha_1 + \beta_1 y_1 + u_1$$

(4.25)

$$c_N = \alpha_N + \beta_N y_N + u_N$$

(4.26)
$$\sum_i^N y_i = \sum c_i + i$$

This model is not yet complete, for it contains $2N$ endogenous variables (the c_i and the y_i) and only $N + 1$ equations. Still needed are $N - 1$ equations to determine how the total income $\sum y_i$ is distributed among the N individuals. There may be some individuals whose incomes are independent of total income $\sum y_i$, but there must obviously be *at least one* individual whose income is positively correlated with the total (otherwise the total could not be correlated with itself, which would be absurd), and in reality there are many such individuals. For an individual with a fixed income, or an income that varies independently of total income $\sum y_i$, his income is clearly exogenous in his individual consumption function, because an increase in that individual's u_i cannot be related to an increase in his own income y_i (though it does raise total income $\sum y_i$ slightly). For an individual whose income is correlated with total income $\sum y_i$, his income is not strictly exogenous in his individual consumption function, because an increase in that individual's u_i causes an increase in total income $\sum y_i$, and hence u_i is correlated with y_i because y_i is correlated

---

[22] The foregoing argument was originally presented in an unpublished note by Koopmans [1949a].

with $\sum y_i$. The more highly an individual's income y_i is correlated with total income $\sum y_i$, the greater is the correlation between that individual's disturbance u_i and his income y_i, and so the less is the justification for regarding his income as exogenous in his consumption equation. See also section 5 below.

4.17   We now present a stochastic model adapted from the exact linear time-series model of III.3.17, equations (3.9)–(3.15). The variables are the same (lower-case letters denoting quantities in real terms): $i =$ private investment, $g =$ government expenditure, $t =$ tax receipts, $r =$ interest rate, $M =$ quantity of money in nominal terms, $n =$ employment, $W =$ money wage rate, $P =$ price level. Random disturbances $u_1, \ldots, u_6$ are attached to the equations that are not identities.

$$(4.27) \qquad y = c + i + g$$

$$(4.28) \qquad c = \alpha(y - t) + \beta + u_1$$

$$(4.29) \qquad i = \gamma r + \epsilon + u_2$$

$$(4.30) \qquad \frac{M}{P} = \zeta r + \theta + u_3$$

$$(4.31) \qquad y = \nu n + \mu + u_4$$

$$(4.32) \qquad n = \xi \frac{W}{P} + \pi + u_5$$

$$(4.33) \qquad n = \rho \frac{W}{P} + \tau + u_6$$

Again the endogenous variables are y, c, i, r, n, W, and P. If the exogenous character of g, t, and M is to be defended, we must argue that each of them meets at least approximately the two criteria mentioned at the end of 4.9. Since they are all assumed to be policy variables, set arbitrarily by legislative or administrative authority, their determination is not via equations that contain any of the endogenous variables, so the segmentability property is present.[23] It is impossible to be sure there is no statistical relationship between g, t, or M on one hand and the disturbances $u_1, \ldots, u_6$ on the other. We can say only that where the theory postulates a relationship among endogenous variables and g, t, or M, we include that variable in the relationship to take care of the postulated influence; and conversely, that if we have left g, t, or M out of an equation, it is because there is no postulated effect of that variable on the relationship described by the equation. Hence the independence (or near independence) of the exogenous variables and the disturbances is supported by the assumptions and experience on which the model is based. Whether such a

---

[23] The equations determining them are not shown in the model (4.27)–(4.33).

model thus set up is correct, or approximately so, is an empirical question that we must defer until we have available the techniques of Chapter X.

4.18 If (4.31)–(4.33) are solved for income, we get as one of the equations of the reduced form the following variation of equation (3.16) in III.3.17:

$$(4.34) \qquad y = v\left(\frac{\rho\pi - \xi\tau}{\rho - \xi}\right) + \mu + u_4 + v\left(\frac{\rho u_5 - \xi u_6}{\rho - \xi}\right)$$

This indicates that even if all parameters are known, and if the probability distribution of the disturbances $u_1, \ldots, u_6$ is known, the resulting value of y will be a random variable. Its mean in any year is the sum of the first two terms, and its variance is the variance of the new random variable appearing as the linear combination of u_4, u_5, and u_6 in the last two terms. Thus even if the theory implied in the model (4.27)–(4.33) is correct, we cannot expect it to predict y exactly. We can, however, expect it to predict y approximately, together with the effects of changes in the policy variables.

4.19 The exact nonlinear Keynesian rigid-wage model of equations (3.1)–(3.6) and (3.8) in III.3.11 can also be made into a stochastic model by the addition of a disturbance to each equation [definitional identities such as (3.1) are not usually written with disturbances]. It is nonsegmentable, and its reduced form is nonlinear with disturbances appearing in nonlinear fashion as well. Hence it is a very inconvenient model to deal with. Its inconvenience provides further justification for the fact that economists use linear models wherever they are plausible.

5   CROSS-SECTION MODELS

5.1 In this section we look briefly at some special features of static stochastic *cross-section* models. There is relatively little to add to the remarks in III.9. The definition of an exogenous variable in a stochastic model, given in 4.9 above, applies to mixed and pure cross-section models as well as to the pure time-series case.

5.2 Let us consider a stochastic version of the pure cross-section model that is described verbally in III.9.5 and expressed symbolically by equations (9.4)–(9.8) in III.9.6. We shall consider this model as of time period t, so all the variables will carry a subscript t. A disturbance u_{it} is added to the ith household's consumption equation, and a disturbance v_{it} is added to the ith household's income-share equation. The symbol U_t refers to $\sum_i u_{it}$. It is assumed that $\sum_i v_{it} = 0$ in order to preserve the interest-rate-determining equation, (5.5) below. Otherwise the notation here is the same as that in III.9.5. It is again assumed that $\sum_i \epsilon_i = 0$. The model is

(5.1) $\qquad c_{it} = \alpha y_{it} + \gamma + \epsilon_i + u_{it} \qquad i = 1, \ldots, M$

(5.2) $\qquad y_{it} = k'_{it} r_t + x_{it} + v_{it} \qquad\quad i = 1, \ldots, M$

(5.3) $\qquad Y_t = C_t + Z_t$

(5.4) $\qquad C_t = \alpha Y_t + M\gamma + U_t$

(5.5) $\qquad Y_t = K'_t r_t + X_t$

This is a pure cross-section model with $2M + 3$ equations. The variables Z_t, X_t, and x_{it} $(i = 1, \ldots, M)$ are assumed to be exogenous. This means by definition that these variables are assumed statistically independent of the disturbances u_{jt} and v_{jt} for *all* values of i and j from 1 to M (it does not matter whether $i \neq j$ or $i = j$). The $2M + 3$ variables r_t, C_t, Y_t, c_{it}, and y_{it} $(i = 1, \ldots, M)$ are endogenous. This means that, as an examination of the equations shows, these variables are not independent of u_{jt} and v_{jt} for *all* values of i and j from 1 to M.

    5.3   Are k'_{it} $(i = 1, \ldots, M)$ and K'_t (which is defined to mean $\sum_i k_{it}$) exogenous in (5.1)–(5.5)? They are if they are statistically independent of u_{jt} and v_{jt} for all i and j from 1 to M, and otherwise they are not. This is a dynamic question. Hence it will be deferred until Chapter VI, but a brief suggestion can easily be given here. Recall [equation (9.12) of Chapter III] that k'_{it}, which is the ith household's net wealth at the beginning of period t, depends on its past wealth and saving behavior.

(5.6) $\qquad k'_{it} = y_{i,t-1} - c_{i,t-1} + k'_{i,t-1}$

Thus k'_{it} depends on disturbances that influence $y_{i,t-1}$ and $c_{i,t-1}$, that is, on $u_{j,t-1}$ and $v_{j,t-1}$. The reader may now guess the answer, namely, that k'_{it} and K'_t are exogenous if the disturbances in one period are independent of those in other periods.

    5.4   In the foregoing pure cross-section model, u_{jt} in particular is not independent of y_{it} for all i and j from 1 to M. This can be seen because y_{it} depends on r_t, which in turn depends on Y_t, which in turn depends on U_t, which includes $u_{1t}, \ldots, u_{Mt}$. Hence this stochastic consumption equation, like its earlier exact version, is not a complete single-equation model, since both c_{it} and y_{it} $(i = 1, \ldots, M)$ are endogenous in it.

    5.5   If data are available for several periods, $t = 1, \ldots, T$, then as in the exact case we can think of T distinct pure cross-section models, one for each period. And if each parameter has a constant value throughout all the periods, we can think of a mixed time-series and cross-section model. As in the exact case, it is then necessary to include explicitly the relation between current net worth and past saving and net worth, given by (5.6) above. Since k'_{it} are thus rendered endogenous in the mixed model, K_t' is too and is defined by

$$(5.7) \qquad\qquad K_t' = \sum_i k'_{it} \qquad t = 1, \ldots, T$$

In the mixed model consisting of equations (5.1)–(5.7) the variables Z_t, X_t, and x_{it} are exogenous, and C_t, Y_t, r_t, c_{it}, y_{it}, K_t', and k'_{it} are endogenous, $i = 1, \ldots, M$ and $t = 1, \ldots, T$. There are $(3M + 4)T$ equations and the same number of endogenous variables. Discussion of the dynamic features of this model will be deferred to Chapter VI.

6 THE ROLE AND SOME LIMITATIONS OF STOCHASTIC THEORY

6.1 Let us review in this section the kind of information about stochastic cases that we can get from theoretical considerations and the kind of information that economists need but cannot get from theory alone.

6.2 We have seen that if we knew the form (as opposed to the numerical values of the parameters) of an economic model, that is, if we knew which variables appear in which equations and which are the endogenous variables, then in principle we could find the reduced-form equations. Furthermore, if we knew the numerical values of the parameters of the model (including the parameters of the probability distribution of disturbances), that is, if the structure were known to us, then we could deduce the numerical values of the reduced-form parameters, and make conditional predictions of the values of the endogenous variables given the exogenous variables. These predictions would be inexact, even if all our information were correct and we made no mistakes, because of the random disturbances that enter into the model. We shall be predicting only the *expected values* of the variables, in which case we should find that our errors will average out algebraically to zero in the long run (i.e., positive ones in some instances would be balanced by negative ones in others). Or we may be stating *intervals* within which we expect the observations to fall, in which case we may expect to be right in a certain percentage of cases, a higher percentage if we use wider intervals and vice versa.

6.3 Having summarized briefly what we could obtain by theoretical analysis if the structure were known, let us turn to the question of what we can learn from theoretical analysis about the structure. Such analysis gives us the same kind of information as in the static case, that is, some

more or less reliable ideas about the nature of the relevant relationships—
the variables that enter each, and sometimes the mathematical form of
each—and which variables are to be regarded as exogenous. In addition,
in the stochastic case theoretical presumptions often provide information
about the average or relative sizes of the disturbances in the various
equations, and the degree of correlation or independence between disturbances and variables (which is relevant in deciding about the
exogenousness of variables).

6.4 Thus while theoretical analysis furnishes some information
about the economic structure relevant to a problem, it cannot furnish all,
and, in general, it cannot tell the values of relevant parameters except in
some cases to say whether they are zero, or whether they are positive or
negative, or very large or very small. Since the solutions to most of the
interesting real economic problems depend on some knowledge of parameters, theoretical analysis is not enough. Empirical work is required. But
before we take up empirical work in Chapters VII to X we shall first
discuss dynamic theories in the next two chapters.

QUESTIONS AND PROBLEMS

2.1. Write the equation of a continuous probability distribution of x, so
that x always falls between a and b, and the density rises linearly from zero at
$x = a$ to a maximum at $x = c$, and then falls linearly to zero at $x = b$. Assume
$a < c < b$.

2.2. What is the conditional probability of drawing a 6 or 7 or 8, given
that a red card is drawn, in shuffled card decks as follows:
  (a) A complete deck.
  (b) A deck that is missing all its aces.
  (c) A deck that is missing all its black aces.
  (d) A deck that is missing all its red aces.
  (e) A deck that is missing all its 5's, 6's, 7's, and 8's.

2.3. Compute the mean and variance of the number of words per line of
running text in a randomly selected page of this book. (You may have to decide
how to count mathematical symbols in order to be able to proceed.)

2.4. Prove equations (2.18), (2.19), (2.20), and (2.23).

2.5. Under what conditions, if any, is $Pb(a < x < b) = Pb(a \leq x \leq b)$?

2.6. In equations (2.26) to (2.28), is it necessary that the midpoint x_i^m of
each interval be used, or will it do to use any arbitrary point within each interval?
Explain.

3.1. Suppose that x is normally distributed with mean 6.2 and variance 0.25.
  (a) What is the value of x that is exceeded with a probability of .8?
  (b) What is the probability that x falls above 6.84?
  (c) What is the probability that x falls between 6.325 and 6.84?

3·2. Suppose that $x_1, \ldots, x_N$ are random variables, all having the same distribution, with a finite variance. Can you construct an example that meets these conditions, for which $\bar{x}$ does *not* approach normality as $N \to \infty$? Explain.

3.3. Prove the statements in 3.4 about the mean and variance of a linear combination of random variables, regardless of whether they are normally distributed.

3.4. Prove equation (3.14).

3.5. Suppose the joint distribution of x and y is given by the following table.

y \ x	-2	-1	0	1	2
10	.09	.15	.27	.25	.04
20	.01	.05	.08	.05	.01

(a) What are the marginal distributions of x and y?

(b) What are the means of x and y?

(c) Are x and y independent?

(d) Are x and y uncorrelated?

3.6. Construct examples to verify the last two sentences of 3.10.

3.7. Prove that (3.17) and (3.18) are equivalent.

3.8. Sketch the graph of the probability density function that u must have in equation (3.33) if the disturbance log u in (3.35) is to be normally distributed.

4.1. Do equations (4.1), (4.2), and (4.6) together form a structure? A model? Explain.

4.2. Discuss the following statement: In a simple two-equation income-consumption aggregate model, the variance of the disturbance in the reduced-form equation for income must exceed the variance of the disturbance in the consumption function, and typically does so by a factor of 2 or more. Hence errors in reduced-form forecasts are likely to be substantially greater than the residuals of the consumption function.

4.3. Can income be exogenous in *all* the demand equations for all goods, as given by (4.21)? Why or why not?

4.4. In the equation $y_t = \alpha + \beta y_{t-1} + u_t$, can y_{t-1} be exogenous? Explain. (This problem is discussed in Chapter VI, but you may enjoy solving it now.)

4.5. Obtain the reduced-form equation for the interest rate from equations (4.27)–(4.33) and discuss the economic meaning of each term it contains.

4.6. Suppose that in a stochastic model G variables including real national income are endogenous and K policy variables are exogenous. Now suppose that policy makers choose an arbitrary target level for real income and exogenously set the values of $K-1$ of the policy variables (all except government purchases), and then solve the system to obtain the value of government purchases that is required to achieve the target level of real income. If you were estimating the parameters of the model using data that were generated by such a policy, would you regard real income as exogenous? Would you regard government purchases as exogenous? Explain. (Recall exercise III.2.6.)

5.1. In the model of 5.2, what restriction is imposed upon the generality of the economic meaning of the model by the assumption that $\sum_i v_{it} = 0$? Explain.

5.2. Can you construct a mixed or pure cross-section model similar to that in Section 5, except modified so that an increase in the stock of capital (because of positive net saving) will lead to an increase of total income? What are the endogenous variables in your model?

CHAPTER V

Dynamic Theory
with Exact Equations

This chapter deals with dynamic nonstochastic theory. Trend variables, lags, rates of change, and differences of variables between periods are introduced. There are brief discussions of linear first-order difference equations and differential equations, and distributed lags. The concept of a predetermined variable is defined for nonstochastic models. Dynamic cross-section models are briefly discussed.

1 INTRODUCTION; THE MEANING OF DYNAMICS

1.1 It has been quipped that there are two kinds of dynamics, one called statics and one called dynamics. There is a certain amount of truth in this, if a quipper's license is granted in interpreting it. In comparative statics we typically study two static equilibrium situations that are alike in the values of all their parameters and exogenous variables except for one parameter or exogenous variable, which has different values in the two situations; we can then infer the effect exerted on the equilibrium values of the endogenous variables by a change in the parameter or exogenous variable concerned. For example, a country's exogenous national expenditure is one billion dollars greater in period 2 than in period 1, and if the appropriate multiplier is 2 in both periods and all other conditions are the same in both, then the equilibrium level of national income will be two billion dollars greater in period 2 than in period 1. This is dynamics in a limited sense, for it deals with the effects of changes in the given conditions. We have discussed such problems in Chapter III. But they do not constitute dynamics in the usual sense because they can be handled entirely by static models in which parameters or exogenous variables are changed.

1.2 By dynamic theory, as opposed to comparative statics as well as other static theory, we shall mean theory that allows for or explains changes in the values of endogenous variables as time passes, even when there are no changes in the economic structure or exogenous variables (except time), that is, no changes in behavior patterns or institutional or technological conditions or policy. Changes that are not due to changes in parameters or exogenous variables (other than time itself) may occur in response to historical trends, to rates of change of variables, to values of variables in the immediately preceding period or periods, etc. A dynamic theory in this sense can be recognized because time appears in it in an essential way, either as an explicit variable itself, or in rates of change, or in the guise of separate variables for different times, such as x_{1959}, x_{1960}, and the like. Dynamic theory, like static, may be either exact or stochastic. In this chapter we shall discuss exact dynamic theory.

1.3 Dynamic theory can arise in several ways. We list four ways, which are not all different and neatly separable, as the ensuing discussion will show:

(1) Belief in trends.
(2) Belief in lagged variables, or in rates of change, as important influences.
(3) Concern for the path that an economic system takes through time from one static equilibrium to another as a result of a change in some parameter or exogenous variable; this may include
(4) Concern for the stability of an equilibrium position.

1.4 An equilibrium position will be said to be "globally stable" if all the variables approach this position in the limit as time passes, no matter what their initial values. An equilibrium position will be said to be "stable in the small" if for sufficiently small deviations from equilibrium all the variables approach this position in the limit as time passes. Clearly if an equilibrium position is globally stable it is stable in the small too, but the converse need not be true.[1] We shall typically be interested in whether an economic process is globally stable, or at least whether it is stable in the small for disturbances as large as any that are likely to occur. Stability in the small is easy to test for, but it is important to remember that it does not guarantee global stability, or stability over any given range of disturbances.

1.5 We should note here that in Chapters V and VI on dynamic theories, we do *not* adhere to the convention set forth in I.5.2, that whenever the word "period" occurs in connection with time series, the word

[1] Samuelson [1947], pp. 261–262.

"region" or "individual" or some such term can be substituted and the discussion can then be understood to apply equally well to cross-section data. In any subsequent discussion of dynamic effects per se, it must be clear that the term "period" usually refers to time; it does not refer to the units for which cross-section data may have been gathered unless these units are connected together by some kind of spatial network that propagates effects from one unit to another.

2 TIME TRENDS

2.1 In this section we discuss trends, the simplest way of introducing dynamic effects into a model. Many of the trends to be presented in the next few pages will occur in the solutions of the dynamic systems that will be presented later in the chapter. A trend is a function of time and enters as an explicit variable. A trend variable may be introduced in a term to be added to others, or multiplied by others, or it may enter in some other way. It may be monotonic (i.e., it may always increase or always decrease) or fluctuating. It may be secular (i.e., long-term) or cyclical with a period[2] from many years down to even a single day in the case of demand for residential electric power. It may have a linear form, or quadratic, or cubic, and so forth, or logarithmic or exponential, or trigonometric, or any one of a large number of other forms. Models that have no dynamic elements other than trend have been called "historical" dynamic models.[3]

2.2 The simplest monotonic trend is a linear function of time. If population, denoted by N, for instance, were regarded as a linear function of time, denoted by t, we could write

$$(2.1) \qquad N = \alpha + \beta t$$

An increasing population would be indicated if $\beta > 0$ and a decreasing one if $\beta < 0$. A quadratic function could be used instead:

$$(2.2) \qquad N = \alpha + \beta t + \gamma t^2$$

This can represent either an increasing or a decreasing population, or one that does both in succession. For any particular value of t we can see which is the case by examining the algebraic sign of the rate of change of population, given by the derivative of (2.2) with respect to t:

$$(2.3) \qquad \frac{dN}{dt} = \beta + 2\gamma t$$

---

[2] This is a different use of the term "period" from that in the foregoing paragraph. Here it means the duration of one complete cycle.

[3] Samuelson [1947], p. 315.

If $\gamma > 0$, then at sufficiently large positive values of t, dN/dt will be positive and N will be increasing, no matter what the value of β; if $\gamma < 0$, then at sufficiently large positive values of t, N will be decreasing, no matter what the value of β. The opposite conclusions apply to large negative values[4] of t. If $\beta > 0$, then for small values of t, dN/dt will be positive and N will be increasing; if $\beta < 0$, then for small values of t, N will be decreasing. N will have either a lowest value or a highest value, and hence a change in the sign of the rate of change, at the time when $t = -\beta/2\gamma$, as can be seen by setting (2.3) equal to zero. Illustrative graphs of the linear and quadratic trends are shown in Figure 2.1.

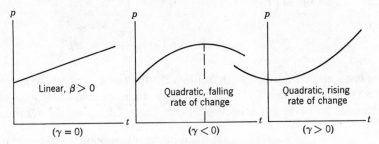

Figure 2.1   Linear and quadratic trends.

2.3   A common type of monotonic trend is the exponential, sometimes called the growth curve. It applies to the growth of a sum of money lent at compound interest, among other things. Suppose M dollars are lent at an annual rate of $100r$ per cent (e.g., 5 per cent) per year. Then at the end of a year, each dollar invested will have earned r dollars (e.g., 0.05 dollar) interest, and the amount M will have grown to $M(1 + r)$ dollars (e.g., to $M \times 1.05$). If this amount is invested for another year, it will grow to $M(1 + r)^2$ dollars. And if M dollars are invested at an annual rate of r, with interest compounded annually, after t years they will have grown to $M(1 + r)^t$ dollars. Observe that the absolute amount of the increase becomes greater each year, since for any year it is a proportion r of the total value of the investment at the beginning of that year. Now suppose that interest is compounded *twice a year* instead of once. The amount after t years is the result of investing for $2t$ 6-month periods, at a rate of $r/2$ per period with interest compounded every 6 months, that is, $M(1 + r/2)^{2t}$. This results in a somewhat higher amount after t years than annual compounding, since newly earned interest now starts to earn interest itself after 6 months instead of having to wait until the end of a year. Now suppose that interest is compounded *monthly*. The result after t years is $M(1 + r/12)^{12t}$, which is still larger than

---

[4] If negative values of t seem strange, think of our calendar with its B.C. era.

$M(1 + r/2)^{2t}$. If interest is compounded n times a year, the result after t years is $M(1 + r/n)^{nt}$. If interest is compounded at shorter and shorter intervals that approach zero in length, then the result approaches the amount

$$(2.4) \qquad \lim_{n \to \infty} M \left(1 + \frac{r}{n} \right)^{nt}$$

In order to understand this expression, we now define a new variable $k = n/r$. We observe that $k \to \infty$ as $n \to \infty$, and we may rewrite (2.4) as

$$(2.5) \qquad \lim_{n \to \infty} M \left(1 + \frac{r}{n} \right)^{nt} = M \lim_{k \to \infty} \left(1 + \frac{1}{k} \right)^{krt}$$

$$= M \left[\lim_{k \to \infty} \left(1 + \frac{1}{k} \right)^{k} \right]^{rt} = M e^{rt}$$

The last step depends upon the fact that the limit as $k \to \infty$ of the expression $(1 + 1/k)^k$ is usually symbolized by e. Its numerical value has been calculated to be approximately 2.71828. Table 2.1 shows the results of

TABLE 2.1   Compound Interest Illustration

Frequency of Compounding	Result of Investing $100 at 3 per cent for a Period of			
	t years	10 years	20 years	30 years
annually	$100\ (1.03)^t$	134.39	180.61	242.73
semiannually	$100\ (1.015)^{2t}$	134.69	181.40	244.32
monthly	$100\ (1.0025)^{12t}$	134.94	182.08	245.69
continuously	$100\ e^{0.03t}$	134.99	182.21	245.96

investing $100 at 3 per cent for 10, 20, and 30 years, compounding annually, semiannually, monthly, and continuously (i.e., at intervals approaching zero). Figure 2.2 shows the results of the continuous compounding.

2.4 Other functions can be made from the exponential function as follows, some increasing and some decreasing. We shall encounter the following types often. Here a, b, and c are positive constants:

$$(2.6) \qquad y = a + be^{ct}$$

$$(2.7) \qquad y = a + be^{-ct}$$

$$(2.8) \qquad y = a + b(1 - e^{-ct})$$

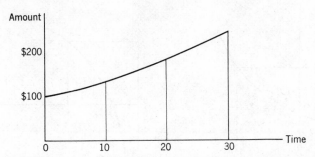

Figure 2.2 Growth of $100 invested at 3% continuously compounded.

Figure 2.3 shows their graphs. The reader should verify their general shapes and limiting values. Still others may be formed by the reader, but these are illustrative of the variety that it possible.

2.5 A close relative of the exponential function is the logarithmic function, defined as the result of solving the exponential function. Thus suppose that

(2.9) $x = e^y$

Then, by the definition of a logarithm,

(2.10) $\log_e x = y$

This is read "the logarithm of x, to the base e, is y." Thus the logarithm of a number is the *exponent* to which the base of the logarithm (in this case the base is e) must be raised in order to make it equal to the given

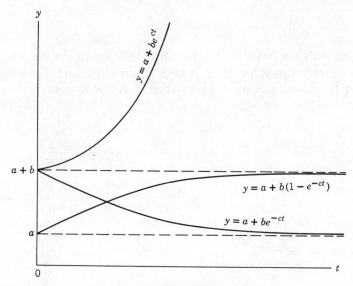

Figure 2.3 Some exponential functions.

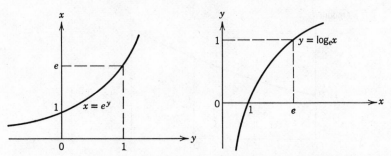

Figure 2.4   An exponential function and its corresponding logarithmic function.

number. The two graphs of (2.9) and (2.10) look just alike, as shown in Figure 2.4, except that one is a mirror image of the other (the axis of symmetry being a 45°-sloped line through the origin). Logarithms to the base e are called natural or Naperian logarithms, and logarithms to the base 10 are called common logarithms. Both types are frequently used and are tabulated in mathematical handbooks. The common logs are most useful for routine computation because the log to the base 10 of any integral power of 10 (such as 0.0001 or 10,000) is an integer. The natural logs are more useful in theoretical problems of growth and in mathematics because the number e occurs in these areas in much the same way as we have seen in 2.3.

2.6   The logistic function, a trend function sometimes useful in describing growth, is related to the exponential, thus:

$$(2.11) \qquad\qquad y = \frac{a}{1 + be^{-ct}}$$

Its graph is shown in Figure 2.5. Its salient characteristic is that the rate of growth begins at a low level, reaches a maximum, and then declines so that the growing quantity approaches a definite maximum value or ceiling, a.

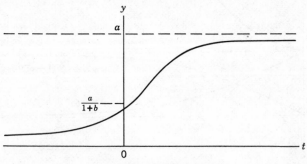

Figure 2.5   Logistic function.

2.7 The most commonly used cyclical or "periodic" functions are trigonometric. Thus, if t is an angle, the function

(2.12) $$y = \sin t$$

varies continuously between -1 and $+1$ in a regular cycle as t increases indefinitely. More complicated functions based on the sine function can be produced, thus:

(2.13) $$y = a \sin (\omega t - \theta) + b$$

where a, ω, and θ are positive constants and b is a constant. Here a is called the *amplitude* of the fluctuation, for y always remains between $b - a$ and $b + a$, inclusive. The *natural period* of the fluctuation is the length of time required for a complete cycle. Since the sine of any angle is the same as the sine of another angle 360° greater, the natural period is the length of time required for ωt to increase by 360°. This is $360°/\omega$. θ is known as the phase angle, for it specifies the stage of the cycle when t is equal to zero or any integral multiple of the natural period, $360°/\omega$. Similar periodic functions can be expressed in terms of the cosine function. It might be noted that if $b = 0$ the function (2.13) satisfies this differential equation of second order:

(2.14) $$\frac{d^2y}{dt^2} = -\omega^2 y$$

This is easily verified. If we differentiate (2.13) twice with respect to time, the results are

(2.15) $$\frac{dy}{dt} = a\omega \cos (\omega t - \theta)$$

(2.16) $$\frac{d^2y}{dt^2} = -a\omega^2 \sin (\omega t - \theta)$$

If (2.13) and (2.16) are substituted into (2.14), b being zero, (2.14) is satisfied. Equation (2.13) is said to be a *solution* of (2.14). Motion described by equation (2.14) is often called simple harmonic motion.

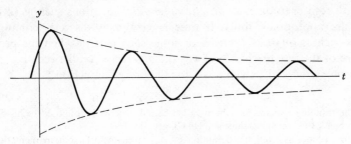

Figure 2.6 Damped periodic fluctuations.

2.8 Sometimes a variable fluctuates with a constant natural period but with a varying amplitude. If the amplitude decreases to zero, the motion is said to be damped or stable; if it increases, antidamped or explosive. An equation describing such a function is

(2.17) $$y = k^t a \sin (\omega t - \theta) + b$$

where k is a positive constant. If $k < 1$, the motion is damped, as shown in Figure 2.6; if $k > 1$, it is antidamped or explosive. The rate of damping or antidamping can be described by the appropriate growth rate or interest rate [as in equations (2.6)–(2.8)] or by the length of time required for the amplitude to be cut in half or doubled.

3 LAGGED VARIABLES, RATES OF CHANGE, AND FIRST-ORDER LINEAR DIFFERENCE EQUATIONS; PREDETERMINED VARIABLES; DEFINITIONS AND A SIMPLE EXAMPLE

3.1 Up to this point we have considered as variables in economic models only economic stocks, flows, prices, and time itself. We here introduce the rate of change of economic variables over time.[5] For example, in a market in disequilibrium where quantities supplied and demanded are not equal, it can be reasonably postulated that the rate at which the price moves toward its equilibrium value will depend on the magnitude of the discrepancy between quantities supplied and demanded. Or it may be assumed, in a national income and consumption model, that consumption depends not only on current income but also on whether income is increasing or decreasing, being less (*ceteris paribus*) if income is rising than if income is falling, because consumers are, in part, still reacting to their earlier level of income.

3.2 Rates of change can be introduced in either of two mathematical forms, depending upon whether time is viewed as a continuous variable or as a discrete variable. If time is viewed as continuous, the appropriate measure for the rate of change of a variable x is the derivative of x with respect to time, dx/dt, and *differential* equations such as (2.14)–(2.16) are appropriate tools. If time is viewed as discrete, coming in chunks such as quarters or years or some such periods, then the proper measure of the rate of change of x is the *difference* Δx_t between its value x_t for one period and its value x_{t-1} for the preceding period:[6]

(3.1) $$\Delta x_t = x_t - x_{t-1}$$

[5] The resulting systems have been called causal systems, as opposed to historical systems. See 2.1 above and Samuelson [1947], pp. 315 ff.

[6] Most economists use the definition of Δx_t given in (3.1), but mathematicians often use $\Delta x_t = x_{t+1} - x_t$ instead, so be careful to understand the notation when you are reading about Δx_t.

Then *difference equations*, that is, equations involving variables such as Δx_t, are appropriate tools. (Difference equations may be appropriate even if time is viewed as continuous, if lagged variables are used; see below.) The question whether to use differential or difference equations is sometimes one of practical convenience only, because the two can be made very much alike—in fact as much as we please—simply by the choice of sufficiently short periods for the difference equations. The reader will recognize that differential equations are the limiting case of difference equations as the period is made to approach zero in length, since dx/dt is defined to be the limit of the ratio $\Delta x/\Delta t$ as Δt approaches zero. Many economic data, particularly concerning flows, are averages over a period such as a year or quarter or day, instead of instantaneous readings such as a speedometer provides. Hence difference equations are appropriate to economic data, even though time is in fact continuous rather than discrete. Accordingly we shall take them up first[7] and shall then digress to consider differential equations briefly.

3.3 We shall first note that using differences as variables is equivalent to using lagged variables, that is, variables pertaining to previous time periods. This is obvious from (3.1), the definition of Δx_t. As an example, consider a consumption function according to which this year's consumption depends on last year's income:

$$(3.2) \qquad c_t = \alpha y_{t-1} + \beta$$

Using the symbol Δ as defined in (3.1), we rewrite (3.2) as

$$(3.3) \qquad c_t = \alpha y_t - \alpha \Delta y_t + \beta$$

Hence an equation involving either lags or differences or both is a difference equation.

3.4 Consider a model consisting of the difference equation (3.2) and the familiar income definition

$$(3.4) \qquad y_t = c_t + i_t$$

where i_t is regarded as an exogenous variable. Suppose that the values of the parameters are $\alpha = 0.5$, $\beta = 120$; that investment i_t is equal to 30 every year; and that income in an initial period is $y_0 = 200$. All quantities are measured in billions of constant dollars per year except α, which is a pure number, that is, a number with no dimensions. Then from (3.2) we find that consumption in the next period, c_1, is $0.5 \times 200 + 120$, or 220. And from (3.4) y_1 is found to be $220 + 30$, or 250. Repeated

---

[7] Several good references are available. See, for example, Allen [1956], Baumol [1951] or [1959], Goldberg [1958], and Samuelson [1947], Appendix B. The last is more difficult than the others.

application of the same procedure will generate a time path for both c and y, as shown in Table 3.1. It will be observed that the increases in y_t in successive years are 50, 25, 12.5, 6.25, . . . , being cut in half each year. Each year the difference between 300 and the previous year's income is halved. Clearly, at this rate, y_t will never exceed or even quite reach 300, no matter how many years pass, but it will nevertheless come arbitrarily close to 300 if enough periods are allowed to pass. In other words, the

TABLE 3.1 Time Paths of Consumption c and Income y (Based on Equations (3.2) and (3.4), and Parameter Values as in 3.4)

t	c_t	y_t
0	—	200
1	220	250
2	245	275
3	257.5	287.5
4	263.75	293.75
.	.	.
.	.	.
.	.	.
∞	270	300

limit of y_t as t approaches infinity is \$300 billion a year. Similarly, the limit of c_t is \$270 billion.

3.5 Now suppose that the parameters and exogenous variable i_t have the same values as assumed in 3.4 but that the initial value of y_0 is 300 instead of 200. Then from (3.2) consumption in the next period, c_1, is equal to $0.5 \times 300 + 120 = 270$. Then from (3.4), $y_1 = 270 + 30 = 300$. Hence 300 billion is an equilibrium for income in these circumstances: if attained, it is maintained. That it is stable is shown by 3.4. Note that this has been indicated by dynamic analysis, following out the time path of the variables.

3.6 The static analysis of Chapter III can demonstrate that 300 billion is the equilibrium value, as follows. Since the equilibrium values of c_t and y_t are by definition the values that are maintained continuously if they are attained, the equilibrium can be described by writing (3.2) and (3.4) without any time subscripts at all, thus:

$$(3.5) \qquad c = \alpha y + \beta$$

$$(3.6) \qquad y = c + i$$

These static equations when solved yield equilibrium values denoted by y^ϵ and c^ϵ, thus:

(3.7)
$$y^\epsilon = \frac{i + \beta}{1 - \alpha}$$

(3.8)
$$c^\epsilon = \frac{\alpha i + \beta}{1 - \alpha}$$

If the above given values of α, β, and i are substituted into (3.7) and (3.8), the results are $y = 300$ and $c = 270$, the same equilibrium values obtained above. Thus the static system (3.5)–(3.6), which we treated in Chapter III, represents the equilibrium position of the dynamic system (3.2) and (3.4). As a general rule we shall find that for every dynamic system having an equilibrium position (whether stable or not) there is a corresponding static system describing that equilibrium position. Interestingly enough, we shall find that a single static system may correspond to several different dynamic systems.

3.7 Any dynamic model generates a time path of its variables, determined by the model, the numerical values of parameters and exogenous variables, and the initial values of endogenous variables. The term "initial conditions" is frequently applied to the given initial values of the endogenous variables. The interest-rate examples of Table 2.1, in 2.3, illustrate these points well. The initial conditions in that case consist simply in the amount of money invested at the beginning, $100 in Table 2.1. The entries in the table show a few points in the time paths of the amounts of money accumulated in the four models having interest compounded annually, semiannually, monthly, and continuously. Table 3.1 provides another example.

3.8 It will be convenient for our further discussion of difference equations to define a new category of variables, consisting of all those whose values are determined in advance of a particular period, t. This new category will be called *predetermined variables as of time t*, though usually for brevity we shall speak simply of predetermined variables. They include, first, the exogenous variables and, second, any lagged values of endogenous variables, that is, values determined in the preceding period $t - 1$ or earlier.[8] The remaining variables will be called "current endogenous" or "jointly dependent" to indicate that their current values are determined by the system.[9] Thus, in the model of (3.2) and (3.4), the current endogenous variables are c_t and y_t; the predetermined variables are y_{t-1} (which is lagged endogenous) and i_t (which is exogenous). Note

[8] This definition is adequate for the exact case, but for the stochastic case it must be modified. The modified definition, which will be used throughout the rest of the book, appears in VI.4.3.

[9] For a slightly fuller discussion of these types of variables, see Christ [1951], p. 37.

that this definition applies to cross-section models as well as to time-series models. Any variable in a cross-section model that is exogenous or that is a lagged value of an endogenous variable is said to be predetermined. (See Section 8.) With these definitions, we can say that any difference-equation model generates a time path of its current endogenous variables if the values of its parameters and predetermined variables are given.

3.9   The definition of the reduced form for static models is given in II.1.12. We now define the *reduced form* of a system of difference equations. It is the result of solving the system for each of the current endogenous variables in terms of the predetermined variables and parameters. The definition now presented is merely a slightly more general form of the earlier one. The reduced form of the model (3.2) and (3.4) is easy to obtain; (3.2) is already in the reduced form for it gives current consumption as a function of predetermined variables only. Current income can be obtained as a function of predetermined variables only, by substituting (3.2) into (3.4). The reduced form is thus:

$$(3.9) \qquad\qquad c_t = \alpha y_{t-1} + \beta$$

$$(3.10) \qquad\qquad y_t = \alpha y_{t-1} + i_t + \beta$$

If the above given values, $\alpha = 0.5$, $\beta = 120$, $i = 30$, are inserted, the reduced form becomes

$$(3.11) \qquad\qquad c_t = 0.5 y_{t-1} + 120$$

$$(3.12) \qquad\qquad y_t = 0.5 y_{t-1} + 150$$

3.10   The reduced form of a system of difference equations expresses the time path of the endogenous variables step by step, as the original difference equations themselves generally do not (unless they already happen to be in the reduced form). A reduced-form equation need not give the time path of each endogenous variable in terms of exogenous variables and past values of *itself only*; note that in (3.9) the path of consumption is expressed in terms of lagged values of income. When the reduced form is further transformed so that each endogenous variable is expressed only in terms of exogenous variables and past values of *itself*, that is, so that each endogenous variable appears in a difference equation without any current or lagged values of other endogenous variables, the result is called the *final equations*.[10] Equation (3.10) is already a final equation, for the only endogenous variable it contains is y. Equation (3.9) can be brought into the final equation form if y_{t-1} is replaced by

---

[10] This term is due to Jan Tinbergen [1939], p. 130. The term "separated form" has been used with the same meaning by Marschak [1950], pp. 34, 40.

$c_{t-1} + i_{t-1}$ from (3.4). The final equations of the model (3.2) and (3.4) are then

(3.13) $$c_t = \alpha c_{t-1} + \alpha i_{t-1} + \beta$$

(3.14) $$y_t = \alpha y_{t-1} + i_t + \beta$$

Of course it does not matter whether it is i_t or i_{t-1} that is used, as long as it is assumed that investment is maintained at a constant level; but if investment changes, then it does matter. If the foregoing given constant values of α, β, and i are inserted in the final equations, they become

(3.15) $$c_t = 0.5c_{t-1} + 135$$

(3.16) $$y_t = 0.5y_{t-1} + 150$$

3.11 We have said in 3.3 that an equation is a difference equation if it involves differences such as Δx_t or lagged values such as x_{t-1}, since either can be expressed in terms of the other. We can cast the final equations (3.13)–(3.14) in terms of differences instead of lags, thus, as the reader may verify:

(3.17) $$c_t = \frac{-\alpha}{1 - \alpha} \Delta c_t + \frac{\alpha i_{t-1} + \beta}{1 - \alpha}$$

(3.18) $$y_t = \frac{-\alpha}{1 - \alpha} \Delta y_t + \frac{i_t + \beta}{1 - \alpha}$$

It is interesting to note that the equilibrium values for c_t and y_t can be obtained very simply from (3.17)–(3.18) by setting $\Delta c_t = 0$ and $\Delta y_t = 0$; these are the conditions for equilibrium. The equilibrium values so obtained are identical with those obtained in (3.7)–(3.8) by static analysis. As might be expected, the same results can also be obtained by dropping time subscripts in the final equations (3.13)–(3.14) and solving each one for its own endogenous variable.

3.12 The concept of the solution of a difference equation is important. Consider a difference equation having one variable whose values are written as a function of a parameter t, $t = -1, 0, 1, 2, \ldots$, which may (but need not) represent points in time as in the economic equations of this chapter. A *solution* of the difference equation, if it exists, is a function of t that, when substituted for the variable in the equation, produces a true statement for every value of t, that is, an identity in t. Let us illustrate with a simple example. Consider the difference equation

(3.19) $$y_t - \mu y_{t-1} = 0$$

This is called a homogeneous linear difference equation of first order with constant coefficient: homogeneous because it equates to zero a homogeneous function of y_t and y_{t-1}; linear because it equates to zero a linear function; of first order because there is just one lag; with constant coefficient because μ is assumed constant. A solution of this equation would be a function of t, for instance, $f(t)$, such that $f(t) - \mu f(t - 1) = 0$ for every value of t. Is the following function of t a solution of (3.19)?

$$(3.20) \qquad\qquad y_t = \mu^t$$

The answer is yes, as can be seen by substituting μ^t for y_t in the first term of (3.19), and μ^{t-1} for y_{t-1} in the second term, thus:

$$(3.21) \qquad\qquad y_t - \mu y_{t-1} = \mu^t - \mu\mu^{t-1} = 0$$

As the last equality in (3.21) shows, the result is indeed an identity in t. Therefore (3.20) is a solution of (3.19). Another solution of (3.19) is

$$(3.22) \qquad\qquad y_t = 7\mu^t$$

This can be verified by substitution of (3.22) into (3.19), in a manner analogous to (3.21). Indeed, if the coefficient 7 in (3.22) is replaced by any number k the result is a solution of (3.19):

$$(3.23) \qquad\qquad y_t = k\mu^t$$

The solutions (3.20) and (3.22) are called *particular* solutions of (3.19). And (3.23) is called the *general* solution of (3.19) because there is no solution of (3.19) that cannot be expressed in the form (3.23), as we shall see in 3.15.

3.13 Consider now another difference equation:

$$(3.24) \qquad\qquad y_t - \mu y_{t-1} - v = 0$$

This is called a linear difference equation of first order with constant coefficients. It is like (3.19) except that if $v \neq 0$ it is nonhomogeneous in the variables y_t and y_{t-1}. Homogeneous difference equations are easier to solve than nonhomogeneous ones, and fortunately nonhomogeneous ones can be solved (if they have solutions) with the aid of solutions to corresponding homogeneous ones, as will be illustrated below. The reader may verify that for any arbitrary number k, the following is a solution to (3.24):

$$(3.25) \qquad
\begin{aligned}
y_t &= k + vt && \text{if } \mu = 1 \\[2mm]
y_t &= k\mu^t + v\frac{1 - \mu^t}{1 - \mu} && \text{if } \mu \neq 1
\end{aligned}$$

If k is assigned a specific numerical value, such as 7, for example, then (3.25) yields a particular solution of (3.24). We shall see in 3.16 that (3.25) is the general solution of (3.24).

3.14 Sometimes, as in some of the preceding examples, initial conditions are given, such as the value of y in some given period, for instance, $y_0 = A$, and we desire to find for a difference equation a particular solution that satisfies the initial conditions. A particular solution of (3.24) that makes y_0 equal to A is easily found: putting $t = 0$ in (3.25) and setting the result equal to A gives

$$A = y_0 = k + v0 = k \qquad\qquad \text{if } \mu = 1$$

(3.26)

$$A = y_0 = k\mu^0 + v\frac{1 - \mu^0}{1 - \mu} = k \qquad \text{if } \mu \neq 1$$

Hence the particular solution provided by setting the arbitrary constant k in (3.25) equal to A will satisfy (3.24) and also satisfy the initial condition $y_0 = A$.

3.15   For a first-order linear difference equation with constant coefficients, such as (3.24), there is *exactly one* particular solution satisfying any single given initial condition, such as $y_0 = A$. This can be seen as follows. First, let us note that there is at least one particular solution satisfying the initial condition $y_0 = A$; it was found in the preceding paragraph. Second,[11] let us see that there is only one particular solution that can satisfy the initial condition $y_0 = A$. This is done by showing that if $y_0 = A$, then the equation (3.24) itself determines uniquely all succeeding (and previous, for that matter) values of y. Setting $t = 1$ in (3.24), we find $y_1 = \mu A + v$, which determines y_1 uniquely. Setting $t = 2$ in (3.24), we find $y_2 = \mu(\mu A + v) + v = \mu^2 A + v(\mu + 1)$, which determines y_2 uniquely. And so on forever. Hence there is exactly one particular solution satisfying $y_0 = A$. And it has been found in 3.14.

3.16   Now it can be seen that (3.25) is the general solution of (3.24). Every possible particular solution of (3.24) leads to some definite and unique value of y_0, obtained by putting $t = 0$ in that particular solution. Every value of y_0 leads to a unique particular solution *of the form of* (3.25), as seen in 3.14–15. Hence there is no solution of (3.24) that is not of the form of (3.25), and hence (3.25) is the general solution. In the special case where $v = 0$, this argument shows that the general solution of the homogeneous equation (3.19) is (3.23).

3.17   Nothing has been said about how we think up functions of t that we can test to see whether they are solutions of a difference equation we want to solve. This is often done by trial and error; it is useful to try functions like ω^t or $k\omega^t$. They usually work if ω is chosen properly. They do not *always* work, as we saw when $\mu = 1$ in (3.25).

3.18   Two useful rules are these. First, if $f(t)$ is a solution of a difference equation, then $kf(t)$ is too, where k is any number. Second, if

---

[11] Strictly, this second argument alone is sufficient to prove the existence and uniqueness of a particular solution satisfying $y_0 = A$.

$f(t)$ and $g(t)$ are solutions of a difference equation, then their sum $f(t) + g(t)$ is too. Proofs of these two rules are left as exercises. From these two rules it follows that any linear combination of two solutions of a difference equation is also a solution.

3.19 An important theorem about linear difference equations with constant coefficients (which is true for linear *differential* equations with constant coefficients too, by the way, and which we will not prove here) is this: The general solution of such an equation is obtainable as the sum of *any* particular solution of it plus the general solution of a homogenous equation that is formed from it by dropping its constant term.   A systematic method of finding the general solution of such a homogeneous equation is available, and various aids to trial and error are available for finding a particular solution of a nonhomogeneous equation. In what follows we deal mainly with trial-and-error methods. There are many sources to which the reader can turn for more systematic approaches and for treatment of second—and higher—order difference equations (i.e., those with two or more lags).[12]

3.20 The final equations (3.13) and (3.14) are first-order linear difference equations with constant coefficients. They have solutions, which can be found by an essentially trial-and-error method. We illustrate for the income equation (3.14). Let y_0 be the level of income in period 0, that is, the initial condition. Since *homogenous* difference equations are the simplest to solve, we shall first eliminate the constant term $(i + \beta)$ in (3.14). This can be done by considering as our variable the *difference* between y_t and the equilibrium value.[13,14] We shall call this difference y^δ, and henceforth the superscript ϵ and δ will denote respectively equilibrium and the deviation from equilibrium:

$$(3.27) \qquad\qquad y_t^{\,\delta} = y_t - y^\epsilon = y_t - \frac{i + \beta}{1 - \alpha}$$

To transform (3.14) in terms of this new variable, we subtract y^ϵ from both sides, and add and subtract αy^ϵ on the right side, thus:

$$(3.28) \qquad y_t^{\,\delta} = y_t - y^\epsilon = \alpha y_{t-1} - \alpha y^\epsilon + \alpha y^\epsilon + i + \beta - y^\epsilon$$
$$= \alpha(y_{t-1} - y^\epsilon) + i + \beta + (\alpha - 1)y^\epsilon$$

Since, from (3.27) $y^\epsilon = (i + \beta)/(1 - \alpha)$, the last three terms add up to zero, and we have

$$(3.29) \qquad\qquad y_t^{\,\delta} = \alpha y_{t-1}^{\,\delta}$$

[12] See the references in footnote 7 of this chapter.

[13] This transformation can be made as long as $\alpha \neq 1$; but if $\alpha = 1$, then we cannot divide by $1 - \alpha$, and then y^ϵ is not defined. .

[14] It can also be done by using the theorem of 3.19, but since that was not proved here the approach of the text above may be more appealing.

Let us now solve this homogeneous difference equation. After we have obtained its solution we shall translate it back into terms of y_t by means of (3.27).

3.21   If we use (3.29) to express y_{t-1}^δ in terms of y_{t-2}^δ, and substitute the result into (3.29) itself, we have

$$(3.30) \qquad y_t^\delta = \alpha(\alpha y_{t-2}^\delta) = \alpha^2 y_{t-2}^\delta$$

If we now express y_{t-2}^δ in terms of y_{t-3}^δ we have

$$(3.31) \qquad y_t^\delta = \alpha^2(\alpha y_{t-3}^\delta) = \alpha^3 y_{t-3}^\delta$$

If the process is continued $t - 1$ times altogether, the result is the solution,

$$(3.32) \qquad y_t^\delta = \alpha^t y_0^\delta$$

The initial condition of this equation is that y_t has the given value y_0 at time 0, from which we find that y_t^δ has the value $y_0^\delta = y_0 - y^\epsilon$ at $t = 0$. Hence we see that (3.32) satisfies the initial condition, for when $t = 0$, $\alpha^t = 1$, so that $y_t^\delta = y_0^\delta$. The other step in verifying that (3.32) is a solution of the difference equation (3.29) is to see whether (3.32) satisfies the difference equation. Substitute for y_t^δ from (3.32) into the left side of (3.29), and substitute for y_{t-1}^δ from a lagged version of (3.32) into the right side of (3.29), and see whether the result is true:

$$(3.33) \qquad y_t^\delta = \alpha^t y_0^\delta \overset{?}{=} \alpha(\alpha^{t-1} y_0^\delta) = \alpha y_{t-1}^\delta$$

The first and last members of (3.33) are indeed equal because the questioned equality holds, and so they do satisfy (3.29). This confirms that (3.32) is indeed a solution of (3.29). This kind of reasoning occurs repeatedly, and the reader should be sure he has followed it.

3.22   We may now use the definition (3.27) of y_t^δ to translate this solution (3.32) back into terms of our original variable y_t, thus:

$$(3.34) \qquad y_t = y^\epsilon + \alpha^t(y_0 - y^\epsilon)$$

We have already seen that (3.32), the form in which we first obtained (3.34), satisfies the initial condition. Let us verify that (3.34) does as well: When $t = 0$, it specifies that income is equal to $y^\epsilon + \alpha^0(y_0 - y^\epsilon) = y^\epsilon + y_0 - y^\epsilon = y_0$, as desired. We have also seen that (3.32) satisfies the homogeneous equation (3.29). Let us verify that (3.34) likewise satisfies the original nonhomogeneous difference equation (3.14) as well: Substituting for y_t and y_{t-1} from the current and lagged versions of (3.34) into (3.14), we have

$$(3.35) \qquad \begin{aligned} y_t &= y^\epsilon + \alpha^t(y_0 - y^\epsilon) \\ &\overset{?}{=} \alpha[y^\epsilon + \alpha^{t-1}(y_0 - y^\epsilon)] + i + \beta \\ &= \alpha y_{t-1} + i + \beta \end{aligned}$$

The questioned equality holds; to see this we use the static solution (3.7). The first and last members of (3.35) are therefore equal and agree with (3.14). Hence we have verified that (3.34) is indeed a solution of (3.14).

3.23 The final equation for consumption, (3.13), has a similar solution, thus:

$$(3.36) \qquad\qquad c_t = c^\epsilon + \alpha^t(c_0 - c^\epsilon)$$

Its derivation and interpretation are analogous to those of (3.34).

3.24 Notice that the solution (3.34) of the final equation (3.14) for income contains two kinds of quantities: those dependent on the structure of the model together with the values of exogenous variables, and those dependent on the initial conditions. The same is true for the solution of any difference equation. For example, in (3.34) the part of the solution that depends on the structure of the model consists of the parameter α and the equilibrium value y^ϵ; the part that depends on initial conditions is the multiplier of the term α^t, namely, the initial deviation $y_0 - y^\epsilon$ from equilibrium.

3.25 Let us examine the solution (3.34) to see what it tells us about the time path of national income. In order to give a definite algebraic sign to $(y_0 - y^\epsilon)$ we shall assume that the initial value y_0 is *above* the equilibrium value. The results of the opposite case will follow easily once we have completed this one. We have just seen that the solution specifies that the initial value of income is y_0, as required. It also specifies the path of y_t as t increases from 0 and the manner of this path's dependence on the value of α. For example, if α is positive,[15] as we expect the marginal propensity to consume to be, then y_t will either rise or fall smoothly (rise if $y_0 > y^\epsilon$, fall if $y_0 < y^\epsilon$) because $\alpha^t(y_0 - y^\epsilon)$ will be monotonic and will not oscillate. And if α is negative, as we do not expect it to be, then y_t will oscillate about y^ϵ because even powers of α will be positive and odd powers negative. Also, if α is numerically less than 1, as we expect the marginal propensity to consume to be, then α^t will approach zero as time passes so that y_t will approach equilibrium, with or without oscillations according to whether α is negative or positive. If α is numerically greater than 1, then α^t will become ever larger numerically, and at an ever-increasing rate, oscillating or not, according to whether α is negative or positive. If α is equal to -1, then y_t will alternate between y_0 in even-numbered periods and $2y^\epsilon - y_0$ in odd-numbered periods, for α^t will be either 1 or -1, respectively.

3.26 If $\alpha = 1$, then the device we used to eliminate the constant term from (3.14), namely, taking deviations from the equilibrium value

---

[15] Recall that (3.34) is not a solution if $\alpha = 1$, for then y^ϵ is undefined. This case will be taken up soon.

$y^\epsilon = (i + \beta)/(1 - \alpha)$, will not work because we cannot divide by zero. But a direct attack will succeed then, for (3.14) becomes

$$(3.37) \qquad\qquad y_t = y_{t-1} + i + \beta$$
$$= y_{t-2} + 2(i + \beta)$$
$$= \cdots$$
$$= y_0 + t(i + \beta)$$

Hence if $\alpha = 1$, y_t increases linearly, adding an amount $i + \beta$ each period. See (3.25) above.

3.27 Thus there are six cases for the value of α as shown in Table 3.2. (We need not consider the case where α is zero, which would imply

TABLE 3.2   Dynamic Behavior of Income in Equation (3.14)

Value of α	Behavior of Income
$\alpha < -1$:	explosive oscillation
$\alpha = -1$:	steady repetitive oscillation
$-1 < \alpha < 0$:	oscillatory convergence to equilibrium
$0 < \alpha < 1$:	monotonic convergence to equilibrium
$1 = \alpha$:	straight-line trend
$1 < \alpha$:	monotonic explosion

y constant and equal to $i + \beta$, for then we would no longer have a difference equation.) Income in these cases may be graphed against time, as in Figure 3.1. If $y_0 < y^\epsilon$ the graphs (except for $\alpha = 1$) will be as shown except for being turned upside down.

3.28 Thus we can say that an economy like that described by (3.2) and (3.4) will have a stable equilibrium (see 1.4 for the definition of stability) if and only if the marginal propensity to consume, α, is numerically less than 1, no matter what the values of the other parameters, the exogenous variables, and the initial conditions. This condition is often expressed in terms of the *absolute value* of α, denoted by $|\alpha|$, and defined as the numerical value of α with a positive sign. Thus the stability condition is $|\alpha| < 1$. We expect such an economy to be stable because we believe the marginal propensity to consume to be less than 1.

3.29 We pause to review the accomplishments of the simple dynamic model, (3.2) and (3.4), and its solution, (3.34) and (3.36). Essentially, it describes the *adjustment* of the corresponding static system (3.5)–(3.6) to an initial disequilibrium. This means, for one thing, that it gives the *time path* followed by the endogenous variables in moving from one static equilibrium to another. These paths are found by the process outlined in 3.4 to 3.6 and 3.20 to 3.25, regarding the original equilibrium values as the initial values (e.g., y_0 and c_0 in the above discussion), and using the *new* values of the parameters and exogenous variables to trace the movement of the system through time. That the dynamic model describes adjustments to disequilibria means, for another thing, that it indicates the *stability or instability* of the equilibrium of the corresponding static system.

3.30   Observe the similarity between Figure 3.1, for $0 < \alpha < 1$ and for $\alpha > 1$, and Figure 2.3 showing exponential functions. Observe also the

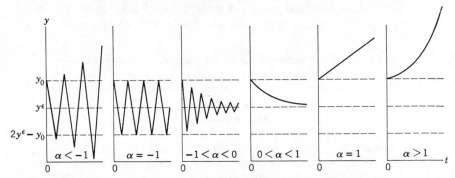

Figure 3.1   Dynamic behavior of income in equation (3.14) if $y_0 > y^\epsilon$.

similarity between (3.34) and (2.6). The graphs are identical in form, and the equations can be made so with the aid of the following transformation, as the reader may verify [in each case we have put on the left the symbols from (2.6) and on the right those from (3.34)]:

$$y = y_t$$
$$a = y^\epsilon$$
(3.38)
$$b = (y_0 - y^\epsilon)$$
$$e^c = \alpha$$

As we shall find, exponential functions appear very often in the solution of difference equations, although as here the number raised to a variable exponent is typically *not* e. That this is a minor difference is shown by the last equation of (3.38).

3.31   We here introduce a *notational convention* that we shall use often henceforth to save time and motion in writing down dynamic models. It is to omit the t in the subscript of all variables, and to agree that any variable with no subscript refers to the current period, while any variable with a subscript -1 or -2 refers to the first or second preceding period, etc. In this notation, for example, the definition

(3.39) $$\Delta x_t = x_t - x_{t-1}$$

is translated into

(3.40) $$\Delta x = x - x_{-1}$$

4 MORE FIRST-ORDER LINEAR DIFFERENCE EQUATIONS; ADJUSTMENT EQUATIONS FOR INCOME MODELS

4.1 We said in 3.6 that a single static system may correspond to several different dynamic systems. In this section we shall illustrate by presenting several dynamic systems, each of which describes a possible adjustment process of the following simple static income-consumption-investment model:

(4.1) $$y = c + i$$

(4.2) $$c = \alpha y + \beta$$

(4.3) $$i = \gamma y + g$$

We have included three equations rather than two, as in (3.5)–(3.6), for in some cases we shall wish to regard investment as being only partly exogenous (g represents this part, such as government expenditures) and partly endogenous as reflected in the term γy, γ being a parameter. In case we wish to regard investment as wholly exogenous, we can either disregard (4.3) altogether or stipulate that $\gamma = 0$ which comes to the same thing since then $i = g$.

4.2 In most of the dynamic systems that we shall set up on the basis of (4.1)–(4.3), we shall replace (4.1) by an equation that specifies, not that aggregate supply (represented by y) is equal to aggregate demand (represented by $c + i$)[16] but that the *rate of change* of supply (represented by Δy) depends upon the discrepancy between $c + i$ and y. This adjustment equation is a structural equation; it describes the behavior of sellers in response to the level of excess supply or demand.[17] All adjustment

---

[16] Recall the discussion in III.3.16, footnote 17, where the usual definition $y = c + i$ is broken down into its components and shown to be a composite of a definition for quantities (or values) demanded and an equilibrium condition.

[17] It is important to realize that there are two time units in the equations we are about to consider: the length of the time period used to express the level of the flow variables, and the length of the lag or period during which the change Δy is measured. We shall nearly always use the same unit for both, usually a year. If either of the two time units is changed, great care must be taken to see that the necessary changes in the units and numerical values of variables and parameters are made. The same caution also applies if the model contains any ratios of stocks to flows. See III.1 for more discussion of units and dimensions.

equations can be regarded as structural equations even though they may not describe the behavior of any single group in the economy such as consumers or investors. They describe the character of the market itself, which is partly institutional and partly the result of the behavior of all groups involved.

4.3 As our first adjustment equation, let us use the following in place of (4.1):

$$(4.4) \qquad \Delta y = c_{-1} + i_{-1} - y_{-1}$$

In other words, this year's income or total supply $(y_{-1} + \Delta y)$ is equal to last year's total demand $(c_{-1} + i_{-1})$; this is a possible behavior pattern of suppliers. Let us regard i as wholly exogenous, thus ignoring (4.3). The dynamic model is then (4.4) and (4.2) (reproduced and renumbered immediately below):

$$(4.5) \qquad c = \alpha y + \beta$$

In this model, income or total supply changes each year by exactly the amount of the discrepancy between $c + i$ and income in the preceding year; and current consumption depends on current income. Clearly the corresponding static model is (4.1)–(4.2), for static conditions require $\Delta y = 0$, and if this is imposed on (4.4) then (4.4)–(4.5) reduce to (4.1)–(4.2). Let us now look at the dynamics of this model. Its final equation for y, obtained by substituting for c_{-1} from (4.5) into (4.4), is

$$(4.6) \qquad y = \alpha y_{-1} + i_{-1} + \beta$$

Its final equation for c, obtained by substituting for y from (4.5) into (4.4), is

$$(4.7) \qquad c = \alpha c_{-1} + \alpha i_{-1} + \beta$$

These final equations are identical with (3.13)–(3.14), the final equations for the model (3.2) and (3.4), except that now in the income equation it is investment as of the *previous* period that enters; in the earlier income equation it is investment as of the *current* period that enters. Since it is usually our concern to trace the time path of a system with parameters and exogenous variables given, exogenous investment will usually be regarded as constant through time, and the two sets of final equations are then identical. Therefore the solution of the model (4.4)–(4.5) is identical with that of the model (3.2) and (3.4), and Figure 3.1 and all the discussion of Section 3 apply equally to both. The equilibrium of the system (4.4)–(4.5) is stable if $|\alpha| < 1$. We expect this condition to be fulfilled, since α is the marginal propensity to consume.

4.4 We now use the same adjustment equation, (4.4), and regard investment as endogenous, dependent on current income. The resulting model consists of (4.4), (4.5), and the following equation:

$$(4.8) \qquad i = \gamma y + g$$

Its static counterpart is the model (4.1)–(4.3). The final equations for this model, as the reader may verify,[18] are

(4.9) $$y = (\alpha + \gamma)y_{-1} + g + \beta$$

(4.10) $$c = (\alpha + \gamma)c_{-1} + \alpha g + \beta - \beta\gamma$$

(4.11) $$i = (\alpha + \gamma)i_{-1} + (1 - \alpha)g + \beta\gamma$$

These equations are like (4.6)–(4.7) and (3.13)–(3.14) in form, since each expresses the value of a variable at time t as a linear function of its value at time $t - 1$. Therefore the reasoning applied above in 3.13–3.18 will establish here as it did there that the solution is stable if and only if the coefficient of the lagged variable is less than 1 in absolute value. Hence the system (4.4), (4.5), (4.8) will be stable if and only if $|\alpha + \gamma| < 1$. The economic meaning of the expression $\alpha + \gamma$ is the marginal propensity to spend; if income rises by one dollar, then total spending, consumption and investment together, rise by $\alpha + \gamma$ dollars.[19] Hence if α and γ are positive, satisfaction of this stability condition implies satisfaction of the previous one, $|\alpha| < 1$.

4.5   Suppose now that the change in income or total supply in a given year is not *equal* to the excess demand or excess supply of the preceding year as in (4.4) but is instead a constant positive multiple of it. And suppose again that investment has an induced component as in (4.8). The model is then

(4.12) $$\Delta y = \theta(c_{-1} + i_{-1} - y_{-1})$$

(4.13) $$c = \alpha y + \beta$$

(4.14) $$i = \gamma y + g$$

and its static counterpart is (4.1)–(4.3) as before. θ is a new positive parameter, indicating the strength of the annual response to a disequilibrium existing in the preceding year. The final equation for income in this model is

(4.15) $$y = [\theta(\alpha + \gamma) + 1 - \theta]y_{-1} + \theta g + \theta\beta$$

and the final equations for c and i are analogous, as the reader may show. These equations are of the same form as (3.13)–(3.14), and accordingly the stability condition is that the coefficient of y_{-1} should be less than 1

---

[18] The final equations can be obtained as follows: First solve the model for its reduced form. The reduced-form equation for y is (4.9), already in final equation form. Lag equation (4.5) one period, solve it for y_{-1}, and substitute the result into the reduced-form equation for c, thus obtaining the final equation for c. Lag equation (4.8) one period, solve it for y_{-1}, and substitute the result into the reduced-form equation for i, thus obtaining the final equation for i.

[19] This explains why $\phi_y + \psi_y$ is assumed to be between zero and one in III.7.8.

in absolute value, that is, that $|\theta(\alpha + \gamma) + 1 - \theta| < 1$. Here the absolute value notation does not simplify matters, since the quantity that must be less than 1 in absolute value is not a simple sum of parameters all having the same sign. More conveniently, but without the absolute value notation, the condition is

$$(4.16) \qquad\qquad -1 < \theta(\alpha + \gamma) + 1 - \theta < 1$$

If each of the two inequalities here is solved for $\alpha + \gamma$, remembering[20] that $\theta > 0$, the result is[21]

$$(4.17) \qquad\qquad 1 - \frac{2}{\theta} < \alpha + \gamma < 1$$

If $\theta = 1$, as in the model of 4.4, this inequality reduces to $|\alpha + \gamma| < 1$, the stability condition of 4.4. If $\theta < 1$, that is, if the change in supply is *less* than the excess supply or demand of the preceding year, then the lower limit of the stable range for $\alpha + \gamma$ is below -1. If $\theta > 1$, that is, if the change in supply *exceeds* the excess supply or demand of the preceding year, the lower limit of the stability range for $\alpha + \gamma$ is above -1, and becomes as high as zero or higher if $\theta \geq 2$. The latter consideration is largely academic, however, for it would indeed be a strange system that responded to a disequilibrium of demand and supply with a change in supply as large as *twice* the discrepancy. This being the case, stability is insured so long as $\alpha + \gamma$ is positive and less than 1.

4.6 The double inequality (4.17) defines a relationship between two parameters, $\alpha + \gamma$ and θ. This relationship can be described by drawing a pair of axes, one for $\alpha + \gamma$ and one for θ, and shading in the part of the plane containing the points (pairs of values) that satisfy (4.17). This is done in Figure 4.1. Points on or outside the boundaries of the shaded region do not provide stability. Such a graph might be called the *stabilogram* of the dynamic system that gives rise to it. It should be noted that the stability condition for the model of 4.4, a special case of the current one when $\theta = 1$, can be read directly from the stabilogram of Figure 4.1 by finding the range of $\alpha + \gamma$ in the Figure at $\theta = 1$; this is from -1 to $+1$, as in 4.4 above.

4.7 If the preceding model is simplified by making investment wholly exogenous, then $\gamma = 0$ and $i = g$, and all the conclusions and conditions developed in 4.5–4.6 will apply if $\alpha + \gamma$ is replaced by $\alpha + 0$, or simply α.

---

[20] If an inequality is divided or multiplied by a number A, the inequality sign must be reversed if $A < 0$ but not if $A > 0$.

[21] The left-hand inequality in (4.16) leads to the left-hand inequality in (4.17), and the right to the right.

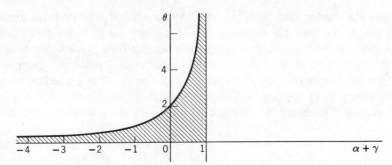

Figure 4.1 Stability condition for equation (4.15). (Shaded area, excluding boundaries, indicates stability.)

4.8   As our last example of a dynamic model corresponding to the simple static model (4.1)–(4.3) we consider one in which it is assumed that the adjustment to disequilibria is immediate, consumption depends on current income, and investment depends on income of the previous period:

(4.18) $$y = c + i$$

(4.19) $$c = \alpha y + \beta$$

(4.20) $$i = \gamma y_{-1} + g$$

The final equation for income is

(4.21) $$y = \frac{\gamma}{1 - \alpha} y_{-1} + \frac{1}{1 - \alpha} g + \frac{\beta}{1 - \alpha} .$$

This equation is similar in form to those above, and hence its solution is stable if and only if the coefficient of y_{-1} is less than 1 in absolute value, that is, if and only if

(4.22) $$-1 < \frac{\gamma}{1 - \alpha} < 1$$

The final equations for c and i are similar to (4.21), and their stability conditions are identical to (4.22). The stabilogram of this system is shown in Figure 4.2. It is obtained from (4.22) as follows. If (4.22) is multiplied by $1 - \alpha$, there are two possible results, depending on the sign of $1 - \alpha$:

(4.23)   if $1 - \alpha > 0$,   then $-1 + \alpha < \gamma < 1 - \alpha$

(4.24)   if $1 - \alpha < 0$,   then $-1 + \alpha > \gamma > 1 - \alpha$

The dividing line between the two cases is $1 - \alpha = 0$, or $\alpha = 1$, and this is shown as a dotted line in Figure 4.2. Equation (4.23) describes the left-hand shaded area, and (4.24) the right-hand one. Hence the system (4.18)–(4.20) would be stable if the parameters α and γ fell anywhere

inside the shaded area in Figure 4.2. Again not all parts of these areas
are interesting from the point of view of the real world. In the first place
marginal propensities to consume and invest can only be positive; hence
only the first quadrant is interesting. In the second place the marginal
propensity to consume cannot reasonably be regarded as exceeding 1, so
only that part of the first quadrant to the left of the dotted line $\alpha = 1$ is
interesting. This being the case, the relevant part of the stabilogram is the

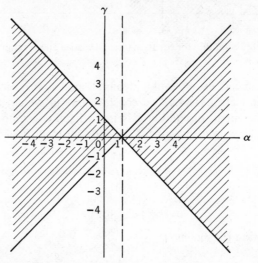

Figure 4.2 Stability condition for equation (4.21). (Shaded area, excluding boundaries,
indicates stability.)

triangle between the origin and the points (0, 1) and (1, 0). The inequalities
describing it are $0 < \alpha + \gamma < 1$, which is in agreement with the relevant
parts of the stabilograms of the dynamic models previously considered.

4.9 The examples above have shown that the stability of equilibrium
of a particular static system may depend upon three things: the type of
dynamic adjustment process that comes into play when the equilibrium
is disturbed; the values of parameters; and the values of exogenous
variables.[22] Recall that the distinction between parameters and exogenous
variables is a minor one on the theoretical level (see again I.5.5).

4.10 We are now in a position to put our results from dynamic
theory to use in helping to answer one of the fundamental questions
about economic models, namely: What kind of *"a priori"* information[23]

[22] It will also depend on the magnitude of the displacement from equilibrium if
there is stability in the small but not perfect stability; see 1.4.

[23] *"A priori"* is put in quotes here for although the information in question is
obtained without detailed observation of the values of the variables, it does make use
of the observed fact of stability. See text below.

is available on the values of parameters in which we may be interested? The reasoning is essentially this: In the real world, we do not usually observe that economic systems are unstable.[24] For any static model we can devise one or more plausible adjustment processes, that is, counterpart dynamic models. The fact of stability enables us to rule out as inadmissible certain sets of values of the parameters in each dynamic model. We can then conclude that the admissible values for the parameters of the original static model consist of only those values not ruled out by all the dynamic models in the process above.

4.11　Suppose we examine the static income-consumption-investment model (4.1)–(4.3) with this in mind. All three of the dynamic processes we examined for this model in 4.4, 4.5, and 4.8 produced different stability conditions. They were, respectively,

(4.25) $$|\alpha + \gamma| < 1 \qquad \text{[in 4.4]}$$

(4.26) $$1 - \frac{2}{\theta} < \alpha + \gamma < 1 \qquad \text{[in 4.5, eq. (4.17)]}$$

(4.27) $$-1 < \frac{\gamma}{1 - \alpha} < 1 \qquad \text{[in 4.8, eq. (4.22)]}$$

These three respective ranges are imposed on the parameters of the static model by the observed fact of the stability of the economic system. But in each case we were able to establish certain presumptions on other grounds, and so to narrow the admissible ranges. First, economic theory suggests that α should be positive and γ should be non-negative, since they represent marginal propensities to spend on consumers' and producers' goods, respectively. Thus in the first dynamic theory used, (4.25) becomes

(4.28) $$\alpha + \gamma < 1$$

In the two other theories, only the first quadrant of the (α, γ) plane is left as admissible. Then in 4.5 it was established that $0 < \theta < 2$, so that (4.26) also becomes (4.28). And last, in 4.8, it was established that usually $\alpha < 1$, since usually not all of an increase in income is spent for consumption; hence (4.27) also becomes (4.28). Thus all three dynamic models, with the aid of these additional presumptions, agree that stability can prevail only if (4.28) holds, that is, if the marginal propensity to

[24] Sometimes it happens that monetary variables, such as prices, and national income in money terms behave in an apparently unstable fashion for a time, as in Germany after World War I, or in Japan after World War II. It should be noted first that these events are due to exogenous circumstances, and second that *real* income and related *real* variables do not participate in them. On the other hand, long-term economic development stretching over decades or centuries may possibly be thought of as an unstable process.

spend (which is presumed to be positive in any case) is less than 1. If there is no other dynamic version of (4.1)–(4.3) that disagrees on this point, then, whenever we observe a *stable* economy whose equilibrium we think is described by the static income-consumption-investment model (4.1)–(4.3), we are entitled to conclude, *without making any further empirical investigations*, that the marginal propensity to spend is less than 1.

4.12 The importance of such a conclusion can be illustrated by the multiplier, $\partial y/\partial g$, in the foregoing static model. It turns out to be $1/(1 - \alpha - \gamma)$ and is seen to be necessarily positive precisely because of (4.28) and the stability of the system. Very often it happens that the algebraic signs of derivatives needed in comparative statics can be determined for stable systems by thus examining the dynamic stability conditions.[25] This explains Samuelson's somewhat paradoxical statement that "One interested only in fruitful statics must study dynamics."[26]

5 ADJUSTMENT PROCESSES IN DEMAND AND SUPPLY EQUATIONS[27]

5.1 We turn now to adjustment processes applicable to the simple market for a single good, where the strictest *ceteris paribus* assumptions are made so that the only variables are prices and quantities of the good in question. The static equations and dynamic adjustments can be phrased either in Walrasian terms with quantities supplied and demanded as functions of the going price[28] or in Marshallian terms with supply price and demand price as functions of the amount traded on the market.[29] The static equations are as follows:

Walrasian:

(5.1)   supply: $x^s = s(p)$

(5.2)   demand: $x^d = d(p)$

(5.3)   equilibrium: $x^s = x^d$

where p = price, x^s = quantity supplied, and x^d = quantity demanded.

[25] But not always. See my comment on a paper of Arthur Smithies, Christ [1951a]. See also Lancaster [1965].

[26] Samuelson [1947], p. 5.

[27] For further treatment of the material of this section, see Samuelson [1947], pp. 17–19, and p. 264, note 9.

[28] See Walras [1926] or [1954], sections 65–66.

[29] See Marshall [1920], p. 346n.

Marshallian:

(5.4)   supply price: $p^s = S(x)$

(5.5)   demand price: $p^d = D(x)$

(5.6)   equilibrium: $p^s = p^d$

where x = quantity sold, p^s = supply price, and p^d = demand price.

The two models have the same static solution, of course; (5.4) is obtained by solving (5.1) for p, and (5.5) is obtained analogously. The corresponding processes described by Walras and Marshall are not equivalent, however, as we shall show.

    5.2   We turn first to the adjustment process envisioned by Walras, in which the price is regarded as set for each period, and changes from

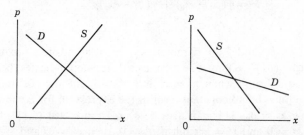

Figure 5.1   Stable situations for Walrasian equations (5.7) or (6.5).

one period to the next in response to the excess supply or demand of the earlier period, increasing if there was excess demand and decreasing if there was excess supply. In order for this system to be stable, the supply curve must cut the demand curve from the left as we move upward along the vertical price axis (see Figure 5.1). This system can be represented by replacing the equilibrium condition (5.3) in the model (5.1)–(5.3) by the price-adjustment equation

(5.7) $\Delta p = \phi(x^d_{-1} - x^s_{-1}) = \phi[d(p_{-1}) - s(p_{-1})]$

where ϕ is a single-valued monotonic increasing function of one variable, such that

(5.8) $\phi(a) \gtreqless 0$ according to whether $a \gtreqless 0$

Condition (5.8) insures that the price increases with excess demand, decreases with excess supply, and does not change if the market is in equilibrium.

    5.3   We now linearize all three functions s, d, and ϕ. We linearize the adjustment function ϕ at the equilibrium point, where both ϕ and its variable $x^d_{-1} - x^s_{-1}$ are zero. We linearize the supply and demand functions

s and d at the equilibrium price p^ϵ, so that our new price variable is the deviation of price from its equilibrium value,[30] $p - p^\epsilon$. We call this new variable p^δ:

$$(5.9) \qquad\qquad p^\delta = p - p^\epsilon$$

The resulting linear model is

$$(5.10) \qquad\qquad x^s = \alpha_0 + \alpha_1(p - p^\epsilon) = \alpha_0 + \alpha_1 p^\delta$$

$$(5.11) \qquad\qquad x^d = \beta_0 + \beta_1(p - p^\epsilon) = \beta_0 + \beta_1 p^\delta$$

$$
\begin{aligned}
(5.12) \qquad \Delta p^\delta = \Delta p &= \gamma(x^d_{-1} - x^s_{-1}) \\
&= \gamma(\beta_0 + \beta_1 p^\delta_{-1} - \alpha_0 - \alpha_1 p^\delta_{-1}) \\
&= \gamma(\beta_0 - \alpha_0) + \gamma(\beta_1 - \alpha_1)p^\delta_{-1} \\
&= \gamma(\beta_1 - \alpha_1)p^\delta_{-1}
\end{aligned}
$$

where α_0, α_1, β_0, β_1, and γ are parameters. γ must be positive because of (5.8). The term $\gamma(\beta_0 - \alpha_0)$ must be zero, as the last step indicates, because of (5.8): At equilibrium when $x^d = x^s$ and $p^\delta = 0$, Δp and Δp^δ must be zero, so there must be no constant term in the expression for Δp in terms of p^δ_{-1}. Hence $\alpha_0 = \beta_0$. This can also be seen from (5.10)–(5.11), for in equilibrium $p^\delta = 0$ and $x^s = x^d$; but if $p^\delta = 0$, then $x^s = \alpha_0$ and $x^d = \beta_0$, whence $\alpha_0 = \beta_0$.

5.4   The difference equation formed by the first and last terms of (5.12) is easily translated into

$$(5.13) \qquad\qquad p^\delta = [1 + \gamma(\beta_1 - \alpha_1)]p^\delta_{-1}$$

This is of the same familiar form as those of Sections 3 and 4, and hence the market in question is stable if and only if the coefficient of p^δ_{-1} is less than 1 in absolute value. An equivalent and more readily interpretable condition is that

$$(5.14) \qquad\qquad -1 < 1 + \gamma(\beta_1 - \alpha_1) < 1$$

that is, that

$$(5.15) \qquad\qquad -2 < \gamma(\beta_1 - \alpha_1) < 0$$

---

[30] Instead of using the equilibrium value p^ϵ, we could use zero. The equilibrium value has two advantages, however: (1) the region in which we are most interested is that near the equilibrium, so we want our linear approximations to be as accurate as possible in that region (this argument also supports the choice of zero as the value around which to expand the adjustment function ϕ); and (2) the choice of p^ϵ makes the linearized adjustment equation have no constant term, which makes it simpler to solve.

Since γ is positive by (5.8), stability requires that

$$(5.16) \qquad\qquad\qquad \alpha_1 > \beta_1$$

$$(5.17) \qquad\qquad\qquad \gamma < \frac{2}{\alpha_1 - \beta_1}$$

The first requirement, (5.16), says that the supply curve must cross the demand curve from the left as we move upward, that is, to larger prices. The stable situations are shown in Figure 5.1, with β_1 negative. The second condition, (5.17), puts an upper limit on the magnitude of the adjustment parameter γ, in terms of the slopes α_1 and β_1 of the supply and demand curves. If γ exceeds this limit, the system will oscillate ever more widely about the equilibrium value.

5.5 We turn now to the adjustment process envisioned by Marshall, in which the quantity available is regarded as set for each period, and

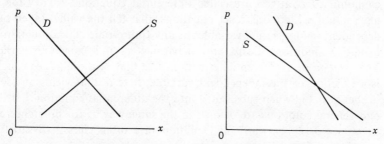

Figure 5.2 Stable situations for Marshallian equation (5.17).

falls or rises in the next period according to whether the supply price was greater or less than the demand price. In order for this system to be stable, the supply curve must cut the demand curve from below as we move to the right along the horizontal quantity axis (Figure 5.2). This system can be represented by replacing the equilibrium condition in (5.6) by the adjustment equation

$$(5.18) \qquad \Delta x = \psi(p^d_{-1} - p^s_{-1}) = \psi[D(x_{-1}) - S(x_{-1})]$$

where ψ is a single-valued function such that

$$(5.19) \qquad \psi(a) \gtreqless 0 \qquad \text{according to whether } a \gtreqless 0$$

If the supply and demand equations (5.4) and (5.5) are linearized at the equilibrium quantity x^ϵ and the adjustment equation (5.18) is linearized at zero, the stability conditions can then be determined by an argument similar to that in 5.1–5.4. Stable situations are shown in Figure 5.2. The examples above further illustrate that the stability conditions for a static model depend upon the character of the dynamic adjustment process that exists or is assumed.

6 CONTINUOUSLY CHANGING VARIABLES; DIFFERENTIAL EQUATIONS

6.1 So far in our discussion of rates of change of economic variables (excluding time itself in Section 2) we have discussed only *discrete* changes from period to period, as from one year to the next. Time has been regarded as a discrete variable that moves ahead in jumps. This view gave rise to lagged variables and to difference equations. We shall now briefly inquire into the situation where time is regarded as a continuous variable. We may then speak of the instantaneous rate of change of a variable, such as income y or price p, with respect to time, that is, the derivatives, such as dy/dt or dp/dt, instead of the change in y or p, occurring in a particular period, such as Δy or Δp. The equations we shall obtain, containing derivatives, are called differential equations.[31] They too may have solutions, like difference equations, that tell the values taken by the dependent (endogenous) variables at any future time t as a function of t, of initial conditions if any, and of parameters and exogenous variables. The *solution* of a differential equation, like that of a difference equation, is a function of the independent variable (here t) that yields an identity in that variable when substituted into the differential equation. Particular and general solutions are defined in the same way as for difference equations (see 3.12 ff.). Particular solutions are often chosen to satisfy the initial conditions, if any are given.

6.2 Differential equations are less used in econometrics than difference equations, probably for two reasons: Economic flow data usually relate to *average* rates over a period such as a week, month, quarter, or year, rather than to instantaneous rates; and a lack of familiarity with calculus is not a barrier to casting economic theories in the form of difference equations. We present a few illustrations involving differential equations because they are more elegant theoretically than difference equations and because their mathematical properties have been more thoroughly investigated, and because some time data may be developed or adapted to suit them sufficiently well.

6.3 It should be clear that derivatives with respect to time, by virtue of their definition as limits of rates of change as the time interval goes to zero, are like differences except that they are evaluated as averages over infinitesimally short periods. This fact has implications about the procedure we must use to deduce, from a given initial position and the knowledge of the instantaneous rates of change at every moment in the

---

[31] Equations containing both derivatives (time being continuous) and lags are called mixed difference-differential equations. We shall not discuss them here.

future, the position that will occur at a specified future time. Consider again the discrete case: If the initial value x_0 of a variable x is known, and the changes Δx_t for the next T periods are known, then the value of x after T periods is easily found as

$$(6.1) \qquad x_T = x_0 + \Delta x_1 + \cdots + \Delta x_T = x_0 + \sum_{t=1}^{T} (\Delta x_t)$$

The procedure is directly analogous in the continuous case, except that there is, so to speak, an *infinite* number of periods from $t = 1$ to $t = T$ because each period is infinitesimally short. Each rate of change dx/dt applies only to a single such short period of duration dt, and, in effect, what we must do to find the value of x at time T is to add to x_0 all the *infinite* number of terms like $(dx/dt)\,dt$. In other words, we must compute the *definite integral* of the function dx/dt between the two values of t, 0 and T, thus:

$$(6.2) \qquad x_T = x_0 + \int_0^T \frac{dx(t)}{dt}\, dt$$

(The reader may wish to refer to the discussion of integrals in IV.2.26 to 2.29). This equation is the analog for the continuous case of the discrete equation (6.1).

6.4 We now frame the Walrasian adjustment process, mentioned in 5.2–4, in terms of derivatives. The model is

$$(6.3) \qquad x^s = s(p)$$

$$(6.4) \qquad x^d = d(p)$$

$$(6.5) \qquad \frac{dp}{dt} = \phi(x^d - x^s)$$

where (6.5) replaces the adjustment equation (5.7). All three variables x^s, x^d, and p are understood to be functions of time. The nature of the adjustment process requires as before that

$$(6.6) \qquad \phi(a) \gtreqless 0 \qquad \text{according to whether } a \gtreqless 0$$

that is, an excess demand makes price rise, an excess supply makes price fall, and a cleared market leads to no change. If the two functions s and d are linearized about the equilibrium point, and ϕ is linearized about zero, and p^δ is used to denote the deviation of p from its equilibrium point p^ϵ as before, the resulting model is

$$(6.7) \qquad x^s = \alpha_0 + \alpha_1(p - p^\epsilon) = \alpha_0 + \alpha_1 p^\delta$$

$$(6.8) \qquad x^d = \beta_0 + \beta_1(p - p^\epsilon) = \beta_0 + \beta_1 p^\delta$$

$$(6.9) \qquad \frac{dp^\delta}{dt} = \frac{dp}{dt} = \gamma(x^d - x^s)$$
$$= \gamma(\beta_0 + \beta_1 p^\delta - \alpha_0 - \alpha_1 p^\delta)$$
$$= \gamma(\beta_0 - \alpha_0) + \gamma(\beta_1 - \alpha_1)p^\delta$$

Since there must be no change of price in equilibrium, we have $\alpha_0 = \beta_0$, and hence

$$(6.10) \qquad \frac{dp^\delta}{dt} = \gamma(\beta_1 - \alpha_1)p^\delta$$

The solution of the latter differential equation is

$$(6.11) \qquad p^\delta = Ae^{\gamma(\beta_1-\alpha_1)t}$$

where A is a constant whose value is determined by the initial conditions. In fact A turns out in (6.11) to be the value that p^δ has when $t = 0$, as we shall presently show.

6.5 The solution (6.11) of (6.10) is obtained as follows. All terms in p^δ are collected on one side, and all terms in t on the other; the differential equation is then said to be separated, thus:

$$(6.12) \qquad \frac{dp^\delta}{p^\delta} = \gamma(\beta_1 - \alpha_1)\, dt$$

Integration being the reverse of differentiation, and the derivative of $\log_e p^\delta$ with respect to t being $(1/p^\delta)\, dp^\delta/dt$, we can *integrate* (6.12) to get

$$(6.13) \qquad \log_e p^\delta = \gamma(\beta_1 - \alpha_1)t + \log_e A$$

The correctness of this step can be checked by differentiating (6.13) with respect to t. The result is

$$(6.14) \qquad \frac{1}{p^\delta}\frac{dp^\delta}{dt} = \gamma(\beta_1 - \alpha_1)$$

which is equivalent to (6.12) or (6.10). The term $\log_e A$, where A is a constant whose value is so far undetermined, is added in (6.13) because any such constant term is consistent with (6.12), as shown by the fact that it disappears in the differentiation of (6.13). Now we transform (6.13). The term $\gamma(\beta_1 - \alpha_1)t$ is the natural logarithm of $e^{\gamma(\beta_1-\alpha_1)t}$ by definition. If this substitution is made we see that the logarithms of p^δ and of $Ae^{\gamma(\beta_1-\alpha_1)t}$ are equal; hence we can equate p^δ and $Ae^{\gamma(\beta_1-\alpha_1)t}$ directly, and this yields the solution (6.11). Then, as noted above, the value of A is determined to be $p_0^\delta = p_0 - p^\epsilon$, by substituting the initial condition $t = 0$ in (6.11).

6.6 We examine the solution (6.11) to see how the price behaves over time. We find first that

$$(6.15) \qquad p = p^\epsilon + (p_0 - p^\epsilon)e^{\gamma(\beta_1-\alpha_1)t}$$

Now e and γ are positive constants. Hence as t progresses from 0 to infinity, the course of the price p depends on the constant $(\beta_1 - \alpha_1)$: If $\beta_1 - \alpha_1$ is positive, p increases indefinitely; if $\beta_1 - \alpha_1$ is zero, no change in p occurs; and if $\beta_1 - \alpha_1$ is negative, p approaches its equilibrium value p^ϵ since $e^{-\infty}$ is zero. Hence the condition for stability is $\beta_1 - \alpha_1 < 0$. In the normal case of an upward sloping supply curve ($\alpha_1 > 0$) and a downward sloping demand curve ($\beta_1 < 0$) stability is assured. This and the other stable case are as shown in Figure 5.1 above. The stability condition in this Walrasian continuous case is the same as in the corresponding discrete case, except that in the continuous case there is no upper limit imposed on γ; compare 5.2–4.

6.7 The Marshallian adjustment process, in which the quantity bought and sold changes in accordance with the difference between supply price and demand price, can also be phrased in terms of differential equations, and the solution and stability conditions can be obtained. We leave as an exercise for the reader the proof that the result is the same as in 5.5.

6.8 As another example, we choose a differential-equation form of the income-consumption-investment model where current consumption and investment are linear functions of current income and where income changes at an instantaneous rate that is proportional to excess demand, that is, to $c + i - y$. In order to eliminate inconvenient constant terms from the equations, we again regard as our variables the deviations of c, i, and y from the equilibrium values c^ϵ, i^ϵ, and y^ϵ, and denote these deviations by c^δ, i^δ, and y^δ. Then the model is

(6.16) $$c^\delta = \alpha y^\delta$$

(6.17) $$i^\delta = \gamma y^\delta$$

(6.18) $$\frac{dy^\delta}{dt} = \lambda(c^\delta + i^\delta - y^\delta) = \lambda(\alpha + \gamma - 1)y^\delta$$

By separating the equation, as was done with (6.10) to obtain (6.12), and integrating, we have

(6.19) $$\log_e y^\delta = \lambda(\alpha + \gamma - 1)t + \log_e A$$

Hence, taking antilogarithms,

(6.20) $$y^\delta = A e^{\lambda(\alpha+\gamma-1)t}$$

The value of the arbitrary constant A is found from the initial condition that at $t = 0$ the value of y^δ is $y_0 - y^\epsilon$; hence the solution is

(6.21) $$y = y^\epsilon + (y_0 - y^\epsilon)e^{\lambda(\alpha+\gamma-1)t}$$

The stability condition again is that the coefficient of t in the exponent be negative; λ must be positive by the nature of the adjustment process (excess demand causes a rise, not a fall in income), so the condition is $\alpha + \lambda < 1$. This is in agreement with the results of 4.4 for the corresponding difference-equation model.[32]

---

[32] The condition derived in 4.4 was that $|\alpha + \gamma| < 1$, but when it is recalled that both α and γ are positive (being the marginal propensities to consume and invest, respectively), this becomes equivalent to $\alpha + \gamma < 1$.

7 DISTRIBUTED LAGS, EXPECTATIONS, AND ADJUSTMENT

7.1 In many dynamic economic models it is plausible to suppose that the current value of one variable, say y_t, depends on many lagged values of another variable, such as x_{t-1}, x_{t-2}, x_{t-3}, etc. In principle such a relationship is sometimes easier to deal with mathematically if the number of lagged values of x involved is infinite, but in practice the coefficients of distant values of x are negligible so this is not an important empirical issue. Sometimes it is assumed that y also depends on the current value of x, and sometimes it is not. A general *distributed-lag* function is

$$(7.1) \qquad y_t = f(x_t, x_{t-1}, x_{t-2}, x_{t-3}, \ldots)$$

A linear form of this function is easier to deal with and is often assumed.[33]

$$(7.2) \qquad y_t = \delta + \epsilon_0 x_t + \epsilon_1 x_{t-1} + \epsilon_2 x_{t-2} + \epsilon_3 x_{t-3} + \cdots$$

$$= \delta + \sum_{i=0}^{\tau} \epsilon_i x_{t-i}$$

Here τ is some very large number and may be chosen to be infinity if desired (the coefficients ϵ_0, ϵ_1, ... must have a finite sum if (7.2) is to make sense).

7.2 Distributed lags are useful wherever there is a process of gradual adjustment to change. The demand for durable goods is an example. A new and superior type of durable good may not immediately replace the entire stock of durable goods of older and inferior design, even if everyone knows about it, because those durable goods of the earlier inferior design that are still relatively new and have a substantial remaining life may continue to be used for a while until they are more nearly worn out. Also, the new design may require new operations to produce it, and time may be required to get them going at satisfactory cost levels. The transmission of new knowledge is a second example. The demand for a new product, durable or nondurable, may be small at first, or the response of demand to a change in price may be small at first, until people learn about it and learn how to make more use of new or relatively cheapened goods and less use of goods that have risen in relative price. Similar reactions occur on the supply side of the market. Expectations about future events[34] may also involve distributed lags, to the extent that these expectations depend on past events.

---

[33] Recall that nonlinear equations can sometimes be made linear by suitable transformations (see III.10.4–10) or approximately linear (see III.2–5).

[34] This kind of expectation is not the same as the mathematical expectation discussed in IV.2.21.

7.3 Little successful work has been done with distributed-lag equations like (7.2) that have a separate parameter for every different lag. A technique that has been used by many economists[35] is to assume explicitly or implicitly that, except possibly for the first few coefficients, the coefficients of the distributed-lag equation decline in geometric progression in successive periods, forever. If the coefficient of the kth lag is the first one in such a geometrically declining series, we have

$$(7.3) \qquad \epsilon_{k+j} = \theta^j \epsilon_k \qquad 0 \leqq \theta < 1, \quad j \geqq 0$$

The reason for assuming $\theta \geqq 0$ is so that the coefficients will not alternate in sign. (If $\theta = 0$, then of course the longest lag in the equation is the kth.) The reason for assuming $\theta < 1$ is so that the coefficients of more distant lags will be less than those of recent lags. If (7.3) is substituted into (7.2) and an infinite number of lags is permitted, the result is

$$(7.4) \qquad y_t = \delta + \sum_{i=0}^{k-1} \epsilon_i x_{t-i} + \epsilon_k \sum_{j=0}^{\infty} \theta^j x_{t-(k+j)} \qquad 0 \leqq \theta < 1$$

This means that after the first k lags, the coefficients decline in geometric progression, each one being θ times its predecessor where θ is zero or positive but less than 1. If the number of lags τ is not infinite, then the second summation above extends from 0 to $\tau - k$ rather than from 0 to ∞. In the simple case where *all* the coefficients are related geometrically, the value of k in (7.3) and (7.4) is 0, and we have for y_t the following:

$$(7.5) \qquad y_t = \delta + \epsilon_0 \sum_{j=0}^{\infty} \theta^j x_{t-j} \qquad 0 \leqq \theta < 1$$

One great advantage of (7.4) and (7.5) is that they have only a few parameters, namely, $k + 3$; (7.2) has an infinite or at least a very large number, $\tau + 2$.

7.4 The preceding five equations appear difficult to deal with empirically because they all involve an infinite or at least a very large number of different lags extending far back into the past [except in (7.4) and (7.5) if $\theta = 0$]. An advantage of (7.4) and (7.5) is that they can be rewritten so as to have only a few lags. This can be done exactly if the original equation contains an infinite number of lags and approximately if it contains a very large but finite number. It depends on the fact that y_{t-1} is a sum of the same type as y_t with coefficients that decline geometrically in the same ratio, so that the tail of the infinite sum in (7.4) or (7.5) can be replaced by a simple function of y_{t-1}. We illustrate for (7.5);

---

[35] See Koyck [1954], Cagan [1956], Friedman [1957], and Nerlove [1958] and [1958a]. There are differences in notation among these writers, and some make use of differential as well as difference equations.

the process for (7.4) is essentially the same. First use (7.5) to express y_{t-1} as a function of x_{t-1} and all preceding values of x, and then multiply the result by θ. This yields the following:

$$(7.6) \qquad \theta y_{t-1} = \theta \delta + \epsilon_0 \sum_{j=0}^{\infty} \theta^{j+1} x_{t-(j+1)}$$

Now the summation here has as its first term θx_{t-1}, its second term $\theta^2 x_{t-2}$, etc., to infinity. This expression can just as well be written as a sum over j from 1 to ∞ of $\theta^j x_{t-j}$. Doing so gives

$$(7.7) \qquad \theta y_{t-1} = \theta \delta + \epsilon_0 \sum_{j=1}^{\infty} \theta^j x_{t-j}$$

Now subtract (7.7) from (7.5). All the terms in the summation in (7.7) cancel the corresponding terms in the summation in (7.5). If the term θy_{t-1} is transferred to the right side of the resulting equation, we have

$$(7.8) \qquad y_t = \delta(1 - \theta) + \epsilon_0 x_t + \theta y_{t-1}$$

This is an equation involving only three different variables and three parameters. If all of its coefficients are known or estimated, then ϵ_0 and θ are available directly, and δ can be found as $[\delta(1 - \theta)]/(1 - \theta)$.

7.5 A similar process applied to the more general equation (7.4) yields

$$(7.9) \qquad y_t = \delta(1 - \theta) + \epsilon_0 x_t + \theta y_{t-1} + \sum_{i=1}^{k} (\epsilon_i - \theta \epsilon_{i-1}) x_{t-i}$$

If $k = 0$, there are no terms in the summation here so that this reduces to (7.8) as it should.

7.6 An illustration of the use of distributed lags in expectations about the future will now be given. Suppose that a behavior variable y_t depends on the value x_t^e that is expected for the future by those who control y_t at time t, thus:

$$(7.10) \qquad y_t = \alpha + \beta x_t^e$$

One fruitful expectations hypothesis[36] postulates that the currently held expectation about the future value of a variable such as x is a weighted average of the expectation held last period and the actual value observed currently, thus:[37]

$$(7.11) \qquad x_t^e = \gamma x_{t-1}^e + (1 - \gamma) x_t \qquad 0 \leqq \gamma < 1$$

[36] See Cagan [1956], Friedman [1957], and Nerlove [1958] and [1958a].

[37] Sometimes the current expectation is taken as an average of the lagged expectation and the *lagged* (rather than current) observed value, $x_t^e = \gamma x_{t-1}^e + (1 - \gamma) x_{t-1}$. Results are similar.

This leads to relationships like (7.5)–(7.8) as we shall now show. The coefficient γ is assumed to be non-negative and less than 1. If γ were 1, there would never be any change in expectations no matter what values of x were observed, an unrealistic possibility. If γ were zero, expectations would always be equal to the most recent observed value. This expectations hypothesis can be expressed in several equivalent forms. One is (7.11). Another is

$$(7.12) \qquad x_t^e - x_{t-1}^e = (1 - \gamma)(x_t - x_{t-1}^e)$$

Another, obtained by expressing x_{t-1}^e in terms of x_{t-2}^e and x_{t-1} from a lagged version of (7.11) and repeating the process indefinitely, is

$$(7.13) \quad \begin{aligned} x_t^e &= \gamma^2 x_{t-2}^e + \gamma(1 - \gamma)x_{t-1} + (1 - \gamma)x_t \\ &= \gamma^3 x_{t-3}^e + \gamma^2(1 - \gamma)x_{t-2} + \gamma(1 - \gamma)x_{t-1} + (1 - \gamma)x_t \\ &= \cdots \\ &= (1 - \gamma) \sum_{i=0}^{\infty} \gamma^i x_{t-i} \end{aligned}$$

This formulation shows the connection between the expectations hypothesis and the distributed-lag equation (7.5). Note that the weights in (7.13) add up to 1 as long as $0 \leq \gamma < 1$, which is assumed.

    7.7   This expectations hypothesis at first seems clumsy to deal with because in (7.11) or (7.12) it involves the unobservable lagged expectation x_{t-1}^e and in (7.13) it involves an infinite number of lags. But it can be transformed into an equivalent equation containing only three variables and three parameters by the same process used to derive (7.8). An even more direct process is to start with (7.11), and then from a lagged version of (7.10) use actual lagged behavior y_t as an indicator of what x_{t-1}^e must have been last period. Specifically, substitute (7.11) for x_t^e in (7.10) to get

$$(7.14) \qquad y_t = \alpha + \gamma\beta x_{t-1}^e + (1 - \gamma)\beta x_t$$

Now substitute for βx_{t-1}^e in (7.14) its value $(y_{t-1} - \alpha)$ as obtained from the lagged version of (7.10):

$$(7.15) \qquad y_t = \alpha(1 - \gamma) + \beta(1 - \gamma)x_t + \gamma y_{t-1}$$

This equation is identical with (7.8) provided that we relate the parameters in the two equations thus:

$$(7.16) \qquad \begin{cases} \alpha = \delta \\ \beta(1 - \gamma) = \epsilon_0 \\ \gamma = \theta \end{cases}$$

7.8 If more than one variable's expectations enter the behavior equation, then (7.10) may be replaced by

$$(7.17) \qquad y_t = \alpha + \sum_{n=1}^{N} \beta_n x_{nt}^e$$

If expectations hypotheses like (7.11) apply to $x_{1t}^e \cdots x_{Nt}^e$, then it is possible to transform (7.17) to an equation analogous to (7.8) or (7.15), but the number of lags required is larger unless the same coefficient γ applies to all the variables $x_1 \cdots x_N$.[38]

7.9 An important feature of the expectations hypothesis (7.11) is that if it is applied directly to a variable x that has been increasing every period for a long time, then although x_t^e will increase through time, the formula will always dictate an expected decrease in x, that is, $x_t^e < x_t$, because x_t^e is a weighted average of current and past values of x whose weights add up to 1 (see 7.6 above). However, if the expectations hypothesis is applied to Δx (or to dx/dt) instead of to x itself, then when x has been increasing for a long time the hypothesis will dictate a further rise in x, at a rate which is an average of past rates of rise.[39]

7.10 Equation (7.15) above has been derived on the assumptions that the behavior variable y depends on expectations x^e about x, and that these expectations are formed on a distributed-lag basis according to the three equivalent equations (7.11) and (7.12) and (7.13). The same equation (7.15) can be obtained from quite a different model. Assume that there is an unobservable *desired* level of y, denoted by y^*, which depends on x thus:

$$(7.18) \qquad y_t^* = \alpha + \beta x_t$$

And assume that the adjustment of the actual level y_t toward the desired level y_t^* is not an instantaneous process, perhaps for the reasons suggested in 7.2. In particular, assume that during a given period t only a fraction $1 - \gamma$ of the difference between the desired level y_t^* and the initial level y_{t-1} is made up, thus:

$$(7.19) \qquad y_t - y_{t-1} = (1 - \gamma)(y_t^* - y_{t-1}) \qquad 0 \leqq \gamma < 1$$

If $\gamma = 0$, the adjustment would be completed in one period; and if $\gamma = 1$, y would never change at all. Now substitute (7.18) for y_t^* into (7.19), and the result is precisely equation (7.15) again. Therefore if equation (7.15) is found to work well, the question remains as to whether an expectations model such as (7.10)–(7.11) or an adjustment model such as (7.18)–(7.19) is operating. Similar remarks apply to more general distributed-lag equations.[40]

---

[38] See Nerlove [1958a], pp. 25–35.

[39] Cagan [1956] uses the hypothesis in this way to obtain expected rates of inflation.

[40] Observation of this duality is due, so far as I know, to Marc Nerlove. See Nerlove [1958a], pp. 14–46.

8   CROSS-SECTION MODELS

8.1 In this section we look briefly at some special features of dynamic exact *cross-section* models. The reader may wish to refer now to earlier remarks on cross-section models in III.9 and IV.5. The definitions of exogenous and predetermined variables in exact models, presented in I.5.5 and V.3.8 respectively, apply to mixed and pure cross-section models as well as to pure time-series models, but with some peculiar results, as we shall see.

8.2 There is an important difference between pure cross-section and pure time-series models, which has not been mentioned until now because its importance emerges most strikingly when lagged variables are introduced. In a pure *time-series* model, on the one hand, the observations are in a natural order, that is, chronological order. Consider a set of time-series data for a variable x_{it}, running from $t = 1$ to $t = T$, namely, $x_{i1}, \ldots, x_{iT}$. The lagged value $x_{i,t-1}$ of this variable is always a member of the same set of data, except only if $t = 1$, in which case the lagged value is x_{i0}, which is not in the set.

8.3 In a pure *cross-section* model, on the other hand, the observations typically have no natural order, though in certain cases we can imagine putting them in order of size, or social status, or distance from some focal point, or what not. Consider a set of cross-section data for the variable x_{it}, running from $i = 1$ to $i = M$, namely, $x_{1t}, \ldots, x_{Mt}$. What variable in this case is analogous to the lagged value $x_{i,t-1}$ in the time-series case? To answer it is first necessary to suppose that there is some meaningful way to arrange the cross-section observations in order. Suppose that social status is the criterion chosen, that it is impossible for two individuals to have the same social status, and that the observations are already in order from the lowest status ($i = 1$) to the highest ($i = M$). Then the variable $x_{i-1,t}$ in this case is directly analogous to the lagged value $x_{i,t-1}$ in the time-series case. $x_{i-1,t}$ stands for the observation corresponding to the individual whose social status is next below that of the individual represented by x_{it}. It represents a kind of "lagged" value, where the ordering in question is now not chronological but hierarchical (hence quotation marks are used). This "lagged" value $x_{i-1,t}$ is always a member of the same set of data as is $x_{it}, i = 1, \ldots, M$, except only if $i = 1$, in which case the "lagged" value is x_{0t}, which in not in the set. A model that involves "lags" of this sort is a "dynamic" model in a sense, and the mathematics describing it may be the same as that describing a dynamic time-series model of the type discussed in earlier sections of this chapter. However, in economics there is usually no meaningful way to

order the M cross-section observations; then the cross-section case has
no analogy to the lagged value in the time-series case.

8.4 What if the lagged value $x_{i,t-1}$ is introduced into a pure cross-
section model that contains x_{it} as a variable? Then it becomes a dynamic
model in the usual (temporal) sense. But notice now that the lagged
value $x_{i,t-1}$ is never a member of the set of data for the unlagged values
x_{it}, for $i = 1, \ldots, M$. Thus if we introduce the lagged value of x_i into a
pure cross-section model that contains x_i, it will be necessary to obtain
twice as many observations of x_i as before: Originally M observations of
x_i in period t were required, but now M observations in period $t - 1$ are
required as well. This is in contrast to the pure time-series case, where it
is necessary only to obtain one additional observation, x_{i0}, in order to
introduce the lagged value $x_{i,t-1}$ into a model containing x_{it} for $t = 1$
to $t = T$.

8.5 Let us now consider a dynamic version of the pure cross-section
model that is described verbally in III.9.5 and expressed symbolically by
equations (9.4)–(9.8) in III.9.6. Each variable now bears subscript t to
locate it in time. The only substantive alteration we make is to assume
now that c_{it}, the ith household's consumption at time t, depends on $y_{i,t-1}$,
its income in period $t - 1$. The variable k_{it} is now replaced by $k_{i,t-1}$.
Both have the same meaning—the ith household's net worth at the end
of period $t - 1$—and the symbol $k_{i,t-1}$ seems preferable only because it
reminds us that the net worth in question is determined by events in
period $t - 1$. Similarly, K_t' is replaced by K_{t-1} (which is defined as
$\sum_i k_{i,t-1}$) with no change of meaning. As before, it is assumed that
$\sum_i \epsilon_i = 0$. Otherwise the notation is the same as in III.9.5. The model is

(8.1) $c_{it} = \beta y_{i,t-1} + \gamma + \epsilon_i \qquad i = 1, \ldots, M$

(8.2) $y_{it} = k_{i,t-1} r_t + x_{it} \qquad i = 1, \ldots, M$

(8.3) $Y_t = C_t + Z_t$

(8.4) $C_t = \beta Y_{t-1} + M\gamma$

(8.5) $Y_t = K_{t-1} r_t + X_t$

This pure cross-section model has $2M + 3$ equations and $2M + 3$
endogenous variables: r_t, C_t, Y_t, c_{it}, and y_{it} $(i = 1, \ldots, M)$. The variables
Z_t, X_t, and x_{it} $(i = 1, \ldots, M)$ are assumed exogenous.

8.6 What of the variables $K_{t-1}, k_{i,t-1}$, and $y_{i,t-1}$ $(i = 1, \ldots, M)$?
Again $k_{i,t-1}$ is a result of saving behavior during period $t - 1$:

(8.6) $k_{i,t-1} = y_{i,t-1} - c_{i,t-1} + k_{i,t-2} \qquad i = 1, \ldots, M$

Thus we see that $k_{i,t-1}$ (and hence also K_{t-1}, which is their aggregate) are
predetermined variables at time t because they depend only on events in

the preceding period (recall the definition in 3.8 above). Similarly $y_{i,t-1}$ are predetermined at time t: They are determined by a set of equations like (8.1)–(8.5) but lagged one period, which describe period $t - 1$ and do not involve period t at all. This much about K_{t-1}, $k_{i,t-1}$, and $y_{i,t-1}$ is presumably obvious. But not only are they *predetermined* in this pure cross-section model; *they are exogenous.* The same properties that render them predetermined insure that they satisfy the definition of an exogenous variable given in I.5.5. Indeed, in exact *pure cross-section* models every temporally predetermined variable is exogenous! (As we shall see later, this remains true in *stochastic* pure cross-section models, but not in mixed or pure time-series models.)

8.7 The fact that $y_{i,t-1}$ is exogenous in the foregoing pure cross-section model means that equation (8.1) constitutes a complete model in itself, determining individual household consumption c_{it} $(i = 1, \ldots, M)$ as a function of exogenous factors and parameters and disturbances. This was not true of the exact *static* consumption equation (9.4) in III.9.6.

8.8 If data are available for several periods, for instance, for $t = 0, 1, \ldots, T$, then we can think of T distinct pure cross-section models, one for each period from 1 to T (data for period 0 are needed for the lagged values of period 1, and so on forward in time). And if each parameter has a constant value throughout all periods, we can think of a mixed time-series and cross-section model. Then (8.6) becomes part of the model, as does the following:

$$(8.7) \qquad K_t = \sum_i k_{it} \qquad t = 1, \ldots, T$$

In the mixed model consisting of equations (8.1)–(8.7) there are $(3M + 4)T$ equations and an equal number of endogenous variables. The variables Z_t, X_t, and x_{it} $(i = 1, \ldots, M)$ are exogenous, the variables r_t, C_t, Y_t, c_{it}, y_{it}, K_t, and k_{it} are endogenous, and the variables K_{t-1}, $k_{i,t-1}$, and $y_{i,t-1}$ are predetermined at time t, $i = 1, \ldots, M$ and $t = 1, \ldots, T$.

9 DYNAMIC SYSTEMS

9.1 We are now in a position to consider briefly the concept of *causation* in dynamic systems. The simplest concept of causation is one according to which one particular event (the "cause") is always accompanied or followed by another particular event (the "effect"); for example, if we flip the proper switch, the electric light goes on, and if we flip it back again, the light goes off. Or if we plant seeds in soil in the spring, flowers or vegetables or some other plants presently come up. Or if it rains heavily in the mountains, the streams and rivers of the foothills swell. This concept of causation can be rendered much more serviceable by admitting into the analysis the possibility of *several* causative events in the past rather than just one, and also the possibility that events of the more remote past may have observable effects. Thus the swelling of the rivers of Colorado or northern Italy follows several prior events: warm weather in the mountains, previous snow fall in the mountains, and, if we wish to go that far, even the existence of mountains (or at least high ground) to begin with. For events that *are* (or to be safer, events that behave as if they were) caused by particular other events, such a concept of causation is ideal. But there are certain types of events that are more fruitfully explained in other terms.

9.2 Consider the motion of a pendulum swinging freely. What is the cause of its change in direction? No outside influence is brought to bear on it just before it stops and begins to move the other way—all external conditions remain the same continuously. Although its motion *can* be explained in terms of changes in the effective force pulling it from side to side, ranging from zero at dead center to a maximum at the height of its swing, there is a more convenient explanation in terms of a dynamic system in which no external changes occur. The given factors in the system are the strength of the force of gravity, the length of the pendulum, the amount by which it was pulled aside from dead center initially, and the magnitude of frictional forces. The situation is the same in dynamic systems represented by difference or differential equations such as we have been discussing. The time path of a variable, whether it be displacement of a pendulum from dead center or of a price or national income from its equilibrium value, is determined by a complex of factors: (1) the model, (2) the parameters and exogenous variables—all of which we have assumed constant as the time path unfolds—and (3) the initial conditions.

9.3 In our work we try to use a concept of causation that combines the dynamic system and the idea of specific external causes. The reader will readily identify the latter with changes of exogenous variables and the changes (we hope less frequent) in structural parameters. With this kind of theoretical framework, providing for both the endogenous aspects and the autonomous aspects (whether fortuitous or deliberate), we hope to be able to understand a widening range of real economic phenomena.

9.4 We now set forth the general form of exact dynamic models, reduced forms, and final equations, respectively. The model is a system of G equations in G endogenous variables $y_1, \ldots, y_G$, with lags from $t - 1$ to $t - \tau$ (τ is then called the *order* of the system), and K exogenous variables $z_1, \ldots, z_K$. It does not matter whether any of the exogenous variables are lagged or not, for they are predetermined in any case, along with the lagged y's; each lagged exogenous variable is represented separately among the z's.[41] The α's are parameters. The model is then

$$(9.1) \quad f_1[y_1, \ldots, y_G; (y_1)_{-1}, \ldots, (y_G)_{-1}; \ldots; (y_1)_{-\tau}, \ldots, (y_G)_{-\tau};$$
$$z_1, \ldots, z_K; \alpha_{i1}, \ldots, \alpha_{iL}] = 0 \qquad i = 1, \ldots, G$$

To be realistic, this system of G equations in G current endogenous variables $y_1, \ldots, y_G$ should have a unique reduced form, that is, a unique solution in terms of the predetermined variables $(y_1)_{-1}, \ldots, (y_G)_{-\tau}$ and $z_1, \ldots, z_K$ and the parameters. Failing a unique reduced form, the reduced form should contain only a few solutions, and it should be possible to tell which one is the relevant one. (See III.6.14–16 for a brief discussion of multiple solutions.) If this is so, then if enough initial conditions are given (i.e., values of each of the y's for τ periods) and if values of the exogenous variables and parameters are given, the system (9.1) will generate values of the y's for all succeeding periods into the indefinite future. The reduced form describing this can be written as

$$(9.2) \quad y_i = g_i[(y_1)_{-1}, \ldots, (y_G)_{-1}; \ldots; (y_1)_{-\tau}, \ldots, (y_G)_{-\tau};$$
$$z_1, \ldots, z_K; \pi_{i1}, \ldots, \pi_{iM}] = 0 \qquad i = 1, \ldots, G$$

where $\pi_{i1}, \ldots, \pi_{iM}$ are reduced-form parameters depending on the α's. The final equation system can be written as

$$(9.3) \quad y_i = h_i[(y_i)_{-1}, \ldots, (y_i)_{-\omega}; z_1, \ldots, z_K; \lambda_{i1}, \ldots, \lambda_{iN}] = 0$$
$$i = 1, \ldots, G$$

where $\lambda_{i1}, \ldots, \lambda_{iN}$ are parameters depending on the π's, and ω is the maximum order of the final equations.[42] In general ω is greater than the order of any of the structural equations or reduced-form equations and may be as great as G times τ.

9.5 In Chapter III we discussed comparative statics, by which is meant the analysis of the differences in the static equilibrium positions of a model under different alternative sets of values of parameters and exogenous variables. In so doing we obtained the derivatives of the equilibrium values of endogenous variables with respect to parameters or exogenous variables; the investment multiplier, $\partial y / \partial i$, is a case in point. However, comparative-static multipliers of this sort are not very useful in practice unless the transition to the new equilibrium is very rapid indeed, requiring at most a year or two, because the exogenous

---

[41] Thus, for example, if government expenditure g were exogenous and g and g_{-1} were both in a model, then g and g_{-1} would be separate exogenous variables, and we can rename them as $z_1 = g$ and $z_2 = g_{-1}$.

[42] See for example Samuelson [1947], Appendix B.

variables of a real economy are typically not held constant for more than a year or two at a time, so that any new equilibrium that takes very long to reach will not be reached. The usefulness of a dynamic theory lies in the fact that it can tell (if it is correct) how long it will be before a new equilibrium position is substantially attained,[43] and also, which is really most important, what position the economy will have reached after one year and after two years. When a policy is being considered, it is very important to know what effects it will have in its first year or two, but less important to know what its effects in later years will be, because in later years other exogenous forces will intervene so that new policies will be required then in any case. Effects of exogenous changes, after one and two years, might be called one- and two-year impact multipliers. It is these that are of practical importance, rather than comparative-static multipliers. Goldberger [1959] presents such impact multipliers.

QUESTIONS AND PROBLEMS

1.1. Can you think of a situation in which the observations in a cross-section sample can be arranged in a natural order so that effects are propagated from one observed point to the next according to a difference equation based on this natural order (rather than on time)?

2.1. What kinds of behavior of x as a function of time are possible with each of the following trend functions?

(a) $(x - \alpha)(t - \beta) = \gamma$.

(b) $x = \alpha + \beta \log \log t$.

2.2. Discuss the contention that the use of a time trend in an economic equation amounts to a confession of ignorance concerning the phenomenon being studied and should be avoided whenever possible.

2.3. Show that if output x depends on capital k and labor l and time t according to the equation $x = f(k, l, t)$, the rate of growth of output is equal to

$$\eta_k \rho_k + \eta_l \rho_l + \rho_t$$

where η_k and η_l are elasticities of output with respect to k and l, respectively, and ρ_k and ρ_l are rates of growth of k and l, respectively, and ρ_t is $\partial f/x \, \partial t$.

3.1. Express $c_t = \alpha y_t + \beta y_{t-1} + \gamma y_{t-2} + \delta$ as a difference equation (i.e., using Δy_t, $\Delta^2 y_t$, etc.).

3.2. Verify that equation (3.13) is one of the final equations of the system (3.9)–(3.10).

3.3. In equations (3.9)–(3.10), if $y_0 = \$200$ billion per year, if $\alpha = 0.5$ and $\beta = \$120$ billion per year, and if $i = \$30$ billion per year for years 1, 2, 3, and

---

[43] It is necessary to say what is meant by "substantially attained." Presumably we would mean that the actual value of the variable has become and will stay within some small distance away from the equilibrium value, say 1 or 10 per cent of the latter.

4 and $i = \$40$ billion per year for years 5 and later, compute and plot against time the values of consumption c and income y for years 1 through 8. Comment on the graphs in connection with the final equations (3.13)–(3.14).

3.4. Show that if $f(t)$ and $g(t)$ are solutions of a difference equation, then $\alpha f(t) + \beta g(t)$ are also solutions where α and β are any arbitrary constants.

3.5. Verify that (3.25) is a solution of (3.24).

3.6. Verify that (3.36) is a solution of (3.13).

3.7. Suppose that the consumption equation is $c_t = \alpha y_t + \beta c_{t-1} + \gamma$, and that $y_t = c_t + i_t$, where $c = $ consumption, $y = $ income, and $i = $ exogenous investment. Find the reduced form. Find the final equations for c and y and their solutions.

4.1. Suppose quarterly data on GNP are available as seasonally adjusted annual rates, in billions of dollars per year, as follows:

1961(I)	1961(II)	1961(III)	1961(IV)	1962(I)
501	513	522	539	545

What are the numerical magnitude *and the units of measurement* of the following:

(a, b) The change, and the rate of change, in GNP from 1961(I) to 1961(II).

(c, d) The change, and the rate of change, in GNP from 1961(I) to 1962(I).

Note: "Change" refers to quantities like Δy, and "rate of change" to quantities like $\Delta y / \Delta t$.

4.2. Derive the final equations for y, c, and i in the model given by equations (4.12)–(4.14).

4.3. Suppose that $c = \alpha + \beta y_{-1}$, and $i = \gamma + \delta \Delta y$, and $y = c + i$. Obtain the reduced form. Obtain the final equation for y, its solution, and its stability condition.

4.4. Can you devise a plausible dynamic version of the static equations (4.1)–(4.3) so that a stability condition *different* from $\alpha + \gamma < 1$ is obtained? (See 4.11.)

4.5. Suppose that $c = \alpha y_{-1}$, $i = \beta \Delta c$, and $y = c + i + g$. Obtain the reduced-form equations for c, i, and y. Obtain the final equation for income. Can you solve it and find its stability condition? (This problem goes beyond the material presented here. You may wish to consult Baumol [1951, 1959], Goldberg [1958], or Allen [1956].)

5.1. Derive the Marshallian stability condition discussed in 5.5.

5.2. Which do you prefer, the Walrasian stability condition shown in Figure 5.1 or the Marshallian shown in Figure 5.2? Why?

6.1. Derive the Marshallian stability condition for the differential-equation adjustment process discussed in 6.7.

6.2. What are the relative merits of difference versus differential equations in economic theory? In empirical economics?

7.1. What if the sum of coefficients, $\sum_0^\infty \epsilon_i$, in (7.2) is infinite?

7.2. Derive equation (7.9). What if $\tau < \infty$ in equation (7.2)?

7.3. Can $\epsilon_0, \epsilon_1, \ldots, \epsilon_k$, δ, and θ be obtained from the parameters of (7.9)? Explain.

7.4. Suppose that (7.11) is replaced by the equation

$$x_t^e = \gamma x_{t-1}^e + (1 - \gamma)x_{t-1}.$$

What modification must be made in (7.15)?

7.5. Suppose that a decision variable y depends on expectations of *two* variables, $y_t = \alpha + \beta x_t^e + \gamma z_t^e$. And suppose that these expectations are formed as follows:

$$x_t^e = \delta x_{t-1}^e + (1 - \delta)x_t$$
$$z_t^e = \epsilon z_{t-1}^e + (1 - \epsilon)z_t$$

Express y_t in terms of a finite number of parameters and a finite number of observed values of x and z and y.

7.6. Suppose that the desired level of y depends linearly upon expectations about the future value of x. Suppose also that the expectations about x are as in equation (7.11), and the adjustment of the actual level of y to the desired level proceeds according to (7.19) but with a speed-of-adjustment coefficient different from γ. Express y_t as a function of a finite number of parameters and a finite number of observed values of x and y. Comment on the empirical usefulness of the result.

8.1. Suppose that a variable z_i in a pure exact cross-section model were spatially predetermined at location i. Would it also be exogenous?

9.1. Evaluate the one-year and two-year dynamic multiplier effects of a change in exogenous expenditure in the following models, and compare the results:

(a) Equations (3.2) and (3.4) discussed in 3.4–29.

(b) Equations (4.4) and (4.5) discussed in 4.3.

(c) Equations (4.4)–(4.5) and (4.8) discussed in 4.4.

(d) Equations (4.12)–(4.14) discussed in 4.5–7.

(e) Equations (4.18)–(4.20) discussed in 4.8.

CHAPTER VI

Dynamic Stochastic Theory

This chapter discusses models that are at once dynamic and stochastic. The effect of stochastic disturbances on forecasting in the distant future is shown. Moments are introduced. The definition of a predetermined variable is modified to apply to stochastic equations, and the assumption of serial independence among disturbances is introduced. Cross-section models are discussed briefly.

1 INTRODUCTION

We now take up briefly the theory of dynamic economic systems in the stochastic case, mainly by bringing together things we have seen in the preceding three chapters. In particular we shall examine the implications of introducing random disturbances into the dynamic analysis presented in Chapter V.[1]

2 DYNAMIC MODELS AND RANDOM VARIABLES; FORECASTING

2.1 The essential character of random variables has been set forth in Chapter IV, and several static stochastic models were exhibited. These models were seen to be obtainable from corresponding static exact models by the introduction of random disturbances in any one of several forms.

---

[1] For a good brief introductory discussion of this subject, see Marschak [1953], pp. 17–24.

We concentrated on additive disturbances, which can be viewed as shifts in the intercepts or constant terms of the (otherwise exact) equations. We shall do the same for dynamic models in this section. That is, we shall begin with dynamic exact models such as those in Chapter V, incorporating into them additive random disturbances and then examining the dynamic solutions obtained by so doing.

2.2 In the dynamic case, just as in the static case, predictions based on reduced-form equations (or final equations) will not be exact even if the underlying structural equations are correct, because of the presence of the random disturbances. Thus, in the following dynamic stochastic model

$$(2.1) \qquad\qquad c_t = \alpha y_t + \beta + u_t$$

$$(2.2) \qquad\qquad \Delta y_t = \theta(c_{t-1} + i_{t-1} - y_{t-1})$$

the final equation for income y_t is

$$(2.3) \qquad y_t = [1 - \theta(1 - \alpha)]y_{t-1} + \theta i_{t-1} + \theta\beta + \theta u_{t-1}$$

Here the endogenous variables are c and y as before; the exogenous variable is i (assumed held constant from year to year); and the random disturbance is u. The parameters are α, β, and θ. It will be seen at once that (2.3) does not determine income in period t *exactly*, when the parameters, investment i, and the income of the preceding year y_{t-1} are known, for there is a random term θu_{t-1}. Apart from this term, the equation describes the value of income exactly. The disturbance u_t is taken to be a random variable with a probability distribution, so that there is a specified probability that u_t will fall in any interval we may care to choose. It is usually assumed that the *mean* of the distribution of u_t is zero (this can be arranged conceptually by altering the value of the constant β until the shifts in the consumption function do have a true mean value of zero). Later in this chapter we shall discuss whether u_{t-1} is independent of the explanatory variables.

2.3 Suppose for example that θ is equal to 0.6, meaning that 60 per cent of any year's excess supply or demand is made up by adjustment in supply in the following year; that α, the marginal propensity to consume, is 0.75; that β is equal to $30 billion per year; and that i is constant and equal to $20 billion per year. Then the final equation becomes

$$(2.4) \qquad\qquad y_t = 0.85y_{t-1} + 30 + 0.6u_{t-1}$$

Now assume that the probability distribution of u_t is the same every year, as follows:

u_t	-2	-1	0	1	2
probability	$\frac{1}{4}$	$\frac{1}{4}$	0	$\frac{1}{4}$	$\frac{1}{4}$

Then the national income in year t will be given by the systematic part of (2.4) *plus* a random component that is either plus or minus $1.2 billion or plus or minus 0.6 billion dollars, each value occurring in about

25 per cent of the cases (years). Of course if we were able to devise a model that could predict annual national income with an error never greater than \$1.2 billion, we would be doing well indeed; the above model is merely illustrative.

2.4 The dynamic solution of (2.4), ignoring the random element for a moment, will give the value of y_t as a function of t and one arbitrary constant [because (2.4) is a first-order difference equation]. This constant depends on the initial conditions; that is, the time path of y_t from a given point of time onward depends on the situation at that point of time. If we call this arbitrary constant A, the solution for the systematic part of y is

$$(2.5) \qquad\qquad y_t = A(0.85)^t + 200$$

That this is indeed the solution can be seen by substituting the values of y_t and y_{t-1} obtained from it into (2.4) (still ignoring the random element) and seeing that (2.4) is satisfied for any value of A whatever.

2.5 The solution (2.5) shows that the systematic part of y_t converges to the equilibrium income \$200 billion as time passes, with the term $A(0.85)^t$ producing a smooth approach to equilibrium as it goes to zero as t increases indefinitely. Suppose we assume a set of initial conditions, for example, that income in an initial period is $y_0 =$ \$100 billion and continue to ignore the random part. Then from (2.1) c_0 must be $0.75 \times \$100 + \$30$ or \$105 billion. From (2.2) y_1 must be \$100 + $0.6(\$105 + \$20 - \$100) = \$115$ billion. Then by substituting this value of y_1 into (2.5) we find the value of A corresponding to the given initial conditions,

$$(2.6) \qquad\qquad A = -100$$

Then the sequence of values of the systematic part of y_t, from (2.5), is

$$
\begin{aligned}
y_0 &= 100 \\
y_1 &= 115 \\
y_2 &= 127.75 \\
y_3 &\cong 138.59 \\
y_4 &\cong 147.80 \\
y_5 &\cong 155.63
\end{aligned}
$$

(2.7)

$$\cdot$$
$$\cdot$$
$$\cdot$$

$$y_{10} \cong 180.31$$

$$\cdot$$
$$\cdot$$
$$\cdot$$

$$y_\infty = 200$$

The rate of convergence depends on the parameters α and θ, as shown in (2.3).

2.6 Now we consider the effect of the random disturbance u_{t-1}, which affects c_{t-1} and hence affects y_t in (2.5). We shall see that it results in an error of prediction that is equal to θ times the disturbance if the prediction is for a period immediately following the sample period, and larger errors for longer-range predictions. Suppose again that income in the initial period is $y_0 = 100$. What will be the value of income in period 1? By the very nature of the stochastic model we are using, it cannot be predicted exactly, even if we assume (as we now do) that predetermined variables at time 0 and all parameters and exogenous variables at all times are exactly known. This is clear from (2.4), according to which (if $y_0 = 100$)

$$(2.8) \qquad\qquad y_1 = 0.85y_0 + 30 + 0.6u_0$$
$$= 115 + 0.6u_0$$

The systematic part of y_1 is thus predictable as in (2.7), but all that can be said in advance about the random part is that it has a 25 per cent chance of being either -1.2 or -0.6 or 0.6 or 1.2 billion dollars. Hence, according to this model, y_1 will be 113.8, 114.4, 115.6, or 116.2 billion dollars, with an equal chance of each. After y_1 is observed, the approximate value of y_2 can be obtained from (2.4) by substituting into it for y_1 whichever one of the four values occurs, but again there will be uncertainty in y_2, even if y_1 is known from observation, because of the disturbance term $0.6u_1$. If we try to predict y_2, knowing y_0 but not y_1, we run into a twofold uncertainty because both of the random disturbances u_0 and u_1 affect y_2. Similarly, all three disturbances u_0, u_1, u_2 affect y_3 if we start from y_0, and in general all the t disturbances u_0, u_1, u_2, ..., u_{t-1} affect y_t. In fact, if y_0 is known but subsequent values of y are unknown, then the value of y_t in the dynamic stochastic case is equal to the value of y_t generated by the corresponding dynamic exact equation, *plus* a random term involving all the intervening disturbances.

2.7 This can be illustrated by referring again to (2.3). For convenience we rechristen some of the coefficients and variables, giving them shorter names, thus:

$$\lambda = 1 - \theta(1 - \alpha)$$
$$(2.9) \qquad\qquad \mu = \theta i_{t-1} + \theta\beta$$
$$v_t = \theta u_{t-1}$$

Then (2.3) becomes

$$(2.10) \qquad\qquad y_t = \lambda y_{t-1} + \mu + v_t$$

If y_0 is given by initial conditions, we have for y_1

(2.11) $$y_1 = \lambda y_0 + \mu + v_1$$

which depends on v_1 and hence on u_0. For y_2,

(2.12) $$y_2 = \lambda y_1 + \mu + v_2$$
$$= \lambda^2 y_0 + (\lambda + 1)\mu + \lambda v_1 + v_2$$

which depends on v_1 and v_2, and hence on u_0 and u_1. For y_3,

(2.13) $$y_3 = \lambda y_2 + \mu + v_3$$
$$= \lambda^3 y_0 + (\lambda^2 + \lambda + 1)\mu + \lambda^2 v_1 + \lambda v_2 + v_3$$

which depends on v_1, v_2, and v_3, and hence on u_0, u_1, and u_2; and so on. In general,

(2.14) $$y_t = \lambda^t y_0 + \mu \sum_{i=0}^{t-1} \lambda^i + \sum_{j=1}^{t} \lambda^{t-j} v_j$$

2.8   Each of the above expressions for $y_1, y_2, \ldots, y_t$ has a systematic part identical to the value of y_t in the corresponding period in the exact case, as can be seen by setting disturbances equal to zero in (2.10)–(2.14), thus reducing the stochastic case immediately to the exact case. The stochastic part of y_t is seen to depend on all values of v from period 1 through period t; it is equal to v_t plus a linear combination of previous disturbances from periods 1 through $t - 1$. Now if the disturbances u_t are serially independent, then so are v_t. Then the variance of the stochastic part of y_t, given y_0, increases as t increases.[2] This means that the uncertainty in forecasting y_t increases with increases in the length of the horizon over which the forecast is to be made. This variance may or may not remain finite as t approaches infinity, depending on the structure involved.[3] Similar conclusions hold for the stochastic version of any dynamic model. The endogenous variables are no longer exactly predictable even if all parameters and exogenous variables and initial conditions are exactly known, and the uncertainty becomes greater as interest is shifted to periods further removed from the initial period.

2.9   The general linear dynamic stochastic equation system with additive disturbances is

(2.15) $$\sum_{i=1}^{G} \beta_{gi0} y_{it} + \sum_{\tau=1}^{T'} \left(\sum_{i=1}^{G} \beta_{gi\tau} y_{i,t-\tau} \right) + \sum_{k=1}^{K'} \epsilon_{gk} x_{kt} = u_{gt} \qquad g = 1, \ldots, G$$

where the β_{gi0} and $\beta_{gi\tau}$ and ϵ_{gk} are parameters; the y_{it} are current endogenous variables at time t; the $y_{i,t-\tau}$ are lagged endogenous variables at

---

[2] Recall the theorems about the variance of a sum in IV.2.25.

[3] See for example Stone [1949]. In our case the variance remains finite if var v_t is bounded and $|\lambda| < 1$. The latter condition, assuming $\theta > 0$, implies $1 - 2/\theta < \alpha < 1$.

time t with lags of τ periods ($\tau = 1, \ldots, T'$, T' being the longest lag in the model); the x_{kt} are exogenous variables at time t; and the u_{gt} are disturbances at time t: Equations (2.15) are only a part of the structure; the remainder is specified by the joint probability distribution of the disturbances $u_{1t}, \ldots, u_{Gt}$, often assumed to be normal and the same for all t and independent of disturbances in the preceding periods. Equations (2.15) can be written in a slightly simpler fashion if the symbols z_{kt} are used to denote all the variables that are either exogenous (x_{kt}) or lagged endogenous ($y_{i,t-\tau}$), and the symbols γ_{gk} are used to stand for the parameters of such z's, and β_{gi} is used instead of β_{gi0}.

$$(2.16) \qquad \sum_{i=1}^{G} \beta_{gi} y_{it} + \sum_{k=1}^{K} \gamma_{gk} z_{kt} = u_{gt} \qquad g = 1, \ldots, G$$

2.10   The reduced form of (2.16) is

$$(2.17) \qquad y_{it} = \sum_{k=1}^{K} \pi_{ik} z_{kt} + v_{it} \qquad i = 1, \ldots, G$$

where $v_{1t}, \ldots, v_{Gt}$ are jointly normally distributed if the u's are. It should be remembered that lagged values of the y's are included among the z's. From the reduced form, the final equations may be obtained, as in V.3.10, thus:

$$(2.18) \qquad y_{it} = \sum_{\tau=1}^{T_i'} \theta_{i\tau} y_{i,t-\tau} + \sum_{k=1}^{K'} \eta_{ik} x_{kt} + w_{it} \qquad i = 1, \ldots, G$$

where $\theta_{i\tau}$ and η_{ik} are parameters, w_{it} are again disturbances (jointly normally distributed if the u's are), and x_{kt} are exogenous. Each of the final equations (2.18) is a linear stochastic difference equation in one variable, similar to (2.3) above, and predictions made from it are subject to the same kind of uncertainty as described in 2.6–8. These dynamic forms (2.15)–(2.18) may be compared with the static stochastic forms (4.8)–(4.11) in IV.4.6.

3 MOMENTS AND SOME NOTATION

3.1   Before going further we pause in this section to introduce some more notation and an important concept, which will be used extensively in the remainder of the book. A standard notation, which is adopted here, for the mean of a set of observations of a variable is the name of the variable with a bar above it. Thus the mean of $y_1, \ldots, y_T$ is denoted by $\bar{y}$, thus:

$$(3.1) \qquad \bar{y} = \frac{1}{T} \sum_{t=1}^{T} y_t$$

It is often useful to consider the deviation of a particular observed value from this observed mean, such as $y_t - \bar{y}$. One of the main reasons for doing this is to obtain a variable whose own observed mean is zero, since many algebraic and arithmetic operations are simpler if the variables have this property. That the deviation of y_t from its mean does indeed have this property is easily seen:

$$(3.2) \qquad \frac{1}{T}\sum_{t=1}^{T}(y_t - \bar{y}) = \frac{1}{T}\sum_{t=1}^{T}y_t - \frac{1}{T}\sum_{t=1}^{T}\bar{y} = \bar{y} - \bar{y} = 0$$

It is convenient to have a briefer notation for this deviation. We shall denote it by sans-serif roman type, thus:

$$(3.3) \qquad \mathsf{y}_t = y_t - \bar{y}$$

Any sans-serif roman-type variable in the remainder of the book will refer to the deviation of the corresponding italicized variable from its observed mean in a set of observations. How will the reader know what set of observations is being used to obtain the mean? He will have to find it from the context.

3.2   Consider what happens when a simple linear bivariate stochastic equation is rewritten in terms of deviations of each variable from its observed mean. Such an equation is the following, identical with (2.1) above:

$$(3.4) \qquad c_t = \alpha y_t + \beta + u_t$$

We proceed as follows. First, write down this equation once for each observed pair of values $(c_1, y_1), (c_2, y_2), \ldots, (c_T, y_T)$, sum these T equations and divide the sum by T. The result is

$$(3.5) \qquad \frac{1}{T}\sum c_t = \alpha \frac{1}{T}\sum y_t + \beta + \frac{1}{T}\sum u_t$$

Using the notation of (3.1) for the mean of a set of values, we can write this as

$$(3.6) \qquad \bar{c} = \alpha\bar{y} + \beta + \bar{u}$$

Note that while $\bar{c}$ and $\bar{y}$ are observable because the c's and y's are observable, $\bar{u}$ is not observable because the u's are not. Next, subtract (3.6) from (3.4). The result is

$$(3.7) \qquad c_t - \bar{c} = \alpha(y_t - \bar{y}) + u_t - \bar{u}$$

Using the notation of (3.3) for the deviation of a variable from its mean, this can be rewritten as

$$(3.8) \qquad \mathsf{c}_t = \alpha\mathsf{y}_t + \mathsf{u}_t$$

This process has resulted in an equation all of whose variables have zero means over the set of values from 1 to T, and also one of the parameters (β) has been eliminated. These simplifications are often important, and we shall make frequent use of them in the pages ahead. When reading material that involves equations like the foregoing, be aware whether each of the variables involved is or is not measured as a deviation from the mean, because the properties of variables and the equations in which they appear depend on this.

3.3 It will often be necessary to deal with the sum of the squares of the deviations of a set of observations of a variable from their mean, or the sum of cross products of deviations of two variables from their means (see the next two equations below). Such an expression is known as a *moment*, or more precisely, as a *second* moment (because each term in the sum is of the second degree) about the *mean* (because deviations from the mean are used).[4] It is often denoted by the lower-case letter m with two subscripts that indicate what variables are involved. The two variables c and y give rise to four such moments, of which two necessarily have identical values. Two of the four are

$$(3.9) \qquad m_{yy} = \sum_{t=1}^{T} (y_t - \bar{y})^2 = \sum_{t=1}^{T} \mathsf{y}_t^2$$

$$(3.10) \qquad m_{cy} = \sum_{t=1}^{T} (c_t - \bar{c})(y_t - \bar{y}) = \sum_{t=1}^{T} \mathsf{c}_t \mathsf{y}_t$$

The other two are m_{cc} and m_{yc}, defined in an analogous manner. Since the order in which two numbers are multiplied does not affect the result, m_{cy} and m_{yc} are necessarily equal. If we also consider the variable u, several other moments can be formed: m_{uu}; m_{uc} and m_{cu}, which are equal; and m_{uy} and m_{yu}, which are equal.

3.4 These moments are not parameters; they are calculated directly from a limited number of observed values of variables. Their *expected* values, if such exist (i.e., if they are finite), can be thought of as parameters, related to the variance and covariance defined in IV.2.22 and IV.3.5. When we use these expected values, we shall denote them by the letter μ with two subscripts, thus:

$$(3.11) \qquad \mu_{yy} = Em_{yy} = E \sum_{t=1}^{T} (y_t - \bar{y})^2$$

$$(3.12) \qquad \mu_{cy} = Em_{cy} = E \sum_{t=1}^{T} (c_t - \bar{c})(y_t - \bar{y})$$

3.5 When we want to compute moments from a set of observations, we can of course do it by performing the operations indicated by (3.9) and (3.10), that is, by computing the mean of each variable, then the

[4] Sometimes one uses moments of first, third, fourth, . . . , degrees, and moments about *zero*. For example, the third moment of c about zero would be Σc_t^3.

deviation of each observation from the corresponding mean, then each square and cross product, and then their sums. But that is a laborious way. There is a short cut, which can be found in the following way. Consider m_{cy} (the same procedure will work for m_{yy}).

$$(3.13) \quad m_{cy} = \sum (c_t - \bar{c})(y_t - \bar{y})$$

$$= \sum (c_t y_t - c_t \bar{y} - \bar{c} y_t + \bar{c}\bar{y})$$

$$= \sum c_t y_t - \bar{y} \sum c_t - \bar{c} \sum y_t + T\bar{c}\bar{y}$$

$$= \sum c_t y_t - \frac{1}{T}(\sum y_t)(\sum c_t) - \frac{1}{T}(\sum c_t)(\sum y_t) + \frac{1}{T}(\sum c_t)(\sum y_t)$$

$$= \sum c_t y_t - \frac{1}{T}(\sum c_t)(\sum y_t)$$

Similarly, we can show that

$$(3.14) \qquad\qquad m_{yy} = \sum y_t^2 - \frac{1}{T}(\sum y_t)^2$$

In other words, we can compute the sum of squares (or cross products) of the observations themselves, and subtract from this sum $1/T$ times the square (or cross product) of the sum(s) of the observations, without computing deviations from the mean at all. The results of the two methods must be the same, but the computations via (3.13) and (3.14) are much more economical than via the definitions (3.9) and (3.10).

   3.6   In computing m_{cy}, or any other such moment, it is preferable to compute T times the sum of squares (or cross products), subtract the square (or cross product) of sums, and then divide the result by T, as follows:

$$(3.15) \qquad\qquad m_{cy} = \frac{1}{T}[T \sum c_t y_t - (\sum c_t)(\sum y_t)]$$

The reason for this has to do with rounding errors. Whenever T is a number such that $1/T$ is an endlessly repeating decimal (such as $1/7$ which is $0.142857142857142857\ldots$), then division by T gives a result that must be rounded off, with a slight error resulting. Ordinarily this is not serious, for the percentage error made by rounding is small. But when we use a short-cut formula such as (3.13) or (3.14) or (3.15) for computing a moment, we typically find that the two numbers whose difference must be taken [e.g., $\sum cy$ and $(\sum c)(\sum y)/T$ in (3.13)] are both very large and are almost the same, differing only after the first 3 or 4 or more digits (such as 1,855,271 and 1,853,130, with a difference of 2,141). Therefore a very small percentage error in $(\sum c)(\sum y)/T$, resulting from division by T and rounding off, might produce a relatively large error in m_{cy}. To avoid this, we use (3.15) instead, which typically postpones the rounding-off until after the subtraction because the typical calculating machine carries enough digits to make rounding unnecessary in the multiplication of $\sum c$ by $\sum y$, and of T by $\sum cy$.

3.7 Some writers define moments as $1/T$ times the expressions in (3.9) and (3.10). The advantage of this definition is that the moments are then the variances and covariances of the set of observations for $t = 1, \ldots, T$. Also then the expected values of the moments become the variances and covariances of the probability distributions of the variables, as can be seen from (3.11) and (3.12). But for algebraic manipulations it is a mild nuisance to carry the factor $1/T$ through all the steps. Hence we adopt (3.9) and (3.10) as definitions of moments. Some writers define moments as T times the definitions we adopt, to gain the computational advantage discussed in the foregoing paragraph. As that paragraph shows, however, that advantage can be gained without altering the definition of moments. When reading, notice what definition is used, because certain important formulae change if the definition is changed.

3.8 Notice that, as a consequence of (*a*) the fact that $\bar{y} = 0$ for any variable y and (*b*) the definition of moments about the mean, the moment about the mean of any two variables (such as c and y) is equal to the moment of their deviations c and y from their sample means, and is also equal to the moment of c with y and to the moment of c with y:

$$(3.16) \qquad m_{cy} = m_{cy} = m_{cy} = m_{cy}$$

This means that in a moment formula about the mean we can always replace a variable by its deviation from its sample mean or vice versa.

4 PREDETERMINED VARIABLES IN DYNAMIC STOCHASTIC MODELS

4.1 The definition of exogenous variables given in I.5.5 had to be modified in IV.4.9 when stochastic models were introduced. Predetermined variables were defined for the dynamic *exact* case, in V.3.8, as variables whose values are already determined as of a given time period; they include exogenous and lagged endogenous variables. Now, to deal with dynamic *stochastic* models, we must modify this earlier definition of predetermined variables.

4.2 Recall that the essential feature of an exogenous variable in either the exact or the stochastic case is that its value can be regarded as fixed and given when we study how the values of endogenous variables are determined. The modification of the definition of exogenousness was not intended to change this feature, but rather to fit it to the stochastic case.

The introduction of the concept of predetermined variables was in the same spirit. And our reformulation of this latter concept, to be given now, has the same motivation.

4.3 Recall that in stochastic models a variable is defined as exogenous if its value in a given period is statistically independent of the values of all the disturbances in the model for all periods (IV.4.9). An analogous condition is needed to adapt the definition of predetermined variables to stochastic models. It is clearly impossible to require that a predetermined variable z_t be independent of all disturbances in *all* time periods, future, current, *and past*. This is because we may want a lagged endogenous variable, such as y_{t-k} with $k > 0$, to be a predetermined variable at time t, and it is clearly not independent of u_{t-k} because the model determines y_{t-k} as a function of u_{t-k}. However, it *is* possible to require that a predetermined variable z_t be independent of disturbances in the *current and future* time periods or, what is the same thing, that all *current and past* values of a predetermined variable be independent of *current* values of the disturbances. Hence the revised definition is this: *A variable z_t is predetermined at time t if it is statistically independent of all current and future disturbances in the model, u_t, u_{t+1}, u_{t+2}, ...* An equivalent requirement of course is that all current and past values of z, namely, $z_t, z_{t-1}, z_{t-2}, \ldots$, be independent of u_t. *This is the definition of predetermined variables that will be used in the rest of this book.* It follows Koopmans and Hood [1953], pp. 117–125. Just as with exogenous variables in the stochastic case, the assumption of *independence* is a little stronger than is required for satisfactory estimation of parameters; but noncorrelation is not strong enough. Independence is made the basis of the definition because it is not much too strong and it is so convenient to deal with mathematically. (See IV.4.10 above and Chapter IX.) A variable that is not predetermined at time t is *jointly dependent* at time t.

4.4 A variable can satisfy this definition of a predetermined variable in either of two ways. First, it can be exogenous; then by the definition of exogenous it is independent of *all* values, past, present, and future, of the disturbances in the model. Second, it can be a lagged endogenous variable *in a model where for every period t each disturbance u_t is statistically independent of all its past values u_{t-1}, u_{t-2}, etc.*[5] If the disturbance u_t is not independent of all its past values, then a lagged endogenous variable such as y_{t-1} need not be independent of the current disturbance u_t, and hence y_{t-1} may fail to satisfy the definition of a predetermined variable.[6] This

---

[5] Note that if u_t is independent of u_{t-1}, for all t, then by symmetry of notation it must be independent of u_{t+1}, as well. Hence it is no more restrictive to say each u_t is independent of all its past and future values than to say that for all t it is independent of all its past values.

[6] See 4.10 below for elaboration.

is important. It is one of the main reasons for assuming that each disturbance in a dynamic model is independent of all its own past values.[7]

4.5 It is important to note that we need *not* assume independence among the values of any observable variable of the model at different times. It is an almost unbroken rule that economic variables themselves are statistically serially correlated or dependent through time, and it would be intolerable to build models in which this was assumed not to be true. That is not the issue here; the issue is whether the values of the *disturbance* to each equation can be assumed to be independent of each other over time. If the disturbance in an equation represents economic variables that have erroneously been left out in writing down the equation, then it is likely that the values of that disturbance will be dependent through time. If the disturbance represents really random shocks, then there is some hope that its values may be independent over time. It is possible to test for such independence; see Chapter X.

4.6 It is also important to note that we often need *not* assume that at any one time t the disturbances in different equations of the model are independent of each other. That is, if a model contains G equations with disturbances at time t denoted by $u_{1t}, u_{2t}, \ldots, u_{Gt}$, we typically do *not* assume that these disturbances at time t are independent of each other. The assumption we do make, to insure that lagged endogenous variables in the model will be predetermined, is that the whole group of disturbances at time t ($u_{1t}, \ldots, u_{Gt}$) is independent of the whole group of disturbances at any other time $t - k$, where $k \neq 0$ ($u_{1,t-k}, \ldots, u_{G,t-k}$).

4.7 Let us illustrate. Consider a simple dynamic model, with a random disturbance u_t, as follows:

(4.1) $$c_t = \alpha y_t + \beta y_{t-1} + \gamma + u_t$$

(4.2) $$y_t = c_t + i_t$$

This model asserts that current consumption can be expected to depend on last period's income as well as on current income. It is similar to the simple static stochastic model of IV.4.11, except that here we have lagged as well as current income in the consumption function. In the static stochastic case we saw that the definition of exogenousness requires that if investment i_t is to be exogenous it must not only be determined in some other model not involving c_t and y_t, but must also be statistically independent of all values of the disturbance $u_t, u_{t\pm1}, u_{t\pm2}, \ldots$. This still applies to the dynamic model (4.1)–(4.2). In addition, if y_{t-1} is to be predetermined in this model it must be independent of $u_t, u_{t+1}, u_{t+2}, \ldots$. We

---

[7] Another reason is that it is then easier to estimate the variances of the estimates of coefficients. See Chapter IX.

now observe that y_{t-1} is indeed determined by a system of equations not including c_t and y_t, namely, the lagged version of (4.1)–(4.2):

(4.3) $$c_{t-1} = \alpha y_{t-1} + \beta y_{t-2} + \gamma + u_{t-1}$$

(4.4) $$y_{t-1} = c_{t-1} + i_{t-1}$$

Now suppose that u_t is statistically independent of all its previous values u_{t-1}, u_{t-2}, ... Then u_t must also be statistically independent of y_{t-1}. This is because u_t is a random drawing from a population that has a probability distribution independent of u_{t-1}, u_{t-2}, etc., so that there can be no relation between u_t and the value of any other variable in the problem that occurs at time $t - 1$ or earlier. (The argument here has an important similarity to that regarding exogenousness in IV.4.9.) Therefore in (4.1)–(4.2) y_{t-1} fulfills the definition of a predetermined variable in the stochastic case.

4.8 A more general example, still linear and with lags of just one period, is as follows. Suppose there are G equations containing G current endogenous variables $y_{1t}, \ldots, y_{Gt}$ and their lagged values and K' exogenous variables $x_{1t}, \ldots, x_{K't}$ and G disturbances $u_{1t}, \ldots, u_{Gt}$, thus:

(4.5) $$\sum_{i=1}^{G} \beta_{gi0} y_{it} + \sum_{i=1}^{G} \beta_{gi1} y_{i,t-1} + \sum_{k=1}^{K'} \epsilon_{gk} x_{kt} = u_{gt}$$

$$t = 1, \ldots, T; \quad g = 1, \ldots, G$$

It will be seen that the y_{it} are determined by the $y_{i,t-1}$ and current exogenous variables and current disturbances. In the next period the $y_{i,t+1}$ will be determined by the y_{it} and the $x_{k,t+1}$ and $u_{g,t+1}$; and again in the next period the $y_{i,t+2}$ will be determined by the $y_{i,t+1}$ and the $x_{k,t+2}$ and $u_{g,t+2}$, and so on indefinitely. This progression can be seen more easily if (4.5) is expressed in a sort of schematic fashion as follows.[8] First, let the boldface symbol $\mathbf{B}_0$ represent the set of all the coefficients $\beta_{110}, \ldots, \beta_{GG0}$ in (4.5). Second, let $\mathbf{B}_1$ represent the set of all the coefficients $\beta_{111}, \ldots, \beta_{GG1}$ in (4.5). Third, let $\mathbf{E}$ represent the set of all the coefficients $\epsilon_{11}, \ldots, \epsilon_{GK'}$ in (4.5). Fourth, let $\mathbf{y}_t'$ represent the set of values at time t of all the endogenous variables $y_{1t}, \ldots, y_{Gt}$ in (4.5), and let this be the case for any value of t. Fifth, let $\mathbf{x}_t'$ represent the set of values of the exogenous variables $x_{1t}, \ldots, x_{K't}$ in (4.5) for any value

---

[8] The schematic form to be presented involves the use of symbols that will later be used for matrices and vectors. However, the reader who is unfamiliar with these concepts need not be dismayed at their appearance here. They are used here merely as abbreviations to exhibit more conspicuously the dependence of values of the y's in one period on the values of the foregoing period. No mathematical manipulation is involved.

of t. And last, let $\mathbf{u}_t'$ represent the set of values $u_{1t}, \ldots, u_{Gt}$ in (4.5) for any value of t. Then (4.5) can be written as follows.[9]

$$(4.6) \qquad \mathbf{B}_0\mathbf{y}_t' + \mathbf{B}_1\mathbf{y}_{t-1}' + \mathbf{E}\mathbf{x}_t' = \mathbf{u}_t' \qquad t = 1, \ldots, T$$

This shows schematically that the y's in period t [$\mathbf{y}_t'$ in (4.6)] depend on the y's in period $t - 1$ and the x's in period t ($\mathbf{y}_{t-1}'$ and $\mathbf{x}_t'$).

4.9 The progression of effects beginning from the y's in period 0 is shown by the following series of equations formed by repeating (4.6) for successive periods, first with $t = 1$, then with $t = 2$, then with $t = 3, \ldots$, and finally with $t = T$.

$$(4.7)$$

$$\mathbf{B}_0\mathbf{y}_1' + \mathbf{B}_1\mathbf{y}_0' + \mathbf{E}\mathbf{x}_1' \qquad = \mathbf{u}_1'$$
$$\mathbf{B}_0\mathbf{y}_2' + \mathbf{B}_1\mathbf{y}_1' \qquad + \mathbf{E}\mathbf{x}_2' \qquad = \mathbf{u}_2'$$
$$\mathbf{B}_0\mathbf{y}_3' + \mathbf{B}_1\mathbf{y}_2' \qquad + \mathbf{E}\mathbf{x}_3' \qquad = \mathbf{u}_3'$$
$$\vdots$$
$$\mathbf{B}_0\mathbf{y}_{T-1}' + \mathbf{B}_1\mathbf{y}_{T-2}' \qquad + \mathbf{E}\mathbf{x}_{T-1}' = \mathbf{u}_{T-1}'$$
$$\mathbf{B}_0\mathbf{y}_T' + \mathbf{B}_1\mathbf{y}_{T-1}' \qquad + \mathbf{E}\mathbf{x}_T' \quad = \mathbf{u}_T'$$

Now the y's in period 0 (i.e., $\mathbf{y}_0'$) are predetermined at time 1 in the first of these equations if the u's in period 1 ($\mathbf{u}_1'$) are independent of the y's in period 0 ($\mathbf{y}_0'$). This is a direct application of the argument in 3.7 and is similar to the argument of IV.4.9. Similarly, $\mathbf{y}_1'$ is predetermined at time 2 in the second equation if $\mathbf{u}_2'$ is independent of $\mathbf{y}_1'$. In general, $\mathbf{y}_{t-1}'$ is predetermined at time t in the tth equation if $\mathbf{u}_t'$ is independent of $\mathbf{y}_{t-1}'$. If $\mathbf{u}_t'$ for all t is independent of $\mathbf{u}_{t-1}'$, $\mathbf{u}_{t-2}'$, $\ldots$, then we can be sure that $\mathbf{u}_t'$ is independent of $\mathbf{y}_{t-1}'$ (and also of $\mathbf{y}_{t-2}'$, $\mathbf{y}_{t-3}'$, etc., if we were interested). As noted above, this is one important reason why it is usually assumed that disturbances in time-series models are independent as between periods.

4.10 So far in this section we have accepted without argument the statement in 4.4 that if not all disturbances in each period are independent of *all* past disturbances, then lagged endogenous variables can fail to be predetermined. Let us take a closer look at this, and see why it is true. Consider what happens in a model containing u_t and y_t and y_{t-1} when u_t and its lagged value u_{t-1} are dependent. Then u_t and y_{t-1} can (and in almost any realistic model will) be dependent. If they are, then by definition y_{t-1} is not predetermined. Consider the model (4.1)–(4.2) and suppose that u_t is dependent on u_{t-1} in the following way:

$$(4.8) \qquad u_t = f(u_{t-1}, v_t)$$

---

[9] We have not yet explained the rules for multiplying $\mathbf{B}_0$ times $\mathbf{y}_t'$ and the like. These are among the rules of matrix algebra. They are not needed here, but they can be found in books on the subject, or in condensed form in Appendix A.

where v_t is a random variable that for all t *is* independent of all its past values (and hence of its future values too). The relation between u_t and y_{t-1} can be examined as follows. Solve the lagged consumption equation (4.3) for u_{t-1} thus:

(4.9) $$u_{t-1} = c_{t-1} - \alpha y_{t-1} - \beta y_{t-2} - \gamma$$

Substitute this for u_{t-1} in (4.8) thus:

(4.10) $$u_t = f(c_{t-1} - \alpha y_{t-1} - \beta y_{t-2} - \gamma, v_t)$$

This equation shows how a dependence between u_t and y_{t-1} can arise. Such dependence is not a logical necessity, but nevertheless it is practically certain in any realistic model. Indeed, the only condition under which u_t and y_{t-1} can be independent, given (4.10), is in case the function relating u_t and u_{t-1} [e.g., the function f in (4.8) and (4.10)] is such as to cancel the effect in (4.10) of the structural relation between u_{t-1} and y_{t-1} [e.g., the structural relation (4.3)]. This could happen only if the function relating u_t and u_{t-1} depends in a particular way on observable variables and on the form of the structural equations, which is most unlikely indeed. Hence it is quite safe to say that in a model where the disturbances u_t for all t are not independent of their lagged values u_{t-1}, lagged values of the endogenous variables will not be predetermined.

4.11 As a very simple example, consider the following single-equation model:

(4.11) $$y_t = \gamma y_{t-1} + u_t$$

Assume that the disturbance u is not serially independent, but that u_t depends on u_{t-1} according to the following simple autoregressive[10] equation:

(4.12) $$u_t = \delta u_{t-1} + v_t \qquad \delta \neq 0$$

where v_t is a random variable that *is* independent of all its past and future values. We shall see whether it is possible in this model for u_t to be independent of y_{t-1}. We shall work out the moment of u_t and y_{t-1} (recall 3.3 above); we shall see that its expected value cannot be zero, so that the joint distribution of u_t and y_{t-1} exhibits a nonzero correlation, so that u_t cannot be independent of y_{t-1}, and hence y_{t-1} cannot be predetermined in (4.11).

4.12 From a lagged version of (4.11), we have

(4.13) $$y_{t-1} = \gamma y_{t-2} + u_{t-1}$$

---

[10] Such an equation is called *auto*regressive because it equates a variable (here u) to a regression on its own (earlier) values.

Using (4.12), (4.13), and (3.10) we have for the moment of u_t and y_{t-1}

$$(4.14) \quad m_{u_t y_{t-1}} = \delta\gamma m_{u_{t-1}y_{t-2}} + \delta m_{u_{t-1}u_{t-1}} + \gamma m_{v_t y_{t-2}} + m_{v_t u_{t-1}}$$

Now by virtue of the fact that v_t is a random disturbance independent of its own lagged values, it is also independent of everything else in the problem occurring at time $t - 1$ or earlier. Hence the last two terms in the last expression in (4.14) must have zero expected values. The expected value of $m_{u_t y_{t-1}}$ must be the same as that of $m_{u_{t-1}y_{t-2}}$. Call this expected value $\mu_{u_t y_{t-1}}$. Denote the expected value of $m_{u_{t-1}u_{t-1}}$ by the symbol μ_{uu}. Then take the expected values of the right and left members of (4.14), and solve the resulting equation for $\mu_{u_t y_{t-1}}$:

$$(4.15) \qquad\qquad \mu_{u_t y_{t-1}} = \frac{\delta\mu_{uu}}{1 - \gamma\delta}$$

This expression cannot be zero unless either δ is zero or γ is infinite, for u is assumed to have a nonzero variance so that μ_{uu} must be nonzero. But the values $\delta = 0$ and $\gamma = \infty$ can be ruled out in this model as follows. If δ is zero, then u_t is independent of u_{t-1}; this removes the serial dependence of u and merely confirms what we said earlier about how lagged endogenous variables are predetermined if disturbances in one period are independent of those in all other periods. If γ is infinite, the model is impossible, because it will yield an infinite value of y immediately following any finite value. Thus we have shown, in the example of the simple model (4.11)–(4.12), how serial dependence of the values of the disturbance u leads to dependence between y_{t-1} and u_t, thus rendering it impossible for y_{t-1} to be a predetermined variable in that model.

4.13 Now suppose that u_t is independent of u_{t-1} for all t, but that u_t is not independent of *all* its more distant lagged values, u_{t-2}, u_{t-3}, etc., for all t. It will suffice to consider a dynamic model where u_t and u_{t-2} are dependent. The first thing to be established is that such a case is possible. This is shown by offering an example of it, as follows. Suppose that the disturbances in successive odd-numbered periods (e.g., periods 1, 3, 5, 7, etc.) are related in a simple autoregressive fashion similar to (4.8) above, thus:

$$(4.16) \qquad\qquad u_t = f_{\text{odd}}(u_{t-2}, v_t) \qquad t = 1, 3, 5, 7, \ldots$$

where v_t is a random disturbance independent of *all* its past and future values. And suppose that the disturbances in successive even-numbered periods (e.g., periods 0, 2, 4, 6, ...) are independent of those in odd periods but are related to each other in a second simple autoregressive fashion, thus:

$$(4.17) \qquad\qquad u_t = f_{\text{even}}(u_{t-2}, v_t) \qquad t = 0, 2, 4, 6, \ldots$$

where v_t is as described above. This case may seem unrealistic, but it might apply if the periods represented seasons, say summer and winter. Summer disturbances might be independent of winter ones but disturbances in successive summers might be related and those in successive winters might be related. Now let the *expected value* of odd-period disturbances be equal to the *expected value* of even-period disturbances. Then whether t is odd or even, u_t will be independent of u_{t-1} for all t, but will not be independent of u_{t-2}. (Furthermore, u_t will be independent of those of its values that are lagged by an odd number of periods, and dependent on values that are lagged an even number of periods.) In this case, a dependence between u_t and y_{t-1} can arise via the chain of dependence leading from u_t to u_{t-2} (autoregressive relation for u) to y_{t-2} (structural equation lagged twice) to y_{t-1} (structural equation lagged once). The reader may verify this by evaluating $m_{u_t y_{t-1}}$ and $m_{u_t y_{t-2}}$. Hence to be assured that lagged endogenous variables are predetermined, we can assume that for all t each disturbance u_t is not only independent of its once-lagged value u_{t-1} but also of *all* its lagged values, u_{t-1}, u_{t-2}, u_{t-3}, ... This assumption is often stated (and tested) in a weak form pertaining only to the relation between disturbances in period t and those in period $t - 1$, even though, strictly speaking, all other periods should be included in its purview. In practice, however, the kind of serial relation most likely to be troublesome is that between disturbances in successive periods, so it is reasonable to concentrate attention on it.[11]

5 CROSS-SECTION MODELS

5.1 In this section we look briefly at some of the special features of dynamic stochastic *cross-section* models. The reader may want now to refer to earlier remarks on cross-section models in III.9, IV.5, and V.8. The definitions of exogenous and predetermined variables in stochastic models, presented in IV.4.9 and VI.4.3, respectively, apply to mixed and pure cross-section models as well as to pure time-series models. The remarks in V.8.2-4 concerning the different roles of lags in cross-section and time-series models are also particularly pertinent here.

5.2 In the last three chapters we have discussed some cross-section models that are neither dynamic nor stochastic, some that are stochastic but not dynamic, and some that are dynamic but not stochastic. Now we are ready to discuss some that are both dynamic and stochastic, which is the most interesting case. We shall use models similar to those described earlier, but to make the present section self-contained we shall begin from scratch.

[11] See Chapter X for appropriate tests.

5.3 Consider first a pure cross-section model, as of time t. Let all stocks and flows be measured in real terms. Let the ith household's consumption c_{it} depend linearly on its own lagged income $y_{i,t-1}$ and a disturbance u_{it}. Let the ith household's income be composed of three parts: a random part v_{it} with $\sum_i v_{it} = 0$, a systematic exogenous part from sources other than property x_{it}, and a systematic property income part that is the product of the current interest rate, r_t, and the household's net worth at the end of the preceding period, $k_{i,t-1}$. Let aggregate consumption C_t depend linearly on aggregate lagged income Y_{t-1} and an aggregate disturbance U_t (which is by definition equal to $\sum_i u_{it}$). Let aggregate income Y_t be equal to aggregate consumption C_t plus aggregate nonconsumption expenditure Z_t, Z_t being exogenous. The two preceding sentences imply that total income is determined by a simple multiplier process. Let the interest rate be determined by the necessity for aggregate income Y_t to equal the sum of aggregate property income $\sum_i k_{i,t-1} r_t$ plus aggregate nonproperty income $\sum_i x_{it}$. Denote $\sum_i k_{it}$ by K_t and denote $\sum_i x_{it}$ by X_t. Assume that $\sum_i \epsilon_i = 0$ (where ϵ_i is part of the intercept in the ith consumption equation below). This model is very crudely Keynesian in its implication that aggregate real income is determined entirely by demand, with no role for supply. Furthermore, it is a strange model in that each household's real nonproperty income is fixed, which might be the case if each household offered a fixed amount of labor, and government policy effectively assured every would-be labor-supplier of employment (or unemployment compensation) at a fixed real wage. A consequence of the two foregoing features is that real property income is a residual, what is left over (whether positive or negative or zero) out of total real income after the exogenous nonproperty incomes have been paid. Individual saving provides a share for the saver in the residual property income but does not lead to any increase in real output by means of the physical productivity of capital, because, as noted, supply considerations have no place in this model. Thus it is an altogether strange economy that we are describing. Nevertheless, it is complex enough to illustrate some of the interesting peculiarities of cross-section models while being simple enough to analyze easily.

5.4 The pure cross-section model just described may be put into the form of a set of $2M + 3$ equations as follows, where M is the number of households (as usual, Greek letters stand for parameters).

$$(5.1) \qquad c_{it} = \beta y_{i,t-1} + \gamma + \epsilon_i + u_{it} \qquad i = 1, \dots, M$$

$$(5.2) \qquad y_{it} = k_{i,t-1} r_t + x_{it} + v_{it} \qquad i = 1, \dots, M$$

$$(5.3) \qquad Y_t = C_t + Z_t$$

$$(5.4) \qquad C_t = \beta Y_{t-1} + M\gamma + U_t$$

$$(5.5) \qquad Y_t = K_{t-1} r_t + X_t$$

The following $2M + 3$ variables are endogenous:

$$r_t, C_t, Y_t, c_{it}, y_{it} \qquad i = 1, \ldots, M$$

The variables Z_t, X_t, and x_{it} are assumed exogenous, which means that the disturbances u_{jt} and v_{jt} are assumed statistically independent of them for *all* i and j from 1 to M (this means it matters not whether $i = j$).

    5.5   Two other equations that will be added to the model later (when it is considered as a mixed model) are

(5.6) $k_{it} = y_{it} - c_{it} + k_{i,t-1}$ $i = 1, \ldots, M$

                                            $t = 1, \ldots, T$

(5.7) $K_t = \sum_i k_{it}$ $t = 1, \ldots, T$

The first of these says that wealth at the end of any period is equal to saving during the period plus wealth at the beginning of the period. Since there is no explicit mention of depreciation, and ·since our wealth must be net not gross in order to make sense out of (5.5) above, we must interpret our incomes as net too. Equation (5.7) simply defines K_t.

    5.6   What of the lagged variables $k_{i,t-1}$ and $y_{i,t-1}$ $(i = 1, \ldots, M)$ and their aggregates K_{t-1} and Y_{t-1}? Are they predetermined at time t in the above *pure* cross-section model? Are they exogenous? Recalling the definitions in VI.4.3 and IV.4.9, we see that (*a*) they are *predetermined* at time t if they are independent of all disturbances in current and future periods, u_{jt}, v_{jt}, $u_{j,t+1}$, $v_{j,t+1}$, $u_{j,t+2}$, etc., for all $i, j = 1, \ldots, M$, and (*b*) they are *exogenous* if they are independent of all disturbances in the current period, u_{jt} and v_{jt}, for all $i, j = 1, \ldots, M$. Let us now apply these definitions.

    5.7   Take K_{t-1} first, because it is so easy to see that it depends only on exogenous factors with no disturbances or unknown parameters, and because the result will be useful in discussing $y_{i,t-1}$. From (5.6)–(5.7) we see that K_{t-1} is equal to $Y_{t-1} - C_{t-1} + K_{t-2}$. From (5.3) we see that $Y_{t-1} - C_{t-1}$ is equal to Z_{t-1}. Therefore

(5.8) $K_{t-1} = Z_{t-1} + K_{t-2}$

This holds for any period. Repeated applications of it in lagged form yield

(5.9) $K_{t-1} = \sum_{q=0}^{\infty} Z_{t-1-q}$

so that the total capital stock at any time is the cumulation of exogenous net investments in the past, and hence can be taken as exogenous itself.

    5.8   Take lagged income $y_{i,t-1}$ next. We shall show in 5.12 that $y_{i,t-1}$ depends on the values of the disturbances $u_1, \ldots, u_M$ and v_i in period $t - 1$, on exogenous factors, and on endogenous factors from period $t - 2$. We shall then show also in 5.12 that the endogenous factors in period $t - 2$ depend on the disturbances $u_1, \ldots, u_M$ and v_i in period $t - 2$, on exogenous factors, and on endogenous factors from period $t - 3$. And so on indefinitely. Therefore for any t, $y_{i,t-1}$ depends on exogenous factors and on the values of $u_1, \ldots, u_M$ and v_i in all periods before (but not including) period t. Using the functional symbol ϕ we may say

(5.10) $\qquad y_{i,t-1} = \phi(\text{exogenous factors},$

$$u_{1,t-1}, \ldots, u_{M,t-1}, v_{i,t-1},$$

$$u_{1,t-2}, \ldots, u_{M,t-2}, v_{i,t-2},$$

$$\ldots \qquad\qquad)$$

5.9 From this we can see two theorems having the same premise, one establishing that $y_{i,t-1}$ is predetermined at time t, and the other establishing that $y_{i,t-1}$ is exogenous in the *pure* cross-section model (8.1)–(8.5). *The premise* of the theorems is: The joint distribution of the disturbances $u_1, \ldots, u_M, v_1, \ldots, v_M$ in any period is statistically independent of every disturbance in every other period. (Somewhat more abstractly, the premise says that u_{it} and v_{it} are independent of u_{js} and v_{js} for *all* i and j from 1 to M and for all s and t such that $s \neq t$.) *The first theorem's conclusion* is: u_{jt} and v_{jt} are independent of $y_{i,t-1-q}$ for all i and j from 1 to M, for all t, and for all non-negative values of $q(0, 1, 2, \ldots)$; that is, u_{jt} and v_{jt} are independent of all incomes in all periods earlier than t, so that $y_{i,t-1}$ is predetermined at time t. For the special case where $q = 0$ the proof of the first theorem consists in noticing in (5.10) that $y_{i,t-1}$ depends on disturbances from periods $t - 1$ and earlier only, and then applying the premise, which implies that disturbances in period t are independent of those in periods $t - 1$ and earlier. For $q = 1$ the proof is the same except that a lagged version of (5.10) is used; for $q = 2$ a twice-lagged version is used; and so on ad infinitum. *The second theorem's conclusion* is implied in the first: u_{jt} and v_{jt} are independent of $y_{i,t-1}$ for all i and j from 1 to M and for all t, so that $y_{i,t-1}$ is exogenous in the *pure* cross-section model (8.1)–(8.5). Y_{t-1} is predetermined and exogenous if $y_{i,t-1}$ $(i = 1, \ldots, M)$ are, since Y_{t-1} is their sum. Notice that neither predeterminedness nor exogenousness is established if we assume that disturbances in one period are independent of those in *some but not all* other periods.

5.10 This argument illustrates the general rule that in *pure cross-section* models every temporally predetermined variable is exogenous.

5.11 The fact that $y_{i,t-1}$ is exogenous given the premise of 5.9 means that equation (5.1) is a complete single-equation model explaining household consumption c_{it} $(i = 1, \ldots, M)$ in terms of parameters and disturbances and exogenous factors.

5.12 This paragraph provides the justification, promised earlier, for some statements made in 5.8. By solving (5.5) for r_t and substituting it into (5.2) and then lagging the result, we find that $y_{i,t-1}$ depends on the disturbance v_i and total income and exogenous factors in period $t - 1$, and on capital stocks at the end of period $t - 2$, thus:

$$(5.11) \qquad y_{i,t-1} = k_{i,t-2} \frac{Y_{t-1} - X_{t-1}}{K_{t-2}} + x_{i,t-1} + v_{i,t-1}$$

Next, express Y_{t-1} in terms of income in period $t - 2$ and the disturbance U and exogenous factors in period $t - 1$ via the lagged reduced form of the two-equation model (5.3)–(5.4); substitute the result for Y_{t-1} in (5.11). This gives $y_{i,t-1}$ in terms of disturbances U and v_i and exogenous factors in period $t - 1$ and total income in period $t - 2$ and capital stocks at the end of period $t - 2$, thus:

$$(5.12)$$

$$y_{i,t-1} = \frac{k_{i,t-2}}{K_{t-2}}(\beta Y_{t-2} + M\gamma + U_{t-1} + Z_{t-1} - X_{t-1}) + x_{i,t-1} + v_{i,t-1}$$

This is the first stage mentioned at the beginning of 5.8. Now by a twice-lagged version of (5.6) it is seen that $k_{i,t-2}$ depends on the ith household's income and consumption in period $t - 2$, which depends in turn on the disturbances $u_1, \ldots, u_M$, v_i in period $t - 2$. Also involved are $k_{i,t-3}$ and K_{t-3} and exogenous factors. So the chain of effects can be pursued backward into the past. At each stage, say the sth, K_{t-s} is in effect exogenous as seen in 5.7; $k_{i,t-s}$ is expressed in terms of $y_{i,t-s}$ and $c_{i,t-s}$ and $k_{i,t-s-1}$ via (5.6); $c_{i,t-s}$ is expressed in terms of $y_{i,t-s-1}$ and $u_{i,t-s}$ via (5.1); $y_{i,t-s-1}$ is expressed in terms of r_{t-s-1} and $v_{i,t-s-1}$ and exogenous factors via (5.2); r_{t-s-1} is expressed in terms of Y_{t-s-1} and exogenous factors via (5.5); and Y_{t-s-1} is expressed in terms of Y_{t-s-2} and U_{t-s-1} and exogenous factors via the reduced form of (5.3)–(5.4). At each stage, disturbances $u_1, \ldots, u_M$, v_i from the next earlier period are seen to be involved. Therefore the assertions in 5.8, including equation (5.10), are established.

5.13 Now consider the status of the variable $k_{i,t-1}$. According to a lagged version of (5.6) it depends on $y_{i,t-1}$ and $c_{i,t-1}$ and $k_{i,t-2}$. This means it depends on the same disturbances that influence $y_{i,t-1}$, namely $u_1, \ldots, u_M$ and v_i in period $t - 1$ and in all preceding periods. Hence we could write $k_{i,t-1}$ as a function of the same disturbances that appear in (5.10). And hence, under the premise stated at the beginning of 5.9, $k_{i,t-1}$ is both predetermined at time t and exogenous in this *pure* cross-section model.

5.14 If data are available for several periods, say for $t = 0, 1, \ldots, T$, then we can think of T distinct pure cross-section models, one for each period from 1 to T (data for period 0 being required for lagged values of period 1, and so on forward through time). If, furthermore, each parameter has a constant value through time, we can think of a mixed time-series and cross-section model consisting of (5.1)–(5.7). There are $(3M + 4)T$ equations in the mixed model, and an equal number of endogenous variables: r_t, C_t, Y_t, K_t, c_{it}, y_{it}, and k_{it}, $i = 1, \ldots, M$ and $t = 1, \ldots, T$. Given the premise in 5.9, the variables Y_{t-1}, $y_{i,t-1}$, and $k_{i,t-1}$ are predetermined at time t, but are no longer exogenous as they were in the pure cross-section model. This is because now the forces determining them have been incorporated into the model by making it a time-series model (though not a pure one), and so it is not true that all the disturbances in the model (u_{js}, v_{js}) are independent of all the values of Y_{t-1}, $y_{i,t-1}$, and $k_{i,t-1}$ for all $i, j = 1, \ldots, M$ and for all $s, t = 1, \ldots, T$. The variables Z_t, X_t, and x_{it} are both predetermined and exogenous as before. K_{t-1} is predetermined and in effect is exogenous too (see 5.7 above) although we have included it as an endogenous variable defined by (5.7).

QUESTIONS AND PROBLEMS

2.1. Using equation (2.4) and the distribution of u in 2.3, find the conditional distributions of y_2 and y_3 given the value of y_0.

2.2. Introduce disturbances into several of the dynamic exact models of Chapter V and deduce the conditional distribution of the endogenous variables at time t, given the values of endogenous variables at times 0 and earlier (where $t > 0$), exogenous variables at all times, and parameters.

2.3. Transform equations (2.1) and (2.2) into the general form (2.15). Indicate the values of G, T', and K' that are needed for this purpose. Assign to each quantity in (2.1) and (2.2) an appropriate symbol from (2.15), and exhibit the resulting list of notational assignments. Then do the same for the general form (2.16), indicating the required values of G and K.

2.4. Prove that under the conditions in 2.7–8 the variance of y_t remains finite as $T \to \infty$ if var v_t is bounded and $|\lambda| < 1$.

3.1. Using a sample of 6 or 7 or 9 or 11 or 12 actual observations for consumption c and income y (or any other closely related variables), compute the moment m_{cy} in several ways as follows:

(a) Use equation (3.10), rounding off $\bar{c}$ and $\bar{y}$ to the same number of significant figures as in the data for c and y, but with no rounding off of cross products.

(b) Use (3.10), rounding off $\bar{c}$ and $\bar{y}$ and all cross products to four significant figures.

(c) Use (3.13), with no rounding off (exception: round off the quotient so that it has as many significant figures as the corresponding sum of cross products).

(d) Use (3.13), rounding off all products and quotients to four significant figures.

(e) Use (3.15), with no rounding off [exception: same as in part (c)].

(f) Use (3.15), rounding off all products and quotients to four significant figures.

Comment on the results.

3.2. Prove equation (3.16). Does all of it hold for moments about zero? Explain.

3.3. (a) Prove that $m_{x,y+z} = m_{xy} + m_{xz}$.

(b) Express the following in terms of moments of the variables w, x, y, and z: (i) $m_{y+z,y+z}$; (ii) $m_{w+x,y+z}$; (iii) m_{ax} where a is a constant; (iv) m_{ab} where a and b are both constants.

4.1. (a) What is the correlation between u_t and u_{t-1} if equation (4.12) is true?

(b) What is the correlation between u_t and u_{t-2}?

(c) Between u_t and u_{t-s} (where $s > 0$)?

(d) Are there any restrictions on the validity of your answer? Explain.

4.2. Prove equation (4.14).

5.1. Construct a simple dynamic pure cross-section model and indicate which variables are exogenous, which are predetermined at time t, which (if any) are predetermined at the ith observation in the cross section, and which are jointly dependent.

5.2. Extend the model of the previous exercise so that it is a mixed time-series and cross-section model, and answer the same questions about it.

Part Three

Empirical Methods

CHAPTER VII

Introduction to Problems
of Statistical Inference
in Econometrics

This chapter forms a bridge between the preceding theoretical chapters and the following chapters, which deal with the making of inferences from a combination of theory and data. Several introductory topics are discussed: the need for knowing the values of structural parameters, the treatment of unobservable variables, disturbances versus errors of measurement, the concepts of population and sample, point and interval estimation, properties of estimators, hypothesis testing, the role of the maintained hypothesis, and prediction.

1 REVIEW AND PREVIEW

1.1 We have now completed our treatment of the theoretical phase of econometrics, and we are about to enter upon the empirical phase, dealing with measurement and statistical inference. Let us pause briefly to take stock. We have seen that economic theories can often be cast in the form of models—systems of equations that purport to explain the values of certain economic variables (called current endogenous or jointly dependent), assuming that certain other quantities (parameters and disturbances and predetermined variables) are fixed. We have presented several examples of such models, which may be static or dynamic, exact or stochastic, the most useful ones being stochastic. We have found that the reduced forms of models (and also the final equations of dynamic models) are useful devices for expressing the expected value of each jointly dependent variable in terms of parameters and predetermined variables only.

1.2   In Section 3 of Chapter I we discussed briefly the fact that the economic models that are used as maintained hypotheses in econometrics are not known with certainty to be correct, and that therefore it makes sense to experiment with several different competing plausible models and to evaluate them in part in terms of how well each one fits a relevant body of data. In I.4 we discussed the relationship between two realms in econometrics, one being a branch of mathematical statistics, the other being an applied empirical field in which the results of the mathematical realm are sometimes useful and sometimes not strictly applicable. Those two sections (I.3–4) are important for the third part of the book and should be read again now.

1.3   One of the chief generalizations to be drawn from the preceding chapters is that many of the interesting and important questions cannot be answered without at least an approximate knowledge of the *numerical* values of the parameters of the reduced form or of the final equation(s). In particular, the parameter values required pertain to the period about which the questions are being asked.

1.4   Having seen that the object of search in an economic problem is often the numerical values of parameters of the relevant reduced-form or final equations, we turned to the question of whether economic theory alone can provide them. The answer we found is that in most cases it cannot. Economic theory has among its premises only qualitative statements such as that consumers maximize utility and firms maximize profits. Hence it tells (ideally) whether or not a given variable (such as income) is important in influencing a given economic relationship (such as demand) and, if so, in which direction; or it sets limits on the values of particular parameters (such as demand elasticities); or it establishes relationships that can be expected to hold among the parameters. As a result, economic theory can often tell us the algebraic signs of important reduced-form parameters (such as multipliers) and can sometimes set upper and/or lower limits on their values, but typically cannot specify numerical values. This is not surprising, after all. It would indeed be strange if all our questions could be answered without the aid of any empirical observations other than those generalizations that lead to the qualitative premises of economic theory.

1.5   And so we turn our attention in the remainder of this book to empirical work, to help us fill in the silences in what economic theory has to say about economic problems. This chapter will discuss several preliminary considerations and will give an introductory view of the general problem of making inferences about unknown parameters on the basis of *a priori* information (known or assumed) and observed data. This topic is known as *statistical inference*. Chapter VIII will discuss the identification problem, which has been introduced in II.6.8–13 and will be referred to again in Sections 2.2 and 7.10 of this chapter. Chapter IX will discuss point estimation of parameters, that is, the choice of a single number as an estimate of a parameter. Chapter X will discuss interval estimation of parameters, that is, the choice of an interval or range intended to bracket the value of a parameter, and also the making of predictions and the testing of hypotheses. Chapter XI presents illustrative computations for a simple econometric model of the United States.

2 THE NECESSITY FOR KNOWING STRUCTURAL PARAMETERS

2.1 The only reason for wanting to know the values of structural economic parameters, apart from the desire to know them as an end in itself, is for the purpose of describing or of predicting economic phenomena. In our earlier discussion of the excise-tax problem in Chapter II, we indicated that if there is no change of structure between the observation period and the prediction period, then the reduced-form parameters relevant to the prediction period can be estimated from observations and it is not necessary to know the structural parameters at all.[1] If a structural change intervenes between the observation period and the prediction period, however, the reduced-form parameters relevant to the prediction period can be obtained only from the new structure, and so the new structural parameters must be known, and this usually requires a knowledge of the old structural parameters plus a knowledge of the character of the structural change. This conclusion holds for any model at all, and its importance lies in the fact that many policy measures that might be proposed are essentially structural changes that affect the old structure in predictable ways; tax and subsidy measures, credit controls, open-market operations, and many direct controls are of this nature. Hence forecasting their effects is much more likely to be successful if the old structure (prevailing before they are instituted) is known.

2.2 This argument can be put in general terms, following the equations in III.10.11–12. The general exact (as distinguished from stochastic) structure may be represented by

$$(2.1) \quad F^i(y_1, \ldots, y_G; z_1, \ldots, z_K; \alpha_{i1}, \ldots, \alpha_{iL}) = 0 \qquad i = 1, \ldots, G$$

where as usual the y's are jointly dependent, the z's are predetermined, and the α's are parameters. The reduced form can be represented as follows, the π's being parameters:

$$(2.2) \qquad y_i = H^i(z_1, \ldots, z_K; \pi_{i1}, \ldots, \pi_{iM}) \qquad i = 1, \ldots, G$$

---

[1] We shall see later, however, in IX.12.4–5, that in some cases a knowledge of the structural parameters contributes to more accurate knowledge of the reduced form than can be obtained otherwise, even if there is no structural change.

The set of all the α's can be denoted[2] by **A**, that of all the π's by **Π**, that of all y's by **y**, and that of all z's by **z**. Since any structural change can be represented as a change in one or more of the parameters[3] in **A**, we can represent the new structure after the change by a new set of parameters denoted by asterisks, **A***, where some of the components of **A*** may be equal to the corresponding components of **A** but at least one is different because of the structural change. Similarly, the new reduced-form parameters are denoted by **Π***. (This use of asterisks occurs in this section only.)

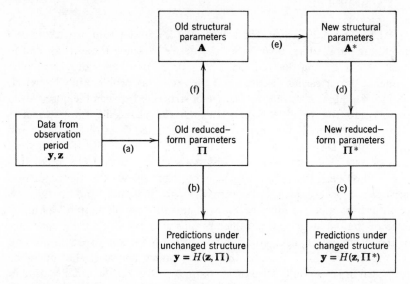

Figure 2.1 The sequence of inferences for making predictions under changed and unchanged structure.

The diagram in Figure 2.1 represents the situation. The arrows indicate the directions in which inferences are to be drawn. First, the set of old (i.e., observation-period) parameters **Π** of the reduced form can always be estimated from data[4] as we shall see in Chapters VIII and IX [see the arrow labeled (*a*) in Figure 2.1]. Second, if there is no structural change,

---

[2] The symbols **A** and **Π** can be thought of as matrices, and **y** and **z** as vectors, but no mathematical operations requiring a knowledge of vector and matrix algebra will be used in this chapter.

[3] That is, it is not necessary to assume that the form of the functions F^i changes, for they can be made general enough so that any desired structural change can be expressed in terms of changes in parameters only, to any desired degree of approximation.

[4] Provided there are enough observations: two are required for locating a straight line, three for a plane, etc.

then **Π** is sufficient for making predictions [arrow (*b*) in Figure 2.1].[5] But if a structural change intervenes just before the prediction period, **Π*** is needed for predictions [arrow (*c*)], and it can be obtained only from **A***, the new structure [arrow (*d*)], which in turn can be obtained through a knowledge of the old structure **A** and of the nature of the change [arrow (*e*)]. Hence it becomes important to deduce the old structure **A** from the old reduced-form **Π** [arrow (*f*)]. Whether this is possible is the core of the identification problem, to be discussed in Chapter VIII below.

2.3 What is there about the structural parameters **A** and **A*** that makes it possible for one knowing the character of the structural change to infer **A*** from **A**, and what is there about the reduced-form parameters **Π** and **Π*** that makes it impossible with the same knowledge to infer **Π*** from **Π** without first passing from **Π** back to **A** and then to **A*** and **Π***? It is simply this: Each structural equation is supposed to apply to some particular fundamental relationship in the economy, describing the behavior of a single fairly homogeneous group of people or organizations, or the limitations imposed by technology, or the effects of an important law or institution. The kind of structural change that is likely to invalidate the parameters of the old reduced form is likely to stem from a change in one or a few of these structural relationships, and to leave other structural relationships unaltered. But *all* the reduced-form relationships are likely to be altered by any single structural change, because typically each is dependent upon every structural relationship.[6] We describe this situation by saying that structural relationships have a high degree of *autonomy*[7] (not many are affected by a single structural change) and that reduced-form equations have only a low degree of autonomy (typically all are affected). This means that it is relatively easy to discover directly what a structural change does to the old structural parameters **A**, but relatively difficult to discover what it does to the old reduced-form parameters **Π** unless one traces the effect via **A** and **A*** as in Figure 2.1.

2.4 Not all policy changes take the form of a structural change; some are merely changes in exogenous variables. Recall for example the excise-tax problem discussed in Chapter II. There a change in the excise-tax rate is a structural change if the tax rate has never been changed before; it is a change in an exogenous variable if the tax rate has been changed before, during the observation period. The reader should trace that example through the steps shown in Figure 2.1. In general, as shown by the chain of arrows (*a*) and (*b*) of the figure, if a policy consists merely in a change of exogenous variables (with no change in structural

---

[5] But see note 1 above.

[6] In segmentable models some structural changes affect only a part of the reduced form.

[7] This term is due to Haavelmo [1944], pp. 26–39. See also II.1.10 above.

parameters) then its results may be predicted from a knowledge of the old reduced form, and it is unnecessary to know the structural parameters at all.[8]

3 OBSERVABLE AND UNOBSERVABLE VARIABLES

3.1 Throughout this book it is assumed that parameters and random disturbances are unobservable. Indeed, it is because parameters are not observable that it is necessary to try to infer their values from other information, and it is because the disturbances are unobservable that these inferences are so troublesome. It has been assumed so far that the endogenous variables y_i and the predetermined variables z_k are all observable. This very convenient assumption will be adhered to throughout except in connection with some of the estimation methods discussed in Chapter IX, but even there it will be assumed that all the y's and z's *in the particular equation being studied empirically* are observable. Actually, it may happen that a variable belonging in a certain equation is in fact not observable, or is very difficult to observe. In this section we shall explore briefly means of maintaining the convenient assumption that all variables are observable when in fact some are not.

3.2 To take an example, in any theory of investment one of the most important variables is the rate of return anticipated by the firm(s) doing the investing, and this is an extremely difficult thing for which to get meaningful figures. Again, the inventory policy of a firm may be affected by the anticipated price of the commodity in question. Futures markets are certainly highly responsive to price expectations, as are security markets. Any such "state-of-mind" variables or "psychological" variables are likely to be in the nonobservable category.

3.3 If observations do not exist for variables that we regard as important, we must either devise ways to obtain these observations or else devise methods of by-passing the need for them. The questionnaire survey technique, which is useful for obtaining data on the states of mind of economic decision-makers, is being increasingly used. The annual Survey of Consumer Finances, conducted by the Federal Reserve Board (formerly jointly with the Survey Research Center of the University of Michigan), is a good example.[9] The quarterly questionnaire sent to firms by the S. E. C. and the Commerce Department, to find out their plans

---

[8] An excellent discussion of this problem will be found in Marschak [1947] or Marschak [1953]. See also Hurwicz [1950], p. 270. And see note 1 again.

[9] See the regular articles in the *Federal Reserve Bulletin* beginning in 1946; Katona [1951], Klein [1951], and Klein [1953].

for investment in plant and equipment, is another example.[10] Interesting problems are then raised about how intentions and anticipations of decision-makers are formed, how they influence events, and how they are revised when frustrated. These problems are not discussed here; they form a whole field in themselves.

3.4 If it is impractical to devise satisfactory measures of psychological variables (or any other unobservable variables, for that matter), it is often possible to express them as functions of other observable variables. Presumably each businessman or consumer forms his intentions and anticipations on the basis of observed facts that come to him, and if we can think of the facts that affect him most we can then incorporate them into an equation that can be tried out to see whether it describes his behavior.

3.5 As an example, consider the inventory policy of a firm that uses a storable raw material, a battery firm using lead, for instance, or a paint firm using linseed oil. The amount of inventory such a firm holds at a given moment must depend in part on the amount and direction by which it expects the price of its material to change over the next month or quarter or year, as well as on its current and anticipated future rates of sales. This statement itself is a hypothesis. The anticipated changes in price and sales are not readily observable, as are actual price and actual sales. But we can form hypotheses as to what kind of data affect the firm's anticipations. A price rise in one period is usually followed by a price rise in the next if the periods are not too long, and a price fall is usually followed by another fall, turning points being less common than continuations of short-term trends. Therefore one simple theory of anticipated price might state that it is equal to a function of current prices and last period's price. The same might be done with sales, anticipated sales being represented by a function of current and lagged sales.

3.6 Let us for simplicity set up linear equations for these hypotheses. Inventory (in real terms) is denoted by v, price by p, and sales (in real terms) by s. The superscript e applied to any quantity in this section denotes the expected or anticipated value of that quantity; thus p^e_{t+1} is the price anticipated for period $t + 1$. Then the hypothesis described at the beginning of 3.5 is

$$(3.1) \qquad v_t = \alpha(p^e_{t+1} - p_t) + \beta s^e_{t+1} + \gamma s_t + \delta$$

$$= \alpha p^e_{t+1} - \alpha p_t + \beta s^e_{t+1} + \gamma s_t + \delta$$

[10] See Friend and Bronfenbrenner [1950], for an analysis of the plans reported in this survey from 1947 to 1950. See quarterly articles in the *Survey of Current Business* for continuing data. See National Bureau of Economic Research [1960] for related papers.

Since p_{t+1}^e and s_{t+1}^e are not observable, we have provisionally adopted two further hypotheses relating them to observable variables:

$$(3.2) \qquad p_{t+1}^e = \epsilon p_t + \eta p_{t-1} + \theta$$

$$(3.3) \qquad s_{t+1}^e = \lambda s_t + \mu s_{t-1} + \nu$$

If these are now substituted into (3.1), the level of inventories is expressed as a function of observable variables alone:[11]

$$(3.4) \quad v_t = \alpha(\epsilon - 1)p_t + \alpha\eta p_{t-1} + (\beta\lambda + \gamma)s_t + \beta\mu s_{t-1} + (\delta + \alpha\theta + \beta\nu)$$

3.7 A more plausible expectations hypothesis is obtained if we replace (3.3) by a distributed-lag equation as in V.7.6, for example:

$$(3.5) \qquad s_{t+1}^e = \omega s_t^e + (1 - \omega)s_t = (1 - \omega) \sum_{i=0}^{\infty} \omega^i s_{t-i} \qquad 0 \leqq \omega < 1$$

A similar distributed-lag equation might be used for p_{t+1}^e instead of (3.2):[12]

$$(3.6) \qquad p_{t+1}^e = \tau p_t^e + (1 - \tau)p_t = (1 - \tau) \sum_{i=0}^{\infty} \tau^i p_{t-i} \qquad 0 \leqq \tau < 1$$

If these are substituted into (3.1) the result is an equation expressing current inventory v_t as a function of present and all past values of sales s and price p. If $\omega = \tau$, it can be expressed in terms of current and once-lagged values of p and s and the once-lagged value of v thus (using the method of V.7.7):

$$(3.7) \qquad v_t = -\dot{\omega}p_t + [\gamma + \beta(1 - \omega)]s_t$$

$$+ \alpha\omega p_{t-1} - \gamma\omega s_{t-1} + \omega v_{t-1} + \delta(1 - \omega)$$

If $\omega \neq \tau$, then the unobservable expected values of both variables s and p can be eliminated and replaced by functions of v_{t-1} and v_{t-2} and other observable variables with lags no greater than 2 periods.

3.8 Suppose that $\omega = \tau$ and that (3.1) and (3.5)–(3.7) are adopted. Then there is a chain consisting of three links between the observable "causes" (v_{t-1}, p_t, p_{t-1}, s_t, and s_{t-1}) and the observable "effect" v_t. The first is the hypothesis that v_t depends on anticipated sales and anticipated price change as in (3.1), and the other two are the pair of hypotheses that the anticipated values of price and sales depend on current and lagged values as in (3.5) and (3.6). These cannot be tested directly, because p_{t+1}^e and s_{t+1}^e are not observed. What can be tested is (3.7), which embodies

---

[11] See Klein [1950], pp. 15–19, for an application of this kind.

[12] Or instead we could assume that expected price *change* $(dp/dt)^e$ obeys a rule like that in (3.6); see V.7.9 for a comment on the merits of this.

all three hypotheses. If (3.7) turns out consistently to accord with observations, all is well with the hypotheses, that is, they are not rejected. But if (3.7) fails, then the chain of hypotheses (3.1) and (3.5)–(3.6) fails as a whole, but it is not possible to tell without further investigation or information which of the three are incorrect and which (if any) are correct. Of course, if we have a high degree of confidence in two of the three, for instance, in (3.5) and (3.6), then the test of (3.7) can be viewed as a test of (3.1) alone, since any failure of (3.7) would then be blamed on (3.1) rather than on (3.5) and (3.6) in which we already believe firmly. In such a case, (3.5) and (3.6) together are the *maintained hypothesis*, and (3.1) is the *tested hypothesis*. The maintained hypothesis concept is thus a useful expedient in case a given empirical result contradicts the theoretical implications of a set of several empirically inseparable hypotheses. The hypothesis to be rejected is the one enjoying the least degree of prior confidence, and the others are "maintained" in the test of the doubtful one. The difficulty with this (or any) procedure for deciding which hypothesis to reject when a chain of several must be tested at once, of course, is that it relies heavily on *a priori* ideas, which are difficult to quantify, though they are useful and necessary. Maintained hypotheses will be discussed at greater length in Sections 5 to 7 below, and again in Chapter X.

4 DISTURBANCES AND ERRORS OF OBSERVATION

4.1 With very few exceptions, this book treats the random components in econometric models as though they came only from disturbances in the equations of the models. Another possible source is errors in economic variables. Such errors may arise because of errors of measurement,[13] or because the measurable quantities are not quite the same conceptually as the relevant theoretical quantities. A good deal of attention has been paid in the statistical literature to the effects of errors in variables,[14] but econometric work has often emphasized disturbances in the equations

---

[13] Notice that if there is an error of measurement in one of the variables in an equation but in no others, and the equation contains no shock, the situation is for many purposes the same as if there is a shock but no errors of measurement. For example, in the equation $y = \sum_i^k \beta_i x_i + u$, suppose y and $x_1, \ldots, x_k$ are observable without error and u is an unobservable random variable. Then there is no way to tell (and it does not matter) whether y is the incorrect measurement of the true variable $y - u$ and the equation holds exactly between $y - u$ and $\Sigma \beta_i x_i$, or whether y is the correct measurement of the true variable y and the equation contains the random shock u. (If the variable that has the measurement error occurs lagged as well as current, then this special case does not apply.)

[14] See, for example, Frisch [1934], Koopmans [1937], Madansky [1959].

and has relegated errors in variables to a less important place, although they are clearly important.

4.2 One of the reasons for the emphasis on disturbances instead of on errors in variables is a belief that disturbances offer more prospect for continued trouble than errors in variables, that is, that there is a better prospect of reducing errors in variables to unimportant proportions than there is of reducing disturbances in economic equations to unimportant proportions.[15] In any case, the magnitudes of the disturbances in economic equations make it clear that disturbances will continue to be an important source of randomness.

4.3 Another reason for the emphasis on disturbances instead of on errors in variables is of course that they are easier to handle with statistical theory, because only one disturbance appears in each equation, while there are usually as many errors as there are variables in each equation. Additional complications arise in dealing with errors in variables in a system of simultaneous equations, for the error attached to the variable y_{it} must appear in every equation where y_{it} appears, so that there is an intricate network of relationships connecting the random elements in different equations.[16]

5 POINT ESTIMATION AND LOSS FUNCTIONS

5.1 In Chapter II, Sections 4–7, a very crude idea was given of how the values of the parameters in the reduced-form equations in the excise-tax problem might be estimated. In the rest of this chapter the problems of statistical inference, that is, inference about parameters on the basis of *a priori* information (known or assumed) and observed data, will be discussed in a somewhat more technical but still introductory fashion, to prepare the way for the material in the remainder of the book. Here we shall discuss in turn point estimation of parameters, testing of hypotheses, interval estimation of parameters and its relation to testing, the use of observed data and (known or assumed) *a priori* information—also called the *maintained hypothesis*—for these types of statistical inference, and prediction. The discussion in this chapter will be in terms of inference concerning a single unknown parameter in a univariate probability distribution, with more complicated cases left to the succeeding chapters, because the object here is to bring out the basic points of an approach.

---

[15] See Morgenstern [1950] and Ames and Reiter [1961] for evidence of the importance of errors in variables.

[16] Expectational models such as are found in 3.7–8 are particularly subject to errors in variables. Friedman [1957] gives a consumption theory using such expectations in an errors-in variables model.

5.2   We shall need to use several statistical concepts that have only been hinted at so far, without being defined. One pair of such concepts is "population" (also called "universe") and "sample." A *population* is any set of individuals, which may be real individual people or objects or numbers or events. The populations we are going to be discussing are those whose elements are *numbers* standing for something in which we have some particular interest as economists, such as the population of amounts spent by consumer spending units, or the population of all possible annual figures for national income, or the population of all possible year-to-year shifts or disturbances in a certain demand equation. When we discuss the individual members of a population we shall mean these *numbers*, not the years or countries or families or business firms that the numbers describe. The individuals in a population are assumed to have a fixed probability distribution, which will usually be expressed as a function with constant *parameters*; examples are the mean, the variance, etc. Populations may be finite or infinite—compare the population consisting of the individual incomes of the (finite) number of people living in a given country in a given period with the population consisting of the outcomes for the number of heads (0 or 1) occurring on (the infinite number of) all possible tosses of a given coin. A *sample* is a set of individuals taken from a population and usually used to make inferences about the parameters of the population from which it is taken. Samples are used when the investigation of the entire population would be too costly (monthly estimates of the United States price level are made from samples), or when the investigation process necessarily destroys each individual investigated (as in the testing of the tensile strength of pieces of material, or the testing of the taste and quality of canned food), or when individual members of the population become available so slowly that to investigate the whole population is to know the result only at Domesday (as in economic time-series analysis, where numbers describing the economy in successive years or quarters are regarded as the individuals making up the population). Samples should be taken at *random*, that is, in such a way that no member of the population has a greater chance of being chosen than any other member.[17] If this is done, then probability theory can be used to draw inferences about what kinds of samples are likely to arise from a given population, and hence—which is really the important thing—about what kinds of population are likely to have given rise to a given sample. It is one of the most surprising and useful facts of statistics that a great deal of information about large or

---

[17] Sometimes it is desirable to divide a population into subgroups and take a random sample from each subgroup, so as to get larger samples from certain subgroups than from others. These subgroups are called strata, and such sampling is called stratified random sampling. See, for example, Cochran [1953].

even infinite populations can be obtained from relatively small samples by the inference methods we shall discuss.

5.3 In time-series work the individuals sampled are numerical characteristics of the world in (usually successive) *years*, or some other periods, and a series of observations from 1 to T (e.g., 1929–1964) is thought of as a sample from the (presumably infinite) population of all such observations from the indefinite past into the indefinite future. Data must be assumed to be selected at random if formal statistical tools are to be used. The randomness is assumed to be a property not of the selection of the *observations themselves* but of the selection of disturbances or shifts in the equations we are interested in. We analyze the data *as if* the disturbances for each year were numbers drawn at random from a hat, on New Year's Eve, for instance, and were then inserted into the appropriate equations so that their effects would show up in the values taken on by the endogenous variables in the ensuing year. For cross-section work the same general kind of model is used, except that the individuals sampled are numerical properties of persons or families or firms or states or cities or the like; the analysis still proceeds as if the disturbances for each one were drawn at random from a hat. It is usually assumed that the probability distribution is the same for all drawings.

5.4 In discussing inference about parameters we shall use the concept of a *sample statistic*, sometimes called simply a *statistic*. If a sample consisting of several observed values of a random variable x is contemplated, say $x_1, \ldots, x_T$, then any function of those observed values is known as a sample statistic. In problems where two or more variables $x, y, \ldots$ are involved, any function of some or all of their observed values is a statistic. Just as it is useful to distinguish between a *function* (which is a rule associating to each possible set of values of the function's arguments a value of the function) and a *value* of that function, so it is useful to distinguish between a statistic and a value of that statistic. An interesting and important statistic for a sample containing the data $x_1, \ldots, x_T$ is the sample mean. Its value is denoted by $\bar{x}$, and it is obtained as $1/T$ times the sum of the observed values in the sample:

$$(5.1) \qquad \bar{x} = \frac{1}{T} \sum_{t=1}^{T} x_t$$

Unfortunately, in common usage the term "sample mean" refers sometimes to the function (i.e., the rule directing the computation of $1/T$ times the sum of the observations) and sometimes to the value $\bar{x}$ so obtained. We shall follow this ambiguous usage because it is so nearly universal, and the reader will have to tell from the context which is meant. The same is true of many other sample statistics such as the variance, covariance, and correlation.

5.5 In order to apply probability theory to the disturbances in our models, we shall always be assuming that they are random variables and that therefore the observed endogenous variables in our sample, which depend in part on these disturbances, are also random variables.[18] Since any function of a set of random variables is a random variable, any statistic [such as $\bar{x}$ in (5.1) above] is a random variable, and as such has a probability distribution. This probability distribution, of course, has parameters of its own, such as its mean and variance. It is important to distinguish conceptually the parameters of the distribution of the data $x_1, \ldots, x_T$ from the parameters of the distribution of any statistic that may be used in connection with those data. For example, the parameter that is the mean of the distribution of the data (which parameter we shall denote by μ) is conceptually different from the parameter that is the mean of the distribution of $\bar{x}$, although it is easy to prove by the rules of mathematical expectation (IV.2.24) that the two have equal values. Similarly, it is important to distinguish the parameter representing the variance of the distribution of the data $x_1, \ldots, x_T$ from the parameter representing the variance of $\bar{x}$, and these two are *not* equal (unless in very special cases, such as when $T = 1$; see IV.2.25).

5.6 An important kind of sample statistic is the *point estimator*. A *point estimator* of a parameter is a single-valued statistic (meaning a statistic that, for any given sample, takes on exactly one value, rather than a range of values or any other set of two or more values) intended, in some as yet undefined sense, to yield a value close to the true value of the parameter. A *point estimate* is a value of a point estimator. Consider again the sample mean. It can be thought of as a point *estimator* of the population mean μ, in which case the sample mean is thought of as the *function or rule* that associates to each sample of T observations the sum of their values divided by T. Or the sample mean can be thought of as a point *estimate* of μ, in which case it is thought of as the *value $\bar{x}$* obtained when (5.1) is applied to a sample.

5.7 In what sense can a point estimator be said to yield estimates that are close to the true parameter? A point estimator is, in general, a random variable, so its value cannot be expected in all cases (or perhaps in any but a few cases) to *equal* the parameter, though of course that would solve (or remove) the statistical inference problem at one stroke if it were possible. The evaluation of the worth of an estimator can be based in part on properties of the probability distribution of estimates that it generates, in part on *a priori* views about the value of the parameter, and in part on judgments about the seriousness of the consequences of having an estimate that misses the value of the parameter by various

[18] Some of the exogenous variables may be random too, and others may be fixed as by policy decisions.

amounts in either direction.[19] A function that assigns a numerical value to the loss incurred by the user of an estimate as a result of any given pair of values of the estimate and the parameter is called a *loss function*. Such losses may be measured in terms of money or any other relevant quantifiable terms, but it is most general to think of them as measured in terms of a utility index. Losses can be positive or zero, or (in the case of gains) negative, but it is conventional to set equal to zero the loss incurred by a perfect estimate (i.e., an estimate equal to the parameter) and to measure other losses relative to that.

5.8   Let α denote a parameter and let a denote a point estimate of α. Then such a loss function may be denoted by

$$(5.2) \qquad L = L_1(a, \alpha) \qquad L_1(\alpha, \alpha) = 0$$

If, as is commonly true, the loss can be said to depend only on the difference between a and α, the loss function may be written as

$$(5.3) \qquad L = L_2(a - \alpha) \qquad L_2(0) = 0$$

If in addition (as is by no means always true) the loss depends on the absolute difference $|a - \alpha|$ but not on whether a exceeds or falls short of α, the loss function is symmetric and can be written as

$$(5.4) \qquad L = L_3(|a - \alpha|) \qquad L_3(0) = 0$$

Suppose the loss due to an overestimate $(a > \alpha)$ depends on $|a - \alpha|$ as in (5.4), and that the loss due to an underestimate $(a < \alpha)$ also depends on $|a - \alpha|$ but in a different way. Then the loss function may be written

$$(5.5) \qquad \begin{aligned} L = L_3(|a - \alpha|) \text{ if } a \geqq \alpha \qquad L_3(0) = 0 \\ L = L_4(|a - \alpha|) \text{ if } a \leqq \alpha \qquad L_4(0) = 0 \end{aligned}$$

Suppose that $L_4(|a - \alpha|)$ is proportional to $L_3(|a - \alpha|)$ with a positive constant of proportionality k. This would mean that the loss due to an overestimate was proportional to the loss due to an underestimate.

$$(5.6) \qquad \begin{aligned} L = L_3(|a - \alpha|) \text{ if } a \geqq \alpha \qquad L_3(0) = 0 \\ L = kL_3(|a - \alpha|) \text{ if } a \leqq \alpha \qquad k > 0 \end{aligned}$$

[19] These matters are discussed systematically and with considerable success in the modern field of statistical decision theory and in Bayesian or subjective statistics. We shall pay implicit attention to such criteria for choices among statistical procedures, but we shall not go into them systematically in this book. The basic original work in decision theory is Wald [1950]. A good account is in Blackwell and Girshick [1954]. Both those books are quite technical. Simpler accounts are given by Bross [1953] and Chernoff and Moses [1959]. Important works in Bayesian or subjective statistics are Savage [1954] and Raiffa and Schlaifer [1961] (both fairly technical) and Schlaifer [1959], which is relatively simple. Econometric ventures in this direction include Theil and Goldberger [1961], Theil [1963], and Drèze [1962]. These are discussed briefly in X.5.8–13. See also Savage [1962], Roberts [1965], Lindley [1965], and Zellner and Chetty [1965].

An alternative to $kL_3(|a - \alpha|)$ is $L_3(k\,|a - \alpha|)$. Of course if L_3 is homogeneous of degree one, they are equivalent. Any symmetric function of the form of (5.4) can be altered as in (5.5) or (5.6) to reflect differences between the consequences of over- and underestimates. If $k = 1$, then (5.6) reduces to (5.4).

5.9   In choosing among estimators on the basis of a loss function, it is a common practice to seek to minimize the mathematical expectation of the loss. This can be done in principle if the probability distribution of each estimator is known, for then the expected loss associated with each estimator can be computed. If the loss function is $L_2(a - \alpha)$ as above and the distribution of the estimator a is represented by the density function $\phi(a)$, then by using the integration technique we see that the expected loss EL for the estimator a is

$$(5.7) \qquad EL = \int_{-\infty}^{\infty} L_2(a - \alpha)\phi(a)\,da$$

5.10   As in many situations, simple functional forms are appealing and are tried out first. A simple and plausible symmetrical loss function is one specifying that the loss is simply proportional to the absolute error. This function is a special case of (5.4). Since the units in which losses are measured can be chosen arbitrarily, just as money amounts can be measured in dollars or nickels, the loss units can be chosen so as to make the constant of proportionality unity. The function is then

$$(5.8) \qquad L = |a - \alpha|$$

As anyone knows who has tried to perform mathematical operations on a function containing absolute values, the resulting discontinuities can be a nuisance. The loss function (5.8) has a sharp corner where $a = \alpha$, so that its first derivative is not continuous at that point, which interferes with the use of differential calculus to minimize its expected value. It has another difficulty too, which it shares with the loss function to be discussed next.

5.11   Another simple plausible symmetrical loss function is the square of the error,

$$(5.9) \qquad L = (a - \alpha)^2$$

This function has no sharp corners and has continuous derivatives, so it is easy to deal with mathematically. Also, as we shall see, it arises naturally in connection with the normal distribution. Minimization of its expected value is closely related to the least-squares estimation method (to be discussed in Chapter IX) under appropriate assumptions. It practically ignores very small errors but is increasingly sensitive to error as the size of the error increases, which has an intuitive appeal.[20] It has been recommended or adopted by many statisticians and economists for many applications.[21] The squared-error loss function (5.9) has a difficulty, however, shared with the absolute error (5.8): It has no bound to the loss that can be sustained, that is, as the error $a - \alpha$ increases without limit, so does the loss. Since the loss is to be interpreted as a negative utility, this means that utility itself is not bounded, which is absurd.[22] Therefore if an unbounded loss function such as (5.9) is to be used, it must be understood as an approximation to the actual loss, not intended to hold for extremely large errors. Such errors in the typical estimation problem are so unlikely that the inaccuracy of the approximate loss function in dealing with them is minor compared with the gain in simplicity resulting from the use of the approximation (5.9).[23]

5.12   In some problems, there is a kind of threshold involved: If the error made is below the threshold level there is no loss, but if the error is greater than the threshold level there is a large loss that is not increased by further increases in the error. Economic losses are not usually of this type, but consider the shipment of a fragile article without shattering it, or the delivery of a message on or before a deadline, or the avoidance of a death from an overdose of a purported remedy. Such a loss function is

(5.10)
$$L = 0 \text{ if } |a - \alpha| \leqq k \qquad k > 0$$
$$L = 1 \text{ if } |a - \alpha| > k$$

The threshold need not be the same for over- and underestimates, and indeed need not be finite for both (though if it is infinite for both then no estimate, however bad, can lead to any loss, a prospect too Utopian—or

[20] See Savage [1954], pp. 232–234, for discussion of this point.

[21] See Mood [1950], p. 149 ("relative efficiency"); Koopmans and Hood [1953], p. 130 ("efficiency"); Savage [1954], pp. 81–82, 232–234.

[22] The celebrated St. Petersburg paradox shows the absurdity of an unbounded utility function for wealth. Suppose you are offered, for a positive price, the chance to play the following game once. A fair coin will be tossed repeatedly until a tail appears, and the total number of tosses made (including the first one showing tail) will be called n. Then you will get a prize of 2^n dollars. Clearly the expected value of the prize in dollars is $\frac{1}{2} \cdot 2 + \frac{1}{4} \cdot 4 + \frac{1}{8} \cdot 8 + \ldots$, which is infinite. Therefore, for any person with an unbounded utility function, the utility of the prize is infinite, and such a person might be expected to be eager to pay any finite price, however large, in return for the chance to play the game once. But surely there is no one who would pay more than a few dollars, perhaps $100, to play this game. What price would you pay? See Savage [1954], pp. 93–95, for further discussion.

[23] See Savage [1954], pp. 81–82. Savage is one of the few writers explicitly recognizing the unbounded-utility implications of (5.9).

too trivial—to study seriously). Then the loss function would be

$$L = 0 \text{ if } k_1 \leqq a - \alpha \leqq k_2 \qquad k_1 < 0, k_2 > 0$$

(5.11)

$$L = 1 \text{ otherwise}$$

If $k_1 = -k_2$, this reduces to (5.10).

5.13   The squared error loss function (5.9) and the threshold loss function (5.11) can be combined to make a loss function that behaves like the squared error for all errors below certain wide limits on either side of zero and shows no further increase in the loss if the error exceeds those limits. This truncated squared-error loss function has the advantages of the squared error except for very large errors and has bounded losses. It has two sharp corners, however, so some smoothed approximation to it might be preferable. Without any such smoothing, it is[24]

$$L = (a - \alpha)^2 \text{ if } k_1 \leqq a - \alpha \leqq k_2 \qquad k_1 \ll 0, k_2 \gg 0$$

(5.12) $$L = k_1{}^2 \text{ if } a - \alpha < k_1$$

$$L = k_2{}^2 \text{ if } a - \alpha > k_2$$

A symmetrical truncated squared-error loss function results if $k_1 = k_2$. Rather than adopting this formally, we adopt the squared error (5.9) and keep in mind that it is not a good approximation for extremely large errors. Some consequences are mentioned in 6.11 below.

6   PROPERTIES OF POINT ESTIMATORS; LIMITING DISTRIBUTIONS, CONSISTENCY, AND OTHER ASYMPTOTIC PROPERTIES[25]

6.1   We now present a brief discussion of several properties of estimators that have sometimes been regarded as desirable by statisticians and economists. Some of these properties have standard definitions that are adopted by practically everyone concerned. We shall discuss the ones known by these terms: *unbiased, minimum-variance, best unbiased, best linear unbiased, minimum expected squared error,* and *consistent.* Some of the properties are defined in slightly different ways by different writers so that the literature about them can be confusing; the ones we shall discuss we shall call *efficient, asymptotically normally distributed, asymptotically unbiased,* and *asymptotically efficient.*

[24] The symbols $\ll$ and $\gg$ in (5.12) mean "is much smaller (greater) than."
[25] This section draws heavily on Cramer [1946], pp. 213–214 and 478–490; Koopmans and Hood [1953], pp. 128–130; and Savage [1954], Chapter 15, on point estimation, pp. 220–245. It also owes much to discussions with David L. Wallace, whose advice I did not always follow, however.

6.2 If the probability distribution of an estimator a of a parameter α has a mean, and not every one does, it is denoted by Ea. If for every sample size Ea exists and is equal to the parameter α, then the estimator a is an *unbiased* estimator of the parameter α. If Ea exists and is not equal to α, then $Ea - \alpha$ is the *bias* of a. As an example, for any distribution of x having a mean μ, the mean $\bar{x}$ of a sample of T random observations (independent or not) is an unbiased estimator of μ, since

$$(6.1) \qquad E\bar{x} = E\frac{1}{T}\sum_1^T x_i = \frac{1}{T}\sum_1^T Ex_i = \frac{1}{T}T\mu = \mu$$

As an example of an estimator that has no mean, consider a sample of T random independent observations from a normal population having constant mean and variance, μ and σ^2, with μ unknown but not zero and σ^2 known, and suppose it is desired to estimate not μ but $1/\mu$. Situations similar to this arise in econometrics all the time when we have made reduced-form estimates and want to transform them into structural estimates, for then we typically need quotients in which the denominators involve parameters. A natural and indeed a good estimator for $1/\mu$ is $1/\bar{x}$. However, the expected value of $1/\bar{x}$ does not exist in this case; it is infinite. This is because (since $\bar{x}$ itself is normally distributed) there is a positive probability density for $\bar{x}$ at the point $\bar{x} = 0$. Therefore the integral of $1/\bar{x}$ times the probability density of $\bar{x}$ (which integral gives the expectation of $1/\bar{x}$) contains the product (at $\bar{x} = 0$) of $1/0$ times a positive number, so it must be infinite. Of course, because $E(1/\bar{x})$ does not exist, $1/\bar{x}$ is not an unbiased estimator of $1/\mu$ (nor can we say it is biased).[26] This is a nuisance, but it does not prevent $1/\bar{x}$ from being a good estimator of $1/\mu$. On the other hand, an estimator is not necessarily good just because it is unbiased. Consider an asymmetrically distributed unbiased estimator that has a high probability of falling far outside a central range near the parameter, as shown by curve (A) in Figure 6.1; it is not a very desirable estimator when viewed from the point of view of minimizing the expected loss. In sum, unbiasedness *taken alone* is not a particularly important property for an estimator to have. However, Theil shows that if the utility function is cardinal (not merely ordinal), and quadratic in the endogenous variables, and if the decision-maker seeks to maximize the mathematical expectation of utility, then unbiased *predictions* are adequate; see Theil [1958], pp. 418–419, or [1961], pp. 415–416.

6.3 If an estimator a of a parameter α has a variance, it is denoted by var a, defined as usual as $E(a - Ea)^2$. To have a variance, it must of

---

[26] We shall see below in 6.9 that even if Ea does not exist, it may be possible to approximate the distribution of a by a distribution that *does* have a mean equal to the parameter α. If so, the nonexistence of Ea is unimportant. This is true, for example, of $1/\bar{x}$ in the context above.

course have a mean Ea. If for every sample size var a exists, and is as small as or smaller than the variance of any other estimator based on the same size of sample, then a is a *minimum-variance* estimator of α. To seek simply for an estimator that has the smallest possible variance among all possible estimators is foolish, because any constant whatever, chosen as an estimator of α, has zero variance, which is as small as a variance can ever be. Taken alone, small (or even zero) variance is not particularly desirable. Consider the highly biased small-variance estimator shown by curve (B) in Figure 6.1. On the other hand, an estimator need not have a

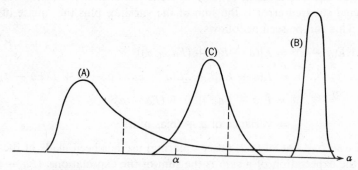

Figure 6.1 Distributions of estimators for (A) an unbiased estimator with large variance, (B) a highly biased estimator with small variance, and (C) a biased estimator with smaller expected squared error than (A) or (B).

variance at all in order to be satisfactory. When $\bar{x}$ is normally distributed with nonzero finite variance and mean μ where $\mu \neq 0$, $1/\bar{x}$ is a good estimator of the parameter $1/\mu$ even though its variance does not exist (is infinite).

6.4 We have seen that an unbiased estimator with large variance is undesirable, and that a small-variance estimator with large bias is too. It seems reasonable, however, that of two estimators having equal variances the one with the smaller bias would be preferable, and that of two estimators having equal biases the one with the smaller variance would be preferable, other things being the same. This suggests two things. First, that among all unbiased estimators, the one(s) with minimum variance would be preferable. Such an estimator is called a *best unbiased estimator*; we shall also call it *efficient*.[27] Note that on these definitions, an estimator cannot be best unbiased or efficient unless it is unbiased; the terms are not defined for estimators that are biased or for estimators that have no mean. Also note that the terms are not defined for estimators whose

[27] This definition of efficiency is not universal. It follows Cramer [1946], pp. 481 and 487, except that he considers only a class of estimators that he calls regular and unbiased; regularity implies certain kinds of differentiability.

variances do not exist.[28] Among the class of estimators that are unbiased and are linear functions of a so-called dependent variable, the one(s) with minimum variance are called *best linear unbiased estimators*, sometimes abbreviated b.l.u.e.

6.5 The second suggestion resulting from the remark at the beginning of 6.4 is that the minimization of some increasing function of both bias and variance might be a useful criterion for selecting among estimators. Thus, we might be willing to tolerate some bias if we could thereby obtain a very small variance, or vice versa. The minimization of expected squared error as in (5.9) above is just such a criterion,[29] for the expected squared error is the sum of the variance plus the square of the bias. This can be seen as follows:

$$(6.2) \quad E(a - \alpha)^2 = E[(a - Ea) + (Ea - \alpha)]^2$$
$$= E(a - Ea)^2 + 2E(a - Ea)(Ea - \alpha) + E(Ea - \alpha)^2$$
$$= E(a - Ea)^2 + 0 + (Ea - \alpha)^2$$
$$= \text{variance of } a + (\text{bias of } a)^2$$

[In the second line of (6.2) (after squaring) use has been made of the fact that the expectation of a sum is the sum of the expectations. $(Ea - \alpha)$ is a constant, so the third term in the second line becomes $(Ea - \alpha)^2$ and the second term becomes $2(Ea - \alpha)E(a - Ea)$, which is zero because $E(a - Ea) = 0$.] Curve (C) in Figure 6.1 describes an estimator that has a relatively small expected squared error, though it is biased and its variance is not zero. Note that although the preceding paragraph makes clear that an efficient estimator is preferable to an unbiased estimator that is not efficient, the use of the expected squared error criterion means that there may be biased estimators that are preferable to efficient estimators. This will be so whenever there is a biased estimator whose variance and squared bias added together are smaller than the variance of an efficient estimator. Note that the term minimum expected squared error is not defined for estimators whose mean and variance do not exist.[30]

[28] Even if var a does not exist, we shall see below in 6.10 that it may be possible to approximate the distribution of a by a distribution that does have a mean equal to the parameter α and a relatively small variance. Then the nonexistence of var a is unimportant.

[29] Koopmans and Hood [1953], p. 130, use the term "efficiency" for this property. Theil [1958], p. 236, uses a related combination of bias and variance, |bias| plus 2 times the standard error, which is mathematically less tractable; in his second edition [1961], pp. 235–240, he has abandoned this proposal.

[30] We shall see below in 6.11 that even if Ea and var a do not exist, it may be possible to approximate the distribution of a by a distribution that does have a mean and a variance, and that has a relatively small expected squared error. Then the nonexistence of Ea and var a is not important.

6.6 The remaining properties to be discussed are properties that appear only in the limit as the sample size T tends to infinity. These are called asymptotic properties. The most important ones are *consistency*, *asymptotic normality*, and *asymptotic efficiency*. They are of interest not because economists ever have, or expect technological progress to furnish, infinite samples, but rather because in many problems convenient approximations hold in the limit and can be used as some kind of guide even for small samples. If and when the behavior of econometric estimators in small samples becomes well understood, then their asymptotic properties will become much less interesting from a practical point of view.

6.7 One of the most important asymptotic properties is *consistency*. In rather rough terms, a is a consistent estimator of a parameter α if, in the limit as the sample size T goes to infinity, the distribution of a approaches a degenerate distribution that has all the probability concentrated at the point $a = \alpha$. This can be true even if Ea and var a both fail to exist. More formally, an estimator a of a parameter α is said to be consistent if, for every value of α, the probability that a differs in absolute value from α by less than some preassigned positive number ϵ (however small) can be made as close to 1 as desired by choosing a suitably large sample size. In symbols, a is a consistent estimator of α if, for all α and all $\epsilon > 0$,

$$(6.3) \qquad \lim_{T \to \infty} \text{Pb}\,(|a - \alpha| < \epsilon) = 1$$

This equation is sometimes read "a converges in probability to α" and sometimes "the probability limit of a is α." The latter is often expressed symbolically as

$$(6.4) \qquad \operatorname*{plim}_{T \to \infty} a = \alpha$$

Thus consistency of a as an estimator of α means that for all α, the probability limit of a is α, or equivalently that for all α, a converges in probability to[31] α. A common way of proving that an estimator is consistent is to make use of the following sufficient conditions (which are quite a lot stronger than necessary because its expectation and variance may fail to exist, but are easy to satisfy in many cases nevertheless): If $\lim_{T \to \infty} Ea$ exists and is equal to α, and $\lim_{T \to \infty}$ var a exists and is equal to zero, then a is a consistent estimator of α. The proof[32] rests on the convergence of the

----

[31] The qualification "for all α" is important, for it insures that if the parameter α changes then the distribution of the estimator a will change accordingly. Without the qualification the definition would say (unreasonably) that any statistic with a probability limit is a consistent estimator of any unrelated parameter that just happens to be equal to that probability limit.

[32] See, for example, Wilks [1943], p. 134.

distribution of $a - \alpha$ to a degenerate distribution with all of the probability concentrated at the point $a - \alpha = 0$. Consistency is a comforting property, because it guarantees the possibility of reducing to an arbitrarily low level the probability of making an absolute error greater than any given size, however small, by choosing a suitably large sample.[33] Of course if nothing is known about an estimator except that it is consistent, there is no guarantee that it will perform well with samples of the sizes that we can afford to use. In this respect consistency is like all asymptotic properties.

6.8　We continue our discussion of asymptotic properties with a description of the idea of the *limiting distribution* associated with an estimator and a definition of an *asymptotically normally distributed* estimator.[34] Consider an estimator a of a parameter α, and let a be a function of the random observations $x_1, \ldots, x_T$. Not every statistic has an associated *limiting distribution* in the sense used here, but if the estimator a has one, it is a probability distribution (a density function) $D(x)$ with the following three properties: (1) it is a *fixed* distribution, that is, for any x, $D(x)$ has a fixed value independent of the sample size T as $T \to \infty$;[35] (2) it is *nondegenerate* in the sense that if it has a variance, that variance is not zero;[36] (3) a *constant*[37] β and a *function* c_T of T can be found such that for every T, c_T is positive and greater than some positive lower bound,[38] and such that the distribution of the statistic $c_T(a - \beta)$ approaches

[33] Savage [1954], pp. 230–232, gives some additional reasons why consistency is valuable.

[34] This will be followed immediately by a discussion of *approximations* to the *mean*, *variance*, and *expected squared error*, and a definition of *asymptotic efficiency*. Then some simple examples will be given in 6.13–14, to give the feel of the several definitions. Relative to the rest of the book, 6.8–14 are rather hard going, but mastery of them will be helpful later.

On a first reading of this section, the reader may wish to skip the rest of the footnotes, for they all concern variations of definition that are used in the literature or that could be used.

[35] This simplifying requirement is not used in all definitions of a limiting distribution. Cramer [1946], pp. 214–215, permits his "limiting distribution" to change without limit as $T \to \infty$. In return for accepting this complication, he is able to simplify property (3) below so that c_T is a constant equal to 1.

[36] This assumption has one minor disadvantage, i.e., it precludes the existence of a limiting distribution in the case of a population with zero variance, but we shall not be interested in such a case.

[37] Instead of a constant β, we could use a function of T, say $\beta(T)$, which has a finite limit as $T \to \infty$, with no change in substance. A constant is simpler. We could go further and permit $\beta(T)$ to grow without limit as $T \to \infty$. This is more complicated so we avoid it, but it would have the advantage of defining a limiting distribution for a statistic like Σx_i, which our definition does not.

[38] For all of the estimators that we shall find desirable, the required function of T is $c_T = \sqrt{T}$. Hence little of practical importance would be lost by framing the defini-

the fixed nondegenerate distribution D in the limit as T goes to infinity. This means that, as $T \to \infty$, for every interval the probability that $c_T(a - \beta)$ falls in the interval approaches the probability assigned to the interval by the distribution D; it also means that for every value of $c_T(a - \beta)$, the density approaches $D[c_T(a - \beta)]$. The mean and variance of the limiting distribution will be called μ_0 and σ_0^2; they may or may not exist. If the statistic whose distribution approaches the fixed nondegenerate distribution D is $c_T(a - \alpha)$ (i.e., if $\beta = \alpha$) and if the associated function c_T approaches infinity in the limit as $T \to \infty$, then a is a *consistent* estimator of α. (This is a weaker sufficient condition for consistency than the one given in 6.7 above, but it is harder to apply. Its sufficiency rests on the convergence of the distribution of $a - \alpha$ to a degenerate distribution at the point $a - \alpha = 0$; the convergence is assured by the existence of the limiting distribution for $c_T(a - \alpha)$ and the fact that $c_T \to \infty$ as $T \to \infty$.) If the limiting distribution is normal, then both $c_T(a - \beta)$ and a are said to be *asymptotically normally distributed*.[39] An estimator can be asymptotically normal with or without being consistent.

6.9 If the mean μ_0 of the limiting distribution associated with an estimator a exists and if Ea also exists, then $Ec_T(a - \beta)$ is approximately equal to μ_0, so that an approximation to Ea for a sample of size T is given by $\beta + \mu_0/c_T$, and the corresponding *approximate bias* of a as an estimator of α for a sample of size T is

$$(6.5) \qquad Ea - \alpha \cong \beta - \alpha + \frac{\mu_0}{c_T}$$

This approximate bias has two parts, $\beta - \alpha$, which is a constant, and μ_0/c_T, which depends on T. For all desirable estimators we shall encounter, c_T approaches infinity as $T \to \infty$, which implies that the approximate bias approaches $\beta - \alpha$ as $T \to \infty$. (Example 3 in Table 6.1 below illustrates.) This approximation is very useful, though it ignores any estimating errors that go to zero faster than does $1/c_T$ in the limit as $T \to \infty$. If μ_0 exists but Ea does not, the expression (6.5) can be regarded as the exact

---

tion of a limiting distribution in terms of $\sqrt{T}$ instead of the more general c_T. Still, pedagogically, I prefer to use c_T because it permits the undesirable estimator in example 4 of Table 6.1 below to have a limiting distribution.

Another point: if β were replaced by a possibly *unbounded* function $\beta(T)$ as mentioned in the preceding footnote, the required c_T should be allowed to approach zero as $T \to \infty$.

[39] Many writers define asymptotic normality in such a way as to require that $c_T = \sqrt{T}$; see Koopmans and Hood [1953], p. 129, and Savage [1954], p. 227. I dislike this (even though $c_T = \sqrt{T}$ in the most important cases) because it requires us to say that certain normal variables are not asymptotically normal; see example 4 in Table 6.1. The definition in Cramer [1946], pp. 213–214, is more general than any of these, including mine.

bias of a distribution that *does* have a mean and that is an approximation to the distribution of a. For practical purposes, even if Ea does not exist, such an approximation makes good sense if T is sufficiently large. If μ_0 exists, we define the *asymptotic mean* and *asymptotic bias*[40] of a respectively as $\beta + \lim_{T \to \infty} \mu_0/c_T$, and $\beta - \alpha + \lim_{T \to \infty} \mu_0/c_T$, and we say that a is an *asymptotically unbiased* estimator of α if $\beta - \alpha + \lim_{T \to \infty} \mu_0/c_T = 0$, regardless of whether Ea exists. These concepts are of less practical importance than the approximations mentioned just above. It may be thought that asymptotic unbiasedness and consistency are the same, but they are not. Consistency is much more important. An example of an asymptotically unbiased estimator that is not consistent is the estimator $\dfrac{1}{2}x_1 + \dfrac{1}{2T}\sum_{2}^{T} x_i$ in example 4 of Table 6.1, below. A consistent estimator may fail to be asymptotically unbiased because the mean of its limiting distribution may fail to exist, in which case its asymptotic bias is not defined. A consistent and asymptotically normal estimator, however, must be asymptotically unbiased.

6.10 If var a and the variance σ_0^2 of the limiting distribution associated with a both exist, then var $c_T(a - \beta)$ is approximately equal to σ_0^2, so that an *approximate variance* of a for a sample of size T is given by

$$(6.6) \qquad \text{var } a \simeq \frac{\sigma_0^2}{c_T^2}$$

For all our desirable estimators, $c_T = \sqrt{T}$ as noted before, which implies that σ_0^2/c_T^2 vanishes as $T \to \infty$. It is often useful to know which of two estimators has the more rapidly vanishing variance as $T \to \infty$, and the fact that $c_T = \sqrt{T}$ suggests comparing the value of σ_0^2 for one estimator with that for another; this is done in 6.12 below. If σ_0^2 exists but var a does not, the expression (6.6) can be regarded as the exact variance (which *does* exist) of a distribution that is an approximation to the distribution of a. For practical purposes such an approximation makes good sense if T is sufficiently large. If σ_0^2 exists, we define the *asymptotic variance*[41] of $c_T(a - \beta)$ (not of a) as σ_0^2, regardless of whether var a exists. No definition of the asymptotic variance of a itself is offered here (a reasonable definition would be $\lim_{T \to \infty} \sigma_0^2/c_T^2$, but in most important

---

[40] This definition is compatible with that of Koopmans and Hood [1953], p. 129, but theirs is stated only for a normal limiting distribution with $c_T = \sqrt{T}$. Sometimes asymptotic bias is defined simply as $\lim (Ea - \alpha)$ (Theil [1958], p. 226, [1961], p. 230), but then asymptotic bias is undefined if Ea does not exist. I therefore prefer the definition in the text.

[41] This definition is in the spirit of Savage [1954], p. 227, except that he gives a definition only for a normal limiting distribution with $c_T = \sqrt{T}$.

cases this is zero, so such a definition would not distinguish among different rates of approach to zero).

6.11 If the mean and variance μ_0 and $\sigma_0{}^2$ of a's associated limiting distribution exist and Ea and var a exist, then an *approximate expected squared error* of a for a sample of size T, following (6.2), is given by the sum of the approximate variance of a from (6.6) plus the square of the approximate bias of a from (6.5), as follows:

$$(6.7) \qquad E(a - \alpha)^2 \cong \frac{\sigma_0{}^2}{c_T{}^2} + \left(\beta - \alpha + \frac{\mu_0}{c_T} \right)^2$$

As noted earlier, $c_T \to \infty$ as $T \to \infty$ for all our desirable estimators, which implies that this expression approaches $(\beta - \alpha)^2$ as $T \to \infty$. Thus (6.7) suggests how with *small* samples an estimator whose (approximate or exact) distribution is biased may be preferred to one whose (approximate or exact) distribution is unbiased, but not with sufficiently large samples. If μ_0 and $\sigma_0{}^2$ exist but Ea and var a do not, (6.7) can be regarded as the exact expected squared error of a distribution that *does* have a mean and a variance and that is an approximation to the distribution of a. For practical purposes such an approximation makes good sense if T is sufficiently large. If μ_0 and $\sigma_0{}^2$ exist, we define the *asymptotic expected squared error* of $c_T a$ (not of a) as the sum of the asymptotic variance and square of asymptotic bias of $c_T(a - \beta)$ from 6.10 and 6.9, thus:

$$\sigma_0{}^2 + [\lim_{T \to \infty} c_T(\beta - \alpha) + \mu_0]^2.$$

It may seem strange to discuss the *approximate* and the *asymptotic* expected squared error of a statistic whose actual variance, and hence *actual* expected squared error, are infinite,[42] as we do here. However, in the light of our earlier discussion of the truncated squared-error loss function in 5.13, it makes good sense in the case of a statistic that has a limiting distribution whose mean and variance exist. Recall that in adopting the squared-error loss function, we did so only for errors smaller in absolute value than some upper limit, such as k; for errors larger than k in absolute value we adopted k^2 as the loss function [see (5.12)]. This means that if the actual distribution of the statistic a is tolerably approximated except in the tails by a distribution that does have a mean and variance, as described in 6.9–10 above, then the expected loss from using the statistic a will be tolerably approximated by the actual expected squared error (6.7) of this approximate distribution of a. This may be seen with the aid of Figure 6.2. The solid line shows the actual distribution of an estimator a of a parameter α for some fixed sample size; it has thick tails and its variance is infinite. The dotted line shows an approximate distribution of

[42] Indeed, Basmann [1961], p. 620, has asserted that it is meaningless.

a; it has thin tails and a finite variance. The approximation is good except in the tails, that is, except for errors larger than the upper limit k specified in the loss function (5.12). The expected squared error of the solid-line distribution (the actual distribution of a) is infinite. The expected squared error of a distribution that is like the solid line, except for having the area in the tails piled up at the points $\alpha \pm k$, is the actual expected loss. The expected squared error of the dotted line (the approximate distribution) approximates (and probably typically even exceeds) this expected loss.

6.12 If an estimator a of a parameter α is consistent and asymptotically normal, then we shall say that it is *asymptotically efficient*[43] if

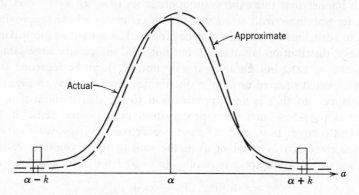

Figure 6.2 Actual and approximate distributions of a statistic showing consequences of using bounded squared-error loss function (5.12) with $k_1 = k_2 = k$.

the asymptotic variance $\sigma_0{}^2$ of its associated statistic $c_T(a - \beta)$ is smaller than or as small as that of any other consistent and asymptotically normal estimator. Note that the term is not defined for estimators that fail to be consistent or asymptotically normal or both. For an asymptotically efficient estimator, the asymptotic expected squared error of the associated statistic $c_T a$ is smaller than or as small as that of any other consistent and asymptotically normal estimator. This can be seen by considering the definition of asymptotic efficiency and the fact that for a consistent asymptotically normal estimator the term $[\lim c_T(\beta - \alpha) + \mu_0]$ in 6.11 is zero. The concept of asymptotic efficiency is similar to that of efficiency defined in 6.4 above, except that (a) it is an asymptotic property, and (b) it can be useful as a guide in dealing with estimators (such as $1/\bar{x}$) that have no mean or variance but that have approximate distributions that *do* have means and variances (see 6.9–11).

---

[43] This definition follows Koopmans and Hood [1953], p. 129. Mood [1950], p. 150, calls this same concept efficiency, and in effect so does Savage [1954], p. 227. Cramer [1946], pp. 489–490, gives a slightly different definition.

6.13 We now consider five examples. They share several features. A sample of independently and identically distributed observations is taken from a population with known finite variance σ^2 and unknown finite mean μ. Table 6.1 summarizes this information, and other conditions assumed in each example: whether x_i is normally distributed, what parameter is to be estimated (μ in most examples, and $1/\mu$ in the last), and what estimator is used. The table also indicates for each example whether a limiting distribution exists for the estimators, and, if so, what are the following: β, c_T, and $c_T(a - \beta)$; μ_0 and σ_0^2 if they exist; the approximate bias and the approximate variance of a if they exist; and whether a is consistent (see 6.8) and asymptotically efficient. In examples 2–5 the approximate expected squared error can be computed from (6.7). In all the examples given, the limiting distribution, if it exists, is normal; no others have been included because the normal is by far the most important limiting distribution, because of the central limit theorem.

6.14 A few remarks may be in order about each example. In example 1 the statistic $\sum x_i$ has no fixed limiting distribution because the limit of its variance is infinite as $T \to \infty$ (but see footnote 35 above). In example 2 $E\bar{x} = \mu$ so $\bar{x}$ is unbiased; it is also efficient and of minimum expected squared error. The central limit theorem insures that $\bar{x}$ has an asymptotic normal distribution. Since observations are independent, var $\bar{x} = \sigma^2/T$ and hence var $\sqrt{T}(\bar{x} - \mu) = \sigma^2$. Therefore $\bar{x}$ is consistent (by the weak condition given in 6.8). Furthermore, $\bar{x}$ is asymptotically unbiased and asymptotically efficient. The same remarks are true of $\bar{x}$ itself in example 3, but here a crazy estimator has been formed by adding $1 + 2/\sqrt{T} + 3/T$ to $\bar{x}$ for didactic reasons. The 1 requires that the value of β be $\mu + 1$ rather than μ; this imparts a bias of 1 to the estimator and destroys consistency. The $2/\sqrt{T}$ gives the limiting distribution a mean μ_0 of 2 rather than zero, and hence adds $2/\sqrt{T}$ to the approximate bias. The $3/T$ goes to zero faster than $1/\sqrt{T}$ as $T \to \infty$ so it does not appear either in the mean of the limiting distribution or in the approximate bias. The variances are not affected by the addition of $1 + 2/\sqrt{T} + 3/T$ because this expression is not a random variable. In example 4 an estimator is contrived (again for didactic reasons) whose variance exists but does *not* go to zero as $T \to \infty$. This is done by giving the first observation in the sample (x_1) a fixed weight in the estimator: $a = \dfrac{1}{2}x_1 + \dfrac{1}{2T}\sum_2^T x_i$. Here $c_T = 1$ (not $\sqrt{T}$ this time) and so the limiting distribution of $c_T(a - \mu)$ is the limit of the distribution of $a - \mu$ itself, which limit is the exact distribution of the statistic $\frac{1}{2}(x_1 - \mu)$, whose mean is 0 and whose variance is $\sigma^2/4$. This is a bad estimator since it is not consistent or efficient; and yet its approximate and asymptotic biases are zero. In example 5, where

TABLE 6.1 Examples Regarding Limiting Distributions Associated with Several Estimators Based on Samples of Independent Observations from a Population with Mean $\mu < \infty$ and Known Variance $\sigma^2 < \infty$

Assumed Conditions				Properties of the Limiting Distribution Associated with the Estimator a								
				Value of					Approx. Bias of a	Approx. var a	Is the Estimator a	
Example No.	Is x_i Normally Distributed?	Desired Parameter, α	Estimator, a	β	c_T	$c_T(a - \beta)$	μ_0	σ_0^2	$\beta + \dfrac{\mu_0}{c_T} - \alpha$	$\dfrac{\sigma_0^2}{c_T^2}$	Consistent?†	Asymptotically Efficient?
1	no	μ	$\sum_1^T x_i$	[A fixed limiting distribution of $\sum x_i$ does not exist]								
2	no	μ	$\bar{x}$	μ	$\sqrt{T}$	$\sqrt{T}(\bar{x} - \mu)$	0	σ^2	0	$\dfrac{\sigma^2}{T}$	yes	yes
3	no	μ	$\bar{x} + 1 + \dfrac{2}{\sqrt{T}} + \dfrac{3}{T}$	$\mu + 1$	$\sqrt{T}$	$\sqrt{T}(\bar{x} - \mu) + 2 + \dfrac{3}{\sqrt{T}}$	2	σ^2	$1 + \dfrac{2}{\sqrt{T}}$	$\dfrac{\sigma^2}{T}$	no	no
4	yes	μ	$\dfrac{x_1}{2} + \dfrac{\sum_2^T x_i}{2T}$	μ	1	$\dfrac{x_1}{2} + \dfrac{\sum_2^T x_i}{2T} - \mu$	0	$\dfrac{\sigma^2}{4}$	0	$\dfrac{\sigma^2}{4}$	no	no
5‡	yes; $\mu \neq 0$	$\dfrac{1}{\mu}$	$\dfrac{1}{\bar{x}}$	$\dfrac{1}{\mu}$	$\sqrt{T}$	$\sqrt{T}\left(\dfrac{1}{\bar{x}} - \dfrac{1}{\mu}\right)$	0	$\dfrac{1}{\mu^4}$	0	$\dfrac{1}{T\mu^4}$	yes	yes

* *Source*: See text, sections 6.8-13. † See 6.7-8. ‡ See Savage [1954], pp. 228–229.

270

$1/\bar{x}$ estimates the inverse $1/\mu$ of the nonzero mean of a normal population, neither $E(1/\bar{x})$ nor var $(1/\bar{x})$ exists, so $1/\bar{x}$ is neither unbiased nor efficient nor of minimum expected squared error. However, $\sqrt{T}(1/\bar{x} - 1/\mu)$ has a normal limiting distribution with mean 0 and variance $1/\mu^4$, so $1/\bar{x}$ is consistent and asymptotically normal. It is also asymptotically efficient, and its approximate distribution is unbiased and of small expected squared error relative to the (exact or approximate) distributions of other consistent and asymptotically normal estimates; see Savage [1954], pp. 228–229.

7. HYPOTHESIS TESTING AND INTERVAL ESTIMATION; OPERATING CHARACTERISTICS AND THE DESIGN OF A TEST; SIGNIFICANCE

7.1 An *interval estimator* (as opposed to a point estimator) is a statistic, each of whose values is an interval (rather than a single number) intended to capture the true value of the parameter between its end points or on one of them. Interval estimation is intimately related to *hypothesis testing*, which will be discussed first.

7.2 In statistical inference the typical hypothesis to be tested is a statement that a parameter, such as a population mean μ, is equal to some chosen value, say θ. Data and *a priori* information are then combined in order to reach one of two decisions: to accept or reject the hypothesis being tested.[44] For example, we might use survey data to test the hypothesis that the mean of the population of family personal incomes in the United States in a certain year was \$6500, or that the interest elasticity of demand for capital goods is zero. In any practical problem, a hypothesis so stated, if taken literally, is virtually certain to be false, because it is almost inconceivable in a complex world that the value θ chosen for the test should turn out to be *exactly* equal to the parameter that the test is about. It must be understood, therefore, that the economist has in mind a range of values extending some distance on either side of θ, from $\theta - \gamma$ to $\theta + \delta$, for example, such that if he knew that μ was in that interval his decision would be the same as if he knew that $\mu = \theta$ exactly. The numbers γ and δ, which may but need not be equal, express the economist's view about how great a deviation of the true parameter μ from θ in each direction would be small enough to ignore.

7.3 How might values be assigned to γ and δ? We can think of a loss function $L_A(\mu)$ showing the loss that will occur as a function of μ when the decision is made to accept the hypothesis that $\mu = \theta$, and another

---

[44] Sometimes a third decision is allowed: collect more data. The study of such situations is known as sequential analysis. We shall not discuss it.

loss function $L_R(\mu)$ showing the loss that will occur as a function of μ when the decision is made to reject the hypothesis.[45] Presumably $L_A(\mu)$ has a minimum where $\mu = \theta$ and rises (or does not fall) as μ moves away from θ, and presumably $L_R(\mu)$ has a maximum where $\mu = \theta$ and declines (or does not rise) as μ moves away from θ; or at least the difference $L_R(\mu) - L_A(\mu)$ has a maximum where $\mu = \theta$. (Otherwise it would be better to choose a new value of θ to make this so.) For all values of μ

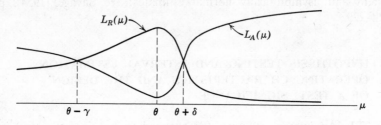

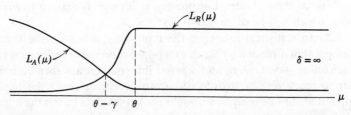

Figure 7.1 Two possible pairs of loss functions $L_A(\mu)$ and $L_R(\mu)$ for tests of hypotheses. See 7.3 in text.

such that $L_A(\mu) < L_R(\mu)$ the appropriate (i.e., loss-minimizing) decision is to accept the hypothesis, and for all values of μ such that $L_A(\mu) > L_R(\mu)$ the appropriate decision is to reject it. Therefore if the two functions cross at a value of μ below θ, that value of μ should be chosen for $\theta - \gamma$, thus determining γ; and if they do not, $\theta - \gamma$ should be assigned the value $-\infty$ (i.e., $\gamma = \infty$). Similarly, if the two functions cross at a value of μ above θ, that value should be chosen for $\theta + \delta$, thus determining δ; and if they do not, $\theta + \delta$ should be assigned the value ∞ (i.e., $\delta = \infty$). Clearly if both γ and δ were assigned the value ∞, this would mean we should always accept the hypothesis that $\mu = \theta$ no matter what the value of μ, a case not worth discussing (recall k_1 and k_2 in 5.12 above). Some possible pairs of loss functions are shown in Figure 7.1, together with the corresponding values of $\theta - \gamma$ and $\theta + \delta$.

---

[45] There are two loss functions because we have suggested that there are just two actions to choose from.

7.4 Clearly if the value of the parameter μ were *known*, there would be no need for statistical inference concerning its value, and we would simply and correctly decide to accept or reject the hypothesis that $\mu = \theta$ by looking at the loss functions L_A and L_R; as indicated in 7.3. In the econometric problems we shall discuss, many of the interesting parameters are not known, but information about them can be obtained from sample data. We continue to illustrate with the case of a population mean μ; for other parameters the principles are the same. The procedure is: Decide the value of T, the sample size;[46] observe the sample data $x_1, \ldots, x_T$; use the sample mean $\bar{x}$ as a point estimator of μ; and then accept the hypothesis that $\mu = \theta$ if the observed value of $\bar{x}$ is not "too far" from θ, and reject the hypothesis that $\mu = \theta$ if the observed value of $\bar{x}$ is "too far" from θ. (How far is "too far", and the sample size T are, of course, crucial features of the test; criteria for deciding them will be discussed presently.) In other words, an *acceptance region* is laid out on the $\bar{x}$-axis, extending some distance away from θ on both sides. Let us call its lower and upper limits $\bar{x}_l$ and $\bar{x}_u$ respectively. Then the value of $\bar{x}$ is computed from the observed sample. If $\bar{x}$ falls within the acceptance region or on its boundary (i.e., if $\bar{x}_l \leq \bar{x} \leq \bar{x}_u$) the decision is to accept the hypothesis that $\mu = \theta$; and if $\bar{x}$ falls outside the acceptance region (i.e., in the *rejection region*) the decision is to reject the hypothesis. The acceptance region need not extend the same distance on both sides of θ; indeed in some problems the best choice is to let it extend to infinity on either the positive or the negative side of θ (but not on both sides, unless we wish to accept the hypothesis regardless of what the sample data reveal).[47] Usually it will not turn out that $\bar{x}_l$ should be chosen equal to $\theta - \gamma$, or that $\bar{x}_u$ should be chosen equal to $\theta + \delta$.

7.5 This test procedure introduces the possibility that the wrong decision about the hypothesis will be made. Suppose that the parameter μ *is* in the interval from $\theta - \gamma$ to $\theta + \delta$ or at one of its end points; then the appropriate decision is to accept the hypothesis that $\mu = \theta$ (see 7.3). In such a case, if the result of applying the test procedure to the sample is to *accept* the hypothesis, there is no error; but if the result is to reject the hypothesis, it is said that an *error of type I* has been made. Suppose instead that μ *is not* in the interval from $\theta - \gamma$ to $\theta + \delta$; then the appropriate decision is to *reject* the hypothesis that $\mu = \theta$. In such a case, if the result of applying the test procedure to the sample is to reject the hypothesis,

---

[46] Recall footnote 44 and accompanying text.

[47] In most cases the best choice for the acceptance region is a one-piece region, that is, one that can be described simply as all points between and including two stated limits. Occasionally an acceptance region with two pieces or more is desirable. In most cases the best acceptance region will include the tested value θ, but sometimes all of it will lie to one side of θ.

there is no error; but if the result is to accept the hypothesis, it is said that a *type II error* has been made. The probability that a test will reject the hypothesis when μ is actually equal to θ is called the probability of type I error and will be denoted by P_I. It is of course a property of the test procedure and is the probability that a sample will arise in which $\bar{x} < \bar{x}_l$ or $\bar{x} > \bar{x}_u$, when $\mu = \theta$. (The probability of rejecting the hypothesis when $\mu \neq \theta$ is not well defined unless the value of μ is stated, because of course the distribution of $\bar{x}$ depends on μ since $\mu = E\bar{x}$; see 7.9 below.)

7.6   The aim is to choose the sample size T and the acceptance limits $\bar{x}_l$ and $\bar{x}_u$ in the best way, which we take to mean in such a way as to *minimize the expected value of the net loss to be incurred*. If extra observations are purchased at an additional cost, this cost must be reckoned as part of the loss, and any observations will be judged worthwhile if and only if the information they yield reduces the expected loss by more than the cost of the observations. Let us approach the choice of T, $\bar{x}_l$, and $\bar{x}_u$ in three stages. In the first stage, in 7.8–15, we shall consider as given the sample size T and the probability P_I of type I error (defined in 7.5) and discuss the best choice of $\bar{x}_l$ and $\bar{x}_u$ as functions of the given T and P_I. This will yield in principle a rule for choosing the best $\bar{x}_l$ and $\bar{x}_u$ whenever T and P_I are fixed; the choice of course will depend on T and P_I. In the second stage, in 7.16–17, we shall consider T as given and discuss the best choice of P_I as a function of the given T. In so doing we associate with each value of P_I the pair of values of $\bar{x}_l$ and $\bar{x}_u$ that is best for the given T and the value of P_I according to the rule obtained in the first stage. This will yield in principle a rule for choosing the best P_I, $\bar{x}_l$, and $\bar{x}_u$ whenever T is fixed. The choice of course will depend on T. In the third stage, in 7.18–19, we shall discuss the best choice of T, and in so doing we associate with each value of T the values of P_I and $\bar{x}_l$ and $\bar{x}_u$ that are best for the given T according to the rules in stage two. This will yield in principle a rule for choosing the best T and $\bar{x}_l$ and $\bar{x}_u$, which is what is wanted (note that when T, $\bar{x}_l$, and $\bar{x}_u$ are chosen, then P_I is determined). A summary of the three stages is given in 7.20.

7.7   To make matters more concrete, suppose we seek to test the hypothesis that a population mean μ is equal to 10, that is, $\theta = 10$. And suppose the maintained hypothesis, not questioned during the test, says that the observations x_1, x_2, x_3, ... are independent random drawings from a normal population with constant mean (μ) and constant variance known to be equal to 4, that is, $\sigma^2 = 4$. Then $\bar{x}$ is normal with mean μ and variance $\sigma^2/T = 4/T$. Arrow [1960] discusses these issues for a similar case.

7.8   *For the first of the three stages in the choice of a test* mentioned in 7.6, suppose the sample size T has been tentatively set at 25, and the probability P_I of type I error has been tentatively set at 10 per cent, or .10.

This means (recalling 7.7) that $\bar{x}$ is normal with mean μ and variance $4/25 = .16$ and standard deviation $2/5 = .4$, and that we must choose an acceptance region such that when $\mu = 10$ the probability of $\bar{x}$ falling in the region is .90. There are infinitely many such regions, some consisting of one piece and some of more than one. Three of the one-piece ones are shown in Figure 7.2. Panel (a) shows a region symmetrical around the tested value 10, panel (b) shows an asymmetrical one with finite limits,

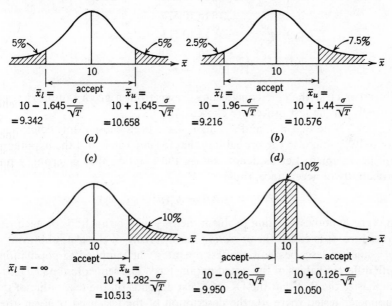

Figure 7.2 Four possible acceptance regions (unshaded) for testing the hypothesis $\mu = 10$, with $P_{\rm I} = .10$ (shaded areas), $T = 25$, and $\sigma = 2$.

and panel (c) shows the asymmetrical one that has $\bar{x}_l = \infty$. A symmetrical two-piece region is shown in Figure 7.2(d), although such a region would never be chosen for this test. The tests in Figures 7.2(a) and (b) are called two-tailed, the one in Figure 7.2(c) one-tailed. The values of $\bar{x}_l$ and $\bar{x}_u$ in each of the four panels of Figure 7.2 have been chosen with the aid of the normal distribution table[48] so as to make $P_{\rm I} = .10$. Now suppose that of four different statisticians, each for his own reasons has chosen a different one of the four tests depicted in Figure 7.2. And suppose that the same random sample of 25 observations is presented to all four statisticians, and that the mean of that sample is $\bar{x} = 10.54$. Then the statistician using the test of Figure 7.2(a), whose acceptance region runs from 9.342

[48] See the last line (the line for an infinite number of degrees of freedom) of Table 1 of Appendix C, and use the standard normal variable $z = (\bar{x} - \mu)/(\sigma/\sqrt{T})$. One may deal with z and the corresponding z_l and z_u instead of $\bar{x}$, $\bar{x}_l$ and $\bar{x}_u$ if desired.

to 10.658, accepts the hypothesis that $\mu = 10$ because the sample mean is inside the acceptance region. This decision and the decisions of the other three statisticians can be summarized thus:

Test as in Figure	Acceptance Region for $\bar{x}$	Decision if $\bar{x} = 10.54$
7.2(a)	9.342 to 10.568	accept
7.2(b)	9.216 to 10.576	accept
7.2(c)	$-\infty$ to 10.513	reject
7.2(d)	$\begin{cases} -\infty \text{ to } 9.950 \\ 10.050 \text{ to } +\infty \end{cases}$	accept

Thus it is clear that the conclusions drawn from a given sample depend crucially on the test procedure chosen.

7.9 Note that if T and $\bar{x}_l$ and $\bar{x}_u$ have been chosen, this determines not only P_I, but also the probability that for *any* value of μ the hypothesis will be accepted. Let us denote by ϕ_A the function that determines this probability of acceptance, thus:

$$(7.1) \qquad \mathrm{Pb}(\bar{x}_l \leqq \bar{x} \leqq \bar{x}_u) = \phi_A(\mu; T, \bar{x}_l, \bar{x}_u)$$

In every hypothesis-testing problem there is such a function for each test procedure. It is called the *operating characteristic* of the test, abbreviated OC, since it describes how the test operates when applied to populations with different values of the tested parameter.[49] The semicolon in (7.1) is to emphasize the fact that the OC of a test depends on the true value of the parameter tested (here μ); the description of the test used is given after the semicolon. In our example, where $\bar{x}$ is normally distributed, the OC is the following function of μ:

$$(7.2) \qquad \mathrm{Pb}\,(\bar{x}_l \leqq \bar{x} \leqq \bar{x}_u) = \int_{\bar{x}_l}^{\bar{x}_u} \frac{\sqrt{T}}{\sqrt{2\pi}\sigma} \exp\left[-\frac{T(\bar{x} - \mu)^2}{2\sigma^2}\right] d\bar{x}$$

It is of course at its maximum when $\mu = \frac{1}{2}(\bar{x}_l + \bar{x}_u)$, and it declines as μ moves further away from that value. The operating characteristic curves of the four tests shown in Figure 7.2 are sketched in Figure 7.3. Of course the value of the operating characteristic when $\mu = 10$ is $1 - P_\mathrm{I}$, that is, .90.

7.10 The problem now in stage one (recall 7.6) is to choose the best test among all those having $T = 25$ and $P_\mathrm{I} = .10$. This must clearly be done in the light of three kinds of information: the operating characteristics of the various tests as illustrated in Figure 7.3, the loss functions $L_A(\mu)$ and $L_R(\mu)$, and any *a priori* ideas that the maintained hypothesis

[49] The *power function* of the test is 1 minus the OC; it shows the probability of *rejecting* the hypothesis as a function of μ.

contains about which values of μ are possible and which impossible (or about how likely it is that μ lies in various ranges of values). All these things are important.[50] The operating characteristic of each test summarizes its relevant features. The loss functions express our views as to the seriousness of the consequences of wrong decisions about the hypothesis and hence are important in choosing a test. And if we have any *a priori* views as to where the true value of μ will be found, they will be in the maintained hypothesis and will affect our choice of a test. The given

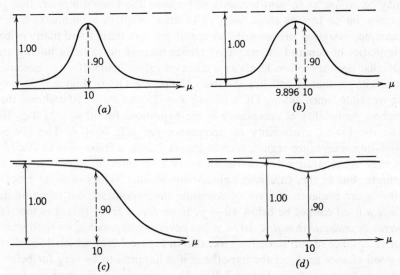

Figure 7.3 Operating characteristics for the four tests shown in Figure 7.2. (The vertical axis shows the probability of accepting the hypothesis that $\mu = 10$.)

values of T and P_{I} of course affect the choice too. Let us try to illustrate with four examples.

7.11 First, we can rule out the two-piece acceptance region of Figure 7.2(d), because although it has the desired P_{I} of 0.10, it has an even *lower* probability of rejecting the hypothesis when the hypothesis is grossly false, as seen in Figure 7.3(d). To use such a test here would be foolish (but see X.7.16).

7.12 Second, suppose that both $L_A(\mu)$ and $L_R(\mu)$ are symmetrical about the point $\mu = 10$, so that $\gamma = \delta$ and the consequences of any act depend on the absolute difference $|\mu - 10|$ but not on the sign of that difference. Suppose also that little or nothing is known *a priori* about the value of μ. Then it is reasonable to choose an acceptance region symmetrical about the value 10, as in Figure 7.2(a). This region (like all those in Figure 7.2) would have a chance of .90 of accepting the hypothesis

[50] See again note 19 in 5.7.

when $\mu = 10$ and it is the shortest such region. Unlike any of the others its probability of accepting the hypothesis whenever $\mu \neq 10$ would be less than .90 and would depend only on $|\mu - 10|$.

7.13 Third, suppose that both $L_A(\mu)$ and $L_R(\mu)$ are symmetrical about the point $\mu = 10$, but that we are certain *a priori* that μ is not less than $10 - \gamma$. This means that *either* the correct decision is to accept the hypothesis $\mu = 10$, *or* μ is so *high* that the correct decision is to reject the hypothesis; there is no need to protect against the possibility that μ may be so *low* as to justify rejection, because it is known *a priori* that μ cannot be so low as that. Such cases arise often in econometrics, for example, marginal propensities to spend are less than 1 and many price elasticities of demand are negative. Hence there is no value in having an OC that declines to low levels as μ takes on values below $10 - \gamma$, because it is known that μ will not do that. Hence the OC in Figure 7.3(c) is appropriate, since among OC's having $T = 25$ and $P_I = .10$ it shows the highest probability of acceptance of the hypothesis for $10 - \gamma \leqq \mu \leqq 10$ and the lowest probability of acceptance for $\mu \geqq 10 + \delta$. The corresponding acceptance region, seen in Figure 7.2(c), is from $-\infty$ to 10.513. It may seem strange to choose an acceptance interval whose length is infinite, but in this case it is appropriate because values of $\bar{x}$ far below $10 - \gamma$ are evidence in favor of accepting the hypothesis, not rejecting it, since μ itself cannot be below $10 - \gamma$. If we feel *a priori* that it is merely *highly improbable* that $\mu < 10 - \gamma$, but nevertheless *possible*, we shall want an acceptance region something like that in Figure 7.2(b), which does offer a good chance to reject the hypothesis if μ happens to be very far below $10 - \gamma$, as indicated in Figure 7.3(b). The examples in this and the foregoing paragraph bring out forcefully the critical role played by *a priori* views about the value of the parameter being tested, for they can lead us to choose any of the acceptance regions in the first three panels of Figure 7.2, or any intervening region, or any similar region off center to the right.

7.14 Fourth, suppose that as in the second example little is known *a priori* about μ, but that the loss functions $L_A(\mu)$ and $L_R(\mu)$ are such that it is much more important to reject the hypothesis that $\mu = 10$ in case μ exceeds 10 slightly than it is in case μ falls short of 10 slightly, as in the top panel of Figure 7.1. In such a case we want an asymmetrical acceptance region like that in Figure 7.2(b), which would be more likely to reject the hypothesis if $\mu > 10$ than if μ falls short of 10 by the same amount, as seen in Figure 7.3(b). If the loss functions $L_A(\mu)$ and $L_R(\mu)$ never cross below the value $\mu = 10$, so that $\gamma = \infty$ (as in a figure like the bottom panel of Figure 7.1 but reversed right to left), then no value of μ below 10 (no matter how far) would justify rejecting the hypothesis. Hence a rejection region extending to $-\infty$ as in Figure 7.2(c) would be correct. Its OC curve is in Figure 7.3(c). The examples in this paragraph and 7.12 bring out forcefully the critical importance of the loss functions. In case the loss functions are not symmetrical about the tested value of μ (as they are not in this paragraph), and also one has *a priori* views about the value of μ (as in 7.13), both the loss functions and these *a priori* views may militate against choosing an acceptance region that is centered on the tested value, possibly in opposing directions, and the task of choosing the best acceptance region becomes more complicated.

   7.15 Paragraphs 7.8–14 have suggested how to choose an acceptance region when T, P_{I}, L_A, L_R, and prior ideas about μ are given. Denote the acceptance limits so chosen by the symbols $\bar{x}^*_{l.T,P_{\mathrm{I}}}$ and $\bar{x}^*_{u.T,P_{\mathrm{I}}}$, the asterisk indicating that these are the chosen limits, and the subscripts after the period $(.T, P_{\mathrm{I}})$ indicating that T and P_{I} are still to be taken as given. If the prior ideas about μ are expressed by a subjective probability distribution $\psi(\mu)$, then the best acceptance region can be expressed as depending on T, P_{I}, L_A, L_R, and ψ as follows:

$$\bar{x}^*_{l.T,P_{\mathrm{I}}} = f_l(T, P_{\mathrm{I}}, L_A, L_R, \psi)$$
(7.3)
$$\bar{x}^*_{u.T,P_{\mathrm{I}}} = f_u(T, P_{\mathrm{I}}, L_A, L_R, \psi)$$

It is to be understood that f_l and f_u depend on the *functions* L_A, L_R, and ψ themselves, *not* on the *values* of those functions at some particular value of μ. Thus f_l and f_u do not depend on μ. (Of course, however, if μ were known then we should dispense with the whole inference apparatus and simply decide what to do by comparing $L_A(\mu)$ and $L_R(\mu)$ as described in 7.3.)

   7.16 *The second stage in the choice of a test* starts with the assumption that the sample size T is given, but the probability P_{I} of type I error is not (recall 7.6). Here we note that for any value of P_{I}, the best acceptance region for the given T and that value of P_{I} will depend on T and P_{I} as in (7.3), and accordingly the best acceptance region for the given T will be obtained by varying P_{I} in (7.3) and choosing the best of the resulting regions, in a way to be discussed presently. No region is eligible for consideration in this second stage unless it is the best region for the given T and *some* value of P_{I} according to (7.3). The best acceptance limits for the given T will be denoted by $\bar{x}^*_{l.T}$ and $\bar{x}^*_{u.T}$ to indicate that they are chosen when T is still given. The value of P_{I} that leads to the best acceptance region for the given T will be denoted by $P^*_{\mathrm{I}.T}$ to indicate that it is the chosen value when T is still given. The acceptance limits that are best for given T and for the value $P^*_{\mathrm{I}.T}$ are thus at least as good as any of those obtainable by letting P_{I} vary arbitrarily for the given T. Hence we have, using (7.3), the following relations:

$$\bar{x}^*_{l.T} \equiv \bar{x}^*_{l.T,P_{\mathrm{I}.T}} = f_l(T, P^*_{\mathrm{I}.T}, L_A, L_R, \psi)$$
(7.4)
$$\bar{x}^*_{u.T} \equiv \bar{x}^*_{u.T,P_{\mathrm{I}.T}} = f_u(T, P^*_{\mathrm{I}.T}, L_A, L_R, \psi)$$

Schematically, we can think of (7.3) as resulting from assigning a gain or loss index to every acceptance region for given T and P_I, and then for each pair T and P_I choosing the region having the highest gain index. If the relation between this highest gain index and the value of P_I is graphed as in Figure 7.4, for given T, we can then see that the best choice of P_I leads to the region with the highest point on the graph; that is what is described by (7.4).

7.17   Now how might we try to apply this scheme to the decision as to what level for P_I is best? Consider the example of 7.12 and Figures

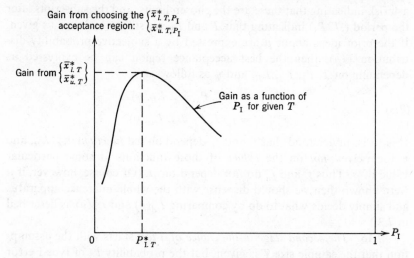

Figure 7.4   Illustrating the choice of the probability P_I of type I error when the sample size T is given. See equation (7.4).

7.2(a) and 7.3(a), in which the best acceptance interval given $T = 25$ and $P_I = .10$ was one centered on the tested value 10. The effect of decreasing P_I to a lower level is to widen the acceptance region shown in Figure 7.2(a) so that less of the probability distribution of $\bar{x}$ falls outside it in each tail when $\mu = 10$. This wider acceptance region will have a higher probability of accepting (and therefore a lower probability of rejecting) the hypotheses than does the centered region whose $P_I = .10$, *no matter what the value of μ.* Hence the OC curve of the test corresponding to the wider acceptance region will lie *above* the OC curve shown in Figure 7.3(a), for every value of μ. Is it wise to decrease the probability of type I error (and accordingly increase the probability of a type II error for every value of μ) by thus widening the acceptance region? The answer must be yes if we feel, in the light of our loss functions, that the reduction of expected loss due to the decrease in P_I is larger than the increase in expected loss due to the rise in the probability of type II error. Thus when it is particularly important to prevent a type I error, we are likely to play safe against this risk and choose a small P_I; and when it is particularly important to avoid a type II error, we are likely to play safe against *this* risk and choose a large P_I. In every case a compromise must be reached between the two when the sample size is given, since a reduction in the probability of one type of error can only be had at the expense of a rise in the probability of the other. When this has been done, the resulting P_I is $P^*_{I.T}$, and the resulting acceptance limits are none other than $\bar{x}^*_{l.T}$ and $\bar{x}^*_{u.T}$ in (7.4) above. It may happen that the best acceptance region, given $T = 25$, is not centered on the tested value, 10, but is off center, as in Figure 7.2(*b*) or (*c*). It may happen that for $P_I = .10$ the best region is centered, and for a lower or higher P_I it is not, and so forth. These cases are handled in the same way as the one described in this and the preceding paragraph.

7.18   *The third stage in the choice of a test* starts with neither the sample size T nor the probability P_I of type I error fixed (recall 7.6). Here we note that the best acceptance region for a given value of T depends on T, and indeed is the one whose limits are $\bar{x}^*_{l.T}$ and $\bar{x}^*_{u.T}$ in (7.4). Accordingly, the best acceptance limits of all are found by varying T in (7.4) and choosing the best resulting limits, in a way to be described presently. The best acceptance limits of all, so chosen, will be denoted by $\bar{x}_l{}^*$ and $\bar{x}_u{}^*$. The corresponding best sample size will be called T^*. Then, using (7.3) and (7.4), we have the relationship

$$(7.5) \qquad \bar{x}_l{}^* \equiv \bar{x}^*_{l.T^*} \equiv \bar{x}^*_{l.T^*, P^*_{I.T^*}} = f_l(T^*, P^*_{I.T^*}, L_A, L_R, \psi)$$
$$= g_l(L_A, L_R, \psi)$$

and an analogous relationship for $\bar{x}_u{}^*$. The expressions $g_l(L_A, L_R, \psi)$ and $g_u(L_A, L_R, \psi)$ indicate that $\bar{x}_l{}^*$ and $\bar{x}_u{}^*$, the optimal acceptance limits, depend on L_A, L_R, and ψ, that is, on loss functions and prior ideas about the value of the parameter being tested. The optimal sample size depends on these too:

$$(7.6) \qquad\qquad\qquad T^* = h(L_A, L_R, \psi)$$

7.19   How do we apply this scheme to the decision as to what sample size T is best? Consider the example of 7.17, in which the best acceptance region given $T = 25$ was found to be centered on the tested value, 10, and to have some particular value of P_I, namely, $P^*_{I.25}$, not necessarily .10. The effect of increasing T is to make possible a new test that is related as follows to the old test with $T = 25$: The new test can be more likely to *accept* the hypothesis when μ is equal to or near 10, and more likely to *reject* the hypothesis when μ is far from 10. The OC curve of a possible new test with $T > 25$ is shown by a dotted line in Figure 7.5, as compared with the solid line that represents the OC curve of the best test obtainable given $T = 25$. This may be verified by studying (7.2), which expresses the OC. Without question the OC corresponding to the larger sample size is better, for it offers lower probabilities of both type I and type II errors. The only question is whether it is enough better to justify the extra costs incurred by increasing the sample size. Like the determination of $P^*_{1.T}$ in 7.16–17, the choice of sample size must be based on expected gains and losses and the attempt to maximize the net gains, where costs of obtaining data are included among the losses. When this has been done, the resulting sample size is T^* and the resulting acceptance limits are the $\bar{x}_l{}^*$ and $\bar{x}_u{}^*$ of (7.5). T^* may be greater or less than 25. It is likely to be large if data are cheap and if γ and δ are small so that accuracy

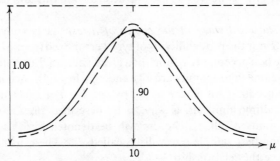

Figure 7.5 Operating characteristics for $T = 25$ (solid line) and for $T > 25$ (dotted line) for tests of the hypothesis that $\mu = 10$.

is important; it is likely to be small if data are costly and if γ and δ are large so that no great accuracy is needed.

7.20 The discussion of 7.6–19 concerning the choice of the sample size T and the acceptance limits $\bar{x}_l$ and $\bar{x}_u$ may be summarized thus. We have at our disposal three kinds of adjustments: changing the sample size, changing the probability of type I error P_I, and changing the location of the acceptance region along the $\bar{x}$-axis (the location may be characterized by the lower limit $\bar{x}_l$, since $\bar{x}_u$ is determined when T, P_I, and $\bar{x}_l$ are specified). Increasing the sample size (keeping P_I constant) incurs costs but permits a desirable change in the shape of the OC curve, raising it near $\mu = 10$ where the hypothesis should be accepted, and lowering it in regions where the hypothesis should be rejected. Increasing P_I (keeping T constant) permits the whole OC curve to rise everywhere, thus making type II error less likely and type I error more likely. Moving the lower acceptance limit to the right (keeping T and P_I constant) raises the probability of acceptance for high values of μ and lowers it for low values of μ, and vice versa (see Figures 7.2 and 7.3). The best choice of these three things—T, P_I, and $\bar{x}_l$—is the one that offers the greatest expected net gain or the least expected net loss, in the light of our ideas about the gains and losses to be had if we accept or reject the hypothesis for various values of μ (the loss functions L_R and L_A) and our prior views about the value of μ. We want to place the acceptance region where $\bar{x}$ is *likely* to fall if $\theta - \gamma \leqq \mu \leqq \theta + \delta$, and at the same time where $\bar{x}$ is *unlikely* to fall if μ has some other value that it would be costly to mistake for θ. The sample size should be chosen so that the marginal gain from increasing it is equal to the marginal cost of so doing. In any practical problem, and especially in econometric inference problems, the choices can be only approximate, since prior ideas about parameters and loss functions can be spelled out only vaguely.

7.21   The terms "significant" and "significance level" are often used in describing statistical tests. The *significance level* of a test is simply the probability P_I of rejecting the hypothesis under test if it is true. Thus a low significance level corresponds to a wide acceptance region, and a high level to a narrow region, *ceteris paribus*. The difference between the observed value of a statistic and the tested value of the parameter is said to be *significant* if the statistic falls outside the acceptance region. It is said to be *very* or *highly significant* if this is the case even for a *low* significance level. The discussion of the OC above makes it clear that the significance level P_I of a test, taken alone, gives a woefully incomplete description of the test. The significance level is equal to 1 minus the height of the OC curve at the point where the parameter is equal to the tested value ($\mu = 10$ in the foregoing examples). As the OC curves in Figures 7.3 and 7.5 suggest, for any hypothesis there is an infinite variety of tests all having the same significance level, some with large sample sizes and some with small, some with acceptance regions centered on the tested value of the parameter and some with off-center regions of either finite or infinite length, and so forth. Hence in reporting the results of a test, it is helpful to give not only the significance level P_I but also at least a rough description of the OC curve of the test. Then the user of the report is in a better position to interpret it in the light of his own opinions and purposes.

7.22   Let us now briefly discuss *interval estimation*, as promised at the beginning of this section. An interval estimator of a parameter is an interval constructed from the observed data so as to have a specified probability of catching within its limits the unknown fixed value of the parameter in question. It is often called a *confidence interval* or a *confidence region*, the specified probability being known as the *confidence coefficient*. The lower and upper limits of a confidence interval for a parameter μ are denoted by μ_l and μ_u respectively. If the confidence interval for the population mean μ is made symmetrical around the sample mean $\bar{x}$, its upper and lower limits are given (when σ is known) by an expression $\bar{x} \pm k\sigma_{\bar{x}}$, that is,

(7.7)
$$\mu_l = \bar{x} - k\sigma_{\bar{x}}$$
$$\mu_u = \bar{x} + k\sigma_{\bar{x}}$$

where $\sigma_{\bar{x}}$ is the standard deviation of $\bar{x}$, and k is a number to be determined. If the interval is not symmetrical about $\bar{x}$, its limits are given by $\mu_l = \bar{x} - k_1\sigma_{\bar{x}}$ and $\mu_u = \bar{x} + k_2\sigma_{\bar{x}}$. Such an estimator is a random variable because through $\bar{x}$ it depends on the sample observations $x_1, \ldots, x_T$. Therefore some confidence intervals for the parameter μ do catch μ within their limits, and some do not. If a set of confidence intervals is constructed for a single parameter, μ, for instance, all with the same confidence coefficient, one interval being constructed for each of the possible (and equally likely) random samples of size T that could be drawn, then the proportion of these confidence intervals that do catch the parameter will be equal to the given confidence coefficient. Indeed, that is the meaning of the confidence coefficient.

7.23 Consider as an example the construction of a 90 per cent confidence interval for the mean μ of the normal population with known variance referred to above. The interval must be constructed, that is, the numbers μ_l and μ_u must be chosen so that in 90 per cent of all samples the interval will catch μ. From the normal table it is easily seen that this is true for a symmetrical interval $\bar{x} \pm k\sigma_{\bar{x}}$ when k is equal to 1.645, the value that leaves 5 per cent of the area under the curve in each tail. (An asymmetrical interval could also be made.) Recall that in the example of 7.7–8 above, $\bar{x} = 10.54$, $\sigma = 2$, and $T = 25$. Then the 90 per cent confidence interval for μ is $10.54 \pm 1.645(2)/\sqrt{25}$, that is, 10.54 ± 0.658. The lower and upper limits of the interval are therefore $\mu_l = 9.882$ and $\mu_u = 11.198$. Of course, either μ is between these numbers once for all, or it is not; μ is not a random variable but a parameter. The random variables here are the confidence limits μ_l and μ_u, and the meaning of the 90 per cent confidence coefficient is that an infinite number of repeated samples, 90 per cent of the confidence intervals constructed by this method will catch μ within their limits, and 10 per cent will not. No one knows for sure, without measuring μ directly, whether a particular interval such as (7.7) does or does not contain μ, just as no one knows for sure, even after a test has been performed, whether the tested hypothesis is true or not.

7.24 There appears to be a close relation between testing hypotheses and constructing interval estimators, for the calculations look much alike. Indeed there is a close relation, and a very simple one. For example, a symmetrical confidence interval for a parameter μ is simply an interval containing exactly those hypotheses about μ that would be accepted in a two-tail symmetrical test with the same sample, using a significance level equal to 1 minus the confidence coefficient. This can be seen by reflecting on the following two statements relating to inferences about the population mean μ: (a) In a two-tail symmetrical test, any hypothetical value of μ will be accepted if it differs from the observed $\bar{x}$ by less than $k\sigma_{\bar{x}}$ and will be rejected if it differs from $\bar{x}$ by more than $k\sigma_{\bar{x}}$, where k is an appropriate number found by looking up the significance level in the normal table. (b) Any hypothetical value of μ will be inside the confidence interval if it differs from the observed $\bar{x}$ by less than $k\sigma_{\bar{x}}$ and will be outside if it differs from $\bar{x}$ by more than $k\sigma_{\bar{x}}$, where k is an appropriate number found by looking up the confidence coefficient in the normal table. Similarly, any interval estimator, whether symmetrical around the sample mean $\bar{x}$ or not, is equivalent to the set of hypotheses accepted by an appropriately constructed test applied to the same sample, the significance level of the test being equal to 1 minus the confidence coefficient of the interval estimator.

7.25   Interval estimators have been advocated on the ground that, since point estimators are almost never correct, we need to know how far in error they are likely to be if we are to know how much faith to put in them. An interval estimator gives a range that is likely (with whatever degree of probability is specified) to catch the true value of the parameter, and thus meets this objection to point estimators. Interval estimation is a standard and generally accepted tool in the practicing statistician's kit. However, at least one able and eminent statistician[51] would leave interval estimation aside in favor of point estimation on the ground that nearly always the action that is to be taken, as a result of estimation, consists of choosing a *single* number for each variable under our control rather than an interval. For example, a firm must decide how many new machines to order, what size of plant to build, what price to charge, and so forth; a government must decide what tax rates to impose, what expenditures to authorize, and so forth. Even granting this, confidence intervals may be useful if the estimates are to be used by different people for different purposes, or by someone whose opinions and purposes are not known. On this problem, see Hildreth [1963].

8   FURTHER REMARKS ON THE MAINTAINED HYPOTHESIS

8.1   Sometimes there is a conflict, apparent or real, between the sample data and the maintained hypothesis. How is such a situation to be dealt with? Consider point estimation first. Again, suppose that a point estimator of a population mean μ is needed, and that it is known

---

[51] See Savage [1954], Ch. 17, pp. 257–262.

that the observations $x_1, \ldots, x_T$ are independently normally distributed with constant known variance σ^2 and constant but unknown mean μ. Suppose it is known *a priori* that μ cannot be less than some particular value, for instance, 9.9. (Of course individual observations x_t may be less than 9.9.) What point estimator should be used? In Section 6, in such a problem without the restriction that $\mu \geqq 9.9$, we saw that the sample mean $\bar{x}$ is the recommended estimator for μ. But what if we know that $\mu \geqq 9.9$, and (as may happen) we get a sample whose mean is *less* than 9.9? We cannot then both (a) choose an estimate meeting the restriction that $\mu \geqq 9.9$ and (b) use the value of the sample mean as the estimate. In such a case, an appropriate estimator is:

(8.1)   est $\mu = \bar{x}$ if $\bar{x} \geqq 9.9$

          est $\mu = 9.9$ if $\bar{x} < 9.9$

This means that whenever there is a sample whose mean does not conflict with the restriction $\mu \geqq 9.9$, that sample mean is adopted as the estimate; but whenever there is a sample whose mean is less than 9.9, it is decided that that sample mean is below the true mean μ, and the value nearest to the sample mean among all the permitted values is chosen as the estimate, namely, 9.9.

8.2   The general approach typified by this example is quite simple in principle; but it is very important that it be clearly understood, because it will be used later in more involved estimation problems where technical details may obscure the principle. The basic idea can be restated as follows: *For any sample in which the unrestricted point estimate does not conflict with the restrictions imposed, the unrestricted point estimate is chosen; for any sample in which the unrestricted point estimate does conflict with the restrictions imposed, we choose to believe the restrictions rather than the sample, and from among all numbers meeting the restrictions, we choose the one that is closest*[52] *to the unrestricted estimate.* This procedure incorporates the rule given above for estimating the population mean μ subject to the restriction that $\mu \geqq 9.9$, and it also incorporates other estimation methods we shall take up in Chapter IX for the parameters of econometric equations.

8.3   Consider now the possibility of conflict between data and maintained hypothesis in *interval estimation*. We continue to use the example of a set of 25 random independent normal observations from a population with a fixed known variance $\sigma^2 = 4$ and a fixed unknown mean μ, which is to be estimated subject to the *a priori* information that $\mu \geqq 9.9$. Consider a symmetric (about $\bar{x}$) 90 per cent confidence interval, whose limits are $\bar{x} \pm 1.645\sigma/\sqrt{T} = \bar{x} \pm 1.645(2)/5 = \bar{x} \pm 0.658$, as in

[52] In complex multivariate cases there may be a choice as to how to measure this "closeness."

7.23. Whenever $\bar{x}$ is not less than 10.558, the lower limit μ_l of this confidence interval is not less than 10.558–0.658 = 9.9, and then the entire confidence interval lies in the range $\mu \geqq 9.9$, so there is no conflict between the maintained hypothesis that $\mu \geqq 9.9$ and the sample data. However, in any sample whose $\bar{x}$ is less than 10.558, the lower limit μ_l of the confidence interval will be less than 10.558 − 0.658 = 9.9. In other words, our sample leads us to an interval for μ, part of which interval lies in the forbidden region below the value $\mu = 9.9$. We cannot sensibly (a) adhere

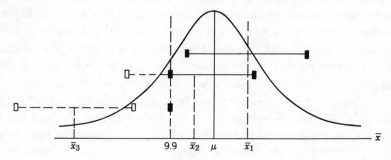

Figure 8.1 Three possible sample means $\bar{x}_1$, $\bar{x}_2$, $\bar{x}_3$, and the associated confidence intervals when the mean is known to be at least 9.9 and $\bar{x}$ is normal. See text, 8.4.

to the restriction that $\mu \geqq 9.9$ and at the same time (b) use the conventional confidence interval as the estimate.

8.4 In such a case, one approach is simply to cut off and discard any portion of the conventional confidence interval that lies in the proscribed region below 9.9. If $\bar{x}$ should be so low that the entire confidence interval falls below the prior limit 9.9, one can choose the point 9.9 as the estimate; this is an interval that has degenerated to a single point. The estimator is then described as follows:[53]

$$\text{if } \bar{x} \geqq 9.9 + 1.645\sigma/\sqrt{T} \qquad \begin{cases} \mu_l = \bar{x} - 1.645\sigma/\sqrt{T} \\ \mu_u = \bar{x} + 1.645\sigma/\sqrt{T} \end{cases}$$

$$(8.2) \quad \text{if } 9.9 - 1.645\sigma/\sqrt{T} \leqq \bar{x} < 9.9 + 1.645\sigma/\sqrt{T} \begin{cases} \mu_l = 9.9 \\ \mu_u = \bar{x} + 1.645\sigma/\sqrt{T} \end{cases}$$

$$\text{if } \bar{x} < 9.9 - 1.645\sigma/\sqrt{T} \qquad \mu_l = \mu_u = 9.9$$

Figure 8.1 shows three possible confidence intervals based on three different sample means, each representing one of the alternatives of (8.2). The figure is drawn for the case where μ is actually somewhat larger than

---

[53] An analogous procedure applies if an asymmetrical confidence interval is wanted.

9.9. The three values of $\bar{x}$ are denoted by $\bar{x}_1$, $\bar{x}_2$, and $\bar{x}_3$, on the $\bar{x}$-axis. The associated truncated confidence intervals are denoted by thin solid horizontal lines whose end points are marked by heavy solid rectangular dots. The end points of the conventional symmetrical (about $\bar{x}$) intervals that would be obtained without the restriction that $\mu \geqq 9.9$, where they differ from the truncated intervals, are shown by hollow rectangular dots. (The height of these horizontal lines above the $\bar{x}$-axis has no meaning; properly speaking they belong *on* the $\bar{x}$-axis but we can see them better if they are displaced upward or downward and separated.) It is easy to verify that the truncated confidence interval estimator of (8.2) and Figure 8.1 does indeed have a 90 per cent chance of capturing μ within it. In 5 per cent of the possible samples, $\bar{x}$ will exceed $\mu + 1.645\sigma/\sqrt{T}$ so that all of the interval will fall on the high side of μ; in 90 per cent of the samples $\bar{x}$ will fall in the range $\mu \pm 1.645\sigma/\sqrt{T}$ and the interval will catch μ; and in 5 per cent of the samples $\bar{x}$ will be below $\mu - 1.645\sigma/\sqrt{T}$ and all of the interval will fall below μ.[54] However, this approach has a peculiar feature. Suppose you are first allowed to observe the value of $\bar{x}$ resulting from a sample, and then you are offered the chance to bet that the truncated confidence interval based on that sample actually contains μ, giving odds corresponding to the chosen confidence coefficient (9 to 1 that μ is in the interval, for a 90 per cent confidence coefficient). Whenever the value of $\bar{x}$ is below $9.9 - 1.645\sigma/\sqrt{T}$ so that the interval reduces to the point 9.9, you will do well to refuse the bet because it is almost inconceivable that μ should be *exactly* 9.9.

8.5 Since a confidence interval is meant to convey some idea of the uncertainty attaching to a point estimate, it might be better to use the following interval estimator instead of (8.2) when it is known that $\mu \geqq 9.9$: cut off any portion of the conventional confidence interval that falls below 9.9 so that $\bar{x}_l \geqq 9.9$ as before, but if $\bar{x} < 9.9$ then let $\bar{x}_u = 9.9 + 1.645\sigma/\sqrt{T}$. This would yield a confidence coefficient of 90 per cent if $\mu \geqq 9.9 + 1.645\sigma/\sqrt{T}$, and a confidence coefficient greater than 90 per cent otherwise (rising to 95 per cent as μ declines to 9.9), but still it is a more reasonable estimator than (8.2) in case $\bar{x} < 9.9$, in the sense that a person is more likely to be willing to use it than (8.2) if he finds that his sample has $\bar{x} < 9.9$. With either of the two estimators, or indeed with any estimator that always has $\bar{x}_l \geqq 9.9$ in deference to the restriction that $\mu \geqq 9.9$, some

---

[54] There is a slight technical difficulty if μ happens to be exactly 9.9, that is, if the *a priori* restriction happens to be *barely* fulfilled with no room to spare. Then whenever $\bar{x}$ is below $9.9 - 1.645\sigma/\sqrt{T}$ as in the third case in (8.2), the point estimate (degenerate interval estimate) 9.9 will be exactly correct. Such a value of $\bar{x}$ would arise in 5 per cent of the samples, so that if $\mu = 9.9$ exactly, the confidence coefficient would actually be .95, rather than .90 as intended.

samples will occur that lead to intervals that do not contain $\bar{x}$ at all. This is not strange *provided* we believe with certainty that $\mu \geqq 9.9$.

8.6   Let us now reconsider briefly the apparent conflict that may arise between a sample and an *a priori* restriction, still using the example in which the point estimator, that is, the sample mean $\bar{x}$, is less than 9.9 and the *a priori* restriction says that $\mu \geqq 9.9$. There are two possibilities. One (not mentioned in this section until now) is that the restriction may be incorrect. The other, of course, is that the restriction is correct but the sample has unusually many individuals below 9.9 in it, or some individuals unusually far below 9.9. Either of these might be true when such an apparent conflict occurs, and it is terribly important to know which is true. If the restriction is incorrect it should be discarded in favor of a correct one (or none at all), and if the restriction is correct it should be adhered to and the sample should be overruled. If we are *absolutely certain* of the correctness of the restriction, we can be absolutely certain that any sample "violating" it is an unusual sample and is not to be trusted on any matter over which the restriction and the sample disagree. Suppose (as is common in econometrics) that we are less than absolutely certain about the restrictions we use. Then there is difficulty whenever a sample occurs that is in violent disagreement with the restrictions, that is, whenever a sample occurs that would have only a very small chance of occurring if the restrictions were correct. When such a conflict occurs, we are led to suspect the correctness of the restrictions, and this is quite proper (unless we are certain that they are correct). What must be done then, loosely speaking, is to balance our *a priori* confidence in the restrictions against the conditional probability with which the observed sample would occur if the restrictions were true. A restriction in which we have a high degree of *a priori* confidence will be adhered to except in the face of a sample that would be highly unlikely if the restriction were correct; a restriction in which we have little *a priori* confidence will be abandoned or modified in the face of a sample that would be highly or even moderately unlikely if the restriction were correct. For example, we might be quite certain that the marginal propensity to consume is between 0 and 1, fairly certain that it exceeds .5 and is less than .95, and so forth.

8.7   Ideally, if we are not absolutely certain about an *a priori* restriction stating flatly that a certain parameter is greater (or less) than a given number, we could specify as part of a more general maintained hypothesis an *a priori* subjective probability distribution for the parameter, expressing the degree of our confidence as to its value, as suggested in 7.15. Systematic methods are available for choosing an estimate of the parameter in the light of the *a priori* probability distribution and other *a priori* presumptions and the observed sample together.[55] In principle these methods

[55] See note 19 in 5.7 again.

are more precise in minimizing the risk of loss than is the simpler method of using restrictions such as $\mu \geqq 9.9$ and then modifying any such restriction that makes the sample result appear too unlikely, because in principle they can incorporate all of our *a priori* presumptions (including *a priori* probability distributions) that bear on the parameters to be estimated. In order to use these methods, however, it is necessary to spell out explicitly and in detail all of our relevant *a priori* presumptions—a very difficult and time-consuming task—and then it is necessary to use more complicated mathematical techniques to obtain estimates that are compatible with these presumptions. For these reasons, most econometric work is conducted with the use of simple restrictions (such as $\mu \geqq 9.9$), and we shall conduct most of our discussion in these terms.

8.8 By now it is clear that the maintained hypothesis or *a priori* information used in solving a problem in statistical inference is of central importance, because the nature of this information influences the result, in both testing and estimation. For example, consider again the test of the hypothesis that $\mu = 10$, discussed beginning in 7.7 above. There a part of the maintained hypothesis was that σ, the standard deviation of the population, was equal to 2. With $\bar{x} = 10.54$ and $T = 25$, the hypothesis under test, which stated that $\mu = 10$, was rejected in a one-tail test at the 90 per cent significance level with the rejection region in the upper tail of the distribution (see 7.8). If the value of σ had been given as a sufficiently large number, 3, for instance, the hypothesis would have been accepted because the acceptance region would then have extended from minus infinity to a point farther to the right than the observed value of $\bar{x}$, 10.54, so that $\bar{x}$ would have fallen in the acceptance region. The given value of σ thus influences the test result. And if no value of σ is given, it must be estimated,[56] and that will affect the result. The other bits of *a priori* information influence the result too. If it were not specified that the distribution of x is normal, we could not use the table of the normal distribution to determine the limits of the acceptance region. If it were not specified that the 25 observations were taken independently, we could not replace $\sigma_{\bar{x}}$ by $\sigma/\sqrt{T}$, because these two quantities are equal only if the T observations are independent. If it were not specified that μ cannot be less than 9.9, we might not place all of the rejection region in the upper tail of the distribution. And so on. *A priori* information plays an equally important role in the point or interval estimation of μ, for the desirable properties of $\bar{x}$ exist because of the independent random character of the observations $x_1, \ldots, x_T$, and the restrictions on the value of the parameter in question of course influence the result of the test or estimation too.

8.9 When several mutually consistent hypotheses are under consideration at once, it is possible to make a choice as to which hypothesis

---

[56] See Chapters IX and X.

shall be tested and which shall be maintained during the test. Earlier, the hypothesis $\mu = 10$ was tested, using as part of the maintained hypothesis the statement that $\sigma = 2$. It is possible instead to reverse matters and test the hypothesis that $\sigma = 2$, using as part of the maintained hypothesis the statement that $\mu = 10$. For either of these two tests, the maintained hypothesis might also include the following: The population is normal, and the observations are drawn independently and at random. It would be possible as a third alternative to test the hypothesis that the population is normal, using as the maintained hypothesis the statements that $\mu = 10$, $\sigma = 2$, and the observations are independent random drawings.[57] And so on. We may wonder how to decide among such a variety of alternatives. The general principle is again to try to decide so as to minimize the risk of losses resulting from our decision. Therefore we should include in the maintained hypothesis those statements that merit the most trust in both of the following senses taken together, namely, trust in the sense that we have a high degree of confidence in the truth of the statement, and trust in the sense that even if the statement is untrue we do not stand to lose much by acting as though it were true. Similarly, the tested hypothesis should include the statements that merit the least trust in both senses together. For example, it would be unwise to include the statement that $\mu = 10$ in the maintained hypothesis of a test if we were very uncertain whether μ is approximately 10, and if it would lead to costly errors to act as if $\mu = 10$ when in fact [58] $\mu > 10 + \delta$. If we were highly confident that $\mu = 10$ approximately, but still it were costly to believe $\mu = 10$ when in fact μ differs much from 10, we would be faced with the problem of balancing the high cost of error against our belief that the chance of μ differing much from 10 is very small. The techniques for doing this, as noted earlier, cannot be taken up in detail here.

8.10 In econometric models the hypotheses to be tested are more complex and the parameters to be estimated are more numerous than in the simple univariate example we have been considering in Sections 5 to 8. Similarly, the maintained hypotheses are more complicated and often more important to the results than those considered here. However, the principles illustrated here apply. It may sometimes happen that the maintained hypothesis used in the estimation of the parameters of a model is not sufficiently restrictive to allow point estimates to be obtained; it is in such cases that the parameters in question are said to be unidentified (recall the discussion of the excise-tax problem in II.6.8–13). The question of identification is so important in econometrics that a whole chapter (VIII) will be devoted to it.

---

[57] These alternative tests will not be discussed here; see any standard statistical inference text.

[58] For example, μ might be the optimum capacity output to be planned for a certain type of product when a new multi-product plant is being designed.

9 PREDICTION

9.1 In this book the terms "prediction" and "forecast" are used interchangeably to refer to statements about behavior that has not yet been observed by the maker of the statements at the time when he makes them. The behavior in question may be future behavior, or it may be past behavior that he does not know about yet. An example of the latter might be a prediction about what would be revealed by a study of historical events in an unfamiliar period and country. (This paragraph repeats part of I.2.1.)

9.2 Some predictions are unconditional (Sally G. will win the fifth race this afternoon) and some are conditional (Sally G. will win the fifth race this afternoon if the track is not muddy). The most useful predictions, if they are accurate, are unconditional. But often it is easier to make accurate conditional predictions than accurate unconditional ones, because particularly uncertain matters (e.g., whether the track is muddy) can be incorporated into the conditions. Conditional predictions permit a small part of a large problem to be isolated for separate study. Most of the predictions we shall deal with are conditional, the conditions involving values of variables whose values are given as of the time when the prediction is made.

9.3 There are *point* predictions or forecasts and *interval* predictions or forecasts, just as there are point estimates and interval estimates. A *point prediction* of a variable is a statement that the value of that variable will be found to be equal to a given number, perhaps under specified circumstances, for example, the United States gross national product next year will be $750 billion. An *interval prediction* is a statement that the value of the variable in question will be found to be between two given numbers (i.e., in a given interval), perhaps under specified circumstances, for example, GNP next year will be between $730 and $760 billion. The remarks in 7.25 about the relative merits of point and interval estimation are applicable to point and interval prediction, for there is a great deal in common between estimating a parameter and forecasting the value of a variable. One important difference is that there is usually an opportunity to observe the actual value of the predicted variable some time after the prediction is made; the implications of this are touched on in 9.6 below. Another difference in practice is that forecasts are more likely to come to the attention of laymen than are estimates, and so there is a particularly strong case for using *interval* forecasts as a means of discouraging misinterpretation of the results.

9.4 It is important to realize that the random or stochastic character of economic variables has two distinct effects on econometric point predictions, one stemming from disturbances in the *prediction* period and one from disturbances in the *observation* period. In the first place, even if all the relevant parameters were known, predictions would not be exact, because of the stochastic disturbances entering during the prediction period into the economic relationships determining the variables. A prediction of any variable should be in the form of a probability distribution, for this reason. This is true even though sometimes for brevity only the expected value of this distribution is given as a point prediction, and is called *the* predicted value. In the second place, the values of the relevant parameters are not known, but must be estimated. The stochastic disturbances of the observation period produce stochastic errors in the estimates. (This error will be even worse if a wrong model is used in estimation.) Thus the point prediction of an economic variable contains two sources of stochastic error. First, the disturbances in the prediction period produce a random deviation of the actual value from the expected value; second, the disturbances in the observation period produce a random deviation of the point prediction from the true expected value. In expressions for the variance of the error of a point prediction, which will be derived in Chapter X, these two sources of random error will be represented by separate mathematical terms, each easily traceable to its own source. It will be helpful in analyzing these formulas to distinguish the error due to incorrect estimation of parameters (which is due, in turn, to the disturbances of the observation period, and which can be made smaller by using larger samples) from the error due to stochastic disturbances in the prediction period (which can only be made smaller, if at all, by revising the model so that the variation not explained by it is reduced).

9.5 Economic predictions can be made for the guidance of economic policy making, or for the purpose of testing the hypotheses on which the predictions are based, that is, for fruit or for light. For *policy-making* purposes, forecasts conditional on predetermined variables are typically required, for the policy maker wants to know the future effects on certain endogenous variables (e.g., national income) of each available alternative exogenous policy.[59] (As we have just seen, the best he can hope to know is the probability distribution of effects of each alternative policy, and in practice even this must be estimated.) For this purpose, estimates of either the reduced form or the final equations of the model are appropriate, since they express endogenous variables in terms of quantities that are autonomous and that can be expected to be known or estimated at the time the policy maker wants to make his forecast.

9.6 For *testing* the hypotheses involved in a model, as well as for evaluating policy, we can use predictions of endogenous variables

[59] For an excellent brief exposition of the relation between prediction and policy, see Marschak [1947] or [1953].

conditional on predetermined variables, made from the *reduced-form* or *final* equations. These predictions are typically a test of the whole model at once because each reduced-form or final equation typically depends on all the structural equations (unless the model is segmentable in which case the test may cover only a segment of the model). It is essential to produce models that can be shown to have performed well on such tests if policy makers are to be persuaded that econometric models should be used as important quantitative guides to policy making. For testing the hypotheses embodied in the model we can also use predictions based on an individual *structural* equation, by inserting into the estimated equation the actual values of all its predetermined variables and all but one of its endogenous variables, and solving the equation for the remaining endogenous variable, thus obtaining a prediction for it. Such predictions are not very useful for policy purposes. By the time we know the actual values of all but one of the endogenous variables as of period t in a structural equation, period t will have come and gone, and it will be too late to make a prediction of the remaining variable that is helpful for policy purposes. These predictions based on an individual structural equation can be extremely useful for testing a model, however, for they enable the economist to test each structural equation individually and thus find and concentrate on the weak parts of a model. Such tests and others are the subject of Chapter X.

QUESTIONS AND PROBLEMS

1.1. In what contexts in economics does economic theory lead to relatively strong or specific *a priori* restrictions on the form of econometric equations? In what contexts do relatively weak or vague *a priori* restrictions arise? Give examples and discuss them.

2.1. Suppose that a structural change modifies a formerly linear equation and makes it nonlinear in the same variables. Can this structural change be represented by a change in one or more parameters in an equation of fixed form? Explain.

2.2. Can you think of examples of structural change where the effect on the structural parameters is easy to quantify? Difficult to quantify?

2.3. Can you think of any reasons for wanting to know the structural parameters if you are sure there will be no structural change? (This question anticipates Chapters IX and X.)

3.1. Analyze the consequences of assuming that the expectation held at present about the future value of a variable x is given by the following equation instead of (3.5):

$$\frac{x^e_{t+1}}{x_t} = \omega \frac{x_t^e}{x_t}.$$

3.2. Derive equation (3.7) from (3.1) and (3.5).

3.3. Carry out the transformation suggested in the sentence following equation (3.7).

4.1. Suppose that a linear equation holds exactly between the *true* values of x_t and y_t, but that x_t and y_t are measured with randomly distributed errors.

(a) Write down the equation that relates the *true* values of x_t and y_t, and the equation that relates their *observed* values. Choose and define your notation carefully.

(b) Under what conditions can it be said that one of the variables in the latter equation is exogenous?

5.1. (a) Prove that $Ex_t = E\bar{x}$ if $\bar{x}$ is the mean of a sample consisting of independent random drawings $x_1, \ldots, x_T$. What if the drawings are not independent?

(b) Is it true that var $x =$ var $\bar{x}$? Explain.

5.2. What is the relationship (if any) between loss functions and utility functions?

5.3. What is appealing about an estimator that minimizes the *expectation* of the loss function? Does this imply ignoring the *variance* of the error of estimation? Explain.

5.4. Is the choice of an estimator a (of a parameter α) to minimize $E|a - \alpha|$ the same as minimizing $|Ea - \alpha|$? Explain.

6.1. Suppose that $x_1, \ldots, x_T$ are normally distributed with unknown mean, and that they are statistically dependent according to the rule $x_t = x_1$ for all $t = 1, \ldots, T$. Can you find a consistent estimator of the mean? Explain.

6.2. Does the consistency of an estimator imply that its variance approaches zero as the sample size increases without limit? Explain.

6.3. Revise the definition of a limiting distribution given in 6.8, by replacing the function c_T with $\sqrt{T}$. Correspondingly, revise the definitions of asymptotic normality, approximate and asymptotic bias, approximate and asymptotic variance, and approximate and asymptotic expected squared error. (The results are simpler than those in the text, and just as useful in most practical cases.)

6.4. Can you give examples of estimators that are (a) consistent and asymptotically normal, (b) asymptotically normal but not consistent, (c) neither consistent nor asymptotically normal?

6.5. Consider a parameter α and its estimator a, and the asymptotic variances of a, of $\sqrt{T}a$, and of $\sqrt{T}(a - \alpha)$. What is the meaning and the usefulness of each of these?

6.6. Consider an estimator a of a parameter α, and the approximate and asymptotic expected squared errors of a, of $\sqrt{T}a$, and $\sqrt{T}(a - \alpha)$. What is the meaning and usefulness of each?

6.7. Why is asymptotic efficiency defined only for consistent estimators?

6.8. How could the definition of a limiting distribution in 6.8 be revised so that Σx_i would have a limiting distribution, where $x_1, \ldots, x_T$ are independent drawings from a normal population with constant mean and variance?

6.9. Consider the estimation of the mean μ of a univariate population, based on a sample $x_1, \ldots, x_T$ of independent observations where both μ and the population variance σ^2 exist. Consider the estimator $\bar{x} + A + B/\sqrt{T} + C/T$, where A, B, and C are constants. What are its approximate and asymptotic expected squared errors? For what sample size (if any) are the approximate variance and the approximate squared bias equal?

7.1. In what kinds of situations might a loss function of the difference $(a - \alpha)$ between an estimate and a parameter be an appropriate tool, and in what kinds of situations might a pair of loss functions $L_A(\alpha)$ and $L_B(\alpha)$ be appropriate? (Recall the discussions in 5.7–13 and 7.2 ff.)

7.2. For each of the four tests of the hypothesis $\mu = 10$ shown in Figure 7.2:

(a) Compute the probability of acceptance if $\mu = 8$, 9, 9.5, 10, 10.5, 11, and 12, and plot the OC curve.

(b) If possible, find the value(s) of μ for which the probabilities of acceptance are .8, .9, and .95, and plot them on the OC curve.

(c) Repeat steps (a) and (b) for a symmetrical two-tail test of the hypothesis $\mu = 10$ using a 20% significance level and a sample size of 25 where it is known that $\sigma = 2$.

(d) Repeat step (c) for a test differing from the immediately preceding case (c) only in having a sample of size 100.

7.3. Describe the effect of each of the following on the operating characteristic of a test, *ceteris paribus*, and indicate in what circumstances each would be desirable or undesirable.

(a) Decrease the sample size.

(b) Decrease the significance level toward zero.

(c) Move the acceptance region toward lower values of the parameter(s) while maintaining the significance level unchanged.

7.4. Discuss the proposition that hypothesis testing is the appropriate inference procedure when a decision must be made between *two* alternative actions, and that estimation is appropriate when there is a *continuous* range of alternative decisions.

7.5. How does the preceding question relate to the proposition that every confidence-interval estimate corresponds to the set of hypotheses that would be accepted by an appropriate test applied to the same sample? (See 7.24.)

7.6. Construct the test that accepts the set of hypotheses given by the 85% asymmetrical confidence interval from 15.065 to 23.846, for the mean of a normal population based on a sample of 100 with $\bar{x} = 2.0$ and standard deviation *known* to be 3. (See 7.24.)

8.1. Give examples, from your own work or from the literature, of conflicts between empirical results and *a priori* ideas concerning the parameters, and indicate what action you think is appropriate and why.

8.2. Does the relationship between hypothesis testing and interval estimation, discussed in 7.24, have any counterpart in situations where the estimation is carried out subject to an *a priori* restriction limiting the value of the parameter to a certain range? Explain.

9.1. For each of the econometric functions described, indicate:

(a) Whether (and if so, how) it can be used to obtain conditional predictions.

(b) Whether (and if so, how) it can be used to obtain unconditional predictions.

(c) The uses to which its predictions can be put in econometrics.
The functions are:

(i) Consumption as a function of income, wealth, and one or more lagged variables.

(ii) Investment as a function of beginning-of-year capital stock and lagged profits.

(iii) GNP as a function of government policy variables and one or more lagged variables.

(iv) Total private output as a function of labor and capital inputs.

(v) Inputs of fuel and manpower in railroading as a function of traffic volume and beginning-of-period capital stock.

(vi) Others of your choice.

CHAPTER VIII

Identification

This chapter discusses the problem of identification of economic parameters. This is the problem of whether the model is restrictive enough so that, given sufficiently large samples, the values of parameters can be determined. Definitions and examples are given. There is an exposition of the rank and order conditions for identification in linear models containing restrictions that exclude certain variables from certain equations. It is shown that these conditions require modification if they are to apply to models nonlinear in variables but linear in unknown parameters. Identification via restrictions on the probability distributions of disturbances is discussed.

1 THE CONCEPT OF IDENTIFICATION;[1]
MODEL EQUATIONS AND STRUCTURE EQUATIONS

1.1 It is a truism that any given observed fact, or any set of observed facts, can be explained in many ways. That is, a large number of hypotheses can be framed, each of which if true would account for the observance of the given fact or facts. Therefore an appeal to the facts alone is not sufficient to enable the investigator to decide among alternative hypotheses, for after he has appealed to the facts he is still likely to have before him

---

[1] Some basic references on identification (in increasing order of difficulty) are Koopmans [1949]; Koopmans and Hood [1953], pp. 135–142; and Koopmans, Rubin, and Leipnik [1950], pp. 69–110. Wald [1950a] gives a more general framework that has proved useful in recent work, e.g., F. M. Fisher [1959] and [1961a]. Hurwicz [1950] furnishes a more abstract treatment. The early literature includes E. J. Working [1927], Frisch [1933], Mann and Wald [1943], and Haavelmo [1944]. See also Ch. II, 6.8–13.

many different hypotheses that have not been ruled out. The purpose of a model, embodying *a priori* information (sometimes called the maintained hypothesis), is to rule out most of the hypotheses that are consistent with the observed facts. The ideal situation is one in which, after appeal has been made both to the facts and to the model, only one hypothesis remains acceptable (i.e., is consistent with both). If the "facts" have been correctly observed and the model is correct, the single hypothesis that is consistent with both facts and model must be correct; this chapter studies the role of the model in the attempt to achieve this ideal. [In practice, of course, we are never sure about the conditions in the preceding sentence, so it is wise to accept a hypothesis (if at all) only provisionally.] In a typical econometrics problem the hypothesis we accept or reject is a statement about the relevant structure or a part of it or a transform of it.

1.2 When stochastic models are used it is important to distinguish and keep separate two kinds of gaps, either of which alone, if not covered, can permit *more than one* hypothesis to be consistent with both data and model. One of these gaps has to do with limitations on the quantity and variety of the data used. With only a finite sample, it is not possible to obtain exact knowledge of the probability distribution of the stochastic variables, because of sampling variation and because of the impossibility of covering the entire range of possible values of each variable (in principle, for example, national income even in real terms might take on values that are far outside the range of values observed so far). Therefore with only a finite sample we often cannot be sure whether a given hypothesis is consistent with the data or not.

1.3 Throughout this chapter we shall proceed as if this gap were closed: We shall analyze only situations in which it is assumed that we have exact and complete knowledge of the conditional probability distribution of the jointly dependent variables (the y's) given the predetermined variables (the z's), that is, of the reduced form and all its parameters (including the numerical values of all the parameters of the probability distribution of reduced-form disturbances as well as the coefficients of the reduced-form equations).

1.4 We shall assume throughout the book that none of the predetermined variables can be expressed as an exact linear function of other predetermined variables alone (if in a particular model this assumption should be violated, the offending predetermined variable can be deleted and replaced by the linear function of others). With this assumption, the knowledge of the conditional distribution of the y's given the z's is equivalent to the information contained in a properly chosen infinite sample, that is, an infinite sample that includes every possible combination of values of the z's and includes an infinite number of observations of the y's for every such combination, so that no corner of the possible range of the variables escapes representation in the sample. The reason for making the unrealistic assumption that the reduced form is perfectly known is to permit concentration throughout this chapter on the second of the two gaps, which must be closed (if at all) by means quite different from taking a larger sample. (We defer to IX.4.13 consideration of the case where there is an *approximate* linear relation among predetermined variables; this is known as multicollinearity.)

1.5 In this chapter whenever we speak of implications of the data, or of hypotheses consistent with the data, we shall be using the expression "the data" as shorthand for just the foregoing kind of infinite sample that yields perfect knowledge of the reduced form (i.e., of the conditional distribution of the y's given the z's).

1.6 The second of the two gaps, which if not covered will permit *more than one* hypothesis to be consistent with both data (cf. 1.5) and model, has to do with the restrictiveness of the model. If the model is not very restrictive, there may be many hypotheses (e.g., structures) consistent with both the data and the model; we may fail to learn very much about the structure by juxtaposing the data and such a model. On the other hand, a model may be extremely restrictive, so much so that *no* hypothesis can be consistent with both the data and the model. In that case the model must be incorrect (or there must be errors in the data). As mentioned in 1.1 the ideal situation is one in which the model is just restrictive enough so that exactly one hypothesis is consistent with both data and model. After giving some formal definitions, we shall say that in this ideal situation the structure (or the part of the structure in question) is *identified* (or, equivalently, *identifiable*). Thus the idea of identifiability refers to the issue of whether the model is just sufficiently restrictive so that when it is confronted with the data (in the sense of 1.5), just one hypothesis is consistent with both model and data. This issue is important and is in a sense logically prior to the issue of statistical estimation (taken up in Chapter IX), because there is little point is attempting to estimate structural parameters from a finite sample if even an infinite sample could not give the desired information about the parameters. That is why we discuss identification now, before estimation.

1.7 In discussing identification it will be extremely useful to have names for several concepts that will recur repeatedly. The following three pairs of terms will be used. (1) A system of equations is unambiguously called a *structure* or a *model*, depending on whether all its parameters have been assigned specific numerical values or not. (2) The coefficient of a variable in an equation (or a variance, etc.) is unambiguously called a *parameter value* or a *parameter*, again depending on whether it has been given a specific numerical value or not. But usually in the literature an equation is ambiguously called an equation in either case. (3) We shall use the terms *structure equation* (*not* structural equation, which has a different and accepted meaning given in II.1.12) and *model equation*, the former for an equation in which all of the parameters have been assigned specific numerical values and the latter for an equation in which some or all have not. Usually it will not be necessary to be explicit about this distinction, but in discussing the identifiability of an equation it is important to do so. Using this terminology, we may note that, in a wide class of econometric problems, we are interested in statements about either an entire structure or a structure equation or a parameter value; we are interested in the numerical values of structural parameters.

1.8 What happens when a structure equation is multiplied by a nonzero constant? All the numerical values of its parameters change (are multiplied by the constant), but of course the content of the equation is not changed. Hence we shall say that it remains the same structure equation as before. This means that if two structure equations differ only by virtue of the fact that one is equal to the product of the other times a nonzero constant, they are really the same structure equation. Similarly, if one or more structure equations of a structure are multiplied by (possibly different) nonzero constants, the structure is not affected; it is still the same structure as before. The process of normalization of an equation (now to be described) is often useful to deal with this situation. Consider (as we typically do in this book) an equation linear in unknown parameters α_i and linear in observable variables x_i, with u as a disturbance, thus:

$$(1.1) \qquad \sum_{j=1}^{N} x_j \alpha_j = u$$

The standard deviation of u is also a parameter; denote it by α_{N+1} for the present. Now choose some i ($1 \leq i \leq N + 1$) for which $\alpha_i \neq 0$, and divide the equation by α_i. The result is

$$(1.2) \qquad \frac{\sum_{j=1}^{N} x_j \alpha_j}{\alpha_i} = \frac{u}{\alpha_i}$$

The parameters of the new equation are $\alpha_1/\alpha_i, \ldots, \alpha_N/\alpha_i, \alpha_{N+1}/\alpha_i$. Of course $\alpha_i/\alpha_i = 1$. This means that if $i \neq N + 1$ the coefficient of x_i has been made equal to 1; this is called *normalizing* the equation by setting the coefficient of x_i equal to 1. If $i = N + 1$ the equation is normalized by setting the standard deviation (or variance) of the disturbance equal to 1. (Other normalizations are possible, such as making the sum of squared coefficients equal to 1, etc.) Now it is easy to tell whether two structure equations are the same structure equation or not: Normalize them both with the *same* normalization rule, and then look at them. If, and only if, after such normalization they are identical, they are the same structure equation.

1.9 For a given set of data (in the sense of 1.5) there is a corresponding set of just those structures that are consistent with the given data.
These are precisely the structures whose reduced forms are identical
(including parameter values) with the reduced form that is obtained from
our hypothetical infinite sample. It will be useful to have a name and a
symbol for this set of structures. We shall call them the *data-admissible*
structures.[2] The model itself is a set of structures; we shall call them
model-admissible.

1.10 A structure equation will be called data-admissible if it is
consistent with the data in the sense of 1.5, that is, if, for every set of
values of the predetermined z's, those values of the z's and the conditional
expectations of the jointly dependent y's given the z's satisfy the structure
equation exactly (with the disturbances set equal to their expected values,
assumed zero). In symbols, let equation (1.1) be rewritten in a form that
separates the variables into the jointly dependent y's and predetermined
z's and renames the parameters β's and γ's, thus:

$$(1.3) \qquad \sum_1^H \beta_i y_i + \sum_1^J \gamma_k z_k = u$$

We shall henceforth usually use β's for the coefficients of jointly dependent
variables y_i and γ's for coefficients of predetermined variables z_k. If (1.3)
has a constant term, one of the z's (say z_K) will be a dummy variable
always equal to 1, so that its coefficient γ_K will be the constant term.
Assume $Eu = 0$ and denote the conditional expectation of y_i given
$z_1, \ldots, z_K$ by $E_c y_i$ (where $K \geqq J$, and K is the number of predetermined
variables in the whole model, and the subscript c is to remind us that the
expectation is conditional). Then if for all possible sets of values of the
z's the following structure equation is true, we say that the structure
equation (1.3) [or equivalently (1.4)] is consistent with the data, that is,
data-admissible:

$$(1.4) \qquad \sum_1^H \beta_i E_c y_i + \sum_1^J \gamma_k z_k = 0$$

1.11 The model typically states certain restrictions that must be
met by the first equation (e.g., the supply equation must have a positive
slope and must not depend on consumer income), certain restrictions
that must be met by the second equation (e.g., the demand equation must
have a negative slope), and so forth; and of course there may be some
restrictions that apply to the relationships between equations (e.g., the
sum of the marginal propensities to consume and to invest must be less
than 1). We shall say that a structure equation that satisfies the restrictions

---

[2] Koopmans [1949], Section 3, uses the term "observationally equivalent" for
structures that belong to the same data-admissible set.

placed by the model on the *g*th equation is *model-admissible as the *g*th equation*. Thus if a model specifies that the first (supply) equation for a good contains as variables only the price *p* and quantity supplied *q* and has a positive slope, then the set of equations that are model-admissible as the first (supply) equation consists of all equations containing *p* and *q* only and having a positive slope.

1.12 The foregoing definitions may be summarized as follows. In this chapter *the data* means an infinite sample that discloses the true reduced form. We call the coefficient of a variable in an equation (or a variance, etc.) a *parameter value* or a *parameter* according to whether or not is has been given a specified numerical value. We use the following terminology for an equation and an equation system to distinguish whether or not all parameters therein have been assigned specified numerical values:

	for an equation	for an equation system
All parameters have specified numerical values	*structure equation*	*structure*
Not all parameters have specified numerical values	*model equation*	*model*

It is understood that if a structure equation is *normalized* by multiplying it by a nonzero constant, it remains the same structure equation, and the structure remains the same structure. A structure or a structure equation that is consistent with the data (in the sense of "the data" defined above) is said to be *data-admissible*; see 1.9–10. A structure that is consistent with (i.e., belongs to) the model is said (rather trivially) to be *model-admissible*. A structure equation that is consistent with the restrictions placed by the model on the *g*th equation is said to be *model-admissible as the *g*th equation*.

1.13 Now we are ready to define identifiability.[3] A *structure* is *identified* (or, equivalently, *identifiable*) with respect to a given model and a given type of data if and only if there is exactly *one* structure that belongs to both the data-admissible set of structures and the model. The *g*th *structure equation* of a model is identified with respect to the model and a given type of data if and only if there is exactly *one* structure equation that belongs to both the data-admissible set of structure equations and the set of structure equations that are model admissible as the *g*th equation.

[3] The definitions to be given here are equivalent to those in Koopmans [1949], Section 3, but are stated differently by means of the terms "structure equation," "data-admissible," and "model-admissible as the *g*th equation."

A *parameter value* for a particular parameter θ is identified with respect to a given model and a given type of data if and only if every structure that is both data-admissible and model-admissible has the same value for θ. A model is *structure-identifying* with respect to a given type of data if and only if the structure is identified with respect to that model and that type of data. In econometric discourse we shall often find people writing and speaking of the identifiability of a model, an equation, or a parameter. We shall sometimes lapse into this somewhat loose usage. It is generally accepted and is interpeted to mean the same thing as the identification of a structure, a structure equation, and a parameter value, respectively.

1.14   The foregoing definitions imply that a parameter of an equation can never be identified unless some particular normalization rule is applied, for the multiplication of a structure equation by a nonzero constant does not change its admissibility or nonadmissibility according to either the data or the model but does change all its parameter values. But take heart: The only interesting parameters in an equation such as (1.1) are of course the normalized parameters given by ratios such as $\alpha_1/\alpha_i, \ldots, \alpha_N/\alpha_i, \alpha_{N+1}/\alpha_i$ as in (1.2); with a suitable model and data these may be identified. The foregoing definitions also imply that a structure equation is identified if and only if *after normalization* all its parameters are identified.[4]

1.15   The qualifying phrase in the definitions, "with respect to a given model and a given type of data," is important. The identification of a parameter or structure or equation is accomplished by a model, if at all, in the light of certain types of data. We cannot decide whether a parameter or a structure or an equation is identified without a specification of the model that we have in mind and a specification of the types of data that are to be used. Specific examples will illustrate this later on.

1.16   Using the foregoing definitions, we can see that whatever can be determined with the aid of the model from an exact complete knowledge of the reduced form is identifiable, and whatever cannot is not. This approach is sometimes useful in studying identifiability, and it will be used below in a few examples. In particular, it establishes the important point that all reduced-form equations and all final equations are identifiable.[5]

1.17   The concept of identification is usually defined in the literature in terms of whether a structure or a parameter value can be inferred *uniquely*[6] from the model and (a suitable infinite sample of) data, and we

[4] A statement similar to this one is used by Koopmans [1949], Section 3, to define an identified equation.

[5] This is true only if no predetermined variable is an exact linear function of other predetermined variables, as assumed in 1.4.

[6] Koopmans [1949], Section 3.

have followed this procedure. As we shall see below in Section 5 it is sometimes possible to infer that the structure is in a certain subclass of the structures permitted by the model, even though it is not possible to infer the structure uniquely. This non-unique type of identification may be sufficient for the solution of certain problems.

2   A SUPPLY-AND-DEMAND EXAMPLE; THE REDUCED FORM AND IDENTIFIED STRUCTURAL PARAMETERS

2.1   Let us review briefly the supply-and-demand model used in the excise problem in Chapter II, paragraph 6.3, for the case in which it is desired to predict the price and quantity of a commodity under a known excise tax of E dollars per unit, when no previous experience with an excise tax on the commodity is available, that is, when the imposition of the tax represents a structural change because a structural parameter (the tax rate) is changed from 0 to E dollars per unit between the observation and prediction periods. This structural change may also be viewed as a change in the constant term of the supply equation, corresponding to the upward shift of the price intercept by an amount equal to the value of the excise tax per unit of output.

2.2   The demand equation, the original (pre-tax) supply equation, and the post-tax supply equation in stochastic form are as follows:

$$(2.1) \quad q = \beta_0 + \beta_1 p + u_\beta \qquad \beta_0 > 0, \beta_1 < 0 \qquad \text{(demand)}$$

$$(2.2) \quad q = \alpha_0 + \alpha_1 p + u_\alpha \qquad \alpha_1 > 0, \alpha_1 \beta_0 / \beta_1 < \alpha_0 < \beta_0 \quad \text{(old supply)}$$

$$(2.3) \quad q = \alpha_0 + \alpha_1(p - E) + u_\alpha \qquad \text{(new supply)}$$

The expected values of u_α and u_β are zero. In order to predict the expected values of price and quantity after the imposition of the tax, it is necessary to know the values of the parameters of the reduced-form equations after the imposition of the tax. These equations are

$$(2.4) \quad p = \gamma_0 + \gamma_1 E + v_\gamma = \frac{\beta_0 - \alpha_0 + \alpha_1 E}{\alpha_1 - \beta_1} + \frac{u_\beta - u_\alpha}{\alpha_1 - \beta_1}$$

$$(2.5) \quad q = \delta_0 + \delta_1 E + v_\delta = \frac{\alpha_1 \beta_0 - \beta_1 \alpha_0 + \alpha_1 \beta_1 E}{\alpha_1 - \beta_1} + \frac{\alpha_1 u_\beta - \beta_1 u_\alpha}{\alpha_1 - \beta_1}$$

The reduced-form equations *before* the tax is imposed are given by setting $E = 0$ in the foregoing two equations; thus data from the sample period (with no tax) can yield knowledge of the reduced-form parameters γ_0 and δ_0, but not of γ_1 and δ_1 unless indirectly by yielding knowledge of all the structural parameters after the tax: α_0, α_1, β_0, β_1, and E. E is known by hypothesis, and the α's and β's are the old structural parameters prevailing before the tax. Hence the problem is to find the values of the old structural parameters.[7]

2.3 The old reduced-form parameters γ_0 and δ_0 are identified. But, as we concluded, it is impossible to deduce the needed values of the old structural parameters α_0, α_1, β_0, β_1 from the values of the old reduced-form parameters γ_0 and δ_0. This conclusion results from either of two equivalent arguments. Geometrically, there is an infinite number of pairs of linear supply and demand curves that might intersect at $p = \gamma_0$, $q = \delta_0$ and have the right slopes [i.e., have $\alpha_1 > 0$ and $\beta_1 < 0$ and satisfy the other inequalities in (2.1) and (2.2)]. Algebraically, there is an infinite number of sets of values of α_0, α_1, β_0, β_1 that can satisfy the equalities obtained by setting $E = 0$ in (2.4) and (2.5) and can still have $\alpha_1 > 0$ and $\beta_1 < 0$ and satisfy the other inequalities. Hence we say that the old structural parameters in the model (2.1)–(2.2) are unidentified, and for that reason the quantitative effect of a given excise tax on price and quantity cannot be found in this context.

2.4 We now go beyond the introductory formulation given in II.6 to consider different possible situations that might lead to the identification of the old structure. The basis of the analysis to be presented in the next few paragraphs is this: *If* we know or believe that a linear two-equation model of price and quantity is appropriate to the excise problem, *and if* price and quantity are not both found to be constant while the excise-tax rate is constant during the observation period, *then* we can be absolutely certain that one or both of the equations have been shifting from year to year during the observation period. If we can assign causes for these shifts, or if we can discover other things about them, we may learn something about the structural parameters, and we may even find that all are identifiable when new information is brought to bear.

2.5 Suppose that we still believe in linear equations, and that p and q vary in the observation period in such a way as to trace out a straight line in the pq plane. If the line has a positive slope, we know that at least the demand curve must have shifted; if it had not shifted, the only straight line that could be observed would be the demand curve itself, but it has a negative slope by hypothesis. Either this observed positive-sloping straight line must be the supply curve itself—and this will be the case if the supply curve did not shift at all during the observation period—or else it must be a hybrid resulting from simultaneous shifts of the supply and demand

---

[7] Where the excise-tax rate had been varied during the observation period, the reduced-form parameters after the tax (they are identified) could be found directly by observation. Hence the need for the values of the structural parameters (either before or after tax) would not arise at all, and their identifiability would be of no concern.

curves. The two situations are shown in Figures 2.1(*a*) and 2.1(*b*) respectively. The observed straight line is *AB* in each case. In the first case, *AB* is the supply curve and is traced out by shifts in the demand curve among the positions *D*, *D'*, *D''*, and *D'''*. In the second, *AB* is traced out by shifts in both the demand and supply curves, as shown, *D* and *S* shifting simultaneously to *D'* and *S'*, to *D''* and *S''*, and so forth. If we are prepared to assert that the demand curve is the only one that shifts, that is, that in (2.2) var $u_\alpha = 0$, then we can conclude that the supply curve is identifiable; and indeed it can be read from a graph such as Figure 2.1(*a*). Note that we have no information about the demand curve

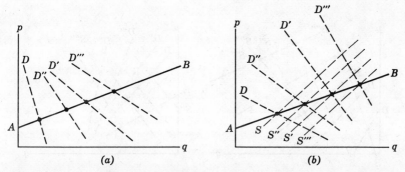

Figure 2.1   Two possible situations leading to data that fall on a straight line *AB*.

here. If we are not prepared to assert that the supply curve stays put, we do not have such an easy time, for we may be looking at a line *AB* generated as shown in Figure 2.1(*b*), where we cannot deduce any further properties of either curve. Even here, perhaps, something may be salvaged. Suppose we knew or believed that the *slopes* of the two curves were constant, so that each curve shifted among positions parallel to each other; and that in addition the shifts (measured in the horizontal direction, i.e., parallel to the quantity axis) were always smaller than some fixed upper limit in the case of the demand curve, and were "very small" in the case of the supply curve as compared with the demand curve. Then we could conclude that the supply curve was "very close" to the observed line *AB*, the "closeness" being dependent on the "smallness" aforementioned and on the limit to the size of the demand curve shifts, as the reader may verify by experimenting with graphs that meet these assumptions. In such a case, although the supply curve could not be found exactly, it could be found approximately. Such non-unique identification will be discussed later, in Section 5.

    2.6   Analogous results follow if price and quantity are observed to trace out a *negatively* sloping straight line. Then it is certain that at least the supply curve has shifted. If the demand curve has not shifted, *it* is the curve observed; if it too has shifted, the observed curve is a hybrid of both supply and demand curves and more information is needed to untangle them.

2.7 If p and q change so as to trace out a curve or an irregular scatter diagram, then on the assumption that both equations are linear, we must conclude that both have shifted. This is the typical case in practice. Examples are shown in Figure 2.2. The discussion of the last few paragraphs has shown that nothing can be learned about the price-quantity supply or demand slopes in equations (2.1) and (2.2) unless something is known or believed about the shifts of one or both

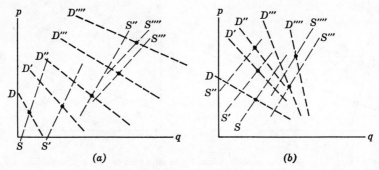

Figure 2.2 Two possible situations of data not on a straight line.

equations in the pq plane. Thus in the absence of such information, the supply and demand slopes are unidentified.

2.8 Let us consider four hypothetical cases, in each of which certain information is assumed to be at hand concerning the shifts, in the pq plane, of the supply curve or the demand curve, or both. In the first case we shall assume that the supply curve does not shift systematically, that is, the expected quantity supplied depends only on prices, while there are systematic shifts in the demand curve in response to exogenous changes in money income, denoted by Y. In the second case we shall assume that the demand curve does not shift systematically while there are systematic shifts in the supply curve in response to exogenous changes in the money wage rate, denoted by W. In the third case we shall assume that each curve shifts systematically, the demand curve in response to exogenous changes in Y and the supply curve in response to exogenous changes in W. In the fourth case we shall assume that each curve shifts systematically in response to changes in *both* Y and W. We shall continue to assume that each equation is linear in all the variables it contains and that the parameters do not change.

2.9 *Case* 1. If the demand curve shifts systematically but the supply curve does not, the model (2.1)–(2.2) may be written so as to show the shifts induced by exogenous income changes, thus:

$$(2.6) \qquad q = \beta_0 + \beta_1 p + \beta_2 Y + u_\beta \qquad \text{(demand)}$$

$$(2.2) \qquad q = \alpha_0 + \alpha_1 p \qquad\qquad + u_\alpha \qquad \text{(supply)}$$

Here we assume that $\beta_2 > 0$, $\beta_1 < 0$, and $\alpha_1 > 0$, and that for all values of Y, $\beta_0 + \beta_2 Y > 0$ and $(\beta_0 + \beta_2 Y)\alpha_1/\beta_1 < \alpha_0 < \beta_0 + \beta_2 Y$. If such a model is correct, what will be observed and what can be deduced? Since the supply curve does not shift systematically, the point corresponding to the expected values of price and quantity for any given value of income must lie on the supply curve, which accordingly is identified. But nothing further can be learned about the slope of the demand curve, for an infinite number of negative slopes are compatible with the data and the assumptions of the model.

2.10 The same conclusions can be established by an algebraic argument. The assumed complete knowledge of the reduced form provides, for each possible value of Y, the conditional expectations of p and q given Y; denote them by $Ep|Y$ and $Eq|Y$. For each value of Y, these conditional expectations and Y itself must satisfy the exact structure equations that would result if disturbances were set equal to zero in (2.6) and (2.2):[8]

$$(2.7) \qquad Eq|Y = \beta_0 + \beta_1 Ep|Y + \beta_2 Y$$

$$(2.8) \qquad Eq|Y = \alpha_0 + \alpha_1 Ep|Y$$

where the α's and β's are restricted by the inequalities stated in 2.9. This being true, $Ep|Y$ and $Eq|Y$ and Y must satisfy any new structure equation obtained by multiplying (2.7) by a number h (not zero or one) and multiplying (2.8) by $1 - h$ and adding the two together, thus:[9]

$$(2.9) \qquad Eq|Y = (1 - h)\alpha_0 + h\beta_0 + [(1 - h)\alpha_1 + h\beta_1]Ep|Y + h\beta_2 Y$$

$$0 \neq h \neq 1$$

In other words, we can say that (2.7) and (2.8) are data-admissible structure equations, and so also is (2.9). The sum of multiples of two things, such

[8] The exact conditional form of structure equations, such as (2.7)–(2.8), is most convenient when discussing identification, and we shall often use it. The stochastic form can always be obtained by inserting disturbances and replacing $Eq|Y$ by q, and $Ep|Y$ by p.

[9] The reason for choosing $h \neq 0$ and $h \neq 1$ is so that (2.9) will not be the structure equation (2.7) or (2.8) but will be a different equation.

as we formed with the two equations (2.7) and (2.8) to obtain (2.9), is called a *linear combination* of those two things if not all the multipliers used are zero. Linear combinations may be formed of more than two things, and may involve positive or negative weights. We chose weights whose sum is 1, that is, h and $(1 - h)$, in obtaining (2.9), so that q would still have a coefficient equal to 1, that is, so that (2.9) would be normalized as are (2.7) and (2.8).

2.11 Now the point of constructing this linear combination of the supply and demand structure equations is to determine whether each of them is identified. If the linear combination (2.9) is a model-admissible supply structure equation, that is, if it satisfies the assumptions that the model imposes on the supply equation, then the supply equation cannot be identified, because *two different* supply structure equations, namely (2.9) and (2.8), will be data-admissible and model-admissible. Let us see whether (2.9) does satisfy the assumptions imposed on the supply equation. It does not, for these assumptions require that the supply equation not shift in the pq plane when Y changes, that is, Y is excluded from the supply equation; but Y appears with a nonzero coefficient, $h\beta_2$, in equation (2.9). Hence there is no structure equation other than (2.8) itself that is consistent at the same time with the data and with the restrictions imposed on the supply equation. Hence (as shown in the next section, 3.5) the supply equation is identified in this model.

2.12 The demand equation, on the other hand, is not identified in this model, for two different structure equations, namely (2.7) and (2.9), are consistent with both the data and the restrictions on the demand equation. Let us verify this by considering these restrictions in turn. First, can equation (2.9) have a negative price slope as required of the demand equation? Yes, for $(1 - h)\alpha_1 + h\beta_1$ in (2.9) will be negative if h is not too small—specifically, h need only be larger than $\alpha_1/(\alpha_1 - \beta_1)$, which itself is less than 1. Second, can equation (2.9) have a positive income slope as required of the demand equation? Yes, if $h > 0$, because $h\beta_2$ in (2.9) will be positive if h is positive. Third, can the three inequalities that involve the demand intercept [stated just following (2.2) in 2.11 be satisfied by (2.9)? Yes, if h is positive. Accordingly, if h is any positive number less than 1 but greater than $\alpha_1/(\alpha_1 - \beta_1)$, then (2.9) will satisfy the restrictions on the demand equation. There is an infinity of such values of h, and hence an infinity of demand structure equations that are at once data-admissible and model-admissible. Thus, although the data and the restrictions of the model are sufficient to narrow the field of admissible supply curves down to *one*, that is, to identify the supply curve, the demand curve is *not* identifiable in this model. However, the same demand equation is identifiable in another model, as we shall see shortly.

2.13   *Case* 2. If it is only the supply curve that shifts systematically, and it does so in response to exogenous wage-rate changes, the model becomes

$$(2.1) \qquad q = \beta_0 + \beta_1 p \qquad\qquad + u_\beta \qquad\qquad \text{(demand)}$$

$$(2.10) \qquad q = \alpha_0 + \alpha_1 p + \alpha_3 W + u_\alpha \qquad\qquad \text{(supply)}$$

The usual assumptions are made regarding the signs of parameters, and also $\alpha_3 < 0$. In this case the demand structure equation does not shift systematically, and no linear combination of the demand and supply structure equations (other than itself) can be confused with it since it includes no term in W; hence (as shown in the next section, 3.5) it is identified. And the supply structure equation is not identified, since an infinity of linear combinations of it and the demand structure equation are indistinguishable from it. The proof of this is similar to that given in 2.12.

2.14   *Case* 3. If both curves shift systematically, each as above, the model is

$$(2.6) \qquad q = \beta_0 + \beta_1 p + \beta_2 Y \qquad\quad + u_\beta \qquad\qquad \text{(demand)}$$

$$(2.10) \qquad q = \alpha_0 + \alpha_1 p \qquad\quad + \alpha_3 W + u_\alpha \qquad\qquad \text{(supply)}$$

Now what will be observed, and what can be deduced? The expected values of the observed price and quantity points for given Y and W almost certainly will not lie exactly on a straight line in the price-quantity plane[10] (recall Figure 2.2), and hence neither the supply curve nor the demand curve will be observed directly. But it is known that the demand curve shifts systematically only with income changes (a rise in income causes a shift to the right) and that the supply curve shifts systematically only with wage rate changes (a rise in the wage rate causes a shift to the left). These facts enable us to identify the price-quantity slopes of both curves.

2.15   The supporting algebraic argument, which is similar to that of 2.10–12, involving linear combinations of the true structure equations, is as follows. For each pair of values of Y and W, the assumed perfect knowledge of the reduced form gives the conditional expectations $E(p|Y, W)$ and $E(q|Y, W)$. Because these expressions are cumbersome we replace them by $E_c p$ and $E_c q$ as in 1.10 above (the subscript c is to

---

[10] I say "almost certainly will not" because the points can lie on a straight line in the pq plane only if throughout the observation period Y is exactly equal to a linear function of W such as $Y = a + bW$, and this is almost certain not to happen in reality. In 1.4 we have assumed that it does not.

remind us that they are conditional). For each pair of values of Y and W, these conditional expectations must satisfy the structure equations:

(2.11) $E_c q = \beta_0 + \beta_1 E_c p + \beta_2 Y$

(2.12) $E_c q = \alpha_0 + \alpha_1 E_c p \qquad + \alpha_3 W$

Hence $E_c p$ and $E_c q$ must also satisfy any linear combination of (2.11) and (2.12), and in particular they must satisfy any linear combination whose weights are h and $1 - h$ where h is not 0 or 1, thus:

(2.13) $E_c q = (1 - h)\alpha_0 + h\beta_0 + [(1 - h)\alpha_1 + h\beta_1]E_c p + h\beta_2 Y$

$\qquad\qquad + (1 - h)\alpha_3 W \qquad 0 \neq h \neq 1$

Now no such structure equation as (2.13) can satisfy the model's restrictions on either the supply curve or the demand curve because the demand equation excludes W and the supply equation excludes Y, whereas (2.13) includes them both. Hence (as shown in the next section, 3.5) there is no structure equation other than the demand equation itself that is consistent with both the data and the restrictions imposed on the demand equation, that is, the demand equation is identified. The analogous statement holds for the supply equation. Observe that each equation is identified by virtue of the fact that it excludes one of the variables in the model; this was true of the demand equation in 2.9–12 and true of the supply equation in 2.13 too.

2.16   *Case* 4. If (implausibly) each curve were assumed to shift in response to both Y and W, the model would be

(2.14) $q = \beta_0 + \beta_1 p + \beta_2 Y + \beta_3 W + u_\beta$ (demand)

(2.15) $q = \alpha_0 + \alpha_1 p + \alpha_2 Y + \alpha_3 W + u_\alpha$ (supply)

Here neither structure equation is identifiable; nothing can be learned about any of the parameters, for there is an infinity of linear combinations of (2.14) and (2.15) that satisfy the data and the restrictions placed on the demand curve (e.g., $\beta_1 < 0$, $\beta_2 > 0$), and the same is true of the supply curve. The situation is exactly parallel to that in the model (2.1)–(2.2) as discussed in 2.1–3.

2.17   The question of estimating identified parameters in the stochastic case will be taken up in Chapter IX. However, it will be helpful in understanding the identification problem if we pause here to indicate how the values of the identified parameters in some of the four preceding cases could be determined if the reduced form were exactly known, and to see just where the attempt to determine the values of the unidentified parameters breaks down. The method is to try to work back from the parameters of the reduced form to the structural parameters.

2.18 We first take up Case 3 (discussed in 2.14–15). The model is (2.6) and (2.10). There are two endogenous variables, p and q, and two exogenous variables, Y and W. The simultaneous solution of the equations yields the reduced form as follows:

(2.16) $\quad p = \dfrac{\beta_0 - \alpha_0}{\alpha_1 - \beta_1} + \dfrac{\beta_2}{\alpha_1 - \beta_1} Y - \dfrac{\alpha_3}{\alpha_1 - \beta_1} W + \dfrac{u_\beta - u_\alpha}{\alpha_1 - \beta_1}$

(2.17) $\quad q = \dfrac{\alpha_1\beta_0 - \alpha_0\beta_1}{\alpha_1 - \beta_1} + \dfrac{\alpha_1\beta_2}{\alpha_1 - \beta_1} Y - \dfrac{\alpha_3\beta_1}{\alpha_1 - \beta_1} W + \dfrac{\alpha_1 u_\beta - \beta_1 u_\alpha}{\alpha_1 - \beta_1}$

It is convenient to rechristen the reduced-form parameters and rewrite (2.16)–(2.17) thus:

(2.18) $\qquad\qquad p = \pi_{10} + \pi_{11} Y + \pi_{12} W + v_1$

(2.19) $\qquad\qquad q = \pi_{20} + \pi_{21} Y + \pi_{22} W + v_2$

where

(2.20)

$$\pi_{10} = \frac{\beta_0 - \alpha_0}{\alpha_1 - \beta_1}, \quad \pi_{11} = \frac{\beta_2}{\alpha_1 - \beta_1}, \quad \pi_{12} = -\frac{\alpha_3}{\alpha_1 - \beta_1}, \quad v_1 = \frac{u_\beta - u_\alpha}{\alpha_1 - \beta_1}$$

$$\pi_{20} = \frac{\alpha_1\beta_0 - \alpha_0\beta_1}{\alpha_1 - \beta_1}, \quad \pi_{21} = \frac{\alpha_1\beta_2}{\alpha_1 - \beta_1}, \quad \pi_{22} = -\frac{\alpha_3\beta_1}{\alpha_1 - \beta_1}, \quad v_2 = \frac{\alpha_1 u_\beta - \beta_1 u_\alpha}{\alpha_1 - \beta_1}$$

Then if the reduced-form parameters are known from our infinite sample, α_1 can be found immediately as the ratio π_{21}/π_{11}, as may be seen by comparing the expressions for π_{21} and π_{11} in (2.20). Similarly, β_1 can be found immediately as the ratio π_{22}/π_{12}. Then, again in (2.20), since α_1 and β_1 have now been found, α_3 can be found from the expression for π_{12}, and β_2 can be found from the expression for π_{11}. Only α_0 and β_0 remain to be found; their values can be determined by solving simultaneously the equations for π_{10} and π_{20} in (2.20). It turns out that $\alpha_0 = \pi_{20} - \alpha_1\pi_{10}$, and that $\beta_0 = \pi_{20} - \beta_1\pi_{10}$. We have now shown how the values of each of the structural parameters in the model (2.6) and (2.10) are found from knowledge of the reduced-form parameters. This establishes the identifiability of both the supply and demand equations of this model in a different way.

2.19 In Case 1 (discussed in 2.9–12) the supply curve does not shift systematically, and the demand curve shifts systematically with income. We saw in 2.9 that the supply parameters α_0 and α_1 can be read from the graph of the conditional expectations of price and quantity for given income. The demand parameters cannot; let us see what happens if we try to deduce them algebraically from the reduced form. The model in this case is equations (2.6) and (2.2). Hence the relevant reduced form is again (2.16)–(2.17), except that now $\alpha_3 = 0$ because the model does not include W as a variable. Hence, π_{12} and π_{22} in (2.18)–(2.19) are zero as well, and all the terms in W disappear from the reduced form. This being the case, α_1 still emerges from (2.20) with the definite value π_{21}/π_{11} as before, and α_0 still emerges with the definite value $\pi_{20} - \alpha_1\pi_{10}$ as before; these are the values that can be read from the pq graph. The four relevant equations of (2.20) thus do show that the supply parameters α_0 and α_1 can be deduced from the reduced form, and hence they are identified. But this is true of none of the β's, the demand parameters. Something can be learned about the β's, nevertheless. A linear relation between β_2 and β_1 is given by the expressions for π_{11} and π_{21} of (2.20), thus:

$$(2.21) \qquad\qquad \beta_2 = \pi_{21} - \beta_1\pi_{11}$$

and a linear relation between β_0 and β_1 is given by the expressions for π_{10} and π_{20} of (2.20), thus:

$$(2.22) \qquad\qquad \beta_0 = \pi_{20} - \beta_1\pi_{10}$$

Hence if β_1 were known, β_0 and β_2 could be found immediately; or if any one of the β's were known, the others could be found. But none of them is known, and so there is an infinite number of trios of values for β_0, β_1, and β_2 consistent with the reduced form and the model. This shows once again that in the model (2.6) and (2.2) the demand equation is *not* identified.

2.20   To sum up the results of this section: In the two-equation linear models considered here, any equation that excludes a variable appearing in the other equation is identified, and any equation that includes all the variables appearing in the model is unidentified. Information that excludes certain variables from certain equations is a powerful aid to the identification of those equations. There are other types of information that aid identification as well, but before we take them up we shall systematically analyze the exclusion-of-variables-from-equations type of information.

3   THE THEORY OF IDENTIFICATION IN LINEAR MODELS; THE ORDER AND RANK CONDITIONS; OVERIDENTIFICATION

3.1   The examples of the preceding section lead us to inquire: Under what conditions is an equation of a linear model rendered identifiable by the knowledge that certain variables of the model are excluded from certain equations (i.e., that these variables have zero coefficients in these equations)?[11] A general theory has been worked out, chiefly by Koopmans and Rubin,[12] answering this question. Toward the end of this section, beginning with 3.37, again following Koopmans, we shall show how the theory is easily extended to take account of knowledge that certain coefficients in a structure equation satisfy a linear and homogeneous relation. Section 4 discusses models linear in parameters but not in variables. Section 5 discusses other kinds of identifying information besides linear relations among coefficients.

3.2 The definition of an identified equation provides the key to the approach. A particular structure equation of a model is identified if, among all the structure equations that are compatible with the data, there is *only one* that is also compatible with the restrictions imposed by the model on that equation.[13] Of course that one is the structure equation in question itself. We shall see that in a linear model any linear combination of the true structure equations is compatible with the data (i.e., is data-admissible), and no linear equation that is not such a linear combination is compatible with the data. The problem of whether a given equation of the model is identified will then reduce to this: Under what conditions does *only one* linear combination of the true structure equations (after normalization) meet the restrictions placed on the given equation of the model? (That one, of course, is the given structure equation itself).[14] There will be much algebra in the next few paragraphs, but to ease matters we shall stop often to take stock.

3.3 Let us now consider a general linear two-equation model and show in 3.3–4 that any linear equation that is a linear combination of the true structure equations must fit the observed data, and in 3.5 conversely. We shall then indicate the proof in 3.6 for the case of G equations. Let the two structure equations be

$$(3.1) \qquad E_c y_1 + \beta_1 E_c y_2 + \sum_1^K \gamma_{1k} z_k = 0$$

$$(3.2) \qquad E_c y_1 + \beta_2 E_c y_2 + \sum_1^K \gamma_{2k} z_k = 0$$

---

[11] Later on, in 3.10, 3.13, 3.15, and 3.19–25, we shall see that this kind of knowledge must be supplemented by restrictions to the effect that certain determinants, formed from the coefficients of the model, are not zero, if identifiability is to be assured with certainty.

[12] Koopmans [1949]; Koopmans and Hood [1953], pp. 135–142; and Koopmans, Rubin, and Leipnik [1950], pp. 53 and 69–85. These three references are here placed in increasing order of difficulty.

[13] Recall that if two apparently different structure equations can be made identical by normalization, they are by definition the same structure equation.

[14] This is a special case of the general linear combination, for it has a coefficient of 1 (or some other nonzero constant) for the equation in question and coefficients of zero for all others.

where $E_c y_1$ and $E_c y_2$ are conditional expectations of y_1 and y_2 given the z's. The endogenous variables are y_1 and y_2. The predetermined variables are $z_1, \ldots, z_K$ (one of these, say z_1, is equal to 1, i.e., is a "constant variable," if there is a constant term in either equation; then its coefficients γ_{11} and γ_{21} are the constant terms). The true values of the parameters are $\beta_1, \beta_2, \gamma_{11}, \ldots, \gamma_{1K}$, and $\gamma_{21}, \ldots, \gamma_{2K}$. They are unknown in practice, except that the coefficients of y_1 are normalized to be equal to 1 as a matter of convenience, and except that certain of the other coefficients may be known or assumed equal to zero (this *is* a restriction, of a sort that is relied on to identify the equations). We assume that the determinant of coefficients of the y's is not zero, that is, $\beta_1 \neq \beta_2$, so the structure has only one solution; a realistic assumption for a linear model.[15]

3.4 Now, by assumption, (3.1) and (3.2) are true for every observed point in the $(K + 2)$-dimensional space whose coordinate axes measure the variables $E_c y_1, E_c y_2, z_1, \ldots, z_K$. If (3.1) is multiplied by a constant h_1 it will remain true, as will (3.2) if multiplied by a constant h_2. And if these multiples are added together, the resulting linear combination [with the coefficients of (3.1) and (3.2) being h_1 and h_2 respectively] must also be true:

$$(3.3) \quad (h_1 + h_2)E_c y_1 + (h_1\beta_1 + h_2\beta_2)E_c y_2 + \sum_{k=1}^{K}(h_1\gamma_{1k} + h_2\gamma_{2k})z_k = 0$$

Hence every linear combination of (3.1) and (3.2) is true for all observed points. This is the first half of the proof we seek. [Note in particular that the set of all such linear combinations includes (3.1) itself (here $h_1 = 1$ and $h_2 = 0$); and also includes (3.2) (here $h_1 = 0$ and $h_2 = 1$). Any linear combination having $h_1 \neq 0$ and $h_2 = 0$ yields (3.1), because (3.1) is the same structure equation as any constant nonzero multiple (h_1) of itself. Similarly, any linear combination having $h_1 = 0$ and $h_2 \neq 0$ yields (3.2).]

3.5 It remains to provide the second half of the proof, that is, to show that any linear structure equation that satisfies the data must be a linear combination of (3.1) and (3.2). Let a devil's advocate choose a structure equation satisfying the data, and suppose the equation chosen is

$$(3.4) \quad \alpha_1 E_c y_1 + \alpha_2 E_c y_2 + \sum_{1}^{K} \delta_k z_k = 0$$

Let the reduced form of the model (3.1)–(3.2), obtained by solving for $E_c y_1$ and $E_c y_2$, be denoted by

$$(3.5) \quad E_c y_1 = \sum_{1}^{K} \pi_{1k} z_k$$

$$(3.6) \quad E_c y_2 = \sum_{1}^{K} \pi_{2k} z_k$$

[15] See Chapter III, 6.10–11.

where the π_{ik} are the familiar functions of the β's and γ's of the model. Recall that $\beta_1 \neq \beta_2$ whence the model has a unique solution, and that the z's are linearly independent (cf. 1.4). Then the reduced form is the only pair of expressions (solutions) for $E_c y_1$ and $E_c y_2$ that satisfies the data. Thus, since (3.4) satisfies the data, it must be obtainable by taking α_1 times equation (3.5) and adding it to α_2 times equation (3.6). That is, (3.4) is a linear combination of (3.5) and (3.6); and this is true no matter what (3.4) is like as long as it satisfies the data. But since (3.4) is a linear combination of (3.5) and (3.6), it is thereby also a linear combination of the structure equations (3.1) and (3.2), for each of the reduced-form equations (3.5) and (3.6) is itself a linear combination of (3.1) and (3.2). Hence every linear structure equation satisfying the data is a linear combination of (3.1) and (3.2). The reader should test his understanding of these points by working out some examples.

3.6 For a model with G linear equations and G endogenous variables, the proof that any linear combination of the structure equations must be a linear structure equation satisfying the data and conversely is quite similar to the proof just given for the special case of the two equations. The model is

$$(3.7) \qquad \sum_{i=1}^{G} \beta_{gi} E_c y_i + \sum_{k=1}^{K} \gamma_{gk} z_k = 0 \qquad g = 1, \ldots, G$$

Since each of these equations holds for every observed point, any multiple of each must hold, and also the sum of any multiples must hold; hence any linear combination holds. This completes the first half of the proof. The reduced form of (3.7) is

$$(3.8) \qquad E_c y_i = \sum_{k=1}^{K} \pi_{ik} z_k \qquad i = 1, \ldots, G$$

It is unique provided that the determinant of the coefficients of the y's in (3.7) is not zero.[16] This assumption is always made and is highly realistic, for the economic systems we try to describe do have determinate values of the variables, and the reduced-form parameters are uniquely determined by the data provided that (as assumed in 1.4) the z's are linearly independent. Hence any linear structure equation satisfying the data is a linear combination of (3.8), which is, in turn, a linear combination of (3.7); hence any linear structure equation satisfying the data is itself a linear combination of (3.7). This completes the second half of the proof.

3.7 We have now shown that *in a linear model the linear structure equations consistent with the data are just those equations that are linear combinations of the true structure equations.* This is a very important

16 See III.6.10–11.

milestone on our way, for because of it we know that we must consider all the equations that are such linear combinations, and no others. *If more than one of this set of linear combinations (after normalization) is consistent with the restrictions applied to a particular equation of the model, then that equation is not identifiable, and conversely.*

3.8 Suppose we now concentrate, until almost the end of this section, on restrictions that exclude certain variables from certain equations[17] (what we have said in 3.2–7 applies to any kind of restrictions on a linear model). We shall use the terms "excluded variables" and "included variables," meaning by the latter all those variables that are not excluded from the equation in question by the model's restrictions, even though it may turn out that some of the so-called included variables have zero coefficients and in fact do not appear in the equation in question. Now if a given linear structure equation is to be identified by this kind of restriction, it must be *impossible* to find any linear combination of the *other* structure equations of the model that excludes all the variables excluded by the given equation. The reason for this is implied above but may be repeated. Any structure equation that could possibly be confused with the given structure equation must have two features: First, it must be satisfied by all the observed points that are generated by the true structure, and second, it must exclude exactly the same variables as the given structure equation. We have seen that the first condition can be met only by a linear combination of the true structure equations and will, in fact, be met by *every* such linear combination. Hence if there is any linear combination of the *other* equations that excludes exactly the same set of variables as the equation in question, then that linear combination is indistinguishable from the equation in question, which accordingly is not identified.

3.9 The problem then is: How can we tell easily whether it is possible to form a linear combination (of the equations other than the given equation) that is restricted to exclude the same variables as the given equation? That is, how can we tell whether there is any linear combination of the other equations that is restricted to have *zero* parameters in just the places where the given equation is required to have them? Let us consider a few examples and see what they suggest. First, we consider a three-equation model of joint demand for two commodities. The demand for each commodity depends on the prices of both, p and p', and on money income Y, which is assumed exogenous for illustrative purposes. The supply of the first commodity, q, depends on its price p and on the money wage rate W, which is assumed exogenous. The supply of the second commodity is completely inelastic at a fixed quantity, q', and this amount

---

[17] But see note 11 above.

is sold each period. The model is then as follows, in the exact form conditional on the predetermined variables:

$$(3.9)\quad E_c q \quad = \alpha_0 + \alpha_1 E_c p \qquad\qquad\qquad\quad + \alpha_4 W \quad \text{(supply of 1)}$$

$$(3.10)\quad E_c q \quad = \beta_0 + \beta_1 E_c p + \beta_2 E_c p' + \beta_3 Y \qquad\qquad \text{(demand for 1)}$$

$$(3.11)\qquad q' = \gamma_0 + \gamma_1 E_c p + \gamma_2 E_c p' + \gamma_3 Y \qquad\qquad \begin{array}{l}\text{(equilibrium}\\ \text{demand for 2)}\end{array}$$

The variables q, p, and p' are endogenous; Y and W are exogenous; q' is an autonomous quantity, but it is not a variable in the model since by assumption it is fixed.[18] The terms have been arranged in columns, one corresponding to each variable, for convenience.

3.10   Is the supply equation (3.9) identified in this model? If so, there must be no linear combination of (3.10)–(3.11) that excludes the variables excluded by (3.9), namely Y and p'. Clearly there are many linear combinations that exclude Y: Any linear combination assigning weights to (3.10) and (3.11) in the ratio of $-\gamma_3$ to β_3 will exclude Y. Also there are many linear combinations that exclude p': Any linear combination that assigns weights to (3.10) and (3.11) in the ratio of $-\gamma_2$ to β_2 will exclude p'. But notice now that no linear combination of (3.10) and (3.11) can do both at once, unless it should happen that $\gamma_3/\beta_3 = \gamma_2/\beta_2$. (Such an equality among the coefficients would be very unusual, and for practical purposes the possibility can be ignored, but more will be said about the matter in 3.13.) Hence, as long as $\gamma_3/\beta_3 \neq \gamma_2/\beta_2$, the supply equation (3.9) is identified. Note that this inequality is equivalent to the condition that the determinant $\begin{vmatrix} \beta_2 & \beta_3 \\ \gamma_2 & \gamma_3 \end{vmatrix}$ be different from zero. This is an example of the points made in note 11.

3.11   What about the demand equation (3.10) for the first commodity? If it is identifiable, there must be no linear combination of (3.9) and (3.11) that excludes W. Looking at the model, we can see that any linear combination assigning a zero weight to (3.9) will exclude W, no matter what weight is assigned to (3.11). Hence any linear combination of (3.10) and (3.11) with a nonzero coefficient for (3.10) will exclude just W. For example, the equation obtained by adding 1 times (3.10) to $\frac{1}{2}$ times (3.11) excludes W. Hence the demand equation (3.10) is not identifiable in this model. The reader should decide whether (3.11) is identifiable, using the same method.

3.12   We have seen enough to begin to generalize. The identified equations in the three-equation model of 3.9 are those that exclude two

---

[18] The role of q' in this model becomes clear when we estimate the constant terms in the equations, which are α_0, β_0, and $\gamma_0 - q'$. After $\gamma_0 - q'$ has been estimated, γ_0 may be estimated via the observed value of q'.

variables; to exclude only one is not enough, as shown by the example of (3.10). If an equation in a three-equation model excluded more than two variables it would still be identified (except if certain determinants are zero; see the end of 3.10 above). The identified equations in two-equation models such as in 2.9–14 exclude at least one variable. Those excluding no variables are not identifiable, as shown by the examples of paragraphs 2.9, 2.13, and 2.16. And every equation in a one-equation model (i.e., a reduced-form or final equation) is identified.[19]

3.13 The foregoing examples suggest a rule that *to be identified, an equation in a model of G linear equations must exclude at least G − 1 of the variables that appear in the model.*[20] This rule is called the *order condition* for identifiability, and it is correct, as we shall explain shortly. But it does not tell the whole story, for an equation may satisfy it and still be unidentifiable. (It is a necessary but not a sufficient condition for identification.) Recall the supply equation (3.9) in the three-equation model (3.9)–(3.11), discussed in 3.10 above. That equation excludes two variables, but it is identified only if, in addition, a certain two-rowed determinant is not zero. This requirement is quite general. *An equation in a linear model of G equations is identified if and only if at least one nonzero determinant of G − 1 rows and columns is contained in the array of coefficients formed as follows: Starting with the row-and-column array of coefficients in the model, omit all columns not having a prescribed zero in the equation in question, and omit the row of coefficients of that equation.* (See footnote 20 again.) This rule is called the *rank condition* for identifiability, as will be explained shortly. Notice that if the rank condition is satisfied, the order condition must be satisfied (if there is such a nonzero determinant of G − 1 rows and columns, then because there are G − 1 columns there must be at least G − 1 prescribed zeros in the equation in question), but the converse is not true (if there are G − 1 or more zeros and hence at least one determinant of G − 1 rows and columns, there may still be no *nonzero* determinant).

3.14 Before giving a general argument in support of these conditions, let us illustrate their use in a four-equation model of joint demand and separate supply, with quantities q and q', prices p and p', money income Y, and money wage rate W, as follows:

$$(3.12) \quad -q \quad + \alpha_0 + \alpha_1 p \qquad\qquad\qquad + \alpha_4 W = u_\alpha \quad \text{(supply of 1)}$$

$$(3.13) \quad -q \quad + \beta_0 + \beta_1 p + \beta_2 p' + \beta_3 Y \qquad = u_\beta \quad \text{(demand for 1)}$$

$$(3.14) \qquad\quad -q' + \gamma_0 \qquad + \gamma_2 p' \qquad\qquad = u_\gamma \quad \text{(supply of 2)}$$

$$(3.15) \qquad\quad -q' + \delta_0 + \delta_1 p + \delta_2 p' + \delta_3 Y \qquad = u_\delta \quad \text{(demand for 2)}$$

---

[19] Again the assumption of 1.4 that the z's are linearly independent is used here.

[20] Assuming that no type of identifying information is used other than the prescribed locations of zero coefficients.

Endogenous are q, q', p, and p'; exogenous are Y and W. There are four equations. Hence the order condition says that if an equation excludes two or fewer variables it is not identified, but if it excludes three or more it may or may not be identified. It is good to apply the order condition first, before the rank condition, because it is easier and it may give the answer. Let us do so. Equations (3.13) and (3.15) exclude only two variables, so they are not identified, and it is unnecessary to examine the rank condition for it clearly cannot be satisfied in their cases. Equation (3.12) excludes three variables and (3.14) excludes four, so they may or may not be identified.

3.15   Let us see whether each equation gives rise to a nonzero 3×3 determinant according to the statement of the rank condition in 3.13. The array of all the coefficients in the model is as follows, each column being headed by its variable (the column of constant terms is headed by the dummy variable "1," as explained in 1.10):

q	q'	1	p	p'	Y	W	
-1	0	α_0	α_1	0	0	α_4	(3.12)
-1	0	β_0	β_1	β_2	β_3	0	(3.13)
0	-1	γ_0	0	γ_2	0	0	(3.14)
0	-1	δ_0	δ_1	δ_2	δ_3	0	(3.15)

Each of the equations may be read off by setting equal to its disturbance the sum of products of q times the parameter in the q column, q' times the parameter in the q' column, 1 times the parameter in the 1 column, and so forth, right across the array. The reader should do this for each equation. For equation (3.12) the array of coefficients relevant to the rank condition is (as the reader should verify)

(3.16)
$$\begin{pmatrix} 0 & \beta_2 & \beta_3 \\ -1 & \gamma_2 & 0 \\ -1 & \delta_2 & \delta_3 \end{pmatrix}$$

Its determinant is $\beta_3(-\delta_2 + \gamma_2) + \beta_2\delta_3$, and except in the event that this is zero, equation (3.12) is identified. For (3.13), the corresponding array of coefficients is

(3.17)
$$\begin{pmatrix} 0 & \alpha_4 \\ -1 & 0 \\ -1 & 0 \end{pmatrix}$$

This array does not have three columns and so cannot yield a nonzero 3×3 determinant (or indeed any 3×3 determinant); hence (3.13) is unidentifiable, as the order condition showed us in the preceding paragraph. For (3.14) the corresponding array is

$$(3.18) \qquad \begin{pmatrix} -1 & \alpha_1 & 0 & \alpha_4 \\ -1 & \beta_1 & \beta_3 & 0 \\ 0 & \delta_1 & \delta_3 & 0 \end{pmatrix}$$

This array has four columns; hence there are four 3×3 determinants obtainable from it, one by dropping the first column, one by dropping the second, and so forth. If one or more of these determinants is not zero, then (3.14) is identified; but if all are zero, (3.14) is unidentified. Equation (3.15) has been shown to be unidentified by the order condition.

3.16 In practice, we never know the true values of structural parameters, so it is impossible to find the true values of the determinants that are involved in the rank condition. Hence the rank condition cannot be applied with absolutely certain results. Two expedients are available, however. First, it is usually safe to proceed as if the order condition were sufficient for identification, even though in strict logic it is not sufficient, because there is almost no prospect of encountering a real problem whose structure is such that all the relevant determinants are zero when the order condition is satisfied.[21] An exception to this general rule may arise if the coefficients in the determinant in question are necessarily mathematically related, for that relation might be such as to make the determinant zero. This is especially likely to occur in a segmentable model (recall III.3.4). Such relations among the coefficients of different equations can be looked for by examining the theory underlying the model, and can be checked against the relevant determinants.[22] Second, it is possible to construct a statistical test of the hypothesis that the relevant determinant is zero, based on estimates of the structural parameters, if desired.[23]

3.17 Rectangular arrays of numbers such as (3.16)–(3.18) are called *matrices* (singular: *matrix*). They are much used in dealing with systems of linear equations, and they will be used considerably in the remainder of this book (especially in Chapters IX and X) because once their simple properties are mastered they make many of the things we are interested in much easier. The reader who is unfamiliar with them should turn,

[21] We can think of structural parameters as continuous random variables, at least subjectively, and then the particular sets of values that make the relevant determinants zero, such as (3.16) above, are seen to have a probability of zero.

[22] As another example, if several factors $x_1, \ldots, x_n$ are used to produce a product, and we consider the firm's demands for them in terms of their prices $p_1, \ldots, p_n$ and the quantity of output, it is known that the partial derivatives $\partial x_i / \partial p_j$ and $\partial x_j / \partial p_i$ from these demand functions are equal; see Samuelson [1947], p. 64. In such a problem we should check whether this requires relevant determinants to be zero.

[23] See Koopmans and Hood [1953], pp. 183–185.

preferably now, but at any rate before coming to Section IX.4, to Appendix A, where he will find a brief introduction to the theory of matrices. The investment of time and energy required will be amply rewarded, for the reader will find it much easier to read Appendix A, and then to read the remainder of the book, than he would have found it to read the same subject matter if written without the aid of matrix terminology.

3.18   The *order* of a matrix such as (3.16) or (3.17) or (3.18) is the pair of numbers telling respectively how many rows and how many columns it has; the order of a square matrix is given by either of these numbers (which are equal for a square matrix); the *rank* of any given matrix[24] is the order of the largest-order square matrix that is contained in the given matrix and that has a nonzero determinant. Hence the names "order" and "rank" conditions for identifiability of an equation; the former requires the order of a certain criterion matrix to be $G - 1$ by at least $G - 1$; the latter requires the rank of the criterion matrix to be exactly $G - 1$, where as before G is the number of equations in the model.[25]

3.19   Let us turn to a general argument in support of the order and rank conditions. The identifiability of a structure equation in a linear model hinges on whether any linear combination of the other structure equations of the model can be made to have zeros in the places where the given equation has prescribed zeros. The coefficients belonging to variables that are permitted to enter the given equation are of no consequence for this purpose. The criterion matrix obtained by omitting the columns of such coefficients is thus the relevant one. Suppose that in a particular linear model of G equations, the first equation excludes a certain number F of the variables. F may be less than, equal to, or greater than $G - 1$. Let the coefficients associated with these excluded variables in the second equation of the model be called $\alpha_{21}, \ldots, \alpha_{2F}$; in the third equation $\alpha_{31}, \ldots, \alpha_{3F}$, and so forth, up to $\alpha_{G1}, \ldots, \alpha_{GF}$ in the Gth equation. Then the criterion matrix for the first equation, denoted by $\mathbf{A}_1$, is

$$(3.19) \qquad \mathbf{A}_1 \equiv \begin{pmatrix} \alpha_{21} & \alpha_{22} & \cdots & \alpha_{2F} \\ \cdot & \cdot & & \cdot \\ \cdot & \cdot & & \cdot \\ \cdot & \cdot & & \cdot \\ \alpha_{G1} & \alpha_{G2} & \cdots & \alpha_{GF} \end{pmatrix}$$

The first equation is then not identified if and only if there is a set of weights $h_2, \ldots, h_G$, not all zero, such that, when each row of $\mathbf{A}_1$ is multiplied by its corresponding h_g and the rows are then added together column by column, every column adds to zero. In other words, the first equation

---

[24] These two properties are also defined in Appendix A, with examples.

[25] Note that the criterion matrix always has $G - 1$ rows and may have $G - 1$ columns or more or less.

is not identified if and only if there is a solution $h_2, \ldots, h_G$, not all zero, to the following system of linear homogeneous equations, one obtained from each column of $\mathbf{A}_1$:

$$\alpha_{21}h_2 + \alpha_{31}h_3 + \cdots + \alpha_{G1}h_G = 0$$

$$\alpha_{22}h_2 + \alpha_{32}h_3 + \cdots + \alpha_{G2}h_G = 0$$

(3.20)

$$\alpha_{2F}h_2 + \alpha_{3F}h_3 + \cdots + \alpha_{GF}h_G = 0$$

These equations can be written equivalently and more concisely as follows:

$$(3.21) \qquad \sum_{i=2}^{G} \alpha_{ij}h_i = 0 \qquad j = 1, 2, \ldots, F$$

3.20 A solution of a set of equations is called a nonzero solution if *not all* the unknowns have zero values in the solution, and a solution is said to be zero if *every* unknown has the value zero in the solution. [Observe that (3.21) does have a zero solution, i.e., $h_2 = h_3 = \cdots = h_G = 0$ satisfies all the equations in (3.21).] Using the term "nonzero solution," we can recapitulate 3.19 thus: If there is a nonzero solution of (3.21) for $h_2, \ldots, h_G$, it can be used as weights to obtain a linear combination of the 2nd through the Gth equations that is model-admissible as the 1st equation because it has zero coefficients in all the places where the model requires the 1st equation to have zeros; in that case the 1st equation *is not* identified. On the other hand, if there is no nonzero solution of (3.21) for $h_2, \ldots, h_G$, then there is no linear combination of the 2nd through the Gth equations that is model-admissible as the 1st equation, and in that case the 1st equation *is* identified.

3.21 We shall now prove a theorem, which together with the argument of 3.20 will establish the necessity and sufficiency of the rank condition for identification stated in 3.13. The theorem is: The rank of the first equation's criterion matrix $\mathbf{A}_1$ is equal to $G - 1$ if and only if (3.21) has no nonzero solution for $h_2, \ldots, h_G$. To prove this theorem, we first recall that (3.21) always has at least one solution, for $h_2 = h_3 = \cdots = h_G = 0$ is always a solution. Hence if (3.21) has a unique solution, that unique solution is zero, so that there is no nonzero solution, which means that the 1st equation is identified. Furthermore, if (3.21) does not have a unique solution, then it must have an infinity of solutions,[26] which means it must have an infinity of nonzero solutions (because only one of its infinity of solutions can be zero), and hence the 1st equation is not

---

[26] For linear equations the only other possibility besides a unique solution and an infinity of solutions is no solution, as shown in III.6.10–11, but that is ruled out here because (3.21) always has a zero solution.

identified. Therefore the theorem will be proved when it is shown that the rank of $\mathbf{A}_1$ is equal to $G - 1$ if and only if (3.21) has a unique solution. This is quite easy, using the results of III.6.10–13 and the definition of rank in 3.18. We shall do it by examining three exhaustive cases, namely, $F < G - 1$ (the order condition is not satisfied), $F = G - 1$ (the order condition is just satisfied), and $F > G - 1$ (the order condition is satisfied with room to spare). Note that the rank of $\mathbf{A}_1$ is either $G - 1$ or less, because $\mathbf{A}_1$ always has $G - 1$ rows.

3.22 *Case* 1: $F < G - 1$. In this case the matrix $\mathbf{A}_1$ has fewer columns than rows, so (3.21) is a system of fewer equations than unknowns and the rank of $\mathbf{A}_1$ is less than $G - 1$. Since the equations are linear, there cannot be a unique solution (see III.6.13). Hence in Case 1 the rank of $\mathbf{A}_1$ is not $G - 1$, and there is an infinity of solutions (recall the preceding footnote).

3.23 *Case* 2: $F = G - 1$. In this case the matrix $\mathbf{A}_1$ is square with $G - 1$ rows and columns, so (3.21) is a system of $G - 1$ equations in $G - 1$ unknowns. A necessary and sufficient condition for the existence of a unique solution to (3.21) is then that the determinant of $\mathbf{A}_1$ not be zero (see III.6.13). Hence in Case 2 if the rank of $\mathbf{A}_1$ is $G - 1$ there is a unique solution to (3.21), and conversely.

3.24 *Case* 3: $F > G - 1$. In this case the matrix $\mathbf{A}_1$ has more columns than rows, so (3.21) is a system of more equations than unknowns. It has a solution so its equations are not inconsistent. If there is a subset of (3.21) containing $G - 1$ equations that has a unique solution, then the whole system (3.21) has a unique solution; and if there is no subset of $G - 1$ equations with a unique solution, then (3.21) does not have a unique solution. But under what conditions is there a subset of $G - 1$ equations with a unique solution? If and only if there is a subset of $G - 1$ equations with a nonzero determinant, that is, if and only if the rank of $\mathbf{A}_1$ is $G - 1$. Hence in Case 3, too, the rank of $\mathbf{A}_1$ is $G - 1$ if and only if there is a unique solution for (3.21).

3.25 Looking back at these three cases (which exhaust the possibilities), we see that whenever the rank of $\mathbf{A}_1$ is $G - 1$, there is a unique zero solution for (3.21) and hence no nonzero solution, and hence the first equation is identified. Whenever the rank of $\mathbf{A}_1$ is not $G - 1$, there is an infinity of nonzero solutions for (3.21), and hence the first equation is not identified. Thus the theorem of 3.21 is proved, and the necessity and sufficiency of the rank condition for the identification of an equation in a linear model are established (when the restrictions consist of statements that certain coefficients are zero and that certain $G - 1$ by $G - 1$ matrices of coefficients have nonzero determinants).

3.26 In econometric parlance, we often say that an equation is identified if the order condition for its identifiability is satisfied, even if the rank condition has not been applied. This is logically dangerous, because the order condition alone is not sufficient, but in practice it is usually safe (recall 3.16).

3.27 If the order condition is just satisfied for an equation, that is, if the equation excludes just $G - 1$ variables, that equation is often said to be *just identified*. If the order condition is satisfied with room to spare, that is, if the equation excludes more than $G - 1$ variables, that equation is often said to be *overidentified*. The distinction between just identified and overidentified equations becomes important when we consider techniques for estimating parameters, as we shall see in Chapter IX.

3.28 In what follows we shall consider the general linear model, which can always be written thus, where the y's are jointly dependent and the z's are predetermined:

$$\beta_{11}y_1 + \cdots + \beta_{1G}y_G + \gamma_{11}z_1 + \cdots + \gamma_{1K}z_K = u_1$$

(3.22)

$$\beta_{G1}y_1 + \cdots + \beta_{GG}y_G + \gamma_{G1}z_1 + \cdots + \gamma_{GK}z_K = u_G$$

Let us consider the gth of these equations, where g may be any number from 1 to G. Suppose that certain of the y's, H in number, are permitted to appear in the gth equation, and the remainder of them, $G - H$ in number, are excluded. Suppose further that certain of the z's, J in number, are permitted to appear, and the remainder of them, $K - J$, are excluded. It is always possible for the y's to be numbered in such a way that $y_1, \ldots, y_H$ are the ones that appear and $y_{H+1}, \ldots, y_G$ are the ones that are excluded, and for the z's to be so numbered that $z_1, \ldots, z_J$ appear and $z_{J+1}, \ldots, z_K$ are excluded. Then the gth equation appears thus:

$$(3.23) \quad \beta_{g1}y_1 + \cdots + \beta_{gH}y_H + 0 + \cdots + 0$$
$$+ \gamma_{g1}z_1 + \cdots + \gamma_{gJ}z_J + 0 + \cdots + 0 = u_g$$

3.29 Before continuing, we make two related remarks about the identifiability conditions. First, there is no distinction made in either the rank condition or the order condition between endogenous and exogenous variables, or between jointly dependent and predetermined variables; and if any of the equations of the model has a constant term, then the constant dummy variable (e.g., $z_{Kt} \equiv 1$ for all t) is to be regarded as a variable for purposes of the rank and order conditions for identification. Second, however, by distinguishing jointly dependent and predetermined variables we can state the order condition in a form that is equivalent but is more convenient for dealing with a single equation when we have not taken the trouble to specify the whole model. The order condition says that the number of variables excluded from an equation [which is $G - H + K - J$, using the notation of (3.23) above] should be at least as great as the number of equations less one, thus:

(3.24) $$G - H + K - J \geq G - 1 \qquad \text{(order condition)}$$

G can be canceled out; rearrangement yields

(3.25) $$K - J \geq H - 1 \qquad \text{(order condition)}$$

In other words, the order condition says that the number of predetermined variables in the model but not in the equation in question should be at least as great as the number of jointly dependent variables in the equation less one, regardless of how many equations the model has altogether. Hence it is not necessary to know how many equations there are in the model (except of course that there are at least H) in order to apply the order condition to an equation. Furthermore, we can sometimes establish that an equation satisfies the order condition even if we do not know how many predetermined variables there are in the model, as long as the number we *do* know about is at least as great as $J + H - 1$ so that (3.25) is sure to be satisfied.

    3.30   An additional remark: Each reduced-form equation satisfies the order condition in either of the two versions given above. Consider (3.24) first: A reduced-form equation can be regarded as a complete one-equation model of $1 + K$ variables with $G - 1 = 0$, so the number of these variables that must be excluded for it to be identified is at least zero, which condition is met of course. Consider (3.25): It says that the number of predetermined variables excluded from a reduced-form equation (which of course is zero) must be at least zero, which is always true.

    3.31   Instead of directly applying the order and rank conditions to test the identifiability of an equation, we can instead try to deduce the values of the coefficients of the equation from the parameters of the reduced form, as done in 2.17–19. This method is not used in practice to determine identifiability, but it *is* often used to determine structural parameters. We shall illustrate how this is done in an equation like (3.23) in the general linear model, and how the determination fails in the absence of identification. The equations of the reduced form that are relevant to the determination of the coefficients of (3.23) are those containing the variables $y_1, \ldots, y_H$, thus:

(3.26)

$$y_1 = \pi_{11} z_1 + \cdots + \pi_{1J} z_J + \pi_{1,J+1} z_{J+1} + \cdots + \pi_{1K} z_K + v_1$$

$$\vdots$$

$$y_H = \pi_{H1} z_1 + \cdots + \pi_{HJ} z_J + \pi_{H,J+1} z_{J+1} + \cdots + \pi_{HK} z_K + v_H$$

All the parameters of the reduced form are always identified. They can therefore all be determined from data. Let us suppose that the π's in (3.26) represent numerical values so determined. If equation (3.23) can be obtained from the reduced form (3.26), it is clear that this must involve multiplying the first equation of (3.26) by β_{g1}, the second by $\beta_{g2}, \ldots,$ the Hth by β_{gH}, and adding up the results. If this is done, the coefficients of the y's turn out as they should: $\beta_{g1}, \ldots, \beta_{gH}$ for the included y's and zeros for the excluded y's. If the attempt is to be successful the coefficients γ_{gk} of the z's must also come out right, thus:

(3.27)

$$\gamma_{g1} = \beta_{g1}\pi_{11} + \cdots + \beta_{gH}\pi_{H1}$$

$$\cdot \quad\quad \cdot \quad\quad\quad\quad \cdot$$

$$\cdot \quad\quad \cdot \quad\quad\quad\quad \cdot$$

$$\cdot \quad\quad \cdot \quad\quad\quad\quad \cdot$$

$$\gamma_{gJ} = \beta_{g1}\pi_{1J} + \cdots + \beta_{gH}\pi_{HJ}$$

$$0 = \beta_{g1}\pi_{1,J+1} + \cdots + \beta_{gH}\pi_{H,J+1}$$

(3.28)

$$\cdot \quad\quad \cdot \quad\quad\quad\quad \cdot$$

$$\cdot \quad\quad \cdot \quad\quad\quad\quad \cdot$$

$$\cdot \quad\quad \cdot \quad\quad\quad\quad \cdot$$

$$0 = \beta_{g1}\pi_{1K} + \cdots + \beta_{gH}\pi_{HK}$$

3.32   The first set, (3.27), contains J equations expressing the coefficients of the *included* z's in terms of β's and π's. The π's are known (having been determined from the data; see 3.31), but $\beta_{g1}, \ldots, \beta_{gH}$ and $\gamma_{g1}, \ldots, \gamma_{gJ}$ are unknown. This set of equations can be used to determine $\gamma_{g1}, \ldots, \gamma_{gJ}$ once these β's have been determined, but it is of no use until then. The second set, (3.28), contains $K - J$ equations expressing the zero coefficients of the *excluded* z's in terms of the β's and π's. This set of equations can show us something, because the left sides contain not unknowns, as in (3.27), but known constants, in fact zeros. The procedure is then to try to solve the equations (3.28) for $\beta_{g1}, \ldots, \beta_{gH}$ in terms of the previously determined π's.

3.33   The first step is to normalize (3.23) by choosing an arbitrary value for one of the β's, say $\beta_{g1} = 1$. This can be done by dividing (3.23) through by β_{g1} to make the coefficient of y_1 equal to one.[27] Then (3.28) becomes a set of $K - J$ equations in the $H - 1$ unknowns $\beta_{g2}, \ldots, \beta_{GH}$, thus:

(3.29)

$$\beta_{g2}\pi_{2,J+1} + \cdots + \beta_{gH}\pi_{H,J+1} = -\pi_{1,J+1}$$

$$\cdot \quad\quad\quad \cdot \quad\quad\quad\quad \cdot$$

$$\cdot \quad\quad\quad \cdot \quad\quad\quad\quad \cdot$$

$$\cdot \quad\quad\quad \cdot \quad\quad\quad\quad \cdot$$

$$\beta_{g2}\pi_{2K} + \cdots + \beta_{gH}\pi_{HK} = -\pi_{1K}$$

[27] Recall 1.8.

Now clearly there can be no unique solution for $\beta_{g2}, \ldots, \beta_{gH}$ unless there are at least as many equations as variables, namely, unless the order condition (3.25) is fulfilled, $K - J \geqq H - 1$. Hence the order condition is once again seen to be necessary for identification.

3.34 But the order condition is not sufficient. Suppose it is just satisfied, that is, $K - J = H - 1$. Then (3.29) is a set of $H - 1$ equations in $H - 1$ unknowns, and there is a unique solution for $\beta_{g2}, \ldots, \beta_{gH}$ if and only if the determinant of that system is not zero, that is, if and only if the rank of the following matrix is $H - 1$:

(3.30)
$$\begin{pmatrix} \pi_{2,J+1} & \pi_{3,J+1} & \cdots & \pi_{H,J+1} \\ \cdot & \cdot & & \cdot \\ \cdot & \cdot & & \cdot \\ \cdot & \cdot & & \cdot \\ \pi_{2K} & \pi_{3K} & \cdots & \pi_{HK} \end{pmatrix}$$

Since this matrix is square and of order $H - 1$ when $K - J = H - 1$, it is usually safe to proceed as if its determinant were not zero (see 3.16).

3.35 Now suppose the order condition is oversatisfied, that is, $K - J > H - 1$. Then (3.29) contains more equations $(K - J)$ than unknowns $(H - 1)$, and there is the possibility of an inconsistency among the equations. If the model used is correct and if the β's and π's in (3.29) are the true values, however, there can be no inconsistency because all the equations in (3.29) are consequences of the model.[28] Once again (cf. 3.24) there will be a unique solution for $\beta_{g2}, \ldots, \beta_{gH}$ if and only if the rank of the matrix in (3.30) is $H - 1$. Since that matrix has $H - 1$ columns and more than $H - 1$ rows when $K - J > H - 1$, it is usually safe to proceed as if its rank were $H - 1$ (see 3.16 again).

3.36 The necessary and sufficient condition for identification of (3.23) that has been found in 3.35, namely, that the rank of the matrix in (3.30) be $H - 1$, is equivalent to the rank condition stated in 3.13, since both are equivalent to the identification of (3.23).[29] If (3.23) is identified, $\beta_{g1}, \beta_{g2}, \ldots, \beta_{gH}$ can be obtained with $\beta_{g1} = 1$ by solving (3.29) for $\beta_{g2}, \ldots, \beta_{gH}$ on the basis of the known values of the π's. When that has been done, $\gamma_{g1}, \ldots, \gamma_{gJ}$ can be found directly from (3.27), using the newly found values of the β's.

3.37 At the beginning of this section, in 3.1, it was said that the foregoing theory of identification in linear models can be and has been

[28] If, as is always the case in practice, the π's are estimated, there may be a contradiction among the equations due to random disturbances. This case will be treated in Chapter IX.

[29] The explicit direct derivation of each rank condition from the other, however, is not very simple, as this book goes. It is found in Koopmans and Hood [1953], pp. 185–186.

extended to apply to homogeneous linear restrictions on the coefficients. Consider a linear structural equation involving $y_1, \ldots, y_H$ and $z_1, \ldots, z_K$, but rewritten for convenience so that its coefficients are called $\alpha_1, \ldots, \alpha_{H+J}$, thus:

$$(3.31) \qquad \alpha_1 y_1 + \cdots + \alpha_H y_H + \alpha_{H+1} z_1 + \cdots + \alpha_{H+J} z_J = u$$

A homogeneous linear restriction on the coefficients of this equation is a homogeneous linear equation that the coefficients $\alpha_1, \ldots, \alpha_{H+J}$ must satisfy. Its general form is as follows, where the λ's are known *a priori*:

$$(3.32) \qquad \sum_{i=1}^{H+J} \lambda_i \alpha_i = 0$$

A few simple examples of the general form (3.32) are $\alpha_1 + \alpha_2 = 0$, $\alpha_3 = 2\alpha_4$, and of course $\alpha_{H+J+1} = 0$ (which is an example of the special case that excludes a variable from a certain equation). Notice that there is never any constant term in any of these linear restrictions. This may seem odd; for example, we might wish to assume for a production function that the sum of the elasticities of output with respect to labor and to capital was equal to 1. Thus, if y_1 is output, y_2 labor input, and y_3 capital input, the production function might be

$$(3.33) \qquad \log y_1 = \log \alpha_0 + \alpha_2 \log y_2 + \alpha_3 \log y_3 + u$$

and we might wish to postulate constant returns to scale, that is, $\alpha_2 + \alpha_3 = 1$. But reflection shows that no constant term is in fact present in such a restriction. The restriction actually says that the sum of the two elasticities is equal to the coefficient of output in the logarithmic form of production function, (3.33); it does *not* say that $\alpha_2 + \alpha_3 = 1$, for if (3.33) were normalized so that the coefficient of $\log y_1$ were 2 it would still be the same equation, but then we would want $\alpha_2 + \alpha_3$ to equal 2 instead. Hence the restriction must be stated as $\alpha_1 = \alpha_2 + \alpha_3$, where α_1 is the coefficient of $\log y_1$, which is 1 by normalization in (3.33). See Nerlove [1965] for a thorough treatment of such production functions.

    3.38 As another example, consider again the excise-tax problem of Chapter II, and assume that the excise tax varies during the observation period (and hence is an exogenous variable). The model is

$$(3.34) \qquad\qquad q = \beta_0 + \beta_1 p \qquad\quad + u_\beta$$

$$(3.35) \qquad\qquad q = \alpha_0 + \alpha_1 p + \alpha_2 E + u_\alpha$$

The ratio of p's coefficient α_1 to E's coefficient α_2 in the supply equation (3.35) is -1, that is, $\alpha_2 = -\alpha_1$, because the supplier responds to an excise tax of E dollars just as he would to a rise of E dollars in his costs per unit of output. If we did not know this, we could not identify the supply equation (recall the discussion of 2.3). But because we *do* know it, we *can* identify the supply equation, as follows. The reduced form of (3.34) and (3.35) is

$$(3.36) \qquad p = \frac{\beta_0 - \alpha_0}{\alpha_1 - \beta_1} - \frac{\alpha_2}{\alpha_1 - \beta_1} E + \frac{u_\beta - u_\alpha}{\alpha_1 - \beta_1}$$

$$(3.37) \qquad q = \frac{\alpha_1\beta_0 - \alpha_0\beta_1}{\alpha_1 - \beta_1} - \frac{\alpha_2\beta_1}{\alpha_1 - \beta_1} E + \frac{\alpha_1 u_\beta - \beta_1 u_\alpha}{\alpha_1 - \beta_1}$$

The parameters of the reduced form can, as usual, be readily obtained. β_1 can be found immediately as the ratio of E's two coefficients in the reduced form, and β_0 can then be found from the two constant terms. In the absence of the knowledge that $\alpha_2 = -\alpha_1$, this is as far as we can go. But since we know that $\alpha_2 = -\alpha_1$, our knowledge of E's coefficient in (3.36) and of β_1 enables us to find α_1, and then α_0 can be obtained from either of the constant terms. Hence with the aid of the knowledge that $\alpha_2 = -\alpha_1$, we can identify an otherwise unidentifiable equation.

3.39   For our purposes it will suffice to say that the order condition for identification still applies, suitably restated, if the identifying restrictions are homogeneous linear restrictions like (3.32) instead of all being restrictions excluding certain variables from certain equations. The "suitable restatement" is this: A necessary condition for the identification of an equation in a model of G linear equations is that the number of independent[30] homogeneous linear restrictions on the parameters of that equation be at least $G - 1$. The rank condition still applies too, also suitably restated, but as its restatement is more complicated we shall be content with the fact that the rank condition is satisfied in nearly every case when the order condition is (cf. 3.16 again). The theory of identification can be similarly extended (with difficulty) to bilinear restrictions involving the parameters of two or more equations.[31]

4   IDENTIFICATION IN MODELS LINEAR IN UNKNOWN PARAMETERS

4.1   In III.10.9 we discuss the general form of an exact model linear in unknown parameters but not in variables. The corresponding stochastic

[30] A set of N linear restrictions contains less than N independent restrictions if some of the restrictions add nothing to what the others say. Thus, given $\alpha_2 = 2\alpha_1$ and $\alpha_3 = 2\alpha_2$, the restriction $\alpha_3 = 4\alpha_1$ is not independent. See Appendix A for a discussion of independent linear equations.

[31] Concerning linear restrictions and identification, see Koopmans, Rubin, and Leipnik [1950], pp. 80–82. Concerning bilinear restrictions relating the parameters of two or more equations, see *ibid.*, pp. 93–106. For more recent advances concerning identification, see F. M. Fisher [1959], [1961], [1965a], and [1966], and Konijn [1958].

model is

(4.1)

$$\sum_{i=1}^{G} \beta_{gi}y_i + \sum_{j=1}^{L} \beta_{g,G+j}f_j(y_1, \ldots, y_G) + \sum_{k=1}^{K} \gamma_{gk}z_k = u_g \qquad g = 1, \ldots, G$$

The $y_1, \ldots, y_G$ are endogenous variables, the $f_j(y_1, \ldots, y_G)$ are nonlinear functions of the endogenous variables having no unknown parameters (these functions may or may not depend on any of the predetermined variables), the $z_1, \ldots, z_K$ are predetermined variables (some may be nonlinear functions of others,[32] as long as there are no unknown parameters in the functions), and the β's and γ's are parameters. New endogenous variables may be defined to represent the f's, thus:

(4.2) $$f_j(y_1, \ldots, y_G) = y_{G+j} \qquad j = 1, \ldots, L$$

Let us assume that the new endogenous variables $y_{G+1}, \ldots, y_{G+L}$ are chosen in such a way that there are no linear relations connecting any of them. (If there were one or more linear relations among them, one or more of them could be eliminated in favor of a linear function of the others.[33]) Equations (4.1) can then be expressed linearly in terms of $y_1, \ldots, y_G$, $y_{G+1}, \ldots, y_{G+L}$ and the z's, thus:

(4.3) $$\sum_{i=1}^{G+L} \beta_{gi}y_i + \sum_{k=1}^{K} \gamma_{gk}z_k = u_g \qquad g = 1, \ldots, G$$

The model (4.1) has then been transformed into a model with G linear stochastic equations (4.3) and L nonlinear definitional equations (4.2).

4.2   The nonlinear equations (4.2), which define the new endogenous variables $y_{G+1}, \ldots, y_{G+L}$, are automatically identified because by hypothesis they contain no unknown parameters to start with. The identification of the model then rests with the identification of the G linear equations (4.3). Before the rank and order conditions can be applied to (4.3) as in Section 3, the following general theorem must be established: If (4.3) are the true structure equations apart from nonlinear identities, then any structure equation that is both linear in $y_1, \ldots, y_{G+L}, z_1, \ldots, z_K$ and consistent with the data is a linear combination of the true structure equations (4.3), and conversely. Compare 3.2–7 above. The converse part of the theorem is true and is easily proven as in 3.4. But the first part of

---

[32] But we exclude linear relations among the z's; see 1.4.

[33] Consider a two-equation nonlinear model with endogenous variables y_1 and y_2. Suppose that it contained three nonlinear functions like (4.2) as follows: $y_3 = y_1^2$, $y_4 = y_2^2$, and $y_5 = 2y_1^2 - 5y_2^2$. Then the three new variables y_3, y_4, and y_5 would be related by the linear equation $y_5 = 2y_3 - 5y_4$. Hence our assumption in the text above requires that one of the three new variables be eliminated and replaced by the equivalent linear function of the other two. Compare 1.4 above.

the theorem is *not* true for all nonlinear models linear in parameters, and hence in general the rank and order conditions as stated in 3.13 are not applicable to nonlinear models linear in parameters. In certain special cases where the theorem mentioned above holds, the rank and order conditions are applicable.

4.3   As an example, consider a demand-supply model in which the demand equation has constant elasticity, thus:

$$\log q = \beta_0 + \beta_1 \log p + u_\beta \qquad \text{(demand)}$$
(4.4)

$$q = \alpha_0 + \alpha_1 p + u_\alpha \qquad \text{(supply)}$$
(4.5)

This pair can be made linear in new variables by rewriting (4.4) and defining r and s as follows:

$$s = \beta_0 + \beta_1 r + u_\beta$$
(4.6)

$$r = \log p$$
(4.7)

$$s = \log q$$
(4.8)

But the *model* has not been made nonlinear: It now contains the two linear equations (4.5) and (4.6) in the variables p, q, r, s, and the two nonlinear identities (4.7) and (4.8). As in a linear model, no linear combination of the true linear structure equations (4.5) and (4.6) can satisfy the restrictions placed by the model on the supply and demand equations (i.e., the demand equation must exclude p and q, and the supply equation must exclude r and s). But the preceding sentence no longer establishes the identifiability of either the demand or the supply equation, because in nonlinear models we no longer have the general theorem mentioned above (valid for all linear models) that every data-admissible linear equation is a linear combination of the true structure equations. This fact destroys the general applicability of the approach of Section 3 to the case of nonlinear models, and hence the rank and order conditions as stated in 3.13 do not apply to nonlinear models.

4.4   In the model consisting of (4.4) and (4.5), it is not difficult to see that if the two equations have a single intersection point in the positive quadrant (note that the demand equation is not defined elsewhere), then neither equation is identified, whereas if they have two intersection points in the positive quadrant, then both are identified. Either situation is possible in the absence of further restrictions on the coefficients, but if the demand and supply curves are known to have negative and positive slopes respectively, then there can be only one intersection in the positive quadrant, and neither equation is identified. Thus nonlinearities such as are in (4.4), when coupled with other restrictions, can sometimes bring about identification, but the other restrictions that would be required in this example are implausible.

4.5 F. M. Fisher [1965] has developed a general approach to the treatment of identifiability of nonlinear equations that are linear in parameters. He shows that if the model contains at least one exogenous variable that varies (i.e., the constant dummy exogenous variable will not do here), then a suitable technique for transforming the matrix of coefficients in equations (4.3) above will yield a matrix to which the rank condition of 3.13 can be applied to give a necessary and sufficient condition for identification. It shows that if into both equations (4.4) and (4.5) above are introduced linear terms in a nonconstant exogenous variable, then both become overidentified. Thus nonlinearities often do aid identification.

5 IDENTIFICATION BY INFORMATION OTHER THAN LINEAR RESTRICTIONS ON COEFFICIENTS

5.1 In our discussion of identification running from paragraph 2.8 through Section 4, we have considered only one type of identifying information, namely, linear homogeneous restrictions on the parameters. The most common type of linear restriction is that stating that certain variables in the model do not appear at all in certain equations of the model; such restrictions can also be expressed by saying that the parameters attached to certain variables in certain equations are zero. Thus, for example, income does not appear in supply equations. Most of the existing literature on identification deals with this type of restriction (but see F. M. Fisher [1963], [1965a]). But it is extremely important to realize that there are other kinds of restrictions that can provide identifying information, and that in some econometric problems these other kinds of restrictions are essential to a solution. Hence they should not be overlooked. It is probable that the current emphasis on restrictions excluding certain variables from certain equations is due to the fact that they have been given an elegant mathematical treatment. In this section we shall discuss briefly several other types of identifying information, namely, various kinds of restrictions on the probability distribution of the disturbances. The treatment will be neither exhaustive nor very systematic, for the purpose is to consider several kinds of relatively neglected identifying information and indicate how they might be used.

5.2 We shall continue to proceed, as in the foregoing part of this chapter, as if the conditional probability distribution of the jointly dependent variables, given the predetermined variables, were completely known. We shall consider a two-equation supply-and-demand model, in which for simplicity price p, quantity q, the money wage rate W, and the disturbances are measured as deviations from their respective means in the hypothetical infinite sample; hence they will be denoted by sans-serif roman type (this notational convention was explained in VI.3.1), and the equations will have no constant terms. Sometimes we shall consider that the money wage rate enters the supply equation as in (5.1) below, and sometimes we shall not, as in (5.2). The demand equation is given by (5.3):

(5.1) $q = \alpha p + \alpha' W + u_\alpha$ $\alpha > 0, \alpha' < 0$ (supply, with wage)

(5.2) $q = \alpha p + u_\alpha$ $\alpha > 0$ (supply, without wage)

(5.3) $q = \beta p + u_\beta$ $\beta < 0$ (demand)

Without further restrictions neither supply curve here is identified (cf. 2.7 and 2.13). The symbols $\sigma_\alpha{}^2$, $\sigma_\beta{}^2$, and $\sigma_{\alpha\beta}$ will refer respectively to the variances of u_α and u_β and their covariance. We shall inquire into the identifiability of the supply equation, sometimes considering (5.2) and sometimes (5.1). We shall discuss four kinds of restrictions on the distribution of the disturbance u_α after normalization: restrictions on the range of u_α, on σ_α, on the ratio $\sigma_\alpha/\sigma_\beta$, and on $\sigma_{\alpha\beta}$.

5.3   Some of the restrictions to be discussed are equalities and some are inequalities. If they are equalities, it will sometimes happen after normalization that two, or three, or some larger but finite number of values of a parameter are both model-admissible and data-admissible. Then we shall say[34] that identification is not *unique*, but is *multiple*. If the restrictions are inequalities, it will sometimes happen after normalization that an infinite number of values of a parameter are both model-admissible and data-admissible, but that all these values are contained in an interval with known end points, at least one of which is finite. Then we shall speak of *interval* identification. Clearly the narrower the interval, the more we know about the parameter in question.

5.4   *Restrictions on the range of u_α.* Suppose that the range R_α of the supply disturbance u_α in (5.2) is finite, and known; denote the known value by[35] k. Then the difference between the largest and smallest possible values of u_α is k. A large and varied sample will yield a scatter diagram like Figure 5.1, in which each dot represents a pair of observations of price and quantity. The axes of the graph show p and q, not the deviations p and q. No two points on the same horizontal line (i.e., at the same price) can be more than k quantity units apart because the range R_α is equal to k; but if the sample is infinite and u_β has varied as well as u_α, the sample points will lie within and on the borders of a region bounded by two parallel straight lines of positive slope whose separation measured horizontally is exactly k units, as shown. The slope α of the supply curve must then be equal to the observable positive slope of the boundary lines,

[34] Following Koopmans, Rubin, and Leipnik [1950], p. 96.

[35] Note that k is not meaningful unless the equation is normalized; we have set the coefficient of q equal to 1.

because any line with either greater or lesser slope would correspond to a disturbance with a range greater than k. Hence the supply slope α is uniquely identified by this restriction, though it would not be identified without it (or some substitute). The special case where $R_\alpha = 0$, in which all points lie on a straight-line supply curve, was discussed earlier in 2.5.

5.5 Now suppose as in 5.4 that the range R_α of u_α is finite, but that it is unknown; all that is known is that it is less than some number k_1. Figure 5.1 still describes the data. Then the supply slope is no longer

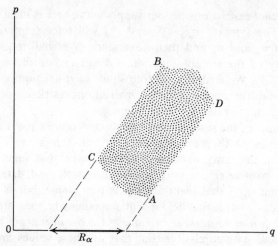

Figure 5.1 Observed points when the model is equations (5.2)–(5.3) and the range R_α of the supply disturbance is finite.

uniquely identified, but it is interval identified. This may be seen as follows. Let the letter a denote the slope of any would-be supply curve permitted by the restrictions. Then if a is larger than the slope depicted in Figure 5.1 (i.e., if we consider a curve appearing flatter),[36] the curve must shift enough to pass through the lower-right extreme point A and again through the upper-left extreme point B. The larger a is, the larger the range of shifts must be, and as $a \to \infty$ the range of shifts approaches infinity too. Hence to place any upper limit k_1 on R_α is to place an upper limit on α. Similarly, if a is less than the slope depicted (i.e., if we consider a curve that appears steeper, or is negatively sloped), the curve must shift enough to pass through extreme points such as C and D; and as $a \to -\infty$, the range of shifts must approach infinity too. Hence the restriction $R_\alpha < k_1$ also places a *lower* limit on α. This lower limit may be negative, in which case it tells us nothing new because we already know that $\alpha > 0$.

[36] Recall that $a = dq/dp$, not dp/dq.

5.6   Note that the restrictions $R_\alpha = k$, or $R_\alpha < k_1$, might well be refuted by the data. This would happen whenever the scatter diagram is spread out so far in a horizontal (quantity) direction that no straight positively sloping line that shifts horizontally by as little as k or k_1 can reach all the observed points.

5.7   In what follows we shall need the reduced form of the model (5.2)–(5.3). Here it is:

$$(5.4) \qquad\qquad q = \frac{\alpha u_\beta - \beta u_\alpha}{\alpha - \beta} = v_q$$

$$(5.5) \qquad\qquad p = \frac{u_\beta - u_\alpha}{\alpha - \beta} = v_p$$

We shall also use the variances of v_p and v_q and their covariance, denoted respectively by $\omega_q{}^2$, $\omega_p{}^2$, and ω_{pq}. These may be expressed as follows (recall the rules given in IV.2.25 and IV.3.8):

$$(5.6) \qquad \omega_q{}^2(\alpha - \beta)^2 = \alpha^2\sigma_\beta{}^2 - 2\alpha\beta\sigma_{\alpha\beta} + \beta_2\sigma_\alpha{}^2$$

$$(5.7) \qquad \omega_{pq}(\alpha - \beta)^2 = \alpha\sigma_\beta{}^2 - (\alpha + \beta)\sigma_{\alpha\beta} + \beta\sigma_\alpha{}^2$$

$$(5.8) \qquad \omega_p{}^2(\alpha - \beta)^2 = \sigma_\beta{}^2 - 2\sigma_{\alpha\beta} + \sigma_\alpha{}^2$$

Our hypothetical infinite sample will yield the numerical values of the reduced-form parameters $\omega_p{}^2$, ω_{pq}, and $\omega_q{}^2$.

5.8   *Restrictions on σ_α.* Suppose that in the model (5.2)–(5.3) the variance of the supply disturbance, $\sigma_\alpha{}^2$, is known. To see whether this knowledge identifies the supply slope, we proceed as follows. Again let the letter a be the slope of any would-be supply equation. The disturbance of such an equation must then be $q - ap$. The variance of this disturbance is the following expression, which we set equal to the known number $\sigma_\alpha{}^2$ because of our knowledge that the supply equation's variance is $\sigma_\alpha{}^2$:

$$(5.9) \qquad \text{var } (q - ap) = \omega_q{}^2 - 2a\omega_{pq} + a^2\omega_p{}^2 = \sigma_\alpha{}^2$$

The center and right-hand members of (5.9) are a quadratic equation in the unknown slope a, and all the coefficients of this quadratic are known: the ω's from observation and $\sigma_\alpha{}^2$ from the model. Hence it is possible to calculate a pair of roots for a. One of them will be the true supply slope α, and we hope that the other will either be equal to it or else be distinguishable from it in some way (perhaps by being negative) so that the supply slope will be uniquely identified. To see whether this is so, we express the ω's in (5.9) in terms of structural parameters. This can be done either by inserting the reduced-form values of p and q from (5.4)–(5.5) into $q - ap$ and then taking the variance of the result, or by inserting the expressions for the ω's from (5.6)–(5.8) into (5.9). In either case the result is

(5.10)
$$\text{var}\,(\mathsf{q} - a\mathsf{p}) = \frac{(a - \beta)^2\sigma_\alpha{}^2 + 2(a - \beta)(\alpha - a)\sigma_{\alpha\beta} + (\alpha - a)^2\sigma_\beta{}^2}{(\alpha - \beta)^2} = \sigma_\alpha{}^2$$

Suppose we try substituting $a = \alpha$ into (5.10) to see whether the center member of (5.10) then becomes equal to $\sigma_\alpha{}^2$. It does, as the reader should verify. (It is easy, for everything else cancels out.) This shows that $a = \alpha$ is indeed one of the roots of the quadratic and establishes that at worst the supply slope is multiply identified, with at most two possible values being both data-admissible and model-admissible.

5.9 Let us find the other root of the quadratic (5.10). First multiply by $(\alpha - \beta)^2$ to clear fractions, and then subtract $(\alpha - \beta)^2\sigma_\alpha{}^2$ from both the center and right-hand terms. The result is that a quadratic function of a is set equal to zero. Dividing this quadratic equation by $a - \alpha$ yields a linear equation in a, which after simplifying gives the other root. The two roots, denoted by a_1 and a_2, are

(5.11) $$a_1 = \alpha$$

(5.12) $$a_2 = \beta + \frac{(\alpha - \beta)(\sigma_\beta{}^2 - \sigma_\alpha{}^2)}{\sigma_\beta{}^2 - 2\sigma_{\alpha\beta} + \sigma_\alpha{}^2}$$

If the roots should be equal,[37] clearly both equal α. If one of the roots should be positive and one negative, then clearly the positive one is α. If both are positive, it may not be easy to tell which one is α without more *a priori* information about the other parameters. If both are negative with an infinite sample, this is a sign that the model is incorrect (sampling variation in a *finite* sample might result in two negative roots even if the model is correct; see VII.8.1–6 again). Clearly, if $\sigma_\alpha{}^2$ and $\sigma_\beta{}^2$ are nearly equal, the last term in (5.12) will be near zero and so the root a_2 will be near β, which is negative, so in that case a_2 is likely to be negative. Thus we have established that if $\sigma_\alpha{}^2$ is known in the model (5.2)–(5.3), at most two numbers are both data-admissible and model-admissible as values of the supply slope α. If one of those two should be negative, then the other one is α, and α is uniquely identified.

5.10 Suppose that in the model (5.2)–(5.3) $\sigma_\alpha{}^2$ is not known, but lower and upper limits for it are known, that is, $k_1{}^2 \leqq \sigma_\alpha{}^2 \leqq k_2{}^2$. Then the variance of the disturbance of any would-be supply equation is again given by the center member of (5.9) or (5.10), but now this variance is restricted to lie between the two quantities $k_1{}^2$ and $k_2{}^2$. This means that at best (i.e., if $k_2{}^2/k_1{}^2$ is close to 1) it may be possible to deduce that α lies

---

[37] This would happen if $\sigma_\alpha{}^2 = \sigma_{\alpha\beta}$.

in one of two intervals whose end points can be calculated; if fortunately one of those intervals contained nothing but negative numbers, then it would be clear that α lay in the other. The nearer to 1 is the ratio $k_2{}^2/k_1{}^2$, the more closely does this situation resemble the case where $\sigma_\alpha{}^2$ is known (treated in 5.8–9) and the narrower are the intervals within one of which α must lie. If $k_2{}^2/k_1{}^2$ is far from 1, then the intervals may become so wide as to be quite uninformative. Thus the restriction $k_1{}^2 \leqq \sigma_\alpha{}^2 \leqq k_2{}^2$ may lead to the interval identification of α but may fail to provide very useful information.

5.11 *Restrictions on the ratio $\sigma_\alpha/\sigma_\beta$.* Suppose in the model (5.2)–(5.3) the ratio of the variances of the supply and demand disturbances is known, say $\sigma_\alpha{}^2 = k^2\sigma_\beta{}^2$, where k is known. Then the disturbance of any would-be supply curve with slope equal to a is $q - a p$, and its variance is given by (5.9). The disturbance of any would-be demand curve with slope equal to b is $q - b p$, and its variance is given by an expression analogous to (5.9) and displayed inside the square brackets in (5.13) below. Applying the restriction that the variance of the supply disturbance is k^2 times the variance of the demand disturbance yields the following:

$$(5.13) \quad \operatorname{var}(q - ap) = \omega_q{}^2 - 2a\omega_{pq} + a^2\omega_p{}^2$$
$$= k^2[\omega_q{}^2 - 2b\omega_{pq} + b^2\omega_p{}^2] = k^2\operatorname{var}(q - bp)$$

This equation states a relationship between a and b, such that if b were fixed there would be two roots for a, or if a were fixed there would be two roots for b; but in this case neither is fixed so a and b have great freedom to vary. The only roots for a, given b, that make sense are real and positive. Hence the admissible values of b are those that lead to real roots for a, of which at least one is positive. Similarly, the only values of b, given a, that make sense are real and negative. Hence the admissible values of a are those that lead to real roots for b, of which at least one is negative. Depending on the ω's and k^2, the restriction $\sigma_\alpha{}^2 = k^2\sigma_\beta{}^2$ may or may not provide useful interval identification for a and b. If we have the restriction $k_1{}^2 \leqq \sigma_\alpha{}^2/\sigma_\beta{}^2 \leqq k_2{}^2$ instead, the chances for useful identification are still less favorable.

5.12 Suppose now that the model is (5.1) and (5.3), that is, the money wage rate W appears in the supply equation but not in the demand equation. Therefore the demand equation is identified (see 2.13). Therefore the demand disturbances u_β can be calculated from our infinite sample as $q - \beta p$, and their variance $\sigma_\beta{}^2$ is identified. If $\sigma_\alpha{}^2 = k^2\sigma_\beta{}^2$ where k^2 is known, $\sigma_\alpha{}^2$ itself becomes known. Then, as in the case where $\sigma_\alpha{}^2$ is known in the model (5.2)–(5.3), α is at worst multiply identified with two possible values, and if one of those is negative then α is uniquely identified. The parameter α' is, at worst, multiply identified with four possible values, and may be uniquely identified. This may be seen in two stages as follows. The first stage concerns α and the second, α'.

5.13 Let a and a' respectively denote the coefficients of price p and wage rate W in any would-be supply curve. The disturbance of such a curve must be $q - a\mathsf{p} - a'\mathsf{W}$. The variance of this disturbance conditional on a given value of W is independent of W, because for given W the term $a'\mathsf{W}$ is constant; this conditional variance is the conditional variance of $(q - a\mathsf{p})$ for given W and is equal to the second (center) member of (5.9) above. This conditional variance is also equal to σ_α^2 itself (whose value is known from $k^2\sigma_\beta^2$) since u_α is by definition statistically independent of the exogenous variable W. Hence the equality

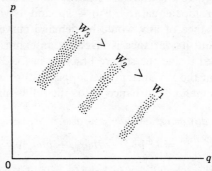

Figure 5.2 Hypothetical data from the model (5.1) and (5.3), showing three wage rates, when the supply curve shifts stochastically much less than the demand curve.

between the center and right members in (5.9) holds in this case too. Hence there are again two solutions for a, and they are the same expressions as derived in 5.8–9 and given by (5.11) and (5.12). One of them is equal to α; if the other is negative, it can be distinguished from α so that α is then uniquely identified.

5.14 This case sheds further light on the identifying role of a variable that appears in one equation but not in the other in a two-equation model. In 2.13 we saw that a variable such as wage rate W that appears only in the supply equation serves to identify the *demand* equation by separating the observed price and quantity points into clusters, one cluster corresponding to each value of W, such that the demand curve is approximately traced out as W changes by a line joining the centers of the clusters, as suggested by Figure 5.2. The figure is drawn for the case in which the shifts of the quantities demanded and supplied *at a given price* are of the same order of magnitude, but the supply shifts are to a very large extent explained by changes in W among three values, so that σ_α^2 in (5.1) is much smaller than σ_β^2 in (5.3). That is, $\sigma_\alpha^2 = k^2\sigma_\beta^2$, where k^2 is much. less than 1. The fact that the shifts in supply at a given price are so well explained by W helps to identify the supply equation too, and indeed Figure 5.2 suggests that the supply equation for given W will be approximately given by a line drawn to fit the cluster of points corresponding to the given value of W. Look again at (5.11) and (5.12), which give the two solutions for a, the would-be supply slope, and imagine that k^2 is near zero. One root is the true supply slope α, as stated in (5.11). The expression $\sigma_\beta^2 - \sigma_\alpha^2$ in the numerator of (5.12) is near σ_β^2. The expression $\sigma_\beta^2 - 2\sigma_{\alpha\beta} + \sigma_\alpha^2$ in the denominator of (5.12) is also near σ_β^2 since it is the variance of $u_\beta - u_\alpha$, and u_β varies much more than u_α. Hence the root a_2 is near $\beta + (\alpha - \beta)$, that is, near α too. Hence no matter which root we choose, the result will be either α or some number near α.

5.15 Now consider the identification of α'. The unconditional variance of the disturbance $q - ap - a'W$ is the following, which must be equal to σ_α^2 by an argument similar to 5.13:

$$(5.14) \quad \mathrm{var}\,(q - ap - a'W) = \omega_q^2 - 2a\omega_{pq} + a^2\omega_p^2$$
$$+ a'^2\sigma_W^2 - 2a'\sigma_{qW} + 2aa'\sigma_{pW} = \sigma_\alpha^2$$

where σ_W^2, σ_{qW}, and σ_{pW} are the variance and covariances involving W. This equation is quadratic in a' for given a, and its coefficients (the ω's and σ's) are known from the model and the hypothetical infinite sample. Thus for each of (5.10)'s two roots ($a_1 = \alpha$ and a_2), (5.14) gives two roots for a'. Hence at worst α' is multiply identified with four possible values. At best, α will be uniquely identified, which eliminates two of the four values of α'. And at best just one of the remaining two will be negative and will thus be admissible, so that α' will be uniquely identified.

5.16 Suppose in the model (5.1) and (5.3) that the ratio $\sigma_\alpha^2/\sigma_\beta^2$ is not known, but is known to lie between the two limits k_1^2 and k_2^2, both non-negative. Then two intervals for α and four intervals for α' will result from inequalities analogous to (5.9) and (5.14), and parts or the whole of some of these intervals may be inadmissible because of the restrictions $\alpha > 0$ and $\alpha' < 0$.

5.17 *Restrictions on* $\sigma_{\alpha\beta}$. Suppose in the model (5.2)–(5.3) the covariance of the supply and demand disturbances, $\sigma_{\alpha\beta}$, is known. Does this identify the supply equation? Let a and b be the slope of any would-be supply and demand equations, respectively. The disturbances to such equations are $q - ap$ and $q - bp$. The covariance of these disturbances is as follows, and it must be equal to the known value of $\sigma_{\alpha\beta}$:

$$(5.15) \quad \mathrm{cov}\,(q - ap, q - bp) = \omega_q^2 - (a + b)\omega_{pq} + ab\omega_p^2 = \sigma_{\alpha\beta}$$

The center and right-hand members here are a linear equation in a if b is given, or a linear equation in b if a is given; the coefficients (ω's and $\sigma_{\alpha\beta}$) are known. But until either a or b becomes known, we can go no further so both are unidentified [except that because of (5.15) some restriction stricter than $\alpha > 0$ may be placed on α by the fact that we must have $\beta < 0$, and some stricter restriction than $\beta < 0$ may be placed on β by the fact that $\alpha > 0$]. In particular, this paragraph shows that it is not very helpful to know that u_α and u_β are uncorrelated ($\sigma_{\alpha\beta} = 0$) if no other restrictions are available.

5.18 Suppose that in the model (5.1) and (5.3), with W in the supply equation, the value of $\sigma_{\alpha\beta}$ is known. Then β is identified (see 2.13), and σ_β^2 also becomes known from the true disturbances $q - \beta p$. Then the conditional covariance of the true demand disturbance and the would-be supply disturbance $q - ap$ for given W is as follows (it must be equal to the known $\sigma_{\alpha\beta}$ because u_α and u_β are statistically independent of W):

$$(5.16) \quad \mathrm{cov}\,(q - ap,\, q - \beta p \mid W) = \omega_q^2 - (a + \beta)\omega_{pq} + a\beta\omega_p^2 = \sigma_{\alpha\beta}$$

This a linear equation in a, which has a solution unless $\omega_{pq} = \beta\omega_p^2$ (an event that occurs only with zero probability). On substitution of the values of the ω's from (5.6)–(5.8) it can be seen that this solution is indeed equal to α. Thus except in zero-probability case, α is uniquely identified. By setting the unconditional covariance of $(q - ap - a'W)$ and $(q - \beta p)$ equal to $\sigma_{\alpha\beta}$ we can see that there results a linear equation in a' given a, which has a solution unless $\sigma_{qW} = \beta\sigma_{pW}$, so a' is uniquely identified if a is, except in that zero-probability case.

5.19 Suppose that in the model (5.1) and (5.3), $\sigma_{\alpha\beta}$ is unknown, but we know it lies between the limits k_1 and k_2 (which may each be positive or negative). Then α and α' are at best interval identified, because the equation (5.16) and its unconditional counterpart for a' are replaced by inequalities.

5.20 Suppose that in the model (5.2)–(5.3) both $\sigma_{\alpha\beta}$ and the ratio $\sigma_\alpha^2/\sigma_\beta^2 = k^2$ are known. Then both (5.13) and (5.15) apply. These are two nonlinear simultaneous equations whose unknowns are a and b, and whose coefficients are known (ω's, k^2, and $\sigma_{\alpha\beta}$). The equations do not have a unique solution; they have a finite number of solutions for a and b; hence at worst α and β are multiply identified in this case (unless certain peculiar relations having zero probability hold among the parameters, making solution impossible). If $\sigma_{\alpha\beta}$ and $\sigma_\alpha^2/\sigma_\beta^2$ are not known, but if upper and lower limits enclosing each are known,[38] then several intervals for α and β may result.

5.21 Using a simple two-equation model as in 5.2, we have illustrated how knowledge about the probability distribution of disturbances (either alone or in conjunction with knowledge about which coefficients in the model are zero) can lead to the identification of equations. Sometimes the resulting identification is unique, sometimes it is multiple, and sometimes it is interval (recall 5.3 for the meanings of these terms). In

[38] See Marschak and Andrews [1944] for an important related discussion.

principle this kind of identifying information can be just as important as the knowledge of which coefficients are zero, but estimation methods using it have not been so well worked out as have estimation methods that use the locations of zero coefficients.

QUESTIONS AND PROBLEMS

1.1. Is it true that every structure equation is a structural equation? Is the converse true? Why?

1.2. Is it true that every model equation is a structural equation? Is the converse true? Why?

1.3. Suppose that a consumption function in real terms is estimated to be $c_t = 5.35 + 0.661y_t + 0.275c_{t-1}$, and that the estimated standard deviation of the coefficient of disposable income y_t is 0.06. (See Table XI.6.1.) Then at the 10% level one cannot reject the hypothesis that the true value of the coefficient is 0.60. Then one might say that values of 0.60 and 0.661 are *both* consistent with observed data. Does this imply that the parameter is not identified? Explain.

1.4. In the reduced-form equation $\pi_0 y_t + \sum_{k=1}^{K} \pi_k z_{kt} = v_t$, are the parameters $\pi_0, \pi_1, \ldots, \pi_K$ identified? Is your answer consistent with the assertion in 1.16 that all reduced-form equations are identified? Explain.

1.5. In the model consisting of the following two equations, (1) $c_t = \alpha + \beta y_t + u_t$ and (2) $y_t = c_t + i_t$, what are the model's restrictions on the gth equation for $g = 1$? For $g = 2$?

2.1. Show that if income Y and wage rate W are exactly linearly related, the expected values of price p and quantity q (given Y and W) in equations (2.6) and (2.10) lie on a straight line in the p,q plane, and conversely.

2.2. Give an intuitive explanation of why, in a two-equation model, an equation is identified if it excludes a variable that appears in the other equation.

2.3. Using the models of 2.9, 2.13, and 2.14, show how each of the identified structural parameters can be obtained as functions of reduced-form parameters in 2.18.

2.4. In the arguments of 2.10 and 2.15, could one work with *actual* values of the endogenous variables p and q instead of with their conditional expectations? Explain.

3.1. Equations (3.1) and (3.2) are both normalized so that they have unit coefficients for y_1. Might the model restrict the coefficient of y_1 to be zero in one of the equations? In both? How should those cases be treated?

3.2. Consider the following income-consumption-investment model, where u_1 and u_2 are disturbances:

$$c = \alpha + \beta y + u_1$$
$$i = \gamma + \delta y + u_2$$
$$c + i = y$$

(a) Can you find a linear combination of the three equations that is different from the consumption equation but that satisfies the model's restriction on the consumption equation, namely, that investment is excluded? If so, do it, and if not, show why not. Is the consumption equation in this model identified?

(b) Use the rank and order conditions to test identifiability of the consumption equation.

(c) Explain why the equation $y = c + i$ is identified, even though it excludes only one variable (the dummy constant variable whose coefficient is the constant term).

3.3. Use the rank condition to show that every reduced-form equation is identified.

3.4. Consider the following income-consumption-investment model:

$$c = \alpha + \beta x + u_1$$
$$i = \gamma + \delta y + u_2$$
$$t = y - x$$
$$c + i = y$$

The exogenous variable is tax receipts t. Disposable income is denoted by x.

(a) Test the identifiability of the investment equation.

(b) Test the identifiability of the consumption equation.

3.5. Consider the following model, equivalent to that of the preceding question:

$$c = \alpha + \beta y - \beta t + u_1$$
$$i = \gamma + \delta y + u_2$$
$$c + i = y$$

(a) Test the identifiability of the investment equation.

(b) Test the identifiability of the consumption equation.

(c) Do your results agree with those of the preceding question? Should they? Explain.

3.6. Show whether α and β in each of the two preceding exercises can be obtained from the reduced form, and explain how or why not. Comment on the result.

3.7. The order condition for identification of an equation in a linear system, given the knowledge that certain coefficients of individual equations are zero, is often stated as $K - J \geqq H - 1$. State it correctly in each of the following cases, where K_1 and J_1 are the number of predetermined variables in the model and in the equation, respectively, *not* counting a dummy variable whose coefficient is the constant term.

(a) There is no constant term in the model.

(b) There is at least one constant term in the model, but none in the equation.

(c) There is a constant term in the equation.

3.8. Obtain the values of β_0, α_1, α_2, and α_0 in terms of reduced-form parameters from equations (3.36)–(3.37).

3.9. Suppose the quarterly equation

$$\alpha_0 + \Sigma \alpha_i x_{it} + \delta_1 d_{1t} + \delta_2 d_{2t} + \delta_3 d_{3t} + \delta_4 d_{4t} = u_t$$

is fitted to seasonally unadjusted quarterly data, where α's and δ's are unknown parameters, x's are ordinary economic variables, and d's are seasonal dummy variables such that $d_{1t} = 1$ in the first quarter of each year and 0 otherwise, and similarly $d_{kt} = 1$ in the kth quarter and 0 otherwise for $k = 1, 2, 3, 4$. Do these seasonal dummies present identification problems? If so, what should be done? If not, why not?

3.10. Consider the following linearized segmentable model. Endogenous variables are c = real consumption, i = real investment, n = employment, P = price level, r = interest rate, y = real income, W = money wage rate. Exogenous variables are g = real government purchases, t = real tax receipts, and M = nominal money stock.

consumption:	$c = \alpha + \beta y - \beta t + \gamma r + u_1$
investment:	$i = \delta + \epsilon y + \zeta r + u_2$
income:	$y = c + i + g$
liquidity preference:	$M = \eta + \theta y + \lambda r + \mu P + u_3$
production:	$y = v + \pi n + u_4$
labor demand:	$n = \rho + \sigma W + \tau P + u_5$
labor supply:	$n = \phi + \xi W + \omega P + u_6$

Consider the identifiability of the equations, especially the liquidity preference equation, in three models as follows:

(a) Apply the order and rank conditions in the context of the whole model. For each nonidentified equation in the model, find a linear combination of the other equations that satisfies the model's restrictions.

(b) In the context of a submodel consisting of the first four equations, with income y as an exogenous variable, apply the order and rank conditions again.

(c) In the context of a submodel consisting of the first five equations, with employment n as an exogenous variable, apply the order and rank conditions again.

(d) Comment on any disparities.

3.11. Test the identifiability of the equations in a model of your choice. (Suggestion: Try some of the models in earlier chapters.)

4.1. Prove the statement in the first sentence of 4.4.

4.2. Test the identification of both equations in each of the following models:

(a) demand: $\log q = \beta_0 + \beta_1 \log p + u_\beta$
 supply: $q = \alpha_0 + \alpha_1 p + \alpha_2 W + u_\alpha$

(b) demand: $\log q = \beta_0 + \beta_1 \log p + \beta_2 \log Y + u_\beta$
 supply: $q = \alpha_0 + \alpha_1 p + u_\alpha$

5.1. (a) Derive equation (5.10).

(b) Which quantities in (5.10) would be known to an investigator, and which would be estimated from the reduced form, if the method of 5.8 were applicable to the estimation of the supply slope α with an infinite sample?

(c) Make up a possible but hypothetical set of numerical values for the quantities in part (b) and estimate α from them. How many estimates did you get? Can you reject any as incorrect? Explain.

5.2. Construct the intervals within which the supply slope α must lie according to the method of 5.10.

5.3. (a) Is not equation (5.13) true if a and b are replaced by α and β respectively?

(b) Why are the symbols a and b used in (5.13) instead of α and β?

(c) Make up possible hypothetical values of the known and reduced-form-estimated quantities in (5.13), and use them to find whether or not in your case the restriction $\sigma_\alpha{}^2 = k^2\sigma_\beta{}^2$ leads to any restrictions on the supply and demand slopes α and β.

5.4. Write out expressions for the four possible solutions for the wage slope α' discussed in 5.15. Make up a possible numerical example and determine which if any of the four can be rejected as incorrect.

5.5. Consider equations (2.1)–(2.2) and assume that their disturbances at any time are known to be uncorrelated. Find two linear combinations of the two equations, with weights h and $1 - h$ and k and $1 - k$, where h and k are neither 0 nor 1, such that the two linear combinations also have uncorrelated disturbances. What does this show about the identifiability of (2.1) and (2.2) given this restriction?

CHAPTER IX

Point Estimation
of Economic Parameters

This chapter discusses the point estimation of parameters of econometric equations. Relevant concepts from earlier chapters are listed with cross references. The assumptions to be used are stated. Three basic models to be discussed are described. Least-squares estimation for single-equation models is discussed in three sections, and its properties in the three models are set forth. Simultaneous-equations methods—including indirect least squares, instrumental variables, limited-information and full-information maximum likelihood, and two-stage and three-stage least squares—are discussed, together with their properties. Least-squares structural estimation, though not consistent in general, is discussed. The several methods are compared and crudely evaluated. The role of serial independence of disturbances in time-series models is discussed.

1 INTRODUCTION; CONCEPTS AND NOTATION; RESIDUALS

1.1 In this chapter we come to grips with the problem of point estimation of economic parameters, both reduced form and structural. In the following chapter we take up interval estimation, testing, and prediction. In all that follows, stochastic models will be used, and inference procedures based on sample data will be presented and discussed.

1.2 We shall make use of many important concepts defined in earlier chapters. For convenience, some of the main concepts with cross references are listed in Table 1.1 below.

1.3 In the rest of the book it will be useful to have some standard notation. Parameters as heretofore will be denoted by Greek letters. The estimate or estimator of a parameter will be denoted in some cases by a corresponding Latin letter (such as $a = $ est α, $b = $ est β, etc.) and in some cases by the Greek letter with some distinguishing extra mark such as $\hat{\alpha}$, $\beta^{(1)}$, $\gamma^{(k)}$, etc. Disturbances will usually be denoted by the letters u and v. The calculated value of a variable is obtained by solving a structural or reduced-form equation for that variable, substituting estimates for parameters in the equation, and ignoring the disturbance. This calculated value is denoted by placing a caret (or "hat") over the variable's symbol, as $\hat{x}$ for the calculated value of x. Suppose an equation connects the variables $x_0, x_1, \ldots, x_K$ as follows, where δ's are parameters and u is a disturbance, and observations are available for periods from $t = 1$ to $t = T$:

$$(1.1) \qquad x_{0t} = \delta_0 + \sum_{k=1}^{K} \delta_k x_{kt} + u_t \qquad t = 1, \ldots, T$$

TABLE 1.1   Some Important Concepts to Be Used in Chapter IX and Cross References to Their Definitions in Earlier Chapters

Concept	Section Containing the Definition
approximate mean, variance, expected squared error	VII.6.9–11
asymptotic efficiency	VII.6.12
asymptotic mean, variance, expected squared error	VII.6.9–11
asymptotic normal distribution	VII.6.8
autonomous equation	II.1.10
bias	VII.6.2, 6.9
best linear unbiased estimator	VII.6.4
consistent	VII.6.7
correlation	IV.3.9
covariance	IV.3.5
determinant	III.6.3–8
distributed lag	V.7
disturbances	II.2.1–7; IV.3.17–22
efficient	VII.6.4, 6.12
endogenous	IV.4.9
estimate and estimator	VII.5.6
exogenous	IV.4.9
expected squared error	VII.6.5, 6.11
expected value	IV.2.21, 26
identification	VIII.1.6, 1.13
identity	III.5.10
independence (statistical)	IV.2.16
jointly dependent	VI.4.3
just identified	VIII.3.27

TABLE 1.1 (Continued)

Concept	Section Containing the Definition
limiting distribution	VII.6.8
linear combination	IV.3.4; A.4.4
loss function	VII.5.7–13
matrix	A.1.3
mean	IV.2.21, 2.26; VII.6.9
model	IV.4.4
model equation	VIII.1.7
moment	VI.3.3
normal distribution	IV.3.1, 3.11
overidentified	VIII.3.27
parameter	I.5.3; VIII.1.7
parameter value	VIII.1.7
predetermined	VI.4.3
probability limit	VII.6.7
reduced form	IV.4.6–7
regression	IV.3.14, 17
squared error	VII.5.11–13
statistic	VII.5.4
structural equation	II.1.12; III.3.16
structure	IV.4.2
structure equation	VIII.1.7
unbiased	VII.6.2, 6.9
variance	IV.2.22; VII.6.10

Then if estimates of the δ's are denoted by d's, the calculated value of x_0 in period t is

$$(1.2) \qquad \hat{x}_{0t} = d_0 + \sum_{k=1}^{K} d_k x_{kt}$$

The *residual* of x_0 in period t is the difference between the actual and calculated values of x_{0t}. It is a calculated value of u_t and is denoted by $\hat{u}_t$, thus:

$$(1.3) \qquad \hat{u}_t = x_{0t} - \hat{x}_{0t} = x_{0t} - \left(d_0 + \sum_{k=1}^{K} d_k x_{kt} \right)$$

Note that although u_t and the δ's are unknown, numerical values can be assigned to their estimates $\hat{u}_t$ and the d's.

1.4 Given a set of data for the x's for periods $1, \ldots, T$, and any set of estimates $d_0, \ldots, d_K$, equation (1.3) determines a set of residuals $\hat{u}_1, \ldots, \hat{u}_T$. This is true no matter how the estimates were arrived at, even if they were selected arbitrarily. If the estimates are changed, with given data, the residuals change correspondingly. Thus any set of estimates can be judged by looking at the residuals it generates. If the residuals obtained are implausible, this suggests that the set of estimates that led to them is implausible too—or worse, that the specifications expressed by the model [e.g., equation (1.1)] are incorrect. We could say that any set of residuals is implausible if the range or mean square of the residuals exceeds a certain *a priori* magnitude. These estimation procedures would be appropriate to the kind of *a priori* information that was discussed in VIII.5.4–10. Most well-developed estimation methods yield residuals that are uncorrelated with the variables designated as exogenous. How this is done, and why it is useful, will appear in due course.

1.5 The remainder of this chapter is organized as follows. Section 2 discusses the assumptions and models to be used. Sections 3–5 discuss the least-squares estimation method as applied to single-equation models, first in a simple case where there is just one explanatory variable and then in more general terms. Section 6 discusses the maximum-likelihood method for a simultaneous-equations model. Section 7 discusses simultaneous-equations methods for a just-identified equation, and Section 8 discusses what difficulties they encounter in an overidentified equation. Sections 9 and 10 discuss the limited-information and two-stage least-squares methods respectively. Section 11 discusses the attempt to estimate structural parameters by least squares. Section 12 compares several structural estimation methods. Section 13 discusses estimation when disturbances are not independent through time. Bayesian estimation is discussed briefly in X.5 along with other procedures for evaluating *a priori* information.

2 ASSUMPTIONS UNDERLYING ESTIMATION METHODS DISCUSSED IN THIS BOOK; MODELS 1, 2, AND 3

2.1 This section lists almost all the assumptions about econometric models that will be used in the remainder of the book. In 2.2 the assumptions are stated in detail, and in 2.3 they are recapitulated with the aid of brief descriptive phrases. We shall discuss several different linear models, each one characterized in 2.4 below by the list of assumptions that it incorporates. Every model we discuss uses assumptions (a) through (h) except that sometimes (a) and (b) and (d) will be modified by adopting either (l) or (m).

2.2 The assumptions are as follows. (In connection with some of the assumptions, explanatory comments are added, indented and in parentheses.)

(a) The model is linear, with G equations, and contains as variables $y_1, \ldots, y_G, z_1, \ldots, z_K, u_1, \ldots, u_G$. It contains parameters, including β_{gi} and

γ_{gk}, that are coefficients in the equations $(g, i = 1, \ldots, G; k = 1, \ldots, K)$. The equations are

$$(2.1) \quad \sum_{i=1}^{G} \beta_{gi} y_{it} + \sum_{k=1}^{K} \gamma_{gk} z_{kt} = u_{gt} \quad g = 1, \ldots, G \quad t = 1, \ldots, T$$

The y's and z's are observable for T periods, $t = 1, \ldots, T$.

(One of the z's, say z_K, may be a dummy variable whose value is always equal to 1; if so, its coefficient γ_{gK} represents a constant term in the gth equation.)

The u's are not observable. The parameters are constant, and the unknown parameters are unobservable.

(If the model specifies that an equation has no unknown parameters, and that its disturbance is always zero so that all data satisfy it, then such an equation is called an identity.)

Some of the β's and γ's may be assigned zero values *a priori*; for example, if $\beta_{12} = 0$ then y_2 does not appear in the first equation. In matrix terms,[1] the equations (2.1) can be written as in (2.2) below, where the boldface symbols for matrices and vectors are defined after (2.2):

$$(2.2) \qquad\qquad \mathbf{B} \mathbf{y}_t' + \mathbf{\Gamma} \mathbf{z}_t' = \mathbf{u}_t'$$

$$(2.3) \qquad \mathbf{y}_t' = \begin{pmatrix} y_{1t} \\ \cdot \\ \cdot \\ \cdot \\ y_{Gt} \end{pmatrix}, \quad \mathbf{z}_t' = \begin{pmatrix} z_{1t} \\ \cdot \\ \cdot \\ \cdot \\ z_{Kt} \end{pmatrix}, \quad \mathbf{u}_t' = \begin{pmatrix} u_{1t} \\ \cdot \\ \cdot \\ \cdot \\ u_{Gt} \end{pmatrix}$$

(2.4)

$$\mathbf{B} = \begin{pmatrix} \beta_{11} & \beta_{12} & \cdots & \beta_{1G} \\ \beta_{21} & \beta_{22} & \cdots & \beta_{2G} \\ \cdot & \cdot & & \cdot \\ \cdot & \cdot & & \cdot \\ \cdot & \cdot & & \cdot \\ \beta_{G1} & \beta_{G2} & \cdots & \beta_{GG} \end{pmatrix}, \quad \mathbf{\Gamma} = \begin{pmatrix} \gamma_{11} & \gamma_{12} & \cdots & \gamma_{1K} \\ \gamma_{21} & \gamma_{22} & \cdots & \gamma_{2K} \\ \cdot & \cdot & & \cdot \\ \cdot & \cdot & & \cdot \\ \cdot & \cdot & & \cdot \\ \gamma_{G1} & \gamma_{G2} & \cdots & \gamma_{GK} \end{pmatrix}$$

(The y's will be the jointly dependent variables and the z's will be predetermined; see assumption (g) below.)

(b) The system of equations (2.1) [or (2.2)] can be solved uniquely for $y_{1t}, \ldots, y_{Gt}$ given the values of the other quantities as of period t. This is equivalent to saying that the determinant of the β's in (2.1) is not zero. *(model is "complete")*

---

[1] Matrix operations will be used beginning in Section IX.4.

(This determinant has G rows and G columns; it is the determinant of the matrix **B**. Note that if $G = 1$, that is, if the model has just one equation and one jointly dependent variable, this assumption (b) is automatically satisfied, for the determinant in question is simply the coefficient of the endogenous variable.)

(c) The vectors of predetermined variables

$$(z_{11} \ldots z_{1T}), \ldots, (z_{K1} \ldots z_{KT})$$

are a linearly independent set. That is, there is no set of K constants $c_1 \ldots c_K$ (not all zero) such that the linear combination $\sum_{k=1}^{K} c_k \cdot (z_{k1} \ldots z_{kT})$ is the zero vector. This assumption requires in particular that $T \geqq K$.

(If T is indeed $\geqq K$ but nevertheless the vectors are a linearly dependent set, the dependent one(s) should be eliminated by replacing them by linear functions of the others so that the remaining vectors *will* be a linearly independent set. This assumption is important because it implies that the reduced form is identified; we have used it in VIII.1.4 and VIII.3.)

This assumption (c) is equivalent to the nonsingularity of the following matrix (see the last theorem in A.4.6):

$$(2.5) \qquad \mathbf{M}_{zz}^{0} \equiv \begin{pmatrix} \sum z_{1t}^2 & \cdots & \sum z_{1t} z_{Kt} \\ \cdot & & \cdot \\ \cdot & & \cdot \\ \cdot & & \cdot \\ \sum z_{Kt} z_{1t} & \cdots & \sum z_{Kt}^2 \end{pmatrix}$$

(If one of the z's, say z_K, is a dummy variable, with $z_{Kt} = 1$ for all t, then assumption (c) is equivalent to the nonsingularity of the following moment matrix $\mathbf{M}_{zz}$, where the moment $m_{z_k z_l}$ is defined as in VI.3.3 as $\sum_{t=1}^{T} (x_{kt} - \bar{x}_k)(x_{lt} - \bar{x}_l)$.

$$(2.6) \qquad \mathbf{M}_{zz} \equiv \begin{pmatrix} m_{z_1 z_1} & \cdots & m_{z_1 z_{K-1}} \\ \cdot & & \cdot \\ \cdot & & \cdot \\ \cdot & & \cdot \\ m_{z_{K-1} z_1} & \cdots & m_{z_{K-1} z_{K-1}} \end{pmatrix}$$

The inverse of (2.5) or (2.6) is used in solving the so-called normal equations of the least-squares method to be encountered below. Note that assumption (c) is about the *sample* values of the z's, not the population; cf. (h) below.)

(d) The equations to be estimated are identified.

(In most of the cases we discuss, the identifying information takes the form of restrictions that exclude certain variables from certain equations, as discussed in VIII.3. Other kinds of identifying information are discussed in VIII.3.37 and VIII.4–5. Note that in a one-equation model, with $G = 1$, this assumption is automatically satisfied if (c) is satisfied.)

(e) The u's are random variables with $Eu_{gt} = 0$ for $g = 1, \ldots, G$ and $t = 1, \ldots, T$; the variances and covariances of the u's are finite for each t.

(f) The joint distribution of $(u_{1t}, \ldots, u_{Gt})$ is the same for every t from 1 to T. The variance of u_{gt} for given g and for every t is therefore by (e) a *constant* finite parameter; we shall denote it by $\sigma_g{}^2$ or by σ_{gg}. The covariance of u_{gt} and u_{ht} is also a *constant* finite parameter for given g and h, denoted by σ_{gh}. The parameters $\sigma_1{}^2, \ldots, \sigma_G{}^2$ (or $\sigma_{11}, \ldots, \sigma_{GG}$) and σ_{gh} ($g \neq h$) are not observable.

(Note that $\sigma_g{}^2$ is not required to equal $\sigma_h{}^2$ if $g \neq h$; that is, the disturbances in different equations may have different variances. Similarly, different pairs of equations' disturbances may have different covariances.)

The matrix of variances and covariances of the u's is denoted by $\mathbf{\Sigma}$ thus:

$$(2.7) \qquad \mathbf{\Sigma} = \begin{pmatrix} \sigma_{11} & \cdots & \sigma_{1G} \\ \cdot & & \cdot \\ \cdot & & \cdot \\ \cdot & & \cdot \\ \sigma_{G1} & \cdots & \sigma_{GG} \end{pmatrix}$$

Since the σ's are variances and covariances, the matrix $\mathbf{\Sigma}$ must be symmetric, that is, $\sigma_{gh} = \sigma_{hg}$ for all g and h, and must be positive semi-definite.[2] If the system contains no identities, $\mathbf{\Sigma}$ is assumed to be positive definite.[2]

(Note that for a one-equation model in which var u_{1t} is positive and constant for all t, the condition about $\mathbf{\Sigma}$ is trivially satisfied, for then $\mathbf{\Sigma}$ has one row and one column and is equal to $\sigma_1{}^2$.)

(g) The z's are predetermined. This means (by the definition in VI.4.3) that u_{gt} is statistically independent of $z_{k,t-s}$ for every s that is $\geqq 0$ and for every g, k, and t. Equivalently, we may say $u_{g,t+s}$ is independent of z_{kt} for every $s \geqq 0$ and for every g, k, and t. Again equivalently, we

---

[2] See A.1.23 for an explanation of this term.

may say $(u_{1t}, \ldots, u_{Gt})$ is independent of $(z_{1r}, \ldots, z_{Kr})$ for all t and r that satisfy $t \geqq r$.

(See also assumption (i) and the next to last remark under (j) below.)

(h) The matrix $\mathbf{M}_{zz}^0$ of moments of predetermined variables about zero, reproduced here for convenience,

$$(2.8) \qquad \mathbf{M}_{zz}^0 \equiv \begin{pmatrix} \Sigma z_{1t}^2 & \cdots & \Sigma z_{1t}z_{Kt} \\ \cdot & & \cdot \\ \cdot & & \cdot \\ \cdot & & \cdot \\ \Sigma z_{Kt}z_{1t} & \cdots & \Sigma z_{Kt}^2 \end{pmatrix}$$

is *well behaved in the limit*, in the sense that it has the following properties,[3] where all inferences are conditional on the pre-sample values of the lagged endogenous variables and on all values of the exogenous variables:

(1) $\lim\limits_{T \to \infty} E \dfrac{1}{T} \mathbf{M}_{zz}^0$ exists and is nonsingular.

(2) $\plim\limits_{T \to \infty} \dfrac{1}{T} \mathbf{M}_{zz}^0$ exists and is nonsingular.

(3) The two aforementioned nonsingular matrices are equal. If we call their common value $\mathbf{M}^0$, we can write

$$(2.9) \qquad \mathbf{M}^0 \equiv \lim_{T \to \infty} E \frac{1}{T} \mathbf{M}_{zz}^0 = \plim_{T \to \infty} \frac{1}{T} \mathbf{M}_{zz}^0$$

$$(2.10) \qquad \det \mathbf{M}^0 \neq 0$$

(If z_K is a dummy variable always equal to 1, then assumption (h) can be stated equivalently in terms of the matrix $\mathbf{M}_{zz}$ of moments of the nondummy predetermined variables about the means, that is, recalling (2.6) above, as follows.)

$$(2.11) \qquad \mathbf{M} \equiv \lim_{T \to \infty} E \frac{1}{T} \mathbf{M}_{zz} = \plim_{T \to \infty} \frac{1}{T} \mathbf{M}_{zz}$$

$$(2.12) \qquad \det \mathbf{M} \neq 0$$

Assumption (h) requires that the time series of the *exogenous* variables (which are conceptually held fixed in repeated samples, and on which all our inferences are conditional) be such that $1/T$ times the matrix of their moments should have a *nonstochastic* limit as the sample size grows without limit. It also requires that the conditional probability distribution of *predetermined but not exogenous* variables (if any), given the exogenous variables and the pre-sample values of the lagged endogenous variables, be such that $1/T$ times their moments with each other and with exogenous variables have conditional expected values, and that these conditional

---

[3] It has already been assumed in (c) above that $\mathbf{M}_{zz}^0$ is nonsingular.

expected values have limits as $T \to \infty$, and that $1/T$ times these moments also have conditional probability limits equal to their conditional expected values. And it further requires that the nonsingularity of $1/T$ times the moment matrix (assumed for finite samples in (c) above) hold in the limit as $T \to \infty$. The effect of assumption (h) is to assure that $1/T$ times the sample moment matrix will be a consistent estimator of $1/T$ times the population moment matrix, and that the latter can be inverted. This assumption, or one like it, is a very important part of many proofs of consistency of estimators.[4]

(i) The z's are exogenous. This means (by the definition in IV.4.9) that u_{gt} is statistically independent of z_{kr} for all g, k, t, and r. Equivalently, we may say that $(u_{1t}, \ldots, u_{Gt})$ is independent of $(z_{1r}, \ldots, z_{Kr})$ for all t and r.

(Note that in a time-series model (i) implies (g), but not vice versa; (i) cannot hold in a time-series model if any of the z's are lagged endogenous. Note also that if a model is segmentable in the sense of III.3.4, and if also all the disturbances in one segment are independent of all those in the other, then the variables that appear in both segments are determined in the logically prior segment and are exogenous in the other (logically dependent) segment. See Koopmans [1950a].)

(j) The u's in every period are independent of those in every other period. That is, u_{gt} and u_{hr} are independent for all g, h, t, and r, provided $t \neq r$. Equivalently, we may say that $(u_{1t}, \ldots, u_{Gt})$ is independent of $(u_{1r}, \ldots, u_{Gr})$ if $t \neq r$.

(Note that if there are any lagged endogenous variables in the model, assumption (j) is used to make them predetermined; see VI.4.10–12. Note that the u's in different equations for the same period are *not* assumed independent.)

(k) The joint distribution of the u's is normal.

(l) Assumptions (a) and (b) together are accepted after being modified as follows: The stochastic equations may be nonlinear in variables, but are linear in unknown parameters; the identities contain no unknown parameters. Therefore the *stochastic* equations can be brought into the same form as (2.1), but if that is done there will be nonlinear identities; see III.10.4–10. The system of equations can be solved for the jointly dependent variables given the other quantities; the number of solutions is finite but because of nonlinearities may be greater than 1. There is

---

[4] Further discussion of this assumption, and of the substitutes for it used by other writers in discussions of consistent estimators, will be found in Sections 9.23–24, where several of the important contributions to the literature on consistency are mentioned.

no matrix **B** as in (2.2) and (2.4) because the system is not linear in variables.

(m) Assumptions (a) and (d) together are accepted after being modified as follows: One of the model's equations is to be estimated; it is over-identified; observations for $t = 1, \ldots, T$ are available for all the variables included in it, and also for a subset of excluded predetermined variables chosen so as to insure its identifiability. Observations are not necessarily available for a subset of excluded predetermined variables that is not needed for its identification. (There may be more than one way to divide the excluded predetermined variables into an observed subset and an unobserved subset so as to preserve the equation's identifiability.) Also, observations are not necessarily available for any of the excluded jointly dependent variables.

2.3 For ready reference, short descriptive phrases may be used for the various assumptions, as follows, but of course these phrases are only *incomplete* descriptions of the assumptions.

(a) Model linear.
(b) Model's determinant not zero.
(c) z's linearly independent.
(d) Equations identifiable.
(e) u's random with zero mean and finite variances and covariances.
(f) Distribution of u's the same in all time periods; their covariance matrix nonsingular.
(g) z's predetermined.
(h) Moment matrix of predetermined variables well behaved in limit.
(i) z's exogenous.
(j) u's serially independent.
(k) u's normal.
(l) Model linear in unknown parameters.
(m) Some z's not observed, but equation in question still identified.

2.4 The models we shall discuss most are characterized by assumptions as follows:

Name of Model	Assumptions Used
Model 1	(a)–(h), (i)
Model 1 (normal)	(a)–(h), (i), (k)
Model 2	(a)–(h), (i), (j)
Model 2 (normal)	(a)–(h), (i), (j), (k)
Model 3	(a)–(h), (j)
Model 3 (normal)	(a)–(h), (j), (k)

Thus all these models are linear, have unique linear reduced forms, and have well-behaved predetermined variables in the limit. In Model 1 the

z's are exogenous and the u's need not be serially independent. In Model 2 the z's are exogenous and the u's are serially independent. In Model 3 the z's are predetermined but not necessarily exogenous; the u's are serially independent as in Model 2. The assumption of normal disturbances may be added to Models 1, 2, and 3. Eventually we shall consider the effect of modifying assumptions (a) and (b) by (l) to obtain nonlinear models that are linear in unknown parameters, or the effect of modifying (a) and (d) by (m) to ignore data for certain variables.

2.5   For ready reference, the differences among the three models can be briefly characterized as follows, but of course these characterizations are incomplete as descriptions of the models.

Model 1: z's are exogenous.

Model 2: z's are exogenous and u's are independent between periods.

Model 3: z's are predetermined and u's are independent between periods.

The three models with the normality assumption are of course similar to the three above except for the presence of that assumption.

2.6   Note that assumptions (a)–(h) in all three models imply that a unique reduced form exists whose disturbances and predetermined variables have the same properties as those of the structural equations (2.1). The reduced-form equations can be written as follows, with the π's being parameters and the v's disturbances:

$$(2.13) \qquad y_{it} = \sum_{k=1}^{K} \pi_{ik} z_{kt} + v_{it} \qquad i = 1, \ldots, G, \quad t = 1, \ldots, T$$

Equations (2.13) and the distribution of the v's express the conditional probability distribution of $y_{1t}, \ldots, y_{Gt}$ given the reduced-form parameters (π's) and the predetermined variables $z_{1t}, \ldots, z_{Kt}$. It will be recalled from IV.3.14 that the conditional mean of y_i in this distribution is known as the *regression* of y_i on $z_1, \ldots, z_K$; it is expressed by $E(y_i \mid z_1, \ldots, z_K)$ and because of assumptions (e) and (g) it is given by the right side of (2.13) *without* the disturbance v. In matrix terms the reduced form is as follows (new symbols are defined below):

$$(2.14) \qquad \mathbf{y}_t' = \mathbf{\Pi} \mathbf{z}_t' + \mathbf{v}_t' = -\mathbf{B}^{-1}\mathbf{\Gamma}\mathbf{z}_t' + \mathbf{B}^{-1}\mathbf{u}_t'$$

$$(2.15) \qquad \mathbf{v}_t' = \begin{pmatrix} v_{1t} \\ \cdot \\ \cdot \\ \cdot \\ v_{Gt} \end{pmatrix}, \quad \mathbf{\Pi} = \begin{pmatrix} \pi_{11} & \cdots & \pi_{1K} \\ \pi_{21} & \cdots & \pi_{2K} \\ \cdot & & \cdot \\ \cdot & & \cdot \\ \cdot & & \cdot \\ \pi_{G1} & \cdots & \pi_{GK} \end{pmatrix}$$

3　LEAST-SQUARES ESTIMATION IN A SINGLE EQUATION WITH ONE DEPENDENT AND ONE PREDETERMINED VARIABLE (SIMPLE REGRESSION); THE MAXIMUM-LIKELIHOOD METHOD; CONSISTENCY AND OTHER PROPERTIES

3.1　Some of the main ideas and techniques of estimation in econometrics can be introduced and illustrated by means of a simple equation having two variables, one dependent[5] and one predetermined. That will be the task of this section. Such an equation can arise if a single-equation model is appropriate, but this is a rather special case not often encountered in economics. Such an equation also arises if we have a reduced form that contains only one predetermined variable. Much of what we shall say in this section applies with suitable modifications to reduced-form equations having several predetermined variables, as will be seen in Section 4; indeed that is the motivation for beginning with this special case. In the early part of this section we shall deal with Model 1 (characterized by assumptions (a)–(h) and (i); see 2.2–4 above), and sometimes we shall restrict the discussion to Model 2, which is a special case of Model 1 produced by adding assumption (j). Later we will use Model 2 (normal) and Model 3.

3.2　Let y be the dependent and z the predetermined variable, v be the disturbance, and π and α be parameters (π_1 and π_2 could be used instead but in most of the section the benefits of such a notation do not seem worth the trouble of carrying subscripts on parameters). By virtue of assumption (f) the variance of v_t is the same for all t; denote it by ω^2. The equation to be estimated is then[6]

$$(3.1) \qquad y_t = \pi z_t + \alpha + v_t \qquad t = 1, \ldots, T$$

In this form the equation has an explicit constant term, α, and nothing is said about whether the sample means $\bar{y}$ and $\bar{z}$ are zero or not (in the absence of such a restriction, it would be most unusual to obtain a sample with either $\bar{y} = 0$ or $\bar{z} = 0$ or both).

3.3　There are three alternative equivalent forms in which (3.1) can be cast, depending on how the constant term is treated and whether the

[5] When an equation has only one jointly dependent variable, it is not necessary to use the word "jointly." (Historically, the idea of jointly dependent variables is newer than that of a single dependent variable.)

[6] We use the symbols π, v, and ω^2 rather than respectively γ, u, and σ^2, because the former notation is like our reduced-form notation and the latter is like our structural notation; as noted in the text just above, the results of this section are more easily generalized to all reduced forms than to all structural models. This generalization will occur later in the chapter.

variables are restricted to have zero sample means. Equation (3.1) and its three alternative forms are all useful, each for certain special purposes. All appear in the statistical and econometric literature. Therefore we shall present them all, so that the reader can become familiar with them.

3.4 The first alternative equivalent form of (3.1) is obtained by transforming z_t into a new variable $z_t - \bar{z}$, whose sample mean is necessarily zero as the reader can easily verify. This new variable is denoted by the sans-serif symbol z_t, following the notational convention introduced in VI.3.1:

(3.2)
$$\mathsf{z}_t = z_t - \bar{z} \qquad \sum_1^T \mathsf{z}_t = 0$$

Define a new constant term thus:

(3.3)
$$\alpha' = \alpha + \pi\bar{z}$$

Now rewrite (3.1) according to the first equality below, and apply (3.2)–(3.3) to obtain the second:

(3.4)
$$y_t = \pi(z_t - \bar{z}) + (\alpha + \pi\bar{z}) + v_t = \pi\mathsf{z}_t + \alpha' + v_t$$

This form of (3.1) will prove convenient whenever it is useful to have the mean of the predetermined variable be zero without altering the dependent variable or the disturbance.

3.5 The second alternative equivalent form of (3.1) is obtained by transforming z_t as in (3.2), and also y_t and v_t in the same way:

(3.5)
$$\mathsf{y}_t = y_t - \bar{y} \qquad \sum_1^T \mathsf{y}_t = 0$$

$$\mathsf{v}_t = v_t - \bar{v} \qquad \sum_1^T \mathsf{v}_t = 0$$

Now observe that if (3.1) is written T times, once for each period, and summed over T and divided by T, the result is

(3.6)
$$\bar{y} = \pi\bar{z} + \alpha + \bar{v}$$

Subtract (3.6) from (3.1), and obtain

(3.7)
$$y_t - \bar{y} = \pi(z_t - \bar{z}) + v_t - \bar{v}$$

Substitute (3.2) and (3.5) into (3.7) to get

(3.8)
$$\mathsf{y}_t = \pi\mathsf{z}_t + \mathsf{v}_t$$

This form of (3.1) has no constant term, and the sample means of its variables, $\bar{y}$ and $\bar{z}$, are constrained to be zero. From (3.5) it is seen that $\bar{\mathsf{v}} = 0$; hence $\mathsf{v}_1, \ldots, \mathsf{v}_T$ cannot all be independent of each other, although $v_1, \ldots, v_T$ are if assumption (j) is used.

3.6 The third alternative equivalent form of (3.1) is obtained by writing its constant term as if it were another variable term, and using a uniform notation for all variable terms so that the summation sign (or a vector or matrix) can encompass them all. Define two new parameters, π_1 (equal to π) and π_2 (equal to α). Define two new variables, z_{1t} (equal to z_t) and z_{2t} (a dummy exogenous variable equal to 1 in every period). Substituting these new parameters and variables into (3.1) yields

$$(3.9) \qquad y_t = \pi_1 z_{1t} + \pi_2 z_{2t} + v_t = \sum_{k=1}^{2} \pi_k z_{kt} + v_t$$

This form of (3.1) is convenient for mathematical manipulations where a separate constant term would be notationally inconvenient. Note, however, that the price we pay for getting rid of an explicit constant term is either to transform the variables to obtain zero sample means as in (3.8) or to increase the number of predetermined variables by 1 as in (3.9). The former is more convenient for arithmetic computation by hand or with a desk calculating machine, where an extra variable appreciably lengthens the computing time; the latter is more convenient for algebraic manipulation, where an extra variable makes no substantial difference but where uniform notation simplifies the algebra.

3.7 For comparison, the four equivalent forms are assembled here:

$$(3.1) \qquad y_t = \pi z_t + \alpha + v_t$$

$$(3.4) \qquad y_t = \pi(z_t - \bar{z}) + (\alpha + \pi\bar{z}) + v_t = \pi \mathbf{z}_t + \alpha' + v_t$$

$$(3.7), (3.8) \qquad y_t - \bar{y} = \pi(z_t - \bar{z}) + v_t - \bar{v} = \mathsf{y}_t = \pi \mathbf{z}_t + \mathsf{v}_t$$

$$(3.9) \qquad y_t = \pi_1 z_{1t} + \pi_2 z_{2t} + v_t = \sum_{k=1}^{2} \pi_k z_{kt} + v_t$$

Equations containing more than two variables can be, and often are, expressed in four analogous alternative forms, and when we encounter them we shall use notation similar to that set forth here. Equations analogous to (1.2) and (1.3) above (defining calculated values and residuals) can be written for each of the four forms.

3.8 In discussing the properties of estimators in Sections 3–10, we shall almost always make assumptions (a)–(h), stated in 2.2 and summarized in 2.3. Occasionally we shall modify them by (l) and (m). We shall sometimes use Model 1 [which adds assumption (i), making the z's exogenous], sometimes Model 2 or Model 2 (normal) [both of which add (i) and (j), making the u's serially independent], and sometimes Model 3, which is dynamic; see 2.4 for a description of these models. All of these assumptions apply to a simple one-equation two-variable model such as (3.1), with certain simplifications: in (3.1) assumption (b) is automatically satisfied; and so is (c) if $T \geqq 2$ and not all the values of z_t in the sample are identical; and so is (d) if (c) is.

3.9 We shall now describe the least-squares method of estimating the parameters π and α in (3.1) or its alternative forms. This subject is known as *regression analysis* because it deals with the estimation of parameters in *regressions* (defined in IV.3.14). (Later, when the properties of the least-squares estimators are discussed, the merits and limitations of this notorious estimation method will become clear.) The least-squares method in effect considers all possible pairs of numerical values of π and α; chooses a direction in which to measure the distance of each sample point (z_t, y_t) from the estimated line;[7] and then chooses as estimates of π and α that pair of values (denote them by p and a respectively) for which the sum of the squares of the distances in the chosen direction from all the sample points (z_t, y_t) to the estimated line $(\hat{y}_t = pz_t + a)$ is as small as or smaller than the corresponding sum of squares for any other pair of estimates.[8] Since the disturbance v_t in (3.1) is independent of z_t by assumption (g), y is dependent and z is predetermined. In least-squares terminology z is called an independent variable and y *the* dependent variable. It is then best (for reasons which will appear when the properties of the least-squares estimators are discussed below) to measure the distances in the direction of v_t itself, namely, parallel to the y-axis. If the estimates p and a are used, the calculated value of y_t is

$$(3.10) \qquad \hat{y}_t = pz_t + a$$

and the distance, measured parallel to the y-axis, from the point (z_t, y_t) to the estimated line is the residual $\hat{v}_t$, which is equal to each of the following expressions:

$$(3.11) \qquad \hat{v}_t = y_t - \hat{y}_t = y_t - pz_t - a$$

[Residuals in the direction of the z-axis could be obtained, if they were desired, by dividing (3.11) by $-p$ to get $-\hat{v}_t/p = z_t - y_t/p + a/p$.]

3.10 The sum of squared residuals to be minimized will be denoted by S:

$$(3.12) \qquad S = \sum_t \hat{v}_t^{\,2} = \sum_t (y_t - pz_t - a)^2$$

---

[7] This direction may be parallel to one of the axes, either y or z, or it may be at any angle between them.

[8] It will be recalled from IV.2.23 that the sum of squared deviations of any given number of observations of a single variable x_t from their average value $\bar{x}$ is less than the sum of their squared deviations from any other number (denoted by a), that is, $\Sigma(x_t - \bar{x})^2 < \Sigma(x_t - a)^2$ if $a \neq \bar{x}$. This suggests that least-squares estimation of π and a in (3.1) can be regarded as a kind of generalized averaging procedure.

To find the values of p and a that minimize S, we reverse the roles of the variables and the constants, that is, we regard S as a function of the "variables" p and a with the given observed values $z_1, \ldots, z_T, y_1, \ldots, y_T$ being "constant." Then we perform the minimization by setting the partial derivatives $\partial S/\partial p$ and $\partial S/\partial a$ equal to zero and solving the resulting two equations for p and a. Assumption (c) implies that this solution is unique. S (being a sum of squares) must be positive or zero and so must have a minimum value. Therefore, the unique values of p and a found from solving the equations $\partial S/\partial p = \partial S/\partial a = 0$ must be the minimizing values desired. The partial derivatives lead to this pair of equations for p and a:

$$(3.13) \qquad 0 = \frac{\partial S}{\partial p} = 2 \sum_{t=1}^{T} (y_t - pz_t - a)(-z_t)$$

$$(3.14) \qquad 0 = \frac{\partial S}{\partial a} = 2 \sum_{t=1}^{T} (y_t - pz_t - a)(-1)$$

Divide each of the above by 2 (ignoring the center member of each), perform the indicated multiplication, and put all terms containing y on the left side of each equation. The result is the so-called *normal equations* for least squares with y as the dependent variable:

$$(3.15) \qquad \sum y_t z_t = p \sum z_t^2 + a \sum z_t$$

$$(3.16) \qquad \sum y_t = p \sum z_t + aT$$

3.11 Solving these normal equations for p and a (by determinants or by any other method) yields the least-squares estimators of π and α in (3.1) with y as the dependent variable:

$$(3.17) \qquad a = \text{est } \alpha = \frac{(\sum y_t)(\sum z_t^2) - (\sum z_t)(\sum y_t z_t)}{T \sum z_t^2 - (\sum z_t)^2}$$

$$(3.18) \qquad p = \text{est } \pi = \frac{T \sum y_t z_t - (\sum y_t)(\sum z_t)}{T \sum z_t^2 - (\sum z_t)^2}$$

Thus to compute from data the values of the least-squares estimators with y as the dependent variable, we need to compute only the sum of the T observations on z, namely, $\sum z_t$; the sum of the y's, namely, $\sum y_t$; the sum of the squares of the z's $(\sum z_t^2)$, and the sum of the cross products of each pair of observations $(\sum y_t z_t)$, and then apply (3.17) and (3.18). Actually the value of the estimator a is much easier to compute from the following formula, which is equivalent to (3.17):

$$(3.19) \qquad a = \bar{y} - p\bar{z}$$

Since the least-squares residual $\hat{v}_t$ is equal to $y_t - pz_t - a$ [see (3.11) above], (3.19) implies that the sample mean of these residuals is zero,[9] that is,

$$(3.20) \qquad \hat{\bar{v}} = \frac{1}{T} \sum_{t=1}^{T} \hat{v}_t = 0$$

This will turn out to be true of the residuals in every estimation method we shall discuss. It is worth remembering. One useful implication of it is that, given the estimated slope(s) of an equation, the corresponding estimated intercept can be quickly found by setting it at that value that makes the algebraic sum of the residuals zero.

3.12 The foregoing estimators can be obtained by starting from any of the three alternative equivalent forms of (3.1). Consider, for example, (3.8), which says $y = \pi z + v$, with no constant term and with variables measured from their sample means. The sum of squared deviations to be minimized in this case is $\sum \hat{v}_t^2$, which equals $\sum (y_t - pz_t)^2$. Will this really yield the same value of p as before? It must, for $\sum \hat{v}_t^2 = \sum (\hat{v}_t - \hat{\bar{v}})^2$ by definition, and $\hat{\bar{v}} = 0$ from (3.20), so $\sum \hat{v}_t^2 = \sum \hat{v}_t^2$; therefore, the same sum of squares is being minimized in both cases. In this case there is only one estimator (p) in the expression, however, not two, for the constant term has been eliminated in (3.8):

$$(3.21) \qquad S = \sum \hat{v}_t^2 = \sum \hat{v}_t^2 = \sum (y_t - pz_t)^2$$

Setting $dS/dp = 0$ yields the single equation

$$(3.22) \qquad 0 = \frac{dS}{dp} = 2 \sum (y_t - pz_t)(-z_t)$$

Multiplying out, we get the single normal equation $\sum y_t z_t = p \sum z_t^2$; and solving for p, we get (recalling from VI.3.3 the definition of second moments about the mean):

$$(3.23) \qquad p = \frac{\sum y_t z_t}{\sum z_t^2} = \frac{m_{yz}}{m_{zz}}$$

Let us show that the two estimators in (3.18) and (3.23) are equivalent. Recall from VI.3.5 that these moments can be more economically computed by the expressions on the right of the equations below:

$$(3.24) \qquad m_{yz} = \sum y_t z_t = \sum y_t z_t - \frac{1}{T}(\sum y_t)(\sum z_t)$$

$$(3.25) \qquad m_{zz} = \sum z_t^2 = \sum z_t^2 - \frac{1}{T}(\sum z_t)^2$$

[9] Note that the sample mean $\bar{v} = \Sigma v_t/T$ of the *true* disturbances is typically *not* zero.

TABLE 3.1   Some Properties of the Least-Squares Estimators p, a, a', ω^2, w^2 of the Parameters π, α, α', ω^2, and ω^2, Respectively, Taking y as the Dependent Variable, in Equations (3.1) and (3.4), $y_t = \pi z_t + \alpha + v_t = \pi z_t + \alpha' + v_t$, in Several Different Models

Model Assumed (see 2.4)	Property	Reference to Proof
1	p is unbiased ($Ep = \pi$)	3.15
	a and a' are unbiased	—
	$\text{cov}(p, a' \mid z_1, \ldots, z_T) = 0$	3.16
1 (Normal)	p and a' are independent	3.16
	See also Model 1 above	
2	$\text{var}(p \mid z_1, \ldots, z_T) = \omega^2 / \sum z_t^2$	3.17
	$\text{var}(a' \mid z_1, \ldots, z_T) = \omega^2 / T$	3.18
	$\text{var}(a \mid z_1, \ldots, z_T) = \omega^2 \sum z_t^2 / T \sum z_t^2$	3.18
	w^2 is unbiased ($Ew^2 = \omega^2$)	3.19
	p is consistent ($\plim_{T \to \infty} p = \pi$)	3.20
	a, a', w^2, and $\hat{\omega}^2$ are consistent	—
	p is best linear unbiased	3.21-22
	a and a' are best linear unbiased	—
3 (Normal)*	p, a, a', and $\hat{\omega}^2$ are maximum likelihood	3.24
	p, a, and a' are normal	3.24
	p, a, and a' are asymptotically efficient	6.8
	See also Model 3 below	
3*	p, a, a', and $\hat{\omega}^2$ are quasi-maximum likelihood	3.25
	p is consistent	3.26-33†
	a, a', w^2, and $\hat{\omega}^2$ are consistent	—
	p, a, and a' are asymptotically normal	6.8
	asymptotic var $\sqrt{T}(p - \pi)$ $= \omega^2 \plim_{T \to \infty} (T / \sum z_t^2)$	3.34‡

* Inferences in Model 3 are conditional on exogenous variables and the presample values of lagged endogenous variables.

† The proof given is for a simpler equation than (3.1), namely (3.59) below, which has no constant term.

‡ The proof given is not strictly complete because it does not prove that $\sqrt{T}(p - \pi)$ has a limiting distribution.

Substitution of (3.24) and (3.25) into (3.23) yields (3.18), which shows that the two estimators of p are equivalent. To estimate α, we use (3.19). To estimate α', the constant term in (3.4), note that $\alpha' = \alpha + \pi\bar{z}$, so that an estimator of α' is obtained by adding $p\bar{z}$ to the estimator of α:

$$(3.26) \qquad a' = \text{est } \alpha' = \bar{y}$$

3.13 The variance ω^2 of the true disturbances v_t can be estimated by means of the minimized sum of squared residuals $\sum \hat{v}_t^2$. It seems reasonable to divide $\sum \hat{v}_t^2$ by the sample size T to get an estimator of ω^2, and indeed (as we shall see below) a fairly good estimator results. Denote it by $\hat{\omega}^2$:

$$(3.27) \qquad \hat{\omega}^2 = \frac{1}{T}\sum \hat{v}_t^2 = \frac{1}{T}\sum (y_t - \hat{y}_t)^2 = \frac{1}{T}\sum (y_t - pz_t - a)^2$$

Another estimator, which as we shall see is somewhat better, is obtained by dividing by $T - K$, where K is the number of coefficients to be estimated, including the constant term if any; in this section $K = 2$. Denote this estimator by w^2:

$$(3.28)$$
$$w^2 = \frac{1}{T - K}\sum \hat{v}_t^2 = \frac{1}{T - K}\sum (y_t - \hat{y}_t)^2 = \frac{1}{T - 2}\sum (y_t - pz_t - a)^2$$

When it is desired to compute $\sum \hat{v}_t^2$, to get $\hat{\omega}^2$ or w^2 or for any other purpose, it is more convenient to use a different formula, which is derived by the following steps:

$$(3.29) \qquad \begin{aligned} \sum \hat{v}_t^2 &= \sum \hat{\mathsf{v}}_t^2 = \sum (\mathsf{y}_t - p\mathsf{z}_t)^2 \\ &= \sum (\mathsf{y}_t^2 - 2p\mathsf{y}_t\mathsf{z}_t + p^2\mathsf{z}_t^2) \\ &= \sum \mathsf{y}_t^2 - 2p\sum \mathsf{y}_t\mathsf{z}_t + p\sum \mathsf{y}_t\mathsf{z}_t \\ &= \sum \mathsf{y}_t^2 - p\sum \mathsf{y}_t\mathsf{z}_t = m_{yy} - pm_{yz} \end{aligned}$$

The fourth equality uses (3.23). The last expression is easy to compute, recalling the short-cut rules for computing moments, given in VI.3.5.

3.14 We now present a catalogue of some of the properties of the least-squares estimators p, a, a', $\hat{\omega}^2$, and w^2 of the parameters π, α, α', ω^2, and ω^2, respectively, taking y as dependent in equations (3.1) and (3.4), under several of the models mentioned in 2.1. The catalogue is in Table 3.1. The first column of the table indicates what model is being assumed as a basis for each of the several properties discussed. The second column states properties that apply to the estimators in the given model. The third column gives references to proofs later in this section.

If in the least-squares computations the deviations in the direction parallel to the z-axis rather than the y-axis are used in the minimization process when in fact z is predetermined, then the estimators of π and α obtained are biased and inconsistent and are not maximum-likelihood estimators. This is the explanation, promised in 3.9, for measuring deviations parallel to the axis of the dependent variable. See 9.23–24 for related literature and Tables 12.1–2 for a summary.

3.15 *Unbiasedness of p in Model* 1. Consider the expression for p given in (3.23). For y_t in the numerator substitute from (3.8). The result is

$$(3.30) \qquad p = \frac{\sum y_t z_t}{\sum z_t^2} = \frac{\sum (\pi z_t + v_t) z_t}{\sum z_t^2} = \pi + \frac{\sum v_t z_t}{\sum z_t^2}$$

Therefore the least-squares estimator of π is necessarily equal to the sum of π itself plus a random error, $\sum v_t z_t / \sum z_t^2$. The denominator of this ratio is observable, but the numerator is not because it depends on the unobservable true disturbances $v_1, \ldots, v_T$. Clearly if $E(\sum v_t z_t / \sum z_t^2) = 0$, then $Ep = \pi$ and p is an unbiased estimator. Recall from assumption (i) that $v_1, \ldots, v_T$ are all independent of $z_1, \ldots, z_T$, and from assumption (e) that $Ev_t = 0$ $(t = 1, \ldots, T)$. Then apply to $E(\sum v_t z_t / \sum z_t^2)$ the rules for operations with mathematical expectation given in IV.2.24 (the expectation of a sum is the sum of the expectations, and if two variables are independent then the expectation of their product is the product of their expectations; note that since v_t and z_s are independent for all s and t, v_t and $z_t / \sum_s z_s^2$ are independent for all t), with the following result:

$$(3.31) \qquad E \frac{\sum_t v_t z_t}{\sum_t z_t^2} = E\left(\sum_t v_t \frac{z_t}{\sum_s z_s^2} \right) = \sum_t \left(Ev_t \cdot E \frac{z_t}{\sum_s z_s^2} \right) = 0$$

[The first equality in (3.31) changes the dummy subscript but not the substance of the denominator, and for later convenience reverses the order of division and summation. The second equality applies the expectation rules. The third equality applies the fact that $Ev_t = 0$.] Hence $Ep = \pi$ and p is unbiased in Model 1. Similar arguments show that a and a' are also unbiased, assuming Model 1. Note that in this proof of unbiasedness, it need not be assumed that the disturbances v_t are normal, or that v_s and v_t are independent for $s \neq t$. Even assumption (i), that z is exogenous, is stronger than necessary; it would be sufficient to assume instead that the *conditional mean* of v_t, given $z_1, \ldots, z_T$, is zero for all t, that is, that $E(v_t \mid z_1, \ldots, z_T) = 0$ for all t. But it is not sufficient to assume simply that v and z are uncorrelated, that is, that $Ev_t z_t = 0$ for all t. This matter was discussed earlier in IV.4.10 and recurs in 5.3 below.

3.16 *Noncorrelation of p and a′ in Model* 1. The joint distribution of $a′$ and p will clearly depend on the values of $z_1, \ldots, z_T$. The conditional covariance of p and $a′$, given $z_1, \ldots, z_T$, can be expressed as follows, using (3.23) and (3.26):

$$(3.32) \qquad \text{cov}\,(p, a′ \mid z_1, \ldots, z_T) = \text{cov}\left(\frac{\sum y_t z_t}{\sum z_t^2}, \bar{y} \mid z_1, \ldots, z_T\right)$$

Using the conditional expectations of $\sum y_t z_t$ and $\bar{y}$ and the definition of covariance, this covariance becomes equal to the following expressions:

$$(3.33) \qquad = \frac{1}{\sum z_t^2} E[(\sum v_t z_t)\bar{v}] = \frac{1}{\sum z_t^2} \sum z_t E v_t \bar{v}$$

Now the expression $E v_t \bar{v}$ must be a constant independent of t by virtue of assumption (f); hence the whole expression is zero because $\sum z_t = 0$. Hence in Model 1 p and $a′$ are uncorrelated, given $z_1, \ldots, z_T$. In Model 1 (normal), p and $a′$ are jointly normally distributed given $z_1, \ldots, z_T$ since each is a linear function of $v_1, \ldots, v_T$; therefore p and $a′$ are independent given $z_1, \ldots, z_T$, since uncorrelated normal variables are independent (see IV.3.12).

3.17 *The variance of p in Model* 2. The variance of p is of course equal to the variance of $p - \pi$. The first and last members of (3.30) imply that $p - \pi = \sum v_t z_t / \sum z_t^2$. We shall find the variance of this to derive an expression for var p. This variance will clearly depend on the values of $z_1, \ldots, z_T$ in the sample. Therefore it is appropriate to consider the conditional variance of p, given the observed values of $z_1, \ldots, z_T$. This does not affect the contribution of the disturbances in Model 2 because according to assumption (i) the distribution of $v_1, \ldots, v_T$ is independent of all the variables $z_1, \ldots, z_T$. In effect we consider all possible samples of data (y_t and z_t) for which $z_1, \ldots, z_T$ are the same as those in the sample in question and obtain the variance of p in that set of samples. Before proceeding, we note that when confronted with the variance of a sum, it is most convenient to try to arrange matters so that the terms in the sum are uncorrelated or statistically independent, in order that we may use the rules (see IV.2.25 and 3.8) that the variance of a sum of uncorrelated or independent variables is equal to the sum of their individual variances. To arrange this, note that $v_t = v_t - \bar{v}$ by definition and that $\sum z_t = 0$; then rewrite $\sum v_t z_t$ thus:

$$(3.34) \qquad \sum v_t z_t = \sum (v_t - \bar{v}) z_t = \sum v_t z_t - \bar{v} \sum z_t = \sum v_t z_t$$

(This procedure is applicable to any second moment about the mean, and is often useful.) Using (3.34) and the first two sentences of this paragraph, we obtain the following argument (some of the steps are explained just below):

$$\text{var}\,(p \mid z_1, \ldots, z_T) = \text{var}\,\frac{\sum v_t z_t}{\sum z_t^2} = \text{var}\left(\sum_t v_t \frac{z_t}{\sum_s z_s^2}\right)$$

(3.35)

$$= \sum_t \left(\frac{z_t}{\sum_s z_s^2}\right)^2 \text{var}\,v_t = \frac{\omega^2}{\sum_t z_t^2}$$

The first equality sign has been explained in the preceding sentence. The second equality changes the dummy subscript but not the substance of the denominator of the fraction, and then for later convenience reverses the order of summation and division. The third equality uses assumption (i), that v_t is independent of $z_1, \ldots, z_T$, and assumption (j), that v_s and v_t are independent for $s \neq t$, and also the rules about the variance of a sum and the variance of kx where k is constant (see IV.2.24). The fourth and last equality again changes the dummy subscript and uses the fact mentioned in 3.2 that var v_t is denoted by ω^2. Thus under Model 2, the variance of p is equal to the variance of the disturbance v divided by the sum of squared deviations of $z_1, \ldots, z_T$ from their sample mean. The variance of p therefore is small if the disturbance v has a small variance, if the z's in the sample have a large variance $\sum z_t^2/T$, and if the sample size T is large.

3.18 *The variances of a' and a in Model 2.* Since a' is equal to $\bar{y}$, the conditional variance of a' given $z_1, \ldots, z_T$ is equal to the variance of $\bar{v}$, whence

$$(3.36) \qquad \text{var}\,(a' \mid z_1, \ldots, z_T) = \frac{\omega^2}{T}$$

The conditional variance of a given $z_1, \ldots, z_T$, using (3.19) and (3.26), is

$$(3.37) \qquad \text{var}\,(a \mid z_1, \ldots, z_T) = \text{var}\,(a' - p\bar{z} \mid z_1, \ldots, z_T)$$

We have just seen in 3.16 that p and a' are conditionally uncorrelated given $z_1, \ldots, z_T$; hence the rule about the variance of a difference of two uncorrelated variables applies (see IV.3.8). The result is that (3.37) is equal to the following:

$$(3.38) \qquad = \text{var}\,(a' \mid z_1, \ldots, z_T) + \text{var}\,(p\bar{z} \mid z_1, \ldots, z_T)$$

$$= \frac{\omega^2}{T} + \frac{\bar{z}^2 \omega^2}{\sum z_t^2} = \frac{\omega^2(\sum z_t^2 + T\bar{z}^2)}{T \sum z_t^2}$$

$$= \frac{\omega^2 \sum z_t^2}{T \sum z_t^2}$$

(The next-to-last step results from obtaining the common denominator $T \sum z_t^2$, and the last step from applying the moment-computing rule derived in VI.3.5.)

3.19 *Unbiasedness of w^2 in Model 2.* The conditional expectation of $\sum \hat{v}_t^2$ given $z_1, \ldots, z_T$ is as follows (some explanatory remarks appear below):

(3.39)

$$
\begin{aligned}
E \sum \hat{v}_t^2 &= E \sum (\alpha' - a' + (\pi - p)z_t + v_t)^2 \\
&= E \sum [(\alpha' - a')^2 + (\pi - p)^2 z_t^2 + v_t^2 + 2(\alpha' - a')(\pi - p)z_t \\
&\quad + 2(\alpha' - a')v_t + 2(\pi - p)z_t v_t] \\
&= T \operatorname{var} a' + \sum z_t^2 \operatorname{var} p + T \operatorname{var} v_t + 0 \\
&\quad - 2E\bar{v} \sum v_t - 2 \sum_t E \frac{\sum_s v_s z_s}{\sum_r z_r^2} z_t v_t \\
&= \omega^2 + \omega^2 + T\omega^2 - 2\omega^2 - \frac{2 \sum_t E z_t^2 v_t^2}{\sum_r z_r^2} \\
&= (T - 2)\omega^2
\end{aligned}
$$

[The first equality arises from the definition of $\hat{v}_t$; the second results from squaring; the third from applying $E \sum$ to each of the six terms in square brackets and applying our previous results concerning $\operatorname{var} a'$, $\operatorname{var} p$, $E \sum v_t^2$, $\operatorname{cov}(a', p)$, $\hat{\bar{v}} = 0$ (which implies that $\alpha' - a' = -\bar{v}$), and $p - \pi = \sum v_t z_t / \sum z_t^2$; and the fourth and fifth from the rules of mathematical expectation in IV.2.24 and the assumptions of Model 2.] On dividing the first and last members of (3.39) by $T - 2$ we obtain the result that w^2 is an unbiased estimator of ω^2 in Model 2:

(3.40)
$$
Ew^2 = E \frac{1}{T - 2} \sum \hat{v}_t^2 = \omega^2
$$

Accordingly $\hat{\omega}^2$, which equals $\sum \hat{v}_t^2 / T$, is biased, but its bias approaches zero as $T \to \infty$ so that it is asymptotically unbiased. Note that unbiased estimators of $\operatorname{var} p$, $\operatorname{var} a'$, and $\operatorname{var} a$ (for given $z_1, \ldots, z_T$) can be obtained by inserting w^2 into equations (3.35), (3.36), and (3.38) respectively. These estimators are useful in connection with tests to be described in Chapter X.

3.20 *Consistency of p in Model 2.* In VII.6.7 it was explained that an estimator a of a parameter α can be proved consistent if it can be shown that $\lim_{T \to \infty} Ea$ exists and is equal to α, and that $\lim_{T \to \infty} \operatorname{var} a$ exists and is equal to zero. Adopt Model 2. Then 3.15 shows that $Ep = \pi$ for all T, so

$\lim_{T \to \infty} Ep = \pi$. And 3.17 shows that var $p = \omega^2 / \sum z_t^2$; now $\sum z_t^2$ is not zero, according to assumption (c); furthermore $\sum z_t^2$ will approach infinity as $T \to \infty$ since $\sum z_t^2 / T$ approaches a nonzero constant as $T \to \infty$ because of assumption (h); hence $\lim_{T \to \infty} \text{var } p = 0$. Hence p is a consistent estimator of π under Model 2.

3.21 *Best linear unbiasedness of p in Model 2.* Recall from VII.6.4 that if a parameter α is estimated by an estimator a that is unbiased and is linear in the observations of a dependent variable, then a is said to be *best linear unbiased* if var a is as small as or smaller than the variance of any other linear unbiased estimator. To prove that p is a best linear unbiased estimator of π in (3.1), it is convenient (though not necessary) to use the equivalent equation (3.4), that is, $y_t = \alpha' + \pi z_t + v_t$, in which $\bar{z} = 0$. The proof proceeds by first obtaining a pair of equations characterizing all estimators of π that are linear in $y_1, \ldots, y_T$ and unbiased, then obtaining an expression for the variance of such an estimator, and then minimizing that variance subject to the conditions that characterize linear unbiased estimators. Let q be any estimator of π. If q is unbiased, $Eq = \pi$ for every value of π. If q is linear in $y_1, \ldots, y_T$, then there must be a set of coefficients $c_1, \ldots, c_T$ (which do not depend on the y's) such that $q = \sum_1^T c_t y_t$. Hence if q is a linear unbiased estimator of π, we must have the following as an identity in π and α':

$$(3.41) \qquad \begin{aligned} \pi = Eq = E \sum c_t y_t = \sum c_t E y_t = \sum c_t (\alpha' + \pi z_t) \\ = \alpha' \sum c_t + \pi \sum c_t z_t \end{aligned}$$

Since the foregoing is an identity in π and α', the coefficients of π in the first and last members must be equal, and so must the coefficients of α'. Therefore we have respectively:

$$(3.42) \qquad\qquad 1 = \sum c_t z_t$$

$$(3.43) \qquad\qquad 0 = \sum c_t$$

This pair of conditions must be satisfied by any set of coefficients $c_1, \ldots, c_T$ for which $\sum c_t y_t$ forms a linear unbiased estimator of π, and by no other set.

3.22 *Best linear unbiasedness, cont'd.* Now the conditional variance of the estimator q, that is, of $\sum c_t y_t$, given $z_1, \ldots, z_T$ is

$$(3.44) \qquad \begin{aligned} \text{var } (q \mid z_1, \ldots, z_T) = \text{var } (\sum c_t y_t \mid z_1, \ldots, z_T) \\ = \text{var } \sum c_t v_t = \sum c_t^2 \text{ var } v_t = (\sum c_t^2) \omega^2 \end{aligned}$$

Thus if $\sum c_t^2$ is minimized with respect to $c_1, \ldots, c_T$ subject to the conditions (3.42)–(3.43), the resulting estimator $\sum c_t y_t$ will be best linear unbiased; we proceed to the minimization, by the method of Lagrange multipliers.[10] First form the following expression, where λ and μ are numbers known as Lagrange multipliers, whose values are to be determined:

$$(3.45) \qquad F \equiv \sum c_t^2 - \lambda(\sum c_t z_t - 1) - \mu(\sum c_t)$$

This quantity F is equal to $\sum c_t^2$ if the two conditions mentioned are satisfied, for then the two expressions in parentheses, by which λ and μ are multiplied, are zero. According to the method of Lagrange multipliers, F is now regarded as a function of the $T + 2$ variables $c_1, \ldots, c_T, \lambda, \mu$, and its partial derivatives with respect to all these variables are set equal to zero. The resulting equations are solved for the values of $c_1, \ldots, c_T$, which minimize $\sum c_t^2$ subject to the two given conditions. There is no need to write down explicitly the equations $\partial F/\partial \lambda = 0$ and $\partial F/\partial \mu = 0$, for (3.42)–(3.43) already express them. The derivatives with respect to c_t are

$$(3.46) \qquad \frac{\partial F}{\partial c_t} = 0 = 2c_t - \lambda z_t - \mu \qquad t = 1, \ldots, T$$

This set of T equations (ignoring the left-hand member) can readily be rewritten as

$$(3.47) \qquad c_t = \frac{\lambda}{2} z_t + \frac{\mu}{2} \qquad t = 1, \ldots, T$$

On substitution of this into the two conditions (3.42)–(3.43) we get respectively

$$(3.48) \qquad 1 = \frac{\lambda}{2} \sum z_t^2 + \frac{\mu}{2} \sum z_t = \frac{\lambda}{2} \sum z_t^2 + 0$$

$$(3.49) \qquad 0 = \frac{\lambda}{2} \sum z_t + \frac{\mu}{2} T = 0 + \frac{\mu}{2} T$$

The values of λ and μ are obtained respectively from the two foregoing equations:

$$(3.50) \qquad \lambda = \frac{2}{\sum z_t^2} \qquad \mu = 0$$

Substituting this into (3.47) gives us the solution we want, namely, the variance-minimizing values of the c's subject to the two conditions (3.42)–(3.43) that characterize linear unbiasedness:

$$(3.51) \qquad c_t = \frac{z_t}{\sum z_t^2}$$

[10] This is a method of maximizing or minimizing a function of several variables when the behavior of those variables is constrained by one or more restricting equations. See Patinkin [1956], pp. 285–288, or [1965], pp. 399–402; Courant, Vol. 2 [1936], pp. 188–199.

Accordingly, the best linear unbiased estimator of π is

$$(3.52) \qquad \text{b.l.u.est } \pi = \sum c_t y_t = \frac{\sum y_t z_t}{\sum z_t^2} = \frac{\sum y_t z_t}{\sum z_t^2}$$

[The last step here is the result of the same kind of procedure used to get (3.34) above; see the remarks before and after it.] Compare (3.52) with the least-squares estimator p given in (3.23); they are identical. Hence under Model 2 the least-squares estimator p is best linear unbiased. This is a special case of the famous Markov theorem.[11] The estimators a and a' are also best linear unbiased in Model 2.

    3.23 We now introduce the *maximum-likelihood* estimation method, and we shall then show that in Model 2 (normal) the least-squares estimators of the parameters of (3.1) are maximum-likelihood estimators. The maximum-likelihood method is widely used and is important because in many applications it yields estimators that are consistent, asymptotically normal, and asymptotically efficient.[12] The method chooses a set of values for the parameters that is at least as likely to generate the observed sample as is any other set of values of the parameters. Somewhat more formally, for the univariate case with one parameter α, express the joint probability of observing the values $x_1, \ldots, x_T$ when the parameter is α as follows:

$$(3.53) \qquad F(x_1, \ldots, x_T; \alpha)$$

Now regard this as a function of α with $x_1, \ldots, x_T$ fixed at the sample values actually observed; then F is called a *likelihood function* (as opposed to a probability distribution function when α is fixed and $x_1, \ldots, x_T$ vary). Now maximize the likelihood function with respect to α for the given x's and obtain as the maximizing value of α a function of $x_1, \ldots, x_T$ known as the maximum-likelihood estimator, which is often denoted by $\hat{\alpha}$.

    3.24 *Maximum-likelihood estimation of* π, α, *and* ω^2 *in Model* 2 *(normal) or Model* 3 *(normal).* Let us find the maximum-likelihood estimators $\hat{\pi}$, $\hat{\alpha}$, and $\hat{\omega}^2$ of the parameters in (3.1). (The notation $\hat{\omega}^2$ used here indicates part of the answer, for $\hat{\omega}^2$ has already been defined in (3.27); we shall soon see that the expression given there is indeed the maximum-likelihood estimator of ω^2.) Because of equation (3.1), which transforms v_t into y_t (some important mathematical features of this transformation are discussed in 6.5 below), the joint conditional probability distribution of $y_1, \ldots, y_T$ given $z_1, \ldots, z_T$ is normal in Model 2 (normal) and in

[11] See David and Neyman [1938].

[12] Maximum-likelihood estimation for the case of a sample of independent observations from a univariate population is discussed in Mood and Graybill [1963], pp. 178–185, Cramer [1946], pp. 498–506, Wilks [1943], pp. 136–142, and Wilks [1962], pp. 358–365.

Model 3 (normal). By assumption (j) it is the product of the individual conditional distributions of y_t given z_t. Each of these has mean $\pi z_t + \alpha$ and variance ω^2 here. Hence the likelihood function of π, α, and ω^2 given the sample data is as follows (to avoid notational confusion we here denote by π the ratio of the circumference of a circle to its diameter):

$$(3.54) \quad F(\pi, \alpha, \omega^2; y_1, z_1, \ldots, y_T, z_T)$$

$$= \frac{1}{(2\pi)^{T/2}\omega^T} \exp\left[- \frac{1}{2\omega^2} \sum_t (y_t - \pi z_t - \alpha)^2\right]$$

The next step is to maximize this likelihood function with respect to π, α, and ω^2. First note that since $\log_e F$ is a monotonic increasing function of F, the values of the parameters that maximize $\log_e F$ will also maximize F. We choose to maximize $\log_e F$ because it is a somewhat simpler expression to differentiate. Denoting $\log_e F$ by L, we have

$$(3.55) \quad L \equiv \log_e F = - \frac{T}{2} \log_e 2\pi - T \log_e \omega - \frac{1}{2\omega^2} \sum_t (y_t - \pi z_t - \alpha)^2$$

The equations to be solved for the maximum-likelihood estimators $\hat{\pi}$, $\hat{\alpha}$, and $\hat{\omega}^2$ are

$$(3.56) \qquad \frac{\partial L}{\partial \pi} = 0 = - \frac{1}{\hat{\omega}^2} \sum_t (y_t - \hat{\pi} z_t - \hat{\alpha})(-z_t)$$

$$(3.57) \qquad \frac{\partial L}{\partial \alpha} = 0 = - \frac{1}{\hat{\omega}^2} \sum_t (y_t - \hat{\pi} z_t - \hat{\alpha})(-1)$$

$$(3.58) \qquad \frac{\partial L}{\partial \omega} = 0 = - \frac{T}{\hat{\omega}} + \frac{1}{\hat{\omega}^3} \sum_t (y_t - \hat{\pi} z_t - \hat{\alpha})^2$$

Observe that the center and right-hand members of (3.56) and (3.57) are identical in form with the corresponding members of the least-squares equations (3.13) and (3.14). Hence the least-squares estimators p and a are identical with the maximum-likelihood estimators $\hat{\pi}$ and $\hat{\alpha}$ respectively, in Model 2 (normal) or Model 3 (normal). If (3.58) is solved for $\hat{\omega}^2$, ignoring the first member, the result is the same as the expression given for $\hat{\omega}^2$ in (3.27), so that $\hat{\omega}^2$ is the maximum-likelihood estimator of ω^2 in Model 2 (normal) or Model 3 (normal). Note also that in Model 2 (normal) the estimators p and a are themselves normally distributed random variables for a given set of sample values of z, for by (3.23) and (3.19) each is a linear function of $y_1, \ldots, y_T$, which are normal given $z_1, \ldots, z_T$ because of (3.1) and the normality of $v_1, \ldots, v_T$.

3.25 If disturbances in a model are not normal, the estimators obtained from the maximum-likelihood method for a model with normal disturbances have no direct connection with the likelihood function for the non-normal model. However, the same estimators may still be used, and sometimes they have some desirable properties (e.g., see 3.15–22 above). They have been called *quasi-maximum-likelihood* estimators by Koopmans, Rubin, and Leipnik [1950], p. 135. The least-squares estimators of π and α under Models 2 and 3 are examples of quasi-maximum-likelihood estimators.

3.26   Let us now let z in (3.1) be the lagged value of y, that is, $z_t = y_{t-1}$, and thus obtain a dynamic equation in which y_{t-1} is predetermined by virtue of assumption (g) but is no longer exogenous. Hence assumption (i) must be abandoned. We adopt Model 3. In this model inferences are conditional on any exogenous variables as before *and also* on the pre-sample values of any predetermined variables that are not exogenous. Under Model 3 the least-squares estimators p and a of π and α do not have means and variances in general, but they are consistent and they have asymptotic variances. The proofs are rather involved even though (3.1) is a very simple equation, and no doubt that is why expository works on econometrics typically offer no proofs of consistency or derivations of asymptotic variance in dynamic models, but refer instead to relatively advanced statistical publications.[13] Rather than follow this example, we shall at least present a proof of consistency of least-squares estimation in a dynamic equation simpler than (3.1), and also obtain the asymptotic variance, so that the reader can get some idea of such

[13] For a proof of the consistency of a maximum-likelihood estimator in the simple case of a single unknown parameter, see Cramer [1946], pp. 500–504; on p. 504 he says a similar theorem can be proved for the case of several unknown parameters. Wilks [1943] treats the same material on pp. 134–135, 136–139, 142. Wilks [1962] treats it on pp. 358–365.

Goldberger [1964] gives a proof of consistency of least squares and a derivation of its asymptotic variance under conditions similar to our Model 3; see his pp. 272–274, which refer back to pp. 266–272.

Mann and Wald [1943], which is rather more difficult than this book, proves the consistency of least-squares estimators for an equation containing only y_t and any number of its lagged values (y_{t-1}, y_{t-2}, etc.) and a constant term and a disturbance, under conditions corresponding to Model 3, except that Mann and Wald prove our assumption (h) as a lemma, assuming that *all* moments of the distribution of disturbances are finite and that the difference equation to be estimated is dynamically stable. They also prove the consistency of maximum-likelihood estimators of a structural equation in a simultaneous system under similar assumptions.

Koopmans, Rubin, and Leipnik [1950], pp. 56–60, 70–72, 112–113, 133–148, give an extremely difficult proof of the consistency of maximum-likelihood estimators for a simultaneous system containing both exogenous and lagged endogenous variables under assumptions similar to Model 3, except that they, like Mann and Wald, treat our assumption (h) as a lemma to be proved.

Durbin [1960] proves consistency of least-squares estimators of a single equation containing both exogenous and lagged endogenous variables under a set of assumptions similar to our Model 3.

See 9.23–24 and Tables 12.1–2 below for further remarks on this and related literature.

proofs in dynamic models. And even so, the proofs to be presented are rather involved, occupying paragraphs 3.27–34 below.

3.27   Consider a first-order difference equation in which the constant term is known to be zero and the disturbances v_t and v_s are independent for $s \neq t$, thus:

$$(3.59) \qquad\qquad y_t = \lambda y_{t-1} + v_t$$

[Note that this is *not* a special case of (3.8) above, for although (3.8) has no constant term, its disturbances must have a sample mean of zero and so they cannot be independent.] Adopt Model 3. As the reader may easily verify, the least-squares estimator of λ with y as the dependent variable (denote it by l) is [14]

$$(3.60) \qquad\qquad l = \frac{\sum y_t y_{t-1}}{\sum y_{t-1}^2} = \lambda + \frac{\sum v_t y_{t-1}}{\sum y_{t-1}^2}$$

Under Model 3, we shall prove that l is a consistent estimator of λ and obtain its asymptotic variance.

3.28   To discuss the consistency of l (and, below, the associated asymptotic variance) we shall use probability limits and limiting distributions, introduced in VII.6.7–8. We shall use two powerful theorems concerning the probability distribution of a function of two random variables based on a sample of size T. Let one of the variables be denoted by e_T; it is assumed to have a *probability limit* ϵ as $T \to \infty$. Let the other variable be denoted by d_T (this notation is temporary and will not be used elsewhere in the book unless reference is made to this context). For one of the theorems d_T will be assumed to have a *probability limit* as $T \to \infty$. For the other theorem d_T will be assumed to have a *limiting distribution* in the sense of VII.6.8 but not necessarily a probability limit. In this case the distribution of $c_T(d_T - \beta)$ will be denoted by $D_T(x)$ and the limiting distribution by $D(x)$; the probability density for any value x of $c_T(d_T - \beta)$ is $D_T(x)$ and its limit as $T \to \infty$ is $D(x)$.

3.29   The theorems are as follows (their proofs are mentioned below):

Theorem (a). *If f is a rational function (i.e., involving only multiplication, division, addition, and subtraction), and if* $\plim_{T \to \infty} d_T$ *and* $\plim_{T \to \infty} e_T$ *and* $f(\plim_{T \to \infty} d_T, \plim_{T \to \infty} e_T)$ *all exist, then the probability limit of $f(d_T, e_T)$ exists and is equal to the same function of the probability limits of d_T and e_T, that is,*

$$(3.61) \qquad\qquad \plim_{T \to \infty} f(d_T, e_T) = f(\plim_{T \to \infty} d_T, \plim_{T \to \infty} e_T)$$

For example, theorem (a) implies that $\plim (1/d_T)$ is equal to $1/\plim d_T$ if $\plim d_T$ exists and is not zero; and that $\plim d_T e_T$ is equal to $\plim d_T$

---

[14] The symbols l and λ will be used for a different purpose in Section 9.

times plim e_T if the latter two exist. It is *not* necessary that d_T and e_T be independent.

Theorem (b). *If e_T has a probability limit ϵ that is positive;[15] and if d_T has a limiting distribution $D[c_T(d_T - \beta)]$, denoted for brevity by $D(x)$, where β is constant and where c_T exceeds some positive lower bound as in VII.6.8; and if the mean and variance μ_0 and σ_0^2 of $D(x)$ exist so that the asymptotic mean of d_T is $\beta + \lim_{T \to \infty} \mu_0/c_T$ and the asymptotic variance of $c_T(d_T - \beta)$ is σ_0^2, then $d_T e_T$ has the limiting distribution $D(x/\epsilon)$, whose mean and variance exist so that the asymptotic mean of $d_T e_T$ is $\epsilon(\beta + \lim_{T \to \infty} \mu_0/c_T)$ and the asymptotic variance of $c_T(d_T - \beta)e_T$ is $\epsilon^2 \sigma_0^2$.*

Note that in theorem (b), as in theorem (a), it is *not* necessary for d_T and e_T to be independent. The theorems are intuitively plausible, for a probability limit is a number showing the value at which all the probability becomes concentrated in a degenerate distribution as $T \to \infty$. The theorems are generalizations of the simple theorems stating that $Exy = ExEy$ if x and y are independent, and that $E\beta x = \hat{\beta} Ex$ and var $\beta x = \beta^2$ var x if β is a constant (see IV.2.24–5). Proofs of theorems equivalent to (a) and (b), and of two related theorems regarding the sum and ratio of two random variables, are given or sketched by Cramér [1946], pp. 254–5.[16,17]

3.30 *Consistency of least squares in Model 3.* We now proceed to prove that the least-squares estimator l is a consistent estimator of λ in (3.59) in Model 3. We apply theorem (a) above to plim $(l - \lambda)$ from (3.60), choosing the function $f(d_T, e_T)$ as d_T/e_T, putting $\frac{1}{T}\sum v_t y_{t-1}$ as d_T and putting $\frac{1}{T}\sum y_{t-1}^2$ as e_T. Thus when we have shown that plim $\frac{1}{T}\sum v_t y_{t-1}$

---

[15] If $\epsilon < 0$, the only alteration in theorem (b) is that $-d_T e_T$ rather than $d_T e_T$ has a limiting distribution, and that distribution is $D(-x/\epsilon)$ rather than $D(x/\epsilon)$.

[16] The proofs are most easily given in terms of cumulative distributions, and Cramér's theorems are so stated (rather than via densities as is done here). Also he uses a somewhat different definition of a limiting distribution. Except for the latter difference, his method of proof for theorem (b) is to show that as

$$T \to \infty, \ \text{Pb}[c_T(d_T - \beta)e_T \leqq x]$$

approaches $\text{Pb}[c_T(d_T - \beta) \leqq x/\epsilon]$, which by hypothesis approaches the cumulative distribution associated with the density $D(x/\epsilon)$.

[17] Cramér gives two other theorems stating that if the assumptions of theorem (b) above hold, then d_T/e_T (but *not* e_T/d_T, notice) and $d_T + e_T$ have respectively the limiting distributions $D(x\epsilon)$ and $D(x - \epsilon)$ whose means and variances exist, so that d_T/e_T and $d_T + e_T$ have asymptotic means given by the asymptotic mean of d_T divided by ϵ and added to ϵ respectively; and the associated asymptotic variances are σ_0^2/ϵ^2 and σ_0^2 respectively. If $\epsilon < 0$, then $-d_T/e_T$ has the limiting distribution $D(-x\epsilon)$. The proof of theorem (a) follows directly from theorem (b) and the two theorems just stated.

and plim $\dfrac{1}{T} \sum y_{t-1}^2$ both exist and that the latter is not zero, we shall be able to evaluate plim $(l - \lambda)$ from the following:

$$(3.62) \qquad \text{plim}\,(l - \lambda) = \frac{\text{plim}\,\dfrac{1}{T} \sum v_t y_{t-1}}{\text{plim}\,\dfrac{1}{T} \sum y_{t-1}^2}$$

Let us take the denominator first. Assumption (h) assures that plim $\dfrac{1}{T} \sum y_{t-1}^2$ exists and is not zero. Hence if the plim in the numerator of (3.62) exists, (3.62) holds.

3.31   Now let us turn to the numerator of (3.62). We want to show not only that plim $\dfrac{1}{T} \sum v_t y_{t-1}$ exists, but also that it is zero, in order to show in (3.62) that plim $(l - \lambda)$ must be zero and hence l must be a consistent estimator of λ. As pointed out in VII.6.7, we can show that plim a equals α if we can show that as $T \to \infty$ two things occur: lim Ea exists and equals α, and lim var a exists and is zero. Hence we shall proceed in two steps, showing first that $\lim E \dfrac{1}{T} \sum v_t y_{t-1}$ exists and is zero, and second that $\lim \text{var} \dfrac{1}{T} \sum v_t y_{t-1}$ exists and is zero.

3.32   The *first step* is easy because $Ev_t y_{t-1}$ is equal to zero for $t = 1, \ldots, T$ by virtue of assumptions (e) and (g), so $\lim E \dfrac{1}{T} \sum v_t y_{t-1} = 0$.

3.33   The *second step*—showing that $\lim \text{var} \dfrac{1}{T} \sum v_t y_{t-1}$ is zero—is as follows. First, since $Ev_t y_{t-1} = 0$, we have the first equality below; others are explained further below.

$$
\begin{aligned}
(3.63) \quad \text{var}\,\frac{1}{T} \sum_t v_t y_{t-1} &= E \frac{1}{T^2} \left(\sum_t v_t y_{t-1} \right)^2 \\
&= E \frac{1}{T^2} \left(\sum_t v_t^2 y_{t-1}^2 + 2 \sum_{s<t} \sum v_t v_s y_{s-1} y_{t-1} \right) \\
&= \frac{1}{T^2} \sum_t Ev_t^2 Ey_{t-1}^2 + \frac{2}{T^2} \sum_{s<t} \sum Ev_t E(v_s y_{s-1} y_{t-1}) \\
&= \frac{\omega^2}{T^2} \sum Ey_{t-1}^2 + 0 \\
&= \frac{\omega^2}{T} E \frac{1}{T} \sum y_{t-1}^2
\end{aligned}
$$

The second equality above results from squaring. The third results because v_t is independent of y_{t-1} and earlier values of y, and also of earlier values of v. The fourth results from $Ev_t{}^2 = \omega^2$ and $Ev_t = 0$. And the fifth results from rearranging. Taking the limits of the first and last expressions in (3.63), and noting that by virtue of assumption (h) $\lim E \dfrac{1}{T} \sum y_{t-1}^2$ exists, we see that ω^2/T goes to zero as $T \to \infty$, so that $\lim \operatorname{var} \dfrac{1}{T} \sum v_t y_{t-1} = 0$ as required. This completes the second step of the proof that $\operatorname{plim} \dfrac{1}{T} \sum v_t y_{t-1}$ is zero, and on substituting the latter result into (3.62) we find that, for Model 3,

$$(3.64) \qquad\qquad \operatorname{plim} (l - \lambda) = 0$$

In other words, l is a consistent estimator of λ under Model 3. The proof that p, a, a', w^2, and $\hat{\omega}^2$ are consistent estimators of π, α, α', ω^2, and ω^2 respectively in equation (3.1) under Model 3 proceeds in a fashion similar to the above, but is somewhat more complex because the disturbances $v_1, \ldots, v_T$ that enter into (3.30) are not independent of each other, since their sample mean must be zero.

3.34 The asymptotic variance of $\sqrt{T}(l - \lambda)$ in Model 3 can be obtained with the aid of theorem (b) of 3.29 above. We shall consider the limiting distribution[18] of $\sqrt{T}(l - \lambda)$. First we express this statistic as the following product, using (3.60):

$$(3.65) \qquad\qquad \sqrt{T}(l - \lambda) = \frac{T}{\sum y_{t-1}^2} \frac{\sum v_t y_{t-1}}{\sqrt{T}}$$

Now $\dfrac{1}{T} \sum y_{t-1}^2$, which is the inverse of the first factor, has a nonzero probability limit by assumption (h), and therefore by theorem (a) above the first factor itself, $T/\sum y_{t-1}^2$, has a probability limit. The second factor, conditional on the pre-sample values of y, has a limiting distribution[19] because it is $1/\sqrt{T}$ times a sum of T terms involving successive values of independent disturbances. The mean of this limiting distribution of $\sum v_t y_{t-1}/\sqrt{T}$ is zero, because $Ev_t = 0$ and v_t is independent of y_{t-1} by assumptions (e) and (g). The variance of this limiting distribution is as

---

[18] Strictly speaking, we do not prove here that such a limiting distribution exists under Model 3, nor do most other works in econometrics except Durbin [1960], but we do obtain its mean and variance.

[19] Durbin [1960] obtained his result in a somewhat different way; see especially his pp. 144, 146–148. See 9.23–24 below for related remarks and references.

shown below. [Most of the steps here follow (3.63); the last step uses assumption (h).]

(3.66) asymptotic var $\dfrac{1}{\sqrt{T}} \sum v_t y_{t-1}$

$$= \lim \operatorname{var} \frac{1}{\sqrt{T}} \sum v_t y_{t-1}$$

$$= \lim \frac{1}{T} E(\sum v_t y_{t-1})^2$$

$$= \lim \frac{1}{T} E\left(\sum v_t^2 y_{t-1}^2 + 2 \sum_{s<t} \sum v_s v_t y_{s-1} y_{t-1}\right)$$

$$= \lim \frac{1}{T}\left[\sum Ev_t^2 Ey_{t-1}^2 + 2 \sum_{s<t} \sum Ev_t E(v_s y_{s-1} y_{t-1})\right]$$

$$= \omega^2 \lim \frac{1}{T} E \sum y_{t-1}^2 + 0$$

$$= \omega^2 \operatorname{plim} \frac{1}{T} \sum y_{t-1}^2$$

Now applying theorem (b) of 3.28, treating $T/\sum y_{t-1}^2$ as e_T and treating $\sum v_t y_{t-1}/\sqrt{T}$ as d_T, we have the following result:[19]

(3.67)

asymptotic var $\sqrt{T}(l - \lambda) = \left(\operatorname{plim} \dfrac{T}{\sum y_{t-1}^2}\right)^2 \cdot$ asymptotic var $\dfrac{1}{\sqrt{T}} \sum v_t y_{t-1}$

$$= \omega^2 \operatorname{plim} \frac{T}{\sum y_{t-1}^2}$$

In a similar way, it can be shown that the asymptotic variance of $\sqrt{T}(p - \pi)$ from (3.1) in Model 3 is

(3.68)   asymptotic var $\sqrt{T}(p - \pi) = \omega^2 \operatorname{plim} \dfrac{T}{\sum (z_t - \bar{z})^2}$

When ω^2 has been estimated, by w^2, for example, the approximate variance of l or p can be estimated using (3.67) or (3.68). For p it is

(3.69)   est approx var $p = \dfrac{w^2}{\sum (z_t - \bar{z})^2}$

What this expression actually gives is an estimate of the exact variance of a distribution that approximates the distribution of p. The distribution of p itself may fail to have either mean or variance in general in Model 3; see VII.6.2 and 6.9–10.

4 LEAST-SQUARES ESTIMATION IN A SINGLE EQUATION WITH ONE DEPENDENT VARIABLE AND SEVERAL PREDETERMINED VARIABLES (MULTIPLE REGRESSION); NOTATION FOR MATRICES OF MOMENTS ABOUT THE MEAN AND ABOUT ZERO; MULTICOLLINEARITY

4.1 This section is similar to the preceding one except that here we consider an equation with *several* predetermined variables. As before there is assumed to be just one dependent variable in the equation. Let y be the dependent variable; $z_1, \ldots, z_K$ (with $z_{Kt} = 1$ for all t if the equation has a constant term) be predetermined variables (called independent in least-squares terminology); v be a disturbance; ω^2 be var v_t (the same for all t); and $\pi_1, \ldots, \pi_K$ be parameters in the equation. Again there are four commonly used equivalent forms for the equation (cf. 3.7 above). They are as follows. The form with a constant term and no special restrictions is

$$(4.1) \qquad y_t = \pi_K + \sum_{k=1}^{K-1} \pi_k z_{kt} + v_t \qquad t = 1, \ldots, T$$

The form having zero sample means for all predetermined variables is

$$(4.2) \qquad y_t = \left(\pi_K + \sum_{k=1}^{K-1} \pi_k \bar{z}_k \right) + \sum_{k=1}^{K-1} \pi_k (z_{kt} - \bar{z}_k) + v_t$$

$$= \pi_K{}' + \sum_{k=1}^{K-1} \pi_k \mathsf{z}_{kt} + v_t \qquad t = 1, \ldots, T$$

where as usual sans-serif roman type denotes deviations from the mean. The form having zero sample means for all variables (including the disturbance) and no constant term is

$$(4.3) \qquad \mathsf{y}_t = \sum_{k=1}^{K-1} \pi_k \mathsf{z}_{kt} + \mathsf{v}_t \qquad t = 1, \ldots, T$$

The form having no explicit constant term, but otherwise similar to (4.1), is

$$(4.4) \qquad y_t = \sum_{k=1}^{K} \pi_k z_{kt} + v_t \qquad t = 1, \ldots, T$$

4.2 Again in this section we shall adhere to assumptions (a)–(h), adding various others to get Model 1, Model 2, or Model 3; see 2.2–4 above. Again assumption (b) is automatically met since there is only one jointly dependent variable, and (d) is met if (c) is.

4.3 Since y is the dependent variable, consider the sum of squared residuals measured in the y-direction. This sum can be formed from any of the four forms (4.1)–(4.4), and from its minimization a set of normal equations will result that can be solved for $p_1, \ldots, p_K$. Let us choose (4.3) since it permits us to solve a system of only $K - 1$ simultaneous normal equations (rather than K) and this is helpful when the computations are done on a desk calculating machine. Denote estimators of the π's by p's with corresponding subscripts. Recall from (3.20) that $\hat{\bar{v}} = 0$, so that $\hat{\mathbf{v}}_t = \hat{v}_t$ for all t. Then using (4.3), we obtain the sum of squared residuals in the y-direction:

$$(4.5) \qquad S = \sum_t \hat{v}_t^2 = \sum_t \hat{\mathbf{v}}_t^2 = \sum_t (y_t - \hat{y}_t)^2 = \sum_t \left(y_t - \sum_{k=1}^{K-1} p_k z_{kt} \right)^2$$

Taking the first partial derivatives with respect to $p_1, \ldots, p_{K-1}$ and setting each of the results equal to zero, we obtain the following set of normal equations (after division of each result by 2 and some rearrangement of terms):

(4.6)

$$\sum y_t z_{1t} = p_1 \sum z_{1t}^2 + p_2 \sum z_{1t} z_{2t} + \cdots + p_{K-1} \sum z_{1t} z_{K-1,t}$$

$$\vdots \qquad\qquad \vdots \qquad\qquad \vdots \qquad\qquad\qquad \vdots$$

$$\sum y_t z_{K-1,t} = p_1 \sum z_{K-1,t} z_{1t} + p_2 \sum z_{K-1,t} z_{2t} + \cdots + p_{K-1} \sum z_{K-1,t}^2$$

There are $K - 1$ equations in this system, and $K - 1$ unknowns, $p_1, \ldots, p_{K-1}$. The "coefficients" are moments of the variables $y, z_1, \ldots, z_{K-1}$ about their means. Using the moment notation of VI.3.3, we can write (4.6) somewhat more concisely as

$$
\begin{aligned}
m_{yz_1} &= p_1 m_{z_1 z_1} + p_2 m_{z_1 z_2} + \cdots + p_{K-1} m_{z_1 z_{K-1}} \\
&\vdots \qquad\qquad \vdots \qquad\qquad \vdots \qquad\qquad\qquad \vdots \\
m_{yz_{K-1}} &= p_1 m_{z_1 z_{K-1}} + p_2 m_{z_2 z_{K-1}} + \cdots + p_{K-1} m_{z_{K-1} z_{K-1}}
\end{aligned}
$$

(4.7)

The other normal equation yields p_K (the estimated constant term) after (4.7) has been solved, as follows (see 3.19):

$$(4.8) \qquad\qquad p_K = \bar{y} - \sum_{k=1}^{K-1} p_k \bar{z}_k$$

4.4 From this point onward, this book will make fairly extensive use of matrix algebra, because it is a very economical and convenient language when one has become fluent in it. The reader unfamiliar with matrix algebra should at least read Appendix A before proceeding, and preferably should work through the main part of an introductory book on the subject. Some references are given in Appendix A. Boldface type will denote matrices and vectors. Lower-case letters will be used for vectors and capital letters for matrices (usually).[20] A boldface lower-case letter with a "prime" (e.g., $\mathbf{z}'$) will denote a column vector, and without a "prime" it will denote a row vector.[21] A row lifted out of a matrix will typically be denoted by the lower-case letter corresponding to the capital letter that symbolizes the matrix; thus, if $\mathbf{M}$ is a matrix, $\mathbf{m}_2$ might stand for its second row.

4.5 To apply matrix methods to the solution of (4.7) we need some notation. We use the following:

$$\mathbf{z}_t = (z_{1t} \quad \cdots \quad z_{K-1,t})$$

$$\bar{\mathbf{z}} = (\bar{z}_1 \quad \cdots \quad \bar{z}_{K-1})$$

(4.9) $$\mathbf{z}_t = (z_{1t} \quad \cdots \quad z_{K-1,t})$$

$$\boldsymbol{\pi} = (\pi_1 \quad \cdots \quad \pi_{K-1})$$

$$\mathbf{p} = (p_1 \quad \cdots \quad p_{K-1})$$

$$\mathbf{m}_{yz} = (m_{yz_1} \quad \cdots \quad m_{yz_{K-1}})$$

(4.10)
$$\mathbf{M}_{zz} = \begin{pmatrix} m_{z_1 z_1} & \cdots & m_{z_1 z_{K-1}} \\ \cdot & & \cdot \\ \cdot & & \cdot \\ \cdot & & \cdot \\ m_{z_{K-1} z_1} & \cdots & m_{z_{K-1} z_{K-1}} \end{pmatrix}$$

where as usual in this book m_{yz_i} stands for $\sum_{t=1}^{T} (y_t - \bar{y})(z_{it} - \bar{z}_i)$ and other moments are defined similarly. With this notation, equation (4.3) becomes

(4.11) $$y_t = \boldsymbol{\pi} \mathbf{z}_t' + v_t$$

The set of normal equations (4.7) can be written as

(4.12) $$\mathbf{m}_{yz}' = \mathbf{M}_{zz} \mathbf{p}'$$

Premultiplying (4.12) on the left by the inverse of $\mathbf{M}_{zz}$ gives the solution for $p_1, \ldots, p_{K-1}$, the least-squares estimators of $\pi_1, \ldots, \pi_{K-1}$ with y as the dependent variable:

(4.13) $$\mathbf{p}' = \mathbf{M}_{zz}^{-1} \mathbf{m}_{yz}'$$

---

[20] Sometimes, in special cases, a matrix may have only one row or one column and hence may be a vector, but a capital letter will be used for a matrix that is not necessarily of only one row or column.

[21] Note that Koopmans and Hood [1953] follow this convention, but some writers follow the opposite convention.

It may be helpful to display in detail the determinant form of the solution for one element of the vector $\mathbf{p}$, for instance, p_1, as follows:

$$(4.14) \qquad p_1 = \frac{\begin{vmatrix} m_{z_1 y} & m_{z_1 z_2} & \cdots & m_{z_1 z_{K-1}} \\ m_{z_2 y} & m_{z_2 z_2} & \cdots & m_{z_2 z_{K-1}} \\ \cdot & \cdot & & \cdot \\ \cdot & \cdot & & \cdot \\ \cdot & \cdot & & \cdot \\ m_{z_{K-1} y} & m_{z_{K-1} z_2} & \cdots & m_{z_{K-1} z_{K-1}} \end{vmatrix}}{\begin{vmatrix} m_{z_1 z_1} & m_{z_1 z_2} & \cdots & m_{z_1 z_{K-1}} \\ \cdot & \cdot & & \cdot \\ \cdot & \cdot & & \cdot \\ \cdot & \cdot & & \cdot \\ m_{z_{K-1} z_1} & m_{z_{K-1} z_2} & \cdots & m_{z_{K-1} z_{K-1}} \end{vmatrix}}$$

The other elements of $\mathbf{p}$ are expressed analogously. If (4.2) is used instead of (4.3), the estimator $\mathbf{p}$ is not affected, and the estimator p_K' of the parameter π_K' is

$$(4.15) \qquad p_K' = \bar{y}$$

4.6 The minimized sum of squared deviations corresponding to (4.5) can be expressed in any of the following ways [compare (3.29) and use (4.12) and (4.13)]:

$$(4.16) \quad \sum_t \hat{v}_t^2 = \sum_t \hat{\mathbf{v}}_t^2 = \sum (y_t - \hat{y}_t)^2 = \sum_T \left(y_t - \sum_{k=1}^{K-1} p_k z_{kt} \right)^2$$

$$= m_{\hat{v}\hat{v}} = m_{yy} - \mathbf{p} \mathbf{M}_{zz} \mathbf{p}' = m_{yy} - \mathbf{p} \mathbf{m}_{yz}' = m_{yy} - \mathbf{m}_{yz} \mathbf{p}'$$

$$= m_{yy} - \mathbf{m}_{yz} \mathbf{M}_{zz}^{-1} \mathbf{m}_{yz}'$$

An estimator of ω^2 (the variance of v_t) can be obtained by dividing $\sum \hat{v}_t^2$ by either the actual sample size T or by an adjusted sample size $T - K$. The two results are

$$(4.17) \qquad \hat{\omega}^2 = \frac{1}{T} \sum \hat{v}_t^2 = \frac{1}{T} (m_{yy} - \mathbf{m}_{yz} \mathbf{p}')$$

$$(4.18) \qquad w^2 = \frac{1}{T - K} \sum \hat{v}_t^2 = \frac{1}{T - K} (m_{yy} - \mathbf{m}_{yz} \mathbf{p}')$$

4.7 The properties of these least-squares estimators ($\mathbf{p}$, p_K, p_K', $\hat{\omega}^2$, and w^2) are analogous to the properties of the corresponding estimators in the simple regression case, catalogued in Table 3.1; proofs are not given in this section. Under Model 1, $\mathbf{p}$ and p_K and p_K' are unbiased,[22] and

---

[22] See 5.3 below for proof.

also **p** and p_K' are uncorrelated.[23] Under Model 2, the matrix of conditional variances and covariances of $p_1, \ldots, p_{K-1}$ given the z's is[24]

(4.19) $\text{cov}(\mathbf{p}', \mathbf{p}) = E(\mathbf{p} - \boldsymbol{\pi})'(\mathbf{p} - \boldsymbol{\pi}) = \omega^2 \mathbf{M}_{zz}^{-1}$

and the variance of p_K' given the z's is

(4.20) $$\text{var } p_K' = \frac{\omega^2}{T}$$

Also under Model 2, w^2 is an unbiased estimator of ω^2, and by inserting w^2 for ω^2 in (4.19)–(4.20) we obtain unbiased estimators of the corresponding variances and covariances of the p's. Also under Model 2, **p** and p_K and p_K' are best linear unbiased. Under either Model 2 (normal) or Model 3 (normal), **p** and p_K and p_K' and $\hat{\omega}^2$ are maximum likelihood. Under either Model 2 or Model 3, the estimators **p**, p_K, p_K', $\hat{\omega}^2$, and w^2 are consistent. Under Model 3, the asymptotic covariance matrix of $\sqrt{T}(\mathbf{p} - \boldsymbol{\pi})$ is

(4.21) asymptotic cov $[\sqrt{T}(\mathbf{p} - \boldsymbol{\pi})', \sqrt{T}(\mathbf{p} - \boldsymbol{\pi})] = \omega^2 \text{ plim } T\mathbf{M}_{zz}^{-1}$

An estimator of the approximate covariance matrix of **p** in Model 3 is

(4.22)   est approx cov $(\mathbf{p}', \mathbf{p}) = w^2 \mathbf{M}_{zz}^{-1}$

even though cov $(\mathbf{p}', \mathbf{p})$ itself does not exist in general in Model 3. See 9.23–4 and Tables 12.1–2 for related remarks and literature.

    4.8 The foregoing method, starting from (4.3) and based on a set of $K - 1$ normal equations involving moments about the mean, does not lead easily to an expression for the variance of the estimated constant term p_K, or for its covariances with $p_1, \ldots, p_{K-1}$. This lack is the price we pay for having reduced the size of the system from K to $K - 1$ equations. Suppose we do not do so, and start instead from (4.4). The sum of squared deviations is then

(4.23) $$S = \sum_t \hat{v}_t^2 = \sum_t \left(y_t - \sum_{k=1}^{K} p_k z_{kt} \right)^2$$

The normal equations resulting from minimizing this form of S are K in number, since K estimators $(p_1, \ldots, p_K)$ appear in (4.23):

$$\sum_t y_t z_{1t} = p_1 \sum_t z_{1t}^2 + \cdots + p_K \sum_t z_{1t} z_{Kt}$$

(4.24)

$$\sum_t y_t z_{Kt} = p_1 \sum_t z_{Kt} z_{1t} + \cdots + p_K \sum_t z_{Kt}^2$$

[23] This means that p_k and p_K' are uncorrelated for $k = 1, \ldots, K - 1$.
[24] See 5.5 below for proof.

The "coefficients" in this equation are moments of the variables y, z_1, ..., z_K about *zero* (not about their means).

4.9 To express their solution in matrix terms, we temporarily let a superscript 0 attached to a vector of variables or parameters denote the inclusion in the vector of another component corresponding to the constant term $\pi_K z_{Kt}$ in (4.4). We also let the same superscript attached to a vector (or matrix) of moments denote the inclusion of another element (or row and column) corresponding to the variable z_K, and also denote the taking of moments about *zero* instead of about the *mean*. Thus we have

$$\mathbf{z}_t^0 = (z_{1t} \quad \cdots \quad z_{Kt})$$

(4.25)
$$\boldsymbol{\pi}^0 = (\pi_1 \quad \cdots \quad \pi_K)$$

$$\mathbf{p}^0 = (p_1 \quad \cdots \quad p_K)$$

$$\mathbf{m}_{yz}^0 = (\Sigma \, y_t z_{1t} \quad \cdots \quad \Sigma \, y_t z_{Kt})$$

(4.26)
$$\mathbf{M}_{zz}^0 = \begin{pmatrix} \Sigma \, z_{1t}^2 & \cdots & \Sigma \, z_{1t} z_{Kt} \\ \cdot & & \cdot \\ \cdot & & \cdot \\ \cdot & & \cdot \\ \Sigma \, z_{Kt} z_{1t} & \cdots & \Sigma \, z_{Kt}^2 \end{pmatrix}$$

If this notation is used, the normal equations (4.24) are

(4.27)
$$\mathbf{m}_{yz}^{0\prime} = \mathbf{M}_{zz}^0 \mathbf{p}^{0\prime}$$

The least-squares estimators $p_1, \ldots, p_K$ are therefore obtained from (4.27) as

(4.28)
$$\mathbf{p}^{0\prime} = (\mathbf{M}_{zz}^0)^{-1} \mathbf{m}_{yz}^{0\prime}$$

The first $K - 1$ elements of $\mathbf{p}^0$ are the same as $\mathbf{p}$ in (4.13), and the Kth element is the same as p_K in (4.8). The minimized sum of squares can be expressed in any of the following ways, all of which are equivalent to (4.16):

(4.29)
$$\sum_t \hat{v}_t^{\,2} = \sum_t \left(y_t - \sum_{k=1}^K p_k z_{kt} \right)^2$$
$$= m_{vv}^{\wedge\wedge} = m_{yy}^0 - \mathbf{p}^0 \mathbf{M}_{zz}^0 \mathbf{p}^{0\prime} = m_{yy}^0 - \mathbf{m}_{yz}^0 \mathbf{p}^{0\prime}$$
$$= m_{yy}^0 - \mathbf{m}_{yz}^0 (\mathbf{M}_{zz}^0)^{-1} \mathbf{m}_{yz}^{0\prime}$$

Hence estimators of ω^2, equivalent to $\hat{\omega}^2$ in (4.17) and w^2 in (4.18), can be obtained by dividing (4.29) by T and $T - K$ respectively.

4.10 The properties of the least-squares estimator $\mathbf{p}^0$ are as described in 4.7. The variance of p_K and its covariances with $p_1, \ldots, p_{K-1}$ are found along with other variances and covariances (given the z's) when the matrix $\mathbf{M}_{zz}^0$ is inverted. The result is, using Model 2,

(4.30) $\text{cov}(\mathbf{p}^{0\prime}, \mathbf{p}^0) = E(\mathbf{p}^0 - \boldsymbol{\pi}^0)'(\mathbf{p}^0 - \boldsymbol{\pi}^0) = \omega^2(\mathbf{M}_{zz}^0)^{-1}$

or, using Model 3,

(4.31)   asymptotic cov $[\sqrt{T}(\mathbf{p}^0 - \boldsymbol{\pi}^0)', \sqrt{T}(\mathbf{p}^0 - \boldsymbol{\pi}^0)] = \omega^2 \text{ plim } T(\mathbf{M}_{zz}^0)^{-1}$

The *estimated approximate* covariance matrix of $\mathbf{p}^0$ is of course $w^2(\mathbf{M}_{zz}^0)^{-1}$, obtained from (4.31) as in 4.7. Expressions for the covariance of the vector $\mathbf{p}^0$ (which includes the constant term) can also be obtained from the matrix $\mathbf{M}_{zz}$ of moments about the mean, by replacing $(\mathbf{M}_{zz}^0)^{-1}$ in (4.30)–(4.31) by its equivalent in terms of $\mathbf{M}_{zz}$. For example, in Model 2, the result is

(4.32) $\text{cov}(\mathbf{p}^{0\prime}, \mathbf{p}^0) = \omega^2 \begin{pmatrix} \dfrac{1}{T} + \bar{\mathbf{z}}\mathbf{M}_{zz}^{-1}\bar{\mathbf{z}}' & -\bar{\mathbf{z}}\mathbf{M}_{zz}^{-1} \\ -\mathbf{M}_{zz}^{-1}\bar{\mathbf{z}}' & \mathbf{M}_{zz}^{-1} \end{pmatrix}$

The reader may wish to verify that the latter matrix when multiplied by $\mathbf{M}_{zz}^0$ does indeed yield the identity matrix of order K.

   4.11   This section has used a clear but cumbersome notational device to distinguish between the two approaches where (1) the constant term is mentioned explicitly and separately as in (4.1), and where (2) it is hidden by means of a dummy exogenous variable always equal to 1 as in (4.4). The device has been to use $\mathbf{M}$ and $\mathbf{m}$ for moments about the sample mean, and $\mathbf{M}^0$ and $\mathbf{m}^0$ for moments about zero; to use $\mathbf{z}$ and $\mathbf{z}^0$ for the vectors of exogenous variables excluding and including the dummy respectively; and to use $\mathbf{p}$ and $\mathbf{p}^0$ (or $\boldsymbol{\pi}$ and $\boldsymbol{\pi}^0$) for the vectors of parameters excluding and including the constant term respectively. Explicitness would be aided by continuing to use this device. Readability would not. I have decided in favor of readability. Accordingly *the notation* $\mathbf{M}^0$, $\mathbf{m}^0$, $\mathbf{z}^0$, $\mathbf{p}^0$, *and* $\boldsymbol{\pi}^0$ *will no longer be used, and the context will be relied upon to tell whether the constant term is included explicitly or implicitly.* Notice that except for the presence or absence of the superscript zeros, the following pairs of equations in this section are identical in form, one member of each pair referring to the explicit and one to the implicit treatment of the constant term:

equations' subject matter	*treatment of constant term*	
	explicitly	*implicitly*
variables and parameters	(4.9)	(4.25)
moments	(4.10)	(4.26)
normal equations	(4.12)	(4.27)
least-squares coefficients	(4.13), (4.15)	(4.28)
minimized sum of squares	(4.16)	(4.29)
covariance matrix, Model 2	(4.19), (4.20)	(4.30)
asymptotic covariance matrix, Model 3	(4.21)	(4.31)

This means that the whole mathematical exposition for implicit treatment of the constant term, in equations (4.25)–(4.31), is already contained in equations (4.9)–(4.21) for the explicit treatment, *provided* we reinterpret the vectors of variables and parameters ($\mathbf{z}$, $\mathbf{p}$, and $\boldsymbol{\pi}$) to include a dummy constant exogenous variable and the constant term, and reinterpret $\mathbf{m}$ and $\mathbf{M}$ to be moments about zero rather than about the mean. *In the rest of the book, such equations as these can be interpreted in either of these two ways*, as convenience dictates. This paragraph is very important and should be kept in mind from now on.

4.12   We conclude this section with a few remarks about difficulties that can arise if covariances among estimated parameters in an equation are too high. Consider for example the estimated equation

$$(4.33) \qquad \hat{y}_t = p_0 + p_1 z_{1t} + p_2 z_{2t} + p_3 z_{3t}$$

The covariance of two estimators here, p_1 and p_2, for example, indicates the degree to which they are likely to err in the same or in different directions because of sampling fluctuations (i.e., variations of the disturbance v_t during the observation period). If cov (p_1, p_2) is positive, this means that in samples that yield an overestimate of π_1 the estimate of π_2 is likely to be *too large also*, and in samples that yield an underestimate of π_1 the estimate of π_2 is likely to be *low*. If cov (p_1, p_2) is negative, overestimates of π_1 will usually be accompanied by *under*estimates of π_2, and vice versa. If cov (p_1, p_2) is near zero, relative to $\sqrt{\text{var } p_1 \text{ var } p_2}$, then there is no appreciable relationship between p_1 and p_2; they are approximately uncorrelated.

4.13   A principal cause of high positive or negative covariance between two estimators such as p_1 and p_2 is high correlation between the corresponding independent variables z_1 and z_2. The reason can be seen from an extreme example. Suppose for simplicity that Model 1 applies. (If Model 3 applied instead, the following would hold except for insertion of the words "asymptotic" or "approximate" regarding covariances.) Suppose that the true equation is

$$(4.34) \qquad y_t = 20 + 0.5 z_{1t} + 0.3 z_{2t} - 12 z_{3t} + v_t$$

and suppose that z_1 and z_2 are two variables that *always* happen to be *equal* during the sample period (this is the extreme feature of the example). This being so, we could never discover the coefficient of either z_1 or z_2, for both variables would always change together, and all we could tell is that when z_1 (and hence z_2 too) changes by one unit, y usually changes by about 0.8 unit in the same direction. We could not rule out the possibility that π_1 is 0 and π_2 is 0.8, or that their values are respectively 0.8 and 0, or 0.4 and 0.4, or even 100 and -99.2, or -100 and 100.8. This is an example of extreme negative covariance—if p_1 is high, then p_2 must be low, and vice versa. In this particular situation of course neither π_1

nor π_2 is identified because assumption (c) is violated; only their sum is identified. But in the less extreme case in which z_1 and z_2 are different variables that are still highly correlated—such as, for example, income and lagged income in a consumption function—it is likely that the estimators p_1 and p_2 will have a high covariance. This is known as the problem of *multicollinearity* among the variables.

4.14 If any equation contains only two independent variables [e.g., if $\pi_3 = 0$ in (4.34) so that only z_1 and z_2 appear], then the sign of the covariance of p_1 and p_2 depends exclusively on the sign of the covariance between z_1 and z_2: When $m_{z_1 z_2} > 0$, then cov $(p_1, p_2) < 0$ and vice versa. This can be seen by applying (4.19), for it shows that in such a case cov (p_1, p_2) is equal to $-\omega^2 m_{z_1 z_2}/\det \mathbf{M}_{zz}$, and recalling that the determinant of a moment matrix satisfying assumption (c) is positive. However, if there are three or more independent variables this simple rule no longer applies, for as (4.19) shows, each off-diagonal element of cov $(\mathbf{p'}, \mathbf{p})$ depends on a set of moments involving *all* the independent variables.

4.15 A related problem may arise when a variable is erroneously omitted from an equation. Suppose Model 1 is assumed and the true equation is

$$(4.35) \qquad y_t = \pi_0 + \pi_1 z_{1t} + \pi_2 z_{2t} + \pi_3 z_{3t} + v_t$$

But suppose that erroneously the variable z_3 is left out and the following equation is estimated instead:

$$(4.36) \qquad y_t = \pi_0 + \pi_1 z_{1t} + \pi_2 z_{2t} + v_t'$$

The true disturbance in the equation actually estimated is not v_t, but is $\pi_3 z_{3t} + v_t$, which has been denoted by v_t' in (4.36). If v_t' is independent of z_{1s} and z_{2s} for all s and t in the sample period, then assumption (i) is satisfied by (4.36), and the least-squares method applied to (4.36) will yield unbiased estimators of π_1 and π_2. But if z_3 is correlated with z_1 and z_2 in the sample period, then v' will be also (for $v' = \pi_3 z_3 + v$), and so assumption (i) is *not* satisfied by (4.36), and the estimators of π_1 and π_2 in (4.36) acquire a bias.

4.16 To take a more concrete example, suppose that the consumption expenditure c of a family depends slightly on current income y, and very heavily on the average level of income expected over the remainder of the breadwinner's working years, y_e, with a disturbance u, thus:

$$(4.37) \qquad c = \beta_2 y + \beta_3 y_e + \gamma + u$$

Suppose[25] that the true value of β_2 is about 0.05, and the true value of β_3 is about 0.7. Suppose further that y_e and y are strongly (but not perfectly) positively correlated. Then if equation (4.36) is fitted by least squares

[25] This hypothesis and the quantitative suppositions are presented in Modigliani and Brumberg [1954].

omitting the variable y_e, the estimate of β_2 will be much larger than 0.05, because the large rise in consumption due to a rise in y_e is attributed by the fitting process to the variable y because y rises more or less in unison with y_e. In this situation y is made to be a kind of proxy for the correlated but ignored variable y_e.

4.17 Notice that the same difficulty does not arise in reverse if a variable that does *not* belong in an equation is erroneously *included*; even if it is correlated with the other independent variables, bias in the estimates of the other variables will not result.

4.18 These difficulties occur all the time in econometrics. High covariances among estimated parameters in an equation can be reduced by taking large samples,[26] for these covariances are inversely proportional to the sample size. Sometimes we are lucky enough to find a model whose independent variables are not very much correlated with each other so that the problem of high covariances does not arise.

4.19 Large samples will not affect the bias due to incorrect exclusion of variables that are correlated with the actual independent variables. The only recourse is to choose the correct model to begin with. Unfortunately it is almost never possible to be sure we have done so. In view of this uncertainty, and in view of the difficulties posed by highly correlated independent variables, there is a strong temptation to use equations whose independent variables are not very highly correlated, even when this means excluding from an equation a theoretically plausible variable just because that variable is highly correlated with the other included independent variables. Presumably there is some critical subjective rate of exchange, so to speak, between the two "goods," low correlation among explanatory variables, and inclusion of an explanatory variable if we have some confidence in its relevance, such that if our confidence is greater than the critical rate of exchange specifies, we should include the variable; and if our confidence is less than that, we should exclude it. This "rate of exchange" of course will depend on the purpose at hand, and perhaps even on the tastes of the decision maker.

4.20 Suppose the aim is not to estimate parameters such as the π's in the regression equations we have been discussing, but is instead to forecast the values of the dependent variable. If the joint distribution of the independent variables stays the same in the forecasting period as it was in the sampling period, high covariances among the estimated coefficients are no disadvantage. We may get good forecasts even without being able to discover the *separate* influences of the independent variables, provided they continue to vary together as in the sample period. But if the sample-period relationship among the independent variables is much altered

---

[26] Unless there is a *perfect* correlation among the independent variables, in which case even an infinite sample would not reduce all the covariances; see 4.13, for example.

during the forecasting period, then accurate forecasting demands accurate knowledge of the separate effects of the explanatory variables. This matter anticipates Chapter X somewhat.

4.21　The comments in 4.12–20 apply (with suitable minor adjustments) to estimation of equations having two or more jointly dependent variables, as well as to equations having just one dependent variable. Estimation in such cases is discussed later, but the discussion of 4.12–20 will not be repeated.

5　THE MULTIPLE-REGRESSION ANALYSIS OF SECTION 4 IN ANOTHER MATRIX NOTATION; AITKEN'S GENERALIZED LEAST SQUARES

5.1　This section repeats the assertions of the previous section regarding equations having just one dependent variable, in terms of an elegant notation used by Aitken [1934] and many others since,[27] and gives some proofs. Here a vector is used to denote all the observed sample values of any single variable and a matrix is used to denote the sample values of the predetermined variables. We include a dummy predetermined variable (always equal to 1) among the $z_1 \cdots z_K$ if the equation has a constant term, to bring it into the same notation as is used for variable terms, as in (4.4). The notation is

$$\boldsymbol{\pi} = (\pi_1 \quad \cdots \quad \pi_K)$$
$$\mathbf{p} = (p_1 \quad \cdots \quad p_K)$$
$$\mathbf{y} = (y_1 \quad \cdots \quad y_T)$$
$$\mathbf{v} = (v_1 \quad \cdots \quad v_T)$$
(5.1)　$$\hat{\mathbf{v}} = (\hat{v}_1 \quad \cdots \quad \hat{v}_T)$$

$$\mathbf{Z} = \begin{pmatrix} z_{11} & z_{12} & \cdots & z_{1T} \\ z_{21} & z_{22} & \cdots & z_{2T} \\ \cdot & \cdot & & \cdot \\ \cdot & \cdot & & \cdot \\ \cdot & \cdot & & \cdot \\ z_{K1} & z_{K2} & \cdots & z_{KT} \end{pmatrix}$$

The notational convention of 4.11 *remains in use.* Notice that in defining $\mathbf{Z}$ we have maintained the usual practice of letting the first subscript of an element denote the row and the second denote the column. Also we represent row vectors by unprimed symbols and column vectors by primed symbols. Aitken [1934] and most writers following him have reversed

[27] E.g., Wold [1953], Theil [1958] and [1961], Stone [1954], and Durbin [1960].

this practice and have used primed symbols for *row* vectors, but for the sake of consistency with our notational conventions we have not done so.[28]

5.2 Consider the equation

$$(5.2) \qquad \mathbf{y}' = \mathbf{Z}'\boldsymbol{\pi}' + \mathbf{v}'$$

This expresses equation (4.4) T different times, once for each of the T sample points. It may be helpful to write (5.2) in more detail, thus:

$$(5.3) \qquad \begin{pmatrix} y_1 \\ \cdot \\ \cdot \\ \cdot \\ y_T \end{pmatrix} = \begin{pmatrix} z_{11} & \cdots & z_{K1} \\ \cdot & & \cdot \\ \cdot & & \cdot \\ \cdot & & \cdot \\ z_{1T} & \cdots & z_{KT} \end{pmatrix} \begin{pmatrix} \pi_1 \\ \cdot \\ \cdot \\ \cdot \\ \pi_K \end{pmatrix} + \begin{pmatrix} v_1 \\ \cdot \\ \cdot \\ \cdot \\ v_T \end{pmatrix}$$

The set of residuals $\hat{\mathbf{v}}$ corresponding to the estimator $\mathbf{p}$ is

$$(5.4) \qquad \hat{\mathbf{v}}' = \mathbf{y}' - \hat{\mathbf{y}}' = \mathbf{y}' - \mathbf{Z}'\mathbf{p}'$$

The sum of squared residuals to be minimized is ·as follows (note the similarity to (4.5) and (4.23) above):[29]

$$(5.5) \qquad S = \sum_t \hat{v}_t^{\,2} = \hat{\mathbf{v}}\hat{\mathbf{v}}' = (\mathbf{y} - \mathbf{pZ})(\mathbf{y}' - \mathbf{Z}'\mathbf{p}')$$

$$= \mathbf{yy}' - \mathbf{yZ}'\mathbf{p}' - \mathbf{pZy}' + \mathbf{pZZ}'\mathbf{p}'$$

Differentiating this last scalar with respect to the vector[30] $\mathbf{p}$ and setting the result equal to the zero vector we obtain the following system of

---

[28] Both Basmann [1957] and Theil [1958], [1961] use notation that violates accepted convention in minor ways. Basmann writes z_{tk} instead of z_{kt} for the value of the kth predetermined variable in period t. Theil lets the first subscript of a matrix element denote the column, and the second denote the row. I have adopted the usual conventions instead on these two points.

[29] Note that $\mathbf{ZZ}'$ is symmetric, since it is a moment matrix. Hence later we shall often write $\mathbf{ZZ}'$ instead of $(\mathbf{ZZ}')'$.

[30] The partial differentiation of S with respect to $\mathbf{p}$ proceeds as follows. The first term, $\mathbf{yy}'$, does not depend on $\mathbf{p}$ at all so it yields zero. The second and third terms are equal, and their sum is $-2\mathbf{pZy}'$; this is a multiple of $\mathbf{p}$ and hence by an extension of the ordinary rules of differentiation it yields $-2\mathbf{Zy}'$. The only difficulty here is in deciding whether the derivative of a scalar with respect to the row vector $\mathbf{p}$ is a row or a column, for we must consider $\partial S/\partial \mathbf{p}$ as either $(\partial S/\partial p_1, \ldots, \partial S/\partial p_K)$ or its transpose; it is convenient to let it be a column vector because the third term comes out that way. The fourth term, $\mathbf{pZZ}'\mathbf{p}'$, presents a little more difficulty. But if we remember that any change in $\mathbf{p}$ is accompanied by a similar change in $\mathbf{p}'$, we can use the product rule to get $\partial \mathbf{pZZ}'\mathbf{p}'/\partial \mathbf{p}$ as $\mathbf{ZZ}'\mathbf{p}' + (\mathbf{pZZ}')'$, the latter term being transposed because otherwise it would be a row; if it is remembered that $\mathbf{ZZ}'$ is symmetric, these two terms can be added to give $2\mathbf{ZZ}'\mathbf{p}'$. It is instructive to try out an example with $K = 2$ to verify this result. For a summary of general rules regarding differentiation of matrices, see Koopmans, Rubin, and Leipnik [1950], p. 115; Dwyer and Macphail [1948]; and Anderson [1958], pp. 346–349.

normal equations (one for each of the derivatives $\partial S/\partial p_k$, $k = 1, \ldots, K$; compare (4.12) and (4.27), which say the same thing):

$$(5.6) \qquad \mathbf{Zy'} = \mathbf{ZZ'p'}$$

The matrix $\mathbf{ZZ'}$ is precisely the same as the matrix of moments denoted by $\mathbf{M}_{zz}$, and the vector $\mathbf{Zy'}$ is the same as $\mathbf{m}'_{yz}$; compare (4.10) and (4.26). Solving (5.6) for the least-squares estimator we have this result [compare (4.13) and (4.28)]:

$$(5.7) \qquad \mathbf{p'} = \mathbf{(ZZ')^{-1}Zy'}$$

Substituting (5.6) or its transpose into the last member of (5.5) shows that the minimized sum of squares is equal to any of the following [compare (4.16) and (4.29)]:

$$(5.8) \qquad \sum \hat{v}_t^2 = \mathbf{vv'} = \mathbf{yy'} - \mathbf{pZZ'p'}$$
$$= \mathbf{yy'} - \mathbf{yZ'p'} = \mathbf{yy'} - \mathbf{yZ'(ZZ')^{-1}Zy'}$$

Hence ω^2 can be estimated by dividing (5.8) by T or by $T - K$ to get $\hat{\omega}^2$ or w^2 respectively, as before. For example,

$$(5.9) \qquad w^2 = \frac{\hat{v}\hat{v}'}{T - K} = \frac{\mathbf{yy'} - \mathbf{yZ'p'}}{T - K}$$

5.3 Under the assumptions of Model 1 it is easy to show that $\mathbf{p}$ is an unbiased estimator of $\boldsymbol{\pi}$, as follows. Substitute (5.2) for $\mathbf{y'}$ in (5.7) to obtain

$$(5.10) \qquad \mathbf{p'} = \mathbf{(ZZ')^{-1}ZZ'\pi'} + \mathbf{(ZZ')^{-1}Zv'}$$
$$= \boldsymbol{\pi'} + \mathbf{(ZZ')^{-1}Zv'}$$

Now by assumption (i) $\mathbf{v}$ and $\mathbf{Z}$ are independent, so the expectation of the last term in (5.10) is the product of $E\mathbf{(ZZ')^{-1}Z}$ and $E\mathbf{v'}$, and accordingly is the zero vector, so that $E\mathbf{p'} = \boldsymbol{\pi'}$, as was to be shown. This notation makes it quite clear that (as remarked at the end of 3.15 for the simple case) $\mathbf{p'}$ is still unbiased if $\mathbf{v}$ and $\mathbf{Z}$ are dependent, *provided* that $E(\mathbf{v} \mid \mathbf{Z}) = \mathbf{0}$ (recall the rule for the expected value of a product in IV.2.24).

5.4 Under the assumptions of Model 2 it is not hard to show that $E\hat{v}\hat{v}' = \omega^2(T - K)$, so that $Ew^2 = \omega^2$. Proceed as follows, but first derive an alternative equivalent form for $\hat{v}\hat{v}'$ (the steps are explained briefly below):

$$(5.11) \qquad \hat{v}\hat{v}' = \mathbf{(y - pZ)(y' - Z'p')}$$
$$= \mathbf{y[I_T - Z'(ZZ')^{-1}Z][I_T - Z'(ZZ')^{-1}Z]y'}$$
$$\equiv \mathbf{yAAy'}$$
$$= \mathbf{yAy'}$$
$$= \mathbf{(\pi Z + v)A(Z'\pi' + v')}$$
$$= \mathbf{vAv'}$$

The first step above comes from (5.4). The second step comes from (5.7) (I_T is an identity matrix of order T). The third step defines A as the matrix in square brackets. The fourth step takes advantage of the fact that $A^2 = A$ as the reader may verify (A is therefore said to be *idempotent*). The fifth step comes from (5.2). The last step comes from applying the definition of A, multiplying out, and canceling like terms. Now denote the typical element of A by a_{st} ($s, t = 1, \ldots, T$). Then the conditional expectation of $\hat{v}\hat{v}'$ given Z is (using Model 2)

$$(5.12) \qquad E\hat{v}\hat{v}' = EvAv' = E \sum_{s=1}^{T} \sum_{t=1}^{T} a_{st} v_s v_t$$

$$= \sum_s \sum_t a_{st} E v_s v_t = \omega^2 \sum_t a_{tt}$$

(The last step uses assumption (j) that $E v_s v_t = \omega^2$ if $s = t$, and $= 0$ if $s \neq t$.) The sum $\sum_t a_{tt}$ of the diagonal elements of A is called the *trace* of A and denoted by tr A (see A.5.2). (The trace is not defined for a matrix that is not square.) By the definition of A, tr A is equal to tr $I_T -$ tr $Z'(ZZ')^{-1}Z$. It is easy to show that if B and C are matrices of order $M \times N$ and $N \times M$, then BC exists and is square of order M, and CB exists and is square of order N, and tr $BC =$ tr CB. Letting $Z'(ZZ')^{-1}$ take the place of B, and Z take the place of C, we can continue with (5.12) as follows:

$$(5.13) \qquad E\hat{v}\hat{v}' = \omega^2 \text{ tr } A = \omega^2 \text{ tr } [I_T - Z'(ZZ')^{-1}Z]$$

$$= \omega^2[T - \text{ tr } ZZ'(ZZ')^{-1}]$$

$$= \omega^2(T - \text{ tr } I_K)$$

$$= \omega^2(T - K)$$

as was to be proved. Hence from (5.9) we see that $Ew^2 = \omega^2$ in Model 2.

5.5   Under the assumptions of Model 2 it is easy to derive the conditional covariance matrix of the estimator p given Z:

$$(5.14) \qquad \text{cov } (p', p) = E(p - \pi)'(p - \pi)$$

$$= E(ZZ')^{-1}Zv'vZ'(ZZ')^{-1}$$

$$= (ZZ')^{-1}Z(Ev'v)Z'(ZZ')^{-1}$$

$$= (ZZ')^{-1}Z\omega^2 I_T Z'(ZZ')^{-1}$$

$$= \omega^2(ZZ')^{-1}$$

The first step applies the definition of the covariance. The second uses (5.10). The third uses assumption (i) that v and Z are independent. The fourth uses assumption (j) that $Ev'v = \omega^2 I_T$. The fifth factors out the constant ω^2 and performs the multiplication. Compare the result with (4.19) or (4.30).

5.6 The other properties stated in 4.7 clearly apply here, since Sections 4 and 5 deal with the same situation, merely using different notation. Proofs of consistency and best linear unbiasedness and the derivation in Model 3 of the asymptotic covariance matrix are not given here for the case of two or more predetermined variables. The former two are given for the case of one predetermined variable in 3.20–23, and all are found in more advanced works for the more general case.[31] A consistency proof for a more general case is given below in 10.10–13.

5.7 Aitken [1934] proposed a generalized least-squares estimator, suitable for estimating the parameter π in the linear equation (5.2) when the disturbances are not independent. Aitken's conditions are similar to our Model 1, where the explanatory variables are exogenous (see 2.3–5 above), but Aitken assumed in addition that the variance-covariance matrix Λ of the disturbance $\mathbf{v}$ is known except for an unknown multiplicative constant ω^2. That is, we have

$$(5.15) \qquad E\mathbf{v}'\mathbf{v} = \Lambda$$

where Λ/ω^2 is known, but Λ and ω^2 are unknown. In that case, as Aitken has shown, because Λ is positive definite, a nonsingular matrix can be found (denoted *in this context only* by Φ) such that

$$(5.16) \qquad \Lambda^{-1} = \Phi\Phi'$$

If the variables in (5.2) are now transformed by multiplication on the left by Φ', we have the equation

$$(5.17) \qquad \Phi'\mathbf{y}' = \Phi'\mathbf{Z}'\pi' + \Phi'\mathbf{v}'$$

Now the variance-covariance matrix of this equation's disturbance $\Phi'\mathbf{v}'$ is

$$(5.18) \qquad E\Phi'\mathbf{v}'\mathbf{v}\Phi = \Phi'\Lambda\Phi = \Phi'\Phi^{-1'}\Phi^{-1}\Phi = \mathbf{I}$$

This means that equation (5.17) has uncorrelated disturbances and suggests that least squares is a suitable method for estimating it. Aitken applied least squares, as in equations (5.6) and (5.7) above, and got the following estimator for π' (denoted by $\mathbf{p}_1'$):

$$(5.19) \qquad \mathbf{p}_1' = (\mathbf{Z}\Lambda^{-1}\mathbf{Z}')^{-1}\mathbf{Z}\Lambda^{-1}\mathbf{y}'$$

It is known as Aitken's generalized least-squares estimator. Aitken showed that under the conditions of this paragraph it is best linear unbiased, and its covariance matrix is

$$(5.20) \qquad E(\mathbf{p}_1 - \pi)'(\mathbf{p}_1 - \pi) = (\mathbf{Z}\Lambda^{-1}\mathbf{Z}')^{-1}$$

[31] See 3.26, 3.34, and 9.23–4 for references, and further remarks thereon, and Tables 12.1–2 for a summary.

If $\Lambda = \omega^2 I$, as assumed in Model 2, the two preceding equations reduce to the ordinary least-squares case; compare (5.7) and (5.14).

5.8 Aitken's generalized least-squares method has two kinds of application of interest to us. One is to the case of serially correlated disturbances; this is discussed in Section 13. The other is to the case of simultaneous-equations estimation, where it turns out to be a very useful general framework into which the two-stage and three-stage least-squares methods fit as special cases; see Section 10, especially 10.25–28.

6   THE MAXIMUM-LIKELIHOOD METHOD APPLIED TO JOINT CONDITIONAL DISTRIBUTIONS; THE FULL-INFORMATION METHOD

6.1 The last three sections have dealt at some length with the least-squares method, and it has been shown that under the assumptions of Models 2 (normal) and 3 (normal), described in 2.2–4 above, least-squares estimators are maximum-likelihood estimators (and therefore have certain desirable properties) *when we are interested in the parameters of a conditional distribution of just one variable given the values of a set of other (predetermined) variables.* We shall now discuss the application of the maximum-likelihood method to *joint* conditional distributions of *two or more* jointly dependent variables given the values of a set of other (predetermined) variables. The method is essentially as follows: Write down the structural equations; solve them simultaneously for the reduced form, which shows the joint conditional distribution of each of the jointly dependent variables y_{it} given the values of the predetermined variables z_{kt}; write the reduced-form equations so that each one has its v_{it} on its left side and has its y_{it} minus a linear function of the z's with unknown parameters on its right; write down the joint normal distribution of all the v_{it}; substitute for each v_{it} in this joint distribution its value from the reduced form, to get a joint conditional distribution function of y's given z's and reduced-form parameters; express each reduced-form parameter in terms of structural parameters to get a joint conditional distribution function of y's given z's and *structural* parameters; regard the latter function as a likelihood function of structural parameters given the observed values of the y's and z's; and maximize this likelihood function jointly with respect to the several structural parameters, subject to the *a priori* restrictions.

6.2 We shall discuss this maximum-likelihood procedure briefly, omitting much of the technical detail. Following Koopmans, Rubin, and Leipnik [1950], especially pp. 70–72, 112–113, and 133–148, we shall conduct the discussion under the assumptions of our Model 3 (normal), that is, assumptions (a)–(h) and (j) and (k) of Section 2. Recall from 2.5 that these assumptions imply the existence of a reduced form whose equations obey similar assumptions. The structure is expressed conveniently in matrix terms, following equations (2.2)–(2.4), as follows:

$$(6.1) \qquad \mathbf{B}\mathbf{y}_t' + \boldsymbol{\Gamma}\mathbf{z}_t' = \mathbf{u}_t'$$

Among the components of $\mathbf{z}$ is a dummy element, always equal to 1, if there are any constant terms in the model. The reduced form is expressed in matrix terms, following (2.14):

$$(6.2) \qquad \mathbf{y}_t' = -\mathbf{B}^{-1}\boldsymbol{\Gamma}\mathbf{z}_t' + \mathbf{B}^{-1}\mathbf{u}_t' = \boldsymbol{\Pi}\mathbf{z}_t' + \mathbf{v}_t'$$

The variance-covariance matrix of the structural disturbances will be denoted by $\boldsymbol{\Sigma}$, thus:

$$(6.3) \qquad \boldsymbol{\Sigma} = \begin{pmatrix} \sigma_{11} & \cdots & \sigma_{1G} \\ \cdot & & \cdot \\ \cdot & & \cdot \\ \cdot & & \cdot \\ \sigma_{G1} & \cdots & \sigma_{GG} \end{pmatrix} = E\mathbf{u}_t'\mathbf{u}_t$$

The variance-covariance matrix of reduced-form disturbances will be denoted by $\boldsymbol{\Omega}$, thus:

$$(6.4) \qquad \boldsymbol{\Omega} = \begin{pmatrix} \omega_{11} & \cdots & \omega_{1G} \\ \cdot & & \cdot \\ \cdot & & \cdot \\ \cdot & & \cdot \\ \omega_{G1} & \cdots & \omega_{GG} \end{pmatrix} = E\mathbf{v}_t'\mathbf{v}_t$$

$$= E\mathbf{B}^{-1}\mathbf{u}_t'\mathbf{u}_t\mathbf{B}^{-1'} = \mathbf{B}^{-1}E\mathbf{u}_t'\mathbf{u}_t\mathbf{B}^{-1'} = \mathbf{B}^{-1}\,\boldsymbol{\Sigma}\,\mathbf{B}^{-1'}$$

The fourth expression here results from substituting $\mathbf{B}^{-1}\mathbf{u}_t'$ for $\mathbf{v}_t'$; the fifth from the constancy of $\mathbf{B}$; the sixth from applying the definition of $\boldsymbol{\Sigma}$. $\boldsymbol{\Omega}$ is nonsingular because assumptions (b) and (f) make $\mathbf{B}$ and $\boldsymbol{\Sigma}$ nonsingular if all identities have been removed from the model (see 6.9 below).

    6.3   Let us illustrate with a relatively simple two-equation supply-and-demand model. Here y_1 will denote quantity of a good sold, and y_2 will denote its price; z_1 will denote the wage level in its production, z_2 income, and z_3 the constant variable 1. The y's are endogenous and the z's exogenous.

$$(6.5) \qquad \text{(supply)} \qquad y_1 + \beta_{12}y_2 + \gamma_{11}z_1 \qquad\qquad + \gamma_{13}z_3 = u_1$$

$$(6.6) \qquad \text{(demand)} \qquad y_1 + \beta_{22}y_2 \qquad\qquad + \gamma_{22}z_2 + \gamma_{23}z_3 = u_2$$

The reduced-form equations are

(6.7)

$$y_1 = \frac{-\beta_{22}\gamma_{11}}{\beta_{22} - \beta_{12}} z_1 + \frac{\beta_{12}\gamma_{22}}{\beta_{22} - \beta_{12}} z_2 + \frac{\beta_{12}\gamma_{23} - \beta_{22}\gamma_{13}}{\beta_{22} - \beta_{12}} z_3 + \frac{\beta_{22}u_1 - \beta_{12}u_2}{\beta_{22} - \beta_{12}}$$

(6.8) $$y_2 = \frac{\gamma_{11}}{\beta_{22} - \beta_{12}} z_1 + \frac{-\gamma_{22}}{\beta_{22} - \beta_{12}} z_2 + \frac{\gamma_{13} - \gamma_{23}}{\beta_{22} - \beta_{12}} z_3 + \frac{u_2 - u_1}{\beta_{22} - \beta_{12}}$$

This reduced form may be rewritten by renaming the reduced-form parameters in it, thus:

(6.9) $$y_i = \sum_{k=1}^{3} \pi_{ik}z_k + v_i \qquad i = 1, 2$$

where the parameters π_{ik} are

(6.10)
$$\begin{cases} \pi_{11} = \dfrac{-\beta_{22}\gamma_{11}}{\beta_{22} - \beta_{12}}, & \pi_{12} = \dfrac{\beta_{12}\gamma_{22}}{\beta_{22} - \beta_{12}}, & \pi_{13} = \dfrac{\beta_{12}\gamma_{23} - \beta_{22}\gamma_{13}}{\beta_{22} - \beta_{12}} \\[3mm] \pi_{21} = \dfrac{\gamma_{11}}{\beta_{22} - \beta_{12}}, & \pi_{22} = \dfrac{-\gamma_{22}}{\beta_{22} - \beta_{12}}, & \pi_{23} = \dfrac{\gamma_{13} - \gamma_{23}}{\beta_{22} - \beta_{12}} \end{cases}$$

and the reduced-form disturbances are

(6.11) $$v_1 = \frac{\beta_{22}u_1 - \beta_{12}u_2}{\beta_{22} - \beta_{12}}, \qquad v_2 = \frac{u_2 - u_1}{\beta_{22} - \beta_{12}}$$

These equations are very similar to equations (2.16) to (2.20) in Chapter VIII. The next step is to rewrite the reduced-form equations (6.9) so that v_i appears on the left and $y_i - \sum \pi_{ik}z_k$ appears on the right; the reader may do this for himself.

6.4   The next step is to set forth the joint normal distribution of v_1 and v_2. The parameters of this distribution are the means of v_1 and v_2, which are zero by assumption (e); the variances of v_1 and v_2, which we have called ω_{11} and ω_{22}, respectively; and the covariance of v_1 and v_2, called ω_{12} or ω_{21}. The joint normal distribution function of v_{1t} and v_{2t}, following the general discussion of IV.3.11, is

(6.12)

$$\psi(v_{1t}, v_{2t}) = \frac{1}{2\pi(\omega_{11}\omega_{22} - \omega_{12}^2)^{1/2}} \exp\left[-\frac{\omega_{22}v_{1t}^2 - 2\omega_{12}v_{1t}v_{2t} + \omega_{11}v_{2t}^2}{2(\omega_{11}\omega_{22} - \omega_{12}^2)} \right]$$

This distribution is for a single observation. The distribution corresponding to a series of observations over periods 1 to T is the product of T distributions such as (6.12), because the v's for any period are independent of those in other periods [assumption (j)]:

(6.13) $\Psi(v_{11}, \ldots, v_{1T}; v_{21}, \ldots, v_{2T})$

$$= \frac{1}{(2\pi)^T(\omega_{11}\omega_{22} - \omega_{12}^2)^{T/2}} \exp\left[-\frac{1}{2} \sum_{t=1}^{T} \frac{\omega_{22}v_{1t}^2 - 2\omega_{12}v_{1t}v_{2t} + \omega_{11}v_{2t}^2}{(\omega_{11}\omega_{22} - \omega_{12}^2)} \right]$$

In matrix terms, the joint normal distribution of v_{it} and v_{2t} in (6.12) is

$$(6.14) \qquad \psi(v_{1t}, v_{2t}) = \frac{1}{2\pi(\det \mathbf{\Omega})^{1/2}} \exp\left[-\tfrac{1}{2}\mathbf{v}_t \mathbf{\Omega}^{-1}\mathbf{v}_t'\right]$$

where $\det \mathbf{\Omega}$ is the determinant of $\mathbf{\Omega}$. The distribution in (6.13) corresponding to observations over periods 1 to T is

$$(6.15) \quad \Psi(\mathbf{v}_1, \ldots, \mathbf{v}_T) = \frac{1}{(2\pi)^T(\det \mathbf{\Omega})^{T/2}} \exp\left[-\frac{1}{2}\sum_{t=1}^{T} \mathbf{v}_t\mathbf{\Omega}^{-1}\mathbf{v}_t'\right]$$

6.5 In the next step, the parameters in the reduced-form equations are introduced explicitly by substituting for v_1 and v_2 from (6.9) into (6.13) to get the joint conditional distribution of the y's, given the z's and the reduced-form parameters:[32]

$$(6.16) \quad \Phi(y_{11}, \ldots, y_{1T}; y_{21}, \ldots, y_{2T} \mid z_{11}, \ldots, z_{KT})$$

$$= \frac{\exp\left[-\displaystyle\sum_{t=1}^{T} \frac{\omega_{22}(y_{1t} - \sum \pi_{1k}z_{kt})^2 - 2\omega_{12}(y_{1t} - \sum \pi_{1k}z_{kt})(y_{2t} - \sum \pi_{2k}z_{kt}) + \omega_{11}(y_{2t} - \sum \pi_{2k}z_{kt})^2}{2(\omega_{11}\omega_{22} - \omega_{12}^2)}\right]}{(2\pi)^T(\omega_{11}\omega_{22} - \omega_{12}^2)^{T/2}}$$

[32] The transformation from (6.13), which is the distribution of the v's, to (6.16), which is the conditional distribution of the y's, looks very simple. Apparently all that is done is to replace each v_{it} by its equivalent, $y_{it} - \Sigma\pi_{ik}z_{kt}$ from (6.9). There is really more to it in principle, however, and it is only because this transformation is a special case that the complications seem to disappear. In general, the mathematical problem is this: A function of a set of variables such as the v's is to be transformed into a function of a different set of variables such as the y's, by the use of a set of equations like (6.9) that expresses the v's in terms of the y's, as is done in obtaining (6.16). In symbols, we are to transform $F(v_1, \ldots, v_N)$ into a function of $y_1, \ldots, y_N$ with the aid of N equations such as $v_i = f_i(y_1, \ldots, y_N)$. To do this correctly it is necessary not only to make the substitution of the f's for the v's; it is necessary also to multiply the whole resulting expression by the so-called Jacobian determinant of the f's, to obtain

$$\begin{vmatrix} \dfrac{\partial v_1}{\partial y_1} & \cdots & \dfrac{\partial v_1}{\partial y_N} \\ \cdot & \cdot & \cdot \\ \cdot & \cdot & \cdot \\ \cdot & \cdot & \cdot \\ \dfrac{\partial v_N}{\partial y_1} & \cdots & \dfrac{\partial v_N}{\partial y_N} \end{vmatrix} F[f_1(y_1, \ldots, y_N), \ldots, f_N(y_1, \ldots, y_N)]$$

In the problem in the text above, the relevant Jacobian is obtained from the reduced form (6.9). As the reader may readily verify, it has 1's on its main diagonal and zeros elsewhere and so is necessarily equal to 1. Hence it is not apparent explicitly in the transformed function (6.16). We could as well treat this problem in terms of the structural disturbances u_i instead of the reduced-form disturbances v_i (see Klein [1953], pp. 104–112), but since the Jacobian of the structural equations relating the u's to the

In matrix terms, this is, from (6.2) and (6.15),

$$(6.17) \quad \Phi(\mathbf{y}_1, \ldots, \mathbf{y}_T \mid \mathbf{z}_1, \ldots, \mathbf{z}_T)$$

$$= \frac{1}{(2\pi)^T (\det \boldsymbol{\Omega})^{T/2}} \exp\left[-\frac{1}{2} \sum_{t=1}^{T} (\mathbf{y}_t - \mathbf{z}_t \boldsymbol{\Pi}') \boldsymbol{\Omega}^{-1} (\mathbf{y}_t' - \boldsymbol{\Pi} \mathbf{z}_t') \right]$$

This is the joint conditional distribution of the y's given the z's and the reduced-form parameters. If we wish to estimate the *reduced-form* parameters, we treat (6.16) or (6.17) as a likelihood function and maximize it with respect to the reduced-form parameters ω_{ij} and π_{ik}, treating the observed values of the y's and the z's as given. In 6.11 there are a few more remarks about this.

    6.6   It is our purpose here to describe the estimation of the *structural* parameters, the β_{ij}, γ_{ik}, and σ_{ij} of equations (6.5) and (6.6). Therefore we pass on to the next step, which is to substitute for each reduced-form parameter in (6.16) its value in terms of structural parameters, from equations (6.4) and (6.10). This expression would be very cumbersome to write down using scalars; therefore only the matrix version will be presented. It is obtained by substituting for $\boldsymbol{\Pi}$ and $\boldsymbol{\Omega}$ from (6.2) and (6.4) into (6.17):

$$(6.18) \quad \Phi(\mathbf{y}_1, \ldots, \mathbf{y}_T \mid \mathbf{z}_1, \ldots, \mathbf{z}_T)$$

$$= \frac{\exp\left[-\frac{1}{2} \sum_{t=1}^{T} (\mathbf{y}_t + \mathbf{z}_t \boldsymbol{\Gamma}' \mathbf{B}^{-1'}) \mathbf{B}' \boldsymbol{\Sigma}^{-1} \mathbf{B} (\mathbf{y}_t' + \mathbf{B}^{-1} \boldsymbol{\Gamma} \mathbf{z}_t') \right]}{(2\pi)^T (\det \mathbf{B}^{-1} \boldsymbol{\Sigma} \mathbf{B}^{-1'})^{T/2}}$$

In evaluating $\boldsymbol{\Omega}^{-1}$ in this distribution function in terms of $\mathbf{B}$ and $\boldsymbol{\Sigma}$, the rules of matrix transposition and inversion have been used.

    6.7   Equation (6.18) is the likelihood function of the structural parameters that comprise the matrices $\mathbf{B}$, $\boldsymbol{\Gamma}$, and $\boldsymbol{\Sigma}$, given the observations $\mathbf{y}_1, \ldots, \mathbf{y}_T$ and $\mathbf{z}_1, \ldots, \mathbf{z}_T$. As in our earlier discussion of the maximum-likelihood method in 3.24, we maximize its logarithm to the base e because that is easier and leads to the same values of the parameters:

$$(6.19) \quad L \equiv \log_e \Phi = -T \log_e 2\pi - \frac{T}{2} \log_e \det \mathbf{B}^{-1} \boldsymbol{\Sigma} \mathbf{B}^{-1'}$$

$$- \frac{1}{2} \sum_{t=1}^{T} (\mathbf{y}_t + \mathbf{z}_t \boldsymbol{\Gamma}' \mathbf{B}^{-1'}) \mathbf{B}' \boldsymbol{\Sigma}^{-1} \mathbf{B} (\mathbf{y}_t' + \mathbf{B}^{-1} \boldsymbol{\Gamma} \mathbf{z}_t')$$

---

y's is not 1 but is the determinant of $\mathbf{B}$, such a treatment would give the appearance of being more technical, though it would give the same final result, (6.18) below. Jacobians are discussed in works on advanced calculus; see, for example, Burington and Torrance [1939], p. 133, and p. 262, equation (8); see also Courant [1936], pp. 133–157.

Estimators obtained by maximizing this logarithmic likelihood function L subject to all the *a priori* restrictions built into the model are called *full-information maximum-likelihood* estimators (to distinguish them from *limited-information* estimators, which do not use all the *a priori* restrictions —see Section 9 below).

6.8 In Model 3 (normal) the full-information estimators of identified elements of **B**, **Γ**, and **Σ** [which are obtained from maximizing (6.19)] are consistent, asymptotically normally distributed, and asymptotically efficient. The assumption that the u_{it} are normally distributed can be relaxed without destroying consistency and asymptotic normality. See Koopmans, Rubin, and Leipnik [1950], pp. 56–60, 70–72, 112–113, 133–148.[33]

6.9 If a model contains exact definitional equations (e.g., disposable income equals consumption plus net private investment plus government deficit), the covariance matrix **Σ** of disturbances will be singular so that Σ^{-1} will not exist, and so L cannot be formed as in (6.19). In that case several equivalent approaches are available. One is to eliminate definitional equations (and one endogenous variable for each) by substitution before estimation is begun. For example, consider the following familiar three-equation national income model, where c = consumption, i = net private investment, y = disposable income, and d = government deficit:

$$(6.20) \qquad c = \beta_1 y + \gamma_1 + u_1$$

$$(6.21) \qquad i = \beta_2 y + \gamma_2 + \gamma_3 y_{-1} + u_2$$

$$(6.22) \qquad y = c + i + d$$

In this model, the consumption equation is overidentified because two predetermined variables (y_{-1} and d) are excluded from it, and the investment equation is just identified because one predetermined variable (d) is excluded from it. The three current endogenous variables are c, i, and y. There are only two stochastic equations, and the model can thus be reduced to two stochastic equations in two current endogenous variables if (6.22) is used to eliminate one variable. Since the definitional equation (6.22) is exact, the estimators obtained will be the same no matter which variable is eliminated; let us eliminate i. The model then contains (6.20) in unchanged form plus the following equation:

$$(6.23) \qquad c = (1 - \beta_2)y - \gamma_2 - \gamma_3 y_{-1} - d - u_2$$

One of the identifying restrictions now takes the form of a homogeneous linear relationship among the parameters of (6.23), rather than a statement excluding certain variables from certain equations. As before, (6.20) is

[33] Mann and Wald [1943], a less difficult paper, proved consistency of such estimators for a more restricted case in which there are no exogenous variables (except for a constant term) and no unidentified parameters. See also 9.23–24 and Tables 12.1–2.

overidentified because it excludes y_{-1} and d. Equation (6.23) is just identified, even though it does not exclude any predetermined variables, because it does have to satisfy the restriction that the coefficient of d must be equal to -1 times that of c. The full-information method can deal with such restrictions as well as with the type specifying that certain parameters are zero.

6.10 The maximization of (6.19) involves such complex and burdensome computation procedures that until the advent of electronic computers the full-information method was used hardly at all except for experimental computations.[34] If the simplifying but dubious assumption is made that all structural disturbances in any period are uncorrelated with each other, so that the matrix Σ is diagonal (i.e., has zeros in all positions except along the main diagonal), the computations are simplified somewhat.[35] However, they are still too cumbersome for easy execution with desk calculators. Almost no further discussion of the full-information method will be given in this book (but see 10.36 ff. below). An exception is the special case where all structural equations are just identified; in this case there is a much simpler computation procedure that gives the same results. This will be taken up in 7.3. Some related methods are discussed briefly at the end of Section 10.

6.11 Section 6 has indicated how the maximum-likelihood method of estimation may be applied at once to all the parameters of a system of several linear difference equations, following the steps listed in 6.1 above. At one stage in this process, the likelihood function (6.16) of the reduced-form parameters (the π's and ω's) was derived. The maximum-likelihood estimators of the π's and ω's obtained by maximizing (6.16) *without regard to the a priori restrictions on the structural parameters* are the least-squares estimates of the reduced form, as would be expected on the basis of the argument in 3.24. The reader may verify this for himself by taking the logarithm of (6.16) to the base e and then differentiating it partially with respect to the π's and ω's and setting the resulting expressions equal to zero; the normal equations of the least-squares method can be obtained by setting the derivatives with respect to the π's equal to zero, after a certain amount of manipulation of the resulting equations. This verification provides another confirmation of the conclusion that least-squares estimators of the reduced form are maximum-likelihood estimators if Model 3 (normal) is used.

[34] A specimen computation for a time-series model with three stochastic equations, and an observation period of 21 years, is given by Chernoff and Divinsky [1953], pp. 255–261 and 278–288. The former six pages are filled by a terse mathematical description of the computation procedure, and the latter eleven pages are filled by the work sheets themselves, reproduced in fairly small print. The fact that so much space is required for such a small model gives an idea of the complexity of the method.

[35] Chernoff and Divinsky [1953], pp. 266–267 and 298–302.

7 MAXIMUM-LIKELIHOOD ESTIMATION OF STRUCTURAL PARAMETERS IN A SINGLE JUST-IDENTIFIED EQUATION: THE INDIRECT LEAST-SQUARES AND INSTRUMENTAL-VARIABLES METHODS

7.1 The import of this section has already been partially indicated in the guided tour and in the chapter on identification (Chapters II and VIII): If a structural equation is just identified, the number of known predetermined variables that influence it *without* appearing in it $(K - J)$ is one less than the total number (H) of jointly dependent variables that do appear in it, as seen from equation (3.25) in VIII.3.29:

$$(7.1) \qquad\qquad K - J = H - 1$$

Hence there is just the right number of equations to enable us to obtain estimators of the structural parameters from the least-squares estimators of the reduced-form parameters: neither too few (no identification) nor too many (overidentification), as discussed in VIII.3.31–35. We shall call this the *indirect least-squares method* of estimating structural parameters and shall restrict its use to the just identified case only.[36] In this section we shall first indicate why structural estimators, so obtained under Model 3 (normal) when *all* equations are just identified, are full-information maximum-likelihood estimators. Second, we shall show for a just-identified equation, even if other equations are overidentified, (a) that such estimators are consistent and (b) a simple commonsense way to get them, which will also throw some light on the discussion of overidentified equations in the next section.

7.2 To review the indirect least-squares method for a just-identified equation whether or not all other equations are just identified: Suppose that the equation to be estimated is

$$(7.2) \qquad y_1 + \beta_2 y_2 + \cdots + \beta_H y_H + \gamma_1 z_1 + \cdots + \gamma_J z_J = u$$

where $y_1, \ldots, y_H$ are jointly dependent and $z_1, \ldots, z_J$ are predetermined variables in the equation. Again a dummy variable, always equal to 1, is included among $z_1, \ldots, z_J$ if the equation has a constant term. The other predetermined variables, $H - 1$ in number, are $z_{J+1}, \ldots, z_K$; hence (7.1) expresses the fact that (7.2) is just identified. The relevant part of the reduced form, that is, the part containing the endogenous variables $y_1, \ldots, y_H$ appearing in the given equation, is

$$(7.3) \qquad y_i = \sum_{k=1}^{K} \pi_{ik} z_k + v_i \qquad i = 1, \ldots, H$$

---

[36] Following Koopmans and Hood [1953], pp. 140–141. See also Sargan [1958].

Now the fact that the original structural equation (7.2) must be a linear combination of the equations of (7.3), with coefficients $1, \beta_2, \ldots, \beta_H$, is expressed by the following K equations, each of which says that the coefficient of one of the z's in the original equation is equal to the same linear combination of the coefficients of that z in the reduced form:

$$\text{for } z_1: \qquad -\gamma_1 = \pi_{11} + \sum_{i=2}^{H} \beta_i \pi_{i1}$$

(7.4)

$$\text{for } z_J: \qquad -\gamma_J = \pi_{1J} + \sum_{i=2}^{H} \beta_i \pi_{iJ}$$

$$\text{for } z_{J+1}: \qquad 0 = \pi_{1,J+1} + \sum_{i=2}^{H} \beta_i \pi_{i,J+1}$$

(7·5)

$$\text{for } z_K: \qquad 0 = \pi_{1K} + \sum_{i=2}^{H} \beta_i \pi_{iK}$$

The equations in (7.5), which are $H - 1$ in number because the just identification of (7.2) requires that $K - J = H - 1$ as in (7.1), can be solved uniquely (with probability 1) for the $H - 1$ unknowns $\beta_2, \ldots, \beta_H$ in terms of the π's.[37] And then the equations (7.4) give values of $\gamma_1, \ldots, \gamma_J$ in terms of the π's and the β's just obtained from (7.5). Hence, once the reduced-form parameters π_{ik} have been estimated by least squares, (7.5) and (7.4) will translate the estimated π's into estimated β's and γ's, respectively.

    7.3   The least-squares method in Model 3 (normal) gives maximum-likelihood estimators of the reduced form, as indicated in 3.24. The indirect least-squares method gives the full-information maximum-likelihood estimators of the parameters if *all* structural equations are just identified, but not if any are overidentified, as shown by the following nonrigorous argument. To obtain either the maximum-likelihood or the indirect least-squares estimators, we start with the likelihood function (6.16) of the reduced-form parameters, given the observed values of the y's and z's. For the maximum-likelihood estimators, we *first transform* the likelihood function (6.16) into (6.18) so that it is in terms of structural parameters $\mathbf{B}$ and $\mathbf{\Gamma}$, and *second* we *maximize* it with respect to $\mathbf{B}$ and $\mathbf{\Gamma}$, subject to the restrictions that are just identifying on $\mathbf{B}$ and $\mathbf{\Gamma}$ (see 6.1–7). For the indirect least-squares estimators, we *first maximize* (6.16) with

[37] See VIII.3.34 and 36. A proof is in Koopmans and Hood [1953], pp. 185–186.

respect to the reduced-form parameters subject to *no* restrictions, and *second* we *transform* the reduced-form estimators to structural estimators, using the just-identifying restrictions. The two procedures differ only in that one transforms first and then maximizes, and the other maximizes first and then transforms. They give the same results in case all equations are just identified, because then the reduced-form parameters can be obtained uniquely from the structure (as usual) *and vice versa*, so that there is a unique relationship between the likelihood-maximizing values of the reduced-form parameters and those of the structural parameters. Hence the indirect least-squares estimators for a just-identified model have all the desirable properties of full-information maximum-likelihood estimators.

7.4 That structural estimators obtained in Model 3 for a just-identified equation via the indirect least-squares method as in 7.2 are consistent (but not unbiased in general), whether or not all other equations are just identified, can be seen in another way: The least-squares (quasi-maximum-likelihood) estimators of the reduced form are consistent; and consistency survives rational operations (i.e., addition, subtraction, multiplication, and division) such as are applied to the π's to get the β's and γ's in this case. The latter point follows from the discussion of probability limits in 3.28–29 and references given there. The reader will find it reasonable if he considers the definition of consistency, which runs in terms of the probability limit of an estimator as the sample grows indefinitely, and if he further considers that probability limits (being ordinary numbers) can safely be put through rational operations according to 3.28–29.

7.5 We now present a simple alternative estimation method, called the method of instrumental variables, directly analogous in computational procedure to the ordinary least-squares method of structural estimation but different in the variables that are used to obtain the moment matrix involved. We will see that for a just-identified equation this simple procedure yields exactly the same estimators as does the indirect least-squares method summarized in 7.2, whether or not other equations are over-identified, without the necessity of computing any reduced-form estimates at all. We shall illustrate with an elementary two-variable example, namely, a simple consumption equation. The variables are consumption c and income y, and the equation is

$$(7.6) \qquad\qquad c = \beta y + \gamma + u$$

7.6 To show the analogy between the ordinary least-squares method and the method that we shall now present, we recall that the former uses a normal equation obtainable by first taking the moment of each term in the original equation with the independent variable (typically income y

is treated as independent in the consumption equation), and then dropping the term containing u because of the assumed independence between y and u in the population. The normal equation, with β replaced by its least-squares estimator b, is as follows (using moments about the mean):

$$(7.7) \qquad\qquad m_{cy} = bm_{yy}$$

so that

$$(7.8) \qquad\qquad b = \text{est } \beta = \frac{m_{cy}}{m_{yy}}$$

The second normal equation, giving the estimator g of the constant term γ, is

$$(7.9) \qquad\qquad g = \text{est } \gamma = \bar{c} - b\bar{y}$$

7.7   We have seen in 3.20–30 that the least-squares method for (7.6) would be consistent in Model 2 or 3 if u and y were independent, so that m_{uy} would be zero. This is *not* the case with (7.6), which suggests using some other variable in the model instead of y to take moments with, a variable that *is* independent of u. Such a variable is called an *instrumental variable*. Suppose that investment i is in the model and is actually exogenous; then it is independent of u. Let us take moments of (7.6) with this instrumental variable i and again drop the term containing u (this time justifiably). The result, with β replaced by its new estimator, which we call $\hat{\beta}$, is

$$(7.10) \qquad\qquad m_{ci} = \hat{\beta}m_{yi}$$

so that

$$(7.11) \qquad\qquad \hat{\beta} = \frac{m_{ci}}{m_{yi}}$$

Then the corresponding estimator of γ, which we call $\hat{\gamma}$, is given by an equation analogous to (7.9):

$$(7.12) \qquad\qquad \hat{\gamma} = \bar{c} - \hat{\beta}\bar{y}$$

Let us call equations (7.10) and (7.12) the *quasi-normal equations* of the instrumental-variables method, by contrast to the least-squares normal equations (7.7) and (7.9). The estimators $\hat{\beta}$ and $\hat{\gamma}$ obtained from the instrumental-variables method fit right in with the assumption that the consumption equation is just identified: The number of endogenous variables in it is 2 (namely, c and y), and just identification means that the number of known predetermined variables that affect it without appearing in it must be $2 - 1$, that is, 1. We have chosen investment as that one predetermined variable, and we should expect to find it influencing the estimates. Observe that no use is made of any structural equation other than the one being estimated, *except* that the instrumental variable i is assumed to be in the model and hence related to c and y in the population underlying the sample. This assumption is important, for if i were unrelated to c and y in the population, then plim $\frac{1}{T} m_{ci}$ and plim $\frac{1}{T} m_{yi}$ would both be zero; plim $\hat{\beta}$, therefore, would not exist, and $\hat{\beta}$ would not be consistent.

7.8   We now show that if i is the only predetermined variable in the model [in which case the equation (7.6) is just identified], the indirect least-squares method of 7.2, proceeding from the least-squares estimates of the reduced form back to the structural estimates, yields exactly the same estimator of β, namely, m_{ci}/m_{yi}. The relevant part of the reduced form is the pair of equations expressing the current endogenous variables c and y in terms of the related exogenous variable i:

$$
\begin{aligned}
c &= \pi_{10} + \pi_{11}i + v_1 \\
y &= \pi_{20} + \pi_{21}i + v_2
\end{aligned}
$$
(7.13)

and the least-squares estimator of it is (using moments about the mean):

$$
(7.14) \quad
\begin{cases}
\hat{c} = \left(\bar{c} - \dfrac{m_{ci}}{m_{ii}} \bar{\imath} \right) + \dfrac{m_{ci}}{m_{ii}} i \\[2ex]
\hat{y} = \left(\bar{y} - \dfrac{m_{yi}}{m_{ii}} \bar{\imath} \right) + \dfrac{m_{yi}}{m_{ii}} i
\end{cases}
$$

The linear combination of these that yields the consumption equation is 1 times the first minus β times the second, thus [we now replace β by its estimator, which we again call $\hat{\beta}$ because it turns out presently to be the same as the $\hat{\beta}$ in (7.11)]:

$$
(7.15) \quad \hat{c} - \hat{\beta}\hat{y} = \bar{c} - \hat{\beta}\bar{y} - (m_{ci} - \hat{\beta}m_{yi}) \frac{\bar{\imath}}{m_{ii}} + (m_{ci} - \hat{\beta}m_{yi}) \frac{i}{m_{ii}}
$$

Now, recalling (7.5) and (7.6), we see that this can be the consumption function only if the coefficient of i is zero, that is,

$$
(7.16) \quad m_{ci} - \hat{\beta}m_{yi} = 0
$$

But this is equivalent to (7.10) and yields exactly the same estimator $\hat{\beta}$ as does the shorter method of instrumental variables. The corresponding estimator $\hat{\gamma}$ of the constant term γ can be obtained from (7.12) as before. Notice that here no use is made of information about any structural equation besides the one being estimated, *except* that the instrumental variables used must be the only predetermined variables in the model. If there are predetermined variables in the model besides those used as instrumental variables (i.e., if the equation is overidentified), then the indirect least-squares method is not defined.

7.9   In the foregoing example, $H = 2$ (the endogenous variables are c and y); $J = 1$ (the single exogenous variable in the equation is 1, for there is a constant term γ); $K = 2$, and $K - J = H - 1 = 1$ (the exogenous variable from outside the equation is i). There are just two $(H - 1 + J)$ unknown parameters, β and γ, and there are two (K) quasi-normal equations (7.10) and (7.12) to determine them. If the indirect least-squares method is used instead, the relevant facts are these: $H - 1 = 1$ so that there is just one unknown parameter of endogenous variables, β, and $K - J = 1$ so that there is just one equation like (7.5) to determine it, namely, (7.16). Then $J = 1$ so that there is one unknown parameter of exogenous variables, γ, and one equation like (7.4) to determine it, namely, (7.12).

7.10   By this time the reader should have a strong suspicion that for a just-identified equation the longer indirect least-squares method and the shorter method of instrumental variables are mathematically equivalent ("mathematically" meaning "logically" in this context, and not having anything to do with the number of arithmetical computations involved). The suspicion is quite correct, provided that the instrumental variables chosen are predetermined variables in the model (there are then no other predetermined variables in the model). That it should be so is suggested by the following nonrigorous argument. The indirect least-squares method makes all the *reduced-form* residuals $\hat{v}_i$ have zero means and be independent of the z's; it accordingly gets a single estimator of each structural parameter. The method of instrumental variables makes all the *structural* disturbances $\hat{u}_i$ have zero means and be independent of the z's; it accordingly gets a single estimator for each structural parameter. The estimators obtained by the two methods are therefore identical, because the operations on which they are based are logically equivalent: If the $\hat{u}$'s have zero means and are independent of the z's, then the same is true of the $\hat{v}$'s and conversely, for the $\hat{u}$'s are a unique linear combination of the $\hat{v}$'s and vice versa. For a just-identified equation, both the indirect least-squares and the instrumental-variables methods are special cases of the other methods to be considered below. See 9.23–24 for related remarks and references and Tables 12.1–2 for a summary.

8   ESTIMATION OF STRUCTURAL PARAMETERS IN AN OVERIDENTIFIED EQUATION: INTRODUCTION

8.1   In this section we shall ask what happens if we try to apply the indirect least-squares or the instrumental-variables estimation method of Section 7 to an *overidentified* equation. Suppose the equation is

$$(8.1) \qquad y_1 + \beta_2 y_2 + \cdots + \beta_H y_H + \gamma_1 z_1 + \cdots + \gamma_J z_J = u$$

Again if there is a constant term, we let one of the $z_1, \ldots, z_J$ be a dummy that is always equal to 1. This looks exactly like the just-identified equation (7.2); the difference is that now the number $K - J$ of known predetermined variables that influence it without appearing in it is greater than the number $H - 1$ of endogenous variables appearing in it less 1. In symbols,

$$(8.2) \qquad K - J > H - 1$$

The $K - J$ predetermined variables excluded from the equation are $z_{J+1}, \ldots, z_K$. If the equation has no constant term but the model has one or more, then one of the $z_{J+1}, \ldots, z_K$ (say z_K) is always 1.

8.2 Suppose we try to obtain estimators of the parameters of (8.1) by using instrumental variables taking moments (about the mean) of (8.1) with predetermined variables. There are K predetermined variables in all, and hence K quasi-normal equations. Suppose that γ_1 is the constant term, so that $z_1 = 1$ always.[38] The $K - 1$ quasi-normal equations generated by $z_2, \ldots, z_K$ are then

$$(8.3) \qquad m_{y_1 z_k} + \hat{\beta}_2 m_{y_2 z_k} + \cdots + \hat{\beta}_H m_{y_H z_k} + \hat{\gamma}_2 m_{z_2 z_k} + \cdots + \hat{\gamma}_J m_{z_J z_k} = 0$$
$$k = 2, \ldots, K$$

The other quasi-normal equation, expressing $\hat{\gamma}_1$ in terms of the estimators $\hat{\beta}_2, \ldots, \hat{\beta}_H, \ \hat{\gamma}_2, \ldots, \hat{\gamma}_J$, is

$$(8.4) \qquad \hat{\gamma}_1 = -\bar{y}_1 - \hat{\beta}_2 \bar{y}_2 - \cdots - \hat{\beta}_H \bar{y}_H - \hat{\gamma}_2 \bar{z}_2 - \cdots - \hat{\gamma}_J \bar{z}_J$$

The difficulty is that in (8.3) there are more equations than unknowns to solve for: There are $K - 1$ equations, but only $H + J - 2$ estimators ($K - 1$ is indeed greater than $H + J - 2$ because of (8.2), the fact of overidentification). And with a finite sample of size $T \geqq K$, the probability is zero that all the equations in (8.3) are perfectly consistent with each other.

8.3 A possible response to this dilemma is simply to choose $H + J - 2$ of the equations of (8.3) and solve them for $\hat{\beta}_2, \ldots, \hat{\beta}_H$, $\hat{\gamma}_2, \ldots, \hat{\gamma}_J$, disregarding the other equations entirely. This amounts to ignoring all but $H - 1$ of the predetermined variables from outside the equation, pretending that the equation is just identified, and using the instrumental-variables method, choosing instrumental variables from among the predetermined variables in the model. The method will provide consistent estimators. It makes a fine method for exploratory computations before all the predetermined variables are selected; it should be particularly valuable when it is easy to see which of the z's are most important and which can most safely be ignored. But it does not seem very satisfactory, once all the predetermined variables to go into the model are selected,

---

[38] If there is no constant term, all K equations will be of the same form, similar to (8.3) except that moments will be from the origin ($\sum_t z_i z_j$) instead of from the means [$\sum_t (z_i - \bar{z}_i)(z_j - \bar{z}_j)$], and the kth equation will contain $\hat{\gamma}_1 \sum_t z_1 z_k, \ k = 1, \ldots, K$.

for two reasons. For one thing, the estimators we get will be different, depending on which z's are used and which are ignored; and if all the z's appear to be about equally important considering what we know before estimating, it is hard to justify any choice of which variables are to be ignored. For another thing, it seems unwise to ignore any *a priori* information we may have, and the presumed relationships between the "surplus" z's and the other variables might very well lead to better estimators if this information could be used properly.

8.4 Suppose we were to try to estimate (8.1) from the least-squares estimators p_{ik} of its reduced form,

$$(8.5) \qquad \hat{y}_i = \sum_{k=1}^{K} p_{ik} z_k \qquad i = 1, \ldots, H$$

We would find $K - J$ equations like (7.5) signifying that $z_{J+1}, \ldots, z_K$ do not appear in (8.1):

$$\sum_{i=2}^{H} \hat{\beta}_i p_{i,J+1} = -p_{1,J+1}$$

$$(8.6) \qquad \qquad \qquad \cdot \qquad \qquad \cdot$$
$$\qquad \qquad \qquad \cdot \qquad \qquad \cdot$$
$$\qquad \qquad \qquad \cdot \qquad \qquad \cdot$$

$$\sum_{i=2}^{H} \hat{\beta}_i p_{iK} = -p_{1K}$$

These equations have only $H - 1$ unknowns, $\hat{\beta}_2, \ldots, \hat{\beta}_H$. Again there are more equations than unknowns because of (8.2), and again there is zero probability that a set of values of $\hat{\beta}_2, \ldots, \hat{\beta}_H$ exists that will satisfy all $K - J$ equations. As before, a possible response is to choose $H - 1$ of the equations and solve them, ignoring the others altogether, in effect pretending that the equation is just identified and that certain of the z's do not exist. If this is done, then afterward $\gamma_1, \ldots, \gamma_J$ can be estimated from (7.4). Consistent estimators of both the β's and γ's may be obtained thus, but in general they are not the same estimators that we get by ignoring the corresponding quasi-normal equations, as discussed in 8.3, except if the equation is just identified as discussed in 7.10.

8.5 Let us illustrate with an example, an aggregate consumption function in a model intended to represent the entire United States economy in a few equations. Important policy variables that affect the economy in the absence of direct controls are real tax collections t, real government outlay g, real Federal Reserve liabilities outstanding F, and the required bank reserve ratio Q. Suppose we choose a consumption function specifying that real consumer expenditures c depend on real disposable income $y - t$ and on the previous period's level of consumer expenditure c_{-1}:

$$(8.7) \qquad c = \beta_2(y - t) + \gamma_1 c_{-1} + \gamma_2 + u$$

This type of function, allowing for cyclical variations in the average propensity to consume, has been used with considerable postwar predictive success, relative to most other consumption functions.[39] It shows a greater proportion of income consumed in depression than in prosperity (γ_1 being positive), which is what we would expect. For convenience in what follows we denote $y - t$ by x. If this equation were estimated by least squares with c as dependent, the normal equations would be (using moments about the mean and *temporarily* denoting least-squares estimates by primes):

(8.8)
$$\begin{cases} m_{cx} = \beta_2' m_{xx} + \gamma_1' m_{c_{-1}x} \\ m_{cc_{-1}} = \beta_2' m_{xc_{-1}} + \gamma_1' m_{c_{-1}c_{-1}} \end{cases}$$

8.6 If the method of instrumental variables were used instead, we should have five predetermined variables with which we might take moments in (8.7): c_{-1}, t, g, F, and Q, and hence these five quasi-normal equations:

(8.9)
$$\begin{aligned} m_{cc_{-1}} &= \hat{\beta}_2 m_{xc_{-1}} + \hat{\gamma}_1 m_{c_{-1}c_{-1}} \\ m_{ct} &= \hat{\beta}_2 m_{xt} + \hat{\gamma}_1 m_{c_{-1}t} \\ m_{cg} &= \hat{\beta}_2 m_{xg} + \hat{\gamma}_1 m_{c_{-1}g} \\ m_{cF} &= \hat{\beta}_2 m_{xF} + \hat{\gamma}_1 m_{c_{-1}F} \\ m_{cQ} &= \hat{\beta}_2 m_{xQ} + \hat{\gamma}_1 m_{c_{-1}Q} \end{aligned}$$

γ_2 can be estimated from the remaining quasi-normal equation:

(8.10)
$$\hat{\gamma}_2 = \bar{c} - \hat{\beta}_2 \bar{x} - \hat{\gamma}_1 \bar{c}_{-1}$$

There is no reason to expect that the estimators of β_2 and γ_1 obtained from any pair of equations (8.9) will agree with those from any other pair, for even though all such estimators are consistent in the statistical sense, equations (8.9) are all but certain to be logically inconsistent. Suppose we decide to use just two of them, and ignore the other three. Since c_{-1} appears in the equation, it is one of the more important z's and should be retained. Certainly t is an important variable, but its major influence in reducing total income to disposable income is already accounted for by the definition of x, so probably it is better to use c_{-1} and g. However, if government outlay has been nearly constant over the observation period and gold flows and/or open market operations have resulted in substantial changes in Federal Reserve liabilities, then the equations involving c_{-1} and F will be preferable.

[39] The chief early users of such functions are Friedman [1957], Modigliani and Brumberg [1954], and Brown [1952].

8.7 If the indirect least-squares method were attempted, the reduced form would first be estimated:

$$(8.11) \quad \begin{cases} \hat{c} = p_{11}c_{-1} + p_{12}t + p_{13}g + p_{14}F + p_{15}Q + p_{16} \\ \hat{x} = p_{21}c_{-1} + p_{22}t + p_{23}g + p_{24}F + p_{25}Q + p_{26} \end{cases}$$

Then there would be four equations like (8.6), signifying that the four variables t, g, F, and Q do not appear explicitly in the equation (8.7):

$$(8.12) \quad \begin{array}{ll} \text{for } t: & p_{12} = \hat{\beta}_2 p_{22} \\ \text{for } g: & p_{13} = \hat{\beta}_2 p_{23} \\ \text{for } F: & p_{14} = \hat{\beta}_2 p_{24} \\ \text{for } Q: & p_{15} = \hat{\beta}_2 p_{25} \end{array}$$

Then one equation like (7.4) would give an estimator of γ_1, in terms of $\hat{\beta}_2$ and the p's:

$$(8.13) \quad \text{for } c_{-1}: \quad \hat{\gamma}_1 = p_{11} - \hat{\beta}_2 p_{21}$$

There are four equations in (8.12) to solve for one unknown, $\hat{\beta}_2$. If we choose as in 8.6 to retain c_{-1} and g, and ignore the other z's, then we use the second equation of (8.12) together with (8.13) to get estimators of β_2 and γ_1. They will differ from the estimators obtained from the corresponding equations (8.9).

8.8 What can be done to avoid wasting any of the information provided by the z's? If a sort of "compromise" set of values for $\hat{\beta}_2, \ldots, \hat{\beta}_H$ could be found (e.g., for $\hat{\beta}_2$ in the example above) that would *almost* satisfy each of equations (8.6) [(8.12) in the example], even though failing to satisfy any of them exactly, then none of the z's would need to be ignored. A method for doing essentially that, on the maximum-likelihood principle, has been worked out by Anderson and Rubin [1949] and [1950]. It has come to be called the *limited-information* method. We shall devote the next section to it. Another method for doing the same thing on a different principle has been developed by Theil [1958] and by Basmann [1957]. Theil calls it the two-stage least-squares method, and Basmann calls it the generalized classical linear method. We shall devote Section 10 to it and related methods.

9 THE LIMITED-INFORMATION METHOD: ITS DERIVATION FROM THE LEAST-VARIANCE RATIO PRINCIPLE; COMPUTATION; PROPERTIES

9.1 The *limited-information single-equation maximum-likelihood* method, often called the *limited-information* method for short, provides estimators of the parameters of a single just-identified or overidentified structural equation on the maximum-likelihood principle, the likelihood-maximizing being done subject only to the *a priori* identifying restrictions imposed *on the equation being estimated*.[40] The so-called *least-variance-ratio* principle, to be explained below, gives the same estimators in this situation as the maximum-likelihood principle, for indeed it can be derived from the maximum-likelihood principle given the assumptions of Model 3 (normal). That derivation is beyond the scope of this book.[41] Instead we shall present a relatively simple nonrigorous justification of the least-variance-ratio principle, which I hope will be convincing, based on the fact that in Model 3 (normal) the least-squares method yields maximum-likelihood estimators for equations having only one dependent variable (all the others being predetermined). After having thus justified the least-variance-ratio principle, we shall follow the rigorous derivation of the limited-information estimators from it. The section will conclude with a discussion of the properties of these estimators under various assumptions.

9.2 We begin by adopting Model 3 (normal), which incorporates assumptions (a)–(h), (j), and (k) summarized in 2.3 above. It is important to go back and read those assumptions again now. Later on in this section, in 9.29 ff., some of these assumptions will be relaxed somewhat, in particular (a), (b), (d), and (k).

9.3 We proceed now to the least-variance-ratio principle for estimating the parameters $\beta_2, \ldots, \beta_H, \gamma_1, \ldots, \gamma_J$ in equation (9.1) below, subject to the *a priori* identifying restrictions on (9.1) and ignoring such restrictions on other equations in the model. We do make assumptions (a)–(c), (e)–(h), (j), (k) about those other equations, but it is not necessary to know how many other equations there are or whether they are identified.

$$(9.1) \qquad y_{1t} + \sum_{i=2}^{H} \beta_i y_{it} + \sum_{i=H+1}^{G} 0 \cdot y_{it} + \sum_{k=1}^{J} \gamma_k z_{kt} + \sum_{k=J+1}^{K} 0 \cdot z_{kt} = u_t$$

---

[40] The method was developed by Anderson and Rubin [1949] and [1950], following a suggestion by M. A. Girshick. They called it the reduced-form method. The term "limited-information method" was applied by later writers (e.g., Koopmans and Hood [1953], p. 162), and the latter name has become general. It is apt because the method ignores all identifying restrictions on equations other than the one being estimated, and ignores data for certain variables that are excluded from the equation being estimated. The method has been adapted by Rubin to estimate simultaneously the parameters of a subset of two or more structural equations of a model; it is then called the limited-information *subsystem* (not *single-equation*) method; see Koopmans and Hood [1953], pp. 164–166 and 170–171; we shall not discuss this.

[41] See Koopmans and Hood [1953], pp. 159–170 and 190–195.

Note that there is no explicit constant term here. If the equation has a constant term, we denote it by γ_J and let z_{Jt} be a dummy variable always equal to 1. We could then rewrite (9.1) in any of the three alternative equivalent forms analogous to (4.1)–(4.3), if desired. We shall adhere to (9.1) in this section and maintain the notational convention of 4.11. The number of predetermined variables in (9.1) is J, and the number of jointly dependent variables in (9.1) is H. If (9.1) has a constant term, the number of nondummy predetermined variables in it is $J - 1$.

9.4   The starting point of our discussion is the fact that, given Model 3 (normal), for an equation having only one current endogenous variable (all other variables being predetermined) the least-squares method yields maximum-likelihood estimators. How can equation (9.1) be altered so that this condition will apply? Looking at (9.1), we see that the expression $y_1 + \beta_2 y_2 + \cdots + \beta_H y_H$ is the current endogenous part of it, and $\gamma_1 z_1 + \cdots + \gamma_J z_J$ is the predetermined part. This suggests that we should define a single new synthetic endogenous variable to stand for the entire endogenous part, denoted say by $\tilde{y}$, thus:

$$(9.2) \qquad \tilde{y}_t \equiv y_{1t} + \beta_2 y_{2t} + \cdots + \beta_H y_{Ht}$$

and then rewrite (9.1) so that it *does* have only one current endogenous variable, thus:

$$(9.3) \qquad \tilde{y}_t = -\gamma_1 z_{1t} - \cdots - \gamma_J z_{Jt} + u_t$$

Now (9.3) meets the condition for least-squares estimators to be maximum-likelihood estimators, and therefore it would be appropriate to estimate the γ's in (9.3) by the ordinary least-squares regression of $\tilde{y}$ on $z_1, \ldots, z_J$. This looks like a successful solution to the problem, except that it does not appear to tell how to estimate $\beta_2, \ldots, \beta_H$, which we want to estimate along with the γ's. What is more, if the β's are not known or at least estimated, then we cannot find the values of $\tilde{y}$ to use in computing its regression on $z_1, \ldots, z_J$.

9.5   The next problem, then, is to find point estimators of the β's. Recall the restrictions that are crucial in the unsuccessful attempt of Section 8 to determine the β's from the estimated reduced form in the case of an overidentified equation. These are the restrictions that the coefficients of $z_{J+1}, \ldots, z_K$ in (9.1) are all zero. These restrictions imply that if we were to compute the regression of $\tilde{y}$ on *all* the z's in the model [*including $z_{J+1}, \ldots, z_K$, which do not appear in* (9.1)], we should expect (with an infinite sample) to get zeros for the estimated coefficients of $z_{J+1}, \ldots, z_K$, because (9.1) does not contain $z_{J+1}, \ldots, z_K$. The import of Section 8 is that, because of sampling variation, it is impossible to choose a set of values of the β's that will make all the estimated regression coefficients of $z_{J+1}, \ldots, z_K$ be exactly zero for a finite sample in an overidentified equation. The next best thing is that values of the β's be chosen so as to make $z_{J+1}, \ldots, z_K$ as unimportant as possible in the regression of $\tilde{y}$ on $z_1, \ldots, z_K$. This can be done by choosing values of the β's so that the excluded variables $z_{J+1}, \ldots, z_K$, when introduced into the regression of $\tilde{y}$ on the included variables $z_1, \ldots, z_J$, will add as little as possible to the explanation of the variation of $\tilde{y}$.

9.6   Following this line, we shall choose the β's so that the sum of squared residuals of $\tilde{y}$ from its regression on $z_1, \ldots, z_J$ shall be as nearly as possible the same size as the sum of squared residuals of $\tilde{y}$ from its regression on $z_1, \ldots, z_J, \ldots, z_K$. In other words the β's are to be chosen so that the following ratio, denoted by l, is as close to 1 as possible:

(9.4)

$$l \equiv \frac{\text{sum of squared deviations of } \tilde{y} \text{ from its regression on } z_1, \ldots, z_J}{\text{sum of squared deviations of } \tilde{y} \text{ from its regression on } z_1, \ldots, z_K}$$

This ratio l is called the *variance ratio*, because it is equal to the ratio of the unexplained variance of $\tilde{y}$ in its regression on the z's *included* in (9.1) to the unexplained variance of $\tilde{y}$ in its regression on *all* the z's in the model.

9.7   The variance ratio l can never be less than 1, that is,

(9.5) $l \geqq 1$

This is because the denominator must always be equal to or less than the numerator, for the introduction of additional independent variables $(z_{J+1}, \ldots, z_K)$ in a regression (of $\tilde{y}$ on $z_1, \ldots, z_J$) cannot possibly increase the sum of squared residuals. At the extreme, the additional variables will show no relationship to the dependent variable,[42] and l will be equal to 1. Indeed, it is just for that reason that we want to choose values of the β_i so that l will be as close to 1 as possible. Since $l \geqq 1$,

---

[42] The simplest example is the comparison of (1) a regression of a variable y on *no* independent variables except a constant and (2) a regression of y on one independent variable z and a constant. The two equations are $y = \gamma_1 + v_1$ and $y = \gamma_2 z + \gamma_3 + v_2$. The estimated "regression line" in the first case will simply be $\hat{y} = \bar{y}$, and in the second case it will be $\hat{y} = (m_{yz}/m_{zz})z + \bar{y} - (m_{yz}/m_{zz})\bar{z}$. One of two possibilities must hold: Either m_{yz} is zero or it is not zero. If m_{yz} is zero, the second regression line is horizontal, the same as the first, and the variable z does not explain any of the variance of y. If m_{yz} is not zero, the second regression line slopes (whether positively or negatively does not matter for our purpose now), and the sum of squared deviations from the second line is less (not greater) than from the first, so that z does explain some of the variance of y.

this procedure is equivalent to minimizing l with respect to the β's, which can be done readily by the use of differential calculus. The minimizing values $\hat{\beta}_2, \ldots, \hat{\beta}_H$ will be the estimates that we seek. This principle of estimation is called the *least-variance-ratio principle*. The corresponding estimates of the γ's can then be obtained from $\hat{\beta}_2, \ldots, \hat{\beta}_H$ via the regression of $\tilde{y}$ on $z_1, \ldots, z_J$ as suggested by equation (9.3).

9.8 In summary, then, the least-variance-ratio principle for estimating the parameters of a single structural equation (9.1) entails the following general procedure: Regard the expression $y_1 + \beta_2 y_2 + \cdots + \beta_H y_H$ as a single endogenous variable $\tilde{y}$, thus transforming (9.1) into a least-squares-type equation (9.3); choose the estimates $\hat{\beta}_2, \ldots, \hat{\beta}_H$ so as to minimize the variance ratio l, that is, so as to make the regression of $\tilde{y}$ on all the z's in the model conform as closely as possible to the restriction that

$$z_{J+1}, \ldots, z_K$$

do not appear in (9.1); obtain estimates of the γ's from the regression of $\tilde{y}$ (evaluated by using the $\hat{\beta}$'s) on $z_1, \ldots, z_J$ as suggested by (9.3). The reader is referred elsewhere[43] for proof that in Model 3 (normal) the least-variance-ratio principle can be derived from the maximum-likelihood principle and that the estimators so obtained are the limited-information maximum-likelihood estimators. Now that the motivation behind the minimization of the variance ratio l with respect to $\beta_2, \ldots, \beta_H$ has been set forth, the next order of business is to express l explicitly as a function of $\beta_2, \ldots, \beta_H$ and observable quantities, and then to perform that minimization. Paragraphs 9.10–14 will do the former.

9.9 First it will be convenient to have some notation in which to express the regressions of $y_1, \ldots, y_H$ on $z_1, \ldots, z_J$ and on $z_1, \ldots, z_J, \ldots, z_K$. As explained in 4.11, we are using vector and matrix notation that can be interpreted in two ways, as describing either one or the other of the following: (a) an equation with an explicit constant term γ_J, and with $J - 1$ nondummy predetermined variables, where vectors and matrices are taken to exclude the dummy z_{Jt} and its parameter γ_J, and variables and moments are taken about the mean; (b) an equation with no explicit constant term, and with J predetermined variables of which the Jth is a dummy if the equation has a constant term, where vectors and matrices are taken to include all J of the predetermined variables in the equation, and variables and moments are taken about zero. The notation is then as follows, the choice of column (a) or column (b) being made according to the interpretation adopted:

[43] Koopmans and Hood [1953], pp. 159–170 and 190–195.

(a) *Explicit constant term*   (b) *No explicit constant term*

$$\mathbf{y} = (y_{1t} \quad \cdots \quad y_{Ht})$$ same as in (a)

$$\mathbf{z}_t^* = (z_{1t} \quad \cdots \quad z_{J-1,t}) \quad \text{or} \quad (z_{1t} \quad \cdots \quad z_{Jt})$$

(9.6) $$\mathbf{z}_t = (\mathbf{z}_t^* \quad z_{J+1,t} \quad \cdots \quad z_{Kt})$$ same as in (a)

$$\boldsymbol{\beta} = (\beta_1 \quad \cdots \quad \beta_H)$$ same as in (a)

$$\boldsymbol{\gamma} = (\gamma_1 \quad \cdots \quad \gamma_{J-1}) \quad \text{or} \quad (\gamma_1 \quad \cdots \quad \gamma_J)$$

$$\mathbf{M}_{z*z*} = \begin{pmatrix} m_{z_1 z_1} & \cdots & m_{z_1 z_{J-1}} \\ \cdot & & \cdot \\ \cdot & & \cdot \\ m_{z_{J-1} z_1} & \cdots & m_{z_{J-1} z_{J-1}} \end{pmatrix} \quad \text{or} \quad \begin{pmatrix} \Sigma z_1^2 & \cdots & \Sigma z_1 z_J \\ \cdot & & \cdot \\ \cdot & & \cdot \\ \Sigma z_J z_1 & \cdots & \Sigma z_J^2 \end{pmatrix}$$

$$\mathbf{M}_{yz*} = \begin{pmatrix} m_{y_1 z_1} & \cdots & m_{y_1 z_{J-1}} \\ \cdot & & \cdot \\ \cdot & & \cdot \\ m_{y_H z_1} & \cdots & m_{y_H z_{J-1}} \end{pmatrix} \quad \text{or} \quad \begin{pmatrix} \Sigma y_1 z_1 & \cdots & \Sigma y_1 z_J \\ \cdot & & \cdot \\ \cdot & & \cdot \\ \Sigma y_H z_1 & \cdots & \Sigma y_H z_J \end{pmatrix}$$

(9.7) $$\mathbf{M}_{yy} = \begin{pmatrix} m_{y_1 y_1} & \cdots & m_{y_1 y_H} \\ \cdot & & \cdot \\ \cdot & & \cdot \\ \cdot & & \cdot \\ m_{y_H y_1} & \cdots & m_{y_H y_H} \end{pmatrix} \quad \text{or} \quad \begin{pmatrix} \Sigma y_1^2 & \cdots & \Sigma y_1 y_H \\ \cdot & & \cdot \\ \cdot & & \cdot \\ \cdot & & \cdot \\ \Sigma y_H y_1 & \cdots & \Sigma y_H^2 \end{pmatrix}$$

$$\mathbf{M}_{yz} = \begin{pmatrix} \mathbf{M}_{yz*} & \begin{matrix} m_{y_1 z_{J+1}} & \cdots & m_{y_1 z_K} \\ \cdot & & \cdot \\ \cdot & & \cdot \\ m_{y_H z_{J+1}} & \cdots & m_{y_H z_K} \end{matrix} \end{pmatrix} \quad \text{or} \quad \begin{pmatrix} \mathbf{M}_{yz*} & \begin{matrix} \Sigma y_1 z_{J+1} & \cdots & \Sigma y_1 z_K \\ \cdot & & \cdot \\ \cdot & & \cdot \\ \Sigma y_H z_{J+1} & \cdots & \Sigma y_H z_K \end{matrix} \end{pmatrix}$$

$$\mathbf{M}_{zz} = \begin{pmatrix} \mathbf{M}_{z*z*} & & \begin{matrix} m_{z_1 z_{J+1}} & \cdots & m_{z_1 z_K} \\ \cdot & & \cdot \\ \cdot & & \cdot \end{matrix} \\ m_{z_{J+1} z_1} \cdots & m_{z_{J+1} z_{J+1}} & \cdots & m_{z_{J+1} z_K} \\ \cdot & & & \cdot \\ m_{z_K z_1} \cdots & m_{z_K z_{J+1}} & \cdots & m_{z_K z_K} \end{pmatrix} \quad \text{or} \quad \begin{pmatrix} \mathbf{M}_{z*z*} & & \begin{matrix} \Sigma z_1 z_{J+1} & \cdots & \Sigma z_1 z_K \\ \cdot & & \cdot \\ \cdot & & \cdot \end{matrix} \\ \Sigma z_{J+1} z_1 \cdots & \Sigma z_{J+1}^2 & \cdots & \Sigma z_{J+1} z_K \\ \cdot & & & \cdot \\ \Sigma z_K z_1 \cdots & \Sigma z_K z_{J+1} & \cdots & \Sigma z_K^2 \end{pmatrix}$$

$$\mathbf{m}_{y_i z*} = (m_{y_i z_1} \quad \cdots \quad m_{y_i z_{J-1}}) \quad \text{or} \quad (\Sigma y_i z_1 \quad \cdots \quad \Sigma y_i z_J)$$

(9.8) $$\mathbf{m}_{y_i z} = (\mathbf{m}_{y_i z*} \quad m_{y_i z_{J+1}} \quad \cdots \quad m_{y_i z_K}) \quad \text{or} \quad (\mathbf{m}_{y_i z*} \quad \Sigma y_i z_{J+1} \quad \cdots \quad \Sigma y_i z_K)$$

Thus $\mathbf{y}$ and $\mathbf{z}^*$ represent variables *included* in the equation to be estimated, and $\boldsymbol{\beta}$ and $\boldsymbol{\gamma}$ are their coefficients, estimators thereof being denoted by $\hat{\boldsymbol{\beta}}$ and $\hat{\boldsymbol{\gamma}}$; $\mathbf{z}$ represents all the predetermined variables in the model. $\mathbf{M}_{yy}$, $\mathbf{M}_{zz}$, and $\mathbf{M}_{z*z*}$ are square symmetric matrices; $\mathbf{M}_{yy}$ has H rows and columns; $\mathbf{M}_{zz}$ has $K - 1$ or K rows and columns; and $\mathbf{M}_{z*z*}$ has $J - 1$ or J rows and columns, being the first $J - 1$ or J rows and columns of $\mathbf{M}_{zz}$. $\mathbf{M}_{yz}$ has H rows and $K - 1$ or K columns; $\mathbf{M}_{yz*}$ has H rows and $J - 1$ or J columns, being the first $J - 1$ or J columns of $\mathbf{M}_{yz}$. The row vectors $\mathbf{m}_{y_i z*}$ and $\mathbf{m}_{y_i z}$ are the ith rows of $\mathbf{M}_{yz*}$ and $\mathbf{M}_{yz}$ respectively.

9.10 Recall that we seek two sums of squared residuals, from the regressions of $\tilde{y}$ on z and on z^*. Since $\tilde{y}$ is defined as $\beta y'$, this means we shall want residuals of the regressions of all its components y_i on z, and also residuals of the regressions of all the y_i on z^*. The residuals from the regression of y_i on z and on z^* are then respectively as follows, where $p_{i1}, \ldots, p_{iK}$ and $p_{i1}^*, \ldots, p_{iJ}^*$ are the estimated regression coefficients:

$$(9.9) \qquad \hat{v}_{it} = y_{it} - \sum_{k=1}^{K} p_{ik} z_{kt} \qquad i = 1, \ldots, H$$

$$(9.10) \qquad \hat{v}_{it}^* = y_{it} - \sum_{k=1}^{J} p_{ik}^* z_{kt} \qquad i = 1, \ldots, H$$

If we use matrix notation and the results of 4.5 above, these can be expressed respectively by (9.11) and (9.12) below, where $\hat{v}_t$, $\hat{v}_t^*$, P, and P^* are implicitly defined by the same two equations:

$$(9.11) \quad \hat{v}_t' \equiv \begin{pmatrix} \hat{v}_{1t}' \\ \cdot \\ \cdot \\ \cdot \\ \hat{v}_{Ht}' \end{pmatrix} = y_t' - \begin{pmatrix} p_{11} & \cdots & p_{1K} \\ \cdot & & \cdot \\ \cdot & & \cdot \\ \cdot & & \cdot \\ p_{H1} & \cdots & p_{HK} \end{pmatrix} z_t' \equiv y_t' - P z_t'$$

$$(9.12) \quad \hat{v}_t^{*'} \equiv \begin{pmatrix} \hat{v}_{1t}^* \\ \cdot \\ \cdot \\ \cdot \\ \hat{v}_{Ht}^* \end{pmatrix} = y_t' - \begin{pmatrix} p_{11}^* & \cdots & p_{1J}^* \\ \cdot & & \cdot \\ \cdot & & \cdot \\ p_{H1}^* & & p_{HJ}^* \end{pmatrix} z_t^{*'} \equiv y_t' - P^* z_t^{*'}$$

Note that typically P^* differs from the first J columns of P, though in some special cases they may be equal, for example, if $z_{J+1}, \ldots, z_K$ are uncorrelated with $z_1, \ldots, z_J$ during the sample period.

9.11 Now since $\tilde{y} = \beta y'$, we can express the value of $\tilde{y}_t$ in terms of its estimated regression on z via (9.11) as follows (we shall return to its regression on z^* in a moment):

$$(9.13) \qquad \tilde{y}_t = \beta y_t' = \beta(P z_t' + \hat{v}_t') = \beta P z_t' + \beta \hat{v}_t'$$

Therefore the desired sum of squared residuals from this regression is

$$(9.14) \qquad \sum_t (\tilde{y}_t - \beta P z_t')^2 = \sum_t (\beta \hat{v}_t')^2 = \sum_t \beta \hat{v}_t' \hat{v}_t \beta'$$

$$= \beta \left(\sum_t \hat{v}_t' \hat{v}_t \right) \beta'$$

The sum in the last term above is a symmetric matrix of squares and cross products of the deviations $\hat{v}$ in the estimated reduced form, an estimator of the relevant rows and columns of the variance-covariance matrix $\boldsymbol{\Omega}$ of reduced-form disturbances, except for a factor $T - K$. We shall call it $\mathbf{W}$, thus:

(9.15)

$$\mathbf{W} \equiv \begin{pmatrix} w_{11} & \cdots & w_{1H} \\ \cdot & & \cdot \\ \cdot & & \cdot \\ \cdot & & \cdot \\ w_{H1} & \cdots & w_{HH} \end{pmatrix} \equiv \begin{pmatrix} \Sigma\,\hat{v}_{1t}^2 & \cdots & \Sigma\,\hat{v}_{1t}\hat{v}_{Ht} \\ \cdot & & \cdot \\ \cdot & & \cdot \\ \cdot & & \cdot \\ \Sigma\,\hat{v}_{Ht}\hat{v}_{1t} & \cdots & \Sigma\,\hat{v}_{Ht}^2 \end{pmatrix} = \sum_t \hat{\mathbf{v}}_t{'}\hat{\mathbf{v}}_t$$

Hence the sum of squared deviations from the regression of $\tilde{y}$ on $\mathbf{z}$ from (9.14) is

(9.16) $$\boldsymbol{\beta}\mathbf{W}\boldsymbol{\beta}'$$

This expression is the desired denominator of the variance ratio l in (9.4). The matrix $\mathbf{W}$ can be expressed in terms of moments of observable variables $\mathbf{y}$ and $\mathbf{z}$ as follows, by an argument similar to that used in obtaining (4.16):

(9.17) $$\mathbf{W} = \mathbf{M}_{yy} - \mathbf{M}_{yz}\mathbf{M}_{zz}^{-1}\mathbf{M}_{yz}'$$

9.12 In a similar fashion, using (9.12), we see that $\tilde{y}_t$ in terms of its estimated regression on $\mathbf{z}^*$ is

(9.18) $$\tilde{y}_t = \boldsymbol{\beta}\mathbf{y}_t' = \boldsymbol{\beta}(\mathbf{P}^*\mathbf{z}_t^{*\prime} + \hat{\mathbf{v}}_t^{*\prime}) = \boldsymbol{\beta}\mathbf{P}^*\mathbf{z}_t^{*\prime} + \boldsymbol{\beta}\hat{\mathbf{v}}_t^{*\prime}$$

Then, by analogy to (9.14), the desired sum of squared deviations from this regression is as follows, where $\mathbf{W}^*$ is defined in (9.20):

(9.19) $$\sum (\tilde{y}_t - \boldsymbol{\beta}\mathbf{P}^*\mathbf{z}_t^{*\prime})^2 = \boldsymbol{\beta}(\sum_t \hat{\mathbf{v}}_t^{*\prime}\hat{\mathbf{v}}_t^*)\boldsymbol{\beta}' = \boldsymbol{\beta}\mathbf{W}^*\boldsymbol{\beta}'$$

(9.20)

$$\mathbf{W}^* \equiv \begin{pmatrix} w_{11}^* & \cdots & w_{1H}^* \\ \cdot & & \cdot \\ \cdot & & \cdot \\ \cdot & & \cdot \\ w_{H1}^* & \cdots & w_{HH}^* \end{pmatrix} \equiv \begin{pmatrix} \Sigma\,\hat{v}_{1t}^{*2} & \cdots & \Sigma\,\hat{v}_{1t}^*\hat{v}_{Ht}^* \\ \cdot & & \cdot \\ \cdot & & \cdot \\ \cdot & & \cdot \\ \Sigma\,\hat{v}_{Ht}^*\hat{v}_{1t}^* & \cdots & \Sigma\,\hat{v}_{Ht}^{*2} \end{pmatrix} = \sum_t \hat{\mathbf{v}}_t^{*\prime}\hat{\mathbf{v}}_t^*$$

Then the desired numerator of the variance ratio l is given by (9.19). The matrix $\mathbf{W}^*$ can be expressed in terms of observable moments as follows, by analogy to (9.17):

(9.21) $$\mathbf{W}^* = \mathbf{M}_{yy} - \mathbf{M}_{yz^*}\mathbf{M}_{z^*z^*}^{-1}\mathbf{M}_{yz^*}'$$

9.13 As pointed out earlier, $\mathbf{W}$ represents the part of the sample variances and covariances of the y's that is not explained by their regression on $\mathbf{z}$. And $\mathbf{W}^*$ represents the part of the sample variances and covariances of the y's that is not explained by their regression on $\mathbf{z}^*$. With the background provided by the three preceding paragraphs, we can now express the variance ratio l in (9.4) in terms of $\boldsymbol{\beta}$ and the matrices of residuals, $\mathbf{W}$ and $\mathbf{W}^*$. Accordingly we rewrite (9.4) thus, by substituting (9.16) and (9.19) into (9.4):

$$(9.22) \qquad l = \frac{\boldsymbol{\beta}\mathbf{W}^*\boldsymbol{\beta}'}{\boldsymbol{\beta}\mathbf{W}\boldsymbol{\beta}'} \geqq 1$$

To review: $\boldsymbol{\beta}\mathbf{W}\boldsymbol{\beta}'$ represents that part of the variation of the synthetic variable $\tilde{y}$ that is unexplained by regression on *all* the z's, $z_1, \ldots, z_K$. Similarly, $\boldsymbol{\beta}\mathbf{W}^*\boldsymbol{\beta}'$ represents that part of the variation of the synthetic variable $\tilde{y}$ that is unexplained by regression on *just those z's that appear in the equation to be estimated,*[44] $z_1, \ldots, z_J$.

9.14 Let us turn to the mechanics of minimizing l with respect to $\boldsymbol{\beta}$. Since $\boldsymbol{\beta}$ is a vector, we must minimize l simultaneously with respect to all its components. Hence we must differentiate l with respect to each component of $\boldsymbol{\beta}$, set the results equal to zero, and solve the equations for the components of $\boldsymbol{\beta}$. We shall temporarily treat β_1 as a variable instead of as 1; this will be all right because l is not changed if $\boldsymbol{\beta}$ is multiplied by a constant; $\boldsymbol{\beta}$ can be normalized later to make $\beta_1 = 1$ again. This minimization process is as follows. First l is differentiated partially with respect to each β_i by the quotient rule, and the results are set equal to zero. If we let $(\mathbf{W}\boldsymbol{\beta}')_i$ stand for the ith element of the column vector $\mathbf{W}\boldsymbol{\beta}'$, and $(\mathbf{W}^*\boldsymbol{\beta}')_i$ for the ith element of $\mathbf{W}^*\boldsymbol{\beta}'$, we obtain:[45]

$$(9.23) \qquad \frac{\partial l}{\partial \beta_i} = \frac{\partial}{\partial \beta_i}\left(\frac{\boldsymbol{\beta}\mathbf{W}^*\boldsymbol{\beta}'}{\boldsymbol{\beta}\mathbf{W}\boldsymbol{\beta}'}\right)$$

$$= 2\frac{\boldsymbol{\beta}\mathbf{W}\boldsymbol{\beta}'(\mathbf{W}^*\boldsymbol{\beta}')_i - \boldsymbol{\beta}\mathbf{W}^*\boldsymbol{\beta}'(\mathbf{W}\boldsymbol{\beta}')_i}{(\boldsymbol{\beta}\mathbf{W}\boldsymbol{\beta}')^2} = 0 \qquad i = 1, \ldots, H$$

Then the last equality is divided by 2 and multiplied by $(\boldsymbol{\beta}\mathbf{W}\boldsymbol{\beta}')$ so that the left side's right-hand term contains $\boldsymbol{\beta}\mathbf{W}^*\boldsymbol{\beta}'/\boldsymbol{\beta}\mathbf{W}\boldsymbol{\beta}'$, which is equal to l:

$$(9.24) \qquad (\mathbf{W}^*\boldsymbol{\beta}')_i - l(\mathbf{W}\boldsymbol{\beta}')_i = 0 \qquad i = 1, \ldots, H$$

Since this is to hold for each component of the vectors $\mathbf{W}^*\boldsymbol{\beta}'$ and $\mathbf{W}\boldsymbol{\beta}'$, it may as well be written in terms of the vectors themselves:

$$(9.25) \qquad \mathbf{W}^*\boldsymbol{\beta}' - l\mathbf{W}\boldsymbol{\beta}' = (0 \cdots 0)' = \mathbf{0}'$$

[44] In what follows, difficulty would arise if either $\mathbf{W}$ or $\mathbf{W}^*$ were singular. However, there is zero probability of this, for the reduced-form covariance matrix $\boldsymbol{\Omega}$ is necessarily nonsingular (see 6.2), and $\mathbf{W}$ and $\mathbf{W}^*$ are estimators of a principal minor of $\boldsymbol{\Omega}$, so in samples with $T \geqq H$, $\mathbf{W}$ or $\mathbf{W}^*$ can be singular only with zero probability. (Recall we have assumed $T \geqq K > H + J - 1$ because we are dealing with an overidentified equation, so that indeed T will be $\geqq H$.) Since $\mathbf{W}$ and $\mathbf{W}^*$ are moment matrices, they must be positive semidefinite, and with probability 1 they must be positive definite.

[45] Compare note 30 in 5.2 regarding the derivative of a scalar with respect to a vector.

Now $\boldsymbol{\beta}'$ can be factored on the right, with the result that we must have

$$(9.26) \qquad\qquad (\mathbf{W}^* - l\mathbf{W})\boldsymbol{\beta}' = \mathbf{0}'$$

9.15   Here we find a system of homogeneous simultaneous equations whose unknowns are $\beta_1, \ldots, \beta_H$, and whose coefficients depend on $\mathbf{W}$ and $\mathbf{W}^*$ [which are matrices that can be calculated directly via (9.17) and (9.21) from observed values of the y's and z's] and on l (which we are trying to minimize). We seem to be going in a circle, for in trying to minimize l we have come to a set of equations that we cannot solve until we find the minimum value of l. But it is not as bad as it seems, for indeed we can now find the minimum value of l. We insist that (9.26) must have a solution $\boldsymbol{\beta}$ that is not a row of zeros, because not all the parameters $\beta_1, \ldots, \beta_H$ are zero; therefore the determinant of coefficients in (9.26) must be zero:[46]

$$(9.27) \qquad\qquad \det\,(\mathbf{W}^* - l\mathbf{W}) = 0$$

This equation, if written out in rows and columns, looks like this:

$$(9.28) \qquad \begin{vmatrix} w_{11}^* - lw_{11} & \cdots & w_{1H}^* - lw_{1H} \\ & \cdot & \\ & \cdot & \\ & \cdot & \\ w_{H1}^* - lw_{H1} & \cdots & w_{HH}^* - lw_{HH} \end{vmatrix} = 0$$

If this determinant is expanded, it yields a polynomial of degree H, with l as its variable, and with coefficients that we may denote by $a_0, a_1, \ldots, a_H$, to avoid spelling them out in terms of the w's and the w^*'s:

$$(9.29) \qquad\qquad a_0 l^H + a_1 l^{H-1} + \cdots + a_{H-1} l + a_H = 0$$

This polynomial equation has H numerical roots, just as a quadratic equation has two roots, a cubic three, and so forth. All the roots must be real numbers greater than or equal to 1, because of the definition of l.[47] Any one of these roots will make the determinant in (9.27) be zero, and no other value of l will do so.

9.16   Suppose we call the smallest root l_1; it is the one we want, for we are minimizing l. Then if the number l_1 is substituted for the variable

---

[46] A system of H homogeneous linear equations in H variables has a row of zeros as its only solution if the determinant of the system is not zero, and has a nonzero solution only if the determinant is zero. See Appendix A.3.

[47] As shown in 9.7, l is the ratio of two real positive numbers and must be ≥ 1, so no root of (9.27) makes sense for us unless it is real and ≥ 1. For the ingredients of a proof that *all* the roots of (9.27) are real and ≥ 1, see Koopmans and Hood [1953], pp. 186–189, especially theorem 1. It will be easier to get this proof from theorem 1 *after* reading on in the text above through 9.17, for the proof results from applying theorem 1 to the matrices $(\mathbf{W}^* - \mathbf{W})$ and $\mathbf{W}$ to show that $l - 1$ must be real and ≥ 0, and that hence l is real and ≥ 1. See also Appendix A.5.

l in the set of equations (9.26), the result is a set of *H* homogeneous equations,

$$(9.30) \qquad (\mathbf{W}^* - l_1\mathbf{W})\hat{\boldsymbol\beta}' = \mathbf{0}'$$

with a zero determinant, in the *H* unknowns $\hat{\beta}_1, \ldots, \hat{\beta}_H$. Then there is an infinite number of nonzero solutions[48] for $\hat{\boldsymbol\beta}$, which is to be expected because we have not yet applied the normalization rule $\beta = 1$. Of course we hope that *after* this normalization, all the solutions will be identical. If so, then we have a unique set of estimators $\hat{\beta}_2, \ldots, \hat{\beta}_H$ that are the limited-information estimators we seek. Fortunately, if the order condition for the identifiability of $\boldsymbol\beta$ is met, it turns out that, except in samples that occur only with probability zero,[49] all of the infinite number of solutions of (9.30) are constant multiples of each other, so that after normalization the limited-information estimators $\hat{\beta}_2, \ldots, \hat{\beta}_H$ are indeed unique. The limited-information estimator of $\boldsymbol\gamma$ can then be obtained as suggested by (9.3), thus:

$$(9.31) \qquad \hat{\boldsymbol\gamma} = -\hat{\boldsymbol\beta}\mathbf{P}^* = -\hat{\boldsymbol\beta}\mathbf{M}_{yz^*}\mathbf{M}_{z^*z^*}^{-1}$$

If there is a constant term and it is being treated explicitly (recall 4.11 and 9.9), then its estimator $\hat{\gamma}_J$ will not be included in (9.31). In that case it is estimated, as is usual with constants, by requiring that the mean values of the variables **y** and **z*** satisfy the estimate of equation (9.1), thus:

$$(9.32) \qquad \hat{\gamma}_J = -\bar{y}_1 - \sum_2^H \hat{\beta}_i \bar{y}_i - \sum_1^{J-1} \hat{\gamma}_j \bar{z}_j = -\hat{\boldsymbol\beta}\bar{\mathbf{y}}' - \hat{\boldsymbol\gamma}\bar{\mathbf{z}}^{*'}$$

9.17 Let us now review this procedure briefly before proceeding to discuss amendments that will permit the identical results to be computed more cheaply. First, the moment matrices $\mathbf{M}_{yy}$, $\mathbf{M}_{yz}$, and $\mathbf{M}_{zz}$ are calculated directly from observed data (note that $\mathbf{M}_{yz^*}$ is a part of $\mathbf{M}_{yz}$, and $\mathbf{M}_{z^*z^*}$ is a part of $\mathbf{M}_{zz}$). Second, the matrices **W** and **W*** are calculated from (9.17) and (9.21). Third, equation (9.27), $|\mathbf{W}^* - l\mathbf{W}| = 0$, is solved for its smallest root l_1. Fourth, l_1 is substituted for *l* in equation (9.26), to get $(\mathbf{W}^* - l_1\mathbf{W})\hat{\boldsymbol\beta}' = \mathbf{0}'$. Fifth, the preceding equation is solved for the estimators $\hat{\boldsymbol\beta}$, the components of the solution being normalized so that $\hat{\beta}_1 = 1$.

---

[48] If any root *other than* the smallest l_1 is substituted for *l* in (9.26), we also get a system of *H* homogeneous equations of the same form as (9.30) with an infinite number of solutions for $\boldsymbol\beta$, but these do not interest us because we seek to *minimize l*.

[49] If the order condition for the identifiability of $\boldsymbol\beta$ is met, then except for samples that occur with probability zero the smallest root l_1 of (9.27) will be a single root; see Koopmans and Hood [1953], p. 173, for this assertion without proof. If a root l_i is a single root, the rank of $\mathbf{W}^* - l_i\mathbf{W}$ is just equal to $H - 1$ (see a proof in Koopmans and Hood [1953], pp. 195–196), so that (9.30) indeed has a unique solution for $\hat{\boldsymbol\beta}$ after normalizing.

Sixth, and last, the estimators $\hat{\boldsymbol{\beta}}$ are substituted into (9.31) above to get $\hat{\boldsymbol{\gamma}}$ and if necessary into (9.32) to get $\hat{\gamma}_J$.

9.18 The procedure just described and summarized will indeed lead to the limited-information estimators $\hat{\boldsymbol{\beta}}$ and $\hat{\gamma}_1 \cdots \hat{\gamma}_J$. However, as is often the case, the computation method that follows the steps of the derivation is not the most economical of time and effort. It happens to be much easier to find the *largest* root than the smallest root of an equation like (9.27), because a repetitive process has been devised in which successively higher and higher powers of all the roots are added together, so that eventually the largest root comes to dominate the result and can be isolated with any desired degree of accuracy.[50] Thus (9.26) will now be recast in a different form, (9.37) below, whose *largest* root λ_1 is $1/(l_1 - 1)$, which we shall seek in order to estimate $\boldsymbol{\beta}$. In order to do this we shall first rewrite (9.26) by adding and subtracting $\mathbf{W}$ in the matrix $\mathbf{W}^* - l\mathbf{W}$, and multiplying by the scalar $1/(l - 1)$. The result is as follows (if $l_1 = 1$, the last step above is impossible[51]):

$$(9.33) \qquad \frac{1}{l-1}[\mathbf{W}^* - \mathbf{W} - (l - 1)\mathbf{W}]\boldsymbol{\beta}' = \mathbf{0}'$$

Now we multiply on the left by $(\mathbf{W}^* - \mathbf{W})^{-1}$ and perform the indicated multiplication by $1/(l - 1)$ to obtain the following (if $\mathbf{W}^* - \mathbf{W}$ is singular we cannot multiply by its inverse[51]):

$$(9.34) \qquad \left[\frac{1}{l-1}\mathbf{I} - (\mathbf{W}^* - \mathbf{W})^{-1}\mathbf{W}\right]\boldsymbol{\beta}' = \mathbf{0}'$$

Now define two new symbols:

$$(9.35) \qquad \lambda = \frac{1}{l-1}$$

$$(9.36) \qquad \mathbf{Q} = (\mathbf{W}^* - \mathbf{W})^{-1}\mathbf{W}$$

Substituting λ and $\mathbf{Q}$ into (9.34) yields

$$(9.37) \qquad (\lambda\mathbf{I} - \mathbf{Q})\boldsymbol{\beta}' = \mathbf{0}'$$

In order for this equation system to have a nonzero solution for $\boldsymbol{\beta}$, as we insist it must, its determinant must be zero:

$$(9.38) \qquad \det(\lambda\mathbf{I} - \mathbf{Q}) = 0$$

9.19 Several remarks about the two preceding equations are in order. *First*, the roots of (9.38), that is, the values of λ that satisfy it, are known as the *characteristic roots* of the matrix $\mathbf{Q}$. For each of these roots

---

[50] This proceess is described in Appendix A.5.

[51] In an overidentified equation it cannot happen except with probability zero that $l_1 = 1$ or that $\mathbf{W}^* - \mathbf{W}$ is singular. In a just-identified equation both of these must happen; this is discussed in 9.21.

there is a corresponding solution of (9.37) for β; each such solution is a vector known as a *characteristic vector* of Q. The characteristic vector corresponding to a given root λ_i is not uniquely determined because $\det(\lambda_i I - Q) = 0$, but if the rank of $\lambda_i I - Q$ is $H - 1$, then the ith characteristic vector is unique except for multiplication by a constant. *Second*, the largest characteristic root λ_1 of Q is equal to $1/(l_1 - 1)$ because of (9.35). If l_1 should be at its minimum possible value of 1, then λ_1 is infinite. If l_1 increases to infinity, then λ_1 decreases to zero. *Third*, if the order condition for the identification if β is met, λ_1 will be a single root and $\hat\beta_2, \ldots, \hat\beta_H$ obtained from solving (9.37) will be unique after normalization makes $\hat\beta_1 = 1$, except for samples that occur with probability zero.[52] We assume that such exceptional samples do not occur. *Fourth*, the iterative procedure mentioned earlier will give numerical values not only for the largest characteristic root λ_1 of Q, but also directly for the characteristic vector associated with λ_1. When this vector is normalized to make $\hat\beta_1 = 1$, its other components are $\hat\beta_2, \ldots, \hat\beta_H$, the limited-information estimators. The iterative procedure is described in Appendix A.5. It is economical whenever $H \geqq 3$. (When $H = 2$, i.e., when the equation to be estimated contains only two jointly dependent variables, then (9.38) is simply a quadratic equation and it can easily be solved for its two roots λ_1 and λ_2.)

9.20 Let us now review the computation procedure involving the quicker method described in 9.18–19 for the limited-information estimators of the parameters β and $\gamma_1 \cdots \gamma_J$ in a structural equation such as (9.1) under the assumptions of Model 3 (normal). The steps are:

1. Compute the moment matrices M_{yy}, M_{yz}, and M_{zz} defined in (9.7). (Note that M_{yz*} and M_{z*z*} are included in M_{yz} and M_{zz} respectively.)

2. Compute the square matrix W, given in (9.17) as

$$M_{yy} - M_{yz}M_{zz}^{-1}M_{yz}'$$

3. Compute $M_{yz*}M_{z*z*}^{-1}$ (to be used in getting the estimate of γ in step 7).

4. Compute $W^* - W$, which by (9.17) and (9.21) is equal to

$$M_{yz}M_{zz}^{-1}M_{yz}' - M_{yz*}M_{z*z*}^{-1}M_{yz*}'$$

(Note that the first term is already available from step 2.)

5. Compute[53] $Q = (W^* - W)^{-1}W$.

---

[52] The rank of $\lambda_1 I - Q$ is equal to the rank of $W^* - l_1 W$ if $l_1 \neq 1$ and $W^* - W$ is nonsingular, because the rank of a matrix is not changed if it is multiplied by a scalar or by a nonsingular matrix. Then footnote 49 (suitably interpreted) applies to (9.37) as well as to (9.30).

[53] If $W^* - W$ is singular, this cannot be done; see 9.21 below.

6. Compute λ_1 [the largest root of (9.38), $\det(\lambda\mathbf{I} - \mathbf{Q}) = 0$] and solve $(\lambda_1\mathbf{I} - \mathbf{Q})\hat{\boldsymbol{\beta}}' = \mathbf{0}'$ for $\hat{\boldsymbol{\beta}}$ and normalize the solution so that $\hat{\beta}_1 = 1$, to obtain the limited-information estimators[54] $\hat{\beta}_2, \ldots, \hat{\beta}_H$.
7. Compute $\hat{\boldsymbol{\gamma}}$ from (9.31), $\hat{\boldsymbol{\gamma}} = -\hat{\boldsymbol{\beta}}\mathbf{M}_{yz*}\mathbf{M}_{z*z*}^{-1}$.
8. If necessary, compute $\hat{\gamma}_J$ from (9.32), $\hat{\gamma}_J = -\hat{\boldsymbol{\beta}}\bar{\mathbf{y}}' - \hat{\boldsymbol{\gamma}}\bar{\mathbf{z}}*'$.

This completes the derivation of the limited-information estimators of the parameters $\boldsymbol{\beta}$ and $\gamma_1 \cdots \gamma_J$ in a structural equation such as (9.1).

9.21 Additional light will be thrown on the limited-information method by the examination of two special cases. First, consider the case in which (9.1) contains two or more y's but is *just identified*. From the discussion in Sections 7 and 8, we know that then the values of the β's can be chosen so that in the estimated regression of the composite endogenous variable $\tilde{y}$ on all the z's in the model, the coefficients of the excluded z's $(z_{J+1}, \ldots, z_K)$ turn out to be *exactly* zero. Therefore $\mathbf{W}^* = \mathbf{W}$, so that $\mathbf{W}^* - \mathbf{W}$ is singular and (9.34) has no meaning. Also in this case $\boldsymbol{\beta}\mathbf{W}^*\boldsymbol{\beta}' = \boldsymbol{\beta}\mathbf{W}\boldsymbol{\beta}'$, and the variance ratio l is equal to 1, so that equation (9.26) reduces to the identity $\mathbf{0}' = \mathbf{0}'$, and no information about $\boldsymbol{\beta}$ can be obtained from it. But do not despair, for then the indirect least-squares method will work and will make $l = 1$ so that the variance ratio is minimized as required. The procedure is then to estimate the reduced form by least-squares regressions of y_i on z as in (9.11), substitute the resulting estimator $\boldsymbol{P}$ for $\boldsymbol{\Pi}$ in (7.4)–(7.5), solve (7.5) for $\hat{\beta}_2, \ldots, \hat{\beta}_H$, and use these estimators in (7.4) to obtain $\hat{\boldsymbol{\gamma}}$. If *every* equation in a model is just identified, then limited-information estimators, full-information estimators, indirect least-squares estimators, instrumental-variables estimators, and two-stage least-squares estimators (see Section 10) are identical. See 9.23–24 for related remarks and references, and Tables 12.1–2 for a summary.

9.22 As the second special case, consider what happens to the limited-information method when the equation to be estimated has *only one current endogenous variable*, that is, $H = 1$. In this case the least-squares estimators of the equation are maximum-likelihood estimators, and we should expect that the limited-information method will yield the least-squares estimators. Let us see whether it does. Since $H = 1$, $\tilde{y}$ is simply equal to y_1. The vector $\boldsymbol{\beta}$ reduces to a scalar, β_1, and we always choose $\beta_1 = 1$ as our normalization, so there is no difficulty in estimating $\boldsymbol{\beta}$; we have simply $\hat{\beta}_1 = 1$. Then we can pass directly to step 7, the computation of $\hat{\boldsymbol{\gamma}}$ from (9.31). This reduces to the least-squares regression of y_1 on $-\mathbf{z}^*$, as expected:

$$(9.39) \qquad \hat{\boldsymbol{\gamma}} = -\mathbf{m}_{y_1z*}\mathbf{M}_{z*z*}^{-1}$$

[54] As stated in 9.19, if $H \geq 3$ step 6 can be done most quickly by a repetitive process described in Appendix A.5.

9.23 So far in this section we have dealt only with the problem of obtaining point estimators $\hat{\beta}_2, \ldots, \hat{\beta}_H$ and $\hat{\gamma}_1, \ldots, \hat{\gamma}_J$, of the parameters in equation (9.1). Because of our assumption (e) that the disturbances u_{it} are random variables, these limited-information estimators are random variables too, with probability distributions. What are their properties? Table 9.1 (p. 426) gives some of the results that are known and gives references to assertions and proofs concerning these properties in the published literature. The table is an integral part of this section, and its substance is not repeated in the text. The proofs are in some cases exceedingly inaccessible, partly because of being written in very concise and relatively advanced mathematical language, and in some cases because of being in unpublished form, particularly the proof of asymptotic efficiency in Model 3 (normal), which is given in Rubin [1948a]. Note of course that Table 9.1 applies also to least-squares estimators in single-equation models (including reduced-form equations); this is shown in 9.22.

9.24 In reading the literature cited in Table 9.1, and in comparing it with our assumptions and models and our discussion of limited-information estimators' properties in Table 9.1, some difficulties of translation and interpretation will almost certainly be encountered. The following remarks may be helpful in avoiding or facing these difficulties. *First*, our Model 3 and Model 3 (normal) are adapted from the assumptions made by Koopmans, Rubin, and Leipnik [1950], pp. 56–60, 70–72, 112–113, and 133–134. The only difference in substance is that whereas we *assume* that moments of all predetermined variables are well behaved in the limit [see assumption (h)], they treat this property as one to be *proved* from the following assumptions: (1) The system of difference equations formed by the model is dynamically stable; (2) there exist finite limits of all second-order moments of strictly exogenous variables as $T \to \infty$ (where "moments" is used in their sense, equivalent to $1/T$ times ours); (3) there exist finite moments (again in their sense of the term), of some order greater than 4, of the distribution of disturbances, and their distribution obeys our assumptions (e) and (f).[55] *Second*, our Model 3 (normal) is equivalent to the set of assumptions made by Koopmans and Hood [1953] on their pp. 117–121, 124, and 149 (note 54) for their model $\mathfrak{S}_T$, except that apparently through an oversight they neglected to mention any assumption like (h) about the asymptotic behavior of the moment matrix of predetermined variables.[56] *Third*, our Model 3 (normal) is essentially

---

[55] They do not give their proof; see their pp. 133–136, including Theorem 3.3.4. Durbin [1960] has remarked (p. 140) that they neglect to mention one further necessary condition for this proof, namely, that the matrix of moments (in their sense) of predetermined variables is nonsingular in the limit as $T \to \infty$.

[56] The assumption that $\mathbf{M}_{zz}$ has a finite probability limit is apparently not necessary for consistency in all cases (see Rubin [1950] for a proof of consistency in a simple unstable equation), but I know of no general proofs that do not use it.

TABLE 9.1 Some Properties of the Limited-Information Estimators $\hat{\beta}$ and $\hat{\gamma}_1 \cdots \hat{\gamma}_J$ of the Parameters β and $\gamma_1 \cdots \gamma_J$ in Equation (9.1) under Different Models

Model Assumed (see 2.4)	Properties of Limited-Information Estimators under Assumed Model	References (see note below)
3	quasi-maximum-likelihood	K & H pp. (117–125, 149), 144–146, 162–163
	consistent and asymptotically normal	KR & L pp. (56–60, 70–72, 112–113, 133–134), 133–148 K & H pp. (117–125, 149), 146–147, 163 C & R pp. 201–202, 207–210 A & R pp. (570–579), 574–580 Durbin [1960] pp. 139–150
3 (normal)	maximum-likelihood	K & H pp. (117–125, 149), 144–146, 162–163
	consistent and asymptotically normal	same as for Model 3
	asymptotically efficient as compared with other estimators using the same *a priori* and observed information (not as compared with full-information estimators)	K & H pp. (117–125, 149), 146–147, 163
	a consistent estimator of the related asymptotic variance-covariance matrix is available	KR & L pp. (56–60, 70–72, 112–113, 133–134), 133–153 K & H pp. (117–125, 149), 177–178 C & D pp. (238–245), 245–246, 268–269, 276

Note concerning references cited above:
A & R stands for Anderson and Rubin [1950].
C & D stands for Chernoff and Divinsky [1953].
C & R stands for Chernoff and Rubin [1953].
K & H stands for Koopmans and Hood [1953].
KR & L stands for Koopmans Rubin and Leipnik [1950].
Page numbers in parentheses refer to descriptions of the models and assumptions used.

equivalent to that assumed by Chernoff and Rubin [1953], except that apparently through an oversight on pp. 201–202 (but not on pp. 207–210) they neither give a substitute for nor mention the assumption that $1/T$ times the matrix of moments (as defined in this book) of predetermined variables has an *expectation* that in the limit is equal to its assumed probability limit. *Fourth*, it appears that the assumptions made by Anderson and Rubin [1950], pp. 570–579, and by Chernoff and Rubin [1953], pp. 207–210, are somewhat weaker than Model 3 in some respects but are satisfied by Model 3, so that the consequences of those assumptions follow from Model 3. *Fifth*, Anderson and Rubin [1949] (which derives the limited-information estimators) and [1950] use a somewhat different approach from that taken by the other references in Table 9.1 and by this book, and their exposition is accordingly least similar to the others; that is why we have referred to it so seldom. *Sixth*, corresponding summary statements about related estimation methods and relevant literature can be found elsewhere in this chapter as follows: for least squares, 3.14, 3.26, 3.34, and Section 11; for the full-information method, 6.8 and 7.3; for indirect least squares and instrumental variables, 7.3–5 and 7.10; for two-stage least squares, 10.16 and 10.19–20. For remarks concerning several methods, see also 9.21, 10.20, and Section 12, especially the summary in Tables 12.1–2.

9.25 We turn now to a brief account of the asymptotic variances and covariances associated with $\hat{\beta}$ and $\hat{\gamma}_1 \cdots \hat{\gamma}_J$. The fundamental theorem concerning the asymptotic properties of the maximum-likelihood estimator $\hat{\theta}$ of a single parameter θ in a *univariate* distribution with *independent* observations states the following.[57] Let $F(x_1, \ldots, x_T \mid \theta)$ be the joint density or likelihood function for a sample of size T, the T observations of x being *independent* of each other. Let L stand for $\log_e F$, in conformity with our earlier use of the symbol L. Note that L, considered as the logarithm of the likelihood function, depends on T. Then under quite general conditions, the probability distribution of the variable $\sqrt{T}(\hat{\theta} - \theta)$ has a fixed normal limiting distribution whose mean is zero[58] and whose variance is a constant, thus:

$$(9.40) \qquad \text{asymptotic var } \sqrt{T}(\hat{\theta} - \theta) = - \plim_{T \to \infty} T\left(\frac{\partial^2 L}{\partial \theta^2}\right)^{-1}$$

---

[57] Cramér [1946], pp. 500–503. Observe that his notation differs from that used here; he works with the logarithm of the distribution of a *single* observation, rather than with the logarithm of the *joint* distribution of observations from 1 to T. See also Koopmans and Hood [1953], pp. 177–178, who work with $1/T$ times the logarithm of the joint distribution. Doss [1962] extends Cramér's result to several parameters under weaker conditions.

[58] Hence $\hat{\theta}$ is an approximately and asymptotically unbiased estimator of θ.

where the plim is based on $F(x_1, \ldots, x_T \mid \theta)$ and the derivative is evaluated at the true value of θ. The approximate variance of $\hat{\theta}$ for finite samples (meaning the exact variance of the approximating distribution of $\hat{\theta}$) is $1/T$ times (9.40), which is approximated by

$$(9.41) \qquad \text{approx var } \hat{\theta} = -\left(\frac{\partial^2 L}{\partial \theta^2}\right)^{-1} = -\left(\frac{\partial^2 \log_e F}{\partial \theta^2}\right)^{-1}$$

It may be estimated consistently by evaluating the derivative at the estimated value $\hat{\theta}$. It approaches zero as $T \to \infty$.[59]

9.26 This result can be readily generalized to the *joint* likelihood function of the maximum-likelihood estimator $\hat{\boldsymbol{\theta}}$ of a vector of parameters $\boldsymbol{\theta}$. Let $F(\mathbf{x} \mid \boldsymbol{\theta})$ be the joint density or likelihood function of $x_1, \ldots, x_T$, $\theta_1, \ldots, \theta_K$, with the observations x_t being independent of each other. Now redefine L to stand for $\log_e F(\mathbf{x} \mid \boldsymbol{\theta})$. Then under quite general conditions $\sqrt{T}(\hat{\boldsymbol{\theta}} - \boldsymbol{\theta})$ has a joint normal limiting distribution with zero mean and with

$$(9.42) \quad \text{asymptotic cov } [\sqrt{T}(\hat{\boldsymbol{\theta}} - \boldsymbol{\theta})', \sqrt{T}(\hat{\boldsymbol{\theta}} - \boldsymbol{\theta})] = -\plim_{T \to \infty} TL^{-1}$$

where $\mathbf{L}$ is defined as the matrix whose typical element is $\partial^2 L / \partial \theta_i \, \partial \theta_j$. In analogy to (9.41) we also have

$$(9.43) \qquad \text{approx cov } (\hat{\boldsymbol{\theta}}', \hat{\boldsymbol{\theta}}) = -\mathbf{L}^{-1}$$

This approximate covariance matrix may be estimated by evaluating the derivatives in $\mathbf{L}$ at the point of estimated values $\hat{\theta}_1, \ldots, \hat{\theta}_K$. Its elements approach zero as $T \to \infty$.

9.27 The generalization of the results given in the foregoing paragraph to cases in which the observations are *not* independent (which are the interesting cases in economics) has been accomplished gradually. Wald [1948] deals with the estimation of a single parameter from non-independent data for a single observable random variable. Mann and Wald [1943] deal with a system of simultaneous equations having no exogenous variables (other than a constant term). Koopmans, Rubin, and Leipnik [1950] deal with a case similar to what we call Model 3 (normal). Other references relevant to Model 3 and Model 3 (normal) are given in Table 9.1. We shall defer further discussion of the asymptotic variance-covariance matrix associated with limited-information estimators until Section 10, which deals with the two-stage least-squares method, since (a) the two methods have the same asymptotic variance-covariance matrix (see 10.19) and (b) its estimation is easier via two-stage least squares.

---

[59] Hence $\hat{\theta}$ is a consistent estimator of θ.

9.28 The limited-information estimators' properties we have discussed so far, stated in Table 9.1, are all asymptotic properties, meaning that they are only approximately relevant for samples of finite size. Some results are beginning to emerge for the so-called small-sample properties of these and related estimators; more will be said about this in 12.9 ff.

9.29 As suggested early in this section, some of the assumptions of Model 3 stated in Section 2 can be relaxed without destroying all the desirable properties of the limited-information estimators. Table 9.1 has already noted that assumption (k), requiring disturbances to be normally distributed, is not necessary to obtain consistency and asymptotic normality of the limited-information estimators.

9.30 Assumptions (a) and (b) can be modified as indicated in assumption (l), to permit in the model stochastic equations that are *non-linear in variables* but *linear in unknown parameters*. If Model 3 is altered in this way, the limited-information estimators remain consistent.[60] The application of the limited-information method in this case requires the introduction of a new set of variables so chosen that the equation to be estimated will be linear *in those variables*. This technique has already been discussed and illustrated in III.10.4–10, and again in VIII.4. Those ten paragraphs are to be considered as part of this section and should be reread now.

9.31 As an additional example, consider the following nonlinear production function (where x is real output, n is employment, and k_{-1} is real capital stock at the end of the preceding period):

$$(9.44) \qquad x = \alpha_0 + \alpha_1 n + \alpha_2 n^2 + \alpha_3 nk_{-1} + \alpha_4 k_{-1}^2 + \alpha_5 k_{-1} + u$$

Here x and n are jointly dependent and k_{-1} is predetermined. This equation is linear in the unknown parameters $\alpha_0, \ldots, \alpha_5$ and can be made linear in variables if new variables are defined equal respectively to n^2, nk_{-1}, and k_{-1}^2. Both n^2 and nk_{-1} are jointly dependent, for both have their current values determined by the current-period operation of the system, even though nk_{-1} involves the predetermined variable k_{-1} as well as the jointly dependent variable n [see note 47 in III.10.8, and the definition of $f_j(y_1, \ldots, y_G)$ in III.10.9, for remarks explaining this]. Accordingly we can rechristen the variables in (9.44) as follows, using y's for jointly dependent variables and z's for predetermined variables as usual (we now treat the constant term explicitly and so use no dummy variable):

$$(9.45) \qquad \begin{aligned} y_1 &= x & z_1 &= k_{-1}^2 \\ y_2 &= n & z_2 &= k_{-1}^{\,} \\ y_3 &= n^2 & y_4 &= nk_{-1} \end{aligned}$$

---

[60] See Anderson and Rubin [1950], Theorem 2, p. 574; Chernoff and Rubin [1953], pp. 210–212.

The nonlinear production function (9.44) now can be written as a linear equation, thus:

$$(9.46) \qquad y_1 = \alpha_0 + \alpha_1 y_2 + \alpha_2 y_3 + \alpha_3 y_4 + \alpha_4 z_1 + \alpha_5 z_2 + u$$

The limited-information method can be applied directly to (9.46), using $(z_1 \ z_2)$ as the vector $\mathbf{z}^*$ of included predetermined variables, and using the vector of all predetermined variables appearing in the model as $\mathbf{z}$. There may be some exact *nonlinear* relations among the variables $z_1, \ldots, z_K$ that make up $\mathbf{z}$, similar to the relation $z_1 = z_2{}^2$ in (9.46), but assumption (c) requires that there be no exact *linear* relations among them. In this case the first step in the limited-information estimation process is to estimate by least squares the parameters of a set of linear approximations to certain equations of the nonlinear reduced form of the model (in analogy to the case of a linear model, where the first step is to estimate by least squares the reduced-form equations for the y's that appear in the equation, as in steps 1 and 2 of 9.20). For each of the jointly dependent variables $y_1, \ldots, y_4$ in the linearized structural equation (9.46) being estimated (including the newly defined variables $y_3 = n^2$ and $y_4 = nk_{-1}$), a linear approximate reduced-form equation is estimated by least squares. The predetermined variables in these linear approximate reduced-form equations are z_1 and z_2 (i.e., k_{-1}^2 and k_{-1}) from the structural equation being estimated, and the predetermined variables from the rest of the model too. That is, the matrices $\mathbf{M}_{yy}$, $\mathbf{M}_{yz}$, and $\mathbf{M}_{zz}$ are computed using $y_1, \ldots, y_4, z_1, z_2$, and the predetermined variables in the rest of the model; then the steps listed in 9.20 are carried out just as described there. Other cases of equations linear in parameters but not in variables may be handled the same way.

9.32   The defining of new variables may be resorted to even when there are no nonlinearities in the equation to be estimated, if the equation contains any term(s) in which a coefficient is applied to a linear function of several variables (this function itself having no unknown parameters). For example, if x is real income before tax and t is real tax payments, a consumption equation might contain a term such as $\alpha(x - t)$. We could then define a new variable, real disposable income $x - t$, denoted perhaps by y_1. Then when the consumption function is estimated, by whatever method, the term αy_1 would be used in place of $(x - t)$.[61]

9.33   Assumptions (a) and (d) can be modified as indicated in assumption (m), to permit the omission of observations on a subset of the variables, *provided* that that subset is not necessary for the identification of the equation to be estimated. (All variables included in the equation must be observed, and in general some excluded z's, to satisfy this

---

[61] See also Chernoff and Divinsky [1953], pp. 237–241.

assumption.) If Model 3 is modified in this way, the limited-information estimators remain consistent.[62] (Note that if Model 3 is modified by adopting *both* assumptions (m) and (l) *at the same time*, however, consistency is not guaranteed.)[63] As an example, turn back to equation (3.14) of VIII.3.14. It is overidentified by virtue of excluding four variables in a model where the required number $G - 1$ is 3, as shown by its criterion matrix (VIII.3.18). The predetermined variables excluded are Y and W. If observations are available for its included variables q' and p', and for *one* of the excluded predetermined variables Y or W, chosen so that the criterion matrix (3.18) is not singular after the column in it corresponding to the *unobserved* predetermined variable is removed, then (VIII.3.14) can be consistently estimated by the limited-information method.

9.34 There are at least three reasons why we might not use all the excluded z's in estimating a single equation like (9.1). *First*, we might not have enough *a priori* information to specify what they all are. When this is the case it is very good to be able to estimate a single equation anyway, without having first to specify the complete list of all the predetermined variables in the whole model. *Second*, even if we have listed all the z's in the model, some of the ones excluded from the equation being estimated may not be observable.[64] *Third*, the sample size T may not be large enough to make it desirable or even possible to use all the excluded predetermined variables in estimating a single equation. This third possibility is particularly relevant if the number of predetermined variables that appear to have a bearing on a particular problem is quite large, that is, larger than or almost as large as the number of observations available. We have seen in 5.4 that the effective or adjusted sample size in a regression involving K independent variables (including a constant term if any) is $T - K$ where T is the actual number of observations. Accordingly in a reduced-form regression of an endogenous variable on K predetermined variables, the effective number of observations is $T - K$. Therefore if T does not exceed K by very much, accuracy of estimation will be very poor; and if T is less than K, our assumption (c) will be violated, and there will be no unique estimates at all. In such a situation the estimated variance of shifts in the regression line may actually be decreased rather than increased by the omission of one of the predetermined variables, if the variable omitted has a small enough effect on the sum of squared residuals to be overcome by the change in $T - K$. For this reason, if the sample is small it is sometimes wise *not* to use all the excluded z's that appear to be relevant

[62] See Anderson and Rubin [1950], Theorem 1, p. 574.

[63] See Anderson and Rubin [1950], Theorem 2, p. 574, and note that this theorem assumes that all of the z's are observed (in their notation, $r_t = 0$).

[64] In VII.3 the problem of unobservable variables in the equation to be estimated was discussed.

for the limited-information estimation of an equation, but to use only as many as (or a few more than) are necessary for identification.

9.35 Certain of the assumptions of Model 3 cannot be relaxed without destroying the consistency of the limited-information estimators of (9.1). In particular, if the true means of the disturbances at period t are not independent of the values of all the z's at periods t and earlier, the estimators are not consistent, nor do they have any other of the desirable properties discussed above.

10   THE TWO-STAGE LEAST-SQUARES METHOD AND RELATED METHODS: PROPERTIES, COVARIANCES, AND COMPUTATION

10.1 At the end of Section 8 we noted that an alternative to the limited-information method for estimating an overidentified equation containing two or more jointly dependent variables was put forward by Theil and also by Basmann. Basmann [1957], p. 77, calls it a *generalized classical linear estimation method*. Theil [1958], p. 225, and [1961], p. 228, calls it the *two-stage least-squares method*, and he also develops in the succeeding two or three pages a class of related methods that he calls the *k-class*. For a useful interpretation, see Klein [1955]. We discuss the methods under the assumptions of Model 3.

10.2 Let us first give a brief and simple description of the estimation technique that is used by the two-stage least-squares method. The steps are these: (a) From among the jointly dependent variables in the equation to be estimated, select the *one* that is to be used as *the* dependent variable in the second stage of the process described below. (b) Compute the least-squares estimates of the reduced-form equations for the *remaining* jointly dependent variables in the equation [all but the one selected in step (a)], using all the predetermined variables in the model (this step is the "first stage" of the two-stage process). (c) Replace the observed data for these remaining jointly dependent variables (all but one of those in the equation) by their *calculated* values from the reduced form as estimated in step (b). (d) Compute the least-squares regression of the selected dependent variable on the set of variables consisting of the *calculated* values of the other jointly dependent variables obtained in step (c) and the *observed* values of the predetermined variables in the equation (this step is the "second stage" of the process). The resulting estimates are the two-stage least-squares estimates of the parameters of the equation to be estimated. Regarding two-stage least-squares residuals, see 10.21 below.

10.3 To give an explicit mathematical account of the two-stage least-squares method, it will be convenient to have some special notation. We shall use many of the same symbols used in the preceding section on the limited-information method and a few additional ones growing out of and consistent with them. Matrix notation analogous to that in Section 5 is used. For the purpose of facilitating comparisons between this book and Theil [1958] and [1961] and Basmann [1957], we present their notation along with ours in Table 10.1. Henceforth the discussion will be conducted in terms of our own notation only. Table 10.1 (except the last two columns) is to be considered an integral part of the text, for much of what is given there is not repeated in the text. Notice that equation numbers are attached to certain of the entries for reference. Notice also that y stands for the vector of data for the variable y_1, and that Y and V are defined for the set $y_2, \ldots, y_H$ omitting y_1.

(10.1)–(10.9)   (These equations are in Table 10.1.)

10.4   The structural equation to be estimated is given by (10.1) in extended (nonmatrix) form and by (10.2) in matrix form; it is identical with (9.1), which was the basis of the discussion of the limited-information method. The symbols for parameters and variables are presented in (10.3)–(10.8). The two-stage least-squares method proceeds from the reduced-form equations for all except one of the jointly dependent variables in the equation. Let that one variable be denoted by y_1. Then the reduced-form equations for $y_2, \ldots, y_H$ are

(10.10) $$y_{it} = \sum_1^K \pi_{ik} z_{kt} + v_{it} \qquad i = 2, \ldots, H$$

In matrix notation this can be written as follows, where Π_1 and V are implicitly defined by the context:[65]

(10.11)

$$Y' = Z'\Pi_1' + V' = Z'\begin{pmatrix} \pi_{21} & \cdots & \pi_{H1} \\ \cdot & & \cdot \\ \cdot & & \cdot \\ \cdot & & \cdot \\ \pi_{2K} & \cdots & \pi_{HK} \end{pmatrix} + \begin{pmatrix} v_{21} & \cdots & v_{H1} \\ \cdot & & \cdot \\ \cdot & & \cdot \\ \cdot & & \cdot \\ v_{2T} & \cdots & v_{HT} \end{pmatrix}$$

Now substitute for Y' from this into (10.2), as follows:

(10.12) $$y' = -(Z'\Pi_1')\beta_1' - Z^*'\gamma' + (u' - V'\beta_1')$$

If the reduced-form parameters Π_1 were *known*, then (10.12) could be regarded as an equation expressing y' as a linear function of the explanatory variables $Z'\Pi_1'$ and Z^*', and its disturbances at time t would be independent of these explanatory variables at time t because by the assumptions of Model 3 both u_t and $v_{2t}, \ldots, v_{Ht}$ are independent of z_t.

---

[65] The subscript 1 is attached to Π here, because earlier Π itself was defined to include another row corresponding to the reduced-form equation for y_1.

TABLE 10.1 Notation for Two-Stage Least-Squares and k-class Estimators of Structural Parameters in a Single Equation from a System of Simultaneous Equations

	Notation Used in This Book	Equivalent Notation[a] in Theil [1958], [1961]	Equivalent Notation[a] in Basmann [1957]
Equation to be estimated: in extended form (10.1)	$y_{1t} + \sum_{2}^{H} \beta_i y_{it}$ $+ \sum_{1}^{J} \gamma_k z_{kt} = u_t$	$y(t) - \sum_{1}^{m} \gamma_\mu y_\mu(t)$ $- \sum_{1}^{l} \beta_\lambda x_\lambda(t) = u(t)$	$\sqrt{N}\left(y_{t1} - \sum_{2}^{m} \beta_{1h} y_{th}\right.$ $\left. - \sum_{1}^{p} \gamma_{1k} x_{tk}\right) = \sqrt{N} e_{t1}$
in matrix form (10.2)	$y' = -Y'\beta_1' - Z^{*'}\gamma' + u'$	$y = Y\Gamma + X_1\beta + u$	$\sqrt{N} y_1 = \sqrt{N}(Y_1\beta_1 + X_1\gamma_1 + e_1)$
Sample size	T	T	N
Variables: jointly dependent { included	$y_1 \cdots y_H$	$y \quad y_1 \cdots y_m$	$\sqrt{N}(y_1 \cdots y_m)$
dependent { excluded	$y_{H+1} \cdots y_G$	$y_{m+1} \cdots y_{M-1}$	—
predetermined[b] { included	$z_1 \cdots z_J$	$x_1 \cdots x_l$	$\sqrt{N}(x_1 \cdots x_p)$
predetermined[b] { excluded	$z_{J+1} \cdots z_K$	$x_{l+1} \cdots x_q$	$\sqrt{N}(x_{p+1} \cdots x_q)$
disturbance	u	u	$\sqrt{N} e_1$
Parameters of: jointly dependent variables[c] (10.3)	$\beta_1 = (\beta_2 \cdots \beta_H)$	$-\Gamma' = -(\gamma_1 \cdots \gamma_m)$	$-\beta_1' = -(\beta_{12} \cdots \beta_{1m})$
predetermined variables (10.4)	$\gamma = (\gamma_1 \cdots \gamma_J)$	$-\beta' = -(\beta_1 \cdots \beta_l)$	$-\gamma_1' = -(\gamma_{11} \cdots \gamma_{1p})$
Data matrices (10.5)	$y = (y_{11} \cdots y_{1T})$	$y' = [y(1) \cdots y(T)]$	$\sqrt{N} y_1' = \sqrt{N}(y_{11} \cdots y_{N1})$
(10.6)	$Y = \begin{pmatrix} y_{21} & \cdots & y_{2T} \\ \vdots & & \vdots \\ y_{H1} & \cdots & y_{HT} \end{pmatrix}$	$Y' = \begin{pmatrix} y_1(1) & \cdots & y_1(T) \\ \vdots & & \vdots \\ y_m(1) & \cdots & y_m(T) \end{pmatrix}$	$\sqrt{N} Y_1' = \sqrt{N} \begin{pmatrix} y_{12} & \cdots & y_{N2} \\ \vdots & & \vdots \\ y_{1m} & \cdots & y_{Nm} \end{pmatrix}$

(10.7)	$Z^* = \begin{pmatrix} z_{21} & \cdots & z_{2T} \\ \vdots & & \vdots \\ z_{J1} & \cdots & z_{JT} \\ z_{K1} & \cdots & z_{KT} \end{pmatrix}$	$X_1' = \begin{pmatrix} x_1(1) & \cdots & x_1(T) \\ \vdots & & \vdots \\ x_i(1) & \cdots & x_i(T) \end{pmatrix}$	$\sqrt{N}X_1' = \sqrt{N}\begin{pmatrix} x_{11} & \cdots & x_{N1} \\ \vdots & & \vdots \\ x_{1p} & \cdots & x_{Np} \end{pmatrix}$
(10.8)	$Z = \begin{pmatrix} z_{11} & \cdots & z_{1T} \\ \vdots & & \vdots \\ z_{J1} & \cdots & z_{JT} \\ z_{K1} & \cdots & z_{KT} \end{pmatrix}$	$X' = \begin{pmatrix} x_1(1) & \cdots & x_1(T) \\ \vdots & & \vdots \\ x_\Lambda(1) & \cdots & x_\Lambda(T) \end{pmatrix}$	$\sqrt{N}X' = \sqrt{N}\begin{pmatrix} x_{11} & \cdots & x_{N1} \\ \vdots & & \vdots \\ x_{1q} & \cdots & x_{Nq} \end{pmatrix}$
Reduced-form calculated disturbances (10.9)	$\hat{V} = \begin{pmatrix} \hat{v}_{21} & \cdots & \hat{v}_{2T} \\ \vdots & & \vdots \\ \hat{v}_{H1} & \cdots & \hat{v}_{HT} \end{pmatrix}$	$V' = \begin{pmatrix} v_1(1) & \cdots & v_1(T) \\ \vdots & & \vdots \\ v_m(1) & \cdots & v_m(T) \end{pmatrix}$	$\sqrt{N}[Y_1' - Y_1'X(X'X)^{-1}X']$
Two-stage least-squares estimators	$\begin{pmatrix} \beta_1^{(1)\prime} \\ \gamma^{(1)\prime} \end{pmatrix}$	$\begin{pmatrix} \mathbf{c} \\ -\,\mathbf{b} \end{pmatrix}$	$\begin{pmatrix} \hat{\beta}_1 \\ -\,\hat{\gamma}_1 \end{pmatrix}$
k-class estimators	$\begin{pmatrix} \beta_1^{(k)\prime} \\ \gamma^{(k)\prime} \end{pmatrix}$	$\begin{pmatrix} \mathbf{c} \\ -\,\mathbf{b} \end{pmatrix}_{/k}$	—

[a] The notation given in the 3rd and 4th columns is equivalent to that given in the 2nd column in the sense that the entry in either the 3rd or the 4th column has *precisely* the same meaning in Theil's or Basmann's work as does the corresponding entry in the 2nd column in this book. See Theil [1958], pp. 208 and 224–227; [1961], pp. 208–209 and 226–231. See Basmann [1957], esp. pp. 77–78 and 80.

[b] Note that if there are any constant terms in the equations, one of the predetermined variables is a dummy always equal to 1.

[c] Basmann [1957] does not explicitly mention the components of his vectors β_1 and γ_1, so I have taken the liberty of assigning subscripts to them in a manner consistent with his explicit usage.

Therefore if $\mathbf{\Pi}_1$ were known, least squares applied to (10.12) would yield consistent estimators of $\boldsymbol{\beta}_1$ and $\boldsymbol{\gamma}$.

10.5 Of course $\mathbf{\Pi}_1$ is not known. But in Model 3 it can be estimated consistently by least squares because (10.11), being in the reduced form, fulfills the sufficient conditions for consistent least-squares estimation. Using the approach of Section 5, we see that the least-squares estimator of $\mathbf{\Pi}_1$ is $\mathbf{P}_1$, which is implicitly defined by the following equation:

$$(10.13) \quad \mathbf{Y}' = \hat{\mathbf{Y}}' + \hat{\mathbf{V}}' = \mathbf{Z}'(\mathbf{Z}\mathbf{Z}')^{-1}\mathbf{Z}\mathbf{Y}' + \hat{\mathbf{V}}' = \mathbf{Z}'\mathbf{P}_1' + \hat{\mathbf{V}}'$$

Thus $\mathbf{Y}'$ from (10.13) can be substituted into (10.2):[66]

$$(10.14) \quad \begin{aligned} \mathbf{y}' &= -\hat{\mathbf{Y}}'\boldsymbol{\beta}_1' - \mathbf{Z}^{*'}\boldsymbol{\gamma}' + (\mathbf{u}' - \hat{\mathbf{V}}'\boldsymbol{\beta}_1') \\ &= -(\mathbf{Y}' - \hat{\mathbf{V}}')\boldsymbol{\beta}_1' - \mathbf{Z}^{*'}\boldsymbol{\gamma}' + (\mathbf{u}' - \hat{\mathbf{V}}'\boldsymbol{\beta}_1') \end{aligned}$$

(In place of $\hat{\mathbf{Y}}'$ or $\mathbf{Y}' - \hat{\mathbf{V}}'$ above, we could have used either of the equivalent expressions $\mathbf{Z}'\mathbf{P}_1'$ or $\mathbf{Z}'(\mathbf{Z}\mathbf{Z}')^{-1}\mathbf{Z}\mathbf{Y}'$; the latter is convenient when the time comes for computation.) $\hat{\mathbf{Y}}'$ or $\mathbf{Y}' - \hat{\mathbf{V}}'$ in (10.14) is the matrix of calculated values of $y_2, \ldots, y_H$ from the reduced form. The two-stage least-squares method consists in applying the least-squares method to the estimation of $\boldsymbol{\beta}_1$ and $\boldsymbol{\gamma}$ in (10.14).

10.6 A heuristic argument concerning the consistency of the two-stage least-squares method under Model 3 is: (a) We know that if $\mathbf{\Pi}_1$ were known, least-squares estimation of $\boldsymbol{\beta}_1$ and $\boldsymbol{\gamma}$ in (10.12) would be consistent. (b) We know that least-squares estimation of $\mathbf{\Pi}_1$ via (10.13) is consistent, so that as the sample size T grows without limit the estimator $\hat{\mathbf{Y}}'$ in (10.14) approaches $\mathbf{Z}'\mathbf{\Pi}_1'$ and the disturbance $\mathbf{u}' - \hat{\mathbf{V}}'\boldsymbol{\beta}_1'$ in (10.14) approaches $\mathbf{u}' - \mathbf{V}'\boldsymbol{\beta}_1'$, so that (10.14) approaches (10.12). (c) Putting the two preceding points together, we see that as $T \to \infty$ the two-stage least-squares estimators of $\boldsymbol{\beta}_1$ and $\boldsymbol{\gamma}$ in (10.14) approach the consistent least-squares estimators of (10.12), and so are themselves consistent, under the assumptions of Model 3. A proof is given below in 10.10–13.

10.7 Let us now proceed to apply least squares to (10.14), following Theil but using our notation. The normal equations, in analogy to (5.6) above, are as follows, where $\boldsymbol{\beta}_1^{(1)}$ and $\boldsymbol{\gamma}^{(1)}$ denote two-stage least-squares estimators[67] of $\boldsymbol{\beta}_1$ and $\boldsymbol{\gamma}$:

$$(10.15) \quad \begin{pmatrix} \mathbf{Y} - \hat{\mathbf{V}} \\ \mathbf{Z}^* \end{pmatrix}\mathbf{y}' = \begin{pmatrix} \mathbf{Y} - \hat{\mathbf{V}} \\ \mathbf{Z}^* \end{pmatrix}(\mathbf{Y}' - \hat{\mathbf{V}}' \quad \mathbf{Z}^{*'})\begin{pmatrix} -\boldsymbol{\beta}_1^{(1)'} \\ -\boldsymbol{\gamma}^{(1)'} \end{pmatrix}$$

The product of the first two matrices on the right contains terms involving $\mathbf{Y}\hat{\mathbf{V}}'$, $\hat{\mathbf{V}}\mathbf{Y}'$, $\hat{\mathbf{V}}\hat{\mathbf{V}}'$, $\hat{\mathbf{V}}\mathbf{Z}^{*'}$, and $\mathbf{Z}^*\hat{\mathbf{V}}'$. These can be simplified as follows.

---

[66] The last member of equation (10.14) can also be thought of as the result of adding and subtracting $\hat{\mathbf{V}}'\boldsymbol{\beta}_1'$ in (10.2).

[67] The reason for this notation will be clear when k-class estimators are described.

First, consider $Z\hat{V}'$ and apply (10.13) to express $\hat{V}'$ as a function of Z and Y:

(10.16) $Z\hat{V}' = Z[Y' - Z'(ZZ')^{-1}ZY'] = ZY' - ZY' = 0$

Hence we have $Z*\hat{V}' = 0$ because it is a submatrix of $Z\hat{V}'$. Also the transposes $\hat{V}Z'$ and $\hat{V}Z*'$ are zero. Second, consider $\hat{V}Y'$ and apply (10.13) to eliminate Y':

(10.17) $\hat{V}Y' = \hat{V}Z'P_1' + \hat{V}\hat{V}' = \hat{V}\hat{V}' = Y\hat{V}'$

The next to last equality above employs the fact that $\hat{V}Z' = 0$ as in (10.16), and the last equality comes from a similar argument applied to the transpose $Y\hat{V}'$. Using (10.16) and (10.17) and multiplying together the first two matrices on the right in (10.15), we have as the normal equations:

(10.18) $$\begin{pmatrix} Y - \hat{V} \\ Z* \end{pmatrix} y' = \begin{pmatrix} YY' - \hat{V}\hat{V}' & YZ*' \\ Z*Y' & Z*Z*' \end{pmatrix} \begin{pmatrix} -\beta_1^{(1)'} \\ -\gamma^{(1)'} \end{pmatrix}$$

For notational simplicity, define the matrix X as

(10.19) $$X \equiv \begin{pmatrix} Y - \hat{V} \\ Z* \end{pmatrix} = \begin{pmatrix} \hat{Y} \\ Z* \end{pmatrix}$$

The two-stage least-squares estimator is therefore, from (10.18),

(10.20) $$\begin{pmatrix} \beta_1^{(1)'} \\ \gamma^{(1)'} \end{pmatrix} = -\begin{pmatrix} YY' - \hat{V}\hat{V}' & YZ*' \\ Z*Y' & Z*Z*' \end{pmatrix}^{-1} \begin{pmatrix} Y - \hat{V} \\ Z* \end{pmatrix} y'$$

$$= -(XX')^{-1}Xy'$$

The results obtained in this paragraph can be used to show that the two-stage least-squares estimator is a special case of the instrumental-variables estimator that was introduced in 7.5–8. The variables that must be chosen as instruments to obtain the two-stage least-squares estimator are the calculated values of $y_2, \ldots, y_H$ and the observed values of $z_1, \ldots, z_J$. Thus if the equation to be estimated, (10.2), is premultiplied by the matrix X of instrumental variables, defined in (10.19), and if the disturbance term is suppressed as usual, the resulting estimating equations for the instrumental-variables method are equivalent to the two-stage least-squares equations (10.18).

10.8 The two-stage least-squares estimator will not exist unless the matrix X above exists and XX' is nonsingular. The proof that X exists is as follows. Assumption (c) says that the rank of Z is K, which is necessary and sufficient for the existence of $(ZZ')^{-1}$, which implies that $Y - \hat{V}$ exists [see equation (10.13)], Q.E.D. The proof that XX' is nonsingular is as follows. First, note that X has $H - 1 + J$ rows and T columns. Next, note that $\mathbf{X}$ can be expressed as $\begin{pmatrix} \mathbf{P}_1 \\ \mathbf{I}_J & \mathbf{0} \end{pmatrix} \mathbf{Z}$ where $\mathbf{I}_J$ is the identity of order J, and $\mathbf{0}$ has J rows and $K - J$ columns. The matrix $\begin{pmatrix} \mathbf{P}_1 \\ \mathbf{I}_J & \mathbf{0} \end{pmatrix}$ has $H - 1 + J$ rows and K columns, with $K \geqq H - 1 + J$ by assumption (d); its rank will then be $H - 1 + J$ with probability 1, because a linearly dependent set of rows will occur only with probability zero. Now $\mathbf{Z}$ is K by T, with $T \geqq K \geqq H - 1 + J$. Hence $\mathbf{X}$ has rank $H - 1 + J$ with probability 1, so $\mathbf{XX}'$ is nonsingular with probability 1. Hence the two-stage least-squares estimator in (10.20) exists with probability 1.

10.9   The error of the two-stage least-squares estimator is obtained by subtracting the true parameter vector from the estimator in (10.20), thus:

$$(10.21) \qquad \mathbf{e}' = \begin{pmatrix} \boldsymbol{\beta}_1^{(1)'} \\ \boldsymbol{\gamma}^{(1)'} \end{pmatrix} - \begin{pmatrix} \boldsymbol{\beta}_1' \\ \boldsymbol{\gamma}' \end{pmatrix} = -(\mathbf{XX}')^{-1}\mathbf{Xu}'$$

The last step above comes from substituting for $\mathbf{y}'$ from (10.14) in (10.20). This error *does not* have zero expectation in Model 3, because $\mathbf{Y}$, which enters into it, is stochastically dependent on the disturbance $\mathbf{u}$. Indeed, in the general case the expectation of the error, and of the two-stage least-squares estimator itself, may fail to exist, because the inversion of $\mathbf{XX}'$ involves division by a determinant that is a random variable having a nonzero probability density at zero.

10.10   We now show (in 10.10–13) that in Model 3 the two-stage least-squares estimator given by (10.20) is consistent.[68] This will be done by showing that the probability limit of its error given by (10.21) is zero. If the probability limit of $\dfrac{1}{T}\mathbf{Xu}'$ is zero and if the probability limit of

---

[68] So far as I am aware, Theil in [1958] and [1961] does not prove consistency of two-stage least-squares estimators, though under assumptions similar to our Model 3 he asserts it; see his [1958], pp. 223–228 and 343, and [1961], pp. 225–232 and 343–344. Basmann [1957] presents a proof of consistency for ordinary least squares on p. 79, and a proof for two-stage least squares on pp. 79–82. Both of these proofs are offered for the case where there are no lagged endogenous variables. His proof for ordinary least squares does not do the job for models containing lagged endogenous variables, because the equality in his expression (15) on p. 79 requires that (in our notation) the conditional expectation of $u_s u_t$ given $z_{ks} z_{lt}$ be equal to $Eu_s u_t$ for all $s,t = 1, \ldots, T$ and for all $k,l = 1, \ldots, K$, which is not true if $z_{kt} \equiv y_{i,t-1}$. His method of proof for two-stage least squares is adaptable to the case where there are lagged endogenous variables. Goldberger [1964] presents a proof of consistency in a case similar to our Model 3, on pp. 272–274, but his argument for consistency in a more general case on pp. 278–280 requires stronger assumptions than he makes explicit. See 9.23–24 for related remarks and references, and Tables 12.1–2 for a summary. See also Basmann [1965].

$T(\mathbf{XX}')^{-1}$ exists, then we have[69]

$$(10.22) \quad \plim_{T \to \infty} \mathbf{e}' = -\plim (\mathbf{XX}')^{-1}\mathbf{Xu}'$$

$$= -\plim T(\mathbf{XX}')^{-1} \plim \frac{1}{T}\mathbf{Xu}' = \mathbf{0}'$$

Both of the provisos are fulfilled: First, $\plim \frac{1}{T}\mathbf{Xu}' = \mathbf{0}'$ because $\plim \mathbf{P}_1$ exists and $\mathbf{Z}$ is predetermined.[70] Second, we shall see that $\plim T(\mathbf{XX}')^{-1}$ exists when we have shown that $\plim \frac{1}{T}\mathbf{XX}'$ exists and is nonsingular,[71] a task to which we turn in the next two paragraphs.

10.11 First let us see that $\plim \frac{1}{T}\mathbf{XX}'$ exists. The matrix $\mathbf{XX}'$ can be expressed as follows [see (10.19) and (10.13)]:

$$(10.23) \quad \mathbf{XX}' = \begin{pmatrix} \mathbf{P}_1\mathbf{ZZ}'\mathbf{P}_1' & \mathbf{P}_1\mathbf{ZZ}^{*\prime} \\ \mathbf{Z}^*\mathbf{Z}'\mathbf{P}_1' & \mathbf{Z}^*\mathbf{Z}^{*\prime} \end{pmatrix}$$

Assumption (h) assures that $\frac{1}{T}\mathbf{ZZ}'$ and $\frac{1}{T}\mathbf{ZZ}^{*\prime}$ and $\frac{1}{T}\mathbf{Z}^*\mathbf{Z}^{*\prime}$ have probability limits and that $\plim \frac{1}{T}\mathbf{ZZ}'$ is nonsingular. We already have seen that in Model 3 $\mathbf{P}_1$ is a consistent estimator of $\mathbf{\Pi}_1$, that is, $\plim \mathbf{P}_1 = \mathbf{\Pi}_1$. Therefore for Model 3 we have established the existence of

$$(10.24) \quad \plim \frac{1}{T}\mathbf{XX}' = \begin{pmatrix} \mathbf{\Pi}_1 \plim \dfrac{1}{T} \mathbf{ZZ}'\mathbf{\Pi}_1' & \mathbf{\Pi}_1 \plim \dfrac{1}{T} \mathbf{ZZ}^{*\prime} \\ \plim \dfrac{1}{T} \mathbf{Z}^*\mathbf{Z}'\mathbf{\Pi}_1' & \plim \dfrac{1}{T} \mathbf{Z}^*\mathbf{Z}^{*\prime} \end{pmatrix}$$

---

[69] Recall the properties of probability limits from theorem (a) of 3.29.

[70] Using the definition of $\mathbf{X}$ above, we have

$$\plim \frac{1}{T}\mathbf{Xu}' = \plim \frac{1}{T}\begin{pmatrix} \mathbf{P}_1\mathbf{Z} \\ \mathbf{Z}^* \end{pmatrix}\mathbf{u}' = \begin{pmatrix} \plim \mathbf{P}_1 \cdot \plim \dfrac{1}{T}\mathbf{Zu}' \\ \plim \dfrac{1}{T}\mathbf{Z}^*\mathbf{u}' \end{pmatrix} = \mathbf{0}'$$

since $\plim \frac{1}{T}\mathbf{Zu}'$ is zero by the same kind of arguments used in 3.31 to show that $\plim \frac{1}{T}\Sigma v_t y_{t-1}$ is zero.

[71] See note 69.

10.12   Next the nonsingularity of (10.24) is to be shown. It is helpful for this purpose to rewrite (10.24), as follows:

$$(10.25) \qquad \operatorname{plim} \frac{1}{T} \mathbf{XX'} = \operatorname{plim} \frac{1}{T} \begin{pmatrix} \mathbf{\Pi_1 Z} \\ \mathbf{Z^*} \end{pmatrix} (\mathbf{Z'\Pi_1'} \quad \mathbf{Z^{*\prime}})$$

$$= \operatorname{plim} \frac{1}{T} \begin{pmatrix} \mathbf{\Pi_1} \\ \mathbf{I_J} \quad \mathbf{0} \end{pmatrix} \mathbf{ZZ'} \begin{pmatrix} \mathbf{\Pi_1'} \quad \mathbf{I_J} \\ \mathbf{0} \end{pmatrix}$$

$$= \begin{pmatrix} \mathbf{\Pi_1} \\ \mathbf{I_J} \quad \mathbf{0} \end{pmatrix} \operatorname{plim} \frac{1}{T} \mathbf{ZZ'} \begin{pmatrix} \mathbf{\Pi_1'} \quad \mathbf{I_J} \\ \mathbf{0} \end{pmatrix}$$

where both identity matrices are $J \times J$, the first zero matrix is J by $K - J$, and the second zero matrix is $K - J$ by J. The matrix whose first $H - 1$ rows are $\mathbf{\Pi_1}$ and whose last J rows are $(\mathbf{I} \quad \mathbf{0})$ has $H - 1 + J$ rows and K columns, with $K \geqq H - 1 + J$. Its rank will be $H - 1 + J$ if the equation is identified, because the only way for its rank to be less than $H - 1 + J$ is for the last $K - J$ columns of $\mathbf{\Pi_1}$ to contain a linearly dependent set of rows, and this cannot occur for an identified equation; recall VIII.3.36. Plim $\frac{1}{T} \mathbf{ZZ'}$ is $K \times K$ and nonsingular by assumption (h). Hence the rank of plim $\frac{1}{T} \mathbf{XX'}$ will be $H - 1 + J$, that is, plim $\frac{1}{T} \mathbf{XX'}$ will be nonsingular, for an identified equation.[72]

10.13   Therefore, from (10.22) and the surrounding text, we see that in Model 3 the two-stage least-squares estimators are consistent, that is, that

$$(10.26) \qquad \operatorname*{plim}_{T \to \infty} \begin{pmatrix} \boldsymbol{\beta}_1^{(1)\prime} \\ \boldsymbol{\gamma}^{(1)\prime} \end{pmatrix} = \begin{pmatrix} \boldsymbol{\beta}_1' \\ \boldsymbol{\gamma}' \end{pmatrix}$$

10.14   For computing purposes, it is helpful to have the two-stage least-squares estimators expressed in terms of observable data only. Using (10.13) and (10.15), we obtain

$$(10.27) \qquad \begin{pmatrix} \boldsymbol{\beta}_1^{(1)\prime} \\ \boldsymbol{\gamma}^{(1)\prime} \end{pmatrix} = - \begin{pmatrix} \mathbf{YZ'(ZZ')^{-1}ZY'} & \mathbf{YZ^{*\prime}} \\ \mathbf{Z^*Y'} & \mathbf{Z^*Z^{*\prime}} \end{pmatrix}^{-1} \begin{pmatrix} \mathbf{YZ'(ZZ')^{-1}Z} \\ \mathbf{Z^*} \end{pmatrix} \mathbf{y'}$$

10.15   Theil has proposed a class of estimators that he calls the k-class,[73] each member of the class being characterized by a (constant or

---

[72] Dr. Takeshi Amemiya gave valuable assistance concerning the arguments in 10.8 and this paragraph.

[73] Theil [1958], pp. 227–228; [1961], pp. 231–232.

variable) value of the scalar k. The general expression for the k-class estimators of equation (10.2) is to be denoted by a superscript k in parentheses; it is

$$(10.28) \quad \begin{pmatrix} \beta_1^{(k)\prime} \\ \gamma^{(k)\prime} \end{pmatrix} = - \begin{pmatrix} \mathbf{YY}' - k\hat{\mathbf{V}}\hat{\mathbf{V}}' & \mathbf{YZ}^{*\prime} \\ \mathbf{Z}^*\mathbf{Y}' & \mathbf{Z}^*\mathbf{Z}^{*\prime} \end{pmatrix}^{-1} \begin{pmatrix} \mathbf{Y} - k\hat{\mathbf{V}} \\ \mathbf{Z}^* \end{pmatrix} \mathbf{y}'$$

Ordinary and two-stage least squares are members of the k-class with k chosen equal to 0 and 1 respectively. Theil states that another member of the k-class is the limited-information estimator, the value of k being equal to the smallest root l_1 of our equation (9.27) above.

10.16 Provided k is such that plim $k = 1$, the k-class estimator is consistent in Model 3.[74] This can be seen from the fact that the consistency proof given in 10.10–13 for two-stage least squares (for which $k = 1$) will hold for any k-class estimator for which plim $k = 1$. Ordinary least squares has $k = 0$ and when applied to a member of a system of simultaneous equations it gives inconsistent estimators in general. The limited-information method has plim $l_1 = 1$.

10.17 The two-stage least-squares estimator is asymptotically normal, at least in Model 2 where all z's are exogenous,[75] and we may conjecture that it is so in Model 3 also. The statistic $\sqrt{T}e$, that is, $\sqrt{T}$ times the error of the two-stage least-squares estimator, has a limiting distribution in Model 3, and its asymptotic covariance matrix can be found as follows (the steps are explained in 10.17–18):[76]

$$(10.29) \quad \text{asy cov}\,(\sqrt{T}e', \sqrt{T}e) = \text{asy cov}\left[T(\mathbf{XX}')^{-1} \frac{\mathbf{Xu}'}{\sqrt{T}}, \frac{\mathbf{uX}'}{\sqrt{T}} T(\mathbf{XX}')^{-1} \right]$$

$$= \text{plim}\; T(\mathbf{XX}')^{-1} \left[\text{asy cov}\left(\frac{\mathbf{Xu}'}{\sqrt{T}}, \frac{\mathbf{uX}'}{\sqrt{T}} \right) \right] \text{plim}\; T(\mathbf{XX}')^{-1}$$

$$= \text{plim}\; T(\mathbf{XX}')^{-1} \cdot \sigma^2 \,\text{plim}\, \frac{1}{T} \mathbf{XX}' \cdot \text{plim}\; T(\mathbf{XX}')^{-1}$$

$$= \sigma^2 \,\text{plim}\; T(\mathbf{XX}')^{-1}$$

[74] This is asserted in Theil [1958], p. 228, [1961], p. 232.

[75] Basmann [1960] proves the asymptotic normality of two-stage least-squares estimators in a case similar to our Model 2. Zellner and Theil [1962], p. 60 n., indicate a proof of asymptotic normality in a similar case.

[76] Theil gives (without proof, and in our notation) $\lim_{T\to\infty} E(Te'e) = \sigma^2 \text{plim}_{T\to\infty} T(\mathbf{XX}')^{-1}$, in [1958], p. 227, or [1961], p. 231. I prefer the asymptotic covariance approach in (10.29) because in general $Ee'e$ fails to exist in the two-stage least-squares method, and hence the meaning of $\lim_{T\to\infty} E(Te'e)$ is not clear. What follows in the text is not strictly a complete proof because we do not show here that $\sqrt{T}e$ has a limiting distribution in Model 3 (nor does Theil [1958] or [1961], nor Goldberger [1964]).

where σ^2 is the variance of the structural disturbance u. The first equality results from (10.21). The second equality is correct by Theorem (b) of 3.29 if the asymptotic covariance matrix of $\mathbf{Xu'}/\sqrt{T}$ and the plim of $T(\mathbf{XX'})^{-1}$ exist. The latter does exist (see 10.11–12). The existence of the asymptotic covariance matrix of $\mathbf{Xu'}/\sqrt{T}$ and the third equality are by no means simple to demonstrate, but they follow from Model 3; see below. The fourth equality is correct since the probability limits exist.

   10.18   Accordingly the next problem is to show that

$$(10.30) \qquad \text{asy cov} \left(\frac{\mathbf{Xu'}}{\sqrt{T}}, \frac{\mathbf{uX'}}{\sqrt{T}} \right) = \sigma^2 \, \text{plim} \, \frac{1}{T} \mathbf{XX'}$$

in order to establish the conclusion in (10.29). We have already evaluated $\text{plim} \frac{1}{T} \mathbf{XX'}$ in (10.24), so we turn to the expression on the left side of (10.30). First note that $\mathbf{X'}$ can be written as

$$(10.31) \quad \mathbf{X'} = (\mathbf{Z'P_1'} \quad \mathbf{Z^{*\prime}}) = \mathbf{Z'} \left(\mathbf{P_1'} \quad \begin{matrix} \mathbf{I}_J \\ \mathbf{0} \end{matrix} \right) = \mathbf{Z'} \left((\mathbf{ZZ'})^{-1}\mathbf{ZY'} \quad \begin{matrix} \mathbf{I}_J \\ \mathbf{0} \end{matrix} \right)$$

$$= \mathbf{Z'} \left((\mathbf{ZZ'})^{-1}\mathbf{Z}(\mathbf{Z'\Pi_1'} + \mathbf{V'}) \quad \begin{matrix} \mathbf{I}_J \\ \mathbf{0} \end{matrix} \right)$$

$$= \mathbf{Z'} \left[\left(\mathbf{\Pi_1'} \quad \begin{matrix} \mathbf{I}_J \\ \mathbf{0} \end{matrix} \right) + ((\mathbf{ZZ'})^{-1}\mathbf{ZV'} \quad \mathbf{0}) \right]$$

The second equality here follows because $\mathbf{Z^*}$ is a submatrix of $\mathbf{Z}$. The third follows from substituting for $\mathbf{P_1}$ from (10.13). The fourth results from substituting from (10.11) for $\mathbf{Y}$. And the fifth comes from performing the indicated multiplication. Therefore asy cov $(\mathbf{Xu'}/\sqrt{T}, \mathbf{uX'}/\sqrt{T})$ can be written as

$$(10.32) \quad \text{asy cov} \left\{ \left[\begin{pmatrix} \mathbf{\Pi_1} \\ \mathbf{I}_J \quad \mathbf{0} \end{pmatrix} + \begin{pmatrix} \mathbf{VZ'}(\mathbf{ZZ'})^{-1} \\ \mathbf{0} \end{pmatrix} \right] \frac{\mathbf{Zu'}}{\sqrt{T}}, \right.$$

$$\left. \frac{\mathbf{uZ'}}{\sqrt{T}} \left[\begin{pmatrix} \mathbf{\Pi_1'} \quad \begin{matrix} \mathbf{I}_J \\ \mathbf{0} \end{matrix} \end{pmatrix} + ((\mathbf{ZZ'})^{-1}\mathbf{ZV'} \quad \mathbf{0}) \right] \right\}$$

Now by theorem (b) of 3.29 this expression is equal to the following product: The probability limit of the expression in the left-hand square bracket, times the asymptotic covariance matrix of $\mathbf{Zu'}/\sqrt{T}$ (whose existence we shall discuss presently), times the probability limit of the expression in the right-hand square bracket. The probability limits of

$(\mathbf{ZZ}')^{-1}\mathbf{ZV}'$ and its transpose exist and are zero,[77] so that (10.32) becomes

$$(10.33) \quad \text{asy cov} \left(\frac{\mathbf{Xu}'}{\sqrt{T}}, \frac{\mathbf{uX}'}{\sqrt{T}} \right) = \begin{pmatrix} \mathbf{\Pi}_1 \\ \mathbf{I}_J \quad \mathbf{0} \end{pmatrix} \left[\text{asy cov} \left(\frac{\mathbf{Zu}'}{\sqrt{T}}, \frac{\mathbf{uZ}'}{\sqrt{T}} \right) \right] \begin{pmatrix} & \mathbf{I}_J \\ \mathbf{\Pi}_1' & \\ & \mathbf{0} \end{pmatrix}$$

A generalization of the argument of 3.34[78] shows that in our Model 3 the asymptotic covariance matrix of $\mathbf{Zu}'/\sqrt{T}$ exists and is

$$(10.34) \qquad \text{asy cov} \left(\frac{\mathbf{Zu}'}{\sqrt{T}}, \frac{\mathbf{uZ}'}{\sqrt{T}} \right) = \sigma^2 \, \text{plim} \, \frac{1}{T} \mathbf{ZZ}'$$

On substituting (10.34) into (10.33) and multiplying out, we get σ^2 times the same result as on the right side of (10.24); that is, (10.30) is proved. Therefore (10.29), which gives the asymptotic variance-covariance matrix of $\sqrt{T}$ times the error of the two-stage least-squares estimators, is established.

10.19 The asymptotic variance-covariance matrix of $\sqrt{T}$ times the error of the k-class estimator, according to Theil,[79] is given by (10.29) provided k is such that plim $\sqrt{T}(k-1) = 0$. This proviso is met by two-stage least-squares and limited-information estimators, so that both (when multiplied by $\sqrt{T}$) have the same asymptotic variance-covariance matrix.

10.20 For an equation that is just identified, the two-stage least-squares and limited-information estimators are necessarily identical. This follows from the fact that in such an equation the variance ratio of the limited-information method [i.e., the smallest root l_1 of (9.27) above] is equal to 1; see 9.21. We have already seen that in that case the limited-information and indirect least-squares and instrumental-variables methods give identical estimators. For a system in which *every* equation is just identified, the two-stage least-squares and full-information methods and all the methods mentioned in the preceding sentence give identical results, as noted in 9.21.

10.21 In order to compute the two-stage least-squares estimate, two matrices must be inverted. One, associated with the "first stage," is $\mathbf{ZZ}'$, with K rows and columns. The other, associated with the "second stage," is $\mathbf{XX}'$, with $H - 1 + J$ rows and columns (identification requires $H - 1 + J \leq K$). When these inversions have been done, the two-stage least-squares estimate is readily available, and the approximate covariance matrix of the two-stage least-squares estimator will be estimated by

[77] $(\mathbf{ZZ}')^{-1}\mathbf{ZV}'$ would be the least-squares estimator of the zero parameters in the equation $\mathbf{V}' = \mathbf{Z}'\mathbf{0} + \mathbf{V}'$, and since in Model 3 least-squares estimation of such an equation is consistent, this estimator is a consistent estimator of zero, that is, its probability limit is zero!

[78] Durbin [1960], especially pp. 144, 146–148, obtains the same result.

[79] See note 76.

$\sigma^2(\mathbf{XX}')^{-1}$, except that σ^2 is replaced by the mean square of the calculated residuals from the equation. If these two-stage least-squares residuals are denoted by $u_t^{(1)}$, $t = 1, \ldots, T$, we have[80]

$$(10.35) \qquad \text{est approx cov } (\mathbf{e}', \mathbf{e}) = \frac{\sum (u_t^{(1)})^2}{T - H + 1 - J} (\mathbf{XX}')^{-1}$$

We could divide by T instead of $T - H + 1 - J$. On the one hand, $T - H + 1 - J$ is more in keeping with the number of degrees of freedom that is relevant for reduced-form equations. On the other hand, Nagar [1961] has shown that under conditions similar to Model 2 (normal), there is a particular member of the k-class of estimators, *not* two-stage least-squares but asymptotically identical thereto, such that division of its sum of squared residuals by T yields an estimator of σ^2 that is approximately unbiased. Since the value of k for which this is true is not observable, and since division by the smaller number $T - H + 1 - J$ is less likely to underestimate σ^2, $T - H + 1 - J$ may be preferable to T as a divisor for the two-stage least-squares case.

10.22 By contrast, to compute the limited-information estimator, we must invert three matrices: $\mathbf{M}_{zz}$ (also known as $\mathbf{ZZ}'$) with K rows and columns as in the two-stage least-squares case, and $\mathbf{M}_{z*z*}$ (i.e., $\mathbf{Z*Z*}'$) with J rows and columns, and $\mathbf{W}^* - \mathbf{W}$ with H rows and columns. The matrix $\mathbf{M}_{yy}$ of moments of included jointly dependent variables is needed to obtain $\mathbf{W}$. When these inversions and the iterations are done, the approximate covariance matrix of the limited-information estimator is not yet readily available. For that, we must invert one more matrix, of $H - 1$ rows and columns.[81] Or we may use (10.35) instead (see 10.19), if two-stage least-squares estimation is being done too. The computing required for the limited-information method is much less straightforward than that for two-stage least-squares, and may be somewhat more time-consuming, especially if the iterative process with the matrix $\mathbf{Q}$ converges slowly.

10.23 Nagar [1962] has introduced a related but more general class of estimators, which he calls the double k-class, because there are two parameters, k_1 and k_2, instead of the single-parameter k as in the k-class. For equation (10.2) the double k-class estimator is (in our notation)

$$(10.36) \qquad \begin{pmatrix} \boldsymbol{\beta}_1^{(k_1,k_2)\prime} \\ \boldsymbol{\gamma}^{(k_1,k_2)\prime} \end{pmatrix} = - \begin{pmatrix} \mathbf{YY}' - k_1\hat{\mathbf{V}}\hat{\mathbf{V}}' & \mathbf{YZ}^{*\prime} \\ \mathbf{Z*Y}' & \mathbf{Z*Z}^{*\prime} \end{pmatrix}^{-1} \begin{pmatrix} \mathbf{Y} - k_2\hat{\mathbf{V}} \\ \mathbf{Z}^* \end{pmatrix} \mathbf{y}'$$

---

[80] The two-stage least-squares residuals $u_t^{(1)}$ are of course obtained by substituting observed data for all the equation's variables and the two-stage least-squares estimates into the equation. Note that they are *not* the same as the residuals from the "second-stage" regression described in step (d) in 10.2 of the text.

[81] See Chernoff and Divinsky [1953], p. 245.

The k-class estimator is a special case of the double k-class, as can be seen by the fact that when we put $k_1 = k_2 = k$ in (10.36), the k-class estimator of (10.28) results. If we put $k_1 = k_2 = 1$, the two-stage least-squares estimator results. The so-called h-class of estimators (introduced by Theil in [1958], pp. 355–6, and [1961] pp. 353–4) is also a special case of the double k-class, obtained by putting $k_1 = 1 - h^2$ and $k_2 = 1 - h$ in (10.36).

10.24 In Model 3 the double k-class estimator is consistent if plim $k_1 = $ plim $k_2 = 1$; its associated asymptotic covariance matrix is given by (10.29) if plim $\sqrt{T}(k_1 - 1) = $ plim $\sqrt{T}(k_2 - 1) = 0$. The proofs of these statements are similar to the arguments in 10.10–13 and 10.16–18. Some approximate small sample properties of the k-class and double k-class estimators have been worked out by Nagar [1959a] and [1962] under a set of assumptions similar to our Model 2 (normal), that is, with serially independent normal disturbances and with all predetermined variables being nonstochastic and exogenous. He also assumed that k_1 and k_2 are nonstochastic. These results are discussed further in Section 12.

10.25 The two-stage least-squares method can be regarded as an application of Aitken's [1934] generalized least-squares method described in 5.7, as shown by Zellner and Theil [1962], pp. 55–56, as follows. Consider (10.2) as the equation to be estimated. Then form a set of estimating equations by multiplying (10.2) on the left by the matrix $\mathbf{Z}$ of data for all the predetermined variables in the model, thus:

$$(10.37) \qquad \mathbf{Zy'} = -\mathbf{Z}(\mathbf{Y'} \quad \mathbf{Z^*}')\begin{pmatrix}\boldsymbol{\beta_1}' \\ \boldsymbol{\gamma'}\end{pmatrix} + \mathbf{Zu'}$$

If the equation being estimated is *just identified*, the number of equations in (10.37) is equal to $H - 1 + J$, the number of elements of $(\boldsymbol{\beta_1} \quad \boldsymbol{\gamma})$ to be estimated; then by suppressing the disturbance term $\mathbf{Zu'}$ and solving for values of $(\boldsymbol{\beta_1} \quad \boldsymbol{\gamma})$ we obtain the instrumental-variables estimator (in this case the same as the indirect least-squares estimator). If an *overidentified* equation is being estimated, then (10.37) contains more estimating equations than its $H - 1 + J$ unknown parameters, and (with probability 1) the equations are inconsistent and have no solution [compare equations (8.9) and the discussion in 8.6]. But now (10.37) can be regarded as a set of K equations with $H - 1 + J$ parameters $(\boldsymbol{\beta_1} \quad \boldsymbol{\gamma})$ and a "disturbance" vector $\mathbf{Zu'}$ whose elements are not independent. It is amenable to estimation by Aitken's method under our Model 2 because the variance-covariance matrix $\boldsymbol{\Lambda}$ of the "disturbance" vector can be expressed as an unknown constant times a known matrix, thus:

$$(10.38) \qquad \boldsymbol{\Lambda} = E(\mathbf{Zu'uZ'}) = \mathbf{Z}(E\mathbf{u'u})\mathbf{Z'} = \sigma^2\mathbf{ZZ'}$$

If Aitken's estimator as given in (5.19) is applied to (10.37), where the "dependent variable" data vector is Zy' and the "independent variables" data matrix is $Z(Y' \quad Z^{*'})$, σ^2 and $(\sigma^2)^{-1}$ cancel out, and the resulting estimator of $(\beta_1 \quad \gamma)'$ is the following, which is equivalent to two-stage least squares:

$$(10.39) \qquad -\left[\binom{Y}{Z^*} Z'(ZZ')^{-1}Z(Y' \quad Z^{*'})\right]^{-1} \binom{Y}{Z^*} Z'(ZZ')^{-1}Zy'$$

Thus the two-stage least-squares method can be regarded as a way of "averaging" the too many contradictory estimating equations that arise when we try to apply the instrumental-variables method to an overidentified equation, using all the predetermined variables in the model as instruments as in 8.6.

10.26 The remainder of this section discusses the three-stage least-squares method devised by Zellner and Theil [1962] for estimating an entire structure subject to all the identifying restrictions simultaneously. Some relationships between it and other methods are pointed out. Most of our discussion will assume Model 2 (normal) (see 2.3–5).

10.27 The three-stage least-squares method begins by estimating each structural equation of the model separately by two-stage least squares, subject only to identifying restrictions on that equation; the two-stage least-squares estimates of the coefficients are then used to calculate residuals $\hat{u}_{it}^{(1)}$ in each stochastic structural equation, and those residuals are used to obtain an estimate $\widetilde{\Sigma}$ of the variance-covariance matrix Σ of the structural disturbances (where these disturbances are assumed to have an unchanging distribution for $t = 1, \ldots, T$ so that Σ is the same for all t, as in assumption (f) of 2.2). Then the "third stage" consists of estimating the coefficients of all equations simultaneously by means of Aitken's [1934] generalized least-squares method (see 5.7), using the estimated variance-covariance matrix $\widetilde{\Sigma}$ and the identifying restrictions on all the coefficients in the model.

10.28 In order to prepare for the third-stage estimation, the *whole model* is written in a form analogous to the matrix equation (5.2), namely, $y' = Z'\pi' + v'$, all the *unknown* coefficients in all the equations being arranged in a single vector that will occupy a place analogous to that of π' in the foregoing equation. The steps in so writing the model are as follows: Let the ith structural equation of the model be written as in (10.2), but with a subscript i on each symbol to distinguish it from the other equations. H_i and J_i will then denote the number of dependent and predetermined variables in the ith equation.

$$(10.40) \qquad y_i' = -Y_i'\beta_{1i}' - Z^{*'}\gamma_i' + u_i'$$

Let the $H_i - 1 + J_i$ by T data matrix for the ith equation be denoted (in this context only) by Q_i thus [compare the meaning of X in (10.19)]:

(10.41) $$Q_i = \begin{pmatrix} Y_i \\ Z_i^* \end{pmatrix}$$

Let the vector of $H_i - 1 + J_i$ coefficients in the ith equation be denoted by δ_i, thus:

(10.42) $$\delta_i = (\beta_{1i} \quad \gamma_i)$$

Then the ith equation given in (10.40) can be written as

(10.43) $$y_i' = -Q_i'\delta_i' + u_i' \qquad i = 1, \ldots, G$$

Now multiply on the left by the $K \times T$ data matrix Z for the model's predetermined variables [just as was done to obtain (10.37) in preparing to apply Aitken's method]:

(10.44) $$Zy_i' = -ZQ_i'\delta_i' + Zu_i' \qquad i = 1, \ldots, G$$

Then (10.44) can be rewritten for all the model's equations at once:

(10.45)

$$\begin{pmatrix} Zy_1' \\ \cdot \\ \cdot \\ \cdot \\ Zy_G' \end{pmatrix} = - \begin{pmatrix} ZQ_1' & 0 & \cdots & 0 \\ 0 & ZQ_2' & & \cdot \\ \cdot & & \cdot & \cdot \\ \cdot & & \cdot & 0 \\ 0 & \cdots & 0 & ZQ_G' \end{pmatrix} \begin{pmatrix} \delta_1' \\ \cdot \\ \cdot \\ \cdot \\ \delta_G' \end{pmatrix} + \begin{pmatrix} Zu_1' \\ \cdot \\ \cdot \\ \cdot \\ Zu_G' \end{pmatrix}$$

10.29 Note that this is a system of GK equations, for the left-hand vector in it has GK elements (so has the extreme right-hand disturbance vector). The number of parameters in the vector of δ's is $\sum_1^G (H_i - 1 + J_i)$. This is the number of unknown coefficients in the model; let us denote it in this context by L. Then the block diagonal matrix in (10.45) is $GK \times L$. Note that the identifying restrictions, prescribing that certain coefficients in the model must be zero, are taken account of in this notation because the vectors δ_i' include only such coefficients as are not required to be zero (and not required by the normalization rule to be 1). For this context only, we adopt the following compact notation for the four matrices in (10.45): $\vec{y}'$ is the $GK \times 1$ vector on the left side; $\vec{u}'$ is the $GK \times 1$ vector on the extreme right; $\vec{Q}'$ is the $GK \times L$ block diagonal matrix on the right side; and δ' is the $L \times 1$ parameter vector on the right side of (10.45). Then (10.45) can be written compactly, in a manner analogous to (5.2):

(10.46) $$\vec{y}' = -\vec{Q}'\delta' + \vec{u}'$$

10.30 The model in the form (10.46) or (10.45) is now almost ready for estimation by Aitken's generalized least squares. Recall from (5.7) that the variance-covariance matrix of the disturbances must be known (except possibly for multiplication by an unknown constant). In (10.46) or (10.45) the last vector in the equation is the disturbance vector; its mean is zero, and its $GK \times GK$ variance-covariance matrix (denoted here by Λ) is

(10.47)

$$\Lambda = E\vec{u}'\vec{u} = E\begin{pmatrix} \mathbf{Zu_1}' \\ \cdot \\ \cdot \\ \cdot \\ \mathbf{Zu_G}' \end{pmatrix}(\mathbf{u_1 Z'} \cdots \mathbf{u_G Z'}) = \begin{pmatrix} \sigma_{11}\mathbf{ZZ'} & \cdots & \sigma_{1G}\mathbf{ZZ'} \\ \cdot & & \cdot \\ \cdot & & \cdot \\ \cdot & & \cdot \\ \sigma_{G1}\mathbf{ZZ'} & \cdots & \sigma_{GG}\mathbf{ZZ'} \end{pmatrix}$$

The last equality above follows from multiplying out and taking the expectation, making use of the facts that the predetermined variables are exogenous and disturbances are serially independent in Model 2 so that $E(\mathbf{Zu_i'u_j Z'}) = \mathbf{Z}E(\mathbf{u_i'u_j})\mathbf{Z'} = \mathbf{Z}(\sigma_{ij}\mathbf{I})\mathbf{Z'} = \sigma_{ij}\mathbf{ZZ'}$. Note that σ_{ij} here as usual is the covariance of disturbances u_{it} and u_{jt} in the ith and jth equations of the model, that is, σ_{ij} is an element of Σ. In order to obtain numerical values for the elements of Λ so that the third-stage estimation of (10.46) by Aitken's method may proceed, Zellner and Theil call upon the first two stages by replacing the unknown parameters σ_{ij} in (10.47) by their two-stage least-squares estimates $\tilde{\sigma}_{ij}$ (i.e., by elements of $\tilde{\Sigma}$, the two-stage least-squares estimate of Σ). Thus the two-stage least-squares estimator of Λ to be used (denoted here by $\tilde{\Lambda}$) is

(10.48)

$$\tilde{\Lambda} = \begin{pmatrix} \tilde{\sigma}_{11}\mathbf{ZZ'} & \cdots & \tilde{\sigma}_{1G}\mathbf{ZZ'} \\ \cdot & & \cdot \\ \cdot & & \cdot \\ \cdot & & \cdot \\ \tilde{\sigma}_{G1}\mathbf{ZZ'} & \cdots & \tilde{\sigma}_{GG}\mathbf{ZZ'} \end{pmatrix}$$

$$= \begin{pmatrix} \tilde{\sigma}_{11}\mathbf{I}_K & \cdots & \tilde{\sigma}_{1G}\mathbf{I}_K \\ \cdot & & \cdot \\ \cdot & & \cdot \\ \cdot & & \cdot \\ \tilde{\sigma}_{G1}\mathbf{I}_K & \cdots & \tilde{\sigma}_{GG}\mathbf{I}_K \end{pmatrix}\begin{pmatrix} \mathbf{ZZ'} & 0 & \cdots & 0 \\ 0 & \mathbf{ZZ'} & & \cdot \\ \cdot & & \cdot & \\ \cdot & & & 0 \\ 0 & \cdots & 0 & \mathbf{ZZ'} \end{pmatrix}$$

$\tilde{\Lambda}$ and the three large matrices in (10.48) are square of order GK. The last equality here may be verified by the reader; it will be used later. $\mathbf{I}_K$ is the identity matrix of order K.

10.31 When Aitken's generalized least-squares method is applied to (10.46), using the two-stage least-squares estimator $\tilde{\Lambda}$, the result is the following equation for the Zellner-Theil three-stage least-squares estimator, denoted here by $\tilde{\delta}$:

(10.49) $\vec{\mathbf{Q}}\tilde{\Lambda}^{-1}\vec{\mathbf{y}}' = -\vec{\mathbf{Q}}\tilde{\Lambda}^{-1}\vec{\mathbf{Q}}'\tilde{\delta}'$

Each side of this equation is an $L \times 1$ vector. The three-stage least-squares estimator $\tilde{\delta}'$ is computed by premultiplying the equation by the inverse of the $L \times L$ matrix $\vec{\mathbf{Q}} \tilde{\mathbf{\Lambda}}^{-1} \vec{\mathbf{Q}}'$. This method is much simpler computationally then the full-information method (see Section 6); the biggest part of the job is the inversion of the $L \times L$ matrix in (10.49).

10.32 Zellner and Theil [1962] show that under conditions similar to our Model 2 (recall 2.3–5), the three-stage least-squares estimator is consistent and asymptotically normal, and that it yields higher asymptotic efficiency than two-stage least squares for any structural equation that is embedded in a model containing both (a) overidentifying restrictions on its other equations and (b) a nondiagonal covariance matrix $\mathbf{\Sigma}$ of disturbances. We may conjecture that these results hold also for Model 3. Zellner and Theil also show that the three-stage least-squares estimator is identical to the two-stage one if either or both of the conditions (a) and (b) stated above fail to apply.

10.33 Under conditions similar to our Model 3 (normal) (see 2.3–5) Durbin [1963] offers a simplified derivation of the estimating equations for the full-information method (the method itself is described above in Section 6), and in the process he shows very clearly the relationship between the three-stage least-squares and full-information methods. If we use the notation of 10.26 ff., Durbin's treatment of three-stage least squares becomes equivalent to the following development, ending with (10.55) below. We begin by writing all the large matrices in (10.49) except $\tilde{\delta}'$ in a different way. First, factor the $GK \times L$ matrix $\vec{\mathbf{Q}}'$, which appears in (10.45) and (10.46), as follows:

$$(10.50) \quad \vec{\mathbf{Q}}' = \begin{pmatrix} \mathbf{Z} & \mathbf{0} & \cdots & \mathbf{0} \\ \mathbf{0} & \mathbf{Z} & & \cdot \\ \cdot & & \cdot & \cdot \\ \cdot & & & \mathbf{0} \\ \mathbf{0} & \cdots & \mathbf{0} & \mathbf{Z} \end{pmatrix} \begin{pmatrix} \mathbf{Q}_1' & \mathbf{0} & \cdots & \mathbf{0} \\ \mathbf{0} & \mathbf{Q}_2' & & \cdot \\ \cdot & & \cdot & \cdot \\ \cdot & & & \mathbf{0} \\ \mathbf{0} & \cdots & \mathbf{0} & \mathbf{Q}_G' \end{pmatrix}$$

The left-hand factor here is $GK \times GT$, and the right-hand factor is $GT \times L$. Next, factor the $GK \times 1$ vector $\vec{\mathbf{y}}'$ in (10.45) and (10.46), thus:

$$(10.51) \quad \vec{\mathbf{y}}' = \begin{pmatrix} \mathbf{Z} & \mathbf{0} & \cdots & \mathbf{0} \\ \mathbf{0} & \mathbf{Z} & & \cdot \\ \cdot & & \cdot & \cdot \\ \cdot & & & \mathbf{0} \\ \mathbf{0} & \cdots & \mathbf{0} & \mathbf{Z} \end{pmatrix} \begin{pmatrix} \mathbf{y}_1' \\ \cdot \\ \cdot \\ \cdot \\ \mathbf{y}_G' \end{pmatrix}$$

The left-hand factor here is $GK \times GT$ as in (10.50), and the right-hand factor is $GT \times 1$. Next, apply the rule that the inverse of a matrix product $\mathbf{AB}$ is $\mathbf{B}^{-1}\mathbf{A}^{-1}$ to find $\tilde{\mathbf{\Lambda}}^{-1}$ from (10.48) thus:

(10.52)

$$
\tilde{\mathbf{\Lambda}}^{-1} =
\begin{pmatrix}
\mathbf{ZZ'} & 0 & \cdots & 0 \\
0 & \mathbf{ZZ'} & & \cdot \\
\cdot & & \cdot & \cdot \\
\cdot & & \cdot & \cdot \\
\cdot & & \cdot\;0 & \cdot \\
0 & \cdots & 0 & \mathbf{ZZ'}
\end{pmatrix}^{-1}
\begin{pmatrix}
\tilde{\sigma}_{11}\mathbf{I}_K & \cdots & \tilde{\sigma}_{1G}\mathbf{I}_K \\
\cdot & & \cdot \\
\cdot & & \cdot \\
\cdot & & \cdot \\
\tilde{\sigma}_{G1}\mathbf{I}_K & \cdots & \tilde{\sigma}_{GG}\mathbf{I}_K
\end{pmatrix}^{-1}
$$

$$
=
\begin{pmatrix}
(\mathbf{ZZ'})^{-1} & 0 & \cdots & 0 \\
0 & (\mathbf{ZZ'})^{-1} & & \cdot \\
\cdot & & \cdot & \cdot \\
\cdot & & \cdot & \cdot \\
\cdot & & \cdot\;0 & \cdot \\
0 & \cdots & 0 & (\mathbf{ZZ'})^{-1}
\end{pmatrix}
\begin{pmatrix}
\tilde{\sigma}^{11}\mathbf{I}_K & \cdots & \tilde{\sigma}^{1G}\mathbf{I}_K \\
\cdot & & \cdot \\
\cdot & & \cdot \\
\cdot & & \cdot \\
\tilde{\sigma}^{G1}\mathbf{I}_K & \cdots & \tilde{\sigma}^{GG}\mathbf{I}_K
\end{pmatrix}
$$

Here all the large matrices are square of order GK, and the scalar $\tilde{\sigma}^{ij}$ is the element in row i and column j of the inverse $\widetilde{\mathbf{\Sigma}}^{-1}$ of the two-stage least-squares estimate of the variance-covariance matrix $\mathbf{\Sigma}$. We have now made one transformation of each matrix in (10.49) except $\tilde{\mathbf{\delta}}'$. Before continuing, the reader may wish to substitute (10.50)–(10.52) into (10.49) and write out the result.

10.34 Next, note that the $GK \times GT$ product of the last matrix in (10.52) times the first matrix in (10.51) can be written as a different product, thus:

(10.53)

$$
\begin{pmatrix}
\tilde{\sigma}^{11}\mathbf{I}_K & \cdots & \tilde{\sigma}^{1G}\mathbf{I}_K \\
\cdot & & \cdot \\
\cdot & & \cdot \\
\cdot & & \cdot \\
\tilde{\sigma}^{G1}\mathbf{I}_K & \cdots & \tilde{\sigma}^{GG}\mathbf{I}_K
\end{pmatrix}
\begin{pmatrix}
\mathbf{Z} & 0 & \cdots & 0 \\
0 & \mathbf{Z} & & \cdot \\
\cdot & & \cdot & \cdot \\
\cdot & & \cdot & \cdot \\
\cdot & & \cdot\;0 & \cdot \\
0 & \cdots & 0 & \mathbf{Z}
\end{pmatrix}
$$

$$
=
\begin{pmatrix}
\mathbf{Z} & 0 & \cdots & 0 \\
0 & \mathbf{Z} & & \cdot \\
\cdot & & \cdot & \cdot \\
\cdot & & \cdot & \cdot \\
\cdot & & \cdot\;0 & \cdot \\
0 & \cdots & 0 & \mathbf{Z}
\end{pmatrix}
\begin{pmatrix}
\tilde{\sigma}^{11}\mathbf{I}_T & \cdots & \tilde{\sigma}^{1G}\mathbf{I}_T \\
\cdot & & \cdot \\
\cdot & & \cdot \\
\cdot & & \cdot \\
\tilde{\sigma}^{G1}\mathbf{I}_T & \cdots & \tilde{\sigma}^{GG}\mathbf{I}_T
\end{pmatrix}
$$

Here the extreme right-hand matrix is square of order GT. Next note, from (10.49)–(10.53), that the products $\vec{Q}\tilde{\Lambda}^{-1}\vec{Q}'$ and $\vec{Q}\tilde{\Lambda}^{-1}\vec{y}'$ in (10.49) both contain an L by GT block diagonal matrix whose $H_i - 1 + J_i$ by T diagonal is $Q_i Z'(ZZ')^{-1}Z$. This matrix can be written as follows (the steps are explained below):

$$(10.54) \qquad Q_i Z'(ZZ')^{-1}Z = \begin{pmatrix} Y_i \\ Z_i{}^* \end{pmatrix} Z'(ZZ')^{-1}Z = \begin{pmatrix} \hat{Y}_i \\ Z_i{}^* \end{pmatrix} \equiv X_i$$

Here the first equality makes use of the definition of Q_i in (10.41); the second equality expresses the fact that $Y_i Z'(ZZ')^{-1}Z$ is the calculated value $\hat{Y}_i$ of Y_i obtained from the least-squares reduced-form equations as in (10.13) above (note that $Z_i{}^* Z'(ZZ')^{-1}Z = Z_i{}^*$ if the columns of Z' are arranged in suitable order, which we assume); the last equality denotes the resulting matrix by X_i as in (10.19).

10.35 Durbin's three-stage least-squares equations can now be found by using the preliminaries given in 10.33–34. Substitute (10.50)–(10.52) into (10.49), and into the resulting equation substitute (10.53)–(10.54). This yields Durbin's expression (in our notation) for the three-stage least-squares estimating equations thus:

$$(10.55) \quad \begin{pmatrix} X_1 & 0 & \cdots & 0 \\ 0 & X_2 & & \cdot \\ \cdot & & \cdot & \cdot \\ \cdot & & & 0 \\ 0 & \cdots & 0 & X_G \end{pmatrix} \begin{pmatrix} \tilde{\sigma}^{11} I_T & \cdots & \tilde{\sigma}^{1G} I_T \\ & & \\ \cdot & & \cdot \\ \cdot & & \cdot \\ \tilde{\sigma}^{G1} I_T & \cdots & \tilde{\sigma}^{GG} I_T \end{pmatrix} \begin{pmatrix} y_1' \\ \cdot \\ \cdot \\ \cdot \\ y'_G \end{pmatrix}$$

$$= - \begin{pmatrix} X_1 & 0 & \cdots & 0 \\ 0 & X_2 & & \cdot \\ \cdot & & \cdot & \cdot \\ \cdot & & & 0 \\ 0 & \cdots & 0 & X_G \end{pmatrix} \begin{pmatrix} \tilde{\sigma}^{11} I_T & \cdots & \tilde{\sigma}^{1G} I_T \\ & & \\ \cdot & & \cdot \\ \cdot & & \cdot \\ \tilde{\sigma}^{G1} I_T & \cdots & \tilde{\sigma}^{GG} I_T \end{pmatrix}$$

$$\times \begin{pmatrix} Q_1' & 0 & \cdots & 0 \\ 0 & Q_2' & & \cdot \\ \cdot & & \cdot & \cdot \\ \cdot & & & 0 \\ 0 & \cdots & 0 & Q_G' \end{pmatrix} \tilde{\delta}'$$

The seven large matrices here are, respectively, $L \times GT$, $GT \times GT$, $GT \times 1$; $L \times GT$, $GT \times GT$, $GT \times L$, and $L \times 1$. Of course (10.55) is equivalent to (10.49). It is useful to recall that in (10.55) the matrices $\mathbf{y}_i'$ and $\mathbf{Q}_i'$ are directly observable data $[\mathbf{Q}_i'$ being equal to $(\mathbf{Y}_i' \quad \mathbf{Z}_i^{*'})]$; that the matrices $\mathbf{X}_i'$ are partly observable and partly calculated by least squares from the reduced form $[\mathbf{X}_i'$ being, so to speak, the least-squares estimator of $\mathbf{Q}_i'$, equal to $(\hat{\mathbf{Y}}_i' \quad \mathbf{Z}_i^{*'})]$; and that the estimates $\tilde{\sigma}^{ij}$ of elements of $\mathbf{\Sigma}^{-1}$ are calculated from the residuals of the two-stage least-squares estimates of the structural equations. The three-stage least-squares estimator $\tilde{\mathbf{\delta}}'$ for all unknown coefficients in the model is computed simply by solving the linear system (10.55) for $\tilde{\mathbf{\delta}}'$.

    10.36   Durbin's [1963] derivation of the full-information maximum-likelihood estimator (denoted by $\hat{\mathbf{\delta}}'$) uses the same notational format as (10.55), and indeed, using assumptions similar to Model 3 (normal), Durbin obtains full-information estimating equations that look just like (10.55), with these exceptions: (a) The estimator $\tilde{\mathbf{\delta}}'$ in (10.55) is of course replaced by the full-information estimator $\hat{\mathbf{\delta}}'$; (b) the least-squares estimator $\mathbf{X}_i$ of $\mathbf{Q}_i$ in (10.55) is replaced by the full-information estimator (say $\hat{\mathbf{Q}}_i$) computed from the reduced form that results from solving the structural equations as estimated by $\hat{\mathbf{\delta}}'$; and the two-stage least-squares estimator $\tilde{\sigma}^{ij}$ in (10.55) is replaced by the full-information estimator (say $\hat{\sigma}^{ij}$) calculated from the residuals that are obtained from the structure as estimated by $\hat{\mathbf{\delta}}'$. The resulting full-information estimating equations are

$$
(10.56) \quad
\begin{pmatrix} \hat{\mathbf{Q}}_1 & 0 & \cdots & 0 \\ 0 & \hat{\mathbf{Q}}_2 & & \cdot \\ \cdot & & \cdot & \cdot \\ \cdot & & & \cdot & 0 \\ 0 & \cdots & 0 & \hat{\mathbf{Q}}_G \end{pmatrix}
\begin{pmatrix} \hat{\sigma}^{11}\mathbf{I}_T & \cdots & \hat{\sigma}^{1G}\mathbf{I}_T \\ \cdot & & \cdot \\ \cdot & & \cdot \\ \hat{\sigma}^{G1}\mathbf{I}_T & \cdots & \hat{\sigma}^{GG}\mathbf{I}_T \end{pmatrix}
\begin{pmatrix} \mathbf{y}_1' \\ \cdot \\ \cdot \\ \mathbf{y}_G' \end{pmatrix}
$$

$$
= -
\begin{pmatrix} \hat{\mathbf{Q}}_1 & 0 & \cdots & 0 \\ 0 & \hat{\mathbf{Q}}_2 & & \cdot \\ \cdot & & \cdot & \cdot \\ \cdot & & & \cdot & 0 \\ 0 & \cdots & 0 & \hat{\mathbf{Q}}_G \end{pmatrix}
\begin{pmatrix} \hat{\sigma}^{11}\mathbf{I}_T & \cdots & \hat{\sigma}^{1G}\mathbf{I}_T \\ \cdot & & \cdot \\ \cdot & & \cdot \\ \hat{\sigma}^{G1}\mathbf{I}_T & \cdots & \hat{\sigma}^{GG}\mathbf{I}_T \end{pmatrix}
$$

$$
\times
\begin{pmatrix} \mathbf{Q}_1' & 0 & \cdots & 0 \\ 0 & \mathbf{Q}_2' & & \cdot \\ \cdot & & \cdot & \cdot \\ \cdot & & & \cdot & 0 \\ 0 & \cdots & 0 & \mathbf{Q}_G' \end{pmatrix}
\hat{\mathbf{\delta}}'
$$

These estimating equations are *not* linear in $\hat{\delta}'$ because both $\hat{Q}_i$ and $\hat{\sigma}^{ij}$ depend upon $\hat{\delta}'$ in the manner just indicated. Hence the use of an iterative method of solution is proposed by Durbin.

10.37 Madansky [1964] and Sargan [1964] have also discussed the relation between three-stage least-squares and full-information estimators and shown that both are asymptotically efficient if there are no *a priori* restrictions on the covariance matrix Σ of structural disturbances. Chow [1964] presents a generalization of the ordinary least-squares principle that incorporates full-information, three-stage least-squares, k-class, two-stage least-squares, limited-information, and canonical correlation as special cases.

10.38 Rothenberg and Leenders [1964] have proposed another estimator for all the coefficients of a complete system and have derived some of its properties and some further properties of three-stage least squares. Their method is called linearized maximum likelihood (LML). Their results are based on assumptions similar to our Model 3 (normal). The LML method is based on equating to zero not the *actual* partial derivatives of the likelihood function, but Taylor-series linear approximations of them, each Taylor expansion being taken at a point where the parameter vector is set equal to any consistent estimator whose variances and covariances go to zero as $1/\sqrt{T}$ does. This method is simpler computationally than the full-information maximum-likelihood method but has the same asymptotic distribution, even when the covariance matrix Σ of disturbances is restricted by the *a priori* information. This method is more troublesome computationally then three-stage least squares. Rothenberg and Leenders show that if not all the predetermined variables are exogenous and if the covariance matrix Σ of structural disturbances at time t is restricted by *a priori* information, then the asymptotic efficiency of three-stage least squares becomes less than that of LML and full information, but that three-stage least squares is asymptotically efficient (like LML and full information) if Σ is not restricted by *a priori* information, or if all the predetermined variables are strictly exogenous,[82] or both. Thus three-stage least squares appears preferable if Σ is unrestricted or if all predetermined variables are exogenous or both, and LML appears worth its extra computational burden otherwise.

11 LEAST SQUARES AS A METHOD OF ESTIMATING STRUCTURAL PARAMETERS: LEAST-SQUARES BIAS

11.1 In this section we shall discuss the consequences of attempting to estimate the parameters of *structural* equations directly by the

[82] On this point, see Rothenberg and Leenders [1964], p. 72, and also Zellner [1962].

least-squares method, even though we have already seen that least squares does not yield estimators with desirable statistical properties such as consistency unless all but one of the variables in the estimated equation are predetermined. But least squares is such a commonly used technique for fitting equations of all kinds that we shall consider it. And we may find circumstances in which it is useful even if the statistical assumptions ensuring its consistency are not strictly valid.

11.2 If we propose to estimate a structural equation by least squares, for example, the equation

$$(11.1) \qquad x_0 = \sum_1^K \alpha_k x_k + u$$

then we have to decide in what direction to minimize the sum of squares. We can take any of the $K + 1$ coordinate directions corresponding to the axes of $x_0, x_1, \ldots, x_K$. Or we can take some other direction not parallel to any coordinate axis.[83] We shall confine ourselves to the coordinate directions, but even so there are $K - 1$ sets of estimators, depending upon which direction is chosen. (Of course if the sum of squares is zero in any one direction, all points must fit the equation exactly, and so the sum of squares must be zero in *every* direction—but this never happens in practice except when the number of parameters to be estimated equals or exceeds the number of observations, in which case we can have no confidence in the estimates.) Which direction should we choose? The statistical assumptions of any of our three models (if they are accepted) bid us choose the one for which the shifts are believed to be independent of the other variables and of each other, but if our equation is part of a system this requirement cannot typically be met, for then each equation typically contains at least two endogenous variables on which the distribution of shifts depends.

11.3 The only kind of system of simultaneous equations in which each does have just one dependent variable (apart from the special case of a system of reduced form or final equations, in which each equation can just as well be treated separately anyway) is the so-called *recursive form*,[84] in which the structural disturbances u_{gt} are independent of u_{hs} for all $g \neq h$, and the matrix of coefficients of the jointly dependent

---

[83] The latter procedure is sometimes used when it is believed that there are random errors in observing the variables as well as random shifts in the equation. See Frisch [1934], Koopmans [1937], and Madansky [1959].

[84] I believe this term was introduced by Bentzel and Wold [1946]. For discussion of such systems see Strotz and Wold [1960], Basmann [1963a] and [1965a], and Bergstrom [1966].

variables has nothing but zeros to one side of the diagonal:

$$y_1 \hspace{8em} = \sum_1^K \gamma_{1k} z_k + u_1$$

$$\beta_{21} y_1 + y_2 \hspace{5em} = \sum_1^K \gamma_{2k} z_k + u_2$$

(11.2) $\hspace{2em} \beta_{31} y_1 + \beta_{32} y_2 + y_3 \hspace{3em} = \sum_1^K \gamma_{3k} z_k + u_3$

$$\vdots \hspace{12em} \vdots$$

$$\beta_{G1} y_1 + \beta_{G2} y_2 + \beta_{G3} y_3 + \cdots + y_G = \sum_1^K \gamma_{Gk} z_k + u_G$$

In the model as a whole the jointly dependent variables are $y_1, \ldots, y_G$ and the predetermined variables are $z_1, \ldots, z_K$, but, under an additional assumption to be stated in a moment, in any one equation—say the gth—there is only *one* dependent variable y_g, all the variables $y_1, \ldots, y_{g-1}$ being predetermined successively by equations earlier in the hierarchy, and $z_1, \ldots, z_K$ being predetermined for the whole system.

11.4 The assumption that u_g is independent of $u_{g-1}, \ldots, u_1$, that is, that u_g and u_i are independent for $g \neq i$, is not made in this book except for this discussion of the recursive form. In such a situation, the parameters γ_{gk} and β_{gj} can be consistently estimated in recurrent steps by least squares. In the first equation y_1 is the dependent variable and $z_1, \ldots, z_K$ are predetermined, so γ_{1k} ($k = 1, \ldots, K$) can be estimated by minimizing the sum of squares in the y_1-direction (see 4.7). Then similarly in the second equation, y_2 is dependent and $y_1, z_1, \ldots, z_K$ are predetermined, so its parameters can be consistently estimated by minimizing the sum of squares in the y_2-direction. Then in the third equation, y_3 is dependent, and $y_1, y_2, z_1, \ldots, z_K$ are predetermined, so its parameters can be consistently estimated by minimizing the sum of squares in the y_3-direction. And so on.

11.5 We shall next try to find out what happens in a few simple cases if the least-squares method is used where assumptions that could guarantee its consistency are not strictly valid.[85] The approach here will be similar to that adopted in 1.4, where the process of estimating the parameters in

---

[85] The approach to be presented in these next few sections (through 11.8) is in large part due to Arnold C. Harberger and is to be found in greater detail in Harberger [1954]. Marschak and Andrews [1944] used the same type of analysis in estimating production functions; see esp. pp. 161–168, 180–182.

an equation was shown to be equivalent to the process of ruling out as impossible or unlikely certain patterns of shifts or disturbances in the equation. In particular, we shall inquire whether least-squares estimators, where they are not consistent, can nevertheless provide some information about the parameters in question, when coupled with some assumptions about the shift pattern. It will turn out that information can sometimes be gained in this way, even when the assumptions used are not restrictive enough to specify a complete model or to permit the use of a consistent method.

11.6 Let us first take a simple two-variable equation, without specifying a complete model and without classifying its variables as endogenous or exogenous (of course at least one must be endogenous, but we do not go beyond this just yet):

$$(11.3) \qquad\qquad y_1 = \alpha y_2 + \beta + u$$

where u is a nonobservable shift or disturbance, taking on whatever value is necessary each year to make the equation true. The least-squares estimator of α is [compare equation (3.23)]

$$(11.4) \qquad\qquad a = \frac{m_{12}}{m_{22}}$$

where for convenience we have written m_{12} and m_{22} instead of $m_{y_1 y_2}$ and $m_{y_2 y_2}$. What can be said about the error in this estimator? We can take moments of our equation (11.3) with y_2 and get

$$(11.5) \qquad\qquad m_{12} = \alpha m_{22} + 0 + m_{u2}$$

On dividing by m_{22} and recalling (11.4), this becomes [compare (3.30)]:

$$(11.6) \qquad\qquad a = \alpha + \frac{m_{u2}}{m_{22}}$$

This equation is of course exactly true for a given set of data, and everything in it can be calculated from the data except α, the parameter to be estimated, and m_{u2}, the sample moment of y_2 with the unobservable shifts u. If m_{u2} could be known, α could be determined accurately. But of course this is impossible; shift variables such as u are introduced precisely because there are unrecognizable factors that make economic equations approximate at best. In any particular set of data, u may be positively or negatively correlated with y_2, that is, m_{u2} may be either greater or less than zero, and the least-squares estimate may be either too large or too small. It may even be correct, but there is no way of telling.

11.7 Even though m_{u2} cannot be measured for any particular sample, it may still be that something is known about its usual behavior. Perhaps it is nearly always positive, or nearly always negative, or nearly always numerically less than some particular magnitude. If we know anything at all about its typical behavior, we immediately know something about the typical relationship of a to α. In the three cases above we would know, respectively, that a is usually an overestimate of α, or usually an underestimate, or rarely off by more than the magnitude given. And possibly a piece of information of this sort can provide the answer to an economic problem with sufficient accuracy to indicate the appropriate policy. Suppose that it is necessary to know whether the supply of a particular product is elastic or inelastic. If a least-squares estimate indicates an elasticity of 1.2, and if it can be established that the least-squares estimate is usually low, then the supply in question is highly likely to be elastic.

11.8 Where can the economist get information about the usual behavior of the moment of a shift variable with one of his measurable variables? He must get it, if at all, from an analysis of the economic environment surrounding his equation. This does not always mean that he must specify a complete model; a few salient features may suffice. Let us look again at equation (11.3), supposing it to be a supply equation, and for simplicity let us require it to have a constant elasticity, denoted by α:

$$y_1 = \log_e q$$

(11.7)
$$y_2 = \log_e p$$

$$\log_e q = \alpha \log_e p + \beta + u$$

where u is a shift accounting for all changes in quantity supplied that are not attributable to price changes along a constant-elasticity curve. Thus u may incorporate the effects of changes in costs, expected future prices, or anything else that may influence the quantity supplied at a constant price. Another way of expressing (11.7), without logarithms, is

(11.8)
$$q = p^\alpha e^{\beta + u}$$

This version is shown, for $u = 0$, in Figure 11.1; the three positively sloping curves indicate three possible elasticities, above, equal to, and below 1. A possible demand curve is shown as a dotted line, DD. Now clearly a positive value of u will rotate the supply curve clockwise about the origin, thus lowering the price, and a negative value will rotate it counterclockwise, thus raising the price. Hence, the moment m_{u2} will usually be negative.[86] Hence the least-squares estimate of α will usually be too low, by (11.6), and hence if the least-squares estimate a exceeds 1 the supply is very likely to be elastic. (Of course if $a < 1$, this argument does not help to answer the original question of whether the supply is elastic.)

[86] If the demand curve did not shift at all m_{u2} would necessarily be negative. Since the demand certainly shifts too, m_{u2} might be positive in some samples, but this will be rare unless there is a link-up insuring that clockwise supply shifts are associated mainly with rightward demand shifts.

11.9 We have seen that if we can establish the probable sign of a moment such as m_{u2}, we can establish that the least-squares estimate of the slope in a linear two-variable equation is probably a limiting value, either upper or lower, for that parameter. Other limiting values for the parameter can be obtained if other upper and/or lower limiting values besides zero can be found for m_{u2}/m_{22}. If these limits narrow the range of possible or likely values of m_{u2}/m_{22} sufficiently close to zero, the least-squares estimators may be usable even though biased; see VII.6.5.

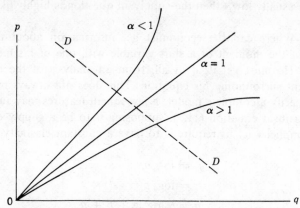

Figure 11.1　Three possible supply curves with constant elasticity α.

11.10 Let us return to m_{u2}. It is proportional to the correlation coefficient r_{u2} between u and y_2 (recall that y_2 is $\log p$) in the sample, thus:

$$(11.9) \qquad m_{u2} = r_{u2}\sqrt{m_{uu}m_{22}}$$

so that

$$(11.10) \qquad \frac{m_{u2}}{m_{22}} = r_{u2}\sqrt{\frac{m_{uu}}{m_{22}}} = r_{u2}\frac{s_u}{s_2}$$

where s_u and s_2 are the standard deviations of u and y_2 in the sample.[87] Here s_2 is positive and measurable, and r_{u2} cannot possibly exceed 1 or be less than -1, so that if some upper limit s_u^{U} can be set for s_u (which is also positive), then the error term m_{u2}/m_{22} will be confined between the two limits $\pm s_u^{U}/s_2$, and α will be correspondingly confined:

$$(11.11) \qquad a - \frac{s_u^{U}}{s_2} < \alpha < a + \frac{s_u^{U}}{s_2}$$

It is difficult to decide on a plausible upper limit for s_u, because there is nothing very concrete to rely on. Of course, s_u must necessarily be greater than or equal to $\sqrt{\sum(y_1 - ay_2 - b)^2/(T-1)}$, the least-squares estimate

---

[87] Note that s_u is not the least-squares estimate of $\sqrt{\operatorname{var} u}$ here; it is the standard deviation of the *actual* shifts occurring in the sample period, and it is unobservable.

of $\sqrt{\text{var } \underline{u}}$, for the least-squares line is by its construction the one whose shifts have the smallest possible variance. And s_u must be less than s_1, the standard deviation of y_1, if the variable y_2 accounts for any of the variation of y_1 at all. And the limits on s_u must be set wider apart for small than for large samples, because of sampling variation. But beyond this, deciding on an upper limit $s_u{}^U$ is largely a matter of judgment based on an examination of the data and an analysis of the economic relationships involved. The same kind of judgment may lead us to set upper and lower limits r_{u2}^L and r_{u2}^U, more stringent than -1 and $+1$, respectively, on the correlation between the shift and y_2 and thus narrow the range of error of the least-squares estimate:

$$(11.12) \qquad a + r_{u2}^L \frac{s_u{}^U}{s_2} < \alpha < a + r_{u2}^U \frac{s_u{}^U}{s_2}$$

Observe that there is no minus sign in the left member of this inequality; that is taken care of by the sign of r_{u2}^L. Indeed, r_{u2}^L and r_{u2}^U may be both positive or both negative, the only general requirement being that $-1 \leqq r_{u2}^L \leqq r_{u2}^U \leqq 1$. Naturally, the degree of confidence we place in such limits on the estimated value of α depends directly on the degree of confidence we put in the presumptions about r_{u2} and s_u.

11.11   The preceding example showed how we might set up an interval, based on observed data, that is likely to include the true value of an unknown parameter. We could not say definitely how large the bias in the least-squares estimator would be, even in an infinitely large sample where all random variation is smoothed out, because we did not know enough about the distributions of s_u and r_{u2}. We shall now shift to another example, for which Haavelmo has derived the asymptotic value of the least-squares bias for an infinite sample, assuming the validity of a particular complete model.[88] He sets up the familiar simple consumption function

$$(11.13) \qquad c = \alpha y + \beta + u$$

Let us first apply the approach just suggested to this problem. The least-squares estimator of α, as we have seen in (11.6), is

$$(11.14) \qquad a = \frac{m_{cy}}{m_{yy}} = \alpha + \frac{m_{uy}}{m_{yy}}$$

By the kind of argument used above, we can show that a is likely to be an overestimate of α. The situation is shown in Figure 11.2. The solid line AB shows the familiar 45° line indicating that consumption c is equal to

---

[88] Haavelmo [1947] tries three alternative sets of assumptions, of which we shall discuss the simplest.

income y minus investment i, where investment is OA. The line $A'B'$ shows the same, where investment is increased to OA'. CD shows the consumption function for $u = 0$. Positive shifts ($u > 0$) lead to higher consumption at any given income, as shown by $C'D'$. Negative shifts would yield the reverse. Hence u and y are likely to be positively correlated, so that $m_{uy} > 0$ and $a > \alpha$. Graphically, we can see that least squares applied to the four points P_1, P_2, P_3, P_4 would lead to an estimated slope a that is steeper than the true slope α of the lines CD and $C'D'$, as suggested by the dotted line. Notice that this conclusion makes use of the

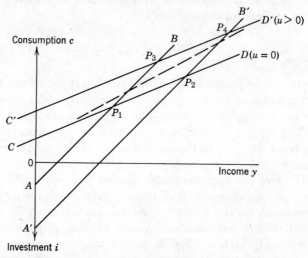

Figure 11.2   Least-squares bias in a simple consumption function $c = \alpha y + \beta + u$.

familiar Keynesian income theory but requires no other assumptions about the equations in the rest of the model.

11.12   Haavelmo uses a different approach, similar in that it uses assumptions about the behavior of disturbances to derive information about parameters, but different in that its assumptions specify a complete model (or at least specify enough about a complete model so that the limited-information method can be used). He shows under his assumptions that the probability limit (as the sample size goes to infinity) of the least-squares estimator of the marginal propensity to consume is greater than the true value, *and* by how much. Instead of using the moment equation (11.14) and arguing from the probable sign of m_{uy}, he assumes a complete model of two equations, incorporating investment i as an exogenous variable, and derives the probability limit of a ($= m_{cy}/m_{yy}$). The other equation, which with (11.13) forms a complete model, is

(11.15) $$y = c + i$$

It is *impossible* to derive the probability limit of a exactly without making quite specific assumptions about the structure that determines c and y; (11.15) plus the exogeneity of i are the assumptions Haavelmo uses in his simplest case, though others may be used instead, with correspondingly different results. The reduced form of Haavelmo's model (11.13) and (11.15) is

$$(11.16) \qquad c = \frac{1}{1 - \alpha}(\alpha i + \beta + u)$$

$$(11.17) \qquad y = \frac{1}{1 - \alpha}(i + \beta + u)$$

and from these he obtains the moments involved in the estimator a (this is one of the points where the specific assumptions of the model enter):

$$(11.18) \quad m_{cy} = \sum (c - \bar{c})(y - \bar{y})$$
$$= \left(\frac{1}{1 - \alpha}\right)^2 \sum [\alpha(i - \bar{\imath}) + (u - \bar{u})][(i - \bar{\imath}) + (u - \bar{u})]$$
$$= \left(\frac{1}{1 - \alpha}\right)^2 [\alpha m_{ii} + (1 + \alpha)m_{iu} + m_{uu}]$$

and similarly

$$(11.19) \qquad m_{yy} = \left(\frac{1}{1 - \alpha}\right)^2 [m_{ii} + 2m_{iu} + m_{uu}]$$

By substituting these two expressions into the least-squares estimator a, we obtain

$$(11.20) \qquad a = \frac{m_{cy}}{m_{yy}} = \frac{\alpha m_{ii} + (1 + \alpha)m_{iu} + m_{uu}}{m_{ii} + 2m_{iu} + m_{uu}}$$
$$= \alpha + \frac{(1 - \alpha)\, m_{iu}/T + (1 - \alpha)m_{uu}/T}{m_{ii}/T + 2m_{iu}/T + m_{uu}/T}$$

where, in the last step, α has been set out by itself so that the error term is clearly shown (of course this error term is equal to m_{uv}/m_{yy}, as the reader may verify). Now as the sample size T increases without limit, the terms in m_{iu}/T converge to zero in probability because u is assumed independent of i (this is another point where the previously mentioned assumptions of the model enter), and m_{uu}/T and m_{ii}/T converge in probability to the true variances of u and i, respectively, T being the sample size:

$$(11.21) \qquad \underset{T \to \infty}{\text{plim}}\ a = \alpha + \frac{(1 - \alpha)\sigma_u^{\ 2}}{\sigma_i^{\ 2} + \sigma_u^{\ 2}}$$

The second term on the right is the asymptotic least-squares bias in Haavelmo's model; it is positive since all variances are positive and α

is less than 1. This does not say what the approximate bias is in finite samples, but that can be inferred roughly from (11.20).

11.13 A more general version of Haavelmo's approach to the problem is provided by Jean Bronfenbrenner.[89] She begins with an example simpler than Haavelmo's and proceeds gradually to a model with two endogenous and two exogenous variables. We shall take up her model with two (endogenous) variables in the equation to be estimated and three variables in the other equation, for it shows some interesting complications:

(11.22) $$y_1 + \beta_{12} y_2 + \epsilon_1 = u_1$$

(11.23) $$\beta_{21} y_1 + y_2 + \gamma z + \epsilon_2 = u_2$$

where (11.22) is the equation to be estimated, and z is assumed exogenous. As usual the least-squares estimator of β_{12} (with y_1 "dependent") is the ratio of $m_{y_1 y_2}$ to $m_{y_2 y_2}$, this time with a negative sign because both y_1 and y_2 are on the same side of the equation. The reduced form of the model is

(11.24) $$y_1 = \frac{1}{1 - \beta_{12}\beta_{21}} (\beta_{12}\gamma z - \epsilon_1 + \beta_{12}\epsilon_2 + u_1 - \beta_{12} u_2)$$

(11.25) $$y_2 = \frac{1}{1 - \beta_{12}\beta_{21}} (-\gamma z + \beta_{21}\epsilon_1 - \epsilon_2 - \beta_{21} u_1 + u_2)$$

From these we can find the requisite moments:

(11.26) $$\frac{(1 - \beta_{12}\beta_{21})^2 m_{y_1 y_2}}{T} = \frac{(1 - \beta_{12}\beta_{21})^2 \sum (y_1 - \bar{y}_1)(y_2 - \bar{y}_2)}{T}$$

$$= \frac{-\beta_{12}\gamma^2 m_{zz}}{T} - \frac{\beta_{21} m_{u_1 u_1}}{T} + \frac{(1 + \beta_{12}\beta_{21}) m_{u_1 u_2}}{T}$$

$$\frac{-\beta_{12} m_{u_2 u_2}}{T} + \text{(terms whose probability limits are zero)}$$

(11.27) $$\frac{(1 - \beta_{12}\beta_{21})^2 m_{y_2 y_2}}{T} = \frac{\gamma^2 m_{zz}}{T} + \frac{\beta_{21}^2 m_{u_1 u_1}}{T} - \frac{2\beta_{21} m_{u_1 u_2}}{T} + \frac{m_{u_2 u_2}}{T}$$

$$+ \text{(terms whose probability limits are zero)}$$

Hence the probability limit of the least-squares estimator of β_{12} obtained by using y_1 as dependent, denoted by b_{12}, is

(11.28) $$\text{plim } b_{12} = \frac{\beta_{21}\sigma_1^2 - (1 + \beta_{12}\beta_{21})\sigma_{12} + \beta_{12}\sigma_2^2 + \beta_{12}\gamma^2\sigma_z^2}{\beta_{21}^2\sigma_1^2 - 2\beta_{21}\sigma_{12} + \sigma_2^2 + \gamma^2\sigma_z^2}$$

$$= \beta_{12} + \frac{(1 - \beta_{12}\beta_{21})(\beta_{21}\sigma_1^2 - \sigma_{12})}{\beta_{21}^2\sigma_1^2 - 2\beta_{21}\sigma_{12} + \sigma_2^2 + \gamma^2\sigma_z^2}$$

---

[89] Jean Bronfenbrenner (now Jean Bronfenbrenner Crockett) [1953]. We shall discuss her Case V, pp. 230–232. She also gives the solution for the general linear model with any number of equations, in matrix terms and without the proof, on p. 235.

where in the last step we have set β_{12} out by itself so that the asymptotic bias will be clearly shown by the remainder. (This remainder must be equal to $-m_{u_1 y_2}/m_{y_2 y_2}$, by an argument similar to that of 11.6.)

11.14 Now let us inquire with Bronfenbrenner: When will the asymptotic bias in the least-squares estimator of β_{12} be zero? Only when the numerator of the asymptotic bias term in (11.28) is zero. The factor $1 - \beta_{12}\beta_{21}$ will never be zero in any model that is realistic enough to use, for if this factor is zero then the solution of (11.14) and (11.15) for y_1 and y_2 must be either impossible or indeterminate. Hence, from the other factor in the numerator, the condition for zero asymptotic bias is

$$(11.29) \qquad\qquad \sigma_{12} = \beta_{21}\sigma_1{}^2$$

We shall see what this means. $\sigma_1{}^2$ will never be zero, for it is the variance of y_1, whose behavior we seek to explain. One possible case in which the condition will be met is when both β_{21} and σ_{12} are zero. In that case, the model becomes

$$(11.30) \qquad\qquad y_1 + \beta_{12}y_2 + \epsilon_1 = u_1$$

$$(11.31) \qquad\qquad y_2 + \gamma z + \epsilon_2 = u_2$$

$$(11.32) \qquad\qquad \sigma_{12} = 0$$

Here we have a recursive system (see 11.3), and y_2 satisfies the definition (see IV.4.9) of an exogenous variable in the one-equation model (11.30), for it is determined in a separate equation (11.31) not involving y_1, and the shifts u_1 in (11.30) are uncorrelated with y_2 because they are uncorrelated with the shifts u_2 in (11.31). *Of course* the least-squares estimator is asymptotically unbiased if y_2 is exogenous! We already know this from Section 3, where the least-squares estimator in this situation was proved to be unbiased for *any* sample size. On the other hand, if σ_{12} or β_{21} is not zero, then y_2 is not strictly exogenous in the equation to be estimated, and the asymptotic bias will be zero only if the two biases introduced by β_{12} and σ_{12} just offset each other as required by (11.29). (It might be added that if $\beta_{21} = 0$ and u_2 is independent of z, then γ in (11.31) can also be consistently estimated by least squares.)

11.15 The least-squares error for equations containing more than two variables can be analyzed by essentially the same methods as we have illustrated. We may use the approach of Harberger, which is to obtain the *actual* error in the estimate obtained from a particular sample, as a function of observed variables and the unobservable shifts u in the equation, and then deduce probable ranges of that error on the basis of presumptions about the behavior of u. Or we may use the approach of Haavelmo and Bronfenbrenner, which is similar except that assumptions about the whole model are used to obtain exact values of the asymptotic bias. In either case, the method shows that least-squares estimators are not consistent if the disturbances are not independent of the "independent" variables and also shows that the least-squares estimators may be quite useful if other appropriate information about the disturbances is available.

12   RELATIVE MERITS OF SEVERAL ESTIMATION METHODS FOR STRUCTURES AND FOR REDUCED FORMS

12.1   In this section we discuss briefly the relative merits of some of the methods of economic parameter estimation that have been presented earlier in the chapter. Usually we shall work implicitly within the framework of Model 3 (see 2.4). Both structural and reduced-form estimation will be considered. For convenience the following abbreviations will be used for structural-estimation methods:

LS: least squares, with some arbitrarily chosen dependent variable.

2SLS: two-stage least squares, with some arbitrarily chosen dependent variable.

k-class: k-class, with some arbitrarily chosen dependent variable.

LI: limited-information maximum likelihood.

FI: full-information maximum likelihood.

3SLS: three-stage least squares.

LML: linearized maximum likelihood.

Reduced-form parameters can be estimated directly by least squares. Also, each of these methods of structural estimation gives rise to reduced-form estimates if the estimated structural equations are solved to get the reduced form. The abbreviations to be used are:

LSRF: least squares, with the ith equation's jointly dependent variable y_{it} used as its dependent variable.

solved LS:
solved 2SLS:
solved k-class:
solved LI: estimate the structure by the method indicated,
solved FI: and then solve for the reduced form.
solved 3SLS:
solved LML:

12.2   Our previous discussion (Sections 6, 7, 9–11) has taught us a good deal about the properties of the foregoing structural-estimation methods. For example, *for structural equations in Model* 3: LS is in general inconsistent, and (if its expectations exist) biased for every sample size and in the limit, but it has the minimum variance (or approximate variance) among the methods discussed here; 2SLS, LI, FI, 3SLS, and LML are consistent; LI, FI, 3SLS, and LML are asymptotically normal; 2SLS and LI have the same asymptotic covariance matrix for $\sqrt{T}$ times the estimators. *For structural equations in Model 3 (normal), FI and LML are asymptotically efficient, and 2SLS and LI are asymptotically efficient compared with consistent estimators using the same a priori* information. See Table 12.1 for more detail.

12.3 Our previous discussion (Sections 3–5) has also taught us a good deal about the properties of LSRF for reduced-form estimation. In Model 3 this method is consistent and asymptotically normal, and in Model 3 (normal) it is asymptotically efficient *compared with* any consistent method that uses the same data and *a priori* information. It is certainly the simplest method to use, for it does not require the computation of any structural estimates at all. That is at once its strength and— in the case of overidentifying models—its weakness: strength because its computations are so simple, and weakness because it ignores all the *a priori* information built into the model telling which variables appear in which equations. This is a weakness only in overidentifying models because only there does the *a priori* information mentioned above affect the estimates of the reduced form. To see this, consider two structure-identifying models, each satisfying the assumptions of Model 3, each containing G structural equations in the same G endogenous variables $y_1, \ldots, y_G$, and each containing the same K predetermined variables $z_1, \ldots, z_K$. Suppose that the variable y_1 describes the expenditure of consumers, and that in the first model the consumption equation is over-identified and contains y_1, y_2, and z_1 only, whereas in the second model the consumption equation is just identified and contains y_1, y_2, y_3, z_1, and z_2. The two models then will differ as to the estimates of the structural parameters of y_3 and z_2 in the consumption equation: The first model will have zeros for these two parameters, but the second in general will not. And yet the least-squares estimators of their reduced forms *must* be identical, because the two reduced forms are alike in expressing each of the y's as a linear function of the same set of z's.[90] Thus the least-squares estimators of the reduced form do use the model's specifications concerning linearity, the properties of the disturbances, and the list of endogenous and predetermined variables appearing *in the model*, but do not use any of the assumptions concerning the particular endogenous and exogenous variables appearing *in each structural equation*.[91]

---

[90] This remark applies equally well to the reduced form of an *unidentified* model.

[91] If samples were infinite this would not create difficulty, for then the least-squares reduced-form estimates would be correct.

TABLE 12.1   Some Mathematically Known Properties of Structural Estimators in Model 3 and Other Models[a,b]

Estimator, and cross references to sections in this chapter regarding their properties	Some known properties in model 3 (lagged endogenous variables permitted; disturbances serially independent but not necessarily normal[b])	Some known properties in Model 3 (normal) and in Model 2 (like Model 3 except that all predetermined variables are strictly exogenous[b])
Least squares 3.14, 4.7, 5, 10.16, 11	inconsistent in general; small variance	
Indirect least squares[c] 7.3–4, 10.20	consistent	
Instrumental variables[c] 7.10, 10.20	consistent	
Limited information[e] 9.21, 9.23–30, 9.33, 9.35; 10.15–16, 10.19–20	consistent; asymptotically normal; approximate covariance matrix available	In Model 3 (normal): asymptotically efficient[f]
2-stage least squares[e] 10.10, 10.15–17, 10.19–20	consistent; asymptotic covariance matrix available	In Model 3 (normal): asymptotically efficient[f] In Model 2: asymptotically normal[g]
k-class[d] 10.16, 10.19	consistent if plim $(k-1) = 0$; approximate covariance matrix available if plim $\sqrt{T}(k-1) = 0$	In Model 3 (normal): asymptotically efficient[f] if plim $\sqrt{T}(k-1) = 0$
3-stage least squares[e] 10.32, 10.37–38	consistent; same as 2-stage least squares if covariance matrix of disturbances is diagonal	In Model 3 (normal): asymptotically efficient if covariance matrix of disturbances is unrestricted In Model 2: asymptotically normal[g] In Model 2 (normal): asymptotically efficient
Linearized maximum likelihood[e] 10.38		In Model 3 (normal): consistent;[f] asymptotically normal; asymptotically efficient
Full information[e] 6.8, 10.37–38	consistent; asymptotically normal	In Model 3 (normal): asymptotically efficient

[a] This catalog of properties does not purport to be exhaustive.

[b] For full descriptions of Models 2, 3, 2 (normal), and 3 (normal) see 2.4–5 above. See also 9.23–24 for related remarks and references concerning the assumptions used in these models.

[c] The four estimators marked "c" in the table are identical in the case of a just-identified equation. See also note e.

[d] See also 10.23–34 regarding the double k-class.

[e] If the entire model is just identified, then all seven estimators marked either "c" or "e" in the table are identical for that model.

[f] Compared with other estimators using the same incomplete *a priori* information.

[g] We may conjecture that for this estimator this property holds also in model 3.

12.4   By ignoring the overidentifying *a priori* information, we obtain, to be sure, the smallest possible residual variance for each estimated reduced-form equation. To see this, consider that any set of reduced-form parameter estimates is compatible with the restrictions imposed by the model on a *just-identified* structural equation.[92] Hence the model's restrictions permit (do not conflict with) the absolute minimization of residual variance that is the basis of LSRF. But there is a probability of 1 that an arbitrarily chosen set of reduced-form parameter values will be incompatible with the restrictions imposed by the model on an *over-identified* structural equation.[93] Therefore, if the estimated reduced-form parameters are required to be compatible with overidentifying structural restrictions, they are not free to take on whatever values will minimize the residual variances in reduced-form equations, and there is a probability of 1 that the resulting residual variances will be larger than those of LSRF.

12.5   The ignoring of *correct* overidentifying restrictions by the LSRF method is a weakness of the method, in spite of the fact that the smallest residual variances are obtained by LSRF. The situation is directly analogous to the one described in VII.8.1–2, where a population mean μ was known to be ≥ 9.9, and the chosen estimator was (a) the sample mean $\bar{x}$ whenever $\bar{x} \geq 9.9$, and (b) 9.9 whenever $\bar{x} < 9.9$. In that example, whenever $\bar{x} < 9.9$ the estimate 9.9 will have a larger sum of squared deviations than will the estimate $\bar{x}$, that is,

$$(12.1) \qquad \bar{x} < 9.9 \text{ implies } \sum_t (x_t - 9.9)^2 > \sum_t (x_t - \bar{x})^2$$

Nevertheless, if we are certain that $\mu \geq 9.9$, then the estimator that minimizes the residual variation *subject to the restriction* is preferable to (i.e., has smaller expected squared error than) the estimator that violates the restriction while freely minimizing the residual variation. In the present case, similarly, it is better to make the reduced-form estimates compatible with *correct* overidentifying restrictions and then choose their values to minimize the residual variation subject to those restrictions, rather than to use LSRF, which minimizes the residual variation without regard to the overidentifying restrictions.[94] Of course, if the overidentifying restrictions used are *incorrect*, it may be harmful rather than helpful to use them. Since in practice we are not usually sure about all of the *a priori* restrictions, LSRF may be a good method just because it does ignore them.

[92] This is shown in effect in VIII.3.34 and IX.7.2 by the fact that a set of model-admissible values of the parameters of a just-identified equation can be obtained from an arbitrary set of reduced-form parameter values.

[93] This is shown in effect in VIII.3.35 and IX.8.4.

[94] Klein [1960], [1960a] deals with this issue. See also Christ [1960] and Liu [1960]. Cragg [1966] discusses a related problem.

TABLE 12.2 Some Mathematically Known Properties of Reduced-Form Estimators in Model 3 and Other Models [a,b,c]

Estimator	Some known properties in Model 3 (lagged endogenous variables permitted; disturbances serially independent but not necessarily normal[c])	Some known properties in Model 3 (normal) and in Model 2 (like Model 3 except that all pre-determined variables are strictly exogenous[c])
LSRF	consistent; asymptotically normal; ignores overidentifying restrictions; cannot handle structural change	In Model 3 (normal): asymptotically efficient if the model is just identified
solved LS	inconsistent in general; uses overidentifying restrictions; can handle structural change	
solved LI solved 2SLS solved k class if plim $\sqrt{\overline{T}}(k-1) = 0$ solved LML solved FI	consistent; uses overidentifying restrictions; can handle structural change	In Model 3 (normal): asymptotically efficient compared with other estimators using the same *a priori* information
solved 3SLS	consistent; uses overidentifying restrictions; can handle structural change.	In Model 3 (normal): asymptotically efficient if covariance matrix of disturbances is unrestricted. In Model 2 (normal): asymptotically efficient

[a] This catalog of properties does not purport to be exhaustive.
[b] This table is based on Table 12.1 and Sections 12.3-7.
[c] For full descriptions of Models 2, 3, 2 (normal), and 3 (normal), see 2.4-5.

12.6 Another weakness of the ordinary least-squares estimators of the reduced form, where a structural change is known or believed to have occurred between the observation and prediction periods, is that they cannot take advantage of this knowledge or belief. This point has been made repeatedly earlier, in II.6–8 and in VII.2.

12.7 Next consider solved LS, that is, the reduced-form estimates obtained from the solution of the structural equations after the latter have been estimated by least squares directly. Least-squares structural estimators are inconsistent if there are two or more jointly dependent variables in the structural equation. Hence the reduced-form estimators that are derived by simultaneously solving structural equations so estimated will partake of the same inconsistency. However, they satisfy *a priori* overidentifying restrictions on the appearance of particular variables in particular structural equations, and they allow account to be taken of structural change. The preceding sentence also applies to solved 2SLS, solved k-class if plim $k = 1$, solved LI, solved FI, solved 3SLS, and solved LML. These six methods are consistent in Model 3. See Table 12.2.

12.8 It has been noted that the structural equations need not be linear in variables but must be linear in unknown parameters, if the estimation methods of this book are to be applied. If the structure is linear in variables, so will be the reduced form obtained by solving it. But suppose the structure is linear only in parameters and nonlinear in variables; then the reduced form obtained by solving it will be nonlinear in variables and nonlinear in structural parameters. Such a nonlinear reduced-form equation must itself be solved for its endogenous variable, and the solution may involve multiple roots. If so, it will usually be immediately clear from the types and magnitudes of the several roots which one corresponds most closely to the data. For example, complex and negative roots are irrelevant for most economic magnitudes such as incomes and prices. Net investment, trade balance, and certain other variables of course may in some cases be negative, but usually only within fairly well-known limits. See III.10.7–12.

12.9 Most of the desirable properties that have so far been proved for the foregoing estimation methods are *asymptotic* properties. This means they are properties that appear only in the limit as the sample size becomes infinite. We do not know, from the mathematical theorems about these asymptotic properties, much about how the estimators will behave when the sample size is 20 or 30, or 100, or even several thousand. But of course this is what we want to know. So far, few theoretical attacks on this problem using mathematical statistics have been very successful, but Nagar and Basmann have made significant contributions. Before discussing them, we recall that most of the estimators considered in this section typically do not possess finite variances or even finite means. This is because in most cases the estimator involves quotients with stochastic denominators that have nonzero probability densities at the value zero, so that the integral defining the mean of the estimator is infinite. Therefore in discussing the nonasymptotic properties of these estimators, we shall find it useful to proceed in terms of the means and variances of the approximate distributions suggested in VII.6.8–11. This is Nagar's approach, to which we now turn.

12.10 Nagar [1959a] and [1962] has analyzed small-sample properties of approximate distributions of the k-class and double k-class estimators (described in 10.15 and 10.23), respectively, under assumptions similar to our Model 2 (normal), that is, with all predetermined variables being exogenous. He assumed that k and k_1 and k_2 are nonstochastic functions of time that approach 1 in the limit as $T \to \infty$, specifically that $k = 1 + \kappa/T$ and that $k_i = 1 + \kappa_i/T$ where κ and κ_i ($i = 1, 2$) are real constants. Therefore his results have not been shown to apply to LI estimators, which belong to the k-class with a stochastic k.

12.11 Nagar under these conditions obtained the approximate bias to order $1/T$, and the approximate matrix of squares and cross products of errors to order $1/T^2$ (neglecting terms in higher powers of $1/T$), for both classes of estimators. The diagonal elements of the matrix are the approximate expected squared errors of the estimators of individual structural parameters, in the sense of VII.6.11. For the double k-class Nagar [1962] shows that the approximate bias to order $1/T$ is as follows (unfamiliar terms are defined below):

$$(12.2) \qquad (\bar{\mathbf{X}}\bar{\mathbf{X}}')^{-1}[(\kappa_1 - \kappa_2)\mathbf{q}^{*\prime} + (-\kappa_1 + K - J - H)\mathbf{q}']$$

where $(\bar{\mathbf{X}}\bar{\mathbf{X}}')^{-1}$ is the parent analogue of the matrix $(\mathbf{X}\mathbf{X}')^{-1}$ defined in 10.7 above, that is,

$$(12.3) \qquad (\bar{\mathbf{X}}\bar{\mathbf{X}}')^{-1} \equiv \begin{pmatrix} \mathbf{\Pi}_1 \mathbf{Z}\mathbf{Z}'\mathbf{\Pi}_1' & \mathbf{\Pi}_1 \mathbf{Z}\mathbf{Z}^{*\prime} \\ \mathbf{Z}^* \mathbf{Z}'\mathbf{\Pi}_1' & \mathbf{Z}^* \mathbf{Z}^{*\prime} \end{pmatrix}^{-1}$$

and where $\mathbf{q}'$ is the column vector of population covariances of u with $y_2, \ldots, y_H, z_1, \ldots, z_J$ (the last J elements being zero), and $\mathbf{q}^{*\prime}$ is the column vector of population covariances of y_1 with $y_2, \ldots, y_H, z_1, \ldots, z_J$ (the last J elements being zero). For the k-class where $\kappa_1 = \kappa_2$, the coefficient of $\mathbf{q}^{*\prime}$ is zero above. For two-stage least squares where $\kappa_1 = \kappa_2 = 0$, the term in square brackets above becomes simply $(K - J - H)\mathbf{q}'$. Hence the two-stage least-squares estimate is approximately unbiased in the sense of VII.6.9 if the estimated equation has just one overidentifying restriction (i.e., $K - J = H$). And a k-class estimator is unbiased to order $1/T$ if its value of k is $1 + (K - J - H)/T$.

12.12 The approximate matrix of expected squares and cross products is a somewhat more involved function of the data and specifications, even for the k-class. Let the matrix of true reduced-form disturbances $\mathbf{V}'$ be written as a linear combination of the normal disturbances $\mathbf{u}$ of the equation to be estimated, plus a matrix $\bar{\mathbf{V}}'$ of random variables also normal but independent of $\mathbf{u}$, thus:

$$(12.4) \qquad\qquad \mathbf{V}' = \mathbf{n}'\mathbf{u} + \bar{\mathbf{V}}'$$

where $\mathbf{n}'$ is a column vector of $H - 1$ constants. Let

$$(12.5) \qquad\qquad \mathbf{C}_1 \equiv \frac{1}{\sigma^2}\mathbf{q}'\mathbf{q}$$

where $\sigma^2 = \operatorname{var} u_t$ as usual, and $\mathbf{q}$ is defined in 12.11, and let

$$(12.6) \qquad\qquad \mathbf{C}_2 \equiv \begin{pmatrix} \dfrac{1}{T}E\bar{\mathbf{V}}\bar{\mathbf{V}}' & \mathbf{0} \\ \mathbf{0} & \mathbf{0} \end{pmatrix}$$

Note that both $\mathbf{C}_1$ and $\mathbf{C}_2$ are square of order $H - 1 + J$, and that the last J rows and columns of each are zero. Then under the conditions mentioned in 12.10, Nagar [1959a] finds that the approximate matrix of expected squares and cross products of errors of the k-class estimators, to order $1/T^2$, when $k = 1 + \kappa/T$, is as follows:

$$(12.7)$$
$$\{[-2(-\kappa + K - J - H) + 1]\operatorname{tr}[\mathbf{C}_1(\bar{\mathbf{X}}\bar{\mathbf{X}}')^{-1}] + \operatorname{tr}[\mathbf{C}_2(\bar{\mathbf{X}}\bar{\mathbf{X}}')^{-1}]\}\mathbf{I}$$
$$+ [(-\kappa + K - J - H - 1)^2 + 2\kappa + 2]\mathbf{C}_1(\bar{\mathbf{X}}\bar{\mathbf{X}}')^{-1}$$
$$- (-2\kappa + K - J - H - 1)\mathbf{C}_2(\bar{\mathbf{X}}\bar{\mathbf{X}}')^{-1}$$

For two-stage least squares, we set $\kappa = 0$ in (12.7). Nagar [1962] derives a similar but more general result for the double k-class. For the k-class he also shows [1959a] that the value of κ (i.e., of $T(k - 1)$) that is optimal, in the sense of minimizing the value of the determinant of the matrix (12.7), is

$$(12.8) \qquad\qquad \kappa = K - 2(H + J) - 1 - \frac{\operatorname{tr}[\mathbf{C}_2(\bar{\mathbf{X}}\bar{\mathbf{X}}')^{-1}]}{\operatorname{tr}[\mathbf{C}_1(\bar{\mathbf{X}}\bar{\mathbf{X}}')^{-1}]}$$

This is likely to be negative unless K, the number of predetermined variables in the whole model, is very large. This means that k is likely to be less than 1, rather than greater than 1 as with LI estimators. Nagar [1959a] presents some examples for a three-equation model taken from Klein [1950].

12.13 Basmann [1961] and [1963] takes a different approach. Instead of working with the approximate distribution of 2SLS estimators of an equation in a fairly general linear model as Nagar does, he derives the exact distributions of certain 2SLS estimators in three particular special cases, each of which is an equation of a model similar to our Model 2 (normal). Case I, in [1961], is the following overidentified equation in a two-equation model containing endogenous variables y_1 and y_2, exogenous variables $z_1, \ldots, z_4$, and disturbances u_1 and u_2:

$$(12.9) \qquad y_1 = \beta_{12} y_2 + \gamma_{13} z_3 + \gamma_{14} z_4 + \gamma_{10} + u_1$$

Case II, also in [1961], is the same equation in the same model except that $\gamma_{13} = 0$ and z_3 does not appear in the model. Case III, in [1963], is the following overidentified equation in a three-equation model containing three endogenous variables $y_i{}'$ and K exogenous variables z_k and three disturbances $u_i{}'$ (we use primes here to distinguish between notation for the first two cases and that for the third):

$$(12.10) \qquad y_1{}' = \beta_{12}{}' y_2{}' + \beta_{13}{}' y_3{}' + \sum_{4}^{K} \gamma_k z_k + u_1{}'$$

In each case Basmann assumes that the sample mean of each variable is zero (in effect measuring each variable as a deviation from its sample mean; recall 4.11 above), that the z's are uncorrelated in the sample, *and* that the units in which the z's are measured vary with the sample size T so that the sample sum of squares of any exogenous variable is 1 whatever the sample size, that is, that

$$(12.11) \qquad \sum_{t=1}^{T} z_{kt}^2 = 1 \qquad k = 1, \ldots, K, \qquad \text{for all } T$$

This requires that any nonzero reduced-form coefficient must be a function of T that approaches infinity in absolute value as $T \to \infty$.

12.14 Under the conditions stated in the foregoing paragraph, Basmann [1961] derives the exact finite-sample probability density function of the 2SLS estimator of β_{12} in Case I, that is, in equation (12.9). We denote this estimator by $\tilde{\beta}_{12}$ in this context only. Its density function turns out to be a rather involved infinite series whose typical term contains $(\beta_{12}\tilde{\beta}_{12} + 1)^{2m_2}/(1 + \tilde{\beta}_{12}{}^2)^{m_2+3/2}$, where m_2 is an index of summation from 0 to ∞; see Basmann [1961], p. 631, equation (3.46), for a somewhat more complex equivalent version, and Kabe [1963], p. 536, equation (12), for the version described here. This density function as given by Basmann or by Kabe does not appear at first sight to depend on the sample size, until we recall that the adoption of (12.11) requires that reduced-form parameters (which appear in the density function) depend on the sample size. Basmann shows that this density function has a finite mean but not a finite variance. Basmann then considers the density in case the true value of β_{12} is zero (unknown to the statistician) and shows that it still has a finite mean but not a finite variance. For a set of illustrative numerical values of the relevant parameters, including $\beta_{12} = 0$, he presents a graph of the density (p. 623); it appears approximately normal but with a taller peak and thicker tails than the normal.

12.15 In Case II, under similar assumptions, including $\beta_{12} = 0$, plus the assumption that z_4 is actually the only exogenous variable in the model so that (12.9) is not identified [unknown to the statistician, who tries to estimate (12.9) on the assumptions that z_1, z_2, and z_4 appear in the model but that z_3 does not so that $\gamma_{13} = 0$], Basmann [1961] derives the exact density function of the 2SLS estimator of β_{12}. If this estimator is denoted by $\bar{\beta}_{12}''$ (in this context only), his result for its density is

$$2/\pi(1 + \bar{\beta}_{12}''^2)^2.$$

This has a finite mean equal to zero, and a finite variance; see his pp. 633–34.

12.16 In Case III, under similar assumptions, including $\beta_{12}' = \beta_{13}' = 0$, plus the assumption that all reduced-form parameters of z_1, z_2, and z_3 are zero except the coefficient of z_3 in the reduced-form equation for y_3', Basmann [1963] obtains the exact density functions of the 2SLS estimators of β_{12}' and β_{13}' in (12.10). Let us call these estimators $\bar{\beta}_{12}'$ and $\bar{\beta}_{13}'$ in this context only. Then Basmann obtains for the density of $\bar{\beta}_{12}'$ the following: $2/(1 + \bar{\beta}_{12}'^2)^{3/2}$. For the density of $\bar{\beta}_{13}'$ Basmann obtains an infinite series whose typical term contains $(1 + \bar{\beta}_{13}'^2)^{m+3/2}$, where m is an index of summation from 0 to ∞; see his p. 168, equation (4.18). See also Kabe [1964] and Bergstrom [1962].

12.17 Nagar's and Basmann's theorizing on small-sample properties constitute important first steps. Nagar's approach is so far the more useful for general models, though it gives only approximate results, and Basmann's is so far limited to special cases, though common features appear in the results obtained so far, and the results are exact.

12.18 We turn now to empirical evidence of two kinds about the small-sample properties of various estimators. One kind is given by econometric studies of real-world data in which two or more estimation methods have been used for the same structural equation or equations. In most cases to date, it is the LS and LI and 2SLS methods that have been used. Comparisons of this kind cannot be conclusive, because the true values of the parameters are not known; hence all we have are two or more estimates of each structural equation, made by different methods. I have not seen all the studies that provide such comparisons. My subjective impression from what I have seen is that in many cases the LS and LI and 2SLS estimates do not differ grossly from each other—by the order of their estimated standard deviation or less—but that where they differ strikingly, particularly where they have opposite signs or very different magnitudes, it is more often the LI estimates that are unreasonable in sign and magnitude, and the LS and 2SLS estimates that are reasonable, in the light of economic theory and other empirical evidence.[95]

12.19   This strange behavior of the LI estimator may be due to peculiar behavior, in some samples, of the LI equation (9.27), which requires that $\det (\mathbf{W}^* - l\mathbf{W}) = 0$, and whose smallest root l_1 is used in LI estimation. Theil [1958], pp. 233–236, or [1961], pp. 235–237, gives some graphs of the behavior of k-class estimators for the model in Girshick and Haavelmo [1947], as functions of the value of k. Quandt [1962] gives similar results for a different model; see 12.33. In most cases the k-class estimator is quite insensitive to the value of k as long as k is less than 1 or 1.05 or 1.1, but the estimator changes very rapidly to infinity and then changes sign and recedes from infinity again if k increases very much beyond 1.   Since k in the LI method is l_1 [where l_1 is the smallest root of the above-mentioned equation (9.27); see 10.15], the behavior shown by Theil's graphs may explain the occasional unreasonable behavior of the LI estimators.

12.20   Klein and Nakamura [1962] show that both 2SLS and LI estimators misbehave if the matrix $\mathbf{W}^* - \mathbf{W}$ is nearly singular (see 9.20–21 for the role of this matrix in LI estimation), and that if $\mathbf{W}^* - \mathbf{W}$ is not nearly singular but if the two smallest roots l_1 and l_2 of the equation $\det (\mathbf{W}^* - l\mathbf{W}) = 0$ are nearly equal, then the LI estimator misbehaves but the 2SLS estimator does not.

12.21   So-called Monte Carlo experiments provide the second kind of empirical evidence about the relative merits of different estimation methods when sample sizes are small. A Monte Carlo experiment is essentially an empirical method of learning about the probability distribution of a statistic. It consists in drawing a large number of samples from the population in question, computing the value of the interesting statistic for each sample, and recording the empirically observed sampling distribution of that statistic. This method is sometimes used when mathematical attacks have not succeeded, and it has become more practical with the advent of electronic computers. In the case of a comparison between estimation methods for structural parameters, it works in this way. First, an artificial structure is set up, consisting of a model such as the following (see 2.2):

$$(12.12) \qquad\qquad \mathbf{B}\mathbf{y}_t{}' + \mathbf{\Gamma}\mathbf{z}_t{}' = \mathbf{u}_t{}'$$

[95] See, for example, Table XI.6.2′ below and Christ [1951], equations 1.0 and 4.0, pp. 72–73. I have seen similar results in several unpublished studies, but not in many published works. Apparently it is not common practice to include an account of one's unsuccessful trials in published reports, but would not other workers in the field gain by learning of them?

with *known* parameters **B** and **Γ**, and with a *known* distribution function of the disturbance vector $\mathbf{u}_t$ including its covariance matrix **Σ** (and any other parameters it may have). Second, a set of values of exogenous variables (i.e., those z's that are not lagged values of the y's) for $t = 1, \ldots, T$ is chosen, and a set of initial values of the y's for $t = 0, -1, -2, \ldots$, is chosen. Then a large number of samples of size T are chosen and observed from the known distribution of $\mathbf{u}_t$. For each of these samples, the reduced-form equations are used to generate a set of values of the jointly dependent variables $\mathbf{y}_t$ and the predetermined variables for $t = 1, \ldots, T$, in terms of the known parameters **B** and **Γ**, the known exogenous variables and initial values of predetermined variables, and the observed values of the random disturbances $\mathbf{u}_t$. This yields a large number of artificial samples of data for $\mathbf{y}_t$ and $\mathbf{z}_t$ for $t = 1, \ldots, T$ that have been generated by the artificial structure that was set up to begin with.

    12.22   Then the known values of **B**, **Γ**, and **Σ** and the values of $\mathbf{u}_t$ are, so to speak, locked up in a drawer, and we pretend they are not known. We then use the artificial sample data for $\mathbf{y}_t$ and $\mathbf{z}_t$ to estimate the parameters **B**, **Γ**, and **Σ** by each method that is in question. This can be done using the correct model, that is, using *a priori* restrictions that correctly describe the artificial structure that was used, or it can be done with an incorrect model. The incorrect model is useful for studying the consequences of using a wrong model to estimate parameters we want. Most studies so far have used the correct model. When the estimated values of the parameters have been computed by each method for each sample, we can then, so to speak, unlock the drawer, and compare each estimation method's sampling distribution of estimators of any parameter with the true value of that parameter, and hence arrive at a judgment as to which estimation method we prefer for that parameter with a sample of size T.

    12.23   Of course it is to be emphasized that the Monte Carlo method does not give the *true* probability distribution of the estimators but rather an empirical estimate of that distribution. It is analogous to determining the probability of heads with a coin by tossing it a large number of times and recording the proportion of heads that occurs. The Monte Carlo method is subject to sampling error itself. But if the number of samples used is large, the error is likely to be small.

    12.24   In order to compare a parameter with several probability distributions of estimators to see which estimator is preferred, we need a scalar measure of closeness between a parameter and a distribution. In principle, as pointed out in VII.5.7–13, this requires a loss function describing our preferences regarding errors of different magnitudes (and possibly directions). For reasons discussed in VII.5.11–13 and 6.11, we adopt the following loss function:[96] (a) the squared error, as long as the error is less in absolute magnitude than some upper limit, say M; (b) M^2, if the error is larger in absolute value than M. In applying this truncated squared-error loss function to Monte Carlo experiments, we should begin by choosing the value of the upper limit M for each parameter to be estimated. Whenever a sample occurs in which the error of the ith parameter exceeds in absolute value the corresponding limit M_i, then M_i itself rather than the actual error should be squared and entered in the sum of squared losses that is to be divided by the number of samples to arrive at the observed mean loss.[97] In many cases the Monte Carlo experimenter has not done this, but instead he has simply computed the mean square error for all the samples in the experiment [or has given the mean and variance of the error, which can be used to compute the mean square error, which is equal to the bias squared plus the variance; compare (VII.6.5) for population values]. The observed mean square error for the ith parameter equals the loss under our chosen loss function provided that the chosen upper limit M_i equals or exceeds in absolute value the largest error that occurred in estimating the ith parameter in the experiment. Thus the observed mean square error can be regarded as at least approximately equal to the loss, for large values of the chosen upper limit M_i.

12.25 A comparison of LS and simultaneous-equations methods of estimating individual *structural* parameters is clearly what is wanted when the problem at hand depends on knowledge of individual structural equations or parameters. Sometimes we want a comparison of the *reduced-form* equations estimated by different methods. And sometimes we want a comparison of *forecasts* made from reduced forms estimated by different methods. Most of the Monte Carlo studies that have been done so far are confined to the estimation of structural parameters. Although there is a relationship between the quality of structural estimators and the quality of reduced-form estimators obtained by solving the estimated structure, it is difficult to make very simple statements about this that are useful for the case of small samples and biased estimators in which economists usually find themselves. If structural parameters are known exactly, then of course reduced-form parameters can be computed exactly. If structural estimators are consistent, then reduced-form estimators obtained by solving the estimated structure are also consistent. If LS

---

[96] See equation (VII.5.12) for a slightly more general loss function. In that equation the letter k is used to describe this kind of upper limit, but we use M here because k here refers to the parameter of k-class estimators.

[97] This implicit procedure for dealing with "outliers" (i.e., occasional estimates that are much further away from the parameter than the others) is a compromise between dropping them and treating them like all other observations.

structural estimators have smaller expected squared errors than other
, structural estimators, there is no general presumption that reduced-form
estimators obtained from the solved LS structure will have smaller
expected squared errors than other reduced-form estimators. The difficulty
with the solved LS structure method is that it has no necessary connection
with maximizing the likelihood function of the reduced form or minimizing
some increasing function of the reduced form's errors.

12.26 The results of several Monte Carlo studies may be briefly
summarized here.[98] Harvey Wagner [1958] compared LS, LI, and instrumental variables estimators of an overidentified "consumption" equation
of the form $c = 0.25 + 0.5y + u$ in two simple three-equation models.
He used 100 samples of size 20 for each model. He found that the three
methods gave about the same mean square error for the marginal propensity to consume, with LS more often best than not; that the bias of
LS was greater than that of the other methods; and that the variance of
LS was smaller than that of the other methods. A. L. Nagar [1960] used
Wagner's models with a new set of synthetic data, also with 100 samples
of size 20 for each model, and compared LS with 2SLS and two other
members of the k-class (see 12.11–12), for the marginal propensity to
consume and for the partial derivatives of "investment" with respect to
current and lagged "income." The mean square errors of all methods
were very similar for the "consumption" equation. For the "investment"
equation they varied more widely: In one model the unbiased method
was best, the 2SLS method almost equally good, the minimum-determinant
method next with mean square errors about 50 per cent larger, and LS
worst with mean square errors more than twice as large as 2SLS; in the
other model the minimum-determinant method was best, followed in
order by LS, the unbiased method, and 2SLS, the ratio of the largest to
the smallest mean square error being about 1.3. It is interesting that
2SLS gave the smallest bias in every case, and the minimum-determinant-
of-second-moments method gave the smallest mean square error in four
of the six cases.

12.27 In papers presented at the Econometric Society's 1958 annual
meetings, Basmann and Summers reported on Monte Carlo experiments.[99]
Basmann compared LS, LI, and 2SLS estimators of an overidentified
equation, $y_1 = -2y_2 + 1.5y_3 + 3x_1 - 0.6x_5 + 10 + u_1$, in a three-
equation model that is a special case of our Model 2 (normal), with no
lagged endogenous variables. He used 200 samples of size 16. For each
of the five parameters, the LS mean square error was much less than that
of LI; and for four of the five it was less than that of 2SLS, but differences

---

[98] A somewhat fuller summary of some of these studies appears in Christ [1960].
[99] Basmann [1960b] describes part of his experiment; a full description is in
Basmann [1958]. See also Summers [1965].

between LS and 2SLS here were small (ratios of LS to 2SLS mean square errors all fell between 3/4 and 4/3).[100]

12.28 Summers [1965] conducted 12 experiments, with two over-identified or just-identified equations that might represent demand and supply of a single good. He used 50 samples of size 20 or size 40. He varied some of the parameters from experiment to experiment, and in two experiments deliberately based his estimates on a model that incorrectly excluded one predetermined variable from one of the equations. He also varied the degree of multicollinearity among exogenous variables. In each experiment he compared (a) LS, LI, 2SLS, and FI estimates of the structure; (b) LSRF and solved LS, solved LI, solved 2SLS, and solved FI estimates of the reduced form; and (c) conditional forecasts of his two endogenous variables based on those five sets of reduced-form estimates.[101] For some comparisons he used the mean square error as a criterion of quality of the estimators, and for some comparisons he used the median absolute error; the two criteria gave very similar results, except regarding the LI method for those few cases in which some of its estimates were *very* far off. For LS structural estimation, variances were small, but biases were so large that LS errors were larger than those of the other three methods in most cases. The differences among the other three structural estimating methods were usually small, with FI being best, except that in the misspecification experiments LI and FI became worse than 2SLS, and in the presence of multicollinearity LI was inferior. The 2SLS structural estimators were the least bothered by misspecification and multicollinearity. For conditional forecasts of endogenous variables, solved LS was almost always substantially worst, and the other four methods of reduced-form estimation yielded forecasts of very similar quality. L'Esperance [1964] finds that real forecasts for the watermelon market are better made by the solved structure in his model than by the least-squares reduced form.

12.29 Neiswanger and Yancey [1959] used a two-equation model under several sets of conditions and found LI somewhat better than LS when the correct model was used; they found both very poor when certain types of misspecification were introduced.

12.30 Ladd [1956] used a two-equation model to compare LI and LS estimation when errors of measurement of variables were present. He used only one sample of disturbances, and all of his thirty-odd samples drawn from the distribution of errors of measurement were used in connection with this single sample of disturbances, so that we do not have

---

[100] Basmann prefers an alternative loss function based on the probability of occurrence of an error greater than some critical size. According to this loss function, LS did poorly. Such a loss function is discussed in VII.5.11–13.

[101] Forecasts are discussed at greater length in Chapter X.

much evidence about the effect of disturbances in his model. He found that errors of measurement impart little bias but increase the variances of structural estimates.

12.31 Quandt [1965] presents results of a Monte Carlo experiment to estimate the equation $y_1 = 0.2y_2 - 2y_3 + y_4 + z_1 + 0.5z_2 - z_3 + u_1$. He used two different four-equation models, one having six exogenous variables (including constant) and one having seven, so that the estimated equation is just identified in one model and overidentified in the other. He used two sets of data for the exogenous variables, one more multi-collinear than the other. He used two normal populations of disturbances, one with a diagonal covariance matrix Σ and one without. He used five different matrices $\mathbf{B}$ of coefficients of endogenous variables, differing in the degree to which off-diagonal elements are numerically much smaller than diagonal elements (he calls the $\mathbf{B}$ matrix *sparse* if it has this property to an extreme degree). He used samples of size $T = 20$, and for each run he took 100 such samples. He grouped his runs into what he calls logical sets, each logical set being characterized by a particular choice of $\mathbf{B}$ and Σ. There were six logical sets chosen; five of them combine one of the five matrices $\mathbf{B}$ with the nondiagonal Σ, and one of them combines the least sparse matrix $\mathbf{B}$ with the diagonal matrix Σ. Each logical set contains four runs, corresponding to the four possible combinations of the two models and the two data sets. He estimated the six parameters in the equation above by least squares and by two-stage least squares for each of the 100 samples in each of the 24 runs.

12.32 Quandt used eight different measures of the quality of estimators: (1) the mean error, (2) the median error, (3) the standard deviation, (4) the mean square error, (5) the proportion of estimates falling within 20 per cent of the true value, (6) the proportion of estimates having the wrong sign, (7) the largest absolute error among the 100 samples, and (8) a conditional forecast of one of the endogenous variables, made from the estimated structural equation given the true values of the other three endogenous variables and of the predetermined variables in the equation. Results regarding structural estimation are summarized in tables in Quandt [1965] and are presented in more detail in an unpublished report, Quandt [1962]. Drawing upon both of these sources, we may construct the following summary of structural estimation: In terms of either mean or median error, LS is usually better than 2SLS for the highly collinear z's, and almost always poorer than 2SLS for the less collinear z's. LS had a much smaller standard deviation than 2SLS, the ratio varying from about 0.01 to 0.7 but usually being less than 0.2. LS usually had a smaller mean square error than 2SLS. The distribution of 2SLS has more concentration within 20 per cent of the true value, but also thicker tails, than LS; the latter is shown by 2SLS' poorer score than LS on wrong signs and on largest errors. High multicollinearity among the z's worsens the estimates; this effect is greater for 2SLS than for LS. Sparseness of the coefficient matrix **B** improves the estimates, as does triangularity of **B**. Diagonality of the covariance matrix Σ improves the estimates, especially for LS. An estimator constructed as follows is recommended by Quandt: Compute 2SLS and LS, and note whether the absolute value of the difference between the two exceeds the absolute value of the LS estimate; if so, adopt LS, and if not, adopt 2SLS. This strategy is likely to take some advantage of both the higher concentration of 2SLS near the true value and the thinner tails of LS.

12.33 In Quandt [1962] are reported k-class estimates computed for 4 of his logical sets (16 runs, omitting those with the diagonal covariance matrix Σ and the triangular coefficient matrix **B**), for 25 values of k ranging from -0.4 to $+2.0$ in steps of 0.1. The manner in which the k-class estimator varies with k is very interesting. Typically there are two or more violent oscillations in the mean estimate over 100 samples as k passes through the region from about 1.05 to 1.3, but apart from that the average of the 100 estimates varies quite smoothly with k as k goes from -0.4 to 1.0, and again from about 1.3 to 2.0. In about two-thirds of the cases the slope of the relationship is small so that the estimator appears insensitive to k over the range from $k = 0$ to $k = 1$, but in about one-third of the cases there is a substantial slope in the neighborhood of $k = 1$. In a few cases the oscillations are felt at values of k as low as 0.8 or as high as 2.0, and in a few cases they are negligible. These results are quite consistent with the findings of Theil ([1958], pp. 233–236, or [1961], pp. 235–237); see 12.19–20 above.

12.34 These Monte Carlo studies do not cover much ground. They suggest, however, that although there will be cases in which the simultaneous equations methods of structural estimation do not give sufficient (if any) improvement over LS to make their extra cost worthwhile, especially for the purpose of getting the structural parameters per se, there will also be cases in which the 2SLS and LI methods are worthwhile, and in which the FI method gives still better results. It might be noted that as the services of high-speed computers become available to more economists, the cost advantage of ordinary least squares will dwindle.

12.35 In summary, it is not yet clear that the least-squares method for structural estimation is dead and should be discarded. It is clear, however, that even for small samples least squares sometimes will not do as well as simultaneous-equations methods. The important task ahead is to learn more about how to decide which estimation method is likely to be best for any given actual econometric problem. For the present, the situation appears to be as follows: For structural parameters, least squares sometimes is preferable to simultaneous-equations methods (probably especially where samples are small and specification error is present), and sometimes is not (probably especially in the reverse case). For reduced-form parameters and forecasts in just-identified models, ordinary least-squares estimation of the reduced form is good; in this case it is equivalent to solving the structure as estimated by two-stage least-squares, limited-information, or full-information methods. For reduced-form parameters and forecasts in *overidentified* models, it seems well to begin by estimating structural parameters by simultaneous-equations methods, and then to solve the estimated structure to get estimates of the reduced form. This appears to be true even in some of the cases where least-squares estimators of the structure are better than simultaneous-equations estimators of the structure, as suggested in 12.25.

13   SERIAL CORRELATION OF DISTURBANCES, FIRST DIFFERENCES, AND LAGS[102]

13.1   As the reader will recall, the preceding pages have made frequent use of the assumption (j) that the disturbance u_t in the equation to be estimated is independent of the disturbances in any period other than t. If there are any lagged endogenous variables among the prede-termined variables, then estimators that would be consistent given inde-pendent disturbances may lose consistency if the disturbances are not independent in different periods. If all the predetermined variables are exogenous, then estimators that would be consistent and asymptotically efficient given independent disturbances may or may not lose consistency, but do lose asymptotic efficiency, if the disturbances are not independent. Many estimation methods have been criticized for assuming independent disturbances, and rightly so, because it is an assumption justified as much by statistical convenience as by economic plausibility. There are several responses that can be made to this criticism. One is to perform a test to see whether serial correlation is present in the shifts, with the idea that if the test shows little or no serial correlation everything is all right; such tests will be discussed in X.4. But if serial correlation is present to any important degree, everything is not all right and something further should be done. We shall discuss several possibilities briefly.

13.2   Two possibilities begin by revising the assumption of serial independence to try to take account of whatever serial dependence there might be. The simplest form of such a revised assumption is that the shift in any period is the sum of two parts, one of which is a constant multiple

[102] This section applies to time-series studies and to those cross-section studies in which the individuals observed are connected in a definite rank order so that dis-turbances are, so to speak, propagated from one to another *in that order*; see X.4.4.

of the previous period's shift, the other being a random disturbance u with the same properties as were assigned to u before. The shift in period t will now be called e instead of u, and as before u stands for a serially independent random disturbance:

$$(13.1) \qquad e_t = \alpha e_{t-1} + u_t$$

In other words, the shifts are assumed to be generated by a linear first-order difference equation with an unobservable random disturbance. Such an equation is also called an *autoregressive* equation, for e_t is determined by a regression on its own lagged value.[103]

13.3 The series of disturbances "explodes" if α is greater than 1 in absolute value, for then e_t incorporates a larger value αe_{t-1} than the preceding value e_{t-1}. It turns out that e_t has a finite and constant variance if and only if $|\alpha| < 1$. This may be seen as follows. We express e_{t-1} in (3.1) in terms of e_{t-2} and u_{t-1}, then express e_{t-2} in terms of e_{t-3} and u_{t-2}, and so on in infinite regress, so that e_t becomes a function of successive u's only, thus:

$$(13.2) \qquad \begin{aligned} e_t &= \alpha e_{t-1} + u_t = \alpha(\alpha e_{t-2} + u_{t-1}) + u_t \\ &= \alpha^2 e_{t-2} + \alpha u_{t-1} + u_t \\ &= \alpha^3 e_{t-3} + \alpha^2 u_{t-2} + \alpha u_{t-1} + u_t \\ &= \cdots \\ &= \alpha^\infty e_{t-\infty} + \sum_{i=0}^{\infty} \alpha^i u_{t-i} \end{aligned}$$

It does no harm to let the "initial" value of e, namely, $e_{t-\infty}$, be equal to zero, for this amounts only to changing the value of the constant term in the equation that has e as its disturbance. Hence

$$(13.3) \qquad e_t = \sum_{i=0}^{\infty} \alpha^i u_{t-i}$$

From this it is easy to see that the expected value of e_t is zero, for the expected value of every term in the sum is zero because Eu_t is assumed to be zero. That is,

$$(13.4) \qquad Ee_t = 0$$

[103] More complex assumptions can be made, for instance that the shifts satisfy an autoregressive equation of the second or higher order, but the economic justification is dubious. Treatments of this general topic will be found in Cochrane and Orcutt [1949], Orcutt and Cochrane [1949], Durbin and Watson [1950] and [1951], Wold [1950], Stone [1954], pp. 284–291, Durbin [1960], Sargan [1961], Zellner [1961], Amemiya [1964], and Taylor and Wilson [1964].

The variance of e_t is

$$(13.5) \qquad \text{var}(e_t) = E(e_t - Ee_t)^2 = Ee_t^2 = E\left(\sum_{i=0}^{\infty} \alpha^i u_{t-i}\right)^2$$

$$= \sum_{i=0}^{\infty} \alpha^{2i} Eu_{t-i}^2 = \sigma^2 \sum_{i=0}^{\infty} \alpha^{2i}$$

The reason for the next to last step is that the expected value of any cross product such as $u_t u_{t-1}$, or $u_{t-j} u_{t-k}$ where $j \neq k$, is zero by the assumption of no serial dependence of u. The last step uses the assumption that u has a constant variance, σ^2. The last expression in (13.5) is an infinite geometric progression in α^2 and hence has a finite and constant value only if $\alpha^2 < 1$, that is, if $|\alpha| < 1$. Let us assume that $|\alpha| < 1$. Then by the standard formula for the sum of an infinite geometric progression, the variance of e_t in (13.5) becomes the finite constant

$$(13.6) \qquad \text{var}(e_t) = \frac{\sigma^2}{1 - \alpha^2} \qquad \text{where } |\alpha| < 1$$

13.4 The serial correlation coefficient of e_t is the ratio of $Ee_t e_{t-1}$ to $\sqrt{Ee_t^2 Ee_{t-1}^2}$, but since e_t and e_{t-1} are typical terms in the same series, Ee_t^2 and Ee_{t-1}^2 must be equal, and this may be written as $Ee_t e_{t-1}/Ee_{t-1}^2$. To find this expression, it is only necessary to multiply (13.1) by e_{t-1} and take the expected value of each side. The result is

$$(13.7) \qquad Ee_t e_{t-1} = \alpha Ee_{t-1}^2 + Eu_t e_{t-1}$$

The last term is zero because u_t is an independent random variable. Hence the serial correlation of e is

$$(13.8) \qquad \rho(e_t e_{t-1}) = \frac{Ee_t e_{t-1}}{Ee_{t-1}^2} = \alpha \qquad \text{where } |\alpha| < 1$$

It is important to realize that this serial correlation is defined only if e_t has a finite constant variance, that is, only if $|\alpha| < 1$. In particular, (13.8) does not apply if $\alpha = \pm 1$.

13.5 The first two possibilities that we consider for dealing with serially correlated disturbances are based on (13.1). The first is to estimate α, along with the other unknown parameters. We may attempt to estimate all the parameters of the equation simultaneously by the maximum-likelihood method. This is extremely cumbersome, and little practical econometric work has been based on it, although some exploratory work has been carried out.[104] Instead of a simultaneous estimation process for

[104] See Koopmans and Hood [1953], p. 120, note 14, and Klein [1953], pp. 85–89. In the latter place estimation of a fairly simple equation requires the solution of a polynomial of high degree.

α and other parameters, we could try an iterative process as follows: First estimate the equation in question, using raw data, that is, as if the disturbances were serially independent. Compute the residuals and call them $u^{(0)}$. Then compute the autoregression coefficient of the series $u^{(0)}$ according to (13.1) and call this computed value $\alpha^{(0)}$. Then transform each variable to a new series whose current value is the current value of the raw data minus $\alpha^{(0)}$ times the lagged value. This is the end of the first iteration. Then estimate the equation, using the transformed data based on $\alpha^{(0)}$. Compute its residuals and call them $u^{(1)}$. Compute the autoregression coefficient of $u^{(1)}$ and call it $\alpha^{(1)}$. Transform the original raw data as above but use $\alpha^{(1)}$ now in place of $\alpha^{(0)}$. This is the end of the second iteration. Repeat as many times as desired. The properties of this method are not well known, but it seems a reasonable one.

13.6 The second possibility we consider is to *assume* a value of α in (13.1) and proceed from there to derive estimators of the other parameters. Good examples of this for $\alpha = 0$ are all the above-mentioned methods described in Sections 3–10, which use assumption (j). What value of α *should* be assumed? There is usually no case for assuming a value outside the range from -1 to $+1$, for in most problems there is no evidence that shifts grow steadily larger at an exponentially increasing rate. There is rarely a case for assuming a negative value of α either, because we do not often observe relationships that appear to shift alternately from one extreme to the other with any regularity. The eligible range is then from 0 to 1. After $\alpha = 0$, which we have already discussed (and which does not always work out, or else we would not be discussing this topic), the next simplest choice is $\alpha = 1$. What are the meanings of these two values? $\alpha = 0$ means that the shift that comes in any particular year exerts its influence for just that year, and then is gone, after which the curve or surface returns to its usual or "average" position, from which it is moved again by the next year's shift. Thus the curve or surface fluctuates about its "average" or usual position, always being separated from it by exactly the amount of the current year's shift. $\alpha = 1$ means that when a shift occurs in a particular year, it stays forever, moving the curve or surface to a new position, from which the next year's shift is received. There is no average position of the curve or surface, for it can be pushed back or forth quite a distance if several successive shifts should all come in the same direction.[105] The difference can be illustrated by the game of matching pennies: $\alpha = 0$ means that the winner gives the penny back to the loser before they match again, so that they always start where they were at first; but $\alpha = 1$ means that the winner keeps the penny and they match again, so that one of them may eventually win quite a

[105] The thing that *does* have an average position in this case is the size of the year-to-year change; it fluctuates randomly about zero.

large sum from the other.[106] Values of α between 0 and 1 correspond to shifts that diminish in effect gradually from year to year instead of dying out immediately after one year or lasting forever. It should be recalled from 13.4 that the shifts u_t have a finite constant variance only if $|\alpha| < 1$.

13.7 The appropriate technique, if we believe that $\alpha = 1$, is to use the estimation methods described in the foregoing sections of the chapter, but first to transform all the time-series data for the variables into first differences, that is, to use Δy's instead of y's, and Δz's instead of z's. Let us illustrate with an example. Suppose we have this equation:

$$(13.9) \qquad x_t = \beta_2 p_t + \beta_3 y_t + \gamma + e_t$$

in which e is believed to be generated by an autoregressive equation such as (13.1) with $\alpha = 1$, where u_t is serially independent, thus:

$$(13.10) \qquad e_t = e_{t-1} + u_t$$

Let us now write (13.9) down twice, once for period t with e_t replaced by (13.10), and once for period $t - 1$, thus:

$$(13.11) \qquad x_t = \beta_2 p_t + \beta_3 y_t + \gamma + e_{t-1} + u_t$$
$$(13.12) \qquad x_{t-1} = \beta_2 p_{t-1} + \beta_3 y_{t-1} + \gamma + e_{t-1}$$

These two equations are identical in form except for the disturbances, which differ only by u_t. Let us subtract (13.12) from (13.11):

$$(13.13) \qquad \Delta x_t = \beta_2 \, \Delta p_t + \beta_3 \, \Delta y_t + u_t$$

We have now devised an equation whose shifts u_t conform to our earlier assumptions, including serial independence, so that it can be estimated by any of the methods described in earlier sections. (Observe that the constant term of an equation disappears if it is transformed into first-difference form. If there is to be a constant term in a first-difference-form equation, there must be a linear time trend in the ordinary equation from which it is derived; the parameter of that term indicates by how much the variable being explained changes every period.)

13.8 We have found that equations using raw economic data are appropriate to a world in which shifts come and last for just one period, and equations using first differences of economic data are appropriate to a world in which shifts come and last forever. Which kind of world most nearly resembles the real world in which any particular equation is embedded (if indeed either comes very close) is a difficult question. It often cannot be settled satisfactorily without trying out the equation, using

---

[106] Indeed, there is a statistics theorem to the effect that if they play long enough the chances approach 100 per cent that one or the other of them will go broke, no matter how rich either was at first. This has important consequences for predicting; see Chapter X, Section 6.4.

both raw and first-difference data and comparing the results.[107] How this is done will be taken up in Chapter X. Caution should be observed in using any of the estimation techniques of 11.5–10 that depend on presumptions about the behavior of the shifts: If raw data are used, then the relevant presumptions pertain to the shifts such as e_t in (13.9), but if first-difference data are used, then of course the relevant presumptions pertain to the shifts such as u_t in (13.11).

13.9 A third possibility for dealing with serial correlation of disturbances, similar to the first two but more general, is to use Aitken's generalized least-squares method described in 5.7. Recall that the variance-covariance matrix Λ of the disturbances of the equation to be estimated is assumed to be proportional to a known matrix Λ/ω^2, where the constant of proportionality ω^2 is not known. Prior to least-squares estimation, the data are transformed by multiplying by a nonsingular matrix Φ, having the property that $\Phi\Phi' = \Lambda^{-1}$; the first-difference transformation discussed in 13.7 above is approximately a special case. The major practical difficulty in applying Aitken's approach in this context is that Λ/ω^2 is typically not known.

13.10 A fourth possibility is to introduce into the equation the lagged value of some variable whose current value already appears there. In practice, if the serial correlation of calculated shifts is positive (as is usual), this device often reduces it. The reason is that almost every *economic* variable is serially correlated, so that the presence of both current and lagged values of a variable in an equation provides a sort of hook on which the serial correlation can be hung, instead of being pushed onto the disturbances. This device often creates just the kind of difficulty described in 4.13, however, that is, the confounding of the effects of two explanatory variables due to correlation between them, and is not always effective. Furthermore, this device is illegitimate if we really know what the correct model for the problem at hand is, because then we should use the correct model regardless of whether its disturbances are independent in different periods or not. But in practice, as noted earlier, we do not

---

[107] Hildreth and Lu [1960] have done this for a number of demand equations for farm products, omitting the lagged value of the dependent variable. They have also found by a trial-and-error method for each equation the value of α that minimizes the sum of squared deviations of the transformed dependent variable $x_t - \alpha x_{t-1}$ from the regression equation whose explanatory variables have been transformed in the same manner. Their "optimum" values of α so obtained are positive in about two-thirds of the cases, ranging from -0.66 to $+0.87$. The sum of squared deviations using $\alpha = 0$ (i.e., no transformation) was never more than 2.2 times that for the "optimal" α, and in about two-thirds of the cases it was less than 1.2 times that for the "optimal" α. The sum of squared deviations for $\alpha = 1$ (the first-difference transformation) exceeded twice that for the "optimal" α in about half the cases, and it was seven times as large in the worst case. In about five cases out of six, the sum of squares for $\alpha = 0$ was less than for $\alpha = 1$. These results suggest using $\alpha = 0$.

really know the correct model, and in particular we may not know whether the lagged value of a certain variable appears in an equation along with its current value or not. In such a case it is tempting to put it in simply to reduce the serial correlation of calculated disturbances, and in the absence of other information bearing on the question there is no good way to decide the issue.

13.11 One reason for introducing into an equation the lagged value of its dependent variable is to deal with unobservable expectations about the future on the part of economic decision-making units. This was discussed in V.7.6 ff., but in a nonstochastic manner. For example, suppose that the decision about the variable y depends linearly on the expected future value x^e of the variable x, with a disturbance u, thus:

$$(13.18) \qquad y_t = \alpha + \beta x_t^e + u_t$$

Suppose also that expectations about x are unobservable and formed with a disturbance v as follows:

$$(13.19) \qquad x_t^e = \gamma x_{t-1}^e + (1 - \gamma)x_t + v_t \qquad 0 \leqq \gamma < 1$$

Then by the same kind of transformation used in V.7.7 we obtain the following equation, in which all the variables (except disturbances) are observable:

$$(13.20) \qquad y_t = \alpha(1 - \gamma) + \beta(1 - \gamma)x_t + \gamma y_{t-1} + (\beta v_t + u_t - \gamma u_{t-1})$$

This treatment is the same as that of V.7.7 except that here stochastic disturbances u and v are included. Notice that if we believe that the disturbances u_s and u_t are independent for $s \neq t$, as in assumption (j), then the disturbance in the empirically estimatable equation (13.20) does *not* have this property as long as $\gamma \neq 0$, for the disturbance in (13.20) includes $u_t - \gamma u_{t-1}$, which must be serially dependent on $u_{t-1} - \gamma u_{t-2}$ because both contain u_{t-1}. Hence y_{t-1} cannot be predetermined in (13.20). On the other hand, suppose (as would seem most unlikely) that the disturbance u were serially autocorrelated as in (13.1) with an auto-regression coefficient precisely equal to the expectation coefficient γ, where w_t is a random disturbance independent as among different time periods:

$$(13.21) \qquad u_t = \gamma u_{t-1} + w_t$$

Then $u_t - \gamma u_{t-1}$ would be serially independent, and if v were serially independent also, then so would be the disturbance in (13.20).

13.12 If the lagged value of the dependent variable is introduced because of belief in an adjustment model (see V.7.10) instead of an expectations model, the stochastic problems are different. Let the unobservable desired level y_t^* of y depend on x as follows:

$$(13.22) \qquad y_t^* = \alpha + \beta x_t + u_t$$

where u_t is random with mean zero and no serial dependence. And let the adjustment of the actual to the desired level occur with an adjustment coefficient γ, thus:

$$(13.23) \qquad y_t - y_{t-1} = (1 - \gamma)(y_t^* - y_{t-1}) + v_t \qquad 0 \leqq \gamma < 1$$

where v_t is also random with mean zero and no serial dependence. Then substituting for y^* into (13.23) yields the following equation in observable variables and disturbances:

$$(13.24) \qquad y_t = \alpha(1 - \gamma) + \beta(1 - \gamma)x_t - \gamma y_{t-1} + [(1 - \gamma)u_t + v_t]$$

Here the disturbance $[(1 - \gamma)u_t + v_t]$ is free of serial dependence if both u_t and v_t are. Note that if not, y_{t-1} is not predetermined and so a bias in estimating γ will occur if y_{t-1} is nevertheless treated as predetermined. When dealing empirically with distributed lags as suggested in V.7, the stochastic implications illustrated here should be kept in mind.[108]

QUESTIONS AND PROBLEMS

1.1. State the definitions of all the concepts listed in Table 1.1.

1.2. Express the difference between an equation's true disturbance u_t and its calculated residual $\hat{u}_t$ in terms of observed data and any other necessary quantities.

2.1. Which (if any) of the assumptions (a) to (k) in Section 2 are definitely violated by the following specifications? Explain.

(a) Among the exogenous variables are total government purchases, government purchases of labor services, and government purchases other than of labor services.

(b) One of the equations is $y_t = \alpha + \beta y_{t-1} + \gamma z_t + u_t$, where y_t is dependent, y_{t-1} and z_t are predetermined, and u_t is a disturbance.

(c) In the preceding equation, the variance of the disturbance u_t is $\sigma^2 z_t^2$, where σ^2 is a constant.

(d) In the preceding equation, $\beta = 2$ and $\gamma = 3$.

(e) A disturbance u_t obeys the rule $u_t = \alpha u_{t-1} + e_t$, where e_t is serially independent and $\alpha > 0$.

(f) A linear time trend term is included in one of the equations of the model.

(g) In a two-equation model with disturbances u_1 and u_2, the correlation between u_{1t} and u_{2t} is high, nearly 1.

(h) The distribution of disturbances $u_{1t}, \ldots, u_{Gt}$ is not independent of z_{ks} for all k, s, and t, but $E(u_{it} \mid z_{ks})$ is zero for all i, k, s, and t.

[108] Estimation of distributed lags is discussed in Klein [1958], Nerlove [1958], [1958a], [1958b], Nerlove and Addison [1958], Griliches [1961], Malinvaud [1961], Mundlak [1961], Liviatan [1963], Hannan [1965], and Jorgenson [1966].

2.2. Prove that the linear independence of the K vectors $(z_{11} \cdots z_{1T}), \ldots,$ $(z_{K1} \cdots z_{KT})$ is equivalent to the nonsingularity of the $K \times K$ matrix of moments of the z's about zero.

2.3. Some proofs of consistency of estimation, in a system of difference equations, employ the assumption that the solution of the system is dynamically stable. What is the relation of that assumption to this book's assumption (h) that the predetermined variables have a moment matrix that is well behaved in the limit?

3.1. Which of the following are correct under the assumptions of Model 3? Explain.

(a) $\bar{v} = 0$

(b) $\hat{v} = 0$

(c) $\operatorname{var}(v_t - \bar{v}) = \operatorname{var} v_t$

(d) $\displaystyle\sum_1^T (\hat{v}_t - \hat{\bar{v}})^2 = \sum_1^T \hat{v}_t{}^2$

(e) $Ev_t\bar{v} = E\bar{v}^2 = \omega^2/T$

3.2. Show that the estimators of α in equations (3.17) and (3.19) are equivalent.

3.3. From equation (3.9) form the sum of squared deviations and minimize it with respect to p_1 and p_2. Show that $\sum z_{2t} = \sum z_{2t}^2 = T$, $\sum z_{1t}z_{2t} = \sum z_{1t}$, $p_1 = p$, and $p_2 = a$ [for p and a, you can use (3.18) or (3.23), and (3.17) or (3.19), respectively].

3.4. Prove that least-squares estimation is unbiased for a simple regression in Model 1 if the assumption of an exogenous z is replaced by the assumption that $E(v_t \mid z_1, \ldots, z_T) = 0$ for all t from 1 to T.

3.5. Does the expression for the sum of squared residuals in (3.29) still hold if z is predetermined rather than exogenous? Explain.

3.6. Suppose that, in a simple regression in Model 1, Eu_t is not zero but is equal to an unknown constant θ. Obtain the expectation of the least-squares estimators of the slope p and intercept a.

3.7. Under the assumptions of Model 1, suppose that in a simple regression u_t is exactly dependent on u_1 according to the rule $u_t = u_1$ for $t = 2, 3, \ldots$. Will the least-squares estimators of the intercept and slope be unbiased? Consistent? Explain.

3.8. Prove that in the equation $y_t = \lambda y_{t-1} + v_t$, where $v_t = \alpha v_{t-1} + e_t$, with $0 < |\alpha| < 1$ and with e_t random and independent with zero mean and constant variance, the least-squares estimator of λ is inconsistent.

3.9. Consider theorem (b) in 3.29. Do its assumptions, either as they stand or strengthened, imply that the statistic d_T/e_T has a limiting distribution? What about e_T/d_T? Explain.

3.10. Consider the equation $y_t = \alpha + \pi z_t + v_t$. Under what conditions (if any) would the least-squares method with z as the dependent variable lead to maximum-likelihood estimators?

4.1. Verify the expressions for the minimized sum of squared deviations in equation (4.16) and in equation (4.29).

4.2. Verify equation (4.32).

4.3. Suppose that two explanatory variables are exactly related according to $z_{2t} = 3.0 + 0.5z_{1t}$, and that $y_t = -1.8 + 2.0z_{1t} - 0.7z_{2t} + v_t$.

(a) Find an equation for y_t that is equivalent to the foregoing and that has an arbitrary value α for the coefficient of z_{2t}.

(b) What are the numerical coefficients if α is set at 0? At 1.5?

4.4. Suppose that w and z are exogenous and are correlated. Consider the two equations

(i) $y_t = \alpha + \beta z_t + \gamma w_t + u_t$

(ii) $y_t = \delta + \epsilon z_t + v_t$

Will the least-squares method yield an unbiased estimator of the coefficient of z (a) if (i) is correct and the investigator assumes (ii), (b) if (ii) is correct and the investigator assumes (i)? Explain. (The approach of 5.3 may be helpful.)

4.5. Under what conditions will the two numerical estimates of the coefficients of z in the preceding problem be identical for a particular sample of data?

5.1. Show that $\mathbf{ZZ}'$ is symmetric, where $\mathbf{Z}$ is a $K \times T$ matrix of data for $z_1, \ldots, z_T$.

5.2. Show that $\mathbf{ZZ}'$ is the same as $\mathbf{M}_{zz}$.

5.3. Verify the expressions in equation (5.8) for the minimized sum of squared deviations.

5.4. Show that if $\mathbf{A}$ is $M \times N$ and $\mathbf{B}$ is $N \times M$, then tr $\mathbf{AB} =$ tr $\mathbf{BA}$.

5.5. Suppose that under Model 1 we have $\mathbf{y}' = \mathbf{Z}'\boldsymbol{\pi}' + \mathbf{v}'$, where $E\mathbf{v}' = \mathbf{0}$ and $E\mathbf{v}'\mathbf{v} = \alpha^2\boldsymbol{\Psi}$, and that $\boldsymbol{\Psi}$ is known but α^2 and $\boldsymbol{\pi}$ are not. Apply Aitken's generalized least-squares method to obtain an estimator of $\boldsymbol{\pi}$, and write down the expressions for its expected value and variance. Compare with (5.19)–(5.20).

6.1. In maximizing a likelihood function, would you expect to obtain a larger value of the likelihood if you *ignored* the identifying restrictions, or if you *maximized subject to* them? Explain.

6.2. Show that the reduced-form estimators obtained by maximizing the logarithm of the likelihood function (6.16) or (6.17), disregarding restrictions on the structural parameters, are the least-squares estimators of the reduced form.

7.1. Show that for a just-identified equation the indirect least-squares estimators and the instrumental-variables estimators are equivalent.

7.2. Why are indirect least-squares estimators not unbiased in general?

7.3. Consider the model

$$c = \alpha + \beta y + u$$
$$i = \gamma + \delta y + \epsilon r + w$$
$$c + i = y$$

where c, i, and y are endogenous, r is exogenous, u and w are disturbances, and Greek letters are unknown parameters. Express the indirect least-squares estimators and the instrumental-variables estimators of the consumption equation in terms of observable data, and show whether the two methods yield the same estimators. Comment on the result.

7.4. At what point does the argument of 7.10 fail if applied to an over-identified equation?

8.1. Consider an overidentified equation, with $K - J > H - 1$. Suppose that $K - J - (H - 1)$ endogenous variables that are known to be in the model, but not in the equation, are nevertheless permitted to enter the equation, thus increasing the number of included endogenous variables to $K - J$. (Is this always possible?) Suppose the indirect least-squares method is then applied. Comment on the quality of the estimators obtained. (This question was suggested to me by Dr. William Poole.)

8.2. What happens when one tries to apply the indirect least-squares or instrumental-variables method to an unidentified equation?

8.3. Consider equations (8.6) which contain $K - J$ conditions upon the $H - 1$ estimates $\hat{\beta}_2, \ldots, \hat{\beta}_H$ of coefficients of jointly dependent variables in an overidentified equation (8.1), that is, $K - J > H - 1$. Comment on the consequences of two alternative methods of reducing (8.6) to only $H - 1$ equations in $\hat{\beta}_2, \ldots, \hat{\beta}_H$, as follows:

(a) Simply ignore $K - J - (H - 1)$ of the equations in (8.6) and solve the remaining $H - 1$ equations for $\hat{\beta}_2, \ldots, \hat{\beta}_H$.

(b) Estimate the reduced form using only $J + H - 1$ predetermined variables, namely the J variables that appear in the equation to be estimated and $H - 1$ of the others; then form $H - 1$ equations like (8.6) and solve them for $\hat{\beta}_2, \ldots, \hat{\beta}_H$.

9.1. Compare, contrast, and interpret the following two equations:

$$(5.4) \quad \hat{\mathbf{v}}' = \mathbf{y}' - \mathbf{Z}'\mathbf{p}'$$

$$(9.11) \quad \hat{\mathbf{v}}_t' = \mathbf{y}_t' - \mathbf{P}\mathbf{z}_t'$$

9.2. Verify equations (9.17) and (9.21) for $\mathbf{W}$ and $\mathbf{W}^*$.

9.3. Comment on the differences between these two estimation procedures for $\boldsymbol{\beta}$:

(a) Minimize the variance ratio $\boldsymbol{\beta}\mathbf{W}^*\boldsymbol{\beta}'/\boldsymbol{\beta}\mathbf{W}\boldsymbol{\beta}'$ which must always be ≥ 1.

(b) Minimize the "variance difference" $\boldsymbol{\beta}\mathbf{W}^*\boldsymbol{\beta}' - \boldsymbol{\beta}\mathbf{W}\boldsymbol{\beta}'$ which must always be ≥ 0.

9.4. Express a_0 and a_H, which appear in equation (9.29), in terms of elements of $\mathbf{W}$ and $\mathbf{W}^*$. Do the same for a_1 and a_{H-1} if you wish.

9.5. Tabulate the function (9.35) $\lambda = 1/(l - 1)$, showing the largest and smallest possible values of l consistent with its definition in equation (9.22), and showing several values in between. What does it mean if λ_1 [the largest root of equation (9.37)] is close to its largest possible value? To its smallest possible value?

9.6. Suppose that for an equation containing two jointly dependent variables it was found that

$$\mathbf{W} = \begin{pmatrix} 200 & 110 \\ 110 & 100 \end{pmatrix} \quad \text{and} \quad \mathbf{W}^* = \begin{pmatrix} 206 & 112 \\ 112 & 101 \end{pmatrix}$$

Compute the smallest root l_1 and the largest root λ_1 of equations (9.27) and (9.38), respectively, and the limited-information estimator of (β_1, β_2).

9.7. Consider the limited-information estimation of an equation that is linear in unknown parameters but not linear in variables, according to the method of 9.31. This involves the least-squares estimation of linear approximations to certain reduced-form equations. Such a linear approximation will of course be different at one point in the sample space from what it is at another. What are the consequences of this difference for (a) small-sample properties of the estimators, (b) asymptotic properties of the estimators?

9.8. Comment on the prospects for the proof or disproof of the conjecture that limited-information estimators are consistent if Model 3 is modified by adopting both assumptions (*l*) and (*m*) at the same time, i.e., by permitting nonlinearities in variables (but not in parameters) and by ignoring some of the predetermined variables that are not required to assure identification.

10.1. Rewrite equation (10.13), expressing each of the matrices $\mathbf{Y}'$, $\hat{\mathbf{Y}}'$, $\hat{\mathbf{V}}'$, and $\mathbf{P}_1'$ as a set of column vectors, thus showing the relationship between the least-squares estimation of a single reduced-form equation as in (5.7) and the least-squares estimation of a number of reduced-form equations as in (10.13).

10.2. Rewrite the two-stage least-squares normal equations (10.15) in three equivalent forms, using in place of $\mathbf{Y}' - \hat{\mathbf{V}}'$ the following in turn: $\hat{\mathbf{Y}}'$, $\mathbf{Z}'\mathbf{P}_1'$, and $\mathbf{Z}'(\mathbf{ZZ}')^{-1}\mathbf{ZY}'$.

10.3. Rewrite the two-stage least-squares normal equations (10.18) in three equivalent forms corresponding to the preceding question.

10.4. Discuss the merits of defining the vector and matrix notation in such a way that equation (5.2) would be written as $\mathbf{y} = \mathbf{Z}'\boldsymbol{\pi} + \mathbf{v}$, and equation (10.2) would be written as $\mathbf{y} = \mathbf{Y}'\boldsymbol{\beta}_1 + \mathbf{Z}^{*'}\boldsymbol{\gamma} + \mathbf{u}$. How would each symbol then be defined? And how would the formulas for the least-squares estimator of (5.2) and the two-stage estimator of (10.2) be written?

10.5. Show explicitly the relationship between the instrumental-variables method and the two-stage least-squares method. (*Suggestion:* see 10.7.)

10.6. Verify that least squares and two-stage least squares are members of the *k*-class with $k = 0$ and 1, respectively.

10.7. Verify that in Model 3 the limited-information estimator is a member of the *k*-class with $k = l_1$, where l_1 is the minimum value of the variance ratio, computed as the smallest root of equation (9.27).

10.8. Show that the *k*-class estimator is consistent in Model 3. (*Suggestion:* see 10.16.)

10.9. State clearly and correctly the meaning that must be given to the following equation if it is to hold when lagged dependent variables are present among the predetermined variables:

$$\lim_{T \to \infty} E(T e'e) = \sigma^2 \plim_{T \to \infty} T(\mathbf{XX}')^{-1}$$

10.10. Derive equation (10.39) and show that it is equivalent to the two-stage least-squares estimator in Model 2. (*Suggestion:* see problems 10.2 and 10.3.) What modifications, if any, are needed if Model 3 is used instead?

10.11. What is the relation of the matrix $\mathbf{Q}_i$ in 10.28 to the matrix $\mathbf{X}$ in 10.7?

10.12. Verify equation (10.48).

10.13. Substitute equations (10.50)–(10.52) into (10.49) and write down the result.

10.14. Verify equation (10.55).

10.15. Can you give intuitive plausibility to the theorems referred to in 10.32 and 10.37–38 regarding comparisons of properties of several simultaneous-equations estimators?

11.1. Show that in each equation of a recursive system as defined in 11.3, all but one of the included variables at time t are statistically independent of the equation's current and future disturbances (and are therefore predetermined).

11.2. What arguments can you give for and against the proposition that all correct econometric models are recursive? (See Wold [1953], pp. 49–53 and 64–71, for an affirmative view. See also Strotz and Wold [1960].)

11.3. Can you state a general conclusion about the identification of equations in recursive models? Explain.

11.4. Show that the last members of equations (11.14) and (11.20) are equal under the conditions of 11.12.

11.5. Consider the demand equation $q = \alpha + \beta p + u$, and suppose that a sample of data yields $m_{pq} < 0$. Find a probable inequality (or inequalities) relating β to its two least-squares estimators, m_{pq}/m_{pp} and m_{qq}/m_{pq}.

11.6. It has sometimes been argued, e.g., by Waugh [1961], that least-squares estimators are unbiased (or consistent), even in a simultaneous-equations model, *provided* one chooses the proper parameters to estimate, namely the expectations (or probability limits) of the least-squares estimators. Comment on (a) the correctness and (b) the applicability of this view. Then consult F. Fisher [1962] and comment again.

12.1. For each of the LS, 2SLS, LI, k-class, FI, 3SLS, and LML estimation methods, indicate the following.

(a) Do its small-sample estimators depend on some choice of a normalization rule or of a "dependent" variable? Or are they independent of any such choice?

(b) What data are required for its use?

(c) What *a priori* specifications are required for its use?

12.2. Construct a two-equation linear model with one equation over-identified. Derive its reduced form, and show what restriction(s) on the reduced form are implied by the overidentification of the structure.

12.3. How would you design a Monte Carlo experiment to learn more about small-sample properties of estimators?

12.4. Suppose that two estimation methods are being compared, and that method A yields smaller expected squared errors than method B for the structural parameters in a model. Can it happen that when estimated reduced forms are obtained by solving the two estimated structures, the estimated reduced form based on method B will have smaller expected squared errors than the one based on method A? Explain.

13.1. Suppose it is known that an equation's disturbance e_t is equal to $\alpha e_{t-1} + u_t$, where u_t is random with mean zero, and where u_s and u_t are independent for $s \neq t$. Suppose α is *known*, and $-1 < \alpha < 1$.

(a) What transformation of the data, if any, will yield an equation whose disturbances are serially independent?

(b) Find $Ee'e$ and the transformation matrix Φ and the vector $\Phi'e'$ for use in Aitken's generalized least-squares method of 5.7 and 13.9.

13.2. Answer the preceding question on the supposition that the disturbance e_t follows a second-order autoregressive equation $e_t = \alpha_1 e_{t-1} + \alpha_2 e_{t-2} + u_t$ rather than the first-order equation given in the preceding question.

13.3. Discuss the possibility of consistent estimation of parameters in an equation whose disturbances are serially correlated. (You may wish to discuss Model 2 and Model 3 separately.)

CHAPTER X

Appraising Econometric Models
and Estimates; Prediction

This chapter discusses the appraisal of econometric models and estimates, and the related topic of prediction. First the distributions of statistics known as t, χ^2, and F are described briefly, together with their use in testing hypotheses. Nonpredictive tests of several types are discussed. They include some tests based on regression and correlation coefficients and their simultaneous-equations counterparts; some other tests of residuals including serial-correlation tests; and some "tests" of *a priori* restrictions. Point prediction and interval prediction, and tests based on the goodness of predictions, are discussed, both for least-squares regression and for simultaneous-equations estimators.

1 INTRODUCTION; THE NORMAL, CHI-SQUARE, t, AND F DISTRIBUTIONS

1.1 This chapter is about the appraisal of econometric models and estimates of their parameters, and about econometric prediction or forecasting (the two terms will be used interchangeably). These topics are closely interrelated. Some appraisal techniques are not related to prediction, but some of the most interesting ones are. Predictions may be made for policy purposes; they may also be made in order to test the models and parameter estimates on which they are based. See VII.9 for some introductory remarks concerning predictions.

1.2 The appraisal techniques to be discussed will be called tests, for brevity, though not all of them are actually tests of hypotheses in the statistical sense introduced in VII.7. These tests may be conveniently divided into two classes, which we shall call predictive and nonpredictive tests, according to whether they depend on making predictions and testing them, or not. Nonpredictive tests will be discussed first, in sections 2–5, and predictive tests in the remainder of the chapter.

1.3 The terms *prediction* (or *forecast*) and *predictor* will be used in analogy to the terms *estimate* and *estimator* (see VII.5.6). That is, a prediction (or forecast) is a specific point or interval that is meant to equal or include the actual observed value of the variable to be predicted. A predictor is a statistic, that is, a function of observed sample data that describes the rule for obtaining a prediction from any given sample of data. A prediction is a value of a predictor. The foregoing two sentences have already made it clear that there are interval predictors as well as point predictors.

1.4 For certain tests, some in each of the two just-mentioned groups, the close relation (discussed in VII.7) between a test and an interval estimator (also applicable to an interval predictor) will be evident and will be used. For brevity in section headings, the interval estimators and interval predictors associated with the various tests and discussed along with them will not be mentioned in the section headings.

1.5 The basic approach of statistical inference was described in VII.6–7, and hypothesis testing and interval estimation were illustrated with reference to a normally distributed variable x with mean μ. Of course the normal probability distribution is not directly applicable to all problems; we have seen that less restrictive assumptions about the relevant probability distribution are often used instead. But in statistical inference the general procedure is the same and may be reviewed here quickly. The hypothesis to be tested or the parameter to be estimated or the variable to be predicted must be specified. A statistic must be chosen, that is, a function of the observed variables, for example, the sample mean $\bar{x}$ if the relevant parameter is the population mean Ex. The probability distribution of the statistic must be specified as completely as possible and, in the case of a test, completely specified under the assumption that the hypothesis to be tested is true. Then for a test, an acceptance region should be constructed with due regard to the *a priori* information about the parameter in question and the losses involved in errors of type I and type II. The hypothesis is accepted if the observed value of the statistic falls in the acceptance region and rejected otherwise. For an interval estimate or an interval forecast, an interval is constructed based on the data, usually surrounding the relevant statistic, in such a way that the required proportion of all such intervals constructed for all samples from the population in question will catch the true value of the parameter being estimated or variable being forecast.

1.6 Other distributions often used besides the normal are the distributions of statistics known as t, χ^2, and F. Their distributions are known as the t, χ^2, and F distributions, respectively. These three statistics are all closely related to z, the standardized normally distributed variable with mean 0 and variance 1, which was defined in IV.3.2.[1] Thus, if x is any normally distributed variable with mean μ and variance σ^2, we have

$$(1.1) \qquad z = \frac{x - \mu}{\sigma}$$

We shall next define F in terms of z, and then set out the theoretical relationships among F, z, t, and χ^2. Good tables of these distributions and good brief descriptions of their use, with examples, are given in two standard collections of statistical tables, Fisher and Yates [1938] and Pearson and Hartley [1954]. Appendix B also tabulates the distributions. For theoretical discussions see Mood [1950], Mood and Graybill [1963], Cramér [1946], and Wilks [1943].

1.7 F is defined as a statistic formed by taking a ratio whose numerator is the mean of the squares of a number N_1 of independent random variables distributed as z is; and whose denominator is the mean of the squares of a number N_2 of random variables, independent of each other and of those in the numerator, distributed as z is. Since the distribution of F clearly depends on the numbers N_1 and N_2, F is often written $F(N_1, N_2)$. Thus, if $z_1, \ldots, z_{N_1+N_2}$ are independent random normal variables with mean 0 and variance 1, we have

$$(1.2) \qquad F(N_1, N_2) \equiv \frac{\dfrac{1}{N_1} \sum\limits_{1}^{N_1} z_i^2}{\dfrac{1}{N_2} \sum\limits_{N_1+1}^{N_1+N_2} z_i^2}$$

The numbers N_1 and N_2 are called the degrees of freedom of the numerator and of the denominator, respectively. One of the major uses of F is in the comparing of two variance estimates s_1^2 and s_2^2 to test the hypothesis that the corresponding true variances σ_1^2 and σ_2^2 are equal. $F(N_1, N_2)$ is then calculated as s_1^2/σ_1^2 divided by s_2^2/σ_2^2, N_1 and N_2 being the degrees of freedom of s_1^2 and s_2^2 respectively.

1.8 The standard normal variable z with mean zero and variance 1 can be thought of as a special case of F, thus:

$$(1.3) \qquad z = \sqrt{F(1, \infty)}$$

---

[1] Be careful not to confuse the statistic t with the T sometimes used to denote the sample size, or with the t sometimes used to denote time. (Some writers use $\frac{1}{2} \log_e F$ instead of F; this statistic is known as Fisher's z. Since $z = \frac{1}{2} \log_e F$, $F = e^{2z}$. We do *not* use z here in this sense.)

This may be seen by considering that $\dfrac{1}{N_2}\sum_1^{N_2}(x_{2i} - Ex_2)^2$ has a probability limit equal to var x_2 as $N_2 \to \infty$ (i.e., it is a consistent estimator of $\sigma_2{}^2$; this is not proved here) so that the term $\dfrac{1}{N_2}\sum z_i{}^2$ in the denominator of F has a probability limit equal to 1; and the numerator of F for $N_1 = 1$ is equal to z^2.

1.9 The statistics χ^2 and t can be defined as special cases of F as follows; each depends on its own number of degrees of freedom as denoted by N_1 and N_2 respectively:

(1.4) $$\chi^2(N_1) = N_1 F(N_1, \infty)$$

(1.5) $$t(N_2) = \sqrt{F(1, N_2)}$$

The four statistics can be shown schematically on a square as in Figure 1.1, the vertical axis representing the numerator's number of degrees of freedom

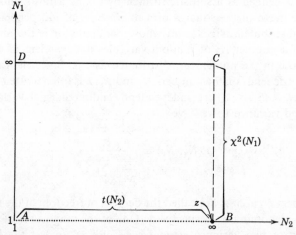

Figure 1.1   Numbers N_1 and N_2 of degrees of freedom for numerator and denominator of the statistic $F(N_1, N_2)$, points on the horizontal axis showing the statistic $t(N_2)$, and points on the vertical line BC showing the statistic $\chi^2(N_1)$. [See 1.9 and equations (1.1)–(1.5) in text.]

N_1, from 1 to ∞, and the horizontal axis representing the denominator's number of degrees of freedom N_2, also from 1 to ∞. Any point inside or on the edges of the square $ABCD$ shows a possible pair of numbers of degrees of freedom for $F(N_1, N_2)$. Any point on the right-hand edge BC shows a possible number of degrees of freedom for $\chi^2(N_1)$, since $F(N_1, \infty) = \chi^2(N_1)/N_1$. Any point on the lower edge AB shows a possible number of degrees of freedom for $t(N_2)$, since $F(1, N_2) = t^2(N_2)$. And the point B corresponds to the statistic z, since $F(1, \infty) = z$.

1.10 The statistic χ^2 with N_1 degrees of freedom may be defined equivalently to (1.4) as the sum of squares of N_1 independent variables distributed as z, thus:

$$(1.6) \qquad \chi^2(N_1) = \sum_1^{N_1} z_i^2$$

It can be shown[2] that the statistic $(T-1)s^2/\sigma^2$ has the χ^2 distribution with $T-1$ degrees of freedom, where s^2 is the unbiased estimator of σ^2 based on a univariate normal sample of size T, thus:

$$(1.7) \qquad \chi^2(T-1) = \frac{(T-1)s^2}{\sigma^2} = \frac{\sum_1^T (x_i - \bar{x})^2}{\sigma^2}$$

The center member of (1.7) shows the resemblance of χ^2 to $(T-1)F$. The statistic χ^2 is used to estimate, or test hypotheses about, the variance of a normal distribution.[3] It is approximately normally distributed itself for about 30 or more degrees of freedom.[4] It is tabulated in Appendix B, Table 2, for degrees of freedom from 1 to 30, and then by tens up to 100. It is used in a manner somewhat analogous to that described in VII.7.7-25 for a normal distribution, except that unlike the normal distribution it is not symmetrical, so that separate calculations must be made for the two tails whenever a two-tailed estimate or test is desired.

1.11 Consider the following example of inference using the χ^2 distribution. Let $\chi_\epsilon^2(n)$ be the 100ϵth percentile of the χ^2 distribution for n degrees of freedom, that is,

$$(1.8) \qquad \text{Pb}\,[\chi^2 \leqq \chi_\epsilon^2(n)] = \epsilon$$

Similarly, the probability that χ^2 will fall between its $100\epsilon_1$th and $100\epsilon_2$th percentiles is $\epsilon_2 - \epsilon_1$, where $\epsilon_2 \geqq \epsilon_1$:

$$(1.9) \qquad \text{Pb}\,[\chi_{\epsilon_1}^2(n) \leqq \chi^2 \leqq \chi_{\epsilon_2}^2(n)] = \epsilon_2 - \epsilon_1, \qquad \text{where } \epsilon_2 \geqq \epsilon_1$$

Let σ^2 be the hypothetical value of the variance of x, that is, the hypothesis being tested says $\text{var}\,x = \sigma^2$. Let s^2 be the unbiased estimator of σ^2

---

[2] See Mood [1950], pp. 199–204.

[3] The quadratic form in the exponent of the joint normal distribution function (see IX.6.4 and IV.3.11) has the χ^2 distribution even if the variables are not independent. See Wilks [1943], pp. 103–105.

[4] For 30 or more degrees of freedom, a fairly good approximation (due to Fisher) is provided by treating $\sqrt{2\chi^2}$ as a normally distributed variable with mean equal to $\sqrt{2n-1}$ (where n = number of degrees of freedom) and variance equal to 1. See various statistics books; Kendall [1952], pp. 294–297, is particularly good here, or see Kendall and Stuart [1958].

based on a sample of size T from the normal population with unknown mean μ and unknown variance, as in (1.7); then $(T-1)s^2/\sigma^2$ has the χ^2 distribution with $T-1$ degrees of freedom if σ^2 is the true value of var x, that is, if the hypothesis being tested is true. Suppose it has been decided that the best test is one with a 6 per cent significance level, with 1 per cent of the probability in the lower tail rejection region and 5 per cent of the probability in the upper tail rejection region if the hypothesis is true, and with a sample size of 24. Then in (1.9) we want $\epsilon_2 - \epsilon_1$ to be .94, ϵ_1 to be .01, ϵ_2 to be .95, and n to be 23. The test statistic is $23s^2/\sigma^2$, that is, $\sum_1^{24}(x_t - \bar{x})^2/\sigma^2$, where σ^2 is the hypothetical value being tested. The hypothesis that var $x = \sigma^2$ should be accepted if $\chi^2_{.01}(23) \leqq 23s^2/\sigma^2 \leqq \chi^2_{.95}(23)$, and rejected otherwise. To be still more concrete, suppose that the hypothetical value of var x is $\sigma^2 = 4$ and the sample estimate s^2 turns out to be 2.10; then the test statistic's value is $23(2.10)/4$, that is, 12.1. Then looking in the χ^2 table we find that the end points of the acceptance region are 10.2 and 35.2. The test statistic is in this region, so the hypothesis that var $x = 4$ is accepted with a little room to spare. From these data, the corresponding interval estimate of var x (i.e., the interval including precisely those values of σ^2 for which the foregoing test plan and data would accept the hypothesis that var $x = \sigma^2$) runs from $\sigma_l^2 = 23(2.10)/35.2 = 1.37$ to $\sigma_u^2 = 23(2.10)/10.2 = 4.74$. This is a 94 per cent confidence interval estimate of var x. In general, an interval estimator with confidence coefficient $\epsilon_2 - \epsilon_1$ (where $1 \geqq \epsilon_2 \geqq \epsilon_1 \geqq 0$) can be made with lower and upper limits, thus:

(1.10)
$$\sigma_l^2 = \frac{(T-1)s^2}{\chi^2_{\epsilon_2}(T-1)}$$

$$\sigma_u^2 = \frac{(T-1)s^2}{\chi^2_{\epsilon_1}(T-1)}$$

1.12 The statistic t with N_2 degrees of freedom may be defined equivalently to (1.5) as the ratio of one variable distributed as z (i.e., normally with mean 0 and variance 1) to the root mean square of N_2 other such variables all independent of each other and of the one in the numerator, thus:

(1.11)
$$t(N_2) = \frac{z_1}{\sqrt{\dfrac{1}{N_2} \displaystyle\sum_2^{N_2+1} z_i^2}}$$

Thus the denominator of $t(N_2)$ is the square root of $1/N_2$ times a variable distributed as χ^2 with N_2 degrees of freedom. Put $N_2 = T-1$. Therefore, recalling from 1.10 that $(T-1)s^2/\sigma^2$ has the χ^2 distribution with $T-1$

degrees of freedom if x is independently normally distributed with mean μ and variance σ^2, we see that under the same assumptions about x the following ratio has the t distribution with $T - 1$ degrees of freedom:[5]

$$(1.12) \qquad t(T-1) = \frac{(x-\mu)/\sigma}{s/\sigma} = \frac{x-\mu}{s}$$

Similarly, for the mean $\bar{x}$ of a sample of size T from the same population, we can see that the following ratio has the t distribution with $T - 1$ degrees of freedom:

$$(1.13) \qquad t(T-1) = \frac{(\bar{x}-\mu)/\sigma_{\bar{x}}}{s_{\bar{x}}/\sigma_{\bar{x}}} = \frac{\bar{x}-\mu}{s_{\bar{x}}} = \frac{(\bar{x}-\mu)\sqrt{T}}{s}$$

The second member of (1.12) or (1.13) shows the resemblance of t to $\sqrt{F}$, and the third member shows its resemblance to z. $T - 1$ is the number of degrees of freedom of the estimator s as well as of the associated t distribution. If $T - 1$ becomes infinite, s converges in probability to σ and so t converges in probability to z, as suggested by Figure 1.1 and by (1.3) and (1.5). The statistic t is used to estimate, or test hypotheses about, the mean of a normal distribution when the variance of that distribution is unknown and must be estimated. It is tabulated in Appendix B, Table 1, with a separate row for each number of degrees of freedom from 1 to 30, and also for 40, 60, 120, and infinity (the last row of course is a table of the normal distribution). It is used in a manner analogous to that described in VII.7.7-25 for the normal distribution.

    1.13   Consider the following example of inference using the t distribution. Let Ea be an unknown parameter in which we are interested; then a is an unbiased estimator of it. Let a be normally distributed with unknown variance var a. Let $s^2(a)$ be an unbiased estimator of var a, such that $\dfrac{ns^2(a)}{\text{var } a}$ is distributed as χ^2 with n degrees of freedom. Then $(a - \alpha)/s(a)$ has the t distribution with n degrees of freedom if the hypothesis that $Ea = \alpha$ is true. Let $t_\epsilon(n)$ be the 100ϵth percentile of the distribution of t with n degrees of freedom, that is,

$$(1.14) \qquad \text{Pb}\,[t \leq t_\epsilon(n)] = \epsilon$$

Similarly, if $\epsilon_2 \geq \epsilon_1$ we have

$$(1.15) \qquad \text{Pb}\,[t_{\epsilon_1}(n) \leq t \leq t_{\epsilon_2}(n)] = \epsilon_2 - \epsilon_1, \qquad \text{where } \epsilon_2 \geq \epsilon_1$$

---

[5] To give a proof of this statement and the next, we must show that Σx_i^2 in the denominator's estimator s is independent of x or $\bar{x}$ in the numerator. This is not proved here.

Suppose it has been decided that the best test of the hypothesis that $Ea = \alpha$ is one with a 15 per cent significance level, with 10 per cent of the probability in the lower tail rejection region and 5 per cent in the upper tail rejection region when the hypothesis is true, and with a sample size such that there are 16 degrees of freedom. Then in (1.15) we want $\epsilon_2 - \epsilon_1$ to be .85, ϵ_1 to be .10, ϵ_2 to be .95 and n to be 16. The test statistic is $(a - \alpha)/s(a)$. The hypothesis that $Ea = \alpha$ should be accepted if $t_{.10}(16) \leqq (a - \alpha)/s(a) \leqq t_{.95}(16)$, and rejected otherwise. To be more concrete, suppose we are testing whether $Ea = 0$ (i.e., $\alpha = 0$), and the sample statistics are $a = -31.1$ and $s(a) = 20.8$, so that $(a - \alpha)/s(a) = -31.1/20.8$, that is, -1.50. Then looking in the t table we find that the end points of the acceptance region are -1.337 and $+1.746$. The test statistic falls outside this region, so the hypothesis that $Ea = 0$ is rejected with a little room to spare. From these data, the corresponding interval estimate of Ea (i.e., the interval containing precisely those values of α for which the foregoing test procedure and data would accept the hypothesis that $Ea = \alpha$) runs from $\alpha_l = -31.1 - 1.746(20.8) = -67.4$ to $\alpha_u = -31.1 - (-1.337)(20.8) = -3.4$. This is an 85 per cent confidence interval estimate of Ea. In general, an interval estimator with confidence coefficient $\epsilon_2 - \epsilon_1$ (where $1 \geqq \epsilon_2 \geqq \epsilon_1 \geqq 0$) can be made with these lower and upper limits:

$$\begin{aligned} \alpha_l &= a - s(a)\, t_{\epsilon_2}(n) \\ \alpha_u &= a - s(a)\, t_{\epsilon_1}(n) \end{aligned}$$
(1.16)

1.14 The table of the t distribution is useful for finding the OC (i.e., operating characteristic; see VII.7.9) of this test, including the risk of type I error, and the risk of type II error for any value of Ea other than the hypothetical tested value. The t distribution is asymptotically normal, that is, $t(\infty)$ is normally distributed. As an examination of the t table will show, it is very like the normal distribution table when the number of degrees of freedom is about 30 or more. For example, consider the 95th percentiles: $t_{.95}(\infty)$ is 1.645; $t_{.95}(30)$ is 1.697, about 1.03 times as large. Even $t_{.95}(10)$ is only 1.812, about 1.1 times $t_{.95}(\infty)$. Only when the number of degrees of freedom n is below about 10 does $t_{.95}(n)$ exceed $t_{.95}(\infty)$ by more than 10 per cent. This statement is approximately true for other percentiles. It holds with room to spare near the center of the distribution, and it becomes less and less accurate as we move far into the tails; the difference between the t and the normal distributions becomes more marked as we get farther into the tails. For any number of degrees of freedom that we are likely to have in an econometric problem, 5 or more, for instance, a sample value of t equal to $+2$ or more is an event whose probability would be 5 per cent or less if the hypothesis under test were true (e.g., if Ea above were really zero). The same is true for a sample value of t equal to -2 or less (i.e., $t_{.95}(5) = 2.015$).

1.15 The statistic F has been defined above, in 1.7, and its use in testing the hypothesis that two variances are equal has been mentioned. This particular use has many applications, among them being the so-called *analysis of variance*, whereby many and varied hypotheses can be tested by breaking up the variance of a suitably chosen random variable to determine the significant sources of its variation. A test of the significance of the squared multiple correlation coefficient R^2 is of this type. F may also be used to obtain an interval estimator of the ratio of two variances. See Mood [1950], pp. 204–206, 268–269, 296–297, 302–307, 318–358; Fisher and Yates [1938], where the term "variance ratio" is used instead of the symbol F; and Pearson and Hartley [1954].

2 NONPREDICTIVE TESTS: INTRODUCTION

2.1 In this and the following three sections we shall discuss what we have called nonpredictive tests of econometric estimates and models, and some associated interval estimators. These are inference procedures that do not consist of preparing a prediction of an as-yet-unobserved datum and then checking to see whether the prediction is borne out by the actual observation.

2.2 In Section 3 we shall discuss tests and some associated interval estimators for regression and correlation coefficients in the least-squares approach, and for some of their counterparts in the simultaneous equations approach.

2.3 In Section 4 we shall discuss tests based on the residuals computed for an estimated equation for the sample period, that is, the quantities denoted by $\hat{u}_t$ and $\hat{v}_t$ ($t = 1, \ldots, T$) in the preceding chapter; see for example IX.1.3.

2.4 In Section 5 we shall discuss tests of the *a priori* restrictions that characterize the models used in econometrics.

3 NONPREDICTIVE TESTS, I: REGRESSION AND CORRELATION COEFFICIENTS AND THEIR SIMULTANEOUS-EQUATIONS COUNTERPARTS

3.1 In this section we discuss statistical inference concerning the regression coefficients in equations that contain only one dependent variable, and concerning the parameters in structural equations that contain two or more jointly dependent variables. The discussion in VII.7 is highly relevant and should be read again at this point; in particular the close relationship described there between hypothesis testing and interval estimation will be used below. This section also discusses inferences concerning the multiple and partial correlation coefficients in regression equations (they are multivariate forms of the simple correlation coefficient defined in IV.3.9 and are explained just below).

3.2 To define multiple and partial correlation coefficients clearly, and especially to show their relations to each other and to simple correlation coefficients, a precise notation is very useful. The following has proved to be extremely convenient and informative, and it is widely used. Consider an equation containing one dependent variable x_0, two predetermined variables x_1 and x_2, and an explicit constant term and a disturbance, thus:

$$(3.1) \qquad x_0 = \alpha_{0.12} + \pi_{01.2}x_1 + \pi_{02.1}x_2 + v_{0.12}$$

Here both the constant $\alpha_{0.12}$ and the disturbance $v_{0.12}$ carry the subscript 0.12; the number 0 before the period indicates that the dependent variable carries subscript 0, that is, it is x_0; and the numbers 1 and 2 after the period indicate that the independent variables carry subscripts 1 and 2, that is, they are x_1 and x_2. The coefficients of the independent variables x_1 and x_2 carry subscripts 01.2 and 02.1 respectively. The first number in each of these subscripts identifies the dependent variable as x_0, the second number identifies the independent variable whose coefficient is described (e.g., x_1 for $\pi_{01.2}$), and any numbers appearing after the period indicate what other variables are in the regression (e.g., x_2 is also in the regression in which $\pi_{01.2}$ is the coefficient of x_1 with x_0 dependent). In this same notation, $\alpha_{1.023}$ and $v_{1.023}$ would be the constant term and disturbance in the regression of x_1 on the three variables x_0, x_2, and x_3. And $\pi_{12.03}$ would be the coefficient of x_2 in that same regression. The order of subscripts *after* the period is always immaterial; for example, $\pi_{12.30}$ and $\pi_{12.03}$ are identical.

3.3 Least-squares estimators of α's and π's are as usual denoted by a's and p's with corresponding subscripts. The calculated value of the dependent variable is shown by a caret or hat, plus a set of subscripts after the period to indicate what dependent variables went into its calculation. Calculated disturbances are indicated by carets or hats. Thus equation (3.1) yields the following when the sum of squared deviations in the x_0 direction is minimized:

$$(3.2) \qquad \hat{x}_{0.12} = a_{0.12} + p_{01.2}x_1 + p_{02.1}x_2$$

$$= x_0 - \hat{v}_{0.12}$$

The variance of a disturbance v and two of its estimators are denoted by

η^2 and by $\hat{\eta}^2$ and h^2, respectively,[6] all with the same subscripts as the v has:

$$\eta_0{}^2 = \text{var } x_0; \quad \eta_{0.1}^2 = \text{var } v_{0.1}; \quad \eta_{0.12}^2 = \text{var } v_{0.12}; \quad \text{etc.}$$

(3.3) $\quad \hat{\eta}_0{}^2 = \frac{1}{T}\sum (x_0 - \bar{x}_0)^2; \quad \hat{\eta}_{0.1}^2 = \frac{1}{T}\sum \hat{v}_{0.1}^2; \quad \hat{\eta}_{0.12}^2 = \frac{1}{T}\sum \hat{v}_{0.12}^2; \quad \text{etc.}$

$$h_0{}^2 = \frac{1}{T-1}\sum (x_0 - \bar{x}_0)^2; \quad h_{0.1}^2 = \frac{1}{T-2}\sum \hat{v}_{0.1}^2;$$

$$h_{0.12}^2 = \frac{1}{T-3}\sum \hat{v}_{0.12}^2; \quad \text{etc.}$$

$\eta_{0.12}$, $\hat{\eta}_{0.12}$, and $h_{0.12}$ are all called the standard error of estimate of equation (3.1).

3.4 The correlation coefficient is a device for measuring the degree to which the relation of two variables is exactly linear. For the bivariate population of two variables x_1 and x_2, it was defined in IV.3.9 as their population covariance (which we here denote by η_{12}) divided by the product of their population standard deviations (which we here denote by either $\eta_1\eta_2$ or $\sqrt{\eta_{11}\eta_{22}}$). Thus for the *population* correlation coefficient between x_1 and x_2 we have

(3.4) $$\rho_{12} = \frac{\eta_{12}}{\eta_1\eta_2} = \frac{\eta_{12}}{\sqrt{\eta_{11}\eta_{22}}}$$

A similar formula holds for any pair of variables x_j and x_k. For a sample of size T from this bivariate population, an analogous equation holds for the sample correlation coefficient, except that now the *sample* moments m_{jk} (defined as $\sum(x_{jt} - \bar{x}_j)(x_{kt} - \bar{x}_k)$ in VI.3.3) instead of the *population* covariances η_{jk} appear. The relation between sample moments and estimated population covariances is

(3.5) $$m_{jk} = T\hat{\eta}_{jk}; \quad m_{jj} = T\hat{\eta}_{jj} = T\hat{\eta}_j{}^2$$

The *sample* correlation of x_0 and x_1, for example, is

(3.6) $$r_{01} = \frac{m_{01}}{\sqrt{m_{00}m_{11}}} = \frac{\hat{\eta}_{01}}{\hat{\eta}_0\hat{\eta}_1} = \frac{\hat{\eta}_{01}}{\sqrt{\hat{\eta}_{00}\hat{\eta}_{11}}}$$

The coefficients ρ_{jk} and r_{jk} are called *simple* correlation coefficients (as opposed to multiple or partial, which will be defined presently) because only two variables are involved in each. For any pair of variables, $-1 \leqq \rho_{jk} \leqq 1$ and $-1 \leqq r_{jk} \leqq 1$.

3.5 It will now be shown that the square of the sample correlation coefficient between two variables can be expressed as 1 minus the ratio

---

[6] The usual notation for variances is σ^2 or, in this book and some related literature, ω^2. We have already used up the symbols σ_{jk} and ω_{jk} (see IX.6.2), and hence we shall use η here instead.

of the unexplained variance of the dependent variable to the total variance of the same variable. This is extremely useful and important. (Some writers *define* the correlation coefficient this way.) Another way of saying it, since the total variance of a dependent variable can be broken into the sum of the variance explained plus the variance unexplained by the independent variable, is this: r_{jk}^2 is the fraction of the sample variance of the dependent variable that is explained by the independent variable. The demonstration is as follows; some explanatory remarks appear below:

$$
(3.7) \qquad r_{jk}^2 = r_{kj}^2 = \frac{m_{jk}^2}{m_{jj}m_{kk}}
$$

$$
= \frac{p_{jk}m_{jk}}{m_{jj}}
$$

$$
= 1 - \frac{m_{jj} - p_{jk}m_{jk}}{m_{jj}}
$$

$$
= 1 - \frac{\sum \hat{v}_{j.k}^2}{\sum (x_{jt} - \bar{x}_j)^2}
$$

$$
= 1 - \frac{\hat{\eta}_{j.k}^2}{\hat{\eta}_j^2}
$$

$$
= 1 - \frac{\hat{\eta}_{k.j}^2}{\hat{\eta}_k^2}
$$

The first and second equalities result from the definition of r_{jk} and r_{kj}. (Note that although $r_{jk} = r_{kj}$ and $m_{jk} = m_{kj}$, in general $p_{jk} \neq p_{kj}$.) The third equality uses the fact that the least-squares estimator p_{jk} of the regression slope π_{jk} (with x_j as the dependent variable) is m_{jk}/m_{kk} (see IX.3.12). The fourth equality results from adding and subtracting m_{jj}/m_{jj}. The fifth equality uses the fact that the sum of squared deviations in the x_j-direction in this regression is $m_{jj} - p_{jk}m_{jk}$ (see IX.3.13). The sixth equality uses the definitions given in (3.3). The seventh and last equality shows the corresponding result for x_k as the dependent variable; its proof may be supplied by the reader. The expressions in the first and second lines of (3.7) are the ratio of explained to total variance of x_j. The fifth line expresses 1 minus the ratio of unexplained to total variance of x_j, and the last does the same for x_k. These equations are for the sample; analogous equations hold for the population correlation coefficient ρ_{jk}.

3.6 The *multiple* correlation coefficient is a device for measuring the degree to which the relation of a dependent variable to a set of independent variables is exactly linear. The squared sample multiple correlation coefficient of x_0 as dependent variable and x_1 and x_2 as independent variables, denoted by $R_{0.12}^2$, is defined in analogy to (3.7) as 1 minus the ratio of the unexplained sample variance of x_0 in that regression to the total sample variance of x_0, thus:[7]

$$(3.8) \qquad R^2_{0.12} = R^2_{0.21} = 1 - \frac{\hat{\eta}^2_{0.12}}{\hat{\eta}_0^{\;2}} = 1 - \frac{\sum \hat{v}^2_{0.12}}{\sum (x_{0t} - \bar{x}_0)^2}$$

$$= 1 - \frac{m_{00} - p_{01.2}m_{01} - p_{02.1}m_{02}}{m_{00}}$$

$$= \frac{p_{01.2}m_{01} + p_{02.1}m_{02}}{m_{00}}$$

The first and second equalities give the definition of $R^2_{0.12}$ and $R^2_{0.21}$. The third equality uses sums of squared deviations instead of estimated variances. The fourth equality uses the expression of IX.4.6 for the sum of squared deviations from a regression and uses m_{00} in place of $\sum(x_{0t} - \bar{x}_0)^2$. The fifth equality results from cancellation of 1 against m_{00}/m_{00}. Similar relations apply to larger sets of variables, for example,

$$(3.9) \qquad R^2_{0.123...K} = 1 - \frac{\hat{\eta}^2_{0.123...K}}{\hat{\eta}^2_0}$$

3.7   Note that whereas the simple correlation coefficients r_{jk} and r_{kj} are the same, the first subscript (before the period) in the symbol for the multiple correlation coefficient cannot be interchanged with any of the other ones without changing the meaning and in general also the value of the coefficient; $R^2_{1.02}$ and $R^2_{2.01}$ are in general different from each other and from $R^2_{0.12}$. R^2 is the fraction of the sample variance of the dependent variable that is explained by the independent variables. (Changing the order of the subscripts *after* the period makes no difference, as usual.) The sign of a multiple correlation is conventionally always taken as positive. See also footnote 7. Thus we always have $0 \leqq R \leqq 1$, and of course also $0 \leqq R^2 \leqq 1$. Analogous relations hold for the *population* multiple correlation coefficient, which we do not denote symbolically and do not discuss extensively.

3.8   The *partial* correlation coefficient is a device for measuring the degree to which the residual relationship between two variables is exactly linear, *after* the effects of some set of independent variables have been taken account of in a linear regression (i.e., when the independent variables in that set are held constant). The squared sample partial correlation of x_0 and x_1, with x_2 held constant, denoted by $r^2_{01.2}$, is defined in analogy to

[7] The multiple correlation coefficient $R_{0.12...K}$ can be shown to be equal to the simple correlation coefficient between x_0 and $\hat{x}_{0.12...K}$, that is, between the observed value of the dependent variable and the calculated value based on the regression equation in question. See, for example, Cramer [1946] pp. 307–308 (in this place he is working with population rather than sample values, but the statement is correct in either case).

(3.7)–(3.8) as 1 minus the ratio of the unexplained-by-x_1-and-x_2 sample variance of x_0 to the unexplained-by-x_2 sample variance of x_0. In our notation,

$$(3.10) \qquad r_{01.2}^2 = 1 - \frac{\hat{\eta}_{0.12}^2}{\hat{\eta}_{0.2}^2}$$

This can be regarded as 1 minus the fraction of the residual-variance-of-x_0-unexplained-by-x_2 that is still unexplained after x_1 has been introduced into the regression. It can be shown that[8]

$$(3.11) \qquad r_{01.2} = \frac{r_{01} - r_{02}r_{12}}{\sqrt{(1 - r_{02}^2)(1 - r_{12}^2)}}$$

From this it follows that $r_{01.2}^2$ and $r_{10.2}^2$ are equal, that is, that $1 - \hat{\eta}_{0.12}^2/\hat{\eta}_{0.2}^2$ and $1 - \hat{\eta}_{1.02}^2/\hat{\eta}_{1.2}^2$ are equal. Similar relations hold for larger sets of variables. For example, the partial correlation of x_0 and x_1 when x_2 and x_3 are held constant is

$$(3.12) \qquad r_{01.23}^2 = 1 - \frac{\hat{\eta}_{0.123}^2}{\hat{\eta}_{0.23}^2} = \frac{(r_{01.3} - r_{02.3}r_{12.3})^2}{(1 - r_{02.3}^2)(1 - r_{12.3}^2)}$$

This is like (3.11) except that a subscript 3 is added everywhere after the period. Similarly,

$$(3.13) \qquad r_{01.234}^2 = 1 - \frac{\hat{\eta}_{0.1234}^2}{\hat{\eta}_{0.234}^2} = \frac{(r_{01.34} - r_{02.34}r_{12.34})^2}{(1 - r_{02.34}^2)(1 - r_{12.34}^2)}$$

The progression scheme for passing to higher orders is evident. Note also that the order in which variables are added in the progression scheme need not be that chosen in (3.12). For example, to get $r_{01.234}$ we could start with $r_{01.4}$, instead of $r_{01.2}$ as in (3.11), and then build up via such a progression to $r_{01.34}$ and then to $r_{01.234}$, obtaining a different but equivalent formula instead of (3.13). Or we could start with $r_{01.3}$ and build up, and so forth.

3.9 Simple, partial, and multiple correlations among a set of variables are related to each other in a systematic fashion. Consider first the three variables x_0, x_1, and x_2, and write the following trivial identity:

$$(3.14) \qquad \frac{\hat{\eta}_{0.12}^2}{\hat{\eta}_0^2} = \frac{\hat{\eta}_{0.12}^2}{\hat{\eta}_{0.1}^2} \frac{\hat{\eta}_{0.1}^2}{\hat{\eta}_0^2}$$

By virtue of the definitions of multiple, partial, and simple correlations above, each ratio in the foregoing identity is equal to 1 minus the square of a correlation coefficient, thus:

$$(3.15) \qquad 1 - R_{0.12}^2 = (1 - r_{02.1}^2)(1 - r_{01}^2)$$

---

[8] Kendall [1952], pp. 368–372, or Kendall and Stuart [1958]. See also Cramér [1946], p. 411, for related expressions for partial correlation.

If a new variable x_3 is considered, and if the identity (3.14) is multiplied on both sides by $\hat{\eta}_{0.123}^2/\hat{\eta}_{0.12}^2$ and the relevant correlations are substituted for the ratios, the result is a higher-order version of (3.15), which can be expressed in two ways, thus:

$$(3.16) \qquad 1 - R_{0.123}^2 = (1 - r_{03.12}^2)(1 - r_{02.1}^2)(1 - r_{01}^2)$$

$$= (1 - r_{03.12}^2)(1 - R_{0.12}^2)$$

Again the progression scheme for passing to higher orders is evident. And we can choose any of several different orders in which to build up to $R_{0.123}^2$; for example, we can form $1 - R_{0.12}^2$ as $(1 - r_{01.2}^2)(1 - r_{02}^2)$ instead of as in (3.15), and so forth.

3.10 Every time an estimator of a variance has been used so far in this section, it has been the estimator whose denominator is the sample size T rather than the number of degrees of freedom $T - K$; recall (3.3). We found in IX.3.19 and IX.5.4 that in Model 2 (see IX.2.3–5) unbiased estimators of the variance of the disturbance require the use of $T - K$ rather than T. Correlation coefficients can be defined accordingly, using degrees of freedom rather than sample size. Such correlation coefficients are said to be *adjusted for degrees of freedom*, or simply *adjusted*, and are customarily denoted by a bar over the letter r or R. Some samples of *adjusted* simple, partial, and multiple correlation coefficients are as follows:

$$\bar{r}_{01}^2 = 1 - \frac{h_{0.1}^2}{h_0^2} = 1 - \frac{(T-1)\hat{\eta}_{0.1}^2}{(T-2)\hat{\eta}_0^2} = 1 - \frac{T-1}{T-2}(1 - r_{01}^2)$$

$$(3.17) \quad \bar{r}_{01.2}^2 = 1 - \frac{h_{0.12}^2}{h_{0.2}^2} = 1 - \frac{(T-2)\hat{\eta}_{0.12}^2}{(T-3)\hat{\eta}_{0.2}^2} = 1 - \frac{T-2}{T-3}(1 - r_{0.12}^2)$$

$$\bar{R}_{0.12}^2 = 1 - \frac{h_{0.12}^2}{h_0^2} = 1 - \frac{(T-1)\hat{\eta}_{0.12}^2}{(T-3)\hat{\eta}_0^2} = 1 - \frac{T-1}{T-3}(1 - R_{0.12}^2)$$

Equations (3.15) and (3.16) hold for *adjusted* coefficients just as they do for unadjusted coefficients, as may be seen by substituting into them from (3.17) and canceling out factors such as $T - 1$, $T - 2$, and so forth. We have noted in IX.9.7 that when one or more additional explanatory variables are inserted into a linear regression equation, the sum of squared deviations of the dependent variable from the regression is either unchanged or decreased; it cannot be increased. Therefore, using the definition of the (unadjusted) multiple correlation coefficient R in (3.8), we see that the inclusion of one or more additional explanatory variables in a linear regression cannot decrease R^2; it can either raise R^2 (if the new variables help to explain the dependent variable better) or leave R^2 unchanged (if the new variables do not help at all). However, it is possible for the inclusion of additional variables to decrease the *adjusted* coefficient $\bar{R}^2$, because the ratio $(T - 1)/(T - K)$ decreases as K increases; if R^2 increases not very much or not at all as K increases, then $\bar{R}^2$ will actually decline as a result of the inclusion of an additional variable. In such a case the additional variable so to speak does not yield enough additional benefit (in terms of reduction in $\sum \hat{v}^2$) to cover its cost (in terms of the decrease in $T - K$). Barten [1962] has shown that in Model 2 (normal) the approximate expectation to order $1/T$ of the adjusted multiple correlation coefficient $\bar{R}^2$ defined as in (3.17) differs slightly from the population value of R^2 when the population value differs from $1/2$: $\bar{R}^2$ is on the average an overestimate when the true value exceeds $1/2$, and an underestimate when the true value is less than $1/2$, but the bias is small, its absolute value never exceeding $.096/T$. Hence $\bar{R}^2$ is quite a good estimator. However, as an estimator of the squared multiple correlation coefficient that is unbiased to order $1/T$, Barten proposes

$$(3.18) \qquad \hat{R}^2 = R^2 - \frac{1}{T}(1 - R^2)[K - (1 - R^2)(1 + 2R^2)]$$

where as usual K is the number of regression coefficients to be estimated (including the constant term) and R is the unadjusted multiple correlation coefficient. Barten gives a table of the factor that is multiplied by $1/T$ in (3.18), so that his statistic may be easily obtained when K and R^2 are given.

3.11 Let us denote the ratio of a squared estimated regression coefficient to its (unbiased) estimated variance by the symbol t^2 with the same subscripts as are carried by the regression coefficient. (We shall see presently that under certain conditions the square root of this ratio has the t distribution, so the notation is reasonable.) And let us denote the unbiased estimated variance of any regression coefficient p by $s^2(p)$. Then, for example,

$$t_{01} = \frac{p_{01}}{s(p_{01})}$$

$$(3.19)$$

$$t_{01.2} = \frac{p_{01.2}}{s(p_{01.2})} \text{, etc.}$$

There is a useful relation between this t and the corresponding partial correlation coefficient (or simple correlation coefficient when there are only two variables in the equation). If $T - K$ stands for the number of degrees of freedom in the unbiased estimator of the standard deviation (i.e., if there are K independent variables in the regression *including* the constant term if any), this relation can be stated in either of the following ways, that is, either solved for t^2 or solved for the partial correlation:

$$t_{01}^2 = \frac{(T - K)r_{01}^2}{(1 - r_{01}^2)}$$

$$t_{01.2}^2 = \frac{(T - K)r_{01.2}^2}{(1 - r_{01.2}^2)}, \text{ etc.}$$

(3.20)

$$r_{01}^2 = \frac{t_{01}^2}{(t_{01}^2 + T - K)}$$

$$r_{01.2}^2 = \frac{t_{01.2}^2}{(t_{01.2}^2 + T - K)}, \text{ etc.}$$

The relation between t_{01}^2 and r_{01}^2 is easy to verify from the formulas for t_{01}^2, the simple r^2, the estimated slope of a simple regression, the variance of an estimated regression slope, and the estimated variance of a regression disturbance [see respectively (3.19) and (3.7) and the following equations from Chapter IX: (3.23), (3.35), and (3.40)]. The relation for $t_{01.2}^2$ and $r_{01.2}^2$ and for higher orders of partial correlation is verified in a similar manner, using the definition of partial correlation; see also Cramér [1946], p. 413.

3.12   The relationships set forth so far in this section are extremely useful and important. Notice that as long as the regression equation used is linear, the relations (3.20) hold exactly, regardless of what linear model applies, for example, regardless of the statistical properties of the distribution of disturbances. Thus they can be freely used in linear models for computing partial r's when t's have already been computed, or vice versa, and the like, regardless of the other assumptions made. On the other hand, the probability distributions of simple and partial and multiple correlation coefficients, and of the t's defined in (3.19), depend crucially on the assumptions that apply to the model used, and therefore any statistical inference undertaken must to be meaningful be based on specifications inherent in the model. We shall now discuss statistical inference concerning the population parameters, using as sample statistics the various correlation coefficients and the t's of (3.19). First we shall discuss inference concerning the slope parameters of the equation in question and then inference concerning population correlation coefficients.

3.13   *Inference about slope parameters.* Let us assume that we are dealing with a linear equation describing the value of a variable x_0 in terms of variables $x_1, \ldots, x_K$ (where one of the latter will be a dummy always equal to 1 if the equation contains a constant term) and a disturbance. Let us assume that Model 2 (normal) applies. Model 2 (normal) specifies that equations are linear, that disturbances are normally distributed and independent from one period to another, that predetermined variables are exogenous and in the limit well behaved, and other properties that it would be wise to review by rereading IX.2.2-4. First we shall assume that the equation to be estimated contains only one dependent variable, x_0. The equation therefore is in the reduced form (this may be because it is a complete single-equation model of itself, or because it is one of the equations of the reduced form of a model of two or more equations). Since in Model 2 all predetermined variables are exogenous, $x_1, \ldots, x_K$ are exogenous. Such an equation is as follows (where for brevity the $K - 1$ subscripts belonging after the period on each of the π's have been omitted, and where one of the π's, say π_{0K}, is the constant term if the equation has one, z_K being a dummy equal to 1):

$$(3.21) \qquad x_0 = \sum_{k=1}^{K} \pi_{0k} x_k + v_{0.12 \ldots K}$$

Later on (in 3.19 ff.) we shall discuss the case of a structural equation having two or more jointly dependent variables (the disturbance in such an equation will be denoted by the letter u in accordance with our custom). Least-squares estimators of π_{0k} treating x_0 as dependent are denoted by p_{0k}, $k = 1, \ldots, K$. In Model 2 (normal or not) they are unbiased and consistent and asymptotically normal (see IX.2.3-4, IX.9.23 and IX.5.3).

3.14 For Model 2 (normal or not) the variance-covariance matrix of the p's is given in IX.5.5 as follows, conditional on the values of the exogenous x's:

$$(3.22) \qquad \operatorname{cov}(\mathbf{p}', \mathbf{p}) = \omega^2 \mathbf{M}_{xx}^{-1}$$

where $\mathbf{p}'$ stands for the column vector $(p_{01}, \ldots, p_{0K})'$, and ω^2 is the variance of v, and $\mathbf{M}_{xx}$ is the matrix of moments of $x_1, \ldots, x_K$. (Recall that the moment m_{jk} of x_j and x_k is defined as $\sum(x_{jt} - \bar{x}_j)(x_{kt} - \bar{x}_k)$ or as $\sum x_{jt} x_{kt}$, depending on whether there is an explicitly mentioned constant term in (3.21) or not. If so, then $\mathbf{M}_{xx}$ has $K - 1$ rows and columns; if not, $\mathbf{M}_{xx}$ has K rows and columns. See IX.4.11 for details of this notational convention.) A consistent unbiased estimator of (3.22) is available in Model 2 (whether normal or not): replace ω^2 by its unbiased estimator w^2 given in IX.5.4. Denote the estimator of var p_{0k} so obtained by $s^2(p_{0k})$.

3.15 In Model 2 (normal) the least-squares estimators p_{0k} of the parameters π_{0k} of the reduced-form equation (3.21) are themselves normally distributed for a given set of sample values of the exogenous variables, because each of the p_{0k} is a linear combination of $x_{01}, \ldots, x_{0T}$, which are themselves normal because of (3.21) and the normality of its disturbances. Furthermore, it can be shown[9] that under the assumptions of our Model 2 (normal) the following ratio has the t distribution with

---

[9] Wilks [1943], p. 162; Cramér [1946], p. 410.

$T - K$ degrees of freedom (again the $K - 1$ subscripts $1, 2, \ldots, k - 1$, $k + 1, \ldots, K$ belonging after the period are omitted for brevity):

$$(3.23) \qquad\qquad t_{0k} \equiv \frac{p_{0k} - \pi_{0k}}{s(p_{0k})}$$

Therefore this ratio can be used to test the null hypothesis that π_{0k} in (3.21) has any particular stated value. The procedure is essentially as described in 1.13. The steps are: Substitute the hypothetical value for π_{0k} in (3.23); choose a sample size T and a one-tailed or two-tailed rejection region for the test (i.e., an acceptance region with lower and upper limits t_l and t_u); obtain a sample of T observations on $x_0, x_1, \ldots, x_K$; compute the sample value of t_{0k} from (3.23), using the estimated values of p_{0k} and $s(p_{0k})$ obtained from the sample; accept the null hypothesis if the sample value of t_{0k} falls in the acceptance region or on its boundary, and reject the null hypothesis otherwise. In the most common use of this test, the hypothetical value of π_{0k} is chosen as zero, which means that the test statistic becomes

$$(3.24) \qquad\qquad t_{0k} = \frac{p_{0k}}{s(p_{0k})}$$

and the null hypotheses tested is that the variable x_k *does not* appear in the equation (3.21). If the null hypothesis is rejected by the test (i.e., if the sample value of t_{0k} is far enough from zero to be in the rejection region), the conclusion is that x_k *does* appear in the equation.

3.16 Several remarks are in order concerning the t test described in the preceding paragraph. *First*, it is not necessary that anything be known about the probability distribution of the variables $x_1, \ldots, x_K$ that are treated as independent in the regression, except that they are exogenous. In particular, they need not be normally distributed. *Second*, if Model 2 applies but the disturbances are not normal, then the normal distribution test is appropriate asymptotically since the estimators $p_{01}, \ldots, p_{0K}$ are asymptotically normal (see IX.9.23), and it is approximately appropriate for small samples, the approximation of course being poorer for smaller samples. *Third*, if Model 3 applies with normal or non-normal disturbances (i.e., if there are lagged endogenous variables in the equation), the preceding sentence is still valid on the understanding that $s(p_{0k})$ is now an estimator of the standard deviation of the *approximate* distribution of p_{0k}, and not necessarily an estimator of p_{0k}'s *actual* standard deviation (which may or may not exist).

3.17 Instead of using the statistic t_{0k} for testing a hypothesis about the parameter π_{0k} in (3.21), we may use it for constructing an interval estimator of π_{0k}. The procedure in Model 2 (normal) is as indicated in 1.13. For an interval estimator with n degrees of freedom and a confidence coefficient of $\epsilon_2 - \epsilon_1$ (where $1 \geqq \epsilon_2 \geqq \epsilon_1 \geqq 0$), the lower and upper limits are respectively

(3.25)
$$(\pi_{0k})_l = p_{0k} - s(p_{0k})t_{\epsilon_2}(n)$$
$$(\pi_{0k})_u = p_{0k} - s(p_{0k})t_{\epsilon_1}(n)$$

The remarks in 3.16 apply to this inference procedure as well as to hypothesis testing.

3.18 Joint tests or joint confidence regions for two or more parameters simultaneously are sometimes appropriate, especially when an equation contains two or more parameters whose estimates have high covariance. This situation was described in IX.4.12 ff., and the reader is referred there to refresh his memory. For example, a joint confidence

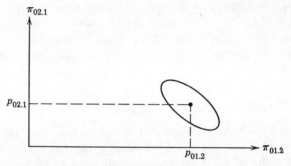

Figure 3.1 Elliptical joint confidence region for two parameters of a regression equation with positively correlated independent variables in Model 2 (normal).

region may be constructed for the two parameters $\pi_{01.2}$ and $\pi_{02.1}$ in (3.1), based on the estimators $p_{01.2}$ and $p_{02.1}$ shown in (3.2). A confidence region for them will turn out to be an area around the point estimate $(p_{01.2}, p_{02.1})$ on a graph of $\pi_{01.2}$ versus $\pi_{02.1}$. The smallest region for a given confidence coefficient turns out in Model 2 (normal) to be elliptical. Suppose x_1 and x_2 are positively correlated; their separate effects are not clearly discernible, and the estimators of $\pi_{01.2}$ and $\pi_{02.1}$ are negatively correlated. Hence the confidence region should show that point estimates of $\pi_{02.1}$ higher than $p_{02.1}$ are usually (i.e., in most samples) accompanied by point estimates of $\pi_{01.2}$ less than $p_{01.2}$. That is, the region should be an ellipse with its long axis sloping negatively, as suggested in Figure 3.1. The construction of such a joint confidence region or test in two or more dimensions uses the F or the χ^2 distribution. The reader is referred to Haavelmo's paper on the marginal propensity to consume for an example, and elsewhere for the theoretical development.[10]

[10] Haavelmo [1947], pp. 86–87 and 89–91 (in Hood and Koopmans [1953]). Wilks [1943], pp. 234–250; Mood [1950], pp. 227–229, 238–239, 295–296, 302–305.

3.19 *Inferences about structural-equation slopes.* As promised at the beginning of this section and in 3.13, we now turn to inferences about slope parameters in a *structural* equation having two or more jointly dependent variables. Such equations have been extensively discussed in IX.7–12. In the notation used there, such an equation is

$$(3.26) \qquad y_1 + \sum_2^H \beta_i y_i + \sum_1^J \gamma_k z_k = u$$

where the y's are jointly dependent, the z's are predetermined, u is a disturbance, and the β's and γ's are unknown parameters. The parameter σ^2, equal to var u, is also unknown.

3.20 If Model 3 applies, there are several consistent estimation methods available for (3.26), for example, limited information, two-stage least squares, and so forth. In Model 3 the limited-information and full-information estimators are asymptotically normal, and in Model 2 and perhaps Model 3 the two-stage least-squares estimators are also.[11] In Model 3 the asymptotic covariance matrices associated with the limited-information and two-stage least-squares estimators are identical, and estimated approximate variances and covariances of either method's estimators of the β's and γ's in (3.26) can be calculated by the method of IX.10.21. Let us denote the limited-information estimators as usual by $\hat{\beta}_i$ and $\hat{\gamma}_k$, and let us denote their estimated approximate variances mentioned above by $\hat{\sigma}^2(\hat{\beta}_i)$ and $\hat{\sigma}^2(\hat{\gamma}_k)$. Then, since the β's and γ's are consistent and asymptotically normal in Model 3, the following statistics have approximately the normal distribution:

$$(3.27) \qquad \frac{\hat{\beta}_i - \beta_i}{\hat{\sigma}(\hat{\beta}_i)}, \quad \frac{\hat{\gamma}_k - \gamma_k}{\hat{\sigma}(\hat{\gamma}_k)} \qquad i = 2, \dots, H; \quad k = 1, \dots, J$$

Analogous statistics from the two-stage least-squares and full-information methods also have approximately the normal distribution. These statistics have the normal distribution *approximately* (not exactly) for several reasons: $\hat{\beta}_i$ and $\hat{\gamma}_k$ are only *approximately* normal, not exactly, and their expectations in general do not exist and so they cannot be unbiased; the $\hat{\sigma}$'s are estimators of the *approximate* (not the exact) standard deviations of the β's and γ's, and the $\hat{\sigma}^2$'s presumably have the χ^2 distribution only approximately at best. The appropriate number of degrees of freedom for the approximate distribution of (3.27) is not clear. Most practitioners use the sample size diminished by the number of unknown parameters in the equation (i.e., $T - H + 1 - J$) in analogy to the correct number for least-squares estimation of a reduced-form equation.

3.21 Since statistics like (3.27) based on our consistent estimators have approximately the normal distribution, such statistics can be used

[11] See IX.2.4, IX.9.23, IX.10.17, and IX.12.2.

for approximate statistical inference (either testing or interval estimation) concerning the structural parameters of equations like (3.26). The procedures are the same as those described in 1.13 and 3.13–18, except that for structural equations with two or more jointly dependent variables, results must be regarded as approximate because the normal distribution is only approximately appropriate. Joint tests and joint interval estimators may be used, as indicated in 3.18.

3.22 Suppose that the least-squares method is used for estimating the structural equation (3.26). If $H \geqq 2$, that is, if the equation contains two or more jointly dependent variables, then least-squares estimators are not consistent, and also the various other properties given in IX.3–5 for these estimators and for their estimated variances and covariances are no longer guaranteed. It is likely that least-squares computations for such a case are not totally uninformative, but unfortunately it is very difficult to know how to interpret the numerical results they yield. It is plausible to conjecture that if we can establish in a particular case that the least-squares bias is small, then ratios analogous to (3.27) and based on least-squares computations will have very approximately the t distribution, so that tests and interval estimation using such ratios and the t table will give approximately correct results. Perhaps further work with the approaches indicated in IX.11.7 ff. would be helpful here.

3.23 *Inference about correlation coefficients.* Let us again consider a single reduced-form equation like (3.21) under Model 2 (normal); then all predetermined variables are exogenous. We now discuss statistical inference based on sample values of the various correlation coefficients discussed in 3.4–12. Such inference of course presupposes that these sample correlation coefficients are random variables having probability distributions. If some or all of the exogenous variables $x_1, \ldots, x_K$ are not random, but are arbitrarily chosen (for example, by a government policy-making agency), the probability distributions of the sample correlation coefficients will depend on the values chosen for those exogenous variables, and even the expected values and probability limits of the sample correlation coefficients will depend on the values of those exogenous variables.[12] Correlation coefficients are supposed to indicate the degree to which relationships are exactly linear. If the expected value and probability limit

---

[12] For example, consider the simple sample correlation r_{01} between x_0 (dependent) and x_1 (independent and nonrandom). It is equal to $m_{01}/\sqrt{m_{00}m_{11}}$. When the values of m_{01} and m_{00} are expressed in terms of the regression equation $x_0 = \pi x_1 + \alpha + v$, r_{01} is seen to be equal to $(\pi m_{11} + m_{v1})/\sqrt{m_{11}(\pi^2 m_{11} + m_{vv} + 2m_{v1})}$. Under Model 2, plim $m_{v1}/T = 0$ and plim $m_{vv}/T = $ var v, and we have for plim r_{01} the following: $\pi/\sqrt{\pi^2 + (\text{var } v)/\text{plim}\,(m_{11}/T)}$. This expression clearly is an increasing function of plim m_{11}/T, for given values of the parameters π and var v, which illustrates the statement in the text above.

of a measure of the degree of linearity are not constant, but depend on the chosen values of nonrandom exogenous variables, the measure of linearity is quite inconvenient. Presumably this is why the theory of the probability distributions of correlation coefficients is usually restricted to the case where there exists a joint distribution of *all* the variables x_0, $x_1, \ldots, x_K$ in the equation, that is, where all the independent variables are random with probability distributions, arbitrary choice of the values of any of the independent variables being ruled out. Then the sample correlation coefficients are random variables whose distributions depend on the joint distribution of $x_0, x_1, \ldots, x_K$.[13] This case is more restrictive than Model 2, which does not require that $x_1, \ldots, x_K$ be stochastic.

3.24 The stochastic theory of correlation coefficients has been especially well worked out for the case where all the variables $x_0, x_1, \ldots, x_K$ in the equation have a joint *normal* distribution. This case is much more restrictive than Model 2, for it requires that $x_1, \ldots, x_K$ all be stochastic and normally distributed. Regarding 3.25–28 below, see Cramér [1946], pp. 394–415, esp. pp. 398–401, 411–415.

3.25 Consider first the case of a bivariate normal distribution of two variables, x_0 and x_1. Such a distribution has been described in IV.3.11. It has five parameters, namely, the means Ex_0 and Ex_1, which are sometimes symbolized by μ_0 and μ_1; the variances var x_0 and var x_1, which we are here denoting by η_0^2 and η_1^2; and the correlation ρ_{01}. (The covariance η_{01} is equal to $\rho_{01}\eta_0\eta_1$ and so is fixed once the correlation and variances are fixed.) The probability distribution of the sample correlation coefficient r_{01}, computed from a sample of T observations on the jointly normal variables x_0 and x_1, is a function of T and the parameter ρ_{01}, but does not depend on the mean or variance of either x_0 or x_1 (Cramér [1946], p. 398). The shape of this distribution varies greatly with ρ_{01}, being symmetrical about zero when $\rho_{01} = 0$ and being asymmetrical when $\rho_{01} \neq 0$. As the sample size T grows without limit, plim $r_{01} = \rho_{01}$, and the distribution of r_{01} approaches normality, but the approach is rather slow if ρ_{01} is not close to zero.

3.26 The distribution of r_{01} has been tabulated as a function of T for the case where $\rho_{01} = 0$, and it is available in many places (e.g., Fisher and Yates [1938], Pearson and Hartley [1954]). Accordingly this table can be used to test the null hypothesis that $\rho_{01} = 0$ when x_0 and x_1 are thought to have a joint normal distribution. An equivalent test in the same circumstances is a t test of the statistic $\sqrt{T-2}\, r_{01}/\sqrt{1 - r_{01}^2}$, which, in those circumstances if $\rho_{01} = 0$, has the t distribution with $T - 2$ degrees of

---

[13] This is not to deny that in such a case we can form the conditional distribution of a correlation coefficient given the values of $x_1, \ldots, x_K$; it is rather to assert that there exists a marginal distribution (see IV.2.11) of a correlation coefficient not dependent on the values of $x_1, \ldots, x_K$.

freedom. This statistic is equal to the statistic t_{01} defined by (3.19) and (3.20) for equation (3.21) with $K = 2$.

3.27 Whether ρ_{01} is zero or not, tests of hypotheses and interval estimators for ρ_{01} can be obtained approximately by the use of a transformation due to R. A. Fisher (the symbol z here does not have the same meaning as elsewhere in this book):

$$(3.28) \qquad z \equiv \frac{1}{2} \log_e \frac{1 + r_{01}}{1 - r_{01}}$$

This variable z is approximately normal even for moderate sample sizes and has approximate mean and variance as follows:

$$(3.29) \qquad Ez \cong \frac{1}{2} \log_e \frac{1 + \rho_{01}}{1 - \rho_{01}} + \frac{\rho_{01}}{2(T - 1)} \; ; \quad \text{var } z \cong \frac{1}{T - 3}$$

Because the shape of this distribution does not depend on ρ_{01}, this approach has two advantages over that of the preceding paragraph: It requires no special table but can use the normal table, and it applies to cases where $\rho_{01} \neq 0$. But it is approximate, not exact.

3.28 Inference about equation (3.21) based on sample *partial* correlation coefficients can be carried out, when all variables in the equation are jointly normal, by the same methods described in 3.25–27 above for the simple correlations, except that the sample size T must now be replaced everywhere by $T - (K - 2)$ so that in effect the number of degrees of freedom is reduced from $T - 2$ to $T - K$. (Recall that K is the number of independent variables in the equation, *including* the constant term.)

3.29 If all the variables $x_1, \ldots, x_K$ in the equation are joint normal, then plim R^2 is equal to the square of the population value of the multiple correlation coefficient. If that value is zero, all observed sample values of R^2 must be equal to or greater than the population value, because $R^2 \geqq 0$. (The same is true of R.) Hence if the population multiple correlation is zero, R^2 cannot be asymptotically normal because R^2 cannot then be symmetrically distributed about its probability limit; in fact TR^2 is then asymptotically distributed as χ^2 with K degrees of freedom. But when the population multiple correlation is positive, then R^2 is asymptotically normal.

3.30 *Goodness of fit of structural equations.* Let us now briefly consider goodness of fit in the case of a *structural* equation having two or more jointly dependent variables. Consider again the structural equation (3.26) containing $y_1, \ldots, y_H$ (jointly dependent) and $z_1, \ldots, z_J$ (predetermined), and as usual let the limited–information estimators of its parameters be denoted by $\hat{\beta}_2, \ldots, \hat{\beta}_H, \hat{\gamma}_1, \ldots, \hat{\gamma}_J$. Let $\sigma^2 = \text{var } u$. And let the calculated residuals and values of y_1 associated with these estimators be denoted by $\hat{u}$ and $\hat{y}_1$, respectively, as follows:

$$(3.30) \qquad \hat{u}_t = y_{1t} - \hat{y}_{1t} = y_{1t} - \sum_{2}^{H} \hat{\beta}_i y_{it} - \sum_{1}^{J} \hat{\gamma}_k z_{kt}$$

(Observe that while the notation $\hat{u}$ clearly refers to a *structural* residual, the notation $\hat{y}_1$ has been used to refer to the calculated value of y_1 based on estimated *reduced-form* equations in Chapter IX, so henceforth we must rely on the context to tell whether $\hat{y}$ refers to calculated values based on estimated *structural* parameters as in (3.30) or on an estimated *reduced form*.) Then a statistic can be defined that estimates the variance of the structural disturbance by taking the mean square of the residuals $\hat{u}_t$ from (3.30). This estimator is

$$(3.31) \qquad \hat{\sigma}^2 = \text{est } \sigma^2 = \frac{1}{T - H - J + 1} \sum_{1}^{T} \hat{u}_t^2$$

Its square root is analogous to the (estimated form of the) standard error of estimate $h_{0.12}$ in (3.3) above, except that $\hat{\sigma}$ refers to the limited-information estimate of a structural equation, whereas $h_{0.12}$ refers to the least-squares estimate of an equation having just one dependent variable. Analogous estimators of σ^2 can be constructed for the two-stage least-squares method, the full-information method, and so forth; see, for example, IX.10.21. All such estimators of σ^2 must of course be greater than or equal to the least-squares estimator.

3.31 One might think of a statistic, analogous to the squared multiple correlation coefficient R^2, but based on the estimate $\hat{\sigma}^2$ from the limited-information method (or some other simultaneous-equations method), and defined as $1 - \sum \hat{u}_t^2 / \sum (y_{1t} - \bar{y}_1)^2$. However, whereas R^2 must be between 0 and 1 inclusive, Basmann [1962a] has pointed out that the statistic discussed in this paragraph can be negative, because $\sum \hat{u}_t^2$ can exceed $\sum (y_{1t} - \bar{y}_1)^2$, and that this can happen even when a correct model is being used. Hence this statistic is of no value as an indicator of the usefulness of an estimated structural equation.

3.32 Hooper [1959] has proposed a statistic, which he calls the *trace correlation*, to measure the proportion of the total variance of the jointly dependent variables as a group that is explained by the predetermined variables as a group in a structural model. In this context only, let the $G \times T$ matrix of data for the current endogenous variables be $\mathbf{Y}$, the $K \times T$ matrix of data for the predetermined variables be $\mathbf{Z}$, and the $G \times K$ matrix of reduced form coefficients be $\mathbf{\Pi}$. Then the conditional expectation of $\mathbf{Y}'$ given $\mathbf{Z}'$ is given by the systematic part of the reduced form, that is,

$$(3.32) \qquad E\mathbf{Y}' \,|\, \mathbf{Z}' = \mathbf{Z}'\mathbf{\Pi}'$$

The least-squares estimator of the reduced form yields the following calculated value of $\mathbf{Y}'$:

$$(3.33) \qquad \hat{\mathbf{Y}}' = \mathbf{Z}'\mathbf{P}' = \mathbf{Z}'(\mathbf{ZZ}')^{-1}\mathbf{ZY}'$$

The $G \times G$ moment matrix of calculated values of $\mathbf{Y}'$ is as follows, where the symmetric $T \times T$ matrix $\mathbf{S}$ is defined below:

$$(3.34) \qquad \hat{\mathbf{Y}}\hat{\mathbf{Y}}' = \mathbf{YZ}'(\mathbf{ZZ}')^{-1}\mathbf{ZY}' = \mathbf{YSY}'$$

$$(3.35) \qquad \mathbf{S} \equiv \mathbf{Z}'(\mathbf{ZZ}')^{-1}\mathbf{Z} = \mathbf{S}'$$

Hooper defines a $G \times G$ matrix $\mathbf{D}$ thus (in our notation):

$$(3.36) \qquad \mathbf{I} - \mathbf{D} \equiv (\mathbf{YY}')^{-1}\mathbf{YSY}'$$

He then points out that $\mathbf{I} - \mathbf{D}$ computed for a structural model can be regarded as a matrix generalization of the scalar squared multiple correlation coefficient R^2; indeed in the degenerate case where the structural model has only one equation and one dependent variable so that $G = 1$, it is easy to show that $\mathbf{I} - \mathbf{D}$ becomes a scalar equal to R^2.

3.33 Hooper defines his *trace correlation*, denoted by $\bar{r}$, in terms of the trace of the matrix $\mathbf{I} - \mathbf{D}$; specifically:[14]

$$(3.37) \qquad \bar{r}^2 \equiv \frac{1}{G}\operatorname{tr}(\mathbf{I} - \mathbf{D})$$

Since the trace of a matrix equals the sum of its characteristic roots,[15] Hooper shows that his squared trace correlation $\bar{r}^2$ is the simple average of the characteristic roots of $\mathbf{I} - \mathbf{D}$. Hooper also shows that the squares of the canonical correlations[16] between the G dependent variables and the K predetermined variables are precisely the characteristic roots of $\mathbf{I} - \mathbf{D}$, and that therefore $\bar{r}^2$ is also equal to the simple average of the canonical correlations. He derives the asymptotic variance of $\bar{r}^2$ under assumptions similar to our Model 2 (normal). Hooper [1962] develops the concept of *partial* trace correlation.

3.34 The point estimation techniques set forth in Chapter IX, and the tests and interval estimators set forth in this section and the next, are based on the classical statistical approach that takes it for granted that the *a priori* information forming the model or maintained hypothesis is known with certainty to be correct. In practice, there is uncertainty about many of the *a priori* restrictions. Some remarks about this will be found in Section 5.

---

[14] The trace of a square matrix is the sum of its diagonal elements; see A.5.2. The notation $\bar{r}$ has a different meaning here than in 3.10.

[15] See A.5.1–2.

[16] See Hooper [1959], pp. 245–247.

4 NONPREDICTIVE TESTS, II: RESIDUALS; SERIAL CORRELATION

4.1 In this section we discuss several tests based on the residuals computed from an estimated equation for the sample period, other than tests of correlation. We shall illustrate them by means of a reduced-form equation:

$$(4.1) \qquad y_t = \sum_1^K \pi_k z_{kt} + v_t$$

As usual y is dependent and $z_1, \ldots, z_K$ are predetermined. We shall make the assumptions of Model 3 throughout this section (see IX.2.4 for Models 2 and 3), including the independence of v_s and v_t when $s \neq t$; and sometimes we shall strengthen them by assuming Model 2 (where all z's are exogenous) and/or assuming that v is normally distributed. The least-squares estimators of π_k are as usual denoted by p_k, and the residual by $\hat{v}_t$, thus:

$$(4.2) \qquad \hat{v}_t = y_t - \hat{y}_t = y_t - \sum_1^K p_k z_{kt}$$

4.2 The first and simplest test of residuals that we take up (and it is not a real statistical test) consists simply of looking at the residuals $\hat{v}_1, \ldots, \hat{v}_T$ from the calculated equation, to see whether they appear too large by comparison with the average size of shift that we expect the equation to undergo. It is difficult to make this test very precise, because there is no precise measure of how large we should expect the shifts to be. Their squares should be smaller on the average than the variance of the variable to be explained (otherwise the equation would explain nothing), and cannot be smaller on the average than the minimized variance of residuals obtained by least squares. Beyond this nothing much can be said, except that *a priori* notions and the comparison of the given equation with similar ones for other regions or periods or industries or commodities may be helpful. The information we may have about maximum plausible shifts of an equation is fairly easy to incorporate into the estimation process, as illustrated in VIII.5.4 ff., and hence this is a case of information that can be used in the estimation process rather than saved till afterward to provide a test. Examples of its use and of a related method are to be found in the work of Harberger [1954] and of Marschak and Andrews [1944], especially pp. 161–168 and 180–182.

4.3 In case the model used specifies normally distributed disturbances, we can test the residuals $\hat{v}_t$ for normality. After the residuals are computed, they are collected into a frequency distribution. The size of the class intervals should be chosen large enough so that each has several members but small enough so that there are at least four or five (and preferably more) intervals having some members. (If there are not enough observations to permit this, the test cannot say much.) The distribution is then graphed and examined to see whether the sample that it represents might reasonably have been drawn from a normal population. A simple graph on ordinary graph paper, with the values of the residuals on one axis and the frequency of occurrence on the other axis, will show an approximately bell-shaped contour if the residuals are approximately normal. A more convenient and informative way is to graph the cumulative distribution of residuals on the especially constructed normal probability paper; if a straight line results, the residuals are normal. In small samples from a normal population, substantial deviations from normality are not uncommon. A more precise test based on the chi-square distribution is available if desired. It is called the χ^2 test of goodness of fit. It proceeds by comparing the observed frequency in each class interval with the frequency that would appear in that class interval under a normal frequency distribution having the same mean and variance and number of observations as the observed distribution. It is described in most statistical inference textbooks.

4.4 Our Models 2 and 3 assume that disturbances v_s and v_t are independent for $s \neq t$. In time-series models, any dependence between disturbances in different time periods presumably is greater for time periods close together than for time periods two years or more apart. The autoregressive disturbances discussed in VI.4.11 and IX.13.2 have this property: The dependence of v_t on v_{t-1} is greatest, and its dependence on $v_{t-2}, v_{t-3}, \ldots$ becomes successively weaker. In cross-section studies, there is no analog of this kind of dependence unless the individuals in the sample have some natural one-dimensional order analogous to chronological order, such, for example, as distances of cities or markets measured from some point along a trade route on which they are all located, so that disturbances are propagated along the route from one member of the sample to the next in a clear-cut order. Tests have been devised for the null hypothesis that v_t and v_{t-1} are uncorrelated, against the alternative hypothesis that v_t and v_{t-1} are correlated. A very crude but very useful procedure for this problem is to plot the residuals $\hat{v}_1, \ldots, \hat{v}_T$ on the vertical axis against t on the horizontal axis, and examine the graph. If the residuals show a trend from negative to positive or vice versa, or if they show fairly smooth long waves with turning points being less common than continuations of upward or downward movements, then they are almost certainly positively serially correlated. If they show persistent alternations between negative and positive values, they are almost certainly negatively serially correlated. Another use for such a graph will be mentioned later in this section.

4.5   Inspection of a graph of residuals against t is not a very precise test. A statistic known as the *ratio of the mean square successive difference to the variance* is suitable for testing whether or not the distribution of each member if an ordered series of random variables is uncorrelated with the succeeding member. It is usually symbolized by δ^2/S^2, and for a series of T observations $x_1, \ldots, x_T$ it is defined thus:

$$(4.3) \qquad \frac{\delta^2}{S^2} = \frac{\sum_{2}^{T}(x_t - x_{t-1})^2/(T-1)}{\sum_{1}^{T}(x_t - \bar{x})^2/T}$$

Its distribution has been derived by von Neumann [1941] and [1942], and tabulated by Hart [1942], on the assumption that the x_t are random drawings from a normal distribution. We are going to follow them and call it δ^2/S^2, instead of δ^2/s^2, because the unbiased variance estimator s^2 that we are using is based on a different number of degrees of freedom from that in the denominator of δ^2/S^2; we will run less risk of confusion if we do not change our definition of s^2 now. If a high value of x is usually followed by a high value, and a low value is usually followed by a low value, as in a smooth uptrend or downtrend or a smooth wavy pattern, there is positive serial correlation among the x's; then δ^2/S^2 will be small because its numerator will be the mean of squares of small successive differences (small relative to the sample standard deviation S). If a high value of x is usually followed by a low value, and vice versa, there is negative serial correlation; then δ^2/S^2 will be large because its numerator will be the mean of squares of large successive differences (large relative to S). Intermediate values of δ^2/S^2, near 2, indicate little or no serial correlation, for if there is no serial correlation in the population from which the x's come, the distribution of δ^2/S^2 is symmetrical and its mean is $2T/(T-1)$. A table of the distribution of $[(T-1)/T]\delta^2/S^2$, adapted from Hart's table,[17] appears in Appendix B. If $(\delta^2/S^2)_0$ represents the lower acceptance limit for δ^2/S^2, the range of values of δ^2/S^2 is divided into three regions, the center being the acceptance region for the hypothesis of zero serial correlation, running from $(\delta^2/S^2)_0$ to $4T/(T-1) - (\delta^2/S^2)_0$, which is the same distance above the mean $2T/(T-1)$ as $(\delta^2/S^2)_0$ is below it. The left-hand rejection region corresponds to positive serial correlation and the right-hand one to negative. See Figure 4.1.

4.6   As an example, suppose that a sample of 18 observations $x_1, \ldots, x_{18}$ resulted in a value of δ^2/S^2 equal to 1.13. Then $(T-1)\delta^2/TS^2$ is

---

[17] See Hart [1942], esp. pp. 207 and 213. The factor $(T-1)/T$ is applied in Appendix B to make this distribution comparable with the distribution of a similar statistic d to be introduced in 4.8. Note that $(T-1)\delta^2/TS^2 = \delta^2/s^2 = d$.

17/18 times 1.13, that is, 1.07. Suppose it is certain that if x_t and x_{t-1} have any correlation it is positive; then we may use a one-tail test of the hypothesis that the serial correlation in the x's is zero. Accordingly the acceptance region for $(T - 1)\delta^2/TS^2$ runs from the maximum possible value (about 4) down to an appropriate value in the left-hand tail of the distribution. Suppose that 95 per cent has been chosen as the best significance level for the test. Accordingly, from the .05 row of Table 4 in Appendix B we find that the lower acceptance limit for $(T - 1)\delta^2/TS^2$ for a sample of 18 observations is approximately[18] 1.24. Now 1.07 is

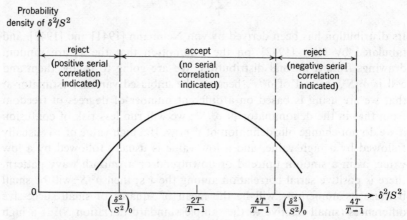

Figure 4.1 Schematic drawing of the distribution of δ^2/S^2 for test of serial noncorrelation of disturbances. See 4.5 in text.

below this, so that the hypothesis of no serial correlation must be rejected for this sample. If the significance level is chosen at 99 per cent instead of 95 per cent, the .01 row of the table gives the lower acceptance limit for $(T - 1)\delta^2/TS^2$ as approximately 0.98; then the conclusion is reversed.

4.7   Hart's table is not strictly appropriate for testing hypotheses concerning serial correlation of the disturbances in an equation,[19] because it is intended to apply to *observable* random variables $x_1, \ldots, x_T$. The disturbances v_t [such as in equation (4.1)] whose serial correlation we are concerned about are never observable; they can be estimated from the calculated equation; we have called these estimated residuals $\hat{v}_t$, as in equation (4.2). The residuals $\hat{v}$ are the variables from which δ^2/S^2 must be calculated in practice for this purpose. That Hart's table is not

[18] The value 1.24 is obtained by interpolating for $T = 18$ between the values of $(T - 1)\delta^2/TS^2$ shown for $T = 15$ and $T = 20$, which are 1.16 and 1.30 respectively.

[19] As pointed out in Christ [1951], p. 68.

appropriate here was forcefully suggested by Monte Carlo sampling experiments conducted by Orcutt and Cochrane [1949]. Artificial models with *known* serial correlation of shifts and *known* parameters were used to generate artificial time-series data, which in turn were used with samples of size $T = 20$ to estimate the parameters of the model. The residuals were then tested for serial correlation by means of Hart's table. In a large number of trials, the hypothesis of no serial correlation was incorrectly accepted too often to justify confidence in the test based on Hart's table of the distribution of δ^2/S^2; this was especially so when the number of variables in the equation was large.

4.8   A test appropriate to testing for serial correlation of disturbances in a regression equation has been worked out by Durbin and Watson.[20] It was specifically designed for regression equations in which all the "independent" variables are strictly exogenous, and so even this test is not strictly appropriate in general to equations that belong to a simultaneous system (but see 4.14 below) or to equations that contain lagged values of dependent variables. The statistic used by Durbin and Watson is called d. It is almost the same as δ^2/S^2, discussed above, differing by the factor $T/(T-1)$, thus:

$$(4.4) \qquad d = \frac{\sum\limits_{2}^{T} (\hat{v}_t - \hat{v}_{t-1})^2}{\sum\limits_{1}^{T} (\hat{v}_t)^2}$$

(It is not necessary to write $\sum (\hat{v}_t - \hat{\bar{v}})^2$ in the denominator of d, because the least-squares estimation process guarantees that $\hat{\bar{v}} = 0$.) Even though, for a given series $\hat{v}_1, \ldots, \hat{v}_T$, their statistic is numerically equal to $(T-1)\delta^2/TS^2$, Durbin and Watson obtained a distribution function different from Hart's for d, because they explicitly took account of the fact that only the *calculated* disturbances $\hat{v}$ are observable, the actual disturbances v being unobservable.

4.9   The exact acceptance limits of this test depend on the observed data for y and $z_1, \ldots, z_K$ in equation (4.2) whose disturbances are being tested. However, for the lower acceptance limit Durbin and Watson worked out and tabulated lower and upper bounds d_l and d_u that are independent of the observed data, such that if d falls below d_l positive serial correlation is indicated, and if d falls above d_u the absence of positive serial correlation is indicated, but if d falls between d_l and d_u the procedure is inconclusive.[21] Since it turns out that the distribution of d is symmetrical

---

[20] Durbin and Watson [1950] and [1951]. The former is theoretical, and the latter contains all that is needed for the actual use of the test.

[21] The nature of these limits, as worked out by Durbin and Watson, may be briefly indicated. Express the equation to be estimated in the matrix notation of IX.5

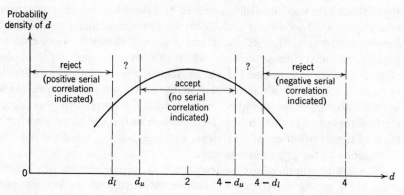

Figure 4.2 Schematic drawing of the distribution of d for test of serial noncorrelation of disturbances; see 4.8 in text.

with a mean of 2, the lower and upper bounds for the upper acceptance limit are $4 - d_u$ and $4 - d_l$, respectively. They are used in testing for negative serial correlation. The range of d is divided into five regions indicating positive, negative, or zero serial correlation or no decision, as shown in Figure 4.2. The points d_l and d_u must of course depend on the number of observations and on the probability assigned to the left-hand tail of the distribution. They also depend on the number

---

thus: $y' = Z'\pi' + v'$. Then the residuals are $\hat{v}' = [I - Z'(ZZ')^{-1}Z]y'$. Write this as Qy', thereby defining Q. Let A be the following $T \times T$ matrix, where elements not indicated (off the three central diagonals) are zero:

$$
A = \begin{bmatrix}
1 & -1 & & & & & \\
-1 & 2 & -1 & & & & \\
 & -1 & 2 & -1 & & & \\
 & & \cdot & \cdot & \cdot & & \\
 & & & \cdot & \cdot & \cdot & \\
 & & & & \cdot & \cdot & \cdot \\
 & & & & -1 & 2 & -1 \\
 & & & & & -1 & 1
\end{bmatrix}
$$

(These definitions of Q and A are used only in this footnote.) Then the statistic d can be expressed as $\hat{v}A\hat{v}'/\hat{v}\hat{v}'$. Durbin and Watson then reduced d to the expression

$$\sum_1^{T-K} v_t x_t^2 \Big/ \sum_1^{T-K} x_t^2,$$

where x_t are normal independent variables with mean zero and variance 1, and where $v_1, \ldots, v_{T-K}$ are the characteristic roots (excluding K zeros) of QA. Thus d depends via Q on the observed data y and Z. Durbin and Watson then showed that v_t has lower and upper limits consisting of certain characteristic roots of A above (which does not depend on the data) and so they obtained d_l and d_u. They also give an approximation procedure for locating the exact acceptance limit more accurately in particular cases as a function of y and Z.

of independent variables in the regression; this number (excluding the constant term) is called $K - 1$ in this book and k' by Durbin and Watson. They are more widely separated from each other if there are many independent variables. Excerpts from Durbin and Watson's tables of d_l and d_u appear in appendix B. The application of the Durbin-Watson test to residuals is quite similar to the application of the Hart–von Neumann test illustrated in 4.6 above.

4.10   In addition to testing time-series residuals for temporal serial correlation, the Durbin-Watson test can be applied to time-series or cross-section residuals arranged in any nontemporal order that is suspected of having nonzero serial correlation. For example, in Nerlove [1963], page 179, the residuals of a cross-section logarithmic total cost function for electricity are arranged in order of increasing output. The Durbin-Watson test is applied, showing strong positive serial correlation and thus indicating that the logarithm of total cost is not linear in the logarithm of output.

4.11   If the equation to be estimated contains the lagged value of the dependent variable, the Durbin-Watson statistic d is biased towards $2T/(T - 1)$, so in that case the test is biased against discovering either positive or negative serial correlation. However, as shown in the next three paragraphs, the Durbin-Watson test using the upper significance limit d_u is approximately suitable for many situations where the lagged dependent variable does not appear, and the use of d_u may even compensate to some extent for the aforementioned bias that is due to the presence of the lagged dependent variable. (Durbin [1957], p. 370, suggests that the same results "may be expected to hold approximately" when lagged endogenous variables appear in the equation.)

4.12   Hannan [1957] has shown that if the explanatory variables $z_1, \ldots, z_K$ in the regression (4.2) are the first, $\ldots$, Kth powers of the same exogenous variable, then the *upper* limit d_u obtained by Durbin and Watson is an extremely good approximation to the correct acceptance limit, differences between the two being of the order of $1/T^2$. This result has not to my knowledge been shown to hold for the general linear regression equation (4.2). But the conjecture that it holds approximately is supported by the following observations. First, recall from 4.7 that in the sampling experiments of Orcutt and Cochrane the Hart table for δ^2/S^2 typically erred on the side of failing to detect serial correlation known to be present. Second, note from Table 4 in Appendix B that the critical value of d in Hart's table is about halfway between the values of d_l and d_u that correspond to the same number of observations and the same significance level, regardless of the number of variables. These two points suggest that the correct acceptance level for d is closer to d_u than to d_l even if the special conditions assumed by Hannan do not hold. Therefore the use of d_u alone can be recommended. If it errs somewhat, it will be by giving false signals of serial correlation slightly too often when no such correlation exists.

4.13 A result similar to Hannan's is obtained by Theil and Nagar [1961]. They assume that all predetermined variables are exogenous and that disturbances are normal. They deal with the one-tail test for zero serial correlation of disturbances against the alternative hypotheses of positive correlation. They show that if the first and second differences of the exogenous variables z_k are small in absolute value by comparison with the ranges of the z_k, the upper limit d_u obtained by Durbin and Watson is a good approximation to the correct acceptance limit. They give a table of approximate 5 and 1 per cent significance points for the Durbin-Watson statistic d under these conditions. In case the sample size T is as small as 15 and the number of parameters to be estimated in the equation (including constant term), K, is as large as 6, the Theil-Nagar approximate 1 per cent significance point is equal to 0.96 times the corresponding value of d_u; for the 5 per cent point the Theil-Nagar value is 0.98 times d_u; for larger samples and/or smaller K, the approximation becomes better rapidly. Theil and Nagar also suggest an estimation procedure if the alternative hypothesis of positive serial correlation is accepted. This procedure is to assume that the disturbance e_t follows the autoregressive rule $e_t = \alpha e_{t-1} + v_t$ where $0 < \alpha < 1$ and v_t is random and serially independent (see IX.13.2–5); to estimate α either by $1 - d/2$ or by a slightly more refined procedure that they describe; to transform the original data for each variable x_{it} into $x_{it} - (\text{est } \alpha)x_{i,t-1}$; and then to apply least squares to the transformed data.

4.14 Durbin [1957] discusses the question whether the Durbin-Watson test, which was designed for single-equation regression models, is applicable to individual structural equations that have been estimated by the limited-information method. He concludes that the answer is strictly yes in a very special case, and approximately yes in the more general cases, and he presents a strictly appropriate test in a not-quite-so-special case. To summarize his results, we recall our expression for the limited-information structural residuals $\hat{u}_t$ in (3.30) above. First, he considers the very special case in which all predetermined variables are *strictly exogenous* (i.e., no lagged endogenous variables appear anywhere in the model) and the structural equation to be estimated is *just identified*. Here he finds that the Durbin-Watson statistic d of (4.4) [redefined in terms of structural residuals $\hat{u}$ from (3.30) instead of reduced–form residuals $\hat{v}$] and the tables of d_l and d_u in Durbin and Watson [1951] are strictly appropriate, entering the tables with their k' set equal to our $K - 1$ (the number of coefficients, besides the intercept, in a *reduced-form* equation). Second, he considers the not-so-special case of an *overidentified* equation, still assuming that all predetermined variables are *strictly exogenous*. Here he recommends the foregoing as "a good approximate test" (p. 377). But he gives a strictly appropriate test for this case, using the table as before but computing the value of the statistic d somewhat differently: In place of the limited-information residuals $\hat{u}_t$ from (3.30), use the residuals from the multiple regression of the synthetic dependent variable $\hat{\beta}\mathbf{y}_t'$ on *all* the predetermined variables in the model ($z_1, \ldots,$ $z_J, \ldots, z_K$). It will be recalled that these residuals appear above in IX.9.11 and that their sum of squares is $\hat{\beta}\mathbf{W}\hat{\beta}'$; see IX.9.10–13.

4.15 We have said that disturbances in econometric equations almost never appear to have negative serial correlation, and hence in the above example we have chosen a one-tailed test with the rejection region in the left-hand tail. However, if first differences of raw data are used in fitting the equation, negative serial correlation of shifts may appear. Suppose the shifts in the equation using raw data are denoted by e and are related to each other by a first-difference equation as discussed in IX.13.2, thus:

$$(4.5) \qquad e = \alpha e_{-1} + v$$

where $0 \leqq \alpha \leqq 1$. Then the shifts in the corresponding equation using first difference data would be the first differences of e, thus:

$$(4.6) \qquad \Delta e = e - e_{-1} = (\alpha e_{-1} + v) - e_{-1}$$
$$= (\alpha - 1)e_{-1} + v$$

If $\alpha = 1$, using first differences would remove the serial correlation from the disturbances, as we saw in IX.13.7. But if α is somewhere between zero and 1, then $\alpha - 1$ is negative, and hence negative serial correlation would be introduced into the shifts Δe. Hence it is wise to test for *negative* serial correlation of shifts as well as positive if first-difference data are used.[22]

4.16 For example, let us look at thirteen United Kingdom demand equations for different classes of commodities, estimated from first-difference data for 1920–1938 by Richard Stone.[23] There are 19 years, and hence 18 first differences. The number of regression coefficients to be

---

[22] Watson and Hannan [1956] give some approximations to the bias of the estimated variance of regression coefficients, some approximations to the loss of efficiency, and some approximations concerning the error of the t and F tests, if an equation like (4.2) is used with erroneous *a priori* information concerning the covariance matrix $Ev'v$. Their results suggest that if the disturbances are known to have a first-order autoregressive nature as in (4.5), and if an incorrect value is assumed for the autoregression coefficient α, in the Aitken method described in IX.13.9, small errors concerning α are not very serious if α is near 0 but become quite serious if α is near 1.

[23] Stone [1951], pp. 71–72.

estimated in addition to the constant term ($K - 1$ in our notation) is three in most of the equations, but is two in one case and four in two cases. The upper limits d_u for the lower 5 per cent points in the Durbin-Watson [1951] table of the distribution of d, for $T = 18$ and for these three values of $K - 1$, are as follows (the corresponding limits for the upper 5 per cent points $4 - d_u$ are shown too):

$$K - 1 \quad 2 \quad 3 \quad 4$$
$$d_u \quad 1.53 \quad 1.69 \quad 1.87$$
$$4 - d_u \quad 2.47 \quad 2.31 \quad 2.13$$

Values of d between the limits d_u and $4 - d_u$ definitely indicate no serial correlation at the 10 per cent (two-sided) level, whereas values below d_u or above $4 - d_u$ suggest positive or negative serial correlation respectively, the suggestion being more forceful for large differences than for small as described in 4.12. Stone gives values of δ^2/S^2, and when these are converted to d by multiplying by 17/18, the results are as follows: For the ten equations having $K - 1 = 3$, the two lowest values of d are 1.56 (somewhat into the "positive serial correlation" region) and 1.74 (no serial correlation); and the three highest values are 2.83, 2.48 (these are far and slightly into the "negative serial correlation" region) and 2.21 (no correlation). For the equation having $K - 1 = 2$, $d = 2.69$ (fairly well into the "negative serial correlation" region). For the two equations having $K - 1 = 4$, the values of d are 1.41 (positive serial correlation) and 2.18 (probably no correlation). Thus the first-difference transformation apparently left no serial correlation among the residuals in eight cases, and indications of negative and positive serial correlation respectively in three and two cases, all at the 10 per cent (two-sided) level.

4.17   Another useful procedure is to investigate whether the residuals from the calculated equation appear to be correlated with any variable (not used in the estimation process) that might have an economic relation to the equation. This procedure is especially important when the residuals have been found to be serially correlated, as by the tests discussed in 4.4–14, for two reasons: (1) because most estimation methods depend on the absence of serial correlation among disturbances; and (2), even more important, because serial correlation among residuals suggests that there are still some unexplained systematic influences, and challenges the economist to try to explain them. This procedure is also very useful in the preliminary stages of an econometric problem when we are not yet certain which variables are going to be of the most value in describing the relationship under study. Graphical methods[24] are excellent for getting a quick impression. The graph of calculated residuals against t is often helpful,

[24] Graphical methods are discussed quite fully in Ezekiel and Fox [1959].

for if its peaks and troughs coincide with (or lead or lag by a constant amount) those of some other economic variable that has not been used in the estimation process, it may be that this economic variable belongs in the equation being estimated (or at least in the model). Also, if residuals are plotted on one axis and a possibly important omitted variable on the other, we can very quickly see about how close a relationship exists between them and also whether it is approximately linear. If an omitted variable can be found that is correlated with the residuals and has good economic reason for being considered as related to the phenomenon described by the equation, it will be helpful to include that variable in the equation. To take a very simple example, if the demand for oleomargarine is estimated as a function of its price and of income, it is very likely that the residuals from this function will be correlated with the price of butter, since high butter prices may drive consumers, *ceteris paribus*, to use more margarine.

4.18 Except for the Durbin-Watson test, all the tests discussed in this section have been described only in terms of the residuals $\hat{v}_t$ from a *reduced-form* equation. In principle, they are all applicable (sometimes with considerable modification) to *structural* equations and their residuals $\hat{u}_t$ as well. See also Theil [1965].

5 NONPREDICTIVE TESTS, III: EVALUATING THE *a priori* INFORMATION

5.1   Most of the statistical inference techniques discussed in Chapters IX and X are based on the notion that the *a priori* information constituting the model is known to be correct. On many occasions throughout this book it has been emphasized that in practice the so-called *a priori* information is far from certain and that it is important to have some means of testing and evaluating this information. That is the subject of this brief section.

5.2   In order to obtain the best possible estimators, meaning by this those with the smallest possible expected squared error,[25] it is of course necessary to use *all* of the *correct a priori* information available. If all of our *a priori* information were known to be correct with no uncertainty, and if economy and simplicity of computation were no object, then it would always be best to incorporate all our *a priori* information into the estimation process. We have earlier considered examples of this kind of estimation: (1) In VII.8.2 the mean of a univariate population was to be estimated from a sample of observations for $t = 1, \ldots, T$, subject to the

[25] A better meaning, in more sophisticated decision-oriented terms, is those with the smallest possible expected loss; see VII.5.11–13.

certain knowledge that the population mean is $\geqq 9.9$. The estimator obtained was: the sample mean $\bar{x}$ or 9.9, whichever is larger. (2) In IX.9 the parameters of a linear structural equation were to be estimated from a sample of observations $y_{1t}, \ldots, y_{Ht}, z_{1t}, \ldots, z_{Jt}, \ldots, z_{Kt}$ for $t = 1, \ldots, T$, subject to the restriction (among others) that the variables $y_1, \ldots, y_H$ and $z_1, \ldots, z_J$ are permitted to appear in the equation with nonzero coefficients but that $z_{J+1}, \ldots, z_K$ do not appear. The estimators obtained were the limited-information estimators. (In IX.10 two-stage least-squares estimators for the same case were discussed.)

5.3 Sometimes difficulties arise in the attempt to include all our *a priori* information in the estimation process. One type of difficulty arises when some of the *a priori* restrictions known with certainty are of a form that is not easy to incorporate in the estimation process. As of 1940 the use of overidentifying restrictions on a structural equation was an example of this kind of problem, and it has been solved through the invention of the limited-information and two-stage least-squares methods. We may expect that other similar problems may be solved by the invention of additional estimation techniques in the future. Another type of difficulty arises when some of the *a priori* information is uncertain. In order that an estimation method can incorporate uncertain information, it is necessary to express the information in the language of uncertainty, namely, in probability terms. One way to do this is to write down the subjective probability distribution (see VII.5.7 and VII.7.10–20) that describes the economist's state of prior knowledge and uncertainty about the structure or reduced form that is to be estimated, and then to build this subjective probability distribution into the estimation process. The development of this approach is still in its infancy, for it is not easy to spell out explicitly our subjective probability distributions, and even when that has been done it is not always easy to build them into an estimation process. Some progress has been made in this direction (e.g., in Theil and Goldberger [1961], Theil [1963], and Drèze [1962], discussed below), and more may be expected.

5.4 Because of these difficulties, it has been common practice in econometrics (and probably will continue to be for some time) to use directly in the estimation process only that set of *a priori* restrictions that can be readily incorporated in an existing estimation method, whether those restrictions are believed with certainty or not. The second set of *a priori* restrictions, that is, those not used directly in estimation, are left aside until the numerical estimates are computed. Then the numerical estimates are confronted with this second set of *a priori* restrictions, and any substantial conflict between the estimates and the second set of restrictions is taken as cause for revising either the first set of restrictions (those used in estimation), or the numerical estimates, or the second set of restrictions, or some combination of three. For example, the estimated income elasticity of demand for a good may turn out to be negative when it is certain that the good has a non-negative income elasticity of demand, with the result that the form of equation originally used may be rejected and a new form tried. A related practice, also widely used, is to formulate several alternative plausible forms of the equation to be estimated, estimate them all, and then choose one of the forms as most promising in the light of the values obtained for estimated parameters and correlation coefficients and in the light of *a priori* restrictions not used in estimation. Let us discuss these two practices in turn, in 5.5 ff. and 5.14 ff., respectively.

5.5   Consider first the estimation of a single plausible form of a desired equation, and the subsequent confrontation of the estimates with the set of *a priori* restrictions not used in estimation. An example may help. Suppose that it is known *a priori* that the demand elasticity of meat with respect to income is not negative but that this knowledge is not directly used in estimation. Suppose a demand equation for meat at retail is estimated, using the *a priori* restrictions that the quantity of meat demanded at retail per capita is a linear function of the relative retail price of meat (relative to the consumer price index), the relative price of protein other than meat, real income per capita, and the proportion of vegetarians in the population; that exogenous variables are the three last-named and a farm real cost-of-production index of meat animals; that disturbances to meat demand are random with zero mean and constant variance and no serial dependence; and other assumptions of Model 2. Suppose that the income elasticity of meat demand as estimated by this equation turned out to be negative. What would the typical empirical economist do? What would you do? The most likely answer is: Decide that the original specification of a linear equation containing the five variables described above is incorrect, and try again. We might drop the income variable out of the equation, keeping the other *a priori* restrictions unchanged, and estimate again; then we would automatically get a non-negative income elasticity (in particular, zero). Or we might change from a linear equation to one linear in logarithms of the variables, or drop out the vegetarian variable, or replace current income by a weighted average of past incomes, or introduce the lagged quantity of meat demanded, and so forth.

5.6   This procedure is a kind of nonrigorous means of evaluating and revising and probably improving upon the set of *a priori* restrictions that seemed most plausible at the beginning of the process but were not known with certainty. It is applicable to restrictions on the magnitudes of parameters as well as their signs, and indeed to any kind of restrictions that are available. It is not easy to give universal rules in such cases. Experience suggests that among the more common difficulties that come to light in this way are special circumstances that either obscure or controvert the relationship that economic theory leads us to expect, inadequate translation of theory into equation form, the use of data that do not really measure the relevant economic magnitudes, and the use of inappropriate statistical methods.

5.7   An economist may have in mind a particular value or finite range of values of a particular parameter (e.g., from 0.6 to 0.8), either because he believes that value or range is approximately correct or because that value or range is a critical one for policy purposes. In either case, he may wish to test the hypothesis that the value or range he has in mind is consistent with the estimates obtained from the data and the model used. The appropriate test has been described in 3.15; the value of the statistic used for the test is obtained by using the economist's hypothetical value of the parameter, or a value near the midpoint of his hypothetical range, in place of π_{0k} in (3.23) above. The operating characteristic of the test will then indicate the probability of acceptance of the hypothesis, as a function of the true value of the parameter in question, so that if the hypothesis involves a range then the probability of acceptance can be determined for both end points of the hypothetical range and for every point within the range. This is a conventional procedure if the *a priori* restrictions forming the maintained hypothesis are known with certainty, but if we contemplate possibly revising these restrictions as a result of the outcome of the test, then the procedure is similar to that of 5.5.

5.8   Theil and Goldberger [1961] have devised an estimation method that can take account of uncertain *a priori* information about the parameters of an equation if that information is in the form of a joint subjective probability distribution, with known means and variances and covariances, of a number of parameters or a number of linear combinations of parameters. Consider a reduced-form equation,[26] written in the matrix notation of IX.5 to show all the observed values of all the variables, thus:

$$(5.1) \qquad \qquad \mathbf{y}' = \mathbf{Z}'\boldsymbol{\pi}' + \mathbf{v}'$$

Here as usual $\mathbf{y}'$ is the $T \times 1$ vector of observations of the dependent variable, $\mathbf{Z}'$ is the $T \times K$ matrix of observations of the predetermined variables, $\boldsymbol{\pi}'$ is the $K \times 1$ vector of parameters, and $\mathbf{v}'$ is the $T \times 1$ vector of disturbances. Make the assumptions of Model 1 (see IX.2.3–5), *and also* assume that the covariance matrix of disturbances is finite, nonsingular, and known except for an unknown scalar factor ω^2, that is, $\boldsymbol{\Lambda}/\omega^2$ is known but $\boldsymbol{\Lambda}$ and ω^2 are not:

$$(5.2) \qquad \qquad E\mathbf{v}'\mathbf{v} = \boldsymbol{\Lambda}$$

---

[26] Theil and Goldberger also show how to deal with a structural equation. A brief description of their method as applied to the reduced form only is in Theil [1961], pp. 232–235.

5.9   Now suppose that there is available *a priori* information about a number L of linear combinations of the parameters of (5.1), consisting of an L-dimensional joint subjective probability distribution of these L linear combinations, with known $L \times 1$ mean $\mathbf{r}'$ and with known finite nonsingular $L \times L$ variance-covariance matrix $\mathbf{\Psi}$, the coefficients of the linear combinations forming a known $L \times K$ matrix $\mathbf{R}'$. That is, the vector of linear combinations $\mathbf{R}'\boldsymbol{\pi}'$ is a random $L \times 1$ vector, thus,

$$(5.3) \qquad\qquad \mathbf{r}' = \mathbf{R}'\boldsymbol{\pi}' + \mathbf{x}'$$

where $\mathbf{R}$ and $\mathbf{r}$ are known and $\mathbf{x}$ in this context is a random $L \times 1$ vector with zero mean and finite nonsingular known covariance matrix $\mathbf{\Psi}$, thus:

$$(5.4) \qquad\qquad E\mathbf{x}' = \mathbf{0}', \qquad E\mathbf{x}'\mathbf{x} = \mathbf{\Psi}$$

Then Theil and Goldberger, assuming that $\mathbf{v}$ and $\mathbf{x}$ are independent, combine the *a priori* and the observational information about $\boldsymbol{\pi}'$ into single set of equations, thus:

$$(5.5) \qquad\qquad \begin{pmatrix} \mathbf{y}' \\ \mathbf{r}' \end{pmatrix} = \begin{pmatrix} \mathbf{Z}' \\ \mathbf{R}' \end{pmatrix} \boldsymbol{\pi}' + \begin{pmatrix} \mathbf{v}' \\ \mathbf{x}' \end{pmatrix}$$

where the "disturbance" vector has zero mean and the following covariance matrix:

$$(5.6) \qquad\qquad E\begin{pmatrix} \mathbf{v}' \\ \mathbf{x}' \end{pmatrix}(\mathbf{v} \quad \mathbf{x}) = \begin{pmatrix} \mathbf{\Lambda} & \mathbf{0} \\ \mathbf{0} & \mathbf{\Psi} \end{pmatrix}$$

5.10   The last two equations are of the same form as (5.1) and (5.2), except that instead of the data matrices $\mathbf{y}$ and $\mathbf{Z}$ we now have matrices $(\mathbf{y} \ \ \mathbf{r})$ and $(\mathbf{Z} \ \ \mathbf{R})$, which combine data and *a priori* opinions, and we also have a "disturbance" that combines the usual disturbance $\mathbf{v}$ with the subjective random variable $\mathbf{x}$. Note that $\mathbf{R}$, $\mathbf{r}$, and $\mathbf{\Psi}$ are assumed known; $\mathbf{\Lambda}$ is not known completely but is known except for a multiplicative scalar constant ω^2. If ω^2 were known so that $\mathbf{\Lambda}$ were completely known, then (5.5) would satisfy the assumptions of Aitken's generalized least-squares method (see IX.5.7), and hence (5.5) could be estimated by that method. The result would be the following estimator of $\boldsymbol{\pi}'$ denoted by $\mathbf{p}_2'$, which makes use of both the observed data and the *a priori* information given by (5.3) and (5.4):

$$(5.7) \quad \mathbf{p}_2' = \left[(\mathbf{Z} \ \ \mathbf{R}) \begin{pmatrix} \mathbf{\Lambda} & \mathbf{0} \\ \mathbf{0} & \mathbf{\Psi} \end{pmatrix}^{-1} \begin{pmatrix} \mathbf{Z}' \\ \mathbf{R}' \end{pmatrix} \right]^{-1} (\mathbf{Z} \ \ \mathbf{R}) \begin{pmatrix} \mathbf{\Lambda} & \mathbf{0} \\ \mathbf{0} & \mathbf{\Psi} \end{pmatrix}^{-1} \begin{pmatrix} \mathbf{y}' \\ \mathbf{r}' \end{pmatrix}$$

$$= (\mathbf{Z}\mathbf{\Lambda}^{-1}\mathbf{Z}' + \mathbf{R}\mathbf{\Psi}^{-1}\mathbf{R}')^{-1}(\mathbf{Z}\mathbf{\Lambda}^{-1}\mathbf{y}' + \mathbf{R}\mathbf{\Psi}^{-1}\mathbf{r}')$$

Theil and Goldberger call this a *mixed estimator* since it uses both prior and sample information.

5.11 An example may be useful. Suppose that $\Lambda = \omega^2 I$ as in Model 2, and suppose that there is *a priori* information about just one component of π, for instance, the first one: π_1 is thought to be approximately equal to the known value r_1, with subjective variance ψ_1^2. Then it is easy to verify, as pointed out by Theil and Goldberger, that the vector $\mathbf{r}'$ becomes the scalar r_1, and the matrix $\mathbf{R}'$ becomes the row vector $(1 \quad 0 \quad \cdots \quad 0)$, and Ψ becomes the scalar ψ_1^2, so that the estimator $\mathbf{p}_2'$ in (5.7) becomes

$$(5.8) \quad \mathbf{p}_2' = \left[\mathbf{ZZ}' + \frac{\omega^2}{\psi_1^2} \begin{pmatrix} 1 & 0 & \cdots & 0 \\ 0 & 0 & & \\ \vdots & & \ddots & \vdots \\ 0 & \cdots & \cdots & 0 \end{pmatrix} \right]^{-1} \left[\mathbf{Z}\mathbf{y}' + \frac{\omega^2}{\psi_1^2} \begin{pmatrix} r_1 \\ 0 \\ \vdots \\ 0 \end{pmatrix} \right]$$

5.12 In order to apply this method we need numerical values for the data matrices $\mathbf{Z}$ and $\mathbf{y}$ of course, but also for Λ, Ψ, $\mathbf{R}$, and $\mathbf{r}$.[27] The last three are the subjective probability distribution's parameters, and hence may be assumed known. The covariance matrix Λ of disturbances is typically *not* known. However, in Model 2, where $\Lambda = \omega^2 I$, we can apply ordinary least squares to (5.1) and obtain a consistent estimator w^2 of ω^2, ignoring the prior information in (5.3), and we can use this to form the estimator $w^2 I$ of Λ for use in the Theil-Goldberger mixed estimator in (5.7). As they point out, the estimate $\mathbf{p}_2'$ of π' obtained from (5.7) implies a new set of calculated residuals, denoted by $\hat{\mathbf{v}}^{(2)}$, which (when summed and squared and divided by the number of degrees of freedom) yields a new estimate of ω^2, denoted by w_2^2, different from w^2. They suggest an iterative process whereby $w_2^2 I$ is substituted for Λ in (5.7); a new estimate, say $\mathbf{p}_3'$, is computed thereby; a third estimate w_3^2 of ω^2 is computed from the residuals implied by $\mathbf{p}_3'$, and so forth. They give some actual examples in which this iterative process appears to converge.

5.13 Theil and Goldberger [1961] is an important early step in bringing uncertain *a priori* restrictions into the estimation process, for it permits the incorporation of *a priori* beliefs that are expressible in terms of a subjective probability distribution with stated means and variances and covariances. It is at best only approximately applicable to cases where we are fairly certain about an upper (or lower) limit for the possible value of a parameter but have no firm idea how far below the upper limit

[27] If all these matrices are known, the mixed estimator $\mathbf{p}_2'$ is the best linear unbiased one, since the conditions of Aitken's [1934] proof are satisfied.

(or above the lower) it might be, as for example where we know the sign but not the magnitude of a parameter. Theil [1963] and Dreze [1962] are also important steps in the same direction. Theil [1963] extends the results of Theil and Goldberger [1961] to provide some asymptotic properties of the estimation method of the preceding paragraph, where $\Lambda = \omega^2 I$ with ω^2 unknown; to provide a test of whether the prior information is compatible with the data; and to give a measure for the relative contributions of prior information and data to the final estimates. Dreze [1962] is a fundamental and important paper showing how probabilistic prior information can be used in simultaneous-equations estimation of the parameters of a whole system, in the Bayesian manner.

5.14   Consider next the estimation of several alternative plausible forms of an equation, the choice among them being made after the estimates corresponding to each are examined. The rationale here is based on the admission that *a priori* information does *not* tell with certainty which variables belong in the equation, or which set of data is the best measure of each desired conceptual variable, or what form the equation has (e.g., linear in variables, linear in logarithms of variables, etc.). If *a priori* information does not fully answer these questions, then empirical information may help. It is for this reason that economists often formulate several forms of an equation, all plausible in the light of the available *a priori* information but differing perhaps in form (some linear, some linear in logs, etc.), or in the set of variables included, or in the particular data used to represent certain variables, and so forth. After all the alternative forms have been estimated, we can examine the numerical estimates obtained for each, and their correlation coefficients, and then we can either (a) accept the equation form that appears best in the light of all this, or (b) reject all the equation forms tried so far, and formulate one or more new ones. To take up again the meat-demand example of 5.5, we might try equations linear in variables and linear in their logarithms; equations with and without the price index of nonmeat protein; equations with and without the vegetarian variable; equations with current income and with a weighted average of past incomes; equations with and without the lagged value of the quantity demanded, and so forth.

5.15   This stage of the work is rendered difficult because there are no fully acceptable criteria that can be applied at the time of estimation to choose among the various versions of the equation. The best version of course is the one that will turn out to make the best predictions or give the best results later on, but this is not known when the choice must be made. It does not do merely to choose the version that fits the data best, for there is always the chance that that version merely fits the peculiar nonrecurring pattern of accidental characteristics of the sample period, without capturing the underlying structure at all; see I.3.5–6. It is at this stage that most econometric studies are made or broken, and there is very little systematic methodology that can be brought to bear.[28]

5.16 Suppose that the confidence we place in an equation is to be determined by a statistical test of the null hypothesis that the population value of its multiple or partial correlation coefficient is zero. Then the process of trying *several* alternatives and choosing the one with the highest correlation coefficient will on the average lead to higher observed correlation coefficients when the null hypothesis is true for all our alternatives than will the process of choosing *one* equation form on *a priori* grounds. Therefore the tests of significance described in 3.13–33 will be too likely to reject the null hypothesis, if they are applied to an equation that has been chosen because of having the highest correlation coefficient among a set of alternative equations.

5.17 The following simple example will make this clear. Suppose that the variable y is to be explained by a single additional variable, and there are 20 possible independent[29] theoretically plausible explanatory variables $x_1, \ldots, x_{20}$, from among which this additional variable is to be chosen. And suppose further that *none* of the variables $x_1, \ldots, x_{20}$ is actually correlated with y in the population, that is, that none of them explains any of the variation of y in its population distribution. Nevertheless, in finite samples, there is a positive probability that a large correlation between y and any of the x's will occur. Suppose that a sample of 12 observations of each variable is used, and the correlation of y with each x_i is computed from such a sample, and the variable x_i with the highest correlation with y is chosen. The probability is 5 per cent that a random sample of 12 (having 10 degrees of freedom) from a bivariate normal population of two uncorrelated variables will have an observed positive correlation coefficient of .497 or more.[30] We might be tempted to think at first that if the variable x_i having the highest observed correlation with y in fact has a correlation of .497, then by choosing this particular x_i we are running only a 5 per cent risk of choosing a variable that is

---

[28] Ragnar Frisch's so-called bunch-map technique fills this gap only partially. It is essentially a device for deciding on statistical grounds alone which variables of a given set belong in an equation and which do not. It proceeds by computing all possible least-squares regressions involving some or all of the variables in the set, and comparing the resulting estimates. It is described in Frisch [1934], especially parts III and IV. It has not been used much in recent econometric work, presumably because its interpretation is not very clear. Simple examples of its use are given in Stone [1954], especially pp. 306–310; see also diagrams, pp. 348–382.

[29] It is unlikely that alternative explanatory variables would be independent, but this assumption simplifies the example without destroying the principle involved.

[30] See Fisher and Yates [1938], Table VI, pp. 54–55 (which gives the area in *both* tails of the distribution of r when $\rho = 0$) or Pearson and Hartley [1954], Table 13, p. 138 (which gives the area in *one* tail and in *both* tails). The same result can be obtained from the distribution of F; see the introduction to either book of tables.

actually uncorrelated with y. But reflection shows that the chance is far higher than 5 per cent, for out of 20 opportunities in which each has a chance of 5 per cent of producing a correlation coefficient exceeding .497, the chance that the *highest* one will equal or exceed .497 is the chance that at least 1 of 20 falls at or above .497, which is 1 minus the chance that all 20 fall below .497, which is $1 - (.95)^{20} = 1 - .358 = .642$ or about 64 per cent, instead of only 5 per cent. Other examples can be constructed.[31] Wallace [1964] and Larson and Bancroft [1963], [1963a] offer interesting results of this kind. See also Hotelling [1940].

5.18   The nonrigorous but common procedures discussed in 5.5 ff. and 5.14 ff., and also the selection of an equation form after studying the residuals obtained from several alternative forms (see 4.17), are not strictly legitimate, as we have pointed out. Perhaps it would be better to say that their operating characteristics are not well understood, because the properties of estimators have been carefully studied only when the *a priori* information used is *correct*. Yet economists have excellent reason to use these approaches, because no appropriate general approach has been well worked out for the case where *a priori* information is uncertain, and because these approaches appear likely to yield fairly close and quite cheap approximations to what such an approach would yield if it were available. Theil [1957] and Griliches [1957] discuss estimation in the presence of specification error.

5.19   There are approximate tests of *a priori* restrictions for the limited-information estimation of an overidentified equation. They are statistical tests in the strict sense. The essential idea of the tests is: If *all* the *a priori* restrictions including the assumptions of Model 3 are correct (which means that the limited-information method has desirable properties; see IX.2.3–5 and IX.9.23), *then* for an overidentified equation, large values of a certain statistic (to be described shortly) are very unlikely, and the appearance of a large value of this statistic is cause for rejecting the hypothesis that all the assumptions are correct. But this does not mean that all the assumptions can be rejected at the same time for, as we shall see, the test requires that at least enough restrictions be imposed *a priori* so that the equation to be estimated is identified. Hence if any particular restrictions are to be rejected, a set of identifying restrictions must be chosen as the maintained hypothesis for the test. Then if a large value of the statistic occurs, the responsibility for this large value will be attached to the set of remaining, overidentifying, restrictions. As pointed out in VII.8.9 in the earlier discussion of maintained hypotheses, there is

---

[31] If *multiple* regressions are used, the distribution of r cannot be used and that of F must be used instead; see note 30 above. If it is supposed that the true correlations are not zero, then a modification of the simple procedure for the uncorrelated case is required; see Kendall [1952], pp. 382–385, or Kendall and Stuart [1958].

a certain arbitrariness in deciding which of the assumptions to maintain and which to test. The identifying set in which we have most trust should be maintained, and the others tested.[32]

5.20   The details of one such test are as follows. (Another is described below.) Recall that in the limited-information method the variance ratio l, equal to $\beta W^* \beta' / \beta W \beta'$, by definition greater than or equal to 1, is minimized in order to get the estimates $\hat{\beta}_2, \ldots, \hat{\beta}_H$ of the parameters of the jointly dependent variables (see IX.9, especially IX.9.3–7). In most overidentified equations l_1 (the minimum value of l) will not be equal to 1 but will be somewhat greater because of sampling fluctuations, especially in small samples. This is because l_1 is a random variable, an estimator of the true variance ratio, which we may call[33] l_1'. If the restrictions excluding certain variables from the equation being estimated are all correct, then $l_1' = 1$ and the random variable l_1 will not exceed 1 by very much except in rare samples. But if there are more than enough restrictions to identify the equation and they are *not* all correct, then l_1' will be greater than 1 and so l_1 will usually exceed 1. Hence l_1 is likely to be the larger, the more incorrect are the restrictions (given an overidentified equation). Here we have the basis for a test of significance, if the distribution of l_1 or some statistic related to it can be found under the null hypothesis.

5.21   The asymptotic distribution of $T \log_e l_1$ has been found by Anderson and Rubin,[34] under conditions similar to our Model 3. In our notation they speak of $1 + 1/\lambda_1$, which is by definition equal to l_1, λ_1 being the largest characteristic root of our equation (IX.9.38). The statistic $T \log_e l_1$ is likely to be small if the null hypothesis is true that all the restrictions used are correct, and likely to be large if the null hypothesis is false. Hence large values of the statistic lead to the rejection of the null hypothesis. Anderson and Rubin showed that if the null hypothesis is true the statistic $T \log_e l_1$ has the χ^2 distribution[35] asymptotically as T increases, with $K - J - H + 1$ degrees of freedom, where K, J, and H as usual stand, respectively, for the number of predetermined variables in the model, the number of predetermined variables in the equation being estimated, and the number of jointly dependent variables in the equation being estimated. The test is no good for just-identified equations, because for them $K - J - H + 1$ is zero, so that there are no degrees of

---

[32] Koopmans [1949], Section 7, third from last paragraph, suggests this.

[33] The natural symbol to use for the parameter of which l_1 is an estimator is λ_1. But λ_1 has already been used to stand for $1/(l_1 - 1)$ in IX.9.18 (in violation of our convention of using Latin letters for random variables and Greek letters for parameters), so to avoid confusion I have used l_1' instead. This quantity l_1' does not appear later on and so need not be remembered.

[34] Anderson and Rubin [1950], esp. theorem 5 on p. 581.

[35] The χ^2 distribution is tabulated in Appendix B, and described briefly in 1.9–10 above.

freedom for the test and l_1 always turns out to be exactly 1. If in a particular overidentified equation the statistic $T \log_e l_1$ takes on a value that is improbably high under the null hypothesis that all restrictions used are correct, then we have only a very generalized alarm signal that cannot point to a specific cause of the trouble, because of the arbitrariness in the choice of the just-identifying restrictions that are to be maintained for the test of the remaining, overidentifying, restrictions.

5.22 Basmann [1960b] has done a Monte Carlo experiment to evaluate the performance of the foregoing Anderson-Rubin characteristic-root test of overidentifying restrictions, and related tests. In IX.12.27 above are described the model [a case of our Model 2 (normal)] and the experiment he used. He found that in 200 samples of size 16, the foregoing Anderson-Rubin test is strongly biased toward rejecting a valid set of overidentifying restrictions; the number of degrees of freedom for his case was $K - J - H + 1 = 6 - 3 - 3 + 1 = 1$.

5.23 Basmann [1960b] also proposes, and tests in the Monte Carlo experiment, two alternative small-sample tests of the hypothesis of overidentification, based on the F rather than the chi-square distribution, one suitable for the limited-information method and one suitable for the two-stage least-squares method. The limited-information version is based on his demonstration that $(l_1 - 1)(T - K)/(K - J - H + 1)$, where as usual l_1 is the minimum value of the variance ratio $\beta W^* \beta'/\beta W \beta'$ in IX.9.3-7, is asymptotically distributed as F with $K - J - H + 1$ and $T - K$ degrees of freedom [see equation (1.4) above regarding the relation of this to chi square]. The two-stage least-squares version is the same, except that instead of l_1 Basmann uses the expression $\beta W^* \beta'/\beta W \beta'$ evaluated by means of the two-stage least-squares estimator of β; denote this alternative estimator by $l'^{(1)}_1$. Basmann's Monte Carlo experiment showed that in 200 samples of size 16 the correspondence between the F distribution and the empirical distribution of $(l'^{(1)}_1 - 1)(T - K)/(K - J - H + 1)$ was excellent, and that for l_1 was quite good. Therefore Basmann's F test may be provisionally recommended for both limited information and two-stage least squares, in preference to Anderson and Rubin's chi-square test for limited information.

5.24 In the few applications made so far it has been relatively unusual for an equation to pass these tests with anything like flying colors, which strongly suggests again that the restrictions used in limited-information estimation are at best approximate descriptions of economic reality. As examples we choose the equations of an aggregate United States model as estimated by the limited-information method.[36] Ten overidentified equations were estimated. The results of both the Anderson-Rubin

[36] Christ [1951], pp. 67–68 and 82–83.

TABLE 5.1   Anderson-Rubin χ^2 and Basmann F Tests of Overidentifying Restrictions as Applied to the Model in Christ [1951]

Equation	l_1	$T - K$	$K - J - H + 1$	$T\log_e l_1$	Pb that $\chi^2(K - J - H + 1)$ exceeds the statistic in col. (5)	$\dfrac{(T - K)(l_1 - 1)}{K - J - H + 1}$	Pb that $F(K - J - H + 1, T - K)$ exceeds the statistic in col. (7)
(1)	(2)	(3)	(4)	(5)	(6)	(7)	(8)
1.0	1.60	13	5	10.3	.07	1.56	.24
2.0	1.86	13	5	13.7	.02	2.24	.12
3.4	3.22	13	6	25.7	<.001	4.81	.01
4.0	2.65	13	5	21.5	<.001	4.28	.02
4.2	3.90	13	6	29.9	<.001	6.28	.004
5.1	2.70	13	4	21.9	<.001	5.52	.01
6.2	1.99	16	2	15.1	<.001	7.9	.004
7.0	10.18	16	2	51.	<.001	73.4	<.001
9.0	2.46	16	2	19.8	<.001	11.7	<.001
10.0	1.077	16	1	1.71	.20	1.23	.27

Sources:

Col. (2): $1 + 1/\lambda_1$, where λ_1 is from Christ [1951], p. 82, col. (3).

Cols. (3)–(4): Christ [1951], pp. 103, 82, 72–6.

Col. (5): $T\log_e$ [col. (2)]; $T = 23$ for eq. (10.0) and $T = 22$ for all others.

Col. (7): col. (2) × col. (3) ÷ col. (4).

Cols. (6) and (8): rough interpolation in χ^2 and F tables.

χ^2 test and the Basmann F test are shown in Table 5.1.[37] They confirm Basmann's findings, that is, they show that the Anderson-Rubin χ^2 test is more prone to reject overidentifying restrictions than is the Basmann F test, for the entries in column (8) are always greater than in column (6). At the 90 and 95 per cent levels, respectively, the Anderson-Rubin χ^2 test rejects all but one and all but two equations. At either the 90 or the 95 per cent level the Basmann F test rejects all but three equations. These results indicate that the whole set of restrictions forming this model are at best approximately correct, and they emphasize again that specification error is a major problem.

6   PREDICTIVE TESTS, I: INTRODUCTION; PREDICTORS BASED ON REDUCED FORMS AND ON STRUCTURES; PREDICTION AS A TESTING METHOD

6.1   This and the following three sections will discuss what we have called predictive tests, that is, tests based on preparing a prediction (also to be called a forecast) and evaluating it by some standard. In some cases the standard will be related to the average size of residuals obtained in the sample period, and in some cases it will be related to the purpose for which the prediction is desired. See VII.9 and X.1.3 for some introductory remarks about prediction.

6.2   Our discussion of predictive tests will depend heavily on the concept of a *point prediction*, which is defined as a *single-valued* prediction of a (scalar or vector) variable. We shall also be interested in this section in *interval predictions*, which give an interval rather than a single value for the predicted variable. Predictions made for the purpose of influencing practical action are typically made from reduced-form rather than structural equations, because in the former but not the latter there is one dependent variable and all the other variables are predetermined as of the period of the prediction. Hence there is a reasonable prospect that when a prediction of the dependent variable is to be made, the values of all the explanatory variables used in the prediction will be at least approximately known.

6.3   Consider a reduced-form equation under Model 3 (defined in IX.2.3-5):

$$(6.1) \qquad y_{it} = \sum_{1}^{K} \pi_{ik} z_{kt} + v_{it}$$

---

[37] Columns (5) and (6) in Table 5.1 are correct. They differ from columns (5) and (7) of Christ [1951], p. 82, which are incorrect because inadvertently logarithms were taken to the base 10 instead of the base e. This error was first called to my attention by George G. Judge.

Consider the least-squares estimators p_{ik} and $w_i{}^2$ of its parameters π_{ik} and $\omega_i{}^2$ (which is the variance of v_i), as derived in IX.3-5, and the calculated values of y_i and the associated computed errors $\hat{v}_i$ for the sample period *and* for the subsequent period, $t = T + 1, T + 2, \ldots$, for which predictions might be made:

(6.2)

$$\hat{v}_{it} = y_{it} - \hat{y}_{it} = y_{it} - \sum_1^K p_{ik} z_{kt} \qquad t = 1, \ldots, T, T + 1, T + 2, \ldots$$

Note that this equation defines not only the calculated values of y_i and of its disturbance during the *sample* period, but also the forecast values and the associated errors of forecast during the *prediction* period. They are distinguished from each other notationally only by the time subscript t carried by $\hat{y}_{it}$ and $\hat{v}_{it}$; $t \leqq T$ in the former case and $t > T$ in the latter case. Predictions can also be made from estimates of the reduced form obtained by solving the system of structural equations after the latter have been estimated by the limited-information or two-stage least-squares or some other method.

6.4   There is a variety of ways in which forecasts can be obtained from a reduced form besides the straightforward method of estimating (6.1) and assigning a value of zero to the prediction-period error as indicated in (6.2). One alternative is to transform all data to first differences before estimating the reduced-form equations, then to use the approach of (6.2) to forecast the *change* Δy_{it}, and then to add the predicted value of Δy_{it} to the lagged value $y_{i,t-1}$ to obtain a forecast of y_{it} itself. Forecasts made in this way become increasingly uncertain as the span is lengthened between the end of the observation period and the period for which the forecast is wanted, *even if the model is correct and the structure does not change.* This is because a forecast made in 1966, for instance, for the year 1970, would be the value of the variable for 1965 plus the sum of the forecast annual changes from 1965 to 1966, 1966 to 1967, . . . , 1969 to 1970, and therefore the standard error of the forecast for 1970 will be the standard error of the sum of the five annual-change forecasts. If the errors of these annual-change forecasts are independent of each other, and if they all have the same distribution, then the standard error of the sum of N annual-change forecasts is $\sqrt{N}$ times the standard error of one such forecast. (If they are positively or negatively correlated, then it will be more or less.) This kind of widening of the standard error of forecast as the forecasts are made longer in advance does not occur in models based on raw data. Nevertheless, the choice between first-difference and raw data cannot properly be made on this ground; it should be made in accordance with whether we believe that the real world is a "first-difference world" or not, as discussed above in IX.13.8.

6.5   Another method is to modify the forecast given by $\hat{y}_{it}$ in (6.2) by adding to it the error made in the previous year, that is, to use as the forecast the quantity $\hat{y}_{it} + \hat{v}_{i,t-1}$. This method would be appropriate if we felt that the expectation of the disturbance occurring in period t would be of approximately the same magnitude as the disturbance in period $t - 1$. It is equivalent to using as the forecast the quantity $y_{i,t-1} + \Delta(\hat{y}_{it})$, that is, to forecasting that y_{it} will be equal to the preceding period's value plus the change in the model's forecast of the systematic (non-random) part of y_i between periods $t - 1$ and t. (Note that this is inconsistent with assumption (j) of serially independent disturbances.) Still another alternative would be to use $\hat{y}_{it} + a\hat{v}_{i,t-1}$, where a is some number between 0 and 1, instead of $\hat{y}_{it} + \hat{v}_{i,t-1}$, to reflect the view that the expectation of the disturbance in period t will be similar to but smaller in absolute size than the disturbance in period $t - 1$. In what follows we shall discuss predictions arising from equations like (6.2) and leave the reader to supply the modifications required if forecasts are made by alternative methods such as those mentioned in this paragraph and the preceding one.

6.6   So far we have considered forecasts made from *reduced-form* equations, given the values of variables that are predetermined as of the forecast period. For some purposes, especially for testing individual structural equations (see VII.9.6), it is useful to make a "prediction" of a jointly dependent variable conditional on the *concurrent* values of the other jointly dependent variables and predetermined variables that appear in a particular *structural* equation, using estimated values of the parameters of that equation. For example, consider the structural equation

$$(6.3) \qquad y_{1t} + \sum_{2}^{H} \beta_i y_{it} + \sum_{1}^{J} \gamma_k z_{kt} = u_t$$

and suppose its limited-information estimated version is used to "forecast" y_{1t} given $y_{2t}, \ldots, y_{Ht}, z_{1t}, \ldots, z_{Jt}$. The "forecast" value $\hat{y}_{1t}$ and the error of "forecast" $\hat{u}_t$ are given by

$$(6.4) \qquad \hat{u}_t = y_{1t} - \hat{y}_{1t} = y_{1t} + \sum_{2}^{H} \hat{\beta}_i y_{it} + \sum_{1}^{J} \hat{\gamma}_k z_{kt}$$

where $\hat{\beta}_i$ and $\hat{\gamma}_k$ are limited-information estimators of β_i and γ_k. Of course estimators of β_i and γ_k obtained by any other method (e.g., two-stage least squares) can be used instead.

6.7   The advantage of a point predictor is like that claimed by Savage for a point estimator,[38] namely, it gives a *single* value for each variable, upon which to base a course of action to achieve desired results. The advantage of an *interval* predictor, in analogy to an interval estimator, is that it gives some idea of the reliability to be expected of the point

---

[38] Savage [1954], Ch. 17, pp. 257–262. See also VII.7.25.

predictor if the underlying model is correct and no structural change has occurred.

6.8 It will be recalled from VII.9.4 that errors in point forecasts arise from two sources (apart from incorrect models or structural changes): One source is the random disturbance during the forecasting period; it would be present even if all the parameters of the model were exactly known. The other source is errors in the estimates of the parameters; it is present because the estimates are based on only a finite sample and is due to the random disturbances in the sample period. In particular, the error of a point predictor of a variable on the average must be at least as large as the standard deviation of the true values of that variable's sample-period disturbances, because one of the components of that error is by hypothesis a disturbance drawn from the same distribution that produced the sample-period disturbances. Furthermore, the error of forecast must on the average be somewhat larger, because its other component [independent of the first under assumption (j) of IX.2] is due to errors in the parameter estimates, which are bound on the average to be greater than zero in absolute value because the samples used are finite. Any interval predictor that we make must reflect both of these sources of error. Similarly, any hypothesis test based on point predictions must do likewise, for as noted in 1.4 and VII.9, predictive tests and interval predictors bear a very close relation to each other just as do ordinary tests and interval estimators.

6.9 It is often said that the acid test of an econometric model or equation is its ability to predict (or even to describe) data that were not used in its construction and estimation. Let us examine this maxim and see in what sense it is true. To do so, we consider the situation faced by an economist who in 1966 has available a set of time-series data for the years 1929–1965 and wishes to devise the best model (and parameter estimates) possible. He is considering two courses of action: (a) to use all the data 1929–1965 to estimate the parameters or (b) to separate the data into two parts, using, for instance, 1929–1959 to estimate the parameters and saving the remainder (1960–1965) for a test of the estimated model's predicting ability. The maxim that prediction is the acid test seems to suggest course (b) as preferable. But no matter which course is followed, the best that could emerge from research done in 1966 using 1929–1965 data would be an estimated model that agrees closely with the data for the entire period 1929–1965. If this close agreement is obtained by choosing a model in 1966 and fitting it to 1929–1959 data and then successfully predicting 1960–1965 data, there is no more assurance that the agreement will extend to post-1965 data than if the close agreement is secured by fitting the model in 1966 to all the 1929–1965 data. Indeed, if we were certain that the *a priori* information underlying the model were correct, and would continue to be correct after 1965, then fitting to all the 1929–1965 data would give estimators with smaller variances because the sample size would be larger. And even if (as is likely) the *a priori* information used is only approximately correct, or is valid for part of the data but not for all, there is nothing that can be learned by saving some data for testing predictions that cannot also be learned by estimating on the basis of all the available data and examining all the residuals. For example, if a demand equation fitted to the prewar period describes the postwar data only after the intercept has been shifted upward, as suggested in Figure 6.1, this could be discovered in the attempt to predict the postwar prices, but it could also be

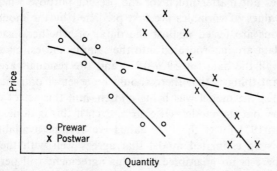

Figure 6.1 Hypothetical prewar and postwar data for price and quantity of a good, with demand curves fitted to prewar, postwar, and combined data.

discovered by an examination of the residuals from the single line fitted to all the data together. Or if a straight line were mistakenly fitted to a parabolic relationship, an examination of the residuals from the line estimated from all the data would show just as much as would the attempt to predict some of the observations from a line estimated from the remaining ones.

   6.10   Is there then any truth in the maxim that prediction provides the acid test? The answer is yes, but the issue lies not in whether we set aside for use in testing predictions some data with which we are already familiar—we have seen that this makes little difference. Rather, the issue lies in whether we confront the model with an *entirely new* set of data with which we were not familiar when the model was chosen.[39] This can be explained as follows. It is well known (though sometimes forgotten) that statistical inference techniques based on the distributions of random variables are not applicable when maintained hypotheses have been chosen so as to conform to the data with which parameters will be estimated or hypotheses will be tested.[40] But it is difficult (*and undesirable,*

[39] Note that in the preceding paragraph no such new set of data was discussed.
[40] See Christ [1951], page 39, note 9, and Koopmans [1949], Section 7, the next to last paragraph. See also I.3.5–6 and X.5.16–17 above.

as argued repeatedly above) to choose our model without making any use of our knowledge of the data to be used in its estimation. Therefore there is danger of choosing an incorrect model that for accidental reasons happens to fit the available data well, in preference to a more nearly correct model that happens not to fit the available data as well. It is this danger against which protection is provided by an entirely new set of data that could not have entered into the choice of the model. In the case of the economist doing his research in 1966, with 1929–1965 data available, such a new set of data could be provided by waiting five years, for instance, and then using the 1966–1970 data to test the model that was chosen in 1966. It does not matter much for the present purpose whether (a) the 1966–1970 values of variables are first predicted by the model and then the predictions are tested against the data, or whether instead (b) the 1966–1970 data are incorporated into the sample and estimates are computed using all the data for 1929–1970 and the residuals are examined. The important thing is that there should be a set of data that were not available when the model was being chosen, and this set of data should be used to try out the model. Of course, even if this is done, the best we can expect in 1971 (after the 1970 data have become available and have been used) is an estimated model that agrees well with the 1929–1970 data, and there is no guarantee that this agreement will persist beyond 1970. But we have more confidence if some of the agreement is for data that appeared *after* the model was chosen and thus provide a genuine test.[41]

6.11   Thus in time-series studies the two main virtues of predictive tests—extending the number of observations with which a model is confronted, and doing so in a way that prevents us from choosing the model in the light of knowledge of the data with which it is to be confronted—can be attained by fitting the model to all the data in question just as well as they can be attained by fitting to some of the data and predicting the rest. However, a compelling practical reason for using predictive tests of a model instead of refitting it, when new data become available, is that the advantages of increasing the sample size from T to $T + 1$ or $T + 2$ may not be judged worth the cost of refitting.

6.12   In cross-section studies the situation may be different. Here the sample is typically very much larger than in time-series studies. We can therefore divide an available sample into two parts, each containing hundreds or thousands of observations, one part to be used initially to help suggest the form of the model and the other part to be used later as a test of the predictive ability of the model chosen. It is not difficult to make that division so as to prevent our knowledge of the *entire* sample from influencing our choice of the model, for the part of the sample that

[41] See Simon [1955] for a concurring view.

is set aside can typically be made so large that if we do not analyze it before choosing the model, we cannot be familiar enough with its characteristics to influence the choice of model seriously.

6.13   Section 7 discusses predictive tests based on sample-period residuals from least-squares estimates of the reduced form. Section 8 discusses predictive tests based on sample-period residuals from structural equations and from reduced-form equations estimated by solving an estimated structure. Section 9 discusses predictive tests not based on sample-period residuals.

7   PREDICTIVE TESTS, II: TESTS BASED ON SAMPLE-PERIOD RESIDUALS FROM A LEAST-SQUARES REDUCED-FORM EQUATION; TOLERANCE INTERVALS

7.1   In this section we consider predictive tests and interval prediction based on least-squares estimators of the reduced form, using the sample-period residuals to obtain estimators of the variance of the point predictors involved. We shall first take up the simple case of a single prediction from a reduced-form equation containing only one predetermined variable (cf. IX.3). Then we shall consider the case of a reduced-form equation with more than one predetermined variable, first dealing with a single prediction from such an equation and then with several predictions for several consecutive periods.

7.2   *A single prediction from a simple regression.* Consider the following reduced-form equation:

$$(7.1) \qquad y_t = \alpha + \pi z_t + v_t$$

Here as usual y is dependent, z is predetermined, v is random with mean zero and variance ω^2, and α and π are unknown parameters. Let us make the assumptions of Model 3 (see IX.2.3-5) for the prediction period as well as the sample period. Then z is predetermined and cannot be treated as fixed in repeated trials, each trial consisting of sample plus prediction. In order to obtain estimators of the slope and intercept that are independent of each other, transform the equation so that the sample mean of the predetermined variable is zero, thus (cf. IX.3.16):

$$(7.2) \qquad y_t = (\alpha + \pi \bar{z}) + \pi(z_t - \bar{z}) + v_t = \alpha' + \pi \mathbf{z}_t + v_t$$

where as before $\alpha' = \alpha + \pi \bar{z}$ and $\mathbf{z}_t = z_t - \bar{z}$. The least-squares estimators of α' and π are a' and p (see IX.3.12). The calculated values of y and v for the sample period $t = 1, \ldots, T$ and the forecast value of y in period

$T + n$ and its error (i.e., $\hat{y}_{T+n}$ and $\hat{v}_{T+n}$) are shown in the following, where n is an integer > 0:

$$(7.3) \qquad \hat{v}_t = y_t - \hat{y}_t = y_t - a' - pz_t \qquad t = 1, \ldots, T, T+n$$

7.3 In order to obtain a predictive test or an interval predictor based on the point predictor $\hat{y}_{T+n}$ implicitly defined by (7.3), it will be necessary to find the probability distribution of the forecast error $\hat{v}_{T+n}$. We shall do this initially under the assumptions that equation (7.2) obeys Model 2 (normal) (whence z is exogenous and can be taken as fixed in repeated trials). We shall find the conditional distribution of $\hat{v}_{T+n}$ given $z_1, \ldots, z_T, z_{T+n}$, rather than its conditional distribution given those z's and $v_1, \ldots, v_T$. To do this we express $\hat{v}_{T+n}$ as follows, using the two preceding equations:

$$(7.4) \qquad \hat{v}_{T+n} = (\alpha' - a') + (\pi - p)z_{T+n} + v_{T+n}$$

Under our assumptions, the true disturbance v_{T+n} is normal, and given $z_1, \ldots, z_T$ the estimators a' and p are also normal. Thus given $z_1, \ldots, z_T$ and z_{T+n} the forecast error $\hat{v}_{T+n}$ is a linear function of the normal variables v_{T+n}, a', and p, and so is itself normally distributed. Its expectation is zero because in Model 2 a' and p are unbiased, and v_{T+n} has zero expectation, thus:

$$(7.5) \qquad E(\hat{v}_{T+n} \mid z_1, \ldots, z_T, z_{T+n}) = 0$$

The variance of $\hat{v}_{T+n}$ is the sum of the variances of the three terms on the right side of (7.4) because all three are independent of each other in Model 2 (normal); see IX.3.17-18 for variances of a' and p:

$$(7.6) \qquad \text{var}(\hat{v}_{T+n} \mid z_1, \ldots, z_T, z_{T+n}) = \frac{\omega^2}{T} + \frac{\omega^2 z_{T+n}^2}{\sum_1^T z_t^2} + \omega^2$$

$$= \omega^2 \left[\frac{1}{T} + \frac{z_{T+n}^2}{m_{zz}} + 1 \right]$$

7.4 Note that there are three additive terms in this variance. Each has a simple interpretation. The first, ω^2/T, is the variance of a' and is the contribution of the error in the estimator of the intercept α' (which equals $\alpha + \pi\bar{z}$); it is a constant independent of the value of z in the forecast period. The second, $\omega^2 z_{T+n}^2/m_{zz}$, is the variance of pz_{T+n} and is the contribution of the error in the estimator of the slope π. It is not independent of z_{T+n} but is proportional to the square of the difference between z_{T+n} and the sample mean of z. Note that the numerator of this second term involves both z_{T+n} and the sample-period values of z, but the denominator involves the sample-period values only. The third term, ω^2, is the variance of v_{T+n} and is the contribution of the forecast-period disturbance. The first two terms reflect the random variation of $v_1, \ldots, v_T$ in the sample period, and the third term reflects that of v_{T+n} in the forecast period. If the model is correct, improved accuracy in estimating α' and π (e.g., by using a large sample) will reduce the variance of $\hat{v}_{T+n}$ but in any case cannot reduce it below ω^2, the variance of v_{T+n}.

7.5 It is important to realize that the distribution of $\hat{v}_{T+n}$ just derived—normal with mean zero and variance as given in (7.6)—applies to the statistical population of errors generated when an infinite number of observations are forecast by the following repeated experiment: Draw an infinite number of samples of size T from a distribution given by (7.2) and Model 2 (normal); for each sample compute estimates a' and p of α' and π; for each sample observe *one* more pair of values z_{T+n} and y_{T+n} and use them and that sample's a' and p as indicated in (7.3) to obtain the forecast error $\hat{v}_{T+n}$. The distribution in question does *not* apply to the repeated experiment of drawing *one* sample of size T and then observing an infinite number of pairs $(z_{T+1}, y_{T+1}), (z_{T+2}, y_{T+2}), \ldots$ and generating an infinite number of forecasts from that single sample.

7.6 The numerical value of the variance of the forecast error $\hat{v}_{T+n}$ is unknown because ω^2, the variance of v, is unknown. But the least-squares estimator $w^2 = \sum_1^T \hat{v}_t^2/(T-2)$ is unbiased and consistent in Model 2, so an unbiased consistent estimator for var $\hat{v}_{T+n}$ is available in Model 2 (normal or not); we denote it by w_{T+n}^2:

(7.7) $$w_{T+n}^2 = \text{est var } \hat{v}_{T+n} = w^2\left(\frac{1}{T} + \frac{z_{T+n}^2}{m_{zz}} + 1\right)$$

7.7 Since $\hat{v}_{T+n}$ is normal with mean zero, and since its variance is estimated without bias by w_{T+n}^2, the statistic $\hat{v}_{T+n}/w_{T+n}$ has the t distribution with $T-2$ degrees of freedom in Model 2 (normal). This means that, given Model 2 (normal), if the structure is the same during the forecast period $T + n$ as it was during the sample period $1, \ldots, T$, there is a probability of $\epsilon_2 - \epsilon_1$ that the statistic $\hat{v}_{T+n}/w_{T+n}$ will fall in the interval whose end points are t_{ϵ_1} and t_{ϵ_2}, where $0 \leqq \epsilon_1 < \epsilon_2 \leqq 1$:[42]

(7.8) $$\text{Pb}\left(t_{\epsilon_1} \leqq \frac{\hat{v}_{T+n}}{w_{T+n}} \leqq t_{\epsilon_2}\right) = \epsilon_2 - \epsilon_1 > 0$$

This means that, in the same situation, an *interval predictor* of y_{T+n} with confidence coefficient[43] $\epsilon_2 - \epsilon_1$ is given by the interval whose limits are $\hat{y}_{T+n} + w_{T+n}t_{\epsilon_1}$ and $\hat{y}_{T+n} + w_{T+n}t_{\epsilon_2}$, thus:

(7.9) $\text{Pb}(\hat{y}_{T+n} + w_{T+n}t_{\epsilon_1} \leqq y_{T+n} \leqq \hat{y}_{T+n} + w_{T+n}t_{\epsilon_2}) = \epsilon_2 - \epsilon_1 > 0$

[42] Recall from 1.13 that t_ϵ is defined as the point of the t distribution that is exceeded with probability $1 - \epsilon$, that is, $\text{Pb}(t \leqq t_\epsilon) = \epsilon$.

[43] We use the term "confidence coefficient" here, for it describes clearly enough the idea at hand, although the interval is not strictly a confidence interval because it is designed to capture not a parameter but a future observable value of a variable.

If a symmetrical interval is desired, we choose $\epsilon_1 < 0.5$ and $\epsilon_2 = 1 - \epsilon_1$; then $t_{\epsilon_2} = -t_{\epsilon_1}$, and the interval becomes $\hat{y}_{T+n} \pm w_{T+n}t_{\epsilon_1}$, and the confidence coefficient becomes $1 - 2\epsilon_1$.

7.8 Equation (7.9) says that if an infinite number of independent samples are drawn at random, and a forecast interval is constructed from each as above, and a single value y_{T+n} is observed for each sample, then a proportion $\epsilon_2 - \epsilon_1$ of all the observed values y_{T+n} will fall in their respective forecast intervals. It does *not* say that if a *single* sample is drawn and forecast intervals are constructed from it as described by (7.9), a proportion $\epsilon_2 - \epsilon_1$ of all future values y_{T+n} (n running to infinity) will fall in the corresponding intervals. The situation can be explained as follows. Because of random variation in the sample-period disturbances, some samples will give unusually good estimates of α' and π, and hence unusually good point forecasts; other samples will give unusually bad. Some samples will give unusually large values of w_{T+n} and hence unusually large intervals; other samples will give unusually small. Therefore some samples will give wide intervals properly centered, which will catch nearly all of the actual values $y_{T+1}, y_{T+2}, \ldots, y_{T+\infty}$ between their boundaries; other samples will give narrow intervals not properly centered, which will catch very few of the actual values $y_{T+1}, \ldots, y_{T+\infty}$; and so on. Therefore we *cannot* proceed from (7.9) to say of each sample: The forecast interval constructed from *this* sample, using $\epsilon_2 - \epsilon_1 = .80$, for instance, will catch about 80 per cent of the actual future values. Some samples will do far better than that, and some far worse. We *can* proceed from (7.9) to say that the average performance of intervals, each associated with a *separate independent* sample, is 80 per cent, if intervals are constructed using $\epsilon_2 - \epsilon_1 = .80$. This point is very important, and the reader should be sure he has it clear.

7.9 The considerations that should determine whether we use a one-tail or a two-tail interval predictor (i.e., whether one or neither of the quantities t_{ϵ_1} and t_{ϵ_2} are chosen to be infinite) are the same here as in the general discussion of VII.7, namely: our *a priori* views about the likelihood of change in the relevant parameters before the prediction period occurs; and the losses that would be incurred from incorrect acceptance or rejection, depending on the true parameter values. As for the losses, in economic forecasting it is often true that the consequences of erring on one side are less serious or costly than those of erring on the other. It is easy to imagine that the government of a country currently enjoying nearly full employment might regard a given drop in money national income as a more serious disaster than an equally large rise, because the drop might be expected to bring unemployment and a fall of real income, whereas the rise might be expected to come with price increases but little or no change in total real income. In that case the government, wishing to forecast what next year's money income would be under a neutral fiscal and monetary policy, in order to decide whether to set anti-inflationary or anti-depression policies in motion, might well ask for a forecast interval extending further below the point forecast than above it. The government might then prepare for depression if the lower limit of the forecast interval fell below a certain point, prepare for inflation if the upper limit fell above a certain (higher) point, and do nothing if neither of these things happened.[44]

7.10   A graphical presentation of the interval predictor of y_{T+n} given by (7.9) may be helpful. The point predictor implicit in (7.3) locates the interval for each value of z_{T+n}; it is shown by the solid straight line in

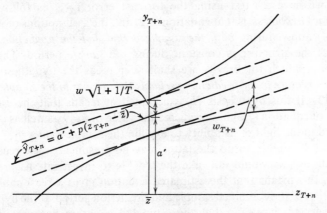

Figure 7.1 Curved limits of the interval regression predictor $\hat{y}_{T+n} \pm w_{T+n}$ for predicting y_{T+n} given z_{T+n}; see 7.10 in text.

Figure 7.1, representing $\hat{y}_{T+n} = a' + pz_{T+n}$. For simplicity let us choose a symmetrical interval such that $t_{\epsilon_1} = -1$ and $t_{\epsilon_2} = 1$. Then the half width of the interval will always be equal to w_{T+n}, which is the square root of the expression given by (7.7). If $z_{T+n} = \bar{z}$, the interval has its minimum width, $w\sqrt{1 + 1/T}$, as shown by the two dotted straight lines in Figure 7.1. If z_{T+n} differs from $\bar{z}$, the interval acquires additional width, because the part of w_{T+n} that depends on $(z_{T+n} - \bar{z})^2$ is not zero; the width of the interval increases at an increasing rate as $z_{T+n} - \bar{z}$ increases. This is shown by the solid curved lines in Figure 7.1. If $t_{\epsilon_1} < -1$, the lower half width shown in the figure is made proportionally greater everywhere (or smaller if $t_{\epsilon_1} > -1$), and correspondingly with t_{ϵ_2} and the upper half width, as required by (7.9).

7.11   The probability distribution of $\hat{v}_{T+n}$ derived in 7.3 can be used for *predictive testing* as well as for interval prediction. When an equation, complete with numerical values of its parameters estimated from a sample, has been obtained that gives a plausible description of

---

[44] If both happened, this would mean that the accuracy of the forecast was insufficient to indicate the appropriate action.

behavior during the sample period, it then becomes desirable to determine whether the equation continues to give a plausible description of behavior during subsequent periods (recall 6.10). In effect we want to test whether an equation with estimated parameters describes the *combined* sample and forecast periods well or not. The probability statement contained in equation (7.8) or equivalently in (7.9) forms the basis for an appropriate test, since this statement is true provided that, during the combined sample and forecast period ($t = 1, \ldots, T, T + n$), the equation (7.2) being estimated obeys Model 2 (normal) and the structure is unchanged. Hence we have a t test using the forecast error $\hat{v}_{T+n}$ as follows. The *maintained hypothesis* is that equation (7.2) and the assumptions of Model 2 (normal) apply during *both the sample period and the prediction period*, and that the structure is constant during the *sample* period. The *tested hypothesis*, which for brevity we shall refer to as the hypothesis H_0, is *that the structure in the prediction period is the same as in the sample period.*

7.12 If this hypothesis H_0 is accepted, it means that the estimated version of equation (7.2) has predicted the value of y_{T+n} as well as could be expected in the light of its ability to explain the sample values $y_1, \ldots, y_T$; and since its ability to do the latter may be presumed to be reasonably good (or else we would not take the trouble to investigate its predicting ability), this means that the estimated equation gives a reasonably good description of the combined sample and prediction period. If the hypothesis H_0 is rejected, it means that the estimated equation has predicted the value of y_{T+n} poorly compared with its ability to explain $y_1, \ldots, y_T$ during the sample period. If H_0 is rejected, it suggests *either* that a structural change occurred between the times T and $T + n$ [with or without destroying the applicability of the *a priori* restrictions that are implied in the form of (7.2) and in Model 2 (normal)] *or* (at least as likely) that the equation (7.2) is inadequate as an explanation of the combined period $t = 1, \ldots, T, T + n$. In the latter case whatever success it had in explaining $y_1, \ldots, y_T$ must have been fortuitous; here the maintained hypothesis is being questioned. In either case, the rejection of H_0 indicates that the equation (7.2) does not represent a theory adequate to explain the behavior of *both* the sample period and the prediction period in one general framework with a constant structure, and that therefore it may be desirable to revise equation (7.2) by including other variables, by changing its form, and so forth. For example, if the slope parameter π appears to vary, it may be helpful to express it as a function (perhaps linear) of some other variable x, thus making (7.2) a linear function of the two variables[45] z and xz. There is an endless variety of possibilities.

7.13 For this t test of the hypothesis H_0, the appropriate statistic is $\hat{v}_{T+n}/w_{T+n}$ and the lower and upper acceptance limits are t_{ϵ_1} and t_{ϵ_2}

[45] In this connection, see III.9.2, note 43.

(equivalently, the statistic y_{T+n} and the acceptance limits $\hat{y}_{T+n} + w_{T+n}t_{\epsilon_1}$ and $\hat{y}_{T+n} + w_{T+n}t_{\epsilon_2}$ can be used). There are $T - 2$ degrees of freedom. The probability of a type I error is $1 - (\epsilon_2 - \epsilon_1)$ since if the hypothesis H_0 is true the probability that the statistic falls in the interval is $\epsilon_2 - \epsilon_1$; see (7.9). The probability of a type II error of course depends on what alternative hypothesis is true if H_0 is false.

7.14   Since there are three parameters (α', π, and ω^2) that are constant according to the tested hypothesis H_0, this test has an operating characteristic (OC) *surface* (rather than the OC *curve* discussed in VII.7.9), showing the probability of acceptance of H_0 as a function of the forecast-period values of all three parameters. *Suppose first* that the value of the intercept α' alone may change after the sample period but before the forecast period. If α' increases, the point forecast $\hat{y}_{T+n}$ is likely to be too low; and if α' decreases, $\hat{y}_{T+n}$ is likely to be too high. Thus if the alternative hypothesis is that α' alone changes, we typically want a two-tail test (i.e., $\epsilon_1 > 0$ and $\epsilon_2 < 1$) if it is not known which way α' will change; if it is known that α' will not decrease, then we want a one-tail test with $\epsilon_1 = 0$; and if it is known that α' will not increase, we want a one-tail test with $\epsilon_2 = 1$.

7.15   *Suppose second* that the slope π alone may change between periods T and $T + n$. If π increases, then for negative values of z_{T+n} the point forecast $\hat{y}_{T+n}$ is likely to be too high, and for positive z_{T+n} it is likely to be too low. The reverse is true if π decreases. Hence if π alone may change, we want a two-tail test if the direction of change of π is unknown. If π cannot decrease, then we want a one-tail test, with $\epsilon_2 = 1$ for negative values of z_{T+n} and with $\epsilon_1 = 0$ for positive values of z_{T+n}; if π cannot increase, the reverse applies.

7.16   *Suppose third* that ω^2 alone may change between periods T and $T + n$. If ω^2 increases, large deviations (both positive and negative) of y_{T+n} from the point forecast $\hat{y}_{T+n}$ become more likely, that is, large values of $(\hat{v}_{T+n}/w_{T+n})^2$ become more likely. If ω^2 decreases, small deviations (positive or negative) of y_{T+n} from $\hat{y}_{T+n}$ become more likely, that is, small values of $(\hat{v}_{T+n}/w_{T+n})^2$ become more likely. A t test can be used, with a two-tailed rejection region ($0 < \epsilon_1 < \epsilon_2 < 1$) if ω^2 cannot decrease, and with the rejection region concentrated in the *center* of the distribution (see Figure VII.7.2(d)) if ω^2 cannot increase. Since $t^2(T - 2)$ is equal to $F(1, T - 2)$ as noted in 1.9, a one-tailed F test for $(\hat{v}_{T+n}/w_{T+n})^2$ can be used equivalently, with the rejection region in the right-hand tail if ω^2 cannot decrease, and in the left-hand tail if ω^2 cannot increase. Note that the F test with the rejection region in the upper tail is also appropriate if the alternative hypothesis shows that α' changes or that π changes; thus this F test is appropriate if the alternative hypothesis says that ω^2 increases and α' and π change, all at once. This F test is particularly important since it can fairly readily be generalized to take account of the forecasting of values of y in *several* periods from the same sample; see 7.20 ff. below.

7.17 *A single prediction from a multiple regression.* Paragraphs 7.2-16 apply to *multiple* regression with only slight modification. Consider now the following reduced-form equation:

$$(7.10) \qquad y_t = \pi_K' + \sum_1^{K-1} \pi_k z_{kt} + v_t$$

As usual y is dependent; $z_{kt} = z_{kt} - \bar{z}_k$ and is predetermined for $k = 1, \dots, K - 1$; v is random with mean zero and variance ω^2; and $\pi_1, \dots, \pi_{K-1}$ and π_K' are unknown parameters. Again we assume that Model 2 (normal) applies both to the sample period $1, \dots, T$ and the forecast period $T + n$, and so the z's become exogenous. Because $z_k = 0$, the least-squares estimator p_K' of π_K' is independent of the least-squares estimators $p_1, \dots, p_{K-1}$ (but the latter are not necessarily independent of each other). The sample-period residuals and the forecast error are given by

$$(7.11) \quad \hat{v}_t = y_t - \hat{y}_t = y_t - p_K' - \sum_1^{K-1} p_k z_{kt}$$

$$= (\pi_K' - p_K') + \sum_1^{K-1} (\pi_k - p_k) z_{kt} + v_t \qquad t = 1, \dots, T; T + n$$

7.18 If there is no structural change during the combined sample and forecast period, an argument similar to 7.3 shows that under Model 2 (normal) the distribution of the forecast error $\hat{v}_{T+n}$ (conditional on all the z's in all periods $1, \dots, T, T + n$) is normal with mean zero and with variance as follows:

$$(7.12) \quad \operatorname{var} \hat{v}_{T+n} = \operatorname{var} p_K' + \operatorname{var} \sum_1^{K-1} p_k z_{k,T+n} + \operatorname{var} v_{T+n}$$

$$= \frac{\omega^2}{T} + \sum_{j=1}^{K-1} \sum_{k=1}^{K-1} z_{j.T+n} z_{k.T+n} \operatorname{cov}(p_j, p_k) + \omega^2$$

$$= \omega^2 \left[\frac{1}{T} + (\det \mathbf{M}_{zz})^{-1} \sum_{j=1}^{K-1} \sum_{k=1}^{K-1} z_{j.T+n} z_{k.T+n} \operatorname{cof} m_{jk} + 1 \right]$$

The second equality applies the familiar results for $\operatorname{var} p_K'$ and v_{T+n}, and applies to the middle term the rule for the variance of a linear combination of random variables (here $p_1, \dots, p_{K-1}$). If we apply to the third equality the result for $\operatorname{cov}(p_j, p_k)$ from IX.4.7, and denote the vector $(z_{1t} \ \cdots \ z_{K-1,t})$ by $\mathbf{z}_t$, and the sample-period matrix of moments of $z_1, \dots, z_{K-1}$ about their means by $\mathbf{M}_{zz}$ (as usual), this variance of $\hat{v}_{T+n}$ conditional on $\mathbf{z}_1, \dots, \mathbf{z}_T, \mathbf{z}_{T+n}$ becomes

$$(7.13) \qquad \operatorname{var} \hat{v}_{T+n} = \omega^2 \left(\frac{1}{T} + \mathbf{z}_{T+n} \mathbf{M}_{zz}^{-1} \mathbf{z}_{T+n}' + 1 \right)$$

This result is directly analogous to (7.6) and reduces to it if $K = 2$ so that there is only one nondummy predetermined variable. The important interpretive paragraphs 7.4 and 7.5 apply to (7.13) and should be read at this point. Of course, all three terms on the right side of (7.12) or (7.13) are non-negative since all are variances; the center term is positive unless $\mathbf{z}$ is zero since $\mathbf{M}_{zz}$ is positive definite by assumption (c) of Model 2 or 3. [If a dummy variable z_{Kt} always equal to 1 is introduced into (7.10) so that the constant term is not treated explicitly (or if there is none), the sum then runs from 1 to K instead of to $K - 1$. Then also the untransformed predetermined variables z (rather than $\mathbf{z}$, which have been transformed to make $\bar{z} = 0$) are used in (7.10)–(7.13), and the moment matrix $\mathbf{M}_{zz}$ acquires a Kth row and column and consists of moments about zero rather than about the sample mean. And in (7.12) and (7.13) the term ω^2/T disappears. In connection with this alternative treatment of the constant term, recall IX.4.11.]

7.19 The variance of $\hat{v}_{T+n}$ can be consistently and unbiasedly estimated in Model 2 (normal) because the least-squares estimator of ω^2, namely, $w^2 = \sum_1^T \hat{v}_t^2/(T - K)$, is consistent and unbiased in Model 2. As in the simple-regression case we denote this estimate by w^2_{T+n}, thus:

$$(7.14) \qquad w^2_{T+n} = \text{est var } \hat{v}_{T+n} = w^2\left(\frac{1}{T} + \mathbf{z}_{T+n}\mathbf{M}_{zz}^{-1}\mathbf{z}'_{T+n} + 1\right)$$

Under our assumptions, $\hat{v}_{T+n}/w_{T+n}$ is distributed as t with $T - K$ degrees of freedom. Therefore equations (7.8) and (7.9) apply to the present multiple-regression case as well as to the simple-regression case, w_{T+n} and the number of degrees of freedom being altered appropriately as explained in this paragraph. Therefore an interval predictor of $\hat{y}_{T+n}$, or a predictive test of the hypothesis H_0 that the prediction-period structure is the same as that in the sample period, can be formed from (7.9) in the manner described in 7.7 and 7.11-16.[46] The interpretive paragraphs 7.8 and 7.9 apply here as well as in the simple-regression case.

7.20 *Several predictions from a multiple regression.* Sometimes, after a sample of T points has been observed and estimates of the parameters have been made from it, we wish to forecast the values of some variable y in *several* periods. For simplicity we shall consider *consecutive* periods, but we shall not require the first forecast to be for the next period immediately after the sample. We shall denote the sample periods by $t = 1, \ldots, T$, and the forecast periods by $t = T + T' + 1, \ldots, T + T' + N$, where

---

[46] For a test, but not for an interval predictor, we can sometimes avoid the necessity of computing the quadratic form involving $\mathbf{M}_{zz}^{-1}$ in (7.14): Substitute $w\sqrt{1 + 1/T}$ for w_{T+n} in forming the limits of the acceptance region; if the test statistic falls within this truncated acceptance region, it is then unnecessary to compute the quadratic form.

$T' \geqq 0$, so that an arbitrary span of T' periods may intervene after the sample ends and before the series to be forecast begins.

7.21 Consider the reduced-form equation (7.10) under Model 2 (normal) as before, with residuals and forecast errors given by (7.11) as before, except that now we consider forecasts $\hat{y}_{T+n}$ for *several* periods, $n = T' + 1, \ldots, T' + N$, made from a single sample. Under these assumptions, and if there is no structural change in the combined period $t = 1$, $\ldots, T + T' + N$, then the distribution of the N forecast errors $\hat{v}_{T+n}$ (conditional on $\mathbf{z}_1, \ldots, \mathbf{z}_T, \mathbf{z}_{T+T'+1}, \ldots, \mathbf{z}_{T+T'+N}$ but not conditional on $v_1, \ldots, v_T$) is joint normal, with means zero. To obtain its variances and covariances, start with expressions for $\hat{v}_{T+n}$ and $\hat{v}_{T+m}$ from (7.11) and proceed as in (7.12)–(7.13), using the symbol δ_{mn} for the so-called Kronecker delta (defined as 1 if $m = n$ and 0 otherwise) and defining a_{mn} by the last equality below:

$$(7.15) \quad \text{cov}\,(\hat{v}_{T+n}, \hat{v}_{T+m})$$

$$= \text{cov}\left\{\left[\pi_K' - p_K' + \sum_{1}^{K-1} (\pi_k - p_k)z_{k,T+n} + v_{T+n}\right],\right.$$

$$\left.\left[\pi_K' - p_K' + \sum_{1}^{K-1} (\pi_k - p_k)z_{k,T+m} + v_{T+m}\right]\right\}$$

$$= \text{var}\, p_K' + \sum_{j=1}^{K-1}\sum_{k=1}^{K-1} z_{j,T+n}z_{k,T+m}\,\text{cov}\,(p_j, p_k) + \text{cov}\,(v_{T+n}, v_{T+m})$$

$$= \omega^2\left[\frac{1}{T} + \mathbf{z}_{T+n}\mathbf{M}_{zz}^{-1}\mathbf{z}_{T+m}' + \delta_{mn}\right] \equiv \omega^2 a_{mn}$$

$$m, n = T' + 1, \ldots, T' + N$$

This expression is of course identical to (7.13) if $m = n$. Thus under this paragraph's assumptions the variance of each of the N forecast errors is the same expression as the variance of the error of a single forecast given by (7.13). Notice that the N different forecast errors based on one sample are *not* independent; the covariances given above for $m \neq n$ are not zero. This is because all the N forecasts depend on the values of the estimates $p_K', p_1, \ldots, p_{K-1}$, and w^2 that occurred in the particular sample.

7.22 Let us denote the row vector of forecast errors from a single sample by $\hat{\mathbf{v}}_f$, thus:

$$(7.16) \qquad \hat{\mathbf{v}}_f = (\hat{v}_{T+T'+1} \quad \cdots \quad \hat{v}_{T+T'+N})$$

(The subscript f distinguishes it from $\hat{\mathbf{v}}$, which is the vector of *sample-period* residuals). And let us denote by $\mathbf{A}$ the $N \times N$ matrix whose elements are a_{mn} [the quantities in square brackets in the next-to-last expression of (7.15)]. Then we have a simple notation for the covariance matrix of the N errors of forecast based on a single sample:

$$(7.17) \qquad\qquad \text{cov}\,(\hat{\mathbf{v}}_f', \hat{\mathbf{v}}_f) = \omega^2\mathbf{A}$$

A consistent estimator of each element $\omega^2 a_{mn}$ of this covariance matrix, or of the whole matrix $\omega^2 \mathbf{A}$, is obtainable by substituting for ω^2 its consistent estimator w^2, as in (7.14). The estimated diagonal element $w^2 a_{nn}$ is what we have earlier called w^2_{T+n}.

7.23 The assumptions and argument of the preceding two paragraphs imply that for a given value of n the distribution of $\hat{v}_{T+n}/w_{T+n}$, that is, of $\hat{v}_{T+n}/w\sqrt{a_{nn}}$ (conditional on all the sample and forecast period z's but not on $v_1, \ldots, v_T$) is the t distribution with $T - K$ degrees of freedom, if Model 2 (normal) applies and the forecast period's structure is the same as the sample period's. Hence under these assumptions, if no structural change occurs, an interval predictor can be made as in (7.9) for each value y_{T+n} ($n = T' + 1, \ldots, T' + N$) that is to be forecast. But it must be remembered that the confidence coefficient $\epsilon_2 - \epsilon_1$ is *not* the proportion of the N forecast intervals *from this particular given sample* that can be expected to enclose the corresponding true values of $y_{T+T'+1}, \ldots, y_{T+T'+N}$.[47] It is instead (as in 7.7 and 7.19) the proportion of the *infinite* number of intervals for y_{T+n}, each based on a separate independent sample, that will enclose the corresponding true value of y_{T+n}, n being fixed at any value between $T' + 1$ and $T' + N$ inclusive.

7.24 The errors of forecast $\hat{v}_{T+n}$ ($n = T' + 1, \ldots, T' + N$) can be used to form a statistic for a predictive test. Analogous to the simple regression case described in 7.2–16, the *maintained hypothesis* here is that equation (7.10) and Model 2 (normal) apply during both the sample period *and* the prediction period, and that the structure is constant during the sample period. The *tested hypothesis*, which again we shall refer to as H_0 for brevity, is that the structure throughout the prediction period is the same as in the sample period (but note that now there are several predetermined variables rather than just one, and several values of y_t to be forecast rather than just one). The test statistic should depend on all of the N forecast errors. A possible statistic involves the mean of the N errors, $\sum \hat{v}_{T+n}/N$, and indeed a test can be based on this statistic. It would have the advantage of being able to distinguish a predominantly negative set of errors from a predominantly positive set, and the disadvantage that an equation that makes huge errors in opposite directions can pass the test if the errors offset each other on the average. (That this is indeed a disadvantage can be seen by considering whether the authorities responsible for countercyclical policy should be satisfied with a real national income forecasting equation that often makes large errors, but whose positive and negative errors average out to about zero over periods as

---

[47] This proportion, instead of being equal to $\epsilon_2 - \epsilon_1$, will vary from sample to sample, being practically 1 for some examples and practically zero for others, for reasons explained in 7.8. The expected value of this proportion over all possible samples, however, is $\epsilon_2 - \epsilon_1$.

long as a decade—such as a simple 3 per cent growth trend, for example.)

7.25 A better statistic for the hypothesis H_0 (stated in the preceding paragraph) in many cases is one involving a suitably weighted sum of squares of the forecast errors (and cross products too, since the errors are correlated), for such a statistic can detect large forecast errors even when they are offsetting on the average. We make use of an F test with N and $T - K$ degrees of freedom, which is a generalization of the F test with 1 and $T - K$ degrees of freedom for the statistic $(\hat{v}_{T+n}/w_{T+n})^2$ described in 7.16 for the case of *one* forecast. To obtain this generalized F test, we call upon a well-known theorem,[48] which proves that if $\hat{\mathbf{v}}_f$ is a row vector of N jointly normally distributed random variables with means zero and with variance-covariance matrix $\omega^2 \mathbf{A}$, then the quadratic form $\hat{\mathbf{v}}_f(\omega^2\mathbf{A})^{-1}\hat{\mathbf{v}}_f{}'$ has the χ^2 distribution with N degrees of freedom. (Observe that this quadratic form is a weighted sum of squares and cross products of the N forecast errors, and that, other things being equal, the larger the variance of any particular error $\hat{v}_{T+n}$ the smaller the weight assigned to its square.) Therefore, if the hypothesis H_0 is true, the quantity $\hat{\mathbf{v}}_f(\omega^2\mathbf{A})^{-1}\hat{\mathbf{v}}_f{}'/N$ is the ratio of an estimator of ω^2 to ω^2 itself, the estimator being based on the N forecast-period observations; if the hypothesis H_0 is false, the quantity $\hat{\mathbf{v}}_f(\omega^2\mathbf{A})^{-1}\hat{\mathbf{v}}_f{}'$ is the ratio of an estimator of a variance different from ω^2 to ω^2 itself. Hence the quantity $\hat{\mathbf{v}}_f(\omega^2\mathbf{A})^{-1}\hat{\mathbf{v}}_f{}'/N$ is an appropriate numerator for an F test. The denominator is provided by the quantity w^2/ω^2, which under the maintained hypothesis (stated in the preceding paragraph) is the ratio of an estimator of ω^2 to ω^2 itself, regardless of whether H_0 is true, this estimator being based on the $T - K$ degrees of freedom available in the sample period. Hence for testing the hypothesis H_0 that the structure throughout the forecast period is the same as the constant structure assumed by the maintained hypothesis for the sample period [including equation (7.10) and Model 2 (normal)], the F statistic, with N and $T - K$ degrees of freedom, is as follows:

$$(7.18) \qquad F(N, T - K) = \frac{\hat{\mathbf{v}}_f \mathbf{A}^{-1} \hat{\mathbf{v}}_f{}'}{Nw^2}$$

7.26 The probability statement associated with this statistic if the hypothesis H_0 and the maintained hypothesis are true is as follows (see footnote 42 above):

$$(7.19) \qquad \text{Pb}\left(F_{\epsilon_1} \leqq \frac{\hat{\mathbf{v}}_f \mathbf{A}^{-1} \hat{\mathbf{v}}_f{}'}{Nw^2} \leqq F_{\epsilon_2}\right) = \epsilon_2 - \epsilon_1 > 0$$

[48] See Wilks [1943], pp. 103–105. This theorem, and the possibility of basing an F test on its implications in this situation, were called to my attention by Leo A. Goodman in a discussion of the problem, for which I express my appreciation.

The choice of ϵ_1 and ϵ_2 will determine the lower and upper acceptance limits F_{ϵ_1} and F_{ϵ_2} for the test, and the probability of type I error will be $\epsilon_2 - \epsilon_1$. The best choice of ϵ_1 and ϵ_2 will depend in part on what alternative hypothesis is thought to be most likely in case H_0 is false. In the unlikely event that we were sure that no structural change could occur except a decrease in ω^2 (the variance of the disturbance v) and we wanted to detect this if it occurred, then it would be appropriate to put all of the rejection region in the lower tail (i.e., $\epsilon_1 > 0$ and $\epsilon_2 = 1$). In the more likely event that we are sure that ω^2 may increase but will *not* decrease, whereas other parameters may change in either direction, it is appropriate to put all of the rejection region in the upper tail (i.e., $\epsilon_1 = 0$ and $\epsilon_2 < 1$). In certain cases where we are sure about the directions in which all slopes and the intercept of the equation may change, it may be desirable to seek a different test statistic, perhaps even one involving $\sum \hat{v}_{T+n}/N$ as suggested in 7.24, that will be more sensitive to the *direction* of forecast errors than is the statistic used here.

    7.27   When more than one value of a variable is to be forecast from a single sample, if the number of postsample observations is large enough to afford enough degrees of freedom, the equation or model can be fitted to the postsample observations alone, and a t test can be used to compare each estimate so obtained with the corresponding sample-period estimate. This is often impractical because we do not like to delay performing the test until the number of postsample observations available exceeds the number of parameters to be estimated, that is, until $N > K$, which we must do with such a test in order to get any degrees of freedom at all.

    7.28   If first differences of data are used instead of raw data in fitting equations like (7.10), all the foregoing remarks in this section continue to apply provided we discuss inference about Δy rather than about y.

    7.29   Suppose the conditions of Model 2 are thought to be satisfied, but the disturbances are not thought to be normal. Then the least-squares estimators of the equation's slope and intercept parameters are asymptotically normal, and hence the forecast errors are asymptotically normal except for the contribution of the forecast-period disturbances v_{T+n} [see the last expression in equation (7.11)]. If the part of $\hat{v}_{T+n}$ that depends on sample results is large relative to v_{T+n}, then the non-normality of v_{T+n} will not itself create any substantial departure of $\hat{v}_{T+n}$ from normality. The inference procedures of this section can be expected to give rough guides in the non-normal case.

    7.30   Suppose Model 3 applies rather than Model 2, that is, there are lagged endogenous variables in the model. Then in general the least-squares estimators of the equation's parameters are not unbiased, and hence the means and variances and covariances of the forecast errors in small samples are only approximately as given earlier in this section for Model 2 (normal). Furthermore, if forecasts are made for periods farther into the future (after the end of the sample period) than the shortest lag in the dependent variable, so that predicted rather than actual values of some of the predetermined variables must be used in some of the forecasts, then these predetermined variables cannot be conceptually held fixed in repeated samples, and the foregoing results are then only approximate at best, even for infinite samples.

7.31 So far in this section we have dealt only with a *single* reduced-form equation such as (7.10), and with forecasts of the value of its one dependent variable in one or more postsample periods. In many cases forecasts of several jointly dependent variables in a model will be made, each from its own reduced-form equation. Each can be dealt with separately according to the methods of this section. Sometimes it will be desirable to make joint interval forecasts of two or more endogenous variables, or joint tests of the forecast errors of two or more such variables, in analogy to the joint estimators and tests mentioned in 3.18. The interested reader may consult Hooper and Zellner [1961].

7.32 *Tolerance intervals* have sometimes been used for the same purposes that the foregoing interval predictors and predictive tests are meant to serve. A tolerance interval is an interval statistic (usually made symmetrical about a point estimator) designed to have a stated probability γ of enclosing *at least a specified proportion P of the individuals in some interesting population.*[49] If we attempt to forecast a future value of y from a sample of size T, we determine the half width of a tolerance interval by a number k chosen so that

(7.20)   Pb [the proportion of samples for which $\hat{y}_{T+n} \pm kw_{T+n}$

$$\text{encloses } y_{T+n} \text{ is} \geqq P] = \gamma$$

Suppose we wish to test the hypothesis H_0 that the forecast-period structure is the same as the structure assumed by the maintained hypothesis for the sample period. The method advocated in the works cited in the preceding footnote is to construct a tolerance interval for y_{T+n} and accept the hypothesis H_0 if and only if the observed value of y_{T+n} falls in the interval.

7.33 The tolerance-interval equation (7.20) does not enable us to find this test's probability of accepting the hypothesis when true; it merely

---

[49] The basic practical statistical reference concerning tolerance intervals for an independent normally distributed variable is Bowker [1947], containing tables for its use as well as a theoretical discussion. Econometric references using or advocating tolerance intervals for testing forecasts include Marshall [1949]; Wallis [1951], esp. p. 50; Christ [1951], esp. pp. 55–58, 68–80; Klein [1953], esp. pp. 257, 272–273. The meanings of P and γ used here will not appear again after this section is ended.

indicates rather widely spaced lower and upper bounds for this probability, namely, $P\gamma$ and $1 - (1 - P)(1 - \gamma)$, respectively.[50] For example, if $P = \gamma = .90$, these limits are .81 and .99. Of course we can find the exact probability of accepting a true hypothesis for such a test by regarding the interval as a forecast interval and applying equation (7.9) above. This amounts to ignoring the tolerance-interval rationale altogether, and is the appropriate choice in the present context.

7.34 It is interesting to compare the size of the tolerance interval in several illustrative cases with the size of a corresponding prediction interval based on the t distribution and equation (7.9). Consider a univariate normal population obeying the equation

$$(7.21) \qquad\qquad y_t = \alpha + v_t$$

where v_t has mean zero and variance ω^2 and is independent of v_s if $s \neq t$. Let w^2 be the unbiased estimator of ω^2, that is, $w^2 = \sum (y_t - \bar{y})^2/(T - 1)$. Then the tolerance interval for the prediction error $\hat{v}_{T+n}$ ($\hat{v}_{T+n}$ equals $y_{T+n} - \bar{y}$) is $0 \pm kw$, where k is tabulated in Bowker [1947],[51] pp. 102–7, for given values of P, γ, and T. Values of Bowker's k are given in Table 7.1 for $P = .90$ and .99, $\gamma = .90$ and .99, and several different sample sizes.

7.35 The prediction interval for $\hat{v}_{T+n}$, given a probability θ of accepting a true hypothesis, is $0 \pm t_{(1-\theta)/2}w\sqrt{1 + 1/T}$ [using the t distribution for $T - 1$ degrees of freedom, using equations (7.7) and (7.9), and noting that z_{T+n} is zero in the present univariate case). Values of $t_{(1-\theta)/2}\sqrt{1 + 1/T}$ for $\theta = .90$, .99 are given in the last two columns of Table 7.1.[52]

7.36 Note that the prediction interval for given θ is narrower than the tolerance interval whose P equals the given θ (except for $T = \infty$);

---

[50] *Proof*: Since under a true hypothesis the probability that $\hat{y}_{T+n}$ lies in the tolerance interval is P or more in a proportion γ of the cases, and is less than P in $1 - \gamma$ of the cases, we have: lower bound $= \gamma$ (lowest value above P) $+ (1 - \gamma)$ (lowest value below P) $= \gamma P + (1 - \gamma)0 = \gamma P$; upper bound $= \gamma$ (highest value above P) $+ (1 - \gamma)$ (highest value below P) $= \gamma(1) + (1 - \gamma)P = 1 - (1 - P)(1 - \gamma)$. Q.E.D.

[51] He denotes it by K, but we have already used that symbol for the number of parameters in a regression.

[52] For a regression equation with $K - 1$ independent variables and K parameters, the tolerance interval for v_{T+n} is

$$0 \pm kw \sqrt{1 + \frac{1}{T} + \mathbf{z}_{T+n}\mathbf{M}_{zz}^{-1}\mathbf{z}_{T+n}'} \Big/ \sqrt{1 + \frac{1}{T}},$$

where k is from the table in Bowker [1947], using $T - K + 1$ rather than the sample size to enter the table. For such a regression, the prediction interval is given by equations (7.14) and (7.9) above. Accordingly Table 7.1 would need modification if applied to such a regression instead of to a univariate population.

TABLE 7.1   Values of k for Tolerance Intervals $(0 \pm kw)$ That Include with Probability γ at Least a Proportion P of a Univariate Normal Population, Compared with Values of $t_{(1-\theta)/2}\sqrt{1 + 1/T}$ for Prediction Intervals $(0 \pm wt_{(1-\theta)/2}\sqrt{1 + 1/T})$ That Include with Probability θ the Observed Value of the Variable to Be Forecast

	k for Tolerance Interval				$t_{(-\theta)/2}\sqrt{1 + 1/T}$ for Prediction Interval	
Proportion P	.90	.90	.99	.99		
Probability γ	.90	.99	.90	.99		
$1 - (1 - P)(1 - \gamma)$	.9801	.999	.999	.9999		
T d.f. $\diagdown^{P\gamma}$	.81	.891	.891	.9801	$\theta = .90$	$\theta = .99$
11 10	2.46	3.40	3.85	5.31	1.89	3.31
21 20	2.14	2.62	3.34	4.10	1.77	2.91
31 30	2.02	2.37	3.16	3.71	1.72	2.79
61 60	1.88	2.10	2.95	3.28	1.68	2.68
121 120	1.80	1.94	2.82	3.04	1.66	2.63
∞ ∞	1.645	1.645	2.58	2.58	1.645	2.58

Source: 7.32–34 in text.

and furthermore is usually narrower than the tolerance interval whose γ equals the given θ, unless P is much larger than γ and/or the sample is quite large. Table 7.1 also shows the upper and lower limits $P\gamma$ and $(1 - P)(1 - \gamma)$ given by the tolerance-interval rationale for the probability of accepting a true hypothesis; they are quite far apart unless P and γ are both very close to 1. Because of these properties of tolerance intervals, we make no further use of them in this book.

8   PREDICTIVE TESTS, III: TESTS BASED ON SAMPLE-PERIOD RESIDUALS FROM A STRUCTURAL EQUATION OR FROM A REDUCED-FORM EQUATION OBTAINED BY SOLVING AN ESTIMATED STRUCTURE

8.1   In this section we first consider the predictive testing of an individual estimated structural equation in a manner analogous to that used for least-squares reduced-form equations in Section 7. Estimated variances and covariances of the estimates of the structural equation's parameters are required. Later in the section we mention inference regarding forecasts made by estimated reduced-form equations obtained by solving the system of estimated structural equations.

8.2 The essential procedure in a predictive test based on sample-period errors is the same whether applied to a reduced-form or a structural equation: The equation's errors (residuals) in the postsample period are compared with errors in the sample period, and if the former exceed the latter by more than can be attributed to chance at some chosen significance level, the conclusion is that the model used for estimation does not hold for the postsample period. The difference between the two sets of tests is very important. The reduced-form tests can test forecasts, whereas the structural-equation tests cannot, because forecasts cannot be made directly from structural equations (except in special cases where they are already in the reduced form). On the other hand, the structural-equation tests can show which equations of a model are at fault and which are not, but the reduced-form tests cannot, because each reduced-form equation is affected by changes in several structural equations (except in the same special cases). Thus for checking forecasts, the reduced-form tests are appropriate; and for testing one or more structural equations individually for validity in the postsample period, the structural-equation tests are appropriate.

8.3 *Testing structural equations.* Consider a structural equation in our usual notation, such as (6.3) above, and the "forecast" of $y_{1,T+n}$ that its limited-information estimator yields for given values of its other jointly dependent variables $y_2, \ldots, y_H$, and its predetermined variables $z_1, \ldots, z_J$, and the error $\hat{u}_{1,T+n}$ of this "forecast,"[53] as follows:

$$(8.1) \quad \hat{u}_{1,T+n} = y_{1,T+n} - \hat{y}_{1,T+n} = y_{1,T+n} + \sum_{2}^{H} \hat{\beta}_i y_{i,T+n} + \sum_{1}^{J} \hat{\gamma}_j z_{j,T+n}$$

$$= \sum_{2}^{H} (\hat{\beta}_i - \beta_i) y_{i,T+n} + \sum_{1}^{J} (\hat{\gamma}_j - \gamma_j) z_{T+n} + u_{1,T+n}$$

Note that there is no explicit constant term here. Make the assumptions of Model 2 (normal) (see IX.2.3–5). Then for given values of all the predetermined variables in the model ($z_{1t}, \ldots, z_{Jt}, \ldots, z_{Kt}$ for $t = 1, \ldots, T, T + n$), if the structure does not change, the "forecast" error $\hat{u}_{T+n}$ has approximately a normal distribution with mean zero and variance obtained by Rubin [1948][54] as follows (terms are explained below):

(8.2)

$$\operatorname{var} \hat{u}_{1,T+n} \cong \sigma^2 (1 + \mathbf{z}^*_{T+n} \mathbf{M}^{-1}_{z^*z} * \mathbf{z}^{*\prime}_{T+n}) + \operatorname{tr} . \Upsilon \Omega + \mathbf{z}^{**}_{T+n} \mathbf{\Pi}^{**\prime} \Upsilon \mathbf{\Pi}^{**} \mathbf{z}^{**\prime}_{T+n}$$

---

[53] This is not a forecast in any practical sense, because to make it we must wait until period $T + n$ so as to be able to observe the values of the other jointly dependent variables in the equation; hence the quotation marks.

[54] He also gives the approximate *covariance* of "forecast" errors $\hat{u}_i$ and $\hat{u}_j$ from two different structural equations in a model.

where

$$\sigma^2 = \operatorname{var} u_{1t}$$

$\mathbf{z}^*_{T+n}$ = row vector of predetermined variables $z_1, \ldots, z_J$ appearing in the equation to be estimated, at period $T + n$.

$\mathbf{z}^{**}_{T+n}$ = row vector of predetermined variables $z_{J+1}, \ldots, z_K$ *not* appearing in the equation, at period $T + n$.

(8.3)
$\mathbf{M}^{-1}_{z^*z^*}$ = matrix of sample moments of $\mathbf{z}^*$ about zero (the typical element is $\sum_1^T z_{jt}z_{kt}$).

$\mathbf{\Upsilon}$ = asymptotic covariance matrix of $\sqrt{T}$ times the limited-information estimators $\hat{\beta}_1, \ldots, \hat{\beta}_H$.[55]

$\mathbf{\Omega}$ = covariance matrix of disturbances $v_1, \ldots, v_H$ in reduced-form equations for $y_1, \ldots, y_H$.

$\operatorname{tr} \mathbf{\Upsilon\Omega}$ = sum of principal-diagonal elements of $\mathbf{\Upsilon\Omega}$.

$\mathbf{\Pi}^{**}$ = matrix (H rows and $K - J$ columns) of parameters of $\mathbf{z}^{**}$ in reduced-form equations for $y_1, \ldots, y_H$.

8.4 Rubin's derivation of the approximate variance of $\hat{u}_{1, T+n}$ is too complex to be given in full here, but its main outline can be sketched. First the vector ($y_1 \ldots y_H$) for period $T + n$ in (8.1) is expressed in terms of $\mathbf{z}^*_{T+n}$ and $\mathbf{z}^{**}_{T+n}$ and reduced-form parameters and disturbances. Then $\hat{u}_{1, T+n}$ becomes the sum of three approximately uncorrelated quantities with approximately zero means: (1) $u_{1, T+n}$; (2) a function of structural disturbances in period $T + n$ for all equations in the model and of the estimating errors $\hat{\beta} - \beta$ for all equations in the model; and (3) a function of $\mathbf{z}^*$ and $\mathbf{z}^{**}$. Hence the approximate variance of $\hat{u}_{1, T+n}$ is the sum of the approximate variances of the three quantities. σ^2 is the variance of the first, $\operatorname{tr} \mathbf{\Upsilon\Omega}$ is the approximate variance of the second, and the two terms in $\mathbf{z}^*$ and $\mathbf{z}^{**}$ are the approximate variance of the third. Note the resemblance of the terms containing σ^2 to equation (7.13), which gives the approximate variance of a least-squares reduced-form forecast error (the resemblance would be more striking if both were put in the same form with respect to the treatment of the constant term). The term containing $\mathbf{M}^{-1}_{z^*z^*}$ is due to errors in estimating $\gamma_1, \ldots, \gamma_J$, which (it will be remembered from IX.9.16) are estimated from the least-squares regression of $\hat{\beta}y'$ on $\mathbf{z}^*$; hence the resemblance. The terms containing $\mathbf{\Upsilon}$ carry the effect of errors in $\hat{\beta}$.

---

[55] Since $\hat{\beta}_1 = 1$ by normalization, the first row and column of this matrix consist only of zeros.

8.5 Estimates of all the unknown quantities in (8.2) (i.e., σ^2, Υ, Ω, Π^{**}) can be obtained from the sample. Hence an estimate of var $\hat{u}_{1,T+n}$ can be obtained; let us denote it by $s_{1,T+n}$. The statistic $\hat{u}_{1,T+n}/s_{1,T+n}$ is then approximately normally distributed, and therefore we can apply an approximate predictive test to the structural equation in question, after the fashion of 7.11–16.[56] The maintained and tested hypotheses here are analogous to those in the least-squares reduced-form case. The *maintained hypothesis* is that Model 2 (normal) and in particular equation (8.1) are correct for both sample and prediction period $t = 1, \ldots, T$, $T + n$, and that the structure is unchanged during the sample period. The *tested hypothesis*, which we may again call H_0, is that the structural parameters of (8.1) are the same in the prediction period $T + n$ as in the sample period. The remarks in 7.12 concerning the implications of acceptance or rejection of H_0 apply here, with obvious necessary modification because here a *structural* equation is being tested rather than a reduced-form equation. The relevant probability statement if H_0 is true is the following, where z_ϵ is the value exceeded with probability $1 - \epsilon$ by a standard normal deviate, analogous to (7.8) and (7.9) above:

$$(8.4) \qquad \mathrm{Pb}\left(z_{\epsilon_1} \leqq \frac{\hat{u}_{1,T+n}}{s_{1,T+n}} \leqq z_{\epsilon_2}\right) \cong \epsilon_2 - \epsilon_1 > 0$$

Accordingly, if the acceptance region runs from z_{ϵ_1} to z_{ϵ_2}, the probability of Type I error is $1 - (\epsilon_2 - \epsilon_1)$. Of course two-stage least-squares estimates can be used instead of limited-information ones, and the remarks of this paragraph still apply.

8.6 If predictive tests are to be made for a structural equation using "forecasts" for several periods rather than just a single period, then the appropriate test procedure would be a modified form of that described in 8.3–5, to take account of the dependence that arises among such "forecasts" because of their being based on the single sample that is used to estimate the parameters of the structural equation. The modification required would be analogous to that described in 7.20–26 for tests of predictions based on least-squares reduced-form equations.

8.7 The remarks of 7.27–31 concerning the relaxation of assumptions to permit the use of first-difference data, non-normal disturbances, dynamic equations, and/or the system of equations as a whole rather than one at a time have application to structural-equation tests as well as to tests of least-squares reduced-form equations.

8.8 *Testing reduced-form equations obtained by solving the structure.* Now consider point predictions made for the single period $t = T + n$

[56] Of course we can also obtain an approximate interval "predictor" for $y_{1,T+n}$, but this is of little interest since predictions for practical use must be made from reduced-form equations rather than structural equations; see 8.2 above.

from an estimated reduced form that has been obtained by solving a set of estimated structural equations. It was pointed out earlier in IX.12.3–5 that if the model is overidentified, then obtaining the estimated reduced form by solving the estimated structure will make use of the overidentifying restrictions, whereas obtaining the estimated reduced form by ordinary least squares will not, and that therefore the former method is likely to be superior when the model is both overidentified and correctly specified.

8.9 In this discussion we shall express the structure, reduced form, and so forth in terms of some symbols defined earlier in IX.2.2a, IX.2.6, and IX.6.1–2, and some new symbols to be defined below. As usual, unprimed symbols for vectors are rows and primed symbols are columns, and estimators of parameters are denoted by "hats" (circumflex accents) on the Greek symbols for the parameters. The true structure is

$$(8.5) \qquad \mathbf{By}_t' + \mathbf{\Gamma z}_t' = \mathbf{u}_t'$$

The estimated structure is

$$(8.6) \qquad \mathbf{\hat{B}y}_t' + \mathbf{\hat{\Gamma} z}_t' = \mathbf{\hat{u}}_t'$$

The true reduced form is

$$(8.7) \qquad \mathbf{y}_t' = -\mathbf{B}^{-1}\mathbf{\Gamma z}_t' + \mathbf{B}^{-1}\mathbf{u}_t' \equiv \mathbf{\Pi z}_t' + \mathbf{v}_t'$$

The estimated reduced form obtained from solving (8.6) is

$$(8.8) \qquad \mathbf{y}_t = \mathbf{\hat{y}}_t + \mathbf{\hat{v}}_t = \mathbf{\hat{\Pi} z}_t' + \mathbf{\hat{v}}_t'$$

The true value of $\mathbf{y}$ in the prediction period is $\mathbf{y}_{T+n}$, the predicted value is $\mathbf{\hat{y}}_{T+n}$, and the error of prediction is $\mathbf{\hat{v}}_{T+n}$. The covariance matrix of $\mathbf{u}_t$ is $\mathbf{\Sigma}$ (constant for all t), and that of $\mathbf{v}_t$ is $\mathbf{\Omega}$ (also constant for all t), thus:

$$(8.9) \qquad \mathbf{\Omega} = E\mathbf{v}_t'\mathbf{v}_t = \mathbf{B}^{-1}\,\mathbf{\Sigma}\,\mathbf{B}^{-1'}$$

The number of jointly dependent variables is G, as is the number of equations; the number of predetermined variables is K. Thus $\mathbf{B}$, $\mathbf{\Sigma}$, and $\mathbf{\Omega}$ are $G \times G$ matrices, and $\mathbf{\Gamma}$ and $\mathbf{\Pi}$ are $G \times K$.

8.10 We seek the $G \times G$ covariance matrix of the forecasts $\mathbf{\hat{y}}_{T+n}$ of the jointly dependent variables in period $T + n$. This will clearly depend on the variances and covariances of all the estimated parameters in the reduced form, that is, of all the elements of $\mathbf{\hat{\Pi}}$. And these variances and covariances in turn will depend on the variances and covariances of all the estimated parameters of the structure, that is, of all the elements of the matrix $[\mathbf{B} \;\; \mathbf{\Gamma}]$. The results have been worked out in Goldberger, Nagar, and Odeh [1961] and are summarized below.[57]

8.11 We first present some notation (a bit different from theirs) for this context only. Let the row vector of all structural coefficients as follows be denoted by $\boldsymbol{\alpha}$:

$$(8.10) \quad \boldsymbol{\alpha} \equiv (\beta_{11} \cdots \beta_{1G} \;\; \gamma_{11} \cdots \gamma_{1K} \;\; \beta_{21} \cdots \gamma_{2K} \cdots \beta_{G1} \cdots \gamma_{GK})$$

Note that $\boldsymbol{\alpha}$ has $G(G + K)$ components. Let $\hat{\boldsymbol{\alpha}}$ denote the estimator of $\boldsymbol{\alpha}$ obtained by some consistent method (e.g., two-stage least squares or limited information), and let $\delta\boldsymbol{\alpha}$ represent the error of estimate, that is,

$$(8.11) \quad \delta\boldsymbol{\alpha} \equiv \boldsymbol{\alpha} - \hat{\boldsymbol{\alpha}}$$

Note that here δ is an operator applied to $\boldsymbol{\alpha}$, not a number multiplied by $\boldsymbol{\alpha}$. Then let $\boldsymbol{\Theta}$ be the square $G(G + K)$th-order matrix of asymptotic covariances and variances of the elements of $\sqrt{T}\delta\boldsymbol{\alpha}$, thus:

$$(8.12) \quad \boldsymbol{\Theta} \equiv \text{asymptotic cov} (\sqrt{T}\delta\boldsymbol{\alpha}', \sqrt{T}\delta\boldsymbol{\alpha})$$

Let $\boldsymbol{\pi}$ be the row vector of all reduced-form coefficients:

$$(8.13) \quad \boldsymbol{\pi} \equiv (\pi_{11} \;\; \cdots \;\; \pi_{1K} \;\; \pi_{21} \;\; \cdots \;\; \pi_{2K} \;\; \cdots \;\; \pi_{G1} \;\; \cdots \;\; \pi_{GK})$$

Note that $\boldsymbol{\pi}$ has GK components. Let $\hat{\boldsymbol{\pi}}$ denote the estimator of $\boldsymbol{\pi}$ obtained by solving the structure using the estimated structural coefficients $\hat{\boldsymbol{\alpha}}$ mentioned above, and let $\delta\boldsymbol{\pi}$ be the error of estimate:

$$(8.14) \quad \delta\boldsymbol{\pi} \equiv \boldsymbol{\pi} - \hat{\boldsymbol{\pi}}$$

Let $\boldsymbol{\Xi}$ be the square GKth-order asymptotic covariance matrix of elements of $\sqrt{T}\delta\boldsymbol{\pi}$, thus:

$$(8.15) \quad \boldsymbol{\Xi} \equiv \text{asymptotic cov} (\sqrt{T}\delta\boldsymbol{\pi}', \sqrt{T}\delta\boldsymbol{\pi})$$

Let $\boldsymbol{\Psi}$ be a matrix of GK rows and $G(G + K)$ columns obtained by multiplying the $K \times (G + K)$ matrix $(\mathbf{\Pi}' \;\; \mathbf{I})$ by the respective scalar elements β^{gi} of $\mathbf{B}^{-1}$ and arranging the results in blocks, thus:

$$(8.16) \quad \boldsymbol{\Psi} \equiv \begin{bmatrix} \beta^{11}(\mathbf{\Pi}' \;\; \mathbf{I}) & \cdots & \beta^{1G}(\mathbf{\Pi}' \;\; \mathbf{I}) \\ \cdot & & \cdot \\ \cdot & & \cdot \\ \cdot & & \cdot \\ \beta^{G1}(\mathbf{\Pi}' \;\; \mathbf{I}) & \cdots & \beta^{GG}(\mathbf{\Pi}' \;\; \mathbf{I}) \end{bmatrix}$$

[57] Brown [1954] obtained some of these results earlier.

Let $\mathbf{F}_t$ be the $G \times GK$ matrix containing values of the model's predetermined variables for period t arranged repetitiously, as follows:

$$(8.17) \quad \mathbf{F}_t \equiv \begin{pmatrix} z_{1t} & \cdots & z_{Kt} & 0 & \cdots & 0 & \cdots & 0 & \cdots & 0 \\ 0 & \cdots & 0 & z_{1t} & \cdots & z_{Kt} & \cdots & 0 & \cdots & 0 \\ \cdot & & \cdot & & & & & & & \\ \cdot & & \cdot & & & & & & & \\ \cdot & & \cdot & & & & & & & \\ 0 & \cdots & 0 & 0 & \cdots & 0 & \cdots & z_{1t} & \cdots & z_{Kt} \end{pmatrix}$$

Let $\boldsymbol{\Phi}_t$ be the $G \times G$ asymptotic covariance matrix of elements of $\sqrt{T}(\hat{\mathbf{y}}_t - \mathbf{y}_t)$, where $\hat{\mathbf{y}}_t$ is the vector of conditional calculated values of $\mathbf{y}_t$ based on the reduced-form estimates $\hat{\boldsymbol{\pi}}$ and given the values of $z_{1t}, \ldots, z_{Kt}$:

$$(8.18) \quad \boldsymbol{\Phi}_t \equiv \text{asymptotic cov } [\sqrt{T}(\hat{\mathbf{y}}_t - \mathbf{y}_t)', \sqrt{T}(\hat{\mathbf{y}}_t - \mathbf{y}_t)]$$

If we consider the $(T + n)$th period then $\boldsymbol{\Phi}_t$ refers to the desired covariances of the forecast errors of $y_1, \ldots, y_G$ in that period.

8.12 Goldberger, Nagar, and Odeh [1961] show that under assumptions similar to those of our Model 3 (see IX.2.3–5) the two asymptotic covariance matrices $\boldsymbol{\Xi}$ and $\boldsymbol{\Phi}_{T+n}$ are the following functions of the data and parameters of the model:

$$(8.19) \quad \boldsymbol{\Xi} = \boldsymbol{\Psi}\boldsymbol{\Theta}\boldsymbol{\Psi}'$$

$$(8.20) \quad \boldsymbol{\Phi}_{T+n} = \mathbf{F}_{T+n}\boldsymbol{\Xi}\mathbf{F}'_{T+n} + \boldsymbol{\Omega}$$
$$= \mathbf{F}_{T+n}\boldsymbol{\Psi}\boldsymbol{\Theta}\boldsymbol{\Psi}'\mathbf{F}'_{T+n} + \boldsymbol{\Omega}$$

Note that a method for estimating $\boldsymbol{\Theta}$ when two-stage least-squares structural estimation is used has been developed by Theil (see [1958], p. 341, or [1961], p. 342); that a consistent estimator of $\boldsymbol{\Psi}$ is available from consistent estimators of $\mathbf{B}$ and $\boldsymbol{\Pi}$; that a consistent estimator of $\boldsymbol{\Omega}$ is available; and that $\mathbf{F}_t$ is observable (or arbitrary values can be assumed as conditions for the forecast); so that consistent estimators of both $\boldsymbol{\Xi}$ and $\boldsymbol{\Phi}_{T+n}$ can be obtained. Approximate covariances for samples of size T can then be obtained from (8.19)–(8.20) in the manner of IX.3.34 and IX.9.25–26. The three authors then give illustrative computations for 1948 forecasts from a simple model devised some years ago by Klein (see Model I in Klein [1950], pp. 58–66).

8.13 An additional suggestion might be made here. Forecasts made from a reduced form whose parameters are obtained by solving the limited-information estimates of the structural equations will be more accurate than forecasts made from the least-squares estimates of the reduced form, provided that there are overidentifying restrictions on the structure *and that they are correct*; this follows from the discussion of IX.12.3–5 above. Therefore we might compare forecasts made by the two methods and use the result as a test of overidentifying restrictions on the structural equations: If the least-squares estimators of the reduced form yield forecasts approximately as good as or better than the solved structure, the overidentifying restrictions are to be rejected.

9 PREDICTIVE TESTS, IV: THE ABILITY OF PREDICTIONS TO IMPROVE DECISION MAKING

9.1 We turn now to predictive tests whose acceptance conditions do not depend on the goodness of fit of the equations in the sample period but depend instead on some idea of the maximum size of error permissible if the equations are to be useful for the decision purpose at hand. Even though an equation or a model may pass the predictive tests described in Sections 7 and 8, its sample-period residuals and its prediction errors may still be larger than those obtainable by some simpler method or may be so large as to render the equation or model useless. This section's tests are meant to show whether this is the case. We first describe the so-called naïve model tests and then offer a few suggestions for other test procedures.

9.2 The naïve model tests are a family of tests consisting essentially of comparing the errors of prediction made by the model or equation in question with the errors made by a "naïve model," that is, by a very simple hypothesis set up as a sort of straw man to see whether the model or equation in question can knock it down. The naïvest of the naïve models, which has been called naïve model I, says simply that next period's value of any variable will be equal to this period's value plus a random normal disturbance; naïve model II says that it will equal this period's value plus the change from last period to this period plus a random normal disturbance.[58] Naïve model II is a reasonable one for any variable that shows monotonic trends for fairly long periods at a time. Naïve model I is a reasonable one for any variable that fluctuates about a fairly steady average value. Both of these naïve models are crude forecasting devices, and hence it is appropriate to set their errors against the forecasting errors made by reduced-form equations. If a reduced-form equation does not make more accurate forecasts for the purpose at hand than a naïve model, it is clearly not a very useful forecasting device.

9.3 Let us formalize naïve model I and the test based on it. This naïve model assumes that the current value of a variable y is equal to

[58] Marshall [1949]; Christ [1951], p. 56.

the preceding value plus a random normal disturbance w^I with zero mean and constant variance, thus:

$$(9.1) \qquad y_t = y_{t-1} + w_t^I$$

If we denote naïve model I's forecast of y_t by $\hat{y}_t^I$, we can express it as follows:

$$(9.2) \qquad \hat{y}_t^I = y_{t-1}$$

Its error of forecast, denoted by $\hat{w}_t^I$, is then

$$(9.3) \qquad \hat{w}_t^I = y_t - \hat{y}_t^I = y_t - y_{t-1} = \Delta y_t$$

The test consists in comparing the forecast error $\hat{w}_{T+n}^I$ of naïve model I in period $T + n$ with the forecast error $\hat{v}_{T+n}$ made in period $T + n$ by the reduced-form equation in question. This is done for each value of n for which forecasts are made. If the reduced-form forecasts are sufficiently more accurate than the naïve model forecasts, the reduced-form equation may be accepted. "Sufficiently more accurate" can be interpreted in terms of the number of cases in which the reduced form's error is less than the naïve model's, or the extent to which the arithmetic mean of the reduced-form errors is less than that of the naïve model's, or the extent to which the sum of squares of the reduced-form errors (perhaps appropriately weighted) is less than that of the naïve model's, and so forth; we can weight the errors in different periods in accordance with some idea of their importance (e.g., see 9.8 below).

9.4 Naïve model II says that y_t is equal to y_{t-1} plus the change $y_{t-1} - y_{t-2}$ plus a random normal disturbance w_t^{II} with zero mean and constant variance, thus:

$$(9.4) \qquad y_t = y_{t-1} + y_{t-1} - y_{t-2} + w_t^{II} = y_{t-1} + \Delta y_{t-1} + w_t^{II}$$
$$= 2y_{t-1} - y_{t-2} + w_t^{II}$$

Its forecast of y_t is

$$(9.5) \qquad \hat{y}_t^{II} = y_{t-1} + \Delta y_{t-1} = 2y_{t-1} - y_{t-2}$$

Its error of forecast is

$$(9.6) \qquad \hat{w}_t^{II} = y_t - \hat{y}_t^{II} = y_t - 2y_{t-1} + y_{t-2} = \Delta y_t - \Delta y_{t-1}$$

Again the test consists in comparing the error of the reduced-form equation for each period with the error of naïve model II for the same period.

9.5 For variables undergoing steady rapid growth, an exponential growth trend would be preferable to the linear one of naïve model II. Accordingly, naïve model III might be set up as follows: This period's value of y is equal to last period's times the ratio of last period's to the preceding period's, plus a random normal disturbance w^{III} with mean zero and variance increasing exponentially with time.

$$(9.7) \qquad y_t = \frac{y_{t-1}}{y_{t-2}} y_{t-1} + w_t^{III}$$

Its forecast of y_t is

$$(9.8) \qquad \hat{y}_t^{III} = \frac{y_{t-1}}{y_{t-2}} y_{t-1} = \frac{y_{t-1}^2}{y_{t-2}}$$

and its error is

$$(9.9) \qquad \hat{w}_t^{III} = y_t - \hat{y}_t^{III} = y_t - \frac{y_{t-1}^2}{y_{t-2}}$$

Its relative error is

$$(9.10) \qquad \frac{\hat{w}_t^{III}}{y_t} = \frac{\hat{y}_t^{III}}{y_t} - 1 = \frac{y_{t-1}^2}{y_t y_{t-2}} - 1$$

9.6 The real power of a naïve model test appears only on occasions when the forecast of the reduced-form equation under test differs substantially from that of the naïve model, for only then is there a chance to discover a substantial difference between the forecasting abilities of the two. Hence if naïve model I is being used, the test should be confined to periods for which the reduced form forecasts a substantial change in the variable. Similarly, if naïve model II or III is being used, the test should be confined to periods for which the reduced form forecasts a substantial deviation of the variable from the linear or exponential trend defined by the two preceding observations.

9.7 If a naïve model test is applied to structural equations instead of reduced-form equations, the test result may depend on the variable that is chosen for the naïve model to predict. This problem does not arise with reduced-form forecasts, for a reduced-form equation contains only one endogenous variable, and hence there is only one appropriate choice of variable for the naïve model to forecast. But a structural equation ordinarily contains more than one endogenous variable. The following example, using naïve model I, will make the point clear. Suppose a consumption equation has been estimated as follows,

$$(9.11) \qquad \hat{c}_t = 28 + 0.8 y_t$$

or what is the same thing normalized on the variable y instead of on c,

$$(9.12) \qquad \hat{y}_t = -35 + 1.25 c_t$$

Now suppose that the observed data for c and y in two succeeding periods are as follows:

period	c	y	Δc	Δy
$t-1$	185	212	—	—
t	180	200	-5	-12

Then the prediction of c_t from the consumption equation would be 28 + 160 = 188, in error by −8, which is worse than naïve model I, whose error is only −5. And the prediction of y_t from the consumption equation would be −35 + 225 = 190, in error by 10, which is better than naïve model I, whose error is −12. What then is the verdict? Is the structural equation's error greater than the error of naïve model I or not? Without some rule for dealing with such cases as this, naïve model tests cannot be applied to structural equations. Most structural equations with unknown parameters are supposed to describe the behavior or operation of some sector or feature of the economy, and we can choose to perform the naïve model test with the variable that that sector or feature of the economy is supposed to affect most directly, for example, consumption in a consumption equation, stock of money in a liquidity preference equation, and so forth.[59]

9.8 For certain purposes it is important to forecast the arrival of turning points in economic time series, such as the peaks and troughs of business cycles. Naïve models I–III are unable to do this at all. If an econometric model forecasts all turning points (i.e., if its forecast value of Δy changes sign at every turning point), and if it also gives no false signals of turning points (i.e., if its forecast value of Δy changes sign *only* at turning points), then the model may be very valuable even though in nonturning-point periods it does considerably worse than any of the three naïve models mentioned. [A naïve model IV could be devised, which simply forecasts that the next turning point will occur after a rise (or fall) of the same duration as the last preceding observed rise (or fall), and the resulting forecasts could be compared with those of the econometric model in question.]

9.9 A related kind of test procedure is simply to inquire whether the prediction errors of the equation or model in question are small enough to permit the equation or model to be useful for the particular purpose at hand. Very little has been done along this line as yet, possibly because econometric model builders have been occupied in attempting to develop models that can successfully meet the other tests of the kinds discussed above. But clearly it is an extremely important type of test procedure. Suppose, for example, that a model were devised for the purpose of forecasting the changes in national income that would take place in the absence of any government influence, so that the government could tell in advance what was the appropriate policy to achieve something like full employment without inflation. If such a model is to be successful, it must at least lead to forecasts that are accurate enough so that national income fluctuates less when policies based on the model's forecasts are

[59] This is what Marshall did in testing the structural equations of one of Klein's models. See Marshall [1949], or a resume in Christ [1951], pp. 56–57.

put into effect than it would if no policy were put into effect.[60] Any model that is to be used for a practical purpose must justify itself on some such pragmatic grounds.[61]

QUESTIONS AND PROBLEMS

1.1. Suppose that $s_1{}^2$ and $s_2{}^2$ are unbiased estimators of two variances $\sigma_1{}^2$ and $\sigma_2{}^2$, based on two independent samples of independent normal observations with N_1 and N_2 degrees of freedom, respectively. Show that if $\sigma_1{}^2$ and $\sigma_2{}^2$ are equal, the ratio $s_1{}^2/s_2{}^2$ has the F distribution with N_1 and N_2 degrees of freedom, and if $\sigma_1{}^2 \neq \sigma_2{}^2$, it does not. How would the distribution of $s_1{}^2/s_2{}^2$ deviate from that of F if $\sigma_1{}^2 > \sigma_2{}^2$? If $\sigma_1{}^2 < \sigma_2{}^2$?

1.2. Suppose that a sample of ten independent normal observations of x yields $\sum (x - \bar{x})^2 = 90$, and that an independent sample of eight independent normal observations of y yields $\sum (y - \bar{y})^2 = 56$. Construct a test of the hypothesis that var $x =$ var y, against the alternative that var $x >$ var y. What statistic would you use? What is the acceptance region if the significance level is to be .05? What is the value of the statistic, given these data? Is the hypothesis accepted or rejected by the given data?

1.3. Using the data of the preceding problem, test the hypothesis that var $x = 12$ against the alternative that var $x \neq 12$, using a significance level of .10. Answer the questions that are asked in question 1.2.

1.4. Consider a sample of 18 independent observations from a normal population, and suppose that $\bar{x} = 11.7$ and $\sum (x - \bar{x})^2 = 153$. Construct a test of the hypothesis that the true mean Ex is equal to 13, with a significance level of .05, (a) against the alternative that $Ex \neq 13$, (b) against the alternative that $Ex < 13$. Answer the questions for each that are asked in question 1.2.

1.5. For what number of degrees of freedom is the acceptance region of a symmetrical two-tail t test about 20% wider than for an infinite number of degrees of freedom (a) at the .02 level of significance, (b) at the .10 level of significance, (c) at the .20 level of significance?

3.1. Using the notation of Section 3, write down in full each of the following regression equations:

(a) The one containing the coefficient $p_{31.245}$.
(b) The one whose correlation coefficient is $R_{4.12}$.
(c) The one whose constant term is $a_{2.134}$.
(d) The one whose disturbance is $v_{2.431}$.

3.2. Express the estimated slope of a simple regression in terms of the sample correlation coefficient and the sample variances of the two variables.

3.3. Under what conditions (if any) are the simple regression coefficients p_{xy} and p_{yx} equal?

---

[60] This point has been developed in Friedman [1953].
[61] Theil [1966] deals with practical economic forecasting.

3.4. For the single-equation regression model $y' = Z'\pi' + v'$ in IX.5.2, verify the following statements:

(a) $1 - R^2 = \dfrac{y[I - Z'(ZZ')^{-1}Z]y'}{yy'}$

(b) $R^2 = \dfrac{yZ'(ZZ')^{-1}Zy'}{yy'}$

3.5. Express the partial correlation of x_1 and x_4, for x_2 and x_3 held constant, in terms of multiple correlations from regression equations (a) where x_1 is the dependent variable, (b) where x_4 is the dependent variable.

3.6. Suppose that your research assistant reported the following results in several different regression problems. In which cases could you be sure that an error had been made?

(a) $R^2_{0 \cdot 12} = .891$ and $R^2_{0 \cdot 123} = .863$.

(b) $\bar{R}^2_{4 \cdot 56} = .760$ and $\bar{R}^2_{4 \cdot 567} = .748$.

(c) $r^2_{01} = .823$ and $r^2_{02} = .792$ and $R^2_{0 \cdot 12} = .891$.

(d) $r^2_{45} = .227$ and $r^2_{47} = .126$ and $R^2_{4 \cdot 57} = .701$.

(e) Same as (d) but with $r^2_{57} = 0$.

(f) $m_{xx}m_{yy} - m^2_{xy} = -1732.86$.

3.7. Verify the relation between t^2_{01} and r^2_{01} in 3.11.

3.8. What value of the squared partial correlation coefficient $r^2_{01 \cdot 2 \ldots K}$ corresponds to a value of 2 for the t statistic $p_{01 \cdot 2 \ldots K}/s(p_{01 \cdot 2 \ldots K})$ when the number of degrees of freedom is 5? 10? 20? 50? 100? Infinite?

3.9. Consider a regression equation $y = \alpha + \pi x + v$, where v is a disturbance that is not known to be normal, and where the assumptions of Model 2 are satisfied, x being exogenous. Consider a test of the hypothesis that π has some particular value π_0, based on the ratio of the least-squares estimate p to its estimated standard error $s(p)$. What can you advise about the use of the t table for choosing the acceptance region of this test? What about the normal table? Explain.

3.10. Answer the preceding question for a structural equation that has been estimated by the limited-information method.

3.11. Perform tests of significance on the parameters of the equations tabulated in Chapter XI, Sections 4 and 6.

3.12. Can the sum of squared residuals from an estimated equation ever exceed the sum of squared deviations of the "dependent" variable from its mean? Explain. (See 3.31.)

3.13. Compare the expression $(YY')^{-1}YSY'$ from the Hooper trace-correlation equation (3.36) with the expression $yZ'(ZZ')^{-1}Zy'/yy'$, which is put equal to R^2 in question 3.4(b). Comment on the relationship.

4.1. Explain why a time series $x_1, x_2, x_3, \ldots$ that alternates between high and low values in successive periods has negative serial correlation, and why one that has long waves has positive serial correlation. Can you devise a regular periodic series that has zero serial correlation? (This question refers to correlation between x_t and x_{t-1}.)

4.2. If $x_1, \ldots, x_T$ are independently and identically distributed, with constant mean μ and variance σ^2, what is the expected value of

$$\sum_2^T (x_t - x_{t-1})^2/(T-1)?$$

4.3. In a reduced form with a sample size of 30, what conclusion would you draw for an equation having a constant term and (a) three predetermined variables where $d = 1.55$, (b) four predetermined variables where $d = 1.55$, (c) four predetermined variables where $d = 2.25$?

4.4. Sketch an intuitive proof of the statement (made in 4.14) that for a just-identified equation containing no lagged endogenous variables, the Durbin-Watson statistic is appropriate for testing for serial correlation of disturbances, where the number of degrees of freedom is the number of nondummy exogenous variables in the reduced form.

4.5. Can the Durbin-Watson statistic be used to test the linearity of a time-series equation that contains no trend variable? Explain.

4.6. Perform tests of serial correlation of disturbances where possible for the equations tabulated in Chapter XI.

4.7. Using as an example the model $y_t = \alpha y_{t-1} + u_t$ where $u_t = \rho u_{t-1} + e_t$ and where e_t is independently and identically distributed with zero mean and constant variance, assess the validity of the Durbin-Watson serial correlation test in the presence of a lagged endogenous variable.

5.1. For the Theil-Goldberger mixed estimator, justify (a) the last step in equation (5.7), and (b) equation (5.8).

5.2. Will the estimated minimum variance ratio $\beta W^* \beta'/\beta W \beta'$ have a distribution whose central location parameter exceeds 1 in the limit for infinite samples if the overidentifying restrictions used in estimating a structural equation are incorrect? Explain.

5.3. Can you reconcile these two statements, made in 5.21 and 5.23, about the estimated minimum variance ratio l_1?

(a) $T \log_e l_1$ is asymptotically distributed as chi square with $K - J - H + 1$ degrees of freedom.

(b) $(l_1 - 1)(T - K)/(K - J - H - 1)$ is asymptotically distributed as F with $K - J - H + 1$ and $T - K$ degrees of freedom.

Hint: If $|x| < 1$, then $\log_e (1 + x)$ can be expressed as the infinite series

$$x - \frac{x^2}{2} + \frac{x^3}{3} - \frac{x^4}{4} + \cdots$$

Comment on the difference between the two approximate distributions that result from (a) and (b).

6.1. Can you think of exceptions to the statement in 6.8 that the error of a postsample forecast from an equation must on the average be *larger* than the standard deviation of the sample-period disturbances of the equation? Explain.

6.2. Are there cases where the forecast $\hat{y}_{it} + \hat{v}_{i,t-1}$ might be appropriate while the transformation of all data to first differences might not? (See 6.4.)

6.3. (a) Defend the proposition that it makes sense to divide the sample data into two parts, using one part to estimate parameters, and using the other part to test the theory underlying the estimates.

(b) Attack the same proposition.

6.4. Compare and contrast forecasts made from a reduced-form equation and from a structural equation. What are the uses of each?

7.1. Consider the error of forecast $\hat{v}_{T+n}$ as given in equation (7.4). What are its mean and variance *conditional upon both the set of disturbances* $v_1, \ldots, v_T$ *and the set of observed values of the exogenous variable* $z_1, \ldots, z_T, z_{T+n}$?

7.2. What assumptions (if any) would be sufficient to guarantee that the N forecasting errors from a regression equation such as (7.10) for the postsample period $(t = T' + 1, \ldots, T' + N)$ are independent, so that their covariances given in (7.15) are zero? Explain.

7.3. Consider an estimate of the regression equation (7.10) under Model 2 (normal), and the use of N forecasting errors $(t = T' + 1, \ldots, T' + N)$ for a test of the hypothesis that the structure during the forecast period is the same as during the sample period. Suppose the alternative hypothesis is that some particular slope π_k (where $1 \leq k \leq K$) is greater during the forecast period than in the sample period. Which of the following tests would you prefer: (a) a t test based on the mean forecast error $\sum \hat{v}_{T+n}/N$, or (b) the F test discussed in 7.25–26? Explain.

7.4. Suppose the regression equation (7.10) obeys Model 2, with non-normal disturbances. What can you say about the asymptotic behavior of the distributions of the following statistics based on a sample of size T, as $N \to \infty$, that is, as both the length of the forecast period and the number of forecasts go to infinity?

(a) The typical forecast error $\hat{v}_{T+n}$, where $1 \leq n \leq N$, conditional on the exogenous variables in periods $t = 1, \ldots, T, T' + n$?

(b) The mean forecast error, $\sum \hat{v}_{T+n}/N$, conditional upon the exogenous variables in all periods $t = 1, \ldots, T, T' + 1, \ldots, T' + N$?

7.5. In what kinds of situations would tolerance intervals be most useful?

7.6. Can you give an intuitive explanation of why the *tolerance interval* for any probability $\gamma < 1$ and a given proportion P, and the *prediction interval* with confidence coefficient equal to P, are (a) the same for infinite samples, (b) different for finite samples, the tolerance interval being wider? (See Table 7.1.)

8.1. What difficulties do you see in the test of overidentifying restrictions that is proposed in 8.13?

9.1. What value of R^2 would be needed in a regression equation for real GNP for 1946 to the present, in order that the root-mean-square residual should be no larger than half of 1% of real GNP for the most recent year?

9.2. What average size of forecast error for GNP, expressed as a percentage of GNP, would you regard as small enough to render an econometric forecasting model useful for policy-making purposes? Explain.

CHAPTER XI

A Simple Illustrative Model
of the United States Economy,
1929–1941 and 1946–1959

This chapter presents some empirical results to illustrate a few of the theoretical points made in earlier chapters. A very simple illustrative seven-equation linear econometric model of the United States for 1929–1941 and 1946–1959 is constructed on the basis of theoretical and empirical considerations, and the construction process is described. The data are described and presented. Estimates of structural equations and reduced forms are obtained by least squares and with the aid of the two-stage least-squares and limited-information methods. Some nonpredictive and predictive tests are applied. They reveal important weaknesses in the simple model presented.

1 INTRODUCTION

1.1 In this chapter we set forth a simple linear model for the United States economy and discuss its construction, analysis, and testing in order to give examples of some of the techniques presented in earlier chapters.

1.2 To show the actual process used in formulating this model, we avoid the rather common practice of beginning with a full-blown model. Instead, we first describe the general features thought to be desirable for our purpose at the time the work was begun and present several theoretically plausible alternative forms for each of the stochastic equations to be included. Then the construction of the data is described (the sample period is 1929–1941 and 1946–1959). Then preliminary estimates of several plausible forms by least squares are described, and the estimates

579

obtained are examined. Then in the light of these estimates and some theoretical considerations, we describe the choice of one form of each stochastic equation (two for the investment equation) as most promising. (This choice was actually made in the spring of 1961.) The limited-information and two-stage least-squares estimation of each of these chosen forms is described. Reduced-form estimates are obtained, and one form of the investment equation is chosen. The estimates are tested by means of forecasts for 1960, 1961, and 1962, and by some of the tests described in Chapter X.

1.3 Readers who wish to jump ahead and examine the chosen model will find it set forth in 5.17 below, in equations (5.10)–(5.16), omitting (5.11′). Variables are defined in 2.3. Structural estimates are given in Tables 6.1, 6.2, 6.3, and 6.4. Reduced-form estimates are in Table 8.1. And forecasts for 1960–1962 are in Table 9.1.

2 SOME THEORETICAL DISCUSSION OF THE MODEL; NOTATION; THE EQUATIONS, INCLUDING ALTERNATIVE FORMS

2.1 The model to be presented here was designed mainly as an illustrative example, and it has not had the resources devoted to it that would be necessary to make it a substantive contribution to knowledge about the United States economy. The number of equations and variables has intentionally been kept rather small. It was decided to include one consumption equation, one equation to explain private domestic investment behavior, and a small number of other equations so as to build a complete model around the consumption-investment nucleus.

2.2 All flows of income and output and expenditure are in real terms, no attempt being made here to explain variations in either absolute or relative prices. Monetary and financial features of the economy are suppressed. This is a major defect that should be corrected in any serious econometric representation of the United States economy. Another major defect is that no production function is included, so that variations in output are explained in the crude fashion adopted by many followers of Keynes, namely, in terms of effective demand only, ignoring resource limitations. Other deficiencies will be clear to the reader.

2.3 The following notation will be used. Variables are listed in an order convenient for computing their values from sources. Detailed definitions of variables in terms of explicit data sources are given below in Section 3. Not all the variables listed below appear in the equations chosen as most promising. Stocks are in billions of 1954 dollars, and flows are in billions of 1954 dollars per year. The GNP deflator is used for most variables, but the National Income Division has prepared deflated values of some variables with their own specific implicit deflators, which we have used (they are c, g, w_g, x_b). The deflator for i is described in 3.4 below.

$$c = y_1 = \text{real consumption expenditures.}$$
$$i = y_2 = \text{real gross private domestic investment.}$$
$$g = z_{16} = \text{real government purchases plus net exports.}$$
$$w_g = z_{17} = \text{real labor income in general government.}$$
$$x_b = y_6 = \text{real gross business product} = \text{GNP} - w_g.$$
$$s_c = y_4 = \text{real net corporate saving.}$$
$$y = y_5 = \text{real disposable personal income (using consumption's}$$
$$\text{implicit deflator).}$$
$$d = z_{20} = \text{real capital consumption at replacement cost.}$$
$$i_n = i - d = \text{real net private domestic investment.}$$
$$k_{-1} = z_{11} = \text{real net private domestic capital stock on December 31}$$
$$\text{of the preceding year (defined as cumulated net}$$
$$\text{investment beginning with 1929, i.e., } k_{1928} = 0).$$
$$w_b = y_3 = \text{real labor income in business including government}$$
$$\text{enterprise and including imputed labor income of}$$
$$\text{proprietors.}$$
$$p = y_7 = \text{real property income net of depreciation and corporate}$$
$$\text{income tax liability (i.e., real national income, less}$$
$$\text{corporate tax liability, and less real labor income).}$$
$$t_p = z_{18} = \text{real personal tax and nontax payments.}$$
$$= p + w_b + w_g - y - s_c.$$
$$t_b = z_{19} = \text{real indirect business taxes and corporate tax liability}$$
$$\text{plus statistical discrepancy less subsidies.}$$
$$= \text{GNP} - (p + w_b + w_g + d)$$
$$a_{-1} = z_9 = \text{stock market price index on December 31 of the}$$
$$\text{preceding year (Standard and Poor) relative to the}$$
$$\text{GNP deflator.}$$
$$i_{-1} = z_8 \quad \text{Lagged value of variable already mentioned.}$$
$$a_{-2} = z_{10}$$
$$c_{-1} = z_{12}$$
$$(w_b)_{-1} = z_{13}$$
$$(s_c)_{-1} = z_{14}$$
$$p_{-1} = z_{15}$$

Each variable has two symbolic names, one being a letter suggestive of its economic meaning (e.g., y for disposable income, c for consumption, a for asset valuation, etc.), and the other being either y_i ($i = 1, \ldots, 7$) or z_k ($k = 8, \ldots, 20$) for use in programming computer work and in distinguishing jointly dependent variables y_i from predetermined variables

z_k. Do not confuse y (disposable income) with any of the y_i (except y_5). In what follows, the word "real" will often be omitted, but it is to be understood that the model is expressed in real terms nevertheless.

2.4 Consumption c is assumed to depend on expected disposable income, which is assumed in turn to follow the exponentially weighted distributed-lag pattern described in V.7.6–7. Hence the observable explanatory variables for the consumption equation are disposable income y and lagged consumption c_{-1}. The equation was tried both with and without lagged consumption. The two forms are

$$(2.1) \equiv (c1) \qquad c = \beta_{15}y + \gamma_{1,12}c_{-1} + \gamma_{10} + u_1$$

$$(2.2) \equiv (c2) \qquad c = \beta'_{15}y \qquad\qquad\quad + \gamma'_{10} + u_1'$$

Each equation carries a second designation, $(c1)$ for the first consumption equation form and $(c2)$ for the second. Here the primes if any and the first subscript of each parameter and disturbance indicate the equation to which it belongs, for example, β'_{15} is in equation $(c2)$. The second subscript of each parameter indicates the variable to which it is attached, for example, $\gamma_{1,12}$ is the coefficient of variable number 12, which is z_{12}, also called c_{-1} (see the list of variables just above). All slopes are expected to have positive signs in these two equations.

2.5 This book is not the place for an extended discussion of the theory of investment behavior. Some brief remarks must suffice to indicate the considerations behind the two dozen alternative forms that were tried for gross investment and the four that were tried (and rejected) for net investment. It was decided to use a gross rather than a net investment equation, because for each of the four net investment equations that were tried by least squares at an early stage, the gross equation obtained by substituting gross for net investment and re-estimating had similar coefficients but a higher R^2 than the net equation.[1]

2.6 It has often been observed empirically that private investment is correlated with business profits or property income and with business output. Theoretical arguments have been advanced to support this result, for example, by Meyer and Kuh [1957] among others: Property income is regarded as a source of investment financing in an imperfect capital market and also as an indicator of future profitability. Output is important because capital stock is needed to produce it. Hence several equation forms were tried using property income p or gross business output x_b

---

[1] The net investment equations used corresponded to equations $(i2)$, $(i4)$, $(i6)$ and $(i15)$ below (Table 4.2). In each case $1 - R^2$ for the net equation was between 3 and 3.3 times the value of $1 - R^2$ for the corresponding gross equation. The coefficient of x_b was always somewhat smaller in the net equations than in the gross, and the coefficient of k_{-1} was somewhat larger in absolute value in the net than in the gross. See 2.7 below for a possible explanation of the latter.

or both. It is sometimes suggested that gross rather than net property income be used, or that depreciation d be included as a separate variable along with net property income p, on the ground that depreciation expense corresponds to a flow of funds that can be used for gross investment. Accordingly several equations incorporating d were tried.

2.7 One approach to investment theory postulates the existence of a *desired* stock of capital, not necessarily equal to the existing stock, and attempts to explain investment in terms of a desired rate of approach to the desired stock. On this view, net investment should be inhibited (for a given value of the desired stock) if the actual stock is large, and gross investment should also be inhibited unless the desired rate of approach to the desired stock is extremely slow. For example, suppose that firms in the aggregate desire to make up in the current year a fraction θ of the difference between the desired stock k^* and the actual stock k_{-1} at the end of the preceding year. Then net investment i_n will be equal to $\theta k^* - \theta k_{-1}$, where k^* depends on such things as anticipated values of aggregate demand and profit rates, and so forth. Now assume that depreciation is approximately a linear function of existing capital stock k_{-1}, containing the term δk_{-1}. Then gross investment i, equal to $i_n + d$, will be a function containing a linear term $(\delta - \theta)k_{-1}$. Now the value of δ is about .04, since d is about 8 per cent of real GNP, which is in turn about half of the real capital stock. Hence if $\theta > .04$, that is, if firms desire to make up in one year more than about 4 per cent of the difference between desired and actual capital, as seems highly reasonable, the coefficient $\delta - \theta$ of k_{-1} can be expected to be negative in a gross investment equation, but it is not expected to exceed or even to equal 1 in absolute value. Hence several equation forms were tried using k_{-1} as a variable. Lagged investment i_{-1} appears in some forms, introduced by the distributed-lag expectations hypothesis.

2.8 In applying the desired-capital-stock approach to investment, Grunfeld [1960] obtained fruitful results in several time-series studies of individual corporations by assuming that desired stock depends on expected rates of return, which are in turn assumed to be reflected by the valuation of the firm's equity in the stock market. This kind of argument suggests including the level of stock prices (relative to the general price level) as of the end of last year, and possibly also as of the end of the year before last, as explanatory variables for this year's investment. In Grunfeld's study, when such expectations variables are included, they are usually significant, and profits usually become insignificant. Hence several equation forms were tried using the relative stock price index at the end of the previous year, a_{-1}, and sometimes also a_{-2}, with and without property income p.

2.9 If the desired-capital-stock approach is ignored in favor of a hypothesis that investment depends on expected levels of output and/or property income, where these expectations have the familiar exponentially weighted distributed-lag form of V.7.6–7, then lagged investment i_{-1} appears in the investment equation with x_b and/or p, just as lagged consumption appears in the consumption equation in a similar case. The sign of i_{-1} should be positive. Accordingly several equations containing i_{-1} without k_{-1} were tried.

2.10 The list of possible explanatory variables for gross investment suggested by the foregoing paragraphs is thus output x_b, property income p, depreciation d, beginning-of-year capital stock k_{-1}, stock market price levels a_{-1} and a_{-2} at the beginning of the current and preceding years, and lagged investment i_{-1}. Note that of these, only x_b and p are jointly dependent; the others are predetermined. The twenty-four equations tried are not reproduced here, in order to save space, but are given below in Table 4.2 when their least-squares estimates are presented.

2.11 The next step taken in the construction of the model was to decide on the accounting identities to be used. Of course there are many equivalent ways to write a given set of identities. For example, we can write (a) "income equals consumption plus investment" and (b) "income equals consumption plus savings"; then (c) "savings equals investment" is implicit in (a) and (b). Or we can write (a) and (c), whereupon (b) is implicit in them. Since our variables include consumption and investment, we shall need to express the fact that real GNP equals the sum of consumption and investment and government expenditure and net exports, $c + i + g$. We express real GNP as the sum of gross business product x_b and employee compensation in general government w_g. Hence one identity can be

$$(2.3) \qquad x_b + w_g = c + i + g$$

This is used below in 3.4 to define x_b. Since our variables also include disposable income y, we shall need to express the fact that real GNP equals the sum of all gross incomes. Thus we have the following adaptation of the National Income Division's identity between GNP and the sum of gross incomes (which is national income, plus adjusting items consisting chiefly of indirect taxes less subsidies, plus depreciation):

$$(2.4) \qquad x_b + w_g = y + t_p + s_c + t_b + d$$

Since our variables include property income p, we must express the division of national income into property and labor income. The following identity does this, each side being equal to real national income net of corporate income tax liability.

$$(2.5) \qquad p + w_b + w_g = y + t_p + s_c$$

2.12   These three identities can be thought of as defining respectively the jointly dependent variables output x_b, disposable income y, and property income p. The consumption and investment equations can be thought of as explaining respectively the jointly dependent variables consumption c and investment i. Of the remaining variables proposed for the model, all can reasonably be regarded as predetermined except two: business labor income w_b and corporate saving s_c. Hence to complete the model we need two more equations to describe the determination of these two endogenous variables.

2.13   The quantity of labor demanded depends in part on the output to be produced (and in part on other things that this model is too simple to deal with, such as the relative prices and marginal productivity schedules of labor and capital). A distributed-lag model may be helpful here, since hiring and layoff decisions depend in part on *expected* output. Or labor demand might be thought to depend on current and lagged output. Accordingly the following three forms of a labor equation were tried:

$$(2.6) \equiv (w1) \qquad w_b = \beta_{36}x_b + \gamma_{3,13}(w_b)_{-1} \qquad\qquad + \gamma_{30} + u_3$$

$$(2.7) \equiv (w2) \qquad w_b = \beta'_{36}x_b \qquad\qquad\qquad\qquad + \gamma'_{30} + u'_3$$

$$(2.8) \equiv (w3) \qquad w_b = \beta''_{36}x_b \qquad\qquad + \gamma''_{3,21}(x_b)_{-1} + \gamma''_{30} + u''_3$$

All slopes are expected to have positive signs here.

2.14   Corporate dividend payments presumably depend upon the expected level of future corporate profits. If expected corporate profits follow the kind of distributed-lag rule that we have been using (see V.7.6–7), we would then find dividends to be a linear function of current profits and lagged dividends. Letting d_c and p_c temporarily represent corporate dividends and after-tax profits, this could be expressed as follows:

$$(2.9) \qquad d_c = \delta_0 + \delta_1 p_c + \delta_2(d_c)_{-1} \qquad (0 < \delta_1 < 1, 0 < \delta_2 < 1)$$

Now since $d_c + s_c = p_c$, both current and lagged dividends can be removed in favor of current and lagged corporate saving s_c, thus:

$$(2.10) \qquad s_c = -\delta_0 + (1 - \delta_1)p_c - \delta_2(p_c)_{-1} + \delta_2(s_c)_{-1}$$

The model does not contain *corporate* profits p_c as an explicit variable, which a useful practical model should do. To keep the model simple, we take advantage of the fact that there has been a very close linear relationship in the United States between our property income variable p and real corporate profits,

$$(2.11) \qquad\qquad p_c \cong \epsilon + .56p$$

When p_c in (2.10) is expressed in terms of p via (2.11) we have (2.12) below, one of the corporate saving equations that were tried. The other three tried were obtained by dropping one or both of the lagged variables. Here are all four alternatives:

$$(2.12) \equiv (s1) \quad s_c = .56(1 - \delta_1)p + \delta_2(s_c)_{-1} \quad - .56\delta_2 p_{-1} + [-\delta_0 + \epsilon(1 - \delta_1 - \delta_2)] + u_4$$
$$\equiv \beta_{47}p \qquad\qquad + \gamma_{4,14}(s_c)_{-1} + \gamma_{4,15}p_{-1} + \gamma_{40} + u_4$$

$$(2.13) \equiv (s2) \quad s_c = \beta'_{47}p \qquad\qquad\qquad\qquad + \gamma'_{4,15}p_{-1} + \gamma'_{40} + u'_4$$

$$(2.14) \equiv (s3) \quad s_c = \beta''_{47}p \qquad\qquad + \gamma''_{4,14}(s_c)_{-1} \qquad + \gamma''_{40} + u''_4$$

$$(2.15) \equiv (s4) \quad s_c = \beta'''_{47}p \qquad\qquad\qquad\qquad\qquad + \gamma'''_{40} + u'''_4$$

In $(s1)$ the expected signs are positive for the coefficients of p and $(s_c)_{-1}$ and negative for the coefficient of p_{-1}, by (2.9).

2.15 Our description of the work of choosing the model has reached the point where it was decided that the model is to have seven equations, consisting of the three identities (2.3)–(2.5) and four stochastic equations: a consumption function to be chosen as (2.1) or (2.2); an investment equation to be chosen from among twenty-four alternative equations containing some or all of the variables i, x_b, p, d, k_{-1}, a_{-1}, a_{-2}, i_{-1}; a labor equation to be chosen as (2.6) or (2.7) or (2.8); and a corporate saving equation to be chosen from among (2.12)–(2.15). The seven jointly dependent variables are x_b, y, p, c, i, w_b, and s_c. The predetermined variables will be those appearing in the chosen equations; they will be some or all of the variables designated as z_j ($8 \leq j \leq 20$) in 2.3 above. An eighth relationship connects the capital stock k with investment and the preceding capital stock:

$$(2.16) \qquad\qquad k = k_{-1} + i - d$$

Since the current k does not appear in the model, and since k_{-1} is predetermined, the equation need not be regarded as part of the model, but for making forecasts more than one year in advance it must be used to obtain the capital stock on which to base these forecasts.

2.16 Since there are to be seven equations in the model, we have $G = 7$, and the order condition for identifiability requires that at least $G - 1 = 6$ variables must be excluded from each equation (if the only kind of identifying restriction used is the kind that excludes certain variables from certain equations; see VIII.3). The three identities we have chosen contain four predetermined variables: w_g, g, t_p, $t_b + d$. (Note that $t_b + d$ is one variable for identification purposes because t_b and d appear in no other way.) It will turn out, below, that the preferred form of the consumption equation contains lagged consumption c_{-1}. Therefore the model will have *at least* thirteen variables, namely, the four predetermined variables in the identities (just listed), plus c_{-1}, plus a dummy always equal to 1, plus the seven jointly dependent variables. (Other lagged variables may turn out to be in the chosen stochastic equations, but we need not inquire about this now.) Therefore any equation that contains seven or fewer variables (counting the dummy as one) will exclude six or more, and so will satisfy the order condition. All of the equations to be discussed below do contain seven or fewer variables (counting the dummy as one) so all do satisfy the order condition for identifiability.

3 DATA

3.1 All data except stock market price indexes are based on the national income and product statistics of the Department of Commerce. The variables are listed below not in alphabetical order but in an order suitable for computing, leading from those requiring no computing to those requiring the most.

3.2 The reading of the following list is likely to be a dull business. However, it contains implicit or explicit details of a few interesting decisions about the variables that are not described elsewhere in the book, for example, the imputation of labor income to proprietors, the conversion of depreciation from historical to replacement cost, the precise definitions used for property income p and for the tax variables t_p and t_b, and the treatment of the statistical discrepancy and of the errors introduced into identities when they are converted from money terms to real terms using different deflators for different components (these appear in t_p and t_b).

3.3 In general the data from the national accounts for various years are taken from the following Department of Commerce publications:

> 1929–1955: *U.S. Income and Output*, Supplement to the *Survey of Current Business*, 1958 (referred to in the bibliography as U.S. Department of Commerce [1958]).
> 1956–1959: *Survey of Current Business*, July, 1960.
> 1960–1962: *Survey of Current Business*, July, 1963.

For a few time series dealing with employment and labor income, the 1954 issue of *National Income* (a supplement to the *Survey of Current Business*) was used for 1929–1945 because *U.S. Income and Output* carries data back only to 1946 for those series.

3.4 The definitions and sources for data based on national accounts are given below. For brevity, only the table and line numbers from *U.S. Income and Output* are given: for example, the entry "I-2.6" for real gross investment refers to Table I-2, line 6. Code numbers in parentheses denote the various time series used as intermediate stages in the process [e.g., (52), (53), (101), (102), etc.]. Units of flows are billions of 1954 dollars per year. Capital stock is in billions of 1954 dollars. Price indexes are equal to 1.00 in the base period, 1954, except for the stock price index (which is not used to deflate anything).

$c = y_1 = (52)$ = real consumption: I-2.2

$i = y_2 = (53)$ = real gross private domestic investment: I-2.6

$\quad\quad\quad (101)$ = real government purchases: I-2.17

$\quad\quad\quad (102)$ = real net exports: I-2.14

$g = z_{16} = (54)$ = (101) + (102)

$w_g = z_{17} = (55)$ = real general government gross product: I-13.3

$\quad\quad\quad\quad (51)$ = real GNP: I-13.1; equal to $c + i + g$

$x_b = y_6 = (56)$ = real business gross product = (51)–(55)

$\quad\quad\quad (117)$ = undistributed corporate net profits after tax: I-17.9

$\quad\quad\quad (118)$ = corporate inventory valuation adjustment: I-17.11

$\quad\quad\quad (119)$ = excess of wage accruals over disbursements: I-17.13

$\quad\quad\quad (121)$ = GNP deflator (1954 = 1.00): VII-2.1

$s_c = y_4 = (60)$ = real corporate net saving = [(117) + (118) + (119)] ÷ (121)

$\quad\quad\quad (122)$ = disposable personal income: II-1.24

$\quad\quad\quad (123)$ = consumption deflator (1954 = 1.00): VII-2.2

$y = y_5 = (61)$ = real disposable personal income = (122) ÷ (123)

$\quad\quad\quad (124)$ = ratio of current cost depreciation to original cost depreciation in manufacturing (1954 = 1.00): V-13.10

$\quad\quad\quad (125)$ = depreciation, original cost: I-17.2

$\quad\quad\quad (127)$ = gross investment in new construction: I-1.7

$\quad\quad\quad (128)$ = gross investment in producers durables: I-1.10

$\quad\quad\quad (130)$ = real gross investment in new construction: I-2.7

$\quad\quad\quad (131)$ = real gross investment in producers durables: I-2.10

$\quad\quad\quad (133)$ = gross private domestic investment deflator (1954 = 1.0)

$\quad\quad\quad\quad\quad$ = [(127) + (128)] ÷ [(130) + (131)]

$d = z_{20} = (62)$ = real depreciation at current cost

$\quad\quad\quad\quad\quad$ = (124)(125) ÷ (133)

$k_{t-1} = z_{11} = (66)$ = real capital stock, end of year $t - 1$, measuring from $k_{1928} = 0$

= cumulation of $i_s - d_s$ from $s = 1929$ through $s = t - 1$

$$= \sum_{s=1929}^{t-1} (i_s - d_s)$$

(103) = total compensation of employees: I-8.2

(104) = general government compensation of employees: I-12.61

(106) = persons engaged in production, all private industries: VI-16.92

(107) = full-time-equivalent employees, all private industries: VI-13.92

(108) = employee compensation, all private industries: VI-1.92

$w_b = y_3 = (57)$ = real labor income in business including government enterprise and including imputed labor income of proprietors (i.e., total real labor income excluding general government)

$$= \frac{(103) - (104) + [(106) - (107)](108)/(107)}{(121)}$$

(113) = national income: I-8.1

(114) = corporate tax liability: I-8.20

$p = y_7 = (58)$ = real property income net of depreciation and of corporate tax liability

$$= [(113) - (114) - (104)]/121 - w_b$$

$t_p = z_{18} = (63)$ $= w_g + w_b + p - s_c - y$

$t_b = z_{19} = (64)$ $= (51) - w_g - w_b - p - d$

(134) = Standard and Poor's index of all common stock prices, December average: Standard and Poor's *Security Price Index Record*, 1960 edition, p. 4 (and later editions for 1960–1962 data).

$a_{t-1} = z_9 = (67)$ $= [(134)/(121)]_{t-1}$

The lagged value of any of these variables is obtained simply by lagging the series.[2] The data themselves appear in Table 3.1.

---

[2] The 1928 (and 1945) values are needed for those variables that appear lagged. The 1928 values of real GNP (51) and w_g appear in Table I-16 of the source. For c and i and the GNP deflator (121), unpublished preliminary estimates in 1939 dollars were used, after conversion to 1954 prices. For the other 1928 values, approximations were used based on the 1928–1929 behavior of related series such as real GNP.

TABLE 3.1   Data Used for Estimation and Testing
(in billions of 1954 dollars, except a_{-1}; see 3.4 in text)

Year	c y_1	i y_2	w_b y_3	s_c y_4	y y_5	x_b y_6	p y_7	a_{-1} z_9	k_{-1} z_{11}	g z_{16}	w_g z_{17}	t_p z_{18}	t_b z_{19}	d z_{20}
1928	125.8	27.4	100.8	4.2	—	—	31.2	30.85	—	—	—	—	—	—
1929	128.1	35.0	106.8	5.1	134.9	171.5	36.2	40.26	0.0	18.7	10.3	13.3	6.4	22.1
1930	120.3	23.6	101.8	0.4	126.1	153.7	25.3	37.28	12.9	20.7	10.8	11.4	5.6	21.0
1931	116.6	15.0	96.4	-6.0	121.3	142.0	12.8	28.00	15.5	21.3	11.0	4.9	12.7	20.1
1932	106.0	3.9	84.2	-10.9	104.7	119.3	-0.2	16.91	10.4	20.2	10.8	1.0	16.3	19.0
1933	103.5	4.0	80.1	-10.4	102.0	115.1	-0.9	15.19	-4.7	19.1	11.5	-0.9	17.6	18.3
1934	108.9	7.4	85.3	-4.7	109.2	125.2	5.8	22.56	-19.0	22.2	13.3	-0.1	15.8	18.3
1935	115.8	16.1	91.6	-1.9	120.0	138.7	14.3	19.74	-29.9	21.1	14.2	2.0	14.6	18.2
1936	127.7	21.0	101.0	-2.1	134.8	156.6	17.0	27.51	-32.0	24.7	16.7	2.0	19.0	19.6
1937	132.1	27.0	110.3	0.0	139.5	167.8	21.4	35.77	-30.6	24.4	15.7	7.9	16.1	20.0
1938	129.9	15.5	103.7	0.0	131.9	158.1	17.5	22.26	-23.6	29.6	17.0	6.3	17.1	19.8
1939	137.3	21.6	112.3	1.0	143.1	172.1	20.4	26.06	-27.9	30.4	17.2	5.8	19.6	19.8
1940	144.6	29.0	118.8	4.5	153.1	188.1	26.4	25.72	-26.1	32.2	17.7	5.3	22.5	20.4
1941	154.3	36.7	133.6	4.5	175.1	216.1	32.1	21.53	-17.5	47.1	22.0	8.1	27.6	22.8

1945	171.4	17.0	161.8	4.4	—	—	37.2	19.70	—	—	—	—	—	—
1946	192.3	42.4	162.7	3.2	209.9	252.6	39.8	25.49	−46.3	47.7	29.9	19.3	27.4	22.7
1947	195.6	41.5	168.3	7.0	201.1	259.5	36.7	20.28	−26.6	45.2	22.8	19.7	28.5	26.0
1948	199.3	49.8	173.2	12.5	211.5	270.3	45.5	18.11	−11.1	44.1	22.8	17.5	22.6	29.0
1949	204.3	38.5	171.8	11.8	213.8	268.8	41.3	17.16	9.7	49.8	23.9	11.4	24.9	30.8
1950	216.8	55.9	184.4	9.6	231.0	293.3	42.7	18.75	17.4	45.3	24.8	11.3	34.0	32.2
1951	218.5	57.7	194.5	10.0	237.0	311.0	44.2	22.07	41.1	65.5	30.8	22.5	36.1	36.2
1952	224.2	50.4	204.3	9.5	243.6	320.3	42.1	24.33	62.6	78.9	33.2	26.5	37.1	36.8
1953	235.1	50.6	217.2	7.9	255.1	336.2	39.0	26.54	76.2	83.4	32.8	26.0	41.7	38.3
1954	238.0	48.9	213.8	6.7	256.9	330.8	38.5	25.08	88.5	76.3	32.3	21.0	37.9	40.6
1955	256.0	62.5	228.5	10.0	273.3	360.5	42.7	34.97	96.8	74.1	32.2	20.1	46.4	42.9
1956	264.3	61.7	238.5	8.2	286.9	368.2	41.8	44.83	116.4	74.8	32.7	17.9	42.3	45.6
1957	271.2	58.1	241.2	7.6	293.8	375.4	42.1	44.40	132.5	79.3	33.2	15.1	44.1	48.0
1958	273.6	48.3	234.4	5.9	296.3	367.6	42.8	37.20	142.6	79.1	33.4	8.4	43.1	47.3
1959	289.4	60.9	249.9	8.9	311.2	394.2	45.2	48.28	143.6	77.8	33.8	8.8	50.0	49.1
1960	298.1	60.2	259.0	6.7	317.8	405.2	43.0	52.45	155.4	81.6	34.7	12.2	53.6	49.6
1961	303.6	57.5	260.7	5.6	328.3	412.0	44.7	49.74	166.0	86.6	35.7	7.2	57.3	49.3
1962	317.6	65.2	273.2	7.1	343.5	437.6	49.2	62.00	178.1	92.0	37.2	9.0	62.1	53.1

Note: 1928 and 1945 data for certain variables were used for 1929 and 1946 lagged values. 1960–1962 data were used for prediction.

4 LEAST-SQUARES ESTIMATES OF ALTERNATIVE STRUCTURAL EQUATION FORMS

4.1 Tables 4.1 through 4.4 show the results of least-squares fitting of alternative forms of the consumption, investment, labor, and corporate saving equations respectively. In each case the format of the table is standardized so as to show one equation form per line. Any of the columns labeled from (1) up to at most (8) contains the estimated coefficient of the variable appearing at the head of the column, together with (in parentheses)

TABLE 4.1　CONSUMPTION Equations (Least Squares)
Dependent variable: c
Period: 1929–1941 and 1946–1959

Equation No. ↓		Coefficient (and t ratio) of		R	Wrong Signs	$\lvert t \rvert < 4.1$ †
		y (1)	c_{-1} (2)			
*(c1)	b_k (t_k)	.661 (11.6)	.275 (4.10)	.9991	none	none
(c2)	b_k (t_k)	.892 (90.9)		.998	none	none
A priori sign of coefficient		+	+			
Simple r		.998	.994			

* Preferred form; see 5.2–3 below.

† All variables with $\lvert t \rvert \geqq 4.1$ (*not* mentioned in this column) have coefficients that would be significant in a single-equation model at about the .0002 level (and of course at any numerically greater level).

Constant terms were computed but are not shown.

the t ratio of the estimate to its standard error. Estimated constant terms are in all equations, but they are not shown. A blank space in any variable's column means that the variable was not included in that equation form. The signs of the estimated coefficients are given as if the dependent variable (c, i, w_b, or s_c) is on the left side of the equality symbol and all other terms including the constant are on the right side. The a priori signs of coefficients and the simple correlations r between the dependent variable and each independent variable are given in the last two lines.

TABLE 4.2 INVESTMENT Equations (Least Squares)
Dependent variable: i
Period: 1929–1941 and 1946–1959

Equation No. →		x_b (1)	k_{-1} (2)	d (3)	i_{-1} (4)	p (5)	a_{-1} (6)	a_{-2} (7)	R	Wrong Signs	Sign OK but $|t| \leqq 1.47$ †
(i1)	b_k	.0894	−.0309	.319	−.0678	.687			.9828	i_{-1}	x_b, k_{-1}, d
	(t_k)	(1.14)	(−.38)	(.33)	(−.60)	(4.08)					
*(i2)	b_k	.245	−.102						.966		
	(t_k)	(13.2)	(−3.56)								
(i3)	b_k	.264	−.0807	−.267					.966	d	k_{-1}
	(t_k)	(2.93)	(−.76)	(−.21)							
*(i4)	b_k	.220	−.109		.164				.969		i_{-1}
	(t_k)	(8.27)	(−3.80)		(1.34)						
(i5)	b_k	.245	−.0790	−.376	.167				.969	d	k_{-1}, i_{-1}
	(t_k)	(2.73)	(−.75)	(−.30)	(1.33)						
(i6)	b_k	.113	−.0067		−.0624	.678			.9827	i_{-1}	k_{-1}
	(t_k)	(3.45)	(−.20)		(−.57)	(4.17)					
(i7)	b_k		.0706			1.070			.973	k_{-1}	
	(t_k)		(4.04)			(14.9)					
**(i8)	b_k	.113	−.0157			.631			.9824		k_{-1}
	(t_k)	(3.50)	(−.55)			(4.55)					

Coefficient (and t ratio) of

TABLE 4.2   (cont.)

Equation No.		x_b (1)	k_{-1} (2)	d (3)	i_{-1} (4)	P (5)	a_{-1} (6)	a_{-2} (7)	R	Wrong Signs	Sign OK but $\mid t \mid \leq 1.47$ †
(i9)	b_k (t_k)		.204 (3.36)				.0610 (.16)		.67	k_{-1}	a_{-1}
(i10)	b_k (t_k)	.251 (14.9)	−.141 (−4.71)				.316 (2.57)		.974		
(i11)	b_k (t_k)		.0744 (3.50)			1.072 (14.7)	−.0407 (−.33)		.973	k_{-1}, a_{-1}	
(i12)	b_k (t_k)	.134 (3.77)	−.0452 (−1.26)			.545 (3.60)	.145 (1.31)		.9837		k_{-1}, a_{-1}
*(i13)	b_k (t_k)	.245 (13.3)	−.128 (−3.87)				.395 (2.61)	−.152 (−.90)	.975		a_{-2}
(i14)	b_k (t_k)		.0909 (4.71)			1.016 (15.3)	.199 (1.47)	−.416 (−2.92)	.9807	k_{-1}	a_{-1}
**(i15)	b_k (t_k)	.107 (3.03)	−.0104 (−.28)			.613 (4.25)	.266 (2.27)	−.275 (−2.11)	.9866		k_{-1}
(i16)	b_k (t_k)		−.0165 (−.35)		.925 (7.21)		.851 (3.44)	−1.032 (−4.07)	.931		k_{-1}
**(i17)	b_k (t_k)	.193 (7.21)	−.127 (−4.27)		.283 (2.50)		.511 (3.55)	−.338 (−2.00)	.9807		

Each data cell shows b_k over (t_k).

Equation								R^2	Add'l variables
(i18)	.108 (5.17)			−.0729 (−.78)	.702 (6.62)			.9827	i_{-1}
*(i19)				.232 (2.23)	.978 (7.41)			.962	
**(i20)	.0975 (6.08)				.682 (6.69)			.9822	
*(i21)	.177 (5.89)			.0795 (.53)				.949	i_{-1}
(i22)				−.0630 (−.48)	1.117 (9.11)			.973	k_{-1}, i_{-1}
(i23)		.0797 (3.05)	−.0175 (−.04)	−.0705 (−.64)	.697 (4.26)			.9827	d, i_{-1}
(i24)	.110 (1.97)		.704 (4.39)	−.123 (−1.09)	.961 (9.65)			.980	i_{-1}
A priori sign of coefficient	+	−	+	+	+	+	−		
Simple r	.948	.67	.87	.87	.954	.44	.17		

*, ** Starred equations are those not ruled out in preliminary screenings; see 5.14 below.
† All variables *not* mentioned in this column either have wrong signs or have $|t| \geq 1.97$ so that coefficients would be significant in a single-equation model at about the .03 level (or of course at any numerically greater level). The variables mentioned have coefficients of the right sign, insignificant at about the .08 level (or of course at any numerically smaller level).
Constant terms were computed but are not shown.

The last three columns give the multiple correlation R, and call attention to any wrong signs in the equation and to any right signs whose t ratio is less than some stated level in absolute value. Thus any equation form with no entry (or "none") in its last two columns is in good accord with *a priori* notions about sign and has no insignificant coefficients at the indicated level.

TABLE 4.3 LABOR Equations (Least Squares)
Dependent variable: w_b
Period: 1929–1941 and 1946–1959

Equation No. ↓		Coefficient (and t ratio) of			R	Wrong Signs	$\lvert t \rvert < 3.91$ †
		x_b (1)	$(x_b)_{-1}$ (2)	$(w_b)_{-1}$ (3)			
*(w1)	b_k (t_k)	.487 (19.0)		.229 (5.34)	.9995	none	none
(w2)	b_k (t_k)	.622 (105)			.9989	none	none
(w3)	b_k (t_k)	.496 (15.3)	.132 (3.91)		.9993	none	none
A priori sign of coefficient		+	+	+			
Simple r		.9989	.9925	.9917			

* Preferred form; see 5.4 below.

† All variables with $\lvert t \rvert \geqq 3.91$ (*not* mentioned in this column) have coefficients that would be significant in a single-equation model at about the .0002 level (and of course at any numerically greater level).

Constant terms were computed but are not shown.

4.2 Some of the equation forms were included because they accord well with theoretical considerations; 2.4–9 and 2.13–14 above describe some of these considerations. Other equation forms, especially (w3) and a few of the investment equations, were tried without a very careful rationale for them, simply to see how well they would work empirically, for such reasons as to learn the effect of omitting a variable previously found to be insignificant, and so forth.

4.3 The matrices of simple correlation coefficients of variables used in these equations are given in Tables 4.5–4.8.

TABLE 4.4   CORPORATE SAVING Equations (Least Squares)
Dependent variable: s_c
Period: 1929–1941, 1946–1959

Equation No. ↓		Coefficient (and t ratio) of			R	Wrong Signs	$\|t\| \leqq 1.7$ †
		p (1)	p_{-1} (2)	$(s_c)_{-1}$ (3)			
*(s1)	b_k (t_k)	.468 (8.02)	−.248 (−3.07)	.450 (2.45)	.973	none	
(s2)	b_k (t_k)	.519 (8.64)	−.104 (−1.70)		.966	none	p_{-1}
(s3)	b_k (t_k)	.408 (6.38)		.0418 (.29)	.962	none	$(s_c)_{-1}$
(s4)	b_k (t_k)	.425 (17.6)			.962	none	
A priori sign of coefficient		+	−	+			
Simple r		.962	.85	.89			

* Preferred form; see 5.5 below.

† All variables *not* mentioned in this column have $\|t\| \geqq 2.45$ and have co-efficients that would be significant in a single-equation model at about the .01 level (and of course at any numerically greater level). The variables mentioned have coefficients insignificant at about the .05 level (and of course at any numerically smaller level).

Constant terms were computed but are not shown.

TABLES 4.5–4.8   Simple Correlation Coefficients, 1929–1941 and 1946–1959

<table>
<tr><td colspan="4">TABLE 4.5
CONSUMPTION</td><td colspan="5">TABLE 4.7
LABOR</td></tr>
<tr><td>c</td><td>y</td><td>c_{-1}</td><td></td><td>w_b</td><td>x_b</td><td>$(x_b)_{-1}$</td><td>$(w_b)_{-1}$</td><td></td></tr>
<tr><td>1.0</td><td>.998</td><td>.994</td><td>c</td><td>1.0</td><td>.9989</td><td>.9925</td><td>.9917</td><td>w_b</td></tr>
<tr><td></td><td>1.0</td><td>.991</td><td>y</td><td></td><td>1.0</td><td>.9893</td><td>.9872</td><td>x_b</td></tr>
<tr><td></td><td></td><td>1.0</td><td>c_{-1}</td><td></td><td></td><td>1.0</td><td>—</td><td>$(x_b)_{-1}$</td></tr>
<tr><td></td><td></td><td></td><td></td><td></td><td></td><td></td><td>1.0</td><td>$(w_b)_{-1}$</td></tr>
</table>

TABLES 4.5–4.8 *(cont.)*

TABLE 4.6 INVESTMENT

i	x_b	k_{-1}	d	i_{-1}	p	a_{-1}	a_{-2}	
1.0	.948	.67	.87	.87	.954	.44	.17	i
	1.0	.82	.964	.901	.88	.45	.26	x_b
		1.0	.937	.78	.53	.63	.55	k_{-1}
			1.0	.89	.76	—	—	d
				1.0	.84	.42	.39	i_{-1}
					1.0	.37	.15	p
						1.0	.72	a_{-1}
							1.0	a_{-2}

TABLE 4.8
CORPORATE SAVING

s_c	p	p_{-1}	$(s_c)_{-1}$	
1.0	.962	.85	.89	s_c
	1.0	.922	.923	p
		1.0	.959	p_{-1}
			1.0	$(s_c)_{-1}$

5 REMARKS ON THE LEAST-SQUARES ESTIMATES; THE CHOICE OF ONE OR TWO PREFERRED FORMS FOR EACH EQUATION

5.1 In this section no estimates except the least-squares ones will be discussed; for brevity the phrase "least squares" will usually be omitted. The "t ratios" discussed are ratios of estimated slopes to their respective estimated standard errors. They do *not* have the t distribution in a simultaneous-equations model, but they are approximately normal as noted in X.3.20, so that large values may indicate a degree of statistical significance in a crude test of whether the relevant variable belongs in the equation. Quotation marks are used in discussing "significance" in this section and later sections because of these difficulties. The use of least-squares estimates (rather than estimates computed by a consistent method) to choose among alternative forms of the equations is not strictly justified in a simultaneous-equations context; however, two-stage least-squares and ordinary least-squares estimators are usually very similar so results would usually be nearly the same if two-stage least squares were used instead.

5.2 *Consumption.* Look at Table 4.1. There are no *a priori* wrong signs. The consumption equation $(c2)$ explains consumption behavior quite well $(r = .998)$, and the marginal propensity to consume is estimated at about .89. Equation $(c1)$ gives a better explanation $(R = .9991$, and the coefficients of both y and c_{-1} are highly "significant" with $t \geqq 4.1)$, but at first sight it appears to give a very different marginal propensity to consume, that is, about .66 instead of .89. Let us examine this. The value .66 is the *short-run* propensity in (c1), for it is the fraction of each additional income dollar consumed in a year when income changes after a period of long-run equilibrium during which y and c and c_{-1} have remained constant. To get the *long-run* propensity implied by $(c1)$, make the assumption of long-run equilibrium in which consumption c and c_{-1} and income y are at their long-run equilibrium values c^ϵ and y^ϵ, respectively, thus obtaining an equation in c^ϵ and y^ϵ only, which when solved for c^ϵ becomes (using the hat on c^ϵ to denote the calculated value of c^ϵ from the estimated equation):

$$(5.1) \qquad \hat{c}^\epsilon = \frac{.661}{1 - .275}\, y^\epsilon + \text{constant} = .913 y^\epsilon + \text{constant}$$

Thus the *long-run* propensity of about .91 implied by $(c1)$ is very close to the propensity of .89 in $(c2)$.

5.3 Another way of obtaining this value .91 is to adopt the distributed lag expectations hypothesis of V.7.6–7 and IX.13.11, according to which consumption depends on expected income y^e (not to be confused with equilibrium income y^ϵ), and current expectations are formed as a weighted average of lagged expectations and the current observation, with the consequence that an empirical equation like $(c1)$ results (note that $u_1 \neq u$ here; see IX.13.11):

$$(5.2) \qquad c = \beta y^e + \alpha + u$$

$$(5.3) \qquad y^e = \gamma y^e_{-1} + (1 - \gamma)y + v$$

$$(5.4) \qquad c = \beta(1 - \gamma)y + \gamma c_{-1} + \alpha(1 - \gamma) + u_1$$

Interpreting $(c1)$ as an estimate of (5.4) we find that our estimates of γ, $\beta(1 - \gamma)$, and β are respectively .275, .661, and $.661/(1 - .275) = .913$. Hence our estimate of the consumption function (5.2) is

$$(5.5) \qquad \hat{c} = .913 y^e + \text{constant}$$

These arguments are reasonably satisfactory, at least for such a deliberately simplified model as this, so we adopt $(c1)$ as the preferred form of the consumption function.

5.4 *Labor.* Look at Table 4.3. There are no *a priori* wrong signs. An argument similar to 5.2-3 leads to the adoption of $(w1)$ as the preferred form of the wage equation: Both x_b and $(w_b)_{-1}$ have highly "significant" coefficients with $t \geq 5.34$, and its R is higher than its rivals' R's. Either the long-term equilibrium approach or the expectations approach can be applied as in 5.2–3. The latter yields the following transformation of $(w1)$:

(5.6) $$\hat{w}_b = \frac{.487}{1 - .229} x_b{}^e + \text{constant} = .632 x_b{}^e + \text{constant}$$

The long-run marginal propensity to use labor in this equation, namely, about .63, is close to the value of about .62 obtained from $(w2)$. Equation $(w3)$ is not used since $(w1)$ is more appealing, but we might note that its long-run propensity of $.496 + .132 = .628$ is near those obtained for the other two equations.

5.5 *Corporate saving.* Look at Table 4.4. There are no *a priori* wrong signs (the *a priori* signs are derived above in 2.14). An argument similar to 5.2–3 leads to the choice of $(s1)$ as the preferred form of the corporate saving equation: All its coefficients are quite "significant" ($|t| \geq 2.45$), and its R is the highest of all the four forms tried. If we compare the estimate of $(s1)$ with (2.12) we find estimates of δ_2 and δ_1 as follows: There are two estimates of δ_2, one from each lagged term in the equation. The $(s_c)_{-1}$ term yields $\hat{\delta}_2 = .450$, and the p_{-1} term yields $\hat{\delta}_2 \cong .248/.56 \cong .443$. This close agreement provides a degree of confirmation of equation (2.11) and indirectly of $(s1)$ itself. From the p term it follows that $\hat{\delta}_1 \cong 1 - .468/.56 \cong .16$. Hence the dividend equation (2.9) is estimated implicitly as

(5.7) $$\hat{d}_c = \hat{\delta}_0 + .16 p_c + .45 (d_c)_{-1}$$

To interpret this equation, we may regard it as the result of a distributed lag expectations model for corporate profits p_c, with dividends linearly dependent on expected corporate profits $p_c{}^e$. Then it can be transformed just as the consumption equation was transformed in 5.3 to obtain the following results, which appear fairly reasonable, although the *long-run* marginal payout propensity of .29 seems a bit low:

(5.8) $$\hat{p}_c{}^e = .45 (p_c{}^e)_{-1} + .55 p$$

(5.9) $$\hat{d}_c = \frac{.16}{1 - .45} p_c{}^e + \text{constant} = .29 p_c{}^e + \text{constant}$$

Note that the distributed-lag expectations theory introduces *both* p_{-1} and $(s_c)_{-1}$ into the empirical relation between corporate saving s_c and property income p, and that both are quite "significant" in $(s1)$. If either one is included without the other, as in $(s2)$ or $(s3)$, the estimated coefficient of the included one is not very "significant," and differs markedly from its value in $(s1)$, where *both* are included; this confirms our decision that both lagged variables belong in the equation. (On the other hand, leaving both out as in (s4) yields about the same coefficient for p, and a quite high value of R.)

5.6 *Investment.* Look at Table 4.2. Here the situation is less simple, and that is why so many different forms of the investment equation were tried. All *a priori* signs are positive except for capital k_{-1} (explained in 2.7) and stock prices at the first of the *preceding* year a_{-2} (i.e., the sign of Δa_{-1} should be positive if a_{-1} and Δa_{-1} are used instead of a_{-1} and a_{-2}). There are many *a priori* wrong signs among the estimates (see the next-to-last column of the table), and even where the signs are not wrong some coefficients are not very "significant" (see the last column). We shall see that none of the twenty-four investment equations is satisfactory in every respect, but as the following observations will show, some are more unsatisfactory than others and can be dismissed quickly.

5.7 First, consider depreciation d. In every equation where it appears, either it or lagged investment has a wrong sign, or both. Furthermore it is "insignificant" whenever the important variable output x_b is in the equation, and its presence or absence affects x_b's coefficient very little. Hence from now on we *dismiss* all equations containing d, since its effect seems to be confused with that of output (which is roughly proportional to d but much larger).[3]

5.8 Next consider output x_b. Recall that we are henceforth ignoring all equations that contain d, as decided in 5.7. No equation that *excludes* x_b was found to be satisfactory; usually there are wrong signs: If capital k_{-1} appears without x_b, its coefficient's sign is wrong in every case but one [(i16), where its value is practically zero and "insignificant"]. In two cases neither x_b nor k_{-1} appears; i_{-1} has a wrong sign in one (i24) and the other, (i19), is rejected because of its relatively low R, as well as because x_b is theoretically important. If x_b is *included*, its coefficient is always positive and quite "significant" ($t > 3$). Its coefficient is affected very little by the presence or absence of capital k_{-1} but is affected substantially by the presence or absence of property income p: *Without p* the x_b coefficient is between .177 and .251, inclusive, with $t \geqq 5.89$, but *with p* the x_b coefficient is smaller, between .0975 and .134, inclusive, with $t \geqq 3.03$. This strongly suggests that x_b should be in the equation, and we shall leave it in. Interaction between x_b and p will be taken up again below, after p is discussed.

5.9 Next consider capital, k_{-1} (d is omitted as above). We have noted that its coefficient's sign should be negative and is wrong (or in one case effectively zero) if x_b is excluded, and we have decided to leave x_b in. With x_b in, the sign of the coefficient of k_{-1} is negative in every case,

---

[3] An alternative not tried was to use gross property income ($p + d$) in place of either or both of p and d as separate variables. The fact that r^2 between p and d is only about .6 suggests that it is not necessary to replace them by their sum.

which is proper, but its magnitude is sharply influenced by the presence or absence of property income p. *Without p* (but with x_b), the k_{-1} coefficient is between $-.102$ and $-.141$, inclusive, with $|t| \geqq 3.56$. *With p* (and x_b), the k_{-1} coefficient is practically zero, between $-.0067$ and $-.0452$ with $|t| \leqq 1.26$. This suggests that if p is included it is difficult to measure the effect of k_{-1} and that perhaps we should not include both. If the depreciation rate were $\delta = .04$ as suggested in 2.7, and if a capital-stock-adjustment theory were adopted, then the coefficient of lagged capital stock would be $.04 - \theta$ as explained in 2.7. Hence a coefficient of $-.10$ to $-.14$ (as obtained in equations *without p*) would imply an annual investment equal to $\theta = .14$ to $.18$ times the discrepancy between desired and actual capital. Similarly a coefficient of $-.007$ to $-.045$ (as obtained in equations *with p*) would imply an annual adjustment equal to $\theta = .047$ to $.095$ times that discrepancy. Hence the small coefficients of $-.007$ to $-.045$ imply unreasonably slow adjustment.

5.10 Now consider property income p (d is excluded as before). Whenever p is included, it is quite "significant" ($t \geqq 3.6$, and this holds whether d is included or not), and always with the *a priori* expected positive sign. The presence or absence of x_b (but not of k_{-1}) makes a substantial difference in the size of its effect: *Without* x_b, the p coefficient is between $.978$ and 1.117, inclusive, with $t \geqq 7.41$. *With* x_b, the p coefficient is smaller, between $.545$ and $.702$, inclusive, with $t \geqq 3.6$. Recall that the x_b coefficient is smaller with p than without. Thus there appears to be a combined effect of x_b and p, which is divided between them if both are included in the least-squares regression but can be represented fairly well by either one alone if the other is excluded. This is not surprising when we note that their simple correlation is $.88$. This makes it difficult to decide which one to exclude, or whether to include both. The difficulties of multicollinearity, as described in IX.4.12–19, are illustrated dramatically by this situation. As already noted, the presence of p appears to reduce to practically zero the estimated effect of k_{-1}. The presence of p also renders i_{-1} "insignificant" except in one case, ($i19$) ($|t| \leqq .78$ except in that case).

5.11 Now consider stock market prices, relative to the GNP deflator, at the end and beginning of the previous year, denoted by a_{-1} and a_{-2} respectively. These variables were introduced to try to see whether the time-series results obtained by Grunfeld [1960] for individual large corporations (and for a small aggregate of eight such corporations) hold for the entire United States economy. Grunfeld found that if he expressed real gross investment[4] as a linear function of (1) real capital stock,[5] (2)

---

[4] His definition of gross investment differs from the one used here since he excluded inventory investment and included maintenance and repair expenditures. Also, he did not exclude the war years 1942–1945.

[5] Defined as cumulated real net noninventory investment.

the real market value of the firm's equity and debt in the preceding December, and (3) real profits, then in most of the corporations investigated the capital coefficient was "significantly" *positive*,[6] the value-of-the-firm coefficient was "significantly" *positive*, and the profit coefficient was "*insignificant*." From this Grunfeld concluded that capital stock is a size variable, and value of the firm is an expectations variable. He concluded further that profits do not belong in the investment function and that the only reason they take on a "significant" positive coefficient in so many empirical investment functions is that the proper size and expectations variables have been left out, so that profits are forced to serve as a surrogate for those proper variables.

5.12   The variables a_{-1} and a_{-2} were introduced in an attempt to explore whether their inclusion in an *aggregate* investment equation would render property income p "insignificant," as the value-of-the-firm variable did in Grunfeld's study of individual corporations. It should be noted that the conditions are not quite the same.[7] The equation in Table 4.2 corresponding most closely to Grunfeld's result is (i11). It, like all the others tried that include p, shows a strongly positive coefficient for p, which contrasts with Grunfeld's result. On the one hand, Grunfeld's argument, which says that for explaining investment *current* profits should be inferior to good measures of expected profitability and access to financing and the size of the market and the like, is a reasonable argument on theoretical grounds. On the other hand, the twenty-four *aggregate* investment equations in Table 4.2 do not demonstrate it empirically. Work by Eisner [1960] and [1963] on corporations confirms Grunfeld's result. See also Jorgenson [1963].

5.13   Stock prices in the preceding December, a_{-1}, should have a positive effect on investment on *a priori* grounds: Higher stock prices suggest optimistic expectations. The twice-lagged value a_{-2} is introduced into some of the equations, because its presence is deduced from an investment theory that assumes the following: (1) Desired capital stock depends on a_{-1} and expected output $x_b{}^e$; (2) expected output depends on present and past outputs with a distributed lag; (3) net investment is a fraction of the difference between desired and actual capital; and (4) depreciation is a simple linear function of actual capital and/or output. In fact such a theory leads to an equation of the form of (i17). The *a priori* sign of the coefficient of a_{-2} is negative. Note that when both a_{-1} and a_{-2} are included, both have the right signs in every case. Also the a_{-1}

---

[6] This usually occurred in our equations too, if output was excluded as in Grunfeld's study.

[7] Grunfeld used the *value* of the firm's equity and debt, whereas a_{-1} is merely the *price* of its equity and thus does not respond to changes in the *quantity* of equity and of debt (debt-*price* changes are negligible by comparison). See also notes 4 and 5 above.

coefficient is larger and more "significant" *with* a_{-2} than without. When a_{-1} is included without a_{-2}, it is often "insignificant" and has the wrong sign in one case [(i11), the equation corresponding to Grunfeld's work mentioned just above]. This suggests that we should either include both a_{-1} and a_{-2}, or exclude both. Their inclusion or exclusion makes very little difference to the other coefficients with one exception: the coefficient of i_{-1} in (i4) is nearly doubled when they are included to obtain (i17); here (i17) is presumably the more reliable because its i_{-1} coefficient is the more "significant." Of the equations including a_{-1} and a_{-2}, the best appear to be (i15) and (i17). The former contains p but not i_{-1}, and the latter contains i_{-1} but not p. Both contain x_b, k_{-1}, a_{-1}, and a_{-2} as well. (A similar equation containing both i_{-1} and p was not tried because whenever i_{-1} and p and any other explanatory variable(s) appear, i_{-1} is "insignificant" with the wrong sign, and its exclusion has little effect on the rest of the equation.)

5.14 A summary of these observations about the twenty-four alternative investment equations is in order. First, eliminate all equations that have wrong signs, or k_{-1} without x_b, or a_{-1} without a_{-2}. This leaves nine equations, which are starred in the left margin of Table 4.2. Next, eliminate (i2) and (i4), since both are improved by the inclusion of a_{-1} and a_{-2} along with i_{-1} to get (i17). Next, eliminate (i13), since it is improved by the addition of either p to get (i15), or i_{-1} to get (i17). Next, eliminate (i21), since in it i_{-1} is "insignificant" ($t < .6$). Next eliminate (i19), since it excludes x_b (see 5.8).

5.15 This leaves four more or less reasonable alternatives, namely, (i8), (i15), (i17), and (i20). They are double starred (**) in the left margin of Table 4.2 and are shown separately in Table 5.1 for easier reference. All four of these equations contain x_b and have $R \geq .9807$. All have *a priori* correct signs, and with two exceptions all coefficients are quite "significant" with $|t| \geq 2$. (The two exceptions are in the equations containing both k_{-1} and p, where—as usual when x_b is included too—the k_{-1} coefficient is very small and not "significant." This suggests that if p and x_b are both included, there is little to be lost or gained by including k_{-1} as well.) The highest correlation R among the four, and indeed among all twenty-four investment equations tried, is .9866 for (i15). The lowest R among the four is .9807 for (i17), which is the only one of the four that does not contain p (no other computed equation excluding p has R above .975). Thus the attempt to explain investment by an equation that excludes property income p has been fairly successful in equation (i17), but it must be noted that (a) somewhat higher correlations are obtained when p is included, even in (i20), which contains *only* x_b and p; and (b) in all of the versions tried the coefficient of p has invariably been highly "significant" ($t \geq 3.6$).

5.16 Because the stock market price variables a_{-1} and a_{-2} are helpful, as shown in 5.13, we *reject* equations (i20) and (i8), which do not contain them. This leaves two preferred forms for the investment equation, namely, (i15), which includes property income p but not lagged investment i_{-1}, and (i17), which includes i_{-1} but not p. On theoretical grounds (i17)

TABLE 5.1   The Four Most Reasonable INVESTMENT Equations (Least Squares)
Dependent variable: i
Period: 1929–1941 and 1946–1959

Equation No. ↓		Coefficient (and t ratio) of						R	$\lvert t \rvert < 2$
		x_b (1)	k_{-1} (2)	i_{-1} (4)	p (5)	a_{-1} (6)	a_{-2} (7)		
(i20)	b_k	.0975			.682			.9822	none
	(t_k)	(6.08)			(6.69)				
(i8)	b_k	.113	−.0157		.631			.9824	k_{-1}
	(t_k)	(3.50)	(−.55)		(4.55)				
*(i15)	b_k	.107	−.0104		.613	.266	−.275	.9866	k_{-1}
	(t_k)	(3.03)	(−.28)		(4.25)	(2.27)	(−2.11)		
*(i17)	b_k	.193	−.127	.283		.511	−.338	.9807	none
	(t_k)	(7.21)	(−4.27)	(2.50)		(3.55)	(−2.00)		
A priori sign of coefficient		+	−	+	+	+	−		
Simple r		.948	.67	.87	.954	.44	.17		

Source: Table 4.2 and text, 5.14
Constant terms were computed but are not shown here.
* The two most reasonable forms tried for the investment equation; see text, 5.16.

is preferable because it excludes p. On the other hand, p has a highly "significant" coefficient when it is included. Therefore both equations will be examined further before a choice is made between them. (The final choice is made in 8.3 below.)

5.17 Accordingly the choice of a model has now been narrowed down to two models, which are identical except for their investment equations. The equations are:

$$(5.10) \equiv (c1) \qquad c = \beta_{15}y + \gamma_{1,12}c_{-1} + \gamma_{10} + u_1$$

$$(5.11) \equiv (i17) \qquad i = \beta_{26}x_b + \gamma_{28}i_{-1} + \gamma_{29}a_{-1} + \gamma_{2,10}a_{-2} + \gamma_{2,11}k_{-1}$$
$$+ \gamma_{20} + u_2$$

$$(5.11') \equiv (i15) \qquad i = \beta'_{26}x_b + \beta'_{27}p + \gamma'_{29}a_{-1} + \gamma'_{2,10}a_{-2}$$
$$+ \gamma'_{2,11}k_{-1} + \gamma'_{20} + u'_2$$

$$(5.12) \equiv (w1) \qquad w_b = \beta_{36}x_b + \gamma_{3,13}(w_b)_{-1} + \gamma_{30} + u_3$$

$$(5.13) \equiv (s1) \qquad s_c = \beta_{47}p + \gamma_{4,14}(s_c)_{-1} + \gamma_{4,15}p_{-1} + \gamma_{40} + u_4$$

$$(5.14) \equiv (2.3) \qquad x_b + w_g = c + i + g$$

$$(5.15) \equiv (2.4) \qquad x_b + w_g = y + t_p + s_c + t_b + d$$

$$(5.16) \equiv (2.5) \qquad p + w_b + w_g = y + t_p + s_c$$

The jointly dependent variables are c, i, w_b, s_c, y, x_b, and p. Other variables are predetermined. See 2.3 above for notation, and Section 3 above for data sources and conceptual details of variables. The following parameters are presumed to be positive on theoretical grounds: β_{15}, $\gamma_{1,12}$, β_{26}, γ_{28}, γ_{29}, β'_{26}, β'_{27}, γ'_{29}, β_{36}, $\gamma_{3,13}$, β_{47}, $\gamma_{4,14}$. The following parameters are presumed to be negative on theoretical grounds: $\gamma_{2,10}$, $\gamma_{2,11}$, $\gamma'_{2,10}$, $\gamma'_{2,11}$, $\gamma_{4,15}$.

6   TWO-STAGE LEAST-SQUARES AND LIMITED-INFORMATION ESTIMATES FOR THE PREFERRED STRUCTURAL EQUATIONS

6.1   In Tables 6.1, 6.2, 6.2', 6.3, and 6.4 we give two-stage least-squares (2SLS) and limited-information (LI) estimates of the preferred forms of the consumption, investment, labor, and corporate saving equations, $(c1)$, $(i17)$, $(i15)$, $(w1)$, and $(s1)$, respectively. Also given are least-squares estimates (LS) from Section 4 for comparison; estimated t ratios for the estimated parameters;[8] the standard error of estimate s (i.e., the estimated value of the standard deviation σ of structural-equation disturbances); the squared ordinary correlation coefficient R^2; the Durbin-Watson d statistic (see X.4.8 and XI.7.3) except for least

---

[8] See 5.1 above regarding their use. The program used computes the estimated approximate variances and covariances of limited-information estimators in terms of the computations used for parameter estimation by that method (see Chernoff and Divinsky [1953]), which is why they differ slightly from the variances and covariances obtained for the two-stage least-squares method, though, as noted in IX.9.27, asymptotically the two are equal.

TABLE 6.1   Alternative Estimates of the Preferred CONSUMPTION Equation
(c1)
Dependent variable: c
Period: 1929–1941 and 1946–1959

Estimation Method	Coefficients (and t ratios) of			s	R^2	d	l_1
	y	c_{-1}	1				
Least squares	.661 (11.6)	.275 (4.1)	5.35 (2.91)	2.671	.998	—	—
Two-stage least squares	.686 (11.6)	.246 (3.5)	5.68 (1.76)	2.682	—	1.76	—
Limited information	.732 (11.8)	.193 (2.64)	6.28 (3.3)	2.756	—	1.69	2.55
A priori sign	+	+					

Source: See text, 6.1–2.

TABLE 6.2   Alternative Estimates of INVESTMENT Equation ($i17$)
Dependent variable: i
Period: 1929–1941 and 1946–1959

Estimation Method	Coefficients (and t ratios) of						s	R^2	d	l_1
	x_b	i_{-1}	a_{-1}	a_{-2}	k_{-1}	1				
Least squares	.193 (7.2)	.283 (2.10)	.511 (3.6)	−.338 (−2.00)	−.127 (−4.3)	−21.78 (−3.7)	4.089	.962	—	—
Two-stage least squares	.189 (7.0)	.296 (2.60)	.518 (3.6)	−.352 (−2.07)	−.125 (−4.2)	−21.16 (−2.96)	4.091	—	2.23	—
Limited information	.176 (6.5)	.339 (2.94)	.540 (3.7)	−.398 (−2.32)	−.118 (−3.9)	−19.11 (−3.2)	4.126	—	2.37	4.18
A priori sign	+	+	+	−	−					

Source: See text, 6.1–2.

TABLE 6.2′ Alternative Estimates of INVESTMENT Equation (i15)
Dependent variable: i
Period: 1929–1941 and 1946–1959

Estimation Method	Coefficients (and t ratios) of						s	R^2	d	l_1	Odd Result for
	x_b	p	a_{-1}	a_{-2}	k_{-1}	1					
Least squares	.107 (3.0)	.613 (4.3)	.266 (2.27)	−.275 (−2.11)	−.010 (−.28)	−7.61 (−1.18)	3.41	.973	—	—	—
Two-stage least squares	.108 (2.36)	.609 (3.8)	.267 (2.26)	−.275 (−2.11)	−.011 (−.28)	−7.65 (−1.02)	3.41	—	2.12	—	—
Limited information	.485 (1.68)	−1.20 (−.88)	.676 (1.49)	−.016 (−.04)	−.317 (−1.30)	−55.4 (−1.42)	10.07	—	.75	5.52	x_b, k_{-1}, p
A priori sign	+	+	+	−	−						

Source: See text, 6.1–2.

TABLE 6.3 Alternative Estimates of the Preferred LABOR Equation ($w1$)
Dependent variable: w_b
Period: 1929–1941 and 1946–1959

Estimation Method	Coefficients (and t ratios) of			s	R^2	d	l_1
	x_b	$(w_b)_{-1}$	1				
Least squares	.487 (19.0)	.229 (5.3)	3.46 (3.1)	1.938	.999	—	—
Two-stage least squares	.490 (18.8)	.223 (5.1)	3.48 (1.58)	1.939	—	1.61	—
Limited information	.494 (18.9)	.216 (5.0)	3.52 (3.1)	1.941	—	1.57	2.33
A priori sign	+	+					

Source: See text, 6.1–2.

TABLE 6.4 Alternative Estimates of the Preferred CORPORATE SAVING Equation ($s1$)
Dependent variable: s_c
Period: 1929–1941 and 1946–1959

Estimation Method	Coefficients (and t ratios) of				s	R^2	d	l_1
	p	p_{-1}	$(s_c)_{-1}$	1				
Least squares	.468 (8.0)	−.248 (−3.1)	.450 (2.46)	−4.64 (−2.48)	1.579	.947	—	—
Two-stage least squares	.488 (7.7)	−.257 (−3.2)	.427 (2.31)	−4.89 (−2.00)	1.584	—	1.93	—
Limited information	.536 (8.1)	−.279 (−3.3)	.374 (1.96)	−5.48 (−2.79)	1.625	—	1.96	2.53
A priori sign	+	−	+					

Source: See text, 6.1–2.

squares; and the smallest root l_1 of the limited-information determinantal equation (IX.9.27). The set of predetermined variables used in computing these two-stage least-squares and limited-information estimates is as follows (recall the notation listed in 2.3 above):[9] i_{-1}, a_{-1}, a_{-2}, k_{-1}, c_{-1}, $(w_b)_{-1}$, $(s_c)_{-1}$, p_{-1}, g, w_g, t_p, t_b, and d. These are also known as $z_8 \cdots z_{20}$ respectively for purposes of computer programming and distinguishing jointly dependent (y) from predetermined (z) variables.

6.2 The estimates given in Tables 6.1–6.4 were computed on an IBM 7090 computer at The Johns Hopkins University, using IBM program number IB9FES prepared by Harry Eisenpress. The writeup is Eisenpress [1961] (see also Eisenpress and Foote [1960], and Eisenpress [1962]). This program transforms all data by multiplying by some power of 10 (the same for all data) before beginning to work, and all outputs are given in terms of the transformed data. Where necessary, the constant terms and their standard errors and the standard error of estimate s have been detransformed before being entered in Tables 6.1–6.4, so these tables show the results corresponding to the data units described in Section 3 above, that is, billions of 1954 dollars as a stock or an annual flow except for price indexes.

6.3 For all four equations, least squares has at least as small a standard error of estimate s as either of the other two methods, as expected. The value of s for two-stage least squares is always almost as small, and the value of s for limited information is always largest; this is typical.

6.4 For the consumption, investment (i17), labor,[10] and corporate saving equations, all three methods give very similar results, with no wrong signs of coefficients, and with all slopes exceeding two standard errors except for one LI estimate that is 1.96 times its standard error. Standard errors of estimate differ almost not at all among the three methods. There are moderate differences in estimated coefficients, the 2SLS estimate in all cases lying between the LS and LI estimates. The

[9] Except that in estimating the investment equation (i15), i_{-1} (i.e., z_8) was not among the predetermined variables used, because when (i15) is used then i_{-1} does not appear in the model. Alternative LI and 2SLS estimates of equations (c1), (w1), and (s1) were computed, *not* using i_{-1} among the predetermined variables, and the results were very similar to Tables 6.1, 6.3, and 6.4; see text, 6.6 below.

[10] Regarding the labor equation, we would expect that if the production function were Cobb-Douglas with constant returns to scale, labor's share of money income would be constant; hence labor's share of *real* income (using the same deflator for both; see 3.4), which is w_b/x_b, would be constant. This suggests that the constant term in the labor equation would be zero in that case. Its value in Table 6.3 is quite small, only about $3.5 billion. When the equation of Table 6.3 is converted to equilibrium form by setting $(w_b)_{-1}$ equal to w_b, its least-squares version becomes $\hat{w}_b = .632x_b + 4.49$, that is, the constant term becomes about $4.5 billion, still quite small, though perhaps "significantly" different from zero in view of the t ratio of 3.1 for the constant term in the least-squares estimate of Table 6.3.

maximum difference between LI and LS estimates for any slope parameter in these four equations is 38 per cent of the larger of the two, and occurs for the coefficient of $(s_c)_{-1}$ in the corporate saving equation (this LI estimate is the one where $t = 1.96$).

6.5 For the investment equation $(i15)$, the least-squares and two-stage least-squares results are almost identical, and reasonable, showing no wrong sign, and no t ratio less than 2 in absolute value except that for k_{-1}. But the limited-information estimates are ridiculous (though not "significant" at moderate levels), with a large negative coefficient for profits, and with much larger coefficients for output and capital stock than with the other two methods, or with least squares for other forms of the same equation. Note the high positive serial correlation of residuals ($d = .75$). Also the fit is poor, s rising to a level of $10 billion a year, which is a very large standard error of estimate. Note, however, that even with the relatively good LS or 2SLS estimates, s is $3.41 billion a year, a rather large standard error of estimate considering that the average value of gross investment in recent years has been about $60 billion (these amounts are in 1954 prices).

6.6 Four models were estimated by both 2SLS and LI, each model using the same consumption and labor and corporate saving equations, and each using one of the four investment equations of Table 5.1 and the associated set of predetermined variables. The results for the model using $(i17)$ are in Tables 6.1, 6.2, 6.3, and 6.4. For the other three models the complete results are not presented here, but it is interesting to note a few features. Consider first the *consumption, labor,* and *corporate saving* equations: (a) For any model and set of predetermined variables, the results of the three estimation methods are very similar, and the 2SLS estimate of every slope coefficient lies between the LS and LI estimates, just as is true of Tables 6.1, 6.3, and 6.4. (b) For any equation, the 2SLS estimates vary less than the LI as we move from one model and set of predetermined variables to another: For 2SLS the ratio of the largest to the smallest estimate obtained for a given parameter in the four different models lies between 1.03 (for the x_b coefficient in the labor equation) and 1.32 (for the $(s_c)_{-1}$ coefficient in the corporate saving equation), while for LI the same ratio lies between 1.06 and 1.57 (the extremes occurring for the same parameters as for 2SLS). (c) All results are reasonable. Consider next the four different *investment* equations: The foregoing picture applies, except that in investment equations $(i8)$ and $(i15)$ the LI estimates are ridiculous, with negative coefficients for profits and with much poorer fit than 2SLS. This unstable behavior of the LI estimators is reminisent of the discussion in IX.12.18–19.

6.7 Since least squares is known to give inconsistent estimators, and since limited information often gives unreliable estimates for one equation (investment), and in the light of IX.12, we adopt the two-stage least-squares method as our preferred method for structural estimation, and we adopt the solved 2SLS method for reduced-form estimation, to be taken up in Section 8 below.

7 SOME NONPREDICTIVE TESTS OF THE
PREFERRED EQUATIONS

7.1 In this section we conduct several nonpredictive tests of the preferred equations, based on the estimates of the five equations given in Tables 6.1–6.4, including 6.2′. We have already noted that all parameter estimates are reasonable in the light of *a priori* views about them (except for certain LI estimates of the investment equation ($i15$) in Table 6.2′), and that all slope parameter estimates equal or exceed 1.96 estimated standard deviations [except for the coefficient of k_{-1} in the investment equation ($i15$) and all of the LI coefficients in that same equation]. Tables 6.1–6.4 show that the standard error of estimate for 2SLS exceeds that for LS by less than one-half of 1 per cent in each equation.

7.2 Graphs of the residuals for the two-stage least-squares estimates are in Figure 7.1. All five graphs have the same scales. The residuals are smallest for the corporate saving equation, but the absolute magnitudes of corporate saving and its fluctuations are small. The residuals in the 2SLS equations are largest for the two investment equations. Like most investment equations in aggregate econometric models of the United States, these two fail to explain the downturns in investment in 1949 and 1958 and the upturns of 1950 and 1955. However, unlike many, they do pretty well in the downturns of 1930–1932, 1938, and 1952–1954 and in the upturn of 1959. The reader is welcome to examine Figure 7.1 to see whether the residuals suggest any other variables that might be included in the equations with improved results.

7.3 In X.4.11–14 it was pointed out that the upper limit d_u for the Durbin-Watson serial correlation test is approximately suitable for the present case, but that the test is biased against discovering serial correlation in all of the preferred equations except ($i15$) because the lagged value of the explained variable appears. The appropriate value for K for the Durbin-Watson test here is the number of explanatory variables in the reduced form, not counting the constant term; thus for equation ($i15$) $K = 12$ and for the other four preferred equations $K = 13$. The Durbin-Watson table (see Appendix B, Table B-4) shows values of K no larger than 5, so it will not provide a conclusive test in most of our cases. However, the table shows that the upper limit d_u increases as K increases, and therefore whenever the observed d is already below the value of d_u tabulated for $K = 5$, we know that the observed d will be below the value taken

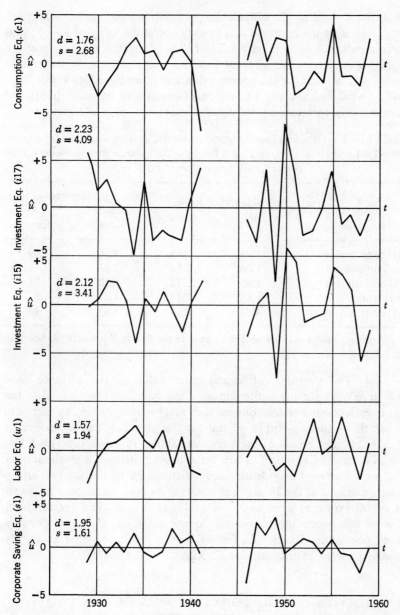

Figure 7.1   Residuals for the 2SLS estimates of the preferred equations in billions of 1954 dollars per year.

by d_u for $K = 12$ or 13, which indicates positive serial correlation. Similarly, whenever the observed d is already above the value of $4 - d_u$ that corresponds to $K = 5$, we have an indication of negative serial correlation. Applying these rules, we see from Table 7.1 that positive serial correlation is indicated at least for the consumption and labor equations (both 2SLS and LI versions) and the LI version of investment equation ($i15$); and negative serial correlation is indicated at least for investment equation ($i17$).

TABLE 7.1   The Observed Durbin-Watson Statistic d for the Preferred Equations, 1929–1941 and 1946–1959, and the 5 Per Cent Acceptance Region Based on the Upper Limit d_u for $K = 5$ and $T = 27$

Equation	Acceptance Region		Observed d	
	d_u	$4 - d_u$	2SLS version	LI version
($c1$) consumption	1.86	2.14	1.76	1.69
($i17$) investment	1.86	2.14	2.23	2.37
($i15$) investment	1.86	2.14	2.12	.75
($w1$) labor	1.86	2.14	1.61	1.57
($s1$) corp. saving	1.86	2.14	1.93	1.96

Source: Tables 6.1–6.4 and 6.2′, and Table B-4 in Appendix B. See also text, 7.3.

7.4   The statistic l_1 (the minimum value of the variance ratio $\beta W^* \beta' / \beta W \beta'$) for the limited-information estimates can be used to test the overidentifying restrictions on each stochastic equation, by means of either the Anderson-Rubin χ^2 test or Basmann's F test (described in X.5.19–24). The results of these tests are shown in Table 7.2. The F test, which Basmann has shown to be a better approximation for small samples, accepts the *a priori* overidentifying restrictions for all but the two investment equations at the 88 per cent level, rejects both investment equations at the 99.4 per cent level, and rejects ($i15$) even at the 99.9 per cent level. The χ^2 test rejects the restrictions for all equations at the 98 per cent level, confirming Basmann's finding that it has a strong bias toward rejecting correct restrictions—see X.5.22.

8   ESTIMATES OF THE REDUCED FORMS OF THE TWO PREFERRED MODELS; THE ADOPTION OF ONE MODEL

8.1   In this section we present estimates of the reduced forms of the two preferred models. We then adopt one of the models. The two models

TABLE 7.2   The Anderson-Rubin χ^2 and the Basmann F Tests Applied to Overidentifying Restrictions in the Preferred Equations (LI Estimates)

Equation (1)	l_1 (2)	$T - K$ (3)	$K - J - H + 1$ (4)	$T \log_e l_1$ (5)	Pb That $\chi^2(K - J - H + 1)$ Exceeds the Statistic in Col. (5) (6)	$\dfrac{(T - K)(l_1 - 1)}{K - J - H + 1}$ (7)	Pb That $F(K - J - H + 1, T - K)$ Exceeds the Statistic in Col. (7) (8)
(c1) consumption	2.55	13	11	25.3	.005	1.83	.17
(i17) investment	4.18	13	7	38.7	<.001	5.16	.005
(i15) investment	5.52	14	8	46.2	<.001	9.04	<.001
(w1) labor	2.33	13	11	22.9	.01	1.57	.23
(s1) saving	2.53	13	10	25.0	.004	1.99	.13

Sources (see also X.5.19–24):

Col. (2): Tables 6.1–6.4.

Col. (3): $T = 27$, $K = 14$ (counting the dummy) except 13 for (i15); see 6.1.

Col. (4): Tables 6.1–6.4.

Cols. (5) and (7): Perform the indicated operations

Cols. (6) and (8): Rough interpolation in χ^2 and F tables.

are stated concisely in 5.17. Recall that the only difference in their *a priori* specifications is in the investment equation: equation (i17) includes lagged investment i_{-1} and excludes property income p; equation (i15) does the reverse.

8.2 In Sections 6 and 7 it was decided that the two-stage least-squares method is preferable to the limited-information method. Accordingly in Table 8.1 are given the two estimated reduced forms for the two models obtained by solving the two-stage least-squares versions of the estimated structures. Also shown for comparison is the least-squares estimate of the

TABLE 8.1 Three Estimated Reduced Forms for Two Models: Least-Squares Solved Two-Stage Least-Squares Version of the Structure, Using Investment Using Investment

Dep. Var.	Row No.	Estimation Method (and Model*)	Coefficient of						
			i_{-1}	a_{-1}	a_{-2}	k_{-1}	c_{-1}	$(w_b)_{-1}$	$(s_c)_{-1}$
c	1	LSRF (i17)	$-.570$	.381	$-.129$	$-.313$	.524	.224	.349
	2	Solved 2SLS (i17)	.515	.900	$-.613$	$-.217$	.675	.205	$-.803$
	3	Solved 2SLS (i15)	—	1.638	-1.685	$-.066$	1.781	$-.257$	-1.896
i	4	LSRF (i17)	$-.382$	.144	.205	$-.235$	.204	$-.336$	**1.393**
	5	Solved 2SLS (i17)	.485	.847	$-.577$	$-.205$	.157	.048	$-.187$
	6	Solved 2SLS (i15)	—	1.621	-1.668	$-.065$	1.266	$-.408$	-1.348
w_b	7	LSRF (i17)	$-.364$	**.474**	$-.151$	$-.212$	**.413**	.289	**.956**
	8	Solved 2SLS (i17)	.490	.856	$-.583$	$-.207$	.407	.347	$-.485$
	9	Solved 2SLS (i15)	—	1.611	-1.657	$-.065$	1.506	$-.112$	-1.603
s_c	10	LSRF (i17)	$-.157$	.060	.015	$-.210$	.183	$-.180$	**.596**
	11	Solved 2SLS (i17)	.249	.435	$-.296$	$-.105$	.207	$-.046$	.181
	12	Solved 2SLS (i15)	—	.861	$-.885$	$-.035$	.805	$-.289$	$-.467$
y	13	LSRF (i17)	$-.786$	**.466**	.058	$-.336$	.539	.075	**1.148**
	14	Solved 2SLS (i17)	.751	1.312	$-.894$	$-.317$	.624	.299	-1.171
	15	Solved 2SLS (i15)	—	2.398	-2.467	$-.097$	2.242	$-.376$	-2.777

reduced form for the model containing equation (i17) and the variable i_{-1}.

8.3 The discrepancies among the three estimated reduced forms in Table 8.1 are substantial. First, compare the two obtained by solving the two different structures. The "multipliers" (i.e., the reduced-form coefficients in Table 8.1) are reasonable when the investment equation (i17) is used, but in many cases are unreasonably large when (i15) is used. For example, consider the multipliers of real gross business product x_b in rows 17 and 18 with respect to government purchases g (government

Estimates of the Reduced Form of the Model Using Investment Equation (i17); Equation (i17); and Solved Two-Stage Least-Squares Version of the Structure, Equation (i15).

p_{-1}	g	w_g	t_p	t_b	d	1	s	R^2
.347	.325	−.660	−.260	**.537**	**2.793**	−28.75	2.07	.999
.483	1.740	.140	−1.880	−.962	−.962	−8.87		
1.327	6.124	−1.260	−4.864	−6.053	−6.053	14.91		
−.103	−.394	−.169	**1.050**	**.687**	**3.032**	−37.70	3.09	.986
.112	.637	−.200	−.437	−.224	−.224	−28.14		
.943	5.063	−1.606	3.457	−5.343	−5.343	−6.17		
−.171	**.466**	**−1.277**	**.524**	**.798**	1.705	−20.13	2.23	.999
.292	1.654	−.519	−1.135	−.581	−.581	−14.64		
1.122	6.024	−1.911	−4.113	−5.633	−5.633	7.84		
−.046	**.404**	**−.893**	.055	−.224	**1.480**	−29.67	1.59	.970
−.109	.841	−.264	−.577	−.784	−.784	−15.81		
.327	3.219	−1.021	−2.198	−3.532	−3.532	−4.84		
.289	.512	.086	−.267	.462	**3.325**	−36.41	3.27	.999
.704	2.536	.204	−2.740	−1.402	−1.402	−21.20		
1.943	8.969	1.845	−7.124	−8.864	−8.864	13.58		

TABLE 8.1

Dep. Var.	Row No.	Estimation Method (and Model*)	Coefficient of						
			i_{-1}	a_{-1}	a_{-2}	k_{-1}	c_{-1}	$(w_b)_{-1}$	$(s_c)_{-1}$
x_b	16	LSRF (*i*17)	**−.943**	**.526**	.073	**−.546**	**.722**	−.105	**1.744**
	17	Solved 2SLS (*i*17)	1.000	1.748	−1.190	−.422	.831	.253	−.990
	18	Solved 2SLS (*i*15)	—	3.259	−3.353	−.131	3.046	−.665	−3.244
	19	Presumed sign (*i*17)†	+	+	−	−	+	+	−
p	20	LSRF (*i*17)	**−.579**	.052	*.223*	**−.334**	*.309*	**−.395**	*.788*
	21	Solved 2SLS (*i*17)	.510	.891	−.607	−.215	.424	−.095	−.505
	22	Solved 2SLS (*i*15)	—	1.648	−1.696	−.066	1.540	−.553	−1.640

* "LSRF" means least-squares estimate of the reduced form. "Solved 2SLS" means the reduced-form estimate obtained by solving the structure after estimating it by two-stage least squares. The two models are the same except for the investment equation; see equations (5.10)–(5.16). The italic or boldface type used for certain LSRF estimates means that in absolute value the t ratio is between 1 and 2, or is 2 or more, respectively. Light type means the t ratio is one or less in absolute value.

wage payments w_g being held constant): they are respectively 3.377 and 12.19. Similarly for personal taxes t_p the respective multipliers of x_b are −2.317 and −8.322; and for business taxes t_b they are −1.185 and −11.40. Because of this the investment equation (*i*17), which contains i_{-1} but not p, is preferable to (*i*15), which contains p but not i_{-1}. Accordingly, (*i*17) is adopted and (*i*15) is rejected [see equations (5.10)–(5.16) above for the rest of the model as well as for the two investment equations].

8.4 Now compare in Table 8.1 the reduced form obtained by least squares with the one obtained by solving the two-stage least-squares estimate of the structure, using the chosen investment equation (*i*17). Again there are large discrepancies. Consider again the equation for gross business product x_b (rows 16 and 17): The two estimates of its multiplier with respect to government purchases g are .916 for ordinary least squares, and 3.377 for the solved structure when (*i*17) is used. The multipliers of x_b with respect to personal taxes t_p are even different in sign, being +.788 and −2.317 respectively, with the positive least-squares estimate having a t ratio exceeding 2. The list of predetermined variables for which the sign of the coefficient in the equation for x_b is different in the least-squares estimate from the sign in the solved preferred structure is:

$$i_{-1},\ a_{-2},\ (w_b)_{-1},\ (s_c)_{-1},\ t_p,\ t_b,\ d$$

(*cont.*)

p_{-1}	g	w_g	t_p	t_b	d	1	s	R^2
.243	.916	−1.807	.788	1.238	5.805	−66.09	3.74	.999
.595	3.377	−1.060	−2.317	−1.185	−1.185	−37.01		
2.270	12.19	−3.865	−8.322	−11.40	−11.40	8.74		
+	+	−	−	−	−			
.414	.450	−.530	.265	−.560	3.100	−45.96	2.83	.981
.304	1.722	−.541	−1.182	−1.605	−1.605	−22.37		
1.148	6.163	−1.955	−4.208	−6.763	−6.763	.89		

† The *a priori* signs (line 19) of reduced-form coefficients using investment equation (*i*17) come from the next-to-last column of Table 8.2. Those using equation (*i*15) are obtainable from a similar analysis of the model when (*i*15) is put in place of (*i*17); they are the same as for (*i*17) with two exceptions: the *a priori* signs for i_{-1} and $(w_b)_{-1}$ are positive, using (*i*17).

For all of these variables except a_{-2} and $(w_b)_{-1}$ the t ratio for the least-squares estimate exceeds 2. Similar discrepancies exist in the reduced-form equations for variables other than x_b.

8.5 To understand these discrepant results it is helpful to obtain the algebraic expressions for the reduced-form equations as explicit functions of the structural parameters. We exhibit the expression in one case, namely, the reduced-form equation for x_b when the investment equation (*i*17) is used [the structural parameter notation for β's and γ's is that of equations (5.10)–(5.16)]:[11]

$$(8.1) \qquad x_b = \frac{1}{\Delta} [\gamma_{28} i_{-1} + \gamma_{29} a_{-1} + \gamma_{2,10} a_{-2} + \gamma_{2,11} k_{-1}$$
$$+ \gamma_{1,12} c_{-1} + \beta_{15}\gamma_{3,13}(w_b)_{-1} - \beta_{15}\gamma_{4,14}(s_c)_{-1}$$
$$- \beta_{15}\gamma_{4,15} p_{-1} + g - (1 - \beta_{15})w_g$$
$$- \beta_{15}t_p - \beta_{15}(1 - \beta_{47})(t_b + d) + \mu]$$

[11] If all structural coefficients of lagged variables are set equal to zero, thus making the model static, then equations (8.1)–(8.3) become identical to equations (III.8.8–10) except that the structural parameters have different names, that is, β_{15} here is the same as α there, β_{47} here is θ there, etc. Compare equations (III.8.1–7) and (XI.5.1–7).

where Δ is the determinant of the system and μ is a function of intercepts, thus:

(8.2) $$\Delta = 1 - \beta_{26} - \beta_{15}[1 - \beta_{47}(1 - \beta_{36})]$$
(8.3) $$\mu = \gamma_{10} + \gamma_{20} - \beta_{15}(\gamma_{40} + \beta_{47}\gamma_{30})$$

8.6 Let us now examine the coefficients in (8.1) to see what can be said about them on the basis of *a priori* presumptions concerning the structure. Consider Δ first since it is the denominator of every coefficient in (8.1). As pointed out in III.8.4, Δ is presumed to be positive, since it is 1 minus the marginal propensity to spend out of an increase in GNP. Hence the multiplier of output x_b with respect to any predetermined variable in (8.1) will have the same sign as the corresponding coefficient inside the brackets in (8.1).

8.7 Consider the multiplier of x_b with respect to government purchases g (with government wages w_g held constant): it is $1/\Delta$. Hence it is presumed positive. Next consider the multipliers of x_b with respect to personal and business taxes: they are $-\beta_{15}/\Delta$ and $-\beta_{15}(1 - \beta_{47})/\Delta$, respectively. Recall that β_{15} is the marginal propensity to consume current disposable income, and hence is presumed to be between 0 and 1; and β_{47} is the marginal propensity of receivers of property income to retain corporate profits, and hence is also presumed to be between 0 and 1. Hence both tax multipliers are presumed negative. These results are summarized in Table 8.2, along with results for all other multipliers in (8.1). The table should be read, as its contents are not repeated in the text. The presumed signs given in Table 8.2 are entered in Table 8.1, row 19, for comparison with the empirical results in rows 16 and 17.

8.8 Notice that all of the signs in the *solved* 2*SLS structure* version of the reduced-form equation for output x_b are *in accord* with theoretical presumptions (compare rows 17 and 19 in Table 8.1).[12] But many of the signs in the *least-squares* version of the reduced-form equation for x_b are the opposite of the presumed signs (rows 16 and 19). Conspicuous here are the tax variables t_p and t_b, which have presumed negative effects on output but have positive coefficients in the least-squares version of the output equation. What can be the reason? It is clearly erroneous to attribute to increased taxes (other predetermined variables held constant) a stimulating effect on output. What has happened is that the cyclical and secular similarity in behavior between output and tax receipts over the sample period has been, so to speak, perceived by the least-squares estimation process, and accordingly that process has assigned positive coefficients to the tax variables. It is in the nature of the least-squares

---

[12] The statement in the text above refers to the model that uses investment equation (*i*17), but the equivalent statement using (*i*15) is also true; see Table 8.1, row 18, and note †.

TABLE 8.2   Presumed Signs of the Multipliers of Gross Business Product x_b with Respect to the Predetermined Variables Based on the Model Using Investment Equation $(i17) \equiv (5.11)$

Predetermined Variable	Multiplier of x_b	Presumed Sign of Multiplier	Reason for Presumed Sign* (Note $\Delta > 0$ and $0 < \beta_{15} = \partial c/\partial y < 1$)
i_{-1}	γ_{28}/Δ	+	$\gamma_{28} = \partial i/\partial i_{-1} > 0$
a_{-1}	γ_{29}/Δ	+	$\gamma_{29} = \partial i/\partial a_{-1} > 0$
a_{-2}	$\gamma_{2.10}/\Delta$	−	$\gamma_{2.10} = \partial i/\partial a_{-2} < 0$
k_{-1}	$\gamma_{2.11}/\Delta$	−	$\gamma_{2.11} = \partial i/\partial k_{-1} < 0$
c_{-1}	$\gamma_{1.12}/\Delta$	+	$\gamma_{1.12} = \partial c/\partial c_{-1} > 0$
$(w_b)_{-1}$	$\beta_{15}\gamma_{3.13}/\Delta$	+	$\gamma_{3.13} = \partial w_b/\partial (w_b)_{-1} > 0$
$(s_c)_{-1}$	$-\beta_{15}\gamma_{4.14}/\Delta$	−	$\gamma_{4.14} = \partial s_c/\partial (s_c)_{-1} > 0$
p_{-1}	$-\beta_{15}\gamma_{4.15}/\Delta$	+	$\gamma_{4.15} = \partial s_c/\partial p_{-1} < 0$
g	$1/\Delta$	+	$\Delta > 0$
w_g (g constant)	$-(1 - \beta_{15})/\Delta$	−	$0 < \beta_{15} = \partial c/\partial y < 1$
t_p	$-\beta_{15}/\Delta$	−	$0 < \beta_{15} = \partial c/\partial y$
t_b	$-\beta_{15}(1 - \beta_{47})/\Delta$	−	$\left. \begin{array}{l} \\ \\ \end{array} \right\} 0 < \beta_{47} = \partial s_c/\partial p < 1$
d	$-\beta_{15}(1 - \beta_{47})/\Delta$	−	

* The partial derivatives in this column are those of individual structural equations in 5.17.

Source: Equation (8.1) and paragraph 5.17.

process to respond to coincidences in behavior, whether or not they have a direct causal connection. This example gives dramatic and important illustration of how a good least-squares fit can sometimes be found even though the numerical values of the regression coefficients may be far from correct. This same example will excite further interest when the forecasts made by the two estimation methods are compared in the next section.

9 FORECASTS FROM THE REDUCED FORM

9.1   In this section are offered three sets of conditional forecasts of the seven jointly dependent variables (c, i, w_b, s_c, y, x_b, p) for 1960–61–62, based on the three sets of reduced-form estimates in Table 8.1, conditional on the actual observed values of the predetermined variables for those years. These forecasts are then compared with the observed values of the dependent variables. The errors are a measure of the one-year forecasting ability of the two models consisting of equations (5.10), (5.11) or (5.11'), and (5.12)–(5.16) when no errors are made in forecasting the predetermined variables.

9.2 Which reduced-form estimation method should be used to make forecasts from the chosen model? If ordinary least squares is used, the unexplained variation during the sample is minimized, but the restrictions placed on the reduced form by the overidentifying structural restrictions are ignored. If a solved structure is used, then the unexplained variation during the sample period is larger than under least squares, but the restrictions on the reduced form are taken into account. (Recall the discussion in VII.8.1–2 and IX.12.3–5.) If we believe the *a priori* restrictions incorporated in the overidentifying model, then clearly we should use the solved estimated structure, which conforms to these restrictions, rather than the ordinary least-squares estimate of the reduced form, which does not. If the latter forecasts better, it will be a kind of indication that the model's restrictions are not correct.

9.3 In Table 9.1 are shown actual values of the model's dependent variables y for 1960–1961–1962, and three forecasts $\hat{y}$ of each, and the corresponding errors of forecast $\hat{v}$. The three forecasts are based on the three different estimates of the reduced form shown in Table 8.1, namely, (1) least-squares estimates of the reduced form corresponding to the choice of investment equation ($i17$); (2) the solved two-stage least-squares version of the structure using ($i17$); and (3) the solved two-stage least-squares version of the structure using investment equation ($i15$) instead of ($i17$). It will be seen that the third, using ($i15$), which was rejected in 8.3 because it has unreasonably large multipliers, gives poorer forecasts than the other two, especially in 1960.

9.4 For the two sets of forecasts corresponding to the preferred investment equation ($i17$), Table 9.2 shows the algebraic mean forecast error $\dfrac{1}{3}\sum\limits_{1960}^{1962}\hat{v}_t$ for each endogenous variable, and the root-mean-square forecast error $\sqrt{\dfrac{1}{3}\sum\limits_{1960}^{1962}\hat{v}_t^{\,2}}$ for each, together with the standard error of estimate s from the sample period for comparison. For all the variables except property income p, the root-mean-square forecast error for LSRF (the least-squares estimate of the reduced form) is better (smaller) than that for the solved 2SLS estimated structure, and the difference is substantially in favor of LSRF in every case except those of labor income w_b and p. This suggests that the simple model used does not correspond sufficiently to the real world (recall the discussion in 9.2). The algebraic mean errors show essentially the same picture; we can see from them that for the solved 2SLS structure the mean error is negative for every variable, indicating a tendency for the model to predict too high on the average in 1960–1962. Note that the root mean square of the LSRF forecast error is of about the same order of magnitude as the sample-period standard error of estimate for every variable except labor and property income w_b and p;

TABLE 9.1   1960-61-62 Conditional Forecasts by Three Estimated Reduced Forms Given Correct Values of the Predetermined Variables; Least-Squares Estimates of the Reduced Form Using Investment Equation (i17) ≡ (5.11); Solved 2SLS Version of the Structure, Using Investment Equation (i17) ≡ (5.11); Solved 2SLS Version of the Structure, Using Investment Equation (i15) ≡ (5.11')

Dep. Var.	Estimation Method and Model*	1960			1961			1962		
		observed y	forecast $\hat{y}$	error $\hat{v}$	observed y	forecast $\hat{y}$	error $\hat{v}$	observed y	forecast $\hat{y}$	error $\hat{v}$
c	LSRF (i17)	298.1	295.8	2.3	303.6	299.8	3.8	317.6	319.6	-2.0
	solved 2SLS str. (i17)		292.1	6.0		308.0	-4.4		320.4	-2.8
	solved 2SLS str. (i15)		274.0	24.1		310.8	-7.2		318.8	-1.2
i	LSRF (i17)	60.2	64.4	-4.2	57.5	53.2	4.3	65.2	65.7	-0.5
	solved 2SLS str. (i17)		63.5	-3.3		62.7	-5.2		72.6	-7.4
	solved 2SLS str. (i15)		45.7	14.5		66.1	-8.6		71.8	-6.6
w_b	LSRF (i17)	259.0	262.8	-3.8	260.7	263.8	-3.1	273.2	281.7	-8.5
	solved 2SLS str. (i17)		256.5	2.5		267.6	-6.9		280.8	-7.6
	solved 2SLS str. (i15)		239.1	19.9		271.1	-10.4		280.1	-6.9
s_c	LSRF (i17)	6.7	7.1	-0.4	5.6	3.4	2.2	7.1	7.4	-0.3
	solved 2SLS str. (i17)		8.2	-1.5		9.9	-4.3		11.1	-4.0
	solved 2SLS str. (i15)		-1.2	7.9		11.8	-6.2		10.8	-3.7
y	LSRF (i17)	317.8	319.8	-2.0	328.3	322.8	5.5	343.5	346.0	-2.5
	solved 2SLS str. (i17)		313.3	4.5		333.4	-5.1		349.4	-5.9
	solved 2SLS str. (i15)		287.1	30.7		337.9	-9.6		347.5	-4.0
x_b	LSRF (i17)	405.2	407.5	-2.3	412.0	404.3	7.7	437.6	440.4	-2.8
	solved 2SLS str. (i17)		402.4	2.8		421.5	-9.5		447.7	-10.1
	solved 2SLS str. (i15)		366.2	39.0		427.4	-15.4		444.9	-7.3
p	LSRF (i17)	43.0	41.2	1.8	44.7	33.6	11.1	49.2	43.2	6.0
	solved 2SLS str. (i17)		42.2	0.8		46.8	-2.1		51.2	-2.0
	solved 2SLS str. (i15)		24.0	19.0		49.9	-5.2		49.8	-0.6

* See note * to Table 8.1.
Source: Tables 3.1 and 8.1

TABLE 9.2 Algebraic Means and Root Mean Squares of Conditional Forecast Errors, 1960–62, from Reduced Form of Preferred Model Using Investment Equation ($i17$), Given Correct Values of the Predetermined Variables; also s (Standard Error of Estimate) from the Least-Squares Reduced Form

Dep. Var.	Estimation Method	1959 Value of Dep. Var.	$\frac{1}{3}\sum_{1960}^{1962} v_t$ Algebraic Mean Error	$\sqrt{\frac{1}{3}\sum_{1960}^{1962} v_t^2}$ Root-Mean-Square Error	s from Reduced Form in Sample Period
c	LSRF	289.4	1.37	2.79	2.07
	solved 2SLS structure		−.41	4.60	—
i	LSRF	60.9	−.14	3.52	3.09
	solved S2LS structure		−5.30	5.56	—
w_b	LSRF	249.9	−5.12	5.65	2.23
	solved 2SLS structure		−4.01	6.11	—
s_c	LSRF	8.9	.52	1.32	1.59
	solved 2SLS structure		−3.25	3.48	—
y	LSRF	311.2	.33	3.66	3.27
	solved 2SLS structure		−2.16	5.21	—
x_b	LSRF	394.2	.86	4.93	3.74
	solved 2SLS structure		−5.57	8.16	—
p	LSRF	45.2	6.27	7.34	2.83
	solved 2SLS structure		−1.10	1.74	—

Source: Tables 3.1, 8.1, and 9.1.

the algebraic mean errors show that the LSRF tended to overestimate labor income and underestimate property income by about the same amount on the average in 1960–1962. (Table 9.1 confirms that this occurred in each of the three years.)

9.5 Figure 9.1 shows the two sets of forecasts based on the preferred model using investment equation ($i17$), together with the actual values. It shows that the LSRF estimates are typically better than the solved 2SLS structure in forecasting the hesitation or near-decline in 1961, although the LSRF forecasts exaggerate its magnitude.

9.6 One of the main weaknesses of this model is that the personal and business tax bills t_p and t_b are treated as exogenous. It would be better to treat the schedules of tax *rates* as exogenous, and let the tax

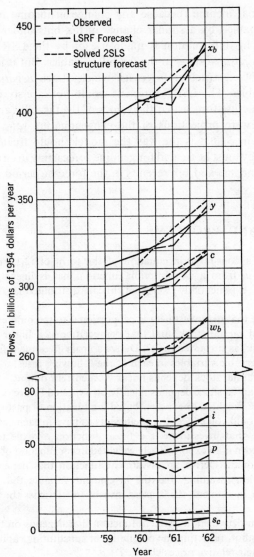

Figure 9.1 1960–61–62 forecasts made by two estimated reduced forms of the pre-ferred model, together with observed data.

bills emerge as endogenous functions of income and the tax rates. Treating tax bills as exogenous gives rise to *positive* coefficients for them in the LS reduced-form equation for gross business product x_b, as noted in 8.8. This helps to explain why the LSRF forecasts are better than the forecasts from the solved structure when correct values of predetermined variables are used. The *correct* values of the tax *bills* contain information about the change in national income (because any change in income next year is typically accompanied by a similar change in tax bills under our actual tax structure). This information is made use of by the LSRF forecasts since they attach *positive* signs to the tax-bill variables. But it is not made use of by the solved-structure forecasts, which attach *negative* signs to the tax-bill variables. The LSRF forecasts would not fare so well relative to the solved-structure forecasts if the values of the tax-bill variables used in the forecasts were projections of the exogenous tax *rates* applied to endogenous income. That is the way the model should treat taxes, and that is the way they must be treated for genuine forecasting in circumstances where national income and tax receipts in the forecast period are not yet known.

QUESTIONS AND PROBLEMS

2.1. Derive a consumption equation of the form of (2.1), namely $c = \beta y + \gamma c_{-1} + \alpha + u$, from a consumption function that is linear in expected income and the exponentially weighted linear distributed-lag expectation hypothesis given in V.7.6–7.

2.2. Assume that net investment is proportional to the difference between desired and actual capital stock, and that depreciation is a linear function of actual capital stock, as suggested in 2.7. Derive a gross investment function that includes only observable variables in each of the following cases.

(a) Desired capital stock depends linearly on current output.

(b) Desired capital stock depends linearly on expected future output, which is an exponentially weighted linear distributed-lag function of past outputs.

What signs would you expect the coefficients to have in each case? Explain.

2.3. Assume that investment is a linear function of expected property income, which in turn is an exponentially weighted linear function of current and past property incomes. Derive an investment function that depends only on observable variables, assuming that the investment variable that behaves as specified (a) is net investment, (b) is gross investment. Discuss the signs of the coefficients.

2.4. Can you derive an investment function that depends on the prices of both capital and labor, reflecting the possibility of substituting capital for labor or vice versa as their relative prices change?

2.5. What should the demand for labor depend on in a model that contains the investment function of the preceding question?

2.6. What economic factors would you expect to find important in the determination of the ratio of corporate profit to total property income?

3.1. In the model used in this chapter,

(a) Where do United States exports and imports appear?

(b) What use is made of relative prices?

Hint: There are several price series, including deflators for GNP, for consumption, and for plant and equipment investment.

(c) How can one defend the use of a time series for capital stock that begins with a zero value for 1928 and is often negative?

(d) How is the income of unincorporated business treated when total income is allocated between labor and property?

(e) How is the "statistical discrepancy" in national accounting treated?

3.2. Examine the time series for t_p (personal tax and nontax payments) in Table 3.1.

(a) Do you find its behavior reasonable?

(b) Can you explain why it behaves as it does, particularly in recent years?

4.1. What meaning can be attached to the so-called t ratios computed for the least-squares estimates in Tables 4.1–4.4?

4.2. Before reading Section 5 and those following, comment on the least-squares equations and indicate which ones are most satisfactory, and why, (a) for consumption (in Table 4.1), (b) for investment (in Table 4.2), (c) for labor (in Table 4.3), (d) for corporate saving (in Table 4.4).

4.3. In which equations of Tables 4.1–4.4 would you expect to find the greatest difficulties due to multicollinearity? (*Hint:* see Tables 4.5–4.8.) Are your expectations borne out? Explain.

4.4. For an equation (or equations) of your choice, prepare data and compute the least-squares estimates, including t ratios, R^2, and standard error of estimate.

5.1. Approximately what value would you expect for the long-run marginal propensity to pay out corporate profits in dividends, in equation (5.9)? Do the results in Table 4.4 require you to reject your hypothesis? Explain.

5.2. Interpret investment equation (i19) in Table 4.2 in terms of the equation $i = \alpha + \beta p^e$ and $p^e = \gamma p^e_{-1} + (1 - \gamma)p$, where p^e is expected property income.

5.3. Derive investment equation (i17) from the theoretical approach indicated in 5.13.

5.4. Compare your results in question 4.2 with the discussion of Section 5.

5.5. List the predetermined variables in each of the two models given in 5.17.

5.6. Examine both of the models in 5.17 to see whether either one is segmentable (in the sense defined in III.3.4).

6.1. Give another possible set of predetermined variables, different from the set given in 6.1, that could appropriately have been used for the limited-information and two-stage least-squares estimation of (a) the consumption equation (c1), (b) the investment equation (i15), (c) the investment equation (i17), (d) the labor equation (w1), (e) the corporate saving equation (s1).

6.2. For an equation such as (w1) whose constant term is expected to be zero, how would you interpret each of the following alternative possible results concerning the estimated constant term?

(a) It is numerically large and statistically "significant."

(b) It is numerically large but not statistically "significant."

(c) It is numerically small and statistically "significant" (which occurred in this case; see 6.4).

6.3. Why should the R^2 column be blank for the simultaneous-equations estimates in Tables 6.1–6.4?

6.4. Comment on the estimates in Tables 6.1–6.4, especially the limited-information estimates of investment equation ($i15$) in Table 6.2′.

6.5. For a simple model of your choice, prepare data and compute the limited-information and two-stage least-squares estimates, including t ratios and the standard errors of estimate. For each equation estimated by the limited-information method, find the value of the smallest root l_1 of the determinantal equation. (Compare question 4.4.)

6.6. For a model of your choice, compute estimates for some member of the k-class other than least squares, limited information, and two-stage least squares.

7.1. What meaning can be given to the results of the Durbin-Watson test of simultaneous-equations-method residuals in Tables 6.1–6.4?

7.2. How large a percentage error does each of the structural equations in Tables 6.1–6.4 make in explaining its dependent variable, on the average?

7.3. What does the Basmann F test in Table 7.2 suggest about the choice between property income p and lagged investment i_{-1} in the investment equation of the model used in this chapter?

8.1. Revise the model of this chapter so that the tax bills t_p and t_b are *endogenous*, determined by exogenous tax *rates* and endogenous taxable bases. Then obtain the reduced-form equation for gross business product in the revised model, and apply *a priori* theoretical presumptions to find the expected algebraic signs of its coefficients.

8.2. Compute the least-squares estimate of the reduced-form equation for gross business product in the model of the preceding question, and compare the signs of its coefficients with your theoretical presumptions about them.

8.3. Are you surprised that all the algebraic signs of the coefficients in the "solved 2SLS structure" version of the reduced-form equation for business product x_b are in accord with theoretical presumptions, as shown in lines 17 and 19 in Table 8.1? Explain.

9.1. How well do the reduced-form equations of Table 8.1 forecast the observed data for 1963 and later? (Note that a major national income data revision occurred in 1965; see the August, 1965 *Survey of Current Business*.)

9.2. What are the main points at which the model of this chapter needs revision? What revisions would you propose?

APPENDIX A

Some Rudiments of Matrix Algebra

1 INTRODUCTION; DEFINITIONS; ELEMENTARY OPERATIONS WITH MATRICES

1.1 In this appendix some of the fundamentals of matrix algebra are set out with a view to aiding the reader of Chapters VIII, IX, and X who is unfamiliar with matrices. The reader interested in further material on matrices, including proofs, is referred to elementary books on the subject.[1]

1.2 Any real number between minus infinity and plus infinity is called a *scalar*. We have all been using scalars all our lives, some of us without knowing it. Examples are -1, 360 billion, $\log_e 2$, $\sqrt{3}$, $1/5$, etc. They can properly be called scalars because they can be measured along a scale from $-\infty$ to $+\infty$.

1.3 Any rectangular array of scalars, arranged in rows and columns, is called a *matrix*. The scalars composing the matrix are called *elements* of the matrix.[2] For convenience we shall often use R to stand for the number of rows, and C or K for the number of columns, in whatever matrix we happen to be talking about in this appendix. An example of a matrix having $R = 2$ and $C = 3$ is

$$(1.1) \qquad \begin{pmatrix} 11 & 0 & 8 \\ -5 & 2 & -7 \end{pmatrix}$$

[1] See for example Aitken [1949], which is particularly useful for beginners, or Albert [1941], or the chapters on matrices and vectors in Allen [1956]. More advanced works are Frazer, Duncan, and Collar [1938], Birkhoff and MacLane [1953], and Bellman [1960].

[2] Matrices whose elements are complex numbers (like $a + b\sqrt{-1}$ where a and b are real numbers) are widely used but not in this book.

The number of elements of a matrix having R rows and C columns is R times C. Such a matrix is said to be of order R by C or $R \times C$. (The number of rows is always given first, by convention.) A matrix is *square* if it has the same number of rows as columns, that is, if $R = C$. If a matrix has $R = 1$ and $C > 1$, the matrix has only one row and is said to be a *row vector*. If a matrix has $R > 1$ and $C = 1$, it is said to be a *column vector*. Hence all vectors are matrices, but not all matrices are vectors. An example of a row vector of order 1 by 4 is (3　−1　0　5). We use specific kinds of symbols to denote matrices and vectors. A boldface capital letter such as **A** or **X** will stand for a matrix. A boldface lower-case letter such as **a** or **x** will stand for a row vector. A boldface lower-case letter with a prime such as **a**′ or **x**′ will stand for a column vector (whose elements reading down the column are the same as the elements of **a** or **x**, respectively, reading left to right). A light italic letter will denote a scalar.

1.4　To discuss a matrix having unknown or numerically unspecified elements, it is often convenient to use a single letter for the unknown elements and attach two subscripts to each, thus:

$$(1.2) \qquad \mathbf{A} = \begin{pmatrix} a_{11} & a_{12} & a_{13} \\ a_{21} & a_{22} & a_{23} \end{pmatrix}$$

In each case (again by convention) the first subscript shows which row the element is in, and the second shows which column. Thus a_{rc} is the element in the rth row and cth column.[3] It is usual to use the same letter of the alphabet to denote the matrix as to denote its elements; thus **A** is the matrix whose elements are a_{rc} $(r = 1, 2; c = 1, 2, 3)$ in equation (1.2). Similarly, **X** would denote a matrix of order R by C whose elements are x_{rc} $(r = 1, \ldots, R; c = 1, \ldots, C)$. Sometimes an R by C matrix with elements such as a_{rc} is expressed as (a_{rc}) or as $\|a_{rc}\|$, as well as in the following way, which we shall use most often:

$$(1.3) \qquad \mathbf{A} = \begin{pmatrix} a_{11} & \cdots & a_{1C} \\ \vdots & & \vdots \\ a_{R1} & \cdots & a_{RC} \end{pmatrix}$$

If two matrices are of the same order and each element of one is equal to the corresponding element of the other, the two matrices are said to be equal.

1.5　We shall discuss the definitions and rules for adding, subtracting, and multiplying matrices in this section and the rules for "dividing" in

---

[3] Most writers use i for row and j for column, but we shall often use r and c in this appendix because they are easier to remember.

Section 3. First and simplest, the rule for multiplying a scalar times a matrix is to multiply each element of the matrix by the scalar. Thus, if the matrix in (1.1) is to be multiplied by -3, the result is

$$(1.4) \quad -3\begin{pmatrix} 11 & 0 & 8 \\ -5 & 2 & -7 \end{pmatrix} = \begin{pmatrix} 11 & 0 & 8 \\ -5 & 2 & -7 \end{pmatrix}(-3) = \begin{pmatrix} -33 & 0 & -24 \\ 15 & -6 & 21 \end{pmatrix}$$

In more general terms, if the matrix $\mathbf{A}$ in (1.3) is multiplied by the scalar λ, the result is

$$(1.5) \qquad \lambda\mathbf{A} = \mathbf{A}\lambda = \begin{pmatrix} \lambda a_{11} & \cdots & \lambda a_{1C} \\ \cdot & & \cdot \\ \cdot & & \cdot \\ \cdot & & \cdot \\ \lambda a_{R1} & \cdots & \lambda a_{RC} \end{pmatrix}$$

Notice that the order of scalar multiplication makes no difference, that is, $\lambda\mathbf{A} = \mathbf{A}\lambda$, and the product $\lambda\mathbf{A}$ always exists if λ is a scalar and $\mathbf{A}$ is a matrix.

1.6 The matrices $\mathbf{A}$ and $\mathbf{B}$ can be added or subtracted if they are of the same order, but they cannot be added or subtracted otherwise. The rule for adding $\mathbf{A}$ and $\mathbf{B}$ if they are of the same order is to add their corresponding elements in pairs, that is, a_{11} is added to b_{11}, a_{12} to b_{12}, a_{13} to b_{13}, and so forth. The result, if we call the sum $\mathbf{S}$, is

$$(1.6) \quad \mathbf{S} = \mathbf{A} + \mathbf{B} = \mathbf{B} + \mathbf{A} = \begin{pmatrix} s_{11} & \cdots & s_{1C} \\ \cdot & & \cdot \\ \cdot & & \cdot \\ \cdot & & \cdot \\ s_{R1} & \cdots & s_{RC} \end{pmatrix}$$

$$= \begin{pmatrix} a_{11} + b_{11} & \cdots & a_{1C} + b_{1C} \\ \cdot & & \cdot \\ \cdot & & \cdot \\ \cdot & & \cdot \\ a_{R1} + b_{R1} & \cdots & a_{RC} + b_{RC} \end{pmatrix}$$

Notice that the order of addition makes no difference, that is, $\mathbf{A} + \mathbf{B} = \mathbf{B} + \mathbf{A}$. The rule for subtraction is similar, the rcth element of the difference $\mathbf{A} - \mathbf{B}$ being $a_{rc} - b_{rc}$. Notice that as in ordinary arithmetic the order of subtraction does make a difference, that is, in general $\mathbf{A} - \mathbf{B} \neq \mathbf{B} - \mathbf{A}$.

1.7 So far matrices seem to have arithmetical rules similar to the rules for ordinary numbers (scalars). Indeed, they are a sort of number system in themselves. And like ordinary numbers, they have a sort of "zero," which when added to any matrix (of the same order) leaves that matrix unchanged, and also a sort of "unity" which when multiplied by any matrix (of the right order) leaves that matrix unchanged. A "zero" matrix is a matrix all of whose elements are zero; zero matrices can differ only in their order. A zero matrix or vector will be denoted by a boldface zero, **0** or **0**′, and the context will tell whether a zero matrix or a zero vector is meant, and of what order. The fundamental property of a zero matrix is that it does not change anything that it is added to. For example, if a zero matrix of order 2 by 3 is added to the matrix in (1.1), the result is

$$(1.7) \quad \begin{pmatrix} 11 & 0 & 8 \\ -5 & 2 & -7 \end{pmatrix} + \mathbf{0} = \begin{pmatrix} 11 & 0 & 8 \\ -5 & 2 & -7 \end{pmatrix} + \begin{pmatrix} 0 & 0 & 0 \\ 0 & 0 & 0 \end{pmatrix}$$

$$= \begin{pmatrix} 11+0 & 0+0 & 8+0 \\ -5+0 & 2+0 & -7+0 \end{pmatrix} = \begin{pmatrix} 11 & 0 & 8 \\ -5 & 2 & -7 \end{pmatrix}$$

A "unit" matrix, or an identity matrix or identity as it is often called, is a square matrix with 1's down the northwest-southeast diagonal and zeros elsewhere. Identity matrices can differ only in their order. They are denoted by **I**. The context usually shows the order of a zero or unit matrix, so the same symbol is usually used for all orders. The 3 by 3 identity is

$$(1.8) \qquad\qquad \mathbf{I} = \begin{pmatrix} 1 & 0 & 0 \\ 0 & 1 & 0 \\ 0 & 0 & 1 \end{pmatrix}$$

1.8 In order to use and understand the identity **I**, it is necessary to learn the rule for matrix multiplication. The rule is that two matrices **A** and **B** can be multiplied in the order **AB** (i.e., **A** on the left and **B** on the right) if the number of columns of **A** is the same as the number of rows of **B**, and not otherwise. Similarly, they can be multiplied in the order **BA** if the number of columns of **B** is the same as the number of rows of **A**, and not otherwise. For example, consider the following three matrices:

$$(1.9)$$

$$\mathbf{X} = \begin{pmatrix} 11 & 0 & 8 \\ -5 & 2 & -7 \end{pmatrix}, \quad \mathbf{Y} = \begin{pmatrix} 1 & 0 \\ -3 & 4 \\ 0 & 9 \end{pmatrix}, \quad \mathbf{Z} = \begin{pmatrix} 2 & 0 & -1 & 3 \\ 5 & 6 & 8 & -2 \\ 10 & -7 & 0 & 4 \end{pmatrix}$$

XY is a permissible product, for **X** has three columns and **Y** has three rows. **YX** is a permissible product, for **Y** has two columns and **X** has two rows. **XZ** is permissible, and **ZX** is not. What about **YZ** and **ZY**?

1.9 The procedure for multiplying two matrices is as follows:[4] The element in the *first row* and *first column* of the product is obtained from

---

[4] If you do not at first understand the ensuing sentence in the text, pass on to the example and return. The type faces in the text are intended to emphasize that *rows* of the *left* factor are combined with *columns* of the *right* factor.

the *first row* of the *left*-hand factor and the *first column* of the *right*-hand factor, and is equal to the sum of the pairwise products of the corresponding elements of that row and column. For example, the first-row first-column element of the product **XY** is as follows, if we denote the product by **P**:

$$(1.10) \qquad p_{11} = 11 \times 1 + 0 \times (-3) + 8 \times 0 = 11 + 0 + 0 = 11$$

Similarly, the element in the *first row* and *second column* of **XY** is obtained from the *first row* of **X** and the *second column* of **Y**, thus:

$$(1.11) \qquad p_{12} = 11 \times 0 + 0 \times 4 + 8 \times 9 = 72$$

And so on. The entire product **XY** is

(1.12)

$$\mathbf{XY} = \begin{pmatrix} 11 & 0 & 8 \\ -5 & 2 & -7 \end{pmatrix} \begin{pmatrix} 1 & 0 \\ -3 & 4 \\ 0 & 9 \end{pmatrix}$$

$$= \begin{pmatrix} 11 \times 1 + 0 \times (-3) + 8 \times 0 & 11 \times 0 + 0 \times 4 + 8 \times 9 \\ -5 \times 1 + 2 \times (-3) - 7 \times 0 & -5 \times 0 + 2 \times 4 - 7 \times 9 \end{pmatrix}$$

$$= \begin{pmatrix} 11 & 72 \\ -11 & -55 \end{pmatrix}$$

This process is sometimes referred to as "row-by-column" multiplication. It may be helpful to think of it by this name, as an aid to remembering that to multiply **X** by **Y**, in that order, we multiply rows of **X** by columns of **Y**. And of course to multiply **Y** by **X** in that order we would multiply rows of **Y** by columns of **X**:

$$(1.13) \qquad \mathbf{YX} = \begin{pmatrix} 1 & 0 \\ -3 & 4 \\ 0 & 9 \end{pmatrix} \begin{pmatrix} 11 & 0 & 8 \\ -5 & 2 & -7 \end{pmatrix}$$

$$= \begin{pmatrix} 1 \times 11 + 0 \times (-5) & 1 \times 0 + 0 \times 2 & 1 \times 8 + 0 \times (-7) \\ -3 \times 11 + 4 \times (-5) & -3 \times 0 + 4 \times 2 & -3 \times 8 + 4 \times (-7) \\ 0 \times 11 + 9 \times (-5) & 0 \times 0 + 9 \times 2 & 0 \times 8 + 9 \times (-7) \end{pmatrix}$$

$$= \begin{pmatrix} 11 & 0 & 8 \\ -53 & 8 & -52 \\ -45 & 18 & -63 \end{pmatrix}$$

To illustrate multiplication by the identity $\mathbf{I}$, consider these products:

$$(1.14) \quad \mathbf{XI} = \begin{pmatrix} 11 & 0 & 8 \\ -5 & 2 & -7 \end{pmatrix} \begin{pmatrix} 1 & 0 & 0 \\ 0 & 1 & 0 \\ 0 & 0 & 1 \end{pmatrix}$$

$$= \begin{pmatrix} 11 \times 1 + 0 + 0 & 0 + 0 \times 1 + 0 & 0 + 0 + 8 \times 1 \\ -5 \times 1 + 0 + 0 & 0 + 2 \times 1 + 0 & 0 + 0 - 7 \times 1 \end{pmatrix}$$

$$= \begin{pmatrix} 11 & 0 & 8 \\ -5 & 2 & -7 \end{pmatrix} = \mathbf{X}$$

$$(1.15) \quad \mathbf{IX} = \begin{pmatrix} 1 & 0 \\ 0 & 1 \end{pmatrix} \begin{pmatrix} 11 & 0 & 8 \\ -5 & 2 & -7 \end{pmatrix}$$

$$= \begin{pmatrix} 1 \times 11 + 0 & 1 \times 0 + 0 & 1 \times 8 + 0 \\ 0 + 1 \times (-5) & 0 + 1 \times 2 & 0 + 1 \times (-7) \end{pmatrix} = \begin{pmatrix} 11 & 0 & 8 \\ -5 & 2 & -7 \end{pmatrix} = \mathbf{X}$$

Note that any matrix $\mathbf{A}$ times the zero matrix of suitable order is zero, that is, $\mathbf{A} \cdot \mathbf{0} = \mathbf{0}, \quad \mathbf{0} \cdot \mathbf{A} = \mathbf{0}$.

1.10 Notice in (1.12) and (1.13) that $\mathbf{XY} \neq \mathbf{YX}$; in fact in that example $\mathbf{XY}$ and $\mathbf{YX}$ are not even of the same order! In this respect matrices are quite different from ordinary numbers, for which the order of multiplication is immaterial. For matrices the order of multiplication is extremely important, and we must be conscious of it all the time in using them. To aid thought about this, special terminology is used to describe multiplication. The product $\mathbf{XY}$ is known as "$\mathbf{X}$ multiplied on the right (or postmultiplied) by $\mathbf{Y}$" or as "$\mathbf{Y}$ multiplied on the left (or premultiplied) by $\mathbf{X}$." Notice also that the product of two matrices (if they can be multiplied) is a matrix having the same number of *rows* as the *left*-hand factor and the same number of *columns* as the *right*-hand factor. What happens is that each row of the left factor gives rise to a row in the product, and each column in the right factor gives rise to a column in the product. The rows of the left factor and the columns of the right must have the same number of elements (as stated earlier in 1.8), so that the rows of the left factor can be multiplied into the columns of the right.

1.11 It is quite easy to express the elements of a product $\mathbf{P}$ of two matrices $\mathbf{A}$ and $\mathbf{B}$ in general algebraic terms. Let $\mathbf{A}$ be R by C, and let $\mathbf{B}$ be C by K. Then the product of $\mathbf{A}$ multiplied on the right by $\mathbf{B}$ will be R

by K, thus:

(1.16)

$$\mathbf{P} = \mathbf{AB} = \begin{pmatrix} a_{11} & a_{12} & a_{13} & \cdots & a_{1C} \\ \cdot & \cdot & \cdot & & \cdot \\ \cdot & \cdot & \cdot & & \cdot \\ \cdot & \cdot & \cdot & & \cdot \\ a_{R1} & a_{R2} & a_{R3} & \cdots & a_{RC} \end{pmatrix} \begin{pmatrix} b_{11} & b_{12} & \cdots & b_{1K} \\ b_{21} & b_{22} & \cdots & b_{2K} \\ b_{31} & b_{32} & \cdots & b_{3K} \\ \cdot & \cdot & & \cdot \\ \cdot & \cdot & & \cdot \\ \cdot & \cdot & & \cdot \\ b_{C1} & b_{C2} & \cdots & b_{CK} \end{pmatrix}$$

$$= \begin{pmatrix} p_{11} & p_{12} & \cdots & p_{1K} \\ \cdot & \cdot & & \cdot \\ \cdot & \cdot & & \cdot \\ \cdot & \cdot & & \cdot \\ p_{R1} & p_{R2} & \cdots & p_{RK} \end{pmatrix}$$

By the rule stated above in 1.9, p_{11}, p_{12}, and so forth must be as follows:

(1.17)

$$p_{11} = a_{11}b_{11} + a_{12}b_{21} + a_{13}b_{31} + \cdots + a_{1C}b_{C1} = \sum_{c=1}^{C} a_{1c}b_{c1}$$

$$p_{12} = a_{11}b_{12} + a_{12}b_{22} + a_{13}b_{32} + \cdots + a_{1C}b_{C2} = \sum_{c=1}^{C} a_{1c}b_{c2}$$

$$p_{rk} = a_{r1}b_{1k} + a_{r2}b_{2k} + a_{r3}b_{3k} + \cdots + a_{rC}b_{Ck} = \sum_{c=1}^{C} a_{rc}b_{ck}$$

$$r = 1, \ldots, R; \quad k = 1, \ldots, K$$

The first two equations of (1.17) describe p_{11} and p_{12}, first in extended form and then in the shorthand $\sum$ (summation) notation explained in III.10.1. The reader should verify and compare them carefully and in detail. The equation for p_{rk} describes the typical element in the product **AB**, that is, the element in the rth row and kth column, where r is any number from 1 to R and k is any number from 1 to K. It says that p_{rk} is obtained by multiplying pairwise the corresponding elements of the rth row of **A** and the kth column of **B** and then adding up all the resulting terms $a_{rc}b_{ck}$, for $c = 1$ up through $c = C$. Therefore another way of writing the product **AB** is

$$(1.18) \quad \mathbf{P} = \mathbf{AB} = \begin{pmatrix} a_{11} & \cdots & a_{1C} \\ \cdot & & \cdot \\ \cdot & & \cdot \\ \cdot & & \cdot \\ a_{R1} & \cdots & a_{RC} \end{pmatrix} \begin{pmatrix} b_{11} & \cdots & b_{1K} \\ \cdot & & \cdot \\ \cdot & & \cdot \\ \cdot & & \cdot \\ b_{C1} & \cdots & b_{CK} \end{pmatrix}$$

$$= \begin{pmatrix} \sum\limits_{c=1}^{C} a_{1c}b_{c1} & \cdots & \sum\limits_{c=1}^{C} a_{1c}b_{cK} \\ \cdot & & \cdot \\ \cdot & & \cdot \\ \cdot & & \cdot \\ \sum\limits_{c=1}^{C} a_{Rc}b_{c1} & \cdots & \sum\limits_{c=1}^{C} a_{Rc}b_{cK} \end{pmatrix}$$

1.12 An important use of matrices in economics is to simplify the handling of systems of linear equations. Consider how the following system of two equations in two variables x_1 and x_2 can be represented in matrix form:

$$(1.19) \quad \begin{aligned} y_1 &= a_{11}x_1 + a_{12}x_2 \\ y_2 &= a_{21}x_1 + a_{22}x_2 \end{aligned}$$

First, this system may be regarded as saying that two particular column vectors are equal, as follows:

$$(1.20) \quad \begin{pmatrix} y_1 \\ y_2 \end{pmatrix} = \begin{pmatrix} a_{11}x_1 + a_{12}x_2 \\ a_{21}x_1 + a_{22}x_2 \end{pmatrix}$$

Next, the column vector on the right side of (1.20) may be regarded as the product of a square matrix of a's multiplied on the right by a column vector of x's, thus:

$$(1.21) \quad \begin{pmatrix} y_1 \\ y_2 \end{pmatrix} = \begin{pmatrix} a_{11} & a_{12} \\ a_{21} & a_{22} \end{pmatrix} \begin{pmatrix} x_1 \\ x_2 \end{pmatrix}$$

Let us now denote the column vector of y's by $\mathbf{y}'$, the matrix of a's by $\mathbf{A}$, and the column vector of x's by $\mathbf{x}'$. Then we have

$$(1.22) \quad \mathbf{y}' = \mathbf{Ax}'$$

Note that we cannot say that $\mathbf{y}'$ is equal to $\mathbf{x}'\mathbf{A}$, for $\mathbf{x}'\mathbf{A}$ does not exist under the rules of matrix multiplication. We can, however, regard (1.19) as saying that two particular row vectors are equal, as follows:

$$(1.23) \quad (y_1 \quad y_2) = (a_{11}x_1 + a_{12}x_2 \quad a_{21}x_1 + a_{22}x_2)$$

and this can be rewritten as a product of a matrix of a's multiplied on the left by a row vector of x's, thus:

$$(1.24) \qquad (y_1 \quad y_2) = (x_1 \quad x_2)\begin{pmatrix} a_{11} & a_{21} \\ a_{12} & a_{22} \end{pmatrix}$$

If the row vectors of y's and x's are denoted by $\mathbf{y}$ and $\mathbf{x}$ respectively, and if this matrix of a's (which is different from $\mathbf{A}$—look closely) is denoted by $\mathbf{A}'$, the system can be written

$$(1.25) \qquad\qquad \mathbf{y} = \mathbf{x}\mathbf{A}'$$

1.13 Any system of linear equations can be expressed in matrix form. The general system of M linear equations in the N variables $x_1, \ldots, x_N$ is

$$y_1 = \sum_{j=1}^{N} a_{1j}x_j$$

$$(1.26)$$

$$y_M = \sum_{j=1}^{N} a_{Mj}x_j$$

Let $\mathbf{y}'$ and $\mathbf{x}'$ now denote column vectors with M and N elements, respectively, and let $\mathbf{A}$ now denote the matrix

$$(1.27) \qquad\qquad \mathbf{A} = \begin{pmatrix} a_{11} & \cdots & a_{1N} \\ & & \\ & & \\ & & \\ a_{M1} & \cdots & a_{MN} \end{pmatrix}$$

Then the system (1.26) in matrix terms is just like (1.22) again. In other words, (1.22) is a quite general formulation of a set of M linear equations in N variables $x_1, \ldots, x_N$, whether $M = N = 2$ as in (1.19) or whether M and N are unspecified integers as in (1.26).

1.14 The operations of adding and multiplying matrices have their counterparts in similar operations performed on systems of equations. If two matrices $\mathbf{A}$ and $\mathbf{B}$ of the same order are added, the resulting matrix $\mathbf{A} + \mathbf{B}$ is the matrix of a system of equations obtained by adding corresponding equations pairwise from the two systems of equations whose matrices are $\mathbf{A}$ and $\mathbf{B}$. Thus, if

$$(1.28) \qquad \begin{aligned} y_1 &= a_{11}x_1 + a_{12}x_2 \\ y_2 &= a_{21}x_1 + a_{22}x_2 \end{aligned} \qquad \mathbf{y}' = \mathbf{A}\mathbf{x}'$$

$$(1.29) \qquad \begin{aligned} z_1 &= b_{11}x_1 + b_{12}x_2 \\ z_2 &= b_{21}x_1 + b_{22}x_2 \end{aligned} \qquad \mathbf{z}' = \mathbf{B}\mathbf{x}'$$

then by addition we obtain

(1.30)

$$y_1 + z_1 = (a_{11} + b_{11})x_1 + (a_{12} + b_{12})x_2$$
$$y_2 + z_2 = (a_{21} + b_{21})x_1 + (a_{22} + b_{22})x_2$$

i.e., $\quad \mathbf{y'} + \mathbf{z'} = (\mathbf{A} + \mathbf{B})\mathbf{x'}$

If two matrices $\mathbf{A}$ and $\mathbf{E}$ of order R by C and C by K respectively are multiplied together, with $\mathbf{A}$ on the left, the resulting matrix $\mathbf{AE}$ is the matrix of a system of equations obtained by substituting the system whose matrix is $\mathbf{E}$ into the system whose matrix is $\mathbf{A}$. Thus, suppose that $\mathbf{y'} = \mathbf{Ax'}$, just as in (1.28) above, and that

(1.31)
$$x_1 = e_{11}w_1 + e_{12}w_2$$
$$x_2 = e_{21}w_1 + e_{22}w_2$$

i.e., $\quad \mathbf{x'} = \mathbf{Ew'}$

Then substitution of the functions of w_1 and w_2 for x_1 and x_2 in (1.28) yields

$$y_1 = a_{11}(e_{11}w_1 + e_{12}w_2) + a_{12}(e_{21}w_1 + e_{22}w_2)$$
$$= (a_{11}e_{11} + a_{12}e_{21})w_1 + (a_{11}e_{12} + a_{12}e_{22})w_2$$

(1.32)
$$y_2 = a_{21}(e_{11}w_1 + e_{12}w_2) + a_{22}(e_{21}w_1 + e_{22}w_2)$$
$$= (a_{21}e_{11} + a_{22}e_{21})w_1 + (a_{21}e_{12} + a_{22}e_{22})w_2$$

or $\quad\quad\quad \mathbf{y'} = \mathbf{AEw'}$

Observe that while $(\mathbf{A} + \mathbf{B})\mathbf{x'}$ and $(\mathbf{B} + \mathbf{A})\mathbf{x'}$ are equal, $\mathbf{AEw'}$ and $\mathbf{EAw'}$ are not equal, in general.

1.15 If the rows and columns of a matrix are interchanged, the result is a new matrix having as many rows as the original matrix had columns, and vice versa. This operation is extremely important in matrix theory, and hence has a name. It is called transposing or transposition, and the resulting new matrix is called the *transpose* of the old. The transpose of $\mathbf{A}$ is usually denoted by $\mathbf{A'}$, called "A transpose." We have already seen examples of this with $\mathbf{A}, \mathbf{y}$, and $\mathbf{x}$ in 1.12. For a more concrete example, consider the transpose of the matrix $\mathbf{X}$, which we used earlier for illustration:

(1.33)
$$\mathbf{X} = \begin{pmatrix} 11 & 0 & 8 \\ -5 & 2 & -7 \end{pmatrix}; \quad \mathbf{X'} = \begin{pmatrix} 11 & -5 \\ 0 & 2 \\ 8 & -7 \end{pmatrix}$$

The transpose of $\mathbf{X'}$ is $\mathbf{X}$ itself, and the same is true of any matrix. The transpose of an R by C matrix is a C by R matrix. Hence only a square matrix can have its transpose of the same order as itself. If a square matrix is equal to its transpose, it is said to be *symmetric*. This is a natural name, for such a matrix must have its first row and column identical, its second row and column identical, and so forth, so that its elements are actually symmetrical about an axis drawn along the northwest-southeast diagonal. This additional is called the *principal diagonal*. An example of a symmetric matrix is

$$(1.34) \qquad \mathbf{W} = \begin{pmatrix} 7 & 0 & 3 \\ 0 & -6 & -5 \\ 3 & -5 & 10 \end{pmatrix} = \mathbf{W}'$$

In general, the distinguishing feature of a symmetric matrix of order N by N is that the element in the rth row and cth column must be equal to the element in the cth row and rth column, that is, $a_{rc} = a_{cr}$, for every choice of r and c, $r = 1, \ldots, N$ and $c = 1, \ldots, N$. Notice that the transpose of a row vector $\mathbf{x}$ is always a column vector $\mathbf{x}'$; this is why the vector notation described in 1.3 was chosen.

1.16 A square N by N matrix whose typical element, in the rth row and cth column, is the moment m_{rc} of x_r with x_c is called the *moment matrix*[5] of the variables $x_1, \ldots, x_N$. Since by definition $m_{rc} = m_{cr}$, all moment matrices are symmetric, thus:

$$(1.35) \qquad \mathbf{M} = \begin{pmatrix} m_{11} & m_{12} & \cdots & m_{1N} \\ m_{12} & m_{22} & \cdots & m_{2N} \\ \cdot & \cdot & & \cdot \\ \cdot & \cdot & & \cdot \\ \cdot & \cdot & & \cdot \\ m_{1N} & m_{2N} & \cdots & m_{NN} \end{pmatrix} = \mathbf{M}'$$

The *correlation matrix* of $x_1, \ldots, x_N$ is similar to the moment matrix except that the rcth element is the correlation coefficient[6] r_{rc} instead of the moment m_{rc} between x_r and x_c, thus:

$$(1.36) \qquad \mathbf{R} = \begin{pmatrix} 1 & r_{12} & \cdots & r_{1N} \\ r_{12} & 1 & \cdots & r_{2N} \\ \cdot & \cdot & & \cdot \\ \cdot & \cdot & & \cdot \\ \cdot & \cdot & & \cdot \\ r_{1N} & r_{2N} & \cdots & 1 \end{pmatrix} = \mathbf{R}'$$

Since $r_{rc} = m_{rc}/s_r s_c$, where s_r and s_c are the standard deviations of x_r and x_c, respectively, the correlation matrix can be obtained from the moment matrix by dividing the first row by s_1 and the first column by s_1, similarly the second row and the second column by s_2, the third row and column by s_3, and so forth.

[5] See 1.20 below, and IX.4.5.
[6] See IV.3.9.

1.17 In using matrices, we often have occasion to transpose a product such as $\mathbf{AB}$. What is the transpose of this product, that is, what is $(\mathbf{AB})'$? Since the rows of $\mathbf{A}$ are multiplied into the columns of $\mathbf{B}$ to get $\mathbf{AB}$, the transpose $(\mathbf{AB})'$ cannot be equal to $\mathbf{A}'\mathbf{B}'$, because $\mathbf{A}'\mathbf{B}'$ requires the columns of $\mathbf{A}$ (i.e., rows of $\mathbf{A}'$) to be multiplied into the rows of $\mathbf{B}$ (i.e., columns of $\mathbf{B}'$), as in $\mathbf{BA}$ instead of $\mathbf{AB}$. Actually the rule is

$$(1.37) \qquad\qquad (\mathbf{AB})' = \mathbf{B}'\mathbf{A}'$$

In $\mathbf{B}'\mathbf{A}'$ the rows of $\mathbf{A}$ (columns of $\mathbf{A}'$) are multiplied into the columns of $\mathbf{B}$ (rows of $\mathbf{B}'$), as in $\mathbf{AB}$. Similarly, $\mathbf{A}'\mathbf{B}'$ is the transpose of $\mathbf{BA}$. The formal proof of (1.37) is short, but confusing if one is not very careful of notation. Let $\mathbf{AB}$ be denoted by $\mathbf{P}$ as before, and $(\mathbf{AB})'$ by $\mathbf{P}'$. Let the rth-row cth-column element of $\mathbf{P}$ be p_{rc}, and let the cth-row rth-column element of $\mathbf{P}'$ be p'_{cr}. By the definition of the transpose, $p'_{cr} = p_{rc}$ for any pair of values of r and c. Similarly, let the rth-row ith-column element of $\mathbf{A}$ be a_{ri}, and the ith-row rth-column element of $\mathbf{A}'$ be a'_{ir} (which is equal to a_{ri}). And let the ith-row cth-column element of $\mathbf{B}$ be b_{ic}, and the cth-row ith-column element of $\mathbf{B}'$ be b'_{ci} (which equals b_{ic}). If this is got straight, the proof is easy:

$$(1.38) \qquad\qquad p'_{cr} = p_{rc} = \sum_i a_{ri}b_{ic} = \sum_i a'_{ir}b'_{ci} = \sum_i b'_{ci}a'_{ir}$$

The first step follows by the definition of $\mathbf{P}'$ and p'_{cr}; the second by the multiplication rule [see (1.17), last line]; the third by the definitions of $\mathbf{A}'$ and $\mathbf{B}'$ and a'_{ir} and b'_{ci}; and the fourth because ordinary numbers like a'_{ir} and b'_{ci} can be interchanged without altering their product. Now the last expression, $\sum b'_{ci}a'_{ir}$, is the typical term (cth row and rth column) of the product resulting if a matrix whose typical term is b'_{ic} is multiplied on the right by a matrix whose typical term is a'_{ir}, namely, the product $\mathbf{B}'\mathbf{A}'$. This completes the proof. The reader should try out a few examples, including the one provided by (1.22) and (1.25). The transpose of a product of three or more matrices is often required. It can be found by applying (1.37). For example, to find the transpose of $\mathbf{XYZ}$, first regard $\mathbf{XY}$ as $\mathbf{A}$ and regard $\mathbf{Z}$ as $\mathbf{B}$, and apply (1.37):

$$(1.39) \qquad\qquad (\mathbf{XYZ})' = [(\mathbf{XY})\mathbf{Z}]' = \mathbf{Z}'(\mathbf{XY})'$$

Then having got this far, regard $\mathbf{X}$ and $\mathbf{Y}$ as the $\mathbf{A}$ and $\mathbf{B}$ of (1.37):

$$(1.40) \qquad\qquad (\mathbf{XYZ})' = \mathbf{Z}'(\mathbf{XY})' = \mathbf{Z}'\mathbf{Y}'\mathbf{X}'$$

Similarly,

$$(1.41) \qquad\qquad (\mathbf{WXYZ})' = \mathbf{Z}'\mathbf{Y}'\mathbf{X}'\mathbf{W}'$$

etc.

1.18 A vector with elements $x_1, \ldots, x_N$ can be multiplied by itself in either of two ways: as a row multiplied on the right by a column, $\mathbf{xx}'$, or as a row multiplied on the left by a column, $\mathbf{x}'\mathbf{x}$. The results are quite different, the former being a 1 by 1 matrix, that is, a scalar, and the other being an N by N matrix, thus:

$$(1.42) \quad \mathbf{xx}' = (x_1 \quad \cdots \quad x_N)\begin{pmatrix} x_1 \\ \cdot \\ \cdot \\ \cdot \\ x_N \end{pmatrix} = x_1{}^2 + \cdots + x_N{}^2 = \sum_{i=1}^{N} x_i{}^2$$

$$(1.43) \quad \mathbf{x}'\mathbf{x} = \begin{pmatrix} x_1 \\ \cdot \\ \cdot \\ \cdot \\ x_N \end{pmatrix}(x_1 \quad \cdots \quad x_N) = \begin{pmatrix} x_1{}^2 & x_1 x_2 & \cdots & x_1 x_N \\ x_2 x_1 & x_2{}^2 & \cdots & x_2 x_N \\ \cdot & \cdot & & \cdot \\ \cdot & \cdot & & \cdot \\ \cdot & \cdot & & \cdot \\ x_N x_1 & x_N x_2 & \cdots & x_N{}^2 \end{pmatrix}$$

Equation (1.42) shows that the row-times-column product of a vector by itself turns out to be the sum of squares of the elements of the vector. This has an obvious use in the theory of least-squares estimation: If $x_1, \ldots, x_N$ are the residuals of observed points from a theoretical curve or surface, then $\mathbf{xx}'$ is the sum of squared deviations that is required to be minimized. This matter is pursued in IX.5.

1.19 Equation (1.43) shows that the column-by-row product of a vector by itself is a symmetric matrix in which the rcth element is the product of the rth and cth elements of the vector. This has a less obvious relation to the moments that occur in statistical analysis. Indeed, the moment matrix $\mathbf{M}_{zz}$ of $z_1, \ldots, z_N$ can be expressed in terms of such products of vectors. It will be recalled[7] that the moment matrix $\mathbf{M}_{zz}$ for observations z_{it} $(i = 1, \ldots, N; t = 1, \ldots, T)$ is defined as

$$(1.44) \quad \mathbf{M}_{zz} = \begin{pmatrix} m_{z_1 z_1} & \cdots & m_{z_1 z_N} \\ \cdot & & \cdot \\ \cdot & & \cdot \\ \cdot & & \cdot \\ m_{z_N z_1} & \cdots & m_{z_N z_N} \end{pmatrix}$$

$$= \begin{pmatrix} \sum_{t=1}^{T}(z_{1t} - \bar{z}_1)^2 & \cdots & \sum_{t=1}^{T}(z_{1t} - \bar{z}_1)(z_{Nt} - \bar{z}_N) \\ \cdot & & \cdot \\ \cdot & & \cdot \\ \cdot & & \cdot \\ \sum_{t=1}^{T}(z_{Nt} - \bar{z}_N)(z_{1t} - \bar{z}_1) & \cdots & \sum_{t=1}^{T}(z_{Nt} - \bar{z}_N)^2 \end{pmatrix}$$

[7] See IX.4.5.

where $\bar{z}_i$ is the mean of $z_{i1}, \ldots, z_{iT}$, i.e., $\sum z_{it}/T$. By the rule for adding matrices, this may be regarded as the sum of T matrices, each pertaining to a different period from $t = 1$ to $t = T$, and each resembling (1.43), thus:

$$(1.45) \quad \mathbf{M}_{zz} = \sum_{t=1}^{T} \begin{pmatrix} (z_{1t} - \bar{z}_1)^2 & \cdots & (z_{1t} - \bar{z}_1)(z_{Nt} - \bar{z}_N) \\ & & \\ & \cdot & \\ & \cdot & \\ (z_{Nt} - \bar{z}_N)(z_{1t} - \bar{z}_1) & \cdots & (z_{Nt} - \bar{z}_N)^2 \end{pmatrix}$$

Because of (1.43) each matrix in the sum of matrices above can be expressed as a column-by-row product of a certain vector by itself, that is, the vector of observations of z_{it} for some particular period t, measured from their sample means $\bar{z}_i$. Let us denote the vector whose elements are $z_{1t}, \ldots, z_{Nt}$ by $\mathbf{z}_t$, denote the vector of means of $z_1, \ldots, z_N$ by $\bar{\mathbf{z}}$, and denote the vector of deviations of $z_{1t}, \ldots, z_{Nt}$ from their respective means by $\mathbf{z}_t - \bar{\mathbf{z}}$, thus:

$$\mathbf{z}_t = (z_{1t} \quad \cdots \quad z_{Nt})$$

$$(1.46) \qquad \bar{\mathbf{z}} = (\bar{z}_1 \quad \cdots \quad \bar{z}_N)$$

$$\mathbf{z}_t - \bar{\mathbf{z}} = (z_{1t} - \bar{z}_1 \quad \cdots \quad z_{Nt} - \bar{z}_N)$$

Then the moment matrix $\mathbf{M}_{zz}$ can be expressed as

$$(1.47) \qquad \mathbf{M}_{zz} = \sum_{t=1}^{T} \begin{pmatrix} z_{1t} - \bar{z}_1 \\ \cdot \\ \cdot \\ \cdot \\ z_{Nt} - \bar{z}_N \end{pmatrix} (z_{1t} - \bar{z}_1 \quad \cdots \quad z_{Nt} - \bar{z}_N)$$

$$= \sum_{t=1}^{T} (\mathbf{z}_t - \bar{\mathbf{z}})'(\mathbf{z}_t - \bar{\mathbf{z}})$$

1.20 The moment matrix $\mathbf{M}_{zz}$ of (1.44) above can be expressed in still a different way with matrices, which is extremely convenient for the type of analysis used in IX.5 and IX.10. Let the matrix of observations of all N variables for periods 1 through T be called $\mathbf{Z}$, thus:

$$(1.48) \qquad \mathbf{Z} = \begin{pmatrix} z_{11} & \cdots & z_{1T} \\ \cdot & & \cdot \\ \cdot & & \cdot \\ \cdot & & \cdot \\ z_{N1} & \cdots & z_{NT} \end{pmatrix}$$

Similarly, let $\mathbf{Z}$ denote the matrix of deviations of each z_{it} from its own sample mean $\bar{z}_i$, thus:

$$(1.49) \qquad \mathbf{Z} = \mathbf{Z} - \bar{\mathbf{Z}} = \begin{pmatrix} z_{11} - \bar{z}_1 & \cdots & z_{1T} - \bar{z}_1 \\ \vdots & & \vdots \\ z_{N1} - \bar{z}_N & \cdots & z_{NT} - \bar{z}_N \end{pmatrix}$$

Then the moment matrix of the z's about their means, $\mathbf{M}_{zz}$, is

$$(1.50) \qquad \mathbf{M}_{zz} = \mathbf{Z}\mathbf{Z}' = (\mathbf{Z} - \bar{\mathbf{Z}})(\mathbf{Z} - \bar{\mathbf{Z}})'$$

Using (1.48) above, we find that the matrix of moments of the z's about zero, $\mathbf{M}_{zz}^0$ (see IX.4.9), is

$$(1.51) \qquad \mathbf{M}_{zz}^0 = \left\| \sum_t z_{it} z_{jt} \right\| = \mathbf{Z}\mathbf{Z}'$$

1.21   A matrix or vector all of whose elements are 1's is useful for expressing sums of sample observations on a variable. Let us define the row vector $\mathbf{1}$ as follows, the number of elements being equal to the sample size T:

$$(1.52) \qquad \mathbf{1} \equiv (1 \quad 1 \quad \cdots \quad 1)$$

Then we have the following relations involving $\mathbf{1}$:

$$(1.53) \qquad \mathbf{1}\mathbf{1}' = T$$

$$(1.54) \qquad \mathbf{1}'\mathbf{1} = \begin{pmatrix} 1 & \cdots & 1 \\ \vdots & & \vdots \\ 1 & \cdots & 1 \end{pmatrix}$$

$$(1.55) \qquad (z_{i1} \quad \cdots \quad z_{iT})\mathbf{1}' = \mathbf{1}(z_{i1} \quad \cdots \quad z_{iT})' = \sum_{t=1}^{T} z_{it}$$

$$(1.56) \qquad \frac{1}{T}(z_{i1} \quad \cdots \quad z_{iT})\mathbf{1}' = \bar{z}_i$$

Hence the matrix $\bar{\mathbf{Z}}$ of sample means in (1.49) is

$$(1.57) \qquad \frac{1}{T}\mathbf{Z}\mathbf{1}'\mathbf{1} = \bar{\mathbf{Z}}$$

Then the moment matrix $\mathbf{M}_{zz}$ about the means can be expressed as

$$(1.58) \qquad \mathbf{M}_{zz} = \mathbf{Z}\left(\mathbf{I} - \frac{1}{T}\mathbf{1}'\mathbf{1}\right)^2 \mathbf{Z}'$$

1.22 The expression $\mathbf{xAx}'$ often occurs in statistical analysis, where $\mathbf{A}$ is a square matrix. Let us see what it means in terms of a simple example. Consider

$$(1.59) \qquad \mathbf{xAx}' = (x_1 \quad x_2)\begin{pmatrix} a_{11} & a_{12} \\ a_{21} & a_{22} \end{pmatrix}\begin{pmatrix} x_1 \\ x_2 \end{pmatrix}$$

This expression must be a 1 by 1 matrix, that is, a scalar, for $\mathbf{xA}$ is a row vector and when it is multiplied on the right by a column vector the result must be a scalar; or to look at it differently, $\mathbf{Ax}'$ is a column and when it is multiplied on the left by a row the result must be a scalar. The result is (via the latter alternative)

$$(1.60) \qquad \mathbf{x(Ax')} = (x_1 \quad x_2)\begin{pmatrix} a_{11}x_1 + a_{12}x_2 \\ a_{21}x_1 + a_{22}x_2 \end{pmatrix}$$
$$= a_{11}x_1{}^2 + (a_{12} + a_{21})x_1x_2 + a_{22}x_2{}^2$$
$$= \sum_{r=1}^{2}\sum_{c=1}^{2} a_{rc}x_r x_c$$

The expression $\mathbf{xAx}'$ or $\sum\sum a_{rc}x_r x_c$ is called a *quadratic form*. A quadratic form can occur in two dimensions like (1.60), or in one dimension ($a_{11}x_1{}^2$), or in three, four, ..., N dimensions. It is a function of $\mathbf{x}$ if $\mathbf{A}$ is numerically specified, and it becomes an ordinary number if numerical values are assigned also to the elements of $\mathbf{x}$. Many uses of quadratic forms involve a symmetric matrix $\mathbf{A}$, in which case (1.60) becomes

$$(1.61) \quad \mathbf{xAx}' = a_{11}x_1{}^2 + 2a_{12}x_1x_2 + a_{22}x_2{}^2 = \sum_r a_{rr}x_r{}^2 + 2\sum_{r<c} a_{rc}x_r x_c$$

1.23 A symmetric matrix $\mathbf{A}$ and the associated quadratic form $\mathbf{xAx}'$ are said to be *positive definite* if $\mathbf{A}$ has the property that for all nonzero vectors $\mathbf{x}$ (of suitable order) the associated quadratic form is positive, that is, if

$$(1.62) \qquad \mathbf{xAx}' > 0 \qquad \text{for all } \mathbf{x} \text{ except } \mathbf{x} = \mathbf{0}$$

Similarly, $\mathbf{A}$ and $\mathbf{xAx}'$ are said to be *negative definite* if $\mathbf{xAx}' < 0$ for all nonzero $\mathbf{x}$. A symmetric matrix $\mathbf{A}$ and $\mathbf{xAx}'$ are said to be *positive semidefinite* if for all $\mathbf{x}$ the associated quadratic form is non-negative, that is, if

$$(1.63) \qquad \mathbf{xAx}' \geqq 0 \qquad \text{for all } \mathbf{x}$$

Similarity, $\mathbf{A}$ and $\mathbf{xAx}'$ are said to be *negative semidefinite* if $\mathbf{xAx}' \leqq 0$ for all $\mathbf{x}$.

1.24 Moment matrices as defined just above are necessarily positive semidefinite. If the vector variables are linearly independent, then their moment matrix is positive definite. The proof of the preceding statement is as follows.[8] Consider the $N \times T$ matrix $\mathbf{Z}$ in (1.48) above, and assume

---

[8] Marc Nerlove suggested this proof.

that its N rows are linearly independent, that is, that its rank is N (of course this requires $T \geqq N$). Then if $\mathbf{x}$ is any row vector of N elements, we see by the definition of linear independence that

(1.64) $\mathbf{xZ} \neq \mathbf{0}$ unless $\mathbf{x} = \mathbf{0}$

Now form the scalar $\mathbf{xZZ'x'}$, and apply (1.64) and the fact that any moment matrix $\mathbf{ZZ'}$ is positive semidefinite, to obtain

(1.65) $\mathbf{xZZ'x'} \geqq 0$, with equality only when $\mathbf{x} = \mathbf{0}$

This proves the positive definiteness of $\mathbf{ZZ'}$ when the rows of $\mathbf{Z}$ are linearly independent, Q.E.D.

1.25   Some other properties of definite and semidefinite matrices are given in Koopmans and Hood [1953], Appendix B, pp. 186–189. These properties will be better understood after the whole of this appendix has been read. They are used in Chapters IX and X, especially in IX.9.13–20, where the limited-information method is discussed.

2 MATRICES AND DETERMINANTS[9]

2.1   *A determinant is a number*, calculated by a specific rule from a square matrix. This rule was explained in III.6.3 and III.6.7–9, but we shall summarize it here, for determinants are useful in order to "divide" one matrix by another. We shall use light italic (not boldface) capital letters to denote determinants, and we shall also sometimes use the symbol "det" to denote the determinant of a square matrix. Vertical lines instead of parentheses will denote a determinant instead of a matrix. Thus,

$$(2.1) \qquad \begin{vmatrix} a_{11} & \cdots & a_{1N} \\ & \cdot & \\ \cdot & & \cdot \\ & \cdot & \\ a_{N1} & \cdots & a_{NN} \end{vmatrix} = \det \begin{pmatrix} a_{11} & \cdots & a_{1N} \\ & \cdot & \\ \cdot & & \cdot \\ & \cdot & \\ a_{N1} & \cdots & a_{NN} \end{pmatrix} = \det \mathbf{A} = A$$

If one row and one column of an N-rowed determinant A are struck out, the resulting determinant is called an $(N - 1)$-rowed *minor* of A. Similarly, if two rows and two columns are struck out, or three, . . . , or $N - 1$, the result is an $N - 2$, or an $N - 3$, . . . , or a one-rowed minor. The *cofactor* of an element a_{rc} of a determinant A is $(-1)^{r+c}$ times the $(N - 1)$-rowed minor obtained by striking out the rth row and cth column of A. The

[9] Concerning this section, see Aitken [1949], pp. 27–50, and III.6 above.

cofactor of a_{rc} is sometimes called cof a_{rc} and sometimes A_{rc}. Thus, for example, if A is a three-rowed determinant,

$$(2.2) \qquad A = \begin{vmatrix} a_{11} & a_{12} & a_{13} \\ a_{21} & a_{22} & a_{23} \\ a_{31} & a_{32} & a_{33} \end{vmatrix}$$

then some of its cofactors are

$$(2.3) \qquad A_{11} = \text{cof } a_{11} = \begin{vmatrix} a_{22} & a_{23} \\ a_{32} & a_{33} \end{vmatrix}, \qquad A_{12} = \text{cof } a_{12} = -\begin{vmatrix} a_{21} & a_{23} \\ a_{31} & a_{33} \end{vmatrix},$$

$$A_{13} = \text{cof } a_{13} = \begin{vmatrix} a_{21} & a_{22} \\ a_{31} & a_{32} \end{vmatrix}, \qquad A_{21} = \text{cof } a_{21} = -\begin{vmatrix} a_{12} & a_{13} \\ a_{32} & a_{33} \end{vmatrix}$$

2.2 The rule for evaluating (i.e., finding the value of) a determinant is to choose any row or column (the result will be the same no matter which is chosen) and move along it, forming the sum of products of each element of that row or column times its cofactor.[10] Then, for example, in (2.2), choosing the first row,

$$(2.4) \qquad A = a_{11}A_{11} + a_{12}A_{12} + a_{13}A_{13} = \sum_{c=1}^{3} a_{1c}A_{1c}$$

or choosing the second column,

$$(2.5) \qquad A = a_{12}A_{12} + a_{22}A_{22} + a_{32}A_{32} = \sum_{r=1}^{3} a_{r2}A_{r2}$$

In the case of the general N-rowed determinant as in (2.1), the sum must run from 1 to N. This rule appears to evade the issue, for it tells how to evaluate a determinant A only if one can evaluate a set of N other determinants such as A_{rc}, the cofactors of A. And how is A_{rc} evaluated? In terms of its own cofactors, by applying the same rule again. But at each stage the cofactors get fewer rows and columns. The process eventually

---

[10] See Aitken [1949], pp. 38–39. There are other rules, but all come to the same result. The intuitive definition of a determinant in the text above is equivalent to the following definition used by mathematical texts (including Aitken [1949], p. 30). First consider the N by N matrix $\mathbf{A} = (a_{rc})$. Now consider a product of N of its elements, $a_{1\alpha}a_{2\beta}\ldots a_{N\nu}$, where all of the column numbers $\alpha, \beta, \ldots, \nu$ are different and lie between 1 and N inclusive. Define the number of inversions in the series $\alpha, \beta, \ldots, \nu$ as the number of pairs that are not in ascending order. (For example, the number of inversions in the series 1 3 2 4 is one, because 3 and 2 are not in ascending order but 1 and 2, 1 and 3, 1 and 4, 2 and 4, and 3 and 4 are. The number of inversions in the series 51324 is five.) Denote the number of inversions temporarily by i. Then the determinant of $\mathbf{A}$ is defined as the sum of the $N!$ different products that can be formed as described, each multiplied by $(-1)^i$, thus:

$$\det (a_{rc}) \equiv \Sigma (-1)^i a_{1\alpha} a_{2\beta} \ldots a_{N\nu}$$

comes down to evaluating 2 by 2 determinants like A_{1c} in (2.4) or A_{r2} in (2.5), and this is done by the same rule. Thus, if B is a 2 by 2 determinant, it can be evaluated along the first row, thus:

$$(2.6) \qquad B = \begin{vmatrix} b_{11} & b_{12} \\ b_{21} & b_{22} \end{vmatrix} = b_{11}B_{11} + b_{12}B_{12} = b_{11}b_{22} + b_{12}(-b_{21})$$

$$= b_{11}b_{22} - b_{12}b_{21}$$

or along the second column, thus:

$$(2.7) \quad B = b_{12}B_{12} + b_{22}B_{22} = b_{12}(-b_{21}) + b_{22}b_{11} = b_{11}b_{22} - b_{12}b_{21}$$

etc. The 3 by 3 determinant A of (2.2) can be evaluated by following (2.4) and expanding each cofactor along its own first row.[11]

$$A = a_{11}\begin{vmatrix} a_{22} & a_{23} \\ a_{32} & a_{33} \end{vmatrix} - a_{12}\begin{vmatrix} a_{21} & a_{23} \\ a_{31} & a_{33} \end{vmatrix} + a_{13}\begin{vmatrix} a_{21} & a_{22} \\ a_{31} & a_{32} \end{vmatrix}$$

$$(2.8) \qquad = a_{11}(a_{22}a_{33} - a_{23}a_{32}) - a_{12}(a_{21}a_{33} - a_{23}a_{31})$$

$$+ a_{13}(a_{21}a_{32} - a_{22}a_{31})$$

$$= a_{11}a_{22}a_{33} + a_{12}a_{23}a_{31} + a_{13}a_{32}a_{21}$$

$$- a_{11}a_{23}a_{32} - a_{12}a_{21}a_{33} - a_{13}a_{31}a_{22}$$

Since a determinant can be expanded either along a row or along a column, the determinants of any matrix and of its transpose must be equal, that is,

$$(2.9) \qquad\qquad\qquad \det \mathbf{A} = \det \mathbf{A}'$$

Both will be denoted by A.

2.3 In III.6.5 these three elementary rules about determinants were set forth as follows (the reader should try them out on a few specific cases):

(a) If any two rows (or columns) of a determinant are interchanged, the sign of the determinant is changed.

(b) If each element of one row (or column) of a determinant is multiplied by a scalar constant, say λ, the determinant itself is multiplied by λ.

(c) If one row (or column) is altered by the addition to it of a scalar constant λ times another row (or column), the determinant is not changed.

2.4 From (a) in 2.3 it follows that any determinant having two identical rows (or columns) must be zero, for interchanging those two identical rows (or columns) cannot change the determinant and yet must change its sign, and the only number that is unchanged when its sign is

---

[11] This means evaluating by elements of the first row and their cofactors.

changed is zero. From this it also follows that if we multiply elements of one row (or column) by cofactors of elements of another row (or column), we shall always get zero as a result. The proof is as follows. Replace the second row by the first; then the resulting determinant is zero, for it has two identical rows. But the expansion of this new determinant is exactly the same as the sum of products of the elements of the second row of the original determinant by the cofactors of the elements of its first row, Q.E.D. This is an important result, and will be used in 3.4.

2.5 In this paragraph a few interesting properties of special determinants are given, without proof, but all the proofs are easy. The determinant of the identity matrix **I** is 1. The determinant of any matrix having zeros for all elements except along the principal diagonal is equal to the product of the diagonal elements, thus:

$$(2.10) \quad \det \begin{pmatrix} a_{11} & 0 & 0 & \cdots & 0 \\ 0 & a_{22} & 0 & \cdots & 0 \\ 0 & 0 & a_{33} & \cdots & 0 \\ . & . & . & & . \\ . & . & . & & . \\ . & . & . & & . \\ 0 & 0 & 0 & \cdots & a_{NN} \end{pmatrix} = a_{11}a_{22}a_{33}\cdots a_{NN}$$

Such a matrix is called a *diagonal* matrix. The determinant of a matrix having zeros for all elements to one side of the principal diagonal is also equal to the product of the diagonal elements:

$$(2.11) \quad \det \begin{pmatrix} a_{11} & a_{12} & a_{13} & \cdots & a_{1N} \\ 0 & a_{22} & a_{23} & \cdots & a_{2N} \\ 0 & 0 & a_{33} & \cdots & a_{3N} \\ . & . & . & & . \\ . & . & . & & . \\ . & . & . & & . \\ 0 & 0 & 0 & \cdots & a_{NN} \end{pmatrix} = a_{11}a_{22}a_{33}\cdots a_{NN}$$

Such a matrix is called a *triangular* matrix.

2.6 A simple way to evaluate a determinant in practice in many cases is to look for a row or column with all zero elements except one, because, if it can be found, the determinant can be expanded along that row or column and is equal to that one element times its cofactor. For example, consider the expansion of the following determinant along its second row:

$$(2.12) \quad \begin{vmatrix} 1 & 4 & -15 \\ 0 & 0 & 3 \\ -5 & 2 & 7 \end{vmatrix} = -3 \begin{vmatrix} 1 & 4 \\ -5 & 2 \end{vmatrix}$$

If there is no such row or column, one can always be made to appear by appropriate use of rule (c) of 2.3. Consider the creation of a zero in row 2, column 3 of the following determinant by the addition of an appropriate multiple (i.e., $-\frac{3}{2}$) of column 1 to column 3:

$$
\begin{vmatrix} 1 & 4 & -15 \\ 2 & 0 & 3 \\ -5 & 2 & 7 \end{vmatrix} = \begin{vmatrix} 1 & 4 & -15 - \frac{3}{2} \\ 2 & 0 & 3 - 3 \\ -5 & 2 & 7 + \frac{15}{2} \end{vmatrix}
$$

(2.13)

$$
= \begin{vmatrix} 1 & 4 & -\frac{33}{2} \\ 2 & 0 & 0 \\ -5 & 2 & \frac{29}{2} \end{vmatrix} = -2 \begin{vmatrix} 4 & -\frac{33}{2} \\ 2 & \frac{29}{2} \end{vmatrix}
$$

Further examples are given in III.7.

2.7 The determinant of a product of two N by N matrices $\mathbf{A}$ and $\mathbf{B}$ is equal to the product of their determinants.[12] This holds regardless of the order of multiplication, even if $\mathbf{AB} \neq \mathbf{BA}$:

(2.14) $\qquad \det(\mathbf{AB}) = AB = BA = \det(\mathbf{BA})$

3 INVERSES AND MATRIX "DIVISION"[13]

3.1 In ordinary arithmetic, the quotient of b divided by a can be expressed as

(3.1) $\qquad b \div a = \dfrac{b}{a} = b\dfrac{1}{a} = ba^{-1} = a^{-1}b$

The symbol a^{-1} is called "a inverse" and is defined by the equation

(3.2) $\qquad aa^{-1} = a^{-1}a = 1$

If the number a, by which we want to divide, has an inverse, all is well and we can go ahead. But if a has no inverse, then we cannot divide by a. There is only one number in ordinary arithmetic that has no inverse, and that number is zero. Division by zero is impossible, but division by any other number is perfectly all right.

3.2 The situation is similar with matrices, except that (1) there are many matrices that have no inverses, and (2) the order in which matrices are multiplied is important. The notation of multiplication by inverses is used rather than that of division, because it is then easier to keep $\mathbf{A}^{-1}\mathbf{B}$

---

[12] For a proof, see Aitken [1949], p. 80.
[13] Concerning this section, see Aitken [1949], pp. 51–57.

and $\mathbf{BA}^{-1}$ separate, which must be done because in general they differ (one or both may even fail to be defined). Let us define the inverse of a matrix, note some of its properties, and then find out how to tell whether a matrix has an inverse and, if so, how to get it. Just as in arithmetic, the inverse of a matrix $\mathbf{A}$ is called $\mathbf{A}^{-1}$ and is defined by the equation

(3.3) $$\mathbf{AA}^{-1} = \mathbf{A}^{-1}\mathbf{A} = \mathbf{I}$$

$\mathbf{I}$ is the identity matrix, corresponding to 1 in arithmetic. Only square matrices can have inverses [if this were not true, $\mathbf{AA}^{-1}$ and $\mathbf{A}^{-1}\mathbf{A}$ would not be equal as required by (3.3)], but not every square matrix has an inverse.[14] Notice that the inverse of a product obeys the same kind of factor-reversal rule as does the transpose of a product as stated in equation (1.37), if the inverses of both factors exist, thus:[15]

(3.4) $$(\mathbf{AB})^{-1} = \mathbf{B}^{-1}\mathbf{A}^{-1}$$

Similarly,

(3.5) $$(\mathbf{ABC})^{-1} = \mathbf{C}^{-1}\mathbf{B}^{-1}\mathbf{A}^{-1}$$

etc. Notice that the inverse of $\mathbf{A}^{-1}$ is $\mathbf{A}$, for any matrix $\mathbf{A}$.

3.3 Before going further, let us look at a couple of examples. The inverse of the matrix $\begin{pmatrix} 3 & -7 \\ 2 & -5 \end{pmatrix}$ is $\begin{pmatrix} 5 & -7 \\ 2 & -3 \end{pmatrix}$. (Do not worry just yet about how it was found.) This may be verified by multiplication with either factor first:

(3.6)
$$\begin{pmatrix} 3 & -7 \\ 2 & -5 \end{pmatrix}\begin{pmatrix} 5 & -7 \\ 2 & -3 \end{pmatrix} = \begin{pmatrix} 15 - 14 & -21 + 21 \\ 10 - 10 & -14 + 15 \end{pmatrix} = \begin{pmatrix} 1 & 0 \\ 0 & 1 \end{pmatrix} = \mathbf{I}$$

$$\begin{pmatrix} 5 & -7 \\ 2 & -3 \end{pmatrix}\begin{pmatrix} 3 & -7 \\ 2 & -5 \end{pmatrix} = \begin{pmatrix} 15 - 14 & -35 + 35 \\ 6 - 6 & -14 + 15 \end{pmatrix} = \begin{pmatrix} 1 & 0 \\ 0 & 1 \end{pmatrix} = \mathbf{I}$$

[14] Mathematics books usually define two inverses, one satisfying $\mathbf{AA}^{-1} = \mathbf{I}$, and the other satisfying $\mathbf{A}^{-1}\mathbf{A} = \mathbf{I}$, and then prove that they must be equal. We shall at the outset assume one inverse satisfying $\mathbf{AA}^{-1} = \mathbf{A}^{-1}\mathbf{A}$, but justify it later. See footnote 16 below. A generalized inverse has been defined for nonsquare matrices, but we do not use it here; see Penrose [1955].

[15] This is easily proved as follows. By definition,

$$\mathbf{AB}(\mathbf{AB})^{-1} = \mathbf{I}$$

Now multiply both sides of this equation on the left by $\mathbf{A}^{-1}$ to get

$$\mathbf{A}^{-1}\mathbf{AB}(\mathbf{AB})^{-1} = \mathbf{A}^{-1}\mathbf{I}$$
$$\therefore \ \mathbf{B}(\mathbf{AB})^{-1} = \mathbf{A}^{-1}$$

Now multiply on the left by $\mathbf{B}^{-1}$ to get

$$\mathbf{B}^{-1}\mathbf{B}(\mathbf{AB})^{-1} = \mathbf{B}^{-1}\mathbf{A}^{-1}$$
$$\therefore \ (\mathbf{AB})^{-1} = \mathbf{B}^{-1}\mathbf{A}^{-1}$$

The last equation is (3.4), Q.E.D.

The inverse of $\begin{pmatrix} 3 & 4 \\ -5 & -6 \end{pmatrix}$ is $\begin{pmatrix} -3 & -2 \\ \frac{5}{2} & \frac{3}{2} \end{pmatrix}$, as may be verified in the same way:

(3.7) $\quad \begin{pmatrix} 3 & 4 \\ -5 & -6 \end{pmatrix} \begin{pmatrix} -3 & -2 \\ \frac{5}{2} & \frac{3}{2} \end{pmatrix} = \begin{pmatrix} -9 + 10 & -6 + 6 \\ 15 - 15 & 10 - 9 \end{pmatrix} = \begin{pmatrix} 1 & 0 \\ 0 & 1 \end{pmatrix} = I$

3.4 To explain how to find inverses, it is useful to define the *adjoint* of a square matrix **A**. The adjoint of **A** is the transpose of the matrix obtained if each element of **A** is replaced by its cofactor. It is denoted by adj **A**. Thus the adjoint of a 3 by 3 matrix **A** is

(3.8)

$$\text{adj } A = \text{adj} \begin{pmatrix} a_{11} & a_{12} & a_{13} \\ a_{21} & a_{22} & a_{23} \\ a_{31} & a_{32} & a_{33} \end{pmatrix} = \begin{pmatrix} A_{11} & A_{12} & A_{13} \\ A_{21} & A_{22} & A_{23} \\ A_{31} & A_{32} & A_{33} \end{pmatrix}' = \begin{pmatrix} A_{11} & A_{21} & A_{31} \\ A_{12} & A_{22} & A_{32} \\ A_{13} & A_{23} & A_{33} \end{pmatrix}$$

As a simple numerical example,

(3.9) $\qquad \text{adj} \begin{pmatrix} 3 & 4 \\ -5 & -6 \end{pmatrix} = \begin{pmatrix} -6 & 5 \\ -4 & 3 \end{pmatrix}' = \begin{pmatrix} -6 & -4 \\ 5 & 3 \end{pmatrix}$

The interesting thing about the adjoint of **A** is what happens when it is multiplied by **A** itself. The result is the same whether the multiplication is on the right or on the left. Let us take **A** adj **A** first:

(3.10) $\qquad A \text{ adj } A = \begin{pmatrix} a_{11} & a_{12} & a_{13} \\ a_{21} & a_{22} & a_{23} \\ a_{31} & a_{32} & a_{33} \end{pmatrix} \begin{pmatrix} A_{11} & A_{21} & A_{31} \\ A_{12} & A_{22} & A_{32} \\ A_{13} & A_{23} & A_{33} \end{pmatrix}$

Let us look first at the diagonal elements of **A** adj **A**. The first-row first-column element is $a_{11}A_{11} + a_{12}A_{12} + a_{13}A_{13}$; this is simply A, the determinant of **A**, expanded along the first row. The second diagonal element of **A** adj **A** is $a_{21}A_{21} + a_{22}A_{22} + a_{23}A_{23}$, which is A again, expanded along the second row. And similarly the third diagonal element of **A** adj **A** is again A, expanded along the third row. Now let us look at the off-diagonal elements of **A** adj **A**. The first-row second-column element is $a_{11}A_{21} + a_{12}A_{22} + a_{13}A_{23}$. This is zero, as pointed out in 2.4, for it is the expansion of A by elements of one row (the first) and cofactors of elements of another row (the second). Similarly, every other off-diagonal element is zero for the same reason. The rth-row cth-column element of **A** adj **A** is the expansion of A by the elements of the rth row and cofactors of elements in the cth row. Thus

$$(3.11) \qquad \mathbf{A} \operatorname{adj} \mathbf{A} = \begin{pmatrix} A & 0 & 0 \\ 0 & A & 0 \\ 0 & 0 & A \end{pmatrix}$$

Similarly, it can be shown that $(\operatorname{adj} \mathbf{A})\mathbf{A}$ is equal to the same diagonal matrix.

3.5 We are now very near the end of the search for $\mathbf{A}^{-1}$, for we have found a matrix (namely, adj $\mathbf{A}$), which when multiplied on either side by $\mathbf{A}$ gives something closely resembling $\mathbf{I}$. It only remains to divide (3.11) by the scalar A to obtain

$$(3.12) \qquad \mathbf{A} \frac{\operatorname{adj} \mathbf{A}}{A} = \begin{pmatrix} 1 & 0 & 0 \\ 0 & 1 & 0 \\ 0 & 0 & 1 \end{pmatrix} = \mathbf{I} \qquad (\text{if } A \neq 0)$$

Is this possible? The answer is yes if A (the determinant of $\mathbf{A}$) is not zero, and no if A is zero. Therefore, if the determinant of a square matrix $\mathbf{A}$ is zero, $\mathbf{A}$ has no inverse; and if the determinant of $\mathbf{A}$ is not zero, $\mathbf{A}$ has an inverse[16] that is equal to

$$(3.13) \qquad \mathbf{A}^{-1} = \frac{\operatorname{adj} \mathbf{A}}{A}$$

A square matrix is said to be *singular* if its determinant is zero, and *nonsingular* if not. Thus all nonsingular matrices have inverses, and no singular matrices have inverses. The terms "singular" and "nonsingular" are not used for matrices that are not square.

3.6 An important use of inverses is in solving systems of simultaneous linear equations. The analogy with ordinary numbers is instructive here. If we have an equation involving scalars

$$(3.14) \qquad ax = y$$

and wish to solve it for x, we multiply the equation by a^{-1} to get the solution:

$$(3.15) \qquad x = a^{-1}ax = a^{-1}y = ya^{-1}$$

Because these are ordinary numbers, we can multiply on either the right or the left by a^{-1}. Now consider the general system of N linear equations

---

[16] Because $\mathbf{A} \operatorname{adj} \mathbf{A} = (\operatorname{adj} \mathbf{A})\mathbf{A}$, the inverse $\mathbf{A}^{-1}$ defined in the text satisfies both $\mathbf{A}\mathbf{A}^{-1} = \mathbf{I}$ and $\mathbf{A}^{-1}\mathbf{A} = \mathbf{I}$. This disposes of the point raised in footnote 14 in this section.

in N variables, printed here in both nonmatrix and matrix form:

$$y_1 = a_{11}x_1 + \cdots + a_{1N}x_N = \sum_{j=1}^{N} a_{1j}x_j$$

(3.16)

$$y_N = a_{N1}x_1 + \cdots + a_{NN}x_N = \sum_{j=1}^{N} a_{Nj}x_j$$

(3.17) $$\mathbf{y}' = \mathbf{A}\mathbf{x}'$$

Suppose we wish to solve this system for **x** in terms of **A** and **y**. If $\mathbf{A}^{-1}$ exists, we multiply (3.17) on the left by $\mathbf{A}^{-1}$ (*not* on the right, for $\mathbf{A}\mathbf{x}'\mathbf{A}^{-1}$ does not exist under the rules of matrix multiplication). If **A** has an inverse, the result is the solution, *presto:*

(3.18) $$\mathbf{x}' = \mathbf{A}^{-1}\mathbf{A}\mathbf{x}' = \mathbf{A}^{-1}\mathbf{y}'$$

This is conceptually very simple and quite analogous in principle to the case of one equation in one variable shown in (3.15) *except* that multiplication of (3.17) by $\mathbf{A}^{-1}$ *must* be on the left. We must be sure that $\mathbf{A}^{-1}$ exists before proceeding, just as we must be sure a^{-1} exists in (3.15).

    3.7 In practice, the solution of a system like (3.17) can be a great deal of work, for it requires many multiplications and additions. Let us illustrate with a 2 by 2 system based on the matrix whose adjoint was computed in (3.9) above. That system is

(3.19) $$\mathbf{y}' = \begin{pmatrix} y_1 \\ y_2 \end{pmatrix} = \begin{pmatrix} 3 & 4 \\ -5 & -6 \end{pmatrix}\begin{pmatrix} x_1 \\ x_2 \end{pmatrix} = \mathbf{A}\mathbf{x}'$$

or, in nonmatrix form,

$$y_1 = 3x_1 + 4x_2$$
(3.20)
$$y_2 = -5x_1 - 6x_2$$

The inverse of **A** in this case, using (3.9) and (3.13), is

(3.21) $$\mathbf{A}^{-1} = \frac{\text{adj } \mathbf{A}}{A} = \frac{1}{3(-6) - (-5)4}\begin{pmatrix} -6 & -4 \\ 5 & 3 \end{pmatrix} = \begin{pmatrix} -3 & -2 \\ \frac{5}{2} & \frac{3}{2} \end{pmatrix}$$

Hence the solution of (3.19) is

(3.22) $$\mathbf{x}' = \mathbf{A}^{-1}\mathbf{y}' = \begin{pmatrix} x_1 \\ x_2 \end{pmatrix} = \begin{pmatrix} -3 & -2 \\ \frac{5}{2} & \frac{3}{2} \end{pmatrix}\begin{pmatrix} y_1 \\ y_2 \end{pmatrix}$$

or, in nonmatrix form,

$$x_1 = -3y_1 - 2y_2$$
(3.23)
$$x_2 = \tfrac{5}{2}y_1 + \tfrac{3}{2}y_2$$

3.8 This solution can be checked by substituting it back into the original equations. First let us substitute (3.22) into (3.19):

$$(3.24) \quad \mathbf{y}' = \begin{pmatrix} 3 & 4 \\ -5 & -6 \end{pmatrix} \mathbf{x}' = \begin{pmatrix} 3 & 4 \\ -5 & -6 \end{pmatrix} \begin{pmatrix} -3 & -2 \\ \frac{5}{2} & \frac{3}{2} \end{pmatrix} \mathbf{y}'$$

$$= \begin{pmatrix} 3(-3) + 4(\frac{5}{2}) & 3(-2) + 4(\frac{3}{2}) \\ -5(-3) - 6(\frac{5}{2}) & -5(-2) - 6(\frac{3}{2}) \end{pmatrix} \mathbf{y}' = \begin{pmatrix} 1 & 0 \\ 0 & 1 \end{pmatrix} \mathbf{y}'$$

$$= \mathbf{I}\mathbf{y}' = \mathbf{y}'$$

What we have done here is to put the value found for $\mathbf{x}'$ back into (3.19) to see if it works as it should; it does. Next let us do the same thing in nonmatrix form, just to allay any skepticism about the process. We shall substitute (3.23) into (3.20). Let us take y_1 first:

$$(3.25) \qquad y_1 = 3x_1 + 4x_2 = 3(-3y_1 - 2y_2) + 4(\tfrac{5}{2}y_1 + \tfrac{3}{2}y_2)$$
$$= -9y_1 - 6y_2 + 10y_1 + 6y_2 = y_1$$

That comes out as it should, that is, the solution does satisfy the equation. Now y_2:

$$(3.26) \qquad y_2 = -5x_1 - 6x_2 = -5(-3y_1 - 2y_2) - 6(\tfrac{5}{2}y_1 + \tfrac{3}{2}y_2)$$
$$= 15y_1 + 10y_2 - 15y_1 - 9y_2 = y_2$$

That also comes out as it should. Notice that the calculations for y_1 in (3.25) are essentially the same as those involved in computing the first row of the product $\mathbf{A}\mathbf{A}^{-1}$ in (3.24), and the calculations for y_2 in (3.26) correspond to those for the second row of the product $\mathbf{A}\mathbf{A}^{-1}$.

3.9 The practical computation of the inverse of a matrix of order 3 by 3 or larger is aided by means of certain shortcut methods that rely on the creation of zeros in the matrix by the use of rule (c) of paragraph 2.3 above, whether done by hand, or on a desk calculator, or by means of a programmed electronic computer. The Doolittle method makes use of such shortcuts; see any computation-oriented matrix algebra book or Klein [1953], Chapter IV. The solution of systems of equations not having a nonsingular matrix (i.e., not having an invertible matrix) is taken up in the next section.

4 GENERAL LINEAR EQUATION SYSTEMS; RANK AND LINEAR DEPENDENCE[17]

4.1 We have seen in 3.6 that if $\mathbf{A}^{-1}$ exists, the system of equations

$$(4.1) \qquad\qquad \mathbf{y}' = \mathbf{A}\mathbf{x}'$$

---

[17] Concerning this section, see Aitken [1949], pp. 59–73.

has the following solution for **x**:

$$\text{(4.2)} \qquad \mathbf{x}' = \mathbf{A}^{-1}\mathbf{y}'$$

How can $\mathbf{A}^{-1}$ fail to exist? It will fail if **A** is not square [i.e., the number of equations in the system (4.1) is different from the number of variables—the components of **x**]. In this case **A** has no determinant, as well as no inverse. It will also fail if **A**, though square, is singular, that is, has a zero determinant.[18] To analyze these cases, it is useful to define the *rank* of a matrix.

4.2 The *rank* of the matrix **A** is the order of the highest-order nonsingular square matrix contained in **A**. "Contained in **A**" here means obtainable by striking out any rows and/or columns of **A**, or by striking out none (i.e., **A** itself is contained in **A**). Let us give some examples. The rank of the matrix $\begin{pmatrix} 3 & 4 \\ -5 & -6 \end{pmatrix}$ is 2, because the determinant of this matrix is not zero, and hence the matrix contains a 2 by 2 nonsingular matrix, namely, itself. The rank of $\begin{pmatrix} 3 & 4 \\ -4.5 & -6 \end{pmatrix}$ is 1, for there is no non-singular 2 by 2 matrix contained in it, but there is at least one nonsingular 1 by 1 matrix (in fact there are four). The rank of $\begin{pmatrix} 5 & 3 & -10 \\ -2 & 0 & 4 \end{pmatrix}$ is 2, for it contains no nonsingular 3 by 3 matrix, but contains at least one nonsingular 2 by 2 matrix (strike out either the first or third column). The ranks of the following four matrices

$$\text{(4.3)} \qquad \begin{pmatrix} 1 & 0 & 0 \\ 0 & 1 & 0 \\ 0 & 0 & 1 \end{pmatrix} \begin{pmatrix} 1 & 0 & 2 \\ 3 & 1 & 0 \\ 4 & 1 & 2 \end{pmatrix} \begin{pmatrix} 1 & 2 & 4 \\ 2 & 4 & 8 \\ 3 & 6 & 12 \end{pmatrix} \begin{pmatrix} 0 & 0 & 0 \\ 0 & 0 & 0 \\ 0 & 0 & 0 \end{pmatrix}$$

are 3, 2, 1, and 0 respectively, as the reader should verify. Several generalizations are immediately clear. First, the rank of a matrix cannot exceed the number of its rows or the number of its columns. Thus the rank of an R by C matrix is at most equal to the smaller of the two numbers R and C. The rank of a vector is at most 1; the rank of a 3 by 50 matrix is at most 3; etc. Second, the rank of a matrix is at least 1 unless the matrix has all zeros for elements, in which case it is zero. Third, apart from that, the rank of a matrix is not related in any simple way to the number of zero elements in it, as the above examples show. Fourth, if we write down a

[18] Let us be clear about the meaning of "A has no determinant" or equivalently "det A does not exist." It does not mean "det A = 0," for if det A = 0 then det A does exist and is equal to zero. It means that "det A" is not defined and has no meaning.

square matrix at random, its rank is almost certain to be equal to its order, for a very special combination of elements is required to make a determinant zero.

4.3 The straightforward way to find the rank of a matrix[19] is to look for a nonsingular square matrix first among the largest-order square matrices it contains; then (if that fails) among the next largest order, etc. For example, consider the matrix

(4.4)
$$\begin{pmatrix} 1 & 3 & 4 & -2 \\ 2 & 6 & 8 & -4 \\ 3 & 0 & 3 & 3 \end{pmatrix}$$

Its rank is at most 3. To see whether it is actually 3, consider the four matrices obtained by striking out in turn each of the four columns. Each of the four has a zero determinant; hence the rank of (4.4) is at most 2. To see whether it is actually 2, start considering the 2 by 2 matrices. The one in the first two rows and columns is singular, for $1(6) - 2(3) = 0$; hence pass on to another. Indeed, any one in the first two rows is singular. But any one involving two elements from the third row is nonsingular, for example, the one in columns 1 and 2 and rows 1 and 3 is equal to $1(0) - 3(3) = -9$. Hence the rank of (4.4) is 2.

4.4 An equivalent way of looking at the rank of a matrix is in terms of the concepts of *linear combination* and *linear independence*, which are useful in discussing systems of equations. A *linear combination* of N quantities $a_1, a_2, \ldots, a_N$ is a weighted sum of them, *where not all coefficients are zero:*

(4.5)
$$\lambda_1 a_1 + \cdots + \lambda_N a_N = \sum_{i=1}^{N} \lambda_i a_i \qquad \text{not all } \lambda_i = 0$$

We may have a linear combination of vectors, $\mathbf{a}_1, \ldots, \mathbf{a}_N$,

(4.6)
$$\lambda_1 \mathbf{a}_1 + \cdots + \lambda_N \mathbf{a}_N = \sum \lambda_i \mathbf{a}_i \qquad \text{not all } \lambda_i = 0$$

or even a linear combination of matrices. An example of a linear combination of three three-element vectors is

(4.7) $2(8 \quad 0 \quad 3) - 5(1 \quad 2 \quad 6) + 4(0 \quad 0 \quad 1)$

$$= (2 \times 8 - 5 \times 1 + 4 \times 0 \quad 2 \times 0 - 5 \times 2 + 4 \times 0$$
$$2 \times 3 - 5 \times 6 + 4 \times 1)$$
$$= (11 \quad -10 \quad -20)$$

We shall deal most with linear combinations of vectors.

[19] But not the easiest way in practice; see Aitken [1949], pp. 66–67.

4.5   A set of R given vectors $\mathbf{a}_1, \ldots, \mathbf{a}_R$ each with C elements is said to be *linearly dependent* if it is possible to find a linear combination of them that is equal to the zero vector with C elements, that is, to find a set of numbers $\lambda_1, \ldots, \lambda_R$ (not all zero) such that

$$(4.8) \qquad \lambda_1 \mathbf{a}_1 + \cdots + \lambda_R \mathbf{a}_R = \sum_{r=1}^{R} \lambda_r \mathbf{a}_r = \mathbf{0}$$

The set of vectors $\mathbf{a}_1, \ldots, \mathbf{a}_R$ is said to be *linearly independent* if no set of numbers $\lambda_1, \ldots, \lambda_R$ exists (except all zeros) to satisfy (4.8). Furthermore, any vector $\mathbf{a}_s$ whose coefficient λ_s is not zero in (4.8) is said to be linearly dependent on the remaining vectors. This dependence can be shown by solving (4.8) for $\mathbf{a}_s$ as a linear combination of the remaining vectors with coefficients $-\lambda_r/\lambda_s$ (where $r = 1, \ldots, s - 1, s + 1, \ldots, R$). For example, the reader may verify at sight that the three rows of the matrix in (4.4) are linearly dependent because

$$2(\text{first row}) + (-1)(\text{second row}) + 0(\text{third row}) = \mathbf{0}$$

The first row is thus linearly dependent on the other two. Observe also that the first row is linearly dependent on the second row alone.[20]

4.6   There are many theorems concerning the rank of a matrix. One of the more important ones for econometrics is the following: In any matrix $\mathbf{A}$, the number of linearly independent rows is equal to the number of linearly independent columns, and this number is the rank of the matrix. This theorem is used in deriving the rank condition for the identifiability of an equation of a linear model in VIII.3.19–25. We shall not prove it here.[21] A special case of the theorem is this: If a square matrix is singular, its rows (and also its columns) are linearly dependent; and if it is nonsingular, they are linearly independent.[22] Another important theorem concerning rank is:[23] If any matrix $\mathbf{A}$ is multiplied by a nonsingular

[20] In some cases there are two or more nonproportional sets of coefficients $\lambda_1, \ldots, \lambda_R$ that satisfy (4.8). In this case there will be two or more independent linear relations among the vectors, and two or more vectors may be expressed independently as linear combinations of the others. For example, consider the vectors $(1, 0, 0), (0, 2, 0), (1, 2, 0)$, and $(1, -2, 0)$; the third and fourth are respectively the sum and difference of the first two.

[21] See Aitken [1949], pp. 62–65, esp. pp. 63–64.

[22] It is easy to prove that the rows of a nonsingular matrix are linearly independent by proving the equivalent theorem that if the rows of a square matrix are linearly dependent, it is singular. *Proof:* For such a square matrix, there exists a linear combination of rows $\sum_{r=1}^{R} (r\text{th row}) \lambda_r$ that is zero. Replace one of the rows that has a nonzero value of λ_r by this linear combination, which equals zero, thus obtaining a zero determinant. But by rules (b) and (c) of 2.3, this replacement cannot have changed the value of the determinant except to multiply it by the nonzero value of λ_r; therefore the original determinant must have been zero. Q.E.D.

[23] Aitken [1949], pp. 60–61 and 96.

matrix, the product has the same rank as A. And another: Let A be K by T; then if the rank of A is K, the rank of AA' is K, and conversely.

4.7 Let us now consider the solution of a general system of N linear equations in N variables $x_1, \ldots, x_N$:

$$(4.9) \qquad\qquad \mathbf{y}' = \mathbf{A}\mathbf{x}'$$

We have already seen in 3.6 that if A is nonsingular this has a unique solution, as follows:

$$(4.10) \qquad\qquad \mathbf{x}' = \mathbf{A}^{-1}\mathbf{y}'$$

The converse is also true, that is, if $\mathbf{y}' = \mathbf{A}\mathbf{x}'$ has a unique solution, then A is nonsingular.[24] An important special case occurs when $\mathbf{y}' = \mathbf{0}'$; the equations (4.9) are then said to be homogeneous:

$$(4.11) \qquad\qquad \mathbf{A}\mathbf{x}' = \mathbf{0}'$$

In this case, if A is nonsingular, the unique solution given by (4.10) is $\mathbf{x}' = \mathbf{0}'$, and there cannot be any nonzero solution.[25] There are occasions on which we know that a homogeneous system like (4.11) *does* have a nonzero solution, even though we may not yet know what the nonzero solution is;[26] the preceding theorem tells us that in such a case A must be singular.[27]

4.8 Suppose that in (4.9) A is singular. This means that the rows of A are linearly dependent, and hence there is at least one row that can be expressed as a linear combination of the others [to see this, recall equation (4.8) and the discussion following it in 4.5]. Each row of A gives the coefficients of $x_1, \ldots, x_N$ in one of the equations of (4.9). It is always possible to write the equations (and correspondingly the rows of A and $\mathbf{y}'$) in a new order. Let us assume that this has been done so that the last (Nth) row of A is a linear combination of some of the others. Then the existence and character of a solution of (4.9) depend on whether y_N, the constant term in the last (Nth) equation, is equal to the same linear combination of $y_1, \ldots, y_{N-1}$ as is used to obtain the Nth row of A from the first $N - 1$ rows. There are two possibilities: (1) If not, then the Nth equation contradicts the first $N - 1$ equations, and (4.9) has no solution at all. (2) If so, then the entire Nth equation is a linear combination of the first $N - 1$ equations; and hence it says nothing besides what the first

---

[24] For a proof see Aitken [1949], pp. 69–71.

[25] A nonzero solution is a solution vector *not all* of whose elements are zero, though some (even all but one) may be zero.

[26] See IX.9.15.

[27] The converse of this holds too, that is, if A is singular, then $\mathbf{A}\mathbf{x}' = \mathbf{0}'$ has a nonzero solution. See the next paragraph in the text; also Aitken [1949], p. 63, bottom.

$N - 1$ equations say, so it can be neglected.[28] In the latter case there are only $N - 1$ independent equations in N variables $x_1, \ldots, x_N$, and there cannot be a unique solution. There must either be no solution or many solutions: If the $N - 1$ equations contradict each other, there cannot be any solution; if they do not, there are infinitely many solutions. In Chapters VIII–X we deal with systems of equations that are meant to describe the real world, and hence inconsistent systems are not used.

4.9   The only interesting case of a system of equations with a singular N by N matrix of coefficients, from our point of view, is the case of homogeneous equations like (4.11). Then the equations are necessarily consistent with each other (i.e., noncontradictory), for the elements of $\mathbf{y}'$ are all zero and so cannot fail to satisfy any linear combination that may relate the rows of $\mathbf{A}$ to each other. Hence there are effectively only $N - 1$ equations at most, and there are infinitely many solutions. What are they like? Suppose first that the rank of $\mathbf{A}$ is $N - 1$, that is, that $\mathbf{A}$ has $N - 1$ linearly independent rows and $N - 1$ linearly independent columns. Let us rearrange the order of the rows and columns if necessary so that the first $N - 1$ rows and the first $N - 1$ columns are linearly independent, the last row being a linear combination of the others, and the last column being a linear combination of the others. The system then looks like (4.11), and we are assured that the $N - 1$ by $N - 1$ matrix of coefficients of $x_1, \ldots, x_{N-1}$ in the first $N - 1$ equations is nonsingular. Let us neglect the redundant Nth equation, and let us move the terms in x_N to the other side of the equality sign, to obtain the following system:

$$a_{11}x_1 + \cdots + a_{1,N-1}x_{N-1} \qquad = -a_{1N}x_N$$

(4.12)
$$\vdots \qquad\qquad \vdots \qquad\qquad \vdots$$

$$a_{N-1,1}x_1 + \cdots + a_{N-1,N-1}x_{N-1} = -a_{N-1,N}x_N$$

If we denote the $N - 1$ by $N - 1$ matrix of a's on the left side of (4.12) by $\mathbf{A}^N$, and the vector $(a_{1N} \cdots a_{N-1,N})$ by $\mathbf{a}^N$, and the vector $(x_1 \cdots x_{N-1})$ by $\mathbf{x}^N$, this can be written

(4.13)
$$\mathbf{A}^N \mathbf{x}^{N\prime} = -\mathbf{a}^{N\prime} x_N$$

Since $\mathbf{A}^N$ is nonsingular by assumption, there is a unique solution of (4.13) for $x_1, \ldots, x_{N-1}$ in terms of x_N, thus:

(4.14)
$$\mathbf{x}^{N\prime} = -(\mathbf{A}^N)^{-1}\mathbf{a}^{N\prime} x_N$$

---

[28] Another and more general way of saying this is: If the rank of $\mathbf{A}$ is the same as the rank of the so-called augmented matrix of the system, which is of order N by $N + 1$ and is formed by tacking the vector $\mathbf{y}$ onto $\mathbf{A}$ as the $(N + 1)$th column, then the whole set of equations is consistent and has at least one solution. See Aitken [1949], p. 70. The solution is unique if and only if the ranks are both equal to N.

Here any nonzero value whatever can be chosen for the scalar x_N, and once that is done the values of $x_1, \ldots, x_{N-1}$ are determined as proportional to x_N. Hence as long as $\mathbf{A}^N$ is nonsingular, any solution $x_1, \ldots, x_{N-1}, x_N$ of (4.11) must be a vector proportional to every other solution. Therefore, although the *values* of $x_1, \ldots, x_{N-1}, x_N$ are not uniquely determined by the homogeneous system (4.11) when its matrix is singular, nevertheless if the matrix is of rank $N - 1$ then the *ratios* $x_1/x_N, \ldots, x_{N-1}/x_N$ are uniquely determined. This theorem has an important application to the estimation of the parameters of an econometric equation, the unknown x's in (4.14) corresponding to the unknown parameters. It is of course unnecessary and impossible that *all* the parameters of an equation should be determined uniquely, for if the equation is multiplied by a constant factor they will all be changed by that factor while the substantive content of the equation will not be affected. Hence what is wanted is precisely a unique set of ratios of all the parameters to some one of them. See the related discussions of identification in VIII.1.8 and estimation in IX.9.13–20.

4.10 Suppose now that $\mathbf{A}$ is of rank less than $N - 1$. Then even (4.14) does not have a unique solution in terms of a given value of x_N. In that case the values of more than one of the suitably selected components of $\mathbf{x}$ can be chosen at will, and the remaining ones (equal in number to the rank of $\mathbf{A}$) are uniquely determined as linear combinations of the arbitrarily chosen values of those components of $\mathbf{x}$. We shall not have much use for this case.[29]

4.11 In 4.1 it was noted that the matrix of a system $\mathbf{y}' = \mathbf{A}\mathbf{x}'$ fails to have an inverse if it is not square. Conditions for the solution of such a system have also been worked out; everything we have said above about systems with square matrices is a special case of the more general theory. These are some of the important results.[30] Let there be R equations in C variables $x_1, \ldots, x_C$, thus:

$$(4.15) \qquad\qquad \mathbf{A}\mathbf{x}' = \mathbf{y}'$$

Then $\mathbf{A}$ is $R \times C$, $\mathbf{x}'$ is $C \times 1$, and $\mathbf{y}'$ is $R \times 1$. We do not specify whether R is equal to, greater than, or less than C. Of course the rank of $\mathbf{A}$ cannot exceed either R or C. If the rank of the augmented $R \times (C + 1)$ matrix $(\mathbf{A} \ \mathbf{y}')$ equals the rank of $\mathbf{A}$, then all the R equations in (4.15) are logically consistent, and conversely. For the sequel, assume the equations are consistent. If the rank of $\mathbf{A}$ equals C, there is a unique solution of (4.15) for $\mathbf{x}'$, and conversely. If the rank of $\mathbf{A}$ is less than C, there is an infinity of solutions, and there is at least one linearly dependent set of columns in $\mathbf{A}$. C minus the rank of $\mathbf{A}$ tells the number of suitably chosen components

---

[29] It is discussed in general in Aitken [1949], pp. 63–69.
[30] Aitken [1949], pp. 59–70.

of $\mathbf{x}'$ that can be arbitrarily fixed in value without violating the equations. The rank of $\mathbf{A}$ tells how many components of $\mathbf{x}'$ can be expressed uniquely in terms of arbitrary values of the suitably chosen components of $\mathbf{x}'$.

5   CHARACTERISTIC ROOTS AND CHARACTERISTIC VECTORS OF A MATRIX[31]

5.1   In the limited-information maximum-likelihood method of estimation (see IX.9.13–20, especially IX.9.18) and in many other mathematical arguments, an equation of the following form occurs:

$$(5.1) \qquad (\lambda \mathbf{I} - \mathbf{Q})\boldsymbol{\beta}' = \mathbf{0}'$$

where $\mathbf{I}$ and $\mathbf{Q}$ are H by H matrices, $\boldsymbol{\beta}'$ is an Hth-order vector of unknown elements (not all zero) to be solved for, and λ is an unknown scalar. As we saw in 4.7, if (5.1) is to have a nonzero solution for $\boldsymbol{\beta}'$, then the determinant of the system must be zero:

$$(5.2) \quad \det(\lambda \mathbf{I} - \mathbf{Q}) = 0, \quad \text{i.e.,} \quad \begin{vmatrix} \lambda - q_{11} & -q_{12} & \cdots & -q_{1H} \\ -q_{21} & \lambda - q_{22} & \cdots & -q_{2H} \\ \cdot & \cdot & & \cdot \\ \cdot & \cdot & & \cdot \\ \cdot & \cdot & & \cdot \\ -q_{H1} & -q_{H2} & \cdots & \lambda - q_{HH} \end{vmatrix} = 0$$

For some values of λ this is true; for others it is not. If the system (5.1) is to have a nonzero solution, λ must take on a value that satisfies (5.2). Accordingly the next step is to solve (5.2) for λ. If the determinant of $\lambda \mathbf{I} - \mathbf{Q}$ is evaluated, it turns out to be an Hth-degree polynomial function of λ, thus:

$$(5.3) \quad \det(\lambda \mathbf{I} - \mathbf{Q}) = a_H \lambda^H + a_{H-1} \lambda^{H-1} + \cdots + a_2 \lambda^2 + a_1 \lambda + a_0 = 0$$

5.2   For example, suppose the original system is 2 by 2:

$$(5.4) \qquad \left[\lambda \begin{pmatrix} 1 & 0 \\ 0 & 1 \end{pmatrix} - \begin{pmatrix} 3 & 2 \\ 2 & 6 \end{pmatrix} \right] \begin{pmatrix} \beta_1 \\ \beta_2 \end{pmatrix} = \begin{pmatrix} 0 \\ 0 \end{pmatrix}$$

Then the determinant that must be zero for $(\beta_1 \quad \beta_2)$ to have a solution other than $(0 \quad 0)$ is

$$(5.5)$$
$$\begin{vmatrix} \lambda - 3 & -2 \\ -2 & \lambda - 6 \end{vmatrix} = \lambda^2 - (3 + 6)\lambda + (3 \times 6 - 2 \times 2) = \lambda^2 - 9\lambda + 14$$

---

[31] Concerning this section, see Frazer, Duncan, and Collar [1938], pp. 57–83, 133–135.

Note that in the general case of det $(\lambda \mathbf{I} - \mathbf{Q})$, as well as in this example, the coefficient of the highest-order term is 1. The negative of the coefficient of the next term is the sum of the diagonal elements q_{ii} of $\mathbf{Q}$ (this sum is called the *trace* of $\mathbf{Q}$ and is denoted by tr $\mathbf{Q}$; only a square matrix has a trace). The constant term is det $\mathbf{Q}$. The quadratic equation in (5.5) has the two solutions

$$(5.6) \qquad \lambda = \frac{9 \pm \sqrt{9^2 - 4 \times 14}}{2} = \frac{9 \pm 5}{2}$$

$$\lambda_1 = 7 \text{ and } \lambda_2 = 2$$

Hence λ must be either 7 or 2 if (5.4) is to have a nonzero solution for β_1 and β_2. Two solutions will be found, one for each value of λ. Let us continue with the example, first substituting $\lambda = \lambda_1 = 7$ into (5.4):

$$(5.7) \qquad \begin{pmatrix} 7 - 3 & -2 \\ -2 & 7 - 6 \end{pmatrix} \begin{pmatrix} \beta_1 \\ \beta_2 \end{pmatrix} = \begin{pmatrix} 4 & -2 \\ -2 & 1 \end{pmatrix} \begin{pmatrix} \beta_1 \\ \beta_2 \end{pmatrix} = \begin{pmatrix} 0 \\ 0 \end{pmatrix}$$

Now the matrix is singular as required, and is of rank $H - 1$ (i.e., 1), so we can choose β_2 arbitrarily and get a unique solution for β_1 in terms of β_2 as explained in 4.9:

$$(5.8) \qquad \beta_1 = \tfrac{1}{2}\beta_2$$

Thus for $\lambda = \lambda_1 = 7$, the vector $(\tfrac{1}{2} \quad 1)$ or any multiple of it is a solution of (5.4). Now substituting $\lambda = \lambda_2 = 2$ into (5.4),

$$(5.9) \qquad \begin{pmatrix} 2 - 3 & -2 \\ -2 & 2 - 6 \end{pmatrix} \begin{pmatrix} \beta_1 \\ \beta_2 \end{pmatrix} = \begin{pmatrix} -1 & -2 \\ -2 & -4 \end{pmatrix} \begin{pmatrix} \beta_1 \\ \beta_2 \end{pmatrix} = \begin{pmatrix} 0 \\ 0 \end{pmatrix}$$

Again there is a unique solution for β_1 in terms of β_2:

$$(5.10) \qquad \beta_1 = -2\beta_2$$

Thus for $\lambda = \lambda_2 = 2$, the vector $(-2 \quad 1)$ or any multiple of it is a solution of (5.4). The values $\lambda_1 = 7$ and $\lambda_2 = 2$ of λ are called *characteristic roots* of the matrix $\mathbf{Q}$ in (5.4), and the vectors $(\tfrac{1}{2} \quad 1)$ and $(-2 \quad 1)$ or any multiples of each are called *characteristic vectors* of that matrix. Each characteristic root has its own characteristic vector associated with it. The characteristic vector associated with any particular characteristic root of $\mathbf{Q}$ is the vector obtained by solving (5.1) for $\boldsymbol{\beta}'$ after that characteristic root has been substituted for λ in (5.1).

    5.3   Returning to the general form (5.1), the H by H matrix $\mathbf{Q}$ has H characteristic roots $\lambda_1, \ldots, \lambda_H$. All these roots may or may not be different, and they may be real numbers or complex numbers (like

$a + b\sqrt{-1}$). If the matrix is symmetric with real elements, all the roots are real.[32] If all the roots are different, then the characteristic vectors will be linearly independent.[33] The matrices whose roots we deal with, in Chapters IX and X where these methods are applied, all arise from moment matrices, which are necessarily symmetric with real elements, and this assures that the characteristic roots are all real and (except for accidents that can occur only with zero probability) all different.

5.4 For some purposes, in particular for maximizing the likelihood function that leads to the limited-information estimates, it is necessary to compute only one characteristic root of a certain matrix $\mathbf{Q}$ derived from observed data, namely, the largest root, λ_1. The characteristic vector $\hat{\boldsymbol{\beta}}$ associated with the largest root is then the limited-information estimate of the parameters in question.[34] The largest characteristic root of course can be obtained by solving the Hth-degree polynomial equation (5.3) to obtain the H solutions, and then examining them and choosing the largest. But this is extremely laborious, for every coefficient in (5.3) is a numerically complicated function of the elements of the matrix $\mathbf{Q}$. There is a much quicker method, dependent upon the fact that if λ_2 (the second largest root) is less than λ_1, the nth power of λ_2/λ_1 approaches zero as n increases without limit, so that the effect of $\lambda_2{}^n$ can be made negligible as compared with that of $\lambda_1{}^n$, and similarly for other roots. The method consists essentially of taking higher and higher powers of the matrix $\mathbf{Q}$ until the effect of the largest characteristic root λ_1 eclipses the effects of all the others to any desired degree, so that the largest root can be isolated. The process is as follows.[35]

5.5 First, choose an arbitrary nonzero column vector of H elements, and call it $\mathbf{b}^{(0)\prime}$. Any such vector at all will do. But the number of times the subsequent step must be repeated (i.e., the power of $\mathbf{Q}$ that is required) is smaller if $\mathbf{b}^{(0)\prime}$ is somewhere near the characteristic vector $\hat{\boldsymbol{\beta}}{}'$, which we seek to solve for. Hence it is well to choose as $\mathbf{b}^{(0)\prime}$ a vector that is believed to be approximately equal to $\hat{\boldsymbol{\beta}}{}'$. The least-squares estimate of $\boldsymbol{\beta}'$ is usually a good choice for $\mathbf{b}^{(0)\prime}$.

5.6 The next step is a unit consisting of two operations. This step is repeated as many times as necessary to get the desired degree of accuracy in the values of the largest characteristic root λ_1 and its associated characteristic vector $\hat{\boldsymbol{\beta}}{}'$. First, compute a new column vector called $\mathbf{b}^{(1)\prime}$, thus:

$$(5.11) \qquad\qquad \mathbf{b}^{(1)\prime} = \mathbf{Q}\mathbf{b}^{(0)\prime}$$

[32] See Koopmans and Hood [1953], Appendix B, Theorem 1 and Corollary, p. 187; or Bellman [1960], p. 35.

[33] Bellman [1960], p. 54, or Frazer, Duncan, and Collar [1938], pp. 64–66.

[34] See IX.9.18–20.

[35] See Chernoff and Divinsky [1953], pp. 240–245, esp. p. 244.

Second, compute another new vector called $\boldsymbol{\lambda}^{(1)}$ whose elements are quotients of the corresponding elements of $\mathbf{b}^{(1)\prime}$ and $\mathbf{b}^{(0)\prime}$, thus:

$$(5.12) \qquad \boldsymbol{\lambda}^{(1)} = \left(\frac{b_1^{(1)}}{b_1^{(0)}} \quad \cdots \quad \frac{b_H^{(1)}}{b_H^{(0)}} \right)$$

We shall see that the vector $\boldsymbol{\lambda}^{(1)}$ is a first approximation to a vector having identical elements each equal to the largest characteristic root λ_1 of $\mathbf{Q}$, and $\mathbf{b}^{(1)\prime}$ is a first approximation to the associated characteristic vector $\hat{\boldsymbol{\beta}}'$ (considering $\mathbf{b}^{(0)\prime}$ as a "zeroth" approximation).

5.7 The foregoing step is repeated n times; we will see how to tell how big n should be in a moment. The result is[36]

$$(5.13) \qquad \mathbf{b}^{(n)\prime} = \mathbf{Q}\mathbf{b}^{(n-1)\prime} = \mathbf{Q}^n\mathbf{b}^{(0)\prime}$$

$$(5.14) \qquad \boldsymbol{\lambda}^{(n)} = \left(\frac{b_1^{(n)}}{b_1^{(n-1)}} \quad \cdots \quad \frac{b_H^{(n)}}{b_H^{(n-1)}} \right)$$

The process is repeated until all the elements of $\boldsymbol{\lambda}^{(n)}$ are equal within as close an approximation as is desired for the value of λ_1. This common value of the elements of $\boldsymbol{\lambda}^{(n)}$ is approximately λ_1, the largest characteristic root of $\mathbf{Q}$. And the last-computed vector $\mathbf{b}^{(n)\prime}$ is approximately the corresponding characteristic vector $\hat{\boldsymbol{\beta}}'$, the required estimate of the parameters that are the elements of $\boldsymbol{\beta}'$. This vector is usually normalized to make $\hat{\beta}_1 = 1$. Usually about a dozen iterations are sufficient to make all the elements of $\boldsymbol{\lambda}^{(n)}$ alike to four or five significant figures. If the convergence is slow, the square or fourth power of $\mathbf{Q}$ can be computed, and then two or four iterations can be done at once in effect by multiplying $\mathbf{b}^{(n)\prime}$ on the left by $\mathbf{Q}^2$ or $\mathbf{Q}^4$ instead of by $\mathbf{Q}$ only.

5.8 The proof that the elements of the vector $\boldsymbol{\lambda}^{(n)}$ do approach the largest characteristic root λ_1, and that the vector $\mathbf{b}^{(n)\prime}$ does approach the associated characteristic vector $\hat{\boldsymbol{\beta}}'$, is as follows. For notational convenience we shall denote the H characteristic roots of $\mathbf{Q}$ by $\lambda_1, \ldots, \lambda_H$, and since they are all assumed to be different[37] we can safely denote the largest by λ_1. We shall denote the H characteristic vectors associated with these roots respectively as $\hat{\boldsymbol{\beta}}^{(1)\prime}, \ldots, \hat{\boldsymbol{\beta}}^{(H)\prime}$. Note that $\hat{\boldsymbol{\beta}}^{(1)\prime}$ is $\hat{\boldsymbol{\beta}}'$, the one we are really looking for. Now every characteristic root together with its characteristic vector satisfies equation (5.1). Indeed that equation defines the characteristic roots and vectors. Therefore

$$(5.15) \qquad \mathbf{Q}\hat{\boldsymbol{\beta}}^{(i)\prime} = \lambda_i\hat{\boldsymbol{\beta}}^{(i)\prime}$$

---

[36] Be very careful in what follows not to confuse superscripts in parentheses and superscripts *not* in parentheses. Thus $\lambda_i{}^n$ is the nth power of the characteristic root λ_i, while $\lambda_i^{(n)}$ is the ith element of the vector $\boldsymbol{\lambda}^{(n)}$ in (5.14).

[37] This assumption was justified above in 5.3.

We shall need to evaluate $Q^n \hat{\beta}^{(i)'}$. This can be done with the aid of (5.15), thus:[38]

$$(5.16) \qquad Q^2\hat{\beta}^{(i)'} = QQ\hat{\beta}^{(i)'} = Q\lambda_i\hat{\beta}^{(i)'} = \lambda_i Q\hat{\beta}^{(i)'}$$
$$= \lambda_i^2\hat{\beta}^{(i)'}$$

By a repeated application of this argument we can evaluate $Q^3\hat{\beta}^{(i)'}$, $Q^4\hat{\beta}^{(i)'}$, etc.

$$(5.17) \qquad Q^n\hat{\beta}^{(i)'} = \lambda_i^n\hat{\beta}^{(i)'}$$

We shall place this result aside until we need it, and proceed with the proof.

5.9 As noted earlier, the characteristic vectors of a matrix are linearly independent if all the characteristic roots are different. Therefore, our arbitrary vector $b^{(0)'}$ can be expressed as a unique linear combination of the characteristic vectors.[39] If we call the coefficients of this linear combination $\alpha_1, \ldots, \alpha_H$, this shows that

$$(5.18) \qquad b^{(0)'} = \alpha_1\hat{\beta}^{(1)'} + \alpha_2\hat{\beta}^{(2)'} + \cdots + \alpha_H\hat{\beta}^{(H)'}$$

From (5.13) and (5.18) we can express the vector $b^{(n)'}$ as follows:

$$(5.19) \quad b^{(n)'} = Q^n b^{(0)'} = Q^n[\alpha_1\hat{\beta}^{(1)'} + \alpha_2\hat{\beta}^{(2)'} + \cdots + \alpha_H\hat{\beta}^{(H)'}]$$
$$= \alpha_1 Q^n\hat{\beta}^{(1)'} + \alpha_2 Q^n\hat{\beta}^{(2)'} + \cdots + \alpha_H Q^n\hat{\beta}^{(H)'}$$

Because of (5.17), this becomes a linear combination of the characteristic vectors:

$$(5.20) \qquad b^{(n)'} = \alpha_1\lambda_1^n\hat{\beta}^{(1)'} + \alpha_2\lambda_2^n\hat{\beta}^{(2)'} + \cdots + \alpha_H\lambda_H^n\hat{\beta}^{(H)'}$$

Now the ith element $b_i^{(n)}$ of the vector $b^{(n)'}$ is a corresponding linear combination of the ith elements $\hat{\beta}_i^{(1)}, \ldots, \hat{\beta}_i^{(H)}$ of the characteristic vectors $\hat{\beta}^{(1)'}, \ldots, \hat{\beta}^{(H)'}$:

$$(5.21) \qquad b_i^{(n)} = \alpha_1\lambda_1^n\hat{\beta}_i^{(1)} + \alpha_2\lambda_2^n\hat{\beta}_i^{(2)} + \cdots + \alpha_H\lambda_H^n\hat{\beta}_i^{(H)}$$

Let us factor out the expression $\alpha_1\lambda_1^n\hat{\beta}_i^{(1)}$ to get

$$(5.22) \quad b_i^{(n)} = \alpha_1\lambda_1^n\hat{\beta}_i^{(1)}\left[1 + \frac{\alpha_2}{\alpha_1}\left(\frac{\lambda_2}{\lambda_1}\right)^n\frac{\hat{\beta}_i^{(2)}}{\hat{\beta}_i^{(1)}} + \cdots + \frac{\alpha_H}{\alpha_1}\left(\frac{\lambda_H}{\lambda_1}\right)^n\frac{\hat{\beta}_i^{(H)}}{\hat{\beta}_i^{(1)}}\right]$$

[38] Note that the following equations contain powers of λ_i, and not $\lambda_i^{(n)}$, down to (5.23), which contains both. See note 36 above.

[39] The coefficients in this linear combination are the unique solution of the system that equates $b^{(0)'}$ to the product of the matrix whose columns are the characteristic vectors of Q, times an unknown vector, say α'. The solution α' is unique only after normalization of the characteristic vectors.

Now as $n \to \infty$, the expression in brackets in (5.22) approaches 1, because $\lambda_2/\lambda_1, \ldots, \lambda_H/\lambda_1$ are all less than 1 and so their nth powers all approach zero. Hence $b_i^{(n)} \to \alpha_1 \lambda_1^n \hat{\beta}_i^{(1)}$. Hence as $n \to \infty$ the ith element $\lambda_i^{(n)}$ of the vector $\boldsymbol{\lambda}^{(n)}$, which is defined in (5.14) as the ratio of $b_i^{(n)}$ to $b_i^{(n-1)}$, approaches the desired characteristic root, for

$$(5.23) \qquad \lambda_i^{(n)} = \frac{b_i^{(n)}}{b_i^{(n-1)}} \to \frac{\alpha_1 \lambda_1^n \hat{\beta}_i^{(1)}}{\alpha_1 \lambda_1^{n-1} \hat{\beta}_i^{(1)}} = \lambda_1$$

and this must be true for every element of $\boldsymbol{\lambda}^{(n)}$, from $\lambda_1^{(n)}$ to $\lambda_H^{(n)}$. Observe also that the vector $\mathbf{b}^{(n)\prime}$ itself approaches $\hat{\boldsymbol{\beta}}^{(1)\prime}$ as a limit [except for a factor of proportionality $(\alpha_1 \lambda_1^n)$, which can be removed by normalizing so that $\hat{\beta}_1^{(1)}$ is made equal to 1], thus:

$$(5.24) \qquad \mathbf{b}^{(n)\prime} \to \begin{pmatrix} \alpha_1 \lambda_1^n \hat{\beta}_1^{(1)} \\ \cdot \\ \cdot \\ \cdot \\ \alpha_1 \lambda_1^n \hat{\beta}_H^{(1)} \end{pmatrix} = \alpha_1 \lambda_1^n \hat{\boldsymbol{\beta}}^{(1)\prime}$$

This completes the proof.

5.10 If $H = 2$, that is, if $\mathbf{Q}$ is 2×2, it is simplest to solve the characteristic equation (which is then quadratic) directly and select the largest root; but if $H \geq 3$, the above iterative procedure is usually quicker. The foregoing derivation makes it clear that computational difficulty will arise if the *two largest roots* of $\mathbf{Q}$ are very nearly equal; see IX.12.20.

6 FURTHER RESULTS

6.1 Certain other results are introduced in the text above as needed, for example, in VIII.3.21 ff., IX.5.2–4, IX.9.13–20, and IX.10.

6.2 The reader is referred to the works cited at the beginning of this appendix for further results.

APPENDIX B

Probability Tables

TABLE B-1   The *t* Distribution and the Normal Distribution

The smaller probability shown at the head of a column is the area in *one* tail, and the larger probability is the area in *both* tails. *Example:* With 5 degrees of freedom, a positive value of *t* larger than 2.015 has a probability of 5 per cent and a value of *t* greater in absolute value than 2.015 has a probability of 10 per cent. The distribution is symmetrical.

More information may be found in X.1.12–14, in the introduction to Fisher and Yates [1938], in the introduction to Pearson and Hartley [1954], or in any good statistical inference book.

Degrees of Freedom	Pb	.25 .5	.1 .2	.05 .1	.025 .05	.01 .02	.005 .01
1		1.000	3.078	6.314	12.706	31.821	63.657
2		.816	1.886	2.920	4.303	6.965	9.925
3		.765	1.638	2.353	3.182	4.541	5.841
4		.741	1.533	2.132	2.776	3.747	4.604
5		.727	1.476	2.015	2.571	3.365	4.032
6		.718	1.440	1.943	2.447	3.143	3.707
7		.711	1.415	1.895	2.365	2.998	3.499
8		.706	1.397	1.860	2.306	2.896	3.355
9		.703	1.383	1.833	2.262	2.821	3.250
10		.700	1.372	1.812	2.228	2.764	3.169
11		.697	1.363	1.796	2.201	2.718	3.106
12		.695	1.356	1.782	2.179	2.681	3.055
13		.694	1.350	1.771	2.160	2.650	3.012
14		.692	1.345	1.761	2.145	2.624	2.977
15		.691	1.341	1.753	2.131	2.602	2.947
16		.690	1.337	1.746	2.120	2.583	2.921
17		.689	1.333	1.740	2.110	2.567	2.898
18		.688	1.330	1.734	2.101	2.552	2.878
19		.688	1.328	1.729	2.093	2.539	2.861
20		.687	1.325	1.725	2.086	2.528	2.845
21		.686	1.323	1.721	2.080	2.518	2.831
22		.686	1.321	1.717	2.074	2.508	2.819
23		.685	1.319	1.714	2.069	2.500	2.807
24		.685	1.318	1.711	2.064	2.492	2.797
25		.684	1.316	1.708	2.060	2.485	2.787
26		.684	1.315	1.706	2.056	2.479	2.779
27		.684	1.314	1.703	2.052	2.473	2.771
28		.683	1.313	1.701	2.048	2.467	2.763
29		.683	1.311	1.699	2.045	2.462	2.756
30		.683	1.310	1.697	2.042	2.457	2.750
40		.681	1.303	1.684	2.021	2.423	2.704
60		.679	1.296	1.671	2.000	2.390	2.660
120		.677	1.289	1.658	1.980	2.358	2.617
(Normal)	∞	.674	1.282	1.645	1.960	2.326	2.576

Source: Abridged from Pearson and Hartley [1954], p. 138, by kind permission of the Syndics of the Cambridge University Press, publishers for the Biometrika Society.

TABLE B-2   The χ^2 (chi square) Distribution

The probability shown at the head of a column is the area in the right-
hand tail. *Example:* With 5 degrees of freedom, a value of χ^2 larger than
9.236 has a probability of 10 per cent.

More information may be found in X.1.10–11, in the introduction

Degrees of Freedom	Pb	.995	.990	.975	.950	.900
1		$392704 \cdot 10^{-10}$	$157088 \cdot 10^{-9}$	$982069 \cdot 10^{-9}$	$393214 \cdot 10^{-8}$	.0157908
2		.0100251	.0201007	.0506356	.102587	.210720
3		.0717212	.114832	.215795	.351846	.584375
4		.206990	.297110	.484419	.710721	1.063623
5		.411740	.554300	.831211	1.145476	1.61031
6		.675727	.872085	1.237347	1.63539	2.20413
7		.989265	1.239043	1.68987	2.16735	2.83311
8		1.344419	1.646482	2.17973	2.73264	3.48954
9		1.734926	2.087912	2.70039	3.32511	4.16816
10		2.15585	2.55821	3.24697	3.94030	4.86518
11		2.60321	3.05347	3.81575	4.57481	5.57779
12		3.07382	3.57056	4.40379	5.22603	6.30380
13		3.56503	4.10691	5.00874	5.89186	7.04150
14		4.07468	4.66043	5.62872	6.57063	7.78953
15		4.60094	5.22935	6.26214	7.26094	8.54675
16		5.14224	5.81221	6.90766	7.96164	9.31223
17		5.69724	6.40776	7.56418	8.67176	10.0852
18		6.26481	7.01491	8.23075	9.39046	10.8649
19		6.84398	7.63273	8.90655	10.1170	11.6509
20		7.43386	8.26040	9.59083	10.8508	12.4426
21		8.03366	8.89720	10.28293	11.5913	13.2396
22		8.64272	9.54249	10.9823	12.3380	14.0415
23		9.26042	10.19567	11.6885	13.0905	14.8479
24		9.88623	10.8564	12.4011	13.8484	15.6587
25		10.5197	11.5240	13.1197	14.6114	16.4734
26		11.1603	12.1981	13.8439	15.3791	17.2919
27		11.8076	12.8786	14.5733	16.1513	18.1138
28		12.4613	13.5648	15.3079	16.9279	18.9392
29		13.1211	14.2565	16.0471	17.7083	19.7677
30		13.7867	14.9535	16.7908	18.4926	20.5992
40		20.7065	22.1643	24.4331	26.5093	29.0505
50		27.9907	29.7067	32.3574	34.7642	37.6886
60		35.5346	37.4848	40.4817	43.1879	46.4589
70		43.2752	45.4418	48.7576	51.7393	55.3290
80		51.1720	53.5400	57.1532	60.3915	64.2778
90		59.1963	61.7541	65.6466	69.1260	73.2912
100		67.3276	70.0648	74.2219	77.9295	82.3581
(Normal)		−2.5758	−2.3263	−1.9600	−1.6449	−1.2816

Source: Abridged from Pearson and Hartley [1954], pp. 130–131, by kind permission of

and the Normal Distribution

to Pearson and Hartley [1954], in the introduction to Fisher and Yates [1938], or in any good statistical inference book.

The last line of the table shows the value of the standard normal variable that is exceeded with the probability given at the head of the column.

.750	.500	.250	.100	.050	.025	.010	.005
.1015308	.454937	1.32330	2.70554	3.84146	5.02389	6.63490	7.87944
.575364	1.38629	2.77259	4.60517	5.99147	7.37776	9.21034	10.5966
1.212534	2.36597	4.10835	6.25139	7.81473	9.34840	11.3449	12.8381
1.92255	3.35670	5.38527	7.77944	9.48773	11.1433	13.2767	14.8602
2.67460	4.35146	6.62568	9.23635	11.0705	12.8325	15.0863	16.7496
3.45460	5.34812	7.84080	10.6446	12.5916	14.4494	16.8119	18.5476
4.25485	6.34581	9.03715	12.0170	14.0671	16.0128	18.4753	20.2777
5.07064	7.34412	10.2188	13.3616	15.5073	17.5346	20.0902	21.9550
5.89883	8.34283	11.3887	14.6837	16.9190	19.0228	21.6660	23.5893
6.73720	9.34182	12.5489	15.9871	18.3070	20.4831	23.2093	25.1882
7.58412	10.3410	13.7007	17.2750	19.6751	21.9200	24.7250	26.7569
8.43842	11.3403	14.8454	18.5494	21.0261	23.3367	26.2170	28.2995
9.29906	12.3398	15.9839	19.8119	22.3621	24.7356	27.6883	29.8194
10.1653	13.3393	17.1170	21.0642	23.6848	26.1190	29.1413	31.3193
11.0365	14.3389	18.2451	22.3072	24.9958	27.4884	30.5779	32.8013
11.9122	15.3385	19.3688	23.5418	26.2962	28.8454	31.9999	34.2672
12.7919	16.3381	20.4887	24.7690	27.5871	30.1910	33.4087	35.7185
13.6753	17.3379	21.6049	25.9894	28.8693	31.5264	34.8053	37.1564
14.5620	18.3376	22.7178	27.2036	30.1435	32.8523	36.1908	38.5822
15.4518	19.3374	23.8277	28.4120	31.4104	34.1696	37.5662	39.9968
16.3444	20.3372	24.9348	29.6151	32.6705	35.4789	38.9321	41.4010
17.2396	21.3370	26.0393	30.8133	33.9244	36.7807	40.2894	42.7956
18.1373	22.3369	27.1413	32.0069	35.1725	38.0757	41.6384	44.1813
19.0372	23.3367	28.2412	33.1963	36.4151	39.3641	42.9798	45.5585
19.9393	24.3366	29.3389	34.3816	37.6525	40.6465	44.3141	46.9278
20.8434	25.3364	30.4345	35.5631	38.8852	41.9232	45.6417	48.2899
21.7494	26.3363	31.5284	36.7412	40.1133	43.1944	46.9630	49.6449
22.6572	27.3363	32.6205	37.9159	41.3372	44.4607	48.2782	50.9933
23.5666	28.3362	33.7109	39.0875	42.5569	45.7222	49.5879	52.3356
24.4776	29.3360	34.7998	40.2560	43.7729	46.9792	50.8922	53.6720
33.6603	39.3354	45.6160	51.8050	55.7585	59.3417	63.6907	66.7659
42.9421	49.3349	56.3336	63.1671	67.5048	71.4202	76.1539	79.4900
52.2938	59.3347	66.9814	74.3970	79.0819	83.2976	88.3794	91.9517
61.6983	69.3344	77.5766	85.5271	90.5312	95.0231	100.425	104.215
71.1445	79.3343	88.1303	96.5782	101.879	106.629	112.329	116.321
80.6247	89.3342	98.6499	107.565	113.145	118.136	124.116	128.299
90.1332	99.3341	109.141	118.498	124.342	129.561	135.807	140.169
−.6745	.0000	+.6745	+1.2816	+1.6449	+1.9600	+2.3263	+2.5758

the Syndics of the Cambridge University Press, publishers for the Biometrika Society.

TABLE B-3   The F Distribution

The upper 5 per cent and upper 1 per cent points are values of F that will be exceeded with probability 5 and 1 per cent, respectively. n_1 and n_2 are the numbers of degrees of freedom in the numerator and denominator, respectively. *Example:* For 5 degrees of freedom in the numerator and 10 in the denominator, a value of F greater than 3.33 has a probability of 5 per cent; and a value of F greater than 1/4.74, i.e., greater than 0.211, has a 95 per cent probability. (The latter figure is in the lower tail of the distribution and hence is obtained by inverting the F ratio and interchanging degrees of freedom.)

More information may be found in X.1.6–1.9, in the introduction to Pearson and Hartley [1954], in the introduction to Fisher and Yates [1938], or in any good statistical inference book.

Upper 5% points

n_2 \ n_1	1	2	3	4	5	6	7	8	9	10	12	15	20	24	30	40	60	120	∞
1	161.4	199.5	215.7	224.6	230.2	234.0	236.8	238.9	240.5	241.9	243.9	245.9	248.0	249.1	250.1	251.1	252.2	253.3	254.3
2	18.51	19.00	19.16	19.25	19.30	19.33	19.35	19.37	19.38	19.40	19.41	19.43	19.45	19.45	19.46	19.47	19.48	19.49	19.50
3	10.13	9.55	9.28	9.12	9.01	8.94	8.89	8.85	8.81	8.79	8.74	8.70	8.66	8.64	8.62	8.59	8.57	8.55	8.53
4	7.71	6.94	6.59	6.39	6.26	6.16	6.09	6.04	6.00	5.96	5.91	5.86	5.80	5.77	5.75	5.72	5.69	5.66	5.63
5	6.61	5.79	5.41	5.19	5.05	4.95	4.88	4.82	4.77	4.74	4.68	4.62	4.56	4.53	4.50	4.46	4.43	4.40	4.36
6	5.99	5.14	4.76	4.53	4.39	4.28	4.21	4.15	4.10	4.06	4.00	3.94	3.87	3.84	3.81	3.77	3.74	3.70	3.67
7	5.59	4.74	4.35	4.12	3.97	3.87	3.79	3.73	3.68	3.64	3.57	3.51	3.44	3.41	3.38	3.34	3.30	3.27	3.23
8	5.32	4.46	4.07	3.84	3.69	3.58	3.50	3.44	3.39	3.35	3.28	3.22	3.15	3.12	3.08	3.04	3.01	2.97	2.93
9	5.12	4.26	3.86	3.63	3.48	3.37	3.29	3.23	3.18	3.14	3.07	3.01	2.94	2.90	2.86	2.83	2.79	2.75	2.71
10	4.96	4.10	3.71	3.48	3.33	3.22	3.14	3.07	3.02	2.98	2.91	2.85	2.77	2.74	2.70	2.66	2.62	2.58	2.54
11	4.84	3.98	3.59	3.36	3.20	3.09	3.01	2.95	2.90	2.85	2.79	2.72	2.65	2.61	2.57	2.53	2.49	2.45	2.40
12	4.75	3.89	3.49	3.26	3.11	3.00	2.91	2.85	2.80	2.75	2.69	2.62	2.54	2.51	2.47	2.43	2.38	2.34	2.30
13	4.67	3.81	3.41	3.18	3.03	2.92	2.83	2.77	2.71	2.67	2.60	2.53	2.46	2.42	2.38	2.34	2.30	2.25	2.21
14	4.60	3.74	3.34	3.11	2.96	2.85	2.76	2.70	2.65	2.60	2.53	2.46	2.39	2.35	2.31	2.27	2.22	2.18	2.13
15	4.54	3.68	3.29	3.06	2.90	2.79	2.71	2.64	2.59	2.54	2.48	2.40	2.33	2.29	2.25	2.20	2.16	2.11	2.07
16	4.49	3.63	3.24	3.01	2.85	2.74	2.66	2.59	2.54	2.49	2.42	2.35	2.28	2.24	2.19	2.15	2.11	2.06	2.01
17	4.45	3.59	3.20	2.96	2.81	2.70	2.61	2.55	2.49	2.45	2.38	2.31	2.23	2.19	2.15	2.10	2.06	2.01	1.96
18	4.41	3.55	3.16	2.93	2.77	2.66	2.58	2.51	2.46	2.41	2.34	2.27	2.19	2.15	2.11	2.06	2.02	1.97	1.92
19	4.38	3.52	3.13	2.90	2.74	2.63	2.54	2.48	2.42	2.38	2.31	2.23	2.16	2.11	2.07	2.03	1.98	1.93	1.88
20	4.35	3.49	3.10	2.87	2.71	2.60	2.51	2.45	2.39	2.35	2.28	2.20	2.12	2.08	2.04	1.99	1.95	1.90	1.84
21	4.32	3.47	3.07	2.84	2.68	2.57	2.49	2.42	2.37	2.32	2.25	2.18	2.10	2.05	2.01	1.96	1.92	1.87	1.81
22	4.30	3.44	3.05	2.82	2.66	2.55	2.46	2.40	2.34	2.30	2.23	2.15	2.07	2.03	1.98	1.94	1.89	1.84	1.78
23	4.28	3.42	3.03	2.80	2.64	2.53	2.44	2.37	2.32	2.27	2.20	2.13	2.05	2.01	1.96	1.91	1.86	1.81	1.76
24	4.26	3.40	3.01	2.78	2.62	2.51	2.42	2.36	2.30	2.25	2.18	2.11	2.03	1.98	1.94	1.89	1.84	1.79	1.73
25	4.24	3.39	2.99	2.76	2.60	2.49	2.40	2.34	2.28	2.24	2.16	2.09	2.01	1.96	1.92	1.87	1.82	1.77	1.71
26	4.23	3.37	2.98	2.74	2.59	2.47	2.39	2.32	2.27	2.22	2.15	2.07	1.99	1.95	1.90	1.85	1.80	1.75	1.69
27	4.21	3.35	2.96	2.73	2.57	2.46	2.37	2.31	2.25	2.20	2.13	2.06	1.97	1.93	1.88	1.84	1.79	1.73	1.67
28	4.20	3.34	2.95	2.71	2.56	2.45	2.36	2.29	2.24	2.19	2.12	2.04	1.96	1.91	1.87	1.82	1.77	1.71	1.65
29	4.18	3.33	2.93	2.70	2.55	2.43	2.35	2.28	2.22	2.18	2.10	2.03	1.94	1.90	1.85	1.81	1.75	1.70	1.64
30	4.17	3.32	2.92	2.69	2.53	2.42	2.33	2.27	2.21	2.16	2.09	2.01	1.93	1.89	1.84	1.79	1.74	1.68	1.62
40	4.08	3.23	2.84	2.61	2.45	2.34	2.25	2.18	2.12	2.08	2.00	1.92	1.84	1.79	1.74	1.69	1.64	1.58	1.51
60	4.00	3.15	2.76	2.53	2.37	2.25	2.17	2.10	2.04	1.99	1.92	1.84	1.75	1.70	1.65	1.59	1.53	1.47	1.39
120	3.92	3.07	2.68	2.45	2.29	2.17	2.09	2.02	1.96	1.91	1.83	1.75	1.66	1.61	1.55	1.50	1.43	1.35	1.25
∞	3.84	3.00	2.60	2.37	2.21	2.10	2.01	1.94	1.88	1.83	1.75	1.67	1.57	1.52	1.46	1.39	1.32	1.22	1.00

TABLE B-3   The F Distribution (concluded)

Upper 1% points

n_2 \ n_1	1	2	3	4	5	6	7	8	9	10	12	15	20	24	30	40	60	120	∞
1	4052	4999.5	5403	5625	5764	5859	5928	5982	6022	6056	6106	6157	6209	6235	6261	6287	6313	6339	6366
2	98.50	99.00	99.17	99.25	99.30	99.33	99.36	99.37	99.39	99.40	99.42	99.43	99.45	99.46	99.47	99.47	99.48	99.49	99.50
3	34.12	30.82	29.46	28.71	28.24	27.91	27.67	27.49	27.35	27.23	27.05	26.87	26.69	26.60	26.50	26.41	26.32	26.22	26.13
4	21.20	18.00	16.69	15.98	15.52	15.21	14.98	14.80	14.66	14.55	14.37	14.20	14.02	13.93	13.84	13.75	13.65	13.56	13.46
5	16.26	13.27	12.06	11.39	10.97	10.67	10.46	10.29	10.16	10.05	9.89	9.72	9.55	9.47	9.38	9.29	9.20	9.11	9.02
6	13.75	10.92	9.78	9.15	8.75	8.47	8.26	8.10	7.98	7.87	7.72	7.56	7.40	7.31	7.23	7.14	7.06	6.97	6.88
7	12.25	9.55	8.45	7.85	7.46	7.19	6.99	6.84	6.72	6.62	6.47	6.31	6.16	6.07	5.99	5.91	5.82	5.74	5.65
8	11.26	8.65	7.59	7.01	6.63	6.37	6.18	6.03	5.91	5.81	5.67	5.52	5.36	5.28	5.20	5.12	5.03	4.95	4.86
9	10.56	8.02	6.99	6.42	6.06	5.80	5.61	5.47	5.35	5.26	5.11	4.96	4.81	4.73	4.65	4.57	4.48	4.40	4.31
10	10.04	7.56	6.55	5.99	5.64	5.39	5.20	5.06	4.94	4.85	4.71	4.56	4.41	4.33	4.25	4.17	4.08	4.00	3.91
11	9.65	7.21	6.22	5.67	5.32	5.07	4.89	4.74	4.63	4.54	4.40	4.25	4.10	4.02	3.94	3.86	3.78	3.69	3.60
12	9.33	6.93	5.95	5.41	5.06	4.82	4.64	4.50	4.39	4.30	4.16	4.01	3.86	3.78	3.70	3.62	3.54	3.45	3.36
13	9.07	6.70	5.74	5.21	4.86	4.62	4.44	4.30	4.19	4.10	3.96	3.82	3.66	3.59	3.51	3.43	3.34	3.25	3.17
14	8.86	6.51	5.56	5.04	4.69	4.46	4.28	4.14	4.03	3.94	3.80	3.66	3.51	3.43	3.35	3.27	3.18	3.09	3.00
15	8.68	6.36	5.42	4.89	4.56	4.32	4.14	4.00	3.89	3.80	3.67	3.52	3.37	3.29	3.21	3.13	3.05	2.96	2.87
16	8.53	6.23	5.29	4.77	4.44	4.20	4.03	3.89	3.78	3.69	3.55	3.41	3.26	3.18	3.10	3.02	2.93	2.84	2.75
17	8.40	6.11	5.18	4.67	4.34	4.10	3.93	3.79	3.68	3.59	3.46	3.31	3.16	3.08	3.00	2.92	2.83	2.75	2.65
18	8.29	6.01	5.09	4.58	4.25	4.01	3.84	3.71	3.60	3.51	3.37	3.23	3.08	3.00	2.92	2.84	2.75	2.66	2.57
19	8.18	5.93	5.01	4.50	4.17	3.94	3.77	3.63	3.52	3.43	3.30	3.15	3.00	2.92	2.84	2.76	2.67	2.58	2.49
20	8.10	5.85	4.94	4.43	4.10	3.87	3.70	3.56	3.46	3.37	3.23	3.09	2.94	2.86	2.78	2.69	2.61	2.52	2.42
21	8.02	5.78	4.87	4.37	4.04	3.81	3.64	3.51	3.40	3.31	3.17	3.03	2.88	2.80	2.72	2.64	2.55	2.46	2.36
22	7.95	5.72	4.82	4.31	3.99	3.76	3.59	3.45	3.35	3.26	3.12	2.98	2.83	2.75	2.67	2.58	2.50	2.40	2.31
23	7.88	5.66	4.76	4.26	3.94	3.71	3.54	3.41	3.30	3.21	3.07	2.93	2.78	2.70	2.62	2.54	2.45	2.35	2.26
24	7.82	5.61	4.72	4.22	3.90	3.67	3.50	3.36	3.26	3.17	3.03	2.89	2.74	2.66	2.58	2.49	2.40	2.31	2.21
25	7.77	5.57	4.68	4.18	3.85	3.63	3.46	3.32	3.22	3.13	2.99	2.85	2.70	2.62	2.54	2.45	2.36	2.27	2.17
26	7.72	5.53	4.64	4.14	3.82	3.59	3.42	3.29	3.18	3.09	2.96	2.81	2.66	2.58	2.50	2.42	2.33	2.23	2.13
27	7.68	5.49	4.60	4.11	3.78	3.56	3.39	3.26	3.15	3.06	2.93	2.78	2.63	2.55	2.47	2.38	2.29	2.20	2.10
28	7.64	5.45	4.57	4.07	3.75	3.53	3.36	3.23	3.12	3.03	2.90	2.75	2.60	2.52	2.44	2.35	2.26	2.17	2.06
29	7.60	5.42	4.54	4.04	3.73	3.50	3.33	3.20	3.09	3.00	2.87	2.73	2.57	2.49	2.41	2.33	2.23	2.14	2.03
30	7.56	5.39	4.51	4.02	3.70	3.47	3.30	3.17	3.07	2.98	2.84	2.70	2.55	2.47	2.39	2.30	2.21	2.11	2.01
40	7.31	5.18	4.31	3.83	3.51	3.29	3.12	2.99	2.89	2.80	2.66	2.52	2.37	2.29	2.20	2.11	2.02	1.92	1.80
60	7.08	4.98	4.13	3.65	3.34	3.12	2.95	2.82	2.72	2.63	2.50	2.35	2.20	2.12	2.03	1.94	1.84	1.73	1.60
120	6.85	4.79	3.95	3.48	3.17	2.96	2.79	2.66	2.56	2.47	2.34	2.19	2.03	1.95	1.86	1.76	1.66	1.53	1.38
∞	6.63	4.61	3.78	3.32	3.02	2.80	2.64	2.51	2.41	2.32	2.18	2.04	1.88	1.79	1.70	1.59	1.47	1.32	1.00

Source: Abridged from Pearson and Hartley [1954], pp. 159 and 161, by kind permission of the Syndics of the Cambridge University Press, publishers for the Biometrika Society.

TABLE B-4   The Distribution of $d = \dfrac{\delta^2}{s^2} = \dfrac{T-1}{T} \cdot \dfrac{\delta^2}{S^2} = \dfrac{\sum\limits_{2}^{T}(\hat{u}_t - \hat{u}_{t-1})^2}{\sum\limits_{1}^{T}\hat{u}_t^{\,2}}$

The probability shown in the second column is the area in the lower tail. K is the number of independent variables in addition to the constant term. *Example:* With 20 observations, and a regression involving three independent variables and a constant term, Hart gives a probability of 5 per cent for a value of d less than 1.30, and Durbin and Watson give a probability of 5 per cent for a value of d between 1.00 and 1.68. The distributions are symmetrical about the point $2T/(T-1)$.

More information may be found in X.4, in Hart [1942], and in Durbin and Watson [1950], [1951].

Sample Size T	Probability in Lower Tail	Values of d from Hart [1942]	Values of d_L and d_U from Durbin and Watson [1951]									
			$K=1$		$K=2$		$K=3$		$K=4$		$K=5$	
			d_L	d_U	d_L	d_U	d_L	d_U	d_L	d_U	d_L	d_U
15	.01	.89	.81	1.07	.70	1.25	.59	1.46	.49	1.70	.39	1.96
	.025	1.04	.95	1.23	.83	1.40	.71	1.61	.59	1.84	.48	2.09
	.05	1.16	1.08	1.36	.95	1.54	.82	1.75	.69	1.97	.56	2.21
20	.01	1.04	.95	1.15	.86	1.27	.77	1.41	.68	1.57	.60	1.74
	.025	1.18	1.08	1.28	.99	1.41	.89	1.55	.79	1.70	.70	1.87
	.05	1.30	1.20	1.41	1.10	1.54	1.00	1.68	.90	1.83	.79	1.99
25	.01	1.12	1.05	1.21	0.98	1.30	0.90	1.41	0.83	1.52	.75	1.65
	.025	1.26	1.18	1.34	1.10	1.43	1.02	1.54	0.94	1.65	.86	1.77
	.05	1.36	1.29	1.45	1.21	1.55	1.12	1.66	1.04	1.77	.95	1.89
30	.01	1.19	1.13	1.26	1.07	1.34	1.01	1.42	0.94	1.51	0.88	1.61
	.025	1.32	1.25	1.38	1.18	1.46	1.12	1.54	1.05	1.63	0.98	1.73
	.05	1.42	1.35	1.49	1.28	1.57	1.21	1.65	1.14	1.74	1.07	1.83
40	.01	1.29	1.25	1.34	1.20	1.40	1.15	1.46	1.10	1.52	1.05	1.58
	.025	1.40	1.35	1.45	1.30	1.51	1.25	1.57	1.20	1.63	1.15	1.69
	.05	1.49	1.44	1.54	1.39	1.60	1.34	1.66	1.29	1.72	1.23	1.79
50	.01	1.36	1.32	1.40	1.28	1.45	1.24	1.49	1.20	1.54	1.16	1.59
	.025	1.46	1.42	1.50	1.38	1.54	1.34	1.59	1.30	1.64	1.26	1.69
	.05	1.54	1.50	1.59	1.46	1.63	1.42	1.67	1.38	1.72	1.34	1.77
60	.01	1.42	1.38	1.45	1.35	1.48	1.32	1.52	1.28	1.56	1.25	1.60
	.025	1.51	1.47	1.54	1.44	1.57	1.40	1.61	1.37	1.65	1.33	1.69
	.05	1.58	1.55	1.62	1.51	1.65	1.48	1.69	1.44	1.73	1.41	1.77
80	.01	–	1.47	1.52	1.44	1.54	1.42	1.57	1.39	1.60	1.36	1.62
	.025	–	1.54	1.59	1.52	1.62	1.49	1.65	1.47	1.67	1.44	1.70
	.05	–	1.61	1.66	1.59	1.69	1.56	1.72	1.53	1.74	1.51	1.77
100	.01	–	1.52	1.56	1.50	1.58	1.48	1.60	1.46	1.63	1.44	1.65
	.025	–	1.59	1.63	1.57	1.65	1.55	1.67	1.53	1.70	1.51	1.72
	.05	–	1.65	1.69	1.63	1.72	1.61	1.74	1.59	1.76	1.57	1.78

The third column is interpolated from Hart [1942] and multiplied by $(T-1)/T$ to convert to d, by kind permission of the *Annals of Mathematical Statistics*, publisher. The remainder of the table is abridged from Durbin and Watson [1951], pp. 173–175, with the kind permission of *Biometrika*, the publisher, and the authors.

APPENDIX C

References

Aitken, A. C. [1934] On Least Squares and Linear Combination of Observations, *Proceedings of the Royal Society of Edinburgh*, Vol. LV, 1934–1935, pp. 42–48.

Aitken, A. C. [1949] *Determinants and Matrices*. Edinburgh and London, Oliver and Boyd, sixth edition (or later editions).

Albert, A. Adrian [1941] *Introduction to Algebraic Theories*. Chicago, University of Chicago Press. Available in paperback edition.

Allen, R. D. G. [1938] *Mathematical Analysis for Economists*. London, Macmillan.

Allen, R. G. D. [1956] *Mathematical Economics*. London, Macmillan (second edition, 1959; second edition with alterations, 1963).

Amemiya, Takeshi [1964] *Specification Analysis in Econometrics*. Ph.D. thesis (unpublished), Baltimore, Johns Hopkins University.

Ames, Edward, and Stanley Reiter [1961] Distributions of Correlation Coefficients in Economic Time Series, *Journal of the American Statistical Association*, Vol. 56, No. 295 (September), pp. 637–656.

Anderson, T[heodore] W[ilbur] [1958] *An Introduction to Multivariate Statistical Analysis*. New York, Wiley.

Anderson, T[heodore] W[ilbur] and Herman Rubin [1949] Estimation of the Parameters of a Single Equation in a Complete System of Stochastic Equations, *Annals of Mathematical Statistics*, Vol. 20, No. 1 (March), pp. 46–63.

Anderson, T[heodore] W[ilbur], and Herman Rubin [1950] The Asymptotic Properties of Estimates of the Parameters of a Single Equation in a Complete System of Stochastic Equations, *Annals of Mathematical Statistics*, Vol. 21, No. 4 (December), pp. 570–582.

Arrow, Kenneth J. [1960] Decision Theory and the Choice of a Level of Significance for the *t*-Test. In Ingram Olkin, Sudhish G. Ghurye, Wassily

674 References

Hoeffding, William G. Madow, and Henry B. Mann, *Contributions to Probability and Statistics, Essays in Honor of Harold Hotelling.* Stanford, Stanford University Press, pp. 70–78.

Bailey, Martin J. [1962] *National Income and The Price Level,* New York, McGraw-Hill.

Barten, A. P. [1962] Note on Unbiased Estimation of the Squared Multiple Correlation Coefficient, *Statistica Neerlandica,* Vol. 16, No. 2, pp. 151–163.

Basmann, [Robert] L. [1957] A Generalized Classical Method of Linear Estimation of Coefficients in a Structural Equation, *Econometrica,* Vol. 25, No. 1 (January), pp. 77–83.

Basmann, R[obert] L. [1958] An Experimental Investigation of Some Small Sample Properties of (GCL) Estimators of Structural Equations: Some Preliminary Results, processed, 97 pp., presented before the Econometric Society, December, 1958.

Basmann, R[obert] L. [1959] The Computation of Generalized Classical Estimates of Coefficients in a Structural Equation, *Econometrica,* Vol. 27, No. 1 (January), pp. 72–81.

Basmann, R[obert] L. [1960] On the Asymptotic Distribution of Generalized Linear Estimators, *Econometrica,* Vol. 28, No. 1 (January), pp. 97–107.

Basmann, R[obert] L. [1960a] An Expository Note on Estimation of Simultaneous Structural Equations, *Biometrics,* Vol. 16, No. 3 (September), pp. 464–480.

Basmann, R[obert] L. [1960b] On Finite Sample Distributions of Generalized Classical Linear Identifiability Test Statistics, *Journal of the American Statistical Association,* Vol. 55, No. 292 (December), pp. 650–659.

Basmann, R[obert] L. [1961] A Note on the Exact Finite Sample Frequency Functions of Generalized Classical Linear Estimators in Two Leading Overidentified Cases, *Journal of the American Statistical Association,* Vol. 56, No. 295 (September), pp. 619–636.

Basmann, R[obert] L. [1962] Letter to the Editor, *Econometrica,* Vol. 30, No. 1 (January), pp. 207–208.

Basmann, R[obert] L. [1962a] Letter to the Editor, *Econometrica,* Vol. 30, No. 4 (October), pp. 824–826.

Basmann, R[obert] L. [1963] A Note on the Exact Finite Sample Frequency Functions of Generalized Classical Linear Estimators in a Leading Three Equation Case, *Journal of the American Statistical Association,* Vol. 58, No. 301 (March), pp. 161–171.

Basmann, R[obert] L. [1963a] The Causal Interpretation of Non-triangular Systems of Economic Relations, *Econometrica,* Vol. 31, No. 3 (July), pp. 439–448.

Basmann, R[obert] L. [1965] A Tchebychev Inequality for the Convergence of a Generalized Classical Linear Estimator, Sample Size Being Fixed, *Econometrica,* Vol. 33, No. 3 (July), pp. 608–618.

Basmann, R[obert] L. [1965a] A Note on the Statistical Testability of "Explicit Causal Chains" against the Class of "Interdependent" Models, *Journal of the American Statistical Association,* Vol. 60, No. 312 (December), pp. 1080–1093.

Baumol, William J. [1951] and [1959] *Economic Dynamics: An Introduction; with a Contribution by Ralph Turvey*. New York, Macmillan (second edition, 1959).

Beach, Earl F. [1957] *Economic Models: An Exposition*. New York, Wiley.

Bellman, Richard E. [1960] *Introduction to Matrix Analysis*. New York, McGraw-Hill.

Bentzel, R[agnar], and H[erman O. A.] Wold [1946] On Statistical Demand Analysis from the Viewpoint of Simultaneous Equations, *Skandinavisk Aktuarietidskrift*, 29, pp. 95–114.

Bergstrom, A. R. [1962] The Exact Sampling Distributions of Least Squares and Maximum Likelihood Estimators of the Marginal Propensity to Consume, *Econometrica*, Vol. 30, No. 3 (July), pp. 480–490.

Bergstrom, A. R. [1966] Nonrecursive Models as Discrete Approximations to Systems of Stochastic Difference Equations, *Econometrica*, Vol. 34, No. 1 (January), pp. 173–182.

Birkhoff, Garrett, and Saunders MacLane [1953] *A Survey of Modern Algebra*, revised edition. New York, Macmillan (earlier editions in 1941 and 1951).

Blackwell, David, and M. A. Girshick [1954] *Theory of Games and Statistical Decisions*. New York, Wiley.

Bowker, Albert H. [1947] Tolerance Limits for Normal Distributions. Chapter 2 in Eisenhart, Churchill, Millard W. Hastay, and W. Allen Wallis, editors, *Selected Techniques of Statistical Analysis for Scientific and Industrial Research and Production and Management Engineering*. New York, McGraw-Hill.

Bronfenbrenner, Jean [1953] Sources and Size of Least-Squares Bias in a Two-Equation Model. Chapter IX in Hood and Koopmans [1953], pp. 221–235.

Bross, Irwin D.J. [1953] *Design for Decision*. New York, Macmillan.

Brown, T. M. [1952] Habit Persistence and Lags in Consumer Behavior, *Econometrica*, Vol. 20, No. 3 (July), pp. 355–371.

Brown, T. M. [1954] Standard Error of Forecast of a Complete Econometric Model, *Econometrica*, Vol. 22, No. 2 (April), pp. 178–192.

Brown, T. M. [1959] Simplified Full Maximum Likelihood and Comparative Structural Estimates, *Econometrica*, Vol. 27, No. 4 (October), pp. 638–653.

Brown, T. M. [1960] Simultaneous Least Squares: A Distribution Free Method of Equation System Structure Estimation, *International Economic Review*, Vol. 1, No. 3 (September), pp. 173–191.

Brownlee, O[swald] H. [1950] The Theory of Employment and Stabilization Policy, *Journal of Political Economy*, Vol. 58, No. 5 (October), pp. 412–424.

Burington, Richard S., and Charles C. Torrance [1939] *Higher Mathematics, with Applications to Science and Engineering*. New York and London, McGraw-Hill.

Cagan, Phillip D. [1956] The Monetary Dynamics of Hyperinflation. In Milton Friedman, editor, *Studies in the Quantity Theory of Money*. Chicago, University of Chicago Press, pp. 25–117.

Chernoff, Herman, and Nathan Divinsky [1953] The Computation of Maximum-Likelihood Estimates of Linear Structural Equations. Chapter X in Hood and Koopmans [1953], pp. 236–302.

Chernoff, Herman, and Lincoln E. Moses [1959] *Elementary Decision Theory.* New York, Wiley.

Chernoff, Herman, and Herman Rubin [1953] Asymptotic Properties of Limited-Information Estimates Under Generalized Conditions. Chapter VII in Hood and Koopmans [1953], pp. 200–212.

Chipman, John S. [1964] On Least Squares with Insufficient Observations, *Journal of the American Statistical Association*, Vol. 59, No. 308 (December), pp. 1078–1111.

Chipman, John S., and M. M. Rao [1964] The Treatment of Linear Restrictions in Regression Analysis, *Econometrica*, Vol. 32, Nos. 1 and 2 (January–April), pp. 198–209.

Chow, Gregory C. [1960] Tests of Equality between Sets of Coefficients in Two Linear Regressions, *Econometrica*, Vol. 28, No. 3 (July), pp. 591–605.

Chow, Gregory C. [1964] A Comparison of Alternative Estimators for Simultaneous Equations, *Econometrica*, Vol. 32, No. 4 (October), pp. 532–553.

Christ, Carl F. [1951] A Test of an Econometric Model for the United States, 1921–1947, pp. 35–107 in *Conference on Business Cycles* by the National Bureau of Economic Research (Universities-National Bureau Committee for Economic Research), New York, N.B.E.R. (Special Conference Series, No. 2). Reprinted as Cowles Commission Paper, New Series, No. 49.

Christ, Carl F. [1951a] Comment on Arthur Smithies' Business Cycle Analysis and Public Policy, pp. 420–422 in the volume cited under Christ [1951].

Christ, Carl F. [1952] A History of the Cowles Commission, 1932–1952. In Cowles Commission for Research in Economics, *Economic Theory and Measurement: A Twenty Year Research Report, 1932–1952.* Chicago, Cowles Commission, pp. 3–65.

Christ, Carl F. [1956] Aggregate Econometric Models: A Review Article, *American Economic Review*, Vol. 46, No. 3 (June), pp. 385–408. Reprinted in R. A. Gordon and L. R. Klein [1965], editors, *Readings in Business Cycles.* Homewood, Ill., Irwin, for the American Economic Association.

Christ, Carl F. [1957] On Econometric Models of the United States Economy. In Milton Gilbert and Richard Stone, editors, *Income and Wealth*, Series VI, Bowes and Bowes, London (for International Association for Research in Income and Wealth), pp. 1–23.

Christ, Carl F. [1960] Simultaneous Equation Estimation: Any Verdict Yet? *Econometrica*, Vol. 28, No. 4 (October), pp. 835–845.

Christ, Carl F., and (eleven) others [1963] (Milton Freidman, Leo A. Goodman, Zvi Griliches, Arnold C. Harberger, Nissan Liviatan, Jacob Mincer, Yair Mundlak, Marc Nerlove, Don Patinkin, Lester G. Telser, Henri Theil) *Measurement in Economics: Studies in Mathematical Economics and Econometrics in Memory of Yehuda Grunfeld.* Stanford, Stanford University Press.

Cochran, William G. [1953] *Sampling Techniques.* New York, Wiley (second edition, 1963).

Cochrane, Donald, and Guy H. Orcutt [1949] Application of Least Squares Regression to Relationships Containing Auto-Correlated Error Terms, *Journal of the American Statistical Association*, Vol. 44, No. 245 (March), pp.32–61.

Courant, R. [1934] and [1936] *Differential and Integral Calculus* (translated from German by E. J. McShane). London, Blackie & Son, Vol. I, 1934 (second edition 1937); Vol. II, 1936.

Cragg, J. R. [1966] On the Sensitivity of Simultaneous-Equations Estimators to the Stochastic Assumptions of the Models, *Journal of the American Statistical Association*, Vol. 61, No. 313 (March), pp. 136–151.

Cramér, Harald [1946] *Mathematical Methods of Statistics*. Princeton, N.J., Princeton University Press.

David, F. N., and J. Neyman [1938] Extension of the Markoff Theorem of Least Squares, in *Statistical Research Memoirs*, Vol. II (London, Department of Statistics, University College, University of London), pp. 105–116.

Doss, S. A. D. C. [1962] A Note on Consistency and Asymptotic Efficiency of Maximum Likelihood Estimates in Multi-parametric Problems, *Calcutta Statistical Association Bulletin*, Vol. 11, No. 43 (August), pp. 85–93.

Drèze, Jacques [1962] The Bayesian Approach to Simultaneous Equations Estimation. Mimeographed, O.N.R. Research Memorandum No. 67, Technological Institute, Northwestern University, 77 pp.

Durbin, J[ames] [1957] Testing for Serial Correlation in Systems of Simultaneous Regression Equations, *Biometrika* 44, Parts 3 and 4 (December), pp. 370–377.

Durbin, J[ames] [1960] Estimation of Parameters in Time-series Regression Models, *Journal of the Royal Statistical Society*, Series B (Methodological), Vol. 22, No. 1 (January), pp. 139–153.

Durbin, J[ames] [1963] Maximum-likelihood estimation of the parameters of a system of simultaneous regression equations (mimeographed, presented at the Copenhagen meetings of the Econometric Society).

Durbin, J[ames], and G. S. Watson [1950] Testing for Serial Correlation in Least Squares Regression. I. *Biometrika* 37 (December), pp. 409–428.

Durbin, J[ames], and G. S. Watson [1951] Testing for Serial Correlation in Least Squares Regression. II. *Biometrika* 38 (June), pp. 159–178.

Dwyer, Paul S., and M. S. Macphail [1948] Symbolic Matrix Derivatives, *Annals of Mathematical Statistics*, Vol. 19, No. 4 (December), pp. 517–534.

Eisenpress, Harry [1961] *Forecasting by Econometric Systems*, Preliminary Write-Up for IBM 709 Program IB9FES, IBM Corporation, Mathematics and Applications Dept. [Report No.] M & A-9, multilithed, 89 pp.

Eisenpress, Harry [1962] Note on the Computation of Full-Information Maximum Likelihood Estimates of Coefficients of a Simultaneous System, *Econometrica*, Vol. 30, No. 2 (April), pp. 343–348.

Eisenpress, Harry, and Richard J. Foote [1960] Systems of Simultaneous Equations on the IBM 704 and 709, *Journal of Farm Economics*, Vol. 42, No. 5 (December), pp. 1445–1449.

Eisner, Robert [1960] A Distributed Lag Investment Function, *Econometrica*, Vol. 28, No. 1 (January), pp. 1–29.

Eisner, Robert [1963] Investment: Fact and Fancy, *American Economic Review*, Vol. 53, No. 2 (Papers and Proceedings) (May), pp. 237–246.

Ezekiel, Mordecai, and Karl A. Fox [1959] *Methods of Correlation and Regression Analysis, Linear and Curvilinear*, third edition, New York, Wiley.

Feller, William [1957] and [1966] *An Introduction to Probability Theory and Its Applications*. New York, Wiley. Vol. I (second edition), 1957; Vol. II, 1966.

Ferber, Robert [1953] *A Study of Aggregate Consumption Functions*. New York, National Bureau of Economic Research (Technical Paper 8).

Fisher, Franklin M. [1959] Generalization of the Rank and Order Conditions for Identifiability, *Econometrica*, Vol. 27, No. 3 (July), pp. 431–447.

Fisher, Franklin M. [1961] On the Cost of Approximate Specification in Simultaneous Equation Estimation, *Econometrica*, Vol. 29, No. 2 (April), pp. 139–170.

Fisher, Franklin M. [1961a] Identifiability Criteria in Nonlinear Systems, *Econometrica*, Vol. 29, No. 4 (October), pp. 574–590.

Fisher, Franklin M. [1962] The Place of Least Squares in Econometrics: Comment, *Econometrica*, Vol. 30, No. 3 (July), pp. 565–567.

Fisher, Franklin M. [1963] Uncorrelated Disturbances and Identifiability Criteria, *International Economic Review*, Vol. 4, No. 2 (May), pp. 134–152.

Fisher, Franklin M. [1965] Identifiability Criteria in Nonlinear Systems: A Further Note, *Econometrica*, Vol. 33, No. 1 (January), pp. 197–205.

Fisher, Franklin M. [1965a] Near-Identifiability and the Variances of the Disturbance Terms, *Econometrica*, Vol. 33, No. 2 (April), pp. 409–419.

Fisher, Franklin M. [1966] *The Identification Problem in Econometrics*. New York, McGraw-Hill.

Fisher, Ronald A., and Frank Yates [1938] *Statistical Tables for Biological, Agricultural and Medical Research*. Various editions (later ones enlarged). London, Oliver and Boyd, 1938 and later.

Fisher, Walter D. [1962] Estimation in the Linear Decision Model, *International Economic Review*, Vol. 3, No. 1 (January), pp. 1–29.

Fox, Karl A. [1958] *Econometric Analysis for Public Policy*. Ames, Iowa State University Press.

Frazer, Robert A., W. J. Duncan, and A. R. Collar [1938] *Elementary Matrices and Some Applications to Dynamics and Differential Equations*. Cambridge, Cambridge University Press. Also available in paperback edition.

Friedman, Milton [1953] The Effects of a Full-Employment Policy on Economic Stability: A Formal Analysis, in Milton Friedman, *Essays in Positive Economics*. Chicago, Univeristy of Chicago Press, pp. 117–132. (A slightly revised version of a manuscript translated into French by Jacques Mayer and published as Les effets d'une politique de plein emploi sur la stabilité économique: Analyse formelle, *Économie appliquée*, Vol. IV, July-December, 1951, 441–456.)

Friedman, Milton [1957] *A Theory of the Consumption Function*. Princeton, Princeton University Press for National Bureau of Economic Research.

Friend, Irwin, and Jean Bronfenbrenner [1950] Business Investment Programs and Their Realization, *Survey of Current Business* (December), pp. 11–22.

Frisch, Ragnar [1933] *Pitfalls in the Statistical Construction of Demand and Supply Curves*. Veröffentlichungen der Frankfurter Gesellschaft für Konjuncturforschung, Neue Folge, Heft 5. Leipzig, Hans Buske Verlag.

Frisch, Ragnar [1934] *Statistical Confluence Analysis by Means of Complete Regression Systems*. Oslo, Universitetets Økonomiske Institutt.

Girshick, M. A., and Trygve Haavelmo [1947] Statistical Analysis of the Demand for Food: Examples of Simultaneous Estimation of Structural Equations. Chapter V in Hood and Koopmans [1953], pp. 92–111. Also in *Econometrica*, Vol. 15, No. 2 (April, 1947), pp. 79–110.

Goldberg, Samuel [1958] *Introduction to Difference Equations*. New York, Wiley.

Goldberger, Arthur S. [1959] *Impact Multipliers and Dynamic Properties of the Klein-Goldberger Model*. Amsterdam, North-Holland Publishing Co.

Goldberger, Arthur S. [1964] *Econometric Theory*. New York, Wiley.

Goldberger, Arthur S., A. L. Nagar, and H. S. Odeh [1961] The Covariance Matrices of Reduced-Form Coefficients and of Forecasts for a Structural Econometric Model, *Econometrica*, Vol. 29, No. 4 (October), pp. 556–573.

Griliches, Z[vi] [1957] Specification Bias in Estimates of Production Functions, *Journal of Farm Economics*, Vol. 39, No. 1 (February), pp. 8–20.

Griliches, Zvi [1961] A Note on Serial Correlation Bias in Estimates of Distributed Lags, *Econometrica*, Vol. 29, No. 1 (January), pp. 65–73.

Grunfeld, Yehuda [1960] The Determinants of Corporate Investment. In Arnold C. Harberger, editor, *The Demand for Durable Goods*, Chicago, University of Chicago Press, pp. 211–266.

Grunfeld, Yehuda, Studies in Mathematical Economics and Econometrics in Memory of. See Christ and others [1963].

Haavelmo, Trygve [1943] The Statistical Implications of a System of Simultaneous Equations, *Econometrica*, Vol. 11, No. 1 (January), pp. 1–12.

Haavelmo, Trygve [1944] The Probability Approach in Econometrics, *Econometrica*, Vol. 12, Supplement (July), 118 pp.

Haavelmo, Trygve [1947] Methods of Measuring the Marginal Propensity to Consume, Chapter IV in Hood and Koopmans [1953], pp. 75–91. Also in *Journal of the American Statistical Association*, Vol. 42, No. 237 (March, 1947), pp. 105–122.

Hannan, E. J. [1957] Testing for Serial Correlation in Least Squares Regression, *Biometrika* 44, Parts 1 and 2 (June), pp. 57–66.

Hannan, E. J. [1965] The Estimation of Relationships Involving Distributed Lags, *Econometrica*, Vol. 33, No. 1 (January), pp. 206–224.

Harberger, Arnold C. [1954] On the Estimation of Economic Parameters, paper presented before the Econometric Society, Montreal, September, 1954. Duplicated.

Harris, Seymour E. (editor) [1947] *The New Economics: Keynes' Influence on Theory and Public Policy*. New York, Knopf.

Hart, B. I., and John von Neumann [1942] Tabulation of the Probabilities for the Ratio of the Mean Square Successive Difference to the Variance, *Annals of Mathematical Statistics*, Vol. 13, pp. 207–214.

Hicks, J. R. [1937] Mr. Keynes and the "Classics": A Suggested Interpretation, *Econometrica*, Vol. 5, No. 2 (April), pp. 147–159.

Hildreth, Clifford [1963] Bayesian Statisticians and Remote Clients, *Econometrica*, Vol. 31, No. 3 (July), pp. 422–438.

Hildreth, Clifford, and John Y. Lu [1960] Demand Relations with Autocorrelated Disturbances. *Technical Bulletin* No. 276. East Lansing,

Michigan State University Agricultural Experiment Station, Department of Agricultural Economics, November, 1960.

Hood, William C., and Tjalling C. Koopmans (editors) [1953] *Studies in Econometric Method*, Cowles Commission Monograph 14, New York, Wiley.

Hooper, John W. [1959] Simultaneous Equations and Canonical Correlation Theory, *Econometrica*, Vol. 27, No. 2 (April), pp. 245–256.

Hooper, John W. [1962] Partial Trace Correlations, *Econometrica*, Vol. 30, No. 2 (April), pp. 324–331.

Hooper, John W., and Arnold Zellner [1961] The Error of Forecast for Multivariate Regression Models, *Econometrica*, Vol. 29, No. 4 (October), pp. 544–555.

Hotelling, Harold [1940] The Selection of Variates for Use in Prediction with Some Comments on the General Problem of Nuisance Parameters, *Annals of Mathematical Statistics*, Vol. 11, pp. 271–283.

Hurwicz, Leonid [1950] Generalization of the Concept of Identification, Chapter IV in Koopmans [1950], pp. 245–257.

Johnston, J. [1963] *Econometric Methods*. New York, McGraw-Hill.

Jorgenson, Dale W. [1963] Capital Theory and Investment Behavior, *American Economic Review*, Vol. 53, No. 2 (Papers and Proceedings) (May), pp. 247–259.

Jorgenson, Dale W. [1966] Rational Distributed Lag Functions, *Econometrica*, Vol. 34, No. 1 (January), pp. 135–149.

Kabe, D. G. [1963] A Note on the Exact Distributions of the GCL Estimators in Two Leading Over Identified Cases, *Journal of the American Statistical Association*, Vol. 58, No. 302 (June), pp. 535–537.

Kabe, D. G. [1964] On the Exact Distributions of the GCL Estimators in a Leading Three-Equation Case, *Journal of the American Statistical Association*, Vol. 59, No. 307 (September), pp. 881–894.

Katona, George [1951] *Psychological Analysis of Economic Behavior*. New York, McGraw-Hill.

Kendall, Maurice G. [1952] and [1951] *The Advanced Theory of Statistics*, 2 volumes. London, Charles Griffin, Vol. I (fifth edition), 1952; Vol. II (third edition), 1951.

Kendall, Maurice G., and Alan Stuart [1958] and [1961] *The Advanced Theory of Statistics*, Vols. I and II. New York, Hafner.

Keynes, John Maynard [1936] *The General Theory of Employment, Interest and Money*. London, Macmillan.

Klein, Lawrence R. [1947] *The Keynesian Revolution*. New York, Macmillan.

Klein, Lawrence R. [1950] *Economic Fluctuations in the United States, 1921–1941*, Cowles Commission Monograph 11. New York, Wiley.

Klein, Lawrence R. [1951] Estimating Patterns of Savings Behavior from Sample Survey Data, *Econometrica*, Vol. 19, No. 4 (October), pp. 438–454.

Klein, Lawrence R. [1953] *A Textbook of Econometrics*. Evanston, Ill., Row, Peterson.

Klein, Lawrence R. [1955] On the Interpretation of Theil's Method of Estimation of Economic Relations, *Metroeconomica*, Vol. 7, Fascicule 3 (December), pp. 147–153.

Klein, L[awrence] R. [1958] The Estimation of Distributed Lags, *Econometrica*, Vol. 26, No. 4 (October), pp. 553–565.

Klein, Lawrence R. [1960] The Efficiency of Estimation in Econometric Models, in Ralph W. Pfouts (editor), *Essays in Economics and Econometrics in Honor of Harold Hotelling* (*Studies in Economics and Business Administration*). Chapel Hill, University of North Carolina Press, pp. 216–232.

Klein, L[awrence] R. [1960a] Single Equation vs. Equation System Methods of Estimation in Econometrics, *Econometrica*, Vol. 28, No. 4 (October), pp. 866–871.

Klein, Lawrence R. [1962] *An Introduction to Econometrics*. Englewood Cliffs, N.J., Prentice-Hall.

Klein, L[awrence] R., and Mitsugu Nakamura [1962] Singularity in the Equation Systems of Econometrics: Some Aspects of the Problem of Multicollinearity, *International Economic Review*, Vol. 3, No. 3 (September), pp. 274–299.

Konijn, H. S. [1958] A Restatement of the Conditions for Identifiability in Complete Systems of Linear Difference Equations, *Metroeconomica*, Vol. 10, Fascicule 3 (December), pp. 182–190.

Koopmans, Tjalling C. [1937] *Linear Regression Analysis of Economic Time Series*. Haarlem, de Erven F. Bohn, Netherlands Economic Institute.

Koopmans, Tjalling C. [1941] The Logic of Econometric Business-Cycle Research, *Journal of Political Economy*, Vol. 49, No. 2 (April), pp. 157–181.

Koopmans, Tjalling C. [1945] Statistical Estimation of Simultaneous Economic Relations, *Journal of the American Statistical Association*, Vol. 40, No. 232, Pt. 1 (December), pp. 448–466.

Koopmans, Tjalling C. [1949] Identification Problems in Economic Model Construction. Chapter II in Hood and Koopmans [1953], pp. 27–48. Also in *Econometrica*, Vol. 17, No. 2 (April, 1949), pp. 125–144.

Koopmans, Tjalling C. [1949a] The Bias in Single-Equation Methods of Estimating Behavior Equations Relating to a Small Sector of the Economy. Cowles Commission Discussion Paper, Statistics, No. 336 (dittoed).

Koopmans, Tjalling C. (editor) [1950] *Statistical Inference in Dynamic Economic Models*. Cowles Commission Monograph 10. New York, Wiley.

Koopmans, Tjalling C. [1950a] When Is an Equation System Complete for Statistical Purposes? Chapter XVII in Koopmans [1950], pp. 393–409.

Koopmans, Tjalling C., and William C. Hood [1953] The Estimation of Simultaneous Linear Economic Relationships. Chapter VI in Hood and Koopmans [1953], pp. 112–199.

Koopmans, T[jalling] C., H. Rubin, and R. B. Leipnik [1950] Measuring the Equation Systems of Dynamic Economics. Chapter II in Koopmans [1950], pp. 53–237.

Koyck, L. M. [1954] *Distributed Lags and Investment Analysis*. (Contributions to Economics Analysis No. 4.) Amsterdam, North-Holland Publishing Co.

Ladd, George W. [1956] Effects of Shocks and Errors in Estimation: An Empirical Comparison, *Journal of Farm Economics*, Vol. 38, No. 2 (May), pp. 485–495.

Lancaster, Kelvin J. [1965] The Theory of Qualitative Linear Systems, *Econometrica*, Vol. 33, No. 2 (April), pp. 395–408.

Larson, Harold J., and T. A. Bancroft [1963] Sequential Model Building for Prediction in Regression Analysis, I, *Annals of Mathematical Statistics*, Vol. 34, No. 2 (June), pp. 462–479.

Larson, Harold J., and T. A. Bancroft [1963a] Biases in Prediction by Regression for Certain Incompletely Specified Models, *Biometrika*, Vol. 50, Parts 3 and 4 (December), pp. 391–402.

L'Esperance, Wilford L. [1964] A Case Study in Prediction: The Market for Watermelons, *Econometrica*, Vol. 32, Nos. 1 and 2 (January–April), pp. 163–173.

Lindley, D. V. [1965] *Introduction to Probability and Statistics from a Bayesian Viewpoint* (two volumes). Cambridge, Cambridge University Press.

Liu, Ta-Chung [1960] Underidentification, Structural Estimation, and Fore-casting, *Econometrica*, Vol. 28, No. 4 (October), pp. 855–865.

Liviatan, Nissan [1963] Consistent Estimation of Distributed Lags, *International Economic Review*, Vol. 4, No. 1 (January), pp. 44–52.

Madansky, Albert [1959] The Fitting of Straight Lines When Both Variables Are Subject to Error, *Journal of the American Statistical Association*, Vol. 54, No. 285 (March), pp. 173–205.

Madansky, Albert [1964] On the Efficiency of Three-Stage Least-Squares Estimation, *Econometrica*, Vol. 32, Nos. 1–2 (January–April), pp. 51–56.

Malinvaud, E[dmond] [1961] The Estimation of Distributed Lags: A Comment. *Econometrica*, Vol. 29, No. 3 (July), pp. 430–433.

Malinvaud, Edmond [1966] *Statistical Methods in Econometrics*. Chicago, Rand McNally, and Amsterdam, North-Holland Publishing Co.

Mann, H. B., and A[braham] Wald [1943] On the Statistical Treatment of Linear Stochastic Difference Equations, *Econometrica*, Vol. 11, Nos. 3–4 (July–October), pp. 173–220.

Marschak, Jacob [1947] Economic Structure, Path, Policy, and Prediction, *American Economic Review*, Vol. 37, No. 2 (Papers and Proceedings) (May), pp. 81–84.

Marschak, Jacob [1950] Statistical Inference in Economics: An Introduction. Chapter I in Koopmans [1950], pp. 1–50.

Marschak, Jacob [1953] Economic Measurements for Policy and Prediction. Chapter I in Hood and Koopmans [1953], pp. 1–26.

Marschak, Jacob, and Willaim H. Andrews, Jr. [1944] Random Simultaneous Equations and the Theory of Production, *Econometrica*, Vol. 12, Nos. 3–4 (July–October), pp. 143–205.

Marshall, Alfred [1920] *Principles of Economics*, 8th edition, London, Mac-millan and Co. Ltd. (871 pp. incl. index). *Note:* Page references given in this book correspond to the original plates of the eighth edition used in American printings by The Macmillan Co., and in British printings 1920–1947 by Macmillan and Co. Ltd., and in C. W. Guillebaud's variorum edition of 1961. British printings of Macmillan and Co. Ltd. in 1949 and later use new plates with different pagination, but a comparative index is given on pp. 720–731.

Marshall, Andrew W. [1949] A Test of Klein's Model III for Changes of Structure. Unpublished M.A. thesis, University of Chicago.

Meyer, John R., and Edwin Kuh [1957] *The Investment Decision: An Empirical Study*. Cambridge, Mass., Harvard University Press.

Modigliani, Franco [1944] Liquidity Preference and the Theory of Interest and Money, *Econometrica*, Vol. 12, No. 1 (January), pp. 45–88. Reprinted in *Readings in Monetary Theory*, American Economic Association, Homewood, Ill., Irwin, 1951, pp. 186–240.

Modigliani, Franco, and Richard Brumberg [1954] Utility Analysis and the Consumption Function: An Interpretation of Cross-Section Data. Chapter 15 in K. K. Kurihara (editor), *Post-Keynesian Economics*, New Brunswick, N.J., Rutgers University Press, pp. 388–436.

Mood, Alexander M. [1950] *Introduction to the Theory of Statistics*. New York, McGraw-Hill.

Mood, Alexander M., and Franklin A. Graybill [1963] *Introduction to the Theory of Statistics*. Second edition of Mood [1950], New York, McGraw-Hill, 1963.

Moore, Henry L. [1914] *Economic Cycles: Their Law and Cause*. New York, Macmillan.

Morgenstern, Oskar [1950] *On the Accuracy of Economic Observations*. Princeton, N.J., Princeton University Press.

Mosteller, Frederick, and Philip Nogee [1951] An Experimental Measurement of Utility, *Journal of Political Economy*, Vol. 59, No. 5 (October), pp. 371–404.

Mundlak, Yair [1961] Aggregation Over Time in Distributed Lag Models, *International Economic Review*, Vol. 2, No. 2 (May), pp. 154–163.

Nagar, A. L. [1959] *Statistical Estimation of Simultaneous Economic Relationships*, doctoral thesis. Rotterdam, Nederlandsche Economische Hoogeschool.

Nagar, A. L. [1959a] The Bias and Moment Matrix of the General k-Class Estimators of the Parameters in Simultaneous Equations, *Econometrica*, Vol. 27, No. 4 (October), pp. 575–595.

Nagar, A. L. [1960] A Monte Carlo Study of Alternative Simultaneous Equation Estimators, *Econometrica*, Vol. 28, No. 3 (July), pp. 573–590.

Nagar, A. L. [1961] A Note on the Residual Variance Estimation in Simultaneous Equations, *Econometrica*, Vol. 29, No. 2 (April), pp. 238–243.

Nagar, A. L. [1962] Double k-Class Estimators of Parameters in Simultaneous Equations and Their Small Sample Properties, *International Economic Review*, Vol. 3, No. 2 (May), pp. 168–188.

Nagar, A. L., and N. C. Kakwani [1964] The Bias and Moment Matrix of a Mixed Regression Estimator, *Econometrica*, Vol. 32, Nos. 1 and 2 (January–April), pp. 174–182.

Nakamura, Mitsugu [1960] A Note on the Consistency of Simultaneous Least Squares Estimation, *International Economic Review*, Vol. 1, No. 3 (September), pp. 192–197.

National Bureau of Economic Research [1960] (Universities-National Bureau Committee for Economic Research), *The Quality and Economic Significance of Anticipations Data*. Princeton, N.J., Princeton University Press for the N.B.E.R. (Special Conference Series, No. 10.)

Neiswanger, W. A., and T. A. Yancey [1959] Parameter Estimates and Autonomous Growth, *Journal of the American Statistical Association*, Vol. 54, No. 286 (June), pp. 389–402.

Nerlove, Marc [1958] Distributed Lags and Estimation of Long-Run Supply and Demand Elasticities: Theoretical Considerations, *Journal of Farm Economics*, Vol. 40, No. 2 (May), pp. 301–311.

Nerlove, Marc [1958a] *Distributed Lags and Demand Analysis* (Agriculture Handbook No. 141). Washington, U.S. Government Printing Office.

Nerlove, Marc [1958b] *The Dynamics of Supply: Estimation of Farmers' Response to Price*. Baltimore, Johns Hopkins Press.

Nerlove, Marc [1963] Returns to Scale in Electricity Supply. Chapter 7 in Christ and others [1963], pp. 167–198.

Nerlove, Marc [1965] *Estimation and Identification of Cobb-Douglas Production Functions*. Chicago, Rand McNally, and Amsterdam, North-Holland Publishing Co.

Nerlove, Marc, and William Addison [1958] Statistical Estimation of Long-run Elasticities of Supply and Demand, *Journal of Farm Economics*, Vol. 40, No. 4 (November), pp. 861–880.

Orcutt, Guy H., and Donald Cochrane [1949] A Sampling Study of the Merits of Auto-regressive and Reduced Form Transformations in Regression Analysis, *Journal of the American Statistical Association*, Vol. 44, No. 247 (September), pp. 356–372.

Patinkin, Don [1951] Price Flexibility and Full Employment, revised. In American Economic Association, *Readings in Monetary Theory*. Philadelphia, Blakiston, pp. 252–283.

Patinkin, Don [1956] and [1965] *Money, Interest, and Prices: An Integration of Monetary and Value Theory*. First edition, Evanston, Ill., Row, Peterson, 1956; second edition, New York, Harper and Row, 1965.

Pearson, E. S., and H. O. Hartley [1954] *Biometrika Tables for Statisticians*, Vol. I. Cambridge, The University Press for the Biometrika Trustees.

Penrose, R. [1955] A Generalized Inverse for Matrices, *Proceedings of the Cambridge Philosophical Society*, Vol. 51, Part 3 (July), pp. 406–413.

Pigou, A. C. [1943] The Classical Stationary State, *Economic Journal*, Vol. 53, No. 212 (December), pp. 343–351.

Quandt, Richard E. [1962] Some Small Sample Properties of Certain Structural Equation Estimators. (Research Memorandum No. 48, Princeton University Econometric Research Program, December 21, 1962, mimeographed, 69 pp.)

Quandt, Richard E. [1965] On Certain Small Sample Properties of *k*-Class Estimators, *International Economic Review*, Vol. 6, No. 1 (January), pp. 92–104.

Raiffa, Howard, and Robert Schlaifer [1961] *Applied Statistical Decision Theory*. Boston, Division of Research, Graduate School of Business Administration, Harvard University.

Rees, Albert [1951] Postwar Wage Determination in the Basic Steel Industry, *American Economic Review*, Vol. 41, No. 3 (June), pp. 389–404.

Roberts, Harry V. [1965] Probabilistic Prediction, *Journal of the American Statistical Association*, Vol. 60, No. 309 (March), pp. 50–62.

Rothenberg, Thomas J., and C. T. Leenders [1964] Efficient Estimation of Simultaneous Equation Systems, *Econometrica*, Vol. 32, Nos. 1–2 (January–April), pp. 57–76.

Rubin, Herman [1948] The Approximate Distribution of Calculated Disturbances. Cowles Commission Discussion Paper, Statistics, No. 318 (duplicated). Chicago, Cowles Commission.

Rubin, Herman [1948a] *Systems of Linear Stochastic Equations*. Unpublished
Ph.D. dissertation, University of Chicago, March.

Rubin, Herman [1950] Consistency of Maximum Likelihood Estimates in the
Explosive Case. Chapter XIV in Koopmans [1950], pp. 356–364.

Samuelson, Paul A. [1947] *Foundations of Economic Analysis*. Cambridge, Mass.,
Harvard University Press. Available in paperback.

Samuelson, P[aul] A., T. C. Koopmans, and J. R[ichard] N. Stone [1954] Report
of the Evaluative Committee for *Econometrica*, *Econometrica*, Vol. 22, No.
2 (April), pp. 141–146.

Sargan, J. D. [1958] The Estimation of Economic Relationships Using Instrumental Variables, *Econometrica*, Vol. 26, No. 3 (July), pp. 393–415.

Sargan, J. D. [1961] The Maximum Likelihood Estimation of Economic Relationships with Autoregressive Residuals, *Econometrica*, Vol. 29, No. 3 (July),
pp. 414–426.

Sargan, J. D. [1964] Three-Stage Least-Squares and Full Maximum Likelihood
Estimates, *Econometrica*, Vol. 32, Nos. 1 and 2 (January–April), pp.
77–81.

Savage, Leonard J. [1954] *The Foundations of Statistics*. New York, Wiley.

Savage, L[eonard] J. [1962] *The Foundations of Statistical Inference*. New York,
Wiley, and London, Methuen.

Schlaifer, Robert [1959] *Probability and Statistics for Business Decisions: An
Introduction to Managerial Economics under Uncertainty*. New York,
McGraw-Hill.

Schultz, Henry [1938] *The Theory and Measurement of Demand*. Chicago,
University of Chicago Press.

Simon, Herbert A. [1953] Causal Ordering and Identifiability. Chapter III in
Hood and Koopmans [1953], pp. 49–74.

Simon, Herbert A. [1955] Prediction and Hindsight as Confirmatory Evidence,
Philosophy of Science, Vol. 22, No. 3 (July), pp. 227–230.

Stone, [J.] Richard [N.] [1945] The Analysis of Market Demand, *Journal of the
Royal Statistical Society*, New Series, CVIII (Parts III–IV), pp. 286–382.

Stone, J. R[ichard] N. [1949] Prediction from Autoregressive Schemes and
Linear Stochastic Difference Systems, *Econometrica*, Vol. 17, Supplement
(July), pp. 29–37.

Stone, [J.] Richard [N.] [1951] *The Role of Measurement in Economics*. Cambridge,
Cambridge University Press.

Stone, [J.] Richard [N.] [1954] *The Measurement of Consumers' Expenditure and
Behaviour in the United Kingdom, 1920–1938*, Vol. I. Cambridge, Cambridge
University Press.

Strotz, Robert H., and H. O. A. Wold [1960] A Triptych on Causal Systems,
Econometrica, Vol. 28, No. 2 (April), pp. 417–463.

Summers, Robert M. [1965] A Capital Intensive Approach to the Small Sample
Properties of Various Simultaneous Equation Estimators, *Econometrica*,
Vol. 33, No. 1 (January), pp. 1–41.

Suzuki, Yukio [1964] On the Use of Some Extraneous Information in the Estimation of the Coefficients of Regression. *Annals of the Institute of Statistical Mathematics* (Tokyo), Vol. 16, Nos. 1 and 2, pp. 161–173.

Taylor, Lester D., and Thomas A. Wilson [1964] Three-Pass Least Squares: A Method for Estimating Models with a Lagged Dependent Variable, *Review of Economics and Statistics*, Vol. 46, No. 4 (November), pp. 329–346.

Theil, H[enri] [1957] Specification Errors and the Estimation of Economic Relationships, *Revue de L'Institut International de Statistique*, Vol. 25, pp. 41–51.

Theil, H[enri] [1958] and [1961] *Economic Forecasts and Policy*. (Contributions to Economic Analysis No. 15.) Amsterdam, North-Holland Publishing Co., first edition, 1958; second edition, 1961.

Theil, H[enri] [1963] On the Use of Incomplete Prior Information in Regression Analysis, *Journal of the Americian Statistical Association*, Vol. 58, No. 302 (June), pp. 401–414.

Theil, H[enri] [1965] The Analysis of Disturbances in Regression Analysis, *Journal of the American Statistical Association*, Vol. 60, No. 312 (December), pp. 1067–1079.

Theil, H[enri] [1966] *Applied Economic Forecasting*. Chicago, Rand McNally, and Amsterdam, North-Holland Publishing Co.

Theil, H[enri], and A. S. Goldberger [1961] On Pure and Mixed Statistical Estimation in Economics, *International Economic Review*, Vol. 2, No. 1 (January), pp. 65–78.

Theil, H[enri], and A. L. Nagar [1961] Testing the Independence of Regression Disturbances, *Journal of the American Statistical Association*, Vol. 56, No. 296 (December), pp. 793–806.

Tinbergen, Jan [1938] Statistical Evidence on the Acceleration Principle, *Economica*, N.S. Vol. 5 (May), pp. 164–176. Reprinted in Tinbergen [1951], pp. 215–229.

Tinbergen, J[an] [1939] *Statistical Testing of Business Cycle Theories*, Vol. II: *Business Cycles in the U.S.A. 1919–1932*. Geneva, League of Nations.

Tinbergen, Jan [1951] *Econometrics* (translated by H. Rijken van Olst from a Dutch book published several years earlier). Philadelphia, Blakiston.

Tintner, Gerhard [1952] *Econometrics*. New York, Wiley.

U.S. Department of Commerce [1954] *National Income*, 1954 edition (Supplement to the *Survey of Current Business*). Washington, U.S. Government Printing Office.

U.S. Department of Commerce [1958] *U.S. Income and Output* (Supplement to *Survey of Current Business*). Prepared in the Office of Business Economics. Washington, U.S. Government Printing Office. (For newly revised data, see *Survey of Current Business*, August, 1959 and August, 1965.)

Valavanis, Stefan [1959] *Econometrics: An Introduction to Maximum Likelihood Methods*. New York, McGraw-Hill.

Vickrey, William S. [1954] Stability through Inflation. Chapter 4 in K. K. Kurihara (editor), *Post-Keynesian Economics*. New Brunswick, N.J., Rutgers University Press, pp. 89–122.

von Neumann, John [1941] Distribution of the Ratio of the Mean Square Successive Difference to the Variance, *Annals of Mathematical Statistics*, Vol. 12, No. 4 (December), pp. 367–395.

von Neumann, John [1942] A Further Remark Concerning the Distribution of the Ratio of the Mean Square Successive Difference to the Variance, *Annals of Mathematical Statistics*, Vol. 13, pp. 86–88.

Wagner, Harvey M. [1958] A Monte Carlo Study of Estimates of Simultaneous Linear Structural Equations, *Econometrica*, Vol. 26, No. 1 (January), pp. 117–133.

Wald, Abraham [1948] Asymptotic Properties of the Maximum Likelihood Estimate of an Unknown Parameter of a Discrete Stochastic Process, *Annals of Mathematical Statistics*, Vol. 19, No. 1 (March), pp. 40–46.

Wald, Abraham [1950] *Statistical Decision Functions*. New York, Wiley.

Wald, Abraham [1950a] Note on the Identification of Economic Relations. Chapter III in Koopmans [1950], pp. 238–244.

Wallace, T[homas] D[udley] [1964] Efficiencies for Stepwise Regressions, *Journal of the American Statistical Association*, Vol. 59, No. 308 (December), pp. 1179–1182.

Wallis, W. Allen [1951] Tolerance Intervals for Linear Regression, in Jerzy Neyman, editor, *Proceedings of the Second Berkeley Symposium on Mathematical Statistics and Probability*. Berkeley, University of California Press, pp. 43–51.

Wallis, W. Allen, and Harry V. Roberts [1956] *Statistics, a New Approach*. Glencoe, Ill., Free Press.

Walras, Leon [1926] *Éléments d'économie politique pure*, Edition définitive. Paris, R. Pichon et R. Durand-Auzias; and Lausanne, F. Rouge, 1926. See also Walras [1954].

Walras, Leon [1954] *Elements of Pure Economics or The Theory of Social Wealth*. Translated by William Jaffe. London. Published for the American Economic Association and the Royal Economic Society by Allen and Unwin.

Watson, G. S., and E. J. Hannan [1956] Serial Correlation in Regression Analysis. II, *Biometrika* 43, Parts 3 and 4 (December), pp. 436–448.

Waugh, Frederick V. [1961] The Place of Least Squares in Econometrics, *Econometrica*, Vol. 29, No. 3 (July), pp. 386–396.

Wilks, Samuel S. [1943] *Mathematical Statistics*. Princeton, N.J., Princeton University Press.

Wilks, Samuel S. [1962] *Mathematical Statistics*. New York, Wiley. (An expanded version of Wilks [1943].)

Wold, Herman [O. A.] [1950] On Least Square Regression with Autocorrelated Variables and Residuals, *Bulletin de L'Institut International de Statistique*, Vol. 32, No. 2, pp. 277–289.

Wold, Herman O. A. [1953] in association with Lars Jureen. *Demand Analysis: A study in econometrics*. New York, Wiley.

Wold, Herman O. A., and P. Faxér [1957] On the Specification Error in Regression Analysis, *Annals of Mathematical Statistics*, Vol. 28, No. 1 (March), pp. 265–267.

Working, E[lmer] J. [1927] What Do Statistical "Demand Curves" Show? *Quarterly Journal of Economics*, Vol. 41 (February), pp. 212–235. Reprinted as Chapter 4 in G. J. Stigler and K. E. Boulding (editors), *Readings in Price Theory*. Homewood, Ill., American Economic Association and Irwin, 1952, pp. 97–115.

Yule, George Udny, and Maurice G. Kendall [1937] *An Introduction to the Theory of Statistics*. London, Griffin. (Fourteenth edition, revised and enlarged, New York, Hafner, 1950.)

Zellner, Arnold [1961] Econometric Estimation with Temporally Dependent Disturbance Terms, *International Economic Review*, Vol. 2, No. 2 (May), pp. 164–178.

Zellner, Arnold [1962] An Efficient Method of Estimating Seemingly Unrelated Regressions and Tests for Aggregation Bias, *Journal of the American Statistical Association*, Vol. 57, No. 298 (June), pp. 348–368.

Zellner, Arnold, and V. Karuppan Chetty [1965] Prediction and Decision Problems in Regression Models from the Bayesian Point of View, *Journal of the American Statistical Association*, Vol. 60, No. 310 (June), pp. 608–616.

Zellner, Arnold, and H[enri] Theil [1962] Three-Stage Least Squares: Simultaneous Estimation of Simultaneous Equations, *Econometrica*, Vol. 30, No. 1 (January), pp. 54–78.

Zellner, Arnold, and George C. Tiao [1964] Bayesian Analysis of the Regression Model with Autocorrelated Errors, *Journal of the American Statistical Association*, Vol. 59, No. 307 (September), pp. 763–778.

INDEX

Every individual author and co-author in Appendix C is indexed here, but page references to Appendix C are given only if the person would not otherwise be indexed or if he is not the first-named co-author (whose name then appears in parentheses after references to pp. 673 ff.).